Political Biography

Dennis Kavanagh

Oxford Paperback Reference

Abbreviations
ABC of Music
Accounting
Archaeology*
Architecture*
Art and Artists
Art Terms*
Astronomy
Bible
Biology
Botany
Business
Card Games
Chemistry
Christian Church
Classical Literature
Classical Mythology*
Colour Medical Dictionary
Colour Science Dictionary
Computing
Dance*
Dates
Earth Sciences
Ecology
Economics
Engineering*
English Etymology
English Language*
English Literature
English Place-Names
Euphemisms
Film*
Finance
First Names
Food and Nutrition
Fowler's Modern English Usage
Geography
King's English
Law
Linguistics
Literary Terms
Mathematics
Medical Dictionary
Medicines*
Modern Quotations
Modern Slang
Music
Nursing
Opera
Philosophy
Physics
Plant-Lore
Political Biography
Politics
Popes
Proverbs
Psychology*
Quotations
Sailing Terms
Saints
Science
Shakespeare*
Ships and the Sea
Sociology
Superstitions
Theatre
Twentieth-Century Art*
Twentieth-Century History
Twentieth-Century Poetry
Weather Facts
Women Writers
Word Games
World Mythology
Writers' Dictionary
Zoology

*forthcoming

A Dictionary of

Political Biography

Edited by

DENNIS KAVANAGH

Oxford New York

OXFORD UNIVERSITY PRESS

1998

Oxford University Press, Great Clarendon Street, Oxford OX2 6DP

Oxford New York
Athens Auckland Bangkok Bogota Bombay Buenos Aires
Calcutta Cape Town Dar es Salaam Delhi Florence Hong Kong
Istanbul Karachi Kuala Lumpur Madras Madrid Melbourne
Mexico City Nairobi Paris Singapore Taipei Tokyo Toronto Warsaw

and associated companies in
Berlin Ibadan

Oxford is a trade mark of Oxford University Press

British Library Cataloguing in Publication Data
Data available

Library of Congress Cataloging in Publication Data

A Dictionary of political biography/edited by Dennis Kavanagh (Oxford paperback reference)
1. Heads of state—Biography—Dictionaries. 2. Statesmen—Biography—Dictionaries.
3. Biography—20th century—Dictionaries. I. Kavanagh, Dennis.
D412.D53 1998 909.82'092'2—dc21 97-37984

ISBN 0-19-280035-3 (pbk.)

1 3 5 7 9 10 8 6 4 2

Typeset by Best-set Typesetter Ltd., Hong Kong

Printed in Great Britain by
Cox & Wyman,
Reading, England

TO DAVID

Contents

Preface

A dictionary of political biography is a work of reference. Its 1,000 entries describe and assess the lives of the men and women who have shaped political events across the world during the twentieth century. Each entry marries description with analysis and includes an account of the background, career, and achievements of the individual concerned. We have sought a careful balance of fact and critical appraisal. An asterisk (*) before a surname indicates that the person has received an entry in the volume. For all but a handful of entries we have supplied dates of birth and, where appropriate, death. In a few cases our best endeavours have not produced the data.

We had criteria for selection but these were not applied rigidly. We have included only political figures whose main activity took place after 1900. This means that Lord Salisbury, who served as British Prime Minister until 1902, and William McKinley, who was US President in 1900, are omitted, because the greater parts of their political careers took place almost entirely in the nineteenth century. We have covered all the principal office-holders for a number of countries, e.g. all US presidents and vice-presidents, all British prime ministers, chancellors of the exchequer, and foreign secretaries, all USSR Communist Party leaders, all German chancellors, and a large proportion of presidents and prime ministers in the French Fourth and Fifth Republics. Beyond that we have been more selective and chosen office-holders on the basis of their importance in their countries.

The emphasis is on elected politicians. Unless they were also political office-holders we have omitted party organizers, political thinkers and commentators, civil servants, and members of the judiciary. The omission does not belittle their political significance—who could deny the importance of a Keynes or a Hayek? The primary focus is, however, on politicians.

There will of course be criticisms of some of our selections and some of our omissions. Our defence is that we have done what we have done and used our best judgement.

I am indebted to many for helping to bring this dictionary to publication, not least to the contributors and the patience and cheerfulness of April Pidgeon, my secretary at Nottingham University, and Alison Ross and Yvonne Janvier at Liverpool University.

As the volume was going to press the editor and publisher learnt of the death of a major contributor, Professor Peter Morris of Aston University. As a colleague at Nottingham, Peter had provided me with encouragement and wise advice in the early stages of planning the dictionary.

D. K.

University of Liverpool
June 1997

List of Contributors

General Editor

Dennis Kavanagh	*Professor* *Department of Politics and Communication Studies* *University of Liverpool*
Keith Alderman	*Reader* *Department of Politics* *University of York*
David Bell	*Professor* *Department of Politics* *University of Leeds*
Chris Binns	*Visiting Lecturer* *London School of Economics*
Peter Boyle	*Senior Lecturer* *Department of American Studies* *University of Nottingham*
Nigel Brailey	*Lecturer* *Department of Historical Studies* *University of Bristol*
Shaun Breslin	*Lecturer* *Department of Politics* *University of Newcastle upon Tyne*
David Childs	*Emeritus Professor,* *Department of Politics* *University of Nottingham*
Christopher Clapham	*Professor* *Department of Politics and International Relations* *University of Lancaster*
David Corkhill	*Senior Lecturer* *Department of Spanish* *University of Leeds*
Harvey Cox	*Senior Lecturer* *Department of Politics and Communication Studies* *University of Liverpool*
John Craig	*Senior Lecturer* *Department of Politics* *Deakin University, Australia*
Phil Deans	*Lecturer in Politics and International Relations* *University of Kent*
Dionyssis Dimitrakopoulous	*Lecturer* *Department of Politics* *The University of Hull*
Neil Elder	*Reader* *Department of Politics* *the University of Hull*
James Ferguson	*Researcher* *Latin American Bureau* *London*

Henry Finch — *Senior Lecturer*
Department of Economic and Social History
University of Liverpool

Peter Flynn — *Professor*
Institute of Latin-American Studies
University of Glasgow

Paul Furlong — *Senior Lecturer*
Department of Politics and International Studies
University of Birmingham

David George — *Lecturer*
Department of Politics
University of Newcastle upon Tyne

Paul Heywood — *Professor*
Department of Politics
University of Nottingham

Tony Kapcia — *Senior Lecturer*
School of Languages and European Studies
University of Wolverhampton

Dennis Kavanagh — *Professor*
Department of Politics and Communication Studies
University of Liverpool

Walter Little — *Lecturer*
Institute of Latin American Studies
University of Liverpool

David Lowe — *School of Australian and International Studies*
Deakin University, Australia

Peter Lyon — *Professor*
Institute of Commonwealth Studies
London

Jo Magone — *Lecturer*
Department of European Studies
University of Hull

David Morgan — *Emeritus Professor*
Department of Politics and Communication Studies
University of Liverpool

Peter Morris — *Late Professor*
Department of European Studies
Aston University

Andrew Nickson — *Senior Lecturer*
School of Public Policy
University of Birmingham

Philip Norton — *Professor*
Department of Politics
University of Hull

Philip O'Brien — *Senior Lecturer*
Department of Sociology
University of Glasgow

Jenny Pearce — *Lecturer*
Department of Peace Studies
University of Bradford

Gillian Peele — *Fellow*
Lady Margaret Hall
The University of Oxford

Benny Pollack — *Professor*
Institute of Latin American Studies
University of Liverpool

Richard Popplewell — *Lecturer*
Department of Politics
University of Salford

Sue Pryce — *Visiting Lecturer*
Department of Politics
University of Nottingham

Inneke Secker — *Lecturer*
Department of History
University of Leiden
The Netherlands

Rachel Sieder — *Lecturer*
Department of Politics
University of London

Gurharpal Singh — *Senior Lecturer*
Department of Politics
De Montford University
Leicester

David Stansfield — *Lecturer*
Department of Politics
University of Glasgow

Tony Stockwell — *Professor*
Department of History
Royal Holloway
University of London

Ian Talbot — *Reader*
Department of International Studies
University of Coventry

Lewis Taylor — *Lecturer*
Institute of Latin American Studies
University of Liverpool

Robert Taylor — *Professor*
School of Oriental and African Studies
University of London

John Wiseman — *Senior Lecturer*
Department of Politics
University of Newcastle upon Tyne

Contributors and Countries

Alderman, Keith	*Britain*
Bell, David	*France*
Binns, Chris	*Former Soviet Union, Yugoslavia*
Boyle, Peter	*USA*
Brailey, Nigel	*Thailand*
Breslin, Shaun	*China*
Childs, David	*Germany, Austria*
Clapham, Christopher	*Sub-Saharan Africa*
Corkill, David	*Ecuador*
Cox, Harvey	*Eire*
Craig, John	*New Zealand*
Deans, Phil	*Japan, Taiwan*
Dimitrakopoulos, Dionyssis	*Greece*
Elder, Neil	*Sweden, Denmark, Finland, Norway*
Ferguson, James	*Dominican Republic, Trinidad, Grenada, Haiti, Dominica, Barbados, Jamaica*
Finch, Henry	*Uruguay*
Flynn, Peter	*Brazil*
Furlong, Paul	*Italy*
George, David	*Iran, Israel, Turkey, Iraq, Oman, Libya, Lebanon, Syria, Palestine, Jordan, Saudi Arabia, Morocco*
Heywood, Paul	*Spain*
Kapcia, Tony	*Cuba*
Kavanagh, Dennis	*Britain, USA*
Little, Walter	*Argentina*
Lowe, David	*Australia*
Lyon, Peter	*Canada*
Magone, Jo	*Portugal*
Morgan, David	*USA*
Morris, Peter	*France*
Nickson, Andrew	*Paraguay*
Norton, Philip	*Britain, USA*
O'Brien, Philip	*Venezuela, Costa Rica, Colombia*
Pearce, Jenny	*El Salvador*
Peele, Gillian	*USA*
Pollack, Benny	*Chile*
Popplewell, Richard	*Poland, Yugoslavia, Russia, Albania, Czechoslovakia*
Pryce, Sue	*USA*
Secker, Inneke	*Netherlands*
Sieder, Rachel	*Guatemala, Honduras*
Singh, Gurharpal	*India, Philippines, Singapore*
Stansfield, David	*Mexico*
Stockwell, Tony	*Malaya, Indonesia*
Talbot, Ian	*Pakistan*
Taylor, Lewis	*Peru*
Taylor, Robert	*Burma*
Wiseman, John	*Sub-Saharan Africa*

Abbreviations

AFPFL Anti-Fascist People's Freedom League (Burma)
ALP Albanian Labour Party
ALP Australian Labour Party
ANC African National Congress
ANZUS Australia, New Zealand, and United States (treaty)
APRA Alianza Popular Revolucionaria Americana
ARP Anti-Revolutionary Party (Netherlands)
ASEAN Association of South East African Nations

BA Bachelor of Arts
BBC British Broadcasting Corporation
BC British Columbia
BCP Bulgarian Communist Party
BDP Botswana Democratic Party

CCM Chama cha Mapinduzi (Party of the Revolution, Tanzania)
CDP Civic Democratic Party (Czechoslovakia)
CDS Democratic and Social Centre (Spain)
CDU Christian Democratic Union (Germany)
CF Civic Forum (Czechoslovakia)
CGT Confédération Générale du Travail
CIA Central Intelligence Agency (USA)
CIS Commonwealth of Independent States
CMEA Council for Mutual Economic Assistance (USSR)
CP Communist Party
CPCz Communist Party of Czechoslovakia
CPI Communist Party of India
CPI(M) Communist Party of India (Marxist)
CPM Communist Party of Malaysia
CPP Convention People's Party (Ghana)
CPSU Communist Party of the Soviet Union
CSU Christian Social Union (Germany)

DC Democrazi Cristiana (Italy)
DEA Department of Economic Affairs
DEP Department for Employment and Productivity
DFC Distinguished Flying Cross
DFP Dominica Freedom Party

EC European Community
ECSC European Coal and Steel Community
EEC European Economic Community
EFTA European Free Trade Association
ENA École Nationale d'Administration
EPL Popular Liberation Army (Colombia)
ERM Exchange Rate Mechanism
EU European Union

FAO Food and Agriculture Organization (of UN)
FBI Federal Bureau of Investigation (USA)
FDJ Free German Youth
FDP Free Democratic Party (Germany)
FDR Federal German Republic
FI Forza Italia
FLN National Liberation Front (Algeria)
FRELIMO Front for the Liberation of Mozambique
FRTS Regional Federation of Salvadorean Workers

GATT General Agreement on Tariffs and Trade
GDP Gross Domestic Product
GDR German Democratic Republic
GNP Gross National Product
GPU *see* OGPU
GVP All-German People's Party

HCP Hungarian Communist Party
HSWP Hungarian Socialist Workers' Party

IDF Israeli Defence Force
IEP Institut d'Études Politiques
ILP Independent Labour Party
IMF International Monetary Fund
IRA Irish Republican Army
IRB Irish Republican Brotherhood

KADU Kenyan African Democratic Union
KANU Kenya African National Union
KGB Committee of State Security (USSR)
KPD Communist Party of Germany

LDLP Lithuanian Democratic Labour Party
LDP Liberal Democratic Party (Japan)
LEHY Lohamei Herut Yisraeli
LLB Bachelor of Law
LRC Labour Representation Committee
LSE London School of Economics

MA Master of Arts
MCP Malawi Congress Party
MCP Malayan Communist Party
MDF Hungarian Democratic Forum
MDS Movement for a Democratic Union
MEP Member of the European Parliament
MfS Ministry for State Security (GDR)
MIT Massachusetts Institute of Technology
MLP Mauritius Labour Party
MNC Mouvement National Congolais
MP Member of Parliament
MPR Popular Movement of the Revolution (Congo)
MRP Mouvement Républicain Populaire (France)

NAFTA North American Free Trade Agreement
NATO North Atlantic Treaty Organization
NCO non-commissioned officer
NDB National Democratic Bloc (Romania)
NEC National Executive Council (of the Labour Party)
NEP New Economic Policy (USSR)
NHS National Health Service
NJM New Jewel Movement (Grenada)
NKVD People's Commissariat for Internal Affairs (USSR)
NPD National Democratic Party (Germany)
NRA National Resistance Army (Uganda)
NRW North-Rhine Westphalia
NSDAP German Nationalist Socialist Workers' Party
NSW New South Wales
NWFP North-West Frontier Province (Pakistan)

OAU Organization of African Unity
OEEC Organization for European Economic Co-operation
OGPU United state political administration for the struggle against espionage and counter-revolution (USSR)

PAIGC Patrido Africano da Guine e Cabo Verde
PAV Public Against Violence (Czechoslovakia)
PC Progressive Conservative (Canada)

PCB	Brazilian Communist Party
PCF	Parti Communiste Français
PCI	Italian Communist Party
PCS	Communist Party of El Salvador
Ph.D.	Doctor of Philosophy
PKI	Communist Party of Indonesia
PLD	Partido de la Liberación Dominicana
PLO	Palestine Liberation Organization
PLP	Parliamentary Labour Party
PNM	People's National Movement (Trinidad)
PNP	People's National Party (Jamaica)
PPF	Parti Populaire Français
PPI	Partido Popolare Italiano
PPP	Pakistan People's Party
PPP	Polish Peasants' Party
PRC	People's Republic of China
PRD	Partido Revolucionario Dominicano
PRG	People's Revolutionary Government (Grenada)
PRI	Party of Institutionalized Revolution (Mexico)
PS	Partido Socialista (Portugal)
PS	Parti Socialiste (France)
PSD	Partido Social-Democrata (Portugal)
PST	Italian Socialist Party
PSU	Parti Socialiste Unifié
PZPR	Polish United Workers' Party
QC	Queen's Counsel
RAAF	Royal Australian Air Force
RAFVR	Royal Air Force Volunteer Reserve
RCC	Revolutionary Command Council (Egypt, Libya)
RCP	Romanian Communist Party
RDA	Rassemblement Democratique Africain
RNVR	Royal Naval Volunteer Reserve
ROC	Republic of China
ROTC	Reserve Officer Training Corps (USA)
RPF	Rwandan Patriotic Front
RPF	Rassemblement du Peuple Français
RPR	Rassemblement pour la République
RSDLP	Russian Social Democratic Labour Party
RSFSR	Russian Soviet Federative Socialist Republic
SA	Sturm-Abteilung
SAP	South African Party
SAP	Socialist Workers' Party (Germany)
SAS	Special Air Service
SD	Security Service (Germany)
SDAP	Social Democratic Party (Netherlands)
SDP	Social Democratic Party
SED	Socialist Unity Party of Germany
SFIO	Section Français de l'Internationale Ouvrière
SLPP	Sierra Leone People's Party
SPD	Social Democratic Party of Germany
SS	Schutzstaffel
SWAPO	South West Africa People's Organization
TANU	Tanganyika African National Union
TUC	Trades Union Congress
UCD	Union of the Democratic Centre (Spain)
UCLA	University of California at Los Angeles
UDF	Union pour la Democratie Française
UFW	United Farm Workers (USA)
UMNO	United Malays National Organization

UN	United Nations
Unesco	UN Educational, Scientific, and Cultural Organization
UNIP	United National Independence Party (Zambia)
UP	United Party (South Africa)
UPC	Union of the Population of Cameroon
UPC	Uganda People's Congress
UPM	Uganda Patriotic Movement
USA	United States of America
USPD	Independent Socialist Party (Germany)
USSR	Union of Soviet Socialist Republics
VAT	value added tax
ZANU	Zimbabwe African National Union
ZAPU	Zimbabwe African People's Union

Abdul Rahman Putra Al-Haj, Tunku (b. Alor Setar, 8 Feb. 1903; d. Kuala Lumpur, 6 Dec. 1990)

Malaysian; Prime Minister of Malaya 1957–63 and of Malaysia 1963–70

A son of the Sultan of Kedah, the Tunku was educated at schools in Bangkok, Alor Setar, at the Penang Free School and St Catharine's College, Cambridge. He entered Kedah government service in 1931 and in December 1941 prevented the British from taking his father out of the state as they retreated before the Japanese. After the Japanese occupation (1941–5), during which he continued in administration, he resumed legal studies at the Inner Temple. Having been called to the bar, in 1949 he joined the Kedah Legal Department and then the Federal Legal Department, but in August 1951 he resigned to succeed Dato Onn bin Jaafar as leader of the United Malays National Organization.

Lacking flamboyance, abrasiveness, and bureaucratic skill, the Tunku flourished as a consensus politician. From 1952 he deftly guided UMNO in an Alliance (with the Malayan Chinese Association and, later, the Malayan Indian Congress) which became heir apparent to the British colonial regime. Counter-insurgency successes against Communist guerrillas from 1953 encouraged the Alliance to demand, and the British to grant, constitutional concessions. In July 1955 the Alliance won 51 of the 52 electable seats in the Federal Council and the Tunku became Chief Minister of a virtually self-governing Malaya. In December he met, but refused to compromise with, *Chin Peng (leader of the outlawed Malayan Communist Party). He was now in a position successfully to demand independence by 31 August 1957.

Under the Tunku, independent Malaya remained close to Britain. In 1963 Malaya became Malaysia through incorporation with the former British colonies of Singapore, Sarawak, and North Borneo (Sabah). While prospering economically, however, Malaysia was challenged by Indonesian 'Confrontation' (1963–6), the secession of Singapore (1965), and communal riots in May 1969 which left hundreds dead in Kuala Lumpur. The 1969 crisis effectively ended his political career. Having presented himself as the father of a multiracial nation, the Tunku resigned as Prime Minister and leader of UMNO in September 1970.

From 1970 to 1973 the Tunku served as secretary-general of the Islamic Secretariat in Jeddah. In retirement in Penang he contributed to public debate through the *Star* newspaper and became an outspoken critic of Dr *Mahathir. His reminiscences were published in a series of collections starting with *Looking Back* (1977).

Acheson, Dean Gooderham (b. Middleton, Connecticut, 11 Apr. 1893; d. 12 Oct. 1971)

US; Secretary of State 1949–53

Acheson received a privileged education at Groton and Yale and, in 1918, graduated LLB from Harvard Law School. At this time it was customary for distinguished Supreme Court judges to pick the two most gifted men in the graduating Harvard law class to assist them. Acheson was chosen by Justice Brandeis. During the First World War Acheson served for a time in the Navy. On returning to civilian life he became a practising lawyer.

In 1933 he gained his first experience of public office when F. D. *Roosevelt appointed him Under-Secretary of the Treasury. An inability to justify Roosevelt's fiscal unorthodoxy prompted Acheson's early departure from office.

In 1939, when Europe once again became embroiled in war, Acheson, an

Anglophile, became a strong advocate of aid to Britain. He returned to government in 1941 becoming Assistant Secretary at the State Department. In the following six years he gained a wealth of experience serving under four secretaries of state. The tasks for which he was responsible notably included organizing the lend-lease programme and making preparations for the San Francisco Conference which created the United Nations.

Acheson is best remembered for his period as Secretary of State during the second *Truman administration, 1949–53. This was the time in which the Cold War and the policy of containment formed the template of foreign relations, and in which the *McCarthy witch-hunts whipped up a climate of hysteria and suspicion at home. Acheson, a cultured, cosmopolitan intellectual, aroused resentment and suspicion. This suspicion was fuelled by his fierce loyalty to his subordinate, Alger Hiss, who was implicated in the 'pumpkin papers' spy case. For much of his time in office Acheson was a persecuted and perpetually embattled Secretary of State at home. This markedly contrasted with his international reputation. At home he earned the disapprobation of the Republicans for his handling of America's China policy and for allegedly 'inviting' the Korean attack in a speech setting out the American defence line in the Pacific. Abroad, at least among European allies, Acheson was credited with being a principal figure behind the creation of the North Atlantic Treaty. Truman asserted that without Dean Acheson there would have been no NATO. The signing of the treaty in 1949 marked the beginning of America's first military alliance concluded in peacetime. It signalled the end of American isolationism and the beginning of its leadership of the Western world. Acheson was also a prominent figure behind the adoption of the *Marshall aid programme. He played a key role in persuading Republican congressmen to endorse aid to Greece and Turkey thereby putting flesh on the bones of the Truman doctrine.

*Eisenhower's landslide in 1952 signalled the end of Acheson's period in office but not his interest in, or influence upon, America's foreign policy. Throughout his public career Acheson was frequently vilified and was the target of smear tactics. But he was a stoic, reflecting that no man needing an atmosphere of approbation would serve as Secretary of State. He was the author of two books: *A Democrat looks at his Party* (1955); *A Citizen looks at Congress* (1957).

Adamec, Ladislav (b. Bohemia, 10 Sept. 1927)

Czech; Czechoslovak Prime Minister 1988–9

Adamec made a career within the party apparatus of the Czech Republic, where he gained the reputation of a technocrat, critical of economic inefficiency. He prospered through the support of the federal premier, Lubomír Štrougal. In March 1987 he entered the Presidium and became Prime Minister of the Czech Republic. In October 1988 he replaced Štrougal as federal premier. Adamec paid lip-service to the language of economic reform, but never did more than tinker with the existing system. In February 1989 he visited Moscow where he was pressed to take a more liberal course. When the 'Velvet Revolution' broke out in Prague in November 1989, Adamec dissociated himself from the rest of the Communist Party leadership and negotiated with the opposition. On 26 November he joined *Havel and *Dubček to address a vast crowd in Prague's Wenceslas Square. On 3 December he made a last-ditch attempt to salvage the power of the Communist Party by proposing a government headed by himself and in which the Communists would hold sixteen out of twenty-one posts. The opposition rejected this scheme. On 7 December 1989 Adamec resigned as Czechoslovak premier and was succeeded by Marián Čalfa. In March 1990 Adamec took over the newly created post of chairman of the (Communist) Party.

Adams, Grantley Hubert (b. 12 Apr. 1898; d. 28 Nov. 1971)
Barbadian; Premier 1951–8, Prime Minister of West Indies Federation 1958–62

An important figure in the regional movement towards integration, Adams was knighted in 1957. The following year the West Indies Federation of ten English-speaking territories was established and Adams became its first and only Prime Minister. Soon, however, tensions between the larger islands such as Jamaica and Trinidad and the smaller territories emerged, and Adams was accused of weak and indecisive leadership. The Federation finally collapsed in 1962 and Adams returned to national politics in Barbados, which by now was ruled by the rival Democratic Labour Party (DLP). By this time Adams was perceived as having lost much of the radicalism of the 1930s and he remained in opposition for the rest of his political life.

Barbados won its independence from Britain in 1966 with Adams on the political sidelines, but he is now commonly considered one of the fathers of Barbadian nationhood. His son, Tom Adams, took over control of the DLP which still remains the most important political party in the island.

Adenauer, Konrad (b. Cologne, 5 Jan. 1876; d. 19 Apr. 1967)
German; Chancellor of Federal Republic of Germany 1949–63, chief mayor of Cologne 1917–33

Together with *Kohl, Adenauer must rank as the most successful German politician since 1945. He led the West Germans from being the most hated and despised people of Europe in 1945, to being amongst the most repected and successful by the late 1950s. No one could have predicted his rise, or that of the future West German state, in 1945.

Adenauer was the son of a civil servant and, after graduating in law and economics, embarked on a legal career in the public service. He turned later to politics, joining the Catholic Centre Party in 1906. Elected to the Cologne city council, he was put in charge of food supplies after the outbreak of war in 1914. From 1917 to 1933 he was chief mayor of Cologne, guiding his fellow citizens through the shock of defeat, Occupation (1918–26), and then, after brief prosperity, through the crisis years to 1933. His detractors later claimed that during this period he was prepared to make too many concessions to the French and even discuss the setting up of a separate West German state. The Nazis removed Adenauer from office, pensioning him off. He lived quietly until arrested in a general round up after the 20 July 1944 bomb plot against Hitler. He remained in prison for three months.

In 1945 the Americans reinstated Adenauer as mayor but the British, who replaced them, later removed him. Although 69 he was elected chairman of the Christian Democratic Union in the British Zone in 1946. He had helped to found this party which, backed by the Catholic church, was meant to supersede the old Centre Party, and reach out beyond Catholics. It would combat the Marxism of the left, but would tackle the problems of the underprivileged. Adenauer was elected chairman of the Parliamentary Council charged with drawing up a constitution for a new German republic. Unlike the SPD's *Schumacher, he was favoured by the three Western occupying powers as a conciliator. The greater demands made by the SPD helped him to win concessions from the Allies. At 73 he took the CDU and the Bavarian CSU into the first federal election in 1949. Together CDU/CSU emerged as the biggest party with 31 per cent; the SPD achieved 29.2 per cent. Adenauer then built up a non-socialist alliance. He persuaded FDP leader *Heuss to back him as Chancellor in return for the CDU/CSU voting for Heuss as President. Adenauer scraped in as Chancellor by one vote. When in 1951 the Allies revised the Occupation regime to allow the Federal Republic to conduct foreign relations Adenauer became Foreign Minister as well as Chancellor.

Adenauer offered the Western Allies a German defence contribution, set up the Coal and Steel Community, acquiesced in the Saar being separated from Germany, made restitution to the Jews, and much more, Many Germans did not find all of this attractive. Rearmament in particular was not popular. However, economic problems were at the forefront of people's thoughts. When asked about the most important problem facing West Germany in 1951, 45 per cent said economic problems but only 18 per cent mentioned reunification. By 1955 only 28 were concerned with economics, 34 with reunification. In 1950 35 per cent of those questioned named Bismarck as the person who had done most for Germany, Hitler scored 10 per cent. By 1956 Bismarck had fallen to 27 per cent, Hitler to 8 per cent, but Adenauer was mentioned by 24 per cent. By 1967 Adenauer scored 60 per cent.

In 1955 the Federal Republic regained its sovereignty and had its own armed forces. It was recognized by almost all the Western and Third World states and even by the Soviet Union. Communist East Germany was totally isolated. On 1 January 1957 the Saar became part of the Federal Republic. Adanauer was a strong advocate of German co-operation with other West European states and was a founder member in March 1957 of the European Economic Community. West Germany was once again a respected partner abroad and at home the economy was booming. Moreover, various potentially troublesome groups, like the millions of Germans expelled from the 'lost territories' or those who fled from the GDR, were given relatively generous help and Adenauer turned a blind eye to former Nazis in the public service. The CDU/CSU reaped its electoral reward. In 1953 it gained 45.2 per cent of the vote, the SPD only 28.8 per cent. In 1957, after an election campaign built around Adenauer, the slogan 'No experiments!', and one or two dirty tricks, it won 50.2 per cent, the SPD 31.8 per cent, and the FDP 7.7. This is the only time in German history in democratic elections that one party has achieved more than 50 per cent of the vote.

Just before the 1961 elections in August, the Communists cut off East Berlin and started to erect the infamous Wall. Adenauer and the West appeared to be powerless. This weakened Adenauer's thesis that if the West were strong enough it could roll back Communism. At the 17 September election the CDU/CSU percentage vote fell to 45.3, the SPD, led by *Brandt, rose to 36.2, and the FDP to 12.8. The crushing of the East German rising in June 1953 had helped the CDU/CSU in the election of that year, the suppression of the Hungarian revolution in 1956 helped them in 1957. Unexpectedly, this time public opinion had gone the other way.

To remain in office Adenauer needed FDP support. He set a date for his retirement. Yet he still hoped to maintain his influence through election as the next President of the Federal Republic. He found little support among his colleagues for this and agreed to retire in 1963.

The Berlin crisis caused friction between Adenauer and President *Kennedy, Adenauer felt the US administration was weakening its stand and seeking an understanding with the Soviets at the cost of the Germans. Adenauer was a strong advocate of German co-operation with other West European states, and Germany was a founder member of the EC. Adenauer turned therefore to *de Gaulle's France and his last great achievement was the signing of the Franco-German Friendship Treaty (January 1963). It became the cornerstone of relations between the two states and was the culmination of Adenauer's efforts at Franco-German reconciliation. His pro-French policy caused a rift between him and his successor *Erhard, who preferred a greater balance between France, the USA, and Britain.

Agnew, Spiro (b. Baltimore, 9 Nov. 1918; d. 17 Sept. 1996)

US; Vice-President, 1968–73

Agnew was a new 'ethnic' American, born the son of a Greek immigrant father. He dropped out of Johns Hopkins University and then studied law in his spare time.

After war service he became a lawyer and entered Baltimore politics. He rose rapidly and was elected Republican Governor for Maryland in 1966. At this time he was a relatively liberal figure in the party. He achieved national prominence for his tough law and order stand in handling the riots in Baltimore which followed the killing of Martin Luther King. In his bid for the presidency in 1968 the Republican Richard *Nixon selected Agnew to be his running mate. Agnew was a compromise figure, acceptable to conservatives in the south and the border states, as well as to the liberals. Nixon was also aware of private polls which indicated that all leading candidates would on balance hurt his election chances, but Agnew would not. As Vice-President, Agnew carried the attacks to Nixon's critics over the Vietnam War and his speech writers gifted him many colourful phrases. He claimed to speak for the 'silent majority' and attacked the media as 'nattering nabobs of negativism'. These abrasive speeches pleased the right wing and articulated some concerns over the role of the media. Not long after he and Nixon were re-elected in 1972 Agnew was accused of taking bribes, or kick-backs, from contractors in Maryland. He denied the charges but in court did not contest the charges of evading federal income tax and he resigned in disgrace. Only one other Vice-President, J. C. Calhoun in the nineteenth century, had resigned, and that was because of political differences with the President.

Ahidjo, Ahmadu (b. Garoua, Cameroon, Aug. 1924; d. 30 Nov. 1989)
Cameroonian; Prime Minister 1958–60, President 1960–82

A Fula Muslim from the north of the country, Ahidjo received a secondary education and became a radio operator in the post office before his election to the Representative Assembly in 1947. In 1953 he was elected to the Assembly of the French Union in Paris. He rose to be Vice-Prime Minister in 1957 and Prime Minister in 1958, becoming President at independence on 1 January 1960. He remained in office until his voluntary retirement in 1982.

As leader of the moderate Union Camerounaise, Ahidjo was aided in his quest for power by French support against the more radical UPC, and retained close links with France. He was a strong supporter of unification with the former British Cameroons, the southern part of which voted for union with former French Cameroon in 1961. Opposition parties were subsequently banned, and the federal system was replaced by a unitary state in 1972. His style of rule became highly personal and paternalistic, but the country, aided by oil revenues, was relatively prosperous and stable.

Ahidjo's sudden retirement in 1982 was widely ascribed to a belief that he was terminally ill. Once his chosen successor, Paul Biya, started to assert his authority, Ahidjo went into exile and was associated with attempted coups in 1983 and 1984. He died in exile in Senegal.

Aitken, William Maxwell *see* BEAVERBROOK, LORD

Akayev, Askar (b. Kyzyl-Baizak, Kirghiz SSR, 10 Nov. 1944)
Kirghiz; President of the Republic of Kirghizstan 1990–1, President of independent Kirghizstan 1991–

Born on a kolkhoz, Akayev's first career was in science. A Doctor of Technological Sciences, and, from 1987, an Academician of the Kirghiz Academy of Sciences, he was a Professor at Frunze Polytechnical Institute till 1986.

He joined the CPSU in 1981, became a member of the CPSU Central Committee in 1990–1, heading the Kirghiz CP Science and Education Committee; Vice-President of the Kirghiz Republic 1987–9 and President of the Kirghiz Academy of Sciences

1989–90. He was elected to the USSR Congress of People's Deputies in 1989 and elected President of the Kirghiz Republic by the Supreme Soviet in October 1990. When Kirghizstan became independent in October 1991 he was re-elected President. A technocrat rather than the typical Communist functionary, Akayev has promoted market reform and Western trade. He made himself head of the government in February 1992 but was forced to concede the post in May 1993 due to pressure from Communist deputies opposing reform. In 1994 he secured the approval by referendum of constitutional reform reducing the powers of the legislature and increasing those of the President. But the new legislature, elected in December 1994, continued to frustrate Akayev's reforms.

Al-Assad, Hafez (b. Qardaha, Syria, 1928)

Syrian; President 1971–

A member of the minority Alawi sect, Assad joined the Ba'ath party at 16. After the party won power in 1963, he became Air Force Commander in 1965 and Defence Minister in 1966. The power struggle within the party between Dr Atassi's Marxist-orientated faction and Assad's nationalist faction was ended by the military coup of 1970 and Assad's election as President in 1971. Since then, he has ruthlessly repressed internal political opposition, particularly from religious extremists.

Assad has pursued an uncompromising foreign policy in the Middle East based on military aid and close ties with the USSR until its collapse. Its key features have been confrontation with Israel, notably in the war of October 1973 launched in conjunction with Egypt; opposition to repeated Israeli incursions into Lebanon; active support, and attempted control, of Palestinian guerrilla and terrorist groups; attempts to impose a *pax syriana* on Lebanon through the Syrian army and use of the Lebanese militia group Amal as a proxy; and bitter rivalry with Ba'athist Iraq, for example, in Syrian support for Iran in the Iran–Iraq War of 1980–8. Syria's participation in the military defeat and expulsion from Kuwait of Iraq transformed its relations with the West and the moderate Arab states in 1990–1. It opened the way to peace negotiations with Israel and the hope of regaining the Golan Heights, but a more immediate reward was to be given a free hand in Lebanon. Syria was able to suppress the revolt led by General Aoun in 1990 and to implement the 1989 Taif agreement to disarm and disband the Lebanese militia of the civil war period. The Iranian-backed Hezbollah militia was exempted as a resistance force to Israeli occupied south Lebanon and it has since been assisted by Syrian military intelligence.

Albert, Carl Bert (b. North McAlester, Oklahoma, 10 May 1908)

US; member of the US House of Representatives 1947–77, Speaker 1971–7

Carl Albert came from a relatively poor family of German descent in the mining area of Oklahoma. After attending the University of Oklahoma, he won a Rhodes Scholarship to Oxford, where he studied law. After a brief spell in F. D. *Roosevelt's Federal Housing Administration (1935–7) and in the Ohio Oil Co. (1939–40), he practised law until the Second World War broke out. During the war he served in the army until 1946 when he won a seat in the House of Representatives.

Albert was fortunate in that his first committee assignments were light, enabling him to become familiar with the workings of the whole House in depth. His attention to detail caught the eye of Speaker Sam *Rayburn and he became part of Rayburn's intimate circle. He became majority whip in 1955, and in 1962 majority leader, beating Richard Bolling for the post. As majority leader, Albert played a major role in helping Lyndon *Johnson pass his Great Society legislation. He succeeded John *McCormack as Speaker in 1971.

Albert's tactics in Congress had involved the pragmatic appreciation of the needs of individual members and an initial willingness to work with the Southern Democrats, who used their seniority to wield power in the House. Albert was, however, well aware of the pressure for structural reforms of the House which would make it more responsive to majority Democratic sentiment. As majority whip he helped revive the Democratic Caucus to discuss party strategy and as Speaker he facilitated a number of important changes which enhanced the accountability of committees to the House as a whole. Taken together these changes (which included transferring committee assignments from the Ways and Means Committee to the Steering and Policy Committee and requiring that committee chairs be approved by the Democratic Caucus) strengthened party leadership and weakened the independent power of committee chairmen. The reforms also provided the foundation for an increase in the power of the Speaker. Although Albert spearheaded some of the opposition to Republican policies over the years 1971–7, he also had to manage a divided party and found himself increasingly out of touch with its younger members who wanted more vigorous leadership. In 1977 he retired from Congress.

Aldrich, Nelson Wilmarth (b. Foster, Rhode Island, 6 Nov. 1841; d. 15 Apr. 1915)
US; member of the Rhode Island House of Representatives 1875–77, member of the US House of Representatives 1879–83, US Senator 1881–1911

Aldrich was educated at the East Greenwich academy, Rhode Island, after which he gained employment in the wholesale grocery trade with Walden and Wightman of Providence, Rhode Island. During the Civil War he enlisted in the Republican army but after only a few months' active service contracted typhoid fever and was medically discharged. Returning to his former employers, his business acumen soon gained him a partnership in the firm and election to directorships in a variety of banking, railroad, and public utility establishments in Providence.

Aldrich's success in business was complemented by a distinguished political career spanning over forty-five years. In 1869 he gained election as an independent Republican to the Providence Common Council, over which he presided 1972–3. In 1875 he was elected to the Rhode Island House of Representatives, was re-elected in 1876, and served as Speaker 1876–7. He was elected to the US House of Representatives in 1878 and 1880, but, in 1881, before the end of his second term, the Rhode Island state legislature elected him US Senator to complete the term of the late General Ambrose E. Burnside. He represented Rhode Island in the Senate for the next thirty years.

During his long senatorial career, Aldrich became a dominant figure in Republican Party politics. He was recognized as the head of a clique of fellow Republicans known as the senate 'oligarchy' which succeeded in imposing its will on Republican congressmen in both Houses, directing legislation and dictating party policy.

Aldrich's particular sphere of interest was banking and public finance. He was associated with the introduction of several controversial tariff acts at the turn of the century, and with the 1909 Act which led to a split in the Republican Party, and with drafting the 1900 Gold Standard Act. In 1910 he did not seek re-election to the Senate but remained a prominent political figure as chairman of the national monetary commission.

Aldrich was a reticent man who made few concessions to public opinion and who was scornful of political rhetoric. He built his political career on his skill as a parliamentary strategist and a complete mastery of his brief in the field of public finance.

Alfonsin, Raul Ricardo (b. Province of Buenos Aires, 13 Mar. 1927)
Argentine; President 1983–9

Born of a middle-class family, Alfonsin was educated at military academy but went on to study law. In 1963 he was elected as a deputy for the Radical Civic Union. On the left of the party, he achieved prominence under the military regime of 1976–83 as a result of his courageous stance on the human rights issue. In 1983 he was elected President, largely because he was not a *Perónist.

No economist, Alfonsin came to power at the high point of the debt crisis and his response was hesitant. Not until 1985 did he adopt a radical approach to Argentina's difficulties but his heterodox stabilization plan was too late and still too timid to appease the country's creditors or attract investment. Structural reform of the state was never contemplated and subsequent stabilization plans were no more convincing. By the time of his early departure from office Argentina was racked by hyperinflation and deep recession.

He also confronted major political difficulties, often at odds with his own party. Moreover, as the Perónist opposition recovered during the 1980s, his tenuous control of Congress disappeared. In the field of foreign affairs he initiated dialogue with Brazil and Chile but, unlike *Menem, retained the committment to non-alignment and was never strong enough politically to risk rapprochement with the UK.

His greatest achievement was in civil liberties and military relations. Despite criticism from human rights activists and rebellions by disgruntled officers, he reduced military budgets, brought the command structure under civilian control, and gaoled the junta leaders who had overseen the Dirty War of the late 1970s.

Alfonsin disappointed many but his curbing of the military was enough to earn him a place in Argentine history. Under very difficult circumstances he showed himself to be a genuine democrat.

Al-Hashimi, Hussein ibn Talal (b. Amman, Jordan, 14 Nov. 1935)
Jordanian; King 1953–

Great-grandson of Sharif Hussein of Mecca and grandson of King Abdullah, whose assassination in Jerusalem he witnessed in 1951, Hussein's father, Talal, abdicated in his favour in 1952. Hussein was enthroned in 1953. He had been educated in Britain at Harrow School and the Royal Military Academy, Sandhurst.

Hussein asserted his independence of British political influence by refusing to join the anti-Soviet Baghdad Pact in 1955, whilst remaining a stalwart anti-Communist; dismissing the British commander of the Arab Legion and power behind the throne in 1956; preventing Britain using her military bases in Jordan during the Suez conflict of 1956 and ending the 1948 Anglo-Jordanian Treaty in 1957. *Nasser's radical Arab nationalism was a major danger to his throne until 1967, especially during the pro-Nasser, pro-Soviet, Nabulsi government of 1956–7. King Hussein's dismissal of Nabulsi's government precipitated a major crisis that led to the US Sixth Fleet being dispatched to protect Jordan in 1957 and British troops being flown into Amman in 1958. Hussein now realigned Jordan with American Cold War policy in the Middle East, although he never formally endorsed the Eisenhower Doctrine. In June 1967, Hussein opened a third front in the Arab–Israeli war, although this was against US policy and Jordan's material interests. The outcome was disastrous: Israel captured the West Bank and East Jerusalem from Jordan, and the throne, which he had joined the war to protect, was now threatened by the PLO and resulted in the civil war of 1970. After surrendering his claims to the West Bank in 1988, and following the Oslo Accords between Israel and the PLO in 1993, Hussein ended the state of war with Israel, which had existed since 1948, at the White House, in July 1994.

Alia, Ramiz (b. 18 Oct. 1925)

Albanian; head of state 1982–92

Alia is the son of poor Muslim parents from the Gheg clan who fled Kosovo after the Balkan Wars. During the Second World War he fought in the Communist guerrilla organization, the Army of National Liberation, and attained the rank of lieutenant-colonel. In 1949 his political career within the Albanian Labour Party (ALP—the Communist party) was advanced when he became a member of the Central Committee. From 1955 to 1958 he was Minister for Education and Culture. Then he moved to the party post of Central Committee secretary with responsibility for the Agitation and Propaganda Department. In 1966 he was elected as alternate member of the Politburo. At the end of 1981 Albania's leader, Enver *Hoxha decided upon Alia as his heir instead of Mehmet *Shehu. In 1982 he became a full member of the Politburo, and at the same time chairman of the People's Assembly, making him head of state.

On Hoxha's death in 1985 Alia became party First Secretary, with powers as great as his predecessor: he was head of state, head of the party, and Commander-in-Chief. He adopted a less strident style than Hoxha and displayed greater pragmatism in his approach to foreign affairs, improving contacts with the states of Western Europe and the Balkans and restoring diplomatic relations with the Soviet Union and the United States. In public Alia seemed more interested in the Albanian minority in Yugoslavia than Hoxha, but in practice continued his predecessor's policy of non-intervention in Yugoslavia's internal affairs. At home, Alia initially seemed set against reform. He was not able to prevent the militancy of the Yugoslav Albanians from stimulating popular demands inside Albania, nor was he able to improve the disastrous state of the economy. Even limited change was a threat to Alia, who owed his position to Hoxha. It was only after the fall of *Ceauşescu's regime in Romania at the end of 1989 that Alia took measures to prevent the growth of unrest in Albania. In May 1990 he introduced limited economic reforms and in December 1990 conceded a multi-party system of government. In March 1991 the ALP defeated four opposition parties in free elections. Though Alia was defeated in his Tirana constituency, the next month parliament appointed him President. Alia and the ALP were not able to maintain their position in the face of continuing public demands for political change and the deterioration of the economy. The Communist government fell in June 1991 and was replaced by a multi-party coalition. When the Democratic Party won an outright majority in the elections of March 1992, Alia resigned as President.

Aliyev, Geydar Aliyevich (b. Azerbaijan, 1923)

Azeri; First Secretary of Azerbaijan 1968–89, President of Azerbaijan 1993–

Aliyev was the son of Azeri parents. By the 1960s he had a prospering career in the Azerbaijani KGB, serving as its Deputy Chairman for three years under *Brezhnev's corrupt friend, S. K. Tsvigun, eventually succeeding him as Chairman. In 1968 Aliyev gained credit for a successful anti-corruption campaign which brought him the highest Republican Party post—First Secretary of Azerbaijan. Thereafter, Aliyev's career prospered at the all-Union level. In 1971 he became a full member of the Central Committee of the CPSU and in 1976 was elected candidate member of the Politburo. Yuri *Andropov made him a full member of the Politburo in 1982. He was one of the few non-Slavs to attain such high rank in the Soviet Union. His fortunes deteriorated under *Gorbachev, who removed him from the Politburo in 1987, accusing him of corruption. Possibly his main crime was resistance to reform. His political career appeared at an end in April 1989 when he announced his 'voluntary' retirement from the Central Committee.

Aliyev returned to politics after the break-up of the Soviet Union. In October 1993 he was elected President of Azerbaijan by a vote of 98.8 per cent in an uncontested election. He was unable to improve Azerbaijan's performance in the war with Armenia. He defeated an attempted coup in March 1995, after which he banned all opposition parties.

Al-Khomeini, Al-Mussavi Ruhollah (b. Khomein, Persia, 25 Sept. 1902; d. 3 Jun. 1989)

Iranian; Leader-Guardian 1979–89

Khomeini was born a *Sayeed* (descendant of Prophet Mohammed), the son and grandson of mullahs. Educated at Qom's theological seminary, he became a distinguished religious scholar and *mujtahid* (authority on divine law), later teaching there. His first major work, published in 1941, was a factor in the murder of the anticlerical author, Kashravi, by an Islamist terrorist in 1945. Hojjatoleslam Khomeini led a delegation of mullahs to the Shah (*Pahlavi) to ask for the terrorist's pardon. During the 1950s, Khomenei rose to the rank of Ayatollah. He had a large and devoted following, including *Hashemi-Rafsanjani, Khamenei, Montazeri, and Motahari, which formed the Islamic revolutionary movement under his leadership. Khomeini launched their campaign against the Shah's regime in 1962 by assailing its new anti-Islamic electoral legislation. By now convinced that no compromise with the Shah was possible, Grand Ayatollah Khomeini publicly denounced him, attacked his 'White Revolution' for conflicting with Islamic values and issued a *fatwa* forbidding collaboration with his regime. He was arrested in the June riots of 1963, rearrested after anti-American agitation in 1964, then exiled for the next fifteen years.

By now Khomeini was a charismatic figure who used his period of exile to transform Shi'i Islam from quietism into an activist political movement, to devise a revolutionary system of Islamic government and launch a revolution to overthrow the Shah. Many militant followers recognized his charisma by calling him *Imam* Khomeini—suggesting a divinely guided, infallible leader—from 1970 onwards. In 1977, Khomeini issued a public *fatwa* 'deposing' the Shah and 'abrogating' the constitution. He also sent a secret message to Motahari and the radical mullahs ordering the revolution to begin. The first mass demonstration—the principal revolutionary tactic—took place at Qom in January 1978. Khomeini's expulsion to France in 1978 gave access to the world's media, which he skilfully manipulated to discredit the Shah and undermine the legitimacy of his regime. In January the Shah fled, Khomeini formed the Islamic Revolutionary Committee—the provisional government—and returned to Iran in February 1979. The system of Islamic government devised by Khomeini in 1969, and centred on the guardianship of the people by the just and pious jurisconsult in the absence of the occulted twelfth *Imam*, was established by the constitution of the Islamic Republic of Iran of 1979. Ayatollah Khomeini held this guardian-leadership, with its transnational applicability, throughout the war with Iraq until his death in 1989.

Allende Gossens, **Salvador** (b. Santiago 26 July 1908; d. 11 Sept. 1973)

Chilean; President 1970–3, Senator 1945–70

Allende qualified as a surgeon in 1932. One of the founding members of the breakaway Socialist Party. He was elected deputy for Valparaíso and Quillota in 1937. In 1939 he served as Health Minister during the Aguirre Cerda administration, and again under the vice-presidency of Gerónimo Méndez, 1941. From 1945 until 1970 Allende remained a Senator, representing the southernmost provinces and then Valparaíso and Aconcagua. He was presidential candidate on four occasions from 1952. In 1952 he achieved 5.27 per cent of the vote. In 1958 as candidate of the

Revolutionary Front of Popular Action—a coalitation of Socialists and Communists—Allende was second—by only 30,000 votes—to the right's Alessandri. In 1964 he registered 38.93 per cent, losing to *Frei's 56.09 per cent.

Allende finally became President in 1970, with the backing of Popular Unity—a coalition of left-wing forces and the Radical Party—obtaining 36.30 per cent. The right's candidate Allessandri polled 34.9 per cent, the Christian Democrat, Tomic 27.8 per cent. This narrow plurality meant that only a controversial deal with the reluctant Christian Democrats enabled Allende to be ratified as President by Congress.

A Marxist, Allende believed structural reforms including extensive nationalization—starting with the copper industry—and land reform would lay the groundwork for a transition from capitalism to socialism. However, this strategy of changing the constitution by constitutional means divided and weakened the left. The opposition forces—who controlled the mass media and received financial backing from the anti-Communist US government—united. A wave of strikes and extreme levels of polarization served as the pretext for the military coup on 11 September 1973. Regardless of whether Allende died during the bombing of the palace or committed suicide, he remains for many a martyr to the unique experiment in the peaceful road to socialism.

Al-Qadhafi, Muammar Muhammad (b. 1942)

Libyan; President 1977–

Qadhafi was born to a family of desert nomads and expelled from secondary school for pro-*Nasserite political agitation. In 1963, he joined Benghazi Military Academy and launched the Nasserite Free Officers movement to infiltrate the army in 1964. As a junior officer, he led the movement in a bloodless coup which overthrew King Idris in 1969 and headed the ruling Revolutionary Command Council.

In line with the 'third universal theory' of his Green Book, Qadhafi reconstructed Libyan political, economic, and military systems, ostensibly on direct democracy principles and Koranic tenets, to produce the Libyan People's Jamahiriya. From 1975, political power was wielded by People's Congresses and People's Committees at all levels of Libyan society and institutions like the Cabinet and RCC were abolished. In 1979, embassies and diplomats were eliminated and replaced by 'people's bureaux'. The armed and police forces were abolished in 1988 in favour of popular organs and remaining state institutions, including the security apparatus, were similarly abolished and replaced later.

Qadhafi's foreign policy is subversive and pan-Arab. It includes: attempted unions and mergers with Arab states, of which one, the 1989 Arab Maghreb (economic) Union, succeeded; subversive intervention in Egypt, Sudan, and Chad; sponsorship of international terrorism by supplying arms, training, money, and sanctuary to insurgents and liquidation of political opponents in Europe. Since 1992, Libya has been subject to UN economic sanctions over the 1988 bombing of PanAm flight 103 over Lockerbie. A mounting Islamist challenge to Qadhafi's nationalist regime began in 1989.

Al-Sadr, Musa Sayyid (b. Qom, 1928; d. 31 Aug. 1978)

Lebanese; *Imam* (Guide) 1959–78

Al-Sadr was born in Iran's holy city, Qom, the son and grandson of Ayatollahs and a *sayyed* (descendant of the Prophet through the seventh Imam).

In 1959, he was appointed judge at Tyre for members of Lebanon's largest, though oppressed, confessional community, the Shia. During Shihab's presidency (1958–64), he campaigned in support of presidential attempts to redistribute national resources to the neglected Shi'i south, and emerged on the national scene as a reformer and dazzling speaker, with aspirations to organize and lead the Lebanese Shia. Al-Sadr's election as first president of the official Higher Shia Council in 1969 made him effective head of this Lebanese community. Simultaneously, his followers and fellow mullahs began to recognize his religio-political charisma by calling him *Imam*, a title imbued with messianic expectations. Throughout the 1970s, Al-Sadr achieved the revolutionary political mobilization of the hitherto quiescent Shia through his Movement of the Disinherited. When civil war broke out in 1975, he formed the Shi'i militia, Amal (Hope), with Libyan finance, to protect the Shia community against other confessional militias. After Syrian intervention in the civil war in 1976, Al-Sadr secured *Assad's patronage by declaring his Alawi sect to be Muslims. Amal became Syria's proxy in Lebanon thereafter. In August 1978, Al-Sadr vanished in mysterious circumstances while on a visit to Libya, allegedly killed on *Qadhafi's orders. He left a twofold legacy: the belief of many followers that he would 'return', and a factional split in Amal, with one faction, Islamic Amal, seceding to become the joint founder of Lebanon's *Hezbollah* in 1982.

Al-Said, Qaboos bin Said (b. Salalah, Oman, 18 Nov. 1940)

Omani; Sultan 1970–

From the age of 16, Qaboos was educated in Britain, first privately, then at the Royal Military Academy, Sandhurst. He subsequently served on an operational tour of duty with the British army in Germany.

On return to Oman, his domineering and reactionary father kept him a virtual prisoner in the southern city of Salalah for the next six years, while a major insurgency by *Nasserist guerrillas raged in the surrounding Dhofar region. Sultan Said bin Taimur kept Muscat and Oman an isolated and economically backward society, in which slavery was still common and oil revenues were spent exclusively on defence. To defeat the uprising and modernize Oman required a change in government. To that end Qaboos deposed his father in a coup of July 1970 with British assistance and to general public acclaim. Oman's armed forces were supplemented by Iran and Britain, military assistance was received from Jordan, Saudi Arabia, and the Emirates, and an astute policy which encouraged defections from the rebel forces was pursued. The insurgency was defeated in 1975 and the rebels pardoned.

Since 1970, increased oil revenues have been used to modernize Oman rapidly, but in a different way from that of other Gulf oil states. Limited oil reserves are conserved for as long as possible; after defence expenditure, oil revenues are used primarily to educate and employ a youthful population; modernization is pursued to ensure no adverse affects on Islam, on Oman's Islamic traditions and culture, on the natural environment and on external and internal security. In 1991, Sultan Qaboos established a Majlis al-Shoura (National Assembly) which has become the most vigorous and effective of all such political bodies in the Arabian peninsula.

Al-Sa'ud, Abd al-Aziz (also 'called Ibn Sa'ud) (b. Riyadh, c.1880; d. 9 Nov. 1953)

Arabian; ruler of Nejd 1902–21, Sultan of Nejd 1921–32, King of Hijaz 1926–32, King of Saudi Arabia 1932–53

As a boy, Abd al-Aziz was exiled to Kuwait after the deposition of the ruling Al-Saud dynasty of central Arabia (Nejd) in 1891. In 1902 he led a small, but daring, raiding party which recaptured Riyadh and restored the dynasty. By 1914, Ibn Sa'ud exercised full control over all the Nejd and the Hasa coastal area near Bahrain, having defeated the rival Al-Rashid dynasty and their Turkish allies in battle. His final conquests in northern and central Arabia were made in 1921, again at the expense of the House of

Al-Rashid. By then a new and bitter rivalry with the ruling Hashemite dynasty of the western region of Arabia (Hijaz) had arisen. When the king, Sharif Hussein of Mecca, claimed the vacant Caliphate in 1924, Ibn Sa'ud led his incensed and militant Ikhwan warriors to conquer Hijaz and depose him. After Ibn Sa'ud assumed the throne of Hijaz in January 1926, he ruled it separately from the Nejd for the next seven years. Britain recognized his sovereignty in the Treaty of Jeddah of 1927. A rebellion by the Ikhwan from 1928 to 1930, and a smaller revolt in 1932 instigated by Emir Abdullah, the Hashemite ruler of Transjordan, proved the only significant threats to his throne during the period before he merged the kingdom of Hijaz with the sultanate of Nejd to form the Kingdom of Saudi Arabia in September 1932. Thereafter, the priorities of King Abd al-Aziz were to unify fully the new kingdom, secure its economic development, and rescue it from acute financial difficulties—the latter being finally achieved when substantial revenues from crude petroleum production accrued after 1945.

Amin, Idi (b. West Nile, Uganda, 1925)

Ugandan; army commander 1966–71, head of state 1971–9

A member of the Kakwa ethnic group from north-west Uganda, Idi Amin Dada received little formal education and remained largely illiterate. He joined the colonial army in 1946, fought against Mau Mau in Kenya, and was heavyweight boxing champion of Uganda 1951–60. He became an officer as part of the Africanization of the army, and his close association with President *Obote after independence in 1962 led to rapid promotion. Obote used Amin to suppress his domestic opponents, but came to fear him, and was about to replace him when Amin launched a pre-emptive coup in January 1971.

Despite benefiting from widespread dissatisfaction with Obote's rule, Amin soon lost support and ruled almost entirely by terror and coercion. Externally, he became a symbol of brutality, powerfully contributing to a declining sympathy for African rulers and to demands for human rights in Africa. Domestically, an estimated 300,000 Ugandans were killed by his government, and Amin was personally associated with the murder of opponents who included the Anglican Archbishop. The economy collapsed, not least as the result of the expulsion in 1972 of the Asian business community.

His eventual fall resulted from an ill-advised invasion of neighbouring Tanzania in 1978. Despite armed Libyan assistance, his army collapsed in the face of a Tanzanian counter-attack, aided by Ugandan exiles; in April 1979 he fled, first to Libya and then to Saudi Arabia, leaving Uganda in complete shambles.

Anderson, John (b. Edinburgh, 8 July 1882; d. 4 Jan. 1958)

British; Governor of Bengal 1932–7, Home Secretary 1939–40, Chancellor of the Exchequer 1943–5; KCB 1919, Viscount Waverley 1952

Educated at George Watson's College, Edinburgh University, and the University of Leipzig, Anderson had a distinguished career as a civil servant before being called on to serve in government. He rose through the ranks of the civil service, becoming permanent secretary at the Home Office in 1922 at the age of 40. At the Home Office, he was responsible for the preparations for handling the General Strike. After ten years in the post, he was appointed Governor of Bengal, serving five years (1932–7) before returning to England. That might have marked the high point of his career, but the possibility of war resulted in him being brought into government, as Lord Privy Seal in 1938, to handle preparations for air-raid precautions. He entered parliament as a national member, sitting for the Scottish Universities. He was among the ministers who in September 1939 pressed *Chamberlain for a declaration of war following the German invasion of Poland. On the outbreak of war, Anderson was appointed Home

Secretary and Minister of Home Security. When *Churchill became Prime Minister in 1940, he was brought into the War Cabinet as Lord President of the Council and chaired a committee that was largely responsible for civil administration. In 1943, he succeeded Kingsley *Wood as Chancellor of the Exchequer, serving until the end of the parliament. He remained an MP until 1950.

Described by Charles Loch Mowat as 'perhaps the ablest of a distinguished generation of civil servants', Anderson became an indispensable figure at a time when professional expertise was necessary for the prosecution of war. His name was to become a household word with the construction of 'Anderson' air-raid shelters. Though never a party man, and lacking an independent political base, he became a powerful figure during the unique circumstances of war. In 1945, Churchill advised the King that, in the event of Churchill and *Eden both dying, he should send for Anderson.

Anderson, John Bayard (b. Rockford, Illinois, 15 Feb. 1922)
US; Illinois State Attorney 1956–60, member of the US House of Representatives 1961–81, Independent presidential candidate 1980

The son of Swedish immigrants, John Anderson grew up in Illinois and attended college in Rockford and at the University of Illinois, Urbana. His education was interrupted by war service in Europe from 1943 to 1945; but he continued his legal education after the war at Urbana and at Harvard and was admitted to the Illinois bar. Although he began legal practice in Rockford, he spent 1952–5 in West Berlin as adviser to the American Commissioner for Germany. In 1956 he ran successfully for the position of State Attorney of Winnebago County and in 1960 he was elected to the House of Representatives and held the seat until 1980, when he did not seek re-election.

Anderson started his political career on the conservative wing of the Republican Party; but, although he remained a fiscal conservative, he became more liberal on foreign policy issues and civil liberties.

In 1969 Anderson became chairman of the House Republican Conference. Increasingly, however, he found himself out of step with the mainstream Republican Party and its leadership. A strongly religious man, he deplored Richard *Nixon's lack of ethics and was among the first in Congress to call for his resignation after the Watergate tapes were released. Yet he was also uncomfortable with the right-wing style of Ronald *Reagan and in 1980 sought the Republican nomination, basing his campaign on a dispassionate appraisal of the issues and an unwillingness to pander either to party orthodoxy or popular opinion. (He was, for example, an advocate of a gasoline tax to cut dependency on Arab oil.)

Anderson's bid for the Republican nomination failed in a year in which the party was swept by the Reagan crusade. The response to Anderson's serious and principled approach persuaded him to mount an independent bid for the presidency by building a coalition of independent voters, moderate Republicans, and Democrats disenchanted with Jimmy *Carter. Anderson's campaign generated much media interest and enthusiasm among activists. Although Anderson came third and failed to carry a single state, his 6.61 per cent of the vote underlined the depth of dissatisfaction with the two major parties in 1980.

After his failed presidential bid, Anderson held teaching positions at several American universities. He also wrote a number of books, including *Between Two Worlds: A Congressman's Choice* (1970) which highlighted the importance of born-again Christianity in Anderson's life.

Andreotti, Giulio (b. Rome, 14 Jan. 1919)
Italian; Prime Minister 1972–91

The son of a teacher, Andreotti graduated in law at the University of Rome in 1942, and was president of FUCI, the students' branch of Catholic Action, from 1942 to 1945. In this post he succeeded Aldo Moro, another future leader of the Christian Democrats (DC), and his period of office coincided with that of Mgr. G. B. Montini, the future Pope Paul VI, as chaplain appointed by the Vatican to FUCI. He had already met Alcide *De Gasperi, the first general secretary of the emerging Christian Democrat Party, and became his personal assistant. Giulio Andreotti was the youngest deputy elected to the Constituent Assembly in 1946, and was elected to the Chamber of Deputies in the Rome constituency in every election from 1948 to 1987. He was under-secretary in the Prime Minister's office during De Gasperi's prime ministerships (1947–53), a position he used to full advantage to establish his own independent centre-right faction known as 'Primavera' (springtime). From then on he was hardly ever out of office, with a total of over thirty individual ministerial or prime ministerial appointments in his entire career. Until 1972 he was usually either Minister of Defence or had one of the Finance portfolios. In 1972, he headed a short-lived centre-right coalition, and then demonstrated his versatility by leading the minority DC governments which ruled with Communist support during the 'historic compromise' period (1976–9). He re-emerged during the 1980s as Foreign Minister in the governments led by the Socialist Bettino *Craxi. His long influence over Italian politics ended when in 1993 the Senate voted to remove his immunity from prosecution on charges of complicity with the Mafia, charges which he strenuously denied.

Andreotti never sought to dominate the course of events, whether in office or out, and was regarded as a supreme interpreter of the party system, not as a policy initiator. His power rested on three main factors: his unrivalled control of his party faction with its base in the region around Rome, his skill in working with the balance of power within the governing coalition, and his range of contacts abroad, especially in the USA, for whose foreign policy community he was an essential point of reference on Italian developments. Andreotti, who was renowned for his oracular style and dry humour, also found time to establish a reputation as an author of mystery novels, cultured biographies, and political commentaries. He was as representative of the post-war Italian Republic as his predecessor Giovanni *Giolitti was of the Italian Liberal state, and as controversial.

Andropov, Yuri Vladimirovich (b. Nagutskaya, 15 June 1914; d. Moscow, 9 Feb. 1984)

Russian; chairman of the KGB 1967–82, General Secretary of the Communist Party of the Soviet Union 1982–4

Andropov was born in the Stavropol area of southern Russia, the son of a railway clerk. He left school at the age of 16, but continued to study part-time at the Petrazavodsk Institute and at the Party High School, then from 1932 to 1936 was educated at a technical institute. His political career started in 1936 when he became an official of the Young Communist League (Comsomol). In 1940 he was made First Secretary of the newly formed Karelo-Finnish Republic. During the Second World War he was employed in organizational work on the Karelian front.

Andropov moved to Moscow as a party official in 1951. In 1954 he became Soviet Ambassador to Hungary. He warned of the impending uprising, and was instrumental in removing *Rákosi. He was closely involved in the suppression of the uprising and gave strong support to the new Hungarian leader, *Kádár. From 1957 to 1967 he was Secretary of the Central Committee responsible for relations with the Soviet Bloc parties. In 1967 he became chairman of the KGB and candidate member of the Politburo. This move was planned by his rival *Suslov, in order to remove him from the Central Committee Secretariat. In 1973 he was made a full member of the Politburo. In May 1982, shortly after Suslov's death, Andropov returned to the

Central Committee, and started an anti-corruption campaign which undermined *Brezhnev's faction. On 12 November 1982 he succeeded Brezhnev as General Secretary. His leadership of the USSR was marked by the deterioration of relations with the USA and by an unsuccessful attempt to improve the economy. After February 1983 Andropov's health deteriorated rapidly. He died of kidney failure.

Ántáll, József (b. Budapest, 8 Apr. 1932; d. Budapest, 12 Dec. 1993)
Hungarian; President of the Hungarian Democratic Forum 1989–93, Prime Minister 1990–3

During the Second World War Ántáll's father, also named József, was government commissioner for refugees. He became famous for his role in saving the lives of hundreds of Jews. The father's heroism was later an advantage to the son. The younger József Ántáll worked as historian and archivist in Budapest in the early 1950s. He led a revolutionary committee during the Hungarian Uprising of 1956, and was active in the short-lived revival of the Smallholders' Party. *Kádár's regime arrested him in 1957 and banned him from teaching until 1963. Ántáll played no role in politics until the late 1980s when the Kádár regime began to crumble. In 1989 he became President of the Hungarian Democratic Forum (MDF), a broad-based party which drew much of its support from the countryside. It appealed to Hungarian nationalist feeling. By a narrow margin, the MDF did best of Hungary's three main parties in the elections of 1990 and Ántáll became the Prime Minister of a coalition government.

Ántáll was opposed to economic shock therapy on the lines of Poland's *Balcerowicz Plan. But he had no clear alternative policies and during his leadership, Hungarian GNP declined. In the summer of 1990, Ántáll and the MDF supported the introduction of a Catholic religious education into the national curriculum. This led to conflict with the other coalition parties, since only three-quarters of the Hungarian population were Catholics. By 1991 Ántáll was receiving criticism for his authoritarian style, though this contrasted with his uncharismatic presence. Conflict over their powers erupted between him and Hungary's President, Árpád Göncz, who belonged to the opposing party, the Alliance of Free Democrats.

Despite failing health, Ántáll skilfully dealt with the problem of the extreme nationalist wing of the MDF, which had taken up the issue of the Humgarian minorities in Romania and Slovakia. In January 1993 he was re-elected party chairman of the MDF. In June 1993 he brought about the expulsion from the party of his nationalist rival, István Csurka.

Antonescu, Ion (b. Pitešti, 14 June 1882; d. Bucharest, 1 June 1946)
Romanian; dictator 1940–4

Antonescu started a career as a professional soldier, rising to the rank of colonel during the First World War. In the 1920s he was military attaché in Rome and London. From 1934 to 1938 he was Minister of War and was briefly Chief of the General Staff in 1937. Antonescu was a supporter of Romanian Fascism and was close to the Iron Guard. In 1938 *Carol II imprisoned him for plotting against his pro-French government. He was released in 1939 and made premier as a result of the rise of German power in Europe. He was unable to prevent Germany's award of a large part of Transylvania to Hungary in 1940. In Autumn 1940 he drove Carol into exile and set himself up as a Fascist-style dictator, and in June 1941 declared war on the Soviet Union. When Axis forces took Odessa that October, it was renamed 'Antonescu'. During the Stalingrad campaign in 1942–3, the Romanian army was decimated, and Antonescu's position at home deteriorated. In August 1944, King Michael overthrew

Antonescu in a coup which led to Romania's change of sides in the war. In May 1946 he was tried for war crimes and shot.

Aquino, Corazón Maria (b. Tarlac Province, 25 Jan. 1933)
Philippine; President (1986–92)

The daughter of a wealthy sugar baron, Aquino obtained a degree in mathematics from Mount St Vincent College, New York. She married Benigno Aquino in 1956. Benigno Aquino became the main opponent and challenger to the rule of President Ferdinand *Marcos (1965–86) in the Philippines. He was imprisoned on charges of murder and subversion (1972–80).

After Benigno Aquino was assassinated at Manila Airport (August 1983), Mrs Aquino became the main focus of discontent against the Marcos regime. In the February 1986 elections the opposition put forward Mrs Aquino as their joint candidate. Although the National Assembly declared Marcos the victor, widespread vote-rigging and open defiance of the regime led to a political stalemate. Mrs Aquino united the disparate support and obtained the backing of the Roman Catholic Church and powerful factions within the army. Seen as the moral victor of the elections, she launched a series of non-violent civil disturbances that eventually climaxed in the exile of Marcos and the installation of Mrs Aquino as President. Although Marcos did not formally relinquish the presidency, the legitimacy of Aquino's succession was not contested, even by Marcos's former supporters.

Mrs Aquino's presidency marked the beginning of transition from authoritarian rule to democracy. She survived seven coup attempts, the most significant of which was in December 1989 when the intervention of US planes from the Clark base prevented the capture of the presidential palace.

The hopes of social reform, however, remained mainly unfulfilled. Land reform became bogged down in bureaucratic delay and landlord opposition. Some steps were taken to improve health care, schools, and roads and, though these were effective in undermining Communist insurgency, the real changes came through economic improvement as a result of liberalization, the dismantling of Marcos's crony capitalism, and increasing trade and commercial links with Asian countries.

Opposition to Aquino accused her of being naive and indecisive. Corruption continued to be widespread and towards the end of her tenure Mrs Aquino faced more than 100 charges ranging from money smuggling to theft. She decided not to stand for re-election in the May 1992 elections and her nominated successor, Fidel Ramos, successfully fought the campaign.

Mrs Aquino came into politics as result of an accident but played a critical role in the democratic transition of the Philippines from authoritarianism. Her importance lies in neutralizing the army and providing the framework for competitive party elections.

Arafat, Yasser Mohammed (b. 24 Aug. 1929)
Palestinian; chairman of PLO 1969– , President of Palestine National Authority 1996–

Arafat studied engineering at Cairo University 1952–6 and co-founded Al-Fatah (Conquest) in 1956 with *Nasser's support. Abu Amar (Arafat's *nom de guerre*) established his political and military credentials through Fatah's battle against Israeli forces at Karameh in 1968. In 1969, Arafat became chairman of the PLO. Its goal, according to the Palestine National Charter of 1968, was the liberation of Palestine and the destruction of Israel through armed struggle. After Arab defeats in the wars of 1967 and 1973, the guerrilla and terrorist groups of the PLO intensified armed struggle against Israel, by cross-border raids from Lebanon and Jordan and such operations as hijacking an aircraft to Entebbe in 1976. A major setback occurred in September 1970 when the PLO was expelled from Jordan to Lebanon, after provoking civil war. A second devastating setback occurred in 1982, when Israel invaded Lebanon in an attempt to eradicate the PLO. Although the PLO's legitimacy had been recognized since 1974 by the Arab Heads of State and by the United Nations, Arafat now lost most Arab support and the impact of Palestinian armed struggle dwindled. He was forced to rethink the fundamentals of PLO strategy. Early in 1988, Arafat took over the organization of the Palestinian *intifada* (uprising) and, at the UN's Geneva meeting of 1988, he announced the PLO's recognition of Israel and abandonment of terrorism. This paved the way for the Baker peace plan of 1989 and the US-sponsored peace process—interrupted by the Gulf War—which culminated in the Oslo Peace Accords of 1993. Under these, Israel began a staged withdrawal from the West Bank and Gaza in 1994, and limited Palestinian self-rule was achieved, within a highly precarious peace process.

Arbenz Guzmán, Lt. Col. Jacobo (b. Quetzaltenango, Guatemala, 1913; d. Mexico, 1970)

Guatemalan; President 1951–4

Jacobo Arbenz was the organizer of the *coup d'état* which overthrew the short-lived successor of the dictator General *Ubico, General Federico Ponce, on 20 October 1944. Minister of War in the elected government of Juan José *Arévalo from December 1944, Arbenz was elected to succeed Arévalo in 1950. In 1951 he embarked on a more radical programme of nationalist reforms than those of his predecessor, including agrarian reform, which was passed by Congress in 1952. This benefited about 100,000 peasants and affected just over 1,000 plantations, including those of the US transnational United Fruit Co. Some 387,000 acres were expropriated from United Fruit and compensation of $1 million was offered, based on 1952 tax returns. The company, backed by the US State Department, rejected the government's offer.

The USA regarded Arbenz as a 'puppet' manipulated by the Communists. However, although a number of Communists held positions of high office in his administration, his Salvadorean wife, María Villanova, was perhaps closer to the Guatemalan Communist Party (PGT) than Arbenz himself. Trade union organization grew under Arbenz: by 1954 50 per cent of the 600,000 workers and peasants were organized. United Fruit conspired with the CIA, the US State Department, and internal opponents of Arbenz to overthrow him. In June 1954 a US-backed rebel force, led by Colonel Castillo Armas, invaded the country from neighbouring Honduras. However, the main military action was bombing raids by US planes. Arbenz capitulated when army representatives demanded his resignation. His later years were spent in Cuba and Mexico, actively seeking democratization in Guatemala. In 1995 his remains were returned to Guatemala and buried with full state honours.

Arévalo Bermejo, Juan José (b. 1904)

Guatemalan; President 1945–51

Prior to the *Ubico dictatorship, Arévalo worked for the ministry of education. In 1934 he obtained a Ph.D. in education from the University of La Plata, Argentina. He taught at several Argentine universities and founded and directed the Pedagogical Institute in San Luis. Supported by a new political group, the Revolutionary Action Party (PAR), Arévalo was elected President in December 1944, following the overthrow of Ubico's successor, General Ponce. He took office on 15 March 1945.

Arévalo described his politics as 'spiritual socialism', although he was a confirmed anti-Communist (the party was banned under his administration). Reforms carried out under the new constitution included a labour code which afforded the right to strike to urban and rural workers and provided a series of measures for cases of unfair dismissal; health and education programmes; a social security system; a hospital building programme; and some attempts to integrate the indigenous population (over 60 per cent of the national population).

However, although the constitution provided for the takeover of idle land, Arévalo did nothing to reform the highly unequal system of land tenure, a source of mounting discontent. Nonetheless, he was labelled a Communist by domestic landowners. In 1951, he handed over power to his elected successor, Jacobo *Arbenz. Following the overthrow of Arbenz in 1954 he was exiled to Mexico, returning in March 1963 to stand in the presidential elections of that year. The poll was pre-empted by a coup staged by Defence Minister Colonel Enrique Peralta Azurdia against President Miguel Ydígoras Fuentes and the elections were subsequently cancelled. Arévalo was appointed ambassador to France in 1970 but replaced in 1972.

Aristide, Jean-Bertrand (b. Haiti, 15 Jul. 1953)

Haitian; President 1991–6

Aristide trained as a priest and studied in Israel and Europe before working at the Salesian St Jean Bosco church in a slum area of Port-au-Prince in 1975. In the mid-1980s he became an outspoken critic of the *Duvalier dictatorship and was widely identified with the *ti legliz*, the Haitian version of radical liberation theology. His political stance included attacks on Haiti's mulatto élite, US 'imperialism', and the army as well as the dictatorship itself. His fiery sermons and radio broadcasts were an important factor in mobilizing opposition to Baby Doc Duvalier who finally fled Haiti in February 1986.

In the aftermath of the dictatorship, a number of military regimes succeeded one another, and Aristide remained a central figure in the fledgling democratization movement. He survived three assassination attempts from paramilitary forces, enhancing his popular stature. He was expelled from the Salesian Order in 1988 for alleged 'incitement to class struggle' and withdrew to run an orphanage. In 1990, having previously shunned electoral politics, he was nominated as presidential candidate for a left-wing coalition and won the December election with 67 per cent of the vote.

Aristide's period in office was in many ways a failure. Despite his radical campaign pledges, little was achieved to remedy Haiti's poverty or social injustice. His coalition broke up, he was unable to enact significant legislation due to a hostile congress and he was accused of tolerating mob rule among his *lavalas* ('landslide') supporters. In September 1991, after seven months in power, he was ousted in a coup and exiled first to Venezuela and then to the USA. A period of three years in exile ensued, as the USA tried to find a solution to the 'Haitian problem' which would sideline Aristide or at least reduce his influence. After months of abortive negotiations with the *de facto* military regime in Port-au-Prince, the Clinton administration finally led a UN-endorsed occupation, designed to return Aristide to the presidency. A combination of international pressure and the fear of escalating illegal immigration from Haiti into Florida were the main factors in forcing Aristide's return. Both the Bush and Clinton administrations had made it clear that they were suspicious of Aristide himself and would much prefer another Haitian leader.

Despite calls for him to extend his presidency, Aristide agreed to stand down in February 1996. His remaining months in office were dominated by the US occupation of Haiti and allegations among his more radical supporters that he had made concessions to the World Bank and IMF on economic restructuring in return for US military support.

In January 1996 Aristide married, having first renounced the priesthood. He remains enormously popular among the majority of Haitians, despite his chequered record in office, and is a real contender for a future presidency, should Haiti's chaotic political culture allow it.

Arnold, Karl (b. Herrlishöfen, Württemberg, 23 Mar. 1901; d. 29 June 1958)
German; Minister-President of North Rhine-Westphalia 1947–56

For many years Arnold was seen as the potential challenger to *Adenauer on the left of the Christian Democratic Union (CDU). Arnold was a shoemaker who rose to lead the Christian trade unions in Weimar Germany. He was persecuted by the Nazis and imprisoned after the abortive bomb plot against *Hitler on 20 July 1944. He survived the war and took part in founding the CDU and the trade unions. In 1946 he was elected chief mayor of Düsseldorf and led the CDU to victory in 1947 in the first post-war elections in North Rhine-Westphalia (NRW) and was elected Minister-President.

Against the opposition of Adenauer he was elected the first President of the Bundesrat, the upper chamber of the German parliament, in 1949. Although Arnold respected Adenauer's leadership qualities the two men did not see eye to eye. Arnold sided with the trade unions against Adenauer on the issue of industrial co-determination which was introduced in spite of government opposition. He also put more weight behind efforts to restore German unity. However, after winning the NRW elections again in 1950, he bowed to Adenauer's view that he should not enter into another coalition with the SPD. With an increased vote he formed a third administration after the election of 1954. It was a bitter blow to him that he was turned out of office in 1956 when the Liberal FDP withdrew their support and joined a coalition with the SPD. Arnold turned down Adenauer's offer that he join the federal government as Deputy Chancellor, preferring to fight on in regional politics. He died from a heart attack in 1958 just before his party once again won the regional elections this time with an absolute majority.

Ashdown, Paddy (b. 24 Feb. 1941)
British; leader of the Liberal Democrats 1988–

Paddy Ashdown has been called the 'action man' in British politics, a tribute not only to his striking physique and love of exercise, but also to his early experience as a commando in the Marines. He is also a qualified Chinese (mandarin) interpreter. After work in the United Nations, industry, and local government he gained Yeovil for the Liberals in 1983.

Ashdown was elected leader of the Liberal Democratic Party in 1988 with over 70 per cent of the vote. The party resulted from the merger of the Social Democrats and the Liberals. He took over at a bad time in Liberal fortunes. The Alliance of Liberals and Social Democrats had not made a breakthrough in the 1987 general election and a proposed merger of the two parties led to splits in both. Membership fell and support for the new party stood at only 6 per cent in the opinion polls when he took over. Ashdown helped to restore its fortunes and it gained 18 per cent of the vote in the 1992 general election. But the new party did not recapture the electoral heights which the Alliance had done in the 1980s. Ashdown supported traditional Liberal policies of constitutional reform, Europe, and partnership in industry and moved the party towards more market-orientated economic policies. The recovery of the Labour Party after 1992 reduced the prospects for a Liberal revival. A perennial problem for Liberals at general elections was maintaining an even stance between Labour and Conservative parties. By 1995 Ashdown had led his party to a stance more sympathetic to the Labour Party. He was rewarded in the 1997 general election when his party gained 46 seats, its largest total in nearly seventy years. But the party was not significant in a parliament in which Labour had a large majority.

Asquith, Herbert Henry (b. Morley, Yorkshire, 12 Sept. 1852; d. 15 Feb. 1928)
British; Chancellor of the Exchequer 1905–8, Prime Minister 1908–16; Earl 1925

Herbert Asquith was the son of a northern clothing manufacturer. He was educated at the City of London school and Balliol College, Oxford, where he was an academic star and became president of the Union. Like a number of contemporary fellow students he came under the influence of T. H. Green, the Idealist philosopher. He became Liberal MP for East Fife in 1886 and represented it for thirty-four years. Asquith became a successful barrister, and he needed the money because, at an early age, he was left as a widower with five young children to provide for.

Asquith admired Gladstone and supported his stand on Home Rule for Ireland, the issue that split the party in 1886. In Gladstone's final government (1892–4) he was made Home Secretary, a remarkable promotion considering his lack of any previous ministerial experience. In the ten-and-a-half years after 1895 in which the party was in opposition he returned to the bar, removing himself from serious consideration for the leadership of a divided Liberal Party.

Along with fellow Liberal Imperialists *Grey and *Haldane, he was prepared to support the Unionist government's handling of the Boer War, but *Campbell-Bannerman, the party leader, opposed it. When the Liberals had the chance to form a new administration in 1905 the three Lib-Imps demanded that Campbell-Bannerman move to the House of Lords and allow Asquith to be leader of the House of Commons and effective leader (the so-called Regulus Compact) Campbell-Bannerman refused and they gave way. In the new government Asquith was made Chancellor of the Exchequer and proved a loyal deputy leader. As Chancellor he provided for old-age pensions in his final 1908 budget.

There was no doubt that Asquith would succeed Campbell-Bannerman when the latter died in office in 1908. He showed great skill in keeping a number of talented and headstrong ministers in line and dealing with a number of explosive issues. He strongly supported *Lloyd George's radical budget of 1909, and was resolute in insisting that the House of Lords' powers be clipped after their rejection of the budget. He prevailed upon the King to create peers as a last resort if the Lords would not give way. He also had to face industrial disruption, the violent campaign of the suffragettes, the threat of military insurrection in Ulster, and the approach of war in Europe.

Asquith was a rationalist in politics, believing that it was possible to arrive at decisions as a result of reasonable discussions—reflecting the influence of Green. He therefore had great difficulty in understanding the attitudes and methods of minorities who felt so strongly about an issue that they resorted to violence to gain their way. He would not, for example, concede the suffragette demands of votes for women until they explicitly abandoned violence. He was similarly tough-minded about the threats of Ulster to fight against Home Rule for Ireland and opposed the 1926 General Strike as a threat to the constitution.

As peacetime Prime Minister he strongly supported his colleagues and took a lead on the crises of the time. He produced a bill in 1912 to provide for Irish Home Rule. This was eventually passed in 1914, although suspended for the duration of the war.

Asquith has not been given high marks for his conduct of the First World War. It is true that he was exhausted—as were many of his colleagues. He invited other parties to join a coalition government in 1916 but this did not still criticisms from the Unionists, their press allies, or, in particular, Lloyd George. The latter was made Secretary of State for War but continued to call for a more energetic prosecution of the war, with Asquith as his target. Lloyd George promised dynamism, Asquith seemed to be unassertive.

Lloyd George campaigned for the creation of a small War Cabinet, with Asquith retaining the premiership but playing a subordinate role. When this was refused Lloyd George resigned, precipitating a government crisis, and Asquith resigned later the same day. It is still not clear whether he stepped down because he thought, wrongly, that Unionist Cabinet ministers wanted him to go, or whether he expected to be recalled. But it was Lloyd George who was invited to form a coalition government two days later. The Liberal Party was effectively split, with Asquith remaining the official leader but Lloyd George commanding the support of a large minority.

The profoundly divided Liberal Party did badly in the 1918 general election and Asquith lost his seat. He was returned in 1920 and still led the party. It was largely his decision in the deadlocked parliament in 1924 to support the experiment of the minority Labour government. Asquith and Lloyd George fell out again over the General Strike in 1926 and he resigned the leadership.

In retirement he wrote journalism and his memoirs, not least because he needed the money. His reputation for a time was sullied by revelations of his laid-back conduct of the war and interpretations of it fostered by Lloyd George. He served as Prime Minister for the longest continuous spell for nearly a century and his record was not overtaken by any successor until Margaret *Thatcher. His dignified bearing, air of imperturbability, and polished debating style earned him the title of 'Last of the Romans'.

Assad, Hafez *see* AL-ASSAD, HAFEZ

Atatürk, Mustafa Kemal (b. Salonica, 12 Mar. 1880; d. 10 Nov. 1938)
Turkish; President 1923–38

The son of a minor Ottoman official, Atatürk attended the War College at Instanbul, from which he graduated in 1905. He helped to found the Fatherland and Freedom Society in 1906 which merged with the Committee of Union and Progress in the following year and spawned the Young Turks Revolution of 1908. Mustafa Kemal gradually became disenchanted with their policies. He conducted a brilliant defence of Gallipoli during the Great War and fought the Allies on various other fronts.

Allied intentions to dismember the Ottoman Empire and divide up its Turkish core, formalized in the Treaty of Sèvres of 1920, had been opposed from 1919 onwards by Mustafa Kemal and his Turkish nationalist associates in Anatolia. At Erzurum and Sivas the basic Kemalist programme as formulated and issued from Ankara as the National Pact. The pact renounced the empire, but demanded complete independence for all Turkish-speaking territories. It was endorsed by the legal Ottoman parliament and then by the new National Assembly meeting at Ankara, in 1920. The Assembly also deposed the Sultan, promulgated a republican constitution, and proclaimed Mustafa Kemal President. These objectives were secured by the Turkish war of independence against Greece, France, Italy, and Soviet Russia, 1920–22.

Atatürk ('Father Turk'—the name he adopted in 1935) now embarked on an ambitious and radical programme to turn Turkey from a Muslim polity into a modern state. The Republic was proclaimed in 1923, with Ankara as its capital, Kemal as executive President, and a single political party. An elected Parliament was added by the 1924 constitution. The dominance of Islam in public life was ended when the Caliphate was abolished in 1924; religious orders were disbanded; religious property was seized; religious instruction was curtailed and a secular educational system established; the Islamic legal system was replaced by a European one; and, in 1928, Islam itself was disestablished. The fez and the veil were forbidden, the Latin alphabet was substituted for the Arabic, and, in 1934, women were enfranchised. Ataturk revitalized the economy, created mixed state-private banks, protected domestic industry and, on *étatiste* Kemalist principles, responsibility for investment and preventing foreign capital entering Turkey was assumed by the state. Atatürk's reforms provoked Kurdish revolts which were ruthlessly suppressed. The Kurdish language was proscribed and Kurdish ethnic identity denied; in the new dispensation, Kurds became 'mountain Turks'.

Attlee, Clement (b. London, 3 Jan. 1883; d. 8 Oct. 1967)
British; Prime Minister 1945–51; Earl 1955

Clement Attlee's government (1945–51) is widely regarded as Labour's most successful government. The administration decisively shaped post-war Britain, establishing the policies for full employment, the welfare state, mixed economy, and passage from the British Empire to Commonwealth.

Attlee was born into a comfortable middle-class family and there was little in his background to suggest that he would lead a party of the left. His father was a city solicitor, able to send him to Haileybury. Attlee graduated from Oxford University and qualified as a barrister. His shock at witnessing poverty in London's East End, reinforced by his reading, made him into a socialist.

The East End was to be his political base for the next fifty years. In 1907 he began to manage a Boys' Club in Stepney and eventually combined this with lecturing in social administration at the London School of Economics. His distinguished record in the 1914–18 war earned him the title 'Major Attlee' in the 1920s. He became mayor of Stepney in 1919 and was elected as Labour MP for Limehouse in 1922. With a private income from his parents he was able to become a full-time politician. He was a middle-class university graduate in a party still recruited largely from the working class.

Attlee held junior office in the first Labour government in 1924. Between 1927 and 1929 he served as one of two Labour members on the Simon Commission on India. In the second Labour government (1929–31) he replaced Oswald *Mosley as Chancellor of the Duchy of Lancaster, when the latter resigned in 1930, and the following year he became Postmaster-General. When the minority government collapsed in 1931, and Prime Minister Ramsay *MacDonald went off to lead the National Government, Attlee had no doubts about staying in the Labour Party. He regarded MacDonald's act as a betrayal.

Attlee gained from the devastation of the Labour Party in the 1931 general election. Just fifty Labour MPs were returned and only a handful had any ministerial experience. He was elected deputy leader and found himself necessarily speaking on a great variety of subjects in the House of Commons. When the leader George *Lansbury resigned shortly before the 1935 election, Attlee was elected as his successor—obviously, so people thought, as an interim leader. In the new parliament over 150 Labour MPs were returned and in a leadership election Attlee beat the more fancied Herbert *Morrison and held the post for the next twenty years, the longest spell in the party's history. Attlee's election was helped by the fact that he was the man in post. But he was also seen as the antithesis of MacDonald. His modest demeanour and his willingness to subordinate himself to the views of the majority in the party were qualities Labour MPs were looking for.

In the late 1930s Labour was increasingly divided over foreign policy and what to do about the rising menace of Nazism in Germany. The party had a strong pacifist group and was opposed to rearmament. In 1940 Attlee led Labour into *Churchill's wartime coalition. He became Lord President of the Council, Deputy Prime Minister 1942–5, and was a member of the five-man War Cabinet. He chaired a number of Cabinet committees, including an important one on post-war reconstruction. As members of the coalition government, Labour ministers demonstrated both their competence and patriotism.

When Labour won the 1945 general election, unsuccessful moves were made to stop him becoming Prime Minister. The left-wing intellectual Harold Laski was a supporter of the claims of Herbert Morrison, and asked Attlee to wait on the approval of Labour MPs before accepting the King's request to form a government. Attlee ignored the request. In another letter, Laski informed Attlee that he lacked 'the peculiar personal qualities' of a great leader and should step down. Attlee's memorable reply was:

'Dear Laski
Thank you for your letter, the contents of which have been noted.
C R Attlee'

As Prime Minister of the 1945 government, Attlee led an experienced team. The massive majority in the House of Commons ensured the speedy passage of radical legislation including major measures of nationalization of the Bank of England, railways, coal, gas, electricity, and steel. Other measures extended welfare provision and established the National Health Service. The government also speeded up the end of the empire and granted independence to India and Pakistan in 1947. The government had to cope with severe economic difficulties consequent on the shift to a peacetime economy and the ending of American lend-lease. It also began the production of Britain's atomic bomb.

As Prime Minister, Attlee kept his talented colleagues together by acting as a broker between different factions and delegated responsibility to key ministers. His style in Cabinet was to wait for a majority view to emerge; he rarely took an independent stand or a prominent part in the growing left–right controversies. He was in hospital when *Bevan and other ministers resigned over *Gaitskell's 1951 budget.

Labour gained a narrow victory in the 1950 general election but lost another in October 1951. The party showed signs of running out of steam; the manifestos essentially defended its record in office. There then began a battle over future policy and the succession to Attlee. After leading the party to another election defeat in 1955, Attlee resigned at the age of 72. Supporters of Herbert Morrison claimed that Attlee's refusal to step down earlier was motivated by a determination to block their man. In retirement, Attlee described Morrison's appointment as Foreign Secretary as 'The worst appointment I ever made!'

Attlee wrote a brief and unrevealing autobiography, *As it Happened*, in 1954. His reticence was such that he has been called an unknown Prime Minister. In his retirement, he proved to be a pungent and much quoted commentator on the working of British government.

Auriol, Vincent (b. Revel, 27 Aug. 1884; d. 1 Jan. 1966)

French; President of the Fourth Republic 1947–54

Born in 1884 the son of a baker, Auriol grew up in the Southern French town of Revel. He used the educational opportunities provided by the Third Republic for bright working-class boys, studied law, and soon got involved in Socialist Party activism. Like many of his generation, he was inspired by the ideal of democratic socialism unifying Marxism and Republicanism preached by *Jaurès and subsequently by *Blum. Elected to the Chamber of Deputies in 1914, Auriol rose quickly through the ranks of the parliamentary Socialist Party and became recognized as its leading economic expert. In the deteriorating political circumstances of the 1930s, the threat posed by the radical Right to the institutions of the Third Republic led to the formation of the Popular Front and the election in 1936 of a left-wing majority in the Chamber of Deputies. Auriol was appointed Minister of Finance in Blum's 1936 Popular Front government and had the difficult task of trying to reassure the business and finance communities that social reform was compatible with sound money. Having initially refused to devalue the franc, he was compelled to do so in October and to declare a pause in the government's social programme. The Popular Front experiment disintegrated in 1937–8 and Auriol left office.

In the traumatic events of 1940 which culminated in the defeat of France and the installation of *Pétain's Vichy regime, Auriol was one of the few political leaders who refused to spit on the corpse of the Third Republic. He retired to his farm, was (briefly) able to shelter Léon Blum from the vengeful attentions of his newly powerful enemies and made no attempt to conceal his opposition to the regime and its leader. By 1942 he had gone into hiding to avoid detention; later he joined the Free French in Algiers. His credentials as a democratic Socialist and impeccable wartime record thus left him well placed to play a leading role in the complicated politics of liberated France. In 1946, as president of the Constituent Assembly, he did more than anyone to frame the constitutional texts of the Fourth Republic. It was this that led the National Assembly to elect him President of the Republic. His presidency was dominated by the need to defend the new constitutional order against the problems caused by a fragmented party system and the semi-subversive attacks of the Communist Party and *de Gaulle's Rassemblement pour la France. In so doing he relied less on the formal powers of the presidency (which were few) or on appeals to public opinion, than on his insider's knowledge of France's political class and on his remaining constitutional rights over the appointment of governments. His posthumously published diaries reveal the extent of his role in shoring up the fragile ministries of the late 1940s. He also travelled widely in France and its empire.

Auriol's presidency came to an end in 1954 and he made no attempt to stand for re-election. He remained active, however, in Socialist politics and was one of those who negotiated with de Gaulle in 1958 over his return to power. He had initially welcomed de Gaulle's return. But his attachment to the political culture of democratic republicanism meant that he was unable to accept the increased presidentializing of the regime and in particular the 1962 amendment providing for the direct election of the President. Both challenged the principles of democratic republicanism which he had absorbed from Jaurès and Blum. He campaigned vigorously against the 1962 amendment.

Awolowo, Obafemi (b. Ikenne, Nigeria, 6 Mar. 1909; d. 8 May 1987)

Nigerian; leader of the Opposition 1960–2, leader of Unity Party of Nigeria 1978–83

A member of the Yoruba ethnic group, Awolowo graduated from University of London through correspondence courses and in 1946 qualified as a barrister. He worked as a lawyer, journalist, and trade union leader and was heavily involved with the burgeoning nationalist movement in Nigeria. In 1950 he founded and led the Action Group which became the dominant party in Western Region. Following defeat in the pre-independence national elections in 1959 he became leader of the Opposition in the federal parliament until his imprisonment in 1962. He was released following the 1966 *coup d'état* and became Federal Commissioner for Finance and vice-chairman in the military-dominated government. With the lifting of the ban on political parties in 1978 he formed the Unity Party of Nigeria. In the 1979 elections his party received overwhelming support in the Yoruba areas but performed less well elsewhere and he came second in the presidential elections. Following a further coup at the end of 1983 all parties were again banned.

Awolowo was, arguably, the greatest head of state that Nigeria never had. He never quite bridged the gap between being a leader of the Yoruba and a truly national leader. He was never a narrow ethnic sectionalist, but neither was he able to gain the trust of the majority of Muslim northerners or the Ibos of the east.

Azikiwe, Nnamdi (b. Zungeru, Nigeria, 16 Nov. 1904)

Nigerian; Governor-General of Nigeria 1960–3, President of Nigeria 1963–6, leader of Nigerian People's Party 1978–83

A member of the Ibo ethnic group Azikiwe received his higher education in the USA. On returning to Nigeria he played a significant role in the growing nationalist movement, establishing a newspaper, the *West African Pilot*. In 1944 he was a founder member of the National Council for Nigeria and the Cameroons (subsequently National Council of Nigerian Citizens), the country's first major political party. In 1946 he took over the leadership of the party, which rapidly established itself as the dominant force in the Eastern Region, where Azikiwe became Premier. Following independence in 1960 his party was a minor partner in the ruling coalition, which was dominated by the Northern People's Congress. His positions as Governor-General and, following the creation of a republic, first President of Nigeria were semi-honorific and lacking in significant power.

Azikiwe supported the Biafran cause during the civil war and was a member of the secessionist government, but in 1969 he switched his support to reunification. He temporarily retired from politics after the war, but in 1978, following the lifting of the ban on political parties, he formed and led the Nigerian People's Party. In the 1979 general elections his party polled strongly in the Ibo areas of the country and in parts of the Middle Belt but failed to establish itself as a truly national party. The further military coup at the end of 1983 brought an end to his active political life.

Known affectionally as 'Zik', he was a major figure in the nationalist phase of the late colonial period but thereafter he never quite succeeded in combining Ibo leadership with wider Nigerian nationalism.

Babangida, Ibrahim Gbadamosi (b. Minna, Nigeria, 17 Aug. 1941)
Nigerian; President 1985–93

A professional soldier, Babangida received military training in India, Britain, and the USA. He played a major role in the internal politics of the army from the 1970s and, in 1984, was appointed Chief of Staff. In 1985 he led a counter-coup against the incumbent military government and became head of state and the first military figure in that role to adopt the title of President.

Initially he was regarded as a liberalizing force, releasing political prisoners and promising to return the country to democratic civilian rule by 1990. He delayed the transition process by several years and increasingly sought to control it by, for example, creating the two political parties which could participate in elections and designating the ideologies they had to espouse. Following the presidential election in July 1993, which was regarded as the most free and fair to have been seen in the country, he surprised most observers by abandoning the whole democratization process. He installed an interim government which was rapidly overthrown in a further coup led by Sanni Abacha.

Despite his early popularity, which earned him the nickname 'Maradona', Babangida increasingly alienated large sections of the population, and his annulment of the 1993 election produced a dangerous political crisis in Nigeria.

Bahr, Egon (b. Treffurt, Werra, 18 Mar. 1922)
German; special ambassador 1967–72, Minister for Special Tasks 1972–4, Minister for Economic Co-operation 1974–6

Because he had a Jewish grandmother Bahr was not allowed by the Nazis to study, but he was conscripted to serve in Hitler's army. After the war he worked for several West Berlin newspapers before being appointed chief commentator of RIAS, the Radio In the American Sector. In 1960 *Brandt, the governing mayor, appointed him head of the West Berlin press and information service.

When Brandt became Foreign Minister in 1966 he offered Bahr the post of special ambassador and head of the planning staff in his ministry. His brief was to conduct negotiations with the Warsaw Pact states. By that time Bahr was well known as the author of the strategy 'change through rapprochement' of the SPD towards Eastern Europe. By seeking agreement on practical matters West Germany would gradually be able successfully to reach out the hand of friendship to its Eastern Bloc neighbours. Bahr played a decisive role in the setting up of a trade mission in Czechoslovakia (1969), the conclusion of a 'normalization' treaty with Poland (1970), and the agreement over the 1971 Renunciation of Force Treaty with the Soviet Union. He also played a key part in the negotiations leading up to the signing of the Basic Treaty with East Germany in 1972. In December 1972 Brandt appointed him Minister for Special Tasks, a post he retained until Brandt's resignation in May 1974. Bahr had voiced his doubts about Günter Guillaume, the spy who brought down Brandt, as early as December 1969, but to no avail.

In July 1974 *Schmidt recalled Bahr to serve as Minister for Economic Co-operation. In this capacity he was criticized for appeasing Third World élites rather than examining more closely the needs of their peoples. He was a member of the Bundestag from 1972 to 1990.

Bahr served as SPD party manager from 1976 until, increasingly at odds with the moderates over defence policy, he resigned in 1981. He remained influential helping to steer the SPD into its controversial dialogue with *Honecker's SED. Like some of his colleagues, he gave up the aim of German reunification, overestimating the strength of the East German and other Communist regimes.

Baker, Howard Henry, Jr. (b. Huntsville, Tennessee, 15 Nov. 1925)
US; US Senator 1967–85, Senator majority leader 1981–5

Baker came from a family long involved in politics. His father, Howard H. Baker, Sr., served in the US House of Representatives 1951–64, and on his death was succeeded by Baker's mother, Ira Baker, 1964–5. Baker married the daughter of Senator Everett *Dirksen. Following service in the Navy in the Second World War, he took a BA at Tulane University in New Orleans and studied law at the University of Tennessee. He practised law in Tennessee and in 1966 was elected to the US Senate.

He won national attention as a prominent member of the *Ervin Committee investigating the Watergate affair in 1973. In 1976 President *Ford considered him as a vice-presidential candidate. If selected, he might have tipped the balance in Ford's favour in the very close presidential election of 1976 by gaining Tennessee and other states in the upper South which Ford lost to Jimmy *Carter. Had he become vice-president in 1976, he would have been a strong candidate to succeed Ford as President in 1980. But instead Ford chose Robert *Dole as vice-presidential candidate in 1976 and lost the election, and in 1980 Baker's bid for the Republican nomination for President made little headway against the successful candidate, Ronald *Reagan. With the Republican victory in the Senate elections in 1980, he became Senate Majority Leader. He played an important role in arranging compromises which secured the passage of the legislative programme of Reagan's first term. In 1984 Baker decided not to run for re-election. Following the Iran-Contra scandal in 1986 which led to the resignation of White House Chief of Staff Donald Regan, Baker returned to government service as White House Chief of Staff, 1987–8.

Baker was one of the most prominent of the Republican politicians in the South in the post-Civil Rights era. He was a pragmatist who was willing to compromise in order to produce results. As an intelligent moderate, however, he became disenchanted with the new breed of conservative Republicans of the 1970s and 1980s who became increasingly dominant in the Republican Party.

Baker, James Addison III (b. Houston, Texas, 28 Apr. 1930)
US; Secretary of the Treasury 1985–8, Secretary of State 1989–92

From a wealthy Texas family, Baker was educated at Princeton University and practised law in Houston, Texas. He bacame involved in Republican politics in Texas and was a close associate of George *Bush. In 1976 he was campaign manager for Gerald *Ford's re-election campaign and in 1980 he managed Bush's campaign for the Republican nomination for President. He served as White House Chief of Staff in President *Reagan's first term, 1981–5. In Reagan's second term, he served as Secretary of the Treasury, 1985–8. In 1988 he managed Bush's successful campaign for President and served as Secretary of State in the Bush administration, 1989–92. In 1992 he resigned as Secretary of State to manage Bush's unsuccessful campaign for re-election.

Baker was a shrewd political operator who was particularly attentive to winning congressional support for any initiative. He was a distinguished and successful Secretary of State, especially with regard to his relations with his Soviet counterpart, Eduard *Shevardnadze, during the climactic years of the end of the Cold War and the collapse of the Soviet Union. Had Bush won re-election in 1992, Baker had ambitions to succeed him as President in 1996. With Bush's defeat, however, Baker's political fortunes faded and he returned to law practice in Houston.

Baker, Kenneth (b. Newport, 3 Nov. 1934)

British; Secretary of State for Environment 1985–6, Secretary of State for Education 1986–9, chairman of the Conservative Party 1989–90, Home Secretary 1990–2

The son of a civil servant, Baker attended Oxford and became secretary of the university Conservative Association. He entered parliament by capturing the East London seat Acton at a by-election in 1968. It disappeared, due to reorganization, in 1970, and he then managed to win the safe seat of the City of Westminster and Marylebone in a by-election in the same year. He held it until 1983 when it disappeared in another reorganization and was then adopted for a safe seat, Mole Valley in Surrey.

In his early days Baker was a friend and political ally of Ted *Heath and this probably slowed his progress under Margaret *Thatcher. Following spells as Minister of Information Technology (1981–4) and Minister of State for Local Government (1984–5) he entered the Cabinet as Secretary of State for Environment in 1985. In this post he pushed through the abolition of the metropolitan counties and the Greater London Council and began work on what finally emerged as the poll tax, to replace domestic rates. He complained that had his original proposals—to phase in the tax over a number of years, and provide substantial Treasury support—been accepted, then the poll tax would have worked.

He made considerable impact as Secretary of State for Education (a post which he held for three years). His far-reaching Education Reform Act (1988) gave state schools the right to opt out of local authority control, introduced a national curriculum, extended parental rights of choice in schools, and delegated financial responsibility to head teachers. Baker also pioneered the creation of a number of City Technology Colleges, and did much to restructure and expand higher education.

By 1989 he was widely regarded as a likely successor to Margaret Thatcher as party leader. He was 'promoted' to party chairman in July 1989 but this ruined his prospects. The unpopular poll tax, economic recession, by-election disasters, and the resignation of a number of key ministers meant that, as party chairman, he had to explain the government's many misfortunes to the mass media. When Mrs Thatcher was challenged for the leadership by *Heseltine in November 1990, Baker's fortunes were low and her decision not to fight a second ballot inevitably weakened his own standing. When she stood down, there was little support for a Baker candidacy.

John *Major, in part to conciliate the Thatcherites, made Baker Home Secretary in his new government. But in this post he proved to be accident-prone and his stock continued to decline. He introduced an Asylums Act (1992) to stem the potentially large flow of refugees from Eastern Europe and the Third World, and the Dangerous Dogs Act, which followed a number of cases in which dangerous dogs had attacked people. He was also a prime mover in the establishment of the National Lottery.

There was no place for Baker in John Major's second administration, formed in April 1992. It was rumoured that he had been offered the post of Secretary of State for Wales, clearly a demotion, and had refused it. On the back benches he became a spokesman for the growing body of opinion in the party that was concerned about the increasing power of the EC to override national sovereignty. He was even talked of as a potential leadership challenger to, but not replacement for, John Major in 1995. He announced his intention to retire at the end of the parliament in 1997.

Baker had a strong interest in literature. He published a number of anthologies of verse and his memoirs, *The Turbulent Years* (1993).

Balaguer, Joaquín (b. Dominican Republic, 1 Sept. 1906)
Dominican; President 1960–1, 1966–78, 1986–96

A poet and historian, Balaguer served as a diplomat in Spain and Colombia before becoming Education Minister under the dictator Rafeal *Trujillo in 1950. He was subsequently Foreign Minister and Vice-President before assuming the titular presidency in 1960. When Trujillo was assassinated in 1961, Balaguer tried to remain in power, but was ousted by a military coup in 1962 and sent into exile.

In 1964 Balaguer founded the Partido Reformista (PR), returning to the Dominican Republic after Juan *Bosch's brief presidency and the 1965 US invasion. In the 1966 elections he defeated Bosch, beginning a twelve-year period of unbroken political power. During that time Balaguer presided over an impressive economic boom but was also accused of involvement with paramilitary forces which murdered thousands of Bosch's supporters. Finally, in 1978 he reluctantly handed the presidency over to Antonio Guzmán of the Partido Revolucionario Dominicano (PRD), but not before Balaguer loyalists in the military had threatened to annul the election result and stage a coup.

In 1986 Balaguer returned to power, having merged his PR with the Partido Revolucionario Social Cristiano (PRSC). The hallmark of his presidency was a taste for extravagant public works and construction schemes, the most controversial being the Columbus Lighthouse, built to commemorate the 1992 quincentenary. Despite considerable opposition and allegations of fraud, he was re-elected in 1990 at the age of 84. The 1994 elections were again tainted by accusations of cheating, and Balaguer was forced to agree to curtail his term from four to two years. In 1996 he grudgingly retired from the presidency, having ensured that his favoured candidate, Leonel Fernández, succeeded him.

Balaguer dominated Dominican politics for forty years and was largely responsible for perpetuating the authoritarianism and *caudillismo* of the Trujillo period. He invariably outmanœuvred his eternal rival and contemporary, Juan Bosch, and was reputed to have a machiavellian survival instinct within the country's labyrinthine political system.

Balcerowicz, Leszek (b. Warsaw, 19 Jan. 1947)
Polish, Finance Minister 1989–92

In the 1980s Balcerowicz was an economic researcher at the Central School of Planning in Warsaw and an adviser to the trade union movement Solidarity. In 1989 he was appointed Finance Minister and Deputy Premier in the Solidarity government formed after the elections of May 1989. Balcerowicz negotiated with the International Monetary Fund (IMF) for credits to help Poland out of her economic crisis. Balcerowicz had little choice but to agree to the harsh conditions which the IMF imposed. The resultant programme of economic shock therapy involved the first comprehensive implementation of market reforms in the former Soviet Bloc. It was heavily influenced by the theories of the Harvard economist Jeffrey Sachs. The 'Balcerowicz Plan' was introduced on 1 January 1990. Balcerowicz had great success in stabilizing the currency and introducing the first stage of marketization. He played a vital role in sustaining international, particularly IMF support for Poland, but his plan led to a serious collapse in living standards and industrial unrest. President *Wałęsa blamed *Mazowiecki and Balcerowicz for not creating an economic revivial quickly enough. Regarding Balcerowicz and his policies as an electoral liability Wałęsa manœuvred him out of office in 1992.

Baldwin, Stanley (b. Worcestershire, 3 Aug. 1867; d. 14 Dec. 1947)
British; Chancellor of the Exchequer 1922–3, Lord President of the Council 1931–5, Prime Minister 1923–4, 1924–9, 1935–7; Earl 1937

The son of an ironmaster and later Conservative MP for Bewdley, Baldwin was educated at Harrow and Trinity College, Cambridge. After graduating, he spent twenty years working in the family firm. He contested the seat of Kidderminster as a Conservative in 1906 but showed little real passion for politics. His entry to parliament came on the back of personal tragedy. His father died, while still MP for Bewdley, in 1908 and his son was selected to contest the by-election. Baldwin entered the House of Commons fairly late in life, at the age of 40. It was almost ten years before he was to be given office, as joint financial secretary to the Treasury when the existing financial secretary was not a member of the House of Commons. After an unspectacular four years in the post, he was promoted to be president of the Board of Trade. His sudden rise to prominence occurred in 1922 at the meeting of Conservative MPs at the Carlton Club called to discuss the future of the coalition government. His attack on the man who had appointed him to Cabinet, *Lloyd George, effectively destroyed the coalition. The new Prime Minister, Bonar *Law, offered Baldwin the Exchequer, which he wanted but took some time to accept. Baldwin established a reputation as an effective operator in Cabinet and an attractive speaker in the House. The following year the fatally ill Prime Minister resigned and the King sent for Baldwin in preference to *Curzon. Baldwin's first tenure of Downing Street was short; he called a general election on the issue of tariff reform and heralded a short-lived minority Labour government. When the Labour government fell a few months later, another election returned the Conservatives to power. Baldwin then served a full parliament (1924–9) as Prime Minister, presiding over a return to the gold standard and the General Strike. The loss of power in the general election of 1929 was to prove short-lived, the collapse of the minority Labour government in 1931 leading to a National Government dominated by the Conservatives. Ramsay *MacDonald was kept on as Prime Minister but power rested with Baldwin as Lord President of the Council. He held the post until 1935, when he resumed the premiership, retiring in 1937. He was created Earl Baldwin of Bewdley and also made a Knight of the Garter.

His long tenure of office and of the party leadership was far from trouble free. He had to contend with an attempt to oust him as party leader, especially in 1930 and 1931—prompting his famous attack on the press barons for exercising 'power without responsibility—the prerogative of the harlot throughout the ages'—and serious dissension within Conservative ranks over empire free trade, dominion status for India, and rearmament. He was later to be much criticized for his 1935 promise that there will be 'no great armaments'. After leaving office, his reputation was to decline and he was to attract some less than flattering biographies.

More recent years have seen some revisionist interpretations of Baldwin's premiership. He was an effective politician, keeping together a party in difficult times. He handled the difficult and sensitive abdication crisis in 1936 with skill, effectively winning the battle with a determined Edward VIII. He presided over a government that laid much of the groundwork for the welfare state, and his government undertook some modest rearmament at a time when public opinion did not appear to favour a military build-up.

A complex character—on the surface modest, unambitious, and unflappable, while beneath the surface a nervous man not lacking in ambition or self-regard—he was to dominate British politics for fifteen years, serving three times as Prime Minister and retiring at a time of his choosing. An apparently lazy manner hid a capacity for political activity that was to produce the results he sought.

Balfour, Arthur James (b. East Lothian, 25 July 1848; d. 19 Mar. 1930)

British; leader of the House of Commons and First Lord of the Treasury 1891–2, 1895–1902, Prime Minister 1902–5, Foreign Secretary 1916–19; Earl 1922

The grandson on his mother's side of the 2nd Marquess of Salisbury, Balfour was educated at Eton and Trinity College, Cambridge. He was elected to the House of Commons in 1874, aged 26, and combined political activity with scholarship, penning several books on philosophy—his first, *A Defence of Philosophic Doubt*, was published in 1879. In parliament, he was a member of Lord Randolph Churchill's 'Fourth Party' before being appointed private secretary to the Foreign Secretary, his uncle, the 3rd Marquess of Salisbury. He entered government in 1885 as president of the Local Government Board and the following year became Secretary for Scotland. While in that post he was elevated to Cabinet rank. In 1887 he began a four-year tenure as Chief Secretary for Ireland—gaining the sobriquet of 'Bloody Balfour' for the determined way he restored the rule of law—before being appointed in 1891 as First Lord of the Treasury and leader of the House of Commons, leading the Conservative Party in the House of Commons while his uncle served as Prime Minister in the House of Lords. When Salisbury finally retired in 1902, his nephew succeeded him.

His premiership was to be destroyed by the battle within the Conservative Party over protection. In 1903 Joseph *Chamberlain began his campaign for Imperial Preference, encountering the vehement opposition of Conservative free traders. Balfour attempted to reach a compromise but failed. In December 1905 he offered the government's resignation. The Liberal leader *Campbell-Bannerman accepted the King's commission to form a government, did so, and then went to the country and won an overwhelming victory. The Conservatives won only 156 seats. Balfour was among the MPs who were defeated. He was immediately found a new seat and returned to the House as MP for the City of London. In Opposition, he fared little better than in government. The Conservative majority in the House of Lords was used to frustrate government measures and to reject the budget in 1909. The government introduced the Parliament Bill in order to reduce the House of Lords' veto power over legislation. Balfour's handling of the response to the bill encountered criticism from within the party and a 'BMG' (Balfour Must Go) movement got under way. In 1911, citing age as a reason, an exasperated Balfour resigned the leadership. It is perhaps surprising that he held on to the leadership for as long as he did, carrying on for six years after the party had lost office.

Balfour's career was by no means over after he gave up the party leadership. In May 1915 he was brought into the wartime government as First Lord of the Admiralty and then in 1916, with *Lloyd George taking over the premiership in a Conservative-dominated coalition, he became Foreign Secretary. He was the signatory to the Balfour Declaration in 1917, recognizing the right for a Jewish homeland in Palestine, and he was a member of the Paris Peace Conference in 1919. In 1919 he became Lord President of the Council, serving until the fall of the coalition in 1922. A few months before it fell, he was created the Earl of Balfour. He was brought back into government by *Baldwin in 1925, serving as Lord President of the Council for the remainder of that parliament. On his 80th birthday, members of both houses presented him with a Rolls-Royce. He left office in June 1929, at the age of 81, and died ten months later.

Balfour had a lengthy political career—serving in Cabinet for no less than twenty-seven years—and had a distinguished early history as a minister and an even more distinguished history as an elder statesman, but his period as leader proved a disaster. A patrician and detached intellectual, he operated at a level well above that of ordinary party members—he once said he would rather take advice from his valet than from a part conference—and lacked the firm hand of leadership that had characterized his period as Chief Secretary for Ireland. Motivated more by duty than by ambition, he stayed a long course in politics even though his abilities could have taken him in several different directions.

Balladur, Edouard (b. 2 May 1929)

French; Prime Minister 1993–5

Balladur came from a family of French businessmen who had been settled for generations in Turkey. He took the classic civil service route to a career in government and was a protégé of *Pompidou, whose private office he ran. He retreated into well-paid obscurity after Pompidou's death in 1974 and built up close links with a number of industrial magnates, most notably Ambroise Roux. While serving in Pompidou's office he had come into contact with Jacques *Chirac and it was Chirac who brought him into politics as one of his policy advisers. During the 1980s, their relationship prospered, though it never became the close friendship which they pretended—Balladur was a colder, more buttoned-up and snobbish character than the impulsive and warm Chirac. Balladur was convinced that Chirac's presidential ambitions needed to be buttressed by a record of solid governmental competence that would overcome the negative image of erratic and ruthless activism. Thus he conceived the system of cohabitation whereby Chirac would govern France in co-operation with President *Mitterrand. When the 1986 parliamentary elections provided a right-wing Chamber, Chirac became Prime Minister and gave Balladur the key role of Finance Minister with effective control over all aspects of domestic policy. He introduced a wide-ranging privatization programme and introduced a limited amount of deregulation to respect the criteria of the Single European Act.

Although Balladur was widely regarded as Deputy Prime Minister, he remained at this time a loyal Chirac supporter. His haughty manner, and fondness for the company of duchesses, led to his being portrayed as an *ancien régime* aristocrat carried around in a sedan chair. Thus there was little evidence to suggest that he might emerge as a contender for the presidential crown himself. But after Chirac's heavy defeat in the 1988 presidential election, he began to polish up his own credentials. He wrote a number of books and was photographed everywhere looking statesmanlike. The collapse of the authority of the Socialist governments of the early 1990s made it certain that a second cohabitation would take place—and this time Chirac refused point blank to expose himself again to the dangers of governing with Mitterrand. Thus Balladur was appointed Prime Minister in May 1993. His popularity immediately soared. Sober-suited, elaborately courteous, and above all respectable, he reassured an electorate grown weary of political scandal and party games. As Prime Minister, he managed to push through the GATT reforms and to maintain the strong franc policy which was an integral part of France's European strategy. Borne aloft by opinion polls, it was by now clear that he harboured presidential ambitions of his own, and was no longer prepared to act as a deputy to a Chirac who looked like a has-been. A number of erstwhile Chirac supporters, including the populist Interior Minister *Pasqua, backed him for the 1995 presidential elections and for a while he looked unassailable. Once the campaign began, however, things went wrong. A poor public speaker, he lacked the resources of a party machine, and was compelled by his prime ministerial office to moderate the sort of campaign promises which his rival Chirac scattered like confetti. On the first round, he came third, behind the Socialist *Jospin and Chirac and stood down, with morose loyalty, in favour of the latter. He resigned as Prime Minister and was re-elected to the National Assembly.

Ba Maw, Dr (b. Maubin, 8 May 1893; d. Yangon, 1977)
Burmese; premier (1937–9), head of state (1943–5)

After an education at Rangoon College, Calcutta University, Grays Inn where he was called to the bar, and Bordeaux where he earned a doctorate in literature, Dr Ba Maw became one of the towering politicians of late colonial Burma. During the final years of British rule, before the Second World War, constitutional reforms had passed a significant degree of power to indigenous elected politicians and Ba Maw was one of the most astute at seizing the opportunities engendered.

He made his mark initially as a barrister, defending the leader of the 1931 peasant revolt, Hsaya Hsan. On the back of the fame achieved as a politician who stayed within colonial law while defending the downtrodden, his small Hsinyeitha (proletarian) Party was able to form the first coalition Cabinet under the Government of Burma Act (1935) in 1937. His government fell two years later in the face of opposition from students and workers who accused him of being pro-imperialist and of aiding foreign capitalists.

Out of office, Ba Maw joined with student leaders, including the subsequent national hero, General Aung San, and the future Prime Minister U *Nu, in organizing a united front called the Freedom Bloc which opposed continued British rule as well as Burmese co-operation in Britain's war agianst Nazi Germany. Arrested by the British, he was released by the invading Japanese in August 1942. Recognizing Ba Maw's popularity and ability to work with the youthful nationalists of the country, the Japanese made him head of a newly proclaimed independent state. Taking the title of *adipati ashin minkyi*, a title with royalist pretensions, Ba Maw lead a government which was recognized by Japan and the Axis powers. His brother, Dr Ba Han, helped draft a detailed planning document for the future of Burma under his supervision.

At the end of the war, Ba Maw fled Burma with the retreating Japanese army. After his capture in Japan, he was held and then released after being considered for prosecution as a war criminal. Returning to Burma, he attempted to re-establish a political career but had lost out by that time to the former students who he had opposed and worked with in the previous decade. His waning influence was subsequently expressed through occasional newspaper articles.

His memoirs, *Breakthrough in Burma* (1968), give his version of a turbulent political career.

Banda, Hastings Kamuzu (b. 1902, Kasungu District, Nyasaland (Malawi))

Malawian; Prime Minister 1963–6, President 1966–94

Born to poor peasant parents of the Chewa ethnic group, Banda received a mission education and left home at the age of 12 to work in Rhodesia and South Africa. He saved enough to travel to the United States, where he received a first degree in political science and subsequently qualified as a medical doctor. He then moved to Scotland, where he gained British medical qualifications, and from 1945 to 1953 practised as a doctor in London. He then spent five years as a doctor in Ghana.

His political activities were aroused by opposition to the Central African Federation, which in 1953 federated Nyasaland (later to become Malawi) with white-ruled Southern Rhodesia. As a result, he was invited to lead the Nyasaland African Congress, which in 1960 became the Malawi Congress Party (MCP), and returned home in 1958 after an absence of over forty years. After outspoken attacks on federation, including a period in jail, he became Prime Minister, and achieved separate independence for Malawi in 1964.

An autocratic and deeply conservative individual, he quarrelled immediately after independence with the younger and more radical members of his party, whom he ousted from office with the support of the British Governor-General. He became President in 1966 and President for Life in 1971. Malawi under his rule was peaceful but severely repressed, and economic development was slow; a committed capitalist, he used his position to build a large private company of his own. Internationally, he expressed outspoken contempt for the African consensus, and in 1970 established full diplomatic relations with *apartheid* South Africa, earning continental odium but gaining substantial aid. In his later years he became senile, but retained office until international pressure coupled with domestic dissent forced the MCP to allow multiparty elections in May 1994. Banda lost, but though accused by the new government of the murder of political opponents, he was unfit to stand trial.

Barber, Anthony (b. Doncaster, 4 July 1920)

British; Chancellor of the Exchequer 1970–4; Baron (life peer) 1974

Barber was educated at Retford Grammar School and Oxford. As a prisoner of war from 1942 to 1945 (before escaping) he studied for a law degree. He was called to the Inner Temple in 1948 but was intent on a political career. He entered the House of Commons, at the age of 31, as Conservative MP for the marginal seat of Doncaster and held the seat from 1951 until 1964. He returned to the House of Commons at a by-election in 1965 as member for the safe seat of Altrincham and Sale.

His rise was steady but not spectacular. He served as a whip from 1955 to 1958 and then spent a year as the parliamentary private secretary (PPS) to Prime Minister Harold *Macmillan. He was Economic Secretary, and then Financial Secretary, to the Treasury in the remaining years of the Macmillan government. He served in the Cabinet as Minister of Health in the year-long *Douglas-Home government.

He was appointed chairman of the Conservative Party by Edward *Heath in 1967. When the party was returned to power in June 1970, Heath created him Lord Privy Seal in order to conduct the negotiations for British membership of the European Community. The sudden death of Iain *Macleod the following month resulted in his unexpected elevation to the post of Chancellor of the Exchequer. He served in 11 Downing Street for the rest of the parliament, presiding over a difficult economic situation and introducing a statutory pay and prices policy in 1972. He left the House of Commons at the end of the short 1974 parliament in order to become chairman of the Standard Charter Bank.

An honourable and competent man, he was overshadowed by the Prime Minister he served from 1970 to 1974 and may come to be remembered as much for having a future Prime Minister—John *Major—work for him at Standard Charter Bank as for his own achievements in public office.

Barkley, Alben William (b. Graves County, Kentucky, 24 Nov. 1877; d. 30 Apr. 1956)
US; Member of the US House of Representatives 1913–27; US Senator 1927–49, Senate majority leader 1937–47, Vice-President 1949–53

The son of a tobacco farmer, Barkley attended local schools before taking to the road selling kitchen utensils in order to earn enough to continue his education. He graduated BA from Marvin College, Clinton, Kentucky in 1897. Thereafter he attended Emory College, Oxford, Georgia and then the University of Virginia Law School, Charlottesville. He was called to the bar in 1901 and that same year began practising in Paducah, Kentucky. He became prosecuting attorney for McCrachen County, Kentucky, 1905–9 and a McCrachen county court judge, 1909–13. His career in national politics began in 1913 when he was elected Democratic member of the US House of Representatives. He was re-elected for a further seven terms to the House, until, in 1927, he was elected US Senator for Kentucky. His senatorial career spanned the next twenty years, ten of which, 1937–47, he served as majority leader.

Barkley was a stalwart of the Democratic Party who on only one occasion spurned party lines. In 1944, unable to support F. D. *Roosevelt's veto of the Tax Reduction Bill, he resigned his party's leadership in the Senate, but was promptly re-elected. In 1948 his devotion to his party ws rewarded when *Truman invited him to become his running mate. After serving a full-term as Vice-President, Barkley returned to the hustings. He died as he had lived, campaigning for his party. Uttering the words 'I would rather be a servant in the House of the Lord than sit in the seat of the mighty' he collapsed and died whilst making a keynote address at a mock Democratic convention at the Washington and Lee University, Lexington.

Barre, Mohammed **Siyad** (b. Lugh District, Italian Somalia, 1919; d. 2 Jan. 1995)
Somali; head of state 1969–91

Son of a herdsman from the Marehan clan of the Darod branch of the Somali, Barre received only elementary education before joining the police force in 1941. He rose rapidly through the ranks, and by 1950 was a chief inspector, the highest position held by a Somali at that time. He transferred to the army in 1952, becoming vice-commander in 1960 and commander in 1965.

Somalia was at that time receiving substantial Soviet military aid and training, and Barre may have had covert Soviet aid when he seized power in October 1969 from the chaotic civilian government. At all events, Somalia was soon declared a Marxist-Leninist state, with a Somali Revolutionary Socialist Party controlled by Barre which was largely cosmetic. His regime had some achievements in its early years, especially in the field of literacy, where it resolved the vexed question of a script for writing the Somali language.

However, with increasing Soviet military support, it became preoccupied with the long-standing Somali aspiration to wrest territory occupied by ethnic Somalis from Ethiopia. Ironically, the invasion meant to achieve this goal was launched in 1977 at the moment when the Soviets transferred their backing to *Mengistu's Ethiopia, and the Somalis were routed. Thereafter, the regime was bent on little more than survival, and clan rivalries intensified. The regime's human rights record declined from bad to appalling. Eventually controlling little more than his palace compound in Mogadishu, Barre was obliged to flee in a tank as the country collapsed around him. He spent his remaining years in exile, leaving a disastrous legacy of civil war and famine.

Barre, Raymond (b. Réunion, 12 Apr. 1924)

French; Prime Minister 1976–81, Presidential candidate 1988

Barre was born in the Indian Ocean island of Réunion and his early years were traumatized by the bankruptcy and imprisonment of his father. He studied economics at Paris, entered the University, and was the author of a best selling textbook on macroeconomics. In 1967 he was plucked from obscurity by *de Gaulle to become one of France's two commissioners in the European Community. He first acquired prominence in November 1968 when he provided de Gaulle with the arguments to prevent the devaluation of the franc which virtually everybody else, in the aftermath of the May 1968 events, believed to be necessary. After leaving the European Commission, he returned to academic life before being invited by President *Giscard d'Estaing to join the government headed by Jacques *Chirac in 1976. When Chirac took the unprecedented step, in the Fifth Republic, of walkng out, Barre took over as Prime Minister. Giscard had in mind his high professional reputation, ('the best economist in France'), his solid administrative competence, his apparent absence of political ambition, and his image as a prudent technician. He looked in every sense to be the antithesis of the aggressive, and unreliable, Chirac. As Prime Minister, Barre embarked on a policy of sound money and high taxation in order to control France's propensity to inflation; he also made tentative steps to limit economic dirigisme, by decontrolling some prices. His government was relatively successful in moderating the worst effects of the late 1970s recession. Yet he found his political authority constantly under challenge not only from the left-wing opposition headed by *Mitterrand but also from the neo-Gaullist RPR which Chirac had founded in order to further his presidential ambitions. By attacking Barre, Chirac hoped to destabilize Giscard. In 1981, the strategy paid off—Giscard was defeated by the Socialist Mitterrand in the presidential election.

As Prime Minister Barre had endured dreadful opinion poll ratings. In opposition, however, his political stock rose fast. Once the initial euphoria of the left's victory had worn off and the failings of the *Mauroy government became obvious, he was able to draw the dividends of his image of calm authority and economic competence—less unstable than Chirac, more human than Giscard. By the mid-1980s polls regularly identified him as the most popular right-wing political leader, and he stood for the presidency in 1988. His 1988 election campaign was, however, widely regarded as a disaster. He lacked a reliable party base to counter Chirac's RPR, his professorial self satisfaction infuriated younger politicians, his campaigning style seemed curiously casual. He was eliminated in round one, with 16.52 per cent of the vote.

Barre's self assurance was unaffected by defeat. He continued to deliver weighty pronouncements on the state of the nation and to stand ostentatiously aloof from the frantic politicking of the French right. His isolation contributed to his popularity, but also made the hopes he nurtured of a presidential comeback illusory. He withdrew from the pre-campaign for the 1995 presidential election when it became clear that he lacked any solid support. He compensated for his loss of a national destiny by becoming, like many of the politicians whom he affected to despise, a big city baron. In 1995 he was elected mayor of Lyons, France's second city.

Basu, Jyoti (b. 1914)

Indian; Chief Minister of West Bengal 1977– , leader of the Communist Party of India (Marxist)

Educated at St Xavier's School and College, Basu studied in England, where he qualified as a barrister at the Middle Temple. During his stay in England Basu became actively associated with the India League and the Federation of Indian Students in England. He was the Secretary of London Majlis and made contacts with the Communist Party of Great Britain.

Basu returned to Calcutta in 1940 and became a leader of the Eastern Bengal Railroad Workers' Union. He was elected to the Bengal Legislative Assembly in 1946. After partition, he remained member of the Assembly but was arrested when the Communist Party of India was banned following its call for open revolt. He was released upon the orders of the High Court and remained a Legislative Assembly Member between 1952 and 1972.

In the 1950s Basu, with Parmode Das Gupta, became the joint leader of the West Bengal Communists. He became state party secretary and led the parliamentary tactics of the CPI in Bengal against the Congress. The anti-Congress nature of Bengal Communism led Basu to align with the Communist Party of India (CPI(M)) following the division of the Communist Party of India in 1964.

In 1967 Basu became Deputy Chief Minister in a coalition United Front government in Bengal in which the CPI(M) was one of the leading parties. This coalition collapsed after eight months. Fresh elections were held in February 1969 in which the CPI(M) emerged as the largest party. Basu was again Deputy Chief Minister in a United Front government that lasted until 1971.

In 1977 Basu was elected to the Parliament from Satgachia. The CPI(M) also won a majority in the Bengal Legislative Assembly. Basu became Chief Minister of West Bengal and under his leadership the CPI(M) has won successive elections since (1982, 1987, 1992, 1996). It is the largest democratically elected Communist movement in the world.

Basu has been a member of the CPI(M)'s Politbureau since 1964. He has been the main influence in shaping the party's domestic and international policy. Of particular importance, since 1991, has been the tactical support given to parties and groupings opposed to the Hindu revivalist Bharatiya Janata Party. This has brought the CPI(M) closer to Congress but the party has avoided an outright coalition.

Basu is recognized as a clever tactician who through the use of parliamentarism created the conditions for the success of Communism in West Bengal. He has a high reputation as a political leader and, following the national elections to parliament (1996), was considered as one of the possible candidates for the post of Prime Minister.

Batista y Zaldivar, Fulgencio (b. Banes, Cuba, 16 Jan. 1901; d. Madrid, 6 Aug. 1973)

Cuban; President 1940–4, 1952–8

The son of a poor labourer, he joined the Cuban army in 1921, after a string of largely unskilled jobs. There he flourished, graduating from the National Journalism School and being promoted to sergeant at Havana's Campamento Columbia, where, as nationwide dissent finally toppled the dictator *Machado in August 1933, he rose to prominence as a spokesman of the discontented soldiers. On 4 September 1933, he and other sergeants joined student rebels to remove Machado's successor and establish a revolutionary government which, though radical and nationalist, depended on a Batista-led army. Finally, encouraged by a watchful Washington, Batista conspired to bring it down in January 1934.

Until 1940, Batista controlled Cuba through a series of puppet presidents, defeating both the left (especially the Communists) and the traditional élite. Batista, however, realized the depth of discontent behind the 1933 revolution and, through his striking deals with Washington in 1934 to ensure Cuban sugar sales and remove the more blatant aspects of US control, his popularity grew. Forging a skilful alliance with the Communist Party in 1938 and ensuring a Constitution (1940) which reflected the 1933 agenda, he was elected President on a programme of nationalist and social reform, much of which succeeded, thanks to wartime sugar prices and clever political manœuvring and patronage.

In 1994, Batista left office constitutionally, eventually settling, somewhat richer, in Florida, from where, in 1948, he was elected to the Cuban Senate, returning to launch a campaign for the presidential elections of 1952. Certain to be defeated, however, he then prevented these elections with a coup on 10 March 1952.

Thereafter, Batista became a more brutal and less skilful shadow of his former self, controlling through coercion, patronage, corruption, and Washington's tolerance. In 1954, after an abortive rebellion by a then largely unknown Fidel *Castro, he won elections almost unopposed; however, from late 1956, the rebel movement began to grow, especially in the eastern mountains and in Havana. He responded to this, and an assassination attempt in 1957, by ever more widespread repression, eventually alienating allies in the middle class, the United States (which withheld arms in 1958) and the army itself. Finally, on 31 December, army conspirators acted, and Batista fled Cuba to the Dominican Republic (some $300 million richer), finally settling in Madrid, where he died.

Overall, Batista dominated Cuban politics between the 1933 anti-Machado revolution and Castro's 1959 rebellion, rising to power as a key actor in the former and being overthrown by the latter.

Batlle y Ordóñez, José (b. Montevideo, 21 May 1856; d. 20 Oct. 1929)

Uruguayan; President of Uruguay 1903–7, 1911–15

The son of General Lorenzo Batlle (President 1868–72), Batlle y Ordóñez ('Batlle') was born into an eminent family in the Colorado party. He studied law and philosophy, visited Paris in 1880, and engaged in political journalism. In 1886 he founded the newspaper *El Día*, which provided both an income and a political platform.

Batlle was elected as senator in 1898, and President in 1903. The governing Colorados had entered a pact in 1897 with their traditional Blanco opponents allowing Blancos to control certain departments of the country. In 1903 the pact broke down, and Aparicio Saravia's armed rising was defeated by government forces in 1904. Although Batlle's refusal to negotiate was opposed by the propertied classes even of his own party, his victory marked a turning point in Uruguayan history. The succession of civil conflicts in the nineteenth century was now followed by a remarkable period of political and social development, underpinned by rapid economic growth.

Although some reform proposals surfaced in 1905, the first administration was more notable for its fiscal correctness. In 1907 Batlle left Uruguay for a four-year exile in Paris, where his plans to make Uruguay 'a model country' took clearer shape. The second administration was more radical. Economic policy centred on the role of state in promoting the diversification of the economy and resisting the predations of British capital. Social policy protected the defenceless: workers, women, the young, and the aged. Capital punishment and bull-fighting were abolished, while the eight-hour working day and divorce for women were established. Political reform proposals intended to curb abuses of presidential power introduced mass politics and the constitution of 1919 in which executive power was shared between a president and nine-person council (with representation for the minority Blanco party). The executive council, displaced in 1933, was restored between 1952 and 1967.

Batlle's reformism instilled a profound belief amongst Uruguayans in the capacity of the state to resolve social conflict. This legacy remains influential.

Bayh, Birch (b. Terre Haute, Indiana, 22 Jan. 1928)
US; US Senator 1963–81

Educated at the University of Purdue, Indiana State College, and the University of Indiana, Bayh spent time as a farmer and a lawyer before entering politics. From 1954 until 1962 he was a member of the Indiana House of Representatives serving as minority leader (1957–8 and 1961–2) and as Speaker (1959–60). Elected to the Senate in 1962 in a suprise victory, Bayh served as chairman of the Intelligence Committee and as a member of the Judiciary and Appropriations Committee. Although a good campaigner, Bayh's politics had become out of step with an increasingly conservative state. As chairman of the Constitutional Amendments Subcommittee Bayh earned praise for his handling of the 25th and 26th amendments; but he became vulnerable to conservative criticism over the equal rights amendment (which he helped promote) and amendments on a balanced budget, abortion, and school prayer which he helped block. In 1980 the conservative tide which brought Ronald *Reagan to the presidency and saw social issues figuring prominently in the campaign, Bayh was beaten by future Vice-President Danforth *Quayle. Bayh returned to legal practice.

Bayh attempted to secure the Democratic nomination twice. In 1971 he withdrew for family reasons. In 1976 he dropped out after running poorly in New Hampshire and Massachusetts.

Beaverbrook, William Maxwell Aitken, 1st Lord (b. New Brunswick, Canada, 25 May 1879; d. 9 June 1964)
British; press proprietor and government minister 1916–18, 1940–2, 1943–5; Kt. 1914, Baron 1917

Beaverbrook gained success as a financier, journalist, press proprietor, politician, and historian. He was the son of a Presbyterian minister and as a young man made money selling insurance in Canada. He came to England in 1910 and in the same year became Conservative and Unionist MP for Ashton-under-Lyne in the December general election. A close friend and political patron was Bonar*Law, a future Conservative party leader and himself a man with New Brunswick connections. In 1916 Beaverbrook took over the ailing *Daily Express* and eventually made it into a best-selling national newspaper. His newspaper interests soon extended to include the *Sunday Express* and *Evening Standard*.

Beaverbrook was friend and adviser to leading politicians for most of his life, particularly in the World Wars. Although he was a man of independent views his political fame rests on his proximity to major figures like Bonar Law, *Lloyd George, and *Churchill. His role as a go-between in the manœuvres which resulted in Lloyd George replacing *Asquith as Prime Minister in 1916 are told in his *Politicians and the War*. Beaverbrook expected a Cabinet post as a reward for his role. Instead he was offered a peerage (which required him to resign his seat in 1916) and eventually occupied posts as Chancellor of the Duchy of Lancaster and then Minister of Information. Neither post satisfied his ambitions.

Beaverbrook played an important role in persuading Bonar Law to make himself available to lead the Conservative Party and replace Lloyd George as Prime Minister in 1922. He soon fell out with the new Conservative leader *Baldwin. Beaverbrook was a passionate supporter of imperial preference, or free trade within the British Empire. The threat of Beaverbrook and Rothermere, another press proprietor, to run their own candidates unless Baldwin complied with their policy demands, inspired the latter to make one of the most famous political charges in 1931. He said that the proprietors were demanding 'power without responsibility—the prerogative of the harlot throughout the ages'.

Beaverbrook was also close to Churchill—they were on the same side in supporting Edward VIII over the abdication crisis in 1936–7. They shared the same swashbuckling approach to life and a devotion to causes above political party. Beaverbrook's finest hour came when Churchill appointed him as Minister for Aircraft Production in 1940. He played a major role in boosting the number of aircraft. He left government in 1942 (he resigned or threatened resignation a number of times) but was recalled the next year as Lord Privy Seal. Beaverbrook was a man of action, single-minded about the immediate objective, and had little time for the committees or co-operative ways of Whitehall.

Many Conservatives did not see him as a good influence on Winston Churchill during the 1945 election. He is credited with misleading Churchill about the state of public opinion and also with reinforcing the leader's determination to make a bellicose radio broadcast (accusing Labour of 'Gestapo' methods) during the election. In later years he used his newspaper to advance political campaigns. To the end his papers were strongly pro-empire. Not surprisingly, they were also bitterly opposed to British membership of the European Community.

Bebel, August (b. Deutz, 22 Feb. 1840; d. Zurich, 13 Aug. 1913)

German; leader of the Social Democratic Party of Germany (SPD) 1868–1913

There were 50,000 mourners at the funeral of Bebel in Zurich, a remarkable number considering the place and the fact that he had never held official office in Germany. Yet he was the internationally admired leader of Germany's biggest political party, the SPD, and had been an active socialist for fifty years. In 1867 he was the first workers' representative to be elected to the North German parliament. He was a member of the Reichstag from 1883 until his death. He had served the movement in other ways too, having been jailed on two occasions for his political activities. From 1892 on he was one of the two chairmen of the SPD. In the controversy over 'revisionism' in the SPD Bebel steered a middle course between Bernstein and the militant Marxists.

Bebel was not a theorist but wrote a widely read book expressing advanced views on the place of women in society. He had seen his mother struggle against poverty and die of consumption when he was 13. Both Bebel's father and his stepfather also died young of consumption. He was lucky enough to be able to stay at school to 14 and then complete a four-year apprenticeship as a master thresher. His involvement in working-class politics began when he joined a workers' education association in 1861. After bitter controversy he was able to overcome the divisions in the workers' movement and found, with Wilhelm Liebknecht in 1869, the Social Democratic Workers' Party.

Bebel was an internationalist who had played a decisive part in founding the Second International in 1889. At his last national election in 1912 the SPD gained 34.8 per cent of the vote, the largest of any party. The party had one million members. Whether, had he lived, Bebel could have steered the SPD to oppose the war in 1914 is debatable. By agreeing to support 'defence of the homeland' it disappointed the hopes of millions in Europe and beyond.

Begin, Menachem (b. Brest-Litovosk, 16 Mar. 1913; d. 9 Mar. 1992)
Israeli; Prime Minister 1977–83, Defence Minister 1980–1

Begin led the revisionist Zionist youth group *Beitar* in Poland in 1931. He entered Palestine in 1942 as a private in the Free Polish Army and, on his discharge in 1943, took command of the near defunct terrorist group, Irgun Zvai Leumi (National Military Organization). Begin revitalized it and organized its terrorist attacks—they included bombing Jerusalem's King David Hotel in 1946 and killing ninety-eight people—to drive Britain out of Palestine. Later murderous attacks he organized were to promote the ethnic cleansing of Palestinian Arabs, such as the operation of April 1948, mounted jointly with Yitzhak *Shamir's LEHY, in which 254 men, women, and children of Deir Yassin village were massacred. At the height of Israel's war of independence in June 1948, Begin nearly started an Israeli civil war. His motto was: 'We fight, therefore we are.'

He founded and led the Herut party as an instrument of the 'fighting family', winning fourteen Knesset seats in the 1949 general elections. After amalgamating Herut with other right-wing factions to form the populist Likud party, Begin succeeded in capturing the oriental Jewish vote after 1973 and, to general surprise, won power in the 1977 general elections. Begin concluded the Camp David Accords with Egypt in 1978 and signed the first Arab–Israeli peace treaty with President *Sadat in 1979. Begin's Zionist convictions about biblical Israel led him to renege on their agreement over full autonomy and self-government for the West Bank and Gaza. His Likud government's attempt to destroy the PLO in the 1982 invasion of Lebanon proved an abysmal failure which cost 600 Israeli lives and $3,500m., and left a legacy of implacably hostile Islamist terrorists to confront successive Israeli governments.

Beijen (Beyen), Jan Willem (b. Utrecht, 2 May 1897; d. The Hague, 29 Apr. 1976)
Dutch; Foreign Secretary 1952–6

Beyen (as the name is usually written) started a banking career in 1925 after serving as an official of the Ministry of Finance (1918–23), and one year as secretary of the board of NV Philips at Eindhoven. As manager of the Rotterdamsche Bank (1927–35) he frequently took part in international negotiations: he was the delegate of the Dutch government to the World Economic Conference in London (1933). In 1935 he was appointed vice-president, in 1937 president of the Bank for International Settlements in Basle. He found himself in 1940 in London as financial director of Unilever in 1940 and served as financial councillor to the Dutch government in exile. He took part in preliminary negotiations which were to lead to the formation of Benelux. Heading the Dutch delegation in Bretton Woods (July 1944) he presented a proposal for post-war economic and financial regional settlements. In 1946 he was appointed director of the International Bank for Reconstruction and Development in Washington. In 1948 he also became executive director of the International Monetary Fund.

Beyen was surprised by the invitation to become Dutch Foreign Secretary in 1952. He had never been a member of a political party and owed his appointment partly to the refusal of the Socialist Prime Minister Willem *Drees to accept a Catholic candidate for the Foreign Office at a time when all other foreign ministers in the other five EEC member states were Catholics. A compromise was reached in the appointment of Beyen as Minister for Foreign Affairs in charge of European and multilateral affairs, and of the Catholic J. *Luns as Minister without Portfolio charged with matters relating to the United Nations and bilateral affairs. Beyen was an active proponent of economic integration. After the rejection of the European Defence Community, he persuaded P. H. *Spaak (Belgium) and J. Bech (Luxembourg) to join him in a new initiative which led via conferences in Messina in 1955 and Venice in 1956 to the Treaty of Rome (1957). The experiment with two ministers at the Foreign Office, one of whom (Beyen) was an active European while the other (Luns) advocated a more Atlanticist approach, was abandoned in 1956 when Luns was appointed the sole Minister of Foreign Affairs. From 1958 to 1963 Beyen served as Dutch ambassador in Paris. Once retired, he was responsible for a World Bank economic mission to Morocco.

Belaunde, Francisco (b. Lima, 7 Oct. 1912)

Peruvian; President 1963–8, 1980–5

Born into a well-established upper-middle-class family, Belaunde trained as an architect at the University of Texas and was first elected as a deputy in 1945. Building on a widespread post-World War sentiment among middle- and lower-class Peruvians, in favour of economic modernization and socio-political reform, Belaunde decided to contest the 1956 presidential elections as a candidate of the National Front of Democratic Youth. Finding his aspirations blocked by military dictator Manuel Odría, who pressured the electoral authorities into refusing to recognize his candidacy, Belaunde organized a meeting in Lima and marched on the offices of the National Electoral Committee. The protest was dispersed by riot police employing tear gas and water cannon, but carrying a Peruvian flag, Belaunde advanced alone to deliver a petition to the electoral commissioners. Given the strong tide of public opinion these events generated, Odría was forced to relent, the Front was recognized, and Belaunde came a commendable second in the 1956 poll.

Shortly following the election, Belaunde formed Acción Popular, a party that he has led and dominated to the present. In the 1962 presidential campaign he came second to Víctor Raúl *Haya de la Torre and in the fresh elections of 1963, realized his ambition to become President. His image as a new figure outside the political establishment enhanced his appeal, as did his campaign promises in favour of land reform, an improvement in the conditions of Andean peasants, greater national integration, industrialization and democratization. Once in office, however, Belaunde proved unable to deliver: the administration lacked a majority in Congress, with the result that key initiatives (especially land reform) were blocked or watered down. Consequently, sectors of the population became disillusioned and opposition to the government grew, a process that culminated in the October 1968 coup led by general Juan *Velasco.

For most of the ensuing twelve years of military rule, Belaunde lived in exile in the USA, but staged a remarkable political comeback in winning the May 1980 general election. Nevertheless, his second administration (1980–5) was no more successful, being characterized by rapidly growing levels of inflation, unemployment, corruption, and an inability to control an escalating civil war provoked by Sendero Luminoso's insurrection. To this backdrop, Acción Popular suffered a humiliating defeat in the 1985 poll, its leader having acquired the reputation of being an honest democrat, but an incompetent president who lacked the dynamism to effectively perform the difficult task of governing Peru.

Ben Bella, Mohammed Ahmed (b. 25 Dec. 1918)

Algerian; Prime Minister 1962–3; President 1963–5

Ben Bella was conscripted into the French Army in 1937 and served with distinction during the Second World War. When France interfered in the 1947 elections to the Algerian Assembly, the younger nationalists, led by Ben Bella, formed the 'Secret Organization', a clandestine movement dedicated to achieve independence, and a revolutionary Algerian government, by armed insurrection. Shortly after he organized its first terrorist attack in Oran in 1949, most of the group's leaders, including Ben Bella, were arrested. He escaped to Cairo in 1952, after two years of French imprisonment. In 1954, eight of the exiles formed the National Liberation Front (FLN), under Ben Bella's leadership, and launched a revolutionary armed struggle for independence. The insurrection spread throughout Algeria over the next nine months before a major terrorist offensive was agreed in August 1956. The FLN bombing campaign caused extensive loss of life and was only halted temporarily by the French army. From 1957 to 1962, Ben Bella was interned in France following the hijacking of an aircraft carrying him and other FLN leaders. In his absence the FLN renewed the armed struggle and, despite settler and army revolts between 1960 and 1962, it concluded independence negotiations at Evian in 1962.

Serious conflict within the FLN after independence was ended when a majority of its military wing gave political victory to Ben Bella's faction. His government began to implement its 'Algerian socialism' programme in 1962. Under the new constitution of 1963, he was elected executive President and the FLN became the sole legal party. Fears that he planned to reduce their power resulted in his overthrow in a military coup of 1965 led by his former ally, Colonel Boumedienne. Detained until 1979, then exiled, Ben Bella has campaigned since 1984 for pluralist democracy in Algeria. He returned there in 1990.

Beneš, Eduard (b. Kozlany, Bohemia, 17 May 1884; d. Prague, 3 Sept. 1948)
Czech; Foreign Minister of Czechoslovakia 1918–35, President 1935–8 and 1941–8

The son of a peasant Beneš was educated at the universities of Prague, Dijon, and the Sorbonne. He obtained a doctorate in sociology and in 1909 was appointed professor at the Prague Academy of Commerce. In 1915 he escaped from Austria-Hungary to Paris, where he helped T. G. *Masaryk to form the Czech National Council. He was Foreign Minister of the new Czechoslovak state from 1918 to 1935 and represented Czechoslovakia at the Paris Peace Conference from 1918 to 1920. He opposed any revision of the post-World War I settlement. In the 1920s he tried to build 'Little Entente' with alliances between Czechoslovakia and Yugoslavia in 1920 and Czechoslovakia and Romania in 1921. He developed close ties with both France and the Soviet Union. Beneš was a strong supporter of the League of Nations, of which he was six times chairman. The admission of the Soviet Union to the League in 1934 was a triumph of his diplomacy. The following year Czechoslovakia made a pact of mutual assistance with the USSR. When Masaryk retired as President in December 1935, Beneš succeeded him. In 1938 he resigned and went into exile in the United States following the Munich Agreement.

From 1941 to 1945 Beneš was head of the Czech government-in-exile in London. In 1943 he visited Stalin in an attempt to act as mediator between East and West. He returned to Prague as President in March 1945. He tried to keep the presidency above party politics and did not intervene against Communist subversion of the government after 1945. In February 1948 Klement *Gottwald launched a Communist coup in Czechoslovakia. Beneš resigned as President on 6 June 1948, refusing to sign Gottwald's Soviet-style constitution. He died three months later.

Ben-Gurion, David (b. Plonsk, Poland, 16 Oct. 1886; d. 1 Dec. 1973)
Israeli; Prime Minister 1948–53, 1955–63

David Gruen was active in the socialist Po'ale Zion party before emigrating to Palestine in 1906. He edited the party's organ, *Adhuth*, taking the surname Ben-Gurion (one of Jerusalem's last defenders against the Romans). He formed the first Jewish trade union in 1915. Expelled from Palestine by the Turks for his pro-Allied activities in 1915, Ben-Gurion co-established the Hehalutz (Pioneer) youth movement and later joined the war on the Allied side.

From 1921 until 1933, Ben-Gurion led Histradut (General Federation of Labour). In 1930 he became leader of Mapai (Workers' Party) and, from 1933, as chairman of the

Jewish Agency Executive, he worked to build the foundations of a Jewish state. He supported the Peel Commission's proposal of 1937 to partition Palestine to facilitate the creation of this state. Britain's failure to implement the proposal against Arab opposition, and the severe limitations on Jewish immigration and land purchase in Palestine imposed in 1939, led Ben-Gurion to reformulate his policy in the Biltmore Programme of 1942. This demanded removal of restrictions on Jewish immigration, Jewish Agency control of immigration and land settlement, and Palestine becoming 'a Jewish Commonwealth'. It was imposed in two ways. With US government support, the Jewish Agency flouted immigration limitations and by the terrorist violence of its clandestine military wing, Haganah, supported by the Irgun and LEHY terrorist groups, it made Britain's Palestine Mandate unworkable by 1947. Ben-Gurion supported the UN partition of Palestine into Jewish and Arab territories in that year. When Israel achieved independence in May 1948, around 400,000 Palestinians had become involuntary refugees and approximately 400,000 more fled from the additional territories conquered by Israel in the Arab–Israeli war, 1948–9. Ben-Gurion's government introduced an immigration programme that doubled the Jewish population of Israel within three years and, with huge external Jewish financial aid, simultaneously carried out a massive land development programme. His 1948 government also established the new state institutions, including building the Israeli armed forces from Haganah and Irgun, and it originated the Israeli policy of their permanent military superiority to Arab states. In 1956, Ben-Gurion secretly agreed with Britain and France to attack Egypt, with the aim of winning a southern security buffer zone. However, the precipitate withdrawal from Suez of his Anglo-French allies frustrated this ambition. Ben-Gurion quit as premier in 1963 for personal reasons.

Benn, Anthony **(Tony)** Neil Wedgwood (b. London, 3 Apr. 1925)
British; Secretary of State for Energy 1976–9

The son of Viscount Stansgate, a former minister, Benn was educated at Westminster School and New College, Oxford. After service in the RAFVR and RNVR (1943–6) and work for the BBC, he became, in 1950, the youngest member of the House of Commons as Labour MP for Bristol South-East.

His refusal to accept the peerage he inherited in 1960 first thrust him into the national headlines. When his parliamentary seat was declared vacant he contested and won the by-election. An election court's decision to declare the defeated Conservative candidate elected created a furore which resulted in the Peerage Act (1963) permitting hereditary peerages to be disclaimed. Benn was then re-elected for Bristol in 1963. He lost the seat in 1983, after boundary revisions, and re-entered the Commons representing Chesterfield in 1984.

In Harold *Wilson's 1964–70 Labour government Benn was first Postmaster-General (1964–6) and then Minister of Technology, in the Cabinet. In Wilson's next government (1974–6) he was Secretary of State first for Industry (1974–5) and then for Energy—a post he retained under James *Callaghan's premiership (1976–9).

From an early moderate left-of-centre position, Benn moved sharply leftwards during the 1970s. (This ideological progression was paralleled by an abbreviation of his name from Anthony Wedgwood-Benn to 'Tony Benn'.) Wilson's decision to transfer him from Industry in 1975 was partly a response to this. His initial support for British membership of the EEC had also changed to opposition to it by the 1975 referendum. (The referendum was itself, like the renunciation of peerages, a constitutional innovation largely attributable to pressure from Benn.) In opposition, he was vociferously critical of the alleged betrayal of manifesto commitments by Labour governments. He assumed the informal leadership of attempts to 'democratize' the party which eventuated in the extra-parliamentary party acquiring a dominant voice in electing the party leader through an electoral college. His disavowal of the policies of governments of which he had been a member antagonized many in the

Parliamentary Labour Party, where his limited following contrasted with his popularity outside (he was a member of the National Executive Committee 1959–94). So, too, did his resistance to revision of party policy to accommodate to social and electoral change. The disruptive effects of his challenges for the deputy leadership of the party in 1981 and the leadership in 1988 were also resented. Internecine strife over 'Bennism'—the conviction that Labour's electoral failure in the 1980s was attributable to its lack of commitment to socialism—was widely blamed for that lack of electoral success.

Benn became increasingly marginalized under the leadership of Neil *Kinnock, John *Smith, and Tony *Blair. Though he remained politically active, his most notable achievement in recent years has been to add to his numerous publications five volumes of his political *Diaries* covering the years 1963 to 1990.

Bentsen, Lloyd Millard Jr. (b. Mission, Texas, 11 Feb. 1921)
US; Member of the US House of Representatives 1949–54, US Senator 1970–92, Secretary to the US Treasury 1993–4

The son of a wealthy Texas rancher, Bentsen was educated at the University of Texas, where he studied law and business. He spent time in the Army Air Corps in the Second World War and returned to practice law in Texas. From 1945 to 1948 he was a judge in Hidalgo, Texas. In 1948 he was elected to the House of Representatives but, after re-election in 1950 and 1952, he left the House in 1954 to develop his insurance business. In 1970 he defeated a liberal Democrat, Ralph Yarborough, in the primary and went on to win the general election against Republican George *Bush, largely as a result of his ability to organize whites and ethnic minorities in a united campaign.

In the Senate he tended to be conservative on fiscal and security issues and more liberal on social issues. His conservative style of politics served him well both as chairman of the Joint Economic Committee and on the powerful Finance Committee which he chaired from 1987. His legislative expertise enabled him to make major contributions to reform in a variety of areas including pensions and catastrophic health care, as well as tax and trade law. Although generally resistant to protectionism, he urged tougher measures against Japan for failing to amend its trading practices. His key committee positions enabled him to defend the interests of Texas, especially its oil industry and his ingenuity on its behalf earned him the nickname 'Loophole Lloyd'.

Bentsen displayed presidential ambitions but his generally conservative politics and dry manner made him an increasingly unlikely Democratic presidential nominee. In 1976 he withdrew at an early stage of the race because Jimmy *Carter seemed more likely to appeal to the South. Yet when Michael *Dukakis chose him as running mate in 1988, he performed very well against Republican vice-presidential candidate Dan *Quayle. When Bill *Clinton appointed Bentsen Treasury Secretary in 1993 and chief economic spokesman, there was some concern that the job had gone to a politician who was too much identified with the establishment and the oil industry. But Clinton needed Bentsen's expertise, especially given how heavily he had emphasized the economy in his campaign. Bentsen served two years as Treasury Secretary in the first Clinton administration where he provided balance to the President's own coterie of advisers. Bentsen left the administration in December 1994.

Bérégovoy, Pierre Eugène (b. Déville-lès-Rouen, 23 Dec. 1925; d. 4 May 1993)
French; Prime Minister 1992–3

The son of Ukrainian immigrants, Bérégovoy left school at 16 and worked on the railways. He was in the Socialist Party (SFIO) youth movement and in the war joined the Resistance. In 1950 he entered Gaz de France and rose to managerial rank. In 1956 Bérégovoy quit the SFIO in protest at its Algerian policy and in 1958 opposed the return of *de Gaulle to power. He was in the Parti Socialiste Unifié but he joined the refounded Parti Socialiste in 1969. Elected to both its Directing Committee and its Executive Bureau, Bérégovoy was sympathetic to *Mitterrand's policy of uniting the left and collaborated with the new leadership after the Épinay party congress of 1971, most notably as national secretary for negotiations with the Communist Party. He had been an admirer of *Mendès France and was not a member of the Mitterrand circle and, although one of the few top Socialists from humble origins, made slow headway in the Mitterrand-led party. He was, however, elected a deputy for the Nièvre (Mitterrand's department) in 1986 and had become an admirer of the President. Of realistic (Mendésiste) views, Bérégovoy was one of the proponents of restraint in the early Socialist government in 1981–3 and was sceptical of the 'dash for growth' which led to balance of payments problems and a U-turn in 1983. Bérégovoy was the most obvious choice for Prime Minister in 1991 but Mitterrand chose Mme *Cresson—who had only short tenure. By 1992 Bérégovoy had no time to make an impact on a disillusioned public and his term was dogged by a scandal involving an unsecured loan. After the Socialist defeat of March 1993 he committed suicide in despair.

Beria, Lavrenti Pavlovich (b. Merkheuli, Georgia, 17 (29) Mar. 1899; d. Moscow, 23 Dec. 1953)

Georgian; USSR Commissar for Internal Affairs 1938–45, deputy chair of Council of Ministers and full member of Politbureau 1946–53, Minister of Internal Affairs 1953

Of obscure, probably middle-class origins, Beria made his career as a ruthless secret police officer in Georgia. Joining the Cheka in 1921, by 1931 he was heading secret police operations for all Transcaucasia. Becoming *Stalin's trusted confidant, in 1931 he was made First Secretary of the CP of Transcaucasia, an area he controlled directly or through clients till 1953. In 1938 he was transferred to Moscow to replace *Yezhov as Commissar for Internal Affairs. With the German invasion of 1941 he was made deputy chair of the Council of People's Commissars responsible for all security operations (including, for example, the Katyn massacre) and a member of the five-strong State Defence Committee. In 1946 he became a full Politbureau member and deputy chair of the new Council of Ministers. Secret police operations were split into two organizations under different heads, but Beria continued to exercise general supervision of both. He worked closely with *Malenkov (e.g. in purging the 'liberated areas' in 1945 and the supporters of *Zhdanov in 1949) and headed the nuclear weapons project. In 1951 he lost favour with Stalin and narrowly escaped being purged himself.

After the death of Stalin in March 1953 he quickly reunited secret police operations under his leadership and from this powerful base formed a ruling alliance with his ally Malenkov, elaborating with him the liberalizing measures known as the 'New Course'; indeed he outbid his colleagues at this time in daring proposals (the reunification of Germany, granting more powers to the Union Republics, liberalizing the collective farm system). But his colleagues suspected a possible coup and in July 1953 he was arrested and executed in December on spurious treason charges.

Berlinguer, Enrico (b. Sassari, Sardinia, 25 May 1922; d. 11 June 1984)

Italian; leader of the Italian Communist Party (PCI) 1972–84

Son of a Sardinian aristocrat, Berlinguer joined the PCI in 1943 and soon distinguished himself in his local party, including in his early career a period in prison in 1944 for organizing an anti-government demonstration. He was elected to the Central Committee of the PCI in 1945, and rose rapidly through the party organization—secretary of the youth movement 1949 to 1956, regional secretary 1956 to 1958, then member of the national secretariat, where he was responsible mainly for the party's national administration. Elected to the Chamber of Deputies in 1968, in 1969 he became deputy secretary of the PCI, and then in 1972 general secretary in succession to Luigi Longo. He was little known to the wider public, and his reputation within the party was that of a grey apparatchik, who could be relied on to ensure a smooth transition to power for the post-war generation of party leaders.

The problem facing the PCI was that, despite its national vote of over 25 per cent of voters, its mass membership of over 1.5 million, and its deep-rooted cultural support in the central regions of Italy, the party faced apparently permanent isolation and exclusion from national government. In 1973 he broke radically with the PCI's traditional strategy by proposing a 'historic compromise of all progressive forces', to include the ruling Christian Democrats. This was followed by immediate electoral success, and after the 1976 parliamentary elections the Communists kept in power a DC-led government for the first time since 1947. Berlinguer was also associated with the development of Euro-communism with the leaders of the French and Spanish Communists. The period of the historic compromise was marked by a major increase in terrorism and serious economic crisis in Italy. Despite Berlinguer's personal prestige, the PCI lost votes in the 1979 elections, and the PCI found itself again isolated. Berlinguer led the party's radical opposition to changes in the wage-indexation system in the early 1980s, but in foreign policy distanced the party from the Soviet Union, criticizing particularly strongly its intervention in Poland. He died suddenly of a brain haemorrhage while campaigning for the European elections in 1984.

Enrico Berlinguer was an unlikely figure as a charismatic leader, but he exercised a powerful popular appeal which he used to legitimize the Italian Communist Party in the eyes of the electorate and to reform the party's domestic and foreign policies. His appeal was based both on his capacity to express a radical vision for Italy which appealed beyond the traditional Communist electorate, and on his obvious personal integrity.

Berlusconi, Silvio (b. Milan, 29 Sept. 1936)

Italian; leader of Forza Italia 1993– , Prime Minister of Italy May–Dec. 1994

The son of a bank manager, Berlusconi was educated at a private church-run school in Milan and qualified in law at the State University in the same city, financing his studies with the help of part-time employment as a singer and entertainer. After finishing his degree in 1961 he achieved rapid success as a property developer in the expanding suburbs of Milan.

Berlusconi extended his property interests to Rome, Turin, and Sardinia, and by the time the property boom ended in the late 1970s he had already diversified his commercial interests into banking, local television, local radio, publishing, and advertising. His financial control was exercised through a complex network of interlocking companies, centred on his financial holding company Fininvest. By the end of the 1980s Fininvest controlled three of the six national television channels.

Berlusconi had previously shown little interest in party politics or government for its own sake, but the collapse of the Socialists (led by his political ally Bettino *Craxi) and of the the ruling Christian Democrats in 1992–4 threatened his television empire at a time when Fininvest was seriously indebted. In December 1993 Berlusconi announced the formation of his own political party, Forza Italia, a lay centre-right populist party. The ideology of FI was familiar but its party organization was entirely novel, in that it was run initially as a marketing division of Fininvest, having very few ordinary members, its candidates chosen by the central party organization or by Berlusconi himself. In the 1994 elections the candidates were predominantly recruited from within Berlusconi's own media empire. He fought his election campaign mainly through his national television channels, resisting strongly efforts to force him to give more air-time to his opponents. FI emerged as the largest single party, and Berlusconi became the new Prime Minister, leading a coalition comprising the former neo-Fascist grouping National Alliance and the regionalist party Northern League. Differences between these parties over a range of major issues led to the collapse of the coalition in December 1994. Out of office, while magistrates continued to investigate him on charges of corruption of tax officials, Berlusconi switched his attention to constitutional reform, proposing an American-style directly elected President, later modifying this to support for a system more similar to the French. In the 1996 elections, his alliance was defeated narrowly by a new centre-left coalition after a campaign fought by Berlusconi on a relatively radical neo-conservative platform.

Berlusconi was not only a brilliant entrepreneur but also an excellent television communicator, with a gift for popular campaigning. He was much less successful at managing a fractious coalition, and showed little gift for the complex political negotiations and compromises needed by an Italian Prime Minister. He was however a consistent anti-Communist who tried unsuccessfully to pursue low-tax policies and to reform central government bureaucracy. His electoral success contributed significantly to the Christian Democrats' rapid disappearance and helped establish the conditions for radical constitutional reform, without his being able to bring these to immediate fruition.

Bessmertnykh, Aleksandr Aleksandrovich (b. 10 Nov. 1933)

Russian; Soviet Minister of Foreign Affairs 1990–1

Bessmertnykh graduated from the Moscow Institute of State Relations. His political career started in the United Nations; he was a translator in the Secretariat from 1960 to 1962 and worked for the Department of Political and Security Council Affairs from 1962 to 1966. He then returned to Moscow, working for the Ministry of Foreign Affairs. In 1970 Bessmertnykh was posted to the Soviet Embassy in Washington and by 1983 had attained the rank of Minister-Counsellor. His fortunes improved after 1985 when *Gorbachev came to power and *Shevardnadze became Soviet Foreign Minister. He was made Deputy Foreign Minister in 1986, heading the United States and Canada Department and was promoted to First Deputy Foreign Minister in October 1988. In December 1990 he was appointed Soviet ambassador to Washington and then replaced Shevardnadze as Foreign Minister after the latter's resignation in late 1990. During the coup against Gorbachev in August 1991, Bessmertnykh did not openly side with the plotters, nor did he rally to Gorbachev. He chose instead to disappear. When he re-emerged after the failure of the coup, Gorbachev dismissed him and replaced him with Boris Pankin.

Betancur Cuartas, Belisario (b. Amaga, Antioquia, Colombia, 4 Feb. 1923)

Colombian; President 1982–6

The second son of twenty-two children, sixteen of whom died as children, Betancur was born into an extremely poor family. He received secondary education in a seminary, but was later expelled for 'lack of vocation'. He entered the University Pontifica Bolivariana as a student of architecture, and had to sleep rough for two years before he obtained a scholarship. He later switched to law, and received a law degree. He worked as a journalist for a number of years.

As a young man he joined an extreme right-wing movement before joining the Conservative Party. In 1946 he was elected a deputy, and in 1950 was appointed to the Constituent Assembly. He was active in opposition to the dictator, General Rojas Pinilla, who jailed him several times. He supported the National Front Agreement between the Conservatives and Liberals. In the 1960s he served as Minister of Labour, and in 1979 he was appointed as ambassador to Spain. He tried three times for the presidency on the Conservative Party ticket, 1962, 1970, and 1978, but each time unsuccessfully.

Betancur was the leader of the progressive wing of the Conservative Party. In 1982 he was finally successful in his bid to become President of Colombia, thanks in part to divisions in the Liberal Party.

As President of Colombia, Betancur was active in trying to broker a peace with Colombia's many guerrilla movements. He also took an active interest in international affairs, helping form the Contadora peace process for Central America, trying to set up a regional debt cartel, establishing a rapprochement with Cuba. In 1982 Colombia joined the Non-Aligned Movement. And in 1993 Betancur's strong speech in support of developing countries at the United Nations won him much support.

However, the foreign policy successes were more difficult to repeat on the domestic front. In November 1982 Betancur offered an amnesty for guerrilla combatants, and some 2,000 guerrillas accepted. In 1984 Betancur and three main guerrilla groups, the Revolutionary Armed Forces of Colombia (FARC), linked to the Communist Party of Colombia, the 19th of April Movement (M-19), and the Popular Liberation Army (EPL) signed a peace agreement. The other guerrilla groups refused to sign. And the powerful military establishment were not happy. As part of the agreement the government promised a number of social and political reforms such as an agrarian reform, the direct election of majors, and guarantees of equality for parties other than the Liberals and the Conservatives. The Liberals and Conservatives had shared power for twenty-five years under the National Front agreement.

However, the peace was short-lived. In December 1995 the M-19 seized the Palace of Justice. Betancur refused to negotiate, and after a siege, sent in the army. Over 100 people died, including many prominent judges. The M-19 and the ELP then declared the peace process over.

In addition to the guerrilla problem Betancur faced a growing problem with the cocaine traffickers. After years of ignoring the problem, US pressure persuaded Betancur to move against the drug barons, supporting the extradition treaty with the USA. They responded by assassinating his Minister of Justice, Rodrigo Lars Bonilla, in 1984, and in effect declaring war against the Colombian state.

Although Betancur was moderately successful in reducing budget deficits and restoring economic growth, he did this at the cost of high unemployment rates and an increase in poverty. His failure to reduce unemployment, tackle poverty, and achieve peace with the guerrillas and the drug barons reduced his popularity considerably. And later allegations of corruption have tarnished some of his undoubted international achievements.

Bevan, Aneurin (b. Monmouthshire, 15 Nov. 1897; d. 6 July 1960)
British; Minister of Health 1945–51, deputy leader of Labour Party 1959–60

The son of a blacksmith, Bevan began work in the coal mines at the age of 13 and, after active membership of the mineworkers' union, became its sponsored MP for Tredegar (later Ebbw Vale), which he represented from 1929 until his death.

Bevan's time as Minister of Health in the post-war Labour government represented the zenith of his political career. He played a leading part in the establishment of the welfare state and initiated a massive rehousing campaign; he introduced reforms of local government; and he was also a major force behind the institution of a comprehensive National Assistance scheme. But his greatest achievement was the establishment of the comprehensive, free National Health Service inaugurated in 1948.

Though transferred to the Ministry of Labour in 1951, Bevan remained fiercely protective of the NHS in Cabinet. He resisted cuts in its expenditure to meet Cold War rearmament costs. After several threats, he eventually resigned in April 1951 (along with a Cabinet colleague, Harold *Wilson, and a junior minister, John Freeman) over a decision to impose Health Service charges. The resignation itself, and Bevan's subsequent widening of his differences with his former colleagues, provoked deep controversy within the party.

Bevan's political career prior to 1945 had been characterized by rebelliousness. In 1937 he had been a co-founder of the left-wing weekly *Tribune*. In 1939 he had been expelled from the party (along with Sir Stafford *Cripps) for membership of the

United Front movement. Readmitted later that year, after pressure on the party by the Mineworkers' Union, he had been an often virulent critic of Winston *Churchill's wartime coalition government. In 1944 he only narrowly escaped withdrawal of the whip for opposing action against unofficial strikers in essential industries. He resumed this former undisciplined behaviour soon after Labour's defeat in the 1951 general election, and attracted over fifty backbench adherents. Attempts to curb the activities of these 'Bevanites' became a constant preoccupation of the leadership and Bevan was himself temporarily deprived of the whip in 1955.

In the party leadership election following Clement *Attlee's retirement, in 1955, Bevan was easily defeated by Hugh *Gaitskell. Accepting defeat, he re-entered the shadow Cabinet, where his support for the policy of rejection of demands for unilateral nuclear disarmament alienated many of his left-wing adherents. But this latter-day moderation resulted in his unopposed election to the party's deputy leadership in 1959. He died after less than a year.

Bevan had a mercurial and charismatic personality and was one of the most effective parliamentary debaters and platform orators of his day. His verbal imagery was often memorable, such as, for instance, his reference to Gaitskell as a 'dessicated calculating-machine' and his declaration that unilateral nuclear disarmament would 'send a British Foreign Secretary naked into the conference chamber'.

Bevin, Ernest (b. Somerset, 7 Mar. 1881; d. 14 Apr. 1951)

British; Foreign Secretary 1945–51

The illegitimate son of a midwife, Bevin left school at 11, working first as a farm boy and later as a tramdriver.

Bevin had two careers. In his first, he became the most powerful trade unionist of his generation. Starting as chairman of a branch of the Dockers' Union in 1910, he became its assistant general secretary in 1920. He then organized an amalgamation of unions to form the Transport and General Workers' Union, becoming its first general secretary. He was a member of the TUC General Council from 1925 to 1940.

Prominence in the industrial labour movement gave Bevin influence in the Labour Party. He was offered (but declined) the offer of a peerage during the second Labour administration, 1929–31. In the 1930s he advocated Labour support for rearmament to counter the threat from Nazism's rise in Germany. However, it was not until 1940, at the age of 59, that Bevin began his second—ministerial—career when *Churchill appointed him Minister of Labour and National Service. He held the post until 1945.

Bevin was one of the most powerful members of the small War Cabinet. He was also one of the most successful, mobilizing the workforce with a minimum of industrial strife and establishing a framework for consultation between government and industry which persisted after the war. He also participated actively in the post-war reconstruction planning which led to the establishment of the welfare state.

When the post-war Labour government (1945–51) was formed, Bevin expected to be made Chancellor of the Exchequer; but, in a last-minute change of plan, Clement *Attlee sent him to the Foreign Office. Although Britain emerged from the war no longer a world power to rank with the USA and the USSR, he was one of the most influential figures in the immediate post-war world. He took the initiative, in 1947, in the formation of the Organization of European Economic Co-operation and he was one of the prime movers behind the creation of NATO. In these areas his policies received widespread support, but his stance on the Middle East and especially Palestine (then a British protectorate) was more controversial. For this he came under sustained criticism (and even accusations of anti-Semitism), particularly from the left wing of the Labour Party.

Bevin's health deteriorated in the latter part of the government's term and Attlee was eventually reluctantly compelled to move him from the Foreign Office. He spent the last weeks of his life as Lord Privy Seal.

At the peak of his powers, Bevin had immense energy and a forceful personality. He was generally intolerant of criticism. Entering the Commons only in 1940, he was never an accomplished parliamentarian. In Cabinet, however, he was extremely effective and his loyalty to Attlee, with whom he worked very closely, was legendary. Indeed, he shielded the Prime Minister from at least one attempt to oust him.

Beyen, Jan Willem *see* BEIJEN, JAN WILLEM

Bhutto, Benazir (b. 21 June 1953)
Pakistani; Prime Minister 1988–90, 1993–6

The eldest of Zulfiqar Ali *Bhutto's four children, Benazir was educated at Harvard and Oxford Universities. She campaigned for her imprisoned father in 1977–9 along with her mother Nusrat, who became chair of the Pakistan People's Party. From 1977 to 1984 she suffered long periods in detention, during which her health deteriorated. Benazir provided a detailed account of this traumatic period in her acclaimed autobiography *Daughter of the East* (1988).

After two years of British exile, Benazir received a tumultuous homecoming in April 1986. In July 1987 she married Asif Zardari, a member of a landowning family from Sind. General *Zia's death in August 1988 paved the way for elections which the PPP won, although it did not obtain an absolute majority. On 1 December, Benazir Bhutto became the first female leader of a Muslim country.

Much of the ministry's energy was dissipated by her conflict with Nawaz Sharif, Chief Minister of the Punjab, and the leader of the national opposition Islami Jamhoori Ittehad alliance. Following the collapse of the PPP-MQM alliance in October 1989 there was mounting ethnic violence between Sindhis and Mohajirs. The May 1990 Pucca Qila incident in Hyderabad intensified the violence throughout Sind. President Ghulam Ishaq Khan cited the deteriorating law and order situation when he dismissed the Bhutto government on 6 August 1990. Benazir was charged with corruption and misuse of power, while her husband Zardari was arrested on a kidnap charge.

Nawaz Sharif held office after the October 1990 elections. There was continuous conflict between him and Benazir during the next two years. In January 1993 however a more conciliatory atmosphere emerged which saw Benazir elected as chair of the National Assembly's Standing Committee on Foreign Affairs. Zardari was released on bail shortly afterwards.

Benazir Bhutto returned to power following the October 1993 polls. Their background had been the President's dismissal of Nawaz Sharif, his reinstatement by the Supreme Court in May, and the deal brokered by the Army in which both the President and Premier resigned. Conflict continued with Nawaz Sharif's opposition Muslim League. Benazir's relations with Nusrate were strained over her becoming sole PPP chair and by her brother Murtaza's claim to his father's political legacy when he returned from exile in November 1993. The greatest threats to her government however emanated from the 1994–5 unchecked violence in Karachi and the deteriorating economic situation in 1996. She was dismissed from office in late 1996 and her husband was arrested in connection with the death of her brother. Her party was trounced in the elections and she is at present facing charges of corruption.

Bhutto, Zulfiqar Ali (b. Al Murtaza, Larkana, 5 Jan. 1928; d. Rawalpindi, 4 Apr. 1979)
Pakistani; President and then Prime Minister 1971–7

The son of a Sindhi feudal landowner, Bhutto was educated at Bombay Cathedral High School and Berkeley and Oxford Universities. After Ayub *Khan's 1958 coup, Bhutto became Minister of Commerce and Industries. He made his name however as an expert on foreign affairs and held this Cabinet office from 1963 to 1966. His outlook was fervently anti-Indian and pro-Chinese. Bhutto clashed with Ayub over the Tashkent Treaty which followed the 1965 Indo-Pakistan War. In November 1967 he founded the Pakistan People's Party which propounded an ideology of Islamic socialism. The PPP co-ordinated the campaign which led to Ayub Khan's replacement by the army chief Yahya Khan.

The PPP triumphed in the West Pakistan constituencies in Pakistan's first national elections in 1970. Sheikh Mujibur Rahman's Awami League similarly succeeded in East Pakistan. The inability to share power or to meet East Pakistani demands for autonomy resulted in the tragedy of the Bangladesh War. Pakistan's defeat by India ended Yahya's power. Bhutto in December 1971 replaced him, initially as civilian martial law administrator. He became Prime Minister following the introduction of the 1973 constitution.

Bhutto's populism encompassed nationalization, land reform, and administrative reform designed to curb the power of the dominant élites. In foreign affairs, he shifted Pakistan into the Islamic and Third World orbit from its more traditional pro-Western stance. His greatest triumphs were the holding of the 1974 Islamic Summit in Lahore and the return of the 93,000 Pakistani prisoners of war following the June 1972 Simla summit with Indira *Gandhi.

By the March 1977 elections however, Bhutto's popularity appeared to be fading. The opposition Pakistan National Alliance claimed that the PPP's sweeping victory resulted from widespread rigging. Its civil disobedience campaign was linked with the demand for an Islamic social order. Despite Bhutto's concessions, he was forced to introduce martial law in a number of cities. On 5 July *Zia-ul-Huq launched a coup.

Zia cancelled the elections he had promised for October. The Lahore High Court found Bhutto guilty of the charge of conspiracy to murder a political oppponent on 18 March 1978 and sentenced him to death, despite the weakness of the prosecution case. The Supreme Court by a majority of one upheld the sentence. Despite an international clamour for clemency, Bhutto was hastily executed on 4 April 1979 at Rawalpindi Central Jail.

Bhutto remains a controversial figure in Pakistani politics; admirers point to his concern for the downtrodden, his dynamism, and his foreign policy achievements. Detractors emphasize his arbitrariness and vanity and claim that he was directly responsible for the dismemberment of Pakistan.

Bidault, Georges Augustin (b. Moulins, 5 Oct. 1899; d. 26 Jan. 1983)

French; Prime Minister 1946, 1949–50, Foreign Minister 1945–6, 1947–8, 1953–4

Lycée history teacher, editor of the Christian Democratic daily paper *L'Aube* from 1936 to 1939, against *Franco, and an opponent of the Munich agreement, Bidault was taken prisoner and on his liberation started Resistance activities in the Lyons region. In 1943 he became president of the Conseil National de la Résistance, which had been formed to co-ordinate the activities of different groups and movements and organized its commitment to *de Gaulle. Although in August 1945 Bidault was in the Paris insurrection and met de Gaulle at the Hôtel de Ville and was at de Gaulle's side for the famous victory march down the Champs Elysée, he was never an unconditional Gaullist. Bidault was a founder and leader of the centrist Mouvement Républicain Populaire (of which he was president). Bidault became Foreign Minister in the provisional government and held that position from 1944 to 1948 and again from 1953 to 1954—he was almost constantly in power. Bidault at the Quay was at first to express a strong anti-German feeling (against German reconstruction), supported the continuation of the French Empire, and was far from being strongly European (and in this was somewhat out of line with the urgent Europeanism of his MRP associates). Bidault was also strongly Atlanticist and flung France's weight behind the Western camp and into the Cold War in 1947. Bidault and the UK's Ernest *Bevin joined in initiatives to consolidate the West European response to the *Marshall Plan (such as the OEEC and NATO) and to parry the Soviet threat to the West: he was one of the founding fathers of European–American co-operation and when he returned as Prime Minister in October 1949 he was instrumental in promoting the *Schuman plan for a Coal and Steel Community. Foreign Minister again in the Mayer and Laniel governments (1953–4), he had less success and, an imperialist, attempted to prevent the rising tide of nationalism in the colonies (ousting the Sultan of Morocco) and to bring America onto the French side in the Indochina War. The Laniel government fell over the military defeat of Dien Bien Phu. Bidault supported de Gaulle's return to power in 1958 and campaigned for a 'Yes' vote in the September referendum but he had close Algerian connections and with de Gaulle's September 1959 speech on Algerian 'self-determination' he went into opposition. This opposition quickly took an insurrectionary turn. He organized a new 'Resistance Council' and then supported the 1962 Generals' putsch and the terrorist Organisation de l'Armée Secrète. Bidault was forced to flee, first to Spain and then to Brazil in a flight which was desperate and despairing (he never believed the 'French Algeria' cause could prevail). He returned to France after the amnesty of June 1968. He was the author of a number of books of politics and autobiography but he has yet to be the subject of a solid biography.

Biedenkopf, Kurt H. (b. Ludwigshafen, 28 Jan. 1930)
German; Minister-President of Saxony 1990– , Secretary-General of the CDU 1973–7

Biedenkopf was one of the first of the post-war generation of Germans to seek intellectual stimulus at American universities, studying politics in 1949 at Davidson College and gaining an LL M from Georgetown University (Washington) in 1962. By that time he had been awarded his doctorate at Frankurt am Main University. From 1964 to 1970 he was professor of commercial law at the Ruhr University serving as rector 1967–9. After heading the government's commission on industrial co-determination, he was appointed to the board of the Henkel firm in 1971 where he remained until 1973.

At the invitation of *Kohl, Biedenkopf took over as Secretary-General of the CDU in 1973, serving until 1977. His brief was to reorganize the party machinery but the Christian Democrats failed in their challenge to *Schmidt in 1976 and he and Kohl cooled in their relations. He was a member of the parliament of North Rhine-Westphalia (NRW) 1980–7, and chairman of the CDU there 1986–7. He stood down after failing to dislodge the SPD government of NRW. He served as a member of the Bundestag 1976–80 and 1987–90.

Biedenkopf was one of the first West German politicians to understand the changes in East Germany in 1989. He had been a frequent visitor and had taken up hardship cases. The result was that he was invited to lead the CDU in Saxony in 1990. He won the regional election in that year, being elected Minister-President, and again in 1994 in this tradionally socialist stronghold.

Bierut, Bolesław (b. Leczno near Lublin, 18 Apr. 1892; d. Moscow, 12 Mar. 1956)
Polish; President of Poland 1946–52, General Secretary of the Polish United Workers' Party (PZPR) 1948–56

Bierut was the youngest son of a farm labourer. He joined the Polish Communist Party in 1920. From then until 1938, when he went to Moscow, he worked for the Comintern in Poland, Bulgaria, Czechoslovakia, and Austria. In 1943 he was infiltrated into Poland to increase Soviet control over the Communist resistance. His wife was captured and tortured to death by the Gestapo. In 1944 he played a key role in organizing the Communist takeover in Poland. In 1946 he became President in the interim Lublin government, posing as a non-party figure. From 1947 to 1952 he was President of Poland, following the rigged elections which brought the Communists to power. In December 1948 he presided over the congress which led to the merger of the

Communists and the Socialists in the PZPR with himself as head of the new party. At the same time he oversaw the humiliation and resignation of his rival, *Gomułka. From 1952 to 1954 Bierut was Polish premier. He was distressed at Khrushchev's 'Secret Speech' denouncing Stalin in 1956 and died shortly afterwards of a heart attack.

bin Mohammed, Hassan Moulai (b. 9 Jul. 1929)
Moroccan; King 1961–

After studies at Bordeaux University, Crown Prince Hassan commanded the army against the Rif rebels in 1958 and acted as Deputy Prime Minister under his father, Mohammed V, after the King dismissed the radical socialist government in 1960. Claiming the religious prestige and authority of direct descent from the Prophet Mohammed—a claim resisted by Mashreq Arabs—he succeeded to the throne in 1961 as Hassan II.

Hassan established a constitutional monarchy in 1962, which was modified in 1972, 1980, and 1992. Throughout his reign, the King has ruled with extensive prerogative powers and supreme religious authority, aided by a compliant *Majlis an-Nuwab* (parliament) dominated by the 'king's men' and the loyalties of a traditional tribal system. Hassan has encountered persistent opposition to his rule from left- and right-wing republicans, Islamic fundamentalists, and the Polisario Liberation Front of Western Sahara, that included attempted coups in 1971, 1972, and 1985. The current of political dissidence and Islamic opposition has been held in check by a combination of astute populist policies and rigorously effective state security.

Territorial disputes have dogged Hassan's foreign policy. A border dispute with Algeria led to war in 1963, a long-standing claim to Mauritania was only abandoned in 1969, and Morocco's claim to the Western Sahara has been tenaciously pursued to the present day. In 1974, a secret agreement with Mauritania to divide the territory on Spain's withdrawal was reached. King Hassan II reacted to international dismissal of Moroccan-Mauritanian claims by ordering the popular 'Green March' of 350,000 unarmed 'civilians' to seize Western Sahara in 1975. Moroccan armed forces occupied the territory in 1976. This further strained relations with Algeria, by frustrating its territorial claims, and initiated a costly, unresolved, low-intensity armed conflict with Polisario.

Birkenhead, Frederick Edwin Smith**, Lord** (b. Birkenhead, 12 July 1872; d. 30 Sept. 1930)
British; Lord Chancellor 1919–22, Secretary of State for India 1924–8; Kt. 1915, Viscount 1921, Earl 1922

The son of a barrister, Smith was educated at Birkenhead School and Wadham College, Oxford, where he took a first in jurisprudence. He lectured in law at Oxford University before being called to the bar. He established a reputation as a brilliant and combative lawyer, willing to demolish weak judges as well as witnesses. He was elected to the House of Commons as a Unionist (Conservative) in 1906. In 1914 he served with the Expeditionary Force but the following year was brought into government as Solicitor-General and, five months later, was promoted to Attorney-General. In 1916 he led the prosecution for treason of Sir Roger Casement. In 1919 he was appointed Lord Chancellor and moved to the Lords as Viscount Birkenhead. He carried through a significant reform of property law. He served until the fall of the coalition government, refusing to serve in the new government formed by Bonar *Law. Recalled by *Baldwin in 1924, he was given (apparently deliberately) a post inappropriate to his particular talents, that of Secretary of State for India. He gained Baldwin's trust as a man of sound judgement, both on India and on domestic issues. Never a rich man, he resigned in 1928 in order to establish a better income for himself and his family. He took up directorships of ICI and Tate & Lyle, but his business career proved a short one. He died in September 1930 at the age of 58.

Beaverbrook rated him 'the cleverest man in the kingdom', an assessment that Birkenhead probably shared. His inability to suffer fools gladly counted against him, ensuring he had plenty of enemies in the political world. Though ambitious and arrogant, he gained the confidence of both Baldwin and Churchill, the former relying on him more and more during his last years of service in the Cabinet.

Bishop, Maurice (b. Aruba, 29 May 1944; d. 19 Oct. 1983)

Grenadian; Prime Minister 1979–83

Born in the Dutch island of Aruba to Grenadian parents, Bishop trained as a barrister in London before returning to Grenada in 1970 to become involved in radical politics. He was instrumental in merging a number of small left-wing groups into the New Jewel Movement (NJM) in 1973, which campaigned against the autocratic government of Premier Eric Gairy. Gairy repressed the NJM and other opponents and in 1974 Bishop was jailed, two weeks after his father had been shot dead during a demonstration. In 1976 Bishop headed a three-party alliance and was elected to parliament, becoming leader of the opposition.

In March 1979 the NJM staged a bloodless coup when Gairy was abroad and proclaimed a People's Revolutionary Government (PRG), in which Bishop was named Prime Minister. Charismatic and popular, he became the figurehead of the PRG, attracting considerable support both within Grenada and from radical circles in Europe and North America. For all its Marxist rhetoric, the PRG was in reality a pragmatic regime, encouraging co-operation between private and public sectors and attempting to diversify out of the island's dependency on agricultural commodities. It earned the enmity of the USA, however, through its close links with Cuba, which assisted in the building of an international airport.

In 1983 differences between the 'moderate' Bishop faction and hardliners within the NJM broke out into violence. Refusing to share the party leadership, Bishop was arrested and then forcibly released by a crowd of supporters. As he was preparing to address a meeting in the capital, St George's, troops loyal to the opposing faction of Bernard Coard opened fire. Bishop and several prominent ministers and supporters were then executed. In the ensuing chaos a Revolutionary Military Council seized power, providing the Reagan administration with the pretext to invade Grenada on 25 October.

Maurice Bishop was feared by regional conservative governments as a subversive example but was also widely admired for his stance against US domination and in favour of small-island sovereignty. His government won praise for its economic policies from such unlikely sources as the World Bank, but some Grenadians accused him of tolerating human rights abuses. Today, his memory is more revered than reviled in Grenada, even if the small party which carries his name receives little electoral support.

Blair, Anthony Charles Lynton (b. Edinburgh, 6 May 1953)

British; leader of the Labour Party 1994– , Prime Minister 1997–

Blair attended the public school Fettes in Edinburgh, read law at Oxford, and became a barrister. His father was a barrister and university lecturer.

In the 1983 general election, Blair won the safe Sedgefield seat for Labour. The Labour Party had its most left-wing manifesto for over fifty years. Good performances in the House of Commons quickly brought him attention and he was elected to the shadow Cabinet in 1988. He became the party's chief spokesmen on energy and then between 1989 and 1992 on employment. In this post his announcement that Labour would not bring back the closed shop which Conservative legislation had virtually abolished was presented as a *fait accompli* to the trade unions. This was an early signal of his determination to modernize Labour.

With the election of John *Smith as party leader and the retirement of a number of senior figures from the front bench after the 1992 general election a younger generation of Labour politicians had the opportunity to come to the fore. Smith appointed Blair as shadow spokesman on Home Office affairs. He was determined to refute the change that Labour was soft on crime and coined the popular phrase that Labour would be 'tough on crime and tough on the causes of crime'.

When John Smith died in 1994 Blair decided to stand for the leadership and was elected by an overwhelming majority on 21 July 1994. Within a few months he announced that he would review Clause 4 of the party constitution, which committed the party to public ownership. 'Review' meant abolition and he carried the fight to the constituencies and was successful. As part of his drive for modernization of the party (he usually referred to 'New Labour') he took steps to reduce the trade union influence in the party and appeal to the middle class. He moved policies sharply to the centre ground, and tried to shed Labour's image as a tax and spend party. There were complaints from party activitists that he was abandoning socialism and that he failed to consult over policy changes. But he got his way because he was seen as the party's best hope of ending its long spell in the political wilderness. He gained his reward when he led his party to a landslide victory in the 1997 general election. The party gained the largest number of seats and higgest majority in its history. Pollsters reported that he was the most popular Prime Minister since surveys had been conducted.

Blum, Léon (b. Paris, 9 Apr. 1872; d. 30 Mar. 1950)

French; Prime Minister 1936–7, Dec. 1946–Jan. 1947

The second of five brothers, born into a non-practising Jewish family from Alsace, Léon Blum is one of the major political figures of mid-twentieth-century France, although no statesman has been so constantly and viciously attacked from the extreme left and the extreme right. His reputation is only just beginning to recover from a vilification in which he was portrayed as a weak and amateurish man without vision (few politicians have been so consistent and firm of purpose). He was a remarkable student at the *lycées* Charlemagne and Henri-IV and then at the élite École Normale Supérieur. Although he studied law and was by profession an *auditeur* at the Conseil d'État, he was often seen as a literary figure and did write copiously on literary issues. Blum joined the Parti Socialiste Français in 1902 and became a close associate of its leader Jean *Jaurès. He was 'politicized' by the Dreyfus affair, which dramatized the values of republican socialism as Jaurès and Blum saw them. Blum's first taste of office was as head of Minister of Public Works Marcel Sembat's private office from the outbreak of war in 1914 until 1916. Jaurès assassination in 1914 thrust him into the front rank of Socialist leaders and into the battle for the wartime coalition, the 'union sacrée'. He was elected as deputy for the Seine in 1919 but was almost immediately caught up in the battle to preserve the old SFIO ('la vieille maison') from a Bolshevik takeover. At the Congress of Tours of 1920 at which the majority of activists (but few deputies) voted to join the Leninist International, Blum, in a speech of remarkable prescience set out the lines of dispute with the Communists: these were not over revolution as such, but over 'democratic centralism', which he predicted would lead to repression. With Paul Faure Blum rebuilt the party and commented daily on politics in the socialist *Le Populaire*. Blum formulated the pragmatic if scholastic distinction between the 'exercise' of power in the interests of the working class and the 'conquest of power' which would be a revolutionary peaceful break with capitalism. When the Popular Front of Socialists, Radicals, and Communists was elected in 1936, Prime Minister Blum faced a general strike of workers who were impatient with that distinction. The Popular Front is remembered for its extensive programme of reforms but it faced debilitating economic problems and sapping foreign policy issues (the Spanish Civil War). He called for a 'pause' (i.e. halt) to reforms after ten months and resigned after thirteen months. He was briefly Deputy Prime Minister in 1938 but was unable to prevail against mounting Communist hostility. Blum voted against the transfer of power to *Pétain in July 1940 after the fall of France and he was arrested. He was put on trial at Riom (with the Communist Party offering to testify against him) but turned the defence into a political triumph with an electrifying speech from the dock. The trial was stopped. He was deported to Buchenwald in 1943 and liberated in 1945 but his writings had been circulated in the Resistance and through those his influence was considerable. When he returned he continued to be politically active and was Prime Minister at the end of 1946 when he was able to negotiate a loan with the USA and to set the basis for the new institutions of Europe in the Treaty of Brussels. His main battle, to place the old *marxisant* SFIO on a more realistic footing, was not successful and he and his associates were rejected by a new generation of Socialists. He remained an inspiration to Socialist modernizers and he is the subject of many biographies (of which Jean Lacouture's *Léon Blum* is the best example).

Bokassa, Jean-Bedel (b. Bobangui, 22 Feb. 1922; d. 3 Nov. 1996)
Central African; head of state 1965–77, Emperor 1977–9

Orphaned at 6, Bokassa was educated at mission schools, joined the French colonial army in 1939, and fought in the Second World War and Indochina, receiving numerous medals for bravery. Commissioned as lieutenant in 1949, he rose rapidly to become Chief of Staff in the government led by President Dacko, whom he then ousted in a military *coup d'état*.

His regime rapidly degenerated into a brutal personal dictatorship, marked by the murder of numerous opponents in which Bokassa personally participated; he also indulged in ritual cannibalism. Not content with declaring himself President for Life, he decided to become an emperor, in emulation of Napoleon, and in 1977 organized a lavish but bizarre coronation ceremony which was alleged to cost a third of the annual national revenue. Despite these excesses, he retained good relations with successive French governments, and notably that of President *Giscard d'Estaing, until he became too embarrassing to be ignored. Public revelations about his gift of diamonds to Giscard, the value of which was hotly disputed, coupled with Bokassa's physical attack on the French ambassador, resulted in his overthrow in September 1979 in an operation by French paratroops which was thinly disguised as an internal coup.

After taking refuge in France and Côte d'Ivoire, he voluntarily returned home in 1986, saying that he was homesick. His expected welcome proved delusory, and he was put on trial for murder and sentenced to death, but this was commuted to life imprisonment.

Bolger, James Brendan (b. Opunake, 31 May 1935)
New Zealand; Prime Minister, Minister in Charge Security Intelligence Service 1990–

Bolger, a farmer by background, left school at 15. He has said that as a practising Christian, having grown up in a strong Catholic household, the social teaching of the church has been very important in shaping his views on issues with an emphasis on fairness and equity.

A minister in the *Muldoon government and leader of the Opposition since 1968, he took office as Prime Minister on 28 October 1990, the day after the National Party's landslide win in the elections of 27 October 1990. Heavy spending cuts in health, education, housing, and defence were announced by his Finance Minister, Ruth Richardson, in the first mini-budget handed down in December. On 1 April

1991, cutbacks to social security came into force with unemployment and sickness benefits reduced. On the same day the radical Employment Contracts Act, which allowed employees to make their own contracts with employers and abolished the right of unions to negotiate employee wages and conditions, was publicly announced. Widespread strikes followed with protesters clashing violently with police.

In July the 1991/2 national budget announced significant cuts to social welfare, most notably in health, education, housing, and pensions, affecting nearly half of New Zealand's population and effectively ending what prior to 1991 had been one of the most comprehensive welfare systems in the world. When the vote on the budget was put four government members crossed the floor. In August two National Party members resigned to become independents in protest against the budget cuts. In October the Minister for Maori Affairs, Winston Peters, a very popular politician, was sacked from Cabinet for his continuing criticism of the government. In December Bolger recorded a 5.5 per cent popularity rating, making him the most unpopular Prime Minister ever and earning him the title of 'Mr 5 per cent'. Despite these unpromising beginnings the Bolger government went on to win the 1993 elections, albeit with a majority of one. At the same time as the elections the Mixed Member Proportional voting system, based on the German system, was approved by 54 per cent of the voters in a referendum. With the next elections due in October 1996 it was announced that a three-party coalition governed New Zealand consisting of the dominant National Party, the United Party, and the one-seat Christian Democrat Party.

Bondfield, Margaret Grace (b. Somerset, 17 Mar. 1873; d. 16 June 1953)

British; Minister of Labour 1929–31

The daughter of a lace worker, Bondfield left elementary school at 13. Most of her life was devoted to trade unionism. Before the First World War she was organizing secretary of the Women's Labour League and the National Federation of Women Workers. During the war she held official positions on the Central Committee on Women's Employment and the War Emergency Workers' National Committee. Afterwards, she served as vice-president of the International Federation of Working Women and in 1924 was appointed official British representative on the governing body of the International Labour Office of the League of Nations. In 1920 she became the chief women's officer of the Gas and Municipal Workers' Union—a post she held until her retirement in 1938. After her retirement she served as a vice-president of the National Council of Social Service.

Bondfield's excursion into parliamentary politics was brief. She was elected Labour MP for Northampton in 1923, only to lose the seat in 1924. Re-elected for Wallsend, in 1926, she left the Commons for good in the 1931 landslide against Labour. Despite its brevity, her political career was noteworthy. Having achieved a number of 'firsts' in the industrial labour movement—first female TUC council member (1918) and chair (1923)—she established a similar record in national politics. She became one of the first women to hold junior ministerial office—in the first Labour government. She then became the first female Privy Counsellor and Cabinet Minister as Minister of Labour (1929–31).

Bondfield was at her best in the industrial labour movement. She was never an accomplished parliamentarian and adverse economic circumstances made her occupancy of the Ministry of Labour thoroughly thankless.

Bonnet, Georges (b. 1889;–d. 1973)

French; Foreign Minister 1938–9

Georges Bonnet was an ambitious, and controversial, member of the French political class of the 1930s who lingered on in politics until the early 1970s. A lawyer by training, he joined the centre left Radical Party after the First World War and established a durable power base in the Dordogne department.

He entered Parliament in the 1924 Cartel des Gauches victory and held a number of government posts in the short-lived Radical governments of the early 1930s. Although he took part in the electoral pact linking Radicals, Socialists, and Communists known as the Popular Front, he was very far from being a left-winger and was appointed United States ambassador by Leon *Blum to get him out of the way. Back in France, he became Foreign Minister in the 1938 *Daladier government and rapidly became one of the most dedicated supporters of appeasement. He gave no support at all to the Czech government in the Munich crisis and sought subsequently to prevent war at all costs; he was the architect of the official visit Ribbentrop paid to Paris in January 1939 which led to Jewish ministers being excluded from official receptions. When war broke out, he was one of the most active proponents of an early peace and then, after the fall of France, of Marshal *Pétain's policy of diplomatic collaboration with the Germans. He was a member of Vichy's Conseil National.

Despite the series of exculpatory memoirs he subsequently wrote, Bonnet's reputation never recovered from his pre-war and wartime activities. In 1945 he was sentenced to a period of national indignity, the first part of which he spent in exile in Switzerland. He did not, however, abandon his political ambitions and in 1956 succeeded in being re-elected deputy for the Dordogne. He remained a member of the National Assembly until 1968 and was active in Radical Party politics for some years after that. He masterminded the electoral campaigns of his son Alain, who inherited his Dordogne constituency as a Socialist and was a minister in the 1981 *Mauroy government.

Borah, William Edgar (b. Fairfields, Illinois, 29 June 1865; d. 19 Jan. 1940)
US; US Senator 1907–40

The son of a farmer, Borah attended local schools in Wayne County and then the Southern Illinois Academy at Enfield. He graduated from the University of Kansas in 1889, having studied law, was called to the bar that same year, and began practising at Lyon. Two years later he moved to Boise, Idaho, and practised with one of the state's leading law firms. His political career began inauspiciously with an unsuccessful bid for election to the US House of Representatives as a 'Silver' Republican in 1896, followed in 1903 by an unsuccessful attempt to win nomination for US senator. In 1907, however, he was elected Republican Senator for Idaho and was re-elected for each subsequent term until his death.

Although he never travelled abroad, Borah's interest was foreign relations. An isolationist, in 1920 he orchestrated the Senate's opposition to the ratification of the Treaty of Versailles. He was a resolute opponent of America's membership of the International Court of Justice at The Hague. In 1924 he became chairman of the powerful Senate Foreign Relations Committee; this enabled him to play an influential part in the direction and development of America's foreign policy.

In domestic affairs Borah assumed the role of spokesman for the interests of the Midwest. He was a prohibitionist but gained a reputation as a radical by being one of the first leading politicians to champion women's suffrage.

Boris III, King of the Bulgars (*full name* Boris Clément Robert Marie Pie Louis Stanislas, Xavier) (b. 30 Jan. 1894; d. c.28 Aug. 1943)
Bulgarian; King 1918–43

Boris was the eldest son of Ferdinand I and Maria Luisa Bourbon-Parma. He commanded the Bulgarian Army on the Macedonian Front during the First World War.

Though defeated in the Anglo-French offensive of 1918 he retained the respect of his men. He became king after his father's abdication on 3 October 1918 with the army's support against republican opposition. Throughout the 1920s and early 1930s, his position was under threat. He protected himself by feigning disinterestedness in politics. In November 1935 he successfully launched a coup against the military regime of Colonel Georgiev. From 1936 to 1943 Boris was effectively the dictator of Bulgaria.

When the Second World War broke out Boris attempted to maintain Bulgaria's neutrality. In 1941 he declared war on the Soviet Union and the Western Allies, but did not collaborate actively with the Axis Powers. This led to a rift with *Hitler who, in August 1943, summoned him to his headquarters in East Prussia, where he violently criticized Bulgaria's role in the war. Boris refused to change his policy. He died suddenly three days later. It is now believed that he was poisoned. Boris was succeeded by his 6-year old son, Simeon II.

Bosch, Juan (b. Dominican Republic, 30 June 1909)
Dominican; President Feb.–Sept. 1963

Bosch spent much of his early life as an exile from Rafael *Trujillo's dictatorship, living mostly in Cuba and establishing a reputation as a novelist and historian. He founded the social-democratic Partido Revolucionario Dominicano (PRD) in Havana in 1939, but had to wait a further twenty-two years before Trujillo was assassinated and he could return home. In 1963 Bosch became President after the Dominican Republic's first ever free elections.

Although his government proved to be cautious, Bosch was suspected of being a Communist sympathizer by the Dominican élite, and after seven months in power he was overthrown by the military with tacit US support. A further military uprising took place in 1965 with the aim of reinstating him, and as the country verged on civil war, the US invaded and imposed peace. In elections the following year Bosch lost to his conservative rival, Joaquín Balaguer. He would never again win the presidency although he attempted to do so on several occasions.

In 1973 Bosch left the PRD, having lost an internal power struggle with those who opposed his policy of boycotting elections. He then formed the Partido de la Liberación Dominicana (PLD), which espoused a pseudo-Marxist position, arguing for 'a dictatorship with popular support'. Gradually, however, the PLD became more social-democratic in orientation and finally championed neo-liberal economic reform in the 1990 elections. From 1978 to 1990 Bosch contested elections every four years and steadily regained his popularity. It is widely believed that only electoral fraud deprived him of beating Balaguer in 1990.

Bosch's last electoral bid was in 1994, when he finished in third place. Shortly afterwards, he retired from the leadership of the PLD, which went on to win the 1996 elections. Remembered as a writer and historian of considerable talent, he was also the eternal runner-up to his arch-rival, Balaguer.

Bourguiba, Habib ibn Ali (b. Monastir, Tunisia, 3 Aug. 1903)
Tunisian; President 1957–87

After legal studies in Paris, Bourguiba formed the radical Tunisian nationalist Neo Destour (New Constitution) party in 1934. Over the next twenty years he was imprisoned three times by the French before they recognized he was the political leader capable of effecting a smooth transition to the inevitable independence of Tunisia. In March 1956, the nationalist movement, with Bourguiba as the Prime Minister, took effective control of Tunisia, deposing the Bey a year later. In the new Tunisian republic, Neo Destour became the official party and Bourguiba the head of state. He negotiated France's military withdrawal from Tunisia by 1962 and successfully devloped commercial contacts between the two countries. Bourguiba pursued a 'Tunisian socialist' programme of socio-economic development which included expropriation of foreign owned land, collectivization of agriculture, and the education of women. It profoundly antagonized traditionalists. Although Bourguiba was declared President for Life in 1975, he faced mounting unrest. Widespread riots in 1978 led to more than fifty-one deaths; an attack on the town of Gafasa in 1980 by Libyan-backed insurgents of the Tunisian Armed Resistance resulted in French and American military assistance; a state of emergency was declared after looting, riots, and public-sector strikes in 1984–5 and, in 1986, he proved wholly incapable of suppressing a resurgence of the militant fundamentalist groups, Mouvement de la Tendance Islamique and Islamic Jihad, despite numerous arrests, imprisonments, and executions. During this period, Bourguiba's behaviour became increasingly erratic and in 1987 he was deposed on the grounds of his senility by the Prime Minister, Ben Ali.

Boyle, Edward Charles Gurney (b. London, 31 Aug. 1923; d. 28 Sept. 1981)
British; Minister of Education 1962–4; Bt. 1945, Baron (life peer) 1970

The son of a distinguished lawyer and grandson of a Conservative MP, Boyle was educated at Eton and Christ Church, Oxford, where he was elected president of the Oxford Union (1948). He had a short career as a journalist before entering the House of Commons, at the age of 27, as Conservative MP for Birmingham Handsworth in November 1950. He was appointed as a junior minister in 1954, aged 32, resigning from the government in 1956 on the issue of Suez. He was brought back into government by Harold *Macmillan the following year, serving as parliamentary secretary at the Ministry of Education and then economic secretary to the Treasury. In July 1962 he was given his own department, becoming Minister for Education, though without a seat in the Cabinet; he was elevated to Cabinet rank by Sir Alec *Douglas-Home in April 1964, serving until the party lost the general election in the October. In Opposition, he was made shadow Home Secretary by Douglas-Home and shadow Education Secretary by his successor, Edward *Heath. In 1969, at the age of 46, he announced he was leaving politics in order to become vice-chancellor of Leeds University. He left the House of Commons in 1970 and entered the Lords as a life peer. He devoted the rest of his life to the academic world, serving as vice-chancellor at Leeds and, from 1977 to 1979, as chairman of the Committee of Vice-Chancellors and Principals, before dying of a heart attack, following a long illness, in 1981 at the age of 58.

An intellectual, patrician, and private individual—he never married—he was not well suited to the hurly-burly and routine aspects of political life. He preferred the solace of classical music to the small talk of party activists. He served in posts where his liberal credentials clashed with the natural sentiments of those on the right of the Conservative Party. He opposed capital punishment and supported liberal policies on immigration. His willingness to concede a case for comprehensive education while shadow Education spokesman proved a particular irritant at party conferences—in 1967 his critics forced the first ballot at a party conference since 1950—and, sensing that he would not be offered the post of Education Secretary in a future Conservative government, left politics for a life more congenial to a scholar.

Bradley, Tom (b. Calvert, Texas, 29 Dec. 1917)
US; mayor of Los Angeles 1974–94

Educated at Southwest Law School and UCLA, Bradley was for many years (1940–62) a member of the Los Angeles Police Department. From 1963 onwards he was fully involved in Los Angeles elective politics, becoming the city's most prominent black leader and serving as a city council member (1963–73) and as mayor (1974–94).

Bradley was the first black mayor of Los Angeles and one of a group of black mayors who played an increasingly important role in American politics. Race played a part in

Bradley's first attempt to become mayor in 1969. Then populist Sam Yorty beat Bradley; but once Bradley won the mayoralty, he managed to maintain a coalition of blacks, Jews, Latinos, and liberals in support of his policies. Bradley moved to incorporate business into the running of the city and was so successful that Los Angeles for a period became a model of racial co-operation and of partnership between the business community and the public sector. His moderate approach disappointed some of his more radical supporters; and there emerged widespread concern about congestion and growth in the city. Yet Bradley remained personally popular and in 1982 he ran for Governor of California. However, he narrowly lost the general election to the Republican George *Deukmejian. When Deukmejian and Bradley fought each other again for the governorship in 1986 Bradley was more decisively defeated.

Bradley's position in California state politics gave him a high profile in national Democratic politics and in 1976 he co-chaired the Democratic national convention. In 1993 Bradley chose not to run again and he resumed private law practice. In 1996 he suffered a stroke while undergoing heart surgery and, although he survived, his activities were inevitably limited thereafter.

Brandt, Willy (b. Lübeck, 18 Dec. 1913; d. 9 Oct. 1992)

German; Chancellor of Federal Republic of Germany 1969–74, leader of SPD 1964–87

No one did more than Brandt as governing mayor of West Berlin (1957–66), Deputy Chancellor (1966–9), and Chancellor (1969–74) to improve the image of post-war Germany. Yet for most of his career he was reviled by right-wing detractors.

Brandt (baptized Herbert Frahm) was the son of an unmarried shop assistant whose SPD-orientated grandfather greatly influenced him. Unusually for a working-class boy at that time, Brandt achieved his university matriculation exam *Abitur* and turned to journalism. In 1931 he left the SPD to join the left-wing Socialist Workers' Party (SAP) which stood between the SPD and the Communist KPD. After the Nazi takeover in 1933 Frahm called himself Brandt to help his underground activity. In April 1933 he was forced to leave Germany for Norway, whose Socialist government gave generous help to the German exiles. Disguised as a Norwegian student Brandt returned to Berlin for several months in 1936, maintaining contacts with several SAP groups. As a journalist he covered the Spanish Civil War in 1937 in Barcelona and lost any illusions he had harboured about the Soviet Union. Back in Norway in 1939 he made his peace with mainstream Social Democracy, becoming officially a member of the exiled SPD in 1944. He had a narrow escape when the Nazis invaded Norway in 1940, posing as a Norwegian soldier and going into captivity for a few weeks. On release he headed for neutral Sweden, where he very nearly got into difficulties once again for his continued political activities.

In 1948 he regained German citizenship, which the Nazis had removed in 1938, and worked for the SPD press. In 1950 Brandt was elected to the West Berlin parliament, and five years later he was its president. His command of languages, especially English, essential to get on with the US and British officials in Berlin, also helped. Once he was elected mayor, he was often seen on television around the world as the leader of 2 million West Berliners determined to maintain their freedom. His success in this role helped to convince his colleagues that, although not the SPD leader (*Ollenhauer), he should be the party's candidate for Chancellor at the 1961 election. In the run-up to the election the East Germans erected the Berlin Wall and revealed the *Adenauer government's impotence. Although the Christian Democrats (CDU/CSU) won the SPD increased its vote from 31.8 to 36.7 per cent.

At the election in 1965 Brandt faced a new opponent, Ludwig *Erhard, who had taken over from Adenauer in 1963. This gave the CDU/CSU a new lease of life and, although the SPD increased its vote, the Christian Democratic total also went up. The SPD had placed much emphasis on cosmetics, public relations, rather than on substance. Brandt was also attacked as a man who had left Germany in its hour of need, when to stay would have meant the concentration camp or worse! Brandt was disappointed and on the point of giving up but was persuaded to carry on. When the Erhard government got into difficulties negotiations were taken up to form a grand coalition of the two main parties. In this Brandt became Vice-Chancellor and Foreign Minister.

The CDU/CSU and SPD coalition lasted from 1966 to 1969 and proved that the Social Democrats were 'fit to govern'. The fear of Germany's neighbours and allies that the far-right NPD would get into the Bundestag communicated itself to the German voters. As it turned out the SPD gained 42.7 per cent, the CDU/CSU 46.1 per cent, and the FDP 5.8 per cent. Brandt formed a government with FDP support.

Brandt's greatest successes were in relations with the Soviet Bloc. The Federal Republic signed renunciation of force treaties with the Soviet Union, Poland, and Czechoslovakia, greatly improving relations with these states. In 1970 Brandt met the head of the East German government, *Stoph, and was extremely popular with the ordinary East Germans. The meetings were the start of a new relationship between the two German states, finding formal expression in the signing of the Basic Treaty in December 1972.

It was to Brandt's credit that in the 1972 election the SPD gained a higher percentage vote (45.8) than the CDU/CSU (44.9) for the first, and so far only, time (1996). In 1974 he was forced to resign after an East German agent in his office was exposed. Brandt remained a formidable presence in the Bundestag until the end of his life. He remained the chairman of the SPD until 1987. He was elected chairman of the Socialist International in 1976, being regularly re-elected until his death. Unlike some SPD colleagues, he strongly supported the restoration of German unity in 1990.

Branting, Karl **Hjalmar** (b. Stockholm, 23 Nov. 1860; d. 24 Feb. 1925)

Swedish; Prime Minister 1920, 1921–3, 1924–5

The son of a professor (who was also director of the Central Institute for Gymnastics) Branting was educated at a private school in Stockholm, then read natural science at Uppsala University 1877–82 and worked as a mathematics assistant at Stockholm Observatory 1879–80 and 1882–4. He became a socialist while at Uppsala on the basis of extensive reading in the social sciences and contact with socialists (including Bernstein) on travels in France and Germany in 1878 and 1882. He was editor-in-chief of the newspaper *Social-Demokraten* 1886–92, 1896–1908, and 1911–17.

In 1889 Branting served as secretary at the founding congress of the Swedish Social Democratic Labour Party and was elected to the party's national executive. From the first he prioritized tactical co-operation with other parties, and especially with the Liberals in support of universal suffrage. In 1897 he was elected to parliament on the Liberal list for Stockholm as the first Social Democratic MP, and he remained a member for the rest of his life. In 1906 he became leader of the Social Democratic parliamentary group, in 1907 party chairman. In 1908 he took the lead in expelling a revolutionary faction from the party; by 1914 the Social Democrats became the largest single party in the directly elected house of the Riksdag. So Branting played a major part in laying the foundations for the highly successful Swedish Social Democratic Labour Party. He also worked for the peaceful resolution of international conflicts in the Second International before the First World War and in the League of Nations after it. In 1921 he won a share of the Nobel Peace Prize.

Brazauskas, Algirdas-Mikolas (b. Lithuania, 22 Sept. 1932)

Lithuanian; leader of Lithuanian Democratic Labour Party President of independent Lithuania 1990–   , 1993–

A construction engineer and manager, Brazauskas rose rapidly in the Lithuanian Communist Party as an industry and economics specialist, becoming Minister of the

Construction Materials Industry (1965–6), Deputy Chair of Lithuanian Gosplan (1966–77), and CP Secretary for Industry (1977–88). In October 1988 he became First Secretary of the Lithuanian CP, facing the rising tide of nationalism. To establish his nationalist credentials in December 1989 he took the Lithuanian party out of the CPSU, the first move of this kind, and became Chair of the Lithuanian Parliament. However, in March 1990 he was replaced in this post by *Landsbergis, whose nationalist party Sajudis won the parliamentary elections. Brazauskas became leader of the re-formed Lithuanian Democratic Party. With the increasing unpopularity and extremism of the Sajudis government new elections were held in October 1992 which were won by the LDLP and in February 1993 Brazauskas convincingly won the presidential elections. His government has pursued a more moderate pace in economic reform, especially in agriculture, and cultivated better relations with Russia and Poland, while maintaining Lithuania's commitment to joining Western institutions.

Brezhnev, Leonid Ilyich (b. Dneprodzerzhinsk, Ukraine, 19 Dec. 1906; d. Moscow, 10 Nov. 1982)

Russian; General Secretary of the Communist Party of the Soviet Union 1964–82

Brezhnev was the son of working-class parents. He qualified first as a land surveyor then in 1935 graduated from the Dneprodzerzhinsk Metallurgical Institute as a steel engineer. He joined the CPSU in 1931 and embarked on a party career in 1936. He worked in the Dneprodzerzhinsk region, joining the party apparatus in 1938 and benefiting from the patronage of *Khrushchev. During the Second World War he served as a political commissar in the Red Army, attaining the rank of major-general.

In 1947 Brezhnev was made First Secretary of Dnepropetrovsk region, which was to be his power base, and in 1950 became First Secretary in Moldavia. In 1952 he entered the Central Committee as a secretary. In 1954 Khrushchev sent him to Kazakhstan as local party chief to supervise the cultivation of virgin lands. Returning to Moscow in 1956 he became full member of the Presidium of the Central Committee (later the Politburo) the next year. From 1960 to 1964 he was chairman of the Presidium of the Supreme Soviet—the head of state. In 1963 he became secretary of the Central Committee with responsibility for day-to-day party organization, which gave him important powers of patronage. He played a major role in orchestrating Khrushchev's removal in October 1964, succeeding him as General Secretary of the CPSU. In the 1960s and early 1970s, Brezhnev ruled as first among equals in a collegiate leadership, while consolidating his power and became President in 1977.

In foreign policy Brezhnev initially allowed *Kosygin to represent the Soviet Union abroad. In 1968 he played a mediating role between the factions for and against intervention in Czechoslovakia. Thereafter his name was linked to the 'Brezhnev Doctrine' by which the Soviet Bloc states had the right to intervene in one another's internal affairs when the interests of 'socialism' as a whole were threatened. During the 1970s he played a prominent role in the development of détente with the United States, which culminated in the Helsinki Agreements of 1975, by which the United States and its allies recognized the territorial division after the Second World War. In the same period he engaged in prolonged arms limitation talks and attempted to improve trade links with the West. Already by 1975 relations with the West were under strain since the USA and USSR remained rivals in Third World conflicts while Moscow continued to restrict human rights in the USSR and Eastern Europe and to build up its nuclear and conventional forces. The beginning of the 'New Cold War' was marked by the Soviet Union's intervention in Afghanistan in December 1979, which Brezhnev supported.

At home, Brezhnev's rule was marked by stability of personnel within the CPSU, by massive investments in armaments, and by the unbridled subsidizing of an inefficient agricultural sector. At the time of his death in 1982, the Soviet Union was in crisis, desperately in need of economic reform and unable to subsidize the arms race threatened by the revival of US power under *Reagan.

Briand, Aristide (b. Nantes, 28 Mar. 1862, d. 7 Jan. 1932)
French; Prime Minister 1909–11, 1913, 1915–17, 1921–2, 1925–6, 1929

Briand was born in the western city of Nantes and trained as a lawyer. He flirted with the far left, made a reputation defending the anarchist trade unionists of the CGT and entered Parliament as a revolutionary Socialist in 1902. In the Chamber of Deputies he quickly demonstrated the mastery of compromise and manœuvre which would become his trademark. As *rapporteur* of the bill introducing the separation of church and state, he worked hard to defuse the tensions between anticlericals and Catholics. He then moved towards the centre by refusing to accept the Socialist Party's embargo on participation in bourgeois governments. Appointed Minister of Education and Churches in 1906, he was promoted by *Clemenceau to Minister of Justice and became Prime Minister on the latter's defeat in 1909. As Prime Minister, he attacked the Radical Party and outraged his erstwhile Socialist colleagues by dealing toughly with trade union militancy. His shift to the right was confirmed by his support for the presidential bid of the conservative Republican *Poincaré, whose Prime Minister he became, and by his leading role in the campaign for an extension of military service to three years.

It was, paradoxically, the First World War which started the process by which Briand regained the confidence of the parties of the left. He was not a very successful Prime Minister in 1915–17. Out of office, he grew alarmed at the endless slaughter and put out diplomatic feelers to the Austrians. In the short run, this proved dangerous as he came up against the implacable determination of Clemenceau, who became Prime Minister in November 1917. Briand narrowly avoided being swept away by the anti-defeatist campaign led by Clemenceau's henchmen and spent the rest of the war in uncharacteristic silence; to his chagrin he was excluded from any role in the 1919 peace negotiations. Yet he quickly recovered his earlier authority, first by leading the backstairs campaign which led to Clemenceau's failure to be elected President of the Republic and then by demonstrating to the inexperienced Chamber elected in 1919 his superior political talents. By 1921 he was back in office as Prime Minister. His clash with the assertive President *Millerand, which led to his resignation in 1922, did him no harm at all when the left regained power in 1924. In the last phase of his career, he was several times Prime Minister, but devoted most of his energies to the cause of Franco-German reconciliation and the League of Nations. He was Foreign Minister for almost six years. Known as the 'pilgrim of peace', he established close links with *Stresemann, built on the 'pale sunlight of Locarno' and even put forward a plan for a European federation.

By 1931 he was visibly failing. He was deeply upset by his failure to be elected President of the Republic in May 1931 and in January 1932 was evicted from the foreign office by his former protégé, *Laval. He died six weeks later. Nine years later the cause of Franco-German reconciliation to which he had devoted his final years collapsed in disaster and some of the strongest champions of 'Briandism' became prominent collaborators. His own reputation, however, survived, and is perpetuated by the memorial plaque outside the French Ministry of Foreign Affairs.

Bricker, John W. (b. Pleasant Township, 6 Sept. 1893; d. 22 Mar. 1986)
US; State Attorney-General 1933–7, Governor 1938–46, vice-presidential candidate 1944, US Senator 1946–58

John Bricker was a conservative whose values reflected the isolationist wing of the Republican Party associated with Robert A. *Taft. He attended Ohio State University, where he studied law. Although Bricker passed the Ohio bar examination in 1917, his legal training was interrupted by the First World War. Initially declared medically unfit to serve, Bricker became first an army athletic instructor and then, after getting ordained for the purpose, an army chaplain. He practised law in Ohio, becoming state Attorney-General in 1933.

In 1938 Bricker was elected Governor of Ohio, a position he held for three successive terms. In office Bricker was extremely successful at improving the state's finances while expanding its expenditure on social programmes and education. He was instinctively hostile to the New Deal and its expansion of federal government power, which he saw as a threat to the integrity of state government.

In 1944 Republican nominee Thomas *Dewey chose Bricker as his running mate, rather than Everett *Dirksen. Bricker's isolationist values appealed also to the far right but Bricker repudiated the attempt by Gerald L. K. Smith and the America First Party to nominate him as that party's vice-presidential candidate. The Dewey–Bricker ticket was defeated by Franklin *Roosevelt but Bricker emerged as a significant figure in the Republican Party. He was elected to the Senate in 1946 and served two terms until defeated in 1958 as a result of a massive anti-Republican swing in Ohio.

In the Senate, Bricker was a fierce opponent of Communism and anything which ensnared America in international institutions or smacked of world government. He opposed American membership of the International Atomic Energy Agency and was hostile to the United Nations and foreign aid. He repeatedly tried to amend the constitution to limit the power of the President to make international agreements. Although all his efforts failed, the so-called 'Bricker amendment' found support in both parties and underlined the strength of isolationist sentiment in Congress after the Second World War. In 1953, despite Eisenhower's rejection of the philosophy of the Bricker amendment, the Senate came within one vote of the two-thirds majority required to submit the amendment to the states.

Brittan, Leon (b. London, 25 Sept. 1939)

British; Home Secretary 1983–85, Commissioner of the European Community 1989– ; Kt. 1989

Brittan was educated at Haberdashers' Aske's School and Trinity College, Cambridge. He was president of the Cambridge Union and part of a distinguished group of undergraduates who went on to Cabinet office. Trained as lawyer—he was called to the bar in 1962—he became one of the country's leading libel lawyers and took silk in 1978. Active in Conservative politics from student days, he served as chairman of the Bow Group in 1964–5 and, after two unsuccessful attempts, was elected to parliament in 1974.

A friend and supporter of Margarent *Thatcher, his talents were quickly recognized. After a brief and successful stint as the Conservative Party's liaison officer with the academic community, he was appointed in 1976 an Opposition spokesman on devolution and made his parliamentary reputation opposing the Labour government's devolution legislation. In 1979 he was appointed Minister of State at the Home Office and joined the Cabinet in 1981 as chief secretary to the Treasury. Two years later, at the age of 43, he was made Home Secretary. Though he handled a difficult brief well—one of the few holders of the office to have a good grasp of the Home Office—he was moved in 1985 in order to make way for Douglas *Hurd. Appointed Secretary of State for Trade and Industry, he was almost immediately embroiled in a dispute with Defence Secretary Michael *Heseltine over the future of the Westland helicopter company. The leak of part of a letter from the Attorney-General to Heseltine was traced to Brittan's office. After a heated meeting of the 1922 Committee in January 1986, he decided he no longer enjoyed the support of the parliamentary party and resigned.

Though Margaret Thatcher had publicly indicated she wished to see him return in due course to the Cabinet, she instead offered him in 1988 the post of one of the British Commissioners in the European Community. He took up the appointment in

1989. He made his mark as Commissioner dealing with external trade, achieving a notable success in GATT negotiations in 1993. In 1994 he was an unsuccessful candidate for the presidency of the Commission.

He was knighted in 1989, apparently declining a peerage in order to leave open the possibility of a return to the House of Commons.

Brock, William Emerson III (b. Chattanooga, Tennessee, 23 Nov. 1930)
US; member of the US House of Representatives 1963–71, US Senator 1971–7, Secretary of Labor 1985–7

William Brock was educated at Washington and Lee University. Following a period in private business (1956–63), he was elected to the House of Representatives for the 3rd District of Tennessee in 1962, beginning a long association with Republican politics. Brock served in the House until elected to the Senate in 1970. In January 1977 he became chairman of the Republican National Committee, a position in which he was responsible for a range of structural reforms as well as intellectual and policy initiatives designed to revive the Republican Party fortunes following the catastrophic 1976 elections. The years of his chairmanship (1977–81) were years of enormous achievement and provided the foundation for the Republican gains of 1980. Although it was not entirely clear how much sympathy Brock personally had for the *Reagan revolution, he served in both the first and the second Reagan administrations—first as US Trade Representative (1981–5) and then as Secretary of Labor (1985–7).

Brooke, Sir Basil Stanlake, Bt. (b. Co. Fermanagh, 9 June 1888; d. 18 Aug. 1973)
British; Prime Minister of Northern Ireland 1943–63; Viscount (Lord Brookeborough) 1952

An Anglo-Irish Protestant landowner's son, Brooke was educated at Winchester and Sandhurst. During the First World War he served in the army, reaching the rank of captain and being awarded the Military Cross and Croix de Guerre. After the war, in the troubled period leading up to the partition of Ireland, he helped to found the Northern Irish Constabulary, in which he became a commandant. His lengthy membership of the parliament of Northern Ireland at Stormont spanned almost forty years. During that time he established a United Kingdom record by holding ministerial office (in the government of Northen Ireland) continuously for thirty-three years. His first important post (1933–41) was as Minister of Agriculture under the premiership of Sir James Craig. After two years as Minister of Commerce, he became Prime Minister of Northern Ireland in 1943, remaining in that post for almost twenty years.

As Prime Minister, Brooke's principal objective was to secure the future of Northern Ireland and its link with Britain by generating greater economic prosperity there than existed in independent Eire, and he succeeded in attracting significant inward investment. He was not an extreme Unionist, but his government did nothing to ameliorate the sectarian divide in Northern Ireland. Indeed, it perpetuated the exclusion of the Catholic minority from political power. Although more outspoken pressure from the civil rights movement and then the outbreak of violence at the end of the 1960s came after he had retired, his government certainly contributed to the circumstances which precipitated them.

Brooke, Edward William (b. Washington, DC, 26 Oct. 1919)
US; US Senator 1967–79

Educated at Howard and Boston Universities, Brooke practised law in Massachusetts and Washington, DC, before becoming Attorney-General of Massachusetts, a post he filled from 1962 until 1966.

In 1966 Edward Brooke's decisive Senate victory made him the first black elected to the Senate in the twentieth century. The victory was all the more unusual because Brooke was a Republican at a time when the vast majority of blacks identified with the Democratic Party and the Republican Party fielded few black candidates. A liberal on most issues except the economy and national security, he was also a key Senate supporter of allowing abortions funded by Medicaid. Brooke's reputation and liberal politics, together with his political skill and personal charm, meant that he was able for a time to secure support from Democrats as well as Republicans in his state. Following an easy re-election victory in 1972, Brooke's seat seemed secure until 1978 when the *Boston Globe* reported a series of financial and ethical problems including the fact that Brooke had lied about his financial worth in divorce proceedings. He was investigated by the Senate Ethics Committee and, although it emerged that much of the information against Brooke was being leaked by members of his family, he became politically vulnerable. Some also criticized him for failing to promote Massachusetts' interests in the Senate; and Massachusetts' other Senator, Ted *Kennedy, for the first time campaigned on behalf of Brooke's Democratic opponent, Paul Tsongas. Tsongas defeated Brooke in the 1978 election.

Browder, Earl Russell (b. Wichita, Kansas, 20 May 1891; d. 27 June 1973)
US; Communist Party presidential candidate 1936, 1940

The son of an impoverished farmer, Browder was largely forced to finish his formal schooling early to help support the family. He took a law degree by correspondence but mainly earned his living as an accountant.

Browder began his lifelong involvement in radical politics in 1907 when he joined the Socialist Party. From then until 1921, when he became committed to Communism, Browder was involved with a range of left-wing and labour organizations including the Syndicalist League of America and the Co-operative League of America. Browder's opposition to American entry into the First World War earned him a sixteen-month prison sentence, which took effect in 1919. Franklin *Roosevelt granted Browder a pardon on taking office in 1933.

When Browder left prison he again joined the Socialist Party, editing its Kansas-based newspaper *The Workers World*, which took a pro-Communist line. An American Communist Party had been founded while Browder was in prison and in January 1921 Browder, who had moved to New York to work as a bookkeeper, became actively involved in its recruitment activities. He helped recruit trade unionists for the first Congress of the International of Labour Unions and travelled to Moscow where he met *Lenin.

From 1926 to 1929 Browder was in China as General Secretary of the Pan-Pacific Trade Union Secretariat and in 1930 he became the Secretary of the deeply divided and faction-ridden Communist Party. Browder was a prolific publicist and imposed a degree of organizational unity on the party. The party line was decided in Moscow. After initial scepticism about the New Deal, the Communist Party adopted a popular front strategy and supported Roosevelt as well as urging co-operation with sympathetic left and liberal groups. In 1936 Browder was the Communist Party candidate for President and secured 80,869 votes.

Communist membership was buoyant until the Nazi-Soviet Pact destroyed its credibility. Browder himself was arrested in 1940 for the unlawful use of a passport and while in prison he again ran for President but his vote (40,251) was much down on the 1936 figure.

In 1946 Browder was ousted from the Communist Party leadership and expelled from it for having supported Roosevelt's wartime policies which constituted 'ideological deviance'. He spent the remaining years of his life in relative seclusion.

Brown, Edward G. ('Pat') (b. 21 Apr. 1905; d. 16. Feb. 1996)
US; Governor of California 1958–66

The young Brown studied law at evening classes. He was a successful lawyer, though always interested in politics. He started as a Republican and tried for election to the state assembly in 1928. By 1939 he had become a Democrat and was elected District Attorney of San Francisco (1943–50). This was a launching pad for his successful bid to become State Attorney-General for California in 1950. He was the only Democrat to win State-wide office that year and remained in the post for eight years. In 1958 he launched a bid for the governorship which was successful. His 'folksy' manner made him popular with the voters and he was only the second Democrat to be elected to that post. In his spell as Governor, Democrats controlled both Houses of the legislature, the first time this had happened since 1889. Brown was on the liberal wing of the party and his opposition to the death penalty brought him much trouble. His indecisiveness angered both supporters and opponents of the policy. He made clear his abhorrence of executions yet often authorized them on the grounds that he was upholding the law. In 1962 he was challenged by Richard *Nixon, who was trying for a political comeback after his defeat in the 1960 presidential race. Brown won the election by over 300,000 votes. Brown's tenure was marked by impressive economic growth in the state and he could point to expansion of school and higher education, the highway system, and an irrigation scheme which supplied water to the desert areas in Southern California. His second term was marred by race riots in Watts, Los Angeles, in which thirty-four people died and great damage was done to the downtown LA area. There was a backlash against disturbances on California University campuses, rising crime, and protests against the Vietnam War. California opinion was moving to the right and the beneficiary of this was his Republican opponent Ronald *Reagan. In 1966 Reagan beat him decisively in the race for Governor.

Brown returned to his law practice but his name lived on in Californian politics as his son, Jerry, served twice as Governor and his daughter Kathleen tried and failed for the office.

Brown, George Alfred (b. London, 2 Sept. 1914; d. 2 June 1985)
British; Foreign Secretary 1966–8, deputy leader of Labour Party 1960–70; Baron (life peer, Lord George-Brown) 1970

The son of a van driver, Brown left school at 15. After becoming an official of the Transport and General Workers' Union, he made his mark politically as a fierce critic of Labour's left wing.

Brown entered parliament in 1945. He had gained junior ministerial office in Clement *Attlee's government by 1947—despite having been involved in a backbench plot to depose the Prime Minister—but he was still only Minister of Works, outside the Cabinet, when Labour lost the 1951 general election. In opposition his industry and loyalty to the official party line against the left-wing 'Bevanites' brought him promotion as a shadow spokesman. He was elected deputy leader in 1960. However, he was comfortably defeated by Harold *Wilson in the leadership election after the sudden death of Hugh *Gaitskell, in 1963. He remained deputy leader.

When Wilson formed his first government in 1964, Brown was appointed First Secretary of State and Secretary of State for Economic Affairs (and, effectively, deputy Prime Minister). He made prodigious efforts to draw up a National Plan to regenerate the economy and to redress the enormous balance of payments deficit Labour had inherited. But he was overborne when the Cabinet accepted public expenditure cuts and a statutory incomes policy in 1966.

Public awareness of Brown's dissent necessitated his transfer. Moved to the Foreign Office, he devoted much of his energy to unsuccessful negotiations for British membership of the European Economic Community. His attempts to promote peace in Vietnam were also unsuccessful. In March 1968 he resigned over his exclusion from a decision designed to stabilize a precarious financial situation. He retained the deputy leadership of the party and his seat in the Commons, but talk of his return to office was unfounded. After his defeat in the 1970 general election (and therefore his automatic loss of the deputy leadership) he went to the House of Lords. He was not offered office when Wilson again formed a government in 1974 and resigned from the party in 1976 in protest at that government's legislation in favour of the trade union 'closed shop'. In 1982 he joined the breakaway Social Democratic Party.

Brown's political career fell short of the heights that his qualities often seemed to merit. His energy was matched by imagination, administrative ability, and campaigning and debating skills. But his Achilles' heel was a volatile temperament. The frequency with which he threatened resignation was notorious and increasingly embarrassed ministerial colleagues. The occasion for his eventual departure from office and his subsequent criticisms of Wilson's prime ministerial style made it appear almost farcical and prompted more by pique than by principle. By this time his public reputation had already been gravely undermined by reports of his often extravagant behaviour and over-indulgence in alcohol. He soon became an almost-forgotten political figure.

Brown, Gordon (b. 20 Feb. 1951)

British; Chancellor of the Exchequer 1997–

Brown was educated in Edinburgh and graduated from the university with a Ph.D. He worked as a lecturer, and then as a journalist and editor on current affairs programmes in Scottish television. His background shows in his skills as a communicator, both in writing press releases and in broadcast interviews. He entered the House of Commons in 1983, winning the safe Labour seat of Dunfermline East and was elected to the Labour Shadow Cabinet in 1987, on the strength of a number of good parliamentary performances. He then held a number of senior economic posts, starting with the job of shadow Chief Secretary to the Treasury. This post enabled him to substitute for the shadow Chancellor John *Smith during the latter's lengthy convalescence following a heart attack. In 1989 he was promoted to be shadow Trade and Industry spokesman.

Following Labour's 1992 election defeat he succeeded Smith as shadow Chancellor of the Exchequer when the latter was elected party leader. At the time Brown was seen as the next party leader. He was bitterly disappointed when, on Smith's death in 1994, he found that his close friend Tony *Blair had overtaken him. Although Brown agreed not to stand for the leadership, it took some time for him to come to terms with his failure. However, the two continued to work closely in modernizing the party. He also took the view that it was no longer sufficient for Labour to rely on the working class and the trade unions, and that it would have to appeal to the more affluent and aspirational voters. It would also have to relegate the role of public ownership, and its traditional commitment to redistribution by taxation. Brown kept an iron control over the spending promises of his colleagues. This enabled him to make a crucial announcement before the general election that Labour would accept the Conservative public spending plans for the next two years and hold income tax rates for the lifetime of the next parliament. In the new Labour government formed in May 1997 Brown was made Chancellor of the Exchequer.

Brundtland, Gro Harlem (b. Baerum, 20 Apr. 1939)

Norwegian; Prime Minister 1981, 1986–9, 1990–

The daughter of a professor of medicine, Brundtland went to school and university in

Oslo, graduating in medicine in 1963 before going to Harvard to take a master's degree in public health in 1965. She then returned to Oslo to practise as a doctor and from 1968 to 1974 was chief physician to the city's Health Administration. Her interest in politics began early. She became vice-chair of the Socialist Schools Association in 1955–7 and held the same office in the Labour Party's Student Association 1958–60. In 1973–5 she had a spell of service on an Oslo district council.

Brundtland was appointed Minister of the Environment in the Labour government of 1974 and remained in that post through the next Labour administration continuously until 1979. In 1977 she was elected to parliament as one of the members for Oslo. From 1979 to 1981 she was vice-chair of her party's parliamentary group before being elected its leader 1981–6 and again 1989–90. In 1981 she became Norway's first female Prime Minister for the first of her three terms to date.

Brundtland's declared support for Norwegian membership of the EC was rebuffed in the referendum of November 1994 but it has not weakened her position in the country's domestic politics, despite the fact that none of her governments has enjoyed a parliamentary majority. Internationally she became well known when she chaired the United Nations Commission on Environment and Development 1984–6—the 'Brundtland Commission'—which produced the significant concept of 'sustainable development'. This contribution to world affairs led to her receiving in 1988 the *Indira Gandhi Prize for Peace, Disarmament, and Development.

Brüning, Heinrich (b. Münster, 26 Nov. 1885; d. 30 Mar. 1970)

German; Chancellor of Germany 1930–2

Brüning took over as head of the German government at a very critical period in 1930. His right-of-centre mini-coalition replaced the SPD-led grand coalition which had fallen over disagreements about financing unemployment relief in the developing economic crisis. The little-known leader of the Catholic Centre was appointed by President von *Hindenburg on the advice of the armed forces (Reichswehr). The 44-year-old bachelor was the second youngest German head of government since 1871, but looked older in his wing collar. The generals trusted him because of his war service as a much decorated lieutenant of a machine-gun company.

Hindenburg and Brüning were monarchists who rejected the Weimar system. They sought to change the reality of the constitution without altering the letter. They strove for a more presidential system which downgraded parliament. Hindenburg was prepared to use Article 48 of the constitution to secure legislation which Brüning had introduced and the Reichstag had rejected. Hindenburg could also threaten parliament with new elections if it passed a no confidence vote against Brüning. This happened, and in July 1930 elections were held which resulted in a breakthrough for the Nazis. Brüning blackmailed parliament into accepting massive cuts in public spending, reducing pensions, public sector pay, and employment, and cutting unemployment relief.

All this made his government very unpopular. His, and Hindenburg's, hope was the Centre Party could link up with the reactionary, monarchist DNVP and with *Hitler's movement. When it was clear he was not the man to achieve this realignment of the right, Hindenburg dismissed him on 30 May 1932 in a three-minute interview.

After Hitler became Chancellor in January 1933 Brüning remained in parliament, being elected leader of the Centre Party. He presided over its disbandment in July 1933. Although he had been prepared to work with the new regime, he realized by May 1934 that this was not possible and fled to Holland. From 1937 to 1952 he worked as professor of politics at Harvard. From 1951 to 1954 he was professor at Cologne University, but disagreements with *Adenauer led him to return to the USA.

Bryan, William Jennings (b. Salem, Illinois, 18 Mar. 1860; d. 26 July 1925)
US; member of the US House of Representatives 1891–5, Democratic Presidential nominee 1896, 1900, 1908, Secretary of State 1913–15

Son of a baptist minister, Bryan was educated at Whipple Academy and Illinois College, Jacksonville, graduating BA in 1881 and MA in 1884. After gaining an LLB from University College of Law Chicago in 1883, he was admitted to the Illinois bar and began practising law in Jacksonville. Moving to Lincoln, Nebraska, in 1887, he continued to practice law but developed political aspirations under the tutelage of J. Sterling Morton, the local Democratic political agent. In 1890 he began to realize these ambitions by gaining election to the US House of Representative; 1894, however, brought a temporary setback when the Nebraska legislature failed to elect him US Senator. He turned instead to journalism and became editor of the Omaha *World-Herald*.

1896 marked Bryan's dramatic debut as a national political figure when as a little-known former Congressman, he succeeded in capturing the Democratic nomination for the presidency. It was a period of economic depression, exacerbated by an appreciating currency linked to gold, and Bryan passionately articulated agrarian discontent. His famous 'Cross of Gold' speech, which ended on the much quoted peroration 'You shall not press down upon the brow of labour this crown of thorns. You shall not crucify mankind upon a cross of gold', swept the convention delegates off their feet. Despite a punishing campaign, during which Bryan travelled 18,000 miles and made over 600 speeches, he was defeated by Mckinley. But he did secure a position of prominence in the Democratic Party for the next thirty years, gaining his party's nomination for the presidency on two further occasions, 1900 and 1908, and influencing the convention to endorse Woodrow *Wilson in 1912. Wilson repaid this political debt by making Bryan his Secretary of State. Bryan, the campaigner and orator, was ill-suited for the post. A pacifist, he felt unable to accept America's drift from neutrality towards support of Britain in the First World War, and resigned in 1915.

Equally at home in religion and politics, Bryan thereafter turned his attention to Prohibition and Fundamentalism. He became a crusader against evolution. As a prosecuting attorney in the famous 'Scopes Monkey' trial he gained the conviction of John Thomas Scopes for teaching evolution. Bryan's name also became associated with white supremacy. At the Democratic convention of 1924, he failed to support a resolution denouncing the Ku Klux Klan.

Bryan was famous for his splendid voice, impressive personality, and impassioned oratory. He is remembered as a champion of lost causes, such as bimetallism. But many of the reforms he pressed for were introduced including: income tax; popular election of US senators; womens' suffrage; regulation of railroads; and currency reform. He was not an original thinker and had no clearly defined political position but his powerful oratory enabled him to move vast, often hostile, audiences. He was an evangelical politician seeking converts to what he regarded as good causes.

He published numerous articles and several books including: *The First Battle* (1897); *The Menace of Darwin* (1921); *The Bible and Its Enemies* (1921); *In His Image* (1922).

Buchanan, Patrick Joseph (b. Washington, DC, 2 Nov. 1938)
US; politician

Born into a large Roman Catholic family of Irish origins, Buchanan was educated at Georgetown University and the Columbia School of Journalism. His early career was spent working for the St Louis Globe Democrat; but in 1966 he became associated with Richard *Nixon's presidential bid working for him first as a researcher and speech writer, then moving into the White House as a special assistant. During his time in the Nixon White House Buchanan dealt with media issues and spearheaded the conservative attack on the liberal news media.

When Nixon left office Buchanan remained but he began to promote his own conservative agenda through widely syndicated newspaper columns, radio, and television. That agenda emphasized the need to reduce radically the role of government in the economy and welfare and took a very conservative line on social issues such as abortion and school prayer. On foreign policy, Buchanan was a militant anti-Communist; but with the end of the Cold War he moved towards an isolationist position which fitted well with his nativist populism.

Buchanan's conservative activism made him an enthusiastic supporter of President *Reagan but he sometimes found it difficult to adapt his shrill views to the realities of government. Thus in 1985 when Buchanan became Director of Communications at the White House, his ideological interpretation of the role frequently brought him into conflict with Reagan's more pragmatic advisers and indeed exacerbated relationships with Congress.

When Reagan retired, Buchanan increasingly projected himself as the spokesman of the conservative movement. In 1992 he ran against Republican candidate George *Bush in the primaries and although he won 37 per cent in New Hampshire he lost in all of them. Yet his invocation of 'a cultural and religious war' generated substantial organizational and financial support and put in place a network of activists loyal to him rather than the Republican Party. In 1996 he ran again on a populist 'America First' ticket which emphasized anti-abortion and curbs on imports. He achieved just under 22 per cent of the popular vote and lost the Republican nomination to Robert *Dole. Although Buchanan was clearly not enthusiastic about Dole's candidacy he rejected the idea of supporting third-party candidate Ross Perot, or mounting an independent candidacy himself.

Buchanan remains one of the most visible leaders of the conservative movement. But he is also divisive and he has to date failed to translate his support into a successful candidacy for major elective office.

Bulganin, Nikolai Aleksandrovich (b. Nizhni Novgorod, 11 June 1895; d. Moscow, 1 Mar. 1975)

Russian; Member of the Politburo 1947–58

The son of a white-collar worker, Bulganin joined the Bolshevik Party in 1917 and served in the Cheka, from 1918 to 1922, receiving criticism even from the party for his brutality. From 1922 to 1931 he held various administrative posts connected with the economy. From 1931 to 1937 he was chairman of the Moscow City Soviet. In July 1937 he was appointed to the important post of chairman of the RSFSR Council of People's Commissars, and was promoted in 1939 to deputy chairman of the USSR Council of People's Commissars. From 1941 to 1943 he did political work in the Red Army. In 1944 he was made deputy commissar for Defence and deputy chairman of the Council of Ministers. In 1947, after Zhukov's decline, he was made member of the Politburo, Minister of Armed Forces (till 1949), and Marshal of the Soviet Union. Despite his long connection with the military, Bulganin was very much a political general and had no influence on the development of the Red Army. In 1955, he was appointed chairman of the Council of Ministers and often accompanied *Khrushchev abroad. In September 1958 he was removed from office after joining the 'anti-party group' which had unsuccessfully opposed Khrushchev.

Bush, George Herbert Walker (b. Milton, Massachusetts, 12 June 1924)

US; CIA director 1976–7, Vice-President 1981–9, President 1989–93

Born into an established East Coast family—his father was to serve as Senator for Connecticut (1952–63)—Bush was educated at Philipps Academy in Andover, Massachusetts, and then saw war service as a naval carrier pilot. He was the navy's youngest pilot, was shot down three times in combat, and received a DFC and three air medals. In 1944, at the age of 20, he married Barbara Pierce, also from a well-to-do family. After the war, he studied at Yale, graduating in 1948 with a degree in economics. Though from a wealthy family, he sought to make his own way in business and spent thirteen years working in the oil industry in Texas. Imbued with a patrician sense of duty, he sought public office, contesting the Texas Senate race in 1964 and then being elected to the House of Representatives in 1966. He was appointed to the Ways and Means Committee, an unusual achievement for a new member, made possible by the influence of his father. He served two terms before again, at the behest of President Richard *Nixon and other Republican leaders, contesting—and losing—the Texas Senate race to Lloyd *Bentsen.

In 1971 he received his first major public appointment when Nixon appointed him US ambassador to the United Nations. He served two years in the post before becoming—somewhat reluctantly—chairman of the Republican National Committee, heading it at a difficult time for the party, embroiled as its leading figures were in the Watergate scandal. Nixon's successor, Gerald *Ford, then appointed him to head the US liaison office in Beijing, a post preferred by Bush over ambassadorships to France and the United Kingdom. He served in China from 1975 to 1976, returning to the USA to become director of the Central Intelligence Agency. He proved a competent leader and showed some managerial skills. By the end of the 1970s, he had built up a record of public service and in 1980 contested the Republican nomination for President. After a sluggish start, he began to prove impressive as a candidate, coining some memorable phrases—most notably 'voodoo economics' to describe the economic policies of his leading opponent, Ronald *Reagan. When Reagan built up a commanding lead in delegates, Bush withdrew. Reagan chose Bush as his running mate. In the general election, they achieved a clear victory over the lacklustre Democratic incumbent, Jimmy *Carter.

As Vice-President, Bush had—in common with most of his predecessors—a fairly low profile, chairing various bodies, including a task force on regulatory reform and the Crisis Management Team (later renamed the Special Situations Group) to monitor emergencies. When President Reagan was shot, Bush returned to Washington and presided over the Cabinet, though sitting in his own chair rather than the President's. Though implicated in the Iran-Contra affair, involving the use of money from the sale of arms to Iran to fund Contra rebels in Nicaragua, he survived the negative publicity. Serving two terms, he proved a loyal lieutenant to Reagan, in effect earning his right to succeed the President as Republican nominee in 1988. He won the nomination—after fighting off accusations of being a 'wimp'—and presided over a campaign notable for its negative attacks on his Democratic opponent, Michael *Dukakis. Bush chose as his running mate a little known Senator, Dan *Quayle. Given an economy in reasonable shape, and a poor performance by his opponent, Bush won comfortably, winning 48.8 million votes to 41.8 million for Dukakis. He was the first incumbent Vice-President since Martin van Buren to be elected to the presidency. He was inaugurated as President on 20 January 1989.

The Bush presidency epitomized what Aaron Wildavsky characterized as 'the two presidencies', one president but two presidencies—one for domestic affairs and one for foreign and defence policy, the latter achieving greater success than the former. Bush was essentially a foreign affairs president. It was a field in which he was well grounded and in which he showed a particular interest. He dispatched troops to Panama in 1989 to overthrow the regime of Manuel Noriega. He presided over the US response to the fall of the Soviet Union and German unification. Bolstered by British Prime Minister Margaret *Thatcher ('Don't go wobbly on me, George'), he committed US forces to repel Iraqi forces invading Kuwait. The success of Operation Desert Storm—Iraqi forces being driven out quickly by Allied forces—raised Bush to unprecedented levels of public support. Thereafter, his support plummeted as domestic affairs came to the fore. The economy declined and Bush found himself agreeing to a tax increase in 1990, despite having made the declaration 'Read my lips—no new taxes' the centrepiece of his 1988 campaign. He appeared to have no clear agenda for addressing domestic problems. His health also started giving some cause for concern. He was diagnosed as having mild heart trouble and in 1992 in Tokyo he collapsed vomiting in the lap of the Japanese Prime Minister.

Bush's failure to address domestic problems rendered him vulnerable in the 1992 election. He faced a contest for the Republican nomination, the challenge of conservative Pat *Buchanan making him appear vulnerable in the early stages, and in the general election faced both a Democratic opponent, Bill *Clinton, and an independent in the form of Ross Perot. The accusation of being a wimp reappeared and his failure to keep his 1988 promise on taxes counted heavily against him. He won less than 38 per cent of the popular vote, Clinton getting 43 per cent and the rest going to Perot. Bush retired from public life, spending time with his family and vacationing. He appeared visibly much more relaxed once he had given up the reins of office.

Bush was a highly likeable individual who inspired great loyalty on the part of his staff. He was dedicated to public service—Nelson Polsby characterized him as an 'American Tory'—but lacked any clear policy goals, especially in the domestic arena. He had little knowledge of American urban life. He was renowned for his verbal gaffes and his occasional strangulation of the English language, though this hardly made him unique among US presidents. In the course of a toast, he once admitted 'fluency in English is something that I'm not often accused of'. He achieved no new directions in the presidency. He constituted what has been described as a 'guardian President', watching over and protecting what was already in existence. He was limited in achieving any new directions by an essentially hostile Congress and by his own failure to generate future goals. He was wedded to the here and now of politics at a time when the mood of America changed. Americans wanted someone who could offer change. Bush was unable to respond to the new mood.

Butler, Richard Austen (b. India, 9 Dec. 1902; d. 8 Mar. 1982)

British; Chancellor of the Exchequer 1951–5, leader of Commons 1955–61, Home Secretary 1957–62, Foreign Secretary 1963–4; Baron (life peer) 1965

R. A. Butler ('Rab') was born into a family notable for its academic scholarship and diplomatic service. His father was a governor of an Indian province and then master of a Cambridge college. He was a 'nearly man' of British politics, twice narrowly failing to become Conservative Prime Minister, in 1957 and 1963, even though the media regarded him as favoured choice on both occasions. He was educated at Marlborough and Cambridge University. As if this provenance was not prestigious enough Butler married into the great wealth of the Courtauld family and became MP for the safe seat of Saffron Walden in 1929.

Butler served under seven Conservative Prime Ministers, starting with *MacDonald down to *Home. He occupied a junior post in the early 1930s and was responsible for the Government of India Act (1935), which granted a large measure of self-government to India. He became second in command at the Foreign Office at the time of the appeasement of Nazi Germany 1938–9; he was a member of the House of Commons, while the actual Foreign Secretary Lord *Halifax was in the House of Lords. Winston *Churchill recognized his talents and kept him on in government 1940–5.

One of Butler's outstanding achievements was the 1944 Education Act, which he introduced as president of the Board of Education during the wartime coalition government. This is sometimes called the Butler Act and shaped secondary schooling in Britain for the next forty years. It raised the school-leaving age to 15 and provided free secondary schooling for all. After the Conservative's election defeat in 1945 Butler's posts as chairman of the party's Research Department and of the Industrial Policy Committee—which led to the Industrial Charter—made him a key figure in reshaping Conservative policy in the years 1945–51. The party came to terms with the electorate's demand for a positive government role in promoting welfare and full employment.

When Churchill was recalled as Prime Minister in 1951, Butler was appointed Chancellor of the Exchequer. He presided over a number of tax-cutting budgets and an improvement in living standards. His reputation for financial prudence was damaged when he cut taxes in a pre-election give-away budget in 1955 and then had to introduce another, tougher post-election budget in autumn.

Churchill's successor as premier, Anthony *Eden, made Butler leader of the House of Commons in 1955. Butler's doubts about the wisdom of the invasion of Egypt to reopen the Suez Canal in 1956 harmed his chances of succeeding Eden when the latter stepped down as Prime Minister. When Eden was ill and abroad Butler was in charge of the government and had to order the withdrawal of British troops from Egypt. When Eden resigned senior figures in the party advised the Queen to send for *Macmillan in January 1957. He was a liberal Home Secretary (1957–62), introducing prison reforms, changing the laws on prostitution and gambling, but did not manage to achieve abolition of capital punishment. Harold Macmillan piled other duties on him, making him chairman of the party and minister in charge of central African affairs.

When Macmillan was ill and preparing to resign in 1963 Butler was the favourite to succeed. In the end, however, thanks to some manipulation by Macmillan, it was *Home who was sent for. Home refused to accept the Queen's commission to form a Cabinet until Butler agreed to join—a mark of the latter's indispensability. To the disappointment of some of his supporters Butler accepted and became Foreign Secretary. He was not prepared to split the party to gain the ultimate prize. Perhaps he did not want the leadership as intensely as others did.

Butler had a number of legislative achievements to his credit. But above all he was responsible for influencing the direction of post-war Conservative policy. He is often seen as the main exponent of One-Nation, or progressive, Conservatism and a shaper of the post-war consensus. His values were dominant in the Tory Party until Mrs *Thatcher arrived on the scene. He was a witty man, once praising Eden to a journalist with 'He is the best Prime Minister we have'.

He retired from politics in 1965 and became Master of Trinity College, a post he held until 1978. His memoirs, *The Art of the Possible*, were published in 1971.

Byrd, Harry Flood (b. Martinsburg, W. Virginia, 10 June 1887; d. 20 Oct. 1966)

US; member of the State Senate 1915–25, Governor of Virginia 1926–1930, US Senator 1933–65

Harry Byrd was a key figure in Virginia politics for forty years and built a political machine that dominated the state and was remarkable for its combination of effectiveness and relative honesty.

The son of a lawyer who served as Speaker of the Virginia House of Delegates, Harry Byrd came from a long-established, but not especially wealthy, Virginia family. After leaving school at 15 to run the family newspaper, Byrd established a highly successful orchard business which supported and complemented his remarkable political career.

He was elected governor in 1926 and in his early years was relatively progressive, introducing a number of economic and political reforms, including an anti-lynching law and the construction of a state highway system. Most significantly, he turned a state deficit into a surplus.

In 1933 Byrd was appointed to fill the unexpired Senate term of Claude Swanson, who was appointed Secretary of the Navy. Thereafter he was re-elected six times. Although he was initially friendly with F. D. *Roosevelt, he came to oppose the New Deal as an extravagant exercise which endangered state autonomy. Increasingly Byrd found himself out of sympathy with the expansionary trend of Washington and the liberal leadership of the Democratic Party. In Virginia and in the Senate, he promoted the loose coalition of conservatives drawn from Democratic and Republican ranks. Through this coalition he and other Southern senators were able to exercise disproportionate power in Congress and to delay the progress of liberal measures especially civil rights.

In the Senate, Byrd was a member of the Armed Services Committee, chairman of the Committee on Rules, and chairman of the Joint Committee on the Reduction of Non-essential Expenditure. As chairman of the powerful Senate Finance Committee, he opposed federal spending programmes championed by presidents from Roosevelt to Johnson. He attacked the Marshall Plan, foreign aid, and most social programmes including Medicare and was able to delay Lyndon *Johnson's 1964 tax cut.

Byrd's inherent opposition to civil rights caused him to urge a campaign of 'massive resistance' to integration in the South in the 1950s and Virginia for a time pursued a strategy of defiance, in which public schools and other facilities were closed to prevent the implementation of the law. By the 1960s however Byrd was forced to accept change, although to many he remained a symbol of white reaction. He was forced by illness to retire from the Senate in 1965 and his son Harry Flood Byrd Jr. inherited the seat.

Byrne, Jane (née Burke)
US; mayor of Chicago 1979–83

Byrne's father was a businessman of Irish origin and she grew up in Illinois, where she attended Barat College of the Sacred Heart in Lake Forest. In 1960 she worked on the Kennedy campaign in Chicago and in 1964 was appointed by Chicago boss Richard *Daley to organize the Chicago anti-poverty programme. In 1968 Byrne became the first female member of Daley's Cabinet, becoming responsible for consumer affairs.

From then until Daley's death in 1976, Byrne worked to improve services to consumers in the city and to build up her power base within the Democratic Party. Without Daley her power with the party machine (which was suspicious of her) was eroded; but she was able to exploit her independence in the struggle for control of the city. In 1978 she entered the mayoral race and in the Democratic primary beat Michael Bilandic by highlighting the corruption of the Cook County machine and its deteriorating efficiency. She won, helped by expanded voter registration and a winter which highlighted the city's weakening services. In the general election, she won easily, becoming Chicago's first woman mayor.

In office she gave high priority to inner city problems, especially housing and education issues. Highly critical of the Carter administration, she threw her support in the 1980 primary race behind Edward *Kennedy. However, her own political position was increasingly under threat on two fronts: from blacks who had previously supported her and from whites increasingly concerned with law and order. In 1983 in a bitterly contested Democratic primary she lost in a three-way race against black Congressman Harold *Washington and the son of the Chicago boss, Richard M. Daley Jr. Byrne did not immediately disappear from the Chicago scene. In 1987 she again entered the Democratic primary but was beaten by Washington; in 1991 she was defeated in the primary by Richard M. Daley Jr. Jane Byrne then wrote her memoirs *My Chicago*, published in 1992.

Byrnes, James Francis (b. Charleston, South Carolina, 2 May 1897; d. 15 Nov. 1972)
US; US Senator 1931–41, Secretary of State 1945–7, Governor of South Carolina 1951–5

Born into an Irish Catholic family, Byrnes had a limited education but studied law part-time and then practised law in South Carolina. He served in the US House of

Representatives 1911–25 and in the Senate 1931–41. Although a conservative Democrat from a southern state, he acted as a bridge between southern conservative Democrats and progressive New Deal Democrats. In 1941 he was appointed as an Associate Justice of the Supreme Court. After only a year on the Supreme Court, however, in 1942 Franklin *Roosevelt appointed him director of the Office of Economic Stabilization and in 1943 he was appointed director of the Office of War Mobilization. Roosevelt described him as 'Assistant President on the home front'. In 1944 he was a leading contender for the vice-presidential nomination when Roosevelt decided not to renominate Vice-President *Wallace. Since Byrnes was a Catholic and was divorced, however, Roosevelt felt that he would be unacceptable to significant elements in the Democratic coalition, so that Harry *Truman was instead given the vice-presidential nomination and succeeded to the presidency on Roosevelt's death in April 1945.

Truman appointed Byrnes as Secretary of State in 1945. He attempted to reach an agreement with the Soviets in his years as Secretary of State, 1945–7. But his dealings with the Soviets became increasingly acrimonious, while Truman became dissatisfied that he failed to keep the president fully informed. In 1947 he was replaced as Secretary of State by George *Marshall. He returned to law practice in South Carolina and became increasingly conservative. He was elected governor of South Carolina in 1950 and was an outspoken opponent of civil rights during his term of office as governor, 1951–5. In 1952 he supported the Republican candidate for president, Dwight D. *Eisenhower, over his Democratic opponent, Adlai *Stevenson.

Byrnes served in all three branches of the US government—the judiciary, the legislature, and executive. He was a pragmatic conservative, who played a vital role in America's war effort, but whose pragmatism was ineffective in dealing with Soviet negotiators and who became increasingly conservative, especially over the race issue. He wrote important memoirs, *Speaking Frankly* (1947) and *All in One Lifetime* (1960).

Cabral, Amilcar Lopes (b. Bafata, Portuguese Guinea, 12 Sept. 1924; d. Conakry, Guinée, 20 Jan. 1973)

Guinea-Bissau; leader of the PAIGC 1956–73

Born in Portuguese Guinea of Cape Verdean parents, Cabral was educated to secondary level in Cape Verde, and graduated in agronomy from Lisbon University. He returned to Guinea as an agricultural engineer in 1952–5, gaining a thorough knowledge of the countryside, and founded the clandestine Partido africano da Guine e Cabo Verde (PAIGC) in 1956. In the face of Portuguese repression and refusal to consider independence, this opted in September 1959 for a strategy of rural guerrilla warfare. From 1960, Cabral organized the war from Conakry in former French Guinée, and by 1963 the PAIGC had a substantial military presence.

Cabral rapidly emerged as the leading theorist and practitioner of guerrilla warfare in Portuguese Africa. He insisted on close association between the guerrillas and the rural populations, and was prepared to execute those who exploited the peasantry. An ideological pragmatist working within the Maoist tradition, he expected nationalist élites to commit 'class suicide' in order to make common cause with the masses after liberation.

By 1973, the PAIGC controlled by far the greater part of Guinean territory, and was preparing to declare independence. Before that could happen, Cabral was assassinated by a dissident PAIGC faction operating in collusion with the Portuguese secret police. His death deprived Guinea-Bissau of a leader of great stature and integrity, and it is widely argued that the post-independence history of the country would have been markedly happier had he lived to govern it.

Caetano, Marcello José das Neves Alves (b. Lisbon, 17 Aug. 1906; d. 26 Oct. 1980)

Portuguese; Prime Minister 1968–74

Caetano was the son of a primary schoolteacher and graduated in law at the University of Lisbon. As a student he was a right-wing activist. His contributions to the right-wing press were anti-republican, emphasizing monarchist, reactionary, and Catholic views. After the *coup d'état* of 28 May 1926, Caetano became an important figure in the new regime. Protected by *Salazar he made his career in the Ministry of Finance, and was trusted with preparing the new legislation and constitution of the corporatist Estado Novo (New State). He was appointed to the chair of constitutional and administrative law at Lisbon University in 1935.

In 1940 Caetano became head of the Mocidade Portuguesa (Portuguese Youth), the state youth movement, and between 1944 and 1947 was in charge of the Ministry of the Colonies. Afterwards, he played a leading role in trying to revitalize the dormant União Nacional (National Union), the single party of the regime. Between 1949 and 1955, he was president of the Corporative Chamber, the second chamber of the façade Parliament of the regime.

Following disagreements with Salazar he resigned from the government and became chancellor of the University of Lisbon in 1958. He resigned this post following the use of police force by the regime to suppress student protests in 1962. Nevertheless, he remained close to the authoritarian regime as a member of the consultative body of the government, the Council of State.

After Salazar's stroke in 1968, Caetano took over the office of Prime Minister. His main slogan was 'evolution in continuity', suggesting that there would be a reform of the Salazarist system. His so-called 'political spring' included greater religious tolerance and freedom of the press and was regarded as an opportunity by the opposition to gain concessions from the regime. Nevertheless, after the elections of 1969 and 1973 it was clear that the past practices of political repression would continue. In 1973, Caetano was pressured by the ultra-right faction inside the Salazarist élite to abandon his reform experiment. The wars in Portuguese Africa were causing major military and economic problems of legitimacy and leading to international condemnation. In March 1974, Caetano faced a military uprising. The final blow to the authoritarian regime was the so-called 'Revolution of Carnations', which led to its downfall on 25 April 1974. Before Caetano surrendered to the revolutionaries, he resigned personally to General António Spinola, to prevent power falling to the revolutionaries. He went into exile to Brazil and was Professor of Law at a private university in Rio de Janeiro until his death.

Callaghan, James (b. Portsmouth, 27 Mar. 1912)

British; Prime Minister 1976–9; Baron (life peer) 1987

James Callaghan held key posts in Labour governments between 1964 and 1979 and is the only Prime Minister, to date, to have already held the three great offices; Foreign Secretary, Home Secretary, and Chancellor of the Exchequer. He was the son of a naval chief petty officer and left school at 14. He began work as a tax officer and then was employed by the TUC.

After war service, Callaghan was part of Labour's landslide victory in the 1945 general election. Between 1945 and 1950 he was MP for Cardiff South and subsequently Cardiff South East, until his retirement in 1987. By the last date, he was one of only four MPs remaining from the 1945 parliament.

In Labour's thirteen years in opposition, Callaghan rose steadily, on the centre-right of the party. When the Labour leader Hugh *Gaitskell died in 1963, he stood for the vacant post; he finished last of three candidates with a respectable forty votes.

He was Chancellor of the Exchequer in the 1964 Labour government. The initial decision of Harold *Wilson and himself not to devalue the pound from its value of $2.80 proved to be disastrous. The British economy was weak and the pound was regularly under threat for the next three years. Devaluation eventually came in November 1967 and the discredited Callaghan resigned as Chancellor. He was moved to Home Secretary and managed to repair his fortunes. He revoked the right of East African Asians to settle in Britain and postponed the changes to parliamentary boundaries proposed by the impartial Boundary Commission He also sent troops to Northern Ireland in 1969 to cope with the worsening violence. From his position on Labour's national executive he opposed Cabinet policy of reforming the trade unions. Callaghan was a powerful spokesman for trade union resistance and, as one of the few Cabinet ministers from a working-class background, earned the title 'the keeper of the cloth cap'. Harold Wilson saw Callaghan's opposition as yet another plot to unseat himself as leader.

With Labour in opposition again after 1970, Callaghan might have left politics if a post in the World Bank had materialized. He was older than Wilson and was no longer regarded as an obvious successor. As shadow Foreign Secretary he kept apart from the growing faction fighting. He accepted the left's demand for a referendum on Britain's membership of the European Community—as an answer to the party's division. When Labour was returned to office in 1974, it was his task to conduct the renegotiations with Community partners and these were approved in a referendum the following year.

Harold Wilson's unexpected resignation in March 1976 provided Callaghan with a late chance of reaching the top. He was, at 64, the oldest of the six candidates. But he was also most clearly the 'middle of the road' candidate. On the third ballot he defeated Michael *Foot by 176 votes to 137. He was the second choice of many Labour

MPs and the least divisive of all candidates. It was the first time that a British Prime Minister had been elected by MPs.

Callaghan's three-year premiership was always under pressure, political and economic. Yet, only at the end did his sure touch for the mood of the party desert him. Callaghan also had to cope with a strong left wing, which was influential in the party's national executive and Conference and regularly opposed the government's economic policies. His government was soon faced with a sterling crisis which led to negotiations with the IMF for a rescue package. The IMF conditions threatened to split the government, but Callaghan gained high marks for keeping ministers together and getting the loan. The cuts in planned public expenditure and continued pay restraint made the left unhappy. In spite of pressure to bear down on inflation and cut government borrowing, the left-wing conference continued to vote for more spending. Labour's narrow majority in the House of Commons disappeared in March 1977 and the party negotiated a pact with thirteen Liberals. In return for consultation on policy, the Liberals agreed to back the government in any confidence vote in the House of Commons.

When the Lib–Lab pact ended in summer 1978, Callaghan was widely expected to call an election in the autumn. Instead, he decided to soldier on, with a prices and incomes policy to combat inflation. This proved a misjudgement, as workers took industrial action against the pay policy over the winter. The upsurge of industrial unrest, subsequently dubbed 'the Winter of Discontent', destroyed Callaghan's authority and Labour's claim that it could work with the trade unions. Ministers appeared impotent in the face of industrial disruption. In January 1979, on his return from sunny Guadeloupe to strike-bound Britain, a tabloid famously misquoted his reaction as 'Crisis! . . . What crisis?' On 28 March, the government lost a confidence vote in the Commons by one vote and Mr Callaghan was now forced into an election which Mrs *Thatcher won. Callaghan's premiership ended ingloriously. The Conservatives continued to make political capital for many years from the 'Winter of Discontent'.

Callaghan remained as party leader for a further eighteen months, but the left grew in influence and steadily repudiated many of the last Labour government's policies. Callaghan exercised little influence as the left reformed party institutions and nearly thirty Labour MPs departed to form a new party. He was out of sympathy with many new policies, particularly the repudiation of incomes policy and membership of the European Community. He caused a stir in the 1983 general election by expressing his disagreement with the party's new policy of unilaterally giving up nuclear weapons.

Callaghan retired from the House of Commons in 1987 and was given a peerage. He published his memoirs, *Time and Chance*, in the same year.

Campbell, Avril Kim (b. Port Alberni, BC, 10 Mar. 1947)

Canadian; Prime Minister 25 Jun. 1993–4 Nov. 1993

Educated at the University of British Columbia, and the London School of Economics, Campbell was a lecturer in political science at UBC 1975–8, and then at Vancouver Community College 1978–81. She was an articled student 1983–4 and then an Associate for General Litigation in Vancouver 1984–5. Other posts include executive Director, Office of the Premier of British Columbia 1985–6, Member of the Legislative Assembly (Social Credit) for Vancouver Point Grey 1986–8, and then MP (PC) for Vancouver Centre 1988–93.

With his personal popularity and that of his party sinking to unprecedented low levels in public opinion polls, Prime Minister Brian *Mulroney announced his retirement on 24 February 1993. The Conservatives sought a fresh personality to lead them into the general election. They chose Campbell, who had first entered the federal parliament only five years earlier and had risen rapidly to become successively Minister of State for Indian affairs and Northern Development 1989–90, Minister of Justice and Attorney-General 1990–2, and then Minister of National Defence 1993 under Mulroney.

She was articulate and photogenic and seemed to speak for a new generation of voters. She easily won the leadership of her party at a national convention held in Ottawa on 13 June, defeating another young Conservative minister, Jean *Charest, from Sherbrooke, Quebec. Ms Campbell was sworn in as Canada's nineteenth Prime Minister on 25 June, becoming the first woman to hold the office.

Despite enjoying an initial surge of popularity, the odds against her leading the Conservatives to a third successive electoral victory were enormous. The free trade agreement with the United States and, even more, the imposition of a sweeping tax on goods and services were deeply unpopular with many Canadians. It was soon evident that Ms Campbell's inexperience and lack of political judgement made her an inept campaigner, especially in comparison with the veteran Liberal leader Jean *Chrétien.

The election produced a landslide defeat for the Conservatives. Kim Campbell was defeated in her Vancouver riding. All twenty-five members of her Cabinet, except for Jean Charest, lost their seats and only two Conservatives (one in New Brunswick and Mr Charest in Quebec) were elected. Never before in Canadian history had a ruling party suffered such an eclipse. The popular vote for the Conservatives dropped to 16 per cent, compared with 43 per cent in the last general election in 1988. Kim Campbell resigned as Prime Minister on 4 November, after having served 134 days in office, the third shortest term of any Canadian leader of a government. She stepped down as leader on 13 January, handing the task of rebuilding the Conservatives as a national party to Jean Charest.

Campbell-Bannerman, Sir Henry (b. Glasgow, 7 Sept. 1836; d. London, 28 Apr. 1908).

British; leader of the Liberal Party 1900–8, Prime Minister 1905–8

Campbell-Bannerman ('CB') was the son of a lord provost of Glasgow and educated at Glasgow High School and at the universities of Glasgow and Cambridge. He then entered the family business and this wealth made him financially secure for the rest of his life. He won the seat of Stirling Burghs in 1868 for the Liberals and held it until his death forty years later. 'CB' was the first incumbent to be given the official title of Prime Minister and was the last Prime Minister to die in office.

He held junior office under Gladstone (1871–4) and in Gladstone's second administration he was Chief Secretary for Ireland (1884–5), though without a Cabinet seat. In this post he had to face the full fury of the Irish Nationalist MPs. He then became Secretary of State for War in the short-lived 1886 government, and held the same post again during Gladstone's last spell of office (1892–4) and Lord Rosebery's (1895). His range of administrative experience was therefore rather limited.

For most of his career Campbell-Bannerman was not regarded as leadership material—more formidable figures were available. He was an indifferent parliamentary performer, although a steady administrator—seen by colleagues as a proverbial pair of safe hands. He was widely thought to be indolent, and he certainly liked long vacations. In the 1890s the Liberal Party was highly fractious and had already split in 1886 over Gladstone's advocacy of Home Rule (or self-government) for Ireland. Campbell-Bannerman followed Gladstone.

After Rosebery resigned the Liberal leadership at short notice in 1895, the party faced a vacuum. A number of fancied contenders disclaimed any interest in the succession and *Asquith was thought to be too inexperienced. The post fell largely by default in 1899 to Campbell-Bannerman. He was widely seen as a temporary leader—until Rosebery returned. 'CB' had a difficult task keeping the party together during the Boer War. A number of frontbench colleagues supported the war but he and

*Lloyd George opposed it. His task was eased and the Liberals unified when *Chamberlain split the Conservative Party with his campaign for protection in 1903. An increasingly frustrated Prime Minister, A. J. *Balfour resigned in December 1905 and Campbell-Bannerman was invited by the King to form the government. Balfour calculated that the Liberals would be too divided to govern effectively. The leading Liberals *Grey, Asquith, and *Haldane announced that they would not serve unless Campbell-Bannerman agreed to go to the House of Lords and not as only a nominal Prime Minister. He refused and they backed down. The new minority government lasted only a few weeks until he called an election in 1906, which the Liberals won by a landslide.

Campbell-Bannerman led what turned out to be a great reforming administration. It was a tribute to his skill that he kept so many talented colleagues together. His own role in directing the government was minimal; he took a limited view of his role. He was dogged by ill-health and died after two years in office. He was not a dynamic leader and adhered to traditional Liberal ideas of free trade, self-government, and social reform.

Cannon, Joseph (b. Guilford, North Carolina, 7 May 1836; d. 12 Nov. 1926)
US; Speaker of the House of Representatives 1903–11

'Cannonism' refers to Joseph Cannon's arbitrary management of business as Speaker in the US House of Representatives. He is also notable for being dethroned from his post, as a result of rebellion by disaffected Congressmen. When he was a child his family moved to Indiana and he became a lawyer. After serving as a state attorney in the strongly Republican state of Illinois, he was elected as a Republican to Congress in 1873, and served until 1891. He was ousted in the 1890 elections, a good year for the Democrats. Already his abrasive manner had earned him the title of 'foul mouthed Joe'. He was returned to the House in 1893 and served until 1913, and again from 1915 until 1923, when he retired. There was some support from him in 1908 at the Republican presidential convention. He was elected Speaker in the new Congress of 1903 and re-elected until his overthrow in 1910, though continuing in office until 1911. Cannon dominated the business in the house and presidents had to defer to him. At this time the Republican Party was increasingly divided between Progressive supporters of Theodore *Roosevelt and the conservatives. He was deeply reactionary, opposing most progressive measures. His iron rule in the House was matched in the Senate by that of Nelson *Aldrich. Cannon wielded his power through the Congressional Campaign Committee, which granted funds to or withheld them from Republican candidates for the House, and the Rules Committee, which determined the business of the House. He also ruthlessly exploited his power to appoint members and chairs of committees to punish rebellious or reformist congressmen. Increasingly, he alienated sufficient number of Democrats and Republicans to provoke a revolt and he was unseated in 1910 as reformers, led by *Norris, sought to break the hold of the conservative establishment in Congress.

Cardenas del Rio, Lázaro (b. Jiquilpan, Michoacan, 21 May 1895; d. 19 Oct. 1970)
Mexican; President of the Republic 1934–40

The son of a shop/bar owner and a seamstress, Lázaro Cardenas was one of eight children in a poor family living in a small provincial town in the south-western state of Michoacan. He attended school for about four years, then was employed as a bookkeeper in a local tax office and as a printer. The family's situation was modest and made the more so by the father's death in 1911.

Cardenas's involvement in the Mexican Revolution seems to stem from the assassination of Francisco Madero in 1913, when he enlisted with a band of local rebels fighting the regime of Victoriano Huerta. His enthusiasm and clerical skills helped a rapid rise through the ranks of the revolutionary army and he became an important member of a clique associated with Generals Alvaro Obregón and Plutarco Elias Calles. These powerful revolutionary figures from the northern state of Sonora were to become presidents of the Republic, 1920–4 and 1924–8 respectively, and, as a trusted associate, Cardenas was appointed to important military positions during their presidencies.

His first significant elected political experience was as Governor of his home state, Michoacan, in 1928 where he displayed an enthusiasm for agrarian reform, popular education, and the encouragement of peasant organizations. At the national level his *patrón*, Calles, although no longer President, was still the dominant force in politics and he selected Cardenas to be the National Revolutionary Party's candidate for the presidency in the 1933 elections. After an extended and populistic campaign he assumed the presidency in 1934. Although he was initially thought to be another tame client of Calles the friendship deteriorated and within two years Calles was exiled.

As President, Cardenas embarked on a series of major reforms. His commitment to agrarian reform led him to expropriate over 40 million acres of private land for distribution to peasant communities. Schoolteachers were dispatched to the countryside to spread literacy and socialist ideas. The industrial sector was also transformed. A number of mines and the railway system were nationalized and, most famously, foreign oil companies were seized in 1938 and reconstituted as a giant state-owned monopoly, Petroleos Mexicanos (PEMEX). These reforms helped his reorganization of the Revolutionary Party in 1938.

The new organization, the Mexican Revolutionary Party (PRM), was a corporatist structure with four sectors. Beneficiaries of the land reforms were drafted into the National Peasant Confederation (CNC), which was the basis of the Agrarian sector. The government's sympathetic attitude towards strikes and worker's organizations helped the creation of a Mexican Confederation of Labour (CTM), which became the mainstay of the Labour sector. The army's commitment to the Revolution was channelled through a military sector; and a catch-all grouping, the National Confederation of Popular Organizations (CNOP), incorporated teachers, bureaucrats, and small businessmen. This mass-based corporatist party has provided a remarkably flexible and effective political machine for the Mexican revolutionary élite and is operative, if under strain, in the late 1990s.

After his retirement from the presidency Cardenas continued to play a political role, briefly as Minister of War and as the director of regional development projects concerned with rural populations in the poorer states of the republic. But he also served as chairman of the pro-*Castro Movement for National Liberation in 1968 and acted as a focus for left-wing opinion within the Mexican revolutionary family until his death in 1970. That mantle was inherited by his son Cuauhtemoc Cardenas who now plays a leading role in the Democratic Revolutionary Party (PRD)—the main leftist opposition party in Mexico.

Cardoso, Fernando Henrique (b. 18 June 1931)

Brazilian; Senator 1978–94, President of the Republic 1995–

One of Brazil's most distinguished sociologists, Cardoso comes from a military family prominent in the civil and military politics of Brazil. Both his grandfather and great uncle were generals, the latter being Minister of War; but Cardoso's family belonged to the nationalist, reformist tradition in the Brazilian officer corps. His father, General Leônidas Fernandes Cardoso, was associated with the *tenente* movement which, in the 1920s, opposed the coffee-based oligarchy. Later, as a civilian lawyer, especially under the Vargas administration, he strongly defended national control of Brazil's oil industry, as did his brother, General Felicíssimo Cardoso.

With this background, it is not surprising that Cardoso opposed the right-wing military-backed coup in 1964. By this time he was also a member of an outstanding school of social scientists in the University of São Paulo, mainly shaped by the highly respected sociologist and socialist, Florestan Fernandes.

After the 1964 coup, Cardoso taught in universities in Latin America, Europe, and the United States, establishing his reputation as a political sociologist, being best known for his work on dependency theory. He founded, in São Paulo, CEBRAP, the Brazilian Centre for Analysis and Planning and held the Simon Bolivar chair in Cambridge. In 1978, as Brazil's return to democracy gathered pace, Cardoso formally entered politics as the *suplente*, the officially elected substitute, of Senator Franco Montoro, of the MDB, the Brazilian Democratic Movement, in São Paulo. In 1982, when Montoro was elected governor, Cardoso took his Senate seat. In 1986, he was elected to Senate in his own right.

After Brazil's return to civilian government, in 1985, Cardoso gained invaluable experience in congressional negotiation, working with leaders of the PMDB, the Party of Brazilian Democratic Movement. In 1988, he was one of a group of politicians, many of them from São Paulo, who broke away from that party, to form the PSDB, the Party of Brazilian Social Democracy, the '*Tucanos*'.

When President Itamar Franco took over from the discredited Collor de Mello, in late 1992, Cardoso became Minister of Foreign Affairs, then, in May 1993, Minister of Finance. He then began to introduce a phased stabilization and reform programme which finally took shape, on 1 July 1994, as the *Plano Real*. In June, the monthly rate of inflation had been just under 50 per cent, but it now dropped sharply, so that in 1995 annual inflation was below 15 per cent, the lowest since 1957.

It was largely the success of the *Plano Real* which brought Cardoso a sweeping victory in the presidential election of 3 October. He won 54.28 per cent of the vote, in the first round, with over 5.4 million more votes than all seven other candidates.

On the strength of this massive mandate, Cardoso and his team have sought to introduce wide-ranging reforms. They include much-needed fiscal reforms and others affecting the public administration and social security systems. These, however, largely depend on amendments to the constitution of 1988, which require the support of three-fifths of the Congress elected in 1994. In terms of simple arithmetic, Cardoso should be able to marshal such support, but the political realities are more complex, allowing resistance or opposition to his proposals.

After more than two years, the *Plano Real* is still intact and the reform programme is moving forward slowly. Cardoso has been criticized for not moving faster, especially in terms of social reforms. The completion of his whole programme may require a second consecutive term in office for Cardoso, following the presidential election of 1998: but, at present, such immediate succession is not allowed under the 1988 constitution. Once again, it would require the support of three-fifths of a recalcitrant Congress.

Carey, Hugh Leo (b. Brooklyn, New York, 11 Apr. 1919)

US; member of the US House of Representatives 1960–75, Governor of New York 1974–83

Educated at St John's College and St John's Law School, Carey was for a time employed in the family petrochemicals business. Carey became a Democratic member of the House of Representatives in 1960 and served there until 1974, for part of the time acting as deputy whip.

In 1974 Carey was elected Governor of New York, a post to which he was re-elected in 1978. In office Carey had to impose a programme of financial stringency on the state and as a result alienated both liberals (who wanted more public spending) and conservatives who wanted more radical cuts in the public budget. Carey also incurred unpopularity for his opposition to capital punishment. Although Carey was for a time mentioned as a possible presidential candidate, the policies he had had to enact as Governor were not likely to win votes with the wider democratic constituency. On leaving office Carey became executive vice-president of W. R. Grace.

Carías Andino, Tiburcio (b. Tegucigalpa, 1876; d. Tegucigalpa 1969)
Honduran; leader of the National Party 1923–48, President of Honduras 1933–49

Carías Andino graduated in law from the Central University of Honduras in 1898. He participated in the civil war of 1893 on the side of the Liberals and, having distinguished himsely in battle, was promoted to the rank of brigadier-general in 1907. After the Liberals' triumph of the same year he was named Commander of Arms, Political Governor of the northern departments of Copán and (latterly) Cortés, and military chief of the northern region, becoming one of the most powerful political figures in the country.

In 1919 Carías lent his support to the faction of the Liberals which in 1923 formed the National Party. The Liberal and National parties continue to dominate the Honduran political system in the 1990s. In the 1923 presidential elections, Carías polled the most votes but failed to achieve the absolute majority required by the constitution. The ensuing débâcle between different factions in Congress led to the civil war of 1924 which was settled by US intervention. Carías subsequently consolidated his power through his control of Congress and the Supreme Court. In 1928, he was defeated at the polls and gained considerable prestige by peacefully accepting electoral defeat; such behaviour not constituting the norm in Honduran politics during the first half of the twentieth century.

In 1932 Carías was finally elected President for the constitutionally mandated four-year term. In 1936 he convened a constituent assembly to issue a new constitution extending the presidential period from four to six years. In 1940 the constitution was again reformed to permit Carías to remain in power until 1949. His opponents were repressed, exiled, or bought off, and the regime's stability guaranteed by Carías near-total control of the National Party, together with the support of the United Fruit Co. and the US government. After the end of the Second World War, opposition to the regime increased. In 1948 Carías selected his successor, Juan Manuel Gálvez. However, Gálvez distanced his government from the dictatorship, resulting in the division of the National Party into two factions. Carías Andino maintained considerable influence within the National Party until his death in 1969.

During his period in power, Carías achieved economic and political stability, and the extension of state authority throughout the nation. However, this was achieved through the suppression of civil liberties and conservative fiscal policies.

Carlsson, Ingvar (b. Borås, 9 Nov. 1934)
Swedish; Prime Minister 1986–91, 1994–6

The son of a warehouse worker, Carlsson went to school and then to a commercial high school in his native town. He subsequently studied social sciences at Lund University and took a degree in 1958 after five terms instead of the usual eight. At school and university he became chairman of the local Social Democratic Labour Youth/Student clubs. At Lund he came to the attention of Prime Minister Tage *Erlander and was recruited to work as an assistant in the Cabinet office 1958–60. In 1960–1 he took a year out to read economics in the United States. On his return to Sweden in 1961 he was elected chairman of the Social Democratic Youth League and remained in that position until 1967.

In 1965 Carlsson was elected to parliament. In 1967–9 he served as an under-secretary in the Cabinet office. In 1969, when *Palme became Prime Minister, Carlsson was appointed Minister of Education until 1973 and then Minister of Housing until 1976. During his party's years in opposition 1976–82 he was given major policy planning assignments especially in the economic and energy fields.

These services were rewarded on Palme's return to office in 1982 with the specially created post of Deputy Premier. In this capacity Carlsson continued to plan long-term policies for his party. On Palme's assassination in February 1986 it was therefore clear that Carlsson should succeed, and he received unanimous endorsement from the party's national executive committee.

Carlsson won elections in 1988 and 1994 and buttressed his minority government in 1995 by entering into an understanding with the non-socialist Centre Party. In March 1996 he retired from office with the satisfaction of having seen his country vote for EC membership and his party remain essentially united in the face of this and other potentially divisive issues.

Carol II (b.Sinaia, 15 Oct. 1893; d. Paris, 4 Mar. 1953)
Romanian; King 1930–40

Carol II was the eldest son of King Ferdinand of Romania. He married Princess Hélène of Greece in 1921. In 1925 Ferdinand disinherited him because of his dissolute behaviour and he went to France with his Jewish mistress, Magda Lupescu. Carol's 6-year-old son Michael succeeded Ferdinand in 1927. In 1930 Carol returned to Romania and was proclaimed King with the support of the premier, Iuliu Maniu. Lupescu followed him in 1931, to the annoyance of Romania's politicians. From 1930 to 1937 Romania was nominally a democracy, while Carol tolerated *Codreanu's Fascist-style Iron Guard. Concerned at the Iron Guard's power, Carol set up a royal dictatorship in 1938, with his own Fascist-style party, the Front of National Rebirth. He executed Codreanu and the Iron Guard leaders. Carol believed that he could maintain Romania's independence by playing the Western Powers off against Germany. In 1940 *Hitler forced Carol to cede territory to the Soviet Union, Bulgaria, and Hungary. This undermined his position in Romania. He was deposed by *Antonescu with German support, abdicating in favour of his son Michael on 6 September 1940. He went into exile, accompanied by Magda Lupescu, whom he married in 1947.

Carrington, Peter Alexander Rupert (b. London, 6 June 1919)
British; Secretary of State for Defence 1970–4, Foreign Secretary 1979–82; Baron (succeeded to title) 1938

An ancestor, Robert Smith, had been banker and adviser to the younger Pitt at the end of the eighteenth century and was given a peerage. Peter Carrington achieved much in different fields—the military, diplomacy, in government. He was educated at Eton and Sandhurst and inherited his title in 1938. Because of service in the 1939–45 war he did not enter the House of Lords until 1945. Among his early posts were High Commissioner in Australia, First Lord of the Admiralty (1959–63), and leader of the House of Lords (1964–70).

Carrington became a close friend and political ally of Ted *Heath. When the latter formed his government in 1970 Carrington was made Secretary of State for Defence, to which post he added the party chairmanship in 1972 and, briefly, the newly created Energy Department at the time of the energy crisis in early 1974. Carrington was blamed by some Conservatives who thought that the election campaign in February 1974 had been badly managed. The election was forced by the coal miners' strike against the government's statutory pay policy, at a time of acute energy shortage. Carrington was one of those who favoured an early election, earlier than the one that was eventually called.

In Opposition between 1974 and 1979 he had an uneasy relationship with the new party leader, Margaret *Thatcher. She respected his experience, contacts, and tactical advice. But he stood for a different kind of conservatism from hers—he was more internationalist and more pro-European abroad and more conciliatory at home. Appointed Foreign Secretary in 1979 he played a key role in the passage to independence of Rhodesia/Zimbabwe and in maintaining reasonable relations with the EC; the latter were dominated at the time by Mrs Thatcher's strident insistence on eliminating a good part of Britain's net deficit with the Community.

The work of the Foreign Office on a scheme for the leaseback of the Falkland Islands to Argentina was one among many signals which led the military regime in Argentina to think that Britain would acquiesce in its seizure of the islands. When Argentina did so, opinion in Britain regarded the event as a national humiliation and, following party criticisms, Carrington resigned as Foreign Secretary. This was a step that Mrs Thatcher much regretted. But he was offended by the criticism and his resignation probably helped Mrs Thatcher. Subsequent official inquiries into events leading to the war cleared the Foreign Office and Carrington of any blame in the matter.

After leaving government Carrington continued to play a public role. He was Secretary-General of NATO (1984–8), and chaired the peace conference on Yugoslavia (1991–2). Carrington represented the aristocracy's tradition of public service. He was regarded as a politician with a sense of proportion, one who was a good diplomat because he respected other points of view and also had a sense of the limits of what politics could achieve.

He published his memoirs, *Reflect on Things Past*, in 1988.

Carson, Edward Henry (b. Dublin, 9 Feb. 1854; d. 22 Oct. 1935)
British; First Lord of the Admiralty 1916–17; Baron (judicial life peer) 1921

The son of a civil engineer, Carson was educated at Portarlington School and Trinity College, Dublin, before embarking on a career at the bar.

Carson entered the House of Commons in 1892. He held junior ministerial posts under Lord Salisbury and Arthur *Balfour (1892 and 1900–5), but his first Cabinet post was as Attorney-General (1915) in H. H. *Asquith's wartime coalition government. He later served under David *Lloyd-George as First Lord of the Admiralty (1916–17) and Minister without Portfolio (1917–18). Thereafter, he remained on the back benches until 1921, when he became a Lord of Appeal in Ordinary.

Commitment to the union between Britain and Ireland dominated Carson's career. In 1911, he declined to be considered for the leadership of the Conservative Party in order to devote himself to Unionism. He opposed the pre-war Asquith government's Home Rule legislation both in parliament and outside it. His extra-parliamentary activities included preparations for armed resistance to Irish Home Rule. He also drafted a constitution for a provisional Unionist government for Ulster. (Some Liberals urged his indictment for treason.)

Carson was a difficult colleague, reluctant to compromise. He resigned from Asquith's government after five months in disagreement with its Balkans policy. Under Lloyd George, his transfer to a non-portfolio post was prompted by a resignation threat and his departure in 1918 was a resignation over the government's Irish policy. Later, his refusal to follow the convention that a judicial position precluded intervention in political controversy brought a public reprimand from the Lord Chancellor. He eventually retired as a Lord of Appeal in 1929, playing little part in public life afterwards.

Carter, James ('Jimmy') Earl, Jr. (b. Plains, Georgia, 1 Oct. 1924)
US; Governor of Georgia 1971–4, President 1977–81

The son of a farmer and a registered nurse, Carter was educated at local public school in Georgia before spending a year at Georgia Southwestern University and then entering Georgia Institute of Technology as a naval ROTC cadet. In 1943 he entered the US Naval Academy at Annapolis—a childhood ambition—graduating in 1946 and being commissioned as an Ensign in the US Navy. Shortly after graduation, he married Rosalynn Smith, from Plains. After two years of service on experimental radar and gunnery vessels, he switched to submarines. On one occasion, he came close to being lost at sea, after being swept from the submarine bridge during a storm. He subsequently applied, and was accepted, to participate in the nuclear submarine construction programme directed by Admiral Hyman G. Rickover. He took courses in nuclear physics and reactor technology at Union College, New York. His naval career was cut short in 1953 when his father died, at a relatively early age, of cancer. He returned home to Plains to run the family peanut-farming and fertilizer business, despite the protestation of his wife. After some lean years, he built the family concern into a prosperous business. He also began to get involved in civic and church affairs, making a name for himself by being the only person locally to refuse to join the racist White Citizens' Council. He also started to take an interest in elective office. His father had been elected a member of the state assembly the year before he died and had encouraged his son to take an interest in public affairs. The principal spur to seeking office, though, came several years later when Carter served as chairman of the local school board. A proposal from the board was subject to a local referendum and he went round giving speeches in support of the proposal. The proposal was narrowly defeated. He made his first bid for elective office in 1962, seeking election to the State Senate. After a bitter primary contest–in which he had to resort to court action to overturn the corrupt practices of his opponents–he won the general election and served two terms (1963–7). He took a particular interest in election reform and improving the education system. He was also a regular opponent of 'sweetheart bills', giving particular individuals breaks on salary or retirement benefits. His autobiography, *Why Not the Best?*, written before he won national office, also reflected a dislike of lobbyists.

In 1966 he announced his intention to run for the US Congress, but after the leading Democratic contender for governor had a heart attack and withdrew from the race, Carter was persuaded to seek the nomination. He lost the nomination to a segregationist, Lestor Maddox, and resolved to contest the nomination again in 1970. After an intense period of planning and campaigning, he was successful the second time round. In the interim, he became a Born Again Christian.

As Governor, he reorganized government, reducing significantly the number of agencies and streamlining the administration. He implemented a number of public sector reforms and increased the number of blacks appointed to public office. He disliked patronage and compromise, and preferred rallying popular support for his measures among voters to bargaining with members of the state legislature. He also sought to raise Georgia's profile abroad, undertaking ten overseas visits in order to promote trade and inform himself about other countries.

In 1972 he began to think seriously about running for President. He served as chairman of the National Democratic Party 1974 Campaign Committee, giving him experience of campaign organization and strategy. In the autumn of 1974 he announced his candidacy for the 1976 presidential nomination. He completed his term of office as Governor in 1975 and thus had time to campaign unfettered by responsibilities of office. The field of candidates increased but Carter scored a major success early in 1976 by topping the poll in the New Hampshire primary. This established him as the front-runner and generated a bandwagon effect. He won six of the first eight primaries. Despite some setbacks–he polled badly in New York and Massachusetts–his opponents were gradually eliminated. By early June he had enough delegates to be assured of the nomination. He had announced in advance that he would select Senator Walter *Mondale as his running mate. He began the general election with a clear lead over the Republican, President Gerald R. *Ford. Ford was the successor to Richard *Nixon, who had resigned in disgrace over the Watergate scandal. Ford had kept on various Nixon appointees and had pardoned Nixon for any offences he may have committed. The situation favoured the Democratic candidate. However, Carter's support slipped as the campaign progressed–his Southern speaking style worked to his disadvantage and he performed below expectations in the first televised debate with Ford—but he held on to win with a 2 per cent margin of victory. He polled well among blacks and blue-collar workers. He was the first Georgian to be elected President and the first President elected from the deep South since 1848.

In the White House, Carter tried to set a high moral tone. He stressed human rights in international affairs and opposed 'pork barrel' legislation at home. In domestic affairs, he stressed the need for energy conservation and sent a major Energy Bill to Congress. He persuaded Congress to approve a major reform of the civil service, something that his predecessors had failed to achieve. In foreign affairs, he obtained Senate approval—by one vote—for the Panama Canal Treaty, restoring the Canal to Panama. In 1978 he hosted a meeting at Camp David with President Anwar *Sadat of Egypt and Prime Minister Menachim *Begin of Israel, resulting in the Camp David Agreement in which both signed up to a peace framework. In the sector of defence, he departed from past policy and cancelled the B1 bomber project. He also vetoed a measure for a $2 billion dollar nuclear carrier; Congress failed to override his veto. He also persuaded Congress to lift the arms embargo on Turkey.

However, Carter's successes in the office were sporadic rather than consistent. His relationship with Congress was not a harmonious one. He had fought the election as an 'outsider' to Washington and now had to work with the institution that formed part of the establishment he had attacked. His narrow victory had denied him a coat-tails effect. The Democrats were well entrenched in both Houses, but with the members not owing their victory to the President. Carter adopted a high moral stance, assuming that Congress would recognize the rightness of his measures. He sent several measures to Congress at the same time and then failed to lobby for them. His Energy Bill got bogged down and emerged eventually in a somewhat emasculated form. Though most of his measures were passed, his success rate in Congress—just over 75 per cent—was markedly lower than for his Democratic predecessors Lyndon *Johnson and John F. *Kennedy and only marginally better than that achieved by the Republican Dwight *Eisenhower. Carter surrounded himself with advisers drawn from Georgia—dubbed 'the Georgia Mafia'—who had no real grasp of Washington politics. A number of important measures, including a Labour Law Reform Bill, failed. Carter appeared increasingly out of his depth. The Camp David Agreement produced a temporary increase in popular support, but his standing soon fell back to low levels. In foreign affairs, crises appeared to be the norm and he appeared surprised by events. The fall of the Shah of Iran and the Soviet invasion of Afghanistan caused particular difficulties and highlighted the incapacity of the US government to do much about either. Carter cut off grain sales to the USSR and encouraged a boycott of the 1980 Olympic Games in Moscow—neither having much impact—and his decision to allow the former Shah into the USA for medical treatment sparked the seizure of hostages in the American embassy in Tehran. The holding of the hostages dented Carter's already fragile public support. In desperation, he authorized a rescue attempt that ended in failure.

Until 1980, Carter experienced low popular ratings because of poor economic performance. Inflation and unemployment were rising and there was little optimism about future prospects. Perceptions of poor performance were then compounded by Carter's handling of the hostages crisis. In 1980, with his popularity in the opinion polls lower than that of any president since Warren *Harding, he faced a challenge from Senator Edward Kennedy for the Democratic nomination. He fought off the challenge, but it served to demonstrate the turmoil and dissatisfaction within Democratic ranks. In the general election, he was beaten by a clear margin by the Republican candidate, Ronald *Reagan. Carter won 35.4 million votes against 43.9 million for Reagan. It was the first time an incumbent had been defeated since 1932. Carter retired to Plains, but maintained an active public career, involving himself in projects to assist Third World countries and occasionally engaging in some international mediation.

Great things were expected of Carter when he entered the White House. He was a highly intelligent individual, a problem solver, a Democrat with a Congress dominated by fellow Democrats. Yet he proved to be a failure. He never really grasped what was required of the incumbent of the Oval Office. He tried to do too many things at once, failed to focus his activities, and was too obviously influenced by the last person he had spoken to. He was viewed as a good man, but one increasingly out of his depth. His White House staff were generally viewed by members of Congress as lightweight; a number—including the Director of the Office of Management and Budget, Bert Lance—became embroiled in scandals. The White House was both scandal-prone on occasion as well as accident prone. On a visit to Warsaw in 1978, an interpreter was hired who was not up to the job—translating Carter's words on arrival as 'I desire the Poles carnally' and 'When I abandoned the United States, never to return'—and Carter's participation in a jogging marathon in Washington was cut short when he collapsed and had to be carried away. Some members of his family also attracted unwelcome publicity, his brother Billy receiving money to provide advice to the Libyan government. There was little observable enjoyment in the final months of his presidency.

In the 1982 *Tribune* poll, Carter was ranked the tenth worst president in US history. He fared a little better in the Murray poll of the same year, being ranked 25th out of 36, one behind his Republican predecessor, Gerald Ford. His public work since leaving office increased his standing in the eyes of the public, though it did little to affect historians' judgement of his presidency. In the 1995 *Chicago Sun-Times* poll of presidential scholars, he was ranked 22nd out of 38. Though some reassessment of his presidency has occurred, as in John Dumbrell's *The Carter Presidency: A Re-evaluation* (1993), he has not been subject to a new interpretation. Richard Nixon fared better in the 1995 poll than he did.

Castle, Barbara Anne (b. Yorkshire, 6 Oct. 1910)

British; Secretary of State for Social Services 1974–6; Baroness (life peer) 1990

The daughter of a civil servant, Castle was educated at Bradford Girls' Grammar School and St Hugh's College, Oxford. After working as a journalist and as a wartime civil servant, she was elected Labour MP for Blackburn in 1945.

Ideologically, Castle was on the left of the Labour Party. A political protégé of Sir Stafford *Cripps in the 1930s, she was associated with Aneurin *Bevan's criticisms of the leadership in the 1950s. She was a member of the party's National Executive Committee from 1950 to 1979.

Castle was in the Commons for nineteen years before achieving ministerial office. When Harold *Wilson formed his first government in 1964 she joined the Cabinet as Minister of Overseas Development. Her effectiveness led to her promotion, after fifteen months, to the Ministry of Transport. Her best-remembered achievement there was the introduction of the breathalyser test for drivers. Her next post, as First Secretary of State and Secretary of State for Employment and Productivity (1968–70), was the most fraught of her career. She had first to secure the passage of legislation on the government's increasingly unpopular prices and incomes policy. But her real problems arose over the contentious proposals to regulate the activities of trade unions in her White Paper *In Place of Strife*. In 1969, she and Wilson were humiliated by the Cabinet's rejection of legislation. Her most enduring achievement at the DEP was the Equal Pay Act, 1970, improving working women's rights.

On Labour's return to office, in 1974, Castle became Secretary of State for Health and Social Services. Her notable success in securing the passage of the Child Benefit Act was overshadowed by problems arising from her attempt to phase pay-beds out of NHS hospitals. She lost office when James *Callaghan assumed the premiership in 1976. After retiring from the Commons in 1979, she stood for the European Parliament—despite her long-standing opposition to British membership of the

European Community. She served two five-year terms, becoming leader of the British Labour group for six years and vice-chairman of the Socialist group for seven.

Castle was one of the most energetic and widely known politicians of her day. Two volumes of *The Castle Diaries* (1980 and 1984) provide illuminating insights on the Wilson governments.

Castro Ruz, Fidel (b. Biran, Cuba, 13 Aug. 1926)

Cuban; leader of anti-Batista rebellion 1953–9, Prime Minister 1959–76, President 1976–

The son of a Galician sugar planter in eastern Cuba, Castro progressed through Catholic schools to study law at Havana University in 1945, where his involvement in the politically confused and murky world of student politics included a 1947 attempt to overthrow the Dominican dictator *Trujillo, and, in 1948, membership of the newly-formed nationalist Ortodoxo Party, for which, in 1952 (after graduating in 1950, and entering a law practice specializing in poor people's cases), he became a congressional candidate.

When *Batista's March coup prevented those elections, Castro and others attacked the Moncada barracks in Santiago, on 26 July 1953, hoping to galvanize resistance. Castro was arrested, tried, and sentenced to fifteen years on the Isle of Pines, where he organized what became the 26 July Movement, based on his own 1953 defence speech, 'History will absolve me'. Released in 1955, Castro went to Mexico, where he met Ernesto Che Guevara, continued to organize the domestic resistance, and trained a small invasion force.

In December 1956, that invasion (near Manzanillo, Eastern Cuba) took place with eighty-two men on the yacht *Granma*, but was easily defeated, eighteen rebels surviving in the nearby Sierra Maestra, where Castro set up his base and where he remained until late 1958, waging guerrilla war, propagandizing, radicalizing his ideas, and so polarizing Cuban opinion that, when Batista fled on 31 December, he was the sole credible power in Cuba.

This radicalization accelerated after 1959, as Castro, Prime Minister from February, responded to internal, popular, and external pressures, and to his own radical and nationalist agenda. This persuaded him first to break with a hostile United States, then adopt a series of unorthodox policies and, despite his 1961 declaration of Marxism-Leninism, to distance Cuba from his new allies, Moscow and the Cuban Communists, differing especially over economic and Latin American policy. Cuba's unique version of Communism throughout the 1960s was partly attributable to his ideas.

The 1970s, however, saw greater orthodoxy and institutionalization and a reduction in his power as Moscow sought to control its wayward ally, yet his hand was again evident in Cuba's policies in the Third World, designed to gain international leverage and leadership.

The late 1980s saw him return to centre-stage, responding to *Gorbachev, the collapse of Communism, and the resulting economic crisis with a characteristic mix of ideological radicalism (post-1986 'rectification' partly seeking to revive 1960s ideas) and open pragmatism in a post-Communist world. Indeed, Castro's continued leadership and survival have always depended on that mix, together with finely tuned political skills and a sense of global politics.

Cavaco Silva, Anibal (b. Poço Boliqueime, 15 July 1939)

Portuguese; Finance Minister 1979–80, Prime Minister 1985–95

Before he entered politics in the 1980s Cavaco was a successful academic. He graduated in Finance at the Technical University of Lisbon in 1964 and received a Ph.D. at the University of York in England in December 1973. Between 1974 and 1979 he occupied several professorships in Portuguese universities, and was a full professor at the New University of Lisbon.

A member of the Social Democratic Party (Partido Social-Democrata—PSD) since its foundation in May 1974, he was a consultant on economic policy in the party's research institute. In January 1980 he became Minister of Finance and Planning in the sixth constitutional government, under the leadership of Francisco Sá Carneiro, but left the post soon after the tragic death of Prime Minister Sá Carneiro in an aviation accident. As Finance Minister, he gave priority to reducing the budget deficit. In October 1980 he was elected member of parliament, and on the death of the party's deputy Prime Minister Mota Pinto was elected party president in 1985. He led the party in the 1985 elections to victory and became Prime Minister of a PSD minority government one month later. He refused to sign any pact with the other parties in the Assembly of the Republic and in 1987 his government was brought down by a motion of censure. In the postponed election of 19 July 1987, Cavaco Silva won an absolute majority, which he repeated in October 1991. In February 1995, he stepped down after serving ten years as Prime Minister; he had played a significant role in Portugal's transition to a stable democracy. After his failure to be chosen as the PSD official candidate for the presidency of the Republic he returned to academic life.

Ceauşescu, Nicolae (b. Scorniceşti-Olt, 26 Jan. 1918; d. near Bucharest, 25 Dec. 1989)
Romanian; Leader 1965–89

Ceauşescu was born 80 miles north-west of Bucharest, the son of an alcoholic peasant. In 1929, at the age of 11, he went to work in a factory in Bucharest. He joined the illegal Union of Communist Youth in 1933 and the Romanian Communist Party (RCP) in 1936. He was imprisoned for his political activities from 1936 to 1938 and from 1940 to 1944. After the Red Army entered Bucharest in 1944, he was made a secretary of the Central Committee of the Union of Communist Youth. In 1945 to 1948 and from 1952 to 1989 he was a member of the Central Committee of the RCP. From 1948 to 1950 he was Deputy Minister of Agriculture and from 1950 to 1954 he was Deputy Minister of the Armed Forces. He became a secretary of the Central Committee of the RCP in April 1954 and a member of the Politburo in 1955. From 1957 to 1965 he was effectively the second in command in Romania under *Gheorghiu-Dej. When the latter died in March 1965, Ceauşescu became General Secretary of the RCP. In December 1967 he became head of state and in 1969 made himself President of the Defence Council and supreme commander of the armed forces.

Ceauşescu followed a foreign policy partly independent of the Soviet Union. In 1967 Romania broke ranks with the Soviet Bloc, giving vocal support to Israel during the 'Six Day War'. In 1968 Ceauşescu denounced the Soviet intervention in Czechoslovakia. At the beginning of the 1970s he played an important part in the re-establishment of relations between the USA and China. Throughout the 1970s he strove to increase trade with the West. But he made no attempt to take Romania out of the Soviet Bloc.

In domestic policy Ceauşescu's rise to power saw a significant reduction in the repression of the Gheorghiu-Dej period. His policies put great emphasis on Romanian nationalism and repressed the large Hungarian minority in Transylvania. It was marked by nepotism and the cult of personality—Ceauşescu was the only Communist leader to carry a sceptre in public. Opposition was ruthlessly suppressed by the hated secret police, the Securitate. At the beginning of the 1980s Ceauşescu introduced an austerity programme in order to pay off Romania's foreign debt. The great hardship which this caused was increased by his programme of 'systematization', the uprooting of traditional villages at the end of the decade. His position was undermined by the development of economic and political reform in the Soviet Union. In December 1989 the city of Timişoara revolted when human rights protests were brutally suppressed. The unrest spread to Bucharest, where the Soviet Union backed a coup against Ceauşescu by elements of the RCP and the army. He fled the capital with his wife Elena on 22 December, but was captured. The couple were tried by a military tribunal and shot on 25 December 1989.

Césaire, Aimé Fernand (b. Martinique, 26 June 1913)
Martinican; Mayor of Fort-de France 1945– , Député 1946–95

Born into a poor black family in French colonial Martinique, Césaire was educated in the island, winning a scholarship to study in Paris. Active in left-wing and artistic circles in Paris, he returned to Martinique in 1939 as a militant anti-colonialist, poet, and exponent of *négritude*—the positive assertion of African cultural values. In the early stage of the Second World War Martinique supported Vichy France and was blockaded by the US navy. By 1942 Césaire had joined the Parti Communiste Français (PCF) and had attracted a following of intellectuals through his teaching and writing. In 1945 he stood as a PCF candidate for the mayorship of Fort-de-France and was overwhelmingly elected. The following year he was also elected as a Communist *député* to represent Martinique in the French National Assembly.

Césaire was an enthusiastic champion of 'departmentalization', the process by which Martinique (together with Guadeloupe, Guyane, and Réunion) became full *départements* of the French Republic. This, he believed, would raise Martinicans' living standards to a level comparable with those of the metropole. At the same time, he argued for political and cultural autonomy for the island, rejecting the assimilationist impetus of the French state. He also came to reject the centralizing influence of the PCF and left in 1956, forming his own Parti Progressiste Martiniquais (PPM) in 1958.

For half a century Césaire represented Fort-de-France as mayor and Martinique as *député* in Paris. In 1981 he declared support for François *Mitterand's Parti Socialiste (PS) and found in Mitterand's decentralization programme a structure within which he could continue to advocate departmentalization and autonomy. As Martinique became a *région*, with increased political and financial autonomy, Césaire could claim that the island was both part of the French Republic yet autonomous in many respects.

The author of some highly regarded poetry, theatre, and history, Césaire became an institution in Martinique, symbolizing the island's continuing dependence upon France but also its own distinctive culture. He was perhaps more influential in the newly independent French-speaking states of Africa than elsewhere in the Caribbean, where Martinique and Guadeloupe are rarely viewed as parts of the regional community.

Chaban Delmas, Jacques (b. Paris, 1 Mar. 1915)
French; Prime Minister 1969–72

Jacques Delmas (the Chaban was his wartime alias) was born to a middle-class family. He was educated at the École Libre des Sciences Politiques, which he detested, and managed on his second attempt to enter the Finance Inspectorate, an élite division of the higher civil service. His good Resistance record, his charm, and his energy were valuable political assets which he, like his friend *Mitterrand, exploited to the full. He chose the south-west town of Bordeaux as the site for his ambitions, becoming its deputy in 1946 and its mayor the following year. Over the next thirty years he constructed an impregnable power base in Bordeaux and the surrounding region, based on clientelism and the judicious construction of personal alliances which transcended party barriers. In the Fourth Republic he demonstrated the flexibility which became his trademark by combining ministerial office with active, if discreet, participation in the plots which led to the return to power of *de Gaulle in 1958. The following year he was elected president of a National Assembly whose powers had been greatly reduced by the new constitution and which he turned into a reliable auxiliary of the new political order. Yet at the same time he cultivated a reformist image by advocating a 'new society' which would end the rigidities of France's social and political institutions. It was this which made him so attractive a figure to the Gaullist high command in the dangerous political climate produced by the 1968 events. *Pompidou, de Gaulle's successor as President, thus appointed him Prime Minister in 1969. As Prime Minister Chaban tried to institutionalize the 'new society' by liberalizing the state-run broadcasting system and strengthening trade union rights in the public sector. The problem with his reformism was that it made no impact on the left, alienated the powerful right-wing faction in the Gaullist Party, and increasingly irritated President Pompidou, whose private office waged merciless war on him. By 1972 he was under fire in the press for his personal tax arrangements which, though legal, hardly fitted in with his claim to want a more socially just France. The botched referendum on British membership of the EEC, and an injudicious attempt to shore up his position by obtaining a parliamentary vote of confidence, sealed his fate. In June 1972, in a brutal demonstration of presidential power, Pompidou sacked him.

Out of office, Chaban mended his fences with the Gaullist Party and prepared for the next presidential contest which, in view of Pompidou's incurable illness, was likely to come soon. The 1974 election, however, proved to be a disaster. He announced his candidature before Pompidou was in his grave, performed badly on television, and could not shake off the tax story or the rumours about his private life. Faced with the smooth reformism of his rival conservative candidate *Giscard d'Estaing and the implacable hostility of Pompidou's protégé, *Chirac, who held the key post of Interior Minister, his campaign disintegrated. The erstwhile prophet of the new society found his support limited to the Gaullist old guard. On round one he was eliminated with only 15 per cent of the vote. His presidential ambitions were over. Yet Chaban remained a prominent political figure. His Bordeaux fiefdom was untouched by the defeat and he continued to nurse dreams of returning to the premiership, dreams which, in the changed politics of the mid-1980s, might have come true. His real strength was as a manager of the National Assembly, whose president he became in 1978 and again in 1986. By the 1990s there were signs that the Bordeaux political machine which he had controlled for so long was starting to break down and he did not stand in the 1995 municipal elections.

Chamberlain, Arthur **Neville** (b. Birmingham, 18 Mar. 1869; d. 9 Nov. 1940)

British; Chancellor of Exchequer 1923–4, 1931–7, Prime Minister 1937–40

The son of Joseph *Chamberlain, and half-brother of *Austen, Neville was educated at Rugby and Mason College, Birmingham. He worked in the Bahamas for five years before returning to Birmingham to build up a manufacturing company of his own. He threw himself into the civic life of Birmingham, serving as lord mayor in 1915–16 and was brought into the wartime effort as director general of National Service at the end of 1916. His tenure was brief, marked by increasing bitterness between him and *Lloyd George. He served until August 1917 and the following year entered Parliament as Conservative MP for Birmingham Ladywood. He entered government following the collapse of the Lloyd George coalition (which brought about his half-brother's resignation as party leader in the Commons) in 1922, serving as Postmaster-General and Paymaster-General, before being promoted to Minister of Health in March 1923 and then, in August, Chancellor of the Exchequer, serving until the party went out of office.

On the party's return to power in November 1924, he was appointed to his old office—not the Treasury but the Ministry of Health. In this post he introduced a raft of measures that were to lay many of the foundations of the welfare state. He put twenty-five measures of social reform before the Cabinet and achieved the enactment of twenty-one of them. In 1930 he took on, albeit briefly, the chairmanship of the

Conservative Party. He returned to the Health Ministry in 1931 for a few months before being appointed Chancellor of the Exchequer in November 1931, serving until his appointment as Prime Minister in 1937.

His premiership was dominated, and destroyed, by his handling of foreign affairs. He had no grounding in the subject but was driven by a belief in his own rightness. Believing he could handle *Hitler in Germany, he pursued a policy of appeasement, returning from Munich in 1938 with a signed agreement that was popular but ultimately worthless. He was harried by anti-appeasers on the Conservative benches. In September 1939 he found himself in the unenviable situation of having to declare that a state of war existed with Germany and transforming himself into a wartime leader. It was a role for which he was ill-suited. The Labour Party refused to enter into government with him and Conservative dissension reached a peak in 1940 with the failure of the Norwegian campaign. At the end of the Commons' debate on the campaign's failure, 41 Conservatives voted against the government and a further 60 abstained from voting. The government's majority fell from its normal 200 to 80. Chamberlain at first failed to recognize the significance of the vote but then succumbed to the message that the House of Commons had sent him. He submitted his resignation as Prime Minister, though not as party leader. He carried the title of party leader for a few months, before ill-health forced him to relinquish that in *Churchill's favour. He died six months after leaving Downing Street.

Viewed solely in terms of social reform, Chamberlain was an outstanding minister. He was destroyed by a disastrous incapacity to handle foreign affairs. He was unwilling to listen to others. *Macmillan recalled that he was 'quite sure of himself . . . at all times he was a difficult man to argue with . . . He knew he was right on all occasions.' He died a broken man.

Chamberlain, Joseph (b. London, 8 July 1836; d. 2 July 1914)

British; Secretary of State for Colonies 1895–1903

Joseph Chamberlain was famous more for the causes for which he campaigned than for offices which he held. He is also notable for helping to split the two major political parties.

Chamberlain was born into a family of boot and shoe manufacturers and entered the family firm after leaving school at 16. He soon moved to work for an uncle who was a screw manufacturer in Birmingham. He was so successful in the enterprise that he was able to retire at the age of 38, in 1874, and devote himself to politics.

Chamberlain is for ever associated with Birmingham. He rose to prominence as a local councillor and Liberal MP for the city, and his provincial base lent an extra edge to his radical politics. He was elected to the Birmingham council in 1869 and supported many of the radical Liberal and nonconformist policies. He became mayor in 1873 and was re-elected for two further years. He was a reforming leader and his schemes of civic improvement made Birmingham a model city. He also helped to form the remarkable Liberal caucus, the most notable example to date of machine politics in Britain. Through the clever deployment of votes, efficient organization, and campaigning the Liberal Party dominated Birmingham politics. In 1876 he was returned at a by-election as an MP for the city.

The Liberal leader, Gladstone, disliked Chamberlain's mix of populism and radicalism. Chamberlain could not be ignored and entered the Cabinet in 1880 as president of the Board of Trade. He supported such radical policies as manhood suffrage, graduated taxation, pre-primary education, and the disestablishment of state churches. He was anathema to many Conservatives and even the Whigs in his own party.

Gladstone's support for Home Rule for Ireland led to Chamberlain's break with the party. The latter was opposed to a measure that he was sure would lead to the breakup of the United Kingdom. Yet he was not unsympathetic to the Irish demands and proposed a federation with separate parliaments for the constituent parts of the

United Kingdom. He also could see that Home Rule would stifle the cause of social reform. In the short-lived 1886 Liberal government he was a member of the Cabinet and president of the Local Government Board. He then resigned and broke with Gladstone. He risked his political future because he was regarded as a likely successor to Gladsone as party leader. There was some irony that Chamberlain was joined by the Liberal Whigs, given the troubled history of their relations. Eventually the breakaway Liberal Unionists were to fuse with the Conservative Party. His local power was shown by the fact that Birmingham followed him when he broke with the Liberal Party.

In the Conservative government of 1895 he was made Secretary of State for Colonies. He was still a supporter of social reform, notably the introduction of old-age pensions, but was able to do little. In spite of his nonconformist appeal he was prepared to accept the Education Act of 1892. His support for the Boer War furthered his break with radical Liberals.

Chamberlain, convinced that Britain was gradually falling behind Germany and the United States as an economic power, thought that Britain should abandon free trade and protect her domestic markets by erecting tariffs. With the revenues from the tariffs the government could introduce social reforms. He also saw a preferential tariff for the colonies as a way of strengthening the union between Britain and her colonies. He resigned his Cabinet post in September 1903 to campaign for tariff reform. His cause divided and eventually led to the collapse of the Cabinet of A. J. *Balfour.

The campaign was doomed. Any proposal for higher taxes on food courted disaster at the ballot box and the Conservative and Unionist Party lost heavily in the 1906 general election. Although the majority of the Conservative Party supported his stand, this was his last great cause. He was incapacitated by a stroke in 1906 and although he lived on until 1914 his political career was finished.

Chamberlain was the father of a remarkable political family. One son, Austen *Chamberlain, became leader of the Conservative Party, and Neville *Chamberlain became Prime Minister.

Chamberlain, Joseph **Austen** (b. Birmingham, 16 Oct. 1863; d. 16 Mar. 1937)
British; Chancellor of the Exchequer 1903–5, 1919–21, leader of the Conservative Party in the House of Commons 1921–2, Foreign Secretary 1924–9; KG 1925

The son of Joseph *Chamberlain, Austen was educated at Rugby and Trinity College, Cambridge. He joined his father in parliament in 1892 when he was returned unopposed as the Liberal Unionist MP for East Worcestershire. He soon began his rise up the ministerial ladder, serving as Civil Lord of the Admiralty (1895–1900) and Financial Secretary to the Treasury (1900–2) before joining his father in the Cabinet as Postmaster-General. When his father resigned in 1903, he became Chancellor of the Exchequer, serving until the fall of the *Balfour government in 1905. His father's stroke in 1906 left him to carry the Chamberlain mantle. By 1911 he was sufficiently senior to be considered as a successor to Balfour as party leader in the Commons, but both he and the other principal challenger, Walter Long, stood down in favour of a compromise candidate. When a wartime coalition was formed in 1915, Chamberlain was appointed Secretary of State for India, resigning in 1917 following publication of a report into the Mesopotamia campaign for which he was technically responsible. He was brought back into government as a member of the War Cabinet in 1918 and the following year returned to the Treasury as Chancellor of the Exchequer. In 1921, following Bonar *Law's resignation, he was elected as leader of the Conservative Party in the House of Commons. He gave up the Treasury and became Lord Privy Seal and Leader of the House. He resisted backbench pressure to bring the coalition to an end and when the demands became more strident he summoned a meeting of Conservative MPs. The meeting took place at the Carlton Club in October 1922.

Chamberlain put the case for maintaining the coalition, but his speech had little effect and the MPs, influenced by the words of *Baldwin and Bonar Law, voted to end the coalition. Chamberlain promptly resigned as leader and declined to serve in the new administration under Bonar Law. Baldwin brought him into government in 1924, appointing him Foreign Secretary, a post to which he appeared naturally suited. He threw himself into the job with vigour and negotiated the Locarno Pact, for which he is principally remembered, in 1925. It comprised a non-aggression pact between France, Germany, and Belgium, guaranteed by Britain and Italy. Though taken ill in 1928, he served in office until the end of the parliament. He served briefly as First Lord of the Admiralty in the National Government in 1931 before retiring. He remained in the House of Commons until his death in 1937.

A highly sensitive and emotionally insecure individual, affected by the absence of a mother (she died within days of his birth), he was a man of great principle, who—despite his political setbacks—appeared to bear little ill-will. He was denied the highest office, not least because he was not a good judge of others. He joined the list of those politicians comprising the best prime ministers we never had.

Charest, Jean J. (b. Sherbrooke, Quebec, 24 June 1958)

Canadian; politician

After graduation Charest practised law, specializing in Legal Aid and Criminal Law. Elected to the Canadian House of Commons in 1984 as a Progressive Conservative, he was successively Assistant Deputy Speaker of House of Commons 1984; Minister of State (Youth) 1986–90; Minister of State (Fitness and Amateur Sport) 1988–90; Deputy Government Leader in the House of Commons 1989–90; Minister of the Environment 1991–3; Deputy Prime Minister; Minister of Industry, Science, and Technology, and of Consumer and Corporate Affairs.

The October 1993 general election produced an unmitigated disaster for the Conservatives. All twenty-five members of Kim *Campbell's Cabinet, except for Charest, lost their seats. Only two Conservatives (one in New Brunswick and Charest in Quebec) were elected. Never before in Canadian history had a governing party suffered such an electoral defeat. In such an unpropitious moment on 13 December 1993, Jean Charest succeeded Campbell as leader charged with the formidable task of rebuilding the Conservatives as a national party.

Charles, Mary Eugenia (b. Dominica, 15 May 1919)

Dominican; Prime Minister 1980–95

Educated in Canada and Britain, Eugenia Charles practised law in Dominica between 1949 and 1970 and in 1968 founded the conservative Dominica Freedom Party (DFP). She was elected to parliament in 1975 and five years later led the DFP to electoral victory over the discredited Dominica Labour Party (DLP), hence making her the first woman Prime Minister in the Caribbean.

Surviving a series of plots and even an attempted coup, Charles became established as one of the Caribbean's most robust defenders of conservative values. She was the foremost regional supporter of the 1983 US invasion of Grenada and was at President Reagan's side when he announced the invasion to the world. She was also an enthusiastic proponent of privatization and structural adjustment, frequently confronting Dominica's trade unions. Dubbed the Caribbean's 'Iron Lady', she was instrumental, together with Jamaica's Edward Seaga, in setting up the Caribbean Democratic Union of right-wing parties in 1986.

Eugenia Charles won a further overwhelming election victory in 1985 and was narrowly re-elected in 1990. Having announced that she would retire at the time of the 1995 elections, she handed over leadership of the DFP to Bruce Alleyne in 1993. With the DFP losing the elections, Charles duly retired, claiming that her fifteen years in office had amounted to a 'thankless task'. She became a Dame of the British Empire in 1991.

Chavez, Cesar (b. Yuma, Arizona, 31 Mar. 1927; d. 23 Apr. 1993)
US; labour organizer and Hispanic political activist

Chavez became a migrant labourer at age 10 and was entirely self-educated. An avid reader, he was influenced especially by Mahatma *Gandhi's autobiography and, although a radical activist, adopted a philosophy of non-violence which fitted well with his deep Christian commitment. In 1952 he joined a community service organization but left in 1962 when it rejected his ideas for mobilizing itinerant farmers. That year (1962) Chavez founded the United Farm Workers' Union, effectively the first organization of migrant farm workers in American labour history. He also began his campaign to heighten public awareness of the conditions in which many migrant farm workers lived in the USA. In 1965 he launched a grape boycott against the wine producers of the Central Valley of California who refused to give union contracts for their workers. He later embarked on public hunger strikes, tactics which earned him huge sympathy and forced concessions from the employers. In 1970 the UFW signed its first union contract with the growers.

Chavez thereby achieved national prominence becoming the most well-known Chicano leader of his time. Union contracts delivered better wages and working conditions for farmers and their families. His union grew to a peak of about 70,000 members and engaged in a range of other successful boycott campaigns. Largely as a result of Chavez's pressure, California in 1975 enacted an Agricultural Labor Relations Act which recognized the right of farm workers to organize collectively.

Thereafter Chavez's influence declined. His union lost members and economic and political conditions allowed growers to return to employing non-union workers and to cut wages. Nevertheless Chavez remained a heroic figure and an important political strategist among Hispanics and migrant workers, especially in the south-western United States.

Chebrikov, Viktor Mikhailovich (b. 27 Apr. 1923)
Russian; chairman of the KGB 1982–8

Of Russian working-class origin, Chebrikov served in the Red Army during the Second World War, joining the CPSU in 1944. Like *Brezhnev, his career began in the Dnepropetrovsk region, where he trained as an engineer at the famous Metallurgical Institute, and from 1951 to 1967 he held a succession of party posts. From 1961 to 1971 he was a candidate member of the Ukrainian Party's Central Committee. He joined the KGB in 1967 when *Andropov became its chairman—possibly appointed by Brezhnev as a check on Andropov—and from 1968 to 1982 was a deputy chairman of the KGB. In December 1982 he became chairman of the KGB. Andropov, now General Secretary, regarded him as a reliable supporter. From 1983 to 1985 he was candidate member of the Politburo. In March 1985 he lent vital support to Gorbachev in his succession struggle by providing compromising information about his rivals, Romanov and *Grishin. A month later he became a full member of the Politburo. Chebrikov turned against Gorbachev when he realized how radical his reform programme was. In 1988 Gorbachev replaced him as head of the KGB and in September 1989 removed him from the Politburo.

Cheney, Richard Bruce (Dick) (b. Lincoln, Nebraska, 30 Jan. 1941)
US; member of the US House of Representatives 1979–89, Secretary for Defense 1989–92

The son of a government soil conservation agent, Cheney was educated at Yale (where he dropped out), the University of Wyoming, and the University of Wisconsin. His political career began in state government in Wisconsin, where between 1965 and 1969 he served on the staff of Governor Warren Knowles. Cheney served as a special assistant to Donald Rumsfeld at the Office of Equal Opportunity (1969–70) and then became a staff assistant in the Nixon White House (1970–1) and assistant director at the Cost of Living Council (1971–3).

Cheney left government briefly for banking in 1973; but he had established a close rapport with Rumsfeld and when Rumsfeld headed the Ford transition team, Cheney returned as his deputy. From 1975 to 1976 Cheney was Chief of Staff at the White House, a post he discharged in a low key manner.

Elected to the House as Wyoming's Congressman-at-large in 1978, he served in Congress until 1989. He acquired leadership positions early becoming chairman of the Republican Policy Committee in 1981, chairman of the Republican Conference in June 1987 and Republican whip in December of the same year. He combined interest in intelligence and security with concern for Western issues, serving on the Intelligence Committee and Interior.

Cheney's conservative politics combined with integrity and policy competence to make him a very popular party man. Following the failure of George *Bush's nomination of John *Tower as Secretary of Defense in March 1989, Cheney was immediately nominated for the position. Despite some concerns about a series of heart attacks in 1978, Cheney was confirmed. A strong supporter of strengthened defence prior to the collapse of Communist regimes in Eastern Europe, Cheney had the task of reducing the defence budget in the post-Cold War context, a task which inevitably brought him to conflict with the services. His tenure as Secretary of Defense was also marked by the Gulf War. Although Cheney was more sceptical than Bush about the chances of reform succeeding in Russia, his pragmatic approach to these developments corresponded with the President's outlook, enabling him to exercise influence as one of Bush's inner circle of advisers on defence and foreign policy issues throughout the administration.

After Bush's defeat in 1992, Cheney went to the American Enterprise Institute.

Chen Yun (b. Jiangsu, c.1905; d. Beijing, 22 Apr. 1995)

Chinese; economist, economic theorist

Chen Yun is perhaps one of the least well known, but one of the most influential of China's first generation of Communist leaders. He was one of the few post-1949 leaders who had a 'soviet' style background in the urban trade union movement whilst working as a typesetter for Commercial Press in Shanghai in the 1920s. Having joined the party in 1924, Chen was involved in the early part of the Long March, but then left for Moscow for ideological and organizational training. On his return to China, Chen led the Party Organization Department but increasingly turned his attentions towards economic affairs during the 1940s.

Chen's economic theories became a source of considerable conflict with *Mao Zedong. Chen rejected Mao's view that rapid economic development could and should be assured by exploiting the revolutionary enthusiasm of the masses. Instead, he argued for a slower but more sustainable pace of economic development, and that some market mechanisms should be used instead of political mobilization to encourage agricultural production. These markets should be localized and strictly limited in scope and importance, and it was essential that the party retained overall control over the economy through strong centralized planning, co-ordination, and control. This relationship between dominant plan and subordinate local markets became known as the 'bird-cage' theory, where the bird (the market) was allowed freedom to move, but was always constrained by the bars of the cage (the plan).

From 1949 to 1954, Chen Yun led the committee in charge of financial and economic work which successfully managed the first stage of industrialization and economic recovery. This strategy was based heavily on the Soviet model of industrialization, and once the Communist leadership decided to move away from the original Soviet blueprint to a distinctive Chinese road to socialism, then the conflicting approaches of Mao and Chen began to manifest themselves in political conflict.

The first major conflict occurred in 1956–7, when Mao forced through a strategy of rapid collectivization of agriculture and a quick dash for growth, even though the party central committee had earlier endorsed Chen's strategy for the second Five-Year Plan. Mao's radical experiment was ultimately to lead to the disastrous Great Leap Forward, and the deaths of 40 million Chinese from starvation between 1958 and 1961. Chen's criticisms of the Great Leap policies were accepted by other key leaders such as Liu Shaoqi, *Deng Xiaoping, and *Zhou Enlai, and by 1962 Chen's ideas were again the main impetus for economic policy. Chen gradually brought about a significant economic recovery, only for his policies to be overthrown by Mao for a second time in 1966 with the onset of the Cultural Revolution.

Whilst disappearing politically, Chen did not personally bear the brunt of Mao's hostilities during the Cultural Revolution. The Cultural Revolution decade had once again severely damaged the Chinese economy, and in 1978, the party turned to Chen Yun once again. In addition to his economic work, Chen also returned to his leadership origins in party organization, becoming the first head of the Central Discipline Inspection Commission, and for a short time, Chen Yun and Deng Xiaoping developed a strategic partnership in the central élites. However, by 1984 Chen Yun had become one of Deng's fiercest critics as economic reforms moved away from Chen's original bird-cage thesis, and more and more market forces were introduced at the expense of central planning. Like Deng, Chen continued to exert considerable political influence behind the scenes despite gradually relinquishing his formal political offices. He consistently berated the reformers for forgetting the importance of grain production, producing unbalanced regional growth, and for continually failing to balance the national budget. Furthermore, he abhorred the declining socialist morality of party members, complaining as early as 1985 that many cadres seemed to have forgotten that they were meant to be Communists.

Chen remained a constant critic throughout the early 1990s. Stock market shares in Hong Kong dropped dramatically on a number of occasions when rumours of Deng's death prompted fears that Chen Yun would assume power. By the time of his death in 1995, Chen's political influence was much declined, partly due to the deaths of other leading conservatives, and partly because of the success of those very economic policies which Chen so opposed. The Chinese economy had probably already gone too far down the line towards the market to be brought back 'under control' by 1995, but Chen's death nevertheless marked a significant watershed in the transition from socialism in China.

Chernenko, Konstantin Ustinovich (b. Krasnoyarsk province, 11 (24) Sept. 1911; d. Moscow, 10 Mar. 1985)

Russian; General Secretary of the CPSU and President of the USSR 1984–5

Of Siberian peasant stock, Chernenko received little formal education. He made his career first in the Krasnoyarsk region as a propagandist and later, 1948–56, in Moldavia, where he established a close personal relationship with Leonid *Brezhnev when the latter was First Secretary there. From then on he owed his rise to Brezhnev's support, moving to Moscow in the Agitprop Department and later the General Department of the CPSU when Brezhnev became leader in 1964. He became a full member of the Central Committee in 1971. Brought into the Politbureau in 1977, he was very much Brezhnev's right-hand man and natural successor. Defeated by *Andropov in the leadership contest after Brezhnev's death in 1982, with the illness and death of Andropov in February 1984 Chernenko was chosen by his colleagues as a safe pair of hands while the younger *Gorbachev was being 'groomed'. Being 72 when he gained office, he achieved little and soon fell ill and died. A man of limited ability, he was merely a stopgap leader of conservative orientation before the reformist Gorbachev, who was in control while Chernenko was ill, took over.

Chernomyrdin, Viktor Stepanovich (b. Orenburg region, 9 Apr. 1938)
Russian; president of Council of Ministers of Russian Federation 1992–6

An engineer by education, Chernomyrdin made his career in the oil and gas industry in the Orenburg region, where he managed an enterprise 1973–8. A member of the CPSU from 1961, in the 1980s he served as deputy minister, later Minister of the Gas Industry (1985–9) and head of Tyumen gas extraction. He was a member of the CPSU Central Committee 1986–90 and a deputy to the USSR Supreme Soviet 1987–9. Under *Yeltsin in 1992 he was deputy Prime Minister for the fuel and energy complex, and in December 1992 he was appointed Prime Minister as a moderate compromise candidate acceptable to the parliament, following the rejection of the reformer *Gaidar. Backed by the powerful oil-gas and military-industrial lobbies and ensuring their support for the government, he pursued a steady if cautious pace of economic reform and proved able to survive crises such as the parliamentary confrontation of 1993 and the Chechnya invasion of 1995 (from which he emerged with some credit). But he is a rather grey figure with little mass base, as was shown by the poor results of his party 'Our home is Russia' in the December 1995 elections, which persuaded him not to stand against Yeltsin in the 1996 presidential elections.

Chervenkov, Vulko (b. 24 Aug. 1900; d. Sofia, 24 Oct. 1980)
Bulgarian; leader 1949–54

The son of a soldier, Chervenkov joined the Bulgarian Communist Party in 1919. He survived the party's disastrous attempted uprising of 1923 and spent the years 1925–46 in the Soviet Union. He worked for the Comintern as secretary and bodyguard to Georgi *Dimitrov, whose sister he married. Dimitrov saved him from liquidation during the Great Purges at the end of the 1930s. Chervenkov nonetheless worked for Soviet intelligence, reporting on Dimitrov.

Chervenkov returned to Bulgaria in 1946. He rose to supreme power after 1949, following the death of Dimitrov and the fall of his rival, Traichko Kostov. In that year he became Central Committee Secretary responsible for propaganda and Deputy Prime Minister. The next year he became First Secretary of the Bulgarian Communist Party and Prime Minister, as well as chairman of the Communist-dominated mass organization, the Fatherland Front. Chervenkov imposed an uncompromisingly Stalinist programme of nationalization, industrialization, and collectivization on Bulgaria, underpinned by the terror of his secret police.

After *Stalin's death the Soviet Union was ruled by a collective leadership and Bulgaria had to follow suit. In 1954 Chervenkov gave up leadership of the party with *Zhivkov replacing him as First Secretary. His fatal mistake was to look to the wrong patron in the Soviet Union for support, namely *Malenkov. On 17 April 1956, two months after *Khrushchev's denunciation of Stalin at the CPSU's Twentieth Party Congress, Chervenkov was demoted from Prime Minister to Deputy Prime Minister. He was further weakened by the rehabilitation of some of his former rivals. In November 1961 Zhivkov denounced Chervenkov's Stalinist past at the party conference of the BCP and he was removed from office. It was believed that his fall was connected with the Soviet Union's rapprochement with Yugoslavia, for which Tito had made Chervenkov's removal a precondition. Chervenkov was rehabilitated and awarded a state pension in 1969.

Chiang Ching-kuo (Jiang Jingguo) (b. Zhejiang, 18 Mar. 1910; d. 13 Jan. 1988)
Chinese; President of the Republic of China on Taiwan 1978–88

Chiang Ching-kuo was the only son of *Chiang Kai-shek by his first wife. Educated initially in China, he went to study science and engineering in Moscow in 1925, where he stayed until 1937, becoming fluent in Russian and marrying a Russian woman. Chiang's time in the Soviet Union is said to have instilled in him a deep dislike for Communism. Following his return to China, Chiang played an increasingly important role in his father's administration, including negotiating with the Soviet forces that occupied Manchuria in 1945.

After the defeat of the Nationalists (KMT) in 1949 and their retreat to Taiwan, Chiang Ching-kuo rose to be head of the various security apparatuses and political commissars in the army, where he carried out a thorough purge of KMT members (1950–2) while Chiang Kai-shek consolidated his rule over the island. He continued to establish a large power base, and rose to the position of Deputy Premier in 1969, and Premier in 1972, where he played an increasingly important role in the day-to-day running of Taiwan, especially after the death of his father in 1975. He was elected President in 1978 and re-elected in 1984 after which he began a dramatic process of democratization of Taiwan's political system, ending a forty-year period of brutal martial law in July 1987. Chiang also oversaw a significant relaxation of links across the Taiwan Straits, allowing Taiwanese to visit mainland China to see relatives for the first time and also oversaw the introduction of a large number of native Taiwanese into the political life of the island. He was succeeded as President by *Lee Teng-hui.

Chiang Kai-shek (Jiang Jieshi) (b. Ningbo, Zhejiang Province, 31 Oct. 1887; d. 5 Apr. 1975)

Chinese; Head of Kuomintang government in Nanjing 1927–37, Head of government in exile in Chongqing 1937–45, President of the Republic of China on Taiwan 1949–75

Despite many years as leader of the Kuomintang, Chiang was primarily a military man. Initially sent to Japan to study military affairs, Chiang joined, *Sun Yatsen's Revolutionary Alliance. Returning to China in 1910, Chiang spent a number of years on the fringes of the Shanghai underworld, before reviving his military/political career in Canton in the early 1920s. Chiang gained Sun's patronage, and was sent for military training in the Soviet Union in 1923, returning to lead the important Whampoa military academy.

Chiang's military and underworld connections played a crucial role in winning the leadership of the Kuomintang on Sun Yatsen's death in 1925. But this victory was achieved at the expense of considerable damage to party unity which dogged his leadership until 1949. Nevertheless, with the support of a number of allied warlords, the Northern Expedition successfully reunited China under Kuomintang rule, and Chiang established a new national government in first Wuhan and then Nanjing in 1927.

Once in power, Chiang abandoned the United Front with the Communists which had been forced on both parties by their mutual backers, the Soviet Union. The purge of Communist elements was followed in December by Chiang's marriage to Soong Meiling, the younger sister of Sun Yatsen's widow, Soong Qingling. As another sister was married to the wealthy and influential financier H. H. Kung, the marriage combined Chiang's formal leadership with the informal connections that remained an important element of political leadership in nationalist China.

In reality, Chiang's dominance was more apparent than real. The dependence on allied warlords that gained him power also made effective national government virtually impossible. With the exception of the area surrounding Nanjing, the Kuomindang had to exercise power through warlords and landlords. These leaders blocked attempts to alter the existing feudal basis of economics and society, and frequently developed their own economic and fiscal policies at odds with policy in Nanjing. Chiang also faced military threats throughout the Nanjing decade from disillusioned warlords, from the rival Kuomintang leader Wang Jingwei, and from Japanese expansion in the north.

Under these circumstances, it would have been very difficult to implement an effective modernization programme. However, Chiang's leadership credentials were somewhat questionable. His 'New Life' ideology was a strange mixture of Confucianism, Christianity, and Fascism which failed to address the problems facing the Chinese population in the countryside. Furthermore, economic policy was dominated by corruption, and was apparently designed to benefit the nationalist élites rather than to bring about national regeneration. While Chiang may have felt that he could not withstand the might of the Japanese, his suppression of anti-Japanese student movements lost considerable popular support at a time when the Communists were emphasizing their own nationalist credentials. Chiang seemed obsessed with eliminating the Communists, and only changed his policy when the northern warlord, Zhang Xueliang, kidnapped him in Xian in December 1936, forcing Chiang to accept a new united front of nationalists, Communists, and warlords against the Japanese.

The Nanjing rule of the Kuomintang collapsed in 1937 under an extreme and brutal Japanese onslaught. Chiang moved the capital to Chongqing, where the nationalists sat out the war in relative comfort. There was considerable scepticism amongst American advisers in Chongqing regarding Chiang's beliefs and loyalties, and a wide held belief that Chiang diverted American aid for his own use, and stored up weapons for use in the coming civil war with the Communists. Nevertheless, the Americans and indeed the Soviets remained committed to restoring Chiang to power throughout the war years.

Despite an American attempt to broker a peace settlement at the end of the Pacific War, the civil war between the Kuomintang and Communists soon resumed. Chiang's forces were vastly superior in manpower and supplies and soon made inroads into Communist held areas in northern China. However, the bitter internal rivalry, corruption, appalling treatment of conscript soldiers, and trench warfare strategies of the Kuomintang armies compared badly with the unity, cohesion, and guerrilla tactics of the Communists. The Communists had also built a sound popular support base through social and economic reforms through much of northern China, and, crucially, were the first troops into the cities of north-east China after the Japanese surrender. Initial victories gave way to a series of military defeats and defections from 1947 through to 1949, forcing the Kuomintang ever southwards and eventually into a quasi-internal exile on the island of Taiwan.

Despite the proclamation of the new People's Republic in Beijing, Chiang refused to relinquish his claim to be the legitimate ruler of all China. To this end, he was supported by the Americans, who installed the Taiwan regime in the Chinese seat at the United Nations (prompting a Soviet walk-out which enabled the Americans to pass a resolution sending UN troops to Korea) which they held until 1972. Despite some initial reluctance, the Americans also placed Taiwan within their strategic defence parameter, and provided a total of US$5.6 billion of economic and military aid (compared to $6.89 billion for the whole of Africa) between 1945 and 1979.

Chiang's rule on Taiwan also benefited from the centralization of power over a relatively small population and territory. Local opposition to Taiwanese rule had been brutally oppressed in 1947, removing the power of local landlords and leaders that had so obstructed his rule on the mainland. With the collapse of the Kuomintang armies on the mainland, Chiang was also freed from much of the internal factionalism of the past. Chiang, consolidating power under martial rule and by linking closely with the American and later the emerging Japanese economies, facilitated the economic modernization that had eluded the Kuomintang in Nanjing. Nevertheless, he will be first and foremost remembered as 'the man who lost China'.

Chifley, Joseph Benedict **(Ben)** (b. Bathurst, NSW, 22 Sept. 1885; d. Canberra, 13 June 1951)

Australian; Prime Minister 1945–9, leader of the Australian Labour Party 1945–51

The son of a blacksmith, Chifley left school at 16. He joined the New South Wales

Railways and advanced to the position of locomotive driver, while educating himself in the evenings. He sat in federal parliament from 1928 to 1931, and was briefly Minister for Defence in the short-lived Labor government of James Scullin.

Chifley regained his federal seat in 1940, a year later became Treasurer, and, soon afterwards, Minister for Post-war Reconstruction in John *Curtin's Labor government. During the war Chifley established his credentials as a successor to Curtin, managing Australia's war economy and planning for the post-war era. He became Prime Minister after Curtin's death in July 1945 and governed until Labor's defeat in December 1949. Chifley strove for 'the light on the hill': the establishment of a just social order in Australia. He and his economic planners drew on Keynesian theories, extending the functions of government, enshrining the goal of full employment, and broadening the base of social welfare. With his Minister for External Affairs, Dr H. V. Evatt, Chifley also nurtured a new role for Australia in international affairs, which was still as committed a member of the evolving Commonwealth, but also sympathetic to nationalist movements in Asia and prepared to take independent stands in the United Nations.

The economic development of Australia was a high priority for the Chifley governments. Two of the biggest projects were the large-scale immigration scheme and the Snowy Mountains Hydro-electric Scheme, both of which would help shape post-war Australia beyond Chifley's term. His attempts to nationalize essential industries and institutions enjoyed mixed success, and his (unsuccessful) attempt to nationalize banks was seized on by conservative opponents as evidence of a Communist core within the Labor party.

After electoral defeat in 1949, Chifley remained Labor leader until his death from a heart attack in Canberra in June 1951. A pipe-smoking and fatherly figure who privately drew strength from his wife and Catholicism, he was much mourned, and quickly became a Labor legend.

Chin Peng (real name Won Man-wa, otherwise Ong Boon Hua) (b. Sitiawan, Perak, c.1921)

Malaysian; secretary-general of Malayan Communist Party/Communist Party of Malaysia 1947–

Chin Peng, whose father ran a small bicycle business, attended Chinese and English schools in Perak and joined the Malayan Communist Party in 1940. During the Japanese occupation (1941–5) he became secretary of the Perak State Committee of the MCP, a member of the Central Military Committee, and leader of the 5th regiment of the Malayan People's Anti-Japanese Army. He liaised with British officers of Special Operations Executive Far East (Force 136) and was later awarded the OBE.

After the British reoccupied Malaya in September 1945 he joined the MCP's Central Executive Committee. Although he was the lieutenant of its secretary-general, Loi Tak, he became frustrated with the party's slow progress and eventually unmasked Loi Tak as a double-agent. After Loi Tak fled in March 1947, Chin Peng became secretary-general and in March 1948 abandoned the 'united front' strategy for armed struggle. In June the British declared a State of Emergency which lasted until July 1960.

The Communists adopted Maoist techniques, deploying 4,000–5,000 guerrilla fighters, supported by a network of food and intelligence gatherers, in order to undermine colonialism and establish liberated areas. Although it held down many more British, Commonwealth, and Malayan forces, the Chinese-dominated Communist movement was unable to achieve lasting control over rural Malaya: it lacked significant outside assistance, failed to attract Malay support, and was starved of supplies by the counter-insurgency of Generals Briggs and Templer. Losing the shooting war, in December 1955 Chin Peng attempted to gain political recognition at the Baling talks with the recently elected Chief Minister of Malaya, Tunku *Abdul Rahman, but returned to the jungle empty-handed.

By the time Malaya achieved independence (31 August 1957), Chin Peng's force of some 450–500 had retreated to the Thai border from which sporadic incursions were launched. After 1968 the MCP (renamed the Communist Party of Malaysia) split three ways: the CPM, the CPM (Revolutionary Faction), and CPM (Marxist-Leninist). Insurgency revived in urban areas in the 1970s and in the mid-1980s, but by then Chin Peng was living in southern China. In December 1989, as the Cold War ended, Chin Peng returned to southern Thailand to conclude an agreement with the government of Malaysia, whereby the Communists disbanded their military units in return for assistance in peaceful resettlement. At the same time Chin Peng vowed that he was still a Marxist-Leninist.

Chirac, Jacques (b. Paris, 23 Nov. 1932)

French; Prime Minister 1974–6, President of the Republic 1995–

Although Chirac's family origins lay in the rural Corrèze department, which he represented in the National Assembly from 1967 to 1995, his father worked for a private bank in Paris. Chirac was educated at the Institut d'Études Politiques, the École Nationale d'Administration, and Harvard Business School and did his military service in Algeria. His youthful left-wing sympathies were soon abandoned for a job in the higher administration and a career in Gaullist politics. Married to the niece of one of *de Gaulle's oldest associates, he found his patron in Prime Minister *Pompidou, who took him into his private office and backed his successful parliamentary campaign in 1967. Chirac worked closely with Pompidou in the May 1968 crisis and was his patron's eyes and ears in the 1968–9 *Couve de Murville government. He held a series of government posts in the Pompidou presidency and was appointed to the politically influential Interior Ministry just before his mentor died. As Interior Minister he intervened successfully, if controversially, in the 1974 presidential contest against the official Gaullist candidate *Chaban Delmas and in favour of *Giscard d'Estaing. Rewarded with the premiership he soon found himself at odds with the policy—and the style—of Giscard and in 1976 became the only Fifth Republic Prime Minister to slam the door on a President.

He now turned his formidable energies to the task of creating a neo-Gaullist party capable of regaining (for himself) the presidency. In December 1976 he founded, and became president of, the Rassemblement pour la Republique and immediately declared war on Giscard. He defeated the President's candidate to become mayor of Paris, and turned the townhall into the centre of a vast patronage machine for his ambitions. Once the 1978 parliamentary elections were won, he intensified his attacks on what he claimed to be Giscard's betrayal of the Gaullist doctrines of national independence and dynamic government. His frenzied activism led some even in his own camp to dismiss him as an unstable demagogue and the nationalist campaign he ran for the 1979 European elections was a disaster. Yet by 1981, when he came third in the first round of the presidential elections, he had succeeded in his aims of reviving electoral Gaullism and disestablishing Giscard, who lost on the second round to *Mitterrand.

Between 1981 and 1995, Chirac battled to assure his mastery of the French right against the familiar opposition of Giscard's supporters and the new challenge posed after 1983 by *Le Pen and the Front National. Never unduly bothered by programmatic consistency, he adopted the free-market liberalism of *Reagan and moderated Gaullist suspicion of European integration. In the 1986 parliamentary elections he headed a successful Conservative coalition and was appointed Prime Minister of the first cohabitation government. It was another unhappy period in office. Despite some successes with the privatization programme, his government was weakened by internal differences and he himself faced the dangerous opposition of Mitterrand. With the help of the RPR machine, he was able, in the first round of the 1988 presidential contest, to see off the challenge of the centrist *Barre; but he polled only 46 per cent of the vote on the decisive second round. Defeat hit Chirac hard. He was increasingly regarded as a good mayor of Paris but a presidential no-hoper. Even the hitherto reliable RPR showed signs of a restlessness which flared into open factionalism when he declared his support for the Maastricht Treaty. The right's overwhelming victory in the 1993 parliamentary elections resulted in the appointment of his close ally *Balladur as Prime Minister. Wafted aloft by opinion polls, and backed by senior Gaullists, Balladur decided that he would make a better president than his former patron. By the time Chirac announced his third presidential bid he looked almost a forlorn figure.

His unexpected success was due to the strengths of the RPR machine, and to his ability to remind the electorate of the traditional Gaullist themes of social solidarity and of the ability of political will to overcome conventional wisdom. He nudged ahead of Balladur on the first round and comfortably defeated the Socialist *Jospin on the second. Chirac's critics argued that he won on a false prospectus which attempted to reconcile the irreconcilable goals of full employment and the Maastricht criteria for monetary union. His early months as President were marked by criticism abroad of French nuclear tests and protests at home of his government's attempts to reduce welfare costs. He had won the presidency after a long and difficult journey. He took a risk in dissolving the Assembly and calling early elections in 1997. He saw his parliamentary majority wiped out and he had to work with his old opponent Jospin, who became Prime Minister.

Chrétien, Joseph Jacques Jean (b. Shawinigan, Quebec, 11 Jan. 1934)

Canadian; Prime Minister 1993– and leader of the Liberal Party of Canada 1990–

Chrétien trained as a lawyer and was called to the bar of Quebec in 1958. He was first elected to the Canadian House of Commons as a Liberal at the general election of 1963 and re-elected continuously until 1984.

He was appointed Parliamentary Secretary to Prime Minister Lester *Pearson in July 1965 and to the Minister of Finance in January 1966. He was successively Minister of National Revenue January 1968, Minister of Indian Affairs and Northern Development July 1968, President of the Treasury Board 1974, Minister of Justice, Attorney-General of Canada, and Minister of State for Social Development 1980, as well as Minister responsible for constitutional negotiations. He was Minister of Energy, Mines, and Resources 1982, Deputy Prime Minister and Secretary of State for External Affairs 1984.

Whilst out of the House from 1986 to 1990, he reputedly made a lot of money as a businessman and legal and political counsellor, particularly with the law firm Lang, Michener, Lawrence, & Shaw.

Elected MP for Beauséjour, New Brunswick, in 1990, Chrétien became leader of the Liberal Party of Canada and of the Official Opposition Party 1990–3.

When Chrétien was sworn in as Canada's twentieth Prime Minister on 4 November 1993 he possessed more ministerial experience than anyone previously first appointed to the office. Aged 59 years he had spent eighteen years in cabinets under Pearson, Piérre *Trudeau, and John *Turner. A staunch federalist he had played a prominent role in defeating the sovereignty option in Quebec's 1980 referendum on constitutional change and in repatriating the Canadian constitution. A pragmatist in his approach and a shrewd tactician he soon made clear that two dominant motifs of his ministry would be restructuring the Canadian confederation and promotion of Canada's international trade.

Church, Frank (b. Boise, Idaho, 25 July 1924; d. 7 Apr. 1984)
US; US Senator 1957–81

The son of a merchant, Church attended local schools in Boise. During the Second World War he enlisted as a private in the US army and was commissioned in 1944, seeing active service in the Far East. Graduating from Stanford University in 1947, he undertook a year's study at Harvard before returning to Stanford Law School, from which he graduated LLB in 1950. That same year he was called to the bar and began practising law in Boise. His career in national politics began six years later when, in 1956, he was elected Democratic Senator for Idaho.

Church was an active member of the prestigious Senate Foreign Relations Committee. He was an outspoken critic of *Johnson's Vietnam policy and chaired a select committee (1975–6) which investigated the operations of the CIA and FBI and made numerous recommendations for curbing their activities. Between 1979 and 1981 he served as chairman of the Foreign Relations Committee.

In 1976 Church made an unsuccessful bid to gain nomination as his party's presidential candidate. Despite early primary successes in the western states, he withdrew in the face of the growing momentum behind *Carter's candidacy.

Church was a man of liberal views. He was an eloquent speaker who was popular with fellow senators. In 1980 he returned to the law after failing to retain his Senate seat.

Churchill, Winston Leonard Spencer (b. Blenheim, Oxfordshire, 30 Nov. 1874; d. 24 Jan. 1965)
British; Home Secretary 1910–11, Chancellor of the Exchequer 1924–9, Prime Minister 1940–5, 1951–5; KG 1953

The son of Lord Randolph Churchill, Winston had an undistinguished education at Harrow. After Sandhurst, he joined the 4th Hussars and had extensive overseas experience. In 1899, he fought Oldham as the Conservative candidate, lost, and then went as a journalist to cover the Boer War in South Africa. He returned a national hero, having fought to protect British troops and having escaped from a Boer prisoner-of-war camp. He was elected as Conservative MP for Oldham in 1900. In 1904 he crossed the floor of the House to join the Liberals, doing so on the issue of free trade. He was quickly rewarded, being made a junior minister in the new Liberal government in 1906. Two years later he joined the Cabinet as President of the Board of Trade. In 1910 he was appointed Home Secretary. He was 35. He implemented some prison reforms but alienated radicals by his willingness to sanction the deployment of troops in Wales during a coal strike. A year later he was made First Lord of the Admiralty. He helped modernize the navy but his reputation declined in the early years of the First World War and he was blamed for the failure of the attack on the Dardanelles. In 1915 the Conservatives insisted on his removal from the Admiralty as one of the conditions for joining a coalition. He was made Chancellor of the Duchy of Lancaster, but resigned within a matter of months in order to see active service. After a year at the front, he returned to Westminster. Excluded initially (on Bonar *Law's insistence) from the *Lloyd George government, he was brought in as Minister of Munitions in 1917. When the war ended, he was appointed Minister of War and used the post as a platform for attacking the new Bolshevik regime in Russia. He was then promoted to be Colonial Secretary. His ministerial career as a Liberal MP ended in 1922. He lost his seat. He wrote a two-volume work entitled *The World Crisis*, and—believing that the Conservatives were the party best placed to combat the threat of socialism—returned to the Conservative fold. In 1924 he was elected as the 'constitutionalist' candidate in Epping and within days Stanley *Baldwin, wanting to separate him from creating an alliance with Lloyd George, had appointed him as Chancellor of the Exchequer. It was a remarkable political rehabilitation. As Chancellor, Churchill presided over a return to the gold standard and the General Strike. He served as Chancellor throughout the parliament (1924–9). However, he proved a difficult and demanding colleague and Baldwin decided not to appoint him again to government. When the Conservatives returned to office in 1931, dominating the National Government, he was consigned to the back benches.

The 1930s were Churchill's wilderness years. He antagonized his own side by his vehement opposition to the Government of India Bill, giving the country dominion status, and by his demands for more rapid rearmament. He was also unpopular because of his support for the King, Edward VIII, during the abdication crisis. By 1937, wrote one biographer (Virginia Crowe), 'his influence had fallen to zero'.

The failure of the Munich agreement and the declaration of war vindicated the stance taken by Churchill. Neville *Chamberlain brought him into his wartime government as First Lord of the Admiralty. Chamberlain's resignation in 1940 created a vacancy that Churchill was to fill. Though Labour leaders and most Conservative MPs would have supported Lord *Halifax as Prime Minister, Halifax demurred in favour of Churchill. Churchill was appointed Prime Minister and threw himself into the office with vigour. He eventually overcame criticisms and political sniping by critics on the Conservative benches. His carefully crafted speeches proved inspirational. He took the House of Commons seriously. His strategic leadership was sometimes flawed but often brilliant. He dominated a powerful War Cabinet. He overcame some difficult moments in the House of Commons, especially in 1942, when a united house was essential to the war effort. When victory was in sight, he wanted to continue the coalition government until a general election could be held. Labour leaders disagreed, and so a caretaker Conservative government was formed in 1945. It held office until the general election later that year, when the Labour Party was returned to power with its first working majority. The result shocked Churchill. His wife told him it might be a blessing in disguise. He replied that, in that case, it was very well disguised.

In Opposition, Churchill proved a lacklustre leader, making some important pronouncements on foreign affairs, but leaving it to others to prepare the party for a new era. He was fortunate in having lieutenants who were up to the task. His own position was variously criticized and some MPs wanted him to retire gracefully. He rebuffed any suggestions that he should step down and he led his party into the 1950 and 1951 general elections. The latter resulted in a Conservative victory and Churchill forming his first peacetime administration. He had little feel for what should be done. He confided to Oliver Lyttleton that 'In the worst of the war I could always see how to do it. Today's problems's are elusive and intangible.' He was keen to ensure social harmony and was willing to appease the unions to avoid industrial unrest. He had able ministers but he had doubts about *Eden's ability to succeed him. Despite being laid low by strokes, he carried on. He eventually gave up office in April 1955, at the age of 80. He stayed in the House of Commons until the 1964 general election, though making no significant contribution to parliamentary debates. He died on 24 January 1965 and was given a state funeral.

Churchill was difficult, impulsive, prone to depressive moods, extreme at times in pursuing his views, and sometimes plain wrong. He was also brave, determined, at times clear-sighted, and the outstanding Englishman of the century. He provided inspirational leadership as Prime Minister in time of war, towering above his colleagues. He died as the great commoner, having declined a dukedom.

Clarke, Charles Joseph **(Joe)** (b. High River, Alberta, 5 Jun. 1939)

Canadian; Prime Minister 1979–80

Born, raised, and educated in Alberta, with degrees in History and Political Science, Clarke studied law at Dalhousie University, where he first became politically active. He was a journalist with local newspapers in Alberta 1964–6, and then from 1966 to

1967 a member of the political science department at his Alma Mater, the University of Alberta.

His first and intimate exposure to federal politics came as executive assistant to Robert L. Stanfield, when the latter was leader of the Opposition in Ottawa 1967–70. Clarke soon acquired a reputation as an expert back-room operator. He entered the Canadian parliament in 1972 as Progressive Conservative MP for Rocky Mountain (later Yellowhead) Riding (constituency), which he was to represent uninterruptedly to 1993. In 1976 he became leader of the federal Progressive Conservative Party.

He defeated Pierre *Trudeau at the May 1979 general election and was sworn in as Canada's sixteenth and youngest Prime Minister on 4 June, one day before his 40th birthday. Winning only two seats in Quebec, the PCs made major gains in Ontario and Western Canada, electing 136 members, six short of a majority. Clarke's proved to be a rather desultory, accident-prone ministry which did not gain any ground politically. On 18 February 1980 the Canadian electorate returned the Liberals to power, headed again by Trudeau, with a majority government. The Liberals won 146 seats compared to 103 for the PCs. The Clark government had lasted 272 days, the shortest of any elected administration in Canada's history.

Subsequently, though deposed as leader of his party, he maintained a high reputation for competence and integrity. Indeed, as Canada's Foreign Minister 1984–91 and then as Minister for Constitutional Affairs and concurrently President of the Queen's Privy Council for Canada 1991–3, Clarke enjoyed a high reputation nationally and internationally at a time when those of his Prime Minister and most Cabinet colleagues were slumping. Previously unilingual, he worked hard to improve his French and to become bilingual. He was an active chairman of the Commonwealth's Committee of Foreign Ministers on South Africa.

Since leaving parliament in 1993 Clarke has been the UN's Special Representative in Cyprus.

Clarke, Kenneth (b. Nottingham, 2 July 1940)

British; Secretary of State for Health 1988–90, Education 1990–2, Home Secretary 1992–3, Chancellor of the Exchequer 1993–7

Clarke's father started his working life as a colliery electrician and then acquired a jeweller's shop. Clarke was educated at Nottingham High School and Cambridge, where he read law. He was active in the university Conservative Association and president of the Union (1963). A number of his fellow students later became Cabinet colleagues. He entered parliament as MP for Rushcliffe in 1970.

In his early years he was a member of the left-inclined Tory Reform Group and a defender of One-Nation Conservative principles, views which were not to the liking of the new party leader Margaret *Thatcher. His career marked time under her. After a succession of junior posts he finally entered the Cabinet in 1985 as Paymaster-General and Minister of State for Employment. In 1987 he became Chancellor of the Duchy of Lancaster and Minister for Trade and Industry. In both posts he shared responsibilities with Lord Young of Graffham, who was in the Lords and the senior minister. Clarke was the department's spokesman in the House of Commons.

Clarke's opportunity to run his own department came in 1988 when he was appointed Secretary of State for Health. He was the force behind the controversial health service reforms; he rejected schemes for the privatization of health but introduced market-orientated solutions. In many of his posts Clarke found himself battling with what he regarded as the last vested interests—the professions. It was so with the doctors and was to be the case in subsequent posts with teachers and the police. In November 1990 he was moved, against his wishes, to run Education and Science. In this post he simplified the testing and national curriculum arrangements inherited from Kenneth *Baker.

Kenneth Clarke was a key figure in the fall of Mrs Thatcher. When she failed to win sufficient votes in the first ballot in the leadership election in November 1990 he was the first Cabinet minister to tell her she should stand down. In the past he had been regarded as a possible leader, but he was not a serious contender in the leadership contest at the time and on the second ballot worked for Douglas *Hurd.

The new Prime Minister John *Major moved Clarke to the Home Office. His stock rose in this post and John Major came to rely heavily on him. Following the collapse of Britain's membership of the European Exchange Rate Mechanism (ERM) in September 1992 Clarke was widely expected to become Chancellor of the Exchequer. He did so in April 1993 and had to raise taxes and cut public spending, with the aim of balancing the national finance. He was a successful Chancellor, presiding over a steady economic recovery, and his refusals in 1995 and 1996 to raise interest rates against the advice of the Bank of England appeared vindicated; inflation remained at its lowest for many years. He resisted pressures to make election-winning tax cuts in his budgets, believing that it was more important for the party to restore its reputation for economic competence. The Conservative Party was divided over further integration of Britain in Europe, and particularly over the British membership of single currency, with opponents growing in strength in 1995 and 1996. Clarke's support for both was a liability and he was bitterly attacked by Eurosceptics in his party and the press. From being regarded as the obvious successor to John Major in 1992 and 1993, his stock in the party steadily fell. In turn, he thought that Major was offering too many concessions to the anti-European Conservatives. He finished second to William *Hague in the contest for the party leadership in 1997 and retired to the back henches.

Clarke was a tough-minded but liberal Conservative. He supported many of the Thatcherite economic policies, believed in the firm control of public spending, and was determined to improve the quality of public services, while ensuring that the public sector became more competitive and delivered value for money. But he also remained firm to his One-Nation Conservative views and believed in a constructive role for the state in providing welfare.

Clemenceau, Georges (b. Mouilleron-en-Pareds, 28 Sept. 1841; d. 24 Nov. 1929)

French; Prime Minister 1906–9, 1917–20

Clemenceau was born in 1841 in the western department of the Vendée. The son of a gentleman doctor imprisoned for his opposition to the 1851 *coup d'état* of Louis Bonaparte, he inherited from his father a lifelong detestation of Bonapartism and a commitment to democratic Republicanism; one of his most celebrated sayings was that the French Revolution was a bloc which must be accepted in its totality, including the Terror. He studied medicine in Paris, where he engaged in anti-regime politics, and then emigrated to the United States, from which he returned, complete with American wife, shortly before the fall of the Second Empire. His entry into politics coincided with the twin disasters of the Franco-Prussian War and the Commune. As mayor of Montmartre he experienced at first hand the brutalities which accompanied the latter and as a member of the National Assembly he was one of the deputies who refused to accept the loss of Alsace Lorraine to Bismarck's Second Reich. By the late 1870s he was the leader of the advanced Radicals, and acquired national prominence as a champion of social reform and hammer of the Catholic church—and also as the wrecker of the Opportunist governments of the early Third Republic. He never held office, however, and in the 1880s his political judgement was called into question by his flirtation with the demagogic General Boulanger and by his friendship with the crooked financier, Cornelius Herz, who was heavily implicated in the Panama Scandal. Having lost his seat in the 1893 parliamentary elections, he looked for a time to be politically finished. His campaigning zeal blazed up again when the Dreyfus Affair appeared to reopen the war between the supporters and opponents of

Republicanism. He flung himself into the pro-Dreyfus cause, opened the columns of his newspaper to Zola's famous article 'J'Accuse', and in 1903 was elected Senator for the Var.

Though Clemenceau still described himself as a Radical, he took no part in the foundation of the Radical Socialist Party in 1901 and was notably reserved about the government led between 1902–5 by the Radical's favourite Émile Combes. In the run-up to the 1906 elections, he was invited to become Minister of the Interior in a coalition government designed to show the unity of the Republican family against its clerical and nationalist opponents. He dealt effectively with the consequences of a mining disaster in Northern France and with the potentially dangerous First of May campaign organized by France's revolutionary syndicalist movement. Four months later, at the age of 64, he became Prime Minister. His appointment was widely regarded as opening the door to the realization of the social programme of Radicalism and his ministerial programme contained proposals for an income tax, old-age pension, and for the nationalization of the Western Railway. Yet although a number of reforms were passed by a government which was one of the longest lasting in the history of the Third Republic, his first ministry is chiefly remembered for the heavy handed way it dealt with labour unrest and for his implacable opposition to public sector trade unionism. Clemenceau insisted that in a democracy force in the defence of the rule of law was justifiable and that public sector officials owed a duty of obedience to the state. His opponents in the Radical Party condemned his disregard for the pieties of Republican unity and the Socialists claimed that his enthusiasm for police repression demonstrated the inability of bourgeois Radicalism to cope with the reality of class conflict. Thus his government witnessed a breakdown in the Socialist-Radical unity which the Dreyfus Affair had created. It gave Clemenceau a reputation as the enemy of organized labour which he would never subsequently lose.

After the defeat of his ministry in July 1909, Clemenceau appeared to settle for the role of Angry, but Isolated, Old Man. If, in the run-up to the First World War he supported the Three Years Law extending military service, he also attempted, unsuccessfully, to prevent the election in 1913 of *Poincaré as President of the Republic. When the First World War began, he used his presidency of the Senate Army commission, and his newspaper, to launch ferocious attacks on what he regarded as the incompetent management of the conflict by governments and generals alike. Excesses of tone once again contributed to his reputation for irresponsibility. But in 1917, as war weariness set in at—and behind—the front, he began to be seen as the man who might galvanize national energies. By late 1917, there was open talk of a compromise peace and some evidence that prominent politicians were starting to put out feelers to the enemy. Faced with this crisis, Poincaré turned to the man who had been savaging him in the newspaper ever since 1913, and appointed him Prime Minister. Clemenceau's ministerial declaration was simple—'I make war'—and he dominated his government. He made frequent visits to the troops at the front, established effective relations with the military, and managed to persuade the English to accept Marshal Foch as Allied Supreme Commander. The real war he waged was against proposals for a negotiated peace, and those who made them. He sent a number of German agents to the firing squad, imprisoned a number of prominent politicians on charges of defeatism, and cowed his most prominent rival *Briand into silence.

Clemenceau's vigour and determination unquestionably restored France's will to fight. When Germany sued for peace in November 1918, he was greeted with acclamation by the public and was declared by parliament to have deserved well of the country. He remained Prime Minister throughout 1919 and dominated the French delegation to the Versailles Peace Conference. As the last surviving representative of the deputies who had refused to accept the 1871 peace settlement, his aims were straightforward—the return of Alsace Lorraine and the destruction of Germany's potential ever again to threaten France. He insisted on the war guilt and reparation clauses of the Versailles Treaty, but was unable to persuade the Allies of the need to separate the Rhineland from Germany. He defended the treaty against the opposition of hard-line nationalists, who argued that it gave too much away, and of the Socialists who regarded it as too harsh. His national popularity remained high and he lent his authority to the anti-Bolshevik Bloc National which swept to power in the November 1919 elections. Thus his victory in the 1920 presidential election looked assured. But at this moment his past reputation destroyed his political future. His uncompromising anti-clericalism alarmed the Catholic right; his equally uncompromising anti-Socialism alienated the radical left; and his bruising attacks on political rivals made him vulnerable to their resentment. On the preliminary vote for the presidency, he was outvoted by the president of the Chamber of Deputies, Deschenel. He immediately withdrew from the contest and resigned as Prime Minister. Having spent the last years of his life travelling, writing and defending the Versailles Treaty, he died, at the age of 88 in 1929, and was buried in the Vendée.

For most of his fifty-year career, Clemenceau was a deeply controversial figure. Self-opinionated and aggressive, he could be almost wantonly destructive and he certainly helped create the culture of government instability which became a characteristic of Third Republic politics. Yet he was consistent in his anti-clericalism, his advocacy of good relations with Great Britain, his commitment to the Republican ideal, and, above all, his blazing patriotism. The leadership qualities he demonstrated in 1917–19 brought France victory and the photograph of the old, moustachioed man talking at the front to ordinary soldiers (he took to his grave the bunch of wild flowers which one such group gave him) is one of the potent images of the First World War. He remains France's most celebrated civilian politician of the twentieth century.

Clifford, Clark McAdams (b. Fort Scott, Kansas, 25 Dec. 1906)

US; Special Counsel to the President 1946–50, Secretary for Defense 1968–9

A St Louis lawyer, Clifford became assistant to James Vardaman, naval aide at the White House and part of a coterie of Missourians around President Harry *Truman. Clifford succeeded Vardaman and then served as Special Counsel to the President 1946–50.

The relationship with Truman was a close and personal one (he regularly played poker with the President) and it enabled him to influence policy and strategy in a variety of fields. He developed a close interest in security matters, helping to write the 1947 National Security Act and serving from 1961 to 1968 on the Foreign Intelligence Advisory Board. His role in Truman's surprise election victory over Thomas *Dewey in 1948 further strengthened his influence with Truman on civil rights and anti-Communism. Although Clifford left the White House in 1949 his pragmatic approach to politics and his legal skills were called upon by subsequent presidents, especially John *Kennedy, Lyndon *Johnson, and Jimmy *Carter.

Although Clifford served as the director of Kennedy's transition team, he took no formal office in the administration. Under Johnson, however, he took over from Robert McNamara as Secretary of Defense, and helped to begin the de-escalation of war in Vietnam. Under Carter as well as being a special envoy to Greece, Turkey, and India, Clifford helped defend Bert Lance, Carter's budget director who was forced to resign as a result of his involvement in a banking scandal. Ironically, Clifford himself became more closely involved in banking issues in the 1980s and became the target of congressional investigation as a result of his association with the BCCI and First American Bankshares, an episode which undermined Clifford's reputation.

In 1991 Clifford's insights into successive presidencies were published in his memoirs *Counsel to the President* which he wrote with Richard Holbrooke.

Clinton, William **(Bill)** Jefferson (b. Hope, Arkansas, 19 Aug. 1946)

US; Governor of Arkansas 1979–81, 1983–92, President 1993–

At birth Clinton was given the name of William Jefferson Blythe. His father was killed in a road accident four months before he was born. His mother—who worked to put herself through medical school—remarried three times, the young child taking the surname (at the age of 15) of her second husband, a car dealer. Educated at Hot Springs High School, Arkansas, he proved to be a bright student. He was notable for the number of organizations he joined (he served as president of several), his competitiveness, and his apparent desire to please people. He was one of two Arkansans picked for 'Boys Nation', a summer vacation programme for outstanding high school pupils. It was while on this programme that he met President John F. *Kennedy, a meeting captured on film. This meeting is believed to have inspired his interest in politics. He went on to study at Georgetown University in Washington, DC, working part-time in the office of Arkansas Senator William *Fulbright, a leading Democratic opponent of the Vietnam War. With Fulbright's help, he achieved a Rhodes Scholarship and spent two years at University College, Oxford. On his return to the USA, he went to Yale law school, where he met and married a fellow student, Hilary Rodham.

He returned to his home state to teach law at the University of Arkansas and to seek election to public office. A Democrat, he cut his political teeth in 1974 by contesting a safe Republican congressional district. In 1976 he was elected state attorney-general. Two years later—at the age of 32—he contested and won the governorship, the youngest person ever to hold the office. He was defeated at the end of his first term, having attempted to tackle a range of issues without clearly identifying where he was going. He fought back to regain the governorship in 1983 and then served four consecutive terms. During this period, goals were targeted and he spent time visiting all parts of the state. He channelled resources to education. Though liberal on social issues such as abortion, he nonetheless introduced welfare policies that appealed to conservatives, for example requiring single mothers to name the father in order to receive welfare support. In 1987 he served as chairman of the National Governors' Association. He also became vice-chairman, and subsequently chairman, of the Democratic Governors' Association. In 1988 he introduced the presidential nominee, Michael *Dukakis, at the Democratic convention but gave a lengthy, rambling speech. (He won applause only when he said 'In closing . . .'.) By 1992 he was the nation's senior governor.

Clinton announced in October 1991 that he was a candidate for the Democratic nomination for President. His campaign was dogged by accusations of infidelity—one woman, Gennifer Flowers, claimed she had a twelve-year affair with him—and by accusations that he avoided military service in Vietnam. He nonetheless polled well in the New Hampshire primary in February 1992, coming second with 25 per cent of the poll, 8 per cent behind Paul Tsongas, the former Senator from Massachusetts. Clinton then pulled ahead in succeeding primaries—sweeping the South in 'Super Tuesday' primaries on 10 March. He went on to victories in the large eastern states, including New York, and his nomination at the Democratic Convention in New York in July became a formality. He chose Senator Al Gore of Tennessee as his running mate.

In the general election Clinton attacked the economic record of his opponent, President George *Bush, and managed to convey that he had policies to address the nation's social problems and that Bush did not. He out-performed Bush in three television debates, though the debates served also to bolster the campaign of the independent candidate, Ross Perot. Clinton emerged the victor, wining 43 per cent of the popular vote, to 37.4 per cent for Bush and 18.9 per cent for Perot. Clinton had patched together the old Democratic coalition of the poor, blue-collar workers and minorities and had polled well in areas of Republican strength, notably the West. He had become President at the age of 46.

The Clinton presidency got off to a poor start. His first two nominees for Attorney-General had to withdraw after it was revealed they hired illegal aliens. The issue of allowing gays to serve in the military—a policy favoured by Clinton but opposed by the chairman of the Joint Chiefs of Staff, Colin Powell—achieved political prominence, ended in a messy compromise, and obscured other policy initiatives. Clinton reorganized his White House staff after only a few months in office. He battled with Congress on health care reform and lost. His handling of foreign policy—as on Bosnia and Somalia—appeared uncertain. The influence of his wife became a political issue. Both he and his wife were implicated in the Whitewater affair, involving the Whitewater Development Co., in which the Clintons had invested and which was funded by a company being investigated for financial improprieties. He had some notable successes, including approval of the North American Free Trade Agreement (NAFTA), but the overall impression was of a presidency in trouble. In the 1994 mid-term elections the Republicans won control of both Houses of Congress for the first time in forty years. Clinton looked like a probable one-term President. However, his standing improved. He proved to be an adept politician, brokering deals to achieve results. His international standing increased as he began to appear more sure-footed in responding to events abroad. A Bosnian peace treaty was agreed in Dayton, Ohio, between the warring parties. The President visited Northern Ireland and tried to act as an honest broker in attempts to move talks forward. The economy continued to improve, with a significant growth in GDP and falling unemployment. The 'misery index' was the lowest since 1969. Deadlock with Congress over the budget in 1995, resulting in a shutdown of government offices, was blamed on Congress rather than the President. In 1996, Clinton ran unopposed for the Democratic nomination. The only cloud on the horizon was the Whitewater affair, especially following the conviction of key participants in the affair. The Republican contest was initially hard fought and bitter, resulting in the selection of Senate Majority Leader, Robert *Dole, a 73-year-old Washington insider with little obvious interest in propounding a vision of the future. Clinton led in the opinion polls throughout the campaign and achieved a healthy but not spectacular victory, winning 49 per cent of the popular vote to 42 per cent for Dole and 9 per cent for Perot. There was little evidence of a coat-tails effect. The Republicans retained control of both Houses of Congress.

Clinton essentially developed two persona. Clinton the President established respect both in Washington and in the country; by the end of the first term, he was looking presidential. He had carved out a New Democratic coalition (much admired by British Labour leader Tony *Blair), maintaining an appeal to minorities while introducing measures on crime and welfare that drew the support of middle-class Americans. Clinton the man remained controversial. Early controversies over whether he smoked marijuana—he admitted that he experimented with the drug but 'didn't inhale'—and dodged the draft died away, but claims of sexual harassment while Governor of Arkansas continued to appear. The death—an apparent suicide—of White House deputy counsel and old Arkansas associate Vince Foster fuelled questions about the White House handling of the affair and speculation as to the reasons for the death. The Whitewater affair continued to cast a shadow. The return of Republican majorities in the House and Senate in 1996 meant that the issue would continue to be the focus of official investigation.

Clinton gained respect for his persistence and his handling of the office, ploughing on despite the various controversies, determined to rise above them rather than be dragged down by them. His re-election in 1996, following a period of notable unpopularity, appeared to confirm his reputation as 'The Comeback Kid'.

Clynes, John Robert (b. Lancashire, 27 Mar. 1869; d. 23 Oct. 1949)

British; Home Secretary 1929–31, leader of Parliamentary Labour Party 1921–2, deputy leader 1922–31

A gravedigger's son, Clynes left school at 11 to become a textile worker and later a trade union official. He was president of the National Union of Gasworkers and General Labourers from 1912 to 1937.

Clynes was a member of both the Independent Labour Party and the Labour Party from their inception and was on the latter's National Executive Committee from 1909 to 1939. He sat in the Commons with only a four-year break from 1906 to 1945. In 1917 he became Minister of Food in David *Lloyd George's wartime coalition government. After the war he was elected deputy leader and then, in 1921, leader of the Parliamentary Labour Party. But he lacked charisma and was replaced as leader by Ramsay *MacDonald in 1922. He then resumed the deputy leadership.

Clynes held office in the inter-war two minority Labour governments: as Lord Privy Seal (1924) and Home Secretary (1929–31). Neither post reflected his true importance; he was actually one of the most influential figures in both administrations.

Codreanu, Corneliu Zelea (b. Huşi, 1899; d. en route from Rimnicu Sarat to Bucharest, 1 Dec. 1938)

Romanian; leader of the Legion of the Archangel Michael 1927–38

Codreanu was born in Moldavia into a peasant family, the son of a German father and a mother of Ukrainian or Polish extraction. He was a member of the anti-Semitic National Christian Defence League. In 1924 he murdered the police chief of Iaşi, which made him a hero, and went unpunished. In 1927 he formed the Legion of the Archangel Michael, an Orthodox, nationalist, anti-Communist, and anti-Semitic organization, through which he intended to bring about the moral regeneration of Romania. It had Fascist style trappings, though Codreanu rejected the ideas of the corporate state, and acquired considerable support among the peasantry and among Romania's numerous unemployed intelligentsia. In 1930 the Legion acquired a youth movement, the Iron Guard (*Garda de Fier*) by which the organization as a whole was generally known. In the 1930s the Iron Guard committed numerous terrorist acts against leftists and Jews. Romanian government officially dissolved the Legion in 1933, but it continued to operate. In 1937 it gained 17 per cent of the vote. In 1938 King Carol II disbanded the Iron Guard and imprisoned Codreanu and its other leaders, to surprisingly little protest.

Colijn, Hendrikus (b. Burgerveen, 22 June 1869; d. Ilmenau, Germany, 18 Sept. 1944)

Dutch; Prime Minister 1933–9

After a six-year military training Colijn joined the Royal Netherlands Indian Army (KNIL) in 1893, covering colonial administration. Upon his return to the Netherlands he was elected a member of the Lower House for the orthodox-Protestant Anti-revolutionary Party. Two years later he was appointed Minister of War, serving in 1912 also as interim Minister for the Navy. During his two years in office he carried through a successful army reorganization.

In order to acquire financial independence (which he considered to be a prerequisite for successful politicians) Colijn temporarily changed national politics in 1914 for an appointment as a managing director of the oil company Bataafsche Petroleum Maatschappij (from 1919 Royal Dutch Shell). He served as a member of the Upper House (1914–20). In 1922 he voluntarily left Shell to devote the rest of his life to national politics, becoming the undisputed leader of the Anti-revolutionary Party and the dominant political figure nationally. After one year in the Lower House he became Minister of Finance (1923–5). In 1925 and again from 1933 to 1939 he led five governments, occupying either the Ministry of Finance or of the Colonies. The backbone of his coalition consisted of his own ARP and two other religious parties, the Protestant CHU and the Catholic RKSP. This coalition was expanded by two Liberal parties from 1933 to 1937. When not a minister Colijn was a member of the Upper House (1926–9) or of the Lower House (1929–33). As Prime Minister during the depression he emphasized the need for a rigid cutting of government expenditures and balanced budgets. For a long time he remained convinced of the need to retain the gold standard (only left in 1936). Colijn was prominent in League of Nations committees. He presided over the Economic Commission of the World Economic Conference in 1933. His fifth Cabinet, formed without Catholic support, was dismissed by a parliamentary vote in 1939, paving the way to a realignment of Dutch politics by the first-time inclusion of Socialist ministers in the ensuing Cabinet.

Colijn was interned by the German occupying authorities in 1941.

Collins, Michael (b. Woodfield, Co. Cork, 16 Oct. 1890; d. 22 Aug. 1922)
Irish; Director of Intelligence of Irish Republican Army 1919–21, Commander-in-Chief of army of provisional government 1922

Collins began his working life in London in 1906 as an employee of the Post Office Savings Bank, and later worked for finance houses. In 1909 he joined the revolutionary Irish Republican Brotherhood. After participating in the Easter Rising he was imprisoned at Frongoch Camp, north Wales, which the Irish Republicans made into an insurrectionary training camp. In 1917 he became a member of the Supreme Council of the IRB and subsequently its secretary. From March 1918 he was Adjutant-General of the newly emerging Irish Republican Army, and writing in its journal *An t'Oglach* ('The Volunteer') he developed his theories of guerrilla and resistance organization. Elected to the first Dáil Éireann in 1918, he became a member of the provisional government, but his key role in the Irish independence struggle was as Director of Intelligence for the IRA. He developed a squad of volunteers aimed at assassinating key members of the G Division of the Dublin Metropolitan Police. Through a corps of informants strategically placed in the police and in government departments (including even Scotland Yard) Collins obtained copies of all significant government reports. Within a short time the anti-insurrectionary capability of the police forces was neutralized, often by ruthless means. Collins had several narrow escapes but was never captured.

In October 1921, following the Truce, *de Valera sent Collins against his wishes as a member of the Irish plenipotentiary team to negotiate the Anglo-Irish Treaty in London. In effect the chief Irish negotiator, Collins defended the treaty as giving 'not the ultimate freedom that all nations desire and develop to, but the freedom to achieve it'.

It was, however, bitterly contested and Collins confessed privately that in signing it he was signing his own death warrant. He became chairman of the new provisional government, resigning later to devote his energies to military leadership in the Civil War. Abandoning IRA activity designed to undermine the new Northern Ireland state, he attempted two pacts (unsuccessful) with Ulster Unionist leader Craig. Collins was killed by republican anti-treaty forces in Co. Cork in August 1922.

Had he lived he would undoubtedly have been as dominant a figure in the new Irish state as he had been in its gestation.

Connally, John Bowden (b. Floresville, Texas, 27 Feb. 1917; d. 15 June 1993)
US; Governor of Texas 1963–9, Secretary of the Treasury 1969–72

Educated at the University of Texas in Austin, Connally made his fortune in the oil industry in Texas. He became involved in the politics of the Democratic Party in Texas and served as an administrative assistant to Senator Lyndon *Johnson in 1949. In 1961 he was appointed Secretary of the Navy by President *Kennedy. In 1962 he was elected Governor of Texas. He won national attention on the day of Kennedy's assassination in Dallas, 22 November 1963, when he was wounded by one of the shots fired at Kennedy. As Governor of Texas Connally benefited from the patronage of his mentor, Lyndon Johnson, who was President of the United States during the same years as Connally was Governor of Texas. Connally was, however, a conservative Democrat and did not support the liberal reforms in the fields of civil rights and anti-poverty which were introduced by the Democratic Party at the national level by the federal government.

In 1971, though still a Democrat, he was appointed Secretary of the Treasury in the Republican administration of President *Nixon. He made a major impact. To deal with the problems of inflation, recession, and growing trade deficits, he introduced prices and wages controls and devalued the dollar. These measures were successful in the short term and produced economic recovery by the time of Nixon's re-election in 1972.

Speculation arose that Nixon would select Connally as his vice-presidential candidate in 1972 in place of Vice-President Spiro *Agnew. Nixon was a strong admirer of Connally and wished to have him as his Vice-President, but Agnew was retained since Connally was unacceptable in some quarters as a nominal Democrat and a somewhat abrasive, arrogant character. Had Nixon selected Connally as his vice-presidential candidate in 1972, he would have succeeded as President following Nixon's resignation over the Watergate affair in July, 1974.

He served in a general role as special assistant to the President in 1973. He was indicted in 1974 in connection with an alleged illegal contribution from the milk producer's lobby but was acquitted. He resumed his business affairs in the oil industry in Texas but continued to be actively involved in Republican party politics. In 1980 he made an unsuccessful bid for the Republican nomination for President. With the fall in oil prices in the 1980s he lost heavily and was declared bankrupt.

Cook, Robin (b. 29 Feb. 1945)

British; Foreign Secretary 1997–

Cook is one of the formidable group of Scots in the 1997 Labour government. He was educated at schools in Aberdeen and Edinburgh and graduated from Edinburgh University in English. He then worked for a time as an adult education tutor and organizer and served as a local councillor in the early 1970s. Elected MP for Edinburgh Central in 1974, he held the seat until 1983 and then sat for the Livingston seat in Scotland. Cook has always been on the left of the party and has seen the mood of the party move sharply left in the early 1980s and then to the right in the 1990s. But he has always been his own man and his interest in constitutional change and electoral reform makes him distinctive. His appeal across the party is seen in the high ranking he regularly achieved in the annual election to the Shadow Cabinet by Labour MPs and he was a shadow Cabinet member between 1983 and 1997. In the long years of Opposition he held various portfolios including Health and Social Security, Europe, Trade and Industry and Foreign Affairs. Although not personally close to the Labour Prime Minister Tony *Blair he emerged as one of a handful of influential figures in the new Labour government. According to some observers, Cook is, on his day, the best debater in the House of Commons, combining serious argument with devastating wit. He is also a good parliamentary organizer and handled leadership campaigns for Neil *Kinnock in 1988 and John *Smith in 1992. As Foreign Secretary in the new Labour government he promised to seek greater co-operation with European Union member states and follow a more ethical foreign policy.

Coolidge, John **Calvin** (b. Plymouth, Vermont, 4 July 1872; d. 5 Jan. 1933)

US; Governor of Massachusetts 1919–20, Vice-President 1921–3, President 1923–9

Educated at Black River Academy, a private school, and then at Amherst (after initially failing the entrance examination because of illness), Coolidge trained as a lawyer. His father held public office and the son soon took after the father in getting involved in local politics. He became an active worker for the Republican Party in

Massachusetts and was elected to various local offices before serving two terms in the state House of Representatives. He also served as mayor of Northampton before being elected in 1911 to the state Senate. In 1914 he became presiding officer of the Senate and in 1915 was elected as the state's Lieutenant-Governor. Three years later he was elected Governor.

As Governor, he promoted a number of important measures, including limiting the working week for women and children, but made his name nationally by using the state guard to restore order during a police strike. Though he had hesitated before using the guard, his action made him popular. He was easily re-elected Governor. Copies of his speeches were circulated to delegates to the Republican Convention in 1920 by one of his political supporters and led to him being selected as Warren *Harding's running mate, in preference to the candidate favoured by party bosses. The election of 1920 saw a Republican landslide and Coolidge went to Washington, DC, as Vice-President. He did not shine in the office. Though sitting in on Cabinet meetings, he contributed little. He was overshadowed by Cabinet members who were either extremely able (such as Secretary of State Charles Evans *Hughes) or extremely corrupt (such as Interior Secretary Albert Fall). However, on 2 August 1923 President Harding died. Coolidge was on holiday at his family home in Vermont and in the early hours of the morning of 3 August was sworn in as President by his father, a notary public, in the family's farmhouse. At the age of 51 he had become the thirtieth President of the United States.

Coolidge's main contribution to the office lay in what he did not do. Having once observed that 'the chief business of the American people is business', he kept government out of the affairs of business as much as possible. At a time of economic success, it was a popular stance and he was easily elected as President in his own right in 1924. In the election, he won 15.7 million votes against 8.3 million for the Democrat, John W. *Davis, and 4.8 million for the Progressive Robert M. *La Follette. He continued his policy of keeping government out of business. He relaxed business regulations and lowered some taxes. He left it to Cabinet members to get on with their work without troubling the President about it. In so far as there was much activity it was in the field of foreign affairs, where Coolidge and some of his able appointees helped bolster diplomatic ties with other countries.

Perhaps the most significant contribution that Coolidge made to the office was to restore its integrity. He stood in sharp contrast to Harding. Whereas Harding was a drinker and gambler, who brought some dubious characters into government, Coolidge was the epitome of New England reticence and rectitude. He was religious and dutiful, there to serve others.

During his full term, economic prosperity continued. Various economic experts warned him that the prosperity was based on unsure foundations. Though worried by what he was told, he made no significant moves to address the problem, relying instead on public pronouncements to bolster confidence. When the crash came, Coolidge had left the White House.

Though eligible to seek re-election in 1928, Coolidge announced in 1927 that he did not choose to run for election. Though some sources suggest that he hoped that he would be invited to run, the party took him at his word and nominated his Commerce Secretary, Herbert *Hoover. Two reasons have been suggested for Coolidge's decision not to run. One was the warnings about the state of the economy. Believing that government action may be necessary, he was not prepared to be the President that took that action. The other was personal. Coolidge had seen various relatives die while he was very young, including his mother and sister, and in 1924 his own younger son, Calvin, died of blood poisoning at the age of 16. His son's death affected him profoundly and part of him seemed to die at the same time. It was not long after his son's death that he apparently decided not to run for public office again. He retired to Vermont and lived for another four years, dying of a coronary thrombosis on 5 January 1933. He was 60 years of age.

Coolidge was a shy, quiet individual, who never enjoyed the best of health and was once described by Alice Roosevelt Longworth (daughter of President Teddy *Roosevelt) as looking 'as if he had been weaned on a pickle'. He slept long hours and was renowned for his taciturnity. He pre-dated Franklin *Roosevelt in the use of the radio for political broadcasts but was less at ease in facing human beings. When he did speak, he had a nasal twang that was sometimes likened to a quack. He nonetheless achieved great political success. He was at the right place at the right time: a Vice-President when the President died, a non-interventionist President at a time of economic boom. He pursued a religious world view that ensured that his stance was consistent. Well-meaning and, according to some analyses, shrewd in judgement, 'Silent Cal' was a popular and probably underrated President.

Cosgrave, Liam (b. Dublin, 13 Apr. 1920)

Irish; Minister for External Affairs 1954–7, Taoiseach (premier) 1973–7

The son of William T. *Cosgrave, the first Premier of the Irish Free State, Cosgrave was first elected to the Dáil in 1943. He served as a Fine Gael member of the two inter-party governments of 1948–51 and 1954–7; in the latter he was Minister for External Affairs. In 1955, on the Irish Republic's formal admission to the United Nations, Cosgrave headed the first Irish delegation to the General Assembly. In 1964 he chaired a policy committee of the Fine Gael party which produced the progressive-leaning *Just Society* paper. He became Taoiseach on 14 March 1973, following the electoral defeat of the Fianna Fáil party, when, for the third time in the post-war era, his Fine Gael party formed a coalition with Irish Labour.

Cosgrave's leadership style bore a marked resemblance to that of his father in the 1920s, being unflamboyant and consensual, and giving priority to law and order and internal political stability. He supported conservative social policies, voting against his government's own bill to liberalize the law on contraception. An effective party politician, like most at the time in Ireland his aim was more to hold office and patronage than to use it for particular policy purposes.

In December 1973 he led his government's delegation to the Sunningdale conference on the constitutional future of Northern Ireland, which led to the short-lived power-sharing administration. His government may have helped to cause its downfall by pressing for an all-Ireland dimension, the proposed Council of Ireland, which was too much for Unionists to stomach. In late 1976 Cosgrave was a central figure in a constitutional crisis involving the powers of the President and culminating in the resignation of President O'Dalaigh. Following a massive electoral defeat, Cosgrave resigned on 20 June 1977. He was succeeded as party leader by Garret *FitzGerald, and retired from the Dáil in 1981.

Cosgrave, William T. (b. Dublin, 6 June 1880; d. 16 Nov. 1965)

Irish; President of the Executive Council of the Irisch Free State (premier) 1922–32

Cosgrave fought in the General Post Office during the Easter Rising of 1916, for which he was initially sentenced to death, but was released in December 1916. Acting as treasurer of the emergent Sinn Fein movement, he was elected to Westminster as Sinn Fein MP for Kilkenny in 1917 and was returned to the revolutionary 1st Dail in the British general election of 1918. He served in the Sinn Fein provisional government as Minister for Local Government. A supporter of the Anglo-Irish Treaty of December 1921 (though not a signatory), Cosgrave emerged unexpectedly as chairman of the provisional government on 25 August 1922, on the death of Michael *Collins and the earlier death, on 12 August, of Arthur Griffith. On 6 December 1922 Cosgrave became the first President of the Executive Council (i.e. premier) of the Irish Free State. He was also its Minister for Finance. In 1923 he founded the pro-treaty party Cumann na nGaedheal. He was premier until electoral defeat by the Fianna Fáil in February 1932. Following a further defeat in 1933 he stood down in favour of the quasi-Fascist General O'Duffy but re-emerged as president of a reconstituted party, now Fine Gael, in 1935, which he led until his retirement in 1944. His son Liam served as premier (now termed Taoiseach) from 1973 to 1977.

Almost unknown on coming into office, Cosgrave was a quiet and self-effacing man rather overshadowed by the larger figures of his era. His style of leadership was more that of a chairman than a chief, and many of the measures brought forward were institutional and unspectacular. His ministry had to survive several crises, including an army mutiny, the failure of the Irish Boundary Commission, and the assassination of the ministry's strong figure, Kevin O'Higgins, in July 1927. His party and government were politically diverse, held together by little other than adherence to the 1921 treaty, an increasingly wasting position, especially with its failure to accommodate the views of Irish Labour. But it did preside successfully over Ireland's transition from state of bitter civil war to a stable, if highly conservative, democracy. This was by no means guaranteed, but Cosgrave helped to secure it in February 1932 by ensuring an orderly transfer of power to his erstwhile civil war opponent and latterly parliamentary adversary, Éamon *de Valera.

Coty, René (b. Le Havre, 20 Mar. 1882; d. 22 Nov. 1962)
French; President of the Republic 1954–8

René Coty came from Normandy and was the son of the director of a private school. He studied law and philosophy at Caen University, fought in the First World War, and became a well-respected lawyer in Le Havre. He enjoyed a moderately successful career in local government before being elected to the Chamber of Deputies in 1923 and to the Senate in 1935. Conservative without being reactionary, his political views were those of the centre-right and he attracted little attention before or during the war, although his refusal to co-operate with Vichy removed the stigma of his vote for *Pétain in July 1940. Elected to the Constituent Assembly in 1945 and the National Assembly the following year, he returned to the Senate in 1948. He was Minister of Reconstruction in three governments in 1947–8, two of which were led by Robert *Schuman, the architect of France's move towards European integration.

Coty's election as President of the Republic in December 1953 was a surprise and came after twelve exhausting ballots in which more obvious candidates had been eliminated. Chosen for his lack of political identity, he was little known to the general public, many of whom were scandalized by the image of political disunity revealed by the length of time it took to elect him. His manifest charm and integrity meant that he (and his wife, who died in 1955) became extremely popular in the country as a counterweight to the bitterness of party conflict. Yet his conception of the presidency stayed firmly within the constitutional limits set by the Fourth Republic. When the conflict in Algeria exploded into a full-scale crisis of regime authority in May 1958, his order to the French army commanders in Algiers to respect the civil power went unheeded. Thus his one decisive intervention was to tell the National Assembly that if they did not accept the return to power of *de Gaulle he would resign. He handed over the presidency to de Gaulle in January 1959 and died three years later.

Coty's presidency was the last of a line which had begun with the election of Jules Grevy in 1879 and was defined by its lack of any independent political authority. He himself had always been in favour of constitutional measures to strengthen the power of government and it was this that led him to support de Gaulle in 1958. But his opposition, shortly before his death in 1962, to the direct election of the presidency showed how attached he was to the tradition of parliamentary republicanism which the Fifth Republic rejected.

Couve de Murville, Maurice Jacques (b. Rheims, 24 Jan. 1907)

French; Minister of Foreign Affairs 1958–68, Prime Minister 1968–9

A member of the Protestant 'Couve' family ('de Murville' had been added in 1925), Couve studied in Paris, where he read literature and law and graduated from the École Libre des Sciences Politiques. He married the painter Jacqueline Schweisguth (also Protestant). In 1932 he became an *inspecteur des finances* and moved rapidly up the civil service hierarchy (he participated in the negotiations for the Wiesbaden armistice). Couve then worked for the Vichy regime but in 1943 joined General Giraud as Financial Commissioner for Free France. When Giraud was sidelined Couve rallied to *de Gaulle and stayed with exemplary loyalty until the General's death. De Gaulle moved him to diplomatic responsibilities and he seemed destined for an ambassadorial career in the 1950s. However, when de Gaulle returned to power in 1958 he was given one of the key posts in the new Republic: Foreign Minister. From then on Couve was at the centre of the active foreign policy conducted by the General: decolonization, rifts in the Atlantic Alliance, and a struggle with the European Community. The achievements of Couve at the Foreign Ministry were, it can be assumed, largely in the implementation of a policy determined by the General and often leaving Couve in the dark. (Outsiders sometimes had the impression that Couve knew no more than they did about the General's intentions.) 'Ice cold Couve' cut a strange figure in the tempestuous foreign policy set by de Gaulle but he was a faithful follower and put his diplomatic skills at the service of the General's designs—whatever those were. In July 1968 *Pompidou was replaced by Couve as Prime Minister. This was a post for which he was ill suited and, with the General's popularity sliding, he was not a memorable Prime Minister. Couve's talents were technocratic, he had no inclination to intrigue or for political campaigning (he was famously incapable of glad handing electioneering). De Gaulle's defeat at the referendum of April 1969 and Pompidou's election as President caused him to leave office and he became a 'Baron' of the Gaullist movement—a distant, cold but respected figure.

Cranston, Alan (b. Palo Alto, California, 19 June 1914)

US; US Senator 1969–93

Cranston's early career was in journalism. He was the foreign correspondent for *International News* (1936–8); but he moved to become a lobbyist for the Common Council for American Unity before going into the army. From 1947 until 1967 Cranston was involved in the real estate business.

His long political career in California politics started when he became California controller in 1958, a post he occupied until 1966. In 1968 he was elected to the Senate, where he served until 1993.

Cranston was a long-term supporter of world government and disarmament, positions which may have found some echo in California but which put him on the far left of the Democratic Party. His mixture of idealism and pragmatism enabled him to exercise some influence in the Senate. He was a member of the Banking Committee and chairman of the Veterans Committee. He was also Democratic majority whip. In 1984 Cranston made an unsuccessful attempt to secure the Democratic presidential nomination.

After retirement from the Senate Cranston served as chairman of the US Kyrgiz Business Council 1993–4.

Craxi, Benedetto (Bettino) (b. Milan, 24 Feb. 1934)

Italian; leader of the Italian Socialist Party (PSI) 1976–93, Prime Minister 1983–7

Son of a local government official, Craxi moved straight into local politics and journalism after leaving secondary school. From the outset, he demonstrated a capacity for hard bargaining and a belief in the importance of effective management. As a member of the faction supporting the old party leader Pietro Nenni, he was regarded as a centrist within the Socialist Party. After early success in local government, in 1968 he was elected to the Chamber of Deputies in the Milan constituency, and in 1969 became deputy party secretary. In this post he showed little interest in the national party organization, but concentrated on building his position within the Milan organization of the PSI and with establishing his reputation within the Socialist International.

In 1976, after the poor Socialist results in the elections of that year, he became party secretary, in which position he was seen as a compromise candidate between the right and left of the party, subordinate to both. However, he rapidly reformed the party's local organization, imposing on the local associations the principle of self-financing, and putting his own supporters into the key positions of regional organizers. By the time of the party congress of 1981 his leadership of the party was unchallenged. He successfully distanced the PSI from its traditional ideological subservience to the much larger Italian Communist Party, led at this time by Enrico *Berlinguer. Craxi used the party's limited resources to promote the party's pivotal role in government coalitions.

In 1983, following relatively successful elections in which the PSI won 14 per cent of the vote, he became the party's first ever Prime Minister. His government stayed in office until June 1986, the longest continuous period of any post-war government, and he was reappointed for a second term until January 1987. While Prime Minister, Craxi negotiated major reforms of the wage-indexation system and introduced a substantial new regime for the Prime Minister's office. His government was also responsible for radical reforms of the tax and pensions systems.

After the 1987 elections, Craxi had to cede the prime ministership, but he continued to exercise a major influence over Italian coalition politics. From March 1992 on, he and many elected members of his party were major targets of the investigating magistrates' drive against corruption. In March 1993 he was eventually compelled to resign the party secretaryship. He fled to Tunisia where in deteriorating health he resisted attempts at extradition on corruption charges. Faced by increasing popular resentment, he continued to insist that the charges against him and his colleagues were a Communist-led drive to belittle his methods and to exaggerate the extent of corruption.

Bettino Craxi exercised a profound influence on Italian politics from the late 1970s on. Unfettered by traditional socialist ideology, he was willing to consider radical change in a variety of policy areas and to introduce new methods of party management. He exploited his reputation as a combative political manager, and flaunted a lifestyle which he argued reflected the high-spending aspirations of many Italians. His achievements in office as Prime Minister are obscured by the dramatic character of his decline.

Cresson, Edith (b. Boulogne-sur-Seine, 27 Jan. 1934)

French; Prime Minister 1991–2

The daughter of a civil servant, Cresson was active in Socialist politics, educated in Boulogne-Billancourt and then at the business school. She did not get involved in the usual left-wing student groups and joined *Mitterrand's followers in 1965 to help in the presidential campaign. She was promoted to the leadership and joined the Socialist Party in 1971. In 1975 she was promoted to the Socialist secretariat and ran a 'fighting' but unsuccessful campaign for the constituency of Châtellerault. In 1979 she was elected to the European Parliament. When Mitterrand won the elections of 1981 she was made Minister of Agriculture where she ran up against the conservatism of the farmers (sometimes violently—she reacted with courage). She was replaced by Michel *Rocard, who made peace with the farmers and she moved to the Ministry of

Trade and a year later took on industrial restructuring in the phase of Socialist 'realism' which replaced the 'dash for growth'. In 1988 she was made Minister for Europe but began to criticize the Rocard government for its right-wing drift. In 1991 she was made the first woman Prime Minister of France but she was not a success. Despite a left-wing rhetoric she raised social security contributions, increased VAT (despite having declared opposition to indirect tax), and failed to find any solution (other than cosmetic) to youth unemployment and made unguarded remarks about the Japanese (she complained about the translation), about minorities, and illegal immigrants. Her tenure was ended by Mitterrand when the opinion polls plummeted in 1992.

Cripps, Richard **Stafford** (b. London, 24 Apr. 1889; d. 21 Apr. 1952)
British; Chancellor of the Exchequer 1947–50; Kt. 1930

The son of the first Lord Parmoor, Cripps was educated at Winchester and University College, London. Trained as a chemist, he worked for the Ministry of Munitions during the First World War. After the war he won a brilliant reputation at the bar.

Cripps joined the Labour Party in 1929 and in 1930 was appointed Solicitor-General in the second Labour government. He entered the House of Commons at a by-election in January 1931 as MP for East Bristol (and represented it until his retirement from parliament in 1950). Labour's massive defeat in the 1931 general election made Cripps a prominent frontbench spokesman in the subsequent parliament. But his extra-parliamentary activities increasingly diverged from the party line. In 1932 he helped to found the left-wing Socialist League. With the PLP still weak after the 1935 general election, Cripps promoted the formation first of a United Front of the Working Class and then, in 1938, an even wider Popular Front to oppose the government. In 1937 he helped to found the left-wing weekly *Tribune*. These activities won support in the constituency parties and his election to the party's National Executive Committee. But they were condemned by the NEC and in 1939 he was expelled from the party.

When Winston *Churchill formed his wartime coalition government in 1940, Cripps was appointed British ambassador in Moscow. He held the post until January 1942. The ambassadorship brought Cripps public acclaim and in February 1942 he was appointed leader of the House of Commons and a member of the War Cabinet. He was also sent on a mission to secure support for the war from the Indian leaders. The mission's failure and Cripps's own deficiencies in the Commons weakened his position and he was transferred to the non-Cabinet Ministry of Aircraft Production, in which he performed very successfully until the wartime coalition government ended.

Cripps rejoined the Labour Party shortly before the ensuing general election and was made president of the Board of Trade in the new Labour government, holding the post for two years—during which he played a prominent part in the negotiations leading to independence for India and Pakistan. In 1947, the outcome of a curious episode in which dissatisfaction with Clement *Attlee prompted Cripps to urge him to give up the premiership, was that Cripps was given the new position of Minister for Economic Affairs. But after only six weeks, he was promoted to the Chancellorship of the Exchequer, made vacant by Hugh *Dalton's resignation. He remained there until ill-health compelled his resignation in October 1950.

As Chancellor Cripps achieved considerable success in restoring international confidence in the Britsh economy. But the necessarily deflationary policies, post-war scarcities, and his well-known personal abstemiousness created for his chancellorship a lasting reputation for austerity.

Crosland, Charles **Anthony** Raven (b. Sussex, 29 Aug. 1918; d. 19 Feb. 1977)
British; Secretary of State for Education 1965–7, Secretary of State for the Environment 1974–6

A civil servant's son, Crosland was educated at Highgate School and Trinity College,

Oxford. During the Second World War he served in the army, reaching the rank of captain. After three years as a don at Trinity he was elected Labour MP for South Gloucestershire in 1950. He was defeated in the 1955 general election, but returned to the Commons in 1959 as MP for Grimsby, and held this seat until his death.

Crosland was on the Gaitskellite side of the Labour Party's internecine struggles during the 1950s. The publication, in 1956, of his *The Future of Socialism* established him as the party's leading intellectual revisionist. A seminal and highly influential volume, it argued that further nationalization was unnecessary since the socialist goals of greater equality and improved living standards could be achieved through growth under a mixed economy. He returned to this theme in *Socialism Now* (1974).

When Harold *Wilson formed his first government in October 1964, Crosland received only a non-Cabinet post at the Department of Economic Affairs. He entered the Cabinet in a reshuffle in January 1965 as Secretary of State for Education, a post from which he was transferred to become president of the Board of Trade in 1967. In 1969, he took over the newly created Department of Local Government and Planning. He resumed similar responsibilities as Secretary of State for the Environment on Labour's return to office in 1974, but was moved again—to the Foreign and Commonwealth Office—when James *Callaghan assumed the premiership in 1976.

Despite his intellectual distinction, Crosland failed to achieve great political eminence in the party. He came only third when he stood for the deputy leadership in 1972 and was fifth in the leadership election in 1976. The frequency of his moves between ministerial posts precluded his leaving a major legislative mark in any of them (though he played a greater part than any other minister in the comprehensivization of secondary education). He was deeply disappointed not to be made Chancellor of the Exchequer after the devaluation of sterling in 1967, but seemed set to achieve this ambition under Callaghan's premiership. His untimely death of a cerebral haemorrhage was widely interpreted as a consequence of the pressures of high office in a minority government.

Crossman, Richard Howard Stafford (b. London, 15 Dec. 1907; d. 5 Apr. 1974)
British; Lord President of the Council 1966–8

The son of a judge, Crossman was educated at Winchester and New College, Oxford, where he was a don before joining the *New Statesman* as assistant editor in 1938. After distinguished service as a specialist in psychological warfare during the Second World War, he was elected Labour MP for Coventry East in 1945, holding the seat continuously until 1974.

Crossman was a frequent left-wing critic of the foreign policy of Clement *Attlee's government (1945–51), and became a close adherent of Aneurin *Bevan. This stance facilitated his election to the National Executive Committee in 1952 (he remained a member until 1967) but kept him outside the parliamentary party's leadership group until Harold *Wilson became leader in 1963. He held Cabinet office throughout Wilson's 1964–70 government, first as Minister of Housing and Local Government (1964–6) and latterly (1968–70) as first head of the Department of Health and Social Services. But he made his greatest mark as leader of the House of Commons (1966–8) when he introduced experimental select committees which were the progenitors of the present system.

When Labour went into Opposition in 1970, Crossman retired to the back benches to return to iconoclastic political commentary as editor of the *New Statesman*. He also began preparation of his three-volume *Diaries of a Cabinet Minister* (1975, 1976, and 1977). These added to his earlier thesis (in an introduction to Bagehot's *The English Constitution*, 1964) that Cabinet government had been replaced by prime ministerial government and manipulation of ministers by their officials. The unprecedentedly revealing diaries provoked a governmental legal action to prevent their publication. They remain a valuable source for students of British government.

Cuomo, Mario Matthew (b. Queens County, New York, 15 June 1932)
US; Governor of New York State 1983–

The son of Italian immigrant parents, Cuomo was educated at St John's University, from which he graduated BA in 1953 and LLB in 1956. He was called to the bar in New York that same year. After a spell as a professional basketball player for Pittsburg Pirates, he practised law 1963–75. He did not embark upon a political career until his forties when, in 1947, he made an unsuccessful attempt to become Democratic candidate for New York state Lieutenant-Governor. He was, instead, appointed Secretary of State to New York Governor Hugh *Carey. In 1977, electoral success once again eluded him when he ran for mayor of New York City but lost in the primary. In 1978 at his second attempt, he was elected Lieutenant-Governor of New York and, in 1982, gained the governorship. He was re-elected by a record margin in 1986.

In office Cuomo established a reputation as a caring liberal, preaching family values and compassion for the needly. He has been acclaimed for his innovatory policies in higher education, for taking moral leadership on New York's Aids epidemic and for his success in balancing the state budget whilst at the same time cutting taxes. But he is not without critics. Questions have been raised about his management style, in particular his failure to delegate and his excessive reliance on the advice of a 'kitchen cabinet' dominated by his lawyer son.

Cuomo's leadership credentials have also been questioned because of his tendency to self-doubt. He writes a detailed daily journal of his activities and reflections. Several volumes have been published, and provide ample testament to the reflective side of his nature. His reluctance to seek national elective office has also been attributed to this brooding self-doubt. In 1984 he achieved national prominence by delivering an electrifying key-note speech to the Democratic national convention, in which he urged the party to stand by its liberal traditions. In 1987 he was widely expected to make a bid for nomination as Democratic presidential candidate but he shocked the party by insisting he had no intention of running. His reluctance to stand aroused speculation about his Italian roots and the possibility of Mafia connections. He furiously denied these rumours and they were subsequently declared unfounded after investigation by the *New York Magazine*. As the primary campaign drew to a close in 1988 Cuomo remained the non-candidate whose shadow nevertheless loomed over the convention. He disappointed many in the party when he failed to play 'white knight' and deliver the convention from the unenviable task of choosing between the charismatic black candidate, Jesse *Jackson, and the lacklustre Michael *Dukakis.

Cuomo is a man of paradoxes: a charismatic leader able to inspire with his vision, eloquence, authority, integrity, and charm; but also a brooding self-doubter reluctant to seek the nation's highest office. He is the author of several books, including *Forest Hills Diary* (1974) and *Diaries of Mario Cuomo* (1983). Co-authored works include *Lincoln on Democracy* (1990) and *The New York Idea* (1994).

Curley, James Michael (b. Boston, 20 Nov. 1874; d. 12 Nov. 1958)
US; Governor of Massachusetts 1934–8

The son of poor Irish immigrants, Curley's access to formal education was limited by the need to help support his family. His organizational ability and shrewd understanding of the needs of his local community combined to make politics a natural career for him. During his long period in Boston's political life, he built up a formidable Democratic Party machine based on the twin pillars of the welfare support and voter loyalty.

Curley's first electoral effort to secure a place on the Boston Common Council was frustrated by the Democratic regulars causing him to attack the boss system as corrupt. However in 1899 he succeeded in getting onto the Council and was also elected as a ward boss. Politics in Boston (as in many big cities at the time) were largely dominated by the Irish and in 1902 Curley established the Roxbury Tammany Club modelled on the New York Democratic machine. In 1902 Curley was elected to the state legislature and from 1904 to 1909 he served as an alderman. When Boston restructured its city government in 1909 Curley was elected to the new city council.

Although municipal politics was Curley's first love, in 1912 he was elected to Congress from the Massachusetts 12th District. There he became a supporter of Champ Clark and helped his presidential bid of 1912. Curley became House minority whip in 1913 and was re-elected to Congress in 1914. However, he did not serve the full second term since in 1914 he mounted a successful bid to become mayor of Boston.

Despite campaigning against the corruption inherent in the boss system, Curley on becoming mayor moved to mobilize the city's resources behind a highly centralized personal machine distributing jobs and welfare on a partisan basis.

Curley's career as mayor was not continuous. After re-election on a reform ticket in 1921, his grip on the office was broken by a law which prevented mayors enjoying consecutive periods in the job. After his second term (1922–6) (which saw massive public works programmes and an enlarged city payroll) Curley unsuccessfully sought the governorship but was re-elected for a third mayoral term in 1929.

In 1934 Curley was elected as Governor of Massachusetts and extended to the state some of the policies he had applied in Boston. In 1936 Curley ran for the Senate but was defeated by Henry Cabot Lodge. In 1938 he was defeated as governor. He was re-elected to Congress in 1942 and again in 1944, a term which he did not complete in order to enter the mayoral race again. Curley failed and between 1945 and 1949 lost three mayoral bids. His last public appointment was as a member of the State Labor Commission in 1957.

Inevitably Curley's use of patronage made him vulnerable to accusations of corruption. In 1947 he spent a term of five months in prison but was pardoned by *Truman in 1950. His colourful career and the system he established ('Curleyism') formed the basis for Edwin O'Connor's *The Last Hurrah*, which prompted Curley's *I'd Do it Again*, published in 1957.

Curtin, John Joseph Ambrose (b. Creswick, Victoria, 8 Jan. 1885; d. Canberra, 5 July 1945)

Australian; Leader of the Australian Labor Party 1935–45, Prime Minister 1941–5

Curtin was the son of Irish Catholic immigrants. His education was partly self-administered and partly gleaned from his association with prominent Victorian socialists and radicals. Having moved to Perth he became editor of the *Westralian Worker*, organ of the Australian Workers' Union, until winning the seat of Fremantle in 1928. Prior to his becoming leader of the Labor Party in 1935, Curtin gained a reputation for his pacifism. He organized unions against conscription during the First World War, and was jailed and fined for sedition. His drinking problem also became well known, and he had to pledge to abstain from alcohol before being chosen as Labor's leader.

Curtin became Prime Minister in October 1941, shortly before Australian's worst fears were realized with Japanese military victories throughout South East Asia and the Pacific, including the supposedly impregnable fortress of Singapore. His response was to announce that 'Australia looks to America, free of any pangs as to our traditional links or kinship with the United Kingdom', a comment which has since been seized on as signalling Australia's reorientation in world affairs.

As a wartime Prime Minister, Curtin held together an often fractious Labor Party. He agonized over the deployment of Australian troops in Middle Eastern and South Pacific theatres; and at the beginning of 1943 he extended conscription for military service beyond the boundaries of Australian shores. He remained committed, however, to his socialist convictions and introduced unemployment and sickness benefits and a reconstruction programme designed to enlarge on the welfare state. The crisis of the war also enabled Curtin to centralize powers in taxation, banking, and industrial regulation at the expense of the Australian states, a transformation in state–federal relations which would not be reversed after the war.

Curtin was a brilliant speaker who inspired many, including opponents. He continued in office after a serious heart attack in November 1944, but died before he could celebrate the end of the war.

Curzon, George Nathaniel (b. Keddlestone, Derbyshire, 11 Jan. 1859; d. 20 Mar. 1925)

British; Viceroy of India 1899–1905, Foreign Secretary 1919–24, Irish rep. peer 1908, Earl 1911, Marquess 1922

Educated at Eton and Oxford, Curzon became a fellow of All Souls in 1883. Destined—not least in his own eyes—for greatness, he established a reputation for his knowledge of foreign affairs. He travelled extensively—publishing a work on Persia in 1892—and in 1891, five years after entering the House of Commons as Conservative member for Southport, was appointed Under-Secretary of State at the India Office; in 1895 he was made Under-Secretary at the Foreign Office, answering for the department in the Commons while Foreign Secretary (and Prime Minister) Lord Salisbury was in the Lords. In 1898, at the age of 39, he achieved one of his life's greatest ambitions—to be Viceroy of India. An able administrator but a vain man, his viceroyship ended abruptly after a clash with the military commander, Lord Kitchener.

He was created an Irish peer in order to resume his political career, but for several years there was no career to pursue. His wife died in 1906 and he spent much of his time absorbed in interests outside politics. Some compensaton came in 1911 when he was created an earl, but it was to be another four years before he returned to public office.

His restoration to high office came in 1915 when he entered *Asquith's coalition as Lord Privy Seal, before serving briefly as President of the Air Board in 1916 and then for three years as Lord President of the Council. He served as a member of the inner War Cabinet throughout its existence (December 1916 to October 1919). He also took over leadership of the Conservative Party in the House of Lords. In 1919, he succeeded *Balfour as Foreign Secretary. It was a post to which his experience, sense of superiority, and ambition lent itself—he was only one step from his ultimate goal, that of the premiership.

The ultimate goal was denied him in 1923, when the King decided that a Prime Minister could not serve in a house in which the official Opposition party was not represented. He carried on as Foreign Secretary until the party was defeated at the polls. On the party's return to power in 1924, *Baldwin made him Lord President of the Council. He died the following year at the age of 66, a disappointed man. His life was a story of achievement—commoner to Marquess, Viceroy, Foreign Secretary—but not to the extent to which he considered himself destined.

Daladier, Edouard (b. Orange, 18 June 1884; d. 10 Oct. 1970)
French; Prime Minister 1933, 1934, 1938–40

Born in 1884 in the southern city of Orange, Daladier's career—like those of *Herriot and *Laval—provides a good example of the opportunities provided by the state educational system of the Third Republic to talented boys from poor families. The son of a baker, he was educated at the Lyons *lycée*, obtained the prestigious *agrégation*, and entered local politics. He fought throughout the First World War and in 1919 was elected to the Chamber of Deputies. By the mid-1920s he had established himself as a pugnacious, ambitious, and effective spokesman for the left wing of the Radical party, whose president he became in 1926. An advocate of the traditional Radical values of anti-clericalism, social reform, and the property rights of the small man, he favoured co-operation with *Blum's Socialist Party. He held office in a number of governments in the mid-1920s before briefly becoming Prime Minister in 1933. His move to the centre stage, in the 1930s, coincided with a darkening international climate caused by the rise to power of *Hitler and the worsening economic situation. The aims of social progress and social stability with which the Radical Party, and Daladier, had identified were now under pressure. In 1934, when he became Prime Minister for the second time, the regime was under attack from an anti-parliamentary right enraged by economic hardship and evidence of political corruption. On 6 February 1934 a mass demonstration outside the Palais Bourbon degenerated into a riot in which nineteen people were killed. It looked like an open threat to the regime. Daladier stood firm against the disorder, but was forced to resign, in favour of a government of national union headed by former President *Doumergue. He was criticized by the right for the bloodshed and by the left for submitting to street violence. Undaunted by these events, he threw himself into the movement for the defence of the Republic known as the Popular Front. This electoral alliance of Communists, Socialists, and Radicals revived memories of earlier campaigns in the defence of the Republic and restored Daladier's credentials. He was a senior member in Blum's 1936 government and initially backed its programme of social reform. But domestic politics were now hopelessly enmeshed with the ever worsening threat from Nazi Germany. Much of the Radical's electorate was outraged by the social reforms of the Popular Front. When Daladier became Prime Minister in 1938 he appeared to move sharply right. He crushed labour protest movement against austerity measures and he signed the Munich agreement with *Hitler. Daladier was no ideological appeaser, but he felt there was no alternative. The tumultuous reception he received on his return from Munich suggested that most people agreed with him.

In 1939 Daladier's reputation was at its zenith and his party urged him, against all the traditions of the Third Republic, to persuade the President of the Republic to call for early general elections. With the onset of the Second World War, however, came a rapid political decline. He was unable to unite the French political class around the war or to frighten into silence the advocates of a compromise peace. Compelled to resign in February 1940 in favour of the more dynamic *Reynaud he allowed personal bitterness to corrupt his judgment to the extent that he flirted with the advocates of peace at any price. Once the collapse occurred, however, his old patriotic Jacobinism reasserted itself. He was one of the group of regime dignitaries who tried unsuccessfully to carry on the war from North Africa and in 1941 launched a spirited defence of his actions when put on trial by the Vichy regime. He was deported to Germany. On his return he found himself an isolated, even despised figure. He fought back, was re-elected to parliament, and became mayor of Avignon. Though he never again held public office, he played an important, if secondary, role in the party politics of the Fourth Republic. In 1958 he demonstrated his enduring attachment to Republican principles by opposing *de Gaulle's return to power. There was, however, no longer room for men of his age and beliefs. He withdrew from public life and died, ignored if not forgotten, in 1970.

Daley, Richard Joseph, Snr. (b. Chicago, 15 May 1902; d. 20 Dec. 1976)
US; member of the Illinois House of Representatives 1936–8, Illinois state Senator 1939–46, mayor of Chicago 1955–76

The son of an Irish immigrant sheet-metal worker, Daley was brought up in a working-class area of Chicago, where he lived until his death. Educated in the local school, he worked part-time to help support himself. He attended a commercial high school 1916–19 to acquire the office skills that enabled him to gain clerical work in the Chicago stockyard. Whilst holding down a day job he doggedly continued with his studies until, in 1933, aged 31, he graduated LLB from De Paul University.

By the time he was 21, Daley had already set out on what was to be a lifetime in politics. That year he became a precinct captain in the local Democratic Party. Although the lowest rung on the ladder of city politics, the job of precinct captain involved close liaison with individual voters and provided early lessons in the arts of brokerage and patronage. He also became the beneficiary of party patronage himself, gaining appointment to a job on the city council.

Daley gained his first elective office in 1936 as a member of the Illinois House of Representatives. Two years later, on the death of an incumbent, he was appointed to the state Senate. He retained the seat for the next eight years. Senatorial office was followed by a two-year period as state director of revenue, 1948–50, and five years as clerk of Cook Country, 1950–5.

Whilst holding elective office and appointments in the city administration, Daley continued to climb the ladder of advancement within the Democratic Party. He gained election to the Cook County Democratic central committee, the controlling organ of the party in the district in 1948, and became chairman of the Cook County Democratic Party in 1953.

In 1955 Daley was elected major of Chicago and was re-elected to office very fourth year until his death. Often described as 'the last of the big-city bosses' he used his skills in brokerage and patronage acquired during his apprenticeship at precinct level, to wield enormous power within Democratic politics at city, state, and national level. In 1960 he played a crucial role in delivering the Illinois votes that secured *Kennedy's nomination. Throughout the 1960s he was regarded as one of the most influential figures in the party and his endorsement was almost a prerequisite for candidates seeking nomination for state or national office.

During his mayoralty Daley was credited with sponsoring large-scale projects of urban renewal, road building, and police reform. But he was criticized for failing to check racial segregation in housing and schools and for encouraging the construction of too many tall buildings in the city. Daley is also remembered, and criticized, for unleashing a brutal police response to the student demonstrations outside the Democratic Party convention in Chicago in 1968.

Rumours of corruption frequently stirred around Daley but none was substantiated. He was a master of political brokerage, a wheeler-dealer from the smoke-filled rooms. He delivered material benefits to his constituents, they loyally delivered their votes to his party.

Dalton, Edward **Hugh** John Neale (b. Glamorganshire, 26 Aug. 1887; d. 13 Feb. 1962)
British; Chancellor of the Exchequer 1945–7, Baron (life peer) 1960

The son of a Church of England canon, Dalton was educated at Eton and King's

College, Cambridge. After service in the army during the First World War, he taught at the London School of Economics and Political Science and wrote on public finance and international relations.

Dalton entered Parliament in 1924 as MP for Peckham, later moving to Bishop Auckland. In 1929, he and his wife were the first married couple simultaneously to sit in the House of Commons. After junior office in the second Labour government (1929–31) he lost his seat in 1931 (recapturing it in 1935). He nevertheless made a major contribution to the Labour Party throughout the 1930s. He played an important part in weaning Labour from its traditional opposition to expenditure on the armed forces. In Winston *Churchill's wartime coalition government (1940–5) he was initially Minister of Economic Warfare—responsible for establishing the Special Operations Executive to undertake sabotage in Nazi-occupied Europe—and then president of the Board of Trade (1942–5).

By then one of the party's most influential figures, Dalton became Chancellor of the Exchequer in Clement *Attlee's government (1945–51) after a last-minute decision to send Ernest *Bevin and not him to the Foreign Office. His chancellorshop ended abruptly with his resignation over a budget leak, in November 1947. The leak was relatively minor and he returned to the Cabinet in 1948 as Chancellor of the Duchy of Lancaster. After the 1950 general election he was made Minister of Town and Country Planning (later expanded to Local Government and Planning). After Labour lost office Dalton's influence waned rapidly. He was defeated in the NEC elections in 1952 and in 1955 announced his retirement from the shadow Cabinet. He accepted a peerage after leaving the Commons in 1959 but was relatively inactive in the Lords.

Opposition suited Dalton less well than office, where he could exercise his administrative skills. But despite his academic background as an economist, he was no great success as Chancellor: his policies were inflationary and inappropriate to the state of Britain's post-war economy. They were largely reversed by his successor. He was more successful at Local Government and Planning.

When in high office, Dalton displayed a commendable preparedness to bring on the younger generation. But he also displayed less attractive attributes. His propensity for gossip and intrigue was renowned. It has been suggested that Attlee's readiness to accept his resignation in 1947 was influenced by recent intrigues against him by Dalton. He was also egotistical and conscious of his ranking in the Cabinet. All these qualities were displayed in the three volumes of his highly controversial memoirs (1953, 1957, and 1962) which revealed the inner workings of party and government with what was, for their day, unaccustomed frankness.

Davis, John W. (b. Clarksburg, West Virginia, 13 Apr. 1873; d. 24 Mar. 1955)
US; lawyer, diplomat, and presidential nominee

The son of a lawyer, Davis spent much of his own career in private legal practice. His period as Woodrow *Wilson's Solicitor-General (1913–18) and his own private legal practice (as head of the New York firm of Davis, Polk) gave him an unrivalled experience of arguing before the Supreme Court. His career was not entirely that of a lawyer, however. In 1918 he became United States ambassador in London and, in 1924, as a result of a deadlocked convention, Davis secured the Democratic nomination on the 103rd ballot. In the presidential election of 1924 Davis lost overwhelmingly to Calvin *Coolidge. Davis returned to legal practice and only briefly engaged in further political activity. In 1928 he supported the Democratic candidate Alfred *Smith but in 1934 he helped to found the American Liberty League, an organization opposed to the New Deal. Although he had been a Democratic presidential candidate and was an opponent of isolationism, Davis supported Republican presidential candidates after 1928.

Davis's legal skills were highly regarded and during his long career he argued an extremely large number and range of constitutional cases before the Supreme Court.

He was involved in many of the key anti-New Deal cases in the 1930s and in 1952 he was counsel for the steel industry in the *Youngstown Sheet and Tube Co* v. *Sawyer* case, arguing that President *Truman's seizure of the steel mills had been unconstitutional. Davis's opposition to school integration and his conservative approach to legal interpretation made him a fierce critic of the 1954 *Brown* v. *Board of Education of Topeka* decision, a case in which he had argued for the constitutionality of the separate but equal doctrine.

Dawes, Charles Gates (b. Marietta, Ohio, 27 Aug. 1865; d. 23 Apr. 1951)
US; Vice-President 1925–9, US ambassador to Britain 1929–32

The son of an American army general, Dawes attended local schools before graduating from Marietta College, Ohio, 1884 and from Cincinnati Law School in 1886. He was called to the bar that same year and began practising law in Lincoln, Nebraska. In 1894, after publishing *The Banking System of the United States*, he gave up law and combined a career in business and finance with his interests in Republican Party politics. In 1896, he was appointed by President McKinley to the position of Comptroller of the Currency. He retired from office in 1901 and turned his attention once again to his private business interest, gaining a reputation as one of the outstanding financial experts in the country.

Commissioned in 1917, Dawes had a distinguished career in the US army during the First World War. He was promoted to the rank of brigadier-general and decorated both by his own country and by Britain, Italy, France, and Belgium.

In 1921 President *Harding appointed Dawes to the newly created post of Director of the Budget. This led to his selection as head of the American delegation to the Reparation Commission in 1923, the outcome of which, the 'Dawes Plan' made his name famous in international politics and made him a joint winner, with Sir Austen *Chamberlain, of the Nobel Prize for Peace, 1925.

Invited by President *Coolidge to be his running mate, Dawes was elected Vice-President in 1925 and served until 1929. Having failed to gain the Republican party's nomination for President in 1928, he was appointed by President *Hoover to serve as US ambassador to Britain. He held this position until 1932, when he returned to America and the appointment of president of the Reconstruction Finance Corporation.

A solider, banker, politician, and diplomat, Dawes was a cultured and modest man. He refused to accept personal credit for the Dawes Plan, citing instead the contribution made by the British delegates, Lord Stamp and Sir Robert (later Lord) Kindersley. He was the author of numerous books including: *Essays and Speeches* (1915); *A Journal of the Great War* (1921); *Notes as Vice-President* (1935); *Journal of Reparations* (1939); *Journal as Ambassador to Great Britain* (1939); *A Journal of the Mckinley Years* (1950).

Deakin, Alfred (b. Melbourne, 3 Aug. 1856; d. Melbourne, 7 Oct. 1919)
Australian; Attorney-General 1901–3, Prime Minister and Minister for External Affairs 1903–4, 1905–8, 1909–10

Deakin's parents emigrated from England to Australia in 1849–50, where his father established himself in Melbourne's coach and carriage industry. Alfred was educated at Melbourne Grammar School and the University of Melbourne, where he graduated in law. He entered politics via journalism, working for Melbourne *Age*. The paper's editor, David Syme, converted him to protectionist trade policy and sponsored his entry to the Victorian parliament in 1879.

Deakin held several portfolios in a coalition government and was joint leader from 1885 to 1890. He became better known, however, for his successful endeavours with others over the following decade, in Australia and in London, to bring about Australia's federation. Deakin was the pre-eminent political figure in the first decade of the new Commonwealth. During his three terms as Prime Minister he continued to press for greater Australian defence preparations, while protesting the over-readiness of Britain to conclude imperial deals with other Europeans who had interests in Australia's region. Deakin's protests to London did not prevent an Anglo-French Convention on the New Hebrides in 1906 which left French influence there unaffected, but his campaigning illustrated his nationalism in international affairs. Between 1908 and 1910 he introduced compulsory military training and founded an Australian navy.

Deakin is probably best remembered as the architect of 'New Protection'—general tariff protection for Australia's manufacturers, but tied to clear expectations that employers would provide 'fair and reasonable' wages and working conditions for their employees. This liberal protectionist platform, enshrined during his second ministry, 1905–8, became a common social aim of political parties in following decades. It was supported by legislation for old-age pensions and a strong Commonwealth Arbitration Court, which in 1907 ruled on what constituted a 'fair and reasonable' wage.

Nicknamed 'Affable Alfred', Deakin had a charming manner, an engaging style, and a journalist's skill with narrative. A man of diverse interests, Deakin was also a spiritualist, a believer in the virtues of the British race, a lover of literature and drama, and given to deep introspection and prayer.

He resigned from politics in 1913 and was seldom in the public light before his death six years later.

Debré, Michel (b. Paris, 15 Jan. 1912)

French; Prime Minister 1959–62, Presidential candidate 1981

Michel Debré was the son of a prominent and high-minded medical professor. Educated at the École Libre des Sciences Politiques, he joined the prestigious Conseil d'État in 1938, served in the private office of the independent-minded finance minister, *Reynaud, and fought in the disastrous military campaign of 1940. After a brief period working for General Weygand, who had supported the creation of the Vichy regime, he joined the Resistance, where he developed the passion for the issues of constitutional and administrative reform which would dominate his career. At the Liberation he was appointed prefect for the Angers region and in 1945 joined *de Gaulle's private office, where he drew up the plans for the École Nationale d'Administration, which became famous as the nursery for France's administrative and political élite. He became a dedicated supporter of de Gaulle, and a vehement critic of the political system of the Fourth Republic which he denounced in a celebrated pamphlet 'Ces princes qui nous gouvernent'.

As Minister of Justice in the government de Gaulle formed in June 1958, Debré played a central role in the drafting of the constitution of the Fifth Republic. In January 1959 he became first Prime Minister of the new regime. A compulsive reformer, he used his term of office to start the process of adapting French agriculture and industry to the Common Market and to put an end to the long conflict over state financing of private education. His modernization mania did not, however, extend across the Mediterranean and he experienced much torment over de Gaulle's increasing determination to lance the boil of the Algerian War by conceding independence to the provisional government of the Algerian Republic. Loyalty to de Gaulle won out, and he did not resign until the peace negotiations were near completion. After a short period in the political wilderness, he returned to government in 1966 as Minister of Economy and Finances and showed characteristic determination (and, critics said, lack of political judgement) in introducing the tough social security measures which helped provoke the mass demonstrations of May 1968. After *Pompidou's election as President in 1969, he took the Defence portfolio, which he held until 1973, his presence guaranteeing the continuity of de Gaulle's strategic vision. He never again held office, but in 1981 stood for the presidency on a programme of fidelity to the legacy of Gaullism. By this time, however, *Chirac had won control of the Gaullist party machine and Debré obtained only 1.6 per cent of the vote. He withdrew progressively from national politics and wrote a well-received four-volume autobiography.

Debré lacked the skills of the successful politician and his tense, interfering manner annoyed many of his governmental colleagues, including, on occasion, de Gaulle. Yet he played a central role in the creation not only of the Fifth Republic constitution but of the post-war French State. Though his nationalism, and statism made him a somewhat archaic figure by the end of his career, he is recognized as one of the most distinguished of France's twentieth-century statesmen.

Debs, Eugene Victor (b. Terre Haute, Indiana, 5 Dec. 1855; d. 20 Oct. 1926)
US; union organizer and socialist leader

Debs, the son of immigrants from Alsace, grew up in Terre Haute, Indiana, as one of ten children. Any education he had was the result of independent study. In his youth he worked in the railway factories and then became a fireman. In 1875 he became a member of the Brotherhood of Locomotive Firemen, having previously been a member of the Brotherhood of Railway Brakemen. Debs became grand secretary and treasurer of the Brotherhood in 1880.

In addition to developing an interest in union organization, Debs also became more involved with politics; he was elected city clerk of Terre Haute in 1879 and won election to the Indiana State Assembly in 1885. Debs's opinions about both labour and politics evolved in a radical direction during the 1880s and 1890s. Increasingly he believed that industrial unionism was more effective than craft unionism. In 1893 he resigned from his union post with the Brotherhood of Locomotive Fireman to organize a more militant form of unionism in the American Railway Union, of which he became president. Two landmark strikes—the eighteen-day strike against the Great Northern Railway Co. in April 1894 and Pullman strike in 1895 made him a national figure. The Great Northern strike was a victory for organized labour but the danger of rioting during the Pullman strike caused President Cleveland to send troops to Chicago.

Debs was charged with conspiracy as a result of the Pullman strike and although originally acquitted he was rearrested for contempt and jailed for six months. In prison Debs's political vision was influenced by reading the works of Karl Marx, although in 1896 he backed the populist William Jennings *Bryan for the presidency. By 1897 Debs declared himself a socialist and helped form the Social Democratic Party.

Debs stood for the presidency as a socialist five times, in 1900, 1904, 1908, 1912, and 1920, in each case raising his vote until by 1912 it was almost a million votes, or 6 per cent of the total. Debs's 1920 vote was obtained from prison since in 1918 he was sentenced to ten years as a result of a speech made against the draft. Although Woodrow *Wilson refused to reduce his sentence, he was released by President Warren *Harding in 1923 but not fully pardoned or restored to full citizenship. After his release from prison, Debs campaigned for political prisoners as well as for other socialist leaders such as Norman Thomas. However, by 1925, Debs's health was weak and he died in a sanatorium of heart failure.

Defferre, Gaston Paul Charles (b. Marsillargues, 14 Sept. 1910; d. 6 May 1986)
French; mayor of Marseilles 1944–5, Minister of the Interior 1981–4

The son of a rakish lawyer, from the Protestant Cevennes, Defferre was educated at the *lycée* in Nîmes, read law in the University of Aix-en-Provence, and practised at the Marseilles Bar from 1931 to 1951. Defferre was a minor Socialist activist before the war but during the Vichy years rose rapidly through the ranks to join the clandestine SFIO Executive Bureau. Defferre's importance was both as a local politician (as cleaner-up of the notoriously ungovernable city of Marseilles) and as a reformer in brief spells of national office. At the end of the war he took over *Le Petit Provençal* and built up a fiefdom with interests everywhere in the city. As the boss of the powerful Bouches-du-Rhône SFIO federation, Defferre conducted a long war against the Socialist Party leader Guy *Mollet, opposing, for example, the leadership's line on Algeria and taking a resolutely anti-Communist and centrist stance. His plans in 1964 for a centre-left, anti-Communist federation of the left in 1965 came to nothing. Despite this anti-Communism, Defferre was instrumental in bringing *Mitterrand (with his strategy of alliance of the left) to the leadership of the new Parti Socialiste at the 1971 Épinay congress. He supported Mitterrand thereafter with a curious division of loyalties in 1979 between Mitterrand and Mauroy (the federation's vote was divided). Defferre was also presidential candidate in the shambolic Socialist campaign of 1969, when he polled a mere 5.07 per cent of the vote. As Minister for Overseas France he was responsible for the 1956 outline law foreshadowing decolonization. As Minister of the Interior in the Socialist government of 1981 he was responsible for the controversial decentralization laws which substantially reduced central oversight of local government and devolved powers to localities and regions. Defferre was a brutal power broker, who had some success at national level and was typical of big city machine politics. He was a dapper dresser and a duellist as well as something of a 'card'.

De Gasperi, Alcide (b. Trento, 3 Apr. 1881; d. 18. Aug. 1954)
Italian; Prime Minister 1945–53

De Gasperi was born in the village of Pieve Tesino in the province of Trento, at a time when though linguistically Italian it was part of the Austro-Hungarian Empire. His father was a local police officer of limited financial means. De Gasperi was active in the Social Christian movement from 1896, and it was Catholic social organization which gave impetus to his politics rather than Italian nationalism, though he was briefly imprisoned by the Austrian authorities in 1904. He graduated in philology from the University of Vienna in 1905 and helped establish the Partito Popolare Trentino, for whom he was elected to the Austrian Parliament in 1911.

He was firmly neutralist during the First World War, which he spent in Vienna. When the Trentino province passed to Italy in the post-war settlement, he took Italian citizenship, and was a founder-member of the Partito Popolare led by Don Luigi Sturzo. Elected to the Chamber of Deputies in 1921, he initially supported the participation of the Popolari in *Mussolini's first government in October 1922, but was soon in conflict with the Fascists over constitutional changes to the powers of the executive and to the election system, and to Fascist violence against the constitutional parties. The Popolari split, and De Gasperi became secretary of the remaining anti-Fascist Popolari in May 1924. In November 1926, in a climate of overt violence and intimidation by the Fascists, his party was dissolved by order of the Ministry of the Interior. De Gasperi attempted to escape into exile and was arrested and imprisoned. After his release in May 1928, he was unemployed and in serious financial hardship, until in May 1929 his ecclesiastical contacts secured him a job as a cataloguer in the Vatican Library, where he spent the next fourteen years until the collapse of Fascism in July 1943.

Throughout this period he continued to write pseudonymously, but his most important work was 'Ideas for reconstruction' (*Idee ricostruttive*), published in 1943, which amounted to a party programme for a new Christian Democrat Party. He was the first general secretary of the new party in 1944, and after a period as minister in the coalition governments under the allies he became Prime Minister for the first time in December 1945. He remained in office as Prime Minister in eight successive governments until August 1953. After a brief period as party secretary again, he retired from active politics in increasing ill-health and died in 1954.

De Gasperi's involvement in the post-war reconstruction was of critical importance for the future functioning of the new Italian state. During his period of office, Italy voted to become a republic (June 1946), the Peace Treaty was signed (February 1947), the *Marshall Plan and other US support for Italy was agreed, the wartime coalition with the Communists and Socialists was ended (May 1947), the new constitution came into force (January 1948), the DC won a majority in the first parliamentary elections (April 1948), and Italy joined NATO (1949). In all of these the guiding hand of De Gasperi was evident. Though at times his control of the DC appeared almost complete, it was in fact the result of a careful balancing of different factions and interests, especially over relations with the Vatican, over social reform, and over foreign policy. The 1952 party congress overwhelmingly endorsed his authority over the government and over the party, but initiated the period of his decline, as he came under increasing criticism from the emerging left of the party. The main accusations against him were that he was too cautious in social and economic reform, that he stifled debate, and that he subordinated the party to the interests of government.

A gradualist and a firm believer in the importance of international alliances, he was a politician for whom the term 'centrist' could have been coined. He was a good practical administrator and a deeply religious individual who hated dogmatism and anything that smacked to him of extremism. De Gasperi is often regarded as one of the few undoubted statesmen of the post-war Italian Republic.

De Gaulle, Charles (b. Lille, 22 Nov. 1890; d. Colombey-les-deux-Églises, 9 Nov. 1970)
French; Head of the Free French, Prime Minister 1958, President of the Fifth Republic

Though de Gaulle grew up in a family whose aristocratic origins, Catholicism, and monarchism were alien to democratic principles of the Third Republic, his father (a school principal) showed the independence of mind for which his son became celebrated by rejecting the divisive politics of anti-Dreyfusard nationalism. For someone of de Gaulle's class and culture, the army was the obvious, perhaps the only, career. Having attended the military academy of Saint-Cyr, he fought in an infantry regiment, was wounded and captured at Verdun in 1916, and spent the rest of the war in a German prisoner of war camp from which he tried repeatedly, but unsuccessfully, to escape. Between the wars, he taught military history at Saint-Cyr, saw service in Poland and Lebanon, and was for a period close to Marshal *Pétain, who became godfather to one of his children. His lack of respect for the orthodoxies which Pétain incarnated manifested itself in his advocacy, in his 1934 book *Vers l'armée du métier*, of a military strategy based on speed and movement. He was tireless in his advocacy of tanks and armoured divisions and attracted the attention of a number of leading Third Republic politicians, including *Blum and *Reynaud. In 1937, he was appointed colonel of a tank regiment.

De Gaulle's military advancement suffered between the wars from his nonconformity and from what his enemies regarded as arrogance; if he had died in January 1940 he would be unknown today. Thus it was the military catastrophe of 1940, and his connection with Reynaud, which began the process whereby de Gaulle evolved from an isolated maverick into France's most celebrated twentieth-century leader. As France's armies succumbed to the 1940 German offensive, Reynaud appointed him Under-Secretary of War on 5 June in the hope that his strategic talents would stimulate the defence effort. It was, of course, too late to halt the collapse and on 16 June Reynaud handed over power—or what was left of it—to Pétain, who immediately sought an armistice with *Hitler. There was no place for someone of de Gaulle's views in the new political order and he immediately flew to London in an English aircraft. On 18 June (the anniversary of Waterloo) he made the celebrated broadcast in which he announced that the loss of a battle did not mean the loss of war and called on all Frenchmen who were able to do so to join him in continuing the combat. The 18 June speech is the founding moment in de Gaulle's political career. It was a dramatic break with the conventions of his career—an officer must obey his commanding officer—and with the values which Pétain incarnated and which someone of his class could be expected to respect. Yet if the speech is the source of de Gaulle's subsequent legitimacy, it attracted little attention in a France which was stunned by defeat and it certainly did not establish de Gaulle as a leader. The vast majority of his compatriots sought refuge from their distress in Pétain's authority; even those who did not were far from willing to accept de Gaulle's claim to speak for France. Thus the early years of the Free French movement which he founded were far from easy. The humiliating failure of the Dakar Expedition of September 1940 demonstrated the refusal of many officials of the French Empire to accept his authority and so too did the bitter feuds within the Free French. His intransigence infuriated his protector *Churchill and he was regarded with implacable suspicion by *Roosevelt, who saw him as the kind of reactionary militarist against whom the war was being fought. Thus de Gaulle faced enormous problems in asserting his authority. That he was finally able to do so reflected his political skill in marginalizing rivals like General Giraud; his eloquence as a broadcaster to occupied France; and his ability to win over the internal Resistance to his cause by placing himself squarely on the side of democracy and social reform. By the time he returned to France in August 1944 (he had not been told in advance of the D Day landings) his authority as leader of Free France was unquestioned and he received a tumultuous reception when he walked down the Champs Elysées on 25 August. To the status he enjoyed as liberator was added the authority he possessed as head of a provisional government which contained representatives of all France's political forces, including the powerful Communist Party.

His authority was temporary. Resigned (briefly) to the role of the parties in the reconstruction of French democracy, he made no attempt to construct his own political machine in the run-up to the October 1945 election of a Constituent Assembly. The new Assembly was, however, dominated by party leaders who had no intention of introducing a system which would institutionalize de Gaulle's leadership. His relations with the Assembly collapsed and in January 1946 he abruptly resigned as head of the provincial government, in the (mistaken) hope that public pressure would force his return. When it became clear that this would not happen, he launched a fierce attack on the constitutional plans of the Assembly and in the famous Bayeux speech on 16 June 1946 set out his model of a presidential system able to protect the authority of government from the interference of the parties. Nine months later he founded a mass political movement, the Rassemblement du Peuple Français (RPF), whose purpose was to force the newly founded Fourth Republic to abdicate in his favour. The RPF was initially highly successful in attracting a mass public, and in the 1951 elections became the largest grouping in the National Assembly. But it did not succeed in its core aim of terrorizing the other parties into submission and gave de Gaulle a dangerous reputation as an anti-Republican demagogue. In 1954, the RPF had disintegrated and its leader retreated into morose retirement at his country home in Colombey-les-deux-Églises, where he wrote three volumes of well-regarded war memoirs. By the mid-1950s, he had disappeared from the list of those that public opinion believed to have a future in national politics.

He was brought back to power in May 1958 by the collapse of the authority of the Fourth Republic. Unable to find a solution to the brutal war in Algeria, and facing the nightmare scenario of a military coup, or even a civil war, the majority of the party leaders turned, as their predecessors had turned in 1940, to a leader who stood outside the existing system. The dual legitimacy de Gaulle possessed as saviour of French honour (1940) and restorer of French democracy (1944) made him acceptable to the defenders of French Algeria and to (most) of the democratic parties. But if Algeria was the cause of de Gaulle's return, it was not the only, or perhaps even the principal, focus of his ambitions. His goal was, as it had been since 1946, to construct a political order which would enable government to govern—and him to rule. On 28 September the constitution of the Fifth Republic, of which he is correctly seen as Founding Father, gained a massive approval in a referendum and seven weeks later an Electoral College elected him President. The new constitution gave the presidency more powers that it had possessed since 1877 and severely constrained the ability of the National Assembly to impede government.

De Gaulle was no reactionary imperialist and he knew his ambitions for France could not be realized so long as the Algerian crisis continued. He thus embarked upon a policy of self-determination which culminated in 1962 in the grant of full independence to an Algeria run by those whom France had been fighting for eight years. Although bitterly opposed by the French settlers and by the far right, the end of French Algeria received a massive backing from the electorate. Military peace was, however, soon followed by political warfare as the parties rebelled against de Gaulle's conception, and use, of presidential power and in particular against his proposal to base the presidency on universal suffrage. What de Gaulle regarded as the legitimization of the power of presidency, introduced by the impeccably democratic method of a referendum, was seen by the opposition as a direct assault on the principles of Republican democracy introduced by unconstitutional methods. After a bitterly contested campaign, de Gaulle won both the referendum and the parliamentary election which followed it. Three years later he became the first French president since Louis Napoleon Bonaparte in 1851 to be elected by popular vote.

Backed by a supportive National Assembly and a loyal, and competent, Prime Minister *Pompidou, de Gaulle was now free to realize his ambitions for French grandeur. While it is not true that, as his critics claimed, he regarded issues of economic and social policy as unworthy of his attention, it is the case that he was primarily interested in creating a role for France as an independent actor on the world stage and in challenging the right of the two super powers to determine the contours of the international system. He cultivated good relations with Third World countries, vigorously promoted France's independent nuclear deterrent, and sought to make France the leader of a European confederation of nation states. For de Gaulle the nation state was the only genuine political institution. It was this belief which led him, while accepting France's membership of both the Atlantic Alliance and the European Economic Community, to withdraw French troops from the integrated military command structure of NATO and to reject all attempts to turn the EEC into a supranational federation. The aggressive individualism of his foreign policy—vetoing Britain's applications to join the EEC, supporting Quebec separatism, condemning United States military involvement in Vietnam—caused much annoyance in Washington and London. Yet it revived France's status within the international system and unquestionably contributed to a revival of national self-confidence.

Such a confidence was decreasingly accorded to de Gaulle's domestic record. He was forced onto a second ballot in the 1965 presidential contest and nearly lost control of the National Assembly in the 1967 legislative elections. If this decline reflected the economic and social inequalities which industrial growth failed to eradicate, it also derived from what his critics regarded as an elective dictatorship and as the solitary exercise of power. Nothing, however, prepared him—or the public—for the explosion of protest which occurred in May 1968 as students and workers united against his rule. For a few weeks, the crisis left de Gaulle helpless and made a mockery of his boast to have given France the stability it had lacked since 1789. At the end of May he regained the political initiative in a dramatic broadcast in which he declared that the Republic would not abdicate and that he would fight to defend the France he had created. It was to be his last decisive intervention. Although the Gaullist Party won an overwhelming majority in the June parliamentary elections, it was a victory for law and order rather than for de Gaulle. De Gaulle tried to respond to the concerns of 1968, and to reassert his personal authority, by a referendum on Senate and regional reform. The referendum offered nothing to radicals and irritated some conservatives.

What sealed his fate was the emergence of Pompidou as a credible successor and the recognition by erstwhile supporters that dropping the captain no longer threatened the survival of the ship. On 27 April 1969, 52.4 per cent of the electorate voted against the referendum proposal. The following day de Gaulle resigned office. He went back to Colombey-les-deux-Églises, where he died on 9 November 1970 and where, having refused a national funeral, he was buried.

A leader dedicated to order and grandeur, de Gaulle was also a rebel and a modernizer who throughout his life asserted the primacy of will over circumstances. His looming presence dominated France from the Second World War onwards and his legacy continues to shape the contours of French constitutional, and international, politics. In his lifetime, he aroused bitter hostility as well as passionate devotion. Today there is near universal acknowledgement of his greatness, and of his central role in the creation of modern France.

de Klerk, Frederik Willem (b. Johannesburg, 18 Mar. 1936)
South African; President of South Africa 1989–94, Deputy President 1994–6.

Born into a family of leading Afrikaner nationalists (his father was a member of Hendrik *Verwoerd's Cabinet and his uncle J. G. Strijdom was Prime Minister 1954–8) de Klerk trained as a lawyer at Potchefstroom University and was first elected to parliament for the ruling National Party in a by-election for the Vereeniging constituency in 1972. He first joined the Cabinet in 1978 and subsequently held a variety of portfolios. Following the breakaway of the Conservative Party in 1982 he assumed the powerful position of National Party leader in the Transvaal. In 1989 he became leader of the party and President of South Africa.

In the 1989 (whites only) general election he campaigned on a reformist platform but few, if any, observers could have anticipated the degree of change which was to take place following his election victory. In February 1990 he released Nelson *Mandela and other political prisoners and unbanned all the major anti-apartheid organizations including the African National Congress. In 1991 remaining apartheid legislation, including the Group Areas Act, was scrapped and the first meeting of the Convention for a Democratic South Africa (CODESA) was held to discuss the future constitution. In response to criticisms from right-wing whites de Klerk called a whites-only referendum in 1992 which approved continued reform by a significant margin. In 1993 de Klerk and Mandela were jointly awarded the Nobel Peace Prize. Although the personal relationship between de Klerk and Mandela was never entirely harmonious, and occasionally descended to acrimony, it was a relationship which played a crucial role in the transition from apartheid to a democratic non-racial South Africa. Each man recognized the importance of the other and the need to compromise in the national interest. In the 1994 election the National Party, led by de Klerk, came second with a little over one-fifth of the total vote and won power at a regional level in the Western Cape. The ability of de Klerk to project the party as a new force which had abandoned its apartheid past is reflected in the fact that over half of the votes for the party came from non-white voters. Following the election de Klerk became Deputy President in the new government of national unity but withdrew his party from this position in 1996.

Above all de Klerk was a pragmatic politician with a greater sense of vision than any of his predecessors.

Delors, Jacques (b. Paris, 20 July 1925)
French; Minister of Finance 1981–4, European Commission President 1985–94

The son of a Bank of France messenger, Delors entered the Bank of France as a trainee in 1944 and rose rapidly through the ranks to a managerial position. A devout Catholic, he was active in the Catholic union movement and in Catholic social and political action groups. A devotee of the philosophy of personalism and briefly a member of the MRP (for eighteen months), he has been involved in a range of Catholic politics. In 1957 his union nominated him to the Economic and Social Council; in 1962 he helped found the circle 'Citoyens 60' and edited its bulletin under the pseudonym Roger Jacques. Pierre Massé brought him into the Plan Commissariat to head the Social section and he was one of the 'three wise men' who reported on how to end the miners' strike of 1963. *Chaban Delmas, who became Prime Minister in 1969, remembered him from this time and asked him to lead his office in the preparation of the 'New Society'. Delors's 'contracts for progress' were badly received by the unions (suspicious of interference in bargaining) and by the technocratic Gaullists around President *Pompidou. Delors realized the difficulty of putting such 'social-delorism' into practice in the Gaullist Party. Chaban was removed in 1972 and Delors also quit. Remaining loyal to his vision of a new society he founded the *Échanges et Projets* club in February 1974 and joined the Socialist Party, giving it much needed economic expertise. He was a loyal supporter of *Mitterrand (despite great reservations about the alliance with the Communists) and at the congress of 1979, which saw *Rocard pitched against Mitterrand, he flung his weight behind Mitterrand (despite the natural affinity of ideas between Rocard and Delors). In the 1981 presidential campaign he was Mitterrand's chief economics adviser and in the new government Delors was made Minister of Finance. He was sceptical of the Socialist government's reflationary strategy of 'dash for growth' through consumption, accompanied by a shopping list of nationalizations. In November 1981 he called for a 'pause' in reforms (Léon *Blum's phrase) and the government swung round to a strategy of modernization and financial discipline: in 1982 wage and price controls, a devaluation, and a consumer cutback were imposed. In 1983 Delors had his plan for spending cuts and austerity accepted by the President. He was a popular Finance Minister but in the Socialist Party his stock was not high. In 1984 he quit the government when there was a reshuffle and in January 1985 left to head the European Commission (as Margaret *Thatcher's first choice, not Mitterrand's, a decision she may have regretted). He remained for three terms. Delors was the author of Europe's new dynamic to give the Community a real internal market and to create a genuine political power. This was dramatized by the '1992 Act' and was followed up by proposals for a step-by-step realization of economic and monetary union. Delors stint at the Ministry of Finance had confirmed him as a friend of the market system, but Delors had a union background and this was evident in his call for extended social protection made practical in the social charter. As Commission President, Delors was at the forefront of international affairs and detached from the entanglements of domestic politics. Delors could have been the Socialist Party's candidate in 1995 (the polls showed him a probable winner) but, after hesitation, would not stand. In the last resort Delors is an academic or technocratic personality and did not relish the prospect of a bruising election campaign.

de Maiziere, Lothar (b. Nordausen, 2 Mar. 1940)

German; head of government of GDR Mar.–Oct. 1990

The son of a lawyer, de Maiziere studied music and, after successfully pursuing this career, he gave it up to become a lawyer. An active evangelical Christian, he specialized in defending dissidents including Christians and those refusing to do military service. He joined the Christian Democratic Union (CDU) in 1957. The CDU was then a satellite of the SED. Once the party decided to break with the SED in November 1989 de Maiziere was elected its chairman. He was also elected deputy head of government in *Modrow's interim administration leading to the March 1990 election.

De Maiziere headed the Alliance for Germany at the first free elections held in the GDR in March 1990, when the Alliance won 47.9 per cent of the vote. De Maiziere then led the coalition government which negotiated with West Germany and France, the Soviet Union, the UK, and the USA, to restore Germany unity. Once unity was achieved on 3 October 1990, de Maiziere served as Minister for Special Assignments in the government of Helmut Kohl. Later he was forced to resign, because of accusations of having worked for *Mielke's secret police, the *Stasi*. He denied the accusations but left political life to return to his law practice.

Deng Xiaoping (Teng Hsiao-p'ing) (b. Sichuan Province, 24 Aug. 1904; d. 19 Feb. 1997)

Chinese; *de facto* leader of China 1978–97

Deng's political career is one of remarkable ups and downs. Initially a close comrade of *Mao Zedong, he was subsequently purged twice under Mao. However, he returned to take *de facto* control of the political structure and implement a series of radical reform in 1978. For much of the 1980s he was feted in the West as a great leader as he moved China away from its Maoist past to a more Western and market-orientated economic system, until his reputation became tarnished with the massacre of student demonstrators in Beijing in June 1989.

Deng was the youngest of a small group of young Communists who were sent on a work-study programme in France by the Communist International. Deng was prominent in the radical student and labour movement in Lyon, and with *Zhou Enlai recruited young Chinese in Europe to the Communist cause. Returning to China, Deng supported Mao's view that the peasantry were a positive revolutionary force, and was subsequently heavily criticized by Li Lisan—the first and mildest of his official condemnations. A veteran of the Long March, Deng also served as a political commissar in the second Field Army in his native south-west China.

After a brief period in charge of the south-west region after 1949, Deng was brought into the central political apparatus where he served as party secretary-general. Despite his impressive leadership credentials, Deng's rapid promotion to central leadership owed much to Mao's patronage. It is sometimes forgotten that Deng was once a very strong supporter of Mao, particularly during the formative years of the Great Leap Forward. However, when the Great Leap collapsed into the great famine, Deng changed his view, or at least changed his allegiances. Together with Liu Shaoqi and the economist *Chen Yun, Deng oversaw the retreat from the Great Leap from 1961 to 1966, and the reinstatement of more orthodox Leninist political and economic disciplines. Deng argued that if a policy was successful in generating economic recovery, then it should be accepted and not subjected to tests of political correctness. If market mechanisms helped bring about recovery, then market mechanisms were good. This was anathema for Mao, and the start of bitter conflict between the two.

Even though Mao, as chairman of the party, remained theoretically in control, he later claimed that Deng did not consult him once during this period, and that Deng would sit with his deaf ear to Mao at party meetings. Mao also suspected that Deng and Liu had deliberately obstructed his socialist education movement of 1962–4, and that these two men were the single biggest obstacle to the implementation of true (i.e. Maoist) socialist principles in China. Thus, when Mao launched the Cultural Revolution to purify the party of these heretical influences, Deng was designated as the second worst class enemy in the party (behind Liu Shaoqi).

Deng suffered massive humiliation and hardship during the Cultural Revolution, as did the rest of his family (his son, Deng Pufang, was paralysed by a 'fall' from a window). However, his treatment was partly tempered by Zhou Enlai's intervention, and Zhou played a leading role in ensuring Deng's rehabilitation in 1973. From 1973 to February 1976, Deng worked as the deputy to the ailing Premier Zhou Enlai, who saw Deng as a crucial counter-balance to the radical Maoist Gang of Four. The extent to which Deng owed his position to Zhou's patronage became clear in 1976. Once Zhou died in February, the left moved to oust Deng. When a spontaneous mass demonstration occurred in Tiananmen Square in April in support of Zhou (and by implication Deng), Deng was accused of orchestrating a counter-revolutionary movement. The demonstration was brutally suppressed, and for a second time in ten years, Deng was purged.

Deng found a safe haven in the south under the protection of the military leader, Wei Guoqing. After Hua Guofeng's succession to Mao, the clamour for Deng's rehabilitation grew ever louder. Whilst other leaders lobbied for Deng's return, Deng wrote an open letter to the Central Committee explaining that he only wanted to serve under Hua. On a popular level, the Democracy Wall movement in Beijing raised difficult questions about Hua's own Cultural Revolution record and called for a new polity. It is notable that once Deng returned to power he acted to weaken those forced that had helped his own rehabilitation—he reshuffled China's military leaders (including Wei Guoqing) to cut them off from their power bases, and closed down the Democracy Wall.

From 1978, Deng oversaw the radical reformation of the basis of the Chinese economy. For much of this period, Deng acted without any formal position of power. He instead acted as the crucial power broker behind the scenes, making and breaking factional alliances to maintain the reform momentum. Even his closest colleagues were dispensable if they got in the way of greater goals. Thus, Deng promoted both Hu Yaobang and Zhao Ziyang to central leadership, but allowed both men to fall from grace when their actions threatened party unity and undermined the reform process.

The fall of Zhao Ziyang in 1989 accompanied the Tiananmen massacre of 4 June. This event perhaps more than anything epitomized Deng's vision of reform in China. The whole point of reform was to bolster the party's grip on power. Economic reform was essential in that it increased the party's popularity, but political reform that threatened the party could not be countenanced. Those elements of Deng's leadership that the West so supported were part of the same strategy that resulted in the human rights abuses that the West so despised. The party's continued grip on power despite the problems generated by reform and events in the Soviet Union and Eastern Europe show that in his own terms, Deng's leadership has so far been a great success.

Denikin, Anton Ivanovich (b. 4 Dec. 1872; d. 8 Aug. 1947)

Russian; leader of White armies in the south 1918–20

Denikin was the son of a former serf who joined the Tsarist army at the age of 15. He served in the Russo-Japanese War and the First World War. He was critical of the incompetence and corruption at Nicholas II's court. After the February Revolution of 1917 he served the provisional government as commander first of the western then the south-western fronts. He took to arms against the Bolsheviks in 1918 as commander of the White 'Armed Forces of the South'. He initially had great success, advancing to within 250 miles of Moscow by the end of August 1919. But in December 1919 the Red Army defeated him at Orel and pushed his army back into the Caucasus, where it collapsed at the end of March 1920. Denikin was outnumbered by the Bolsheviks, who enjoyed superior communications. But he was also weakened by his determination to maintain the unity of the Russian empire, which meant he would not ally with the Ukrainians, Poles, or Caucasians. Denikin lived in France until 1945, when he settled in the United States.

Desai, Marorji (b. Bhadeli 29 Feb. 1896; d. 10 Apr. 1995)

Indian; Deputy Prime Minister and Minister of Finance 1967–9, Prime Minister 1977–9

Son of a schoolteacher, Desai was educated at Wilson College, Bombay where he obtained a B.Sc. in 1916. In 1918 he qualified for the Bombay Civil Service. He resigned from the civil service in 1930 to join M. K. *Gandhi's Salt *satyagraha*. He rose rapidly up the party machine under the patronage of Patel. From 1937 to 1939 he was

Minister of Agriculture and Revenue in the Congress ministry in Bombay. Following the Quit India Movement, Desai was jailed for thirty-four months.

After the elections in 1946 Desai rejoined the Bombay Congress ministry and became Home Minister, a position he held for six years. In 1952 he succeed B. G. Kher as Chief Minister of Bombay. Desai held this post until 1956 when he was elevated to Minister for Commerce and Industry (1956–8) and for Finance (1958–63). Under the Kamaraj plan Desai resigned to work for Congress party organization in Gujarat.

Denied the prime ministership in 1964 and 1966, Desai challenged Mrs *Gandhi for the leadership in 1967 and lost. He became Deputy Prime Minister and Minister of Finance but neither was comfortable with each other. In 1969 following the split in Congress he left the government.

Desai joined with the opposition in the campaign against Mrs Gandhi in 1975. During the State of Emergency, he spent eighteen months in jail, much of it in solitary confinement. He was released in January 1977 and became the world's oldest Prime Minister at the age of 81 when the Janata Dal came to power. Desai's main achievement was to dismantle the machinery of Emergency and to restore respect for the constitution. He shelved India's nuclear plans and made visits to Beijing and Moscow as well as hosting a visit by President Jimmy *Carter.

Desai was unable to keep the Janata coalition together. The government's declining fortunes were accompanied by caste wars and a police strike. In July 1979, after twenty-seven months in office, Desai resigned and was succeeded by Charan Singh.

Desai retired to Bombay and kept out of politics. In 1989 Pakistan presented him with its highest civilian honour, the Nishan-e-Pakistan in recognition of the 'golden and peaceful' period in relations between India and Pakistan while he was Prime Minister.

Desai was an austere individual who kept to a strict personal regime and was a vegetarian and teetotaller all his life as well as practising urine therapy. He was not a popular leader but was highly respected for his political integrity. In retirement he wrote a two-volume autobiography *The Story of My Life* (1982).

Deukmejian, George Courken (b. Menands, New York, 6 June 1928)

US; Governor of California 1983–91

An Armenian whose father was an oriental rug dealer, Deukmejian gained his education by working his way through Siena College, New York, and St John's College, Brooklyn, where he studied law. Deukmejian moved to California in 1955 following a spell in the army. He entered private law practice and entered politics in 1962 as a Republican state Assembly man for Long Beach. After serving four years in the Assembly (1962–6) he was elected to the state Senate where he rose to become leader of the Republican group. In 1978 he successfully ran for the post of Attorney-General, a position he had sought unsuccessfully in 1969.

During his period in state politics Deukmejian established a strongly conservative record on law and order and promoted a capital punishment bill which passed over Governor Pat *Brown's veto. He also gained support in sections of the business community by his attacks on regulation and his commitment to economic growth even at the expense of environmental concerns.

In 1981 he won the Republican gubernatorial primary and against the trend of the early 1980s went on in 1982 to beat Tom *Bradley narrowly in the general election. Deukmejian's period as Governor saw California hit by a financial crisis and the imposition of a freeze on appointment and spending cuts which hit the state's university network particularly hard. Yet Deukmejian did not raise taxes as the legislature wanted and his record impressed voters so that when he again faced Bradley in a gubernatorial race in 1986 he won overwhelmingly. Deukmejian left the governorship in 1991 and was succeeded by another Republican Pete *Wilson.

de Valera, Éamon (b. New York, 14 Oct. 1882; d. 29 Aug. 1975)

Irish; President of provisional government 1919–21, President of the Executive Council (premier) of the Irish Free State 1932–48 (renamed Taoiseach 1937), Taoiseach 1937–48, 1951–4, 1957–9, President of Republic of Ireland 1959–73

De Valera was born in the USA, the son of a Spanish emigrant father (who left his mother soon after de Valera's birth) and an Irish mother, who took him back, in infancy, to be brought up in Bruree, Co. Limerick. The obscurity of his origins and his aloof personality lent him a powerful mystique. A mathematician, de Valera joined the Gaelic League in 1908 and as a member of the Irish Volunteers commanded its 3rd Brigade at Boland's Mill during the Easter Rising of 1916. His death sentence was commuted in deference to his American birth; he was thus the senior participant in the Rising to survive. In 1917 he was elected Sinn Fein MP for Clare, assumed the presidency of Sinn Fein, and was elected president of the Volunteers (IRA). He was arrested in May 1918, and while he was held in Lincoln jail (till his escape in February 1919) four Irish constituencies returned him as an MP in the 1918 election. In April 1919 the abstentionist MPs, now constituting themselves the first Dáil, elected him its first President. He spent much of the ensuing period of the 'Anglo-Irish War' in the USA securing an external loan and working for recognition of the putative Republic. He remained in Dublin during the negotiations leading to the Anglo-Irish Treaty of December 1921, and then denounced the agreement, resigning his presidency of Sinn Fein and of the Dáil on its being narrowly ratified. He led the anti-treaty forces in the 1922–3 Civil War. He was imprisoned for a year in 1923–4, but led anti-treaty Sinn Fein in the 1923 general election to win 44 abstentionist seats (out of 153). Out of this he formed Fianna Fáil in 1926, and in 1927 led it into the Dáil, setting the oath of allegiance aside as 'an empty formula'. He became premier in 1932 after Fianna Fáil's electoral success. He was president of the Council of the League of Nations in 1932. As premier from 1932 to 1948 de Valera saw through a series of measures completing the transition from the Free State of the treaty to a *de facto* independent Irish Republic. These included establishing a new constitution, 1937, the return of the 'Treaty ports' in 1938, and maintaining Irish neutrality in the Second World War. He lost office in 1948 but later formed two more ministries before resigning in 1959 to contest, and win, the presidency of the Republic, which he held till 1973.

De Valera dominated post-independence Irish politics for forty years. His Ireland was conservative, Catholic, and inward looking. His aim was to complete the task of creating the Republic proclaimed in 1916, drawing on its unique Gaelic, nationalist, and Catholic heritage. He succeeded up to a point, but at two prices. First, the conflict over the treaty led to civil war and a lasting legacy of bitterness; second, his policy of pursuing an end to partition was contradicted by his republicanization of the south, which widened the Irish gulf.

Dewey, Thomas Edmund (b. Oswosso, Michigan, 24 Mar. 1902; d. 16 Mar. 1971)

US; Governor of New York 1943–55, Republican presidential candidate 1944, 1948

Born in Michigan and educated at the University of Michigan, he moved to New York to take his LLB at Columbia University. He spent the rest of his career in New York state. He practised law in New York city and in 1935 was appointed special prosecutor to investigate organized crime. He gained a reputation as a 'rackets buster', which won him prominence and enabled him to advance rapidly in his political career in the Republican Party in New York state. In 1942 he was elected governor of New York and was twice re-elected, in 1946 and in 1950. In 1944 he won the Republican nomination for president but lost to Franklin *Roosevelt. In 1948 he was again the Republican nominee for president but lost to Harry *Truman.

During his three terms as governor of New York, 1943–55, he was regarded as a moderate Republican. He developed the State University of New York, expanded the

New York state highway system, opposed racial discrimination in employment and housing and expanded New York state's unemployment and welfare system. In *The Case against the New Deal* (1940) he expounded his philosophy of moderate Republicanism, opposing the New Deal but favouring limited government intervention in social and economic affairs. In foreign policy he was a moderate internationalist. He supported Roosevelt's wartime policies and also the initiatives to involve the United States in international affairs after the Second World War, especially the United Nations, the Marshall Plan, and NATO. His standpoint as a moderate Republican who won acclaim as an effective governor of New York gave him an excellent prospect of winning the presidency. In 1944 Roosevelt's advantage of incumbency during wartime gave Dewey little chance of success. In 1948, however, he seemed virtually certain to defeat Truman in the presidential election. He chose Earl *Warren, the governor of California, as his vice-presidential candidate, forming a Republican ticket of the governors of the two largest states, both moderate Republicans. Truman's popularity had sunk to a low ebb, while the Democratic Party had split, with Henry *Wallace gaining liberal Democratic support running for President as a Progressive and Strom *Thurmond winning Southern Democratic support running as a Dixiecrat. Opinion polls unanimously predicted a Dewey victory by a comfortable margin, but in one of the greatest upsets in American political history, Truman won re-election. Dewey was an overconfident and bland campaigner, and compared unfavourably to the charismatic Roosevelt or the feisty Truman. More significantly, as the Democratic victory in the congressional elections in 1948 illustrated, the majority of the American people supported the party of the New Deal, which offered them greater security. rather than the Republican Party, which was still associated with the Depression. In retrospect, Dewey's prospects for victory in 1948 were poorer than they appeared at the time.

In 1952 Dewey supported Dwight D. *Eisenhower for the Republican nomination for president over Robert *Taft. Dewey thus had the satisfaction of the victory of a candidate of his political persuasion, namely, Eisenhower, who was a moderate Republican in domestic and foreign affairs, even if he himself never attained the presidency.

Diefenbaker, John George (b. Ontario, 18 Sept 1895; d. 16 Aug. 1979)

Canadian; Prime Minister 1957–63

Diefenbaker was born in Ontario although his boyhood and most of his life was spent in Saskatchewan. In his politics he exemplified the conservative populist loyalism of the prairie provinces. Educated at the University of Saskatchewan, he served with the Canadian army in France (1916–17) but was invalided home, and called to the Saskatchewan bar in 1919. After building up a considerable and lucrative law practice, he entered Canada's House of Commons in 1940 for Lake Centre, Saskatchewan, and became leader of the Progressive Conservatives in December 1956. In June 1957 he became Prime Minister of Canada, forming a minority government, when the Liberal Party was defeated after twenty-two years in office. Diefenbaker came to Ottawa profoundly suspicious of what he regarded as the near indelible pro-Liberal ('Grit') bias of the top levels of the federal bureaucracy and of the 'Pearsonalities', the admirers and acolytes of Lester *Pearson.

As Prime Minister he sought, though unsuccessfully, to reorientate Canadian trade by reducing its strong north-south bias (i.e. towards the United States) and to increase its transAtlantic dimensions, especially with Britain. In foreign policy he was envious of and sought to emulate Pearson's international reputation. Much to Harold *Macmillan's irritation, Diefenbaker played a clamorous role at Commonwealth Prime Ministers' conferences in 1961 and 1962, opposing the continued membership of an apartheid-practising South Africa in the association and criticizing Britain's application to join the European Common Market. His government also introduced a

Bill of Rights, enfranchised the native peoples, and attempted to promote the development of the Canadian North. In the general election of 1958 his party won a sweeping victory, but his popularity soon slumped and his inexperience and maladroitness in a badly divided government soon became clear to insiders. In 1963 the Liberals again took office.

In 1967 he was replaced as party leader by Robert Stanfield (b. 1914), but to his death he remained an influential figure, especially in legal, Progressive Conservative, and prairie province circles.

Dies, Martin (b. Colorado, Texas, 5 Nov. 1900; d. 14 Nov. 1972)

US; Member of the US House of Representatives 1930–44, Congressman-at-large for Texas 1952–9

Dies was the son of a Congressman and was educated at Wesley College, Greenville, the University of Texas, the Hickman School of Speech and Expression in Washington, DC, and National University.

Dies was elected to the House in 1930. Although he was initially a supporter of the New Deal, he became more critical of F. D. *Roosevelt's liberal initiatives, especially the regulation of the coal industry, minimum wage legislation, and measures supportive of organized labour.

Increasingly obsessed with the threat of Commmunist subversion, in 1938 Dies persuaded the House to set up a committee to investigate un-American activities under his chairmanship. Known from 1938 to 1945 as the Dies Committee, this committee (the House Committee on Un-American Activities or HUAC) became the primary instrument for probing Communist (and, to a lesser extent, Fascist) influence in the United States.

The committee's activities (which included inquiries into the Congress of Industrial Organizations and various New Deal agencies) gained Dies temporary national fame. But his attempt to exploit it failed miserably. He lost a Senate bid in 1941 and his cause proved difficult to promote in the midst of a war fought in alliance with the USSR. Dies retired from Congress in 1944 but returned to the House as Congressman-at-large for Texas in 1952. However, by then others had taken up the anti-Communist crusade and Dies was not reappointed to HUAC. He continued to promote anti-Communist legislative measures and to oppose liberal initiatives, especially in the field of civil rights. In 1957 he made a final attempt to enter the Senate but again failed.

In retirement Dies continued to lecture and publish extensively, mainly on the theme of anti-Communism.

Dimitrov, Georgi Mikhailovich (b. Pernik near Radomir, 18 June 1882; d. Moscow, 2 July 1949)

Bulgarian; head of the Comintern 1935–43, Bulgarian leader 1946–9

Dimitrov started his political career within the Bulgarian trade union movement, organizing strikes from 1905 onwards. In 1917 he became a Communist, helping to found the Bulgarian Communist Party (BCP) in 1919. In September 1923 he led an armed rising, which the government suppressed, and fled to Moscow. He worked for Comintern in Vienna and Berlin. In 1993 the Nazis arrested him on a secret mission to Berlin and charged him of complicity in the Reichstag fire. Dimitrov conducted his own defence and brilliantly outmanoeuvred his accusers, including Hermann *Göring. This won his acquittal and gave a fillip to the Communist cause throughout the world. Dimitrov returned to the Soviet Union, where he survived the Purges, helped by his friendship with *Stalin. From 1935 he served as the Secretary-General of the Comintern, until Stalin disbanded it in 1943.

Dimitrov returned to Bulgaria in 1945. In October 1946 he became Prime Minister after rigged elections which established Communist rule. He introduced a ruthless programme of Stalinization. Stalin reprimanded him for following too independent a foreign policy, but he rallied behind the Soviet Union after the Stalin–*Tito split in 1948. He died in Moscow in July 1949.

Dinkins, David (b. Trenton, New Jersey, 10 July 1927)

US; member of the New York State Legislature 1965–7, Mayor of New York City 1990–4

The son of a barber, Dinkins graduated BA from Howard University, Washington, in 1950. After service in the US Marines he returned to his studies in 1953, graduated from Brooklyn Law School in 1956, and joined a Harlem law firm that same year. Thereafter he combined practising law with active involvement in New York's Democratic politics. Gaining his first electoral office in 1965 he served briefly in the New York State Assembly. In 1967 reapportionment denied him the opportunity of standing for a second term. He turned instead to serving in appointed offices in City Hall, including ten years as city clerk, 1975–85. Returning to electoral office in 1985 he became president of Manhattan. Five years later he attracted national and international attention by becoming New York's first black mayor. He achieved a surprise victory in the Democratic primary defeating the sitting tenant, the charismatic Ed Koch, running for an unprecedented fourth term.

Dinkins's leadership style was low key. He was a consummate organization man, skilled in brokering interests and building coalitions. Dubbed 'Mr Nice Guy' and 'Mr Softie', critics doubted he would be tough enough for the rough and tumble of New York City politics. After a turbulent four years in office grappling with the city's perennial problems of crime, corruption, racial tension, homelessness, Aids, and urban decay, his critics seemed to be vindicated. In 1994 he narrowly lost the mayoralty to his former Republican rival, Rudolph Guiliani.

Dirksen, Everett McKinley (b. Pekin, Illinois, 4 Jan. 1896; d. 7 Sept. 1969)

US; Member of the US House of Representatives 1933–48, US Senator 1950–69

Dirksen's parents were German and he grew up in an Illinois farming community. Although enrolled at the University of Minnesota, Dirksen left before finishing his degree, but he later obtained a law degree through night school. After a brief spell in the army in the First World War, Dirksen went into business in Illinois, eventually starting with his brothers a successful bakery. In 1927 he was elected City Commissioner of Finance and developed political ambitions. In 1932 he successfully ran for the House of Representatives having dislodged the incumbent Republican in the primary. In Congress he carefully steered a line between rejecting the New Deal measures of F. D. *Roosevelt and over-enthusiastic endorsement of them. Initially an isolationist, he became more of an internationalist as the Second World War progressed, though he remained suspicious of foreign aid and international entanglements. Illness forced Dirksen to retire at the end of 1948 but he returned to the Congress in 1950 as a Senator.

In the early 1950s Dirksen's loyalty was to Robert *Taft, whom he supported for the presidential nomination in 1952, and it was not until after *Eisenhower's re-election in 1956 that Dirksen closed the gap between himself and the Republican president. In 1959 Dirksen was elected Republican leader of the Senate and thereafter tried to adopt a national rather than purely partisan perspective. He exercised a powerful influence, often in support of measures sought by Democratic presidents *Kennedy and *Johnson. Party unity was always a major consideration for Dirksen and he rallied the party behind *Goldwater in 1964 and *Nixon in 1968.

A shrewd tactician and a good committee man, Dirksen was sometimes mocked for his tendency to change his mind on crucial issues, such as the Civil Rights Act of

1964 (he initially opposed it and then urged support of it). He was also criticized for lacking vision and, as the 1960s progressed, his influence declined and he became increasingly out of touch with the younger more liberal elements in his party. Despite periods of illness, his death was unexpected and he was succeeded as Republican Senate leader by the moderate Hugh *Scott.

Djilas, Milovan (b. Podbivice, Montenegro, 12 June 1911; d. Belgrade, 20 Apr. 1995)
Montenegrin Serb; Secretary of Central Committee of Yugoslav Communist Party heading Propaganda Department 1948–54

After studying literature and law at Belgrade University Djilas became a Communist in 1932 and was imprisoned until 1936 for taking part in demonstrations against King Alexander. When *Tito returned to Yugoslavia to head the Communist Party in 1937 Djilas became one of his closest friends and aides, joining the Central Committee in 1938 and the Politbureau in 1940. He played a prominent role in organizing partisan forces during the War. In 1948 he was made a Secretary of the Central Committee and head of its Propaganda Department, his best-known political role. Initially he was responsible for imposing a ruthless cultural dictatorship, but after the break with *Stalin in 1948 he played a major part in denouncing Stalinism, encouraging greater freedom of literary expression and creating the new ideology of 'self-management'. In 1953 he was made Vice-Premier and Speaker of the parliament, but in January 1954, after publishing articles arguing for a relaxation of party discipline and criticizing the lifestyle of party leaders, he was deprived of all his offices and expelled from the party. He was imprisoned after a secret trial in 1956 for three years, during which time his best-known book *The New Class* was published in New York, for which he was given a further sentence. In 1961 he was released on parole but in 1962 was imprisoned once more for the US publication of *Conversations with Stalin*. Released in 1966 he was allowed to travel abroad for two years, but his increasingly anti-Communist pronouncements (as in *The Unperfect Society*) led to a permanent travel and publication ban. He became a non-person and there was no mention of his name or work in public. He was an embarrassment to the Yugoslav authorities, so East–West negotiations covered cases of human rights abuses. Despite this he published abroad his memoirs and a biography of Tito. Rehabilitated in 1989, he supported the liberal opposition to the Serbian leader *Milosevic. Djilas was famous more as a literary than a political figure, and as a political prisoner.

Dobrynin, Anatoly Fedorovich (b. 16 Nov. 1919)
Russian; Soviet ambassador to the United States 1961–85

Dobrynin joined the Soviet diplomatic corps in 1946 and his first posting abroad was to the UN secretariat, where he worked from 1957 to 1960. From February 1960 to December 1961 he was head of the American Department of the Soviet Ministry of Foreign Affairs. There followed a post as Soviet ambassador to the United States, where he remained until 1986. Dobrynin played an important role in the Cuban Missile Crisis. His abilities were recognized by the Soviet leadership, which made him a candidate member of the Politburo in 1966, and full member in 1971. Dobrynin's career continued to prosper after 1985 under *Gorbachev. In 1986 he played a pivotal role in the formulation of Soviet foreign policy when he was made secretary of the International Department of the Central Committee. This was the first time that Dobrynin had served in the party apparatus, and his appointment represented the relatively low priority which Gorbachev placed on ideology in foreign policy. Dobrynin retired from the Central Committee at the end of 1988, but continued as adviser to the presidency.

Dole, Robert J. (b. Russell, Kansas, 22 July 1923)

US; US Senator 1966– , Senate majority leader 1985–6, 1995– , Republican presidential candidate 1996

In the Second World War Dole served in Italy, where he was wounded, leaving him with permanent injuries including a withered arm. After the war, he attended the University of Kansas and Washburn University. He served in the Kansas House of Representatives 1951–3, and was County Attorney for Russell County, Kansas, 1953–9. He was elected to the US House of Representatives in 1960 and served four terms. In 1968 he was elected to the Senate and was re-elected in 1974, 1978, 1986, and 1992. In 1976 he was selected by President *Ford as the vice-presidential candidate of the Republican Party. He performed poorly in the campaign, coming across as acerbic, especially in a debate with the Democratic vice-presidential nominee, Walter *Mondale. His performance was regarded as one reason for the loss by a narrow margin of the Ford–Dole ticket to the victorious Carter-Mondale Democratic ticket. Nevertheless, he was highly regarded for his legislative skill in Congress and rose to prominence in the Republican Party. A bid for the Republican nomination for president in 1980 was unsuccessful, but in 1985 he became Senate Majority Leader. With the loss of control of the Senate by the Republicans as a result of the 1986 elections he became minority leader, until as a result of the Republican triumph in the 1994 Senate elections he became Senate majority leader again in 1995. In 1988 he sought the Republican nomination for president but lost to George *Bush. In 1996 his third bid for the Republican nomination for President met with success.

He held moderately conservative views on most issues. But his reputation was established above all as a pragmatic political fixer. With Republican victory in the 1994 congressional elections, he attempted to steer through the Senate the measures proposed in the Contract with America in the campaign in 1994. With a Democrat in the White House, however, gridlock developed over such matters as the budget, Medicare reform, and term limits.

Dole's high reputation in the halls of Congress was not matched by success as a campaigner, where he appeared too much as a Washington insider who lacked any overall vision and who spoke in flat, monotonous tones, with a streak of mean-spiritedness. In 1996 he suffered also from the disadvantage that at the age of 73, he appeared to be too old.

Doriot, Jacques (b. 26 Sept. 1898; d. Germany, 23 Feb. 1945)

French; Communist and Fascist leader

Doriot came from a working-class background, fought in the latter stages of the First World War, and in 1920 flung himself into the revolutionary politics of the newly formed Communist Party. Physically courageous and an aggressive speaker, imprisoned several times for his anti-colonial activities, he rose rapidly through the Communist hierarchy. He was elected to the Chamber of Deputies in 1924 and subsequently established a power base as deputy mayor of the working-class Paris suburb of Saint-Denis. His independence of judgement probably explains why he failed to become party leader in the early 1930s; and in 1934 he left the Communist Party when it failed to respond to the resurgence of mass anti-regime movements of the right. The irony is that within three years he was founder and leader of just such a movement, the Parti Populaire Français. The PPF was based on profound anti-Communism, and it was this that led Doriot in 1940 to offer his support to *Pétain. Regarded as a dangerous revolutionary by the bourgeois traditionalists of Vichy, he turned himself into a fanatical supporter of the Nazi vision of a New Europe and saw the PPF as its shock troops. He was a founder member of the Legion of Volunteers against Bolshevism, and donned a German uniform to fight on the eastern front. In 1944 he went to Germany and was killed in 1945 when the car he was travelling in was machine gunned by Allied planes.

Doriot's war experiences left him with a loathing of the established political and social order which led him to try one and then the other of the revolutionary ideologies which rejected it. Regarded as the most authentically Fascist of France's right-wing opponents of Republican democracy, he remains a pariah figure.

Douglas, Helen Gahagan (b. Boonton, New Jersey, 25 Nov. 1900; d. 28 June 1980)
US; member of the US House of Representatives 1944–51

Douglas's father was a wealthy engineer and she grew up in Brooklyn. Educated at Barnard College, she pursued her ambition to become an actress by appearing in plays even during her college years. After Barnard she devoted herself to acting and appeared in a number of theatre and opera productions under the name Helen Gahagan between 1922 and 1938.

Douglas became active in politics after moving from New York to Los Angeles. A supporter of the New Deal, in California she took up a number of liberal causes including environmentalism, civil rights, and the cause of labour. She also served in a number of party posts, including Democratic National committeewoman (1940–4) and vice-chairman of the Democratic state central committee, as well as on the advisory committee of the Works Progress Administration. Her celebrity status enhanced her political appeal and in 1944 she was elected to the House of Representatives for the California 14th District and secured re-election in 1946 and 1948. While in Congress she highlighted those causes which she had championed earlier and was a strong supporter of Franklin *Roosevelt's and Harry *Truman's domestic policies. On foreign policy issues Douglas resisted what she saw as anti-Communist paranoia—by voting against the reauthorization of the House Un-American Activities Committee and attempting to substitute United Nations action for American intervention against Communism in Europe.

In 1950 Douglas ran for the Senate against an incumbent Senator (Sheridan Downey), associated with oil interests, and Richard *Nixon the Republican candidate. Douglas won the primary but lost the general election as a result of a vicious campaign in which Nixon implied that Douglas was a fellow-traveller if not an outright Communist, accusations made more damaging in the light of the North Korean attack on South Korea in June 1950. The tactics used by Nixion earned him the label 'tricky Dick', although in fact both Douglas and Nixon were criticized for their campaign propaganda. Douglas did not seek further elective office but continued to write and lecture. She was appointed by Lyndon *Johnson as special ambassador at the inauguration of President Tubman of Liberia in 1964.

Douglas-Home, Alexander **(Alec)** Frederick (b. London, 2 July 1903; d. 5 Oct. 1995)
British; Foreign Secretary 1960–3, 1970–4, Prime Minister 1963–64; 14th Earl of Home 1951–63, Kt. 1962, Baron (life peer) 1974

Educated at Eton and Christ Church, Oxford, Douglas-Home's career was one of public service. He was elected as Conservative MP for Lanark in 1931 at the age of 28 and, apart from a five-year period, was to spend the rest of his life in parliament. He was appointed parliamentary private secretary to Neville *Chamberlain in 1935, accompanied Chamberlain to Munich, and served him until his resignation in 1940. He then spent part of the war years in plaster, part of the time lying flat on his back, the result of a spinal operation. In 1945, he served briefly as Under-Secretary at the Foreign Office in *Churchill's caretaker government. He lost his seat in the Labour landslide of 1945 but won it back in 1950. The following year he succeeded his father to the earldom and became the 14th Earl of Home.

During thirteen years of Conservative government, he rose from the post of Minister of State at the Scottish Office to Prime Minister. After his stint as Minister of State (1951–5) he joined the Cabinet as Secretary of State for Commonwealth Relations and served concurrently for three years as Lord President of the Council. In 1960 he was *Macmillan's choice as Foreign Secretary. The choice of a peer proved controversial, but the post was the one that he most enjoyed. In 1963, he was a surprise successor to Macmillan as Prime Minister, after Macmillan switched his support from Quintin Hogg to him. He renounced his title and was returned to the House of Commons in a by-election as MP for Kinross for West Perthshire. His 'emergence' proved controversial and, although he was able to form a Cabinet, two members of Macmillan's Cabinet refused to serve under him.

His premiership was short-lived. Overshadowed by a young and effective leader of the Opposition, he had little time to establish himself before calling a general election. In the 1964 general election, he fought well in a difficult situation. Though the party lost the election by a narrow margin, it was nonetheless lost. His period as leader of the Opposition was not a happy one and was marked by backbench criticism. The following year he resigned, his successor being elected by a process that he had initiated and approved. In many respects, his most successful period of public service was yet to come. He served as Foreign Secretary throughout the period of Edward *Heath's government, handling the post with confidence and aplomb.

In 1974 he returned to the House of Lords with a life peerage and was a regular attender for almost twenty years until prevented from further attendance by a stroke. He died peacefully in October 1995 at the age of 93.

An enormously popular figure, he was regarded as a gentleman in politics. He was also a true Tory, always recognizing that politics was important but not the only important thing in life.

Doumergue, Gaston (b. Aigues Vives, Aug. 1863; d. 18 June 1937)
French; President of the Republic 1924–31, Prime Minister 1913, 1934

Born in 1863, Doumergue studied law and became a colonial magistrate before being elected to the Chamber of Deputies. A moderate Radical, he enjoyed a reasonally successful career in government before the First World War and then settled comfortably into the role of regime dignitary. His moderation and respect for constitutional proprieties made him an attractive candidate for the presidency when the right-wing incumbent *Millerand was forced to resign after the victory of the Socialist-Radical coalition in the 1924 elections. Doumergue was an outstandingly successful President for a political system which expected its head of state to behave like a constitutional monarch and allowed him to exercise surreptitious political influence. Jovial, shrewd, reliable, he appealed to the democratic left and reassured the middle classes. The national popularity he gained as President explains why his successor, *Lebrun, invited him to take over the reins of government in the crisis circumstances created by the riots of 6 February 1934. Doumergue formed a government of national unity, which included Marshal *Pétain. As Prime Minister, he offered no solution to the economic problems facing France and embarked instead on a programme of constitutional reform designed to strengthen the Executive. In so doing, he ignited the fears of those who regarded any attempt to constrain the powers of parliament as an assault on the principles of Republican democracy. By November 1934 his usefulness to the system parties of the Third Republic was at an end. Broadcasts to the nation, modelled on *Roosevelt's fireside chats, allowed the political parties to accuse him of incipient Fascism. His coalition government fell apart and he was compelled to resign.

Drees, Willem (b. Amsterdam, 5 July 1886; d. The Hague, 14 May 1988)
Dutch; Prime Minister 1948–58

While attending secondary school Drees became an active practitioner of a new shorthand method developed by A. W. Groote. After serving three years as a bank clerk, he became a professional stenographer reporting for municipal councils and professional associations. He was an official parliamentary stenographer from 1906 to 1919, when he was appointed Alderman (*Wethouder*) of the City of The Hague (1919–33). In this office he enjoyed great prestige, as one of the great inter-war 'municipal socialists'.

Drees had joined the Social Democratic Party (SDAP) in 1904. He became chairman of local party organization in The Hague (serving with a short intermission from 1911 until 1931). In 1913 he was elected a local councillor in The Hague, followed by election in 1919 also as member of the Council of the Province of Southern Holland (1919–41). He became a member of the National Executive of the SDAP in 1927, was elected to the Lower House in 1933, and became leader of the parliamentary party in 1939 when two Socialists became Cabinet ministers for the first time in Dutch history.

During the German occupation he was taken hostage in Buchenwald in October 1940. Freed one year later, he played a prominent role, as vice-chairman and acting chairman of the illegal Executive Committee of the SDAP, and as a prominent participant in secret interparty consultations. In 1944 he became chairman of the Contact Commissie van de Illegaliteit and a member of the College van Vertrouwensmannen which the London government in exile charged with the preparation of steps to be taken at the time of liberation. He was invited by Queen Wilhelmina to form the first post-war Cabinet, together with Willem Schermerhorn. Drees became Minister of Social Affairs (1945–8). His temporary Old Age Pensions Act (1947) earned him nationwide popularity. Between 1948 and 1958 he presided as Prime Minister over four Cabinets consisting of the transformed Dutch Labour Party (PvdA), the Catholic KVP, and two other parties.

Drees's period in office saw at least four major political developments: the traumas of decolonization, economic reconstruction, the beginnings of a welfare state, and international integration and co-operation, including the formation of Benelux, the OEEC, NATO, the ECSC, and the EEC. When his Cabinet broke up in December 1958, he was appointed to the honorary position of *Minister van Staat*. The Socialist PvdA appointed him a member of its Executive Council for life in 1959. Due to impaired hearing he stopped attending its meetings in 1966. He strongly disagreed with New Left tendencies in the membership and strategies of the Dutch Labour Party. He eventually gave up membership of a party he had served for close to sixty-seven years. He remained a very active observer of Dutch politics, publishing a substantial number of books, articles, etc. until the age of 97.

Dubček, Alexander (b. Uhrovec, western Slovakia, 27 Nov. 1921; d. Prague, 7 Nov. 1992)

Slovak; leader of the Slovak Communist Party 1963–8, leader of the Czechoslovak Party 1968–9.

The son of a Communist carpenter, Dubček spent his childhood from 1925 to 1938 in the Soviet Union. He joined the illegal Slovak Communist Party in 1939. In August 1944 he participated in the Slovak National Uprising and was wounded. Until 1949 Dubček held a variety of menial and factory jobs. He then entered the party apparatus full-time, working in Trenčin, and was appointed to the Slovak Central Committee in 1951. Early in 1953 he was promoted to post of regional secretary of the Banská Bystrica area in central Slovakia. In 1958 he was made regional secretary for Bratislava and member of the Central Committee of the Czechoslovak Party. In 1960 he made his only trip to the West, visiting Finland. In June 1960 he became a secretary of the Central Committee of the Czechoslovak Party and entered the Czechoslovak Party Presidium in 1963. In May 1963 he replaced Karol Bacílek as

Slovak Party leader, defeating *Novotný's candidate, Michal Chudík. In June 1966 Chudík and Novotný failed to oust Dubček from leadership of the Slovak Party. In October 1967 Dubček led the revolt against Novotný of reformists and Slovak nationalists within the Czechoslovak Central Committee and replaced Novotný as First Secretary of the Czechoslovak Party in January 1968. Impelled by economic crisis and popular expectations, Dubček's regime enacted a series of far-reaching measures intended to create 'socialism with a human face'. The culmination was the 'Action Programme' of April 1968, by which the party announced reforms including basic civil rights, an independent judiciary, and economic decentralization. From 29 July to 2 August Dubček met the Soviet leaders at Čierna-nad-Tisou in Slovakia. He promised to maintain the one-party system and to keep Czechoslovakia within the Warsaw Pact. On the night of 20–1 August 1968 the forces of the Warsaw Pact intervened in Czechoslovakia. Dubček and five other leaders were arrested and taken to Moscow, but were soon returned to Prague. In 1969 *Husák replaced Dubček as party leader and he became President of the Federal Assembly. In 1970 he was removed from office and expelled from the party. From then until 1989 he worked as a forest warden in Slovakia. He sided with the democratic opposition during the 'Velvet Revolution' of 1989 which brought down the Communist regime in Czechoslovakia, but did not play a significant political role thereafter. He died after a car crash in 1992.

Duclos, Jacques (b. Louey-par-Juillan, 2 Oct. 1896; d. 25 Apr. 1975)
French; presidential candidate 1969

Brought up in a single-parent family by his mother in a strictly religious atmosphere, Duclos became an apprentice pastry cook at the age of 12 and was an adept at this profession before being mobilized in 1915 (and participating in the battle of Verdun). He was taken prisoner in 1917, but had been profoundly marked by the war and took to politics on his release. He quickly associated with the extreme left and then with the Communist Party after the Congress of Tours in 1920. He was an early recruit to the Bolshevik School in Moscow and rose with *Stalin and Stalin's French representative (*Thorez) and was an adept at sectarian actions (to the extent that he was once condemned to forty-seven years in prison and fled the country). Duclos was a Comintern agent in Spain and ran the closely supervised Information Section of the International. He went underground in 1939 when the French Party was outlawed and, with Thorez in Moscow, ran the PCF from Brussels. He was in close contact with Moscow throughout the war and as such the key Communist in France (with Tillon and Frachon he ran the cadres). After the war Duclos stood in for Thorez during his many absences and was sent to receive the dressing-down from the Soviets at the founding meeting of Cominform in September 1947. He was instrumental in purging the Resistance leaders from the PCF. During the anti-American Ridgeway riots of 1952, Duclos was incautious and was picked up by the police, who searched him on the ridiculous pretext that two dead pigeons were meant for communication with Moscow. Notes were discovered but by feigning a diabetic fit he swallowed some others. He then backed Thorez's resistance to de-Stalinization but his influence began to wane as *Khrushchev's power waned. By 1964 he was out of favour. However the change in Soviet leadership brought him back into internal councils and he was a prime force in the rise of *Marchais. He ran as Communist presidential candidate in 1969 and against hopeless odds polled a creditable 21.5 per cent. No picture of the Communist Party leadership of the 1940s and 1950s was complete without the toothy, diminutive figure of the avuncular looking Duclos. He was in reality glacial, hard-line, and sarcastic, but an effective autodidact. Duclos was awarded the Order of Lenin in 1971 but the real activity and influence of this shadowy figure in French and international Communism may never be fully known.

Dukakis, Michael Stanley (b. Brookline, Massachusetts, 3 Nov. 1933)

US; member of Massachusetts House of Representatives 1963–70, Governor of Massachusetts 1975–9, 1983–91, Democratic presidential nominee 1988

The son of Greek immigrant parents (his father was a doctor and his mother a schoolteacher), Dukakis graduated BA from Swarthmore College 1955. After two year's military service with the US army in Korea he returned to his studies in 1957 and graduated LLB from Harvard Law School in 1960. He was called to the bar in Massachusetts that same year and began to practise law in Boston 1960–74. A Democrat, he embarked on his political career in 1962 when he was elected to the lower house of the Massachusetts State Legislature. In 1970 he ran unsuccessfully for the office of Lieutenant-Governor. Already combining a career in law and politics, he added a further string to his bow, 1971–3, by presenting a weekly television news programme, *The Advocates*. He gained election to the state governorship in 1975, but in 1979 returned to Harvard in the role of Director of Intergovernmental Studies in the Kennedy School of Government, when he failed to secure the Massachusetts governorship for a second term. This did not mark the end of his political career. He regained the governorship in 1983 and in 1988 he successfully competed against Jesse *Jackson and Al *Gore for the Democratic Party nomination for the presidency.

Dukakis is described by his critics as an arrogant technocrat who possesses an analytical mind but lacks the passion and vision needed for leadership. His first term as governor was marred by an autocratic style of administration. He set about cleaning up the old political machine in Boston, a course of action almost guaranteed to make enemies. He was accused of being ruthless and insensitive to former allies who had outlived their usefulness. The interlude at Harvard gave him time for reflection. When seeking to regain the governorship in 1983 he promised a more consensual approach if re-elected. His second period in office coincided with the Massachusetts economic miracle of the mid-1980s. Dukakis was the beneficiary of this economic prosperity. He was returned to office with an increased majority in 1986. After receiving the Democratic nomination in 1988 he managed to transform a huge lead in the opinion polls to a landslide defeat. The *Bush camp succeeded in burdening Dukakis with the 'l-word' image. A moderate in terms of social reform, he failed to either clearly embrace or repudiate the liberal label. This left voters confused and unwilling to support him on polling day. The result appears to have drawn a line under Dukakis's career in national politics. The downturn in the Massachusetts economic boom discouraged him from seeking a further term as governor in 1990 and he returned instead to an academic career.

Dulles, John Foster (b. Washington, DC, 25 Feb. 1888; d. 24 May 1959)

US; Secretary of State 1952–9

The son of a Presbyterian minister, Dulles graduated BA from Princeton in 1908, attended the Sorbonne (Paris) for a year, and then graduated LLB from George Washington University in 1911. That same year he began practising law in New York. He served as a captain, and then major, in the US army during the early years of the First World War, and as a member of the American Commission to Negotiate Peace, 1918–19. He briefly experienced political office when, in 1949, he was appointed to complete the term of the late Senator Wagner of New York. His bid for re-election was unsuccessful.

Dulles is best known for his six years' service as Secretary of State in the *Eisenhower administration. Few secretaries can claim to have had a more thorough preparation for office. Foreign policy was in his blood. One grandfather had been Secretary of State under Harrison, and an uncle had served in the same post under *Wilson. Dulles himself had gained early experience in foreign affairs as a member of the American delegation at Versailles in 1918, as a consultant to the US delegation to the San Francisco Conference, 1945, which set up the United Nations, and as acting chairman of the US delegation to the United Nations General Assembly in 1948. He had also served as an adviser to the Secretary of State on various foreign visits, 1947–50 and, in 1950, had been appointed by *Truman to negotiate peace with Japan. Eisenhower described him as the greatest Secretary of State he had ever known and reputedly considered creating a new post—First Secretary to the Government—for Dulles, a post which he already occupied in fact if not in name.

Dulles was a staunch anti-Communist. He believed that freedom would eventually triumph within the Communist empire if the West stood firm. He did not favour intervention for liberation but did favour a policy of deterrence through the threat of mass retaliation. Dulles was known for his reluctance to delegate and this was sometimes a source of misunderstandings arising from poor communications. This is offered by some as an explanation for the rift in Anglo-American relations during the Suez crisis in 1956.

Dulles left office on health grounds two months before his death. He is the author of two books: *War, Peace and Change* (1939); *War or Peace* (1950).

Duvalier, François ('Papa Doc') (b. Port-au-Prince, 14 Apr. 1907; d. 21 Apr. 1971)
Haitian; President 1957–71

The son of a teacher, Duvalier trained as a doctor and worked in the Haitian countryside among poor rural communities. Hostile to the US occupation of Haiti (1915–34), he joined the *Griots*, a group of black nationalist intellectuals, who formulated the theory of *noirisme*, celebrating Haiti's African culture. He joined the *noiriste* Mouvement Ouvrier-Paysan (MOP) and was appointed Minister of Health and Labour in 1949 by President Dumarsais Estimé. When Estimé was overthrown in 1950 Duvalier went underground.

Duvalier re-emerged as the successful presidential candidate in the 1957 elections, defeating the wealthy mulatto businessman, Louis Déjoie in what many viewed as army-controlled elections. But Duvalier was by no means a pawn of the traditionally powerful Haitian military. He swiftly curtailed their influence and built a paramilitary counterweight, the Volontaires de la Sécurité Nationale (known popularly as the Tontons Macoutes), as a private militia. Using a mix of mystic populism and terror, he confronted and subdued all of Haiti's main power brokers—the mulatto business community, the Catholic church, and the military. He also antagonized the neighbouring Dominican Republic and successive US presidents, causing Washington to cut off aid in 1963.

Human rights abuses were commonplace under Papa Doc (a name affectionately used by his supporters), and several thousand opponents were tortured and murdered. Haiti, already the poorest state in the Americas, became poorer still, shunned by the international community. In 1964 Duvalier declared himself President for Life, having survived a number of invasion and coup attempts.

Yet Duvalier also enjoyed significant support among Haiti's majority black rural population who saw in him a champion of their claims against the historically dominant mulatto élite. During his fourteen years in power he created a substantial black middle class, mainly through government patronage and corruption.

In 1971 Duvalier died, having first named his son, Jean-Claude Duvalier ('Baby Doc') as his successor. His reign will be remembered as one of the worst periods in Haiti's troubled history, when the country was memorably described by Graham Greene as a 'nightmare republic'.

Dzerzhinsky (Dzierżyński), Feliks Edmundovich (b. Poland, 12 Sept. 1877; d. Moscow, 20 July 1926)
Polish; Head of the Bolshevik secret police 1917–26

Dzerzhinsky was born in Russian Poland into a family of gentry and intelligentsia. As a boy he hoped to become a Catholic priest before converting to Marxism. In 1896 he joined the Lithuanian Social Democratic Party, working as a revolutionary agitator among the workers, and was regularly imprisoned. In 1900 he was a founding member of the Social Democratic Party of the Kingdom of Poland (SKDPiL). The SKDPiL opposed nationalism and stood for close co-operation with the Russian Marxists.

After the February Revolution of 1917, Dzerzhinsky joined the Bolshevik Party and became the first head of *Lenin's political police (known as the Cheka from 1917 to 1922, and the OGPU from 1923 to 1934). The KGB regarded him as its founding father. He was a member of the Central Committee of the Bolshevik Party from 1917. From 1921 to 1924 he was People's Commissar for Transport and from 1924 to 1926 was Chairman of the Supreme Council of the National Economy (VSNKh). Both these posts in the economic sector were closely associated with the political police and its broader brief of maintaining order. Dzerzhinsky showed a good understanding of economic problems. He was a supporter of the New Economic Policy after 1921, which meant the maintenance of broad sectors of the market economy and sensitivity to the economic needs of the peasantry. In 1924 he was made a member of the Politburo. Dzerzhinsky died of a heart attack in 1926 while delivering a ferocious attack on the Bolshevik's enemies at a meeting of the Central Committee. He was remembered not only for his ability but also as the 'Iron Feliks', an uncompromising man with an almost superhuman capacity for work. Dzerzhinsky became a hallowed symbol of the revolution in the Soviet Union.

Eastland, James Oliver (b. Doddsville, Mississippi, 28 Nov. 1904; d. 19 Feb. 1986)
US; member of the Mississippi State Legislature 1929–32; US Senator 1940–78

Born into a wealthy cotton plantation family, James Eastland was very much a product of the Old South. He grew up in Forest near Jackson, Mississippi, and attended the University of Mississippi, Vanderbilt University, and the University of Alabama; he was called to the Mississippi bar in 1927. In 1928 he was elected to the State Legislature (where he served until 1932) and thus began a lifelong career in politics in which he sought to defend the southern way of life, and especially segregation, loyalties which caused him to bolt the Democratic ticket for the Dixiecrat Party in 1948.

Appointed to the Senate in 1941 after the death of Pat Harrison, Eastland was very much part of the group of Southern Democrats whose seniority in Congress brought them immense authority despite their increasing isolation from the mainstream of the Democratic Party. Eastland rose to the powerful position of chairman of the Judiciary Committee, a position he held for twenty-two years. From this vantage point he could block civil rights initiatives and, because all federal judicial nominations required ratification by the Committee, could impede confirmation of judges whose philosophy or politics seemed too liberal. Given the growing role of the courts in the process of desegregation, Eastland's role was crucial. He was highly critical of both the landmark *Brown* v. *Board of Education* decision of 1954 and its author, Chief Justice Earl *Warren. (Eastland supported Mississippi Governor Ross Barnett in his efforts to prevent the integration of the University of Mississippi.) Yet Eastland was a procedurally fair Judiciary Committee chairman. He scrupulously observed the conventions of senatorial courtesy and used his power pragmatically. Thus, although he held up President *Kennedy's nomination of the black liberal Thurgood Marshall to the Court of Appeals in 1961–2, he ensured that his agreement to the nomination, when finally given, was in exchange for the nomination of a Mississippi friend to the bench.

Eastland was also a violent foe of Communism and served for a time as the chairman of the Internal Security Subcommittee. Part of his opposition to the civil rights movement of the 1960s was a result of his belief that it had been taken over by Communists.

Eastland's opposition to civil rights and desegregation made the passage of Lyndon *Johnson's Great Society programme problematic. Ultimately, however, Johnson and the Senate leadership were able to bypass the Judiciary Committee. Much of this legislation, such as the Civil Rights Act of 1964 and the Voting Rights Act of 1965, eroded Eastland's power. Blacks began to vote in the South and Eastland found he could no longer appeal to this new constituency. Other social and political changes affected the power of southern committee chairmen so that, by the 1970s, Eastland had ceded a substantial amount of influence to subcommittee chairs. Despite his long association with support of segregation, Eastland made friends with traditional liberal Democrats such as Hubert *Humphrey. The changing character of Southern politics made Eastland an anomaly and he retired from the Senate in 1978.

Ebert, Friedrich (b. Heidelberg, 4 Feb. 1871; d. 28 Feb. 1925)
German; President 1919–25, Chancellor 1918–19, SPD leader, 1913–19

Ebert's death in 1925 was a devastating blow to the Weimar Republic. His successor was Field Marshal von *Hindenburg, the man who appointed *Hitler Chancellor in

1933. From 1918 until his death Ebert attempted to keep Germany on a democratic path.

Born into a working-class family, Ebert worked as a saddler but was victimized for his trade union activities. Later he worked as a publican before becoming a journalist for the Social Democratic Party (SPD). In Bremen, where he led the SPD, he was a member of the city council from 1900. In 1912 he was elected to the Reichstag and, on the death of *Bebel in 1913, was elected one of the party's two chairmen. By then the SPD was the largest party in Germany, having secured 34.8 per cent of the vote in 1912, but it was regarded as not fit to govern by the propertied classes.

At the outbreak of war in 1914 Ebert helped to persuade his colleagues to vote with the government for the war credits, which in practice meant for war. The package was sold to the anti-militarist SPD as voting for the defence of Germany against tsarist autocracy. As the war continued with mounting casualties, shortages, and Germany adopting imperialist war aims, the SPD split, with a significant pacifist minority setting up the USPD. Ebert attempted to keep in contact with fellow socialists in Europe through the neutral states and played a decisive part in *Lenin's return to Russia in 1917 and in the peace of Brest Livowsk between Russia and Germany. This peace did not help Germany in the long term and on 3 October 1918 the German military advised the government to seek an immediate ceasefire. Two days later revolution broke out. On 9 November the Kaiser abdicated and appointed Ebert Chancellor. Ebert persuaded the USPD to join his government. On 11 November the armistice was signed between Germany and the Allies.

Ebert worked tirelessly for German democracy against a Bolshevik-style takeover. Unfortunately he had to use the remnants of the old army to achieve this. This brought bitterness on the left, but little gratitude from the right and no help from the Allies. The Versailles Treaty weakened the position of Ebert and his colleagues. Elected President of Germany on 2 February 1919, Ebert faced a hateful campaign against his personal integrity which continued to his death.

Eden, Robert **Anthony** (b. Windlestone, Co. Durham, 12 June 1897; d. 14 Jan. 1977)
British; Foreign Secretary 1935–8, 1940–5, 1951–5, Prime Minister 1955–7; KG 1954, Earl of Avon 1961

Eden was educated at Eton and Christ Church, Oxford, where he took a first in oriental languages. He had a good war record—he was awarded the Military Cross in 1917—and was destined for a distinguished political career. Elected as Conservative MP for Warwick and Leamington in 1923—aged 26—he served as a parliamentary private secretary to Foreign Secretary Sir Austen *Chamberlain before becoming Under-Secretary at the Foreign Office in 1931. Three years later he was made Lord Privy Seal and then in June 1935 Minister for the League of Nations, with a seat in the Cabinet. Six months later, at the age of 38, he was made Foreign Secretary following the dismissal of Sir Samuel *Hoare. He resigned in February 1938, in opposition to the government's policy of appeasement, but was brought back into government by Neville *Chamberlain as Dominions Secretary in 1939 and then returned to the Foreign Office by *Churchill in 1940. He served as Foreign Secretary throughout Churchill's wartime and peacetime administrations and was widely recognized as Churchill's heir apparent. In May 1955 he finally ascended the steps of No. 10 Downing Street as Prime Minister and promptly led his party to victory at a general election. His premiership was short-lived, broken on the back of the Suez expedition the following year. Citing ill-health—his doctors announced publicly that his condition was such that he could not continue in office—he resigned in January 1957. He also left the House of Commons. Four years later, he was elevated to the peerage as the Earl of Avon.

Though great things were expected of him when he became Prime Minister, he was an indecisive and highly strung individual. He was not well physically, the result of a botched surgical operation in 1953, and his mental state at times was fragile, exacerbated by having to wait so long to succeed Churchill as party leader. As Prime Minister, he was unpredictable and meddled in the affairs of departments, his leadership coming in for criticism even before the Suez affair. The nationalization of the Suez Canal by President *Nasser of Egypt induced in Eden the need to prove his strength—he saw in Nasser another *Hitler—and, in collusion with France and Israel, Britain attempted to seize the Suez Canal zone by force. The action, though near to completion, was ended by intense pressure from the United States. The episode destroyed Eden's standing and his health, the Cabinet coming to be dominated by his Chancellor, Harold *Macmillan. His premiership had lasted twenty months. In retirement, he wrote three volumes of autobiography and died in 1977 at the age of 79.

Though popular with party workers, and well regarded during his period as Foreign Secretary, his shortcomings were recognized by many of his colleagues, including Churchill. Churchill's son Randolph was subsequently to write that 'even before the Suez adventure there were many of his colleagues who felt that he was inadequate to the task and that he would have to be replaced as quickly and as kindly as possible by someone with a more robust political stamina'. The Suez expedition was the culmination of poor leadership by Eden rather than an isolated instance of it. He was not cut out for the rough and tumble of party politics. A vain and insecure man, he was out of his depth in the premiership.

Eisenhower, Dwight David (b. Denison, Texas, 14 Oct. 1890; d. 28 Mar. 1969)
US; Supreme Allied Commander 1944–5, Chief of Staff of the US army 1945–8, Supreme Commander NATO 1950–2, President 1953–61

David Dwight Eisenhower—he was later to transpose the first two names—was born in Denison, Texas, the third of seven sons born to parents of German-Swiss Protestant descent. At the age of 2, his family moved to Abilene, Kansas, where his father worked as a mechanic in a creamery. He was keen to have a military career and was admitted to the US Military Academy at West Point. He was also a keen football player, but a knee injury put paid to his playing days. His first military posting was to Fort Sam Houston in Texas, where he met and married Mamie Doud. During the First World War he trained tank battalions in the USA and from 1922 to 1924 was stationed in the Panama Canal. He impressed his superiors and was sent to the Command and General Staff School at Fort Leavenworth, Kansas, graduating first in a class of 275. In 1933 he was appointed as an aide to General Douglas MacArthur. In 1941 he demonstrated a remarkable capacity for co-ordination in battle manœuvres and was soon promoted to the rank of temporary brigadier-general. After the Japanese attack on Pearl Harbor he was appointed Chief of Staff to General George C. *Marshall and helped draft the strategy for the war. In 1942 he became Allied Commander-in-Chief for the invasion of North Africa. In December 1943 he was appointed Supreme Commander of the Allied Expeditionary Force and masterminded the D-Day invasion for the liberation of Europe. Eisenhower—by now holding the rank of General of the Army—proved an effective strategist, co-ordinator, and leader, ensuring that a diverse body of often strong-willed military commanders stayed in line. He entered the war as an unknown soldier and ended it as a national hero.

After the end of the war, Eisenhower became Chief of Staff of the US army and supervised demobilization and a reorganization of the armed forces. After being allowed to retire in 1948, he became President of Columbia University. He turned down an approach from both Republican and Democratic activists to run for President of the USA. In 1950, President Harry S *Truman called him back into the service of his country appointing him Supreme Commander of the new North Atlantic Treaty Organization (NATO), a post he held until 1952, when he was persuaded to run for the Republican nomination for President. He retired from army service in June 1952 and won the nomination against Senator Rober H. *Taft. He won a clear victory in the general election, winning almost 34 million votes against 27 million cast for his Democratic opponent, Adlai *Stevenson. He was inaugurated on 20 January 1953.

Eisenhower's presidency was to be noteworthy as much for what it did not do as for what it did. Eisenhower presided over a period of calm in American life. He saw his presidency as a response to the radicalism of the presidency of Franklin *Roosevelt. He was a conservative, espoused no radical policies, but sought no return to the status quo ante. There was no attempt made to undo the measures of the New Deal. The decade was one essentially of peace. An armistice was achieved in Korea. Domestically, some modest social reforms were implemented, including the passage in 1957 of a Civil Rights Bill. For most of his presidency, Congress was controlled by the Democrats. Of the proposals put before Congress, he had a respectable success rate, most measures getting through, the percentage only dipping at the end of his presidency. The country enjoyed a period of economic prosperity and Eisenhower appeared to epitomize the era.

Problems that Eisenhower encountered were not usually of his own making. The anti-Communist crusade of Senator Joe *McCarthy carried over from the Truman to the Eisenhower presidency. Eisenhower declined to engage publicly in dispute with McCarthy, though disapproving of his tactics. In 1954 the Supreme Court struck down segregation in schools as unconstitutional. Eisenhower disagreed with the decision—and had come to regard his nomination of Earl *Warren as Chief Justice of the United States as the biggest mistake he had made—but realized he was duty bound to uphold it. When rioting broke out in Little Rock, Arkansas, in 1957 after attempts were made to allow black children into the previously all-white high schools, he tried to persuade the state Governor, Orval *Faubus, to take action to ensure that the court's order was enforced. When his attempts at persuasion failed, he dispatched federal troops to restore order.

In foreign affairs, Eisenhower declined to take action to assist uprisings in Eastern Europe but was concerned to prevent the spread of Communism elsewhere. In 1954 the USA pledged to support any member nation of the newly formed South-East Asian Treaty Organization against attack. This formed the basis of the US commitment to South Vietnam and followed the French defeat at Dienbienphu. In 1956 he pressured the UK to cease the military intervention in the Suez Canal Zone. In response to Suez, he promulgated the Eisenhower Doctrine, committing the US to aid any country in the Middle East threatened by international Communism. In 1958 he sent US ships and troops to Lebanon to support the Lebanese government against a rebellion allegedly fostered by President *Nasser of Egypt. At the same time, he sought to ease tensions between the USA and the Soviet Union. However, relations with *Khrushchev did not go well and a final summit meeting in 1960 failed after a US U2 spy plane was shot down in Soviet air space.

Although suffering a heart attack in 1955 and an attack of ileitis in 1956, Eisenhower had successfully sought re-election for a second term in 1956, winning—again over Stevenson—by an increased margin, by 35.5 million votes to 26 million. However, despite the size of the win, he did not have a significant coat-tails effect. His vote was essentially personal. Although his popularity dipped toward the end of his presidency—the result of economic downturn—he nonetheless remained a popular figure. At the end of his presidency, he warned prophetically against the growth of the 'military-industrial complex' and then retired to his farm in Gettysburg, Pennsylvania. He died eight years later at the age of 78.

Eisenhower was subsequently to be criticized for his failure to take more decisive action to address the nation's problems. He was seen as standing aloof from the fray. Partisan attacks were left to his Vice-President, Richard *Nixon. Rather than tackle social problems, he left others to take care of them. His presidency, according to critics, was marked by drift and indecisiveness. Given Eisenhower's popularity, a popularity that constituted a valuable political resource, his presidency was characterized as a lost opportunity. The election of a young, energetic John *Kennedy in 1960—who had attacked Eisenhower for allowing a 'missile gap' to develop in the arms race with the Soviet Union—reinforced the growing view that Eisenhower was an old man who had not tackled key issues facing the United States. In a 1962 poll of historians, Eisenhower ranked equal 20th, at the bottom end of the 'average' presidents. In a 1970 poll, he held the same position.

More recent years have seen revisionist historians argue that Eisenhower was far more effective than critics have allowed. According to revisionists, led by Fred Greenstein, he gave more time than is generally realized to the job and enjoyed doing it. Drawing on previously unavailable papers, Greenstein—in *The Hidden-Hand Presidency*—argues that Eisenhower was active behind the scenes, publicly making little comment or distracting attention from the issue while privately meeting with key actors to influence outcomes. This form of 'hidden hand' leadership allowed Eisenhower to appear detached from partisan or controversial activity, and thus remain popular, while achieving many of the results he wanted. In the 1982 Murray poll, Eisenhower was ranked 11th in the list of presidents. In the 1995 *Chicago Sun-Times* poll of presidential scholars he had moved up to 9th place. The feature on which he scored highest was that of character.

Erhard, Ludwig (b. Fürth, 4 Feb. 1897; d. 5 May 1977)

German; Chancellor of the Federal Republic of Germany 1963–6

Perhaps no other figure is more closely associated with West Germany's post-war economic recovery than Erhard. He returned from the First World War badly wounded and decided to study economics and sociology, achieving his doctorate in 1925. From 1928 to 1942 he worked in market research in Nuremberg, after which he founded his own institute with money from private industry. Intellectually he was thinking about the possible consequences of Germany's coming defeat. From 1945 on he was encouraged by the Americans, working first as Economics Minister in Bavaria, and then in Frankfurt am Main on the currency reform. However Erhard was kept in the dark about the date and conditions of the new mark's introduction (1948). He thought of resigning but was allowed to announce its coming on the radio. With it came the market economy which swept away many of the wartime controls still in place. Prices were high but the shop windows were full again. Long hours of work brought rewards. The German miracle was greatly helped by the outbreak of the Korean War in 1950 which gave West Germany its chance in world markets. The well-trained labour force was ready to be deployed. High unemployment helped to keep wages low.

Erhard was never really a party man and would have been at home in the Liberal FDP but *Adenauer persuaded him to join his CDU. He served as Minister of Economics from 1949 to 1963. By the mid-1950s the German economy had recovered far more rapidly than anyone had foreseen, and Adenauer and Erhard were popular—but not with each other!

The public saw Erhard as the 'crown prince' and felt he should succeed Adenauer. By 1959 Adenauer was 83 but was only willing to give up as Chancellor if he could be President and Erhard, then 62, was restless. The two had other differences. Adenauer was far more political and was looking for a united, Catholic Western Europe whereas Erhard was more pragmatic. Adenauer had his power house in the party, Erhard did not. The losses at the election of 1961 decided the issue of Adenauer's departure in 1963. Erhard seemed to be the man who could steer the CDU/CSU back to popularity. In the election of 1965 he led his forces to an unexpectedly good result against *Brandt's SPD.

As Chancellor of a CDU/CSU and FDP coalition Erhard could not deal with the manœuvring of the different factions. He attempted to stand aside between the quarrels of the so-called Gaullists and the Atlanticists. But he backed the USA against *de Gaulle on defence issues, thus offending German Gaullists. Remarkably, it was not foreign policy but more economic policy which brought him down. In the summer of 1966 West Germany was suffering a mini-recession. Germany's neighbours would have shrugged it off, but the Germans felt insecure with any hint of an economic downturn. The government lost popularity, was defeated in the Hesse regional elections on 6 November 1966, and Erhard resigned on 1 December.

Erlander, Tage Fritiof (b. Värmland county, 13 June 1901; d. 21 June 1985)
Swedish; Prime Minister 1946–69

The son of a teacher, Erlander went to school at Karlstad in his native county and university at Lund, graduating in political science and economics in 1928. In 1930 he joined the Social Democratic Labour Party and was elected to the Lund City Council, where he served until 1936. He entered parliament in 1932 as a Social Democratic representative for the Malmö–Lund area and remained a member of one or other of the two houses until his retirement in 1973. His early political progress was steady and unspectacular: he served on major commissions of inquiry, notably on unemployment at the time of the recession, and progressed via junior office at the Ministry of Social Welfare to become Minister without Portfolio in 1944 and Minister for Education in 1945.

When Prime Minister Hansson died suddenly in office in 1946, Erlander was the surprise beneficiary of his party's wish for a generational change. He proceeded with shrewd authority to set his country's course in the post-war world. Domestically he pursued what he called 'the strong society': large extensions to the welfare state and the public sector financed by high taxation underpinned by co-operation with both sides of industry. In foreign and defence policy he pursued the goal of well-armed neutrality, coupled with strong support for the United Nations and economic aid to the Third World. For Sweden these were in general years of prosperity, and Erlander had the satisfaction of winning a resounding electoral victory in 1968 before stepping down from office in the following year. He was known as 'Sweden's longest Prime Minister' both because of this span in office and because he was some 6 ft. 4 in. tall. Between 1972 and 1982 he wrote six volumes of memoirs.

Ervin, Samuel **(Sam)** James Jr. (b. Morganton, North Carolina, 27 Sept. 1896; d. 23 Apr. 1985)
US; member of the US House of Representatives 1946–7; US Senator 1954–74; chairman of the Senate Select Committee on Watergate 1973–4

Ervin graduated from the University of North Carolina in 1917. After service in France during the First World War, when he was twice cited for gallantry, he graduated LLB from Harvard Law School in 1922 and began practising law in Morganton. He served for several years as a circuit judge at county level.

His political career began in 1923 when he was elected to the North Carolina General Assembly. He was re-elected in 1925 and 1931. His debut in national politics came in 1946 when he was elected US representative to fill a vacancy caused by the death of his brother, Joseph W. Ervin. He did not seek re-election to the lower house but in 1954 was appointed to the US Senate, also to fill a vacancy. Regular re-election followed until 1974 when he decided to retire and return to his Morganton law practice.

Ervin was a Southern Democrat. In the 1950s and 1960s he opposed civil rights legislation designed to improve the position of blacks. He supported the policy of containment, accepted the high levels of military expenditure this entailed, and supported American intervention in Vietnam. His conservatism did not extend to condoning the activities of Senator Joseph *McCarthy, whom he voted to censure in 1954. He also opposed a national system of surveillance of dissidents in 1970.

During his twenty years as a Senator Ervin acquired a reputation as an authority on American constitutional law. This led to his appointment as chairman of Watergate committee hearings. Though a courteous Southerner with a folksy manner, Ervin was determined that constitutional propriety should be upheld. This turned him into a formidable opponent of the perpetrators of the Watergate débâcle and it led to fierce televised clashes with President *Nixon and his aides. Showing characteristic modesty, Ervin described himself as 'just an ol' country lawyer from Dixie' but the part he played in the Watergate investigations transformed him into a guardian of the constitution and American folk hero.

Despite his self-deprecating claims, Sam Ervin was no simple backwoodsman. He was a widely read, erudite man, famed for his inexhaustible store of quotations. He was a shrewd politician, of broadly conservative but independent judgement and unshakeable dedication to constitutional principles. After retiring from the Senate in 1974 he wrote his own account of Watergate and published his autobiography, *Preserving the Constitution*.

Fabius, Laurent (b. Paris, 10 Aug. 1946)

French; Prime Minister 1984–6

The son of a Parisian antiques dealer, Fabius followed the *cursus honorum* of the French upwardly mobile. He attended the Lycée Janson-de-Sailly and Louis-le-Grand then the École Normale Supérieur, and the Institut d'Études Politiques followed by the *agrégation des lettres* exam and finally ENA to start a career as '*auditeur*' in the Conseil d'État. It was *Mitterrand's 'talent spotter' Georges Dyan who noticed Fabius and persuaded him to take up a political career. He joined the party in 1974 and then moved up the hierarchy rapidly as Mitterrand recognized his abilities; he became head of Mitterrand's private staff in 1976, and a party national secretary in 1979. It was Fabius rebuking Rocard at the Congress of Metz in 1979 who exclaimed that 'between the Plan and the market there is . . . Socialism'. After the victory of 1981 Fabius was made Budget Minister, effectively minister for reflation. However, he came to see this policy as mistaken and quickly came round to a 'Rocardian' view to side with *Delors and the Prime Minister *Mauroy in rejecting protectionism and the 'dash for growth' and embracing financial discipline and spending cutbacks. In 1983, as Industry Minister, he became a leading 'modernizer' committed to the virtues of the market, competition, profits, and business independence from government. In July 1984 Fabius became the youngest Prime Minister since Élie Decazes in 1819. The appointment was partly intended to symbolize the new politics of social democracy through financial responsibility, modernization, and social progress. Fabius's government did stop the Socialist decline in the opinion polls but it was hamstrung by a number of problems including the affair of the sinking of Greenpeace's *Rainbow Warrior* by French agents in 1985, a dire TV appearance in debate with Jacques *Chirac, and an ill-considered disagreement with President Mitterrand over the reception of Poland's head of state on a visit to Paris. Fabius, whose ambition was never in doubt, also chose to stake a claim to run the 1986 election campaign against the Party leader *Jospin. The lunge for power was crude and started a long war between the two lieutenants of the Mitterrand camp which could hardly be said to have ended by 1995. All the same the defeat at the elections of 1986 was far from disastrous and prepared the ground for the victory of 1988. However Fabius's quarrel with Jospin made it difficult for him to play a role in the party from 1986 to 1988. In 1988 another lunge for power, this time to be First Secretary of the Socialist Party, was seen off by an unlikely coalition of factions and he took the Speaker's Chair in the Assembly as a consolation prize (it is, however, a very powerful post). Fabius then attempted a second takeover of the Parti Socialiste and succeeded in 1992 in becoming First Secretary. However, he was worn down by accusations that he was involved in a government dispatch of AIDS-contaminated blood to haemophiliacs and had not recovered from that. In 1993, after the Socialists' humiliation at the polls, he was ousted by *Rocard, and has not been in the mainstream since that time. He remains supported by the majority of the party's small number of deputies but his fate will now be determined by the party leader Jospin and whether he has the Nixonesque ability to drag himself off the canvas.

Fanfani, Amintore (b. Arezzo, 6 Feb. 1908)

Italian; Prime Minister six times between 1958 and 1987

A leading member of Catholic Action during the Fascist period, in the 1930s Fanfani was professor of economic history at the Catholic University in Milan and wrote two well-received works on the relationship of Catholicism to industrialization. He was a founder member of the Christian Democrat Party after 1943, and was elected to the Constituent Assembly in 1946. He quickly established himself as a leading proponent of the left within the DC, and was Minister of Labour in the fourth *De Gasperi government (June 1947). Periods of office in the Ministries of Agriculture and of the Interior followed, and after De Gasperi's retirement in 1953 Fanfani emerged as the expected successor, a role confirmed by his appointment as party secretary. It was an early indication of the problems that were to beset his career that his first prime ministership in January 1954 lasted little more than a month. Though he returned several times as Prime Minister and as party secretary he was never again able to combine the two roles. His activist and sometimes authoritarian style, together with his reputation as an economic reformer, ensured he was always regarded with suspicion by the moderates within the DC, and he was rarely able to exploit fully the opportunities which he created. He was largely responsible for setting up the national organization of the Christian Democrats after the dependence on the church and on the government which had characterized the De Gasperi period. Though he established his own party faction in this way, the dominant faction which inherited the party machine was the *dorotei*, representing the conservative wing of the party. In government, he was a leading proponent of opening to the centre-left, which included the Socialists in the governing coalition from 1963, but he was too powerful to be allowed to be the Prime Minister of the first such government. In the later part of his career his ambition was to be elected President of the Republic, but despite the formal nomination of his own party he never secured the wide base of support required in the electoral college. He led the Christian Democrats to narrow defeat in the divorce referendum (1974), which he fought in typically combative style, alienating the pro-divorce groups to a perhaps unnecessary extent, without achieving the victory which would have given him predominance in his own party. Thereafter, he had to content himself with the status of Speaker of the Senate, formally the second office of the state, and with occasional periods as caretaker Prime Minister, the last of which was in 1987.

Amintore Fanfani was one of the dominant figures of the Italian Christian Democrats for over three decades. He represented a particular ideological position, that of socially conservative Catholics who favoured economic interventionism, which was very influential in the 1950s but which gradually lost its appeal. With this decline, his energetic personal style and forceful opinions became more obviously anomalous in an increasingly grey and pluralistic DC.

Faubus, Orval Eugene (b. Greasy Creek, Arkansas, 7 Jan. 1910; d, 14 Dec. 1994)
US; Governor of Arkansas 1957–67

The son of a poor farmer, who was a socialist, Faubus had little education but became a schoolteacher before becoming involved in politics during the Depression. War service in the army (where he rose to the rank of major) was followed after demobilization by a period in state government as State Highway Commissioner. By this stage Faubus had acquired a reputation as a progressive and in 1954 he ran for governor on a moderate populist ticket, promising to use government constructively to improve the infrastructure of Arkansas.

Faubus's gubernatorial period will be remembered primarily for the dramatic resistance to school integration and the confrontation with the federal government over the admission of blacks to Little Rock Central High School in 1957. Yet it was not inevitable that Faubus's career should have been so distorted by the civil rights issue. Although racial questions were explosive throughout the South, Arkansas was relatively tolerant by comparison with other southern states and had in fact desegregated its transport system at the start of Faubus's gubernatorial term. Faubus seemed relatively liberal on race issues and included blacks in his political inner circle.

Faubus apparently took up the segregation issue as much to ward off political challenge from the right as from principle. The courts had ordered the integration of Little Rock schools at a time when Faubus was politically vulnerable because of a tax increase he had imposed. The cause of states rights offered a way of diverting attention from that increase and building support with the local electorate. In September 1957 Faubus ordered the Arkansas National Guard to stop nine black children entering Little Rock Central High School, resistance which met with federal intervention from the courts and President *Eisenhower, who took control of the Arkansas National Guard from Faubus.

Faubus's actions fended off more extreme opponents and he kept the governorship until 1967 despite a tradition of limiting governors to two terms. However, he paid a heavy price as the incident yoked him with last ditch segregationists such as George *Wallace and Ross Barnett, overshadowed his other policies as governor and ensured that he was never seriously considered for national office. Faubus left the governorship in 1967 and worked in routine banking jobs. Despite several attempts at re-election, he never held political office again.

Faulkner, Arthur **Brian** Deane (b. Co. Down, 18 Feb. 1921; d. 3 Mar. 1977)

British; Prime Minister of Northern Ireland 1971–2; Baron (life peer) 1977

The son of a businessman, Faulkner was educated at the College of St Columba, Co. Dublin, and Queen's University, Belfast. He entered the parliament of Northern Ireland at Stormont at the age of 28 as the Unionist member for East Down. After junior ministerial office he held the important posts of Minister of Home Affairs (1959–63), Minister of Commerce (1963–9), and Minister of Development (1969–71) before becoming Prime Minister.

In the late 1960s, Faulkner's staunch Unionism led him to oppose the then Prime Minister of Northern Ireland Terence O'Neill's concessions to the increasingly active civil rights movement and his development of closer links with Eire. He resigned from the government in 1969 in the hope, it was thought, of taking O'Neill's place. But though O'Neill resigned, Faulkner was passed over and he achieved the premiership only after the resignation of O'Neill's immediate successor, James Chichester-Clark, in 1971. His brief tenure of that office was dominated by the growth of violence and terrorist activity. His tough security policy, including the introduction of internment without trial in August 1971, failed and in March 1972 he and his government resigned when the United Kingdom government assumed direct responsibility for law and order in Ulster.

Nevertheless, he participated in the Assembly which the UK government then established and assumed the headship of a power-sharing executive. This moderate approach alienated many Unionists and after a political strike organized by the Protestant Ulster Workers' Council in 1974 he resigned from the executive, which then collapsed. By the time of his death in a riding accident in 1977 he had little political influence in Northern Ireland.

Faure, Edgar (b. 18 Aug. 1908; d. 30 Mar. 1988)

French; Prime Minister 1955

Edgar Faure came from a middle-class family and trained as a lawyer. He first acquired prominence in 1945 as one of the French prosecutors at the Nuremberg trials and then entered the National Assembly for the eastern department of Jura. Able and ambitious, a natural governmentalist unencumbered by strong doctrinal convictions, he held a number of posts in the short-lived coalitions of the Fourth Republic and succeeded *Mendès France as Prime Minister in 1955. In office he continued the decolonization programme of his predecessor and was an early advocate of the EEC. In December 1995, however, he dissolved the National Assembly and called a snap election. His decision, although legal, caused great controversy for its disregard of the constitutional code of French Republicanism. He was expelled from the Radical Party and lost the political, and personal, friendship of Mendès France.

The return to power of *de Gaulle in 1958 ended the ministerial career of many of the party leaders of the Fourth Republic. Faure, however, adapted quickly to the new rules of the political game and put his trouble-shooting skills at the service of de Gaulle. In 1966 he was appointed minister of Agriculture with the task of calming an—electorally important—farming community which had been offended by the rationalization programme of his predecessor Edgard Pisani. The clearest acknowledgement of his talents came when de Gaulle asked him to become Minister of Education in the aftermath of the political chaos of the May 1968 events. Faure's brief was to draw up a plan for higher education which would democratize its structures while maintaining state control over the system. His law alienated the more conservative elements in the National Assembly but succeeded in defusing, if not solving, the crisis in the universities.

Faure never held ministerial office after de Gaulle's resignation in 1969 but he remained an important figure in the parliamentary game. He was president of the National Assembly from 1973 to 1974 and nursed dreams of standing for the presidency in 1974. Towards the end of his life he became a supporter of *Chirac and wrote several volumes of memoirs. A man of great intelligence and energy 'Edgar' (as he was familiarly known) was, in the last analysis, too clever by half to be suitable for the high offices which he craved.

Feinstein, Dianne (b. San Francisco, 22 June 1933)

US; Mayor of San Francisco 1978–88, US Senator 1992–

Feinstein was educated at Stanford University and is a criminologist by training. She was appointed to the California Parole Board 1960–6 before becoming a member of the San Francisco County Board of Supervisors. From 1970–1 she was president of the Board of Supervisors, a post she occupied again from 1974 to 1975 and in 1978. As a moderate she backed stronger law and order measures. She was able to combine this stance with more liberal views on lifestyle issues, though she has annoyed both gay and feminist groups on occasion. In 1978, she became mayor following the murder of Harvey Moscone and served for his expired term plus two full terms of her own, a period in which she displayed political skill and a high degree of administrative competence.

In 1990 Feinstein entered the gubernatorial race against Pete *Wilson but was narrowly defeated. In 1992 she successfully ran for the unexpired portion of Wilson's Senate term and held the seat in 1994 against the challenge of the wealthy Michael Huffington in one of the United States' most expensive Senate campaigns.

Feinstein's political experience in state and local politics as well as in the Senate makes her one of the most visible female politicians in United States and a possible Democratic contender for the governorship of California or the presidency.

Ferraro, Geraldine Anne (b. Newburgh, New York, 26 Aug. 1935)

US; Member of the US House of Representatives 1981–4, vice-presidential candidate 1984

Daughter of Italian immigrant parents, Ferraro graduated BA from Marymount College, Manhattan, in 1956 and LLB from New York Law School, 1978. Called to the New York bar in 1961, she headed a successful law practice until 1974. In that year she began her political career as a Democrat in the post of assistant district attorney of Queens County, New York. Four years later, in 1978, she headed a Supreme Court bureau for the victims of violent crime. Elected to the House of Representatives in

1981 as Congresswoman for 9th District New York, she undertook the role of secretary of the House Democratic caucus.

Ferraro was re-elected for a second term in 1983, and a year later was propelled to the forefront of the national political stage when Walter *Mondale chose her to be his vice-presidential running mate (the first woman to be so selected). At the time of Ferraro's nomination questions were raised not only about her gender, which some Democrats feared might alienate more male blue-collar voters than it would attract radical feminists, but also about the limited extent of her political experience. After only six years in national politics she might be placed only one step away from the Oval Office.

At the outset the 'Ferraro factor' brought glamour and energy to Mondale's rather staged, lacklustre image and plodding campaign. Shortly after the convention, however, controversy erupted about her personal finances. Her reputation was damaged by revelations of tax avoidance, shady business dealings, and possible Mafia connections of her husband, John Zaccaro. There were also allegations that Ferraro herself had been involved in financial impropriety in respect of her 1978 campaign funds. The ensuing scandal doomed the Mondale–Ferraro ticket.

Ferraro retired from politics after the defeat of the Democrats in the 1984 election and returned to private practice. In 1992 she attempted to make a political comeback, contending the Democratic nomination for US Senator for New York. Inevitably the scandals of 1984 overshadowed her campaign and dashed her hopes. She accepted an appointment from President *Clinton to represent the USA at the United Nations Commission on Human Rights Conference in Geneva in 1993.

Ferraro was seen by some as the 'mandatory' woman, chosen for her gender not her political agenda or ability. For others she symbolized a shrewd politician and career woman who was unfairly pilloried by the political establishment.

Figueres Ferrer, José (b. San Ramon, Costa Rica, 25 Sept. 1906; d. 8 June 1990)
Costa Rican; President of Costa Rica as head of a junta government 8 May 1948–8 Nov. 1949, as constitutional President 1953–8, 1970–4

José Figueres, popularly known as 'Don Pepe' was one of Costa Rica's most important political figures. The son of recent Spanish immigrants to Costa Rica, he had little formal education after the secondary level. In 1924 he went to the USA to study electrical engineering, but never matriculated. In 1928 he returned to Costa Rica to take up farming at which he was successful.

In 1942 he was exiled from Costa Rica for criticzing the then President, Rafael Ángel Calderón Guardia. He returned two years later from Mexico. During his exile Figueres and other Caribbean exiles developed the Caribbean Legion, a plan to rid the whole of the Caribbean of dictators. After accusing Calderón Guardia of fraudulently stealing the presidency in 1948, Figureres raised a citizen army and with help from his Caribbean allies waged a successful six-week 'war of national liberation'. In May 1948 Figueres became President as head of the Founding Junta of the Second Republic of Costa Rica. In the eighteen months of the junta, Figueres changed the life of Costa Rica dramatically. He abolished the army, nationalized the banking system, and imposed a 10 per cent wealth tax. He then held elections for a constituent assembly to draft a new constitution in 1949 which made constitutional his earlier reforms and created new autonomous public sector institutions and government regulations for a strong social democratic institutional system. Figueres then resigned.

In 1953 Figueres was democratically elected to the presidency. He created additional public sector autonomous institutions for electricity, banking, health care, telephones, and insurance. He also set up the National Council of Production to support farming and industry through supplying assistance with marketing, credits, and price supports. These reforms consolidated Costa Rica as a haven of peace, democracy, and relative equality in a region, Central America, plagued by violence, dictatorship, and extreme inequalities.

However, Figueres continued his Caribbean Legion objectives in his foreign policies. Exiles flocked to Costa Rica from all over the Caribbean, and received his support. He aided Nicaraguan exiles in their attempts to overthrow the dictator, Somoza. Somoza retaliated by twice supporting 'exile' invasions of Costa Rica from Nicaragua. Figueres had to appeal to the Organization of American States (OAS) for help. They agreed, but only on condition that Figueres expelled the so-called Caribbean Legion from Costa Rica, and stopped supporting the struggles against the dictators. The USA regarded Figueres as a trouble-maker. However, their attitude towards him changed after the Cuban Revolution when the CIA sought his help against *Trujillo, the dictator of the Dominican Republic, and to lessen *Castro's appeal to the Latin American and Caribbean left. Figueres, who had initially supported Castro, had turned against Castro after Castro had entered the USSR sphere of influence. Figueres became an important supporter of President *Kennedy's Alliance for Progress, but after Kennedy's death, and in 1967, when details of his collaboration with the CIA were leaded, his international reputation diminished.

In 1970 Figueres again won the presidency. Controversially he established trade and diplomatic relations with the Soviet Union. He also proposed making Costa Rica an international financial centre. Unfortunately this proposal brought the corrupt international financier, Robert Vesco, to Costa Rica, and not much else. There were accusations of bribes passing from Vesco to Figueres. The ensuing scandals tarnished Figueres' reputation somewhat.

Nevertheless Figueres was a key figure in ensuring that Costa Rica avoided the problems which bedevilled the rest of Central America. Costa Rica's committment to democracy and peace, and to ensuring the economic and social well-being of all its citizens, is in no small part due to Figueres' bold reforms.

FitzGerald, Garret (b. Dublin, 9 Feb. 1926)
Irish; Taoiseach (premier) 1981–2 and 1982–7

FitzGerald was the son of Desmond FitzGerald, Minister for External Affairs 1923–7 and Defence 1927–32. Both his parents had taken part in the Rising of Easter 1916, though his mother was an Ulster Protestant. A planner, journalist, and university lecturer in economics, he became a Senator (Fine Gael) in 1965 and was elected to the Dáil in 1969, becoming frontbench spokesman on education. He served as Minister for External Affairs in the *Cosgrave administration 1973–7. As such he played a leading role in the Sunningdale Conference, December 1973, which paved the way for the short-lived power-sharing administration in Northern Ireland. In June 1977 he became leader of Fine Gael, and Taoiseach in June 1981. In a noted radio interview in September 1981 FitzGerald conceded that there were sectarian elements in the Irish state which were unacceptable to Protestants in Northern Ireland. One of his objects in politics had been to desectarianize southern Irish society, and his pledge to work to this end now became known as his 'constitutional crusade'. His government lost office over a budgetary issue in February 1982, but regained it in December. His 'crusade' failed to take off; Catholic pressure groups, inspired by the Pope's visit to Ireland in 1979, succeeded in getting both major parties to agree a referendum to render abortion unconstitutional as well as illegal, and this passed in September 1983. FitzGerald attempted a second constitutional adendment in June 1986, this time to delete the prohibition on divorce, but once again the conservative Catholic position triumphed at the referendum.

FitzGerald had more success, however, in Anglo-Irish relations and in providing Northern Irish nationalists with an alternative way forward to that held out by militant republicanism. This was in his New Ireland Forum, reporting in May 1984, and his subsequent negotiation with Margaret Thatcher's government of the Anglo-Irish Agreement of November 1985. This marked a major constitutional amendment to the 1920–1 settlement, *vis-à-vis* Northern Ireland, and laid a foundation for future co-operation between the Republic and United Kingdom governments in advancing a 'peace process' in Northerm Ireland. FitzGerald resigned the party leadership after his government lost the February 1987 election.

A fast-talking liberal Catholic intellectual, FitzGerald subsequently produced a characteristically wordy and informative political memoir, *All in a Life* (1991).

Foot, Michael (b. Plymouth, 23 July 1913)

British; Lord President of the Council 1976–9, deputy leader of the Labour Party 1976–80, leader 1980–3

The son of a Liberal MP, Foot was educated at Leighton Park School, Reading, and Wadham College, Oxford, and worked as a journalist before his election as MP for Plymouth, Devonport, in 1945. Defeated in the 1955 general election, he returned to the Commons at a by-election in Ebbw Vale (later Blaenau Gwent) in 1960.

Twenty-nine years elapsed between Foot's first election and his initial experience of ministerial office. On the back benches in the 1940s and 1950s (and, while he was out of parliament, in *Tribune* of which he was then editor) he was a persistent left-wing critic of the Labour leadership. He was deprived of the whip 1961–3. His criticism was much more restrained when Harold *Wilson became party leader, but he nevertheless declined office in the 1964–70 Labour government and attacked its policies on such issues as expenditure cuts, industrial relations, and Vietnam.

In opposition (1970–4) Foot unsuccessfully contested the deputy leadership in 1970, 1971, and 1972 but was regularly elected to the shadow Cabinet. When Labour regained office in 1974 he joined the Cabinet as Secretary of State for Employment, taking responsibility for legislation strengthening trade union rights, particularly over the closed shop. He was also one of the ministers who took advantage of the Cabinet's 'agreement to disagree' with the official government line during the 1975 referendum on continued membership of the European Community.

When James *Callaghan assumed the premiership, Foot (who had been runner-up in the leadership election and was then elected deputy leader) became Lord President of the Council and leader of the House of Commons. He took over the legislation on devolution for Scotland and Wales, but his main responsibility was as the government's principal business manager in an increasingly precarious parliamentary situation. Long known as a most effective debater, he now also proved extremely adept at negotiation with the minor parties.

Foot was reluctant to contest the succession when Callaghan resigned the leadership in 1980. His election (at the age of 67) was the last to be conducted by the PLP alone. The party was deeply divided: the left was intent upon constitutional reform to prevent a repetition of the Wilson and Callaghan governments' alleged betrayals of party policy. Despite Foot's reputation as a unifier, the task was beyond him. (His *Another Heart and Other Pulses* (1983) traces his approach to these problems.) Twenty-eight MPs defected on the launch of the Social Democratic Party in 1981. The activities of the left attracted much adverse publicity. A combination of these factors, plus the Falklands factor, a disastrous manifesto (dubbed 'the longest suicide note in history'), and Foot's own low popular appeal, made Labour's share of the vote in the 1983 general election its lowest since 1918. Foot resigned the leadership, though he remained in parliament until 1992.

Foot had a career outside politics as a journalist, reviewer, and author. Among his many books is a two-volumed biography of his hero Bevan.

Ford, Gerald Rudolph (b. Omaha, Nebraska, 14 July 1913)

US; Vice-President 1973–4, President 1974–7

The son of Leslie Lynch King and Dorothy King, Ford was named at birth as Leslie Lynch King Jr. His parents divorced when he was 2 years old and his mother later married a paint salesman named Gerald Rudolf Ford. His name was changed to

Gerald Rudolph Ford Jr. when he was legally adopted by his stepfather. (He did not discover he was adopted until the age of 17.) He attended South High School in Grand Rapids, Michigan, and the University of Michigan, where he majored in economics. Coming from a modest background, he had to work part-time to maintain himself. He was a star football player and was voted the team's 'most valuable player' in 1934. After graduating from Michigan in 1935, he went on to Yale law school, where he worked on the athletic staff while studying for a law degree, receiving his degree in 1941. He was admitted to the Michigan bar and set up law practice in Grand Rapids. He saw war service and spent four years in the navy aboard the *USS Monterey*. Returning to Grand Rapids, he resumed his law practice and, in 1948, married a divorcee, Betty Bloomer Warren. The same year his stepfather—active in local Republican politics—and the state's senior Republican Senator, Arthur Vandenberg, persuaded him to run for Congress in his home district against the incumbent, an isolationist in international affairs. Ford scored a surprise victory in the Republican primary and went on to win easily in the general election.

Ford served for twenty-five years in the House of Representatives. He was a hard-working member and was appointed to several committees. In 1950 he was given a Distinguished Service Award by the US Junior Chamber of Commerce as one of the ten outstanding young men in the United States. Attentive to the needs of Grand Rapids, he regularly won re-election. In 1963 he was appointed as a member of the *Warren Commission, investigating the assassination of John F. *Kennedy, and in 1965 led a 'young turks' movement against the Republican leadership in the House. Elected as minority leader, he spent much of his spare time campaigning and giving speeches for colleagues. Ford had a reputation for being approachable, willing always to help and working hard to master his duties. In his voting behaviour, he was a conservative. He had a particular dislike of the opinions of liberal Supreme Court Justice William O. Douglas, and sought unsuccessfully to impeach him. He had little grounding in foreign affairs but supported President Richard *Nixon in his policy of détente with China and the Soviet Union.

By the early 1970s, he was considering retiring from Congress. He had served almost a quarter of a century in the House. His wife was conscious that she saw little of him and was keen to return to Grand Rapids. His plans changed suddenly in 1973 when President Nixon nominated him, under the terms of the 25th Amendment to the US constitution, to succeed Spiro *Agnew as Vice-President after Agnew's resignation. Ford was not Nixon's first but he was his safest choice. Ford was a popular figure in Congress and the members were content to approve one of their own as Vice-President. His nomination was confirmed by both chambers and he took the oath as Vice-President on 6 December 1973.

Ford was a loyalist by inclination and promptly proclaimed his faith in the innocence of Richard Nixon in the face of accusations levelled against him in the Watergate affair. He toured the country giving speeches and defending the President, doing so after it became clear that he would be well adivsed to adopt a more aloof stance. After the release of incriminating tape recordings, Richard Nixon announced his resignation as President on 8 August 1974. The following day, Ford and his wife waved goodbye to Nixon as he left the White House by helicopter. Then, at noon, in the East Room of the White House Ford was sworn in as the 38th President of the United States. He became the only President never to have been elected to either the presidential or vice-presidential office.

Ford had to contend with a worsening economic situation and a political environment that was increasingly hostile. A month after his inauguration, he pardoned Richard Nixon for any crimes he may have committed. The pardon was unpopular—Ford's own press secretary resigned in protest—and the President's ratings in the opinion polls plummeted. In November, the Democrats made sweeping gains in the mid-term congressional elections. There was an attempt by the elected Democrats to pursue their own agenda against that of an unelected President.

In domestic affairs, Ford sought initially to tackle inflation. He held a gathering of economic experts and then distributed 'WIN' (Whip Inflation Now') badges. However, he soon changed course and made tackling unemployment the administration's priority. He clashed with Congress, which wanted to go further than he was prepared to go in funding public works projects. Ford used the veto extensively before being advised that it was politically unwise to use it so liberally. In his short term of office, he vetoed 66 measures. Of the 48 regular vetoes, 12 were overridden. He had the lowest average success rate of modern presidents in getting measures passed by Congress (57.6 per cent, compared with 67.2 per cent for Nixon). In his energy policy, Ford supported market pricing and attempted to lift controls on oil prices and to deregulate natural gas rates, but Congress rejected his measures.

Ford also clashed with Congress on foreign policy. Congress denied Ford's attempts to send increased military aid to Cambodia and Vietnam. (Ford subsequently blamed Congress for the fall of the regime in South Vietnam.) Congress also refused Ford's request for more substantial aid to the pro-western forces in Angola. Against Ford's wishes it also imposed an arms embargo on Turkey.

Ford nonetheless was able to claim some successes. He was able to use his veto to achieve some compromise on energy policy and on unemployment programmes. He achieved a ceiling on federal expenditure in return for his approval of a bill authorizing reductions in income tax. In foreign affairs, Secretary of State Henry *Kissinger continued his shuttle diplomacy in the Middle East, achieving disengagement of forces in the Sinai and on the Golan Heights. Ford sent US marines to retake the American merchant ship, the *Mayaguez*, seized—according to American intelligence—by Cambodian forces in international waters. Though it later emerged that the Cambodians were about to release the crew (rendering unnecessary the American casualties sustained in the operation) the action was popular, and Ford's popularity ratings took a sudden, though temporary, upswing.

Ford's greatest contribution to the office, though, was in restoring a sense of stability. By the time of the 1976 presidential election campaign, he had established himself as a serious candidate. Though initially declaring he would not seek election in his own right, he changed his mind and sought the Republican nomination. He was challenged by the former Governor of California, Ronald *Reagan. After a bruising contest, Ford won the nomination. In the general election, Ford did well in the first of two televised debates with his Democratic opponent Jimmy *Carter, but then slipped in the second debate—on foreign policy—when he asserted that the countries of Eastern Europe were not under the domination of the Soviet Union. It took some days before Ford clarified what he meant (that the Soviets had no legal entitlement to dominate Eastern Europe) but the gaffe and the delay in rectifying it harmed his support. In the event, he lost narrowly to Carter, garnering 48 per cent of the popular vote to Carter's 50.1 per cent. Given the circumstances in which he came to the presidency, his performance was a highly creditable one. After his defeat, he retired from politics. A proposal that he become Ronald Reagan's running mate in 1980 was discussed but not pursued. He gave the occasional lecture but seemed at his happiest on the golf course.

Ford was extremely well liked as an individual. He was pleasant and open. His family circumstances aroused sympathy: his wife was rushed into hospital for major surgery shortly after the couple entered the White House and later received treatment for chronic alcoholism (she subsequently established the Betty Ford clinic). Ford was the subject of two assassination attempts; in one, in San Francisco, bullets were fired and just missed him—his life was saved by a bystander who knocked the arm of the woman firing the gun. The White House became more of a home than a fortress and Ford did much to restore the dignity of the office.

As President, though, Ford was not always taken that seriously. A knee injury—the result of his football playing days—left him prone to falling down steps occasionally. He was a master of the verbal gaffe. Much of the humour at his expense he took in good part. He once had to rebuke his own press secretary for appearing on a late-night television show and banging his head against the microphone, recognized by the audience as a take-off of his boss. He had an engaging way of making light of his own misfortunes. During one speech he was giving—not too well—he interrupted himself to announce, 'I told Betty before I gave this speech that I knew it backwards—and that seems to be how I am delivering it.' He was the antithesis of his predecessor. That was probably what the United States needed at the time.

Forrestal, James Vincent (b. Beacon, New York, 15 Feb. 1892; d. 22 May 1949)
US; Secretary of the Navy 1944–7, Secretary of Defense 1947–9

The son of a builder, Forrestal attended local schools before becoming a reporter, first for the *Journal* and then for the *Mount Vernon Argus*. In 1911 he returned to full-time education, attending Dartmouth College as a freshman before transferring to Princeton University in 1912. He acquitted himself well as an athlete at Princeton but he left in 1915 without taking a degree. He gained employment first as a cigar salesman with the Tobacco Products Co. and then as a bonds salesman with the banking house, Dillon, Reed & Co. During the First World War he enlisted in the US Navy Reserve and served in the Navy Department in Washington. After the war, returning to his former employers, he soon became a partner and eventually, in 1939, company president.

Forrestal returned to public service in 1940 when he became an administrative assistant to President *Roosevelt. Later that same year he was appointed to the newly created position of Under-Secretary of the Navy, becoming Secretary of the Navy in 1944. In 1947 he became America's first Secretary of Defense, a position which he held until resigning in 1949.

Forrestal was a quiet, modest man who had a 'passion for anonymity'. He was energetic and dedicated to hard work: a factor which may help to explain the circumstances of his death. Suffering from a serious mental breakdown, he retired from office on 28 March 1949 and flew to Florida in order to take a long rest, having taken only one week's leave since 1940. Less than two months later he jumped from a window on the sixteenth floor of the Bethesda Naval Hospital and died instantaneously.

Franco Bahamonde, Francisco (b. El Ferrol, 4 Dec. 1892; d. 20 Nov. 1975)
Spanish; dictator 1939–75

The least studied of the great European dictators, General Francisco Franco has generally escaped the moral opprobrium heaped upon Adolf *Hitler and Benito *Mussolini, midwives to the birth of his regime through their massive material assistance during the Spanish Civil War (1936–9). Although opponents and critics have dismissed him as nothing more than a repressive Fascist, the more generally accepted picture of Franco, who ruled Spain from 1939 until his death at the age of 82 in November 1975, owes much to the image of a wise and visionary leader presented by supporters and hagiographers.

Franco sought constantly to reinvent his persona, adapting his self-image to the prevailing winds of national and international circumstance. Even at the height of war in Europe, with Spain racked by starvation, Franco found time in late 1940 to write a work of fiction based on his own family history and entitled, significantly, *Raza*. In it, he set out a romanticized vision of his background, in which humble origins are replaced by the status of minor aristocracy and the hero's father, in contrast to his own, was a naval officer killed on active duty. This need to reconstruct his past reflected a deeply unhappy relationship with an authoritarian, dissolute, and philandering father who was dismissively contemptuous of him. In compensation, Franco developed extremely close ties to his mother Pilar, from whom he inherited a lifelong capacity for serenity in the face of turmoil.

A series of contradictions characterized the Caudillo. Franco was deeply cunning, yet remarkably credulous; cruel and impassive, yet easily moved to tears; duplicitous, yet naive; pompous and self-aggrandizing, yet timid. Ultimately, his world-view was simple, shaped by his experiences as a soldier in Africa defending Spain's beleaguered colonial remnants. From these early experiences developed an enduring distrust of politicians. He came to regard parliamentary democracy as synonymous with freemasonry, to which—alongside Communism—he was obsessionally opposed. The constants in his political outlook were order, hierarchy, and discipline, supported through an instrumental attachment to the Catholic church. Lacking the messianic vision which drove Hitler and Mussolini, his political project was summed up instead by the need to remain in power through the exercise of *el mando* (command) and defend Spain from the evils of Communism and freemasonry. He came genuinely to see himself as the providential saviour of a Spain understood in terms of its imperial past.

That Franco was able to survive so long in power is a puzzle. For many—notably his Fascist sponsors, but also various members of his close entourage—Franco was an ineffable mediocrity, utterly lacking in charisma. To some extent, his survival depended upon a consummate ability to detect his rivals' weaknesses and, more importantly, their price. He was possessed of genuine political cunning, which enabled him to play off potential opponents from within the regime against each other as well as to buy loyalty. Against opponents from outside the regime, survival was facilitated by his unhesitating use of terror: Franco's victory in the Civil War was marked by tactics of attrition and revenge. The early years of his dictatorship were viciously repressive. Spain was divided into victors and vanquished and, if the scale of the terror had diminished by the 1950s, its memory still served to induce compliance.

Crucially, Franco appears also to have been blessed with *baraka*, a term used in Morocco to describe a mystical quality of divine protection. Many of his claimed achievements happened in spite of, rather than because of, his best efforts. A central myth of his regime was that Franco employed skilful diplomacy in repelling Hitler's efforts to bring Spain into the war on the Axis side. In fact, Franco was anxious to join the war effort, but wanted to time his entry at a point where victory was assured; he was fortunate that the Führer was not prepared to meet the Spanish leader's price, whilst the Allies' control of fuel and food supplies acted as a further constraint. Franco enjoyed further good fortune in that the emergence of the Cold War transformed his regime from Fascist pariah to bulwark against Communism, with the USA instrumental in sponsoring his reincorporation into the international community. The Caudillo's contribution was simply to survive, confident that the tide would eventually turn.

Similarly, Franco can be accorded little credit for the dramatic economic growth of the 1960s which allowed him to pose as the avuncular overseer of modernization, hunting and fishing as Spain grew rich. His understanding of economic policy was decidedly limited, based on a misplaced belief in autarky. He was, at various points, persuaded of the existence of enormous gold deposits in Extremadura, the invention of synthetic gasoline, and the easing of famine by feeding people dolphin sandwiches. Such credulity was mirrored by his growing belief, reinforced by withdrawal into an ever more rarefied court of sycophantic followers, that he stood comparison with such Spanish heroes as El Cid, Charles V, and Philip II. By the time of Franco's death, his dictatorship represented a political anachronism which would not long survive its founder.

Fraser, John **Malcolm** (b. Melbourne, 21 May 1930)

Australian; Prime Minister 1975–83

The son of a Victorian grazier, Fraser was educated at Melbourne Grammar School and Oxford University. He entered parliament, as a member of the Liberal Party, in

1955, but had to wait more than ten years before entering Cabinet. Fraser's ambition and preparedness to challenge his party's leaders emerged during intra-party politicking between 1967 and 1971. He successfully challenged Billy Snedden for the position of party leader in March 1975.

Fraser will long be remembered for the extraordinary way in which he became Prime Minister. In opposition he used the Senate to block the Labor government's supply bills, thereby precipitating a constitutional crisis. The Prime Minister, Gough *Whitlam, refused to meet Fraser's demand that he hold an election, and the Australian Governor-General, Sir John Kerr, broke the deadlock on 11 November 1975 by dismissing Whitlam and appointing Fraser as a caretaker Prime Minister. In the ensuing election, Fraser's coalition government won control of both houses.

As Prime Minister Fraser presided over a transitional period between the protectionist, high spending of previous governments, and the neo-classical rationalism which took hold in the 1980s. As a consequence, he has been criticized by some for not making sweeping cuts to government expenditure, and by others for imposing austerity on working Australians (employing the memorable phrase, 'Life is not meant to be easy'). Inheriting deep structural economic problems and meeting new ones made his tenure difficult.

Fraser carried further the initiatives of the Whitlam government in broadening Australia's immigration programme and articulating 'multiculturalism'. Fraser is remembered also for his international diplomacy, especially his strong line against South Africa's apartheid policies. Two years after his government's defeat and his resignation from politics in 1983, he was appointed member of the Commonwealth Group of Eminent Persons which attempted to create a dialogue aimed at ending apartheid in South Africa. This, and his work for humanitarian organizations and his criticism of free market reforms, has helped soften his prime ministerial image as patrician and lacking tolerance.

Frei Montalva, **Eduardo** (b. Santiago, 13 Aug. 1911; d. 23 Jan. 1982)
Chilean; President 1964–70, President of Senate 1973

After studying in a seminary and at the Institute of Humanities, Frei read law at the Catholic University of Chile. In 1934 he wrote articles for *El Diario Ilustrado* and took charge of the daily *El Tarapacá de Iquique*. In 1937, Frei returned to academia, teaching Labour Law at the Catholic University and Social Policy at the College of Social Service. He became president of the National Falange Party 1941–6; and in 1945 served under President Juan Antonio Ríos as Public Works Minister. In 1949 he was elected Senator for Atacama and Conquimbo, and for Santiago in 1957. In 1958, as the presidential candidate of the recently formed (1957) Christian Democrats, Frei came third behind *Allende and the victor, Alessandri.

Frei became President of Chile in 1964 when his party won a convincing majority. This was followed by an absolute majority in the Chamber of Deputies—the first party to do so in 100 years—in the congressional election of 1965. The main highlights of his administration were: the strengthening of the Andean Pact; the kindergarten law; the building of numerous schools and the Lo Pardo tunnel; the expansion of union rights in the agricultural sectors; 250,000 new homes; 56 new hospitals; legal cover for work-related accidents and illness; centres for mothers, neighbourhood associations, and the agrarian reform.

In the economic field the Office of National Planning was founded. Chilean Electricity was nationalized. State-controlled telecommunications and television networks were set up. The 'Chileanization' of copper and the extensive Agrarian Reform epitomized Frei's 'Revolution in Liberty'—a programme of extensive social change, nationalism, and economic development often described as communitarianism. Frei wrote prolifically. His last piece being *The Humanist Message* (1981), a year before his death in 1982.

Fulbright, James **William** (b. Sumner, Missouri, 9 Apr. 1905; d. 9 Feb. 1995)

US; Senator from Arkansas 1945–74, Chairman, Senate Committee on Foreign Relations 1959–74

Fulbright took a BA at the University of Arkansas, an LLB at George Washington University, and was a Rhodes Scholar at Oxford University. He taught law at George Washington University and the University of Arkansas and became president of the University of Arkansas in 1939. In 1942 he was elected to the House of Representatives. In 1944 he was elected to the Senate and served as Senator from Arkansas for the next thirty years.

His interests lay very largely in the field of foreign affairs. In 1946 he sponsored the bill which created the international educational exchange programme which bore his name. He supported the general lines of American foreign policy during the Cold War, though he emphasized the importance of economic and cultural issues as well as military and political containment. In 1959 he became chairman of the Senate Committee on Foreign Relations. He supported American policy in Vietnam in the early 1960s and in 1964 he sponsored the Gulf of Tonkin Resolution, which gave broad powers to the President in his conduct of the war in Vietnam. In 1965 he began to question American policy in Vietnam and in 1966 he held hearings on the war in Vietnam before the Senate Committee on Foreign Relations. The hearings provided a major focus for the expression of opposition to the war in Vietnam and he became increasingly marked as a leading dissenter with regard to American policy in Vietnam. His position on Vietnam led him to clash with his fellow Southerner, President *Johnson. After the 1968 election Fulbright encouraged President *Nixon to negotiate an end to American involvement in Vietnam.

On domestic matters Fulbright took the conservative standpoint of a Southern Democrat, especially on civil rights. He adopted this standpoint for reasons of political necessity as much as of conviction, since his intellectual bearing and haughty manner made him vulnerable in his bids for re-election in Arkansas, especially when he became a dissenter on Vietnam. In 1974 he was defeated in his final bid for re-election. Highly regarded as a scholar in politics, he was the author of many books on American foreign policy, such as *The Arrogance of Power* (1966).

Furtseva, Yekaterina Alekseevna (b. Kalinin region of Russia 7 Dec. 1919; d. 25 Oct. 1974)

Russian; Member of the Politburo 1956–61

Furtseva was the daughter of Russian working-class parents and educated as an engineer. Having joined the CPSU in 1930 she held minor posts in the party and Comsomol until 1942, when she was appointed district party secretary for Moscow. In 1950 she became Second Party Secretary for Moscow and from 1954 until 1957 held the key position of First Party Secretary for Moscow. In 1952 she became a candidate member of the Central Committee and her prospects were greatly strengthened by the rise of her close ally, Nikita *Khrushchev. In 1956 she was appointed full member and secretary of the Central Committee, and a full member of the Presidium (later known as the Politburo), of which she was the first female member in 1957. But in 1960 she was removed as secretary of the Central Committee and appointed to the less important state position of Minister of Culture, which she held until her death. Her job was to ensure that the Soviet intelligentsia toed the party's line. In 1961 she was removed as member of the Presidium.

Gaddafi, Muammar *see* Al-Qadhafi, Muammar

Gaidar, Yegor Timurovich (b. 19 Mar. 1956)
Russian; Minister of Economics 1991–3

Gaidar is the son of the well-known writer Arkadi Gaidar and grandson of Vice-Admiral Timur Gaidar. A graduate from the economics faculty of Moscow State University in 1978, he was a postgraduate student supervised by *Shatalin. After working as an economist in a number of academic institutes, Aleksandr *Yakovlev made him the head of the economics section of the journal *Kommunist*. In 1990 he became the head of the economics section of *Pravda*. In spring 1991 he became head of the Institute of Economic Politics within the Soviet Academy of Sciences and in November that year Minister of Economics and first deputy chairman of the government of the Russian Republic. He stood for rapid marketization and had some success in stabilizing the rouble. Although he lost influence with Boris *Yeltsin at the expense of the latter's former associates from Sverdlovsk, Yeltsin appointed him his plenipotentiary when Gaidar visited the USA in search of loans. He was dismissed in 1993.

Gaitskell, Hugh Todd Naylor (b. Kensington, London, 9 Apr. 1906; d. 18 Jan. 1963)
British; Chancellor of the Exchequer 1950–1, leader of the Labour Party 1955–63

Gaitskell was the son of a senior civil servant in India. From a well-to-do family, he was educated at Winchester and Oxford. His studies at Oxford and his experience of the General Strike (1926) converted him to socialism.

Leaving Oxford he was briefly an extra-mural tutor with the Workers' Educational Association in Nottingham and in 1928 became a university lecturer in economics in London, remaining in post until the outbreak of war. During the war he was a civil servant and worked for a time for the leading Labour politician, Hugh *Dalton. Gaitskell acquired a good reputation as an administrator and never lost the air of a civil servant. Socialism for him was about taking practical, pragmatic measures to improve living conditions, particularly for the poor. In 1945 he won Leeds South for Labour and held the seat until his death.

After holding a number of junior posts in the 1945 government he became Minister of State for Economic Affairs in February 1950. He had shown authority in arguing the case for devaluation in 1949 and administrative skill at the Ministry of Supply, coping with the coal shortage during a bitterly cold winter. He succeeded the ailing Sir Stafford *Cripps as Chancellor of the Exchequer in October 1950. His 1951 budget proposed to finance a massive rearmament programme (subsequently reduced by the incoming Conservative government), a course which upset many on the left and made Aneurin *Bevan a long-standing opponent, because it involved the imposition of prescription charges on the health service which the latter had created.

The Labour Party began its thirteen years in opposition after losing the 1951 election. The early 1950s were taken up with divisions over German rearmament (Gaitskell supported it, Bevan opposed it) and a struggle for the succession to the ageing Clement *Attlee. There was also division between them over support for the American alliance against the USSR. In a symbolic contest for the party treasurer in 1954 Gaitskell, backed by the bulk of the trade unions, defeated Bevan. When Attlee retired Gaitskell was elected as his successor in December 1955 by a clear margin over Herbert *Morrison and Bevan. He had been an MP for just over ten years.

Gaitskell, like Attlee, was an upper-middle-class, public school, Oxbridge-educated leader. He was backed by the Labour right and the trade unions against Bevan, the working-class hero of the left and the constituency parties. Eventually, there was an uneasy relationship between the two.

Gaitskell's conduct of the Labour campaign in the 1959 general election increased his stature. But the party lost its third successive general election and he was blamed by some for making an unwise pledge that a Labour government would finance its spending programmes without increasing income tax. After defeat Gaitskell proposed to amend Clause 4 of the party constitution, the clause that committed Labour to public ownership of the means of production, distribution, and exchange. This move was bitterly opposed throughout much of the party. Gaitskell's own proposal which involved the party pledging to promote social justice, planning, and equality was accepted, but Clause 4 remained. It was a defeat. To the left Clause 4 was *the* symbol of socialism.

Gaitskell was immediately faced with a new row over defence. The Campaign for Nuclear Disarmament made progress in the party and the party conference in 1961 carried a unilateralist policy platform. Gaiskell, in a passionate speech, pledged himself to 'fight, fight and fight again to save the party we love' and began a long battle to reverse the decision. This was achieved at the next party conference in 1962. At the same conference Gaitskell made clear his opposition to Britain's membership of the European Community on the terms then offered, warning that a federal Europe would mean 'the end of a thousand years of history'. This helped mend his fences with traditional opponents on the left. By the time of his sudden death in early 1963 Gaitskell was in command of his party and was widely seen as the next Prime Minister.

Gaitskell was a rationalist in politics—famously dismissed by Bevan as a desiccated calculating machine. He was also highly principled and unwilling to compromise on what he regarded as key policies. His efforts to lead the Labour Party to the centre ground led the *Economist* to refer to 'Butskellism', a term for the perceived similarities in economic policies between himself and the Conservative R. A. *Butler. Gaitskell took an instrumental view of public ownership. He thought that the mixed economy was now able to deliver full employment and the welfare state. Socialists should be interested in promoting a better quality of life and greater equality. Within the Labour Party he attracted a number of followers, so-called Gaitskellites, including Roy *Jenkins and Anthony *Crosland.

Gamsakhurdia, Zviad Konstantinovich (b. 1939; d. 31 Dec. 1993 or 1 Jan. 1994)

Georgian; President 1991–4

Gamsakhurdia was a literary scholar by profession. In 1974 he was a founding member of the Initiative Group for the Defence of Human Rights Literary, the aims of which were to defend human rights and the environment, and to expose the misdeeds of *Shevardnadze's government. He was also the founder of two underground journals; in the *Golden Fleece* he published Georgian-language work banned by the censor, and in the *Georgian Messenger* he reported on human-rights violations. He was co-founder of a group monitoring observation of the Helsinki Accords of 1975. Gamsakhurdia's works were a stimulus to the Tbilisi riots of April 1978 when several thousand successfully demonstrated against a proposal to give the Russian language equal status in the republic of Georgia with Georgian itself. Gamsakhurdia was arrested in 1977 and sentenced to three years' imprisonment in May 1978. In 1979 he was released after a partial recantation.

In May 1991 Gamsakhurdia was elected as the newly independent Georgia's first President but his behaviour was erratic and there were doubts about his sanity. He was forcibly driven from office amid well-founded charges of corruption, violation of human rights, and abuse of office. Gamsakhurdia and his followers fought against the new regime. He was killed in action.

Gandhi, Indira (b. Allahabad, 19 Nov. 1917; d. 31 Oct. 1984)
Indian; Prime Minister 1966–77, 1980–4

Daughter of Jawaharlal *Nehru, Indira Gandhi was educated at Visva-Bharati and Cambridge. In 1929 she founded Vanar Sena, the Congress children's organization. She joined the Congress in 1938 and married Feroze Gandhi in 1942. After her mother's death (1936), she became closer to her father.

Gandhi was elected to the Congress Working Committee in 1955 and became party president between 1959 and 1960. During this period she masterminded the collapse of the Kerala Communist state government. She was elected to parliament in 1964 and became the Minister for Information and Broadcasting under Nehru's successor, Lal Bahadur Shastri.

Following the death of Shastri (1966), Gandhi was elected as Prime Minister by the Congress party. She led the party to a fourth successive general election victory, though with a greatly reduced majority. In 1969 her nominee for President of India was successfully elected but precipitated a split within the Congress between the parliamentary and organizational wings. The split was followed by a radical left turn which included the nationalization of banks and insurance companies.

In 1971 Gandhi went into a national election on a slogan of 'eradicate poverty'. Her appeal projected her as a national leader and undermined organizational opposition to her within the party. The successful execution of the Indo-Pak War (1971) under Gandhi's guidance led to the creation of Bangladesh. Her popularity was at an all-time high and was followed by Congress victories in the states.

After the 1973 global increase in oil prices, the opposition parties led a country-wide agitation against inflation and corruption. On 12 June 1975 Gandhi was found guilty of corrupt election practices by the Allahabad High Court. On 25 June 1975, Gandhi, using article 352 of the constitution, imposed a State of Emergency.

The State of Emergency was followed by the suspension of the constitution, arrests of opposition leaders, press censorship, and curtailment of the powers of the judiciary; 110,000 political activists were arrested. A twenty-point programme of economic and social reforms was promoted by Gandhi during the Emergency. Gandhi's son, Sanjay Gandhi, established the Youth Congress, which became notorious for its programme of forcible sterilization. The State of Emergency was lifted in March 1977 and elections were held to the national parliament.

The 1977 elections led to a crushing defeat for the Congress, which won only 154 seats, and the election of a Janata government. Gandhi was tried for the excesses of the Emergency but prosecution backfired on the Janata government as it became riven with factional conflict. In 1980 when a national election was called, Gandhi campaigned on a platform of a government that works. She made a successful comeback, winning 351 seats.

Gandhi's final term as Prime Minister was marked by the centralization and personalization of power. Dissent within Congress was not tolerated. Opposition state governments were regularly undermined by the imposition of President's Rule. Following the defeat of Congress in Andhra Pardesh and Karnataka, Gandhi sought to consolidate her support among the Hindu community.

Following the return to power in 1980, Gandhi dismissed the Akali Dal (Sikh Party) led state government in Punjab. This led to a state-wide agitation by the Akali Dal for regional autonomy. Factions within Congress supported the more militant groups among the Sikhs in order to gain party advantage. Between 1981 and 1983 several rounds of negotiations took place between Sikh leaders and the central government, but Gandhi always blocked a deal. As violence in Punjab increased, central rule was imposed. On 4 June 1984 Gandhi ordered the Indian Army to eradicate militant resistance based in the Golden Temple. Operation Blue Star resulted in the deaths of 1,000 people and the permanent alienation of the Sikh community.

Although Operation Blue Star made Gandhi very popular among the Hindu community, it marked the first major use of the Indian army against civilians and was followed by a mutiny of soldiers. Sikh resentment continued to fester and Gandhi was assassinated by her bodyguard on 31 October 1984. Her death was followed by massacres of Sikhs in Delhi in which 3,000 lost their lives.

Gandhi is often seen as the practitioner of *realpolitik*. What she lacked in intellectual ability she compensated for by a ruthless streak gained from a long apprenticeship in politics. Gandhi began the process of deinstitutionalization of Congress with her plebiscitary politics in the early 1970s and the destruction of the old Congress Party. She is best contrasted with her father, Nehru, and is seen as a centralizer who outmanœuvred more experienced contenders for power.

Gandhi, Mohandas Karamchand (b. Porbandar, 2 Oct. 1869; d. Delhi 30 Jan. 1948)

Indian; leader of Indian National Congress, religious leader

Son of a Prime Minister of a princely state, Gandhi was educated in Gujarat and England, where he qualified as a barrister. On return to India he was unable to secure employment in the legal profession and then left for South Africa in 1883. In South Africa Gandhi was employed by a firm of Muslim lawyers in Pretoria and became involved in number of struggles against the authorities. During these agitations Gandhi perfected the technique of non-violent protest that he was to use later in India.

Gandhi returned to India in 1915. Immediately he joined in the task of building the Indian National Congress (Congress) as a mass movement. His simple style of a white loin-cloth, white shawl, and sandals appealed to rural masses who soon gave him the title 'Mahatma' (great saint).

Gandhi's political philosophy revolved around three key concepts: *satyagraha* (non-violence), *sawaraj* (home rule), and *sarvodaya* (welfare of all). Whereas *satyagraha* was essentially a tactic of achieving political ends by non-violent means, *sawaraj* and *sarvodaya* sought to encourage—through social work, spinning of cotton, rural uplift, and social welfare—ideas of individual and collective improvement and regeneration. Such regeneration, Gandhi insisted, was necessary if India was to rediscover her enduring historical and religious self and throw off British rule.

In 1919 Gandhi persuaded the Congress to launch a Non-Cooperation Movement (1919–22) that soon attracted the support of the Muslim community. This movement snowballed into a country-wide agitation which took a violent turn with the Chauri Chaura incident (1922). Following this incident he suspended the movement and was sentenced to six years' imprisonment. He was released in February 1924.

During the next five years Gandhi devoted himself to the 'constructive programme'—social work aimed at uplift of the poor and building Muslim-Hindu unity. Following the Simon Commission (1927–30) and the *Nehru Report (1928), he launched the Civil Disobedience Movement (1930–3) which began with the famous Dandi Marcha and the Salt *satyagraha*. This movement was suspended for a while as Gandhi participated in the Round Table Conference (1931) in London. During his visit to London he stayed with the poor in the East End. But as the conference failed to produce an outcome satisfactory to Congress, the agitation was resumed upon return to India. The failure of the Round Table Conference led to the announcement of the Communal Award (1932) by the British government which gave communal representation, including untouchable Hindus, in provincial legislatures. This award led Gandhi to undertake a fast that led to the Poona Pact (1932) by which untouchable leaders renounced separate representation for remaining within the Hindu fold.

Gandhi severed formal links with the Congress in 1934 but remained its guiding light. He moved to his ashram in Wardha and concentrated on the 'constructive programme' until 1940 when he briefly resumed leadership of the Congress at a time when India had been declared to be at war. This declaration, made in 1939, was opposed by the Congress, which offered to support the war effort provided it was given a firm guarantee of independence. The rejection of such promise by the colonial government led the Congress to launch a Quit India Movement (1942). This national movement was ruthlessly suppressed and Gandhi was kept in detention at the Aga Khan Palace until 1944.

Between 1944 and 1945 Gandhi engaged in prolonged dialogue with M. A. *Jinnha, leader of the Muslim League, for a political settlement that could accommodate both the Congress and the League. These discussions proved fruitless and, as the end of British rule loomed, Gandhi became increasingly sidelined in the discussions about the post-independence *shape* of India.

Gandhi's last major act as a national political leader was to fast for peace amidst growing sectarian conflict between Hindus and Muslims. Twice he fasted in Calcutta (1946 and 1947) to protest against the religious killing that was taking place. After partition in August 1947, Gandhi returned to Delhi to help restore harmony among Hindus and Muslims. Gandhi's activities had aroused much hostility among Hindu extremists. On 30 January 1948, Nathuram Godse, who was the editor of *Hindu Mahasabah* extremist weekly, shot Gandhi at point blank range while he was on his way to the evening prayer meeting. He died instantly.

Gandhi is revered in India as 'the father of the nation'. Since his death he has become the source of inspiration for non-violent political movements such as the civil rights movement in the USA and Northern Ireland. Gandhi's insistence that means were more important than the ends distinguished him from other great political leaders of the twentieth century, like *Lenin and *Mao, with whom he is often compared.

Critics of Gandhi have argued that his tactics unnecessarily delayed the departure of the British, precipitated the partition of India, and led to the Hinduization of Congress because of his over-emphasis on religion. His defence of caste especially annoyed the untouchable (outcastes) who were denied political independence due to astute political manœuvres. Few of Gandhi's ideas were put into practice by independent India.

Gandhi, Rajiv (b. 20. Aug. 1944; d. Sriperumbudur, 21 May 1991)
Indian; Prime Minister 1984–9

The son of Indira *Gandhi, Gandhi was educated at the élite Doon School in Dehra Dun. In 1961 his interest in engineering took him to Imperial College, London, and Trinity College, Cambridge. He left Cambridge before taking a degree and was married to Sonia Maino in 1964.

After his return to India Gandhi concentrated on flying and in 1967 he joined the staff of the domestic airline. For thirteen years he flew propeller-driven aircraft and developed a reputation as a reliable, rather reticent man. Throughout this period he lived quietly with his family in the residence of his mother, who for most of that time was India's Prime Minister.

During the Emergency and after Gandhi remained aloof from politics. When his brother, Sanjay Gandhi was killed (June 1980), Gandhi entered politics with great reluctance and was elected a Member of Parliament in 1981. Within a few months he was made a general secretary of the All-India Congress Committee and acquired significant party influence.

Gandhi's first major achievement was the organization of the Asian Games (1982). He drew on his experience as a pilot by emphasizing the value of technology and modern business methods. When his mother was assassinated on 31 October 1984, Gandhi was sworn in as Prime Minister.

As Prime Minister Gandhi sought to remove many of the corrupt and criminal elements within Congress, whom he excluded from the candidate list in the general election in late December 1984. The election resulted in a massive 'Indira wave' which gave the Congress a more than two-thirds majority.

On being re-elected Gandhi moved swiftly to deal with the Sikh agitation. In 1985 the Rajiv–Longowal Accord was signed which granted the Sikhs most of their demands. This agreement was also accompanied by accords in Assam and Mizoram. Gandhi also declared that he would hold party elections and denounced the working of Congress at its centenary session (1985). But perhaps the most significant innovation was the emphasis on modernization of the economy and economic liberalization. This created an access to consumer goods that had been largely denied to Indians under Nehruvian planning.

By early 1986 Rajiv had effected a U-turn in domestic policy. Many of the provisions of the Rajiv–Longowal Accord remained unimplemented and thereafter he resorted to using the policy of force. In 1987 Punjab was placed under President's Rule. This reversal was followed by a dispute with President Zail Singh and the constant shuffling of ministers. The most notable casualty was V. P. Singh, who was dismissed as Minister for Defence.

Politically the single largest blow to Gandhi's reputation was the Bofors scandal which clouded the second half of his period in office. It emerged that large commissions had been paid by the Swedish arms manufacturer in connection with a contract for weapons for the Indian army. It was never established that any of the money had come Gandhi's way but he clouded the atmosphere by seeming reluctant to prosecute the issue.

In foreign policy the emphasis on economic liberalization and technology moved India closer to the West. However the military relationship with the Soviet Union remained. Relations with Pakistan remained strained and almost led to conflict during Operation Brass Tacks (1986). In 1987 the Indo-Sri Lankan Peace Accord led to the deployment of over 50,000 Indian troops in Sri Lanka. The Indian army became embroiled in a conflict with Tamil Tigers and, as the casualties mounted, it was withdrawn in 1990.

Gandhi fought the 1989 general election against mounting opposition charges of corruption and incompetence. The Congress suffered a heavy defeat to be replaced by the Janata Dal coalition. In opposition Gandhi sought to revive the party. When the Janata coalition collapsed, Gandhi offered support to a breakaway faction led by Chandra Shekhar that ruled between November 1989 and June 1991. When the arrangement between Shekhar and Gandhi led to a disagreement, the former called for elections in May 1991. While campaigning for his party in Sriperumbudur, Tamil Nadu, Gandhi was killed by a suicide bomber believed to be a member of Tamil Tigers.

Gandhi is remembered as a reluctant politician whose image as 'Mr Clean' and as a modernizer who wanted to take India into the twenty-first century was quickly tarnished by his inability to cope with the realities of Indian politics. He sought technocratic solutions to political problems and, towards the end of his period as Prime Minister, became increasingly out of touch with domestic realities.

Garner, John Nance (b. Red River, Texas, 22 Nov. 1868; d. 7 Nov. 1967)

US; member of the US House of Representatives 1903–33, Speaker of the House 1931–3, Vice-President 1933–41

The son of a Confederate cavalry trooper, Garner received only limited elementary education. Then, after attending Vanderbilt university for one term, he read law whilst employed in the office of Sims and Wright, Clarkesville, Texas. He was called to the bar in 1890 and began practising law at Uvalde Texas, at the same time he edited the weekly *Uvalde Leader*.

His forty-six-year long public career began in 1894 when he was appointed to an unexpired term as Uvalde county judge. Re-elected to a further term in 1895, but defeated in 1897, he turned his attention to the state legislature. After serving two terms in the Texas House of Representatives, 1898–1902, he was elected Democratic Representative for the 15th Texas congressional district, a new seat he had persuaded the state legislature to create. He served in Congress continuously for thirty years, including two years as elected minority leader, 1929–31, and two as Speaker of the House, 1931–3. A candidate for his party's nomination for President in 1932, he agreed to release his delegates in favour of Franklin D. *Roosevelt and was rewarded with the vice-presidency, which he held throughout Roosevelt's first two terms. In 1940 he broke with Roosevelt over the latter's decision to run for a third term and challenged him for the party's nomination. On failing to secure it, he retired to his Texas homestead to live out the rest of his life reading, discussing politics, and regaling people with tales of his Washington years.

Fondly nicknamed 'Cactus Jack' after the inhospitable landscape of his birthplace, Garner was a colourful, independent-minded politician who was renowned in Washington for his somewhat eccentric lifestyle. At election time he refused to campaign for votes and when Speaker of the House he refused use of an official car. His working day began at 7.30 a.m., he went to bed by 9 p.m., and, except in times of dire emergency, would not answer the telephone after 6 p.m. Claiming that he was 'striking a blow for liberty' he openly drank a glass of whiskey a day throughout the Prohibition years. He is alleged to have dismissed the vice-presidency as 'not worth a pitcher of warm piss'.

Geisel, Ernesto (b. Bento Gonçalves, Rio Grande do Sul, 3 Aug. 1907; d. Rio de Janeiro, 12 Sept. 1996)

Brazilian; President of Brazil 1974–9

Ernesto Geisel, like Getúlio *Vargas and Luís Carols *Prestes, was a *gaúcho*, born in Brazil's southernmost state of Rio Grande do Sul, the son of German Lutheran immigrants. Like many *gáuchos*, and many sons of families from the north-east, Geisel and his brothers saw the officer corps of the army as a source of education and a means of social advancement. His brother Orlando eventually became Minister of War, under the military president Garrastazú Médici (1969–74), who, like his predecessor, Artur Costa e Silva (1967–9) was also a *gaúcho*.

Ernesto Geisel's career was typical of many able officers in the Brazilian army, a mixture of military and civilian appointments. In the 1950s, he served on the staff of the National Security Council, but, from 1955 to 1956, was Superintendent of the President Bernardles oil refinery. In 1957, he represented the War Ministry on the National Petroleum Council, then headed the intelligence section of the Army General Staff. Later, he became President of Petrobras, Brazil's state-owned oil industry, the country's biggest company.

Geisel early joined the movement against President João Goulart, which culminated in the coup of 1964, but he belonged to the 'Sorbonne' group of officers, those associated with the ESG, Escola Superior de Guerra, who always wanted a return to civilian government. In this, he was associated with General Golbery do Couto e Silva, yet another *gaúcho*, the *éminence grise* of President Castello Branco and, in time, of Geisel himself, as President.

1974 was a political watershed, with election victories for the opposition. President Geisel spoke of a 'slow, gradual and secure' *distensão*, or political relaxation. Many commentators, then and since, gave insufficient weight to the qualifying adjective, 'secure', showing that he sought a political opening within the priorities of 'national security'.

Geisel also wanted 'relative democracy', within a controlled process of redemocratization; but, he worked steadily for that process, even in his much criticized 'April

Package' of 1977, which, while apparently reactionary, was designed to safeguard *distensão* against its right-wing opponents, especially in the intelligence services. Geisel tried 'slowly' and 'securely' to guide Brazil back to democracy, a process which sometimes eluded his control, but which, eventually, led to restored democratic government, in 1985.

Geisel's economic policies were criticized for pursuing massively expensive projects, which were accused of feeding inflation and pushing up Brazil's foreign debt, but he was, above all, pragmatic, in, for example, promoting the use of alcohol as a substitute for petrol after the 1973 oil crisis and allowing foreign companies access to oil exploration.

After leaving office, Geisel, as a prominent business leader, continued to influence both military and national politics. He was an austere figure, remote and authoritarian, but always pragmatic, not least in steering Brazil back towards more open forms of government.

Genscher, Hans-Dietrich (b. Reideburg bei Halle, 21 Mar. 1927)

German; Vice-Chancellor and Foreign Minister 1973–92, leader of the FDP 1974–85

Born in Reideburg in what was then Middle Germany, Genscher was briefly involved in the fighting in 1945. He studied law in Leipzig in the new Soviet Zone/German Democratic Republic (GDR), fleeing to the West in 1952. Having been a member of the (East German) Liberal Democratic Party he immediately joined the Liberal FDP. He was soon called upon to do service for the FDP as deputy chairman in 1968 and chairman in 1974. He supported the FDP's move to the left and was rewarded with the Ministry of the Interior in 1969 in the *Brandt SDP–FDP government. He was also faced with rising terrorism, including the massacre of eleven Israeli athletes at the Munich Olympics in September 1972 by Palestinian terrorists. Genscher created the GS-9 anti-terrorist corps which later achieved some notable successes.

By 1982 Genscher feared that the FDP could suffer because of the unpopularity of the SPD. Although the party had fought the 1980 election on the clear understanding it would remain with the SPD, he took it out of *Schmidt's government and into a coalition with *Kohl's CDU/CSU. A number of prominent members left the party and, in the election of 1983, the FDP's vote fell and he resigned from the chairmanship in 1985.

The high point of Genscher's career was concluding the negotiations leading to the restoration of German unity on 3 October 1990. After taking over as Vice-Chancellor and Foreign Minister in 1974 he pursued a crippling schedule in his search for international understanding, especially between West Germany and the Soviet bloc. Part of Genscher's enthusiasm was due to the fact that he was himself from East Germany. He remained Foreign Minister to May 1992, a remarkable European record. Although the three chancellors he served under, *Brandt, *Schmidt, and *Kohl, were deeply involved in foreign policy, this should not detract from his efforts. He worked towards the deepening and broadening of the European Community. Serious discussion of monetary union was initiated and Greece (1981), Spain (1986), and Portugal (1986) joined the Community. He worked for closer ties with the Middle East states, was the first Western Foreign Minister to visit Albania (1987), and persuaded the Community to recognize Croatia and Slovenia in January 1992, a move later criticized by some of Germany's allies.

Gerö, Ernö (b. 1898; d. Budapest, 12 Mar. 1980)

Hungarian; General Secretary of the Hungarian Socialist Workers' Party 1956

As a member of the illegal Hungarian Communist Party (HCP), Gerö spent much of the inter-war period either in Soviet exile or working for the Comintern in France, Belgium, and Spain. In 1944 he returned to Hungary as chairman of the HCP's provisional central committee. When *Rákosi returned to Hungary in February 1945, *Stalin insisted that he should have overall control of the HCP. Thereafter Gerö was his loyal second in command. In 1950 he became member of the 'Defence Committee' alongside Rákosi, and Mihály Farkas, the Minister of the Interior. This triumvirate was the real centre of power in Hungary, bypassing the party's Central Committee and Politburo. Gerö had supreme control of the economy and supported a brutal and rapid industrialization programme which did much to destabilize the country by the mid-1950s. In 1952 he announced at the HCP's Second Party Congress that he would transform Hungary from a peasant country to a modern 'country of iron and steel' within four years. In 1953 he became Minister of the Interior, a move which Rákosi intended to stem Imre *Nagy's power. When Rákosi resigned as General Secretary on 18 July 1956 Gerö received Soviet support to replace him. He intended to make concessions to the workers, but to continue with the forced collectivization of agriculture. He was unable to stop mounting unrest and demands for his replacement by Imre Nagy. In early October 1956, Gerö and *Kádár were in Moscow where they pressed for *Nagy's return to the party as the only way of calming the unrest. On 25 October 1956, when the Hungarian uprising had started, the Soviet authorities insisted that Gerö resign as General Secretary in favour of Kádár and follow Rákosi into exile in the Soviet Union. He was expelled from the party in 1962.

Gheorghiu-Dej, Gheorghe (b. Birlap, Moldavia, 8 Nov. 1901; d. 19 Mar. 1965)
Romanian; Leader 1952–65

Gheorghe Gheorghiu worked as a tramway worker in the inter-war period. He joined the illegal Romanian Communist Party in 1929. From 1933 to 1944 he was imprisoned at the town of Dej for organizing a railway strike and added 'Dej' to his surname to commemorate this period. He escaped from prison in August 1944, after which he became Secretary-General of the RCP. With Soviet support, he played a key role in the overthrow of Radescu's coalition government in 1945. After 1946 he held a succession of economic posts. At the same time he built up his control of the organization of the RCP and in 1952 became Prime Minister. In June that year he launched an anti-Semitic campaign which coincided with Stalin's purge of the Jews in the Soviet Union. It enabled him to eliminate the faction of his rival, Ana *Pauker, within the RCP, giving him complete control of the party.

While *Stalin lived, Gheorghiu-Dej was ardently Stalinist in both domestic and foreign policy. After 1953 he adapted to *Khrushchev's doctrine of peaceful coexistence with the West. Convinced of Romania's loyalty, Khrushchev withdrew all Soviet troops from the country in 1958. In 1961 Gheorghiu-Dej became Romanian President and launched an industrialization campaign. This was at odds with the plans of Comecon and led to conflict with the Soviet Union. Gheorghiu-Dej died of lung cancer in 1965.

Gierek, Eduard (b. Bédzin, near Katowice, 6 Jan. 1919, 1913)
Polish; First Secretary of the Polish United Peasants and Workers' Party (PZPR) 1970–80

Gierek was the son a coalminer. In 1923, after his father's death in a mining accident, he and his mother moved to France. There he went to work in the mines at the age of 13. He joined the French Communist Party in 1931, emigrated to Belgium in 1937, and during the Second World War he fought in the Belgian resistance. In 1946 he became chairman of the National Council of Poles in Belgium. He returned to Poland in 1948, joined the PZPR, and embarked on a career in the party *apparat*. He was elected to the Polish parliament, the Sejm, in 1952. In 1954 he was awarded a degree in mining engineering by the Crakow School of Mining. In 1956 he was elected to the PZPR's Central Committee and became Party First Secretary for the province of Katowice, Poland's most important industrial region. In 1970 he replaced *Gomułka as leader of the PZPR amid serious industrial unrest, promising the reversal of recently introduced austerity policies. He represented the PZPR's 'technocrat faction' and in the 1970s he oversaw massive borrowing on the international market. The loans were intended for the modernization of the Polish economy, but were incompetently applied. Often they were used to buy consumer goods to keep the workers quiet. In 1980 Gierek faced economic crisis and another upsurge in worker unrest in response to price rises which led to the birth of Solidarity. After a heart attack he resigned in favour of Stanisław Kania. In July 1981, when the corruption of his regime was exposed he was expelled from the PZPR. *Jaruzelski interned him for a year in December 1981.

Gingrich, Newton **(Newt)** (b. Harrisburg, Pennsylvania, 17 June 1943)

US; Member of the US House of Representatives 1978– ; minority whip 1989; Speaker of the House 1994–

Named after his natural father, Newton McPherson, Newt Gingrich was adopted by his stepfather, army lieutenant Robert Gingrich. He graduated BA from Emory University in 1965 and from Tulane University, New Orleans, he graduated MA in 1968 and gained a Ph.D. in European History in 1971. As a temporary stepping-stone to a career in politics he became a history professor at West Georgia College, chosen for what he regarded as its potential as a future political constituency. In 1974 and again in 1976 he unsuccessfully challenged West Georgia's sitting Congressman, Democrat Jack Flynt. He finally gained the seat for the Republicans in 1978 when Flynt retired.

Gingrich soon achieved prominence as an advocate of confrontational politics and emerged as the principal spokesman for the conservative coalition in the House. Involving himself closely in the process of candidate selection, he set about transforming the Republican Party into a more disciplined, cohesive instrument for revolutionizing the American political agenda.

He is attributed with being the architect of the Republican landslide of 1994 which brought the first Republican majority in the lower house for forty years and the speakership to Gingrich himself. Having fought the election on the basis of his programmatic 'Contract with America' promising balanced budgets, lower taxes, welfare reform, and a crackdown on crime, Gingrich used his disciplined Republican freshmen to try to deliver his promised revolution in American politics.

Described as ruthless, brilliant, obnoxious, Gingrich transformed the House of Representatives and the speakership into instruments of personal and political power. Gifted propagandist and populist, Gingrich introduced a new style into American politics and succeeded in setting the agenda for the 1990s. But his political future is by no means certain. Having ousted the previous Democratic Speaker on ethics charges, he has himself become the subject of investigation by the House ethics committee. He is the author of *To Renew America* (1994).

Giolitti, Giovanni (b. Mondovì, 22 Oct. 1842; d. 17 July 1928)

Italian; Prime Minister five times between 1892 and 1921

Born into a wealthy professional family in Piedmont, Giolitti went to university in Turin where he graduated in law at the age of 19, though he afterwards said that he distinguished himself mainly as a fencer. He became a Treasury civil servant in 1862 and then transferred to the Court of Accounts; in 1882 he became a member of the Council of State, the senior administrative tribunal, and in the same year was elected to the Chamber of Deputies for the constituency of Cuneo (Piedmont). He was nominated as Prime Minister following the government crisis 1892, but had to resign after being implicated in the banking crisis of 1893. This interrupted his political career for nearly a decade. He returned first as Interior Minister in 1901 and then as Prime Minister in 1903, and dominated Italian politics for the next two decades.

Giolitti's method, sometimes referred to as transformism, consisted in the relatively unscrupulous manipulation of the electoral system, so as to ensure the return of deputies sympathetic to his policies or at least to his continuation in power. The transformism consisted in the continual changes in the governmental majority in parliament depending on the particular measure. In this way Giolitti secured relatively stable government in a parliament whose largest grouping, the Liberals, was a collection of notables rather than a modern party.

Giolitti is credited with using these less than transparent methods to secure policy advances in social reform, which resulted in the closer integration of the reformist wing of the Italian Socialist movement; when this broke down over foreign policy, Giolitti developed good relations with the other great excluded group of Italian politics, the Catholic social organizations. He believed in the tactical use of diplomacy and military force to reduce Italy's traditional dependence on the European great powers, and was firmly neutralist during the First World War. He returned to power in 1919 in a parliament dominated for the first time by the Catholic and Socialist parties, for which his methods were much less suitable. Like many others, he underestimated the emerging threat of the Fascists, and believed initially they could be brought into the constitutional fold as the Socialists had been. The dissolution of parliament in 1921 at his behest and the elections which followed mark the end of Giolitti's influence. He opposed the Fascist dictatorship, particularly after 1925.

Giolitti was always a controversial figure during his political career, and he remains so. His two decades of power are known as the Giolittian period by supporter and critic alike, and for better or worse are regarded as typical of what the Liberal state was capable of; he was described (among others by the historian Benedetto Croce) as the greatest statesman of the Liberal period after Cavour, and by the radical Gaetano Salvemini as the 'minister for the underworld'.

Giscard d'Estaing, Valéry (b. Koblenz, Germany, 2 Feb. 1926)

French; Minister of Finance 1962–6, 1969–74, President of the Republic 1974–81

Valéry Giscard d'Estaing came from an upper-class family with close links to business and politics. He attended two of France's élite training schools and, after a brief period as an Inspector of Finances, was elected in 1956 deputy for his grandfather's constituency in the Puy-de-Dôme. A member of the Conservative Independent Party, he broke with the majority of his colleagues by supporting *de Gaulle over Algerian independence and the direct election of the presidency. He was rewarded by being made Minister of Finance in *Pompidou's 1962 government, in which post he prepared a stabilization plan. The plan's austerity measures were blamed by de Gaulle for his relatively poor showing in the first round of the 1965 presidential election and led to Giscard's replacement as Finance Minister. Giscard used his period out of office to create his own political party, the Independent Republicans, and to prepare himself for a future presidential contest. He sought to distinguish himself from the Gaullist Party, by emphasizing his credentials as a European-minded progressive and criticizing the authoritarian style of the Gaullist presidency. In 1969, he played a decisive role in de Gaulle's departure from office by advocating a 'no' vote in the referendum on regional reform, an action which earned him the enduring hostility of de Gaulle's most fervent supporters. Yet he immediately signalled his support for the Gaullist candidate for the presidency, *Pompidou, who in turn recognized Giscard's professional competence and political strengths by making him Minister of Finance. The two men engineered a successful devaluation of the franc in 1969 and co-operated in the industrialization programme which was the hallmark of the Pompidou presidency.

In the early 1970s, Giscard used his position, and his party allies, to prepare himself for the presidential contest which Pompidou's incurable illness was bringing ever closer. When Pompidou died, in March 1974, he was able to present himself as the natural leader of a France which wanted political and social change but was fearful of the consequences of the victory of a Socialist candidate backed by the Communists. He was greatly helped in the first round of the presidential election by the personal weaknesses of his principal rival, *Chaban Delmas, and by the divisions the latter's candidacy aroused in the Gaullist Party. He easily saw off Chaban's challenge in round one and then gained a narrow, but clear, victory over *Mitterrand in the second, decisive ballot. The Giscard presidency began with a flurry of political and social reforms: abortion was legalized and contraception made easier, the voting age was reduced to 18, the role of the Constitutional Council was enhanced, direct elections to the European Parliament were accepted. The president tried to humanize the presidency by visiting prisons and inviting dustmen to breakfast at the Élysée Palace. Giscard's aim, which he outlined in his book *Democratie française*, was to create a France in which the adversarial absolutes of Gaullism and Marxism would give way to a more consensual polity. At the same time, however, he insisted on his right to exercise the full range of his presidential powers and quickly demonstrated an authoritarian style of political management. He established close relations with the German Chancellor Helmut *Schmidt and was able, with him, to determine the agenda of the European Community, including the creation of the European Monetary System.

His presidency faced two major problems. One was the impact on French growth of the worldwide recession which followed the oil price rises of the mid-1970s. The other was his inability to control, let alone eliminate, opposition within the coalition which had elected him. He lacked the support of a majority party in the National Assembly and soon found himself challenged by his first Prime Minister, the Gaullist Jacques *Chirac. In August 1976, Chirac resigned office and immediately set about the task of reviving the Gaullist Party as a vehicle for his own presidential ambitions. Relations between the Gaullist Rassemblement pour la Republique and the Independent Republicans deteriorated and Giscard suffered a major setback when Chirac defeated his candidate in a contest for the Paris townhall. The president fought back by creating a confederation of non-Gaullist parties, the Union pour la Democratie Française, and was able to prevent a left-wing victory in the 1978 legislative elections. The respite was short-lived. Chirac and his supporters waged an unceasing propaganda war on the President, whom they accused of betraying French independence and failing to provide strong leadership. What made Giscard vulnerable was the steadily rising jobless rate, which alarmed an electorate used to virtually full employment, and the growing criticism of his personal style. He was damaged by revelations of the gift of diamonds he had accepted from the crazed 'emperor' of Central Africa, *Bokassa, and by stories of a near monarchical style far removed from the 'citizen president' image he had portrayed in 1974. In the 1981 presidential elections, he faced opposition not only from the left but from the rejuvenated Gaullist Party under Chirac. He obtained only 28 per cent of the vote on round one of the elections and his fate was sealed when Chirac declined to offer him full support on round two. In the second round, he won only 48.25 per cent of the vote to Mitterrand's 51.75 per cent.

Giscard tried throughout the 1980s to re-establish his credentials as the natural leader of the French Right. He was re-elected to the National Assembly in 1984, headed a united conservative list for the European Parliament in 1988–9, and was an energetic proponent of the cause of European unity. But the opposition of Chirac's Gaullists remained implacable and he found it increasingly difficult to control his erstwhile protégés in the UDF. He was unable to muster enough support for a presidential bid in 1988 and 1995, and failed in his 1995 bid to be elected mayor of Clermont-Ferrand.

For all his undoubted talents, Giscard's career ended in disappointment. He had the misfortune to become President just at the time when the 'thirty glorious years' of French economic expansionism was coming to an end. And he never managed to unify the warring factions of the French right as his two predecessors had done.

Goebbels, Josef (b. Rheydt, 29 Oct. 1897; d. 1 May 1945)

German; Minister of Popular Enlightenment and Propaganda 1933–45

Goebbels was born into a Catholic working-class family in the small textile town of Rheydt. Perhaps he sought to excel with his intellect because a childhood illness had left him permanently crippled. Scholarships saw him through grammar school and university. At Heidelberg he was awarded a doctorate in literature. After failing to get his literary works published he took to politics, joining *Hitler's NSDAP in 1922. His propaganda skills were soon recognized in this small party but his career nearly ended in 1926 when he backed the NSDAP left against Hitler. Hitler convinced him and forgave him and promoted his career. From 1927 to 1935 he edited the Nazi weekly *Der Angriff*. Election to parliament followed in 1928. In the following year he was given charge of all NSDAP propaganda.

Shortly after Hitler became German Chancellor, in 1933, Goebbels was appointed Minister of Popular Enlightenment and Propaganda. By that time the German mass media were under virtual Nazi censorship.

Goebbels realized that most people have little interest in politics and ensured that the radio and cinema served the popular desire for entertainment and escapism. He was responsible for many propaganda films, especially during the war, often wrapped up as historical adventures. *Ohm Krüger* sought to expose British crimes in the Boer War, 1899–1901. *GPU* was one of the few anti-Soviet films. Several films were made about the Irish struggle against the British. The popularization of mercy killing was the theme of *Ich klage an* ('I Accuse'). *Der ewige Jude* ('The Eternal Jew') was one of the most grotesque misuses of documentary technique in the history of the cinema. His propaganda prepared the ground for the massacre of the Jews, the useless sacrifices of German youth, and the destruction of German cities. In the end, he fell victim of his own propaganda, sacrificing not only his own and his wife's lives, but those of their six children in the belief 'They belong to the Third Reich and to the Führer, and if these two cease to exist there can be no further place for them.' Goebbels followed Hitler to the end, having himself and his wife killed the day after Hitler's suicide.

Goldwater, Barry Morris (b. Phoenix, Arizona, 1 Jan. 1909)

US; US Senator 1953–65, 1969–87, Republican presidential candidate 1964

Educated at Staunton Military Academy and the University of Arizona, Goldwater began to work for the family firm, Goldwater's Inc., in Phoenix in 1929, rising to become president of the company in 1937. In 1952 he was elected to the Senate and established a reputation as a leading conservative within the Republican Party. In 1964 he won the Republican nomination for President following a bitter contest with his liberal Republican rival, Nelson *Rockefeller, which split the Republican Party asunder. In the 1964 presidential election he lost in a landslide to his Democratic opponent, President *Johnson. Although he was regarded as a man of honesty, integrity, and attractive personality, he was viewed in 1964 by commentators and by public opinion as an extremist who was representative of a minority viewpoint of right-wing conservatives and whose standpoint was outmoded and out of the mainstream of American politics. From his humiliation in 1964, however, he rose to rehabilitation, both in terms of personal stature and growing support for his political philosophy. In 1968 he won election again as Senator from Arizona and became a highly respected senior figure in the Republican Party. In 1974 he was one of the principal senior figures who persuaded President *Nixon to resign in August 1974. In the 1980s his conservative policies on increased military spending and reduced domestic expenditure were largely implemented during the administration of President *Reagan. He published his conservative political views in *The Conscience of a Conservative* (1960).

Gomez, Juan Vicente (b. Tachira, Venezuela, 24 July 1857; d. 17 Dec. 1935)
Venezuelan, President and Dictator of Venezuela 1908–35

Gomez began his career as a butcher and cattle rancher before entering politics. He was exiled to Colombia before returning as an officer in Cipriano Castro's small Army of the Liberal Restoration in 1899. He became Vice-President before carrying out a coup to depose the President, General Cipriano Castro, in 1908. Initially Gomez was supported by both the Liberal and Nationalist parties and the European powers and the USA who believed Gomez would be a puppet for them.

However, Gomez systematically removed all internal challenges to his authority, and built an army and central administration leadership from his followers in Tachira. Between 1914–22 Gomez formally left the presidency in the hands of a provisional president whilst he remained 'President elect' and head of the army, and even leaving Caracas to live in Maracay. He formally returned to the presidency in 1922, though leaving day-to-day matters of government in Caracas to his interior minister. He also appointed his brother as first and his son as second Vice-President. But factions soon formed around these two. In June 1923 Gomez's brother was stabbed to death in the presidential palace, and in 1928 after a wave of protests and a military uprising his son was forced to leave for Europe, and the post of Vice-President was abolished.

In 1929 Gomez again stepped down from the presidency whilst retaining power, but in 1931 in response to another military conspiracy he formally took over the presidency again where he remained until his death in 1935.

Gomez was undoubtedly a ruthless and bloody dictator, savagely repressing the student protests in 1918 and after, the various military uprisings, the frequent attempts at invasions by exiles, and in general all forms of protest. He also monopolized land and concessions for himself and his family and associates, and imposed strict censorship. Nationalist critics see his oil policy as an abject surrender of Venezuela's sovereignty. However, recent reassessments of Gomez have begun to stress his crucial role in Venezuela's modernization. He undoubtedly gave Venezuela a prolonged period of economic growth and relative political stability. He gave very generous concessions to foreign oil interests particularly in the 1922 petroleum law, but this did lead to the rapid development of the oil industry. He modernized and reformed the Venezuelan armed forces by creating a Military Academy. And through a policy of balancing the budget, his various ministers of finance ensured that a centralized tax collection system put Venezuela's public finances on a sound basis.

Gomułka, Władysław (b. Krosno, Austrian Galicia, 6 Feb. 1905; d. Warsaw, 1 Sept. 1982)
Polish; First Secretary of the Polish United Workers' Party (PZPR) 1956–70

As a young man, Gomułka worked first as a locksmith then in an oil refinery. He entered the socialist movement in 1921 at the age of 16 and organized youth groups. In 1926 he joined the illegal Polish Communist Party and was imprisoned twice in the 1930s for his trade union activities. In 1934 he went to Moscow to attend the International Lenin School, returning to Poland in 1935. During the Second World War he was a leader of the Communist resistance, often following a line somewhat independent of Moscow, and in 1943 became leader of the Polish Communist Party.

In January 1945 Gomułka was deputy premier in the interim Lublin government as well as Minister for the Territories taken from Germany as Poland's western border moved to the Oder–Neisse line. The patronage powers which this gave him were of great importance in building up the Communist Party. Gomułka led the campaign to destroy *Mikołajczyk's Peasant Party and planned the merger between the Communists and the Socialists which took place in 1948. However, he incurred *Stalin's displeasure for proposing a 'Polish road to socialism'. Gomułka successfully resisted the collectivization of agriculture and unsuccessfully opposed the formation of the Cominform in 1947. At the founding congress of the PZPR in December 1948 he was forced by Stalin's order to make a confession of his 'errors'. He was replaced as party leader by his old rival, *Bierut, and in July 1951 was placed under house arrest.

In 1956 serious industrial unrest mounted in Poland, reaching a peak with the Poznań Rising in June. Gomułka was now a popular figure because of his resistance to Stalin. In August he was readmitted to the PZPR. In October 1956, despite initial Soviet objections, the PZPR leadership appointed him First Secretary of the party in order to avoid revolution. In 1957 he introduced limited political reforms, reducing the powers of the secret police, reducing the repression of the Catholic church and ending the collectivization of agriculture. However, he was true to his predecessors' policies of austerity and industrialization. His failure to improve living standards led to general popular disappointment with him. By 1968 Gomułka faced growing and cohesive opposition from workers and the intelligentsia. The poor state of the economy made it difficult to make economic concessions. On 20 December 1970 Gomułka resigned after riots against increases in food prices. He was succeeded as First Secretary by *Gierek.

González Márquez, Felipe (b. Seville, 5 Mar. 1942)

Spanish; Prime Minister 1982–96, leader of the Socialist Party 1974–

One of the country's leading political figures in the twentieth century, González first joined the Socialist Party (PSOE) in 1964, having previously been a member of the Socialist Youth. After university studies in Seville and Louvain in Belgium, in 1968 González set up a labour law practice in the Andalucían capital. Together with his friend and subsequent first lieutenant, Alfonso Guerra, González soon established a reputation for trenchant arguments and a highly critical attitude towards the party's 'historic' leadership, based in Toulouse following defeat in the Spanish Civil War. Repeated interference and pressure from the exiled executive led to both their resignations, followed in 1974 by a successful assault on the existing leadership.

Once established in the new executive, González and Guerra consolidated their position. Guerra became editor of *El Socialista*, and González moved to Madrid in 1975, where he largely bypassed the existing PSOE organization and set up his own party machinery, aided by Miguel Boyer (later to become Economy Minister in the first González administration). González was able to attract loyalty and support on the basis of his undoubted political talents: he was intelligent, highly articulate, and charismatic. Equally important, in Guerra he had the perfect partner, who operated behind the scenes to set up and run a dynamic party machine.

As Prime Minister, González dominated Spanish politics. His first period in office saw the consolidation of Spanish democracy and the full incorporation of the country into the international community, as Spain joined the European Community and confirmed its membership of NATO. His second administration (1986–9) reaped the economic rewards of these developments and saw Spain enjoy dramatic levels of growth. However, González appeared to become disillusioned during this period. His presence in the Spanish parliament became increasingly infrequent, and he concentrated ever more on international affairs, apparently seeking to assume a role similar to that of the French president.

Often looking weary, or even bored, with domestic political matters, González announced that the 1989 general election would be the last in which he led the Socialist Party. He was forced to retract this remark as a major struggle developed over the succession. Indeed, his third administration (1989–93) was marked by internal party strife, exacerbated by growing evidence of corruption. After the enforced resignation of Alfonso Guerra—implicated in a scandal involving his brother Juan—as Deputy Prime Minister in 1991, relations between the two PSOE leaders deteriorated sharply. González associated himself ever more closely with the liberal market-orientated version of social democracy espoused by his controversial Economy Minister Carlos Solchaga, against the more populist leftist rhetoric of Guerra and his followers. As the boom of the mid- to late 1980s was replaced by recession in the early 1990s, arguments within the PSOE became increasingly bitter. González remained identified, however, as the party's greatest electoral asset. This was dramatically demonstrated in the 1993 general election, in which he took full charge of the PSOE campaign and defied opinion polls to pull off an unexpected victory, although he was forced to rely on support from Jordi Pujol's Catalan Nationalists to remain in office.

Following the 1993 elections, González came under fire for presiding over a government which seemed increasingly mired in corruption scandals. An escape route seemed to open as the Spanish premier was widely tipped to succeed Jacques *Delors as president of the European Commission in 1995. However, González refused all approaches, insisting that his duty lay in rooting out corruption and in steering Spain through the challenge of meeting the convergence terms for European economic and monetary union. Having lost the support of Pujol, he was forced to go to the polls a year early in March 1996. This time he did lose the election, but by a much smaller margin than had been predicted in opinion polls. Although effectively abandoned by many leading party colleagues, who were convinced that the PSOE was heading for a catastrophic defeat, González won sufficient support to prevent an outright victory for the opposition and thereby secured his own position as leader of the PSOE against any internal challenges.

Gorbachev, Mikhail Sergeyevich (b. Stavropol region of southern Russia, 2 Mar. 1931)

Russian; General Secretary of the CPSU 1985–91

Gorbachev was born into a peasant family. He entered the Law Faculty of Moscow State University in 1950, graduating with top marks in 1955. He joined the CPSU in 1952. From 1956 he followed a career in the Communist Youth League (Comsomol) in the Stavropol region, before joining the local party apparatus in 1962. In 1967 he graduated from Stavropol Agricultural Institute. In 1970 he became First Secretary of the Stavropol region. Next year he was elected to the Central Committee. In 1978 he moved to Moscow as secretary of the Central Committee in charge of agriculture. He enjoyed the patronage of *Andropov, who made him a full member of the Politburo in 1980.

After Andropov was elected Soviet leader in November 1982, Gorbachev became the second most powerful man in the USSR, with a brief covering the whole economy. His powers increased during the brief reign of *Chernenko from 1984 to 1985. After Chernenko's death in March 1985, Gorbachev's bid for the general secretaryship was strongly resisted by the Brezhnevites within the Politburo, whom he defeated with the support of *Ligachev and *Gromyko. Gorbachev became President of the USSR after Gromyko's forced retirement in 1988.

Gorbachev's reforms revolved around the restructuring (perestroika) of the economy and increased freedom of expression (glasnost) in political and cultural affairs. He did not follow a precise blueprint in either area and it is debatable how far his policies were forced upon him by the economic crisis and growth of national unrest within the Soviet Union, which worsened with each year of his rule. He was unwilling to remove the clause of the constitution guaranteeing the 'leading role' of the Communist Party, but after 1988 undermined its power by allowing partially free elections to the legislatures in the union republics and to the Congress of People's Deputies and by augmenting the power of the presidency. This did nothing to prevent the growing self-assertiveness of the Russian (as distinct from) the Soviet Communist Party. By 1990 Gorbachev's hold on power was shaky and he was unable to satisfy the demands of conservative Communists demanding the maintenance of the Soviet Union and the party-state and of the nationalists in the republics at a time when the economy was breaking down. In August 1991, Gorbachev's opponents within the leadership staged a coup to save the union, placing him under house arrest. They surrendered three days later, having failed to win the support of either the people or the army. On his return to power, Gorbachev resigned as party leader. In December 1991 he resigned as President when the Soviet Union was voted out of existence by the representatives of its constituent republics. In 1992 Gorbachev was expelled from the CPSU for causing the collapse of the USSR.

In international affairs Gorbachev oversaw the withdrawal of the Red Army from Afghanistan, a great improvement of relations with the USA and European Community, and the normalization of relations with China. In Eastern Europe in 1989 he accepted the trade union movement Solidarity's electoral victory in Poland and then encouraged the overthrow of hard-line regimes in East Germany, Czechoslovakia, Bulgaria, and Romania, while maintaining a policy of strict non-intervention once revolutions had started. He co-operated with the US-led UN forces during the Gulf War against Iraq in 1990–1, even though it was a former Soviet ally.

Since 1991 Gorbachev has been head of the Moscow-based 'Gorbachev Fund', a centre for the study of international relations.

Gordon Walker, Patrick Chrestien (b. Sussex, 7 Apr. 1907; d. 2 Dec. 1980)

British; Foreign Secretary 1964–5; Baron (life peer) 1974

The son of a judge, Gordon Walker was brought up in India and educated at Wellington College and Christ Church, Oxford. After some years as a don, he worked with the BBC during the Second World War.

Gordon Walker entered Parliament as MP for Smethwick in 1945 and received rapid promotion in Clement *Attlee's government (1945–51). After playing a leading part in negotiating independent India's continued membership of the Commonwealth during two years as a junior minister, he became Secretary of State for Commonwealth Relations. His record there was marred by controversy over the government's refusal to recognize Seretse *Khama as head of the Bamangwato tribe in Bechuanaland after he had married a European woman.

As a firm *Gaitskell supporter, he was approached (but declined) to contest the leadership on Gaitskell's death. When Harold *Wilson formed his first government in 1964, Gordon Walker was given the Foreign Office, in spite of his having lost his seat at the general election. A vacancy in the Commons was created at Leyton, but he lost the by-election there, in January 1965, and resigned. Gordon Walker's misfortunes were largely attributed to the racial issue (he had led Labour's opposition to the Conservative government's Commonwealth Immigrants Bill). But there were also doubts about his effectiveness as a candidate. His career never recovered from this setback. Although he won Leyton in 1966 and Wilson the next year honoured a promise to restore him to ministerial office, his return to the Cabinet was short-lived. He was dropped after a mere sixteen months—divided between a non-portfolio post and the Secretaryship of State for Education. He retired from the Commons in 1974.

Gore, Albert Jr. (b. Washington, DC, 31 Mar. 1948)
US; member of the US House of Representatives 1977–85, US Senator 1985–93, Vice-President 1992–

A member of a prominent political family, Gore could be said to have been earmarked for a political career from birth. Son of the former liberal Southern Democrat Senator from Tennessee, Albert Gore Snr., Albert Jr. had a privileged education and upbringing in Washington, DC. He attended the exclusive St Alban's School and thereafter graduated BA from Harvard in 1969; attended the Graduate School of Religion, Vanderbilt University 1971–2 and Law School 1974–6. As a student he protested against the Vietnam War but was not a draft dodger. He served in Vietnam as an army journalist, 1969–71, after which he returned to Nashville taking up an appointment as an investigative journalist and editor on *The Tennessean*, 1971–6. His political career began in 1977 when he was elected as a Democrat to the US House of Representatives. He was returned to the next three successive Congresses until, in 1985, he was elected to represent Tennessee in his father's former seat in the US Senate. In addition to his work in journalism and politics Gore also retained an interest in the family farm in Tennessee and between 1971 and 1976 had his own house building and land development company.

In 1988 Gore made a bid for his party's nomination as presidential candidate but was eclipsed by front-runners Jesse *Jackson and Michael *Dukakis. In an attempt to woo conservative Southern Democrats back to the party's fold in the presidential race, he changed his stance from liberal to moderate Democrat before the southern primary's Super Tuesday. But to no avail. Lacking appeal in the North, he was routed in the primaries. He declined to run for the presidency in 1992 but by acceptance of Bill *Clinton's invitation to be his running mate, he entered office as Vice-President.

Gore was one of the handful of Democratic Senators who voted in favour of the use of force in the Gulf in 1991. He subsequently challenged the *Bush government's betrayal of the Kurds in Iraq. He has made his name as a prominent environmentalist, acquiring the nickname 'the ozone man' from President *Bush during the 1992 campaign. In association with three Democrats in the lower house, he has sponsored legislation to ease the tax burden on the working poor.

A Congressman by the age of 28, Senator at 36, and Vice-President by 44, it is unlikely that 1988 marked the end of Gore's hopes to become President. Given the Democrats need to recapture the South Gore's incumbent advantage favours his future prospects for gaining his party's nomination. Despite his obvious status as a Washington insider, he has gained popularity as a national politician who is willing to look to state and local politicians for practical policy ideas. Criticized for his lack of passion and rather wooden, pompous style during the 1992 campaign, he nevertheless proved himself to be a sharp debater who paid attention to detail. His supporters claim that Gore is a man of substance with a bright political future.

Göring, Hermann Wilhelm (b. Rosenheim, 12 Jan. 1893; d. Nuremberg 15 Oct. 1946)
German; head of government of Prussia 1933–45, Commander-in-Chief of German air force 1935–45, Plenipotentiary of Four-Year Plan 1936

The son of a colonial official, Göring ended the First World War as the much decorated commander of the famous Richthofen air squadron. He then worked as a show and transport flyer before starting his climb in the NSDAP. He took part in *Hitler's failed Munich putsch (1923) and was elected to the German parliament in 1928. When the NSDAP became the largest party in the Reichstag in 1932 he was elected its president. Once Hitler became Chancellor in 1933, he appointed Göring Minister without Portfolio, Reich Commissar for Aviation, and Prussian Minister of the Interior. Göring ruthlessly exploited these positions in the Nazi cause. On 22 February he appointed the SA, SS, and their Stahlhelm allies police auxiliaries. He later boasted to General Halder that it was he who had set fire (27 February) to the Reichstag. This was blamed on the Communists and was made the excuse for initiating a reign of terror against the left. He set up the first concentration camps in Prussia, arresting 4,000 Communists and banning the left-wing press. From April 1933 he also served as head of the Prussian government. Acting for Hitler, he carried through the bloody purge of the SA in Berlin and north Germany on 30 June 1934. He was by then the second most important man in Germany.

As Plenipotentiary for the Four-year Plan Göring helped to prepare the economy for war in 1939, stripped the Jews of their property, and used his position to amass a personal fortune. He was best known for the part he played in building up the German air force in contravention of the Versailles Treaty. It was first used in Spain to back Franco, 1936–9, and subsequently became an integral part of all Nazi aggressive plans. Göring's most decisive failure was his inability to destroy the British air force in 1940. As the war continued, Germany lost air supremacy to the Allies. Göring also lost ground in the Nazi hierarchy especially to *Himmler and *Goebbels.

Göring's death was as dramatic as his life had been. He cheated the hangman two hours before his planned execution at Nuremberg after being sentenced to death by the International Military Court in 1946.

Gottwald, Klement (b. Dedice, Moravia, 23 Nov. 1896; d. Moscow, 14 Mar. 1953)

Czech; Leader of the Czechoslovak Communist Party 1929–53, Czechoslovak President 1948–53

From a peasant family, Gottwald served in the Austro-Hungarian army on the Eastern Front during the First World War. In 1921 he was a founder member of the Czechoslovak Communist Party; he became its general secretary in 1929 with *Stalin's backing and made the party subservient to Moscow. He also worked for the Comintern in Czechoslovakia. Though organizationally strong and polling up to 10 per cent of the vote in inter-war Czechoslovakia, the Communists were not effective in parliament. After the Munich Agreement of 1938, he fled to Moscow. In December 1943 he had discussions with the Czechoslovak *Beneš, who was visiting Moscow. He returned to Prague at the same time as Beneš in 1945, and became Deputy Prime Minister in the provisional government. In May 1946 he became head of a coalition government following elections in which the Communists won 38 per cent of the vote, becoming the largest party in Czechoslovakia. He annoyed Stalin by agreeing to accept *Marshall Aid in June 1947 and withdrew his decision. By February 1948 the Communists had no chance of winning fair elections. Gottwald launched a coup, using the workers' militia and the Communist-dominated police.

In June 1948 Gottwald succeeded Beneš as President. He commenced the Stalinization of society and economy in 1949. In 1950 Gottwald carried out a purge of the followers of his Minister of the Interior, Rudolf *Slánský at Soviet instigation. This served both to protect Stalin's perceived security needs and to bolster Gottwald's domestic position. Slánský was executed after a show-trial in 1952. In March 1953 Gottwald caught pneumonia in Moscow attending Stalin's funeral, and died.

Gowon, Yakubu (b. Lur, Nigeria, 19 Oct. 1934)

Nigerian; head of state (military) 1966–75

A member of the small Angas ethnic group, Gowon is both a northerner and a Christian, a combination which was important in his political career. A professional soldier, he was trained at Sandhurst, and appointed army Chief of Staff following the January 1966 *coup d'état*. Although he did not participate in the further coup in July of the same year he was chosen, as the senior surviving officer, to become the new military head of state.

He assumed power in a period of major political crisis and, although he worked hard to prevent the secession of Biafra under the leadership of Chukwuemeka Odumegwu *Ojukwu, Nigeria descended into civil war. The federal forces, under Gowon's overall leadership, finally defeated the Biafran secessionists and after the end of the war in 1970 he embarked on a process of reconciliation under the slogan 'no victors—no vanquished' which was largely successful in reintegrating the, predominantly Ibo, rebels into the federal republic. In spite of his considerable personal triumph in this matter his regime became increasingly bogged down in inefficiency and corruption. Although there has never been any evidence to suggest that Gowon was personally corrupt, the legitimacy of his government became seriously eroded and was further damaged by his decision in 1974 to postpone indefinitely a promised return to civilian rule. In July 1975 he was overthrown in a bloodless counter-coup while he was attending an OAU meeting in Uganda. He went into exile in England, where he enrolled as an undergraduate student in political science at the University of Warwick. In 1976 he was accused, without any evidence, of complicity in a further failed counter-coup in Nigeria. He finally returned to Nigeria in 1983.

Gowon was arguably the most important, and certainly longest surviving, of Nigeria's post-independence rulers.

Grechko, Andrei Antonovich (b. near Rostov, 17 Oct. 1903; d. Moscow, 26 Apr. 1976)

Russian; Minister of Defence 1967–76

Grechko served in the Red cavalry during the Russian Civil War, after which he received training at the Frunze Military Academy. He joined the Communist Party in 1928. In 1941 he completed a course at the General Staff Academy and thereafter held senior cavalry commands. From 1943 to 1944 his cavalry armies helped recapture the northern Caucasus and Kiev. From 1944 to 1945 he commanded the First Guards Army, which advanced through the Ukraine to Czechoslovakia. In 1945 he became commander of the Kiev Military District. In 1953 he was appointed Marshal of the Soviet Union and Commander-in-Chief of the Soviet occupation forces in Germany and in the same year he was in charge of the suppression of the uprising in East Germany. In 1957 he became First Deputy Minister of Defence and Commander-in-Chief of Soviet Ground Forces and was promoted in 1960 to Commander-in-Chief of Warsaw Pact Forces. In April 1967 he became Soviet Minister of Defence, holding this position until his death in 1976. In 1973 he was made a full member of the Politburo. In the period of détente he was a hard-liner, overseeing the continuous growth of the Soviet armed forces.

Greenwood, Arthur (b. 8 Feb. 1883; d. 9 June 1954)

British; Minister of Health 1929–31, deputy leader of the Labour Party 1935–45

The son of a decorator, Greenwood was educated at a higher grade school and the Yorkshire College (later Leeds University). After graduating he taught at the university and for the Workers' Educational Association. During the First World War he was a civil servant in David *Lloyd George's secretariat. He became secretary to the Labour Party's Research Department in 1920 and played a leading role in policy formulation there until he gave up the post up, in 1943.

Greenwood entered the Commons as member for Nelson and Colne in 1922 and represented this constituency until the party's decimation in 1931. Returned to parliament at a by-election in Wakefield in 1932, he held that seat until his death. His ministerial career never matched up to the promise many saw in him in his early years or to his great popularity in the party, which resulted in his holding the deputy leadership for ten years and a lengthy membership of the National Executive Committee. After junior ministerial office in 1924, he was Minister of Health, in the

Cabinet, between 1929 and 1931. He then held a non-portfolio post in Winston *Churchill's coalition government for two years (1940–2). He also held non-portfolio Cabinet posts for two years (1945–7) in Clement *Attlee's Labour government (1945–51). His role was mainly policy co-ordination and his primary interest domestic, and especially social, policy. In this sphere his most lasting achievement was his decision (while in the wartime coalition government) to set up the Beveridge Committee, whose report laid the foundation for the post-war welfare state.

Grey, Edward (b. London, 25 Apr. 1862; d. 7 Sept. 1933)

British; Foreign Secretary 1905–16; Bt. 1882, Viscount 1916

The son of an army officer, Grey was educated at Winchester and Balliol College, Oxford, from which he was sent down. At the age of 23 he was elected Liberal MP for Berwick-on-Tweed, and retained the seat until his elevation to the peerage.

As a result of the Conservatives' monopoly of office for the previous two decades, Grey had had only three years' junior ministerial experience (1892–5) when Sir Henry *Campbell-Bannerman appointed him Foreign Secretary in 1905. His subsequent eleven consecutive years' occupancy of the post has not since been equalled.

Grey occupied the Foreign Office at a crucial period and his record was controversial. Even the circumstances of his appointment were curious. Differences within the Liberal Party in opposition had led Grey, H. H. *Asquith, and R. B. *Haldane to agree (in the so-called 'Relugas Compact') to accept office under Campbell-Bannerman only if he undertook to go to the House of Lords and to leave Asquith as leader in the Commons. When Campbell-Bannerman rejected these terms, Grey delayed the formation of the government for several days—despite the obvious risk to party unity this action presented.

Criticism of Grey's foreign secretaryship has focused upon his concealment of the true nature of the understandings reached with France before the First World War and the terms of a secret treaty he made with Italy in 1915. In the former case, neither the public, nor even the full Cabinet, was made aware that the logical implication of the arrangements arrived at was British military support for France in the event of war between the latter and Germany. Indeed, Grey maintained that Britain retained complete freedom of action in the event of the outbreak of such hostilities. Concerning Italy, Grey agreed that it should be ceded substantial rights in Dalmatia in return for declaring war on Germany. Earlier, his negotiation of the 1907 Anglo-Russian agreement over spheres of influence in Asia had had a hostile reception—not least from Liberal backbenchers, many of whom considered his policies too close to the 'imperialism' of the previous Conservative government.

Many of Grey's endeavours were, however, widely praised. He had a leading role in improving conditions in the Belgian Congo, where the treatment of the indigenous population under the rule of the King of Belgium had become an international scandal. He also played a vital part in averting the outbreak of hostilities between France and Germany over the Agadir crisis in 1911 and in helping to prepare the ground for the USA's entry into the war against Germany.

Grey undertook some public functions after his departure from office when David *Lloyd George succeeded Asquith as Prime Minister in December 1916. The most notable of these was his unsuccessful attempt, in 1919 (on the government's behalf), to persuade the USA to join the League of Nations. But his eyesight deteriorated badly and his political activities had become minimal well before his death.

Grimond, Joseph **(Jo)** (b. St Andrews, 29 July 1913; d. 24 Oct. 1993)

British; leader of the Liberal Party 1956–67; life peer 1983

Grimond was born in St Andrews in Scotland and educated at Eton and Balliol College, Oxford. After qualifying as a barrister, and service in the war, he was elected

Liberal MP for the remote islands of Orkney and Shetland in Scotland in 1950. At the time he was one of only nine Liberal MPs and the party seemed to be on its deathbed. He was elected party leader in 1957. His philosophy was that the Liberals should 'get on or get out'. As leader he gave the party a radical edge. It advocated British membership of the European Economic Community, constitutional reform, and co-partnership in industry, and rejected British possession of nuclear weapons. Grimond thought that the only future for the Liberals was to merge with moderates in the Labour and Conservative parties to form a new radical centre party. Although the Liberal party doubled its vote in the 1964 general election the first-past-the-post electoral system meant that it elected only six MPs. There was some informal co-operation with the Labour government elected in 1964 under Harold *Wilson, but a large Labour victory in 1966 ended Grimond's ambitions. He was disappointed that support for the party fell back and resigned as leader in 1967. Only with the party's alliance with the Social Democrats in the early 1980s did his hopes appear to be fulfilled.

Grishin, Victor Vasilyevich (b. Serpukhov, near Moscow, 1914)
Russian; First Secretary of the Moscow City Committee 1967–85

Grishin was the son of a railwayman, who initially followed his father's career. He joined the Communist Party while doing military service in the years 1938–40 and then entered a political career. He worked in the party organization of his home town until 1950, when he moved to Moscow. By 1952 he had reached the rank of second secretary of the Moscow party and had entered the Central Committee. From 1956 to 1967 he was head of the Soviet trade unions. In 1967 he became First Secretary of the Moscow City Committee of the CPSU. In 1971 he was elected full member of the Politburo. From 1976 to 1985 he held the nationally important post of First Secretary of the party organization in Moscow. In 1985 he stood against Gorbachev as a candidate for the post of General Secretary. At the end of the year, Gorbachev replaced him as Moscow First Secretary with Yeltsin and in February the next year removed him from the Politburo.

Gromyko, Andrei (b. Old Gromyki near Minsk, 18 July 1909; d. Moscow, 2 July 1989)
Russian; Minister of Foreign Affairs 1957–85

Gromyko was born in Belorussia, the son of Russian peasants. He studied economics and agronomy in Minsk and at the Institute of Economics in Moscow and joined the Communist Party in 1931. Gromyko worked first as an agrarian economist, writing for the journal *Voprosy ekonomiki* from 1936 to 1939 and joined the diplomatic service which *Stalin had just purged and was aided by the patronage of *Molotov. After serving for four years as counsellor at the Soviet Embassy in Washington he became ambassador to the United States in 1943. He led the Soviet delegation at the Dumbarton Oaks conference in 1944 which paved the way to the foundation of the United Nations, and in 1945 was present at the Yalta and Potsdam conferences. From 1946 to 1948 he was a permanent Soviet Representative at the UN Security Council. In 1949 he returned to Moscow as First Deputy Minister of Foreign Affairs but three years later became Soviet Ambassador to London; this was a demotion, reflecting Stalin's ill-will. Returning to Moscow following Stalin's death, he survived Molotov's disgrace to become Foreign Minister in 1957. He prospered under *Brezhnev after 1964 and became a full member of the Politburo in 1973.

Gromyko's influence on foreign affairs increased even further under *Andropov and *Chernenko in the years 1982 to 1985. He gave *Gorbachev vital backing in his bid to become General Secretary of the CPSU in March 1985 but soon ceased to be Minister of Foreign Affairs and was replaced by *Shevardnadze. He was promoted to the largely honorific post of chairman of the Presidium of the Supreme Soviet—the

USSR's head of state. In 1988 he retired and in April 1989 was removed from the Central Committee.

Grotewohl, Otto (b. Braunschweig, 11 Mar. 1894; d. 23 Sept. 1964)
German; head of government of the GDR 1949–64

Born the son of a master tailor, Grotewohl was a full-time SPD politician before 1933. In the Third Reich he worked as a small businessman, being held in custody in 1938 for seven months for illegal SPD activities.

Many regarded Grotewohl as a duped opportunist when he led the Social Democrats (SPD) in the Soviet Zone into a merger with the Communists to form the Socialist Unity Party of Germany (SED) in April 1946. The SPD was, however, under heavy pressure from the Soviet military authorities, who arrested some Social Democrats. Many activists fled to the West where they were welcomed by Kurt *Schumacher. Grotewohl remained to save what he could of the SPD legacy. His reward was election as co-chairman of the SED and, in 1949, becoming head of government (Minister-President) of the government of the new East German state. Although he remained head of government until his death in 1964 he saw his power steadily decline. The government became secondary to the SED and in that party *Ulbricht was dominant.

Groza, Petru (b. Becia, Transylvania, 1884; d. Bucharest, 7 Jan. 1958)
Romanian; premier 1945–52

Groza was a well-off Transylvanian landowner and industrialist who was regarded as one of Romania's finest classical scholars. In 1933 he founded the Ploughman's Front, a radical agrarian organization which drew its support from the Transylvanian peasantry. In 1944 the Ploughman's Front joined the Communist-dominated coalition party, the National Democratic Front (NDF). Groza stood for three policies: land reform; reconciliation with Hungary and Romania's Hungarian minority; and accommodation with the Soviet Union, on grounds of *realpolitik*. Arguably, his primary motivation was a lust for power and publicity. He was a ready puppet for the Soviet leaders and the RCP. On 27 February 1945, the Soviet Foreign Minister *Vyshinsky arrived in Bucharest to insist that Groza head the government and on 6 March 1945 Groza became Prime Minister. His Cabinet was a coalition, but the non-Communists in it were Communist puppets. Groza's period in office saw land reform, the RCP's takeover of the administration, army, and police as well as the purge of their political opponents. At the same time, there was large-scale Soviet exploitation of the economy. In 1952 Groza ceased to be premier and was given the honorific post of President of the Presidium of the RCP.

Guterres, Antonio (b. Lisbon, 30 Apr. 1949)
Portuguese; Prime Minister 1995–

Born in Santos-o-Velho, Lisbon, Guterres studied electro-engineering at the Higher Technical Institute in Lisbon. His political career started as a Catholic activist and during the revolutionary period in 1974–5 he became a member of the Socialist Party (Partido Socialista—PS). As a leading Socialist MP he held office in several governments during the revolutionary period. After the revolution, he took part in the Committee on European Integration, which negotiated the accession of Portugal to the European Community.

On the international stage, Guterres was the president of the Parliamentary Committee on Demography, Migrations and Refugees of the Parliamentary Assembly of the Council of Europe in 1985. Nevertheless, after 1987 he was increasingly involved in the opposition strategy of the PS, and sought to moderate party policies, and suggest alternatives. In 1992 he was elected secretary-general of the party. In October 1995 the Socialist Party won the legislative elections with a high relative majority and Guterres became Prime Minister. Regarded inside the party as a technocrat, his main policy aims are to give priority to education, social welfare, and administrative decentralization.

Hague, William (b. Rotherham, Yorkshire, 26 Mar. 1961)
British; Conservative Party Leader 1997

When he was elected Conservative Party leader in June 1997, William Hague became the youngest party leader since William Pitt, 200 years earlier, as well as the first party leader to have attended a comprehensive school. He seemed marked out for political stardom ever since his much-lauded address to the Conservative conference at the age of 16 in 1977. As a student at Oxford University, he followed a time-honoured path of becoming president of the Oxford University Conservative Association and president of the Students' Union. After university he took a lucrative job with the management consultants McKinsey.

In January 1989 Hague was elected for the safe Conservative seat of Richmond in a by-election. After a spell as a junior social security minister he joined the Cabinet as Secretary of State for Wales in June 1995, when the holder of the post resigned to challenge John *Major for the party leadership.

Hague is often accused of lacking convictions. This may be the product of calculation, his relative youth, or the short period in which he was been in the House of Commons. Although he is on the centre right of the party it is difficult to associate him with settled views, apart from hostility to the single European currency. This outlook actually worked to his advantage when there was a leadership vacancy after the 1997 election defeat and John Major resigned. Hague was fortunate in the absence of more favoured and senior candidates, due to ill health or to a failure to hold their seats at the general election. Three other candidates were clearly on the right wing of the party and Kenneth *Clarke was clearly on the liberal wing. Hague had no strong enemies and beat Clarke on the third and final ballot by 90 votes to 72. He promised to unify his bruised party. Although he clearly spoke for the Eurosceptic majority in his party there is a considerable Europhile minority and it remains to be seen how he keeps the party united.

Haig, Alexander Meigs, Jr. (b. Philadelphia, 2 Dec. 1924)
US; General US army 1973–9, Supreme Allied Commander Europe 1974–9, White House Chief of Staff 1973–4, Secretary of State 1981–2

Haig was educated at West Point and graduated MA from Georgetown University, 1961. He joined the US army in 1947, serving in Korea 1950–1 and Vietnam 1966–7. In 1973, promoted to the rank of general, he became Vice-Chief of Staff US Army Washington and worked as a junior adviser to Dr *Kissinger in the National Security Council. This latter post brought Haig to the attention of President *Nixon, who appointed him White House Chief of Staff. During the turbulent closing weeks of the Watergate affair, Haig was one of the few officials to have continued access to the President and was perceived as being almost a lone voice of calm in the White House. After Nixon's resignation Haig returned to military duties as Supreme Allied Commander in Europe, 1974–9. Retiring from active service in 1979, he took up a career in private consultancy.

In 1981 Haig became President *Reagan's Secretary of State. But in stark contrast to his reputation for calm and efficiency at the height of the Watergate drama, his period at the State Department was marred by turf wars between himself and other members of the administration. Soon after his appointment Haig gained a reputation for being power hungry and ambitious. He began badly by staking a claim to responsibility for 'everything beyond the water's edge'. Then, in the immediate aftermath of the attempt on the President's life in March 1981, Haig displayed a lack of judgement and political finesse by asserting on television 'I am in control here in the White House, pending the return of the Vice President', thereby encroaching on the territory of Mr Weinburger, Secretary of Defence and second in line of command after the Vice-President in an emergency. This self-inflicted damage compounded an earlier error when he had tried to assume the chairmanship of a new crisis management committee, a task allotted to the Vice-President.

Haig resigned from his post in 1982, blaming lack of consistency in foreign policy, and once again returned to private consultancy work. In 1987 he made a brief return to the public arena when he attempted unsuccessfully to gain the Republican Party's nomination for the presidency.

Haile Selassie I, Emperor (b. Harar, 27 Jul. 1882; d. Addis Ababa, 27 Aug. 1975)
Ethiopian; Regent 1916–30, Emperor 1930–74

Tafari Makonnen, who took the regal name of Haile Selassie (meaning Power of the Trinity) on becoming Emperor in 1930, was the son of Ras Makonnen, first cousin of Emperor Menilek II and governor of Harar in south-east Ethiopia. Educated by Jesuit missionaries and at secondary school in Addis Ababa, he was appointed governor of Harar at the age of 17. In September 1916 Menilek's grandson and successor, Yasu, was ousted in a palace coup, and Tafari became regent and heir to the throne with the title of Ras, thus gaining the name by which he was to be known to the Rastafarians.

Over the next fourteen years he gradually built up his power through a capacity for skilful political manœuvre which he never lost. He was instrumental in securing Ethiopia's admission to the League of Nations in 1923, and became Emperor in 1930. As leader of the modernizing group in the Ethiopian court politics of the time, he sought to expand education and build links with foreign states, but was careful not to alienate powerful domestic interests. He issued a written constitution in 1931, in which he retained all major powers himself. His diplomatic skills however failed to avert invasion by Fascist Italy in 1935; the Ethiopian armies were defeated and Haile Selassie fled to exile in England, impressing the world with his dignity in an address to the League of Nations, protesting at Italian conquest.

Haile Selassie returned to Ethiopia in 1941, and regained the throne with the defeat of the Italians. Initially reliant on the British, he established close relations with the United States, curbed the power of the regional aristocracy, and built a more centralized administration than Ethiopia had ever known. He secured the federation with Ethiopia of the former Italian colony of Eritrea in 1952, and despite a 1955 constitution which introduced universal suffrage he retained close personal control over government. His cautious regime came to seem archaic to younger educated Ethiopians, and his imposition of centralized rule on Eritrea provoked revolt. After an abortive coup led by the commander of his bodyguard in 1960, he was always on the defensive.

He seized the diplomatic opportunity presented by African independence, and hosted the 1963 conference which established the Organization of African Unity, ensuring that the organization would be used to uphold existing states and boundaries. This aided him both against the Eritrean separatists, and against Somali claims on south-east Ethiopia. In the latter part of his reign, his prestige abroad contrasted with a steady loss of authority at home, and he was unable to cope with the creeping revolution which led to his deposition by a radical military regime in September 1974. His apparent indifference to a major famine undermined his position. He was murdered in his palace by his successor, *Mengistu Haile Mariam. Despite his decline in his later years, he remained a symbol of African dignity both within and outside the continent, and is likely to be remembered as one of the greatest of twentieth-century Africans.

Hailsham, Lord *see* HOGG, QUINTIN

Haldane, Richard Burden (b. Edinburgh, 30 July 1856; d. 19 Aug. 1928)
British; Lord Chancellor 1912–15 and 1924; Viscount 1911

Richard Haldane was accomplished as a politician, philosopher, and lawyer. He was educated at the University of Edinburgh, Göttingen, and then Edinburgh again. His family (strongly evangelical) had religious objections to him attending Oxford. He read for the bar in London and built himself a successful practice. In 1885 he became Liberal MP for East Lothian and held the seat until 1911, when he was raised to the peerage. For most of his years as a backbencher he practised at the bar.

Haldane had a particular talent for administration. From 1905 to 1911 he was Secretary of State for War and put in hand a number of army reforms, including the creation of what is now the Territorial Army. In 1911 he entered the House of Lords and the following year was made Lord Chancellor. His fluent German and sympathy for that country made it understandable that *Asquith should authorize him to visit Germany in 1912 with a view to easing tensions between the two countries. It failed and when war broke out he was attacked by a jingoistic press and unionist opposition as pro-German. It was no surprise that Asquith left him out of his first coalition government in 1915.

In 1917 he chaired a committee which reviewed the machinery of government. The following year it produced the *Report of the Committee on the Machinery of Government*, known as the Haldane Report. It proposed that government should be reorganized according to the service provided rather than clients served. This was largely followed. Haldane joined the Labour Party in 1918, and in 1924 he was made Lord Chancellor in the first Labour government. In later years he was showered with honours and wrote a number of well-regarded works on philosophy.

Halifax, Edward Frederick Lindley Wood, **Earl of** (b. Devon, 16 Apr. 1881; d. 23 Dec. 1959)
British; Viceroy of India 1926–31, Foreign Secretary 1938–40, ambassador to the USA 1941–6; Baron Irwin 1925, KG 1931, 3rd Viscount 1934, Earl 1944

The son of the 2nd Viscount Halifax, Wood was born without a left hand. He was educated at Eton and Christ Church, Oxford, entered parliament in 1910 as Conservative MP for Ripon, and saw war service in 1915–17. He got his first ministerial post in 1921 as Under-Secretary for the Colonies. In 1922 Bonar *Law appointed him president of the Board of Education. In 1924 *Baldwin appointed him as Minister of Agriculture and then a year later ennobled him, as Baron Irwin, and sent him to India as Viceroy. He served six years in a post that suited his nature and talents. On his return in 1931 he was made a Knight of the Garter. In 1932, he was again appointed as president of the Board of Education before being appointed Secretary of State for War (1935), Lord Privy Seal (1935–7), and Lord President (1937–8), at the same time serving as leader of the House of Lords. In 1938 he was appointed Foreign Secretary. He supported *Chamberlain's appeasement policy with loyalty but no great enthusiasm. As A. J. P. Taylor was to record, he 'alone emerged from appeasement with a reputation unsullied or even enhanced'.

Well respected in parliament, he came close to succeeding Chamberlain as Prime Minister in 1940. He enjoyed the support of Labour leaders and Conservatives who distrusted *Churchill. He declined the post, saying it would be inappropriate for a peer to serve in such circumstances. Churchill appointed him ambassador to Washington, where his diplomatic skills were put to good effect. He served in

Washington until 1946. Until his death in 1959, he was also chancellor of the Universities of Oxford and Sheffield, and High Steward of Westminster.

An intelligent, dignified patrician, he was a High Tory who served his country while recognizing that there was more to life than politics. Well suited to foreign affairs, he was less attuned to domestic issues. He ended his career as one of the most respected politicians of his generation.

Halleck, Charles Abraham (b. Jasper County, Indiana, 20 Aug. 1900; d. 3 Mar. 1986)
US; member of the US House of Representatives 1935–68

The son of an Indiana lawyer and state politician, Halleck was first elected to Congress in 1935 and rapidly became one of its key leaders in the House of Representatives. In 1943 he was chairman of the Republican Congressional Campaign Committee and became majority leader of the House in 1947. When the Republicans again won control of the House in 1952 Halleck was once more made majority leader. However, when the Republicans became a minority in 1955, Halleck was given the unofficial post of deputy leader under Joseph *Martin's leadership. This device gave Halleck continuing influence and access within the Republican hierarchy.

In 1959 Halleck ousted Martin in a move that suggested there would be new and more dynamic leadership for the House Republicans. In fact, Halleck's period as leader saw substantial Republican unhappiness about the party's electoral and legislative impact. Halleck had originally been an isolationist but after the Second World War he became a supporter of interventionism. He was an adroit legislative tactician but frequently gave more weight to cutting deals with the President than to keeping the party united. He proved a useful ally of Republican President *Eisenhower but also of Democratic Presidents *Kennedy and *Johnson. Thus, for example, in 1963 he played a key role in the passage of civil rights legislation against the wishes of the 'conservative coalition'.

In tandem with Everett *Dirksen he gained wide publicity in the 1960s as a result of their popular television news conferences dubbed the 'Ev and Charlie' show in which contemporary issues and personalities were subjected to partisan analysis.

Although considered vice-presidential material, Halleck was bypassed in 1948 and 1952 when he came closest to being selected by the Republican presidential nominee. Increasingly criticized for his lacklustre performance in the House and for his part in the GOP's electoral disaster of 1964, Halleck was replaced as Republican leader by Gerald *Ford in 1965. Halleck retired from Congress in 1968.

Hanna, Marcus Alonzo (b. New Lisbon, Ohio, 24 Sept. 1837; d. 15 Feb. 1904)
US; US Senator 1897–1904

The son of a doctor who became a wholesale grocery merchant, Hanna attended local schools in Cleveland, Ohio, where his family lived from 1852, and Western Reserve College, Hudson, Ohio. In 1858 he entered a copper and iron ore firm, a subsidiary of his father's business, and rapidly worked his way up from labourer in the warehouse, to bookkeeper, salesman, and purser on one of the firm's ships. After his father's death, in 1862, he became a partner in the business with his uncle. He continued to manage the firm, with an interlude of 100 days devoted to defending Washington during the Civil War, until 1867, when he sold his share and entered a business association with his father-in-law. Thereafter he turned his hand successfully to a wide range of business ventures including: copper; blast furnaces; street railways; shipping; banking and publishing.

Hanna's interest in business was complemented by an interest in Republican party politics. He was one of the new breed of party bosses to emerge after the 1883 Civil Service Reform Act curbed patronage as a source of revenue and prompted politicians to turned increasingly to big business for money and support. He played an active part in every political campaign from 1867 until his death. Between 1888 and 1900 he was *de facto* Republican 'king-maker' managing Senator John Sherman's successful bid for the party's presidential nomination in 1888, William McKinley's in 1892, and persuaded the party to nominate McKinley on the first ballot at the 1896 national convention. Selected as chairman of the Republican national committee in 1896, he became a key figure in national politics. McKinley's victory over William Jennings *Bryan, the choice of both the Populists and the Democrats, in the election that year is widely attributed to Hanna's fund-raising and skills of political management.

A year later, in 1897, Hanna became US Senator for Ohio, appointed to complete a year's unexpired term of John Sherman who had accepted a post in McKinley's Cabinet. The following year he won a full term in the Senate after a contested election in the state legislature, and was re-elected for a further term but died before taking his seat. During his time in the Senate he remained a dominant figure in his party and an influential adviser to McKinley and then Theodore *Roosevelt.

Hardie, James **Keir** (b. Lanarkshire, 15 Aug. 1856; d. 2 Sept. 1915)
British; first Independent Labour MP 1892, first chairman of the Parliamentary Labour Party 1906

A carpenter's son educated at elementary school and evening classes, Hardie started work at the age of 7 as a messenger boy, later becoming a coal miner. Precluded from further work in the coal mines in 1878 because of his attempts to organize miners, he help to found the Scottish Miners' Federation, of which he became the first secretary in 1886, supporting himself largely through journalism. Though he had initially been a Liberal, his first unsuccessful attempt to enter parliament was as an Independent Labour candidate in 1888. He secured election as Independent Labour MP for South West Ham in 1892, but was defeated in 1895. He re-entered the Commons as MP for Merthyr Tydfil in 1900 and represented that constituency until his death.

Hardie has a unique place in the Labour Party's history. Having been founding chairman of the Scottish Labour Party (Britain's first labour political party) in 1888, he became first chairman of the Independent Labour Party in 1893, also setting up the *Labour Leader*, its weekly paper. He was prominent in the formation of the Labour Representation Committee in 1900 and after it became the Labour Party, in 1906, was elected leader of its MPs for two years, though he was never very effective in that role. In 1914 he was chairman of the British section of the International Socialist Bureau.

Hardie's stature in the Labour movement was not matched outside it. His political stance was often highly unpopular. He was an outspoken republican and he risked physical injury for his public opposition to the Boer War. In 1907, he caused a furore by advocating a form of self-government for India during a visit there. In 1914 he opposed British participation in the First World War. Nor was his ability as a public platform speaker matched by his performance in the House of Commons. His interventions often antagonized members of both the major parties as did his provocatively unorthodox dress.

Harding, Warren Gamaliel (b. Corsica, Ohio, 2 Nov. 1865; d. San Francisco, 2 Aug. 1923)
US; US Senator 1915–20, President 1921–3

The son of a farmer, speculator, and doctor, Harding was educated at Ohio Central College and graduated in 1882. After a short stint at a number of jobs, he entered publishing—he bought out an ailing local paper—and established himself as a figure in Ohio politics. A Republican, he was elected to two terms in the state Senate and served for two years as the state's Lieutenant-Governor. Defeated for the governorship of the state in 1910 and again in 1912 he thought about leaving politics, but his forceful wife Florence (known as 'the Duchess') and a political ally and fixer, Harry Daugherty, persuaded him to carry on. In 1914 he was elected to the US Senate. He enjoyed mixing with other members. He did little in terms of legislative activity but towards the end of his term began to give voice to a popular mood of despair. In 1920, he emerged as the presidential candidate of a deadlocked Republican convention. He was the choice of the party bosses, who thought he would be responsive to their wishes. They were to be proved right.

Harding, campaigning on a promise to 'return to normalcy', was elected President by a massive majority. He won 16 million votes, against 9 million for the Democratic candidate, James Cox. He was inaugurated on 4 March 1921 and appointed to office a number of the political cronies to whom he was both indebted and loyal. He did little, although during his term in the White House his government hosted the Washington conference on naval disarmament and his able Treasury Secretary, Andrew Mellon, achieved reform of the budget system. Harding largely left the business of government to others, a number of whom did treat it as a business. Interior Secretary Albert Fall and Attorney-General Harry Daugherty were among several government officials using their positions to enlarge their personal finances. Fall was leasing oil reserves—including at Teapot Dome, Wyoming—in return for kickbacks. In 1922 rumours of corrupt practices began to circulate and two of those involved committed suicide. Charges were levelled against Daugherty and Fall and in March 1923 Fall was forced to resign. Harding conceded that it was his friends rather than his enemies that were keeping him awake at nights.

Harding went on a trip to restore his flagging popularity. He spoke in several states in the Midwest and West before going to Alaska and then Canada. He then travelled to Seattle and San Francisco. On the way to San Francisco he suffered an attack of food poisoning. In San Francisco, he suffered a cerebral thrombosis and died before doctors could reach him. His body was brought back to Washington to lie in state.

Harding was a disaster as President. His credentials for the job appeared to be that he looked presidential and would not go against his backers. His main attributes appeared to be those of ill-health (he suffered several nervous breakdowns during his publishing career), gambling, drinking, and adultery. He was lazy, preferring to play poker with his cronies to getting on with whatever job he was meant to be doing. His marriage was one of convenience and he had a child by his mistress Nan Britton (who later published a book about their affair). He was not a strong personality, wanting to get on with everyone, and had few ideas of his own. His wife was a driving force, influencing some of his decisions and apparently on occasion—like a later First Lady—taking advice from an astrologer. Though popular in office, the scandal engulfing his administration—dubbed the Teapot Dome scandal—robbed his presidency posthumously of any credit. He was not cut out to be President. Left to his own preferences, he would have stayed in the Senate.

Harriman, William **Averell** (b. New York City, 15 Nov. 1891; d. 26 July 1986)

US; US ambassador to Russia 1943–6, ambassador to Britain 1946, Secretary of Commerce 1946–8, ambassador extraordinary and plenipotentiary 1948–50, Special Assistant to the President 1950–1, Governor of New York 1955–8

The son of a railway magnate and self-made millionaire, Harriman was educated at Groton before graduating from Yale in 1913. Having worked as a clerk in the Union Pacific Railroad yards in Omaha, Nebraska, during college vacations, in 1915 he became a vice-president of the company. During the next twenty-five years he built up his own business empire, which included a private bank and one of the largest American-owned merchant fleets. In addition he chaired the boards of both the Illinois Central Railroad and the Union Pacific Railroad, 1932–42.

A staunch Democrat, it was in his capacity as close friend and confidant of Franklin D. *Roosevelt that Harriman entered a career in the public service that was to span thirty-five years and four Democratic presidencies. In 1934, at the invitation of Roosevelt, he became a member of the Business Advisory Council of the Department of Commerce. A further appointment followed in 1941 when Roosevelt sent him to London to negotiate the Lend-Lease arrangements. Thus began a long career in international diplomacy that was to take Harriman to Russia and Britain as US ambassador, 1943–6 and 1946 respectively; to the conferences of the Allied powers at Casablanca, Tehran, and Yalta; gave him a roving brief as ambassador extraordinary and plenipotentiary 1948; ambassador at large in 1961 and 1965, and to include the frustrating and difficult task of representing the USA at the Vietnam peace conference, 1968–9. Sandwiched between these wide-ranging diplomatic posts, he also served as Secretary of Commerce in *Truman's Cabinet, 1946–8.

When the Democrats lost the presidency in 1953 Harriman changed from being an appointed public servant to an elected one. In 1954 he narrowly won the governorship of New York. But his term of office was possibly one of the least successful of his roles. A Republican-controlled State Legislature frustrated his attempts to deliver his election pledges and, in 1958, he lost the governorship to another public-spirited plutocrat, Nelson *Rockefeller. Two years earlier, in 1956, he had also seen his aspirations for becoming his party's presidential candidate dashed when Adlai *Stevenson won the nomination.

In 1961 Harriman returned to the public service as ambassador at large, 1961 and 1965, and Assistant Secretary for Far Eastern Affairs 1961–5 and Under-Secretary of State for Political Affairs 1963–5. When *Nixon became President in 1969 Harriman retired and assumed the role of elder statesman of the Democratic Party. Harriman was an example of a man of great wealth who devoted much of his life to the service of his country. He was a skilled negotiator and a first class administrator.

Hart, Gary Warren (né Hartpence) (b. Ottawa, Kansas, 28 Nov. 1936)
US; US Senator 1976–84

Hart was educated at Bethany Navarene College and Yale's Divinity and Law schools. He practised law between 1967 and 1974 when he ran for the Senate. Hart had managed the primary strategy of the *McGovern presidential campaign in 1972 and projected himself as part of a new generation of Democratic politicians with fresh ideas. He won the Senate seat in 1976 against incumbent Republican Peter Dominick.

In the Senate Hart established himself as an authority on military policy, serving on the Armed Services Committee, where his attention to detail gained respect from both parties and from hawks and doves. He also established effective environmental credentials on the Senate Environment and Public Works Committee and its subcommittees on nuclear regulation and environmental pollution.

Gary Hart made two attempts at securing the Democratic nomination. In 1984 he lost to Walter *Mondale but performed sufficiently well to make him the front runner in 1988. However, press speculation about sexual infidelity after he was seen in the company of model Donna Rice raised a major character issue and forced him to withdraw from the race. He did not seek re-election to the Senate and left politics to practise law.

Hashemi-Rafsanjani, Ali Akhbar (b. Rafsanjan, 25 Aug. 1934)
Iranian; Speaker of the *Majles* (Consultative Assembly) 1980–9, Acting Commander-in-Chief of the Armed Forces 1988–9, President 1989–

Rafsanjani became a pupil and disciple of *Khomeini at Qom theological seminary, reaching the rank of *Hojjatoleslam* in the late 1950s. He organized anti-Shah riots in June 1963 and was imprisoned at least four times for his political activities in the

Islamic resurgence between 1964 and 1978. Rafsanjani was one of Khomeini's chief lieutenants in Iran after his banishment in 1964 and a member of the small group of radical mullahs who led the Islamic revolution in Iran until Khomeini's return in 1979. He was then appointed to the governing Revolutionary Council by Khomeini. Rafsanjani co-founded the Association of Militant Clergy faction and was co-leader of the Islamic Republican party which dominated the Assembly after the general elections of 1980 and elected him as its Speaker. In that capacity he entered into secret negotiations to trade Western hostages for US arms in 1986, but succeeded in avoiding lasting damage to his reputation when the negotiations became public knowledge. After Khomeini's death in 1989, Rafsanjani emerged as the Islamic Republic's first executive President, to which he was re-elected for a final, four-year term in 1993. During his presidency, Iran has undergone widespread and fundamental reforms that have reconstituted it as a Second Republic. Among the more important of these has been a programme of economic reconstruction through liberalization and the state's withdrawal from the economy. A corresponding shift in foreign policy, aimed at Iran's reintegration into the international community, began with the release of Western hostages in Lebanon at Rafsanjani's behest between 1991 and 1992. Rafsanjani's Iran, however, continues to export Islamic revolution and it sponsors militant Islamic fundamentalist groups on a worldwide basis.

Hassan II, King of Morocco *see* BIN MOHAMMED, HASSAN

Hatfield, Mark Odom (b. Dallas, Oregon, 22 July 1922)

US; Governor of Oregon 1959–67; US Senator 1966–96

Mark Hatfield was educated at Willamette University and Stanford University. After naval service in the Second World War, he became a professor of political science and administrator at Willamette University. He was elected to the Oregon House of Representatives serving there until 1955 when he came a member of the Oregon Senate. He was Secretary of State for Oregon from 1957 to 1959 and Governor from 1958 to 1966.

Hatfield secured election to the US Senate in 1966 and was re-elected in 1972, 1978, and 1984, 1990.

In the Senate Hatfield adopted consistently liberal and dovish positions on foreign policy issues, reflecting the distinctive tradition of the state, though increasingly out of line with the Republican Party as a whole. He opposed the Vietnam War, voted against the Gulf War resolution in 1991, and regularly opposed enhanced defence spending and nuclear weapons.

Hatfield was chairman of the Senate Committee on Appropriations from 1981 to 1986 and again from 1995 to 1996. In that role he stood out against the Balanced Budget Amendment, which he saw as a threat to the committee's autonomy.

Despite Hatfield's strong religious commitment, he has been tainted by political scandal and was formally censured by the Senate Ethics Committee in 1992 for failure to report gifts. His independent stance and long service in the Senate enabled him to survive. He retired from the Senate in 1996.

Hattersley, Roy (b. Sheffield, 28 Dec. 1932)

British; deputy leader of the Labour Party 1983–7

Roy Hattersley was born into a Labour political family—his mother was a mayoress of and a major political figure in Sheffield. He was educated at Sheffield Grammar School and Hull University, a scholarship boy from a working-class home which expected him to do well. He had turned 40 before he learnt that his father was a lapsed Roman Catholic priest.

After university he also became active in local Sheffield politics. In 1964 he won the safe seat of Sparkbrook in the centre of Birmingham. The constituency had a large Asian membership and Hattersley was always interested in race and immigration issues. In these years he was on the right of the party and a supporter of Roy *Jenkins.

In 1972 Harold *Wilson appointed him as shadow Education Secretary, to replace Roy Jenkins, who had resigned over the party's decision to call for a referendum on Britain's membership of the European Community. Hattersley believed in greater equality, opposed private education, and was a strong advocate of comprehensive education (or the ending of selection on academic grounds), beliefs which he clung to all his life. He was too radical a figure for Harold Wilson who passed him over when a new Labour government was formed in 1974, and would have been so for Tony *Blair who was elected party leader in 1994.

Promotion to the Cabinet came in September 1976 when the new Prime Minister, James *Callaghan, made him responsible for prices and consumer affairs. This was an important post because the Labour government depended on the co-operation of the trade unions for the success of its anti-inflation policy. Hattersley could not have realized that Labour's defeat in the 1979 election meant that his ministerial career was finished, at the age of 46. Between 1979 and 1983 the left were rampant in the Labour Party, now in opposition. He was a beleaguered figure as many of his political friends left to join the new Social Democratic Party (SDP) and he had little time for the new Labour leader Michael *Foot or Labour's policies of unilateral defence, withdrawal from the EC, and more public ownership. Hattersley agreed with virtually all the policies of the SDP, but did not consider that sufficient reason to leave Labour. Almost inevitably, he was criticized as an opportunist.

In 1983 he stood for the leadership, was easily defeated by Neil *Kinnock, but elected to the post of deputy leader which he held until 1992. Between 1983 and 1987 he was the party's shadow Chancellor of the Exchequer, a post in which he did not make a mark. In the 1987 parliament he moved to be the shadow Home Secretary, a post more to his liking. By now he was the senior figure in the shadow Cabinet. He was not close to Kinnock and there was a certain wariness in their relations. But the two worked to get the party to drop a number of its left-wing policies and helped to bring Labour back into the mainstream. Some reformers in the party were disappointed that Hattersley did not embrace more enthusiastically the cause of constitutional and, particularly, electoral reform. Under the leadership of Tony Blair, Labour moved further to the middle ground, provoking criticism from Hattersley that it was ceasing to be a party of redistribution and equality.

Roy Hattersley was in politics to do things and the fact that the best years of his life were spent in Opposition was a frustration. After the party's fourth successive election defeat in 1992 he decided to stand down from the deputy leadership and become a backbencher again; he retired as an MP in 1997. Hattersley was remarkable for the life he led outside politics. He was a prize-winning author—of novels, essays, biography, and autobiography, e.g. the well-reviewed *A Yorkshire Boyhood* and *Who Goes Home?*—and a prolific journalist. He also wrote a much admired statement of his political philosophy, *Choose Freedom*, which tried to reconcile the principles of political equality and freedom. His media skills, which earned him considerable sums of money, excited resentment and jealousy among some Labour activists. Yet he was a dedicated politician, devoted to the Labour Party and to his constituency.

Haughey, Charles James (b. Castlebar, Co. Mayo, 16 Sept. 1925)

Irish; Taoiseach (premier) 1979–81, 1982, 1987–92

The son of an officer in the Irish army, Haughey's family roots were in northern Irish republicanism. In 1951 he married a daughter of Sean *Lemass, then deputy premier and later Taoiseach, 1959–66. He was elected to the Dáil in 1957, and achieved ministerial rank in 1961, serving in all subsequent Fianna Fáil governments until his dismissal by Jack *Lynch in May 1970 over suspected complicity in an attempt to import arms for the IRA using government money. In a celebrated trial subsequently, Haughey was acquitted. He became wealthy through a development land deal, whose details remained obscure.

He was a highly energetic and effective minister in a succession of posts and was noted for his encouragement of cultural life. His three periods as Taoiseach were marked by persistent criticism and opposition, particularly from within his own party, and from leading journalists. He was widely respected for his ability but also widely distrusted as a shifty and unprincipled self-aggrandizer. His second (February to December) 1982 government was especially scandal ridden, particularly concerning his alleged authorizing of the tapping of journalists' phones.

As Taoiseach Haughey's abilities were much consumed by the problems of political survival and the worsting of opponents within his own party (some of whom broke away to form the Progressive Democrat Party). His capacity to survive became legendary; yet he failed in five successive elections to lead his party to victory with a working majority, and in 1989 had to form Fianna Fáil's first ever coalition government.

In opposition, and at election times, Haughey was disposed to revert to a populist republicanism, but in office he initiated with Mrs *Thatcher a slow rapprochement with Britain in co-operative management of the Northern Irish crisis. Theirs, in 1980, was the decision to explore jointly 'the totality of relationships in these islands'. He at first opposed the 1985 Anglo-Irish Agreement, but toned down his criticism on observing its popularity in the Republic, and in office from 1987 he worked it as if he had fashioned it himself. He was finally forced from office in 1992 by the resurrection of the phone-tapping controversy.

Haughey was a very able minister who, as premier, appeared primarily as a nimble-footed fixer, clever in manœuvre, admired by many for these qualities, and, by many others, equally distrusted. His party and personality difficulties meant that his administrations had little opportunity, even had they had the inclination, to develop creativity in policy.

Havel, Václav (b. Prague, 6 Oct. 1936)

Czech; President of Czechoslovakia 1989–93, President of the Czech Republic 1993–

Havel was born into a family of upper-middle-class origin—his grandfather had been a well-known architect. He was denied entry into university because of his 'bourgeois' origins and attended evening classes at Prague Technical University while working as a laboratory assistant and taxi-driver. He started his career as a writer in 1961. In 1963 his first play was produced: *The Garden Party* was a satire on the Novotný regime. Havel graduated from the Prague theatrical academy in 1967. He worked in Prague for the 'Theatre on the Balustrade' which flourished in the years 1967–8. He wrote plays for this theatre and worked as a stage-hand. In 1968, during the 'Prague Sping' he became chairman of the Czechoslovak Writer's Union. Performance of his work was banned in 1969, but he continued to write and his plays were popular in the West. In April 1975 he wrote an *Open Letter to President Husák* criticizing the regime. He was a founder member of the human rights group Charter 77 whose programme was announced on 1 January 1977. He was gaoled from January to May 1977 and put under house arrest until 1979, when he was again imprisoned. He was released on grounds of health in 1983. In January 1989 he was sent back to gaol, despite an outcry in the West, and released in May 1989. In November 1989 during the 'Velvet Revolution' he played a pivotal role in co-ordinating the popular rising against the Communist regime and in articulating an opposition programme. One month later he was elected President by the Czechoslovak Assembly after *Husák's resignation and confirmed in office by popular vote in 1990. Havel regretted the break-up of

Czechoslovakia in 1992 but believed that there was no way to prevent it. In January 1993 he was elected President of the Czech Republic.

Hawke, Robert **(Bob)** James Lee (b. Bordertown, South Australia, 2 Dec. 1929)
Australian; leader of the Australian Labor Party and Prime Minister 1983–91

Hawke was born to religious parents, his father a Congregational clergyman and his mother a teacher who saw messianic qualities in her son. From the University of Western Australia, Hawke won that state's Rhodes scholarship to Oxford. After distinguishing himself as a tenacious and sophisticated workers' advocate with the Australian Council of Trade Unions, Hawke entered federal politics in 1980, and became leader three years later.

Within one month of becoming ALP leader in 1983 Hawke was Prime Minister, and he remained so until the end of 1991. In this period Hawke, together with his Treasurer, Paul *Keating, transformed the Australian economy and the platform of the ALP. They deregulated the financial sector, floated the Australian dollar, established stronger ties with growing North East Asian economies and began to cut the tariffs which had, for so long, protected Australian manufacturing in particular. They concluded a Prices and Incomes Accord with Australian unions which provided for unions' wage restraint in return for government attention to conditions and inflation. Towards the end of the 1980s Hawke began to attract criticism for his close relationships with prominent Australian businessmen and media barons. His slide from power accelerated from 1990 after he reneged on a promise to hand the leadership to Keating. On his second attempt, Keating succeeded in wresting the position from Hawke at the end of 1991.

For much of his tenure as Prime Minister Hawke enjoyed great popularity. His style was populist and familiar, drawing strength from his 'matey' vernacular speech and his semi-public battles with alcohol. On the other hand critics have commented on his narcissism. After leaving politics early in 1992 Hawke disillusioned many former supporters through his enduring hostility towards the Keating Labor government, his ostentatious financial success, and his divorce of his long-time wife, Hazel, followed by his marriage to his biographer, Blanche d'Alpuget.

Haya de la Torre, Víctor Raúl (b. Trujillo, 22 Feb. 1895; d. Lima, 2 Aug. 1979)
Peruvian; Leader of APRA 1924–79, President of Constituent Assembly 1978–9

Born into a middle-class provincial family, after secondary education Haya de la Torre went to university in Lima, where he became a prominent figure within the movement for university reform and was active in 'popular universities' aimed at consciousness raising among recently unionized industrial workers. Following protests against moves by Augusto *Leguía to secure his re-election as president, Haya de la Torre was deported and founded the Alianza Popular Revolucionaria Americana (APRA) in Mexico in 1924. Intended as a continent-wide political movement, APRA's maximum programme had five central policies: anti-imperialism; Latin American economic and political unity; internationalization of the Panama Canal; the nationalization of large-scale haciendas and industry; and solidarity with oppressed classes.

After travelling throughout Europe and to the Soviet Union, Haya returned to Peru upon the fall of Leguía to fight the 1931 election, having founded the Peruvian section of APRA in 1930. Coming second in a heated contest, he protested that he had been the victim of fraud. When the appeals failed and his supporters became the victims of repression, Haya de la Torre moved into violent opposition: a series of APRA-inspired revolts occurred within the armed forces, rebellions that culminated in the Trujillo uprising of July 1932, when the city was captured and approximately sixty army officers shot. In reprisal, when Trujillo was retaken, around 1,000 *apristas* were placed before the firing squad.

These events were to sour military–APRA relations for four decades. The party, being the main opposition force to oligarchic rule, became the target of repression during the 1930s and 1940s. In response, Haya de la Torre abandoned his earlier radicalism and moved to the right, becoming virulently anti-Communist and seeking accommodation with the establishment in return for the legalization of APRA. This created discontent among the grass roots, but failed to placate the military, who launched a coup when Haya de la Torre won the 1962 election. In response to Fernando *Belaunde's victory in the 1963 poll, he opportunistically entered into an alliance with the main rightist party in an attempt to block reforms. In the Constituent Assembly elections of 1978, APRA emerged as the largest party, Haya de la Torre became president of the Assembly and played a key role in overseeing the return to elected government after twelve years of military rule. He died in 1979, never having realized his ambition to become President.

His significance lies in the fact that he founded the first modern mass party in Peru. He also had organizational capabilities, charisma, and lived an austere lifestyle. His detractors point to his authoritarianism, erratic behaviour, and high ambition, which produced opportunistic policy shifts and led his party into a cul-de-sac during the 1950s and 1960s. For many Peruvians, however, Haya de la Torre is considered the best President the country never had.

Healey, Denis Winston (b. Broadstairs, Kent, 30 Aug. 1917)

British; Chancellor of the Exchequer 1974–9, deputy leader of the Labour Party 1980–3; Baron (life peer) 1992

The son of a teacher, Healey was educated at Bradford Grammar School and Balliol College, Oxford. Serving in the army during the Second World War, he reached the rank of major. After the war he became secretary of the International Department of the Labour Party (1945–52). In this position he drafted policy statements for the Labour Party and advised party leaders. He also gained a close knowledge of European politics and made many contacts with European socialists. He was a bitter opponent of Soviet expansionism in Eastern Europe.

Healey entered the House of Commons at a by-election as member for Leeds South East in 1952; the seat was redrawn as Leeds East in 1955 and he held it until his retirement in 1992. He was a supporter of the Labour leader Hugh *Gaitskell in his battles against the left. Gaitskell sought to wean the party from its commitment to greater public ownership and successfully fought off the proponents of nuclear disarmament.

In Harold *Wilson's Labour government (1964–70) Healey served as Secretary of Defence, one of the few Cabinet ministers to hold the same post throughout the period. He presided over a reorganization of defence and made cuts in commitments and expenditure. In Opposition after 1970, he became shadow Foreign Secretary and then, in 1972, shadow Chancellor. In government between 1974 and 1979 he was Chancellor of the Exchequer for the entire period. This was an unenviable post because at a time of international recession living standards could not be improved. As Chancellor he handled the IMF negotiations in 1976, presided over a pay policy from 1975, made spending cuts after 1976, and abandoned full employment. These policies made him deeply unpopular among the party grass roots and he did badly in elections for the party leadership in 1976 when Harold Wilson retired. In opposition again he was thought to have a good chance of succeeding James *Callaghan when the latter retired as Labour leader in 1980. But he was beaten by Michael *Foot by 139 votes to 129 on the second ballot, and elected as deputy leader. He was challenged in 1981 for the latter post by Tony *Benn and won only by a fraction. The breakaway Social Democrats hoped that Healey would join them and his departure would have been a disaster for Labour. But he firmly opposed the breakaway MPs and thought that they should have remained and fought the left. When Labour lost the election in

1983 he did not stand for the leadership but continued as shadow Foreign Secretary under Neil *Kinnock. He gave up this post in 1987 and retired from the House of Commons in 1992.

Healey was often called the best leader the Labour Party never had. He was tough-minded, direct, and a formidable opponent of the left. He had little time for ideologies but prided himself on being a pragmatic politician. He wrote a well-received autobiography, *The Time of my Life* (1989).

Heath, Edward (b. 9 July 1916)

British; leader of the Conservative Party 1965–75, Prime Minister 1970–4; Kt. 1992

Ted Heath was the only son of a carpenter, later a master builder. He was educated at Chatham School, Ramsgate, and Balliol College, Oxford. At university he was active in the Conservative Party and president of the Oxford Union. After a good war record he sought entry to the House of Commons. He was one of a new breed of young post-war Conservatives, somebody who wanted to be a professional politician. He had no family tradition of political involvement and did not come from a public school, an established profession, business, or the land.

In 1950 Health won the Bexley seat, part of which was renamed Old Bexley and Sidcup in February 1974. Health's maiden speech was, significantly, a call for Britain to respond favourably to attempts to build a united Western Europe. He was quickly appointed to the whips' office and between 1955 and 1959 was chief whip. He was credited with keeping the party together during the Suez crisis (1956) and involved in the emergence of Harold *Macmillan, rather than R. A. *Butler, as leader in 1957.

In 1960 Heath was appointed Lord Privy Seal, charged with handling negotiations for Britain's entry into the European Community. He became Britain's 'Mr Europe' and was bitterly disappointed when General *de Gaulle vetoed the British application in January 1963. Sir Alec *Douglas-Home appointed him to the Board of Trade. In this post he overcame party opposition to achieve the abolition of resale price maintenance. The measure showed his interest in economics competition and did much to improve his leadership prospects.

In Opposition after 1964 the Conservative Party sought a more meritocratic leader than Sir Alec, one who could stand up to Labour's Harold *Wilson. The grammar school Heath seemed to fit the bill. In a leadership contest in July 1965 Heath gained 150 votes to 133 for Reginald *Maudling and Enoch *Powell's 15 votes. Maudling immediately stood down, thus giving the leadership to Heath. At the age of 49 Heath was the youngest Conservative leader for over a century. Considering that many Conservative MPs came from an upper-class background, Heath's rise was noteworthy.

As Opposition leader, Heath was determined to pursue policies for modernizing Britain. His proposals for trade union reform, tax cuts, constraints on public spending, disengagement from industry, and avoidance of incomes policies might be seen as a first shot at Thatcherism. Some part of the shift to the right was a consequence of opposing the economic interventionism of the Labour government. Heath had the opportunity to deliver the programme when the party gained an unexpected election victory in 1970.

The Heath government (1970–4) has been noted for reversals of policy, what were known as U-turns. It was badly hit by the sharp rises in commodity prices in 1971 and then the quadrupling of Arab oil prices in late 1973. The government felt itself forced to rescue firms because of fears of rising unemployment, and adopted a statutory prices and incomes policy to arrest inflation. There were a record number of days lost due to strikes and direct rule was imposed in Northern Ireland, following violence in the province. The incomes policy proved Heath's undoing. The miners disrupted normal life by their strike against the policy in the winter of 1973–4. As industry struggled to cope, Heath felt that there was no option but to call a general election.

Although the Conservatives ended with most votes, Labour had more seats in the February 1974 election.

After leading the party to a second general election defeat in October 1974, his position as Conservative leader was weak. He had lost three out of four general elections and was widely regarded as an electoral liability. Conservative MPs were disenchanted for various reasons—he lacked tact in dealing with backbenchers, had been niggardly with political honours, and some on the right never forgave his abandonment of free market policies in government. In a leadership contest on 4 February 1975 Margaret *Thatcher defeated him on the first round by 130 to 119 votes and he resigned immediately. Heath had been the first Tory leader to be chosen in a contested election and was the first to be defeated in one.

Heath's determination to defend the record of his government brought him into conflict with Mrs Thatcher. He stood for One-Nation Conservatism, incomes policy, and state intervention in the economy, when the party was moving to the right. She clearly was determined to break with policies of the past, including those of Heath, and would not have him in her Cabinet. In the 1980s he was a vehement critic of the Thatcher government's policies on the economy, education, welfare, Europe, and the poll tax. His critics saw him as a bad loser and he was probably counter-productive to the causes he espoused. He welcomed the leadership of *Major but became critical of what he regarded as appeasement of the anti-European right in the party.

Heath's outstanding achievement was entry into the European Community. Support for European unity and integration was a constant theme in his political career. He played a prominent role in the 1975 referendum on EC membership and spoke against the growing Euro-scepticism in his own party in the 1990s. As a leader he was handicapped by an inability to communicate effectively his visions, notably for enterprise and Britain in Europe.

Heathcoat-Amory, Derick (b. Devon, 26 Dec. 1899; d. 20 Jan. 1981)

British; Chancellor of the Exchequer 1958–60; Viscount Amory 1960, KG 1968

The son of a baronet, Heathcoat-Amory was educated at Eton and Christ Church, Oxford, and spent his formative years in the family's textile business. A former Liberal, he was converted to Conservatism by Harold *Macmillan's *Middle Way*. A member of Devon county council for almost twenty years (1932–51), his entry to parliament came relatively late in life. He was elected as the Conservative MP for Tiverton in 1945, shortly before his 46th birthday. He was recruited by R. A. *Butler to assist in drawing up the party's Industrial Charter and on the party's return to office in 1951 was given ministerial office, serving principally as Minister of Agriculture before being made Chancellor of the Exchequer in January 1958, following Peter *Thorneycroft's decision to resign. He had difficulty resisting Macmillan's demands for an expansionary budget in 1959 and was uncomfortable at the dispatch box, looking close to collapse during the budget speech. He gave up office in July 1960, accepting a viscountcy, and the following year became High Commissioner for Canada, a post he held for two years. He subsequently held a number of other business and public posts, including serving as chairman of Voluntary Service Overseas and president of the Association of County Councils. A very private man, who never married, he was motivated by a sense of public duty. He was also noted for his modesty. His biographer aptly titled his biography *The Reluctant Politician*.

Heinemann, Gustav (b. Schwelm, Ruhr, 23 July 1899; d. 7 July 1976)

German; President of Federal Republic of Germany 1969–74

Heinemann was elected third President of the Federal Republic in 1969, the first, and so far only, Social Democrat to hold this position. His election was due to Liberal FDP support. It was seen as a victory of the 'democrats from conviction' rather than of those who were fair-weather democrats.

Heinemann was the son of a Krupp director and, after studying law and economics, worked for Krupp, serving from 1936 to 1949 as a director of the steel company Rheinische Stahlwerke. From 1933 onwards he was also a director of a coal-mining company. Remarkably, he was also an organizer of the anti-Nazi Confessing church.

In common with most of his social class he joined the Christian Democratic Union (CDU) in 1945, and was appointed Justice Minister for North Rhine-Westphalia. *Adenauer, in need of prominent Protestants for his new government, appointed Heinemann Minister of the Interior in 1949. Heinemann held the job for just over a year, resigning because of Adenauer's authoritarian style, the drift to the right in the CDU, and his opposition to German rearmament and Western integration without reunification.

In 1952 Heinemann resigned from the CDU and in the following year established the All-German People's Party (GVP). The party stood for total neutrality of a united Germany. In the 1953 election it attracted only 1.2 per cent of the votes, a result that led to the party being dissolved and most of its members, including Heinemann, joining the SPD. From 1957 until 1969 Heinemann was a member of the Bundestag, serving as Minister of Justice in the grand coalition 1966–9. Heinemann remained a committed Christian, serving on the Executive of the Evangelical Church from 1945 to 1967. This helped in his election as Federal President on the third ballot with only the smallest of margins over his CDU opponent. As President he helped to create a more tolerant atmosphere in West Germany. He served until 1974, not seeking re-election.

Helms, Jesse A. (b. Monroe, North Carolina, 18 Oct. 1921)
US; US Senator 1972–

The son of a police chief, Jesse Helms was educated at Wingate College and Wake Forest University. After a period in the navy (1942–5) he became city editor of the *Raleigh Times* and a member of the Raleigh City Council (1957–61). From 1960 to 1972 Helms was Executive Vice-President of the Tobacco Radio Network. Elected to the Senate in 1972, Helms made a mark as an ideological conservative and as a major fund-raiser where direct mail and tobacco money enabled him to finance not only his own expensive campaigns but also those of like-minded politicians. His conservative crusade pitted him against a range of liberal policies including abortion, affirmative action, civil rights, and high domestic spending. In foreign policy his instinctive opposition to Communist and left-wing regimes made him supportive of dictatorships.

A staunch defender of the tobacco industry, Helms has defended its interest on the Agriculture Nutrition and Forestry Committee. As the senior Republican on the Foreign Relations Committee, Helms became its chair when Republicans recaptured the Senate in 1994. Although Helms has acquired positions of power in Congress he is widely seen as lacking policy and legislative competence and his effect is generally more of an irritant than anything else.

Helms's high-profile conservatism makes him vulnerable in a rapidly changing state. The race against Jim Hunt in 1984 was extremely expensive, as were the 1990 and 1996 races which were also closely fought. Yet Helms survived, a testament to the enduring appeal of his style of conservative politics.

Henderson, Arthur (b. Glasgow, 13 Sept. 1863; d. 20 Oct. 1935)
British; Foreign Secretary 1929–31, chairman of Parliamentary Labour Party 1908–10, 1914–7, and 1931–2

The son of a cotton worker, Henderson started work in a steel foundry at the age of 12 after an elementary education. He gravitated from trade union activism to party politics, first as a Liberal and then with the Labour Representation Committee (later the Labour Party). He was a central figure in the latter's organization for over thirty years as general secretary (1912–35) and treasurer (1903–12 and 1929–35) of the party nationally and, in the Commons, as party chairman (1908–10, 1914–17, and 1931–2) and chief whip (1906–7, 1914, 1920–4, and 1925–7).

Henderson was an unlucky parliamentary candidate. He was first elected (for Barnard Castle) at a by-election in 1903, becoming only the third LRC member to enter the Commons, but he several times lost a seat at general elections and had to secure re-election at by-elections. His ministerial career was less important than his role as the architect of the party organization, but it was a distinguished one nevertheless. He joined H. H. *Asquith's wartime coalition government in 1915, becoming the first Labour Party member to hold Cabinet office. Though nominally president of the Board of Education (later Paymaster-General) his real role was to advise on Labour issues.

When David *Lloyd George became Prime Minister in 1916, he made Henderson Minister without Portfolio in his small War Cabinet. Henderson led a mission to keep post-revolutionary Russia in the war against Germany but was soon afterwards compelled to resign after urging Labour Party attendance at an international socialist conference without prime ministerial approval.

Henderson's next experience of office was as Home Secretary in the short-lived first Labour government (1924). Ramsay *MacDonald (to whom Henderson had never been close) combined the foreign secretaryship—for which many thought Henderson best fitted—with the premiership, but Henderson played a prominent part in foreign affairs, attending the League of Nations Assembly at Geneva. In the second Labour government (1929–31) Henderson became Foreign Secretary. His main work was, again, at the League of Nations, where he was engaged in disarmament negotiations. Before these came to fruition, Henderson was in the forefront of the opposition to the cuts in unemployment benefit that precipitated the government's collapse. When MacDonald formed a national government, Henderson was elected party leader, but resigned after losing his seat at the 1931 general election.

Although soon back in the Commons, Henderson devoted most of the remainder of his life to League of Nations affairs. He presided over the World Conference on Disarmament and it was primarily for this work that he became, in 1934, one of only two serving or former British foreign secretaries to receive the Nobel Peace Prize.

Herriot, Edouard (b. Troyes, 5 July 1872; d. 26 Mar. 1957)

French; Prime Minister 1924–5, 1932–3, President of the National Assembly 1936–40, 1941–55

Edouard Herriot was, like his rival for the leadership of the inter-war Radical Party *Daladier, a product of the state educational system created by the Third Republic and a passionate defender of the principles of the French Revolution. The son of a junior army officer who died when he was a child, Herriot had a brilliant educational career and became a *lycée* teacher at Lyons in 1904. In 1907, he was elected mayor of Lyons, which became his power base for the whole of his life. He was elected to the Senate in 1907 and held a number of ministerial offices during the First World War. His national prominence dates from the early 1920s, when he took control of the near moribund Radical Party and recreated its image as the voice of progressive reformism. In the 1924 general elections he formed a successful coalition with the Socialist Party and was able to force the right-wing President of the Republic *Millerand to resign. Appointed Prime Minister, he embarked on a programme of reconciliation with Germany, recognized the Soviet Union, and gave strong support to the League of Nations. He was, however, much less successful in dealing with France's chronic inflation problems and was forced to resign office when opposition from the privately owned Bank of France threatened to destroy the currency. What Herriot called 'the wall of money' durably shaped his subsequent attitudes. He felt compelled to join the government of national unity formed by *Poincaré in 1926, and bitterly resented the opportunity this gave to Daladier to take over the Radical Party. In the early 1930s, however, he was back in the saddle and formed another successful electoral coalition with the Socialists in 1932. The government he formed was no more able to deal with economic problems than its predecessors and also had to face a worsening international situation. By now the regime itself was under severe pressure from disaffected social groups and Herriot was president of the Chamber of Deputies when it was attacked by right-wing groups on 6 February 1934. He was uneasy about the left-wing alliance of Communists, Socialist, and Radicals and refused to join any of the Popular Front governments formed after the 1936 elections, preferring instead the Chamber presidency.

It was as Chamber president that he participated in the dramatic events of July 1940 which led to the suicide of the Third Republic and the installation of the Vichy regime of *Pétain. Although he made no attempt to lead an opposition to Pétain's legal coup, he did what he could to defend the prerogatives of the French parliament and indicated his disapproval of Vichy's anti-Semitism by sending back his *legion d'honneur* decoration. As the symbol of the Third Republic's political traditions, he was deprived of his Lyons town hall and was placed under house arrest. In the last days of Vichy, he was unwise enough to negotiate with *Laval for a possible summoning of the National Assembly; it was lucky for his subsequent reputation that he was deported to Germany. On his return to France, he earned *de Gaulle's lasting contempt by refusing to join his provisional government and demonstrated his commitment to the political values of his youth by leading the campaign for the restoration of the Third Republic. His efforts in this respect were wholly unsuccessful; over 90 per cent of the electorate rejected a return to the past. But the emergence of a parliamentary regime very similar in practice, if not in principle, to the Third Republic enabled him to return to the centre of politics. He regained his presidency of the National Assembly, and used his office to shore up the shaky authority of the coalition governments of the Fourth Republic. He also intervened in national policy debates by opposing French participation in the European Defence Community and supporting the reformist programme of *Mendès France. By the time of his death in 1957, he was regarded as the patriarch of the Republic.

A compulsive writer with a taste for grandiloquent oratory, Herriot was a vain and touchy man whose affable, pipe-smoking public persona concealed a more complex interior. His ministerial record was hardly distinguished. He remains, however, the most distinguished twentieth-century advocate of the political culture of French Republicanism.

Heseltine, Michael (b. Swansea, 21 Mar. 1933)

British; Secretary of State for Environment 1979–83, Defence 1983–6, Environment 1990–2, Trade and Industry 1992–5, Deputy Prime Minister and Lord Privy Seal 1995–7

Heseltine's father was a steel company manager, wealthy enough to send his son to Shrewsbury School. At Oxford University he was president of the Union. He was first elected as Conservative MP for Tavistock in 1966. As a young MP he made himself financially independent, making money from property development and publishing and founding the Haymarket Press. He was a millionaire by the time he was 30. In February 1974 he became the member for Henley.

In 1979 Mrs *Thatcher made him Secretary of State for Environment. He presided over the popular policy of selling council houses to tenants. Much of the period was spent in conflict with local government as he tried to bear down on its spending. His 1981 green paper ruled out a poll tax as unfair and unworkable. Heseltine also believed that the government had a role to play in helping run-down inner cities.

Following the riots in Liverpool in 1981 he became *de facto* Minister for Merseyside. His call for a major investment to fight urban poverty and regenerate the inner cities was blocked by the Treasury.

In 1983 Mrs Thatcher moved him to defence. She needed a more persuasive spokesman to deal with the Campaign for Nuclear Disarmament and the women protestors at Greenham Common. His relations with Mrs Thatcher were never close. They were different kinds of Conservative, she suspected his political ambitions, and he believed the government should do more to combat unemployment. Rival schemes to rescue the ailing Westland Helicopter Company at the end of 1985 brought the two of them into conflict. Heseltine favoured a European-backed rescue bid, Mrs Thatcher and the Department of Trade and Industry favoured an American-backed one. When Mrs Thatcher, in an effort to contain the public row, insisted that all future statements should be cleared with the Cabinet office, a frustrated Heseltine abruptly collected his papers and left a Cabinet meeting. Cabinet colleagues only learnt subsequently that he had resigned. In subsequent public statements he made his resignation a matter of constitutional principle, claiming that he had been denied the right to put his case to Cabinet.

On the back benches Heseltine kept himself in the public eye. He visited over 200 constituency associations and made clear that he was available—if and when there was a leadership vacancy. Whenever Mrs Thatcher's position weakened his own stock rose. He supported privatization and trade union reform, but was more supportive of the European Community and favoured a more active role for government in the economy. His critics on the right dismissed him as a corporatist.

His opportunity came following the resignation speech of Sir Geoffrey *Howe in November 1990. He stood in the annual leadership election and, although Margaret Thatcher defeated Heseltine by 200 votes to 152, this margin was four short of the required 15 per cent majority and a great achievement for the challenger. Mrs Thatcher was persuaded to stand down and on the second ballot John *Major was elected.

Major made Heseltine Secretary of State for Environment. In this post he ended the poll tax, replacing it with a council tax. In the 1992 parliament he was moved to the Department of Trade and Industry and gave himself the title of president in an attempt to increase the profile of the post. He had long cherished the post, which would enable him to intervene, boost exports, and make industry more competitive. He dismissed proposals that he become party chairman, claiming that over the previous thirteen years his department had had twelve ministers. It needed stability. He remained in post for thirty-nine months.

For a time his political prospects wavered following the controversy over his acceptance of the Coal Board's proposal to close thirty-one uneconomic coal pits and in summer 1993 he suffered a heart attack. He made a recovery and by 1994 was seen as a likely successor to John Major. When Major won a leadership contest in July 1995 his first step was to make Heseltine Deputy Prime Minister and give him a wide-ranging brief. There was much speculation about a 'deal' between the two. Heseltine provided strong support for John Major and was an important link between the pro and anti factions over Europe. When the Conservative Party went down to a heavy defeat in the 1997 general election and John Major announced his intention to stand down, Michael Heseltine was widely thought to be the obvious successor, even though it might be for a spell of a few years. It was his great misfortune that an apparent recurrence of his heart problems found him out of the race. He retired to the back benches.

Hess, Rudolf Walter Richard (b. Alexandria, 26 Apr. 1894; d. 17 Aug. 1987)
German; deputy leader NSDAP 1933–41

Born in Egypt of German parentage, Hess served in the First World War, ending it as an air force lieutenant. He joined the paramilitary Free Corps and soon after the NSDAP. He took part in *Hitler's Munich coup (1923) and was imprisoned with him in Landsberg jail. In prison Hitler dictated to him his *Mein Kampf*. He rose due to his close association with Hitler, who appointed him his Deputy in the NSDAP, a member of the government, and an SS general in 1933. On 30 August 1939 he was included in the Defence Council of the Reich. Despite all these offices his influence was limited, a fact which helped to save his life in 1945.

Hess was held prisoner from May 1941 when he flew alone to Scotland on an abortive peace mission. This was undertaken without Hitler's approval and was not taken seriously by the British. In spite of doubts about his mental state he was put on trial by the Allies at Nuremberg in 1945 and sentenced to life imprisonment. From 1966 he was the only prisoner in Spandau and died in 1987.

The official position is that he was Hess and that he died of natural causes, but in certain circles doubts remain.

Heuss, Theodor (b. Brackenheim, 31 Jan. 1884; d. 12 Dec. 1963)
German; President of the Federal Republic of Germany 1949–59

Although he had been a member of the Reichstag since 1924 on the left-liberal German Democratic Party (DDP) list, Heuss voted for *Hitler's enabling act in 1933. Heuss worked as a liberal journalist before the First World War and as an academic after it. He had denounced Hitler, but, like all the other non-socialist members of parliament, capitulated to him in the decisive moment. His vote did him little good; he worked as a journalist until 1936 when he was banned from writing.

In 1945 he was briefly Minister of Culture in Baden-Württemberg and then professor of politics at the Technical University of Stuttgart. He remained interested in active politics helping to establish the Free Democratic Party (FDP), becoming its leader in 1948. In 1949 he struck a deal with *Adenauer: the Christian Democrats would vote for Heuss as President if his colleagues would vote for Adenauer as Chancellor. The result was that both were elected, Heuss on the second ballot.

Heuss, already 66, had the features of a kindly father-figure. He also acknowledged his past mistakes, which was also advantageous as so many others had made the same political mistakes. He was re-elected in 1954 with a large majority. Never a Nazi, he was able to represent the new state abroad, visiting Greece (1956), Turkey (1957), Canada, the USA, and Britain in 1958.

Himmler, Heinrich (b. Bavaria, 7 Oct. 1900; d. 23 May 1945)
German; Chief of Police 1936–45, leader of the SS 1929–45, Minister of the Interior 1943–45

The son of a Catholic secondary schoolteacher, Himmler served as a cadet in the 11th Bavarian Infantry without seeing action in the First World War. He took up the study of agriculture, but was soon involved in right-wing politics and took part in *Hitler's Munich putsch (1923). He became a poultry farmer in 1928, only to be appointed head of the then small SS a year later by Hitler. In 1931 he set up the SD or Security Service of the Nazi party. When Hitler was appointed Chancellor in 1933 Himmler was appointed Bavarian police chief. He set up the first concentration camp in southern Germany at Dachau near Munich. Himmler's great moment came on 30 June 1934 when, on Hitler's orders, he sent his SS units into action against his erstwhile mentor and boss Ernst Röhm and other SA leaders. Three weeks later the SS was elevated as an independent organization free of SA control. By 1936 Himmler, already head of the SS and SD, was appointed Chief of the German Police including the Gestapo. Although nominally directly under Dr Frick, Minister of the Interior, Himmler was virtually answerable only to Hitler.

The outbreak of war in September 1939 saw a further escalation of Himmler's power. Hitler made him Reich Commissar for the Consolidation of German Nationhood. This involved the compulsory resettlement of Germans from outside the Reich into Germany, and the expulsion or elimination of non-Germans and the mentally sick. His empire expanded as Germany occupied most of Europe. Many members of the Polish intelligentsia were among his first foreign victims. Thousands of others from all nationalities followed. From the summer of 1941 he energetically implemented the 'final solution of the Jewish question' at Auschwitz and elsewhere.

By the time Himmler was appointed Minister of the Interior (25 August 1943) the Third Reich was losing the war. It was disintegrating when he took over as commander of the Volkssturm [Home Guard] in July 1944. Yet his vast army of Waffen-SS, including many foreign volunteers, fought on until the final surrender in May 1945.

Unlike some other Nazi leaders, Himmler was determined to survive the lost war. In April 1945 he took up contact with the Swedish Red Cross, offering to hand over Jewish survivors to their care. He also sought negotiations with the Allies. Furious, Hitler ordered his arrest. Himmler then sought to escape in disguise. He fell into British hands posing as an ordinary soldier; on being recognized, he swallowed the poison capsule in his mouth, dying almost at once.

Hindenburg, Paul von (b. Posen, 2 Oct. 1847; d. 2 Aug. 1934)

German; President 1925–34

Hindenburg was a Prussian from Germany's eastern frontier and had a successful military career in the Austro-Prussian War (1866) and the Franco-Prussian War (1870–1), retiring as a general in 1911. He was recalled in 1914 and achieved spectacular successes against the Russians at Tannenberg and the Masurian Lakes in 1914. He was promoted to field marshal and in 1916 became the supreme military commander.

Hindenburg was elected President on 26 April 1925, on the death of *Ebert. He was the candidate of the right and defeated the candidate of the Catholic Centre, Social Democrats, and Liberals by 14.6 million votes to 13.8 million. In April 1932 he was re-elected as the candidate of the moderates, defeating *Hitler by 19.36 million to 13.4 million. Hindenburg had appointed *Brüning Chancellor in 1930, hoping that together they would introduce a more presidential-style government. His subsequent appointees, *von Papen and General Kurt von Schleicher, shared these views.

By appointing *Hitler Chancellor on 30 January 1933 Hindenburg made the greatest mistake of his career as President. He did so because he did not really believe in the Weimar Republic and hoped for an alliance of all 'national' forces leading, via an authoritarian state, to the restoration of the monarchy. He greatly underestimated Hitler, thinking he could be controlled by the non-Nazi majority in the 'government of national concentration'. Hindenburg, a senile and arrogant old man, was manipulated by Hitler with the help of his son Oskar von Hindenburg.

Hirohito Michinomiya (b. Yokohama, 29 Apr. 1901; d. 7 Jan. 1989)

Japanese; Showa Emperor of Japan 1926–89

Hirohito was the 124th Emperor of Japan and his reign coincided with great changes in Japan. He was the first senior member of the Japanese royal family to make a formal overseas tour when he visited Europe as Crown Prince in 1921, a tour that influenced his food and dress habits thereafter. He married in 1924 and his first child and heir, Akihiko, was born in 1933. Hirohito succeeded to the throne on the death of his father on 25 December 1926, and took the reign name *Showa*, meaning 'Enlightened Peace'. His relationship to the military in Japan remains controversial. In 1936 he ordered his generals to put down a coup that had killed two Cabinet members, but did nothing about the Japanese invasion of China in 1937, or the attack on Pearl Harbor in 1941. Only when the Cabinet was deadlocked over the decision of whether to accept the terms of the Potsdam Declaration in 1945 did Hirohito intervene again, this time in favour of surrender. Hirohito always claimed that he was carrying out his duty as a constitutional monarch and that there was nothing he could do to prevent the militarism of the 1930s.

Hirohito announced Japan's surrender by radio in August 1945 and he told the Japanese people that it was 'time to endure the unendurable'; this was the first time that his voice had ever been broadcast. He visited Douglas MacArthur, the head of the Allied Occupation forces, and offered to take full responsibility for the war; however the US government had already decided that Japan would be easier to administer if the Emperor was maintained as a figurehead, and so Hirohito escaped being tried as a war criminal, despite strong pressure from other Allied countries.

On 1 January 1946 Hirohito officially renounced his divinity and began to restyle himself as a European constitutional monarch, although his attempts at greater openness were constantly stymied by the conservative imperial household which strictly controlled and regulated his life. In 1971 he undertook a controversial tour of Europe, the first overseas visit by a reigning Japanese monarch. He was a distinguished amateur marine biologist who published a number of academic papers.

Hirohito's life was a secretive and enclosed one and little is known about his personal beliefs and opinions. His death after a long illness in January 1989 was regarded by many Japanese as marking the end of a remarkable era of tragedy and success.

Hitler, Adolf (b. Braunau, Austria, 20 Apr. 1889; d. Berlin, 30 Apr. 1945)

German; Chancellor of Germany 1933–45, leader of the German People 1934–45

World history might have been different had the selectors at the Vienna Academy of Fine Arts admitted Adolf Hitler. The son of an over-strict provincial customs official, Hitler left grammar school aged 16 without graduating. After years as an aimless maverick, he tried his hand at painting. His failure to gain admission to the Academy further alienated him from those with formal qualifications. His rejection for compulsory military service in Austria added to his sense of failure and his contempt for the Austrian system. He volunteered for war service in 1914 and joined a Bavarian regiment.

Twice wounded, Hitler resented Germany's defeat, and explained it by reference to treachery. The traitors were the men of the left and the democrats who accepted the Versailles Treaty, forced on Germany by the Allies. In the chaos of post-war Munich he joined the German Workers' Party, a small right-wing group, as an army spy. It was not difficult for him to become its leader, changing its name to the German National Socialist Workers' Party (NSDAP) or Nazi Party.

In 1923 Hitler staged a putsch in Munich, influenced by *Mussolini's March on Rome of 1922. The coup was crushed by armed police and Hitler spent nine months in Landsberg jail for his part in it. He was released as part of a general amnesty. In prison he wrote his political testament, *Mein Kampf* ('My Struggle'). Crudely written, the book was an exposition of Hitler's German nationalism based on blood, imperialism, hatred of Jews, Marxists, and pacifists, and belief in the need for a totalitarian state. It also contained a jumble of 'socialist' proposals.

Hitler's activities gained him support in reactionary circles which helped him in 1926 to smash the left in the Nazi Party led by Gregor Strasser. Despite his efforts the NSDAP gained only 2.6 per cent in the Reichstag election of 1928. In 1930 Germany, in spite of Nazi, nationalist, and Communist opposition, agreed under the Young Plan to pay war reparations until 1988. This campaign brought the Nazis into touch with a much wider nationalist audience than before and the outbreak of the world slump in 1929 also helped. Unemployment soared, small investors lost their savings, the propertied classes feared revolution. In the 1930 election the Communist vote increased to 13.1 per cent, but the Nazi to 18.3 per cent. In the end, however, the

Nazis gained power not by the ballot box but by the help they received from *Von Papen and the reactionary circles close to President von *Hindenburg, who appointed Hitler Chancellor on 30 January 1933. In the previous election (November 1932) the Nazis had attracted only 33.1 per cent. The Reichstag fire on 27 February 1933 was the signal for Hindenburg to suspend civil liberties, and thousands were placed in the newly established concentration camps. The election of 5 March gave the Nazis 44 per cent and with their nationalist allies they held an absolute majority of 52 per cent. A mixture of threats and persuasion saw parliament (except for the Social Democrats and the banned Communists) grant Hitler's government emergency powers for four years. The persecution of the Jews began. After the death of Hindenburg in 1934 Hitler took over as head of state whilst remaining head of government. On 30 June 1934 he wiped out potential opponents in his own party, including stormtroop leader Ernst Röhm.

Hitler is widely credited with having created full employment and prosperity in Germany in the 1930s. But many of the measures he used had been started by previous administrations, and world trade was recovering from the slump, although the rearmament programme certainly helped. In foreign policy at first Hitler preached peace. A concordat was signed with the Vatican in 1933 and a friendship treaty with Poland in the same year. In 1935 he signed the Anglo-German Naval Agreement but also reintroduced conscription. In 1936 he reoccupied the Rhineland in breach of the Versailles Treaty and supported the rebellion of *Franco in Spain. In 1938 he took over Austria by threat of force and gained the Sudetenland from Czechoslovakia by promising peace to Britain, France, and Italy. After he broke his promises by seizing the rest of Czechoslovakia in February 1939, Britain guaranteed Poland. Hitler's invasion of that country on 1 September 1939, his rear secured by the Hitler–*Stalin Pact, led to Britain and France declaring war.

The defeat of Poland was followed by 'lightning war' against Denmark, Norway, Luxembourg, Holland, Belgium, and France with Hitler virtually controlling Western Europe by June 1940. After failing to get Britain to negotiate peace, or to defeat it in the Battle of Britain, he turned his armies against the USSR in June 1941. This was a great mistake. His declaration of war on the USA in December 1941 was another. After gaining massive victories, the German armies were stopped outside Moscow in December 1941 and decisively defeated at Stalingrad in January 1943. The Africa Corps were forced to surrender in May 1943 due to Hitler's indifference to their fate. In Italy Hitler's ally *Mussolini fell from power and in June 1944 the Allies landed in Normandy. Meanwhile Germany's population centres were being devastated by Anglo-American air raids.

Hoping for a compromise peace a group of military plotters attempted to kill Hitler on 20 July 1944. They had been appalled by German suffering at home and Nazi atrocities in occupied Europe. Hitler's mass extermination of the Jews and the Gypsies, and the death of millions of Soviet prisoners of war, were just the two most extreme atrocities. These crimes made no economic, military, or political sense. After show trials Hitler ordered the slow strangulation of those plotters who fell into Gestapo hands.

On 19 March 1945 Hitler gave Albert Speer, his Armaments Minister, the order to destroy everything of value in Germany, even gas, water, and electric supplies. He believed the best Germans had died in the war and those who remained did not deserve to survive. Speer did not carry out the order. As Soviet troops had captured most of Berlin, and realizing the end was near, Hitler took his own life on 30 April 1945. His Third Reich surrendered a week later.

Hoare, Samuel John Gurney (b. London, 24 Feb. 1880; d. 7 May 1959)

British; Foreign Secretary 1935, Home Secretary 1937–9; Bt. 1915, Viscount Templewood 1944

The son of a baronet and member of an old Norfolk farming family, Hoare was educated at Harrow and New College, Oxford, where he graduated with a double first. At the age of 23 he was appointed assistant private secretary to the Secretary for the Colonies and at 26 tried to get elected to the House of Commons. He was elected as Conservative MP for Chelsea in 1910. His first ministerial post came twelve years later, when the *Lloyd George coalition collapsed. He was appointed secretary of State for Air, a post he was to hold in the succeeding parliament (1924–9). In 1931 he was promoted to be Secretary of State for India and handled the passage of the India Bill effectively, despite attacks from critics on the Conservative benches.

In 1935 he was appointed Foreign Secretary. His tenure of the office was short-lived. In need of rest, he went to Switzerland. On the way, he visited French Foreign Minister *Laval and negotiated the Hoare–Laval Pact which, following the attack on Abyssinia by Italy, conceded two-thirds of the country to Italy. The pact came in for immediate attack by MPs and threw the Cabinet into confusion. Hoare, still in Switzerland, broke his nose while skating. At a meeting of the Conservative backbench Foreign Affairs Committee, Sir Austen *Chamberlain attacked the pact and declared, 'gentlemen do not behave in such a way'. According to Harold *Macmillan 'that settled it'. Hoare was forced to resign and the Cabinet repudiated the Pact. Hoare made a dignified resignation speech and was brought back into government the following year (1936) as First Lord of the Admiralty and then, in 1937, was appointed Home Secretary, a post in which he took a particular interest in penal reform. In September 1939 he was made Lord Privy Seal and included in the War Cabinet. A close supporter of Neville *Chamberlain, he was not kept on in government when *Churchill succeeded to the premiership. Instead he was shipped off as ambassador to Spain, a sensitive post in which he served until 1944. On his return, he was created Viscount Templewood and spent several years holding a range of offices in public and voluntary bodies.

An able minister until broken by the Hoare–Laval Pact, Hoare suffered from an element of poor judgement and never fully recovered from the affair. Reflecting his problems, he titled his memoirs *Nine Troubled Years*.

Hogg, Quintin McGarel (b. London, 9 Oct. 1907)
British; Lord Chancellor 1970–4, 1979–87; Viscount 1953–63, Baron (life peer) 1970

Hogg inherited his father's love of the law and a family trait of having slightly deformed hands: he was born with a sixth digit (which was quickly removed) attached to the thumb on his right hand. He was educated at Eton and Christ Church, Oxford, and was destined for a career in the law and politics, following in the footsteps of his father. He was called to the bar in 1932 and practised as a barrister until elected to parliament in a celebrated by-election in 1938, winning Oxford City as a pro-*Chamberlain Conservative. After wartime service in the Rifle Brigade, he served briefly as Under-Secretary for Air in *Churchill's 1945 caretaker government. Seen as a progressive Conservative, he was prominent in the movement to modernize the party and penned an influential book, *The Case for Conservatism*, published by Penguin in 1947.

In 1953 his father died and he moved to the House of Lords as the 2nd Viscount Hailsham, a move he tried to resist, but he was unable to persuade the Prime Minister to change the law. In 1956 he was appointed First Lord of the Admiralty and joined the Cabinet a year later as Minister for Education. In 1959, he was appointed Minister for Science and Technology. He served at the same time as Lord President of the Council (1957–9, 1960–4) and Lord Privy Seal (1960–1), and as deputy leader (1957–1960) and leader (1960-3) of the House of Lords. He combined his ministerial duties with chairmanship of the Conservative Party from 1957 to 1959, his ebullience and energy proving popular with party activists.

When *Macmillan announced his resignation as Prime Minister in 1963, Hailsham used the occasion of the party conference to announce his renunciation of his peerage—made possible by the passage of the 1963 Peerages Act—and in effect campaign publicly for the party leadership. His campaigning apparently resulted in Macmillan withdrawing support from him.

Though returned to the House of Commons in 1963 as member for St Marylebone, his service in the House was to prove relatively short-lived. In 1970, Edward *Heath appointed him to the post once held by his father—that of Lord Chancellor—and he returned to the House of Lords with a life peerage as Lord Hailsham of St Marylebone. He was to serve in the office not only for the lifetime of the Heath government (1970–4) but also for two full parliaments of the *Thatcher premiership (1979–87). He was 80 years of age when he relinquished office. Though responsible for a number of reforms, he was essentially in the mould of a traditionalist Lord Chancellor, defending most of the practices of the bar and the judicial process. Unusually for modern Lords Chancellor, he chose to sit on occasion to hear appeals. Following his retirement, he continued to attend the House of Lords on a regular basis.

His willingness to demonstrate his brilliance, an unwillingness to suffer fools gladly, and a volatile temper did not always commend him to others. Few, though, have doubted his outstanding intellectual capacity. His contribution to politics has combined the practical with the reflective. His writings in his early political life provided intellectual inspiration to a new generation of Conservatives and his 1976 Dimbleby Lecture, advocating the case (which he later refuted) for a written constitution, provided a new phrase to the lexicon of British politics when he warned of the possibility of an 'elective dictatorship'.

Holland, Sidney George (b, Canterbury, 18 Oct. 1893; d. 5 Aug. 1961)
New Zealand; leader of the National Party 1940–57, Prime Minister 1949–57; Kt. 1957

Born and educated in Canterbury, Holland's early employment was in his father's haulage firm. He served as a second lieutenant in the First World War. He then became a Christchurch business man in hardware, transport, engineering, and later a sheep and cattle stud farmer. He was elected National Party member for Christchurch North in 1949. He was now launched on a political career and in 1940 he became leader of the National Party. In that year he refused to join the War Cabinet led by Labour. As the Japanese threat loomed larger he joined the Cabinet in 1942, but left after a few months following disagreement on domestic politics. His party's position improved in the 1943 and 1946 elections, but still trailed Labour.

He led the National Party to its first electoral victory in 1949. The new government, in spite of its anti-socialist rhetoric, did not bring a sharp change to New Zealand. Labour's social welfare programme was accepted by the Nationals, who also accepted the importance of full employment and overseas markets. However, rationing on petrol and butter was removed as were quantative controls on many imports although price control was maintained. Major confrontations with the unions occurred following moves to deregister the Carpenters' Union and the Waterside Workers' Union. The government declared a state of emergency under the Public Safety Conservation Act (1932) and subsequently passed the Police Offences Amendment Bill, which caused widespread concern for its restrictions on civil liberties.

He was a strong supporter of Britain and open access to British markets underpinned the economic system, which depended heavily on handsome prices for primary products. However, fluctuations in prices led to guaranteed prices for dairy products and the Act of 1956 which gave producers a larger majority on the Marketing Commission and the authority to fix their own prices. The success of Deputy Leader *Holyoake in pacifying the farmers ensured his succession to the leadership.

According to historian Keith Sinclair, Holland's bouncy and at times aggressive leadership failed to conceal or compensate for his ineffable mediocracy. Holland was very reluctant to stand down but eventually gave way under pressure from senior

Cabinet colleagues just ten weeks before the elections in which the Nationals were defeated.

Holyoake, Keith Jacka (b. Pahiatua, Feb. 1904; d. 8 Dec. 1984)
New Zealand; Prime Minister 1957, 1960–72, Governor-General 1977 for one term; Kt. 1978

Holyoake left school early and worked on the family farm. He was largely self-educated. When he became an MP by winning a by-election in 1932 for the Reform Party he was the youngest member of the House of Representatives. This began a political career which lasted for nearly fifty years. He lost the seat in 1938, was re-elected in 1943, and in 1946 became deputy leader of the opposition National Party. Three years later his party replaced Labour in office and he was Deputy Prime Minister and Minister of Agriculture.

He became Prime Minister after *Holland was persuaded to stand down in 1957, only to lose office in the following elections. The Nationals returned to power in 1960 with a majority of twelve which at three subsequent elections was strong enough to withstand whatever attacks a broken Opposition could manage.

A master of consensus-making, he happily ran a Cabinet where he listened, quizzed, and quietly commanded for eleven years. Holyoake's style was represented by his handling of right-wing pressure from National Party membership for an end to compulsory unionism. Hearings into a proposed bill to amend existing legislation showed that organizations representing employers, manufacturers, farmers, and unions were against change. The subsequent legislation had provisions for qualified or unqualified preference being given to unionists. Formally compulsory membership was abolished but in practice the situation remained the same with union membership maintained undisturbed.

A far greater threat developed when overseas prices for produce plunged. As Minister for Finance, Holyoake was faced with the possible necessity of introducing a 'Black Budget' similar to that which had contributed to the defeat of the previous Labour government. However, the government did nothing spectacular and eventually prices rebounded. He was able to go to the 1963 election with the slogan 'Steady Does It', which suited his style perfectly. By the late 1960s New Zealand was running into a recession with unemployment and industrial unrest increasing. In the 1969 election the National majority was reduced to six. Cabinet faltered as it tried to cope with Britain's entry into the Common Market, with inflation, and with farmer discontent. In February 1972 a reluctant Prime Minister was persuaded to stand down in favour of his deputy John Marshall. Ten months later the government was defeated by a resurgent Labour Party.

In 1975 Holyoake became a Minister of State in the first *Muldoon government. In 1977 Muldoon moved Holyoake out of his ministry to the Governor-General's chair.

Home, Lord *see* DOUGLAS-HOME, ALEC

Honecker, Erich (b. Neunkirchen, Saar, 25 Aug. 1912; d. Chile, 29 May 1994)
German; first/general secretary of the SED 1971–89, head of GDR 1976–89

Born the son of a coal miner, Honecker was brought up in a Communist (KPD) household. He went through the various stages of the Communist youth movement and, although apprenticed as a roofer, soon became a full-time KPD official. By 1931 he was Communist youth leader in the Saar. Honecker continued underground activities after the Saar was incorporated into Nazi Germany in 1935. He was arrested in that year and sentenced to ten years' imprisonment in 1937. In 1945 he was liberated from Brandenburg jail by the Red Army and immediately resumed KPD youth work.

When the Free German Youth (FDJ) was established in 1946 he was elected chairman and remained in this office until 1955. He was also elected to the Executive Committee (later Central Committee) of the ruling Socialist Unity Party (SED) in 1946, and as a candidate member of the Politburo in 1950. He spent a year on a course in Moscow, 1956–7, a city where he had spent a similar year in 1930. His election to full membership of the Politburo followed in 1958. From 1956 Honecker had been responsible for security matters on behalf of the Politburo, and he is credited with the building of the Berlin Wall in 1961.

Erich Honecker owed his success to the support of *Ulbricht, who at one period looked upon him as his natural successor. However, the relations between the two cooled. Honecker got tired of waiting as the 'crown prince'. He also felt Ulbricht was verging on revisionism with his economic reforms, his attempts to woo the West German Social Democrats, and his arrogance towards the Soviet Union. He sought, and gained, Soviet blessing for the removal of Ulbricht as SED first secretary in 1971. He was then unanimously elected to that office, which he occupied until October 1989. Honecker sought to dispel his austere image. For a time he allowed more freedom in the arts. In 1976 he also announced a mass of social welfare measures designed to increase the birth rate. He followed the Soviet line on détente with West Germany, which paved the way for mutual recognition by the two German states in 1973, and led to the international recognition of the GDR. Détente, and with it millions of West German visitors, made it increasingly difficult for the SED to maintain its hard-line stance within the GDR. Increasingly, intellectuals, environmentalists influenced by the West German Greens, and active Christians challenged its authority. Western television helped East Germans to get a clearer picture of the world. Consumers were increasingly dissatisfied with the poor range and quality of goods on offer and the restrictions of travel.

Honecker followed Ulbricht in amassing power and pursuing the personality cult. He took over as head of state in 1976 and chairman of the Defence Council of the GDR. After 1985 he found himself at odds with the CPSU by rejecting General Secretary *Gorbachev's glasnost reforms. In the summer of 1989 thousands of East German tourists escaped to the West through Hungary, whose Communist rulers had opened their frontier to the West. This, and the fortieth anniversary of the GDR celebrations in October, provoked demonstrations throughout the Republic and calls for free elections. The sickly Honecker was forced out of office in much the same way as Ulbricht. Egon *Krenz replaced him for a few weeks before the whole edifice of the SED state collapsed. After being expelled from the party he had helped to found, imprisoned and forced abroad, Honecker died in Chile.

Hoover, Herbert Clark (b. West Branch, Iowa, 10 Aug. 1874; d. New York, 20 Oct. 1964)

US; President 1929–1933

Raised by Quaker relatives—his father and mother died while he was still a child—Hoover was educated at Newberg Academy and Stanford University (then a new university) and trained as an engineer. After an uncertain start, including a stint when he was without a job, he set up his own company and was a millionaire by the time he reached the age of 30. As an international engineer of renown, he travelled the globe.

During the First World War, he was appointed to head a relief agency in Europe and after US entry into the war he was appointed as US Food Administrator. At the end of the war, he returned to Europe to help tackle food shortages. They were tasks to which Hoover—a highly effective administrator and philanthropist—was ideally suited. His work attracted praise on both sides of the Atlantic and established him as a public figure. In 1921, President Warren *Harding invited him to become Commerce Secretary. Hoover accepted and completely transformed the Department, using it to cut down on bureaucratic waste and to encourage business. He held the post under President Calvin *Coolidge and in 1928 was sufficiently prominent to be a candidate for the Republican nomination for President. He was nominated on the second ballot and won an easy victory over Democrat Al *Smith in the election. He amassed 21.3 million or 58 per cent votes to Smith's 15 million. At a time of economic boom, there was little doubt that the business-oriented Republican would win over the Democrat, and first Roman Catholic, candidate for the office.

Hoover was one of the most able men to be elected as President and also one of the unluckiest. He was inaugurated on 4 March 1929. Seven months later the Stock Market crashed. The new President was a believer in self-reliance and self-help and was loathe to see government intervention in economic affairs. He sought, ineffectually, to encourage expansion through a tax cut and by urging business to expand. Spending measures passed by Congress that threatened a balanced budget were rejected. As the ranks of the unemployed swelled, Hoover's popularity plummeted. Soup kitchens became common sights. Many factories became desolate sites. The production index fell to its lowest point in the country's history.

Settlements of unemployed men sprang up and were dubbed 'Hoovervilles'. The army was used to remove war veterans who had marched to Washington, DC, to ask for advance payment of their war bonuses. Hoover stuck to his principles and continued to urge local and state action. The states proved unable to cope. As conditions worsened, Hoover established the Reconstruction Finance Corporation to lend money to firms that could offer collateral, but it had little impact.

Other issues also served to increase Hoover's unpopularity. He opposed repeal of the Eighteenth Amendment, which imposed prohibition. At one baseball match, he was booed and chants of 'We Want Beer' rang in his ears as he left. The election year of 1932 was a bad one for Hoover. He criticized and later vetoed the *Wagner–*Garner unemployment relief bill, which included provision for $500 million for public works. The Republican Convention was dominated by a debate over prohibition and not by debate over the state of the economy. The Democrats nominated the Governor of New York, Franklin Delano *Roosevelt, and committed themselves to the repeal of prohibition. Roosevelt in his acceptance speech emphasized the need for economic recovery. Hoover was easily beaten in the election. Though he won 15.7 million votes, or 40 per cent, he carried few states—the only large state that he carried was Pennsylvania—and secured only 59 electoral college votes. Roosevelt, with 22.8 million votes, amassed 472 electoral college votes.

Hoover retired to his home in Palo Alto, California, but was to emulate a predecessor, William Howard *Taft, in finding his true vocation after service in the White House. He opposed American entry into the Second World War, but in 1946—two years after the death of his wife—responded to the call of President Harry S *Truman to help the food distribution programme in Europe. He was appointed Co-ordinator of Food Supply for World Famine. A combination of his humanitarianism and organizational skills made him an ideal candidate for the post, and he served with distinction. His service, for which he refused any remuneration, helped restore his reputation at home. In 1947 President Truman appointed him to head a commission on the reorganization of the executive branch, resulting in various changes designed to make government more efficient. President Dwight *Eisenhower recalled Hoover to head a second Hoover Commission in 1953. Hoover was by this time approaching 80 and was looked upon as an elder statesman. He lived for another decade, dying in New York in October 1964 at the age of 90.

Hoover was a dedicated and extremely able individual. He shone in all the public positions he held, bar one. His tenure of the presidency was fated. His ideology clashed with conditions that would not respond to his prescription. A man of great humanity, he was unable to convey that effectively while occupying the White House, but was able to demonstrate it to great effect in later years. When he left the White

House, he was extraordinarily unpopular. By the time of his death, he was a widely respected figure.

Horthy de Nagybánya, Miklós (b. Kenderes, 18 June 1868; d. Estoril, Portugal, 9 Feb. 1957)
Hungarian; Leader 1920–44

Horthy was born into a family of Protestant aristocrats. He entered the Austro-Hungarian Naval Academy at Fiume in 1886 and in 1909 became aide-de-camp to the Emperor Franz-Josef. On active service in 1917, his cruiser broke through the Allied blockade of the Straits of Otranto and returned home to the Adriatic, which made him a national hero. At the end of the war he was Commander-in-Chief of the Austro-Hungarian navy, which he had to transfer to Yugoslavia.

Horthy led the Hungarian resistance to the Communist regime of Béla *Kun. He organized an army which accompanied the Romanians who occupied Budapest in November 1919. He then oversaw the 'White Terror' against those suspected of involvement with Communism. In March 1920 Horthy became regent following the Hungarian Parliament's vote to restore the Habsburg monarchy. However, in 1921 he refused to allow Charles I to ascend the throne. Throughout the inter-war period Horthy headed a conservative regime which was set against social reform.

Horthy's foreign policy centred on the revision of the post-World War I settlement which had created large Hungarian minorities in Romania and Czechoslovakia. Horthy disliked *Hitler, but approved of his anti-Communism and appreciated that Hungary's territorial aims could only be realized with German support. By the First Vienna Award of November 1938 he gained the Hungarian-inhabited areas of Czechoslovakia. By the Second Vienna Award of August 1940 he obtained most of Transylvania from Romania. In November 1940 Hungary joined the Axis side in the Second World War. Horthy tried to keep Hungarian participation on the eastern front to a minimum after 1941. In October 1944 he sought a separate peace with the Western Allies, but was deposed by the Germans, who put him in a concentration camp. In 1945 the Allies imprisoned Horthy, but refused to deliver him to the Yugoslavs, who wanted to try him for war crimes. He was released in 1946 and retired to Portugal.

Houphouet-Boigny, Felix (b. Yamoussoukro, Oct. 1905; d. 7 Dec. 1993)
Ivoirian; President 1960–93

Son of a prosperous Baoule planter, Houphouet-Boigny was trained as a medical assistant, and became a local administrative chief and planter. His involvement in politics dated from his organization of African planters in 1944 against the preferential treatment given to French settlers. He soon formed the Parti Democratique de la Côte d'Ivoire (PDCI), and from 1945 was elected to successive Constituent and then National Assemblies in Paris. Initially aligned with the French Communist Party, he operated skilfully in Fourth Republic French politics, and broke with the Communists in 1950. In 1956 he became mayor of the Ivoirian capital, Abidjan, and gained a seat in the Council of Ministers in Paris which he held for three years.

He opposed plans for a federation of the French West African colonies, not least because Côte d'Ivoire was the wealthiest and would have had to subsidize the others. When *de Gaulle conceded independence to the colonies, he became President virtually unopposed, and ruled the country for the next thirty-three years. Though his style of rule was personalist and even autocratic, it was not especially repressive. Maintaining a capitalist economy in close association with France, Côte d'Ivoire flourished in its first two decades of independence as a prosperous state almost entirely dependent on agriculture, and contrasted sharply with the failures of states which had chosen a socialist orientation. Houphouet-Boigny himself built a massive personal fortune.

Declining primary produce prices in the 1980s brought the end of the Ivoirian 'miracle', and in his later years 'le vieux' (as he was universally known) became obsessed with the development of his home town, Yamoussoukro in central Côte d'Ivoire, and with the construction of a massive Catholic basilica there which was consecrated by the Pope. When the wave of democratization swept Africa after 1989, he remained politically nimble enough to call immediate multi-party elections, which he was able to win before his opponents could effectively organize. Although the country was peaceful and his successor took over by constitutional means, by the time of his death much of his achievement in building a prosperous state was tarnished.

Howard, John Winston (b. Earlwood, NSW, 26 July 1939)

Australian; Leader of the Liberal Party 1985–9, 1995– , Prime Minister 1996–

John Howard grew up in suburban Sydney. His father was a small businessman who ran a petrol service station. Howard was educated at Canterbury Boy's High School and Sydney University. He graduated with a law degree and worked as a solicitor in Sydney. He joined the New South Wales State Executive of the Liberal Party in 1963 and entered federal parliament in 1974.

Howard quickly established his strengths as a policy formulator and as a parliamentary speaker. Ideologically, he emerged as a 'dry' Liberal, emphasizing the central value of market forces in generating economic and social benefits. As Treasurer in the late 1970s and early 1980s, however, he was unable to effect major reforms to Australia's regulated and protected economy.

After the Liberals' electoral defeat in 1983, leadership of the party passed to Howard's party rival, Andrew Peacock. Tension developed between these two dogged conservative politicians throughout the 1980s. A miscalculation by Peacock enabled Howard to seize the leadership in 1985; but his hopes for electoral success were ruined by continued internal fights and an unsuccessful attempt by a group of conservatives to clear a path for Queensland Premier John Bjelke-Peterson to become Prime Minister. Howard was deposed as Liberal leader in 1989.

Two subsequent party leaders later in 1995, Howard re-emerged as a great survivor of Australian politics to lead the Liberal Party to a landslide victory in March 1996, after thirteen consecutive years of Labor rule. By this time much of the financial deregulation and privatization of public assets integral to Howard's planning was well under way. His early priorities were to continue these reforms, overhaul industrial relations, and reduce public spending in order to combat a large budget deficit.

On becoming Prime Minister, Howard's earlier image as a dry advocate of free markets was tempered by respect for his political longevity and, for some, by his commitment to traditional family values and attachment to the monarchy.

Howe, Geoffrey (b. Glamorgan, 20 Dec. 1926)

British; Chancellor of the Exchequer 1979–83, Foreign Secretary 1983–9; Kt. 1970, Baron (life peer) 1992

Howe was born in Port Talbot in south Wales. His father was a solicitor who could afford to send his son to Winchester. Howe then went to Cambridge to read law. He was an early member of the Bow Group, which consisted of members of university Conservative associations, and was chairman in 1955. He was a successful barrister before entering politics.

Howe entered the House of Commons in 1964 as Conservative MP for Bebington, which he held until his defeat in 1966. He then re-entered in 1970 as MP for Reigate and then Surrey East after the reorganization of constituencies in 1974, and held it until his retirement in 1992. Howe was made Solicitor-General (with a knighthood) in Edward *Heath's 1970 government. In this post he played a key part in framing the legislation for the controversial Industrial Relations Act—which embittered relations with the trade unions—as well as the European Communities Act. The latter was a formidable operation because it involved the merger of much British law with the Treaty of Rome. In 1972 he was made Secretary of State for Trade and Consumer Affairs, with a seat in the Cabinet, and was responsible for overseeing the statutory controls on prices and incomes.

When Heath was defeated in the first round of the party's leadership contest in 1975, Howe entered the second ballot. He finished a distant third behind the eventual winner, Margaret *Thatcher. But he had made a mark and she appointed him shadow Chancellor. As Chancellor of the Exchequer in the first Thatcher government (1979–83) he ended exchange controls, cut income tax, and doubled VAT in his first budget. Howe took monetarist ideas seriously and his 1981 budget shocked Cabinet colleagues and Keynesian economists by deflating the economy at a time of severe recession. Sir Geoffrey signalled a decisive break with the incomes policies and corporatism of the 1970s.

Between 1983 and 1989 Howe was Foreign Secretary, the longest tenure of any Foreign Secretary since *Grey (1905–16). He had to cope with Mrs Thatcher's suspicions of the Foreign Office—she regarded it as too compliant to foreigners, particularly to the European Community (EC). Compared to her, Sir Geoffrey was more pro-EC and less Atlanticist, favoured British membership of the Exchange Rate Mechanism (ERM) of the European Monetary System, and was more willing to encourage British contacts with the African National Congress. The agreement to transfer Hong Kong to China in 1997 was largely his policy.

As a minister he joined a capacity for hard work to patience and an interest in working for long-term solutions. He was an effective debater but not an inspiring public speaker. His mumbling monotone style earned him the title 'Mogadon Man'. Europe was to be the cause of his (and Mrs Thatcher's) downfall. Like her he had no time for the bolder schemes of federalism but he did believe in pooling national sovereignty where it would produce more benefits than action by a single government. On the eve of an important summit of European leaders in June 1989, Nigel *Lawson (the Chancellor of the Exchequer) and Sir Geoffrey jointly threatened resignation unless Mrs Thatcher moderated her opposition to Britain's entry to the ERM. She compromised but determined to move Sir Geoffrey at her earliest opportunity.

The next month Howe was demoted to the post of leader of the House of Commons with the title of Deputy Prime Minister. The last was only a gesture. He was not successful in either post, because he had no close relationship with the Prime Minister, and grew increasingly disillusioned. She made it clear that she would not listen to him, and he thought that on Europe she was not only destabilizing the Cabinet but harming the national interest. After more belligerent speeches from Mrs Thatcher on Europe he resigned on 1 November 1990. He judged that only by leaving might he be able to effect a change. His nineteen-minute resignation speech in the House of Commons on 13 November was devastating in its criticism of Mrs Thatcher's handling of Cabinet and her attitude to Europe. It greatly weakened her position, opening the way for the leadership challenge from Michael *Heseltine and her eventual downfall.

Howe played a major role in preparing and delivering many of the economic and foreign policies of the 1980s. Perhaps only Mrs Thatcher herself deserves more credit as an architect of what was known as Thatcherism. He retired from the House of Commons in 1992 and entered the Lords as Lord Howe of Aberavon.

Hoxha, Enver (b. Gjirokaster, 16 Oct. 1908; d. Tirana, 11 Apr. 1985)
Albanian; Leader 1946–85

Hoxha was born into a Muslim landowning family of the Tosk clan. He studied and resided in France from 1930 to 1936, joining the French Communist Party. He then returned to Albania and in 1941 became provisional secretary-general of the Albanian Labour Party, as the Communist party was correctly known. The next year a Communist resistance movement, the Albanian National Liberation Movement, was formed with the help of *Tito's Yugoslav partisans. Hoxha and Mehmet *Shehu were its leaders. At the end of 1944, the Communists were in control of all Albania's main towns and declared Albania a People's Republic in 1946, having eliminated their political rivals. Hoxha was Prime Minister, Foreign Minister, Defence Minister, and head of the party. With particular brutality, his regime imposed a Stalinist one-party system with collectivization of agriculture, nationalization of industry, and suppression of both the Islamic and Christian religions. Thereafter Hoxha stood firmly against the slightest modification of the system.

In 1948 Hoxha fiercely supported *Stalin when he broke with Tito. This greatly strengthened his position, since he was able to use Soviet support to destroy his enemies within the ALP. Relations with the Soviet Union soured after 1956 when *Khrushchev denounced Stalin at the Twentieth Congress of the CPSU and in 1961 Albania was excluded from Comecon and the Warsaw Pact. At the end of the 1960s Albania drew close to China. This relationship deteriorated in the 1970s when Hoxha criticized China's accommodation with his arch-enemy, the United States. In 1978 the Chinese government abruptly broke off relations with Albania. Hoxha's change in foreign policy broadly coincided with purges of his rivals at home. He eliminated different alleged factions in 1973, 1974, 1975, and in 1982. In December 1981 Mehmet Shehu committed suicide in mysterious circumstances after Hoxha had replaced him as his designated heir with Ramiz *Alia. The next year Shehu's supporters were purged.

Hoxha died on 11 April 1985, having ruled for forty-one years—longer than any other Communist leader except North Korea's *Kim Il Sung. His road to socialism had failed long before. Economic growth had stopped in the mid-1970s and Albania was the poorest country in Europe.

Hughes, Charles Evans (b. Glen Falls, New York, 11 Apr. 1866; d. 28 Aug. 1948)
US; Governor of New York 1906–10, Republican presidential candidate 1916

Hughes, the son of a Baptist preacher, was educated at Brown University and Columbia Law School, from which he graduated in 1884. He served as a legal counsel for New York in investigations of insurance firms and utility industries in the state. In 1906 he was elected Governor of New York and re-elected in 1908. In this post he established a Public Service Commission to regulate utilities and railroads. He resigned from his Governorship in October 1910 to become a member of the Supreme Court, nominated by President *Taft. In the court he was part of the liberal voting block. He resigned in 1916 to seek the Republican nomination for the presidency, and won the nomination on the first ballot. The election was fought as the war clouds in Europe were gathering and the Republicans were strongly neutralist. In spite of being the favourite Hughes lost to the incumbent Woodrow *Wilson by 49 per cent to 46 per cent of the popular vote.

Hughes was made Secretary of state by President *Harding and served for a time under his successor *Coolidge. He managed to slow down the legal armaments race and took steps to improve relations with Latin America. He returned to his private law practice in 1925. Between 1928 and 1930 he served as a judge at the International Court of Justice. In 1930 he began an eleven-year spell as Chief Justice of the US Supreme Court. This was a controversial period in legal history as the court ruled several New Deal measures unconstitutional. Hughes was unapologetic in striking down the National Recovery Act but supported a number of other measures. He vigorously opposed President *Roosevelt's plans for 'packing' the court with his own nominees to replace elderly judges.

Hughes, William **(Billy)** Morris (b. Pimlico, London, 25 Sept. 1862; d. Lindfield, NSW, 28 Oct. 1952)

Australian; Prime Minister 1915–23

The son of a Welsh carpenter, Hughes was educated in Wales and London before migrating to Australia in 1884. After several years in a variety of itinerant jobs, he settled in Sydney and became involved in NSW labour politics and shearers' and then waterside unions.

Between 1901 and his becoming Prime Minister in 1915, Hughes established a reputation as a nationalist, an advocate of greater preparations for Australia's defence, and a compelling speaker. As Prime Minister during the First World War he tried twice to introduce conscription, but both referenda failed and his pro-conscription stance led to his expulsion from the Labor Party. This was also the catalyst for a major split which had been looming between industrial and political labour, and Hughes and his supporters joined conservatives to form the Nationalist Party, which Hughes then led as Prime Minister until 1923. In 1931 Hughes helped to form the new conservative party, the United Australia Party. He was narrowly beaten by Robert *Menzies to the prime ministership in 1939, but stayed to join the next political incarnation of Australian conservatism, the Liberal Party. He died in 1952, the longest serving parliamentarian in Australia's history.

Standing only 5 ft 6 ins (167 cm), the diminutive Hughes is also remembered for his aggressive and raucous championing of Australia's interests in the First World War. In London in 1916 he outmanœuvred officialdom to buy fifteen frigates, which formed the core of the new Commonwealth Shipping Line. At the end of the war, in London and Paris, his strident nationalism ('I speak for the 60,000 dead') secured for Australia effective control over former German New Guinea, and earned him a reputation for standing up to greater powers. Hughes did not, however, challenge the imperial framework within which Australian overseas interests were expressed. His protection of Australian interests was founded on a then common vision of Australia's white racial destiny.

Hughes was an outspoken opponent of appeasement during the 1930s and played significant roles in government and then in the Advisory War Council during the Second World War. He retained a capacity both to charm and to launch violent attacks, and made strategic use of his deafness to ignore unwanted views.

Hull, Cordell (b. Olympus, Tennessee, 2 Oct. 1871; d. 23 July 1955)

US; Secretary of State 1934–44

Hull was a successful lawyer by profession. He was elected to the Tennessee House of Representatives in 1892. After service in the Spanish–American war he served as a state judge between 1903 and 1907. He was then elected to serve in Congress as a Democrat in 1907 and served until 1921, suffering defeat in the Republican landslide in 1920. He was a prominent early advocate of the federal income tax and played a major part in framing the income tax and inheritance tax laws of the Woodrow *Wilson administration. Out of Congress, he was chairman of the Democratic National Committee (1921–4). He was re-elected to Congress in 1924 and served until 1931 when he entered the Senate. As a legislator he was interested in tax and tariff matters. His growing reputation led some to think of him as presidential material. In 1928 he had some support for the Democrat presidential nomination, but finished a distant second to Alfred *Smith.

Hull's main political achievements were as the longest-serving Secretary of State. He was in office from 1934, during the momentous Depression and war years, stepping down because of ill-health in 1944. He was a key figure in American diplomacy before the outbreak of the Second World War and an influential adviser to President F. D. *Roosevelt during the war. He concluded the lend-lease agreement with Britain.

He was also a key influence on the emergence of the United Nations and Roosevelt called him 'father of the United Nations'. His contribution earned him the Nobel Prize in 1945. Hull believed that the failure of the League of Nations and the refusal of the United States to enter were major causes of international instability in the 1930s. As Secretary of State, Hull also worker hard to lower tariffs between nations. The Trade Agreement Act (1934) provided for reciprocal foreign trade agreements and the granting of most favoured nation status to trading partners. Agreements were signed with over twenty states. Hull believed that free trade would promote prosperity and peace. He was much respected for his integrity and judgement.

Humphrey, Hubert (b. Wallace, South Dakota, 27 May 1911; d. 13 Jan. 1978)
US; Vice-President 1964–8

Humphrey qualified from the University of Minnesota in pharmacy and political science and practised both. He became an organizer for the Democratic Farmer-Labour Party in the state in 1944 and was elected mayor for Minneapolis in 1945, holding the position until 1949. Always on the party's liberal wing he helped found the Americans for Democratic Action in 1947. At the 1948 Democratic Convention he spoke out for a strong civil rights platform; the adoption of the platform drove some Southern delegates to withdraw and form their own party. Between 1949 and 1965 he represented Minnesota in the Senate. He made a failed bid for the Democratic presidential nomination in 1960; he lacked the resources to compete with John *Kennedy in the primaries and did not have the support of senior party figures. Between 1961 and 1965 he was Senate majority whip and played an important role in the passage of key legislation on civil rights as well as the Nuclear Test Ban Treaty. At the 1964 Democratic convention, President Lyndon *Johnson appeared at the convention rostrum and nominated Humphrey as the party's vice-presidential candidate. Humphrey was loyal to Johnson and, fatally for him, defended America's military involvement in Vietnam. This lost him much liberal party support and the anti-war candidates did well in the Democratic primaries in 1968, which Humphrey avoided. At the party convention in 1968, the party delegates nominated Humphrey on the first ballot. This caused outrage among critics of the war who felt that the nomination had been 'stolen' from them. It was ironic that Humphrey, who had tried to challenge the party establishment in 1960, now relied on it. Because of the party divisions Humphrey was given little chance of winning the election, but he made up much ground on the Republican Richard *Nixon in the last few days of the campaign, only losing by 43.4 per cent to 42.7 per cent of the popular vote. He returned to the Senate in 1971 and served until his death. He made one last effort for the presidential nomination in 1972, but his time was past. Humphrey was in many respects an old-fashioned liberal Democrat, remaining true to New Deal values, a believer in the beneficence of government action.

Huq, Zia-ul- (b. Jullundur, 12 Aug. 1942; d. 17 Aug. 1988)
Pakistani; President 1978–88

Zia came from a lower-middle-class family and was educated at St Stephen's College inn Delhi before joining the British Indian Army in 1944. He was commissioned into the cavalry and saw service in Burma, Malaya, and Java at the end of the Second World War. After his promotion to Brigadier in 1969, Zia was seconded to Jordan where he helped King Hussein's forces in their operations against the PLO. On his return home, Zia commanded the first Armoured Division for three years. He was still relatively unknown however when he became head of the Pakistan army in the spring of 1976.

Zia launched the coup code-named 'Operation Fairplay' against *Bhutto on 5 July 1977. It ushered in Pakistan's longest period of military rule. Even when it was withdrawn on 30 December 1985, Zia retained his post as Chief of Army Staff and continued to wield power through the office of President. Indeed on 29 May 1988, he dismissed his handpicked Prime Minister Mohammed Khan Junejo.

Zia's political survival rested on his skill in wrong-footing opponents, and on the favourable external environment following the December 1979 Soviet occupation of Afghanistan. This transformed him overnight from an international pariah to America's front-line ally in the fight against Communism. The Reagan administration provided $3.2 billion of military and economic assistance, despite concerns over human rights abuses and the nuclear programme.

The martial law era was punctuated by unfulfilled promises of national elections and by discussion of the relevance of democracy for an Islamic state. Zia maintained that a Western-style democracy was unsuitable for Pakistan. He eventually agreed to hold 'party-less' elections in February 1985, following a referendum on his Islamic policies which was linked with his re-election as President. The eleven-party alliance Movement for the Restoration of Democracy, which had mounted a major campaign in Sind in 1983 against the Zia regime, boycotted both the polls.

Zia introduced special *shariat* courts, with Islamic rules of evidence and punishments for certain crimes. Further measures included the provision of Islamic banking facilities and the government collection of *zakat* (alms) and *ushr* (agricultural tax). Islamization which was stoutly opposed by women's groups and human rights activists stirred up sectarian tensions between Sunnis and Shias.

Karachi experienced mounting ethnic violence from 1986 onwards. Clashes between *mohajirs* and Pakhtuns, later extended to the Sindhi community. The growing lawlessness was encourage by the ready availability of weapons and drugs as a result of the Afghan War. Zia justified his dismissal of Junejo in terms of the deteriorating security situation. Party-less elections were scheduled for November 1988. Zia died however on 17 August following the unexplained crash of his C-130 aircraft.

Zia can be viewed as a pious Muslim who halted his country's moral decay and contributed to the collapse of the Soviet Empire, or condemned as an intolerant and vindictive ruler who cynically manipulated Islam to remain in power.

Hurd, Douglas (b. 8 Mar. 1930)

British; Home Secretary 1985–9, Foreign Secretary 1989–95

Hurd came from a political family; his father and grandfather had both been Conservative MPs. He was educated at Eton and Trinity College, Cambridge, where he became president of the Union. He then entered the diplomatic service, rose to a high position in the Foreign Office, and would probably have risen to the top had he remained. He left the service in 1966 and worked for two years as a researcher in the Conservative Party. In 1968 the Conservative leader Ted *Heath invited him to manage his office. When Heath became Prime Minister in 1970 Douglas Hurd served as his political secretary in No. 10 Downing Street until 1974.

In February 1974 Hurd was elected MP for Mid-Oxon, subsequently in 1983 for the Witney constituency. In Margaret *Thatcher's first government, he held a junior position in the Foreign Office in 1979 and became Minister of State in the Home Office in 1983. In 1984, in her second administration, he was made Secretary of State for Northern Ireland with a seat in the Cabinet, and a year later became Home Secretary. In this key position he supported stiffer sentencing for criminals, boosted police resources and manpower, and in 1988 banned broadcasts with suspected terrorists in Northern Ireland and their supporters. He was a reforming Home Secretary and produced important legislation on drugs, public order, and criminal justice, as well as reforming the Official Secrets Act.

Hurd's ambition was realized when he became the Foreign Secretary in October 1989. This appointment was a surprise because it arose as a consequence of the unexpected resignation of the Chancellor of the Exchequer Nigel *Lawson and transfer of John *Major from the Foreign Office to the Treasury. As Foreign Secretary Hurd was aware that although Britain was only a medium-sized power it was able to 'punch above its weight'. In spite of sniping from the Prime Minister he carried on his predecessor's policy of building bridges with the European Community. He welcomed the end of apartheid in South Africa, was more supportive of German reunification than Mrs Thatcher, and, together with John Major, persuaded her to take Britain into the ERM in October 1990.

For a brief period (1985–6) he was seen as a stopgap successor to Mrs Thatcher. Near the end of her premiership he, like a number of Cabinet ministers, was becoming alarmed at her failure to adhere to agreed lines about the European Community and at the resignation of major figures from Cabinet. When she resigned he entered the second ballot of the leadership contest and finished a distant third (57 votes) behind John Major (185 votes) and Michael *Heseltine (131 votes).

He remained as Foreign Secretary under John Major and helped negotiate the Maastricht Treaty in December 1991. In 1992 and 1993 he played a major role in keeping Britain and the European Community from getting involved in the conflict over the break-up of Yugoslavia. Yet as the Conservative Party became increasingly sceptical about the integrationist thrust of the Community, so his position became less comfortable and he gave up his post in 1995 and retired as an MP in 1997. He had other interests to pursue.

Hurd was something of a traditional Conservative, trying to reconcile the Thatcherite emphasis on individualism and enterprise with Tory ideas of community. He wrote a number of thrillers as well as a well-received memoir of his years as political secretary to Mr Heath (*An End to Promises*) in 1979.

Husák, Gustáv (b. Dúbravka near Bratislava, 10 Jan. 1913; d. Bratislava, 18 Nov. 1991)
Slovak; leader of the Communist Party of Czechoslovakia 1969–87, President of Czechoslovakia 1975–89

The son of a Slovak worker, Husák trained as a lawyer in Bratislava. He joined the Communist Party in 1933. He was leader of the Slovak Communist resistance during the Second World War. In December 1943 he and the Communist poet Laco Novomeský ratified the 'Christmas Agreement' with the social-democratic section of the Slovak resistance. The Communists and the social democrats guaranteed the restoration of the pre-war Czechoslovak republic. In August 1944 the resistance started the Slovak National Uprising, which failed.

Husák was elected as a deputy to the National Assembly in 1946. From 1948 to 1949 he was Minister of Agriculture in *Gottwald's government. In 1951 he was arrested in the purge of the Communist party which followed the arrest of Rudolf *Slánský, and accused of being a 'Slovak bourgeois nationalist'. His real crime was to have asserted Slovak interests against the wishes of *Stalin and Gottwald during the war. He was imprisoned from 1954 until 1960 when he was released and rehabilitated. From 1963 to 1968 he worked at the Academy of Sciences in Prague. He became Deputy Premier in 1968 and was associated with the reforms of the 'Prague Spring'. But by the end of the year he had decided to follow a course pleasing to Moscow.

In 1969 Husák replaced *Dubček as leader of the Czechoslovak Communist Party. He initiated a thorough, though non-bloody purge of those associated with the 'Prague Spring'. Thereafter his power was based on a ubiquitous secret police and a level of consumerism which the economy could not afford. He oversaw the introduction of a federal constitution on 1 January 1969, which gave Slovakia autonomy. In 1975 Husák became President of Czechoslovakia. He retained this post after he handed leadership of the party to Miloš Jakeš in 1987. He resigned as President in December 1989 following the 'Velvet Revolution'. He died in 1991, having received Catholic last rights.

Hussein, King of Jordan *see* AL-HASHIMI, HUSSEIN

Hussein, Saddam (b. Takrit, Iraq, 28 Apr. 1937)
Iraqi; President 1979–

Saddam Hussein joined the Ba'ath party in 1957 and was sentenced to death in 1959 for participation in the attempted assassination of Premier Qasim. He escaped to Syria. A year after returning to Iraq in 1963, his relative, Hasan al-Bakr, secured his appointment as principal Ba'athist organizer and Saddam played a prominent role in the 1968 Ba'athist coup. President al-Bakr continued to patronize Saddam, making him deputy-chairman of the decision-making Revolutionary Command Council. Already head of the Ba'ath party organization and militia, Saddam added control of the security services to become the regime's strong man and effective deputy leader by 1971. Oil revenues enabled them to launch an ambitious programme of public-sector industrialization and the building of a welfare state after 1973. Saddam's powers steadily increased and, with al-Bakr in poor health, his rise to supreme leader was only a matter of time. He assumed absolute power as President in 1979.

The threat to his position from Kurdish rebellion in the north and Shi'i unrest in the south, abetted by Iran, caused Saddam to invade the Islamic Republic in 1980 seeking a quick victory and the overthrow of the *Khomeini regime. This failed and Iraq's armed forces withdrew from Iranian territory in 1982. The conflict then became a prolonged war of attrition, increasingly financed by Kuwait and Saudi Arabia, and supported militarily by the USSR, and increasingly by the West too. It ended in 1988 with Iraq in possession of the world's fourth largest army and mountainous debts, but without territorial or security gains. A second monumental military miscalculation was to invade Kuwait in 1990 and provoke a UN multinational force to rout the Iraqi army and end the occupation in 1991. By arousing popular Arab support, however, the war was a political success for Saddam. Post-war uprisings by Kurds and the Shi'i were brutally crushed and the Iraqi people's agony continued under UN economic sanctions, with Saddam Hussein more securely in power than before.

I

Iliescu, Ion (b. Oltenita, near Bucharest, 1930)
Romanian; President 1990–6

Iliescu joined the Communist Youth Union in 1944 and the Communist Party in 1953. He was educated as an electrical engineer at the Bucharest Polytechnic Institute and at Moscow State University, but followed a career within the party apparatus. In 1956 he became Secretary of the Central Committee of the Union of Communist Youth and prospered after his patron, Nicolae *Ceauşescu, became General Secretary of the Communist Party in 1965. The same year Iliescu entered the Central Committee as candidate member and became a full member in 1968. From 1967 to 1971 he was the Minister for Youth. In 1971 Ceauşescu became suspicious of him, stripped him of all his party positions except membership of the Central Committee, and relegated him to the provinces. He served as regional party secretary in Timişoara until 1974 and from then until 1979 in Iasi. He retired in 1984.

By the late 1980s Iliescu was one of a number of senior party officials and army officers disaffected with the Ceauşescu regime. In 1989 they obtained Soviet sanction for his removal, and took direction of the unrest in Bucharest which led to Ceauşescu's downfall in December 1989. Iliescu became President of the National Salvation Front formed to guide the revolution and created a provisional government. In May 1990 he was elected President of Romania with 85 per cent of the vote and despite discontent with the economic situation he was re-elected with 61 per cent in 1992.

However, the economy stagnated and corruption and sleaze were as bad as ever. Iliescu did little to reform the centralized economy and state security apparatus. He was defeated in the elections in November 1996, by the reformist Constantinescu. It was the first time Romania had changed its leader through democratic elections.

Izetbegovic, Alija (b. Bosanski Samac, Bosnia-Herzegovina, 8 Aug. 1925)
Bosnian Moslem; President of Bosnia-Herzegovina 1990–

During the Second World War Izetbegovic joined the Islamic 'Mlada Bosna' organization which opposed the Croat Fascist state of which Bosnia was then part. After the war he was imprisoned for three years by the Communist regime for 'pan-Islamic' activity. On his release he studied law at Sarajevo University and became a legal adviser. After *Tito's death in 1980 he published in Yugoslavia his book *Islamic Declaration* (first published abroad in 1970), for which he was imprisoned in 1983 for five years.

In 1990 he founded and became president of the Party of Democratic Action, representing Bosnian Muslims, which gained 86 of 240 seats in the December 1990 elections, and formed a grand coalition with the Serbian Democratic Party and the Croatian Democratic Community. By inter-party agreement Izetbegovic became President for one year, since when, in spite of the outbreak of civil war in Bosnia in April 1992, he has been regularly re-elected. While his writings favour Islamic fundamentalism, in practical politics he has worked for a multi-ethnic, democratic Bosnia. A survivor both of physical dangers and shifting political alliances, he has gained respect as a symbol of Bosnian, especially Muslim, national integrity.

Jackson, Henry Martin (b. Everett, Washington, 31 May 1912; d. 1 Sept. 1983)
US; member of the US House of Representatives 1940–52; US Senator 1952–83

The son of Norwegian immigrants, Jackson acquired the nickname 'Scoop' as a result of delivering newspapers while a schoolboy. Although he started university at Stanford, he transferred to the University of Washington, where he completed both his undergraduate degree and a law degree. After a brief period as a county prosecutor, he was elected in 1940 to the House of Representatives, where he served until 1952 when he secured election to the Senate.

Throughout his career he was sceptical about the motives of the Soviet Union and a 'hawk' on foreign and security policy. He used his Senate position to urge the United States to achieve arms superiority over the USSR and resist initiatives which might weaken America in relation to Russia. He publicized the missile gap in 1955 and successfully urged amendment of President *Kennedy's test ban treaty with *Khrushchev. His support for Israel prompted the Jackson–Vanik amendment in 1974 linking most-favoured nation status for Russia to a liberalization of its emigration laws; and he was a powerful critic of *Carter's Salt II Treaty. Thus he became a leading member of the neo-conservative group of academics and politicians whose ideas became influential in the late 1970s and early 1980s.

Although Jackson was resolutely opposed to the Soviet Union and Communism, his stance was based on analysis not emotion. He distanced himself from crude anti-Communists and his early career in the Senate was marked by withdrawal from the Permanent Investigations Committee because of Senator Joe *McCarthy's behaviour.

In domestic politics he was a traditional New Deal liberal, supporting welfare and civil rights, though opposing busing. He was a strong environmentalist and sponsored the legislation which created the Environmental Protection Agency.

Jackson twice sought the Democratic presidential nomination. In both 1972 and 1976 his hawkish views on foreign policy (including broad support for the Vietnam War) put him too far to the right of the Democratic Party to win the nomination. His expertise on nuclear and defence issues and his seniority in the Senate ensured, however, that he remained a figure of influence with administrations of both parties and a key figure in the debate about America's relationship with Russia.

Jackson, Jesse (b. Greenville, South Carolina, 8 Oct. 1941)
US; civil rights leader

Jackson was born out of wedlock but his natural mother later married and gave him his adoptive father's name. Jackson's athletic ability won him a scholarship to the University of Illinois. Poor academic progress and a desire to play quarterback made him transfer to an all-black college (North Carolina Agricultural and Technical State College) where he became a prominent quarterback and an active civil rights leader.

After graduation, Jackson worked briefly for North Carolina Governor Terry Sanford and then went to Chicago Theological Seminary. Jackson was more drawn to political activism than the ministry and he left to work for Martin Luther *King's Southern Christian Leadership Conference. (He was, however, ordained in 1968.)

In 1966 King, who took a personal interest in Jackson's career, appointed him to organize Operation Breadbasket (the economic arm of SCLC) in Chicago. Jackson displayed imaginative and dynamic leadership persuading many Chicago firms to improve their job opportunities for blacks. In 1967 he became National Director of Operation Breadbasket.

Jackson was with King when he was assassinated in 1968. Although Jackson saw himself as King's organizational heir, there was opposition to him inside the SCLC and Ralph Abernathy was appointed to succeed King. Organizational tensions heightened as Jackson increasingly developed his own approach to black politics. In 1971 Jackson was suspended from the SCLC and in the same year he founded PUSH (People United to Save Humanity). This initiative was followed in 1976 by PUSH-Excel, a campaign targeted at the problems of black youth, especially drugs and truancy.

His personal charisma and the high-profile organization (which was frequently criticized for administrative incompetence) made Jackson a major black leader and gave him a national reputation. He gained national exposure from high-profile international trips—for example those to South Africa and the Middle East in 1979. In 1983–4 he translated his growing celebrity status into a presidential election bid. The effort proved divisive not just within the Democratic Party but also in the black community as moderate blacks such as Tom *Bradley and Andrew *Young opposed him. He won 458 delegates and came way behind Walter *Mondale and Gary *Hart. He immediately began building a network of support for his next presidential bid. He founded the National Rainbow Coalition in 1986 in an attempt to broaden his political base beyond the black community and urged extended voter registration among blacks and delegate selection rule changes. Despite running well in the primaries, he came second to Michael *Dukakis with 962 delegates or 23 per cent of the total. He had however shown that a black candidate could secure white votes at the national level and had made himself a major force in the Democratic Party.

In 1990 Jackson won the nomination for one of two shadow senator seats from the District of Columbia. Jackson's enhanced political position was seen as potentially damaging to the Democratic Party. In 1992, Bill *Clinton took care to distance himself from Jackson's style of minority politics and policies such as quotas likely to deter voters. Jackson remains the most charismatic leader of America's black community and may yet have further political impact especially if he continues to adapt his agenda and style to the demands of mainstream politics.

Jakeš, Miloš (b. Prague, 12 Aug. 1922)

Czech; leader of the Czechoslovak Communist Party (CPCz) 1987–9

Of working-class origin, Jakeš first worked as an electrical engineer, joining the CPCz in 1945. He was educated from 1955 to 1958 at the Higher Party School in Moscow, where he shared a room with *Dubček. On his return to Czechoslovakia he entered the Ministry of the Interior, where he reached the rank of Deputy Minister in 1966. In 1968 Dubček gave him the influential position of chairman of the Party's Audit and Control Commission. Jakeš was opposed to the reform movement of the 'Prague Spring', and was removed as Deputy Minister. In August 1968 he supported the Soviet intervention in Czechoslovakia.

After 1969 Jakeš supervised the whole-scale purge of reformists. He became a Secretary of the Central Committee and candidate member of the Presidium (equivalent to the Politburo) in 1977. He became full member of the Presidium in 1981. In 1987 he replaced *Husák as General Secretary of the CPCz. His opposition to any meaningful change in the Communist system strained his relations with *Gorbachev. He was caught unawares by the 'Velvet Revolution' and resigned from office along with the rest of the Presidium on 24 November 1989. The following month he was dismissed from the CPCz.

Jaruzelski, Wojciech Witold (b. 6 July 1923)

Polish; Polish leader 1981–9, President 1989

Jaruzelski was born into a middle-class family in eastern Poland. In 1940, following the Red Army's invasion, he and his family were deported to the Soviet Union, where his father died in captivity. Jaruzelski was made to do forced labour. Thereafter he was educated in the Soviet system, becoming a Communist. In 1944 he served in the Polish forces attached to the Red Army during the campaign in Poland. He continued in the army after the war and in 1956 became the youngest general in the Polish army. He became Chief of the Polish General Staff in 1956, Minister of Defence in April 1968, and a full member of the Politburo in 1971. In 1976 he vetoed the use of the army against demonstrating workers.

On 9 February 1981 Party First Secretary Stanisław Kania appointed Jaruzelski Prime Minister. He tried to find a compromise with the trade union movement Solidarity, who put forward demands for a democratic electoral system and a share of state power. On 18 October 1981 Jaruzelski replaced Kania as Party First Secretary. In a masterfully executed coup he introduced martial law and banned Solidarity on 13 December 1981. In the *Gorbachev era Jaruzelski published his autobiography, in which he claimed that he had acted in the national interest in his coup of 1981, since this was the only way left to prevent Soviet military intervention. Because of his early history, he bitterly resented being called 'a Russian in Polish uniform'. In the 1980s he repeatedly tried to find the social consensus necessary for the implementation of major economic reforms. In 1982 he partially lifted martial law. Yet Jaruzelski was unable to reconcile the workers and intelligentsia who resented his continuing repression of Solidarity and his apparent subservience to Moscow. Though innocent of the crime, Jaruzelski was discredited in October 1984 by the murder of Father Jerzy Popiełuszko by members of the Religious Affairs Department of the Ministry of the Interior. Jaruzelski stopped the collapse of the economy, which had started in 1980, without taking on foreign loans. In 1988 a 'second stage' of economic reform was greeted by widespread strikes. At the end of 1988, with Gorbachev's support, he initiated the 'Round Table Talks' with Solidarity and the Catholic church. These led to the elections of 1989 after which the Communists lost power and Jaruzelski became a figurehead President. He resigned in November 1990 and was succeeded by Lech *Wałęsa.

Jaurès, Jean Léon (b. Castres, 3 Sept. 1859; d. 31 July 1914)

French; deputy 1885–9, 1902–14, Deputy Speaker 1902–4

From a down-at-heel section of a wealthy and successful family, Jaurès showed early promise and won a place at the École Normale Supérieur and passed the *agrégation* exam to become a philosophy teacher first in the Lycée d'Albi and then in Toulouse University. In 1885 he was elected on a vague Republican ticket at 25 years of age. He had shaken off his religious affiliations but at that time he did not consider himself to be a 'socialist'. He was defeated in 1889 and returned to teaching. He then began the process of constructing a non-dogmatic and consensus socialism which was to make him one of the intellectual and practical leaders of the French left and for which he is remembered. He was a brilliant speaker and he wrote copiously on a vast range of subjects but never abandoned scholarly interests including an ambitious and weighty history of the French Revolution. The mining strike in Carmaux completed his transformation and he was returned to the Assembly in 1893 as a non-violent Marxist 'Independent socialist'. Although he was a leader in the Assembly he took very much his own path, was not a member of any party, and sometimes (as in his support for the co-operative glassworks in Carmaux) found himself at odds with the rest of the movement. Such was initially the case with the Dreyfus affair. Jaurès was one of those few Socialists who immediately recognized that the socialists had an interest in defence of the rights of the wrongly accused Captain Dreyfus and that it was not just a wrangle between capitalists. The socialist movement had, like the Republic, to ensure justice for all people in all walks of life. When he was defeated in 1898 he flung himself into the Dreyfusard campaign and brought most of the rest of the socialists behind him to the crucial benefit of the Dreyfusards. As a Dreyfusard he became part of the general Republican campaign and brought other socialists in behind him. Jaurès, who sought to unify the socialists in France, was unable to get them all to take his view of the Dreyfus affair and they were split by Alexandre *Millerand's participation in Waldeck-Rousseau's Republican unity government. Jaurès was re-elected in 1902 and joined the *bloc des gauches*, as deputy speaker and supported the Radicals' reform programme. However, forces inside the socialist movement made such continued 'class collaboration' difficult and the 1904 Socialist International condemned experiments such as Millerand's ministerial collaboration in 'bourgeois' governments. Thus somewhat counter to Jaurès general direction the French Socialist movement was united in 1905 as the Section Française de l'Internationale Ouvrière (SFIO) on a 'revolutionary' platform of non-participation. He founded the socialist daily *L'Humanité*, in which he wrote regularly and his writings gave him the stature to make him the evident leader of the new party, but he soon became preoccupied with the looming prospect of war. Jaurès was a forceful campaigner for peace but he did not take the extreme view that war should always be opposed, it was not just a clash of competing capitalisms and hence no business of the working class. Jaurès did recognize the right of self-defence and one of his most famous books is *L'Armée nouvelle*. Jaurès, portrayed as a crazed anti-patriotic extremist by the extreme right, was assassinated on 31 July 1914 as he took a break with colleagues from *L'Humanité*. There is no telling what his outlook on the war would have been but his humanitarian and consensual legacy has made him a recognized founder of French socialism.

Javits, Jacob Koppel (b. New York City, 18 May 1904; d. 7 Mar. 1986)

US; member of US House of Representatives 1947–54; New York Attorney-General 1954–7, US Senator 1957–80

Born the son a Ukrainian immigrant, Javits was forced in his early years to earn money as a salesman. He studied part-time at Columbia and gained a law degree from New York University. After a period in the military in the Second World War, he won a surprise victory in 1946 to the House of Representatives. In 1954 he became Attorney-General of New York. In 1956 he defeated Mayor Robert Wagner (Jr.) for the New York Senate seat.

Despite his father's close association with Tammany Hall, Javits became associated with Fiorella *La Guardia's political club and joined the Republican Party. Throughout his career he was a liberal Republican. His reformist ideals and his Jewish background made Javits an unusual and somewhat isolated figure in Republican ranks. In the Senate, he served on a range of key committees and was a leading supporter of civil rights and a liberal on domestic issues, advocating greater federal involvement in welfare provision and aid for the cities. He helped pass much of Lyndon *Johnson's Great Society programme, including the creation of the Legal Services Corporation, the Comprehensive Education and Training Act, and funding for the education of the handicapped. He made a major contribution to much labour legislation and to pension law reform.

Javits developed a keen interest in foreign policy and was for long the ranking Republican on the Senate Foreign Affairs Committee. Initially a hawk on military spending and supportive of the war in Vietnam, he became a critic and later helped pass the Cooper–Church amendment (which banned funding for military involvement in Cambodia) and the War Powers Act of 1973 which reasserted congressional control over the war-making power by limiting the President's freedom to deploy troops overseas. He was also a strong supporter of the state of Israel and assisted President Carter in promoting the Middle East peace process of 1977.

For most of his career, Javits enjoyed a strong personal vote in New York. Yet his position on the liberal wing of the Republican Party became extremely vulnerable as the party moved right during the late 1970s. In September 1980 he lost to a more conservative candidate, Alfonse D'Amato, in the Republican Senate primary. Javits then ran on the Liberal Party ticket. Although he lost, his 629,000 votes were the highest ever recorded for the Liberal Party.

His departure from the Senate deprived him of the chairmanship of the Foreign Affairs Committee which would have been his as the Republicans took the Senate in 1980. After retirement he taught at Columbia, acted as a government adviser, and wrote his autobiography: *Javits: The Autobiography of a Public Man* (published in 1981). The onset of a fatal nervous disease (Lou Gehrig's disease) prompted him to spend time in his last years participating in the 'living will' debate.

Jawara, Dawda Kairaba (b. Barajally, Gambia, 11 May 1924)

Gambian; Prime Minister 1962–70, President 1970–94

A member of the Mandinka ethnic group Jawara graduated in veterinary medicine from the University of Glasgow in 1953. In 1959 he founded and led the Protectorate People's Party (later People's Progressive Party). After the victory of the party in the 1962 election he became Prime Minister, a post he retained after independence in 1965. With the adoption of a republican constitution in 1970 he became President. From independence until 1994 he retained a democratic multi-party system with freedom for opposition parties, although his own party won a majority of seats in every election. He gained an international reputation as a defender of human rights. In 1981 an attempted *coup d'état* by the para-military police was defeated with assistance from Senegalese troops. Following this a Senegambian Confederation was established but this was dissolved in 1989. In July 1994 Jawara was overthrown by the army in a *coup d'état* and went into political exile.

Under Jawara's rule Gambia remained an isolated example of democracy and stability in the troubled West African region but in the latter part of his rule corruption became a major problem. For a short time before his overthrow he was the very last of that generation of African leaders who had led their countries to independence in the 1960s to remain in power.

Jenkins, Roy (b. South Wales, 11 Nov. 1920)

British; Chancellor of the Exchequer 1967–70, president of European Commission 1976–81; Baron 1987

Jenkins's father was a Labour MP, who served for a time as Parliamentary Private Secretary to the Labour Prime Minister *Attlee. In 1948 Jenkins was elected for a London constituency and, after that disappeared due to redistribution, he was elected for Birmingham Stetchford in 1950. He held the seat until his resignation in 1976. In the 1950s Labour was in Opposition and Jenkins proved himself a skilful advocate for the party on television. He also was a highly regarded author. He supported the revisionist policies of the party leader Hugh *Gaitskell. In 1959 he introduced the Obscene Publications Act, which eased censorship.

Roy Jenkins entered the Cabinet in 1965 as Home Secretary in the Wilson government. He held this post until 1967 and presided over the liberalization of laws on divorce, abortion, and homosexuality. Critics later derided these measures as encouraging the permissive society: Jenkins preferred to call it the civilized society. In 1967 he replaced *Callaghan as Chancellor of the Exchequer, following the devaluation of the pound. He proved to be something of an iron Chancellor and gained control of public spending and brought round the balance of payments. After the 1970 election defeat he was blamed by some Labour MPs for not using his 1970 budget to engineer a pre-election boom. Jenkins was then elected deputy leader of the party and was widely regarded as Wilson's heir apparent. In fact the party was moving to the left and he grew increasingly disaffected with what he regarded as Wilson's pusillanimous leadership. He resigned as deputy leader in 1972 when the party called for a referendum over Britain's membership of the European Economic Community. Europe was always a key issue for Jenkins.

With Labour in government again, he was Home Secretary between 1974 and 1976, although disappointed not to become Foreign Secretary. Again, he was becoming disillusioned with the party's drift to the left. He did badly in the leadership election in 1976 and withdrew from the race after finishing third on the first ballot. He then left to become president of the European Commission.

His call for a realignment in the British party system eventually led to the formation of the Social Democratic Party (SDP) in 1981. The SDP attracted a number of disillusioned right-wing Labour MPs and for a time the party promised to break the mould of British politics. He re-entered the House of Commons in 1982 when he won Glasgow Hillhead at a by-election. After losing his seat in 1987 he entered the House of Lords as Jenkins of Hillhead and became chancellor of Oxford University.

Jenkins had a life outside politics. He was a fine essayist and reviewer. He was also an accomplished biographer and wrote studies of *Baldwin, *Asquith, and Gladstone.

Jiang Jieshi *see* CHIANG KAI-SHEK

Jiang Jingguo *see* CHIANG CHING-KUO

Jinnah, Mohammad Ali (b. Karachi, 25 Dec. 1876; d. 11 Sept. 1948)
Pakistani; Governor-General 1947–8

The eldest son of a hide merchant, Jinnah was educated at the Sind Madrassa and Lincoln's Inn, London, where he qualified as a barrister. The future founder of Pakistan was first known as the ambassador of Hindu-Muslim unity. Indeed Jinnah only resigned from Congress in 1920 when he became disillusioned with the violence and communal passions unleashed by *Gandhi's Congress-Khilafat civil disobedience campaigns. The division widened in 1928 when the Nehru Report rejected Jinnah's 'fourteen points' constitutional proposals.

During 1921–35, Jinnah's political career was in the doldrums. He returned to India in October 1935 after a five-year British exile to reorganize the Muslim League. It nevertheless lost heavily in the 1937 provincial elections. The Congress ministries' insensitivity to Muslim demands rescued it from oblivion, although Jinnah's leadership was equally crucial to its dramatic transformation. From 1940 onwards, he propounded the two-nation theory justification for Pakistan and increasingly embodied the aspirations of the Indian Muslim community which acclaimed him as the *Quaid-i-Azam*, the great leader. Within the fractious politics of the Muslim League, he exerted an unquestioned moral authority which underpinned his formal power as President. Simultaneously he deployed his forensic skills in the complex constitutional negotiations with the British and the Congress.

Jinnah's successful claim to be the sole spokesman of Muslim India at the July 1945 Simla conference greatly strengthened the Pakistan demand. During 1946–7, however, he suffered a series of reversals as the Muslim League lost its wartime bargaining power. He had to abandon his strictly constitutional approach to politics, but the resulting communal riots threatened civil war. Agreement for Partition was finally reached on 3 June 1947: the Pakistan which emerged was not of the full six Muslim provinces of Jinnah's dreams, but a moth-eaten country shorn of West Bengal and East Punjab. Mass migrations and massacres accompanied the Punjab's partition. The refugee crisis increased Pakistan's formidable security and administrative problems.

Jinnah, who was both Pakistan's Governor-General and Constituent Assembly President, assumed much of the burden for laying the state's foundations. He was by now 70 and appeared frailer and more emaciated than ever. It remains doubtful however whether if he had lived longer than September 1948, Pakistan could have avoided its growing crisis of governability.

Jinnah is still revered as Pakistan's founding father. Islamists improbably and secularists more soundly have attempted to claim his mantle. Recent revisionist scholarship, however, has speculated that Partition was the unintended consequence of his trumpeting the Pakistan demand as a bargaining counter for power in a united India.

Johnson, Hiram Warren (b. Sacramento, California, 2 Sept. 1866; d. 6 Aug. 1945)
US; Governor of California 1911–17, US Senator 1917–45

After two years at the University of California in Berkeley, Johnson worked in his father's law office in San Francisco and was admitted to the California bar. He gained prominence as a prosecutor, which enabled him to win the Republican nomination for Governor of California in 1910. In the 1910 campaign he displayed the characteristics which became his hallmark of a feisty progressive reformer with a fiery oratorical style and with a dedication to battle against vested interests on behalf of the people. As governor of California 1911–17 he established himself as one of the major figures of the progressive movement. He enacted reforms of major significance to curb the power of vested interests, such as the establishment of a Railroad Commission to control the power of the Southern Pacific Railroad, and to give more power to the people over the state government, such as by means of the initiative, referendum, and recall.

In 1912 he bolted the Republican Party and was vice-presidential candidate on the Progressive Party ticket led by Theodore *Roosevelt. He was re-elected Governor of California in 1914 as a Progressive, but with the demise of the Progressive Party, he rejoined the Republican Party and won election to the US Senate as a Republican in 1916. He supported with reluctance America's intervention in the First World War but was highly critical of the terms of the Treaty of Versailles and was one of the leading 'irreconcileables' in opposition to American participation in the League of Nations. In 1920 he sought the Republican nomination for President and was bitterly critical of the undemocratic procedure in the 'smoke-filled room' at the Republican national convention in Chicago which led to the nomination of Warren *Harding. He opposed the policies of the conservative Republican presidents of the 1920s and was particularly critical of the policies of President *Hoover. In 1922 and 1928 he was easily re-elected to the Senate but he increasingly took an independent position in support of progressive reform on domestic issues and isolationism in foreign policy.

In 1932 he did not support Hoover's re-election but endorsed the Democratic candidate, Franklin *Roosevelt. He was offered the post of Secretary of the Interior in Roosevelt's administration, but he declined since he preferred to maintain his independence as a Senator. He supported the New Deal in its early years and was one of the most prominent of the progressive Republicans whose support was important for the passage of New Deal legislation. But by 1936–7 he turned against Roosevelt and the New Deal and reverted to his more customary position of opposition. He feared that Roosevelt's landslide re-election victory in 1936 and his plan to pack the Supreme Court were signs of an excessive increase in the power of the President. Even more so, he became increasingly distrustful of Roosevelt's foreign policy. Johnson was one of the most outspoken isolationists during the 1930s. He sponsored the Johnson Act of 1934, which prohibited further loans to nations in default on previous loans from the United States, and he supported the Neutrality Acts of 1935–7. He was fiercely critical of Roosevelt's policies of aid to the Allies in 1939–41, such as Lend-Lease, which he was certain would take America into war. After Pearl Harbor, he accepted that America had no alternative other than involvement in the Second World War, but he opposed American international involvement after the War, especially American participation in the United Nations. Although he had been easily re-elected to the Senate in 1934 and 1940, he was in failing health after 1941 and his position was becoming increasingly isolated and outmoded. His death, which occurred symbolically on the same day as the dropping of the atomic bomb on Hiroshima, marked the death of the isolationist standpoint which he had embodied.

Johnson, Lyndon Baines (b. near Stonewall, Texas, 27 Aug. 1908; d. 22 Jan. 1973)
US; US Senator 1949–61, Vice-President 1961–3, President 1963–9

Though Lyndon Johnson was born into an established Texas family—his paternal grandfather had given his name to Johnson City—his parents were not especially wealthy, having to make a living from largely unproductive farming land. They were hit by the Depression. After leaving high school, Johnson took a range of largely menial jobs, including working on a road gang. He decided he could do better and, encouraged by his mother, he entered the Southwest Texas State Teachers College and graduated in 1930. During his time at College he led the debating team and, to help finance his studies, he worked as secretary to the College principal. As secretary, he developed skills that he was to use throughout his political career. He recognized that organization was power and the principal came to rely on his highly effective secretary. He then went on to teach at the Sam Houston High School in Texas before campaigning for a Democratic candidate for Congress, Richard Kleberg. Kleberg then hired him as his secretary in Washington. Johnson deployed the same skills as he had when working for the College principal. He led a group of secretaries (known as the Little Congress) and came to the attention of House Speaker Sam *Rayburn, who included him in his inner circle. For Johnson, Washington was his natural habitat. He had been born into a world of politics—his father and maternal grandfather had both served in the Texas legislature—and he was to spend the rest of his life in political activity. He was also to do so from a more secure financial base, having married Claudia Alta ('Lady Bird') Taylor, from a well-to-do family, in 1934.

In 1935, Johnson was appointed director of the National Youth Administration in Texas, a post that drew out his administrative talents and brought him to the attention of a wider political community. When a congressional vacancy occurred in 1937 Johnson went after it and, standing as an ardent New Deal Democrat, won election. He was 28 years old. An early meeting with Franklin *Roosevelt secured the President's favour and in 1940 Johnson headed the House Democratic Campaign Committee. In 1941 he sought nomination for a Senate seat, again emphasizing his support for Roosevelt. He narrowly lost the nomination to the state Governor. After volunteering for active service during the war—he was awarded the Silver Star Medal for showing remarkable calm while aboard a bomber aircraft that had come under enemy attack—he returned to Washington to chair the Subcommittee on Naval Affairs. He was later appointed to the Postwar Military Policy Committee, opposing the rapid dismantling of the US war machine. In 1948, he again sought to run for a Senate seat, this time emerging successful in the Democratic primary—but only just. He won it in a run-off election by 87 votes and survived a court challenge to the result. He sailed to an easy victory in the general election.

In the Senate, Johnson established himself as a leading member and a consummate politician. He was appointed to the Armed Services Committee and supported a strong military for the USA. On domestic issues, conscious of his home constituency, he adopted a largely conservative stance. In 1953 he was elected Minority Leader. The following year he was re-elected easily to the Senate and, with the Democrats taking control of the chamber, he became majority leader. He was an accommodator rather than an ideologue. He brokered deals and used his persuasive skills to muster majorities for administration measures that he favoured. He helped *Eisenhower achieve passage of some measures of social reform. One of the most notable achievements was the passage in 1957 of a Civil Rights Bill—the first in the twentieth century—representing an effective partnership between Johnson and the President.

Johnson suffered a serious heart attack in 1955 but made a full recovery within a matter of months. That was the only setback he faced during the decade. He was emerging as a major figure, vital to the passage of important measures. His reputation grew as he achieved mastery of the Senate and was increasingly viewed as one of the most effective majority leaders in its history. Though he had ambitions beyond the Senate, he was clearly at home on Capitol Hill. However, in 1960, he was offered the vice-presidential nomination by John *Kennedy. Although Johnson was a good choice in terms of ensuring a balanced ticket—an established Texan Democrat who could help deliver the South—the choice was problematic. The Kennedys had a low opinion of Johnson and there was little obvious reason why Johnson should give up a position of real power for a largely ceremonial post in which he would have little scope to exercise his particular skills. Johnson accepted the nomination, apparently believing that he could mould the office and, as his biographer Doris Kearns has noted, recognizing that the position of majority leader would be less powerful under an activist Democratic President. In the event, Johnson helped deliver the election to Kennedy, the votes of Texas and Illinois proving crucial in giving Kennedy a narrow majority. Not for the first time in his career, Johnson was to be associated with allegations of Texas vote rigging.

As Vice-President, Johnson was appointed to head various commissions and councils, including the National Aeronautics and Space Council, and sent on various overseas missions. Although he proved loyal to the President—never voicing disagreement with his policies—he came to hate the position. 'I detested every minute of it', he later told Kearns. A proud man, he detested the patronizing attitude taken toward him by the Harvard-educated Eastern sophisticates in the Kennedy circle and was frustrated by his inability to transform the position into one of power. He appeared disillusioned and increasingly disinterested.

The assassination of Kennedy on 22 November 1963 propelled Johnson from the political periphery to the ultimate position of power. He was sworn in as President aboard Air Force One and five days later addressed a joint session of Congress. He immediately adopted an activist stance. He pushed Congress to pass the Civil Rights Bill that Kennedy had introduced. He used his State of the Union message to press for passage. He reverted to the skills he had honed in the Senate to get that and a whole raft of other measures passed. He met members of Congress, phoned them, and cajoled them; if they needed to feel important, he made them feel important; if they wanted favours, he offered them favours. He masterminded the passage of an anti-poverty programme, he achieved passage of a tax cut, he persuaded Congress to vote funds for mass transit facilities. By the time of the 1964 presidential election he already had a record to run on. Aided by his achievements, by the Kennedy legacy, and by the Republicans nominating Senator Barry *Goldwater, a candidate portrayed by opponents as an extremist and warmonger, Johnson sailed to an overwhelming victory. He won 43 million votes to 27 million for Goldwater, the largest winning margin achieved in US history. Equally importantly, he had a coat-tails effect, ushering in a Congress dominated by liberal Democrats.

The period from 1965 to 1967 saw Johnson at his peak. He achieved passage of a programme of social reform, dubbed the Great Society programme. Medicare was introduced, providing medical assistance to the elderly through the Social Security system. Extensive new programmes of federal aid to education, housing, and deprived areas were approved. The Voting Rights Act, providing for federal intervention to ensure black voting rights were enforced, was enacted in 1965. However, what looked like being one of the most successful and reforming presidencies of the twentieth century was soon in trouble. There are three reasons for the presidency turning from success to failure. One was Johnson's techniques. He put pressure on members of Congress to pass his measures. The pressure could be intimidating and unrelenting. Johnson was not averse to using physical intimidation if he felt it necessary. After a time, the president's techniques lost their appeal and members of Congress were less amenable to presidential persuasion. The second reason was that the measures were hastily constructed. Johnson was more concerned with passage than implementation, and some did not work out as intended. The measures also appeared to contribute to growing expectations on the part of the black community that the administration could not meet. The summer of 1965 saw riots in the Watts district of Los Angeles and subsequent summers saw violent disturbances in many of the nation's leading cities, including Washington, DC. The third and most important reason was the Vietnam War.

Johnson inherited his predecessor's commitment to South Vietnam and gradually increased the number of US troops sent to the country to assist the South Vietnamese government against North Vietnam and Vietcong insurgents. By 1967 nearly half-a-million troops had been sent. Johnson authorized bombing raids on targets in North Vietnam. There was little military success. By the summer of 1967 almost 80,000 Americans had been killed or wounded in Vietnam. Though initially supportive of US involvement, the American public turned against the war. Johnson faced a rising tide of hostility. Black riots in the inner cities were superseded by white anti-war riots on college campuses. Johnson's public appearances were increasingly concentrated on US military bases. Congress grew restive, some leading figures coming out in opposition to Johnson's policy. Their number included Senator Robert *Kennedy of New York. It was proving impossible to fund the Great Society programme and the war effort and funding for many domestic programmes was scaled down.

In November 1967 Senator Eugene *McCarthy of Minnesota announced that he would seek the Democratic nomination for President on an anti-war ticket. In January 1968, the Tet offensive in Vietnam—a major assault by the Vietcong—appeared to confirm that the war was unwinnable. In the New Hampshire primary in March, McCarthy—with 42 per cent of the vote—came a close second to Johnson and was able to claim a moral victory. Robert Kennedy announced that he would also seek the Democratic nomination. On 31 March, a haggard-looking Johnson made a television broadcast. He announced a bombing pause in Vietnam and then declared that he would not seek, or accept, his party's nomination that year. His announcement caught the political community unawares. Rather than stand, he chose instead to engineer the nomination of his Vice-President, Hubert *Humphrey. Robert Kennedy was assassinated in Los Angeles and the Democratic nomination in Chicago was a shambles, the police dealing violently with anti-war protesters in the streets. In the election, Humphrey went down to defeat. Johnson retired to the LBJ ranch in Texas to work on his memoirs. He died four years later, on 22 January 1973, after being struck down by another heart attack. He was aged 64.

Johnson was a man who became President but never managed to become presidential. He retained a manner that was vulgar and abrasive. He swore, pushed people around, and held meetings with journalists and others regardless of circumstance. He continued conversations with visitors while in the toilet; he once spoke to journalists while being given an enema. His political techniques were carried over from the Senate. Though his political instincts were liberal, he was an authoritarian in approach. He expected complete loyalty from aides. He was possessive. He spoke of government in the first person. A proud man, insecure as a child and keen to please his mother, he could not tolerate failure. He worked hard but never seemed to achieve personal satisfaction from his efforts—he was always wanting to press on to achieve something more. When the political climate turned against him, he did not know how to respond. He aged in office. Though only 59 when he made his televised withdrawal from the presidential race, he looked closer to 69.

Johnson nonetheless achieved some success in the domestic arena. A former segregationist, he achieved far more than his predecessor in the field of civil rights and showed courage in his pursuit of equality. Though associated primarily with the Vietnam War, historians have not been that unkind to him. In the 1982 Murray poll he was ranked as the tenth best President. By the time of the 1995 *Chicago Sun-Times* poll of presidential historians he had slipped, but was still in the top half, ranking

15th, three places ahead of his immediate predecessor. He was an average President but a first-rate majority leader. His problem was that he could not differentiate between the two.

Jørgensen, Anker Henrik (b. Copenhagen, 13 July 1922)

Danish; Prime Minister 1972–3, 1975–8, 1978–82, Social Democratic party chairman 1973–87

Jørgensen came to political prominence by what the Danes call 'the long road'. He never knew his father; his mother died young, and he received a basic education at the Royal Orphanage School in Copenhagen. He then at the age of 14 became a warehouse worker, joining the Store and Warehouse Union and the Social Democrats' youth wing. He continued his education on trade union courses and by extensive private reading. An able organizer and negotiator, he became vice-chairman of his union in 1950 and chairman in 1956, and in 1968 he became chairman of Denmark's second largest union for general and semi-skilled workers.

In 1961 Jørgensen was elected to Copenhagen City Council, serving until 1964. In 1964, by which time he was a leading trade unionist, he was elected to the Danish parliament. Here he became prominent as a left of centre Social Democrat who was not a maverick and who favoured Danish membership of the EC. On 3 October 1972, the day after the Danish referendum in favour of joining the EC, he was nominated by the retiring Social Democratic Prime Minister—Krag—as the successor to the premiership, notwithstanding the fact that he had never served in government.

Jørgensen dominated the next decade in Danish politics. He had to cope with a severe economic crisis, with an unusual degree of turbulence in domestic politics, and with considerable trade union opposition, and his negotiating skills were called upon to the full in winning support from the non-socialist parties of the centre-right.

Since his resignation as Prime Minister in 1982, Jørgensen has been active on the Nordic Council—resigning as its president in 1992—and he has become something of a legend in his country's political life, respected for being consistently true to his working-class roots.

Joseph, Keith Sinjohn (b. London, 17 Jan. 1918; d. 10 Dec. 1994)

British; Secretary of State for Social Services 1970–4, Industry 1979–81, Education 1981–6; Baron (life peer) 1987

Keith Joseph was that rare British animal, an intellectual in politics. His father was Sir Samuel Joseph, a self-made wealthy man who helped to build up Bovis, the building firm, and became lord mayor of London. He could afford to send Keith to Harrow and then Magdalen College, Oxford. After war service Keith gained a fellowship at All Souls College and passed for the bar but never practised. He became an MP in February 1956, winning the safe Conservative seat of Leeds-North-East at a by-election, a seat he held until his retirement from the Commons in 1987. In the 1970s and 1980s he was one of the few Conservatives to hold a seat in a northern city.

Sir Keith Joseph showed an early interest in social issues, a feature that made him unusual among Conservatives. He was also one of only two Jewish Conservative MPs at the time of his entry to parliament. He was a defender of entrepreneurial capitalism which he saw as a means of improving quality of life for the disadvantaged. But he was not a simple right winger, opposing capital punishment and, surprisingly for a Jew, regretting the Anglo-French invasion of Suez in 1956.

Sir Keith's political career was not advanced under Conservative leader Edward *Heath. In spite of Joseph's interest in economic issues Heath kept him away from economic posts. As Secretary of State for Social Services in the 1970 Heath government, Joseph substantially increased his departmental budget. When the party was in opposition after 1974 he repented of his role in government, claiming in April

1974 that, at the age of 56, he had only just become a true Conservative. He regretted his participation in the Heath government's introduction of statutory controls on incomes and prices and other measures which weakened the market economy. He was influenced by the writings of Hayek and Milton Friedman and the ideas of the free market Institute of Economic Affairs.

Sir Keith was seen as the obvious right-wing challenger to Ted Heath for the leadership in late 1974. But after some ill-judged speeches he withdrew and threw his support behind Mrs *Thatcher. He lacked the popular touch, and realized that he was not cut out for the position. At this time Joseph was an advocate of what came to be known as Thatcherism. He called for big cuts in taxes and public spending, a reduction in the power of the trade unions, firm control of money supply to combat inflation, and encouragement for the free market. In speeches, pamphlets, and press articles Joseph opposed the drift of post-war politics and is properly credited with doing much to change the climate of opinion and shift the political agenda to the right.

When she became party leader in 1975 Mrs Thatcher gave Joseph responsibility in the shadow Cabinet for policy. Some Conservative colleagues were aghast at his claims that government should abandon the goal of full employment—because it was beyond its power to deliver it. They could imagine the charges from political opponents: 'Sir Keith calls for more unemployment.'

In the Thatcher government in 1979 he was made Secretary of State for Industry. In spite of his philosophy he found himself providing large subsidies to troubled firms like British Leyland, British Steel and Rolls-Royce. He bore the brunt of much criticism as employment nearly doubled in the first two years of government. In 1981 he was happy to move to the Department of Education. He launched a number of ideas, many of which were to be embodied in the Education Reform Act (1988) of Kenneth *Baker. Much of this period as a minister, however, was dogged by bad relations with the teachers, strikes, and long-running pay disputes. He left the Commons in 1987 and took a seat in the Lords.

Sir Keith was not given high marks as an administrator. His critics thought that he was indecisive—because he was open-minded—and listened to his civil servants too much. It was said that he was 'a lion in opposition and a lamb in government'. But he was creative and had the talent and courage to question and overturn much of the conventional wisdom of the day.

Jospin, Lionel (b. Meudon, 12 July 1937)

French; First Secretary of the Parti Socialiste 1981–8, 1995–   , Education Minister 1988–92, presidential candidate 1995, Prime Minister 1997

The son of a teacher who was a socialist activist, educated at the prestigious ENA, Jospin was active on the left but not sympathetic to the old SFIO. He went into the diplomatic service and rose through its ranks from 1965 to 1970, when he left to teach economics at the University of Paris. He joined the Parti Socialiste after 1971 and was spotted by *Mitterrand as a potential lieutenant. He rose rapidly up the hierarchy, becoming National Secretary for the Third World 1975–9 and Secretary for International Relations 1979–81 through Mitterrand's patronage and his own energy; always his own man and with a rectitude which was a reflection of a Protestant upbringing. In 1981 he was made First Secretary and loyally held the party behind Mitterrand during the first governmental term and was regularly consulted by the President (the nomination of *Fabius, *Chirac, and *Rocard as Prime Minister, the Gulf war, etc). He never organized a faction of his own and he always disapproved of the party's factionalism. In 1986, however, a quarrel broke out between Fabius and *Jospin over who should lead the party in the elections. In 1988 when Mitterrand wanted to push Fabius to the head of the PS, Jospin blocked the way: this split in the Mitterrand camp was to divide the party over the next six years. Never an unconditional supporter of Mitterrand, his doubts began to grow. The nomination of Mme *Cresson as Prime Minister was a turning point. He wrote a book criticizing the Mitterrand system in which presidentialism was pushed to extremes and in which responsibilities were not taken up and where leadership was lacking. The left, had, in his view been unable to promote the national interest and the left itself had not been given a longterm perspective by Mitterrand. In 1992 he withdrew from the political front line, fell ill, and he thought of returning to diplomatic service. However, the débâcle of the left in 1993 followed by the collapse of both the Rocard and the Delors candidacies led him to promote his own merits as unifier of the left and he ran a last-minute but effective presidential campaign in 1995. The result, despite Chirac's victory, made Jospin the principal personality of the French left and he was able to start to remould the Socialist Party bequeathed by Mitterrand with a virtually free hand. He was rewarded when he led his party to victory in the Assembly elections in 1997 and was made Prime Minister.

Joynson-Hicks, William (b. London, 23 June 1865; d. 8 June 1932)
British; Home Secretary 1924–9; Bt. 1919, Viscount Brentford 1929

Educated at Merchant Taylors' School, Joynson-Hicks became a successful solicitor. He changed his surname from Hicks to Joynson-Hicks (to include his wife's maiden name) in 1896 and was commonly called 'Jix'. He was elected to Parliament as a Conservative MP in 1908, losing his seat in 1910 and then being returned for Brentford in 1911. Interested in transport (he was chairman of the Automobile Association from 1908 to 1923), he served on several committees dealing with transport issues. An opponent of maintaining the *Lloyd George coalition, he tabled a vote of censure, provoking a spirited defence of the coalition by Austen *Chamberlain. He held a number of junior ministerial posts in 1922 and 1923 before being appointed Minister of Health in August 1923. When the Conservatives were returned to power in November 1924 he was appointed Home Secretary and served in the post for the rest of the parliament (1924–9). He was responsible for handling the General Strike in 1926. Described by Roy Jenkins as 'good on penal reform but illiberal on all else', he authorized police raids to seize the works of authors such as D. H. Lawrence. He also persuaded the Prime Minister and Foreign Secretary to authorize a raid in 1927 on the Soviet Trade Delegation and All-Russian Co-operative Society building in Moorgate. The raid showed that the premises had been used for the purposes of Soviet subversion and relations with the Soviet Union were broken off. In June 1929, he was created a viscount. He died three years later, shortly before his 67th birthday.

Juppé, Alain Marie (b. Mont-de-Marsan, 15 Aug. 1948)
French; Prime Minister 1995–

The son of a farmer, Juppé had an impressive school career at the Lycée Louis-le-Grand followed by the IFP and the École Normale Supérieur (where he qualified as a classics teacher) and graduated from the ENA in 1972. By 1976 he was Jacques *Chirac's economic adviser and rapidly became Chirac's second in command. As an impressive administrator (known as 'Amstrad' because of his facility with figures) he was in charge of the Budget for Paris in 1979 and in the 1980s he became identified with free-market ideas as a result (possibly) of visits to America. In the 1980s he was somewhat overshadowed by other personalities but established himself as Chirac's key lieutenant in the 1988 elections. In the wake of Jacques Chirac's 1988 presidential defeat he kept the RPR behind Chirac and out of the orbit of Séguin and Pasqua. He was not so successful on his own count: an attempt to run for president of Île-de-France in 1992 was thwarted. A Europeanist, he was not in tune with the leadership during the Maastricht campaign and threatened to resign (he frequently pulled Chirac back from more adventurous policies), and during his time as Foreign

Minister in the *Balladur government (1993–5) he arbitrated between the unconditional Chirac supporters and the pro-Balladur camp who wanted the Prime Minister to run for President. During 1991–3, while others deserted Chirac, Juppé remained loyal and promoted Chirac's interests inside the government. The worst split in the Balladur government was between Juppé and Interior Minister *Pasqua (a pro-Balladur Gaullist) over Algerian policy and in particular over the response to a hijacked plane. This helped Chirac to win the presidency in 1995. In June Juppé took over the City Hall at Bordeaux from the long-serving Gaullist *Chaban Delmas and became president of the Neo-Gaullist Party in October. Juppé was in a very powerful position but in the autumn of mid-1995 his government was riven with disagreements, hit by scandals, Bordeaux took to the streets, and a seeming lack of direction set in. In a position of extreme unpopularity, Juppé reshuffled the government, turning it from the most feminine ever to a completely male one and took the long postponed decision to reform the French costly social security in the teeth of opposition from user groups, unions, and doctors. This was immediately unpopular but if successful would have enabled future savings and facilitated the meeting of the 'Maastricht criteria' for a single European currency.

Kádár, János (b. Fiume (now Rijeka), 26 May 1912; d. Budapest, 6 July 1989)
Hungarian; Minister of the Interior 1948–51, First Secretary of the Hungarian Socialist Workers' Party 1956–88

Kádár was the illegitimate son of Borbála Csermanek, an illiterate Slovak maid, and János Kressinger, a Hungarian peasant, whom he never knew. He was brought up by foster parents in the Hungarian village of Karpoly, educated in his village school, and trained as an instrument-maker. He joined the illegal Hungarian Communist Party (HCP) in 1931, changing his name to Kádár ('Carter'), and was arrested several times in the 1930s for illegal political work. He was active in the resistance during the Second World War, becoming a member of the Central Committee of the HCP in 1942. In 1945 he entered the Party's Politburo and became Deputy Chief of Police. As Minister of the Interior (1948–51) he was intimately connected with the brutal Sovietization carried out by *Rákosi's regime. He organized the trial of László *Rajk in 1949. In April 1951 he himself was arrested and tortured by the secret police, then charged with treason and imprisoned. He was released in July 1954 when Rákosi's hold on power was weakening. Kádár initially shared in the reformist aims of Imre *Nagy's government which came to power after Rákosi's fall in July 1956. On 25 October 1956 he became First Secretary of the Hungarian Socialist Workers' Party (the HCP-led coalition) and deputy premier. However, he was alarmed at the pace of change, particularly by the party's failure to control reform and the re-emergence of old 'bourgeois' political parties. On the night of 1–2 November 1956 he secretly left Budapest and returned on 4 November 1956 with the invading Red Army.

After the suppression of the Hungarian uprising, Kádár became Prime Minister, resigning in 1958, having followed a repressive course. In his second term as premier from 1961 to 1965 he allowed a cautious liberalization, characterized by his comment on political opponents: 'those who are not against us are for us'. In the economic sphere Kádár followed an inconsistent policy in which he periodically tried to introduce elements of the market economy while retaining the overall structure of the economy. By the end of the 1970s his failure was apparent and Hungary had the largest per capita debt in the Soviet Bloc. In 1988 he was removed as First Secretary by a party revolt engineered by Imre Pozsgay, and given the honorific post of President, which he resigned in May 1989 as his health failed.

Kaganovich, Lazar Moisevich (b. Kabana, 22 Nov. 1893; d. Moscow, 25 July 1991)
Russian; member of the Politburo 1926–57

Kaganovich was born in the Kiev region of the Ukraine into a poor Jewish family. After leaving school at the age of 14 he worked as a tanner. He joined the Bolshevik Party in 1911 and was involved in organizational work. He participated in the October Revolution of 1917 which brought the Bolsheviks to power. From 1925 to 1927 he was head of the Ukrainian Communist Party, becoming a candidate member of the Politburo in 1926. He moved to Moscow in 1928, becoming a Secretary of the Central Committee with responsibility for agriculture. Thus he was closely involved with the brutal collectivization of agriculture after 1929. In 1930 he was made a full member of the Politburo and First Secretary of the Moscow Party Committee (until 1935). Kaganovich's success was based on his reputation as the best administrator in the USSR and his unquestioning support for *Stalin. As chairman of the Commission of Party Control he was responsible for the purge of 1933–4. During the great purges of 1936–8, Stalin asked him whether his brother Mikhail should be shot. He replied that that was a matter for the police to decide. Mikhail committed suicide. From 1936 to 1944 he was People's Commissar for Railways. For a brief period after the Second World War, Stalin sent him to replace *Khrushchev as leader of the Ukrainian Communist Party. Relations between Kaganovich and Khrushchev were bad thereafter. Kaganovich's position weakened in Stalin's last years. After Stalin's death in 1953, he was one of the most important of the new collective leadership. In 1957 he was one of the 'antiparty group' which failed to remove Khrushchev. This was the end of his political career. He first took charge of a Siberian cement works, then retired to live in obscurity in Moscow.

Kamenev, Lev Borisovich (*original name* Rozenfeld) (b. Moscow, 22 July 1883; d. Moscow, 15 Aug. 1936)

Russian; chair of the 2nd Congress of Soviets in 1917, deputy chair of Council of People's Commissars 1922–4, chair of the Supreme Council of the National Economy 1928–32

Kamenev's father was an engineer and he grew up in Moscow and later Tblisi. While studying law at Moscow University he joined the Bolsheviks. A close colleague of *Lenin in the pre-war period, he became editor of *Pravda* in St Petersburg but was deported in 1915. In 1917 he returned to Russia and again became editor of *Pravda*, but was soon in disagreement with Lenin over the policy of 'revolutionary defeatism' and the seizure of power, even resorting (together with *Zinoviev) to denouncing the planned November coup in the press, after which he resigned from the Central Committee. However, he was brought back by Lenin as Chair of the 2nd All-Russian Congress of Soviets (the equivalent of state President) and as first chair of its Central Executive Committee. His main power-base was in Moscow, where he was chair of the Moscow Soviet 1918–26. He was deputy chair of the Council of People's Commissars (Deputy Prime Minister) 1922–4.

After Lenin's death he joined *Stalin and Zinoviev in the 'Triumvirate'; he was the first director of the Lenin Institute and Trade Commissar from 1926. In 1925 he followed Zinoviev in breaking with Stalin over the policy of 'socialism in one country' and in 1926 they joined with *Trotsky to form the Joint Opposition (Kamenev was married to Trotsky's daughter, Olga). He was made ambassador to Italy, but was later expelled from the Party, following Trotsky, in 1927. Denouncing the Trotskyists in 1928, he was readmitted to the party and made chair of the Supreme Council of the National Economy. In 1932 he was again expelled from the party, readmitted 1933 and finally expelled in 1934, imprisoned in 1935 and executed in 1936 as a Trotskyist. He was rehabilitated in 1988.

Karamanlis, Konstantinos (b. Proti, Serres, 8 Mar. 1907)

Greek; President of the Hellenic Republic 1980–5, 1990–5, Prime Minister 1955–8, 1958–61, 1961–3, 1974–80, founder and leader of New Democracy 1974–80

The elder son of a ten-member family, he studied law in Athens where he also became a successful lawyer. Karamanlis entered parliament in the 1930s and after the war he held various posts in different ministries. He became Prime Minister for the first time in 1955 and remained the undisputed leader of the Conservative Party (ERE) until his departure to Paris in 1963 after his electoral defeat by his main political adversary, *Papandreou. He remained in exile until 1974, when he returned to Athens to form the 'government of national unity' which prepared the country's transition to democracy (after the seven-year 'dictatorship of the colonels' 1967–74). He established the conservative New Democracy Party and was elected as Prime Minister. He was responsible for the referendum which abolished the monarchy and established a republic (1974), and a new constitution which enhanced the Prime Minister's powers. He became President in 1980 and was re-elected in 1990.

In his charisma, Karamanlis was typical of a generation of Greek politicians. He represented the conservative political establishment. Yet during his pre-1967 tenures as Prime Minister, Karamanlis was also prepared to oppose the monarchy's interventionist tendencies. Both the parties he has headed and the governments he has formed were characterized by their leader's dominance and intolerance of dissent. His supporters regarded him as the Leader of the Nation (*Ethnarchis*). Even his opponents agree that his main contribution was the initial association (1961) and subsequent accession (1981) of Greece to the European Community, which he considered as the country's natural area of interest. He also calculated that membership would protect Greek territorial integrity against the Turkish threat and promote modernization.

Kardelj, Edvard (b. Ljubljana, Slovenia, 17 Jan. 1910; d. Ljubljana 10 Feb. 1979)
Slovene; Secretary of the Central Committee of the Yugoslav Communist Party and Vice-President of the Yugoslav government 1952–79

Trained as a teacher, at 18 Kardelj became a Communist and in 1930–2 was imprisoned for his activities. In 1934–7 he worked for the Comintern in Moscow, where he met *Tito and became his close colleague. He founded the Slovene Communist Party in 1937 and helped Tito rebuild the Yugoslav Communist Party, but always advocated a balance between national and class approaches in party and state structures. In 1940 he was elected to the party's Central Committee and Politbureau, remaining a member till his death. He was Vice-President of the Provisional Government (AVNOJ) in 1943 and of the subsequent Tito–Subasic government, becoming also Foreign Minister when Subasic resigned in 1946. Later he was appointed secretary of the Central Committee of the League of Communists of Yugoslavia (as it became in 1952) and, after the fall of *Djilas in 1954, Vice-Premier and Speaker of the Yugoslav parliament.

Kardelj made an enormous contribution to the theoretical and institutional development of Yugoslav Communism. In the 1940s he helped to create the new Yugoslav legal system and the 'federal' state structure of 1946. After the disgrace of Djilas in 1954 he became the main theoretician of the party's new ideology of 'self-management'. In the 1960s his ideas for federalizing reform were opposed by Serbian centralists, but after the fall of Rankovic in 1966 they found fruition in the constitutional amendments of 1971 and the new constitution of 1974, which gave decisive power to the Republics and Provinces. It also introduced a complicated 'delegation system' designed to promote 'non-party pluralism' (a sort of one-party corporatism). But this unstable compromise resulted in governmental paralysis after Tito's death in 1980.

Karimov, Islam Abduganievich (b. 30 Jan. 1938)
Uzbek; President of Uzbekistan 1990–

Karimov started his career working in the Tashkent Aviation Factory. He joined the Communist Party in 1964. From 1966 to 1983 he worked on the organization of the state 'five-year' plans (*Gosplan*) for Uzbekistan. From 1983 to 1986 he was Uzbekistan's Minister of Finances. After coming to power in 1985, Gorbachev launched a full-scale purge of the corrupt and conservative Uzbek party leadership. In 1986 Karimov embarked on a party career when he entered one of the posts made vacant thanks to Gorbachev, becoming First Secretary of Kashkadar'ya regional committee. In June 1989 he was made First Secretary of the Uzbekistan Communist Party, replacing Rafik Nishanov, who became chairman of the USSR Soviet of Nationalities. In 1990 Karimov became President of the Uzbek Republic. In July that year he was elected to the Central Committee and to the Politburo.

Kaunda, Kenneth David (b. Lubwa, Zambia, 28 Apr. 1924)
Zambian; President 1964–91

Born to parents of Malawian origin Kaunda qualified and worked as a teacher. In 1951 he joined the Northern Rhodesian ANC and rose to become its secretary-general. After short periods of imprisonment for nationalist activities, and clashes with the other ANC leaders, he became leader of the more militant United National Independence Party (UNIP) in 1960. In the terminal colonial period he became a cabinet member in 1962 and prime minister in January 1964. Following UNIP victory in the pre-independence election he became President with the end of colonial rule in October 1964.

In 1972, following the growth of opposition parties, Kaunda declared Zambia to be a single-party state with UNIP as the only legal party. Although some competition between UNIP candidates was permitted in elections nobody was allowed to contest the presidential election with Kaunda until the return to multi-partyism in 1991. Although he professed an ideology of 'Zambian humanism' and stressed the importance of mass participation his style of rule became increasingly personalized and authoritarian.

He played a significant role in the international affairs of southern Africa as one of the leaders of the Frontline States in opposition to white minority rule in Rhodesia and South Africa. In 1987 be became chairman of the Organization of African Unity (OAU).

Under his rule the Zambian economy declined significantly, a development which was partly explained by drops in world copper prices but which was also due to inefficiency and corruption within government. From around the mid-1980s economic decline and political authoritarianism provoked growing domestic opposition and, in 1990 Kaunda reluctantly agreed to the re-establishment of a multi-party system. In the October 1991 elections Kaunda and UNIP were resoundingly defeated by the opposition Movement for Multi-Party Democracy (MMD) and he accepted defeat with considerable dignity. He continued to lead UNIP in opposition.

An emotional man, who was fond of flamboyant rhetoric, his earlier prestige as 'father of the nation' had worn very thin by the 1990s.

Keating, Paul John (b. Sydney, 18 Jan. 1944)
Australian; Prime Minister 1991–6

Born in Sydney of working-class Catholic parents, Keating left school at the age of 14. He worked for the Sydney County Council and managed a pop group before joining the Australian Labor Party (ALP) and becoming a researcher for the Federated Municipal Employees' Union.

Keating entered parliament aged 25. His political outlook was in tune with the right wing of the ALP in New South Wales, concentrating on economic growth as the basis for governing. Keating was briefly Minister for the Northern Territory before the fall of the *Whitlam government in 1975, and he held a number of shadow portfolios until Labor was re-elected in 1983. Keating then became Treasurer and, under Prime Minister Bob *Hawke, embarked on sweeping financial deregulation.

Having been promised and then denied the leadership position by Hawke, Keating wrested the position from him in a December 1991 challenge. As Prime Minister he continued the move to the right of traditional Labor platforms with further deregulation and the sale of portions of public utilities. His policies fostered strong economic growth, but unemployment was always 8–10 per cent.

Keating encouraged Australians to rethink their national identity in the context of Australia's multiculturalism, its rapid economic enmeshment in the Asia-Pacific region, and the possibility of Australia's becoming a republic. With his Native Title legislation recognizing Aboriginal land rights, he also confirmed a High Court decision overturning the doctrine of *terra nullius*, which had governed against the assumption of original Aboriginal ownership of land prior to white settlement.

He defied commentators' predictions to win the 1993 federal election, capitalizing on uncertainties over the operation of the Liberal Party's proposed goods and services tax. He resigned from parliament soon after Labor's landslide defeat in March 1996.

A master of witty and often venomous riposte, Keating was accused by his opponents of arrogance, but his leadership also attracted admiration across a broad spectrum, and especially from the arts community.

Kefauver, Estes. (b. Tennessee, 26 July 1903; d. 10 Apr. 1963)
US; US Senator 1948–52

Kefauver was brought up in Tennessee and graduated from the state university. He then studied at Yale and became a successful company lawyer. He was elected in 1938 as a Democrat to the House and served for ten years until being elected to the Senate in 1948. He was a liberal Democrat in a conservative state. He was a member of the armed services and judiciary committees. In 1950 he was appointed chairman of a special senate committee to investigate organized crime in interstate commerce. The televising of these hearings in 1950–1 gave him great exposure. He campaigned for the Democratic presidential nomination in 1952 and 1956. At this time it was still difficult for a southerner to gain the Democratic nomination. His victory over *Truman in the New Hampshire primary in 1952 was a factor leading the President to stand down. He entered the 1952 convention with the most pledged votes via the primaries of the candidates, but lost to *Stevenson. At the 1956 convention Stevenson was again nominated but left it to delegates to decide on the vice-presidential candidate. Kefauver narrowly beat J. F. *Kennedy. He would not have got the nomination had it been left to the party leaders.

Kekkonen, Urho (b. Kajana, Finland, 3 Sept. 1900; d. 31 Aug. 1986)
Finnish; Prime Minister 1950–3, 1954–6, President 1956–81

The son of a forestry foreman, Kekkonen attended school in his native township and university in Helsinki. Here he graduated in law in 1926 and took his doctorate in 1936. From 1927 to 1931 he was a lawyer with a local government federation and 1933–6 with the Ministry of Agriculture. From 1936 to 1956 Kekkonen was an Agrarian (Centre) Party member of parliament and served as Speaker 1948–50. In 1936–7 he was Minister of Justice, in 1937–9 Minister of the Interior, and in 1944–6 Minister of Justice again.

In this latter post Kekkonen helped build bridges with the Soviet Union after the two Finnish–Russian wars. Similarly he helped bring about the 1948 Treaty of Friendship, Co-operation, and Mutual Assistance with the Soviet Union that laid the groundwork for Finnish neutrality policy. This reflected a subtle awareness of Soviet security fears and a determination to defend the democratic Finnish political system—though as President Kekkonen was not above using foreign policy considerations to his own domestic political advantage. He was greatly helped by establishing friendly personal relations with successive Soviet leaders, based partly on his earthy realism and partly on his ability to outlast even his hosts when it came to the consumption of hard liquor. In domestic politics Kekkonen skilfully defended the interests of the poorer agricultural areas of Finland, incorporated the Communists into the political system without prejudice to his country's freedom, and dominated the political scene from 1963 to 1975. In foreign policy the presidency gave him large powers which he used to help bring about free trade agreements with EFTA in 1961 and with the EC in 1973 while encouraging trade with the East to show a profit. He also rebuilt Finland's defences and hosted the 1975 Helsinki Conference on Security. In 1981 he was compelled by ill-health to resign office.

Kellogg, Frank (b. New York, 22 Dec. 1856; d. 21 Dec. 1937)

US; Secretary of State 1925–9

Kellogg was brought up in Minnesota, where he practised as a lawyer. He was a Republican, but broke with the party established in 1912 to support Theodore *Roosevelt for the presidency. He was counsel for the government in its fight against trusts and was successful in the case which led to the break-up of the Standard Oil Trust. In 1916 he was elected Republican Senator for Minnesota. After defeat in 1922, he held a number of government appointments. including ambassador to Britain. He served as Secretary of State for the duration (1925–9) of *Coolidge's presidency. His lack of initiative in that post made him, according to many observers, an appropriate colleague for the laid-back President. His main achievement was the Kellogg–*Briand peace pact (1928) in which countries repudiated war as an instrument for settling disputes. The initiative for this 'outlawing of war' lay with the French Foreign Minister. Although it gained Kellogg a share of the Nobel Peace Prize in 1929 it made no provision for punishing aggressors and proved irrelevant in the storms of the next decade. From 1930 to 1935 he served as a member of the Court of Justice at the Hague.

Kemp, Jack French (b. Los Angeles, 13 July 1935)

US; member of the US House of Representatives 1971-89, Secretary of Housing and Urban Development 1989–93, Republican vice-presidential candidate 1996

Jack Kemp was educated at Occidental College, at the University of California at Long Beach, and at Western University. Before entering politics he was a professional footballer, playing quarterback for the San Diego Chargers and the Buffalo Bills.

After a period working for the *Reagan gubernatorial campaign in California in 1966 and as special assistant to Reagan when he was Governor, Kemp in 1969 worked for the chairman of the Republican National Committee. In 1970 Kemp was elected to the House of Representatives for the 38th District of New York and served there until 1989.

In Congress Kemp became increasingly interested in economic ideas and was a keen supporter of supply-side economics and especially of large cuts in direct taxes which, he argued, would pay for themselves as well as an advocate of deregulation and enterprise zones. In 1978, together with Senator Roth of Delaware, Kemp sponsored a 30 per cent across the board tax cut which was in large part enacted in the 1981 Reagan budget. Kemp's vigorous promotion of supply-side economics made him a well-known, if controversial politician, and earned him a popular following among the Republican rank and file. On cultural issues, however, Kemp was highly conservative and was a strong opponent of abortion rights. Despite his preference for ideas over pragmatic institutional politics, Kemp was elected Republican conference chairman in 1981.

In 1988 Kemp made a brief bid for the Republican presidential nomination. He was unsuccessful but in 1989 George *Bush appointed him to be Secretary of Housing and Urban Development when he formed his administration. He was not altogether successful in this role and was perceived by many as a maverick rather than a collegial member of the administration.

The selection of Kemp as Robert *Dole's running mate in 1996 was thus something of a surprise, not least because Kemp and Dole had had policy disagreements in the past and had been political rivals in 1988. Dole had generally been sceptical about massive tax cuts preferring to emphasize deficit reduction but the electoral dynamics of 1996 converted Dole to the merits of tax cuts. In this context Kemp was an ideal vice-presidential choice. He symbolized vigorous tax cuts and was able to generate enthusiasm among Republican activists. Kemp was well known nationally because of his football career; and it was hoped that Kemp's energetic style and manner would balance Dole's age. Dole may also have hoped that Kemp would lure Democrats and uncommitted voters into the Republican camp. In the event the Dole–Kemp ticket was decisively defeated by President *Clinton and his running mate Al *Gore.

Kennedy, Edward Moore (b. Boston, 21 Feb. 1932)
US; US Senator 1962–

Educated at Harvard University and the University of Virginia Law School, Kennedy became assistant district attorney for Suffolk County, Massachussetts, and served on John F. *Kennedy's election campaign in 1960. In 1962 he was elected at the age of 30 to the Senate seat which his brother had vacated in 1960. In 1964 he was re-elected for a full term to the Senate and won subsequent re-election in 1970, 1976, 1982, 1988, and 1994.

As a member of the most celebrated political family in America, he attained prominence and widescale media attention. Following the assassination of President Kennedy in 1963, and especially after the subsequent assassination of Robert *Kennedy in 1968, he was regarded as the standard-bearer of the Kennedy tradition and a very likely future President of the United States. In 1969, however, he was involved in a serious scandal, when he drove a car off a bridge at Chappaquidick, an island vacation resort in Massachusetts, and his young woman companion, Mary Jo Kepechne, was drowned, while he failed to report the accident to the police and gave an unconvincing account of the incident. The scandal destroyed his chance of winning the Democratic nomination for President in 1972 and, more especially, in 1976 when, but for the Chappaquidick affair, his prospects of being elected President would have been very good. In 1980 he challenged President *Carter for the Democratic nomination, but, although he won considerable support, he was unable to take the nomination from an incumbent Democratic President.

He failed to achieve his goal of the presidency and, although elected Democratic Whip in 1969, he was defeated for re-election in 1971. Nevertheless, his accomplishments as a senator were solid. Although media attention focused on a variety of scandals in the Kennedy family which continued to dog his career, he was a hard-working, conscientious, and effective legislator. He rose in seniority and became chairman of the Senate Committee on the Judiciary. He took a consistently liberal position on issues such as civil rights, welfare, education, immigration, health care, and the environment. By the 1980s liberalism became a minority position in America, while the Republican victory in the Senate elections in 1980 resulted in his loss of a Senate chairmanship and minority status for the Democratic Party. Democratic victory in the Senate elections in 1986 restored majority status until 1994, but the tide against liberalism continued to be strong, particularly with Republican control of the White House until 1992. With Democratic victory in the 1992 presidential election, he became an influential congressional supporter of President *Clinton, particularly on the issue of health care reform. The failure of Congress to enact health care reform in 1993–4, however, followed by Republican triumph in the 1994 congressional elections, reduced Kennedy to a more marginal role. Moreover, his narrow re-election victory over his Republican opponent in the Senate election in Massachusetts in 1994 illustrated that he was increasingly regarded as a figure from the past who stood for causes which no longer attracted widespread support.

Kennedy, John Fitzgerald (b. Brookline, Massachusetts, 29 May 1917, d. Dallas, Texas, 22 Nov. 1963)

US; member of the US Congress 1947–60, President of the United States 1961–3

John F. Kennedy was the son of Joseph Kennedy, the first chair of the Securities and Exchange Commission and, later, an ambassador to London. He was educated at the Choate School, the London School of Economics, and Harvard. His undergraduate dissertation at Harvard, a study of British appeasement of *Hitler in the 1930s, was published as a book entitled *Why England Slept* in 1944. In August 1943 the loss of the his ship, PT 109, earned him a decoration for bravery and a reputation as a war hero.

He entered the House of Representatives from the strongly Irish American 11th Congressional District in 1947 and identified himself with traditional Democratic issues such as trade union matters and aid to cities but also spoke on defence and foreign policy matters. In 1952 he defeated Henry Cabot Lodge for a seat in the US Senate and a year later he married Jacqueline Bouvier. Because of a major spinal operation he was absent when the Senate censured Senator Joseph *McCarthy in December 1954. In 1956 he failed to secure the nomination for Vice-President but, by trying, ensured his re-election to the Senate in 1958. In July 1960 after a hard fought primary election campaign to nullify prejudice against his Catholicism, he took the Democratic nomination and on 8 November 1960 was elected President.

Kennedy's presidency was marked by a succession of economic and security crises. Black America demanded desegregation in its search for education, prosperity, and equality of status. During the 1960 campaign Kennedy had cultivated black leaders, but after the election seemed reluctant to support black demands. He appointed a black, Robert *Weaver, to head the Housing and Home Finance Agency and, using Executive Orders, he created the President's Committee on Equal Employment Opportunity which sought to end discrimination in government and, very importantly, covert discrimination among government contractors. At the Justice Department Kennedy's brother, Attorney-General Robert *Kennedy, pressed desegregation at every legal opportunity, sometimes with little help from the FBI. In the autumn of 1962 there was a major crisis involving federal marshals and a southern mob at the University of Mississippi. By early 1963 Robert Kennedy was progressively strengthening a draft bill, a weakened version of which became law after Kennedy's death.

From his inauguration Kennedy pressed Congress to adopt measures to create jobs, alleviate family poverty, assist poor areas, and improve job training opportunities. By late 1962 Congress had appropriated $1.6 billion in a variety of aid programmes and the Housing Act was helping create over 400,000 construction jobs. The President used executive authority to speed federal agency procurements, post office, and highway construction, liberalize federal housing loans, and create a pilot Food Stamp programme. Added to increased defence spending and tax relief for business investment, these steps constituted a moderately successful economic recovery programme which had the effect of sharply increasing the growth rate by 1963. In crucial areas of labour–management relations Kennedy was willing to denounce union 'featherbedding' and was unwilling to seek changes in the unpopular *Taft–Hartley Act. In April 1962, however, he showed himself equally ready to use publicity and Anti-Trust legislation against steel companies which increased their prices having had Kennedy's help to moderate union demands. All in all Kennedy proved to be a conservative in words but an active state interventionist in deeds. Blue-collar and black America had much to thank him for.

Abroad the President faced the consequences of a 'Communist' Cuba and the threat of similar unwelcome regimes in Latin America. Within days of being in office he had to decide not to cancel an invasion of Cuba by exiles trained and financed in the USA. The subsequent 'Bay of Pigs' fiasco in April 1961 scarred the President badly and led him to espouse the Alliance for Progress aimed at economic aid to Latin America. Relations with the USSR were, however, much more important and degenerated after the Vienna Summit with *Khrushchev in June 1961. Two months later the building of the Berlin Wall symbolized a distinct hardening of Soviet–American relations. By the spring of 1962 Kennedy had authorized the expansion of US military involvement in South Vietnam, though commenting, 'It is their war and they must win it'. Most seriously of all, in October 1962, the world seemed on the brink of nuclear war when the USA quarantined Cuba to prevent the arrival of Soviet nuclear missiles. A dangerous impasse was broken only by a secret deal on US missiles in Turkey—a deal which saved Russian face but led eventually to the downfall of Khrushchev. The two powers hastily established a 'hot line' between them and in July of 1963 signed a Nuclear Test Ban Treaty which opened the way to a massive sale of wheat to the USSR. Having thus put Soviet–American relations on a safer footing Kennedy was assassinated, ironically, on a visit which was meant to end chronic feuding between factions of Texas Democrats.

President Kennedy and his wife symbolized a new generation in the White House —he was the first President to be born in the twentieth century. As his inaugural showed he was very conscious of speaking for a generation which had done the dying and not the leading in the Second World War. He never lost a veteran's attitude to 'civilians' and was suitably sceptical of military leadership and its received wisdom. He was genuinely appreciative of intellectuals certainly when it came to using them to frame policies, improve governance, and civilize public service and public attitudes. If he did not share all his wife's artistic tastes and connections few artists doubted their welcome at the restored, period White House. The myth of Camelot, though useful politically, was rooted in this self-conscious civility and high aspiration. For Kennedy 'the business of America was not business'.

It is true to say that, domestically, he would not rank as a very successful President though a second term might well have changed that judgement. Abroad he frightened an ageing Soviet leadership but showed real statesmanship during the Cuban crisis. It is very probable that he would have found it difficult to withdraw from Vietnam and thus would have had to endure the same agonies that he bequeathed to his successor.

Kennedy, Robert Francis (b. Brookline, Massachusetts, 20 Nov. 1925; d. 6 June 1968)
US; Attorney-General 1961–4, US Senator 1965–8

Kennedy served in the navy 1944–5. He then took a BA at Harvard University and an LLB at the University of Virginia. In 1952 he acted as campaign manager for his elder brother John F. *Kennedy's successful race for the US Senate. In 1953 he became Assistant Counsel for the Senate Permanent Subcommittee on Investigations, which was chaired by Senator Joseph *McCarthy, but he joined the walkout of Democratic members of the subcommittee in protest against McCarthy's methods. In 1955–7 he became Chief Counsel to the Subcommittee on Investigations when Senator John McClellan became chairman. In 1957–9 he became Chief Counsel to McClellan's Senate Rackets Committee, which won him national prominence in his aggressive pursuit of Teamsters' Union president Jimmy Hoffa.

In 1960 he acted as campaign manager for John F. Kennedy's successful campaign for President. He was appointed Attorney-General in President Kennedy's administration and took a strong stand in the enforcement of civil rights measures in the South. He was President Kennedy's closest adviser on all matters including, for example, foreign policy issues such as the Cuban missile crisis. After Kennedy's assassination, he continued to serve in President *Johnson's Cabinet as Attorney-General and was disappointed that Johnson did not choose him as vice-presidential candidate in 1964. Instead he ran for election as Senator from New York in 1964. He supported President Johnson on domestic issues, especially the War on Poverty and civil rights, but he disliked Johnson personally and above all clashed with him over the war in Vietnam. By 1968 he was one of the most significant dissenters with regard to American policy on Vietnam, while on domestic policy he became increasing liberal and acquired an unusually close empathy with minorities and the dispossessed. He hesitated to challenge Johnson for the Democratic nomination for President in 1968. When Johnson's weakness was illustrated, however, by the strong support for Senator Eugene *McCarthy in the New Hampshire primary in March, he declared his candidacy for the Democratic nomination. His victory in a string of primaries gave him a strong chance of winning the Democratic nomination over Vice-President Hubert *Humphrey, who was the front runner following Johnson's withdrawal from the race. After his victory in the final primary in California, however, he was shot and killed by Sihran Sihran, a Palestinian who was angered by Kennedy's support for Israel, though it was not an issue on which he had taken a prominent stand.

Kenyatta, Jomo (b. Gatundu, Kenya, c.1893; d. 22 Aug. 1978)
Kenyan; Prime Minister 1963–4, President 1964–78

A member of the Kikuyu ethnic group in central Kenya, his original name was Kamau wa Ngengi and Kenyatta was a nickname. He received some mission education, and was active in Nairobi politics from 1920, becoming General Secretary of the first Kenyan African political organization, the Kikuyu Central Association. In 1931 he went to Britain, where he studied anthropology and wrote a detailed study of the Kikuyu, *Facing Mount Kenya*. In 1945, with others including Kwame *Nkrumah, he organized the Manchester Pan-African Congress.

Returning to Kenya in 1946, he became president of the Kenya African Union and was active in nationalist agitation. He was subsequently suspected by the colonial administration of organizing the Mau Mau movement, which violently attacked white settlers and their African supporters, a charge which he strongly denied. He was however charged and convicted in 1953 of managing Mau Mau, and sentenced to seven years' imprisonment. Once the colonial government was obliged to concede independence, however, his authority was such that no settlement could be reached without his participation; the main nationalist party, KANU, elected him as leader while still in jail. He was released and elected to the legislative council in 1962, becoming Prime Minister in 1963; he retained the position at independence, and became President in 1964.

As a national leader, he showed few of the radical sympathies for which he had long been feared by white Kenyans and colonial rulers. Behind a titular socialism, he was firmly committed to capitalist development and established good relations with the United Kingdom. His political style was monarchical, but he absorbed rather than suppressing any opposition politician who accepted his authority, and was universally known as 'Mzee', a Swahili term meaning 'elder'. Though an undercurrent of violence remained, his regime was not overtly repressive, and Kenyatta retained great personal support. Increasing corruption, in which members of his family were closely involved, did not prevent a constitutional transfer of power to his successor, Daniel arap *Moi, on his death in 1978.

Kerenski, Alexander Fyodorovich (b. Simbirsk, Russia, 22 Apr. (4 May) 1881; d. New York, 15 June 1970)
Russian; leader of the provisional government June–Oct. 1917

The son of the headmaster of a school where *Lenin studied in Simbirsk, Kerenski studied law at St Petersburg University, where he made his reputation defending revolutionaries in the political trials of the later tsarist years. He joined the Socialist Revolutionary Party (former Populists) and was an active, but not disruptive deputy (for Saratov) in the third and fourth Dumas (from 1912), a member of the Trudovik group.

After the February Revolution he became Vice-President of the Petrograd Soviet and also, from March, Minister of Justice in Prince Lvov's provisional government: these posts in both the foci of the 'dual power' gave him considerable political importance as a broker between the two institutions. He became Minister for War and the Admiralty in May and in June became leader of a new coalition. Hoping to retrieve Russia's military fortunes and to please the allies he launched a military offensive in Galicia which ended in failure. In July he helped crush the abortive coup by the Bolsheviks, but was forced to seek their aid in August to deal with Kornilov's attempted coup. Increasingly isolated and discredited from the military failure, the postponement of the Constituent Assembly elections and the lack of progress in land reform, he managed to escape when the Bolsheviks stormed the Winter Palace in October and fled from Murmansk on a British destroyer. In exile he wrote several works of self-justification. He lived initially mostly in France, later moving to Australia and ultimately the USA. Effective as a fiery orator in the pre-revolutionary period, he had no political base and was out of his depth in the polarized politics of 1917.

Khama, Seretse (b. Serowe, Bechuanaland, 21 July 1921; d. 13 July 1980)
Botswana; President 1966–80

Born as the undisputed heir to the Bangwato chieftaincy Seretse was only 4 years old when his father died and his uncle, Tshekedi, was recognized as regent. His marriage to a white woman, Ruth Williams, in London in 1949 was bitterly opposed by the South African government because it contradicted its own apartheid system. Under pressure from the South Africans the British government banned Khama and his wife from his homeland for several years and stripped him of his hereditary rights to the Bangwato chieftaincy. Although the latter action was personally devastating for him at the time it did enable him to develop as a truly national leader and he retained his traditional authority in the eyes of his people without being encumbered with the day-to-day duties of a chief. In 1962 he founded the Botswana Democratic Party (BDP) which has remained the leading party ever since. Following BDP victory in the pre-independence elections he became state President at independence in 1966.

Under his leadership Botswana entered an era of very rapid economic growth combined with the maintenance of a stable and democratic political system which made it an outstanding example of post-independence success in Sub-Saharan Africa. Economic success was due to a mixture of good luck (the discovery of huge deposits of diamonds) and good management (the development of an efficient and largely non-corrupt state structure). Administrative efficiency and political democracy resulted, to a significant extent, from the leadership of Khama.

As the leader of a black majority-ruled state bordering on apartheid South Africa he demonstrated considerable diplomatic skill in combining a pragmatic recognition of vulnerability in relation to a powerful neighbour with a foreign policy based on clear moral principles and a rejection of racism. In his later years he emerged as a respected international statesman and a voice for moderation. At home his political authority remained undiminished in spite of the freedom allowed to opposition groups to criticize as they saw fit. He was deeply mourned following his premature death from cancer. His greatest legacy to Botswana was to have constructed a system which survived his departure and to have made himself dispensable.

Khan, Mohammad Ayub (b. Rehana, NWFP, 14 May 1907; d. 20 Apr. 1974)
Pakistani; President 1958–69

Ayub came from a middling income Pakhtun family from the Hazara district of the North-West Frontier. He was educated at Aligarh College and Sandhurst from where he was commissioned in 1928. He served in Burma during the Second World War and in the Punjab Boundary Force at the time of Partition. After his promotion to major-general he commanded the forces in East Pakistan. In 1951 he became the first Pakistani Commander-in-Chief. From October 1954 to August 1955 he also served as Minister of Defence.

In the coup of 8 October 1958 he became chief martial law administrator; shortly afterwards he deposed Iskander Mirza and became President of Pakistan. Ayub sought to modernize Pakistan by introducing land reform and social reforms such as the celebrated Muslim Laws Family Ordinance of 15 July 1961 and by stressing economic development. In foreign affairs he maintained a pro-Western stance. Political parties were banned however until July 1962 and Ayub favoured the system of guided democracy known as the basic democracy scheme. The 1962 constitution created a powerful President who was to be elected by the 80,000 basic democrats.

From 1965, however, Ayub's fortunes declined as his growth-orientated strategy of channelling resources to an entrepreneurial élite generated increasing social and regional tensions. The 1965 Indo-Pakistani War following the failure of Operation Gibraltar's infiltration of armed volunteers into Kashmir was another major setback. Ayub was never comfortable with his new political role from December 1963 onwards as head of the Convention Muslim League. He had lost the campaign, although he won the tightly controlled 1965 presidential election contest with Miss Fatima Jinnah. Ayub had also created an Achilles' heel when he stood down as Commander-in-Chief of the army. The popular disturbances from November 1968 onwards lost him the support of his former army colleagues. By March 1969 he had no choice but to step down in favour of General Agha Muhammad Yahya Khan.

Ayub is remembered as a hard-headed administrator whose modernizing impulses foundered because his regime never acquired political legitimacy. He wrote a well-received autobiography *Friends Not Masters* (1969).

Khasbulatov, Ruslan Imranovich (b. Groznyi, Chechnya, 22 Nov. 1942)

Chechen; Speaker of the Russian Parliament 1991–3, Opposition leader in Chechnya 1994–6

Coming from a family exiled to northern Kazakhstan under *Stalin, he was educated at Kazan and Moscow universities as an economist and, after working in production in Alma-Ata, became an academic. He is a doctor of economic sciences, professor, and author of many academic works. He taught economics at the Plekhanov Institute of National Economy in Moscow 1979–90, where he headed a department. He was a party member 1966–91.

In 1990 he was elected to the Russian Republic Supreme Soviet, becoming Deputy Speaker. In October 1991 he was elected Speaker (President) of the Supreme Soviet of the Russian Federation. Initially a supporter of *Yeltsin, he became his implacable opponent, leading the opposition to Yeltsin's economic reforms and style of government and asserting the rights of parliament. In October 1993 he was arrested when the parliament was stormed. Later charges were dropped and he returned to Chechnya as a leader of the Opposition to Dudayev, but, though he denounced the methods of the Russian invasion, he failed to gain credibility as an alternative leader, and early in 1996 returned to Moscow to teach at the Plekhanov Institute.

Khomeini, Ayatollah *see* AL-KHOMEINI, AL-MUSSARI

Khrushchev, Nikita Sergeevich (b. Kalinovka, Kursk province, 17 Apr. 1894; d. Moscow 11 Sept. 1971)

Russian; Ukrainian First Secretary 1938–49, CPSU First Secretary 1953–64, Prime Minister 1958–64

Born in a village on the Russian–Ukrainian border, Khrushchev received little formal education and became a metal fitter. He joined the Bolsheviks in 1918 and fought in the Civil War. In 1924 he started working in the Ukrainian Communist Party, then headed by *Kaganovich, who brought him to Moscow in 1929 as his assistant in running the Moscow party; they collaborated on the construction of the Moscow metro in 1933. In 1934 Khrushchev joined the Central Committee and in 1935 succeeded Kaganovich as Moscow party First Secretary. In 1938 he was given the difficult job of Ukrainian First Secretary (and Politbureau membership) to rebuild the party after the purges and in 1940 supervised the sovietization of western Ukraine (acquired by the Nazi-Soviet pact), which involved mass arrests and deportations. During the Second World War he was a senior political commissar, notably at Stalingrad. Resuming his Ukrainian duties in 1943, Khrushchev's toughness was tempered by sensitivity to national feeling in his cultural and personnel policies. He launched an effective economic reconstruction campaign, in which the party was closely involved, and also experimented with his controversial 'agro-towns' idea, designed to improve peasant welfare by merging communities into larger units. These policies made *Stalin and *Malenkov suspect Khrushchev of 'nationalist' and 'narodnik' (pro-peasant) inclinations and for much of 1947 he was demoted to deputy chief of Ukraine. He soon regained Stalin's trust, but was moved from Ukraine in 1949 to head the Moscow party organization once more, perhaps as a check on Malenkov. In 1950 he was also given responsibility for agriculture, when he again promoted his 'agro-towns' scheme, but was openly criticized in 1951–2 by Malenkov, who took over supervision of agriculture. However, Khrushchev was still one of Stalin's most trusted colleagues, even though he had his own ideas and, like others, increasing doubts about his leader.

In the 'collective leadership' following Stalin's death in 1953 Malenkov took the top post of Premier, leaving Khrushchev the apparently lesser post of CPSU Secretary, later elevated to First Secretary. Over the next two years Khrushchev outmanœuvred Malenkov, attacking his economic policies for neglecting heavy industry, encouraging military fears of Malenkov's opening to the West and reliance on nuclear deterrence and exposing the ills of Soviet agriculture. In 1954 he launched the 'Virgin Lands' campaign to boost agricultural output, with great initial success which later ended in ecological disaster. Posing as the defender of Leninist orthodoxy, he launched a revival of party propaganda (including a strident anti-religious campaign), as a necessary complement to the ending of terror. By 1955 he had used his control of the party machine to get Malenkov replaced by his ally *Bulganin and established himself as top leader. He now adopted Malenkov's policy of 'peaceful coexistence', seeing the benefits defence cuts would have for raising living standards. In 1956 he made a sensational attack on Stalin at the 20th CPSU Congress (the 'Secret Speech'), partly to wrongfoot his opponents, but this sparked off a crisis in Poland and especially Hungary, where a national revolution had to be crushed with Soviet troops. In 1957, after initiating a major decentralization of the industrial ministries, he was outvoted in the Presidium (Politbureau), but appealed to the Central Committee and succeeded in ousting Malenkov and other ministers (the 'antiparty group'). In 1958 he assumed the additional post of Premier to control the ministries, which made his powers formally comparable with Stalin's. In 1961 at the 22nd Congress he publicly renewed the attack on Stalin (played down since 1956) in the context of the Sino-Soviet dispute and had Stalin's remains removed from *Lenin's mausoleum. At the same time he introduced an optimistic new party programme, committed to overtaking the USA in per capita production by 1970 and building a Communist society by 1980.

His rule was rocked by external and internal crises, yet there was a coherent strategy, even though marred by contradictions in implementation. Khrushchev was a simple man whose central beliefs were a wish to improve mass living standards, a hatred of bureaucracy, and a deep faith (boosted by Soviet war triumphs and the success of the space programme in the 1950s) in the superiority of the Leninist system, once purged of Stalinist distortions. These beliefs were theorized by ideologists (in the 1961 party programme) into a reassertion of the Leninist project of the stateless, classless Communist society. In domestic policy this meant re-establishing the political primacy of the Communist Party as the co-ordinator of Communist society; regular meetings of the Politbureau, Central Committee, and Congress were re-established and the leadership made more accountable to them; party membership was increased; to promote renewal offices were to be rotated and not duplicated with state posts; the party was to have an increased role in running the economy and, to develop specialized expertise, the regional apparatus was split into industrial and agricultural sections (a reform highly unpopular with party bureaucrats); party control of the secret police (the new KGB) was established. The state apparatus, destined to 'wither away' under Communism, was downgraded (thereby conveniently sidelining his opponents): the central industrial ministries, considered the main source of bureaucratic inertia and inefficiency, were replaced in 1957 by over 100 regional economic councils (*sovnarkhozy*), though the resultant administrative chaos forced Khrushchev to recentralize in 1963 with the Supreme Council for the National Economy. He established 'Comrades' Courts' and volunteer militias (*druzhiny*) as harbingers of the deprofessionalization of the judiciary and the police. He tried to increase mass political involvement by enhancing the powers of the soviets and trade unions. To create a society of convinced Communists he increased general educational levels, insisted on 'polytechnical' education and labour experience for everyone and intensified political and atheistical education (religion had to disappear under Communism); emphasis was placed on egalitarianism and 'moral incentives' in the workplace. Writers and artists were allowed to expose the wrongs of Stalinism, but not to attack the Soviet system—yet there were no 'show trials'. Intellectual life was much freer, yet he continued to favour Stalinist cranks like Lysenko. On the practical side living standards (especially in housing) and the provision of consumer goods were greatly improved (financed by defence cuts), though the emphasis was not on individual consumerism but on the development of free or subsidized collective services for a Communist society based on distribution according to need. In the economy he failed in his attempt to provide new structures for industry and agriculture which would increase motivation and efficiency. Agriculture, despite constant reform and much investment, remained a problem: he was forced to raise food prices, causing protests (in Novocherkassk in 1962 many demonstrators were killed by troops) and later to import Canadian wheat.

In foreign policy, Khrushchev's risky scheme of arming Cuba with nuclear missiles as bargaining pressure on the USA brought the world very near nuclear disaster in 1962. But there was real achievement in East–West relations with the first nuclear test ban treaty and the agreement on Berlin (where the situation was very tense before the building of the Berlin wall in 1961). In Eastern Europe he tried to increase the autonomy and status of his allies, abolishing the Stalinist Cominform, reviving the CMEA, and forming the Warsaw Pact, to develop a sort of Soviet-dominated multilateralism, yet he used force in Hungary in 1956 when autonomy threatened to turn into independence and his attempt to force the pace of CMEA integration in 1962 alienated Romania. In 1956 he admitted the possibility of 'different roads to socialism', a sop mainly to Yugoslavia, which he tried, without success, to lure back into the Soviet camp, even with a personal visit to Belgrade in 1955; he also failed to dislodge *Tito from the leadership of the non-aligned movement, despite wooing India and other ex-colonial countries. His attacks on Stalin provoked a break with the Chinese Communists which also led to Albania's defection in 1961.

By 1964 Khrushchev had alienated the military and party élite by his bullying, arbitrary, and often boorish style and constant administrative tinkering and 'hare-brained schemes', so in October he was sacked. While he became a 'non-person', he was allowed to retire peacefully (a testament to his humanization of Soviet politics), compiling memoirs which managed to reach the West. In his methods Khrushchev remained imprisoned in his Stalinist training, but, nevertheless, he was the most significant Soviet reformer before *Gorbachev, albeit in a very different direction—essentially trying to put the clock back, to make the Leninist dream work. This attempt failed because of bureaucratic resistance and his own impatience and mistakes, but mainly because the ideas were even less practicable in the 1960s than they were in the 1920s. He was buried in the Novodevichii cemetery, where his tomb, with a headstone carved by the modernist sculptor Neizvestnyi, whom he once mocked, became a shrine for the intelligentsia under *Brezhnev, who remembered his tolerance and humour with nostalgia.

Kiesinger, Kurt-Georg (b. Ebingen, Württemberg, 6 Apr. 1904; d. 9 Mar. 1988)
German; Chancellor of the Federal Republic of Germany 1966–9

When Kiesinger was elected Chancellor in 1966, with the support of *Brandt's SPD, millions of Germans were dismayed. Kiesinger had been a member of Hitler's NSDAP from 1933 until 1945 and worked during the war as deputy director of the radio propaganda department of the Foreign Ministry. The Allies interned him for eighteen months.

Kiesinger had worked as a lawyer until 1940; in 1948 he returned to legal practice and joined the CDU. In 1949 he was elected to the first Bundestag, chairing the foreign affairs committee (1954–8). In 1958 he was elected Minister-President of Baden-Württemberg, where he remained until 1966. Kiesinger's past was a disadvantage for him as Chancellor. During this period, 1966–9, the far right National Democratic Party (NPD) succeeded in gaining election to most of the regional parliaments. Kiesinger's own NSDAP membership made it more difficult to attack the Nazi credentials of NPD leaders. This was also the period of student protest. Left-wing students attacked Kiesinger and others like him, questioning their moral authority. They also criticized the Bundestag in which, due to the grand coalition, there was virtually no opposition. The Bundestag adopted for the first time emergency powers laws. From the liberal point of view, this appeared a step in the direction of authoritarianism. One other highly controversial issue was the extension of the period during which Nazi crimes could be prosecuted.

Kiesinger had difficulties with his government as it comprised the leading figures of both major parties. He was most active in foreign affairs, but had to share the glory with Brandt. They sought better relations with the Soviet bloc, establishing diplomatic relations with Romania. However, the Warsaw Pact invasion of Czechoslovakia in 1968 made progress more difficult.

The election of Social Democrat *Heinemann to the presidency on 5 March 1969 marked the end for Kiesinger. By voting for the SPD candidate the FDP showed that its offer of a coalition with Brandt was genuine. The loss of support for the CDU/CSU in the 1969 election led Heinemann to ask Brandt to form a government. Kiesinger served as Chairman of the CDU from 1967 to 1971 and remained in the Bundestag until 1976.

Kilmuir, Lord *see* MAXWELL-FYFE, DAVID PATRICK

Kim Il Sung (b. Mangyongdae near Pyongyang, 15 Apr. 1912; d. 8 Jul. 1994)
Korean; paramount North Korean political leader 1948–94

Kim Il Sung dominated North Korean politics for forty-six years. Official Korean biographies explain the entire history of modern Korea in terms of Kim's family's revolutionary activities, but the reality is slightly more mundane. Kim's family emigrated to Manchuria in the early 1920s, and Kim's revolutionary activities began in exile first in Manchuria and later in the Soviet Far East. Kim was placed in power by the occupying Soviet forces in 1945, but soon established his own power bases by eliminating rival political factions. Kim blamed other factions for the failures of the Korean War, and effectively destroyed all active opposition by 1961.

Kim established an extreme and all pervasive personality cult. He also kept the country on a constant war footing against the American backed South Korea, and is personally blamed for a number of atrocities such as the bombing of the South Korean Cabinet in Rangoon. His refusal to rule out a nuclear strike on the south was a cause of considerable instability in East Asia, and latterly a cause of embarrassment for his 'allies' in Beijing.

Kim's philosophy of *Juche*, or self-reliance, argued that North Korea's economic miracle was entirely due to Kim's genius and the revolutionary zeal of the Korean people. This ignored Korea's actual reliance on the Soviet Union, and the similarity between Kim's Flying Horse economic strategy and earlier Chinese experiments. From the mid-1970s, the Korean economy lurched from decline to the verge of collapse, and a number of senior military leaders began questioning the wisdom of the *Juche* approach. When Kim died in July 1994, he left his son and political heir, *Kim Jong Il, a very unstable economic, political, and diplomatic inheritance.

Kim Jong Il (b. Soviet Union, 16 Feb. 1942)
Korean; second ranked political leader 1980–94, primary leader 1994–

Kim's political career was an accident of birth. As the son of North Korea's paramount leader, *Kim Il Sung, Kim junior was groomed for political succession from an early age. Having sat out the Korean War in Manchuria, he later studied philosophy at the Kim Il Sung University. Some reports suggest that he also spent some time at the East German Air Force Academy.

Kim became his father's secretary while still in his early twenties, and held a number of important posts before becoming the official number two to his father in 1980. He took over an increasing amount of his father's work in the 1980s whilst establishing a basis for succession. Official reports stopped referring to him by name, instead using the title 'Dear Leader' to indicate his political pedigree and seniority. Kim also took over the mantle of ideological legitimacy—he was the only person who truly understood his father's genius, and the only person who could continue the great revolution.

Kim did indeed succeed his father in July 1994, but the succession was far from smooth. Kim only took over because he represented his father's ideas. But this was at a time when many Korean leaders blamed his father's ideas for the near collapse of the economy. Kim's desire to exercise political power is also questionable. He is rumoured to have a massive collection of Western films, and appears happier talking about cultural affairs than making political speeches or inspecting guards of honour. Lacking the charisma, ruthlessness, and political wit of his father, and with floods causing famine and economic collapse in 1995–6, neither Kim nor the North Korean economy is likely to have a particularly rosy future.

King, Mackenzie (b. Berlin (Kitchener), Ontario, 17 Dec. 1874; d. Ottawa, 22 July 1950)
Canadian; Prime Minister 1921–6, 1926–30, 1935–48

King remains Canada's longest-serving Prime Minister and a giant in the country's political history. He spent some time in the Canadian civil service after university. In 1908 he was elected as Liberal MP. By 1909 he was Minister of Labour, serving under Wilfrid *Laurier. After some time out of politics and working at the Rockefeller Foundation, he was returned again as an MP and, on Laurier's death, was made party leader in 1919. His absence from Parliament, at a time when the party was so divided on conscription during the First World War, was a political advantage for him.

Between 1921 and 1926 King was Prime Minister and Minister for External Affairs. His party's majority in parliament had disappeared in the 1925 election and he relied upon the support of the Progressives to carry legislation. He was then involved in the famous King–Byng affair. This arose when his government faced a motion of censure in 1926 which it was sure to lose and his request to Governor General Byng for a dissolution was refused. The main opposition party, the Conservatives, were then given the opportunity to form a government which lasted a short time until it lost a key vote, and Byng agreed to the Conservative request for a dissolution. In the election, King's Liberals gained a clear majority. His party lost the 1929 election—which meant that it escaped some of the responsibility and unpopularity for tackling the economic depression—but returned in 1935. King was influential in shaping the Statute of Westminster (1931), which paved the way to a greater self-government for the dominions in the British Empire. In the late 1930s he supported the appeasement of *Mussolini and *Hitler, until it was clear that war was inevitable.

The question of whether Canada should introduce conscription during wartime was again divisive, as it had been in the First World War. King was originally opposed, not least because of opposition in Quebec, but he gradually coaxed his colleagues and the country to support it. In 1940 his government had introduced conscription for the defence of Canada and a plebiscite in 1942 supported its extension. In 1944 it was finally agreed that Canada would send troops abroad, as opposed to relying on volunteers. The fact that it was near the end of the war prevented the issue from being as divisive as in the past. King's lengthy tenure as Prime Minister is a tribute to his political skills as well as a reflection of the Liberal Party's dominance in Canada. He retired from the premiership in 1948, having been in post since 1935.

King, Martin Luther (b. Atlanta, Georgia, 15 Jan. 1929; d. Memphis, Tennessee, 4 Apr. 1968)

US; civil rights leader

Martin Luther King's role in the American civil rights movement made him the most celebrated black leader of his generation and an international political figure. The son of a Baptist preacher, King was educated at Morehouse College, Atlanta, Crozer Theological Seminary and Boston University, and himself became a Baptist pastor in Montgomery before devoting himself to the nascent civil rights movement.

King first gained political recognition as a result of the successful Montgomery bus boycott of 1955. In 1957 he became president of the Southern Christian Leadership Conference and developed a campaign of direct but non-violent action against segregation across the south. King's involvement in the sit-ins and marches, although themselves non-violent, elicited a violent reaction from southern officials and he experienced periods of imprisonment as a result of his activities. During one such period in 1960, presidential candidate John *Kennedy (advised by Harris *Wofford) made a sympathetic telephone call to King's wife. The initiative was widely seen as an important factor swinging the black vote behind the Democrats. By the time of the Selma Freedom March of 1963 King had become the most visible symbol of black Americans' aspirations and a powerful political figure in a country wrestling with racial inequality. The assassination of Kennedy in 1963 produced the climate in which Lyndon *Johnson could secure passage of the landmark Civil Rights Act of 1964 and the Voting Rights Act of 1965, legislation which spelled the end of *de jure* segregation in the south. Thereafter, King broadened his campaign to encompass the morally more complex issues of *de facto* segregation outside the south, economic injustice, and the increasingly divisive war in Vietnam.

Part of King's power stemmed from his biblically inspired oratory; and his espousal of non-violence (based on the teachings of Christ and *Gandhi) gave him a reputation far beyond the United States. He was awarded the Nobel Peace Prize in 1964.

King's crusades were however at the centre of America's political struggles and he inevitably acquired enemies as well as a devoted following which regarded him as a saint. Despite his record of political achievement and his charismatic personality, some blacks in the 1960s felt that his tactics were too moderate and began to look to the more militant strategies advocated by the Black Power movement. King also faced allegations that his movement had been infiltrated by Communists and he became an object of hatred on the right.

In 1968, while on the balcony of his Memphis motel room he was assassinated by James Earl Ray. The assassination triggered riots across the United States and a battle for the control of the civil rights movement. It also ensured King's pre-eminent position in modern black American history, a position which was later given national endorsement by the creation of a public holiday in his honour.

King, Thomas **(Tom)** Jeremy (b. Somerset, 13 June 1933)
British; Defence Secretary 1989–92

Educated at Rugby School and Emmanuel College, Cambridge, King was a businessman before entering parliament as MP for Bridgwater in 1970. He was quickly talent spotted to serve as a parliamentary private secretary to Christopher Chataway, the Minister for Posts and Telecommunications. He served as Chataway's PPS throughout the parliament. His career progressed after Margaret *Thatcher was elected party leader; he was appointed as an Opposition spokesman on industry in 1975 and subsequently on energy. However, his frontbench status was not translated into Cabinet office in 1979, and instead he had to serve four years as Minister of State for Local Government and Environmental Services before being appointed to the Cabinet as Environment Secretary in January 1983. He was Environment Secretary for six months, being moved to Transport in June and then to Employment in October. After a solid two-year stint at Employment, he was appointed Northern Ireland Secretary in 1985. He took over the Northern Ireland portfolio just in time to preside over the signing of the Anglo-Irish Agreement and had to contend with opposition to the Agreement from the Unionist parties in the province. He developed links with the Irish government and disbanded the Northern Ireland Assembly after the Unionists withdrew from it. After four years in the post, he was rewarded with the post of Defence Secretary. He was responsible for a major defence review and had to endure a troublesome Minister of State in Alan Clark, who was to write both critically and affectionately about King in his published diaries. King was one of the principal supporters of Douglas *Hurd in the party leadership contest in 1990. He stood down from ministerial office in 1992.

An ambitious man, King never quite managed to reach the political heights that he and some of his supporters believed he was capable of achieving. A competent administrator, he was respected but never quite trusted by Margaret Thatcher.

Kinnock, Neil (b. Glamorgan, 28 Mar. 1942)
British; leader of Labour Party 1983–92

Neil Kinnock was the son of a coal miner and brought up in the Welsh valleys. At university he devoted a lot of his energy to student politics. He won a safe Labour seat, Bedwelty in South Wales (much of which remained in the new seat of Islwyn which he represented from 1983), and entered parliament in 1970 aged 28. Kinnock was a brilliant orator and a supporter of most left-wing causes in the next ten years. This was useful as the party moved sharply to the left, particularly after the defeat of the Labour government in the 1979 election.

Kinnock was elected to the party's National Executive in 1978 and then the shadow Cabinet in 1980. After Labour's worst election defeat for fifty years the party skipped a generation and elected him as leader in 1983 in succession to his close friend

Michael *Foot. He was elected under the new electoral machinery which gave 70 per cent of the vote to the constituency parties and trade unions. It was this extra-parliamentary support that helped him to win.

As party leader Kinnock was faced by a formidable Prime Minister in Margaret *Thatcher and huge Conservative majorities in the House of Commons. The Thatcher government broke with the post-war consensus and moved the agenda sharply to the right. Labour had to come to terms with the changes and was dispirited in these years. Kinnock also had to face down challenges from determined left-wing Labour local authorities and trade unions (notably the National Union of Mineworkers) who robustly contested Conservative government policies. He showed great courage in defying activists' demands that he support actions which broke the law. He had few heavyweight supporters in the party. Before the 1987 election Kinnock persuaded the party to accept a number of policy changes including the sale of council houses to tenants and Britain's continued membership of the European Community.

After another clear election defeat in 1987 Kinnock moved party policy further to the centre ground. For Labour to come to terms with the social and cultural changes and win another election, it would have to change itself radically. This involved abandoning a unilateralist defence policy, accepting a number of the Conservative policies on privatization, tax, and industrial relations, and trying to appeal to the skilled working class. The party's left wing criticized the policy changes, as well as the reforms in the party organization, which were designed to weaken the influence of left-wing activists, and the use of public relations. He was challenged in a leadership contest in 1988 by the left-wing Tony *Benn, and won 88 per cent of the electoral college vote. In the 1992 election a Labour victory seemed highly probable and Kinnock was bitterly disappointed when the party failed to win. He knew that he was widely regarded as an electoral liability and resigned the leadership soon afterwards.

Kinnock had done much to make the Labour Party more electable and repudiate the left wing. But much of his energy was spent on internal party battles rather than projecting himself to the nation. It was ironic that, having been elected as the candidate of the left, Kinnock did so much to weaken it. Critics pointed to the number of positions which he had held as a young MP but now repudiated and wondered what he stood for. It was his misfortune that much of his political learning and many of his changes of mind on policy occurred while he was party leader. Apart from a brief spell as Michael Foot's parliamentary secretary, he never held any government post. In 1994 he resigned from the Commons and became a European Commissioner.

Kirov, Sergei Mironovich (b. Urzhum, 28 Mar. 1886; d. Leningrad, 1 Dec. 1934)
Russian; Leningrad Party Secretary 1925–34

Orphaned at an early age, Kirov was brought up by his grandmother. He won a scholarship to Kazan technical college, from where he graduated. As a student he became involved in the revolutionary movement, joining the Bolshevik Party. He was jailed for a year in 1906. Thereafter he served longer periods in prison, finding himself in Siberian exile when the February Revolution broke out in 1917. During the Civil War he was involved in party work in the Caucasus and from 1920 to 1921 was Bolshevik ambassador to the briefly independent government of Georgia. In 1922 he helped form the Transcaucasian Soviet Federated Socialist Republic, which was one of the first four republics to join the USSR. In 1921 he was elected as a candidate member of the Central Committee, becoming a full member in April 1923. He was made head of the Leningrad regional party committee in December 1925 with the task of purging the Party of *Zinoviev's supporters. As a reward, *Stalin made him a full member of the Politburo in July 1930. Kirov received a massive ovation for his speech to the 17th Party Congress in 1934 in which he criticized collectivization and 'extremism' in dealing with the peasants. He was elected to the secretariat and was to have moved to Moscow but was shot and mortally wounded by Leonid Nikolayev, a young

Communist who had penetrated the Leningrad party offices. Stalin used the murder as the pretext for a full-scale purge in Leningrad. His involvement in the murder remains unclear, though in 1956 *Khrushchev suggested that he had instigated it. In his memoirs *Mikoyan claimed that Stalin was relieved by Kirov's death, though he wept for him in public.

Kissinger, Henry A. (b. Fuerth, Germany, 27 May 1923)
US; National Security Adviser 1969–75, Secretary of State 1973–7

Of German Jewish origin, Kissinger's family fled from Nazi Germany to the United States in 1938. He served in the US armed forces 1943–5. After the war he took a BA and Ph.D. at Harvard University and taught Government at Harvard University. As director of the Harvard International Services and director of the Special Studies Project of the Rockefeller Brothers Fund he became acquainted with prominent political as well as academic figures. His book *Nuclear Weapons and Foreign Policy* (1957) won him wide acclaim as a conceptual strategic thinker. He became an adviser on foreign policy to Nelson *Rockefeller. After Richard *Nixon's election as President in 1968, he was appointed National Security Adviser. He provided the intellectual basis for the policy options which were chosen by President Nixon on the vital issues of foreign policy such as Vietnam, China, détente with the Soviet Union, and the Middle East. Following Nixon's re-election as President in 1972, he was appointed Secretary of State, though he continued to serve also as National Security Adviser until 1975. After Nixon's resignation in 1974 and the succession of President *Ford, he continued to be an extremely influential adviser to the President as Secretary of State, though Ford appointed a new National Security Adviser in 1975. After the end of his service as Secretary of State in 1977, he formed a private company, Kissinger Associates, which offered advice on international affairs and foreign investment.

He won acclaim for his intellectual acumen and the sophistication of his thinking. On the other hand, he was criticized as amoral in his approach. With regard to Vietnam, for example, his critics suggest that the extensive use of force by massive bombing of North Vietnam and the invasion of Cambodia was unjustified and futile. His defenders suggest, however, that this strategy brought success in his negotiations with his North Vietnamese counterpart, Le Duc Tho, which ended the war and won Kissinger a joint Nobel Peace Prize in 1973. His ideas on triangular US–Chinese–Soviet diplomacy and the drawing of the Soviet Union into the web of intentional affairs by means of détente similarly earned criticisms and praise. In the Middle East, where he acted as emissary between Israel and Arab countries after the Yom Kippur War in 1973, his critics suggested that he was concerned largely to protect American interests and exclude the Soviet Union, while his defenders praise his step-by-step approach in forwarding the peace process in the Middle East. He set out his views on international relations at considerable length in *White House Years* (1979), *Years of Upheaval* (1982), and *Diplomacy* (1994).

Klaus, Václav (b. Bohemia, 19 June 1941)
Czech; Czechoslovak Minister of Finance 1990–2, Czech premier 1992–

Klaus made a career in Prague's Institute of Economic Forecasting, an organization which became critical of the *Husák regime's failure to introduce economic reforms in the 1980s. When the 'Velvet Revolution' started in November 1989, Klaus joined the Czech opposition organization, Civic Forum (CF). At the beginning of 1990 he became Minister of Finance. With Vladimír Dlouhý, the Minister for Planning, he advocated economic shock therapy. He was opposed by President *Havel and by Valtr Komárek, the first Deputy Prime Minister who favoured a more moderate move towards the market. After the elections of June 1990 Klaus remained Minister of Finance, whereas Komárek left the government. On 1 January 1991 the government introduced a programme of economic shock therapy. In the spring of 1992 Klaus's reforms progressed further when thoroughgoing privatization measures were introduced.

During 1990, Civic Forum splintered into different political groups. The Interparliamentary Group of the Democratic Right backed Klaus's monetarist policies and ensured his election as leader of Civic Forum in October 1990. He stated that his aim was to transform CF into a party of the centre-right, which led to conflict with those who wanted it to remain an umbrella organization. In February 1991 CF split into a Civic Democratic Party (CDP) led by Klaus and a Civic Movement of social-democrat orientation. In June 1992 the CDP was the single largest party in the Czech National Council. Klaus became Czech premier.

The CDP's electoral success in the Czech Republic was paralleled by that of separatist groups led by Vladimír Mečiar in Slovakia. In the subsequent negotiations between the two republics, Klaus refused to yield to Slovak demands which he regarded as excessive and threatening to his economic reforms. No compromise was reached and on 1 January 1993 the Czechoslovak federation was dissolved.

Knowland, William Fife (b. Alameda, California, 26 June 1908; d. 23 Feb. 1974)
US; US Senator 1945–58

Knowland, whose father was a Congressman and part owner of the *Oakland Tribune*, grew up in California and in Washington, DC. He worked for the *Tribune* after graduating from Berkeley. In 1932 he was elected to the California state assembly and in 1934 to the state senate. Knowland became a member of the Republican National Committee in 1938 and was chairman of its executive committee in 1941. Drafted into the army, he returned when he was named to fill a California Senate vacancy created by the death of Hiram *Johnson in 1945. Knowland won re-election in his own right in 1946 and in 1952 he won re-election on both the Republican and the Democratic tickets.

In the Senate Knowland was a supporter of a bipartisan foreign policy and was among those Republicans who challenged Robert *Taft's leadership. He was made acting majority leader of the Senate in 1953 following Taft's illness. He served as Senate majority leader 1953–5 and as minority leader 1955–9. Knowland's period as leader of the GOP forces in the Senate was a difficult one. The party was faction-ridden and he had to work hard to keep it unified behind *Eisenhower. In the partisan struggle, Knowland was hardly the equal of Lyndon *Johnson and was generally criticized for his lack of legislative and political dexterity.

In 1958 Knowland retired from the Senate to run for Governor of California. However, he was beaten by Edward *Brown in a contest in which labour rights and the recession were key issues. Knowland then returned to Oakland and edited the *Tribune* after his father died in 1966. Knowland exercised a good deal of political influence through the press but he was also still involved in Republican politics. He headed the California campaign committee for *Goldwater in 1964 and endorsed *Reagan in 1968. Debts, partly incurred as a result of his second marriage, caused him to commit suicide in 1974.

Kohl, Helmut (b. Ludwigshafen, 3 Apr. 1930)
German; Chancellor of the Federal Republic of Germany 1982– , Minister-President of the Rhineland Palatinate 1969–76

Kohl is one of the most underestimated and most successful of German politicians since 1871. In length of service as Chancellor by 1996 he overtook *Adenauer's record of fourteen years. Yet after his failure to replace *Schmidt as Chancellor in the 1976 elections Kohl's career seemed finished.

Kohl always wanted to be a politician. In 1947 he founded the JU, the youth wing of the CDU, in his home town. His doctorate from Heidelberg University was in political science. In 1959 he was elected to the parliament of the Rhineland Palatinate as its youngest member. Backed by the other JU members he was elected deputy chairman of the CDU group in 1961 and chairman two years later. From 1969 to 1976 he served as Minister-President of the Rhineland Palatinate. Meanwhile he had been building himself up within the party. He joined the federal executive in 1966, was elected deputy chairman in 1969 and chairman in 1973. With the CDU/CSU being out of office in Bonn from 1969 onwards, the prime ministers of the regions (*Länder*) became more important within the party. The failure of Barzel to oust the *Brandt government in the 1972 election gave Kohl his chance.

The election of 1976 revealed some of Kohl's weaknesses. Clearly he was not a gifted public speaker. His lack of English was also a handicap in dealing with foreign correspondents. Schmidt could brief them in English. Kohl could not. Despite some difficulties, West Germany was doing well compared with its neighbours and the SPD could quote the foreign press to emphasize the point. But at that election Kohl did well in southern Germany, and Schmidt did not. The CDU/CSU once again overtook the SPD, increasing their percentage from 44.9 in 1972 to 48.6. The SPD percentage fell from 45.8 to 42.6. This improvement was not enough to oust Schmidt. The defection of the FDP from the Schmidt-led coalition was needed.

Kohl had good contacts within the FDP, especially with *Genscher. By 1980 Genscher himself was worried about the future of his small party given the growing unpopularity of the SPD-led government trying to cope with the oil crisis. However, the process of change was halted when the CDU/CSU picked *Strauss as their Chancellor candidate in 1980. Strauss was defeated and Schmidt stayed in office. The Munich conference of the SPD in April 1982 helped the FDP to decide that it was time for a change. The SPD had turned left on economic policy and defence and the FDP signalled its unhappiness with the government. Schmidt was provoked into asking for the resignations of the FDP ministers. Kohl was then elected Chancellor by the Bundestag on 1 October 1982. Yet he remained much less popular than ex-Chancellor Schmidt. Nevertheless, the elections held on 6 March 1983 vindicated the CDU/CSU. With 48.8 per cent they got their highest score since 1957; the SPD vote fell from 42.9 in 1980 to 38.2 per cent.

To the surprise of some, Kohl's government retained Genscher as Foreign Minister, ensuring continuity in external relations. This was also true of inter-German relations. In 1987 Kohl received *Honecker in Bonn and gave more emphasis to the principle of German reunification than the outgoing government had done. On domestic policy, the moderates dominated and Strauss was not offered a post. Kohl benefited from the continuing divisions in the SPD and by that party's failure to produce a successor worthy of Schmidt. Kohl did however get into difficulties from time to time especially when he spoke bluntly about East Germany or the Soviet Union.

In June 1989 Kohl suffered several setbacks. His party lost ground in the European elections suffering from the new far right Republican Party campaigning on an anti-immigration policy. In regional elections too the CDU did poorly. In the same month *Gorbachev visited West Germany. He was received with great enthusiasm and he too was more popular than Kohl. No one knew how rapidly Kohl's fortunes would change.

In summer 1989 the Communist leaders in Eastern Europe were losing their grip on power. In East Germany in October, Honecker was replaced by *Krenz, but the crisis got worse. After the East German frontiers were opened and hundreds of thousands poured out, Kohl made his first definitive statement on 28 November. In a ten-point programme he cautiously referred to the formation of 'confederative structures' involving the two German states. He was attacked inside and outside Germany for alleged nationalism and not consulting his allies. The truth was that East Germany was nearing collapse and neither Kohl nor anyone else could stop the revolution of expectations of the East German people. His plan helped to reduce panic. On 22 December Kohl and East German reform Communist leader *Modrow jointly opened the Brandenburg Gate in Berlin. In February 1990 Kohl proposed a currency union of the two German states. That month in the East crowds welcomed Kohl with the message, 'Helmut you are also our Chancellor'. Brandt and other Social Democrats supported the East German SPD, a new party, but the doubts expressed by *Lafontaine about reunification had done their work. The Alliance for Germany (mainly Christian Democrats) won a great victory on 18 March. Kohl showed remarkable skill in the negotiations leading up to the achievement of German unity on 3 October 1990.

Perhaps Kohl's greatest moment came in December 1990, when his party won the first elections to a democratic parliament of a united Germany since 1932. In the following years Kohl had to deal with the huge problems of East Germany, the massive help needed by the former Soviet Union, the Gulf War, to which Germany made a hefty financial contribution, the complicated negotiations over the widening and deepening of the EU, and the war in the former Yugoslavia. At home, he faced the political, economic, social, and security problems posed by the continuing influx of people seeking asylum in Germany. Kohl was attacked from all sides and it was no mean achievement for him to get re-elected in October 1994.

Under Kohl, Germany was the driving force for the expansion and greater integration of the European Union, and he was prepared to involve Germany in an emerging Europe federation.

Kolchak, Aleksandr Vasilievich (b. Crimea, 17 Nov. 1870; d. Irkutsk, 7 Feb. 1920)
Russian; Leader of the White forces in Siberia 1918–20

Kolchak was born of Tartar descent. He distinguished himself in the defence of Port Arthur (now Dairen) during the Russo -Japanese War of 1904–5. Thereafter he was involved in the reform of the Russian fleet. In 1916 he was made Vice-Admiral with command of the Black Sea Fleet. Following the October Revolution he was Minister of War in an anti-Bolshevik 'All Russian Government' set up at Omsk in western Siberia. Initially he was successful in fighting the Red Army along the Trans-Siberian Railway. In December 1918 he disbanded the Ufa Directory, a rival anti-Bolshevik government. After November 1918 he styled himself 'Supreme Ruler' of Russia, though he acknowledged *Denikin as overall leader of the White armies. Kolchak failed to win the support of the local population, of the strong Czech Legion or, finally, of his own men. At the end of 1919 his forces collapsed before the Bolshevik offensive which took Omsk. He was overthrown in December 1919. In February 1920 he was betrayed to the Bolsheviks and shot at Irkutsk.

Kosygin, Alexei Nikolaevich (b. St Petersburg 8 (21) Feb. 1904; d. Moscow, 18 Dec. 1980)
Russian; Politbureau member 1948–53, 1957–80, chair of Council of Ministers 1964–80

After serving in the Red Army in the Civil War Kosygin was trained as a textile worker in Leningrad. Benefiting from the rapid promotion associated with the Purges he soon became a textile factory manager and in 1938 chair of the Leningrad City Soviet. In 1939 he was made People's Commissar for the Textile Industry. He played an important part in the organization of Leningrad's war economy during the blockade. In 1946 he became a Deputy Chair of the Council of Ministers and was briefly Minister of Finance in 1948. He narrowly escaped being purged along with the other Leningrad Zhdanovites, but survived to be promoted to the Politbureau in 1948 and made Minister of Light Industry in 1949.

After *Stalin's death he was demoted, having an uneasy relationship with

*Khrushchev, and only in 1957 regained membership of the Politbureau and became deputy chair of the Council of Ministers.

When *Brezhnev replaced Khrushchev as party leader Kosygin was made chair of the Council of Ministers, a post he held for sixteen years till he resigned from ill-health in 1980. Initially he wielded considerable authority, especially in economic matters. In 1965 he introduced an economic reform package designed to promote greater efficiency. Profit was to be a key performance indicator; plan targets were to be expressed in terms of goods actually sold; managers were given greater leeway in using profits; bonuses would raise motivation. But the price system was not reformed and enterprise autonomy proved illusory, so the profit motive could not function. The reforms were in difficulties even before the 'Prague Spring' of 1968 made conservatives fear the link between market-orientated reform and political liberalization. Kosygin's influence rapidly declined in the early 1970s after the failure of his reforms.

Kozyrev, Andrei Vladimirovich (b. Brussels, 27 Mar. 1951)

Russian; Foreign Minister of the Russian Republic 1990–1, Foreign Minister of the Russian Federation 1991–6

The son of a diplomat and born in Brussels, Kozyrev was educated at Moscow State Institute for International Relations, graduating as a Candidate of Historical Sciences. He then joined the Ministry of Foreign Affairs, rising to become its head of the Direction of International Organizations in 1989–90, when he laid the groundwork for the development of Russian diplomacy. In October 1990 he became Russian Foreign Minister and remained in that post when the Russian Federation became independent at the end of 1991. His command of foreign languages (English, Spanish, and Portuguese), diplomatic experience, and loyalty to Yeltsin made him indispensable in the early years. Often criticized by the opposition as a 'liberal' member of Yeltsin's team, he became distinctly more 'Eurasian' after the parliamentary crisis of October 1993, insisting on Russia's prominent role in world affairs, especially in Europe, and in 1995 warning of the possible use of force 'to defend our compatriots abroad'. Regarded as a grey figure and too flexible to have credibility, he was replaced in January 1996 by Primakov after winning a seat in the December 1995 parliamentary elections.

Kreisky, Bruno (b. Vienna, 22 Jan. 1911; d. 29 July 1980)

Austrian; Chancellor of Austria 1970–83

Kreisky was the talented son of a well-to-do Jewish family. A student of law and economics at Vienna University he joined the Socialist Party and was imprisoned for his political activities in 1935. As the Nazis took over Austria in 1938 he managed to escape to Sweden, spent the war years in Britain, and returned to Austria in 1945. He served in the Foreign Ministry (1946–51) and then in the Prime Minister's office (1951–3). Increasingly recognized in the Socialist Party he became Foreign Minister (1959–66) and then Chancellor in 1970, heading Austria's first all-Socialist post-war administration. At home he modernized his party and further extended the welfare state and social partnership with the unions and management. Austria became highly successful economically under his administration, its prestige rose, and Vienna became an international centre of diplomacy. He suffered a setback in 1978, when his government's nuclear energy policy was rejected in a referendum. An election was called shortly afterwards and his party increased its lead, and established a record of winning an absolute majority at three consecutive elections. In 1979 Kreisky broke new ground by inviting the PLO leader Yasser *Arafat to Vienna. He resigned in 1983 not wishing to head a coalition government after his party had lost ground in the elections, although it remained in office.

Krenz, Egon (b. Kolberg, 19 Mar. 1937)
German; General Secretary of the SED, head of state Oct.–Dec. 1989

Krenz was the illegitimate son of a tailor whom he never knew. A refugee from the lost territories, he later found both a home and a father in the GDR and its ruling Socialist Unity Party (SED). Backed by *Honecker he climbed the ladder of the Free German Youth (FDJ), becoming its First Secretary in 1974. On the way he had trained as a teacher and took a course at the CPSU university in Moscow, 1964–7. In May 1976 he was awarded candidate status in the Politburo of the SED. In 1983 his FDJ work ended and he was 'elected' as one of the key secretaries of the Central Committee, at the same time becoming a full member of its Politburo. Trusted by the Soviets, he was seen as the 'crown prince'; his SED function was responsibility for security. The youngest member of the Politburo, his future looked assured, but he saw the increasing dangers from the rising tide of discontent and from Honecker's estrangement from the CPSU under *Gorbachev after 1985. By the time he led the coup against Honecker on 18 October 1989, it was too late. Demonstrations were taking place throughout the GDR. He made matters worse by taking over, like Honecker, as head of state as well as SED chief. This disillusioned some potential supporters. He was forced to resign on 3 December and later expelled from the party and arrested. He was credited with avoiding violence and opening the Berlin Wall.

Kryuchkov, Vladimir Aleksandrovich (b. Volgograd, 29 Feb. 1924)
Russian; Chairman of the KGB 1988–91

Kryuchkov was born into a working-class family. He was a factory worker from 1941 to 1944, having left school early because of the war. In 1944 he joined the Communist Party and held a number of low-level party posts in Stalingrad. He trained as a lawyer by correspondence and graduated in 1949. In 1954 he joined the Soviet Embassy in Hungary working under *Andropov. From 1959 to 1967 he continued to work under Andropov in the apparatus of the Central Committee in Moscow. When Andropov became chairman of the KGB in 1967, Kryuchkov went with him. He served successively as Chief of Secretariat, First Deputy Head, and Head of the First Chief Directorate (responsible for foreign intelligence). In 1985 he supported *Gorbachev's succession. Kryuchkov adapted himself to the language of Gorbachev's 'New Foreign Policy' and mounted a KGB publicity campaign which fitted the requirements of glasnost. In 1988 he became a full member of the Central Committee. On 1 October 1988 he replaced *Chebrikov as chairman of the KGB. In September 1989 he became a full member of the Politburo. Kryuchkov was opposed to the dismantling of the Soviet Union and was one of the main organizers of the unsuccessful coup of August 1991. He was arrested but acquitted.

Kun, Béla (b. Szilagyczeh, Transylvania, 20 Feb. 1886; d. Soviet Union, Aug. 1938)
Hungarian; Communist dictator 1919

Kun was born into a middle-class Jewish family in Austria-Hungary. Before the First World War he worked as a journalist and joined the Social Democrats. He fought in the Austro-Hungarian Army from 1914 to 1916, when he was captured by the Russians. He joined the Bolshevik Party after the October Revolution of 1917, came to Lenin's notice, and was specially trained in revolutionary technique. He returned to Hungary after the war and founded the Hungary Communist Party (HCP) on 20 December 1918. In March 1919 Kun brought about the fall of the liberal provisional government of Count Mihály Károlyi and came to power with the help of the Social Democrats, who joined the Communists in a coalition. The new government was dominated by the Communists, even though the HCP had only 7,000 members at the beginning of 1919. They set up a Bolshevik-style dictatorship based on their secret police. Kun formed a Red Army which regained from Romania and Czechoslovakia most of the territory which Hungary lost in the First World War. However, the Kun regime was generally loathed in Hungary because of its brutality and its policies of collectivization of agriculture and nationalization of industry. After only four and a half months in power, Kun's regime was swept away by the Romanians and the counter-revolutionary forces of *Horthy. In August 1919 Kun fled to Vienna then Moscow.

In 1921 Kun was appointed to the Executive Committee of the Comintern. In 1938 he was arrested by the NKVD, charged with 'Trotskyism', and shot in August. He was formally rehabilitated in 1958.

La Follette, Robert Marion (Jr.) (b. 6 Feb. 1895; d. 24 Feb. 1953)

US; US Senator 1925–46

Robert La Follette Jr. was the son of 'Battling Bob' La Follette, who made Wisconsin synonymous with Progressive politics and whose independent bid for the presidency in 1924 gained him one-sixth of the total vote. Robert Jr. spent his early years acting as his father's secretary in the Senate and when his father died in 1925 Robert Jr. was appointed to fill the unexpired portion of Robert Sr.'s Senate term. Thereafter he was re-elected three times in his own right: as a Republican in 1928 and as a Progressive in 1934 and 1940.

Robert La Follette Jr. devoted much energy in the 1930s to civil liberties and labour issues. As chairman of the Senate Civil Liberties Committee he examined working conditions and especially the freedom of labour to organize across the United States. He was an advocate of farm relief and reform of the tax system. He was also a supporter of streamlining procedure inside the Senate and sponsored a major reorganization of the Senate which only took effect after he had left the legislature. On foreign policy La Follette's opposition to war put him in the broad isolationist tent in the 1930s.

In 1946 La Follette tried to run as a Republican but he lost the primary to Joseph *McCarthy and after leaving the Senate he pursued a career in business in Washington. His defeat, together with health worries, contributed to depression and he committed suicide in February 1953.

Lafontaine, Oskar (b. Saarlouis, 16 Sept. 1943)

German; Minister-President of the Saar 1985– , chief mayor of Saarbrücken 1976–85, deputy chairman of the SPD 1987–

It is remarkable that Lafontaine joined the SPD, given his Catholic, CDU-orientated background and the influence of a Nazi class teacher whom he greatly admired. Lafontaine's father was a baker who, as an NCO, was killed in the war. His mother, a secretary, made great sacrifices to send her twin sons to a Catholic classics-orientated boarding school. However, with a bursary from a Catholic charity, Lafontaine studied physics, chemistry, and maths in Bonn and Saarbrücken.

Lafontaine followed his twin brother when he joined the SPD in 1966. Three years later he was elected to the Saabrücken city council, serving as mayor, 1974–6, and chief mayor, 1976–85. From 1970 to 1975 he was a member of the Saar Landtag (regional parliament). Lafontaine made his way in the SPD as a left-winger strongly opposed to nuclear arms and nuclear energy. He was elected Chairman of the Saar SPD in 1977 and to the SPD's federal executive in 1979. Since 1985 he has been Minister-President of the Saar and since 1987 Deputy Chairman of the SPD. His caution over German reunification provoked angry debates in the SPD leadership.

Lafontaine led the SPD to a defeat in the first democratic elections in East Germany (March 1990), and the first democratic election (December 1990) throughout Germany since 1932. In the case of the March election the early indications were that the SPD was ahead in the polls. Intervening from West Germany, Lafontaine urged caution about German reunification and stressed the economic difficulties and the cost. The East Germans were disappointed and they deserted the new SPD for the ex-Communist satellite CDU which *Kohl supported.

La Guardia, Fiorello (b. New York City, 11 Dec. 1882; d. 20 Sept. 1947)
US; mayor New York 1934–45

La Guardia was born in New York and brought up in Arizona. In his early twenties he spent time in Hungary with his mother and relatives. He returned to New York, graduated in law from New York University and practised. Law led to politics. At his second attempt, he was elected as a Republican to the House of Representatives in 1916. After serving for a few months in 1917 he absented himself to enlist in the war effort. He had promised the voters that if he voted for the war he would enlist. The House kept his seat vacant. He had a good war record, was re-elected, but resigned at the end of 1919 to concentrate on his duties as president of the New York Board of Alderman. He was elected to Congress again in 1923 and served until 1933. He was always an independent outspoken politician, on the Progressive wing of the Republican Party. He supported Woodrow *Wilson in the declaration of war, advocated social welfare reform, and opposed prohibition. In 1924 he supported the Progressive *La Follette for President. Over the year he was elected to Congress successfully as a Republican, independent, and Progressive Republican. His independence made him a national figure. He was the author of the *Norris–La Guardia Act (1932) which outlawed contracts seeking to deny workers the right to belong to trade unions and allowed workers to picket peacefully and strike, except in those services and industries which were essential for public safety. He was defeated in the democratic landslide in the 1932 elections.

In 1929 he ran unsuccessfully as a 'Fusion' party candidate for mayor of New York city. In 1934 he ran again, standing on behalf of a coalition of reformist groups and parties, and won. He served until 1945, being elected three times in all. This was remarkable in a Democratic state and at a time of Democratic electoral ascendency. He was a vigorous supporter of President F. D. *Roosevelt and the New Deal. In turn, Roosevelt intervened to help him by splitting the Democratic vote in the 1934 elections. La Guardia saw many of the policies which he favoured come to fruition in the New Deal. He was a great reforming mayor, presiding over civic improvements, slum clearance, a reduction in corruption, and the balancing of the city budget. La Guardia was a dynamic politician, a visionary with a gift for practical application, and is one of the country's great non-partisan reforming mayors. In 1946 he was director-general of the United Nations Relief and Rehabilitation.

Lamont, Norman (b. Lerwick, Shetland, 8 May 1942)
British; Chancellor of the Exchequer 1990–3

Norman Lamont was educated at Cambridge, becoming president of the Union in 1964. After university he worked for a time in the Conservative Research Department, the nursery of many Conservative ministers, and then as a merchant banker. He gained the Kingston-upon-Thames seat at a by-election in 1972.

He occupied a number of junior posts in the 1979 administration. His expertise was on economic matters and after a spell as Financial Secretary to the Treasury he became Chief Secretary to the Treasury, with a seat in the Cabinet in 1989. This post gave him the opportunity to negotiate spending levels with Whitehall departments. More significant for his future political career was that the Chancellor of the Exchequer, his senior minister, was John *Major. One of Major's last actions as Chancellor was to take Britain into the ERM of the European Monetary System in October 1990.

When Margaret *Thatcher resigned from the Conservative leadership in November 1990, Norman Lamont became campaign manager for John Major. When the latter became Prime Minister he appointed Lamont as Chancellor; the appointment was widely seen as a reward for campaign services. Lamont's misfortune was that Britain had entered the ERM at a rate which could not be sustained without damaging the economy. Membership prolonged the recession and added to unemployment. As Chancellor he defended entry and warned of economic disasters if Britain left.

When Britain was forced out of the ERM in September 1992, it was inevitable that Lamont—and to a lesser extent other ministers—was blamed. He remained in government but was increasingly marginalized and was an unhappy figure. Neither he nor the government admitted that the original policy had been a mistake, although the economy steadily recovered. Indeed he claimed that he was 'singing in his bath' when Britain left the ERM.

In a government reshuffle in May 1993 he was offered an alternative post, which he declined. He left the government and was an increasingly bitter critic of John Major and the government's European policy, calling for British withdrawal. He felt that he had been made a scapegoat and not received credit as economic benefits came on stream. He was a possible challenger for John Major for the leadership in July 1995, but supported John Redwood.

Lamont was an innovative Chancellor. He introduced unified budgets, appointed the panel of so-called wise men who gave advice to the Chancellor, and in 1992 abolished the National European Development Council.

Landon, Alfred (b. West Middlesex, Pennsylvania, 9 Sept. 1887; d. 12 Oct. 1987)
US; Governor of Kansas 1933–7

Landon was brought up in Ohio and moved with his family to Independence, Kansas, when he was 17. His father was an oil prospector and oil was the reason for the move to Kansas. Landon read law at the state university but decided to follow his father into the oil industry and made himself wealthy. In politics he was a progressive Republican and became chairman of the state. In 1932 he was elected Governor, a year of a Democratic landslide and was the only incumbent Republican Governor to be re-elected in 1934. As Governor, he cut state spending and managed to balance the budget. He easily won the party's nomination to fight the 1936 presidential election. He accepted many of the aims of *Roosevelt's New Deal but objected that it was hostile to business and involved too much waste. At the end of the campaign he accused Roosevelt of acquiring so much power that he was subverting the constitution. The election was humiliation for Landon. He carried only Maine and Vermont and lost the popular vote by 67 per cent to 37 per cent. After his term of office as Governor ended, he retired from politics.

Landsbergis, Vytautas (b. Kaunas, 18 Oct. 1932)
Lithuanian; President 1990–2

Landsbergis was born in the still-independent Lithuanian state into a middle-class, intellectual family. He studied music at the Vilnius Conservatorium, where he followed an academic career, rising to become professor. In 1988 he was a founder of Sajudis, the Lithuanian popular front organization, which pressed for independence. In 1989 Landsbergis was elected to the Soviet Congress of People's Deputies. On 15 January 1990 Landsbergis was elected President of the Soviet Republic of Lithuania, defeating the Communist candidate, Algirdas Brazauskas. The next month, the nationalists won two-thirds of the seats in the Lithuanian Supreme Soviet. On 11 March 1990 the Lithuanian Supreme Soviet voted to secede from the USSR.

Landsbergis was unable to maintain the unity of Sajudis, which split over the course of 1990. By the end of 1991, its popularity had considerably decreased as the result of economic crisis. In the parliamentary elections of February 1992 the Lithuanian Democratic Labour Party, as the reformed Communists were known, won a majority of seats. Its leader, Brazauskas, replaced Landsbergis as President.

Lang, Jack Mathieu Émile (b. Miracourt, 2 Sept. 1939)
French; Arts Minister 1981–84, 1988–91

The son of an industrialist, Lang was educated at the Lycée Poincaré in Nancy and the Law Faculty in Nancy as well as at the élite IEP in Paris. He was a professor of law and a dean of the Nancy Law Faculty. He also founded the International Festival of Student Theatre and was made head of the National Theatre of Chaillot (a controversial tenure until he was fired in 1974). His political career started under *Mendès France but he joined the new Socialist Party in 1972 and began a rapid rise. He ran the 1979 European elections for the party and was a long-serving Minister of Culture—a high-profile minister and a zealous defender of President *Mitterrand. As minister he gave the arts a much needed strategy. He also started by attacking American cultural imperialism (he preferred *Castro, he said) but ended by enticing Disneyland to Paris and by presenting the *médaille de la chevalier* to Sylvester Stallone in 1990: 'one culture does not threaten another', he said. He left office a popular figure, especially with the young, and was proposed for the presidency as Socialist candidate in 1995 (but withdrew). His subsequent place within *Jospin's PS was marginal.

Lange, David Russell (b. Otahuhu, North Island, 4 Aug. 1942)
New Zealand; Leader of the New Zealand Labour Party 1983–9, Prime Minister 1984–9

Lange's father was a medical specialist and his mother a nurse. He was educated at Otahuhu College and Auckland University and practised law. In a by-election in 1977 he entered parliament as the Labour member for Mangere. He became deputy leader of the Opposition in 1979 and leader of the Opposition in 1983.

Lange became Prime Minister in 1984 after the defeat of the National Party led by Robert *Muldoon in the general elections. His government was marked by major shifts in both foreign and domestic policies. In July 1984 the New Zealand government, with strong public support, announced that ships carrying nuclear weapons would not be allowed into New Zealand ports. This was a direct challenge to the United States, who declared that it would be difficult to see how the ANZUS treaty could survive if United Ships could not count on New Zealand as a friendly port. Australia was the third party to the treaty and in March 1985 its Prime Minister Bob *Hawke, declared the treaty to be inoperative.

On the domestic scene, with Roger Douglas as Minister for Finance, the new Labour government adopted economic policies more closely identified with the conservatism of Britain's Margaret *Thatcher. The financial market was speedily deregulated. The New Zealand dollar was allowed to float in 1985. All controls on foreign exchange transactions were removed. New banks were allowed. A Goods and Services Tax of 10 per cent later raised to 12.5 per cent was introduced. Agricultural subsidies, consumer subsidies on electricity, export incentives, and import licences were phased out. Forestry, Lands, Coal, and Electricity were turned into commercial state corporations and told to make a profit.

After the 1987 election disagreement between Lange and Roger Douglas weakened Lange's position. The majority of Caucus supported Lange but the majority of Cabinet supported Douglas. In a package of economic reforms Douglas announced a 'flat' tax on 23 per cent instead of the graduated tax on all incomes. Lange unilaterally cancelled this package early in 1988. Douglas was sacked after describing Lange as 'acting irrationally' in August 1989. The Labour Caucus voted to replace the sacked minister and Prime Minister Lange promptly resigned. Sales of state assets went ahead almost as planned.

Lange has acknowledged that the Roger Douglas episodes were the greatest failings of his leadership and believes that he should have accepted Douglas's resignation when it was offered on a number of occasions. Associates considered that Lange failed to achieve the level of 'detachment' the office of Prime Minister requires. Lange liked people, and liked to be liked, which was a problem when a decision required that he go straight down the middle.

Lansbury, George (b. Norfolk, 21 Feb. 1859; d. 7 May 1940)
British; First Commissioner of Works 1929–31, leader of the Labour Party 1931–5

The son of a railway subcontractor, Lansbury received only elementary education before beginning work as a manual labourer. Initially a Liberal, he became a Christian Socialist and joined the Social Democratic Federation, which later affiliated to the Labour Party. Thereafter, Christianity was the core of his approach to politics.

After numerous unsuccessful candidatures Lansbury was eventually elected for Bow and Bromley in 1910. But he resigned his seat in 1912, in protest at the imprisonment of suffragettes. In 1913 he was imprisoned after a speech at a suffrage meeting. Out of parliament (until 1922) he was active in local government in Poplar (London) and was again imprisoned, for 'Poplarism'—refusing to collect local rates from the unemployed. He also co-founded in 1912, and edited, the *Daily Herald* (later the Labour movement's official newspaper).

Lansbury held office in the second Labour government (1929–31), in the unprestigious (though Cabinet) post of First Commissioner of Works. His most enduring achievement was the creation of the Lido in Hyde Park. After the disastrous 1931 general election, Lansbury was the sole member of the previous Cabinet in the forty-six-strong Parliamentary Labour Party and became its leader. The inevitable arduousness of the task was exacerbated by criticism from former senior ministers on the party's National Executive Committee. *Hitler's accession to power made the divergence between Lansbury's Christian pacifism and the party's official support for the League of Nations (and sanctions) increasingly pronounced. He resigned after vociferous criticism of his leadership at the Annual Conference in 1935 and subsequently had little influence on party policy although he remained in parliament until his death.

Lansing, Robert (b. Watertown, New York, 17 Oct. 1864; d. 30 Oct. 1928)
US; Secretary of State 1915–20

The son of a lawyer and banker, Lansing graduated BA from Amherst College in 1886. Thereafter he read law in his father's office, was called to the bar in 1889, and that same year joined his father's practice. Specializing in international law, he acted as counsel for the Chinese and Mexican legations in Washington, DC, 1894–5 and 1900–1; counsel for the US Bering Sea Claims Commission 1896–7; and counsel for the USA at the Alaskan Boundary Tribunal 1903. He was a founder member of the American Society for International Law in 1906 and in 1907 he established the *American Journal of International Law*, which he continued to edit until his death.

In 1902 Lansing made an unsuccessful bid to enter the political arena when he stood as Democratic candidate for mayor of Watertown. Although elective office eluded him he entered the public service as a counsellor for the State Department 1914–15, a role which enabled him to serve as acting Secretary of State during the absences of Secretary *Bryan, and eventually to become Secretary of State in 1915 after Bryan's resignation. In 1920, amid controversy, he left office himself in response to a request from *Wilson that he resign. The President accused Lansing of having usurped his authority by calling Cabinet meetings during the President's illness. After his resignation, Lansing returned to practising international law.

Laurier, Sir Wilfrid (b. Montreal, Quebec, 20 Nov. 1841; d. Ottawa, 17 Feb. 1919)
Canadian; Prime Minister 1896–1911

Laurier was a successful lawyer before he turned to politics. He entered the Canadian

Parliament in 1874 and, as the most prominent Liberal in Quebec, quickly became the nationally recognized leader of the party's Quebec wing. He was made Minister of Inland Revenue in 1878 in a Liberal Cabinet. Defeat in the 1878 election kept the party out of government for the next eighteen years. In 1887 Laurier was elected party leader and held the post for the next thirty-six years. When he became Prime Minister in 1896, he was the first French-Canadian and first Roman Catholic to hold the office. His government resisted pressure from Joseph *Chamberlain for Canada to join a common defence scheme covering the British Empire. Britain's involvement in the Boer War against South Africa was not popular in Canada, and strongly opposed in Quebec. Laurier's confidence in dissolving parliament in 1911 proved to be misplaced. A trade agreement with the United States that year provoked fears among many British Canadians that links with the mother country would be sacrificed in the quest for closer ties with the USA. He supported Canadian participation on the British side in the First World War, but opposed conscription. This issue split the party in 1915, as some Liberal ministers joined the coalition government. In 1917 Laurier was invited to join the coalition, which was introducing conscription. Sensitive to Quebec opposition to the measure he refused. In a pro-British atmosphere the Liberals were heavily defeated in the 1917 elections, doing particularly badly in English-speaking Canada.

Laurier did much to change the Liberal Party. In the late nineteenth century it suffered electorally from being seen as more anti-British than the Conservatives. He also had a formidable election record, winning in 1896, 1900, 1904, and 1908 and his governments presided over important economic developments and fostered a sense of national unity.

Laval, Pierre (b. Châteldon, 28 June 1883; d. 15 Oct. 1945)
French; Prime Minister 1930, 1935, head of government of the French state 1940, 1942–4

Pierre Laval was a classic example of the poor boy who makes good and turns bad. Born in the small town of Châteldon (Puy-de-Dôme), the son of a barkeeper, he was a brilliant schoolboy and managed by hard work to obtain a law degree. Like many of his kind, he decided to make his fortune as a lawyer in Paris and built up a reputation defending radical trade unionists who had fallen foul of the police authorities. His early political sympathies were with the Socialist Party of *Jaurès and he became in rapid succession deputy and mayor of the working-class suburb of Aubervilliers, north of Paris. After the First World War, he began a journey away from the left which led him to swap his parliamentary seat for the more conservative Orne, to start representing companies rather than trade unionists, to build up a business empire based on provincial newspapers, and to buy the château in his home town. He held a number of ministerial portfolios in the late 1920s and in 1930 was briefly Prime Minister. His political skills, like those of his mentor *Briand, were those of the negotiator and manipulator and he prided himself on what he regarded as his peasant cunning. By the mid-1930s, however, when he became Prime Minister for the second time he was clearly identified with deflation at home (public sector pay cuts) and appeasement abroad (the *Hoare–Laval pact of 1935). Neither of these policies was likely to appeal to the left-wing coalition which won the Popular Front elections in 1936. Laval's resentment at exclusion from office fuelled a hostility to the Republican parties which had caused it that would become obvious in 1940. Yet it was foreign policy which proved to be decisive in his political evolution. A committed supporter of appeasement, he nurtured the dream of an alliance with *Mussolini's Italy and was openly critical of the decision to go to war with Germany. He participated in all the parliamentary intrigues designed to end the war in the winter of 1939–40.

Laval played no part in the events which led *Pétain to seek an armistice with *Hitler in June 1940. Once Pétain's intention to proceed to a constitutional revolution became clear, however, he rushed to Vichy to be at his side and his political skills played a decisive role in the French Parliament's decision to vote itself out of existence. When Pétain appointed himself head of the French state, Laval became his Prime Minister. He plunged into the task of establishing good relations with the Nazi Occupier and pledged himself to a policy of collaboration, Laval was indifferent to the reactionary fantasies of the ideologues of the État Français; they, like Pétain, regarded him with a mixture of contempt and fear. In December 1940 he was sacked and briefly detained in a coup organized by Pétain's inner court. His career was saved by the correct belief of the Germans that he was the best defender of the cause of collaboration. Relations with Pétain were patched up and by 1942 he was back in office as the official number two of the regime. It was now that he committed the acts which would eventually destroy him. Convinced both of his indispensability and of the necessity for ever closer collaboration, he co-operated with the Germans in the deportation of the Jews and introduced the hated system of industrial conscription which sent thousands of French workers to German factories in return for a small number of prisoners of war. His government introduced ever more repressive measures against members of the Resistance and underwrote the terror campaign carried out by Joseph Darnand. As the last remnants of Vichy's authority crumbled in the face of the liberating armies, Laval strove to protect his future (it is amazing he thought he had one) by unsuccessfully trying to persuade the president of the Chamber of Deputies, *Herriot, to recall the National Assembly which had been dissolved in 1940. Deported with the rest of the Vichy crew to Germany, he refused, like Pétain, to take any part in the fantasy 'governments of national liberation' set up by the Nazis. At the end of the war, he managed to flee to *Franco's Spain, where he sought exile. Franco, however, handed him over to the French authorities who put him on trial for treason. At his and Pétain's trial, he tried to argue that collaboration had been designed to protect French soil and French lives. After a trial which brought no credit on the French judicial system, he was found guilty of treason and condemned to death. On the day of his execution, he tried to commit suicide by poison, was brought back to life by the prison guards, taken out, and shot. He was still wearing the tricolour sash which was the symbol of his office of mayor of Aubervilliers.

Laval remains to this day an outcast figure in France and no serious attempts have been made to rehabilitate him. His unattractive personal appearance and politican's cunning made him a convenient scapegoat, after his execution, for the error of others. Yet if he cannot be regarded as Vichy's evil genius, his responsibility for some of the worst cruelties of the Occupation, and his enthusiasm for a German victory, are beyond question. A belief that Nazi Germany was the only way to prevent the Bolshevization of France is one part of the answer, sheer lust for office another. But perhaps the principal motivation was his belief that he alone could strike a deal with Hitler. Laval prided himself on his realism and on his peasant's ability to negotiate a good bargain. It was a misplaced pride and one which cost him, and France, very dear.

Law, Andrew **Bonar** (b. New Brunswick, Canada, 16 Sept. 1858; d. 30 Oct. 1923)

Canadian; leader of Conservative Party in the House of Commons 1911–21, Chancellor of Exchequer 1916–19, Prime Minister 1922–23

The son of an Ulster-born Presbyterian minister, Law was educated in New Brunswick and then, after moving with an aunt to Scotland, at Glasgow High School. He made his money as an iron merchant in Glasgow before entering the House of Commons in 1900 as Conservative MP for Glasgow Blackfriars. His business knowledge was used to good effect in his speeches and within eighteen months he was appointed parliamentary secretary to the Board of Trade, serving until the resignation of *Balfour's government in 1905. An effective speaker, addressing meetings without notes, he was a vigorous advocate of tariff reform and became a leading figure in the parliamentary party in Opposition. In 1911, he merged as a compromise candidate for the party leadership in the House of Commons when it looked as if the party might have to vote to choose between Austen *Chamberlain and Walter Long. As party leader, Bonar Law led the party in resisting the Home Rule Bill for Ireland, announcing virtually unconditional support for Ulster Protestant resistance to Home Rule. After the outbreak of war, he joined *Asquith's coalition as Secretary of State for the Colonies. The following year, with *Lloyd George, he engineered Asquith's resignation, resulting in a Conservative-dominated coalition with Law as Chancellor of the Exchequer. Law and Lloyd George worked closely together, almost as joint Prime Ministers, meeting together every morning in Law's office. Law also served as Leader of the House, often spending long hours in the House and making sure he knew its temper. In 1919, he gave up the burden of being Chancellor, taking the title of Lord Privy Seal, but remaining leader of the House and, in effect, Deputy Prime Minister. In 1921, feeling unwell and after consulting his doctor, he resigned from government.

Out of government, Law began to worry about the direction the government was taking and sent out warning signals, including a letter to *The Times*. When a meeting of Conservative MPs was called in October 1922 to discuss the future of the coalition, he decided to attend. His short speech against continuing the coalition sealed its fate. Lloyd George resigned and Law was summoned by the King to form a government. With many of the leading figures in the party unwilling to serve, he formed a Cabinet derided by Winston *Churchill as the 'second eleven'. Law served for only seven months in the office. Gravely ill (he had cancer of the throat, though he was never told this), he resigned on 20 May 1923. He had been Prime Minister for 209 days. He died five months later.

Law had an unusual background for a leader of the Conservative Party. He was a powerful figure whose life was marked by tragedy (his wife died in 1909 and his two eldest sons were killed in the war), leaving him prone to the dark melancholy that afflicted his father. Popular with MPs, he left little mark beyond his period of office, Robert Blacked entitling his biography of him *The Unknown Prime Minister*.

Lawson, Nigel (b. London, 11 Mar. 1932)

British; Chancellor of the Exchequer 1983–89; Baron (life peer) 1992

Educated at Westminster and Christ Church, Oxford, where he took a first in PPE, Lawson had a distinguished career as a journalist before entering parliament. After ten years as a financial journalist and a year spent as a speech writer to Prime Minister Sir Alec *Douglas-Home (1963–4), he was appointed editor of the *Spectator* in 1966, a post he held for four years. In 1970 he stood unsuccessfully as Conservative candidate for Eton and Slough. He entered parliament in February 1974, shortly before his 42nd birthday, as MP for the safe seat of Blaby in Leicestershire. Within two years he had been appointed an Opposition whip and in 1977 was made a spokesman on Treasury affairs. A neo-liberal, he was appointed Financial Secretary to the Treasury when the party was returned to office in 1979. In 1981 he entered the Cabinet as Energy Secretary and in 1983 he began a six-year stint as Chancellor of the Exchequer. He set about simplifying the tax system and reducing the level of direct taxation, actions that made him popular with both the party and the Prime Minister. Though he shared Margaret *Thatcher's economic philosophy, he opposed the introduction of the poll tax and, with the Foreign Secretary, Sir Geoffrey *Howe, pushed the Prime Minister to join the Exchange Rate Mechanism. The Prime Minister's increasing reliance on the advice of her economic adviser Sir Alan Walters resulted in Lawson demanding Walters's departure. When this was refused, he resigned, creating a short period of intense political difficulty for the Prime Minister.

After leaving government, Lawson accepted a directorship of Barclays Bank and wrote a massive volume of memoirs, *The View from Number 11* (1992), providing a fascinating insight into economic policy-making. Though widely recognized—including by Margaret Thatcher—as being intellectually brilliant, he also had a reputation for intellectual arrogance. He was not a clubbable politician and the consequences of his expansionary 1988 budget reduced his support on the back benches. He left the House of Commons in 1992, taking a life peerage as Lord Lawson of Blaby.

Lebrun, Albert (b. 29 Aug. 1871; d. 6 Mar. 1950)
French; President of the Third Republic 1932–40

Albert Lebrun came from a peasant family in eastern France and was educated in Paris at the prestigious École Polytechnique. He was elected to the Chamber of Deputies as a conservative Republican in 1900, held a number of middle-rank ministerial posts before and during the First World War, and in 1920 entered the Senate, whose president he became in 1931. The Senate presidency was a traditional stepping stone to the presidency of the Republic. When President Doumer was assassinated by a Russian anarchist in 1932, Lebrun felt obliged to offer himself as successor and was duly elected by a huge majority of the National Assembly. A conscientious attender of official functions, he lacked personal charisma (his propensity to weep in public made him an easy target for satirists) and made no attempt to challenge the prevailing Republican orthodoxy which prevented the President from asserting an independent political authority. Thus in 1936 he overcame his aversion to the victory of the left-wing Popular Front and dutifully invited the Socialist *Blum to become Prime Minister. Four years later, after a less than triumphal re-election in 1939, he behaved with similar constitutional scruple in the dramatic events surrounding the fall of France. He made no attempt to support those of 'his' ministers who opposed the growing clamour for an end to the war and, by appointing *Pétain Prime Minister, made certain that an armistice would be signed. He was similarly inert in the hectic days leading to the establishment of the Vichy regime and the overthrow of the Republic whose head he was supposed to be. He was deported to Germany during the war and played no part in politics after it.

In his war memoirs, *de Gaulle dismisses Lebrun's role in 1940 with curt brutality. Lebrun personified the weakness of the Third Republic head of state and was the anti-model for the presidency which de Gaulle created in the 1958 constitution.

Lecanuet, Jean (b. 4 Mar. 1920; d. 23 Feb. 1993)
French; Presidential candidate 1965, Minister of Justice 1974–7

Born to a modest family, Lecanuet studied law and history. He joined the Christian Democratic Mouvement Républicain Populaire in 1945 in Paris and was elected to the National Assembly for the Seine Inférieure department in 1951. In the changed political circumstances produced by the establishment of the Fifth Republic and the granting of Algerian independence, he sided with the left-wing MRP against the die-hard supporters of French Algeria. The MRP broke with *de Gaulle over his rejection of the cause of European integration and it was this which gave Lecanuet his chance. He decided to run against de Gaulle in the 1965 presidential elections. Youthful, articulate, possessing a dazzling smile, he modelled himself on John *Kennedy and ran on a pro-European (and pro-NATO) ticket. The 15.8 per cent vote he obtained on round one was lower than the polls had predicted; but it demonstrated that there was a possible future for non-Gaullist conservatism. He spent the next nine years trying to build up a Centrist, anti-Communist political force capable of defeating the Gaullist Party and gave strong support to the presidential bids of *Poher (1969) and *Giscard (1974). The latter's victory brought him into government as Minister of Justice, a post he held, without much distinction, for three years. He never held ministerial office after 1977, but remained a significant figure in the confederation of non-Gaullist parties called the Union pour la Democratie Française. He also became a regional political boss as mayor of Rouen and president of the departmental council of the Seine Inférieure. A committed supporter of European integration, he campaigned actively, shortly before his death from cancer in 1993, in favour of the referendum on the Maastricht Treaty.

Lecanuet's career demonstrates the persistence in the Fifth Republic of a Christian Democratic strain in French conservative politics.

Lee Kuan Yew (b. Singapore, 16 Sept. 1923)

Singaporean; Prime Minister 1959–90

Born in Singapore of a wealthy Chinese family, Lee Kuan Yew was educated at Fitzwilliam College, Cambridge, and was called to the bar at Middle Temple. Upon return to Singapore he became advocate and solicitor and in 1954 founded the moderately anti-Communist People's Action Party whose general secretary he remained until 1992.

Lee Kuan Yew was elected to the Singapore Legislative Assembly in 1955. He became the country's first Prime Minister in 1959, a position he held until November 1990 when he resigned. He was re-elected in 1963, 1968, 1972, 1976, 1980, 1984, and 1988.

Lee Kuan Yew is the architect of modern Singapore since it gained self-government in 1959 and independence in 1965. In 1960 the city state was described by one magazine as being a cesspool of squalor and degradation. Today Singapore's per capita income is second only to Japan and the state has no foreign debts. This rapid economic transformation has been achieved through tight political control. Under Lee Kuan Yew's leadership, Singapore became one of the world's most regulated societies. Its politics, the way government exercised control over virtually every aspect of life, was compared to the defunct Communist regimes of Eastern Europe. The significant difference was that Singapore's anti-Communism, under Lee Kuan Yew, was able to deliver high-value financial rewards to its citizens.

In recent years Lee Kuan Yew has become the main exponent of Asian values and the economic success of Singapore is much admired in South East Asia and the Far East as well as Europe. These values, he has asserted, are closely linked to the values of the Chinese community which has been the main support base of the People's Action Party. Despite these comments, he was able to rule Singapore as a multi-ethnic state.

Critics of Lee Kuan Yew in Singapore and abroad during his tenure pointed to the promotion of an authoritarian political culture that was opposed to dissent, especially when it challenged the ruling party. This was best reflected in his dominating style, the curtailment of civil liberties, and bureaucratic hurdles placed in political mobilization of the opposition.

Lee Kuan Yew resigned in November 1990 after thirty-one years as Prime Minister. His successor, Goh Chok Tong, has promised to carry on the tough, no-nonsense approach, but has been increasingly criticized by Lee Kuan Yew for lacking political assertiveness. Brigadier-General Lee Hasien Loong, Lee Kuan Yew's son, is seen as his eventual successor.

Lee Teng-hui (Li Denghui) (b. Tamsui, 15 Jan. 1923)

Chinese (Taiwanese); President of the Republic of China on Taiwan 1988–

Lee was born and grew up in Taiwan while it was a Japanese colony. He studied agriculture at Kyoto Imperial University, and also studied at National Taiwan University and Iowa State University. He received a Ph.D. in Agricultural Economics from Cornell University. For most of the 1950s and 1960s he was an academic and scholar at the National Taiwan University, becoming a full professor in 1958, and worked on the Joint Commission for Rural Reconstruction from 1957 to 1962.

*Chiang Ching-kuo is reported to have been impressed with Lee's academic work and offered him the position of chief of the Rural Economic Division, where he served from 1970 to 1972. Lee rose quickly both in the hierarchy of the Nationalist Party (KMT) and the state. He was a Minister of State from 1972 to 1978, the mayor of Taipei (Taibei) 1978–81, and Governor of Taiwan Province 1981–4. He was elected Vice-President of the ROC in 1984, and took over as President following the death of Chiang Ching-kuo in 1988, becoming the first native Taiwanese ever to rule Taiwan.

Lee proceeded to consolidate his power and continue the process of democratization and opening to the PRC begun by his predecessor. Under Lee democratic elections have been held at all levels, culminating in his election as President in March 1996, the first democratically elected President in Chinese history. He has come under considerable criticism from the PRC for trying to increase Taiwan's international profile as a separate entity, which Beijing sees as tantamount to moving toward independence, and he has also received criticism from pro-independence groups in Taiwan for moving too slowly. He visited the USA in 1995, the first leader of Taiwan ever to do so, and is mounting a campaign for the island to be admitted to the UN.

Leguía, Augusto (b. Lambayeque, 19 Feb. 1863; d. Lima, 6 Feb. 1932)

Peruvian; Finance Minister 1903, Prime Minister 1904, President 1908–12, 1919–29

Born into a middle-class provincial family of Basque origin, Leguía received his secondary education in the British school in Valparaiso (Chile). Upon returning to Peru, he engaged in commerce, becoming the Lima representative of the New York Life Insurance Company, before being appointed as manager of the Peruvian properties of the British Sugar Co. On the basis of his foreign connections, Leguía became Finance Minister and later Prime Minister in the Partido Civil administration headed by José Pardo. With his reputation suitably enhanced as a result of his administrative competence and energetic debating style in Congress, Leguía was chosen as presidential candidate of the Partido Civil in 1908.

Having attained the presidency, he endeavoured to introduce mild reforms but faced stiff opposition from more conservative 'oligarchic' members within his party. After completing his term in office, Leguía went into voluntary exile, returning to contest the May 1919 general election. To political and élite groups, he argued that if revolution was to be averted it was necessary to pursue a policy of capitalist modernization from above, while simultaneously implementing mild reforms to Peru's archaic social and political system. To the lower classes, Leguía expressed sympathy with their demands for reform and succeeded in forging a coalition strong enough to defeat the official conservative candidate of the Partido Civil. Fearful of being prevented from taking office by powerful enemies from within his own party, Leguía organized a pre-emptive coup with backing from rival parties and sections of the military, but once installed in the presidential palace, strove to undermine all rival political forces, as well as imprisoning or sending into exile prominent members of the *civilista* élite. He then built up a personalist authoritarian regime, based on a large clientelist network, an amenable Congress, allied to a strengthening of the bureaucratic and coercive arms of the state. The constitution was rewritten to facilitate his re-election in 1924 and 1929. On the economic front, Leguía embarked on a policy of rapid modernization from above, financed through foreign loans and the encouragement of outside investment. However, the Wall St. crash of 1929 and the attendant steep fall in commodity prices destabilized his regime and provoked a successful military coup in August 1930. The first conscious attempt in twentieth-century Peru to modernize the country thus ended with Leguía in prison and the military in power. Despite declining health, the incoming regime prevented him from receiving medical attention until it was too late, with the result that the longest serving president in modern Peruvian history died in prison a broken man in February 1932.

Lemass, Sean Francis (b. Co. Dublin, 15 Dec. 1899; d. 11 May 1971)

Irish; Tanaiste (deputy premier) 1945–8, 1951–4, 1957–9, Taoiseach (premier) 1959–66

The son of a Dublin hatter of Huguenot origins, Lemass joined the Irish Volunteers in 1915 and played a minor role in the Easter Rising of 1916. He was interned in the later stages of the Anglo-Irish independence conflict, and in 1922 joined the anti-treaty forces in the Irish Civil War, in which he was again interned, and in which his brother was brutally murdered. Elected to the Dáil in November 1924, it was largely on Lemass's initiative that the Fianna Fáil party was created at Easter 1926 out of the more pragmatic, pro-*de Valera members of third Sinn Fein, and following its entry to the Dáil it was Lemass who coined the description of the Fianna Fáil as 'a slightly constitutional' party. Lemass remained a firm republican, but now pragmatically using parliamentary methods. He served as Minister for Industry and Commerce in de Valera's administrations from 1932 onwards, adding Supplies during the war, and was Tanaiste (deputy premier) in Fianna Fáil governments 1945–59. On de Valera's retirement in June 1959 Lemass was his inevitable successor, and served as Taoiseach until November 1966. He left the Dáil in 1969 and died in 1971.

His period as Taoiseach was marked by the opening up of the country to modernizations possibly delayed by de Valera's prolonged ascendancy. He was associated with the first Programme for Economic Expansion, 1958, with its espousal of tariff demolition, encouragement of inward investment, and the development of a mixed economy. Ireland formally applied unsuccessfully to join the EEC in July 1961. But the sending of an Irish UN contingent to the Congo, and the role there of Conor Cruise O'Brien as UN representative, showed Irish independence and neutrality now translating into positive international terms. In Ireland Lemass's boldest action was his visit to Terence O'Neill at Stormont in January 1965, one of whose results was Lemass's encouragement to the Nationalists to take up the role of official opposition in the Northern Ireland parliament.

Lemass's business-like pragmatism and his new approach to the North appeared at odds with his origins as a revolutionary republican but were not, to him, incompatible with them, being rather logical adaptations of old principles to new times.

Lenin, Vladimir Ilich (real name **Ul'yanov**) (b. Simbirsk, Russia, 22 Apr. 1870; d. Gorki, near Moscow, 21 Jan. 1924)

Founder and leader of the Bolshevik Party, chair of Council of People's Commissars 1917–24

Vladimir Ul'yanov came from a provincial middle-class family of mixed ancestry (Russian-Kalmyk and Jewish-German), his father being a school inspector (hence in the minor nobility). Soon after his father's death in 1886 Lenin's elder brother Alexander, a student, was hanged for participating in a plot by a revolutionary populist group to assassinate Alexander III. This event made a deep impression on the younger Ul'yanov and, after passing his final school exams with distinction, he too joined a populist group when he began studying at Kazan University, for which he was rusticated. His mother bought an estate in Samara province, but there too he joined a populist group, although he became increasingly interested in Marxism. He completed a first class degree in law at St Petersburg University as an external student in 1891. After a period as an assistant advocate in Samara he moved in 1893 to St Petersburg, where he joined the Marxists. In 1895 he was sent to Geneva to make contact with Plekhanov's group. Soon after he returned he was imprisoned and in 1897 sentenced to Siberian exile. While in Siberia he married Nadezhda Krupskaya and completed, in 1899, his first major work *The Development of Capitalism in Russia* in which he argued that Russia had irrevocably embarked on the capitalist road and rejected populism (though his ideas on revolutionary organization remained influenced by it). After his release in 1900 he joined Plekhanov in Switzerland and, now using the pseudonym Lenin, with him launched the newspaper *Iskra* ('The Spark'), in which they attacked the 'Economists' (supporters of incremental reform). In 1902 Lenin published his notorious pamphlet *What is to be done*? in which he argued that a successful revolutionary party in Russian conditions had to be a highly centralized and conspiratorial organization of 'professional revolutionaries' to be an effective vanguard of the workers who would not spontaneously develop revolutionary consciousness. This novel view of the Marxist Party provoked considerable opposition. At the 2nd Congress of the RSDLP, held in Brussels and London in 1903, *Martov's more moderate views on the party won the day, but Lenin's group, with the support of Plekhanov, won the elections to the central party bodies. Lenin termed his group the 'Majoritarians' (*Bolsheviki*) and Martov's group 'Minoritarians' (*Mensheviki*) and increasingly treated his group as the real party.

The revolutionary events of 1905 in Russia caught Lenin unawares, like most other exiled socialists, and he returned to Russia only in November. In his work *Two Tactics of Social Democracy in the Democratic Revolution* he argued that the workers would have to take a leading role in the bourgeois revolution, co-operating with revolutionary elements in the peasantry. This latter point was unusual in Marxist thinking, perhaps showing underlying populist influence on Lenin. He made some moves towards reconciliation with the Mensheviks, putting forward the idea of 'democratic centralism', in which his 1902 model of the party was modified by emphasis on the democratic electivity and accountability of the leadership. But, once in exile again in 1907, he resumed his policy of promoting schisms, designed to strengthen the revolutionary vanguard. Differences with the Mensheviks continued to widen, now reflecting disagreement on the whole approach to revolution, and the split became final in 1912. He spent the war years mainly in Switzerland, arguing for turning the imperialist war into a revolutionary civil war. In *Imperialism* (written 1916) he argued that the capitalist powers were driven into territorial imperialism by capital export and used the 'super-profits' derived from colonial exploitation to bribe the working class into quiescence by wage increases and social benefits, but that Russia, though less developed, could be the 'weakest link' from which general revolution might develop.

Lenin, like other socialists, was surprised by the February Revolution in Russia and the consequent abdication of the Tsar. He obtained German permission to travel across Germany in a sealed train to Russia (where the Germans hoped his anti-war propaganda would help undermine the Russian war effort). Arriving in Petrograd (as St Petersburg had been renamed) in April 1917, he brought out his *April Theses* in which he disconcerted the more gradualist domestic Bolsheviks by urging non-cooperation with the Provisional Government, rejection of any participation in the war, and active propaganda work in the soviets to achieve a Bolshevik-dominated soviet government which would create a revolutionary state. It took some months before these tactics paid off, but gradually the effectiveness of Bolshevik propaganda (with slogans like 'Bread', 'Peace', 'Land') combined with the ineffectiveness of the provisional government and its continuance of the war compromised the Mensheviks and Socialist Revolutionaries who took part in it and increased Bolshevik support in the Soviets. After a near catastrophic premature uprising in July (as a result of which Lenin was forced to go into hiding in Finland) Bolshevik fortunes rose again because of their role in foiling Kornilov's attempted coup in August. In his work *The State and Revolution*, which appeared in the summer of 1917, Lenin argued that the bourgeois state had to be smashed and a 'dictatorship of the proletariat' established which would move rapidly to create a new order, though this was not considered an immediate prospect. However, by October the popular revolutionary mood was intensifying, the Bolsheviks gained majorities in many of the town and military soviets, and *Trotsky and his group had come over to the Bolsheviks. Lenin returned on 10 October and urged an immediate armed uprising against the provisional government. Masterminded by Trotsky, the seizure of power was effected on the night of 25–6 October in the name of the All-Russian Congress of Soviets, to which Lenin announced the setting up of a Council of People's Commissars, led by himself. However, contrary to the expectations of many, Lenin refused to share power with other socialists, though a few left-wing socialist revolutionaries were given minor posts. Some revolutionary decrees were quickly issued: the Decree on Peace withdrew Russia from the war; the Decree on Land sanctioned the peasant takeover of the estates; other decrees separated church and state and established workers' control in the factories (soon to be reversed); the armed forces were disbanded and a voluntary militia established. However, opposition soon made itself felt and Lenin was forced in December to create the Cheka, a secret police force, and to place 'temporary' bans on non-Bolshevik newspapers and parties. Elections were held for the Constituent Assembly on universal suffrage in November, in which the Bolsheviks gained 24 per cent of the votes and the Socialist Revolutionaries 40 per cent. When the Assembly met in January and voiced strong criticisms of the Bolshevik government, it was not allowed to reconvene, an important symbolic act in the creation of the one-party state. In March 1918 Lenin was forced to sign the treaty of Brest-Litovsk, a separate peace with Germany and Austria, ceding huge amounts of territory, including the Ukraine. The Left SRs then resigned from the government and started resistance, soon afterwards foreign forces intervened and the civil war started. There developed a highly authoritarian and centralized system of rule known as 'War Communism': all industrial enterprises were nationalized, all non-Bolshevik activity treated as counter-revolution, the economy run by central command, and military and civilian conscription employed. By 1920 the war was over, but with the economy in a state of collapse and millions dead. Following Trotsky's suggestion, Lenin introduced in March 1921 the New Economic Policy, a 'breathing-space', though one that he thought could last for 'a generation', involving denationalization of small-scale enterprises and restoration of an agricultural market. At the same time political discipline was increased with a ban on factional activity in the party and the maintenance of bans on non-Bolshevik parties and media. This 'tactical retreat' rapidly revived the economy. But Lenin's health was now bad: after surviving an assassination attempt in 1918 he had his first stroke in 1921 and was more or less incapacitated from 1922. His last struggles were against the rising tide of bureaucracy (but his solution was a bureaucratic one—still more committees, like Rabkrin) and to prevent Stalin gaining power after his death (but his recommendation for Stalin's removal as General Secretary was suppressed). He died at the age of 53 in January 1924, his weak constitution broken by overwork.

Lenin had been obsessed with achieving socialist revolution in Russia, for which end he considered any means justified, including terror and deceit, and did not appreciate the long-term dangers of such methods. His emphasis on central direction and the party's vanguard role ('We know best what's good for you') never changed, despite the broadening of party membership, and produced the dangers of 'substitutism' about which Trotsky warned. Once revolution was achieved he seemed trapped in short-term tactical changes, unclear about long-term strategy. Undoubtedly an outstanding political leader whose personal contribution changed the face of the twentieth century, his dogmatism and ruthlessness, even though partly compensated by approachability and rejection of hero-worship, provided a precedent for the excesses of *Stalin.

Le Pen, Jean-Marie (b. 20 June 1928)

French; Presidential candidate 1974, 1988, and 1995

Born in the western department of Morbihan, the son of a fisherman killed at sea in 1942, Le Pen was educated locally. He got involved in extreme right politics while a law student in Paris and then joined a paratroop regiment, arriving in Haiphong just before *Mendès France signed the Geneva accords which saw the end of French Indochina. On his return to France, he joined the anti-system movement led by *Poujade and in January 1956 was elected Poujadist deputy for Paris. He soon broke with Poujade and took leave from the National Assembly to rejoin the paratroopers fighting in Algeria. A fervent defender of the cause for empire, and always mistrustful of *de Gaulle, Le Pen was re-elected to the National Assembly in 1958. He became a vehement critic of the policy of withdrawal from Algeria, was briefly placed under arrest, and in 1962 lost his parliamentary seat. Algerian independence, economic growth, and the consolidation of electoral Gaullism combined to push Le Pen to the margins of French politics for the next eighteen years. He participated in the twilight world of the far right and in 1972 managed to unite a number of its warring factions in the Front National, of which he became president. But in 1974, when he stood for the presidency, he won under 1 per cent of the votes cast and seven years later was unable to obtain the 500 sponsors needed for him to stand.

His political prospects changed markedly in the early 1980s (his personal fortunes had already improved thanks to an inheritance from a rich supporter). As the euphoria produced by *Mitterrand's 1981 victory evaporated, Le Pen was able to capitalize on the resentment felt by many at the government's austerity measures and on the failure of the parties of the system right to provide a convincing alternative. A good performance in the 1983 municipal elections was followed next year by a 10 per cent vote for Le Pen's list in the European elections, and in 1986 by the election of thirty-five Front National deputies. Suddenly Le Pen found himself a media star. To the inhabitants of run-down suburbs, his blunt message—2 million immigrants too many—had considerable appeal. His warnings of an impending Islamic invasion of France and his denunciations of the political Establishment struck a chord with right-wing conservatives and with the former Algerian settlers concentrated in the south-east. The hard core of Le Pen's supporters shared his anti-Semitic, pro-*Pétain views. But it was his populist ability to identify scapegoats—Arabs, bureaucrats, Aids victims—which helped him to win 14 per cent of the vote in the 1988 presidential election and 15 per cent in 1995.

If Le Pen's success demonstrates the persistence in France of a radical right discourse which many thought had disappeared in the Fifth Republic, it also shows the difficulties the mainstream conservative parties have had in maintaining the electoral hegemony they established in the 1960s and 1970s.

Li Denghui *see* LEE TENG-HUI

Ligachev, Yegor Kuzmich (b. near Novosibirsk, 29 Sept. 1920)

Russian; Secretary of Central Committee of CPSU 1983–90, Deputy to USSR Supreme Soviet 1966–89, People's Deputy of the USSR 1989–91

A graduate engineer, Ligachev trained at the Higher Party School and from 1949 worked in the Comsomol and then the party apparatus, mostly in Siberia, where he was First Secretary of the Tomsk Regional Committee 1965–83. He was a full member of the Central Committee from 1976, but only gained prominence when *Andropov brought him to Moscow as head of the party's Organizational Work department and Secretary of the Central Committee in 1983. Initially a close colleague of *Gorbachev, he gained full Politibureau membership when Gorbachev became General Secretary in April 1985 and became 'second secretary', supervising ideology and party organization. A teetotaller and puritan, he promoted the anti-alcohol campaign of 1985–6, which badly misfired. He became increasingly critical of the pace and extent of reform under Gorbachev, especially of the 'excesses' of glasnost in the rewriting of history. Hence from September 1988 his responsibilities were narrowed to agricultural reform. He continued to resist Westernization and 'hasty' change and in August 1990 retired from all his posts after the 26th Congress.

Lindsay, John Vliet (b. New York, 24 Nov. 1921)

US; member of the US House of Representatives 1959–61; mayor of New York City 1965–73

Lindsay was educated at St Paul's Concord, New Hampshire, and graduated from Yale, BA in 1944 and LLB 1948. He was called to the bar in New York, 1949. Serving in the US navy during the Second World War, he saw active service in Sicily, Biak, Hollandia, and the Philippines. He began practising law in 1953, was appointed executive assistant to the US Attorney-General, 1955–6, and thereafter combined a career in law and politics. He was elected US Congressman for the 17th District of New York in 1959, retaining his seat in the next two elections. He gained the position for which he is best known in 1965 when he became mayor of New York City, an office he continued to hold for the next eight years.

Beginning his political career as a Republican, in the early 1960s he was associated with the moderate, liberal Ripon group which was trying to reform the party in the hope of attracting the support of new, young suburbanites and college graduates. Eventually abandoning the GOP as a lost cause, he became a Democrat.

Since leaving office Lindsay has continued to practise law and has become a television commentator.

Li Peng (b. Sichuan Province, 1928)

Chinese; Acting Premier 1987–9, Premier 1989–

Li Peng was born in Sichuan in south-west China in 1928. Orphaned at an early age, Li was taken under the wing of *Zhou Enlai, who looked after him throughout the war years (although not formally adopting him as some accounts suggest). He also provided important political patronage after 1949, and there can be no doubt that his relationship with China's most popular premier did nothing to harm Li's own elevation to the position in 1987. It is also notable that like Zhou, Li escaped the Cultural Revolution unscathed, although his control of energy supplies to Beijing at this time may have been at least as influential as his political connections.

Li's early political career was typical of that of one of the second generation of Chinese Communist leaders. Immediately after the war, he was sent for specialist training in energy and power engineering in Moscow. Returning to China in the early 1950s, his political career was dominated by life in the energy and power bureaucracies, culminating in his appointment as Minister of Electrical Power in 1979.

Li's technocratic/bureaucratic career may not have made him the most well known of Chinese leaders, but did provide him with important specialist knowledge which stood him in good stead in the emerging post-Mao political order. Li also benefited from the support of important figures in the old guard of ageing Chinese revolutionaries, notably *Chen Yun. Nevertheless, it was still something of a surprise (and not just in the West) when he was named acting Premier in November 1987 in succession to Zhao Ziyang.

Zhao had been serving as both premier and party leader since the dismissal of Hu Yaobang in the wake of student democracy demonstrations during the previous year, and a general upsurge in dangerous liberal and 'bourgeois' trends. Zhao later claimed that he had only abandoned the premiership on *Deng Xiaoping's 'advice' and that this was the worst political decision of his career, as he had lost control of the economy to the more cautious and conservative Li Peng. The two clashed bitterly at a party work conference in the autumn of 1988 as the leadership tried to respond to a deepening inflationary crisis. Zhao advocated further liberalization of the economy and more and more market reforms, but Li Peng emerged victorious, and implemented a stark retrenchment campaign which drew China back from the market and restored more central planning controls.

This conflict between Zhao and Li provided the backdrop to the political turmoil in

Beijing during the spring of 1989. Furthermore, the death of Hu Yaobang, which sparked the initial demonstrations, was reportedly brought on during a particularly rancorous debate with Li Peng. As the student demonstrations grew, Li Peng became the target of increasingly bitter attacks, and while Zhao embraced appeasement and reconciliation with the students, Li stood firm and refused to give an inch. It was Li in a televised speech on 19 May who called the students 'counter-revolutionaries' and called on the army to defend the revolution leading to the establishment of martial law the next day.

With Zhao Ziyang's removal and the Tiananmen massacre on 4 and 5 June, Li Peng's position appeared to be stronger than ever. However, with the promotion of Jiang Zemin to the party leadership, and Zhu Rongji's appointment as *de facto* economic chief (both 'outsiders' from the Shanghai party-state machinery), his position was if anything much weaker by the end of the decade. Li's economic retrenchment campaign rather petered out in the face of non-compliance from the newly powerful provinces in the south-east, and when Deng Xiaoping gave his stamp of approval to further reform by touring the 'Gold Coast' in 1992, the era of Li Peng in ascendancy was essentially over. Li's position was further weakened in 1995 with the death of his main patron (and Deng Xiaoping's chief critic), *Chen Yun.

Li Peng has devoted much time and effort subsequently in attacking official corruption, which has become almost endemic in reformist China. Despite his best efforts, and his (apparent at least) conversion to a more reformist economic platform, he will find it extremely difficult to shake off the legacy of the political struggles of 1988 and 1989.

Litvinov, Maximilian (*also known, in Russian, as* **Maksim Maksimovich**)
(b. Bialystok 18 July 1876; d. Moscow, 31 Dec. 1951)
Russian; Commissar of Foreign Affairs 1926–39

Litvinov was born as Meier Wallakh into a poor Jewish family in Russian Poland. He joined the Russian Social Democratic Labour Party (RSDLP) in 1898. He was imprisoned but escaped from Russia in 1902 and settled in France. Having joined the Bolsheviks under Lenin in 1903 he was deported from France in 1908 because of his revolutionary activities, which had involved smuggling arms into Russia. He then moved to London where he worked for a publisher and married an Englishwoman, Ivy Low, in 1916, and after the October Revolution became the Bolsheviks' first representative in Britain. The appointment was brief, for he was deported in September the next year. On his return to Russia he worked for the Commissariat of Foreign Affairs, becoming Deputy Commissar (i.e. Deputy Foreign Minister) and represented the Soviet Union at several disarmament conferences in the 1920s including the *Kellogg-*Briand Pact. Effectively, Litvinov was in charge of the Commissariat of Foreign Affairs from 1926; officially he became Foreign Commissar in July 1930, replacing Chicherin, but did not enter the Politburo. Alarmed by the growth of German and Japanese power, Litvinov supported a policy of collective security and the League of Nations. He also sought better relations with the USSR's Western neighbours and was largely responsible for the Franco-Soviet Pact of mutual defence in 1935.

*Stalin dismissed Litvinov in the May 1939, believing that as a Jew he would be unable to reach agreement with Nazi Germany. From December 1941 to July 1943 he was Soviet ambassador in Washington and then Deputy Commissar of Foreign Affairs from 1943 until his retirement in 1946.

Lloyd, John **Selwyn** Brooke (b. West Kirby, Wirral, 28 July 1904; d. 17 May 1978)
British; Foreign Secretary 1955–60, Chancellor of the Exchequer 1960–3, Speaker of the House of Commons 1971–6; Baron (life peer) 1976

The son of a doctor, Lloyd was educated at Fettes College and Magdalene College,

Cambridge (president of the Cambridge Union 1927). A barrister, he saw wartime service, reaching the rank of brigadier-general, before being elected to the House of Commons in 1945. Though originally a Liberal—he fought Macclesfield as a Liberal in 1929—he had converted to the Conservative cause. On the party's return to office in 1951 he began a rapid progression up the ministerial ladder—Minister of State at the Foreign Office (1951–4), Minister of Supply (1954–5), and then, briefly, Minister of Defence (1955), before being appointed Foreign Secretary in December 1955. Though he was closely linked with the failure of the Suez expedition, Harold *Macmillan decided to keep him in the post, and in July 1960 made him Chancellor of the Exchequer. Associated with unpopular 'stop-go' economic policies, he was the principal victim of Macmillan's 'Night of the Long Knives' in 1962. He returned to government during the *Douglas-Home premiership (1963–4), serving as Lord Privy Seal and leader of the House of Commons, a position in which he showed sensitivity to the needs of backbenchers. In Opposition, he served in the shadow Cabinet for two years before returning to the back benches.

Though his frontbench career ended in 1966, a second political career lay ahead. In 1971 he was elected Speaker of the House and served in the post for five years. The election was contested, some MPs resenting the way that the choice of Lloyd was being pushed by the *Heath government. Though relying heavily at times on the Deputy Speaker to occupy the chair, he proved attentive to the needs of members. He accepted a life peerage on his retirement from the speakership, but lived for only another two years, dying at the age of 73.

Though an able individual and competent minister, he suffered from his association with the Suez expedition and the claim that he was the monkey to Macmillan's organ grinder. He was an unpopular Chancellor, presiding over a period of economic downturn, but restored his parliamentary reputation during his speakership. Having been divorced in 1957, he often cut a lonely figure in the House of Commons. Personally courteous and friendly, he became a source of support to many new MPs.

Lloyd George, David (b. Manchester, 17 Jan. 1863; d. 26 Mar. 1945)

British; Chancellor of the Exchequer 1908–14, Prime Minister 1916–22; Earl 1945

Historians are divided over whether Lloyd George (the 'Welsh Wizard') or Winston *Churchill is the greatest British political figure in the twentieth century. For all his Welshness Lloyd George was born in Manchester. He was the son of a schoolteacher who died when David was only a few months old. The family moved to rural Wales, where he was brought up by an uncle and eventually became a solicitor. He was born in humble circumstances and belonged to a small nation; the background gave a radical edge to his politics.

Lloyd George won the seat of Carnaervon for the Liberals at a by-election in 1890 and remained its member until 1945, when he took an earldom. He never lost his concern for the poor or small nations. In the 1890s he was prominent as a Welsh radical. He achieved some fame, indeed notoriety, as a courageous critic of the Boer War—which aroused his sympathies for a small nation. Lloyd George led a complicated private life for a prominent nonconformist Liberal politician. He lived openly with a mistress, Frances Stevenson, from 1912 until he married her in 1941, soon after the death of his first wife.

In the 1905 Liberal government he was made president of the Board of Trade and then succeeded Herbert *Asquith as Chancellor of the Exchequer in 1908 when the latter became Prime Minister. His famous 1909 budget, which raised taxes to fund welfare reforms and increase naval spending, prompted a constitutional crisis when the House of Lords refused to pass it. In 1911 he introduced the National Insurance Act which provided for contributory health and unemployment insurance. In these years Lloyd George was firmly on the left, or radical, wing of the Liberal Party.

Unionists feared him as a proponent of class hatred and a demagogue. His supporters regarded him as the voice of the ordinary people.

Lloyd George's talents as an administrator and decisive leader came to the fore during the 1914–18 war, even though he decided to support it only late in the day. As Minister of Munitions he brought businessmen into Whitehall and persuaded the trade unions to co-operate in boosting production. As the war made little progress so Lloyd George was increasingly seen as a man who had the necessary energy and drive to achieve victory. He became Secretary of State for War in 1916 and, still frustrated at the lack of direction, proposed a small War Cabinet, with Asquith being relegated to a subordinate role. When Asquith refused to agree Lloyd George resigned on 5 December, prompting a crisis. Asquith resigned later that same day, although he may have hoped to demonstrate his indispensability and be recalled. Instead, it was Lloyd George, supported by the Unionists, who formed a government two days later. The Liberal Party was a casualty of the split between Asquith and Lloyd George and never recovered.

As Prime Minister Lloyd George wielded almost dictatorial powers. He effectively modernized the central government machine. He introduced a small five-member War Cabinet, in place of Asquith's twenty-three-member Cabinet, set up a Cabinet secretariat to take minutes and prepare the agenda, and introduced a 'Garden Suburb' which was effectively his own policy staff.

Yet he was not the leader of the Liberal Party and depended heavily upon the support of the Unionists. And for all his energy, dynamism, and popularity with the public, he failed to get control of the army. He could not get rid of General Haig though he bitterly opposed the heavy loss of manpower in Flanders in 1917. In the 1918 general election Lloyd George led the coalition to a landslide victory, but it was largely a Unionist majority and many in the party had little loyalty to him. The divided Liberals did badly and Labour became the official opposition. Lloyd George's plans to fuse the Unionists and his own Liberal followers into a new centre party came to nothing. Although normal Cabinet government was restored in peacetime, Lloyd George still acted in a presidential manner and treated his Foreign Secretary *Curzon particularly badly. He enjoyed playing the role of international statesman and was out of the country for a large part of the period.

Lloyd George achieved peace in Ireland—for a time. The Government of Ireland Act (1920) gave independence to the South. But it had been preceded by the state-sponsored terrorism of the Black and Tans and further alienated his old Liberal supporters.

Growing discontent among Unionists came to a head when it was feared that Lloyd George was leading Britain into a war against Turkey in 1922. At a famous meeting in the Carlton Club Unionists voted to leave the coalition. *Baldwin warned that Lloyd George was 'a dynamic force' and 'a dynamic force is a terrible thing' and, having split the Liberals, would do the same to the Unionists. There was much concern at the time that he was selling political honours and building up his own war chest with the proceeds. When he fell, he was at the height of his powers and few doubted that he would return. It was not to be. In the general election he was returned at the head of just fifty-five National Liberals.

Lloyd George had an instrumental attitude to political parties. Parties were there to achieve objectives, they were not ends in themselves. But such an attitude made him widely distrusted. He had actually proposed a coalition to the Unionists in 1910 when there were inter-party talks over the constitutional crisis.

He and his National Liberals rejoined the Liberals in 1923 and he succeeded Asquith as leader in 1926 when the latter resigned. In the 1929 election he proposed a bold plan, borrowed from the economist J. M. Keynes, for tackling the unemployment crisis by a public works programme. He was impatient with the feeble attempts of the 1929 Labour government to combat mass unemployment and was negotiating to enter a coalition when the financial crisis produced the collapse of the government in 1931. Lloyd George was ill at the time of the crisis but did not support the decision of the Liberal Party to join the coalition. He was left to lead a small group of Liberals, mainly from his family. The 1930s were spent globe-trotting, earning money from journalism and his best-selling *War Memoirs*, and intervening on the great issues of the day. There was talk of government posts but in 1940 he refused Winston Churchill's invitation to join the wartime coalition government.

Lodge, Henry Cabot Jr. (b. Nahant, Massachusetts, 5 July 1902; d. 27 Feb. 1985)
US; US Senator 1936–52, US delegate to the United Nations 1953–60, US ambassador to South Vietnam 1963–4, 1965–7

Lodge was educated at Middlesex School, Concord, Massachusetts, and graduated from Harvard in 1924. He embarked on a career in journalism, beginning as a trainee on the *Boston Evening Transcript* and then becoming a staff reporter on the *New York Herald Tribune*. At the age of 30 he followed in his grandfather's (Henry Cabot *Lodge Sr.) footsteps and was elected, first to the Massachusetts legislature, and then, four years later in 1936, to the US Senate.

Lodge, a liberal Republican in domestic matters, inherited his grandfather's isolationist views in respect of foreign policy, and, in 1939, voted against amending the Neutrality Act in Britain's favour. His views on foreign policy were changed by his wartime experience. During the Second World War he saw active service in Libya. On returning to the Senate in 1946 he became a convinced advocate of the need for America to participate in the proposed collective security arrangements of the United Nations.

Lodge played an active role in persuading General *Eisenhower to accept the nomination as Republican Party presidential candidate in 1952. Lodge lost his own Senate seat in this election to John F. *Kennedy. Eisenhower repaid his indebtedness to Lodge by appointing him US Permanent Representative to the United Nations at ambassadorial rank with a seat in the Cabinet.

Lodge never ran for the presidency himself but in 1960 agreed to be Richard *Nixon's running-mate. The contest was narrowly lost to Lodge's former political rival, Kennedy, who, in 1963 appointed Lodge ambassador to South Vietnam, a post which he continued to occupy under *Johnson. After this assignment Lodge spent a couple of years as ambassador-at-large and then spent his final years in public service as the President's Special Representative to the Vatican.

Lodge, Henry Cabot Sr. (b. Boston, Massachusetts, 12 May 1850; d. 9 Nov. 1924)
US; member of the US House of Representatives 1887–93; US Senator 1893–1924

Lodge was educated at Dixwell's Latin School, graduated BA from Harvard and LLB from Harvard Law School. He was called to the Boston bar 1874 and, after a brief period as assistant editor of the *North American Review*, he combined a lectureship in history at Harvard with an assistant editorship of the *International Review*. His political career began with his election to the Massachusetts House of Representatives in 1879. In 1887 he was elected to the US House of Representatives. He remained in the House for six years until, in 1893, he followed in the footsteps of his great grandfather George Cabot, and was elected US Senator for Massachusetts.

Lodge, a staunch Republican and patriot, achieved his first political ambition, becoming chairman of the prestigious Senate Foreign Relations Committee. Fulfilment of the greatest ambition, to become President of his country, eluded him, despite Theodore *Roosevelt's strong endorsement of his candidacy for his party's nomination in 1916.

Lodge's patriotism bordered on jingoism. He was an avid believer in the destiny of his country, an unwavering advocate of the Munroe Doctrine and a declared Anglophobe. He is perhaps best remembered for the part he played, as majority leader and chair of the Foreign Relations Committee, in the Senate's refusal to ratify the Treaty of Versailles and, therefore, of America's failure to participate in the League of Nations.

Lodge, lacking charisma and a following outside New England, was never a popular national figure. He did, however, personify the gentleman and scholar in politics. He published *Early Memoirs* (1913)—a volume in which he described and accounted for his deep hostility to England.

Long, Huey Pierce (b. Winnfield, Louisiana, 30 Aug. 1893; d. 10 Sept. 1935)
US; Governor of Louisiana 1928–32; US Senator 1932–5

Long received a state education at grammar and high schools and at the age of 16 became a travelling salesman. He was admitted to the bar and built up a practice in small towns attacking public utility corporations. By the age of 25 he had a gained place on the state Railway Commission. He made an unsuccessful bid to become state Governor in 1924 but was elected in 1928 by a minority vote in a three-cornered fight. In 1932 he relinquished the governorship to a henchman, having himself been elected to represent Louisiana in the US Senate.

Long was a populist. He delighted in the nickname 'Kingfish'—a title borrowed from a popular radio series, *Amos 'n' Andy*. But his enemies and critics described him as a 'spurious Hitler', a 'bullyragging hypocritical swashbuckler', 'the dictator of Louisiana'.

Initially he was a supporter of Franklin *Roosevelt and the New Deal, but he nursed presidential aspiration himself. To this end he created the 'Share Our Wealth' movement. Propaganda clubs were established in every state in the Union to whip up existing resentment about the maldistribution of wealth and to win support for the movement's programme. This included: the liquidation of all personal fortunes above $3,000,000; a $1,000,000 limit on personal incomes; the abolition of poverty by guaranteeing every deserving family $5,000 income; redistribution of wealth to provide every citizen with a job, a car, a radio, and 'two chickens in the pot'; generous old-age pensions; free university education and shorter working hours.

Long was popular. He brought material benefits to many groups in the community. Within the state of Louisiana he improved the roads, abolished tolls on bridges and ferries, introduced mobile libraries to rural areas, forced the utilities to lower their charges, and relieved 70 per cent of the state's population of direct taxation. There was of course a price. In monetary terms it was reflected in the state public debt which had mounted to $145,000,000 at the time of Long's death. The cost was also reflected in the ruthless and undemocratic regime Long established in Louisiana. He centralized the whole state administration under his control including the bar, the police, and the fire department. The State Legislature was in his pocket. In 1934, for example, it passed forty-four of 'his' (the Governor being his creature) bills through all their stages in two-and-a-half hours. The state Bureau of Criminal Investigation was in effect a secret police force engaging in political espionage and suppression of opposition. Had he lived Long would have faced a congressional inquiry into 'whether Louisiana has the Republican form of government guaranteed by the Constitution'.

On 10 September 1935 opposition caught up with Long. He was assassinated by Dr Carl Austin Weiss, who had been outraged by Long's attempt to dislodge a judge, Weiss's father-in-law.

López Arellano, Oswaldo (b. Danlí, Honduras, 1919)
Honduran; Head of the Armed Forces 1958–75, President 1963–71, 1972–5

López Arellano entered the Honduran air force in 1939. In 1956 he played a key role in the *coup d'état* which removed the would-be dictator Julio Lozano Díaz. The coup constituted the first intervention of the armed forces as an institution in national political life. After 1956, López Arellano held the post of Defence Minister. In 1957 the military junta struck a deal with the Liberal Party whereby the former would permit elections in exchange for amendment of the constitution to grant autonomy to the armed forces. The power of military over civilian politicians subsequently increased significantly. In 1958 López Arellano became head of the armed forces, a position he maintained until 1975.

In 1963, López Arellano led an anti-Communist coup which overthrew the mildly reformist government of Ramón Villeda Morales. The aim of the coup was to prevent the ascension of an anti-military Liberal Party candidate to power. In 1965, his *de facto* rule was 'legalized' by a constituent assembly which also promoted him to the rank of general. During the period 1963–71 his government was both conservative and repressive, exiling political opponents and fomenting clientelism and corruption.

Following a brief interregnum of bipartisan civilian government in 1971–2, López Arellano led a further *coup d'état* on 4 December 1972. The subsequent 1972–5 administration adopted a populist tone and introduced a number of socio-economic reforms which aimed to modernize the country through active state intervention. Among the most controversial measures introduced was a programme of agrarian reform. However, this top-down reformism, fiercely opposed by more conservative political sectors, had lost its original impetus by 1975.

In April 1975, López Arellano was removed from power by the military high council in the wake of a bribery scandal known as 'Bananagate', whereby the US multinational United Fruit Co. had allegedly paid large sums to government officials to secure a reduction of the banana export tax. López Arellano subsequently became one of the country's most important businessmen, his interests extending to cattle-ranching, banking, and airlines.

Lott, Trent (b. Grenada County, Mississippi, 9 Oct. 1941)
US; member of the US House of Representatives 1972–88, US Senator 1988–

Educated at the University of Mississippi and at Mississippi Law School, Lott practised law and worked for Democratic Congressman William Colmer between 1968 and 1972. In 1972 he was elected to Colmer's seat in the House of Representatives as a Republican and was elected Republican whip in 1980. Lott became a key figure in Republican politics in the 1980s, and organized the Convention platform committees at the Republican conventions of 1984 and 1988, although in 1988 he supported Jack *Kemp's abortive presidential bid rather than the candidacy of George *Bush.

Lott successfully ran for the Senate in 1988. Once in the Senate he became a natural candidate for Republican leadership positions. Following the 1992 elections, he was elected Republican conference secretary. In 1994, Lott became Senate Republican whip. When in June 1996 Robert *Dole resigned from the Senate majority leadership to concentrate on his presidential campaign, Lott was elected Republican leader. A tax-cutting and cultural conservative by instinct, Lott nevertheless tempered his partisanship and showed an early ability to negotiate both within his own party and with Democrats. There had been a general feeling that the Senate had become gridlocked and it was hoped that Lott would be able to improve its workings by cultivating a more open leadership style and by concentrating on the legislative business rather than campaigning. Lott's election to the post of Senate majority leader also reduced the ideological distance between the Republican leadership in the Senate and the House and put both leadership positions firmly in the hands of conservatives.

Lubbers, Rudolphus (**'Ruud'**) Franciscus Marie (b. Rotterdam, 7 May 1939)
Netherlandish; Prime Minister 1982–94

After studying economics in Rotterdam Lubbers became secretary of the board of Hollandia Machine factory, a family firm of which he became co-director with his brother after the death of their father. He was active as a young Catholic entrepreneur in several associations of Christian employers.

A member of the Catholic party (KVP) since 1964, his political career began in 1970, when he was elected to the Rijnmond Council, a new representative body for Rotterdam, its docklands and surrounding areas. In 1973 at the age of 34 Lubbers became Minister of Economic Affairs in the Den Uyl government, the first Cabinet in which ministers of left parties had a clear majority over ministers drawn from the Catholic KVP and the Calvinist Anti-revolutionary Party. He became a member of the Lower House in 1977. One year later he was elected leader of the newly formed Christian Democratic parliamentary group which issued into the CDA, the merger of the former three denominational parties KVP, ARP, and CHU in 1980.

Between 1982 and 1994 Lubbers led three cabinets in succession, the first two composed of Christian Democrats and Liberals, the last one a coalition between the former and the Social Democrats. During his first governmental period (1982–6) his government decided on severe economic measures (*Time* spoke of a 'Ruud-shock'), which contributed to a consolidation of the Dutch economic position inernationally. He became known as a troubleshooter *par excellence*, often thinking of several solutions at once for any given problem. One important example was the manner in which he solved the political crisis on the stationing of cruise missiles on Dutch soil, which had been the focus of unparalleled mass demonstrations. He became increasingly a senior presence in the international arena. On what is normally called in Dutch diplomatic circles Black Monday (30 September 1991) Dutch proposals for a more federal Europe badly backfired. Only Lubbers's considerable diplomatic skills secured the adoption of a heavily revised Treaty of Maastricht during the Dutch EC presidency in December 1991.

At the end of his long ministerial career—no Dutch Prime Minister remained in office as long as he did—his name figured unsuccessfully for high international posts as chairman of the European Commission and Secretary-General of NATO respectively. After his resignation in 1994 he returned to the family enterprise; he became professor of 'global international economic relations' in Tilburg and director of the Research Bureau of the Christian Democratic Party.

Luk'yanov, Anatoly Ivanovich (b. Smolensk, 7 May 1930)

Russian; CPSU Central Committee member 1986–91 and Secretary 1987–91, chair of the Supreme Soviet 1990–1

Having worked in a factory from the age of 13, Luk'yanov was later educated in law at Moscow University (where he became friends with *Gorbachev) and joined the Communist Party in 1955. He became a Doctor of Juridical Sciences and a legal consultant, first for the Council of Ministers and then the Presidium of the USSR Supreme Soviet. From 1983 he worked in the Central Committee apparatus, first as head of the General Department (assisting the General Secretary) and later as Secretary and head of the Administrative Organs Department (supervising the military and KGB). Elected to the Congress of People's Deputies in 1989, he became deputy chair to (Gorbachev) of the Supreme Soviet and Chair in 1990, when Gorbachev moved to the executive presidency. He was responsible for overseeing much of the new legislation, but became increasingly conservative. In August 1991 he was involved in the putsch against Gorbachev and was arrested and accused of treason, but was later amnestied. He became a prominent force in the Russian Communist Party when it was relegalized.

Lumumba, Patrice (b. Kasai, Belgian Congo, 2 July 1925; d. 13 Feb. 1961)

Zairean; Prime Minister 1960

As the charismatic leader and first Prime Minister of Zaire (the former Belgian Congo, now the Democratic Republic of Congo), Patrice Lumumba has gained a reputation out of all proportion to his brief tenure of power. After primary education, he became assistant postmaster in Stanleyville (now Kisangani) and was imprisoned for a year for embezzlement. In 1958 he formed and led the Mouvement National Congolais (MNC), which sought a unitary state while its main opponents opted for some form of federalism. In the May 1960 elections, the MNC emerged as the strongest single party with thirty-three of the 137 seats, and Lumumba became Prime Minister at independence in June, in uncomfortable coalition with his rival, Joseph Kasavubu. The complete breakdown of order immediately after independence was due in part to Lumumba's intemperate rhetoric, and was followed by the attempted secession of the mineral-rich Katanga region under Moise Tshombe, and by UN intervention. In September the coalition broke down, and Lumumba was ousted in a coup led by *Mobutu. Attempting to escape, he was captured and flown to Katanga, where he was murdered by Tshombe's forces.

Charismatic, idealistic, and entirely unsuited to government, Lumumba's name lives on as a symbol of the tragedy of the Congo, and as a contrast and reproach to his successors.

Lunacharsky, Anatoly Vasilyevich (b. Poltava, 24 Nov. 1875; d. 26 Dec. 1933)

Russian; Commissar for Enlightenment 1918–29

Lunacharsky was the son of tsarist official of radical political views. He became interested in Marxism, while still in his teens and, as a student at Zurich University, met Rosa Luxembourg, who impressed him profoundly. Back in Russia in 1899 he was soon arrested for his political activities. When he returned to Switzerland in 1902 he joined the socialist philosopher A. A. Bogdanov, whose sister he married. Lunacharsky met *Lenin in Paris in 1904, became editor of the Bolshevik newsheets *Vpered* and *Proletary*, and returned to Russia in 1905. He quarrelled with Lenin, who attacked his philosophical outlook in *Materialism and Empiro-Criticism* and returned to Switzerland in 1914, where he joined the 'internationalists' associated with *Trotsky. He rejoined Lenin in Russia in 1917, after the February Revolution, was made a member of Sovnarkom, and became Commissar for Enlightenment (equivalent to Minister of Education and the Arts), holding the position until 1929 when he became head of the Learned Council of the USSR Central Executive Committee. From 1930 to 1932 he and *Litvinov represented the Soviet Union at the League of Nations. In 1933 he was appointed Soviet ambassador to Spain, but died on the outward journey.

Luns, Joseph Marie Antoine Hubert (b. Rotterdam, 28 Aug. 1911)

Dutch; Foreign Minister 1956–71, Secretary-General of NATO 1971–84

After attending secondary schools in Rotterdam and Brussels, Luns studied law in Leiden and Amsterdam. In preparation for a diplomatic career he took a course on political economy in London, and on diplomacy in Berlin.

In 1938 he was appointed to a post in the Ministry of Foreign Affairs in The Hague. He was attaché in Berne (1940–1) and in Lisbon (1941–2), being promoted to Second Secretary (1942–3). He was transferred to London in 1943, where he stayed till 1949. From 1944 he was First Secretary at the Dutch Embassy. He became a Permanent Delegate to the United Nations (New York, 1949–52). In 1952 the Catholic party (KVP) pressed for his appointment as Minister of Foreign Affairs. Prime Minister *Drees resisted the appointment of a Catholic Minister of Foreign Affairs (all other five states in what was sometimes called *l'Europe Vaticane* having Catholic foreign ministers at the time). He favoured instead the appointment of J. W. *Beijen, a non-party diplomat and financier. A compromise was reached in which Beijen became Minister for Foreign Affairs in charge of Europe and multilateral relations, Luns as Minister without Portfolio in charge of Benelux, bilateral affairs, and the United Nations. In 1956 this odd situation of two Ministers of Foreign Affairs ended, with Luns serving as the sole Minister of Foreign Affairs until 1971.

One of the main problems Luns faced as Foreign Minister was negotiations with Indonesia concerning New Guinea, which had not been transferred to Indonesian rule in December 1949. Luns was strongly against the transfer of this territory which had been promised the right to self-determination. Eventually he had to give in when the expected military support of the USA in case of an armed confrontation failed to materialize. After the transfer of the territory in 1962, relations with Indonesia (which had broken down in 1960) were restored.

Luns contributed to the establishment of the EEC in 1957. He became a substantial force opposing *de Gaulle's wish for an *Europe des Nations* under French leadership, insisting on the need to involve Britain as a member of the European Communities, and advocating a greater degree of supranationality in EEC matters. He resigned as Foreign Minister in 1971, after the longest uninterrupted period of any Dutch minister in that position, to take up the post of Secretary-General of NATO.

Luthuli, Albert John (b. near Bulawayo 1898; d. 21 July 1967)

South African; President African National Congress 1952–67

Born in Rhodesia into a Zulu chiefly family who moved to Natal (South Africa) when he was a young boy he was educated in mission schools and qualified as a teacher. In 1935 he inherited a minor Zulu chiefship but was subsequently deposed by the government for political activities. In 1945 he joined the ANC, becoming president of the Natal branch shortly afterwards. Following the defiance campaign in 1952 he was elected national President. From then on his active role within the organization was severely limited due to almost constant restrictions, banning, and imprisonment by the government. His role was predominantly one of symbolic and moral leadership whilst other leaders such as Nelson *Mandela were responsible for day-to-day co-ordination.

Throughout his life he remained committed to the goal of a non-racial South Africa and was a staunch believer in non-violent passive resistance to apartheid. He was awarded the Nobel Peace Prize in 1960. In 1962 he published his autobiography, *Let My People Go*, which vainly called for a peaceful solution to South Africa's conflicts. In 1967 he was killed by a train whilst crossing a railway track in what are regarded by many as suspicious circumstances.

Lynch, John (Jack) (b. Cork, 15 Aug. 1917)

Irish; Taoiseach (premier) 1966–73, 1977–9

Lynch owed much of his success in Irish politics to his immense popularity as a Gaelic footballer and, especially, hurler, as well as to his affable and easy-going character. Initially a civil servant and later lawyer, he entered the Dáil in 1948, and served in Fianna Fáil administrations from 1957 onward as successively Minister for the Gaeltacht, Education, Industry and Commerce, and Finance. His succession as Taoiseach to Sean *Lemass in November 1966 was largely due to his emergence as a third candidate in a contest deadlocked between two stronger contenders. His first period as Taoiseach saw the transition in Northern Ireland from steady state to turmoil. His response to this crisis tended to be largely reactive, infuriating unionists, who saw him as an irredentist republican, while doing little practical to help nationalists or advance their cause. In August 1969 he announced, in response to the severe rioting of the time, that Irish army field hospitals would be set up in border areas, and called for the intervention of a United Nations peacekeeping force. In 1970 he sacked two of his ministers, Charles *Haughey and Neil Blaney, on suspicion of their involvement in a plan to assist the IRA in the acquisition of arms, which led ultimately to a celebrated but inconclusive trial in 1979. In opposition from 1973, Lynch proved his immense vote-winning capability when in the 1977 general election he led his party to its greatest post-war electoral success. Flushed with this, Lynch's government launched an expansionary economic policy which rapidly led to inflation and a balance of payments crisis. Appearing to lose grip, Lynch was ousted from office in December 1979 as a result of pressure from the more republican wing of the Fianna Fáil party, who were incensed at his increasing co-operation with Britain on cross-border security.

A moderate at heart, Lynch's skills lay more in party management and tactics than in policy innovation. He maintained the integrity of his party's constitutional republicanism while successfully steering a course between both British and militant republican attempts to get the Irish Republic more actively involved in assisting their respective causes.

Lyons, Joseph **(Joe)** Aloysius (b. Stanley, Tasmania, 15 Sept. 1879; d. Sydney, 7 Apr. 1939)

Australian; Premier of Tasmania 1916–19, 1923–8, Leader of United Australia Party and Prime Minister 1931–9

Lyons, the son of Irish parents, was forced at a young age to help support his large family after his father proved unsuccessful in small business and then lost the family's money gambling. He attended St Joseph's Convent School and the local state school and graduated from pupil to qualified schoolteacher in 1901.

After entering the Tasmanian parliament in 1909 Lyons was quickly promoted in the Labor Party and he held a number of portfolios, including Treasurer and then Premier in First World War ministries. Lyons's early reformist zeal, which led to free and better education in Tasmania, had been tempered by the time of his second premiership in the late 1920s; and by the time he became acting federal Treasurer in 1930 he was financially conservative. When the Labor government responded to the financial emergency of 1930–1 with orthodox budgetary restraint, Lyons bore the brunt of the left's anger. He refused to entertain thought of postponing overseas loan repayments, aligned himself with an influential group of Melbourne businessmen opposed to Labor and, with their backing, became leader of the new conservative alliance, the United Australia Party. Soon afterwards, Lyons won the December 1931 federal election and remained Prime Minister until his sudden death, from a heart attack, in 1939.

As his party was a loose coalition, Lyons spent much of his premiership trying to co-ordinate its members. His general aim, to put the country on sound business lines, was achieved to some extent, but more specific proposals struggled to find their way through opposition from states, influential key interest groups, or from within parliament where he held only narrow majorities. Despite protracted planning and negotiation he was unable to turn social insurance proposals into law. In foreign policy Lyons was mostly content to follow the lead of Britain, although he briefly and unsuccessfully tried to interest the United States in a Pacific pact.

Through his shrewdness, his parliamentary skills and use of radio, and through a lack of viable contenders, Lyons led his party to three successive electoral victories. Throughout his career he derived great support and advice from his wife, Enid, who in 1943 became the first woman in federal parliament.

McCarthy, Eugene Joseph (b. Watkins, Minnesota, 29 Mar. 1916)

US; member of the US House of Representatives 1949–59, US Senator 1959–70

The son of a cattleman, McCarthy was educated in state schools, graduated BA from St John's University, Collegeville, 1935, and MA from the University of Minnesota, 1939. After three years as a secondary schoolteacher, 1936–9, he returned to St John's as a professor of economics and education. In 1944 he became a civilian technical assistant in the Military Intelligence Division of the War Department, where he remained until 1946. He returned to an academic career as an instructor in sociology and economics at St Thomas's College St Paul.

McCarthy, a Democrat, embarked on a political career in 1949 when he was elected US representative for Minnesota's 4th District. He was re-elected to the next four consecutive congresses and then, in 1958, successfully ran for the Senate, and was re-elected in 1964.

In 1968 McCarthy sought nomination as his party's presidential candidate. His support was shaky in the early stages of the primaries, but after the assassination of rival candidate Robert *Kennedy, he relaunched his campaign. In the growing storm of protest against the Vietnam War, McCarthy, as a liberal and anti-war candidate, attracted the support of the young, the ethnic minorities, and women. At the nominating convention in Chicago, however, party bosses swung the vote in favour of the more orthodox candidate, Vice-President Hubert *Humphrey. This sparked a riot among McCarthy's supporters who had been excluded from the convention. This prompted the Democrats to revise the party's rules for choosing delegates to future conventions.

McCarthy retired from politics in 1970 and returned to a career in teaching and writing. He is the author of numerous books and articles on politics, including: *Frontiers in American Democracy* (1960); *Dictionary of American Politics* (1962); *The Year of the People* (1969).

McCarthy, Joseph Raymond (b. Grand Chute, Wisconsin, 14 Nov. 1908; d. 2 May 1957)

US; US Senator 1946–57

The son of an Irish immigrant farmer, McCarthy attended the local rural school and helped his father on the farm. After working for a while in a grocery store he decided to study law. At the age of 19 he undertook a year's intensive study in high school to gain entrance to Marquette University, Milwaukee, in 1930. He graduated LLB 1935 and practised law in Waupaca 1935–6 and in Shawano until 1939. After successfully contesting an election to circuit judge in 1939 he soon deserted the bench for service in the US Marine Corps during the Second World War. He advanced from the rank of private to captain, seeing active service as a rear-gunner with the marine aviators. In 1945 he returned briefly to the bench but later, as a Republican, he successfully challenged sitting Senator Robert *La Follette, Progressive, for a place representing Wisconsin in the US Senate.

After an initially uneventful start to his Senate career McCarthy gained national attention, leading eventually to notoriety, when, in 1950, he claimed to have the names of 200 Communist Party members employed in the State Department. This became the opening salvo of the McCarthy 'witchhunt' period which dominated American politics 1952–4. After the 1951 victory for the Republicans in the Senate, McCarthy was able to use his position as chairman of the powerful subcommittee of the Appropriations Committee to launch investigations into 'un-American activities' of members of the State Department and public life in general. Even war hero General George *Marshall did not escape McCarthy's censure.

In 1954 McCarthy was himself censured by his fellow Senators. This marked the waning of his influence. He sank into obscurity and alcoholism in his last years. McCarthy is remembered as a bitterly controversial figure in American political life.

McCormack, John William (b. Boston, 21 Dec. 1891; d. Boston, 22 Nov. 1980)
US; Member of the US House of Representatives 1928–71

McCormack's father was an Irish hod carrier from South Boston; but his early death forced John McCormack to work as a newsboy to earn money to support the family. After working in a law office, he studied law privately and began practice as a lawyer in 1913. After army service in the First World War, he entered Democratic politics and served for six years in the Massachusetts Assembly and Senate (1920–6). In 1928 he was elected to fill the congressional vacancy created by the death of James Gallivan and was also elected in his own right to the subsequent Congress. Thereafter he served continuously in the House of Representatives until 1971.

On his first election to the House McCormack established a close friendship with John Nance *Garner (who secured his assignment to the Ways and Means Committee) and Sam *Rayburn and became part of the inner circle of Democrats, many of whom played poker together. In 1936 he helped Rayburn become majority leader and, when Rayburn became Speaker in 1940, McCormack was in a good position to succeed as majority leader. McCormack held that position (apart from brief spells when Republicans controlled the House) until 1961 when he became Speaker on Rayburn's death. Although he never acquired Rayburn's authority and was constrained by the powerful committee chairmen, he was an impartial and avuncular Speaker.

McCormack was a good constituency member, thoroughly at home with the intricacies of Boston politics; and he was a hard-working Congressman. He became an expert on taxation and finance and developed an interest in space, chairing the House Committee on Science and Astronautics and helping to establish NASA in 1958.

He was an ardent supporter of Franklin *Roosevelt's New Deal and of Harry *Truman's Fair Deal as well as a believer in civil rights. He was not a complete supporter of his fellow Bostonian John *Kennedy, however, partly because Kennedy had failed to help secure a pardon for McCormack's Boston crony James Michael *Curley in 1947. In 1961 Kennedy's federal aid to education bill was killed as a result of McCormack's efforts to allow church schools to participate.

A loyal Roman Catholic, McCormack (who was dubbed 'the Archbishop') was an adamant anti-Communist and chaired a forerunner of the House Un-American Activities Committee in the 1930s. He was also a pragmatic politician within the Democratic Party, keen to keep its southern and northern wings together through compromise and personal warmth. He played a key role in securing the passage of much of Lyndon *Johnson's Great Society programme especially the landmark legislation in the field of civil rights, health care for the elderly, education, and anti-poverty measures.

By 1970 McCormack had experienced some criticism from younger Democrats anxious for more vigorous leadership. However, he stepped down of his own accord, choosing not to seek re-election in 1970. He retired to his native Boston.

MacDonald, James **Ramsay** (b. Lossiemouth, Scotland, 12 Oct. 1866; d. 9 Nov. 1937)
British; leader of the Labour Party 1922–31, Prime Minister 1924, 1929–35, Lord President of the Council 1935–7

The political career of Ramsay MacDonald, like that of *Lloyd George, is one of the most remarkable in modern British politics. Both came from humble backgrounds.

MacDonald was the illegitimate son of a farm labourer and, like Lloyd George, did not attend a university. He came to England at the age of 18 to make his name. He studied, did odd jobs, was political secretary to a Liberal candidate, and hoped for a Liberal Party nomination. This was not to be and in 1894 he joined the Independent Labour Party.

MacDonald's secretarial and debating skills proved invaluable in the early years of the Labour Party. He was secretary of the New Labour Representation Committee, formed in 1900. It was thanks to a Lib-Lab pact, which he helped to negotiate, that he became Labour MP for Leicester in 1906 and held the seat until 1918. He was one of twenty-nine Labour MPs to be returned in the 1906 election. At this time Labour was broadly sympathetic to many of the policies pursued by the Liberal Party.

MacDonald was the party's best Parliamentary performer and became leader of the small group of Labour MPs in 1911 and held the post until 1914. He wrote numerous pamphlets and books in which he propounded evolutionary ideas of socialism and firmly rejected the notions of revolution and class conflict. His socialism owed more to Darwin than to Karl Marx and was rarely linked to practical policies.

The outbreak of war in 1914 forced his resignation from the leadership. Most Labour MPs supported the war effort but MacDonald opposed it, although he was not a pacifist. His position remained complex during the war years but be was vilified by jingoistic elements in the country and lost his seat in 1918. His war record gave him a false radical reputation in and out of the Labour Party.

He was returned as Labour MP for Aberavon in 1922 and was elected chairman of the Labour Party. Labour was now the official opposition, thanks to Liberal divisions. In January 1924 he was invited to form the first Labour government—a minority one. MacDonald wielded the full power of the Prime Minister, when it came to making appointments, and insisted on the parliamentary party's autonomy from conference. He also made himself Foreign Secretary, a comment on his interest in international affairs, and his lack of admiration for colleagues, but this only contributed to overwork. The government's minority status provided some excuse for it accomplishing little, although it did recognize the Soviet Union. MacDonald took pride in showing that Labour was 'fit to govern', and reassuring middle-class opinion.

In the 1929 general election Labour were this time the largest party, though again lacking an overall majority. MacDonald formed a second minority Labour government, one that was to prove traumatic for the party and MacDonald himself. The economy worsened and unemployment more than doubled within two years. The government seemed to have no answer to the growing economic crisis. MacDonald argued that the capitalist system had failed, but the country, in effect, had to wait for socialism to come about.

A committee was appointed which recommended increases in taxation and swingeing cuts in public spending, including unemployment benefit. The Conservative opposition and much of the financial opinion demanded the full programme but the Cabinet was split about accepting the recommendations. MacDonald left to tender the government's resignation to the monarch; when he returned he shocked colleagues by revealing that he had been persuaded to stay on and lead a national all-party government which would deal with the crisis. This was the great betrayal in the Labour Party. Only a handful of the party followed MacDonald, who made little effort to court Labour followers. The breach was made irreparable when a general election was called and MacDonald, at the head of a national government, won a huge landslide and Labour was almost wiped out.

MacDonald clung on as an ineffectual Prime Minister, a prisoner of a largely Conservative Cabinet and Conservative parliamentary party. In 1935 he changed jobs with Stanley *Baldwin to become Lord President of the Council. In 1929 he had won Seaham, a Labour stronghold, and in 1931 held it as National Labour. He lost it in 1935. He was then elected to serve as member for the Scottish Universities between 1936 and 1937.

MacDonald formed three governments and was never backed by a party majority of his own. He did not have a practical government agenda and was too passive in the face of adverse circumstances. Labour's rapid growth from a parliamentary pressure group to a party of government was played out in his career. It was his misfortune that, although mainly interested in foreign affairs, his periods in government were dominated by economic issues.

McGovern, George Stanley (b. Avon, South Dakota, 19 July 1922)
US; US Senator 1963–81, Democratic presidential candidate 1972

McGovern took a BA at Dakota Wesleyan University and served in the Second World War as a pilot, winning the Distinguished Flying Cross. He took a Ph.D. at Northwestern University and taught history and political science at Dakota Wesleyan University, 1949–53. He became active in the politics of the Democratic Party in his home state of South Dakota, which was normally Republican. In 1956 he was elected to the US House of Representatives and re-elected in 1958 but defeated in a bid for a Senate seat in 1960. He was appointed Special Assistant to the President in 1961 as Director of the Food for Peace Program. In 1962 he was elected as senator from South Dakota and served for eighteen years in the Senate, winning re-election in 1968 and 1974.

He was a firm supporter of liberal causes. Through the 1960s he supported the domestic programme of the Great Society of President *Johnson on such issues as civil rights, anti-poverty measures, and the environment. He took a liberal position also on social issues such as abortion, homosexuality, and the women's movement. On foreign policy he took a strong interest in the Third World and favoured increased American aid to developing countries. On the war in Vietnam he came to be firmly opposed to American involvement.

He was not a nationally well-known figure until 1968 when, following the assassination of Robert *Kennedy, he declared himself as a candidate for the Democratic nomination for President. He did not achieve success in winning the support of many delegates to the Democratic National Convention and was easily defeated for the nomination by Hubert *Humphrey. He gained widespread recognition and admiration, however, by the manner of his campaign in 1968. In 1972 he sought again the Democratic nomination for President. He appeared initially to have little chance of overtaking the front runner, Senator Edmund Muskie. When Muskie's campaign faltered, however, the path was open for McGovern to gain the Democratic nomination. He faced enormous difficulties, however, in the presidential election in 1972 against his Republican opponent, President *Nixon. Nixon's successes in foreign policy, especially his trip to China in 1972, the initiation of détente with the Soviet Union, and the winding down of the war in Vietnam made the President a formidable opponent. At the same time, McGovern was increasingly associated with the more extreme elements in American society such as within the peace movement and the women's movement. He was overwhelmingly defeated in the 1972 presidential election, winning only one state, Massachusetts, the most liberal state in the Union, and losing every other state, including his home state of South Dakota.

The Watergate investigations of 1973–4 revealed that McGovern had been the victim of smear tactics and campaign dirty tricks in 1972, though his defeat was due largely to more substantive issues. He gained a measure of revenge for his humiliating defeat with Nixon's enforced resignation in 1974. He was not, however, able to regain a position of major influence within the Democratic Party, while the trend of developments in America of the 1970s during the presidencies of Gerald *Ford and Jimmy *Carter were in a conservative direction, which left him a more marginal and outmoded figure. In 1980 he was defeated in his bid for re-election to the Senate in 1980. He thereafter began a successful career in the hotel business in Washington, DC.

Machado y Morales, Gerardo (b. Santa Clara, Cuba, 28 Sept. 1871; d. Florida, 29 Mar. 1939)

Cuban; President 1924–33

The son of a cattle rancher, Machado served as a brigadier-general in the Liberation Army in Cuba's second War of Independence (1895–8). He then entered politics, becoming mayor of Santa Clara and then Inspector of the Armed Forces and then Secretary of the Interior in the Gomez administration (1909–13). After a successful period as farmer and businessman, he returned to lead the traditionally nationalist Liberal Party, in the wake of a disastrous sugar crisis (1921). Capitalizing on widespread unrest at growing dependence on the United States and at rampant corruption, Machado was elected Cuba's fifth president in 1924 after a populist and nationalist campaign. Initially, thanks to a recovery of sugar and the vital US market, much of his public works, social, and protectionist programme was enacted.

In 1928, however, arguing *force majeure*, Machado decreed a two-year extension of his presidency and changed the constitution to allow for his re-election largely unopposed, since dissent was met with a fierce and unprecedented repression.

Eventually, with the Depression, opposition grew, especially from students, the terrorist group ABC, and increasingly militant Communist-led unions. It became so widespread and violent that, despite Washington's attempts to mediate, a student-led rebellion and an NCOs' mutiny succeeded in removing him from power on 12 August 1933. He died six years later in exile in Florida.

Overall, Machado bridged the period between the early Republican generation of political leaders and the later radicalism which he did much to accelerate.

Machel, Samora Moises (b. Xilimbene, Mozambique, 29 Sept. 1933; d. 19 Oct. 1986)

Mozambican; President 1975–86

Born into a poor peasant family Machel never completed his secondary education. In 1963 he joined the main anti-Portuguese nationalist movement, the Front for the Liberation of Mozambique (FRELIMO) and rapidly became one of its main guerrilla commanders after receiving military training in Algeria. Following the death of Eduardo Mondlane he led FRELIMO in bringing an end to Portuguese colonialism. At independence in 1975 he became Mozambique's first state President.

Initially he declared Mozambique to be a Marxist state aligned to the Soviet Union but this position was subsequently substantially modified. The country remained extremely vulnerable to the military and economic strength of South Africa and in 1984 Machel signed the Nkomati Accord with the Pretoria regime and agreed to deny the ANC bases in return for a cessation of South African support for Mozambican dissidents.

In 1986 he was killed when his plane crashed in the eastern Transvaal in circumstances which have never been adequately explained.

McKenna, Reginald (b. London, 6 July 1863; d. 6 Sept. 1943)

British; Chancellor of the Exchequer 1915–16

The son of a civil servant, McKenna was educated at King's College School, London, and Trinity Hall, Cambridge, before becoming a barrister. He entered the Commons in 1895. After a year as a junior Treasury minister in the Liberal government formed by Henry *Campbell-Bannerman in 1905, he spent the following nine years in four separate Cabinet posts: president of the Board of Education (1907–8); First Lord of the Admiralty (1908–11); Home Secretary (1911–15); and Chancellor of the Exchequer (1915–16).

McKenna's ministerial career was often controversial. At the Admiralty, he was at the heart of Cabinet disputes over the seriousness of the threat presented by the growth of the German navy: in 1909 resistance to his demands for many more capital ships led him to threaten resignation. At the Home Office, he had to steer through legislation to disestablish the Welsh church, passage of which was achieved only by invoking the Parliament Act to overcome opposition in the Lords. But the greatest controversy arose over his Prisons (Temporary Discharge for Ill-Health) Act, 1913. This unpopular ('Cat and Mouse') legislation permitted hunger-striking convicted suffragettes to be repeatedly released temporarily and then reimprisoned. McKenna's chancellorship included the immensely difficult problems created by the massive military expenditure necessitated by the war.

When H. H. *Asquith's government collapsed in December 1916 McKenna declined to serve under David *Lloyd George and never again held ministerial office. He was approached to become Chancellor of the Exchequer again in 1922, but no suitable parliamentary seat could be found for him (he had been defeated in 1918). He spent the remainder of his working life as chairman of the Midland Bank.

Macleod, Iain Norman (b. Yorkshire, 11 Nov. 1913; d. London, 20 July 1970)
British; Chancellor of the Exchequer 1970

The son of a Scottish doctor, Macleod was educated at Fettes College and Gonville and Caius College, Cambridge. He saw service during the Second World War in France and Norway, suffering a serious leg injury. He also suffered from a rare form of rheumatoid arthritis that limited his movements and often left him in considerable pain. He served in the Conservative Research Department from 1948 to 1950, before being elected as MP for Enfield West in February 1950. A brilliant debater, he caught *Churchill's eye in March 1952 with a devastating attack on Aneurin *Bevan in the House. Six weeks later he was appointed Minister for Health, a post he held for three years (1952–5) before being promoted to Minister of Labour. In 1959 *Macmillan appointed him Colonial Secretary and two years later made him chairman of the Conservative Party. A supporter of R. A. *Butler, he refused to serve in the administration of Sir Alec *Douglas-Home and took the post of editor of the *Spectator*, writing a damning critique of the 'magic circle' that produced Home as party leader. He was brought into the shadow Cabinet following the 1964 election defeat and in 1965 the new leader, Edward *Heath, made him shadow Chancellor. Though not an economist, he worked hard to master his brief. Following the election of a Conservative government in June 1970 he was appointed Chancellor of the Exchequer. A month later, after being unwell for some time, he collapsed and died of a heart attack in 11 Downing Street.

Regarded as having a brilliant mind—he was an outstanding bridge player—he was widely respected. He was also intellectually arrogant and took little trouble to disguise the fact. Describing himself as a 'liberal Conservative', he was a founder member of the One-Nation group of Conservative MPs. His liberal instincts, especially during his tenure of the Colonial Office, made him unpopular with the right wing of the Conservative Party, the Marquess of Salisbury once describing him as 'too clever by half'. He was regarded as a pivotal figure in the new Heath government in 1970, his sudden death robbing the government of one of its most powerful and capable figures.

Macmillan, Maurice **Harold** (b. London, 10 Feb. 1894; d. 29 Dec. 1986)
British; Foreign Secretary 1955, Chancellor of the Exchequer 1955–7, Prime Minister 1957–63; Viscount Stockton 1984

The son of a publisher (and grandson of a Scottish crofter), Macmillan was educated at Eton and Balliol College, Oxford. He served with the Grenadier Guards during the First World War and was wounded three times, on the third occasion seriously. His wartime experience, surviving when much of his generation was wiped out, had a lasting impact. So too did his experience as Conservative MP for Stockton-on-Tees, representing the depressed industrial town from 1924 to 1929 and from 1931 to 1945. His experiences led him briefly to resign the Conservative whip (1936–7) and to write *The Middle Way*, espousing a moderate brand of Conservatism. His stance was essentially paternalist. He married into the family of the Duke of Devonshire and retained a fascination with the aristocracy.

His first ministerial experience came in 1940 when he was appointed as a junior minister. Two years later he took up the post of Resident Minister at Allied Forces HQ in the Mediterranean theatre, in which post he struck up a friendship with *Eisenhower. He served until the caretaker Conservative government in 1945 in which he served as Secretary of State for Air. He lost his seat at Stockton in the general election but was almost immediately returned at a by-election for the safe seat of Bromley. He was a leading member of the Opposition front bench from 1945 to 1951, speaking on economic and industrial issues, but occasionally contributing to debates on foreign affairs. On the return of a Conservative government in 1951, he was appointed to the Cabinet as Minister of Housing. The post was less than he had hoped for, but he threw himself into it with vigour. He proved an effective minister. By 1953, he could claim that 300,000 new homes had been built. In 1954 he was rewarded with promotion. He was appointed Minister of Defence. His tenure of the post and, indeed, his two subsequent posts was short-lived. In April 1955, the new Prime Minister *Eden appointed him Foreign Secretary. It was the post he wanted, but he served in it only nine months. Eden wanted to remain involved in foreign affairs and in December appointed Macmillan Chancellor of the Exchequer, a move that Macmillan did not appreciate. As Chancellor, he introduced the Premium Bond and variously clashed with Eden. When *Nasser nationalized the Suez Canal, Macmillan was among the more hawkish members of the Cabinet. When the Americans applied economic pressure, he shifted his position and came to dominate the Cabinet. Eden resigned. The majority of the Cabinet and the parliamentary party reportedly favoured Macmillan, rather than *Butler, as his successor and—after taking advice—the Queen sent for Macmillan.

Macmillan quickly restored the morale of the Conservative Party. He exuded an air of calm confidence. When the Chancellor Peter *Thorneycroft and the other Treasury ministers resigned in January 1958, Macmillan dismissed it as a 'little local difficulty'. He was able to cite continuing economic prosperity and in the 1959 budget pushed the new Chancellor *Heathcoat-Amory to adopt an expansionary budget. In 1959 he led the party to a substantial victory in the general election. He was hailed as 'Supermac'. Conditions turned against him in the new parliament. The party's 1959 manifesto offered no clear sense of direction. Facing economic pressures, Chancellor Selwyn *Lloyd adopted an unpopular 'stop-go' economic policy. Macmillan decided to pursue an application for membership of the European Economic Community. The application split the party and was subsequently vetoed by French President Charles *de Gaulle. In 1962, government unpopularity spurred Macmillan into dismissing one-third of the Cabinet, 'the Night of the Long Knives', an act that upset many of his own supporters. The following year, his handling of the Profumo affair—when his War Minister resigned after admitting lying to the House about his affair with a prostitute—left him looking out of touch with events. He looked old, and old-fashioned, in comparison with the new Labour leader, Harold *Wilson. Macmillan and his ministers were on increasingly bad terms with the press. Speculation about his leadership grew. He planned to lead the party into the next general election. His plans were upset in October 1963 when he was taken ill with prostatitis and had to go into hospital for an operation. Believing he was more gravely ill than in fact he was, he resigned the premiership (a decision he quickly regretted). From his hospital bed, he set in train a process of sounding out opinion in the party as to his successor. Initially a supporter of Lord Hailsham (Quintin *Hogg), Hogg's antics at the party conference led him to shift his support to Lord Home (Alec *Douglas-Home). The advice received from the party appeared to confirm this view, though the process of ascertaining the view was to prove highly controversial. The Queen sent for Lord Home.

Macmillan retired from the House in 1964 and declined a peerage. He worked on his memoirs and enjoyed his position—to which he had been elected in 1960—as chancellor of Oxford University. After twenty years out of parliament, he returned in 1984, having accepted a hereditary peerage. He was installed as Viscount Stockton. Despite being 90 years of age and with poor eyesight, he attended the House and, speaking from notes held in front of his face, criticized the economic policies of the *Thatcher government, claiming that privatization was like 'selling the family silver'. His time in the Upper House was short. He died on 29 December 1986.

Macmillan was often portrayed as a great showman in politics. He exuded unflappability and urbaneness, an outward appearance that masked both nervousness and personal unhappiness. His earlier experiences never left his memory, his wife had a long-standing affair with another MP (Robert Boothby), and his son Maurice—an MP to whom he had denied ministerial office—predeceased him. He was committed to ensuring a stable society, free of the misery he had witnessed in Stockton. His misfortune was to be Prime Minister at a time when Britain's economic improvement ran into the buffers.

McNamara, Robert Strange (b. San Francisco, 9 June 1916)
US; Secretary of Defense 1961–8

The son of a wholesale shoe industry executive, McNamara was educated in state schools, graduated BA from the University of California, Berkeley, in 1937 and gained an MBA from Harvard in 1939. He began working for the accountants Price Waterhouse that year, but a year later he returned to Harvard as an assistant professor of business administration. During the Second World War he became a consultant to the US Department of War in 1942, he was commissioned captain in the USAF in 1943, was awarded the US Legion of Merit, and promoted to lieutenant-colonel in 1946. He saw active service in England, India, China, and the Pacific. Retiring from active service in 1946, he has since then held the rank of colonel in the AF Reserve. On returning to civilian life he joined the Ford Motor Co., and between 1946 and 1961 held various managerial posts until eventually becoming company president in 1960 (the first non-member of the Ford family to hold that office). In 1961 *Kennedy appointed McNamara Secretary of Defense. He continued to serve in this post under Lyndon *Johnson until 1968.

McNamara occupied this highly sensitive position during a period of increased tension in East–West relations, marked by the building of the Berlin Wall (1961), the Bay of Pigs fiasco (1961), and the Cuban missile crisis (1962) and the controversial escalation of American involvement in Vietnam. Although admitting to having shared in the responsibility for the latter policy at the time, he subsequently aroused controversy by expressing doubts about the wisdom of America's stance in Vietnam. Whilst in office he was instrumental in setting up the Defense Supply Agency and the Defense Intelligence Agency with the Defense Intelligence School.

On leaving public office in 1968 McNamara became president of the International Bank for Reconstruction and Development.

Mahathir bin Mohamad, Dr Datuk Seri (b. Alor Setar, Kedah, 20 Dec. 1925)
Malaysian; Prime Minister 1981–

The son of a Malay headmaster of an English-medium school in Kedah, Mahathir was educated at Sultan Hamid College, Alor Setar, and the University of Malaya in Singapore where he qualified in medicine. He worked as a medical officer in Kedah and Perlis 1953–7 and as a general practitioner 1957–64 when he was elected Member of the House of Representatives for Kota Setar Selatan.

An 'ultra' in the leading party, the United Malays National Organization, Mahathir was forced into the political wilderness after the 1969 race riots when he accused Prime Minister Tunku *Abdul Rahman of 'giving the Chinese what they demand'. He resumed medical practice and wrote *The Malay Dilemma* (1970) in which he diagnosed the causes for the economically inferior position of Malays in genetic and cultural terms and prescribed positive discrimination to ensure their position as the 'definitive race'. Although the government embarked on a similar course with its New Economic Policy, this book was banned because it touched 'sensitive issues'.

In the 1970s Mahathir was readmitted to UMNO and, after brief membership of the Senate, was elected to the House of Representatives as Member for Kubang Pasu in 1974. He served in the government of Tun Abdul Razak (1970–6) as Minister of Education (1974–7) and under Tun Hussein Onn as Deputy Prime Minister (1976–81) and Minister of Trade and Industry (1977–81). In 1981 he succeeded Hussein Onn as Prime Minister and president of UMNO.

As Prime Minister (an office he has combined with those of Minister of Defence 1981–6 and Minister of Home Affairs since 1986), Mahathir brought a new vigour to government and economic management. The first Malaysian Prime Minister not to have come from the Malay aristocracy nor to have been educated in Britain, he tilted at the special relationship with Britain and the constitutional privileges of Malaysia's king and sultans, while his 'Look East' policy was inspired by Japan's economic success. Commanding an effective party machine, controlling the media, and benefiting from the country's remarkable economic growth, Mahathir has survived leadership contests, splits in UMNO, and challenges from the Islamic Party (PAS). The Barisan National (a coalition dominated by Mahathir's UMNO) has sustained an overwhelming majority in the federal parliament as a result of successive electoral victories.

Major, John (b. 29 Mar. 1941)

British; Foreign Secretary 1989, Chancellor of the Exchequer 1989–90, Prime Minister 1990–7

Although John Major's two immediate predecessors as Conservative Party leader had also come from modest backgrounds, they had at least attended university. Major, the son of a trapeze artist, did not shine at his local grammar school and he left at 16. After some experience of unemployment he worked for a bank. While in Nigeria he had a serious accident which left him with a limp.

In the late 1960s he was a local Conservative councillor in the London Lambeth local authority, the only Conservative leader this century to have had local government experience. He defeated a number of better-known candidates for the safe Conservative seat of Huntingdonshire, which he won in the 1979 general election. There followed spells in the whip's office and in the Social Security Department. He was a middle of the road Conservative, though with liberal views on social issues. There was nothing in his background to mark him out as a man of the right.

Appointed Chief Secretary to the Treasury in June 1987 he became the first of the 1979 intake to enter the Cabinet. He worked with Nigel *Lawson and had responsibility for public spending. In July 1989 Major replaced Sir Geoffrey *Howe at the Foreign Office. From being talked about as a possible next leader but one, he was now widely regarded in the media as the likely successor to Margaret *Thatcher. He was not happy in his few months in the Foreign Office, although it would not have been easy for any incumbent to cope with such a dominant and experienced Prime Minister as Mrs Thatcher.

A few months later he was again, suddenly, transferred to a new post, this time Chancellor of the Exchequer, following the sudden resignation of Nigel Lawson. As

Chancellor he continued with the regime of high interest rates to bear down on inflation. With the support of the new Foreign Secretary, Douglas *Hurd, he persuaded Mrs Thatcher to take Britain into the European Community's ERM in September 1990. This was a fatal decision and subsequent events were to prove that Britain had entered at too high a rate.

During 1990 Mrs Thatcher's leadership was under pressure. She was unpopular with voters and regarded as a vote loser by a number of colleagues. John Major was one of her two proposers when she stood in the annual leadership election in November 1990. He was unwell and absent from the manœuvres which took place following her failure to win an outright victory on the first ballot. When she stood down, John Major entered the contest and, with Thatcher's support and no candidate standing for the right, he was a clear favourite. He won the second ballot with 185 votes, compared to 131 for Michael *Heseltine and 56 for Douglas Hurd. He was two votes short of an outright victory but the other two candidates stood down and he became the new party leader. Only one other twentieth-century Prime Minister had held the two great posts of Foreign Secretary and Chancellor—James *Callaghan. Major's tenure of the two, however, amounted to only seventeen months in total.

As Prime Minister, Major inherited a party divided over Europe and these divisions came to dominate the latter part of his premiership. He gained credit for his conduct during the Gulf War, helped to replace the hated poll tax, and negotiated the Maastricht Treaty, which kept the Cabinet united. One policy firmly identified with him was the Citizen's Charter, designed to improve public services. By 1992, however, he was increasingly criticized on the right of the party. He suffered in comparison with his predecessor, lacking her drive and her radical agenda. Critics said that he had been over-promoted and that his spells at the Foreign Office and the Treasury had been too brief either for him to make a mark or for mistakes to become evident.

By the end of 1995 Major had been in office for over five years and only four post-war prime ministers had enjoyed a longer tenure. Yet there was often an air of impermanence about his premiership. For the first sixteen months there was the likelihood of defeat in a general election whenever it was called. Against the odds he led his party to an election victory in April 1992. Although the Conservative majority over Labour was 65, it was only 21 overall. Because of divisions over Europe and losses in by-elections it was not long before the party lacked an assured majority in the new parliament. Recovery from the economic recession was delayed by membership of the ERM. It was a blow to his prestige when Britain was forced out in September 1992. A bruising battle to pass the Maastricht Treaty through parliament in 1993 showed the government to be at the mercy of events and rebel Tory Euro-sceptics seemed to have the initiative. According to opinion polls, he and the government were the most unpopular since polling began. He surprised his party critics by resigning the party leadership in June 1995 and offered himself for re-election. He decisively beat the challenger John Redwood by 218 votes to 89, with 20 abstentions or spoilt ballots.

By 1997 his government could point to historically low inflation and low interest rates. His pragmatic wait-and-see position on entering a single European currency seemed to match the public mood and was perhaps the only one which could stop the party from splitting outright. He called a general election in May 1997. He was unable to overcome the mood of 'Time for a Change' (his party had been in office for eighteen years) and internal divisions over Europe. The Conservative Party went down to its worst defeat of the century and Major resigned the leadership.

Makarios, Mikhail (b. Pano Panayia, Cyprus, 13 Aug. 1913; d. 3 Aug. 1977)
Cypriot; President 1959–77

The son of a peasant, Makarios studied divinity at an Athens monastery. After being ordained a priest in 1946 he studied in the United States. He became Bishop and then Archbishop of the Orthodox church in Cyprus in 1958. This position of ecclesiastical leadership involved him in the politics of the island. His support for EOKA, a movement which worked for a union of Cyprus and Greece, brought him into conflict with Britain, which wanted Cyprus to become independent within the Commonwealth, and Turkey, which had a large minority population on the island and wanted partition. The British arrested him in 1956 on suspicion of terrorist activities and he was exiled for a time. In 1959 he abandoned the quest for union with Greece, EOKA was disbanded, and Cyprus was granted independence. He was elected President in 1959 and again in 1968 and 1974. His efforts to integrate Greek and Turkish communities on the island were criticized by intransigent supporters of the union with Greece. In 1974, with Greece under military rule, there was an attempted coup in Cyprus by the Greek Cypriot National Guard and Makarios was forced to flee. Shortly afterwards Turkey invaded Cyprus and partitioned the island. Makarios returned to the island at the end of 1974 but was unable to reverse the partition. After his death the posts of primate and head of state in Cyprus were separated.

Maksimovich, Maksim *see* LITVINOV, MAXIMILIAN

Malenkov, Georgii Maximilianovich (b. Orenburg, Russia, 8 Jan. 1902; d. Moscow, 23 Jan. 1988)

Russian; Politbureau member 1941–57, Deputy Prime Minister 1946–53, Prime Minister 1953–5

From a middle-class background, Malenkov joined the Communist Party in 1920 and worked in the Central Committee apparatus after graduation from Moscow Higher Technological Institute in 1925. He became a close associate of *Stalin and *Beria and was heavily involved in the collectivization campaign and the purges of the 1930s. He became a Central Committee member in 1939 and candidate member of the Politbureau and State Defence Committee member in 1941. In 1946 he became a full member of the Politbureau and deputy chair of the Council of Ministers and after *Zhdanov's death in 1948 was regarded as Stalin's natural successor, confirmed by his delivery of the General Report to the 19th CPSU Congress in 1952.

After Stalin's death Malenkov was briefly both chair of the Council of Ministers and party secretary, but soon ceded the latter post, considered less important, to *Khrushchev. Together with Beria he launched a reform programme known as the 'New Course', reviving the idea of 'peaceful coexistence', laying more stress on agriculture and consumer goods and repudiating the 'Doctors' Plot' of 1952. However, he was outmanœuvred by Khrushchev, who stole his liberal policies and managed to install his ally, *Bulganin, as premier in February 1955. Malenkov, still a member of the Presidium (Politbureau), mobilized the state apparatus against Khrushchev, defeating him in the Presidium in 1957. However, Khrushchev appealed successfully to the Central Committee and ousted the 'Anti-Party Group', including Malenkov, from the Presidium and the Central Committee. Malenkov was exiled as manager of a hydro-electric plant in Kazakhstan, but returned to a long retirement in Moscow. Not just a pen-pusher, as depicted by Khrushchev, he was an able and tough politician who started the post-Stalin liberalization.

Mandela, Nelson Rolihlahla (b. Qunu, South Africa, 18 July 1918)

South African; President 1994–

Born into the Thembu (Xhosa) ruling family Mandela studied at Fort Hare University but was expelled for leading a student strike. He subsequently qualified as a lawyer through correspondence courses and in 1952, with Oliver Tambo, he established the country's first black law firm. In 1944 he was a founder member of the Youth League of the African National Congress (ANC). During the 1940s and 1950s he rose rapidly through the ANC hierarchy but was frequently subject to police harassment, detention, and banning. When the ANC was outlawed in 1960 he went underground and organized its military wing, Umkhonto we Sizwe (Spear of the Nation). In 1962 he was sentenced to five years' imprisonment. In 1964, whilst still in detention, he was charged with treason and, after giving a memorable four-and-a-half hour speech criticizing apartheid, he was sentenced to life imprisonment.

In total Mandela spent twenty-seven consecutive years in detention. From 1964 to 1982 he was held on Robben Island, from 1982 to 1988 in Pollsmoor Prison, Cape Town, and from 1988 to 1990 in Victor Verster Prison, Paarl. From 1985 on he rejected several offers of 'conditional' release which would have imposed severe limits on his political activities. In many ways his imprisonment increased his, already considerable, political status and resulted in a worldwide campaign for his release. In February 1990 he was unconditionally released to scenes of joyous celebration at home and abroad.

On his release he became deputy president of the now legalized ANC leaving the ailing Oliver Tambo to hold the presidency for a short time longer, before being elected president of the party in July 1991. Displaying a quite extraordinary lack of rancour towards whites he began to work towards the establishment of a non-racial democracy in South Africa to replace the totally discredited apartheid system. To this end he participated in the Convention for a Democratic South Africa (CODESA), which began work in early 1992 to negotiate the future constitutional arrangements for the country but collapsed in 1992 and was replaced by a new forum at Kempton Park in 1993. In 1993 he and F. W. *de Klerk were jointly awarded the Nobel Peace Prize. Although the negotiations were not without setbacks and delays they eventually produced an interim constitution which led to the first ever non-racial election in April 1994. In recognition of Mandela's huge personal popularity the ANC campaign for the National Assembly elections came close to being a presidential-style campaign with great emphasis put on the leader. With the ANC gaining just under two-thirds of votes cast, Mandela, as leader of the largest party in parliament, was installed as national President.

On coming to power he formed a coalition government of 'national unity' following the requirements of the interim constitution, which included de Klerk as Deputy Vice-President but in which the ANC held the majority of portfolios. Under Mandela's leadership the government embarked on the twin paths of reconciliation and reconstruction in a society which had been badly divided by over a century of racial segregation and apartheid.

Helped by a combination of acute intelligence, total moral integrity, and an approach to politics which combined idealism and pragmatism, Mandela has been the key pivotal figure in a political transformation which few believed was possible.

Manley, Michael Norman (b. Jamaica, 10 Dec. 1924)

Jamaican; Prime Minister 1972–80, 1989–92

The son of Norman Manley, the founder of the People's National Party (PNP) and a 'father' of Jamaican independence, Michael Manley entered a political dynasty, becoming leader of the PNP in 1969. He had previously studied economics at the LSE and worked for the BBC in London, organized Jamaican sugar workers in a PNP-run trade union, and been elected to parliament in 1969.

He led the PNP to victory in the 1972 election and two years later declared himself a democratic socialist, proposing a radical agenda of nationalizations, social reforms, and close ties with Cuba. He introduced legislation on union and women's rights, started a land reform, and spent heavily on health, education, and housing. The PNP was re-elected in 1976 but its second term was characterized by economic crisis and mounting political violence. Manley alleged that the USA and IMF, hostile to his brand of socialism and Third Worldism, destabilized the Jamaican economy, cutting credit, and imposing covert sanctions. The PNP lost the 1980 election to the conservative Jamaica Labour Party (JLP) of Edward Seaga.

After nine years in opposition, Manley returned to power in 1989, inheriting an even more bankrupt economy. By now he had recanted much of his earlier radicalism, made peace with Washington, and broken with the left-wing faction of the PNP. His government presented itself as pro-business and advocated privatization policies, although maintaining cautious links with Cuba.

In 1992 Manley retired from the premiership on grounds of ill-health, handing over power to P. J. Patterson. He has subsequently worked as a consultant and has contributed to various regional commissions and organizations.

Mansfield, Michael (Mike) Joseph (b. New York, 16 Mar. 1903)

US; member of the US House of Representatives 1943–53, US Senator 1953–77, Senate majority leader 1961–76, US ambassador to Japan 1977–88

The son of a grocer, Mansfield dropped out of school before completing eighth grade. During the First World War, at the age of 14, he enlisted in the US Navy and served as a seaman second class. He then enlisted as a private in the army; after serving for one year he joined the Marines and as a private first class saw two years' service in the Philippines, China, and Siberia. From 1922 to 1931 he worked as a miner, and then as a mining engineer, in Butte Montana. Concurrently he attended Montana School of Mines, 1927–8. He graduated BA in 1933 and MA in 1934 from Montana State University, Missoula. In 1933 he joined the faculty of the university as a professor of Far Eastern and Latin American history.

Mansfield, a Democrat, launched his political career in 1940 when he made an unsuccessful attempt to gain election to Congress. He remained in his academic post until 1942 when on his second attempt he was elected representative of the 1st Montana District. He was re-elected to the next four congresses. During his ten years in the House he was a prominent member of the foreign relations committee.

Elected US Senator for Montana in 1952, Mansfield served for twenty-five years in the Senate during the high summer of the Democrat's ascendancy. He became assistant majority leader 1957–61 and majority leader 1961–77. During his first term in the Senate he attempted, unsuccessfully, to bring the activities of the CIA under closer Senate scrutiny. In the early 1970s, before the full extent of the Watergate scandal had become known, he favoured a constitutional amendment that proposed introducing a single six-year presidential term. In the wake of Vietnam, and at the height of the Watergate furore, he supported the War Powers Resolution 1973 limiting presidential authority to wage undeclared wars. Mansfield was a prominent member of the Senate's prestigious Foreign Relations committee.

During his time in Congress, he visited the People's Republic of China on four occasions, served as presidential representative in China in 1944, and US delegate to the United Nations Assembly in Paris 1951–2. He retired from the Senate in 1976 but not from public service. In 1977 he became a member of a commission seeking information about US servicemen missing in Indochina. The same year he was also appointed by President *Carter to the post of US ambassador to Japan. He remained in post during *Reagan's presidency, finally retiring in 1988.

Mansholt, Sicco Leendert (b. Ulrum, 13 Sept. 1908; d. Wapserveen, 29 June 1995)

Dutch; President of the EC 1972–3

Mansholt was born the son of a farmer. Both his parents were politically active in the Labour Party (SDAP). Once a farmer himself, he also joined the SDAP.

He specialized in tropical agriculture, but due to the economic depression of the 1930s he could not afford to buy or rent a farm himself. After working for two years at different places, he decided to try his luck in the Netherlands East Indies. From 1934 till 1936 he was employed at a tea plantation. Not at ease in the colonial world, he returned to the Netherlands as soon as there was an opportunity to become a (tenant-)farmer in the newly reclaimed land of the Wieringermeer. During the Second World War he actively participated in the resistance movement. Immediately after the war he was asked to become Minister of Agriculture, Food Supply and Fisheries, a post he was to retain until 1958. He was chairman of the Dutch delegation to the FAO in 1946. In the 1950s he developed plans for future European agricultural development. Following the *Monnet–*Schuman plans for a European Coal and Steel Community he suggested the creation of a common European agricultural market (first Mansholt Plan).

In 1958 Mansholt was appointed as member of the European Commission for Agricultural Affairs. In 1967 he was elected Vice-President, and from March 1972 he acted as President of the EC until his resignation in 1973. When in the 1960s problems of agricultural surpluses arose, Mansholt came with a second Mansholt Plan to redevelop European agriculture. This plan failed to secure full ministerial backing, however, and was only partially carried out. Years later Mansholt admitted that he regretted not having resigned on that occasion. Impressed by the report of the Club of Rome Mansholt tried in vain to convince the EC of the urgency of solving problems concerning environmental pollution, energy, world food supply, ecology, and the increase of population. After his retirement in 1973 he continued to beg attention for a more ecological approach to economical development. Until his death in 1995 he remained an ardent advocate of the renewal of agricultural policy through a third Mansholt Plan: direct control of production together with guaranteed prices.

Mao Tse-tung *see* MAO ZEDONG

Mao Zedong (Mao Tse-tung) (b. Shaoshan, Hunan Province, 26 Dec. 1893; d. 9 Sept. 1976)

Chinese; chairman of the Chinese Communist party 1935–76, paramount leader of the People's Republic of China 1949–76

Mao Zedong was the single most influential figure in Chinese politics in the twentieth century. Even after his death, his legacy for Chinese politics was immense—indeed the continued use of the term 'post-Mao' China to define the current epoch is testimony to his importance and standing. As Mao was also a crucial player in global politics for three decades, he was quite simply one of the most important leaders in the world.

While many other Chinese Communist leaders spent some time in France or Moscow, Mao's formative political experiences were all in China. The young Mao spent much of his spare time travelling in the local countryside, talking to the local peasants about their problems. Like many of his generation, he was later inspired by opposition to the oppressive Confucian family system. In many ways, the translation of Ibsen's *A Doll's House* was more of an inspiration to Mao's generation than translations of Marx, Engels, and *Lenin. Indeed, Mao did not have a particularly good knowledge of the major Communist texts, and in later life often made a virtue out of his experiences with the Chinese people, extolling the importance of 'seeking truth from facts' at the expense of book-learned socialism.

Whilst enrolled as a mature teacher-training student in Changsha in 1913, Mao first became involved in political organization and mobilization under the influence of his first mentor, the philosopher Yang Changji. In 1918, Yang helped Mao secure a job under the Marxist theoretician, Li Dazhao in the Beijing University library, which marked Mao's conversion from liberal to Marxist. Nevertheless, although Mao was a founder member of the Chinese Communist Party in 1921, he still did not have a firm understanding of the basics of Marxism at this time.

On Moscow's instructions, the Communists joined a United Front with the Nationalists in the early 1920s, and Mao was placed in charge of the peasant work department where he undertook a study of the situation in rural Hunan. Mao became convinced that the peasantry and not the urban proletariat would be the source of revolution in China. This view was antithetical to the official party line, and resulted in much criticism from both Moscow and the party leaders in Shanghai. Mao retained a fierce grudge against his critics during this period, particularly those who he felt were isolated from the real revolution and struggle in the Chinese countryside.

When the Nationalists installed a new national government in Nanjing, *Chiang Kai-shek abandoned the united front and moved against the Communists. Mao led one of a number of failed Communist uprisings (in Changsha), and the defeated troops escaped to the mountains of Jiangxi Province. Joined over the years by other sympathizers, and the remnants of another abortive set of rebellions in 1930, the Communists established a Soviet headquarters at Ruijin, where Mao devised the strategy that was later to bring the Communists to power. In addition to his formula for rural-based revolution, Mao developed a mobile warfare guerilla strategy built on a cohesive, disciplined, and democratic Red Army.

Mao was temporarily displaced from power as the Nationalists increased their attacks and forced the Communists to retreat. The heavy losses of the early days of the Long March out of Jiangxi proved the wisdom of Mao's mobile strategy, and although Wang Ming still claimed the mantle of Communist leadership from the safety of Moscow, Mao was effectively leader of the Chinese Communists from the Zunyi Conference of January 1935 to his death in 1976.

From the end of the Long March in 1935 throughout the subsequent war against Japan, Mao and his colleagues planned their military and revolutionary strategy from Yanan in Shaanxi Province. Through a combination of exploiting their nationalist credentials, moderate social and economic reform, political cohesion and mobilization, effective guerilla military tactics, and the concomitant failings of the nationalists, the Communists surprised perhaps even themselves by establishing a new People's Republic on 1 October 1949.

Having won the revolution in the face of apparently insurmountable odds, Mao became convinced that there was nothing that the Chinese people could not achieve if they were correctly educated and mobilized. Whilst other leaders argued for a slow and stable process of economic development based on Soviet Leninist principles, Mao argued for a Chinese solution entailing mass mobilization to bring about the simultaneous political development of the Chinese people, and rapid economic change.

Mao's first radical experiment saw the rapid collectivization of the countryside. The early successes of this policy led on to the Great Leap Forward—a mass campaign to communize the Chinese population as soon as possible, and in the process unleash the enthusiasm of the masses in economic production. China would surpass Britain's level of development in fifteen years and China would be pushed to the verge of real Communism. The result was somewhat different. The Great Leap collapsed into a great famine, resulting in the deaths of 40 million Chinese between 1961 and 1963.

Instead of accepting the errors of his strategy, Mao instead blamed the failings of local officials, the peasants' poor understanding of socialism, and the failings of some of his leadership colleagues. When these leaders, notably Liu Shaoqi and *Deng Xiaoping, intervened to marginalize his Socialist Education Campaign from 1962 to 1964, Mao became convinced that if his correct vision of the Chinese revolution was to succeed, then the party had to get rid of these 'capitalist roaders'.

Thus, Mao unleashed the revolutionary enthusiasm of the Chinese students who had been indoctrinated in loyalty to his name in a Cultural Revolution against class enemies. The result was chaos. Communist leaders at all levels were arrested, and many lost their lives. Countless others also died as the student Red Guards became ever more vindictive and imaginative in defining ways to identify class traitors, and parts of the country descended into virtual civil war. By 1971, Mao had been forced to rely on the military to restore order, and purged two of his closest political allies, Lin Biao and Chen Boda, as the system lurched uncertainly back towards a semblance of stability.

Mao grew ever more ill during the 1970s, and his political role in these years remains unclear. Many believe that his radical followers, the Gang of Four, exercised power in Mao's name, although it is likely that he still had the final word on major issues. Despite the arrest of the Gang of Four, and Deng Xiaoping's ascension to power in 1978, the party did not feel able to criticize Mao directly for the Cultural Revolution until 1981. Even then, the party took great care to show that his many great deeds vastly outweighed his errors. *Chen Yun's appreciation of Mao's career is closer to the truth: if he had died in 1956, the party could have remembered Mao as a great revolutionary hero. As he died in 1976, 'there is nothing that we can do about it'.

Marchais, Georges (b. La Hoguette, 7 June 1920)
French; Communist Party Secretary-General 1972–94, presidential candidate 1981

The son of a miner, Marchais became a mechanic and went to Paris sometime in the mid to late 1930s to work in the aeronautical industry. After the Occupation he went to work in Messerschmitt (not as conscripted labour). His exact activities between joining Messerschmitt in 1942 and 1947 (when he says he joined the Communist Party) are not known for sure. He then rose under the patronage of leader *Thorez and probably attended the Communist school in Moscow in 1955. He was secretary of Seine-Sud federation in 1956 and the same year was a substitute Central Committee member, and in 1959 a substitute Politbureau member. In 1961 he entered the secretariat with responsibility for organization and, with *Rochet ill, was effective party leader by 1970. He continued the policies of alliance with the Socialists and of 'modernization' inherited from Thorez and Rochet and the mid-1970s were years of movement and when the hope for an 'Italianate' party appeared incarnated in Marchais. This hope was dashed in 1977 when Marchais ended the alliance and returned to a hard-line pro-Sovietism symbolized by support for the invasion of Afghanistan. The party's vertiginous decline then set in starting with the loss of votes in the 1981 presidentials, through the dissidence of the 1980s, to the anti-glasnost, anti-perestroika stance of the late 1980s. In 1989 he regretted the fall of the Eastern Bloc but asserted that 'Socialism' would display its capacity for renewal in the Soviet fatherland itself. The party initially failed to condemn the coup of August 1991. Marchais was by all accounts a limited personality, a party apparatchik, if with a talent for dramatic TV and for clownish aggression.

Marcos, Ferdinand Edralin (b. Ilocos Norte, 11 Sept. 1917; d. 28 Sept. 1989)
Philippino; President 1965–86

The son of a politician, Marcos studied law at the University of the Philippines. As a law student he was accused of murdering a political opponent of his father, but Marcos defended himself and secured his own acquittal. During the Second World War he led a Philippine army unit in the anti-Japanese resistance and was held prisoner in the Bataan prison camp.

Marcos was elected to the Philippines House of Representatives in 1949, standing in Ilocos Norte on behalf of the Liberal Party. In 1959 he secured election to the

Senate and became its presiding officer in 1963. He switched his allegiance to the Nacionalista Party and, promising a 'New Society', was elected President in November 1965.

In November 1969 Marcos became the first President of the Philippines to be re-elected for the second time. Faced with an increasing Communist insurgency, economic mismanagement, and loss of political office, Marcos declared martial law on 21 September 1972.

The early promises of the martial law regime gave way to corruption and rapid political decay. Marcos perpetuated his rule by managed referenda and elections. He experimented with a number of political systems—parliamentary, French-presidential—in order to construct some legitimacy.

Martial law was lifted in 1981 and in June of that year Marcos was elected President for a six-year term in elections which were boycotted by the Opposition. The personal authority of Marcos began to fade rapidly after this, especially following the assassination at Manila Airport (August 1983) of his chief political rival, Benigno Aquino. This triggered widespread opposition to the regime and the combination of American pressure, economic crises, and internal Communist insurgency persuaded the President to call a national election in February 1986.

Although Marcos was declared the victor by the National Assembly, the elections were heavily rigged and sparked a peoples' power movement led by Mrs Corazón *Aquino (wife of Benigno Aquino). Divisions within the army and the withdrawal of American support forced Marcos to leave the Philippines for exile in Hawaii.

Marcos is remembered as someone who established his dominance over the Philippines through his national philosophy of 'new society' and national regeneration. His anti-Communism and American support were key factors in keeping him in power. His wife, Imelda Marcos, symbolized his corrupt and personalized rule, particularly after 1972.

Markovic, Ante (b. Konjic, Bosnia, 25 Nov. 1924)

Croat; Prime Minister of Communist Yugoslavia 1989–91

After studying electrical engineering at Zagreb University Markovic went into economic management, making his reputation as director (1961–86) of the Rade Koncar factory, one of Yugoslavia's largest plants. In 1982–6 he was Croatian premier and in 1986–8 Croatian President. In March 1989 he became President of the Federal Executive Council (i.e. Yugoslav premier). Building on the 1988 constitutional amendments, which had extensively liberalized the economy, he put forward a technocratic programme for a 'completely new type of socialism', involving economic liberalization and stabilization and strengthening of federal decision-making. By December inflation levels forced him to introduce 'shock therapy' measures, involving a wage freeze and tight monetary and fiscal controls, which rapidly brought down inflation and boosted Markovic's popularity with the international political and financial community. However, the disintegration of the country along ethnic lines escalated rapidly after the collapse of the League of Communists in January 1990 and the subsequent nationalist election victories and it became almost impossible to implement federal policy. In July he founded his own federal-technocratic party, the Alliance of Reform Forces, which had some success in Bosnia (5.4 per cent) and Macedonia (9.2 per cent), but failed in Serbia and Montenegro. In 1991 he struggled to maintain republican co-operation and external support but was increasingly sidelined by direct deals between republican leaders. He came to rely on the support of the Yugoslav army and sanctioned, controversially, their intervention in Slovenia in June 1991 to defend Yugoslavia's borders after Slovenia and Croatia declared independence. Shocked at the carnage in Croatia, he tried to bring the army under control by demanding in September the resignation of the Defence Minister and his deputy, but they refused. Faced with a complete breakdown of federal authority he resigned on

20 December, unable to accept a budget in which 86 per cent of expenditure was allocated to the military. An able and well-meaning administrator he was overwhelmed by a tide of nationalism he was powerless to resist.

Marquis, Frederick James *see* WOOLTON, LORD

Marshall, George Catlett (b. Uniontown, Pennsylvania, 31 Dec. 1880; d. 16 Oct. 1959)
US; Chief of Staff 1939–45, Secretary of State 1947–9, Secretary of Defense 1950–1

Marshall was educated at the Virginia Military Institute, 1897–1901, graduated with honours from the US Infantry-Cavalry School 1907 and from the Army Staff College 1908. In 1901 he was commissioned as a second lieutenant of infantry and served first in the Philippines and then as a Staff College instructor. In the First World War he went overseas as chief of operations on the staff of the First Division, services for which he was decorated both by his own country and France.

Franklin *Roosevelt recognized Marshall's qualities and during the Second World War appointed him Chief of Staff, tasked with building up and modernizing the army. After the war, as Special Presidential Envoy to China, Marshall assumed the mission impossible of trying to bring about peace in the civil war between Communists and Kuomintang forces. His failure to do so influenced America's decision to abandon containment in China, and led to Marshall's censure by Senator *McCarthy for betraying America's vital interest.

In 1947, with the unanimous endorsement of the Senate, Marshall became Secretary of State. Many brilliant minds contributed to the Marshall Plan for the reconstruction of post-war Europe. It was Marshall, however, as Secretary of State, who played a key role in persuading Americans to shoulder a major burden in the recovery programme and in persuading Europeans of the need for co-operation with each other.

Marshall retired on health grounds in 1949. During the Korean War, at the urging of *Truman, he returned to office as Secretary of Defense and played an influential part in the demise of General McArthur.

General Marshall was recognized by his own countrymen and by the Allies as a man of courage, vision, and integrity, who made a major contribution to winning the war and the peace. In addition to numerous decorations and honorary degrees, in 1953 he received the Nobel Peace Prize.

Marti, Farabundo, Augustin (d. 30 Jan. 1932)
Salvadorean; revolutionary agitator in Central America in the 1920s, leading member of the Communist Party of El Salvador (PCS)

The son of a landowner of mixed Indian/Spanish (*mestizo*) race, Marti was known as *El Negro* because of his dark complexion. He was educated at the National University of El Salvador, where he became influenced by Marxist-Leninist ideas and subsequently dedicated his life to revolutionary agitation.

Expelled from the country in 1920, Marti travelled throughout Central America, devoting himself to building a revolutionary movement in the region. He was a founder member of the Central American Socialist Party, in Guatemala City in 1925, returning to El Salvador that year to work as a propagandist for the Regional Federation of Salvadorean Workers (FRTS). Marti gained a considerable reputation for his intellect and learning during these years and organized a number of left-wing study groups.

Jailed by President Pio Romero Bosque and released only after a hunger strike, Marti left for New York in 1928, and worked for International Red Aid (Socorro Rojo Internacional). By the end of the year, he was back in Central America, working as the personal secretary of Augusto Cesar Sandino, the Nicaraguan engaged in a struggle against US troops in his country. But the two had ideological differences; Marti claimed that Sandino was only interested in national independence and not in social revolution.

Back in El Salvador in 1930, Marti joined the leadership of the PCS. Political activity centred on the Western coffee estates of Ahuachapan and Sonsonate, where some 80,000 peasants had joined the FRTS. The onset of the Depression and the collapse in coffee prices and coffee-workers wages led to escalating social tension. After a further period of jail and expulsion, Marti was back in El Salvador, leading peasant and worker strikes in 1931. Following a coup in December 1931 by General Maximiliano Hernandez Martinez, Marti was amongst those PCS leaders who felt the party should participate in the elections called for January 1932. But fraud and refusal to allow elected party members to take office, led the PCS to prepare for an armed insurrection to take place on 16 January.

Marti is reputed to have been amongst those who believed there was no hope of victory. The regime discovered the plans, and jailed Marti, along with two students who were helping him. When other leaders found out, they tried to call off the insurrection but it took place on the night of 22–3 January 1932, and resulted in a massacre of some 30,000 peasants. Marti and the two students were tried on 29 January and executed the next day.

Farabundo Marti remains a legendary figure for the Salvadorean left; his memory was kept alive by the revolutionaries of the 1980s, who called their movement, the Farabundo Marti Movement of National Liberation (FMLN)

Martin, Joseph William Jr. (b. North Attleboro, Massachusetts, 3 Nov. 1884; d. 6 Mar. 1968)

US; member of the US House of Representatives 1925–67

The son of a blacksmith, Martin worked as a journalist after attending high school. In 1908 he bought the *North Attleboro Evening Chronicle* and in 1912 was elected to the Massachusetts House of Representatives, where he served until 1914, when he was elected to the state Senate. In 1917 he became chairman of the Massachusetts Legislative Campaign Committee and was from 1922 to 1925 executive secretary of the Republican State Committee. Elected to the US House of Representatives in 1925, Martin became minority leader in 1939, a position he held until 1959. From 1940 to 1942 Martin combined the role of minority leader of the House with the chairmanship of the Republican National Committee. With the Republican congressional victory of 1946, he served as Speaker in the 'do-nothing Eightieth Congress' (1947–49), a role he occupied again when Republicans enjoyed a majority in the House from 1953 to 1955.

Martin played a key part in the 'conservative coalition'. He was able to unite Republicans and conservative southern Democrats to curb the expansion of federal government and to limit the impact of liberal legislative initiatives. In 1946 he helped to pass the *Taft–Hartley Act, limiting the power of organized labour, over President *Truman's veto. For many on his own side his leadership style was too autocratic and there were suspicions that his friendly relationship with Democratic Speaker Sam *Rayburn limited Republican effectiveness in Congress. Discontent with the Republican electoral and legislative performance combined with concern about the neglect of the party's Policy Committee to remove him from the leadership in 1959. In 1966 Martin failed to be renominated and he died two years later.

Martinez, Gral Maximiliano Hernandez (b. 29 Oct. 1882; d. 17 May 1966)

Salvadorean; President of the Republic 1931–44

El Salvador's most colourful and eccentric President came to power in a coup in

December 1931. An officer of humble origins, he had been vice-presidential candidate in the 1930 election of President Araujo and subsequently became Minister of War in the government he replaced.

Martinez is remembered as the President who ordered the massacre of an estimated 30,000 peasants in the wake of the abortive peasant uprising of January 1932. But he is also remembered for his bizarre lifestyle and obsessions. He espoused the causes of temperance, vegetarianism, and theosophy, believing in the transmigration of human souls and reincarnation.

His dictatorial government also saw the establishment of El Salvador's first official party, 'Pro-Patria' (for the homeland), a personal instrument of the President. All other organizations were banned, while Martinez centralized decision-making and replaced civilian with military officers at local and national levels of government. Martinez was attracted by the Axis powers during the 1930s and Salvadorean officers went to train in Germany and Italy. Unable to sustain the economy through trade with these two powers, Martinez was forced for economic reasons to shift allegiances back to the Allies by 1940.

Martinez experienced at least three plots to overthrow him in the 1930s. Disaffection within the army continued to grow as a clique of the President's friends concentrated more and more power and privileges in their hands. Members of the landed oligarchy also grew restive at his economic policies of state interventionism and protectionism. When he tried to alter the constitution and secure a fourth term as President in 1944, a coup was staged. Although he survived the coup and executed all those involved, massive popular protests took place amongst students, workers, and peasants. On 8 May, Martinez announced his resignation, reportedly on the advice of the US President. He fled to Honduras, where he became a landowner; he was hacked to death by one of his workers shortly afterwards.

Martinez was the last of the *caudillo* political leaders of El Salvador, able to stamp their personal whims on public office. He lost power when civilians united against him; henceforth the military made sure of their social and political base of support, most notably from the country's oligarchic landowning class.

Martov, Yulii Osipovich (*real name* **Tsederbaum**) (b. Constantinople, 24 Nov. 1873; d. Berlin, 24 Apr. 1923)

Jewish; revolutionary, a leader of the Mensheviks 1905–7 and official leader 1917–20

Born in Constantinople into a middle-class liberal Jewish family (his father was a foreign correspondent) which moved back to Odessa in 1877 and in 1882 to St Petersburg, Tsederbaum became a populist when he started studying at St Petersburg University in 1891, for which he was expelled. He joined the Russian Social Democratic Labour Party in 1892 and spent two years in Vilnius developing his ideas on mass agitation. Initially he co-operated with *Lenin in founding the St Petersburg Union of Struggle for the Liberation of the Working Class in 1895, and later, after three years in exile, on the *Iskra* newspaper. But at the 2nd Congress of the RSDLP in 1903 they parted company, Martov (as he was now known) favouring a more tolerant and open type of party than that proposed by Lenin in *What is to be done?*; he won the vote on this question, but Lenin's group won the later elections to the main party bodies, which enabled him to dub his opponents the *Mensheviki* (Minoritarians) and his group the *Bolsheviki* (Majoritarians). Martov became, with Dan, one of the Menshevik leaders in 1905–7 and differences, especially over revolutionary strategy, with the Bolsheviks steadily increased; the schism became permanent in 1912. Returning to Petrograd after the February Revolution of 1917 he led a group of left-wing Mensheviks who rejected the 'national defence' line of their leaders participating in the provisional government, while not accepting Lenin's 'revolutionary defeatism'. After the Bolshevik revolution, when he became the official leader of the Mensheviks, he boycotted the 2nd Congress of Soviets in protest against Lenin's refusal to form a coalition; pressure on the Mensheviks increased after the closure of the Constituent Assembly in January 1918 and in June they were expelled from the Congress altogether. With the end of the Civil War in 1920 it became difficult for him to remain in Russia and his health was declining, so he left for Berlin, where he remained, editing the *Socialist Courier* newspaper, till his death from tuberculosis in 1923. Martov was a Marxist idealist who rejected Lenin's 'barracks socialism' and 'Pugachev-style' violent revolutionism as 'Asiatic', but lacked the political skill and will-power to develop a serious alternative.

Marx, Wilhelm (b. Cologne, 15 Jan. 1863; d. 5 Aug. 1946)

German; Chancellor of Germany 1923–5, 1926–8, leader of Centre Party 1922–8

The son of an elementary school headmaster, Marx was brought up in a strongly Catholic home. He studied law at Bonn University and took up a legal career but was soon involved in politics, winning a seat in the Prussian parliament in 1899 and election to the Reichstag in 1910. On the point of retiring he was persuaded in 1921 to take over the chairmanship of the centre group in the Reichstag. In the following year he was elected national chairman. Marx supported Weimar democracy, worked in the Catholic interest, but ignored the Vatican's disapproval of his co-operation with the SPD and strove to build a 'coalition of reason' of moderates. He was a German patriot but worked for international accord. He succeeded at the London reparations conference of 1924 in getting a reasonable agreement for Germany in that Germany accepted the *Dawes Plan in exchange for speedier Allied withdrawal from the Rhineland. His third government took Germany into the League of Nations in 1926.

He was Chancellor from November 1923 to January 1925, and from May 1926 to June 1928, but formed four cabinets during these years. It was a tragedy for Germany that Marx failed to beat von *Hindenburg for the presidency in 1925. Backed by the SPD, his own Centre Party, and other moderates, he attracted 13,751,605 votes against Hindenburg's 14,655,641 and 1,931,151 for the Communist Ernst Thälmann. In December 1926 *Scheidemann (SPD) attacked the government because of the secret co-operation between the armed forces and the Soviet Red Army. The government fell but Marx survived. He remained in the Reichstag until 1932 and then withdrew from political activity.

Masaryk, Jan (b. Prague, 1886; d. Prague, 10 Mar. 1948)

Czech; Czechoslovak Ambassador to London 1925–38, Foreign Minister 1941–8

Jan Masaryk was the son of T. G. *Masaryk. He travelled widely as a young man and was educated at the universities of Prague and Vienna. He emigrated to the United States in 1907. He entered the newly created Czechoslovak diplomatic service in 1918 and from 1919 to 1920 was *Beneš's main aide at the Paris Peace Conference. In 1925 he was appointed Czechoslovak ambassador to London, where his charm and fluent English won him great popularity. He was one of the few commoners allowed to tell rude jokes to George VI. He resigned in 1938 after the Munich Agreement and in July 1941 became Foreign Minister and Deputy Prime Minister of the Czechoslovak government in exile in London.

Masaryk returned to Prague with Beneš in 1945 and was Foreign Minister in the coalition government. He continued in this post after the elections of May 1946, serving without party affiliation. Like Beneš, he hoped that Czechoslovakia might serve as a bridge between East and West. Opposed to the Soviet Union's refusal to allow Czechoslovakia's acceptance of *Marshall Aid in 1947 he criticized the non-Communist ministers' decision to resign from Beneš's government in February 1947, which prompted the Communist coup. At Beneš's request he did not resign as Foreign Minister after the Communist seizure of power. Three weeks later his body was found in the courtyard of the Foreign Ministry beneath an open window. The official verdict was suicide. An official re-examination of his death in 1968 was closed after the failure of the 'Prague Spring'.

Masaryk, Tómas Garrigue (b. Hodonin, Moravia, 7 Mar. 1850; d. Castle Lany, 15 Sept. 1937)

Czech; President of Czechoslovakia 1918–37

Masaryk was born on a Habsburg estate, the son of a coachman. His parents were Czechs who spoke German as their first language. He learned Czech and Slovak as second languages. He displayed intellectual promise at an early age and was educated at the universities of Brno, Vienna, and Leipzig, receiving a doctorate from Vienna in 1876. From 1879 to 1882 he taught philosophy there. In 1882 he became professor of philosophy at the newly founded Czech University in Prague. In his political writings he supported democracy and social reform; in philosophy he sought to combine the Western empirical tradition with Slavonic thought. From 1891 to 1893 Masaryk represented the Young Czech Party and from 1907 to 1914 was the head of the Czech Realist Party in the Austrian parliament. He sought a federal status for Bohemia and Moravia within the Habsburg Empire, but still regarded complete independence for the Czechs as impossible because of their proximity to Germany. Unlike the Czech Pan-Slavists he did not look to Russia as liberator and inspiration, but to the democratic traditions of Britain and France. In 1909 Masaryk became famous throughout Europe when he defended a group of Croat nationalist leaders in a treason trial at Agram (Zagreb) by proving that the Austrian Foreign Ministry had forged the evidence used against them.

In December 1914 Masaryk fled to London. In 1915 he became chairman of the Czech National Council, which he co-founded with *Beneš. It campaigned for an independent Czechoslovak state. Masaryk convinced the British Cabinet that the Czechs and Slovaks should be united. While in London he was a lecturer in Slavonic history at King's College. At the end of 1916 he became editor of the monthly periodical *The New Europe*. In 1917 he visited Russia, where he organized the Czech Legion from prisoners of war. In the United States in 1918 he concluded the Pittsburg Agreement with the local Slovak leaders which provided for the union of Czechs and Slovaks in a new state. Masaryk had great influence on President Woodrow *Wilson's views on the post-war settlement. In September 1918 the US government recognized him as the leader of an Allied country.

In November 1918 Czech independence was declared in Prague and Masaryk was elected President of the new republic. He was re-elected in 1927 and in 1934. Masaryk believed that the presidency should remain above party politics. His attempt to reconcile the national minorities with the new state failed in the cases of the Sudeten Germans and the Hungarians. Nonetheless his great achievement was the maintenance of Czechoslovakia as the only democracy in Eastern and Central Europe in the inter-war period. In foreign policy Masaryk was aware that Czechoslovak independence was dependent upon the backing of the great powers and he was therefore a firm supporter of the League of Nations. He was alarmed by the rise of German strength after *Hitler came to power in 1933. In December 1935 he resigned as President, feeling that a younger man was needed to counter the Nazi threat. He was succeeded by Beneš.

Massey, William Ferguson (b. Londonderry, Northern Ireland, 26 Mar. 1856; d. 10 May 1925)

New Zealand; Prime Minister 1912–25

Massey was the son of small farmers and of Ulster Protestant stock. He was brought up by relatives and emigrated to New Zealand in 1870 to join his parents who had emigrated eight years earlier. Massey was an energetic self-made farmer and active in Auckland farming policies; he remained attentive to the interests of farmers throughout his career. In 1894 he was elected an MP and in 1903 became leader of the conservative Reform Party in opposition. In 1912 he helped to oust the Liberals from a twenty-two-year spell in office, when he successfully moved a vote of no confidence, and attracted sufficient dissident right-wing Liberals to become Prime Minister himself. His government had to tackle bitter industrial disputes and brought in tough anti-strike legislation. He was a strong supporter of Britain during the First World War and triumphed in a jingoistic election in 1914. From 1915 to 1919 he led a coalition national government. A firm believer in the British Empire, he represented New Zealand at the Paris Peace Conference in 1919.

Maudling, Reginald (b. London, 7 Mar. 1917; d. 14 Feb. 1979)

British; Chancellor of the Exchequer 1962–4, Home Secretary 1970–2

Educated at Merchant Taylors' School and Merton College, Oxford, Maudling practised at the bar before entering politics. After an unsuccessful attempt to enter the House of Commons in 1945, he was elected in 1950 as MP for Barnet. Recognized as being among the more able of the new intake, he was appointed a junior minister in 1952 and began a rapid rise up the ministerial ladder, becoming Minister of Supply in 1955, Paymaster-General in 1957, president of the Board of Trade in 1959, and Colonial Secretary in 1961. In July 1962, following the 'Night of the Long Knives', he was appointed to succeed Selwyn *Lloyd as Chancellor of the Exchequer, a post he retained under *Macmillan's successor, Sir Alec *Douglas-Home. When Douglas-Home gave up the party leadership in 1965, Maudling was nominated to succeed him and was widely expected by press commentators to win the contest against Edward *Heath. He got 133 votes to Heath's 150. He was appointed by Heath as deputy leader of the party and on the return of the party to government in 1970 became Home Secretary. His tenure of the post was short-lived. He resigned in July 1972, because he believed that he could not occupy the post while a police investigation was under way into the affairs of the architect John Poulson, with whom he had had a business relationship. He was brought back to the front bench when Margaret *Thatcher was elected party leader in 1975. She appointed him shadow Foreign Secretary. They disagreed about foreign as well as economic policy and a year later she sacked him. Margaret Thatcher recorded in her memoirs (*The Path to Power*) that 'he was increasingly unwilling to disguise his differences with me, and he was laid back. But when I told him he had to go, he summoned up enough energy to be quite rude. Still, out he went'. The following year he was criticized by a Commons Select Committee for 'conduct inconsistent with the standards which the House is entitled to expect' because of his dealings with Poulson. A motion to expel him from the House was defeated by 331 votes to 11 on 26 July 1977. Less than two years later, he died, shortly before his 62nd birthday.

Widely recognized as intellectually able, he was also noted for being lazy, for having recourse too often to liquid refreshment, and for not being discriminating enough in his business dealings. Having once been the great future hope of the Conservative Party, his last years were years of notable decline, a man with a glorious future behind him.

Mauroy, Pierre (b. Cartignies, 5 July 1928)

French; Prime Minister 1981–4, first secretary of the Parti Socialiste 1988–92, President of the Socialist International 1994–

The son of a primary schoolteacher, Mauroy became a technical education teacher and national secretary of the Young Socialists 1950–8. 'Le gros quinquin', he was a product of the socialism of northern France. He was elected federal secretary of the

Nord in 1961 and to the National Bureau of the Socialist Party in 1963. As the leader of one of the biggest socialist federations he was well placed to succeed the ageing leader Guy *Mollet and was elected deputy secretary-general in 1966. However, he failed to take the leadership by one vote in 1969 when Mollet did step down and in 1971 was leader of the coalition which brought *Mitterrand to the head of the new Parti Socialiste. In 1971 he became mayor of Lille and in 1973 was elected to the Assembly from Lille. Despite Mauroy's support for Mitterrand he was temperamentally a social democrat and joined his old friend *Rocard in opposition to Mitterrand in 1979. This caused his stock to fall, although he was never totally out of favour. He played a prominent role in the 1981 elections and was made Prime Minister after the Socialist victory. He was at first in charge of a 'dash for growth strategy' which he rapidly came to see as unrealistic and lobbied the President (with others) for a less reflationary strategy. A U-turn came about in 1983 and for the next year he promoted a programme of restructuring and cutbacks. The fiasco of the attempt to integrate church schools into the state system (Alain Savary's bill) led him to tearfully submit his resignation in July 1984. In 1988 he became first secretary of the Parti Socialiste, a candidate acceptable to all factions, but the wearing in-fighting led him to stand down in 1992.

Maxton, James (b. Glasgow, 22 June 1885; d. 23 July 1946)
British; chairman of the Independent Labour Party 1926–31 and 1934–9

The son of a teacher, Maxton was educated at Hutcheson's Grammar School and the University of Glasgow, before becoming a teacher. After conscientious objection and imprisonment during the First World War, he was elected MP for Glasgow, Bridgeton, in 1922. At Westminster he was one of a group of 'Clydeside Reds' whose uncompromising socialism often led to disorderly behaviour.

Maxton was a persistent critic of the 'gradualist' policies of the Labour governments of 1924 and 1929–31. Under his chairmanship the ILP drifted apart from the Labour Party. Its candidates were refused official endorsement in the 1931 general election and after it ILP members sat separately and Maxton declined an invitation to sit on the Labour front bench. The ILP disaffiliated from Labour in 1932 and rapidly atrophied. Maxton contested the 1945 election as a Labour candidate.

Maxton had a far higher public profile than a career on the back benches and leadership of a minute party might suggest. He was an eloquent and witty speaker and the attractiveness to cartoonists of his gaunt appearance made him widely recognized.

Maxwell-Fyfe, David Patrick (b. Edinburgh, 29 May 1900; d. 27 Jan. 1967)
British; Home Secretary 1951–4, Lord Chancellor 1954–62; Kt. 1942, Viscount Kilmuir 1954, Earl 1962

Educated at George Watsons' College and Balliol College, Oxford, Maxwell-Fyfe was a distinguished barrister before being elected to parliament as Conservative MP for the West Derby division of Liverpool in 1935. He was appointed Solicitor-General in 1942 and Attorney-General in 1945, serving subsequently as Deputy Chief Prosecutor at the Nuremberg war trials (1945–6). In Opposition, he chaired a party committee that produced a report—the Maxwell-Fyfe Report—that opened up candidatures to those without personal fortunes. *Churchill appointed him to the Cabinet in 1951 as Home Secretary and Minister for Welsh Affairs and three years later made him Lord Chancellor. He held the post for eight years, before becoming one of the principal victims of *Macmillan's 'Night of the Long Knives' in 1962, the speed of his removal from office taking him by surprise. He subsequently held various business appointments before his death in 1967.

Though he contributed to a significant reform of the Conservative Party, he was neither a reforming Home Secretary nor Lord Chancellor, adopting a highly traditionalist stance on most issues. Even though it was during his tenure of the Home Office that the Wolfenden Committee to consider prostitution and homosexual offences was established, he reputedly refused to sit at the Cabinet table if homosexual law reform was discussed. He had an unhappy marriage—his wife lived openly with another peer—and he deeply resented the manner of his dismissal from office. Macmillan later described him as 'the stupidest Lord Chancellor ever . . . hopeless in Cabinet—that's why I got rid of him'.

Mazowiecki, Tadeusz (b. Plock, 17 Apr. 1927)

Polish; Prime Minister 1989–90

In the early 1950s Mazowiecki started his career as a journalist and Catholic activist within the official Polish Catholic organization, PAX. He rose to become editor of Wrocław's weekly Catholic newspaper. In 1955 he was expelled from PAX after a row with its leader and the next year founded the Warsaw branch of the Club of the Catholic Intelligentsia. From 1961 to 1972 he played a prominent role in the independent Catholic group, *Znak*. Mazowiecki was a significant figure in forging close bonds between the Polish intelligentsia and the workers' movement. In 1970 he tried to organize a commission to investigate the government's use of violence against workers' demonstrations that year. He was close to the Workers' Defence Committee, acting as its spokesman during a hunger strike in 1977. In August 1980, Mazowiecki became Lech *Wałęsa's adviser when confrontation started between the workers of the Gdańsk shipyard and the government, and continued to advise Wałęsa after the foundation of the trade union movement Solidarity in September 1980.

Mazowiecki did not stand in the partially free elections of May 1989 because he disagreed with Solidarity's refusal to allow candidates from outside its own organization to run on its ticket. Nonetheless, at Wałęsa's insistance, General *Jaruzelski appointed him as the first non-Communist head of government in the Soviet Bloc on 24 August 1989. He formed a Solidarity-led coalition government on 12 September. From then to the end of the year his government enacted a series of decrees removing the coercive apparatus of the former Communist regime. In January 1990 he gave his full support to the radical *Balcerowicz Plan for rapid marketization. This led to conflict with Wałęsa, who on the one hand was concerned at the hardship caused by economic reform and on the other believed that political change ought to be faster. The split in Solidarity came to a head in September 1990 when Jaruzelski resigned from the presidency. In November 1990 Mazowiecki stood against Wałęsa and the hitherto unknown Polish-born émigré businessman Stanisław Tymiński. He gained 18 per cent of the vote and was beaten by both Wałęsa (40 per cent) and Tymiński (23 per cent). After this humiliation, Mazowiecki resigned from the government.

Mečiar, Vladimír (b. 26 July 1942)

Slovak; Slovak Prime Minister 1992–3

Mečiar was a former Communist who before 1989 was distinguished only by his performance as a boxer. During the revolution of 1989 he joined the Slovak anti-Communist umbrella organization, Public Against Violence (PAV). In 1990 Mečiar established himself as the central figure within the PAV faction which stood for greater Slovak autonomy, state intervention in the economy, and cautious economic reform. He was thus opposed to the programme of the Czech politician Václav *Klaus. On 6 March 1991 Mečiar split PAV by forming a Movement for a Democratic Slovakia (MDS), which immediately became the most popular party in the Republic. This reflected partly genuine popular aspirations and partly Mečiar's populist methods. A governmental crisis developed in Slovakia as a result. It was made worse by various allegations of misconduct against Mečiar, including the charge that he had consulted with Soviet generals before he founded the MDS. On 23 April 1991 the Slovak National Council removed him from office. In the elections of June 1992, the MDS gained 37 per cent of the votes to the Slovak National Council as well as a large number of seats in the Federal Assembly. On 17 July 1992 the Slovak National Council issued a declaration of Slovak sovereignty. The subsequent negotiations between Slovakia and the Czech Republic were bedevilled on the one hand by Mečiar's high demands, possibly made in the hope of exacting maximum concessions from the Czechs, and on the other by the Czech government's refusal to compromise. On 1 January 1993 the Czechoslovak state was dissolved. Mečiar took an intransigent line with the representatives of Slovakia's 600,000-strong Hungarian minority.

Meir, Golda (b. Kiev, 3 May, 1898; d. 8 Dec. 1978)
Israeli; Foreign Minister 1956–66, Prime Minister 1969–74

After emigrating to Palestine in 1921, having first emigrated to America, Golda Meir soon became an official in Histradut (General Federation of Labour) and an activist in the Mapai (Workers' Party). In 1946 she became head of the political department of the Jewish Agency.

She was elected to the Knesset in the 1949 general elections and appointed Minister of Labour in *Ben-Gurion's government, holding this position until she became his Foreign Minister in 1956. Mrs Meir retained the office in the Eshkol administration from 1963 to 1966, resigning only to devote the next three years to build the Labour Party from Mapai and other leftist factions. She became Prime Minister in March 1969, following the death of Premier Eshkol. Her administration ignored UN resolutions that invalidated the annexation of east Jerusalem and those which demanded Israel's withdrawal from all other occupied Palestinian territories; it continued (illegally) to build Jewish settlements in the occupied territories; it rejected a peace settlement with Arab regimes, either on the basis of UN Security Council resolution 242 or the Rogers peace plan of December 1969, and it vigorously applied an 'iron fist' counter-terrorism policy against the PLO and its host countries. Israeli intransigence resulted in a renewal of war in October 1973. The Egyptian and Syrian attacks caught the government completely by surprise, however, and showed its defence strategy—wide buffer zones with neighbouring Arab states—to be ineffective. Despite these failures of policy, intelligence, and strategy, Golda Meir managed to lead Labour to a narrow victory in the 1973 general elections. In April of the following year, however, she was forced to resign in disgrace when the official report on the 1973 war was published.

Mendès France, Pierre (b. 11. Jan. 1907; d. 18 Oct. 1982)
French; Prime Minister 1954–5

Pierre Mendès France was Prime Minister of France for a 7½-month period in 1954–5. A professional politician and long-time member of the Radical Party, whose leader he was 1955–7, he was first elected to the Chamber of Deputies in 1932. He became the youngest ever minister in the history of the Third Republic when he joined Léon *Blum's 1938 government and he was a member of *de Gaulle's provisional government in 1944–5. Yet in conventional terms his career was a failure. He was only briefly in government during the Fourth Republic and he never subsequently held office. Only once, after de Gaulle's return to power in 1958, did he manage to win a parliamentary seat, and in the 1969 presidential election the joint campaign he ran with Gaston *Deffere obtained a humiliating 5 per cent of the vote. His intransigent opposition to the new constitutional order of the Fifth Republic (in particular the directly elected presidency) completely failed to mobilize public support.

The paradox is that, for all this apparent failure, Mendès France acquired during his lifetime a political stature that was denied to any of his contemporaries and that even today *mendésisme* has, for some at least, an inspirational quality. How can this be explained? Part of the answer lies in the record of his 1954 government. As Prime Minister, he ended the disastrous colonial war in Indo-China and set Tunisia and Morocco on the path to independence. He showed a dynamic and determined style of leadership that contrasted with the shabby compromises usually associated with Fourth Republic governments and was encapsulated in the famous phrase 'To Govern is to Choose'. His premiership won plaudits from overseas figures like *Churchill and *Dulles and his attempt to substitute issue-centred reformism for the sterile ideological absolutes of French party rhetoric was attractive to many French modernizers. Yet the real source of his appeal lay in the impression of principle and integrity that he conveyed. His personal bravery was never in doubt and was demonstrated during the Second World War when he was persecuted for his refusal to accept defeat and collaboration and subsequently by his resilience in the face of bitter attacks from his opponents. After 1958, his implacable opposition to what he saw as the authoritarian nature of the Fifth Republic appealed not only to defenders of France's republican traditions but to a new generation of political radicals. His (silent) appearance at the huge Charlety meeting during the 1968 Events showed that he was the only established political figure to have the respect of the protesting students: 1968, like Mendès France, failed to overthrow the Fifth Republic. He retired from political life in 1973 but the Mendès name and reputation certainly contributed to the creation of the left-wing coalition that eventually won power, under *Mitterrand, in 1981. The new President was right to say, when embracing Mendès France after the installation in office, 'Without you I would not be here.'

Menem, Carlos Saul (b. La Rioja Province, 2 July 1930)

Argentine; President 1989–95, 1995–

The son of Syrian immigrants, Menem graduated from the University of Cordoba in 1955. Active in the Perónist Youth Movement, he soon attracted the backing of the exiled *Perón. In 1973 he was elected governor of La Rioja but was arrested following the 1976 coup and detained until 1981. A member of the personalist wing of Perónism he made a name for himself as a critic of the military and in 1988 was nominated as presidential candidate.

Menem campaigned in 1989 as a flamboyant populist but, once elected, opted for radical neo-liberalism—what he called 'surgery without anaesthetic'. State companies were privatized, union power reduced, protectionism eliminated, public employment cut, foreign investment encouraged, and the currency dollarized. The result of these changes was dramatic. Inflation fell from 6,000 per cent to single figures; annual GDP growth averaged 5 per cent; foreign investment boomed. The losers in this process were precisely those who had voted for him: the poorer provinces, public employees, and the industrial working class.

Menem also abandoned Argentina's traditional nationalism. Agrentina left the non-aligned movement, restored relations with the UK, joined the non-proliferation agreement, sent ships to the Gulf War, opened up free trade with Brazil, and openly courted the USA.

Politically, Menem ruled in a heavy-handed way. Following a deal with *Alfonsin, he revised the constitution so as to be able to stand again, amnestied officers accused of human rights crimes, and packed the Supreme Court and Cabinet with personal followers. Throughout he ignored the Perónist controlled Congress, relying instead on Presidential decree. Often linked with corruption he simply ignored his critics.

Menem's triumphant win in 1995 showed that—harsh though the remedies were for some—Argentines had come to prefer growth, monetary stability, and political order over stagnation, inflation, and political disorder.

Mengistu Haile Mariam (b. Addis Ababa, 1940)

Ethiopian; vice-chairman of Provisional Military Administrative Council 1974–7, chairman 1977–84, general secretary of Workers' Party of Ethiopia 1984–91

Son of an army corporal from south-western Ethiopia, Mengistu was trained at the Holeta military academy, and was serving as a major in the 3rd Division in Harar when the Ethiopian revolution broke out in 1974. Elected as one of its representatives to the military council (or *Derg*) which seized power in September 1974, he soon became one of its most outspoken radical nationalist members. He became vice-chairman in November 1974, and chairman in February 1977, after a shoot-out in which his predecessor was killed. He ruthlessly eliminated his opponents in the 'red terror' of 1976–8, and sought an alliance with the Soviet Union. He was able to defeat the Somali invasion of 1977–8, with massive Soviet and Cuban military aid, and sought to build a powerful and centralized Ethiopian state on Marxist-Leninist principles.

The culminating point of this process, the formation of the Workers' Party of Ethiopia in September 1984, coincided with a catastrophic famine which cost hundreds of thousands of lives, and made Ethiopia a by-word for human misery. Mengistu's centralizing autocracy aroused increasing opposition, especially from the northern regions of Eritrea and Tigray, where effective guerrilla insurgencies contested his rule. In May 1991, with guerrilla armies closing on Addis Ababa, he fled to exile in Zimbabwe. Remembered as one of Africa's most ruthless dictators, his rule is redeemed only by the fact that he does not appear to have been corrupt, and was apparently guided, however counter-productively, by nationalist rather than merely personal ambitions.

Menon, Krishna Vengalil Krishnan (b. Calicut, 3 May 1897; d. 5 Oct. 1974)

Indian; member of the Indian parliament 1952–67, 1969–74, Minister for Defence 1957–62

A member of the Menon caste from Kerala, Menon was educated at Presidency College, Madras. As a young man he joined the Theosophical Society and became a member of Mrs Annie Besant's inner circle and was a volunteer in her Home Rule campaign. He graduated from the London School of Economics and University College. He also studied law and was called to the bar by the Middle Temple.

In 1927 Menon became the general secretary of the India League. He transformed it from a largely student body to the chief instrument of Congress propaganda in Britain and on the continent. Through the League Menon developed a close relationship with *Nehru which was to last throughout his life. In 1934 he was elected to the St Pancras Borough Council. He became Chairman of the Library Committee on the council. Menon developed close contacts with the Labour Party and became a parliamentary candidate for Dundee. He was forced to relinquish his candidature for speaking at a Communist-inspired meeting in 1941. In addition to his political activities, Menon edited the 'Twentieth Century Library' issued by Bodley Head and was the first editor of Pelican Books.

Following the transfer of power in August 1947, Menon was appointed the first High Commissioner to the United Kingdom by Nehru. His period as High Commissioner was frosty. The one major achievement accredited to Menon during these years was the effort he made to keep India within the Commonwealth. In 1953 he was elected to the upper house of parliament in India and became the country's representative on the General Assembly at the United Nations, a position he held until 1962. In July 1956 when President *Nasser nationalized the Suez Canal, he took a leading part in the negotiations that followed.

In 1956 Menon entered Nehru's Cabinet as Minister without Portfolio. In April 1957 Menon was made the Minister for Defence and became the main protagonist of

Nehru's forward policy on the Sino-Indo border dispute. Menon like Nehru believed that the main threat to India came from Pakistan and found no reason to change this belief in light of the border dispute with China. Menon, with the support of Nehru, continued to maintain that India's defence forces were capable of confronting any challenge posed by the Chinese over the border issue. These assurances became more and more emphatic following the growing tension between India and China after 1959.

As Minister for Defence Menon was suspected of building a clique within the army to give himself a base from which, after Nehru, he could make a bid for power. Throughout he had an uneasy relationship with the armed forces and interfered in operational and personnel matters. Often this interference led to confusion and demoralization.

In the Indo-China War (1962) the inadequacy of India's defence force was brutally exposed. Menon's policy and *ad hoc* intervention in military operations led to a catalogue of disasters which resulted in the humiliating retreat of India's army. Menon became the chief causality of the defeat and, to deflect criticism from Nehru, was dismissed as Minister for Defence. He was offered the post of Minister for Defence Production but also had to resign from this post after a week following heavy criticism in parliament and the press. He remained an MP on the backbenches and wrote his *Autobiography* (1965).

In 1966 Menon resigned from the Congress after a bitter dispute and failed to get elected as MP in the 1967 general elections. He returned to parliament in 1969 after support from Bengali Communists and the United Front government and remained a member until his death.

During his lifetime Menon was described as 'a lone wolf' who was ever the fighter. He, it is said, fought to win using every weapon that his trenchant brain and withering personality could command. He always stood apart and this isolation was usually ascribed to irascible temperament which made him a man of few friends. Menon's left-wing leanings and proximity to Nehru made him an easy target of attack. He worked untiringly for India's independence for twenty-seven years. Despite his prominent position in international diplomacy and as Minister for Defence, he never really received the nation's gratitude or even acceptance, remaining an outsider. His honours included an honorary fellowship of the LSE and Freemanship of the Borough of St Pancras.

Menzies, Robert Gordon (b. Jeparit, Victoria, 20 Dec. 1894; d. Melbourne, 15 May 1978)

Australian; Prime Minister 1939–41, 1949–66

Menzies grew up in the tiny Victorian country township of Jepari, where his Presbyterian parents had a store. His excellence in his studies quickly earned him scholarships to Wesley College, Melbourne, and Melbourne University, where he completed a prize-filled law degree. From constitutional law he entered the Victorian parliament as a conservative, and then shifted to federal politics in the mid-1930s, where he initially rose as rapidly as he fell. As Prime Minister from April 1939 to August 1941 he struggled to control a disintegrating coalition of conservatives and was accused of aloofness. He was forced to resign, but reinvented his political image and helped to redefine conservatism in the form of the new Liberal Party, born in 1944. He led the Liberals, in coalition with the Country Party, to a huge electoral victory at the end of 1949, and remained Prime Minister for more than sixteen years, thereby inspiring the reference, 'the Menzies era'.

Menzies's spectacular reign as Australia's longest serving Prime Minister is attributed to a number of factors. He targeted the suburban middle class, with special attention to women, in his electoral platforms; he fuelled the fires of division within the Labor Party by highlighting the danger of Communism, domestically and in his foreign policy; he presided over a period of strong economic growth and high employment, largely based on exports of Australian primary products; and he employed to full advantage his unrivalled speaking skills and commanding presence. During his reign, Australian military forces fought in Korea and Malaya; and, in his last fourteen months before retirement, he introduced compulsory military service (with liability for service overseas) and committed Australian troops to Vietnam.

Menzies has been criticized for his lack of innovation, for languishing in office during an economically fortunate era while clinging to his strong attachment to the British empire and royalty, rather than initiating economic and other reforms. While these criticisms still surface, in recent years there has also been a trend towards re-examining the Menzies era for its stability, and for Menzies' commitment to socially centred liberal values.

Menzies became Knight of the Thistle in 1963 and succeeded *Churchill as Warden of the Cinque Ports in 1965. Shortly after his retirement he became chancellor of Melbourne University.

Messmer, Pierre August Joseph (b. Vincennes, 20 Mar. 1916)

French; Prime Minister 1972–4

A Doctor of Law and graduate of the School of Oriental Languages in Paris, Messmer embarked on a career as a colonial civil servant in 1938 and was, at the outbreak of war, a colonial administrator. In 1940 he joined the Free French Forces and participated in African and European campaigns. In 1945 he was taken prisoner by the Vietminh in the Indochina campaign. In 1946 he became head of the Interministerial Committee on Indochina and from 1947 to 1948 Chief of Staff to the High Commissioner for Indochina. He then moved to Africa where he became Governor of Mauritania (1953) of the Ivory Coast (1954) and briefly a member of Gaston *Defferre's office preparing an outline law on colonial autonomy. He was High Commissioner of African colonies 1956–9 and in 1960 he was made Minister for the Army at a time of turmoil over the war in Algeria. He applied *de Gaulle's policy of professionalization of the army and the construction of nuclear forces. Loyal Gaullist, he left office when the General did in 1969 to set up the Gaullist Présence et Action du Gaullism as a way of keeping the General's ideals alive. In 1971 he was made Minister of State for Overseas France by President *Pompidou. His combativity probably led Pompidou to nominate him as Prime Minister in 1972 when he replaced *Chaban Delmas with an impeccable orthodoxy and pulled the right together for the battles with the left. President Pompidou's health deteriorated, the government drifted, and Messmer was criticized for not leading it. He was reconfirmed by Pompidou as Prime Minister in February of 1974 but the President died in April. Thereafter he played a backstage role until his defeat in 1988.

Michael, King of Romania (b. Bucharest, 25 Oct. 1921)

Romanian; King of Romania 1927–30, 1940–7

Michael was the son of Crown Prince Carol of Romania, who renounced his claim to the throne in 1925. Michael succeeded his grandfather, King Ferdinand, to the throne in 1927. In 1930 Carol returned from exile and made himself king. Carol II was forced to abdicate by General *Antonescu in 1940 and Michael succeeded him. Power lay in Antonescu's hands and Michael held no responsibility for Romania's declaration of war on the Soviet Union in 1941. He played a major role in organizing the coup which led to Antonescu's overthrow in August 1944. He then accepted Allied peace terms and on 15 August 1944 declared war on Germany. The Soviet authorities awarded him the Order of Victory in 1945. In March 1945 he was forced to appoint the Soviet puppet, *Groza, as premier. When Britain and the United States refused to recognize this government, Michael unsuccessfully tried to manœuvre Groza out of power. In the autumn of 1945, Michael withdrew to his country estate and refused to sign any state papers. On 30 December 1947 he was forced to abdicate and went into exile. President Iliescu's regime refused to allow him to return to Romania after the revolution of 1989.

Michnik, Adam (b. 17 Oct. 1946)

Polish; dissident 1967–89, member of Sejm 1989–

Michnik was born into a Jewish family. In his early years he was a Marxist who hoped that the Communist system in Poland would be able to reform itself. He lectured in history at Warsaw University until March 1967 when he was suspended during a purge of the University's Jewish staff. In January 1968 he was arrested for organizing student demonstrations.

In the early 1970s Michnik became an influential theorist about the relationship between state and society. He put forward the theory of 'new evolutionism', rejecting Communist-led reform as a sham and accurately predicting the gradual emancipation of civil society through a process of self-organization. He claimed that a self-organizing society must insist on 'living as if it were free' and worked to unite the previously antipathetic traditions of the lay left and the Catholic Church in Poland. In 1976 Michnik played a major role in the foundation of the Polish Workers' Defence Committee (KOR) and was a member of the dissident 'Flying University' which provided a non-Communist education to the workers. In 1980–1 Michnik was prominent on the radical wing of the trade union movement Solidarity. He was arrested after *Jaruzelski's imposition of martial law in December 1981 and imprisoned until July 1986.

In January 1989 Michnik was a key Solidarity adviser in the Round Table talks which prepared the way for partially free elections, though Jaruzelski's regime had initially objected to his participation. Thereafter he became editor of *Gazeta Wyborcza* ('Election Gazette'), the newspaper which Solidarity created to prepare for the elections. He was elected to the Sejm (parliament) in May 1989, and originated the compromise between Solidarity and the Communists, whereby there would be a Communist head of state but a Solidarity head of government. At the end of 1989, Michnik lost Wałęsa's support because of his alleged slowness in encouraging political reform. In summer 1990 he joined the Civic Movement-Democratic Action (ROAD), which was comparable to Western social democracy and opposed to Wałęsa.

Mielke, Erich (b. Berlin, 28 Dec. 1907)

German; Minister for State Security of GDR 1957–89

Mielke was not well known before his fall in 1989. Yet his Ministry for State Security (MfS) was perhaps the largest employer in the GDR. Per 10,000 of population there were more full-time operatives of the MfS than there were medical practitioners, and they were backed up by an army of informers of roughly the same size as the professionals. Mielke was proud of this situation and was shocked to be dismissed after being minister since 1957. He had been a member of the Politburo of the ruling Socialist Unity Party (SED) since 1976 and was regarded by his colleagues as the Moscow agent in their midst. He had taken part in the plot which led to *Honecker's removal in October 1989 only to find himself expelled from the SED alongside Honecker on 3 December. He was subsequently arrested for misuse of office. After German reunification in 1990, he was convicted of the murder of two Berlin policemen in 1931 and sentenced to six years' imprisonment.

Mielke was born into a politically conscious working-class family in Berlin. His family joined the Communist Party (KPD). After grammar school, he successfully completed an apprenticeship with a haulage firm. Unemployment soon followed but he supplemented his unemployment pay by working for a Communist paper. Keen on sport, he was soon involved with the paramilitary wing of the KPD. It was on a party assignment that he shot the policemen. To avoid arrest he escaped to Moscow, where he underwent political and military training. He served as an officer in the security service of the International Brigade in the Spanish Civil War where he became notorious in the Stalinist purges. After that war ended in 1939 he was interned in France. Once back in Germany in 1945 he re-established his contacts and was appointed to various police posts. By 1950 he was already a state secretary in the newly established MfS and member of the Central Committee of the SED. Despite the crises in the SED and his ministry he rose steadily. The MfS was reponsible for both internal security and intelligence-gathering abroad. Until 1986 Markus Wolf headed the HVA, which was charged with activities outside East Germany. It was highly successful in West Germany, where it penetrated virtually all political and military bodies. Inside East Germany Mielke was unable to stop the rising tide of discontent despite the lavish resources of the MfS. Few realized the informer net was so widespread and it left a legacy of mistrust long after the fall of Mielke and the MfS.

Mihailovic, Dragoljub **(Draza)** (b. Ivanjica, Serbia, 27 Apr. 1893; d. Belgrade, 17 July 1946)

Serb; Yugoslav general and non-Communist (Cetnik) resistance leader; Minister for War in Yugoslav government-in-exile 1941–4

As a Serbian professional soldier Mihailovic served in the Balkan Wars and the First World War and rose in the Yugoslav army to be lieutenant-colonel in 1929. In the 1930s he served abroad as a military attaché and later in Belgrade as head of the army's educational section. In 1939–40 he opposed official policy on the close relationship with Germany and on defence strategy (arguing that Bosnia, not Slovenia, should be the main line of defence). With the German invasion in 1941 he was given command of the Second Army in Bosnia, but after the Croat capitulation his army disintegrated and he withdrew the loyal remnants to the Ravna Gora area of Serbia.

His strategy was to develop an underground organization, based on royalist and Serbian nationalist values, which, when Allied support became available, would lead a national uprising. In 1941 he refused *Tito's offer to form a joint resistance, regarding the Partisans as a key threat to the monarchy (in 1942–3 he even helped the Germans and Italians against the Partisans). The London-based government-in-exile made him Minister for War and Commander of the 'Yugoslav Army in the Fatherland', with the rank of army general, but having a low opinion of all politicians he had few dealings with them. In 1943 his troops were heavily defeated by the Partisans and, with British support shifting decisively to the Partisans, in 1944 he was dismissed from the government on the eve of the Tito–Subasic agreement. Mihailovic fought on, even after the end of the war, but was eventually cornered in Bosnia by the Partisans in 1946, put on trial in Belgrade accused of war crimes and collaboration, and executed.

Mikołajczyk, Stanisław (b. Westphalia, Germany, 18 July 1901; d. USA, 13 Dec. 1966)

Polish; leader of the Peasants' Party 1931–45, head of the government in exile 1943–4, leader of the Polish Peasants' Party 1945–7

Mikołajczyk was born in Westphalia, the son of an émigré miner. He moved to Poland in 1918, entering politics soon after. From 1931 to 1939 he was head of the Peasant Party, the most powerful political group in inter-war Poland. From 1940 he was a minister in the Polish government in exile in London and its Prime Minister after the death of General Sikorski in 1943.

Mikołajczyk returned to Poland in autumn 1944, resigning as head of the government in exile on 24 November. His arrival stopped Communist attempts to set up the

Peasants' Party as a puppet party of their own. In 1945 he became Deputy Premier in the new coalition government in Warsaw. In August 1945 he left the government to launch the new Polish Peasants' Party (PPP). His hope was that with peasant support he could make Poland ungovernable for the Communists and that the Soviet Union would accept Polish neutrality. By January 1946 the PPP had 600,000 members, making it the largest political party in Poland, and demanded free elections in 1946. The Communists pressed Mikołajczyk to join a 'Democratic Bloc', but he demanded that the PPP should have three-quarters of the seats in any coalition. The Communists thereupon set about the intimidation of the PPP. The PPP's struggle against the Communists was fatally weakened in November 1946 when the Socialists agreed on an electoral pact with the Communists. In the rigged elections of January 1947 the Democratic Bloc won just over 80 per cent of the vote at the elections while the PPP obtained just over 10 per cent. Hearing that he was about to be arrested, Mikołajczyk fled to the West, settling in the USA.

Mikoyan, Anastas Ivanovich (b. Sanain, 21 Oct. 1895; d. Moscow, 21 Oct. 1978)
Armenian; Member of the Poliburo 1922–66

Mikoyan was born in Armenia the son of a carpenter, but was brought up in Azerbaijan. He trained as a priest before joining the Bolshevik Party in 1915. After the February Revolution he engaged in party work in the Caucasus. In 1918 he escaped arrest by local anti-Bolshevik forces and was thus the only one of the 'Twenty-Six Commissars' from Baku who was not shot. *Stalin was Mikoyan's patron and secured his entry into the Central Committee of the CPSU in 1922. Mikoyan was a candidate member of the Politburo from 1922 to 1926 and full member from 1926 to 1966. He moved to Moscow in 1926 and held economic posts for the rest of his career, first replacing *Kamenev as People's Commissar for Trade and then after 1930 as Commissar for Supplies. This post enabled him to raise massive sums of hard currency by selling art treasures on the American market. From 1937 to 1955 he was deputy chairman of the Council of People's Commissars (known as the Council of Ministers after 1946). In 1943 he argued successfully against the whole-scale deportation of the Ingush and Chechen peoples from the Caucasus. He was out of favour in Stalin's last years but then became an ally of *Khrushchev. In 1956 he accompanied Khrushchev and *Suslov to Budapest to determine Soviet policy after the Hungarian Uprising. In 1962 he had the delicate mission of explaining to Fidel *Castro the decision to withdraw Soviet missiles from Cuba. He lost influence after Khruschev's fall and was given the honorific post of chairman of the Presidium of the Supreme Soviet, then in 1966 went into retirement.

Having survived the Purges of the 1930s he justifiably acquired the reputation of the great survivor. On walking into the rain without an umbrella he allegedly told observers 'Don't worry, I can dodge between the raindrops.'

Millerand, Alexandre (b. Paris, 10 Feb. 1859; d. 6 Apr. 1943)
French; Prime Minister 1919–20, President of the Republic 1920–4

Alexandre Millerand was born in Paris and came from a hardworking family of shopkeepers. He studied law, became a barrister, and plunged when still in his twenties into the political life of Paris, which would be his base for over three decades. In 1884, he was elected to the Paris municipal council and the following year entered the Chamber of Deputies. His initial political sympathies lay with the left-wing radicalism of *Clemenceau but in the early 1890s he moved over to the emerging socialist movement. His decision was motivated by his work as a barrister defending workers' rights. In 1896, in a celebrated speech in his Saint Mandé constituency, he set out the elements of a programme which virtually all the socialist factions could accept and which combined the Marxist belief in the collectivization of property with a commitment to patriotism and to the principles of Republican democracy. It was this commitment to Republicanism which led to his controversial decision in 1899 to join the government of Republican defence formed at the height of the Dreyfus Affair by Waldeck-Rousseau. Many Socialists condemned his participation in a bourgeois government. Millerand argued that the Republic was worth defending and used his three years as Minister of Commerce to introduce a number of laws which improved the legal rights of trade unions and the social rights of workers.

By 1914, Millerand had moved far from his political origins and his professional activities increasingly concentrated on highly paid commercial litigation. He opposed the anti-clerical enthusiasms of the 1902 Combes government, and of the Radical Party which supported them, and was expelled from the Socialist Party. His earlier interest in social issues was replaced by a fascination with foreign and defence questions. He was Minister of War in *Poincaré's 1912 government and was a strong supporter of the Three Years Law extending the length of military service. Back at the War Ministry from August 1914 to October 1915, he was criticized for the total backing he gave to the army high command and for his opposition to parliamentary attempts to intervene in the conduct of military operations. In early 1919 he was briefly High Commissioner for the Liberated Regions of Alsace Lorraine and then led the conservative coalition known as the Bloc National for the 1919 elections. His Ba Ta Clan speech which argued for a stronger Executive and denounced the perils of Bolshevism—and by extension socialism—set the tone for a campaign which saw the Bloc National sweep to power. In December 1919 Millerand was appointed Prime Minister with a programme that linked military support for the enemies of the Soviet Union with rigorous insistence on Germany's implementation of the reparation clauses of the Versailles Peace Treaty. Less than a year later he was triumphantly elected President of the Republic, following the enforced resignation of his predecessor.

He immediately showed that his determination to break with the constitutional convention that a president should be a figurehead by involving himself closely with policy-making. He proved to be the most interventionist president in the history of the Third Republic and in 1922 provoked the resignation of his Prime Minister *Briand by criticizing his alleged willingness to be soft on the Germans. He backed the military occupation of the Ruhr carried out by Poincaré in 1924.

So long as the Bloc National remained in power Millerand's assertiveness was not a problem. But in the run-up to the 1924 elections he intervened publicly in favour of the outgoing majority and against the Socialist-Radical opposition headed by *Blum and *Herriott. When the latter won the elections, they turned on a President whom they regarded as a renegade and as a threat to parliamentary democracy. The new majority refused to co-operate with Millerand, declaring that his continuation in office would 'offend the Republican conscience'. Millerand was thus forced to resign. He attempted unsuccessfully to create a mass movement, the National Republican League (the title indicated its politics) and spent the last years of his career in semi-obscurity in the Senate. He died in 1943.

Efficient and uncharismatic, Millerand has never acquired the historical status of Clemenceau or Poincaré and remains a neglected figure. His attempt to strengthen the presidency made him an easy target for the defenders of Republican democracy and his anti-Communism led to comparisons with other Socialist renegades like the German Noske. Yet the reforms he introduced between 1899 and 1902 did inaugurate a new era in French social policy; and even after his move to the right, he never adopted the anti-democratic views to which other former Socialists succumbed.

Mills, Wilbur Daigh (b. Kensett, Arkansas, 24 May 1909; d. 2 May 1992)
US; member of the US House of Representatives 1939–77

Educated at Hendrix College and Harvard Law School, Wilbur Mills was first elected to Congress in 1938 following service as a county judge in Arkansas. As a long-time member of the powerful Ways and Means Committee, which he chaired from 1957 to 1975, Mills exercised massive control over all money bills. He built up a formidable expertise on all aspects of taxation and revenue as well as on tariff and trade legislation and social security and Medicare. Virtually anything touching federal spending had to pass through his hands. In addition to the influence given by Ways and Means policy jurisdiction, during the years of Mills's chairmanship Democratic committee assignments were handled by the chairman of this key committee, giving Mills substantial influence over his Democratic colleagues' careers.

A conservative Democrat whose opposition to civil rights precluded him from national office, Mills used his power autocratically but not ideologically. Ways and Means had no subcommittees so its power was not fragmented; and measures coming from Ways and Means were always voted a closed rule from the Rules Committee, so were not subject to floor amendment. Mills was thus rarely forced to compromise; yet he was a skilled and pragmatic negotiator, whose expertise in the detail of legislation was formidable. After the death of Sam *Rayburn in 1962, there were few rivals to his congressional influence.

However, a bizarre set of events led to his fall from power in 1974, a time when Congress was beginning to revolt against the unfettered power of committee chairmen. When Mills's car was stopped by police, an intoxicated Mills was found with a stripper, Fanne Foxe, 'the Argentine Firecracker', who threw herself into the Tidal Basin. Mills, always a colourful personality, confessed to alcoholism and did not seek re-election the next year as chairman of Ways and Means. In 1976 he retired from Congress.

Milosevic, Slobodan (b. Pozarevac, Serbia, 20 Aug. 1941)

Serb; President of Serbian League of Communists 1986–8, President of Serbia, 1988–

Milosevic joined the League of Communists while studying at Belgrade University, from where he graduated in law in 1964. He went into economic management, becoming deputy director and then director (1973–8) of the gas company Tehnogas. From this time on his career was advanced by Ivan Stambolic, his predecessor as Director of Tehnogas. In 1978 he became President of Beobanka, the largest Serbian bank. In 1983 he entered high politics when he joined the Presidium of the Serbian League of Communists and in 1984 succeeded Stambolic as president of the Belgrade party organization. In 1986 he was elected president of the Serbian League of Communists (again succeeding Stambolic). Up to that time Milosevic was mainly known for his advocacy of greater economic efficiency through strengthened federal decision-making and a liberalized market within a socialist structure (ideas embodied in the recommendations of the 'Milosevic commission' on constitutional reform 1988). But in 1987 Milosevic's career took a decisive nationalist turn when he visited the Serbian community in the Albanian-dominated Serbian province of Kosovo: pressured by a mass rally to give assurances of help for the embattled Serbs, he subsequently exploited the nationalism of the Serbs outside Serbia, rapidly boosting his popularity with a series of huge mass rallies in Serb areas. In 1988 he forced his patron Stambolic to resign as Serbian President over his handling of the Kosovo issue and was elected to succeed him. He then amended the Serbian constitution to impose direct rule over Kosovo.

In 1990, with the break-up of the League of Communists, Milosevic reluctantly accepted multi-party democracy in Serbia and founded the Socialist Party of Serbia, which won 46 per cent of the vote and 78 per cent of the seats in the Serbian parliament in the December elections. In 1992 in the first direct elections for the Serbian presidency Milosevic won in the first round with 56 per cent of the vote. While his support dropped markedly in the 1992 parliamentary elections to 40 per cent of seats, it rose to just under 50 per cent in the 1993 elections, making only a minor coalition partner necessary. His party also has a majority in the parliament of the new Federal Republic of Yugoslavia.

Like his Croat rival *Tudjman, Milosevic is a highly controversial figure, whose ruthless pursuit of personal ambition allied to Serbian nationalist fears played a major part in the escalation of conflict in Yugoslavia in the 1990s.

Mitchell, George John (b. Waterville, Maine, 20 Aug. 1920)
US; US Senator 1980–94

George Mitchell was born to an Irish father and a Lebanese mother and grew up in relative poverty. Educated at Bowdoin and Georgetown Law School, he worked for the Department of Justice before resigning in 1962 to become an assistant to Senator Edmund Muskie, who greatly influenced Mitchell's career. Mitchell left Muskie's staff in 1965 for private law practice but in 1968 he became deputy director of Muskie's vice-presidential campaign. When Muskie ran for the Democratic nomination in 1972 Mitchell served as deputy director. Mitchell served in a number of Democratic Party posts: he was chair of the Maine Democratic National Committee 1966–8 and was a member of the party Commission on Party Structure and Delegate Section where he opposed delegate quotas. Although he lost a bid to become chair of the Democratic National Committee in 1972 he was appointed a member in 1974, a post he resigned when President Jimmy *Carter appointed Mitchell US attorney for Maine in 1977. (He was appointed a judge on the US District Court in 1979.)

Mitchell had made an unsuccessful gubernatorial race in 1974 and might have stayed a judge but for Carter's nomination of Muskie to be Secretary of State in 1980, thus vacating a Maine Senate seat. Through Muskie, Mitchell was appointed and then surprisingly won re-election in his own right in 1982. In 1988 he won re-election easily.

In the Senate Mitchell gained respect for his mastery of legal detail and for his organizational capacity. His major legislative interests were environmental issues (where he proved an able critic of the *Reagan policies) and especially air pollution. In 1984 he was elected chair of the Democratic Senate Campaign Committee and took a lot of the credit for the Democratic recapture of the Senate in 1986. In 1987 Mitchell's impressive performance on the Iran-Contra hearings, enhanced his reputation and in 1989 he was elected majority leader against competition from Daniel Inouye and Bennett Johnson.

Mitchell's low-key style of leadership proved well suited to a period in which Congress and the presidency were frequently in conflict but legislative compromises had to be reached. In 1994 Mitchell retired from the Senate. In retirement he played a key role in attempts to bring about a settlement to the Northern Ireland conflict.

Mittag, Günter (b. Stettin, 8 Oct. 1926; d. 18 Mar. 1994)
German; member of the Politburo of the SED 1963–89, Secretary for the Economy 1962–73, 1976–89

In 1958 *Ulbricht picked out Günter Mittag, a former railway inspector from Stettin, then a 32-year-old economics expert, and put him in charge of transforming the East German economy into a world-class, technologically based vehicle of socialism. After occupying several posts connected with economic management, Mittag was 'elected' secretary of the Central Committee of the ruling SED responsible for the economy in 1962. He headed a team of experts who introduced the New Economic System in 1963. In the same year he became a candidate member of the Politburo. His reforms were meant to reintroduce an element of the market economy, strengthen the remaining private sector, concentrate investment in the new technologies, and put the emphasis on quality rather than quantity. The erection of the Berlin Wall in 1961 had at last secured the labour force and for a few years the GDR seemed to enjoy modest prosperity. When *Honecker overthrew Ulbricht in 1971 what was left of the reforms came to an end. In 1973 Mittag was given a lesser economic post in the state apparatus, remaining a member of the Politburo of which he had been a full member since 1966. With the economy faltering he was returned to his old command in 1976. But this meant his complete submission to Honecker, who understood little of economics. Despite West German assistance, Western loans, and millions of West German visitors, the East German economic situation got steadily worse from at least the late 1970s onwards. Mittag was regarded as a virtual dictator of the economy until in October 1989 he fell with Honecker when he was arrested for misuse of office. He died a sick and broken man in 1994.

Mitterrand, François (b. Jarnac, 26 Oct. 1916; d. 7 Jan. 1996)

French; President of the Fifth Republic 1981–95

François Mitterrand was born in the small south-western town of Jarnac to a comfortably off, conservatively minded business family. He studied law in Paris and was active, if not prominent, in pre-war right-wing politics. He fought in the 1940 campaign and spent eighteen months in a German prisoner of war camp before escaping to France. He immediately went to Vichy to offer his services to *Pétain for whom, as he acknowledged fifty years later, he had great respect. He worked in the Vichy administration before in 1943 joining the Resistance. Having flown to Algeria, he showed the refusal to accept the political legitimacy of *de Gaulle which would characterize his subsequent career by refusing to place his Resistance organization under the General's command. After the war, he was elected to the National Assembly in November 1946 for the rural Nièvre department on a centre-right ticket and first held office in 1947. His career flourished in the Fourth Republic. A leading member of the Union Democratique et Socialiste de la Republique, a small but influential centre grouping, he was a member of eleven governments. Although he lacked a clear ideological profile and was regarded by many as an ambitious opportunist, his political opinions had by the mid-1950s moved to the centre-left. He was Minister of Justice in the administration formed in 1956 by the Socialist Guy *Mollet but was excluded from the last three governments of the Fourth Republic on account of his progressive views on Algeria.

The turning point in Mitterrand's career came in 1958. His opposition to the return to power of de Gaulle led to the loss of his parliamentary seat, and involved him in 1959 in a scandal, the Affaire de l'Observatoire, which nearly destroyed him. Back in the National Assembly in 1962, he was one of the first anti-Gaullist politicians to realize that the direct elections to the presidency introduced by the 1962 referendum could be a mechanism for the left—and him—to win power. Having demonstrated his credentials as a Republican democrat by writing a powerful indictment of the Gaullist regime *Le Coup d'état permanent*, he then announced his intention to stand in the 1965 presidential elections. He obtained the backing of the Socialist and Communist parties and on the second round of the election, in November 1965, won 43 per cent of the total vote. The result established him as the natural leader of the Opposition and demonstrated that the left was capable one day of winning power in a system designed for its opponents. The construction of such a coalition became Mitterand's overriding purpose. It was a hard and long task. Mitterrand's reputation was damaged by his response to the events of May 1968, in which he was rejected by the radical left as a machine politician and denounced by the right as a subversive. In 1971, however, he won control of the Socialist Party, becoming its First Secretary, and the following year created the electoral and programmatic alliance with the Communist Party known as the Union de la Gauche. This gave him a strong base for the 1974 presidential elections which he lost by a whisker to the non-Gaullist conservative, *Giscard d'Estaing.

His long march to power was not yet over. In 1977, the Communist Party took fright at the advance of the Socialist Party. Its decision to pull out of the Union of the Left cost the left its expected victory in the 1978 parliamentary elections and weakened Mitterrand's credibility. Although he was able to maintain his control of the Socialist Party, in the face of a strong challenge from *Rocard, his third bid for the presidency in 1981 was regarded by many commentators as doomed to failure. What transformed his prospects was, first, a skilful campaign in which the radicalism of the Socialist programme was complemented by the reassuring image of the 64-year-old Mitterrand as 'the tranquil force'; secondly, the growing public disenchantment with the incumbent Giscard; and thirdly, the poor first round performance of the Communist candidate *Marchais. The latter removed the fear that a Socialist President would be the plaything of the Communist Party. On the second round, Mitterrand won a comfortable victory against Giscard, a result which produced widespread public euphoria and enabled the Socialists to sweep to power in the subsequent parliamentary elections.

Mitterrand immediately indicated that he intended to make full use of the presidential powers which he had earlier criticized. In the first part of his presidency, he embarked, with his Prime Minister *Mauroy, on a comprehensive programme of change. Civil liberties were strengthened, local government powers extended, welfare entitlements improved. The core aim was to reduce unemployment and increase production by an ambitious programme of nationalization and demand stimulation. The programme failed and Mitterrand's popularity declined. In 1983, faced with soaring inflation and balance of payment deficits, a weakening currency and rising unemployment, Mitterrand made a spectacular economic U-turn. Sound money, industrial competitiveness, profits, and Europe were henceforth to be the cornerstone of economic policy. Mitterrand signalled the second stage of his presidency by replacing Mauroy with the thirty-something technocrat *Fabius, and by abandoning the cherished Socialist project of tighter state control of church schools. He also laid ever greater stress on the European Community as the vehicle of France's economic and political ambitions and—like de Gaulle and Giscard—established a close relationship with the German Chancellor.

The victory of the Conservative coalition in the 1986 parliamentary elections led to a period of power sharing known as cohabitation. While withdrawing from domestic policy-making, Mitterrand maintained control of the core presidential domains of foreign and defence policy and cultivated a successful profile as the defender of national unity. This enabled him to walk to victory over *Chirac in the 1988 presidential contest on a consensus platform very different from that of 1981. In the early 1990s, however, things started to go wrong. The problem of ever rising unemployment was fuelled by growing discontent at the arrogance of Mitterrand's use of power (his decision to replace Prime Minister Rocard with Edith *Cresson was a disastrous miscalculation) and, above all, by a series of corruption scandals involving close presidential associates. Abroad, he dealt skilfully with France's response to the Gulf War but mishandled his response to the attempted coup against *Gorbachev. His enduring commitment to European integration as a means of controlling German power led him to champion the Maastricht Treaty. But the near failure of the 1992 Maastricht referendum showed the decline in his popularity; and the following year the Socialist Party he had done so much to create went down to crushing defeat in the parliamentary elections. No longer able to conceal the truth about his cancer—or his role half a century earlier in Vichy—he was a much weaker though still not powerless figure in the second cohabitation period. He left office in May 1995.

Mitterrand is one of the most controversial of France's twentieth-century leaders. His enemies regarded him as an unprincipled opportunist who would say, and do, anything to advance his personal ambitions. More sympathetic analysts pointed to his physical and political courage, to his success in teaching the left how to win and exercise power, and to his recognition of the changed international realities within which French policy had to operate.

Mladenov, Petur (b. 22 Aug. 1936)

Bulgarian; Foreign Minister 1962–89, leader 1989–90

Mladenov was Bulgaria's long-standing Foreign Minister. He was disgusted by the Bulgarian Communist Party (BCP) leader *Zhivkov's forced Bulgarianization of the Turkish minority in summer 1989. Mladenov first rallied anti-Zhivkov members in the party, then secured Soviet consent for Zhivkov's removal. On 10 November, he removed Zhivkov from office during a session of the central committee, and became leader of the Bulgarian Communist Party and President. He averted revolution by introducing political pluralism and promising free elections.

In 1990 Mladenov was faced with two main tasks: to secure the victory of reformers within the party; and to enable it to win free elections. The reform process began at the BCP's 'Congress of Renewal' at the end of January 1990. In February he announced that he could not be both head of state and leader of the party and was replaced as BCP First Secretary by Aleksandur Lilov, a reformist. Despite the change of faces at the top, Zhivkov's old supporters retained considerable power in the country. In June 1990, the reformed party won free elections, gaining a narrow majority in parliament. Mladenov resigned as President in June 1990 after a videotape was released which showed him proposing the use of tanks against a demonstration in 1989.

Mlynář, Zdeněk (b. Bohemia, 22 June 1930; d. 15 Apr. 1997)

Czech; member of the Central Committee of the CPCz 1968–9

Mlynář joined the Communist Party of Czechoslovakia (CPCz) in 1946. From 1950 to 1955 he studied law in Moscow State University. Upon his return he was made a departmental head in the Office of the Public Prosecutor in Prague and was involved with the supervision of the state administration. In October 1956 he was appointed to the Czechoslovak Academy of Sciences' Institute for the Study of the State and Law, where he researched in the field of political theory. In 1964 he was made secretary to the legal commission of the Central Committee. In January 1968 the *Dubček regime appointed him to a group which prepared the CPCz's 'Action Programme'. Adopted by the CPCz in April 1968, it offered a more responsive relationship between the party and society. On 5 April 1968 Mlynář became a member of the Central Committee secretariat without secretarial function. He was elected to the secretariat of the Central Committee on 1 June 1968. At the beginning of August he was present at the Bratislava meeting between the CPCz and Soviet Bloc leaders. Following the Soviet intervention in Czechoslovakia later that month, Mlynář was forcibly taken to Moscow with the other Czechoslovak leaders. On 16 November 1968 he resigned from all posts in the party leadership, but remained an ordinary member of the Central Committee. In January 1969 he was appointed to work at the National Museum in Prague. He was expelled from the Central Committee in September 1969 and from the party in March 1970. In 1977 he joined *Havel and others to found the Czechoslovak human rights organization, Charter 77. As a result he lost his job and went abroad. His memoirs, *Night Frost in Prague*, appeared in 1978.

Mobutu, Sese Soko Kuku Ngbendu Wa Za Banga (b. Lisala, Belgian Congo, 14 Oct. 1930; d. 7 Sept. 1997)

Zairean; head of state 1960, 1965–97

A Bengala from northern Zaire (now the Democratic Republic of Congo), Joseph Desire Mobutu (as he was then called) joined the Belgian colonial army direct from secondary school. An ally initially of Patrice *Lumumba, he was appointed army

Chief of Staff at independence in June 1960 and Commander-in-Chief in September, launching his first *coup d'état* against his former patron a few days later. At this point he returned power to civilian politicians, but after a further coup in 1965 he installed himself as President.

In his first few years, Mobutu succeeded in imposing some order on the chaos of Congo/Zairean politics, and gained the support especially of the United States. In 1967, he created a notional political party, the MPR. He proved adept at manœuvring between different domestic groups and external patrons, launching a campaign of 'African authenticity' in 1970, in the course of which he changed his own name and that of the country (from Congo to Zaire), and contested the power of the Catholic church. In 1977 and 1978, opposition groups invaded the Shaba (formerly Katanga) region from Angola, and by playing on the danger of a Communist takeover Mobutu was able to gain essential military support from Western states, especially France and Belgium. At other times, relations with Belgium were poor.

Under Mobutu, Zaire became possibly the most corruptly run state in the world, and reports of his wealth ran to massive figures. In 1990, following riots and external pressure, he promised political reform, but was able to stay in power through manœuvre, repression, and a measure of continuing international support until May 1997, when he was ousted by a guerrilla insurgency led by Laurent Kabila; the name of the country was then changed back to Congo.

Moch, Jules (b. Paris, 15 Mar. 1893; d. 31 July 1985)
French; deputy 1928–36, 1937–40, 1946–58, 1962–7

The son of an army officer, Moch trained as a lawyer and an engineer, attending the élite École Polytechnique until 1912. Mobilized for the First World War, he was mentioned in dispatches for bravery, and returned to civil engineering after military service. Elected as a Socialist in 1928 he became a close associate of Léon *Blum but did not participate in the first Popular Front government. He was Minister for Public Works in 1938. He voted against full powers to *Pétain in 1940, was imprisoned and then liberated in 1941 to join the Free French in London. He served as head of François d'Astier de la Vigerie's office in London and then in the consultative assembly from 1943 to 1944. He was again Minister of Public Works in successive governments from 1945–7. Moch was Minister of the Interior during the crucial years of 1947–9. In November of 1947 there were quasi-insurrectional strikes orchestrated by the Communists. Many expected the Republic to buckle under the impact, but Moch played a leading part in imposing the state's authority. An anti-Communist, pro-Nato Socialist, and Minister for Defence in 1950–1, he was also anti-Gaullist and was made Minister of the Interior in 1958 in the hope of bolstering the Republic as in 1947. However, he opposed the return of *de Gaulle and was not re-elected in 1958. During the 1960s he attacked de Gaulle's excessive nationalism (as he saw it) and the nuclear strike force. He was marginalized in the Gaullist Republic and declined to stand in 1967. In the 1970s he fell out with the direction of his own party as it set a course for alliance with the Communists and resigned in 1974. Moch wrote a substantial number of books, articles, and pamphlets and an autobiography *Une si longue vie* (1976).

Moczar, Mieczysław (b. 21. Dec. 1913)
Polish; Minister of the Interior 1964–71

From 1941 to 1945 Moczar served in the Polish Communist resistance, commanding its organization in the Łódź region. After the war he attained the rank of general in the Polish army. He became Minister of the Interior in 1964, and was the main symbol of resistance to *Gomułka's regime within the Communist Party. He had support within the police and security services as well as the party as a whole. Moczar's faction was known as the 'Partisans' after his role in the wartime resistance and that of many of his supporters. The Partisans felt that Gomułka was subservient to Moscow. The group was typified by nationalism, illiberalism, and hostility to intellectuals and Jews. Moczar manipulated anti-Semitism to win support, though he appeared genuinely to believe that the Jews were the root cause of political dissent in Poland.

During the 'Six Day War' in 1967 the majority of Poles sympathized with Israel, regarding the Arabs as Soviet satellites. Gomułka felt threatened by the ensuing wave of anti-Soviet feeling and, to neutralize popular sympathy for Israel, encouraged anti-Semitism. He thus appropriated Moczar's tactics. But the continuance of unrest strengthened Moczar as the representative of law and order. In March 1968 the special police units which he had created brutally put down student demonstrations and it seemed that Moczar was about to seize power. Gomułka was saved by the support of Eduard *Gierek, the powerful party boss of Silesia. In December 1970 there was another outbreak of unrest. Moczar's security forces were responsible for the violent repression of workers' demonstrations. Gomułka then resigned in favour of Gierek, whom he saw as the only counterweight to Moczar. Gierek won over many of Moczar's supporters and in June 1971 replaced him as Minister of the Interior with Stanislaw Kania. Moczar was given an honorific position.

Modrow, Hans (b. Jasenitz, 27 Jan. 1928)

German; head of government of GDR Nov. 1989–Mar. 1990

Modrow completed an apprenticeship as a mechanic before military service in the Wehrmacht. Taken prisoner by the Soviets he was sent to an anti-Fascist indocrination camp. He owed his early success to his work in the Free German Youth (FDJ) and to his contacts with the Soviets.

Modrow headed the government of the GDR at the critical time between the end of the dominance of the Socialist Unity Party (SED), 18 November 1989, and the election of the first democratic government in East Germany in March 1990. Modrow was accepted because he had built up a reputation as a Communist in line with the principles of Soviet leader Mikhail *Gorbachev. He was briefly made a member of the Politburo in an effort to boost sagging party morale. Modrow had previously served as SED first secretary in Dresden and before that in Berlin-Köpenick.

Modrow attempted to save what he could of the SED and the GDR, leading the former Communists (PDS) in the democratic elections of March 1990. After reunification he served as PDS member of the German parliament until 1994.

Moi, Daniel Torotich **arap** (b. Baringo, Kenya, 2 Sept. 1924)

Kenyan; Vice-President 1967–78, President 1978–

A member of the Kalenjin people from the Rift Valley, Daniel arap Moi was a headmaster and vice-principal of a teacher training college, before being nominated by the colonial authorities as a legislative council representative in 1955; he was elected to the position in 1957, and in 1960 became chairman of the Kenya African Democratic Union (KADU), a party formed to represent the smaller ethnic groups. He became leader of the opposition at independence in 1963, but in 1964 KADU merged with the ruling KANU and he became Minister of Home Affairs. He was made Vice-President in 1967, and peacefully took over as President when *Kenyatta died in 1978.

Lacking Kenyatta's charisma and ethnic base, he gradually strengthened his position by easing the main Kikuyu politicians out of office, and as he consolidated his power became increasingly authoritarian and hectoring in manner. An attempted *coup d'état* led by a section of the air force in 1982, and supported by students, was repressed with some difficulty. Levels of corruption grew, and the assassination of potential rivals who included the Minister of Foreign Affairs was ascribed to individuals close to the President. A vigorous pro-democracy movement formed in Kenya after 1989, and Moi was eventually forced by external pressure, notably from the United States, to hold multi-party elections in December 1992; he won these on a minority vote after the opposition split, and subsequently sought to re-establish his control. In foreign policy, he remained pro-Western while engaged in acrimonious conflict with the United States over its pro-democracy and human rights policies.

Mollet, Guy Alcide (b. Flers, 31 Dec. 1905; d. 3 Oct. 1975)
French; secretary-general of the SFIO 1946–69, Prime Minister 1956–7

Of modest origins, the son of a textile worker, Mollet read for a degree in English at the University of Lille and taught English. He wrote an English grammar and knew England well. He was mobilized in 1940, captured, and released. He joined the Resistance in 1941 in Arras and was elected mayor in 1945 at the Liberation and then returned as deputy for Pas-de-Calais. He was a rising star in the Socialist Party (SFIO) but, paradoxically, opposed the modernizers, the old leadership around Léon *Blum and Daniel Mayer with a sectarian Marxism demanding a close alliance with the Communists. He was elected secretary-general in 1946. The onset of the Cold War imposed a reversal of the policy of alliance with the Communists and the Socialist Party became a buttress for the Republic against the challenges from the CP on the one side and *de Gaulle on the other. Minister five times and Prime Minister once, Mollet became an important facilitator or coalition bargainer in the Fourth Republic and managed to get himself a name as a visionless machiavel who cynically manipulated behind a dogmatic Marxist rhetoric; he almost seemed to personify the Fourth Republic in which he was highly influential, but he remarked that he would rather have been SFIO secretary-general than Prime Minister. However, Mollet kept the Socialist Party in the centre of things and accomplished a major raft of social and foreign policy measures (including the launch of the European institutions) and kept the Republic in being against extreme challenge. Mollet's grip on the SFIO leadership was, it seemed unshakeable, and he presided over a party with dwindling membership and diminishing influence. Moreover Mollet was never forgiven for a number of policies during his brief premiership including the decision to prosecute the Algerian war vigorously. It was the Mollet government which in 1956 lost control of events in Algeria and started the long slide to civil war which ended with de Gaulle's return to power—in which he played an important role rallying socialist support for the General. In 1958 Mollet rallied to de Gaulle, was one of the authors of the constitution of the Fifth Republic, and was a Minister of State from 1958 to 1959. However, Mollet did not have a place in the Gaullist Republic and went into opposition. In 1962 he organized the left's *cartel des non* and took the first steps towards alliance with the Communists. In 1965 Mollet at first supported the candidature of *Pinay for the presidency and then Mitterrand's but sabotaged that of his colleague *Defferre (who would have supplanted him in the party). However, he fell out with Mitterrand, who was rapidly dominating the left and during the foundation of the new Parti Socialiste manœuvred to retain power backstage (he did not stand as leader). In 1971, when Mitterrand took over the party in a 'coup', he formed La Bataille Socialiste to oppose the new leadership.

Molotov, Vyacheslav Mikhailovich (real name **Skryabin**) (b. Vyatka province, Russia, 25 Feb. (9 Mar.) 1890; d. Moscow, 8 Nov. 1986)
Russian; Politbureau member 1921–57, Chair of Council of People's Commissars 1930–40, Soviet Foreign Minister 1939–49, 1953–7

Nephew of the composer Skryabin, Molotov was studying at Kazan University when he became a Bolshevik in 1906, taking his revolutionary name ('Hammer') soon afterwards. He became *Stalin's trusted henchman, acting as his assistant in the party secretariat in the 1920s and helping to purge many oppositionists; he joined the Politbureau in 1921 (full member from 1926). Throughout the 1930s he was the formal head of the Soviet government and was the only prominent Old Bolshevik to survive the purges, no doubt for his fanatical loyalty to Stalin, even signing the arrest order for his own wife.

However, it was when he replaced *Litvinov as Soviet Foreign Minister in 1939 that he became internationally known. One of his first acts was to sign the notorious Nazi–Soviet pact, reversing his predecessor's 'collective security' policy. He played a prominent role at the Yalta and Potsdam conferences and in the early Cold War years at the UN, where his constant obstruction of Western proposals earned him the nickname of 'Mr Nyet' in the Western media. He lost favour with Stalin in 1949, when he ceased to be Foreign Minister and became deputy chair of the Council of Ministers.

After Stalin's death he regained his post as Foreign Minister but opposed *Khrushchev's de-Stalinization and supported the 'Anti-party group' in 1957. When the attempt to unseat Khrushchev failed he lost his post and Central Committee membership and was sent as Soviet ambassador to Mongolia. In 1960 he became Soviet delegate to the International Atomic Energy Agency but after renewed attacks on him in 1961 he retired in 1962. In 1964 he was expelled from the party, only being readmitted in 1984.

Mondale, Walter Frederic (b. Ceylon, Minnesota, 5 Jan. 1928)

US; US Senator 1965–77, Vice-President 1977–81, Democratic presidential candidate 1984

Educated at the University of Minnesota, where he took a BA and LLB, Mondale practised law in Minneapolis. In 1960 he was elected Attorney-General of Minnesota. He was a protégé of Hubert *Humphrey in the Democratic Party of Minnesota. In 1964, with Humphrey's election as Vice-President, Mondale was elected to the Senate seat from Minnesota which had been vacated by Humphrey when he became Vice-President of the United States. He supported the liberal measures of President *Johnson on such issues as civil rights, anti-poverty, and the environment. He was re-elected for a second Senate term in 1970 and continued to work for liberal reforms, though with little success in the more conservative mood of America in the 1970s.

In 1976 he was chosen as vice-presidential candidate by Jimmy *Carter. His selection was crucial to the victory by a very narrow margin of the Democratic ticket in the presidential election of 1976. As a liberal from a Northern state he balanced the ticket which was headed by Carter, a conservative Democrat from a Southern state. Moreover, he projected a very favourable image in the 1976 campaign, especially in the vice-presidential television debate with his Republic rival, Robert *Dole. In office as Vice-President, he continued to project a favourable image and he was a very influential adviser within the Carter administration. He retained prestige and popularity while Carter steadily lost respect and popular approval. He was renominated as vice-presidential candidate in 1980, but despite an effective campaign and favourable comparison with his Republican rival, George *Bush, the Carter–Mondale ticket lost heavily to the Republican ticket headed by Ronald *Reagan.

In 1984 he successfully sought the Democratic nomination for President. The mood of public opinion had, however, moved in a conservative direction, and he was identified with a discredited liberal Democratic standpoint. Moreover, his Republican opponent, President Reagan, had won widespread popularity by boosting national morale, pursuing expansionist economic policies and strengthening national defence. As a result Mondale suffered humiliating defeat, winning only his home state of Minnesota. He returned to law practice in Minneapolis, though he continued to be a respected senior figure within the Democratic Party. With the election of a

Democratic President in 1992, President *Clinton appointed him as American ambassador to Japan.

Monnet, Jean Omer Marie Gabriel (b. Cognac, 9 Nov. 1888; d. 16 Mar. 1979)
French; head of French Plan 1946–52, president of ECSC 1952–5

The son of a brandy wholesaler, Monnet was sent to learn English in the City of London at 16 and then travelled Europe and North America selling on behalf of the family firm. In 1914 he joined the private office of Prime Minister René Viviani and helped create the Allied committees to co-ordinate the purchase of vital commodities. He was Deputy Secretary-General to the League of Nations 1920–2 before once again returning to business and spent the next fifteen years in banking. In 1938 he returned to public service and became head of the Anglo-French co-ordinating committee in October 1939. It was Monnet who proposed the unsuccessful plan for Anglo-French union when France was invaded and he then served on the British supply council (1940–3) in Washington acting as a very effective go-between for the Americans and the Allies. After the Allied landings in 1943 he went to Algeria and supported *de Gaulle's leadership of the Resistance. In 1945 he proposed a plan for the economic revival of France and was put at the head of the new Planning Commissariat which distributed *Marshall aid to great effect. For the French the problem of how to manage a reviving Germany was unresolved but Monnet, seeing an opportunity, drew up a plan to pool the coal and steel production of the two countries under the direction of a quasi-federal High Authority. The plan was promoted by Robert *Schuman and formed the basis of future attempts at European integration. In April 1951 the European Coal and Steel Community was set up and Monnet became its president. Monnet also prepared a plan for a European Defence Community which never came to fruition but at the Messina conference of 1955 promoted the ideas of a general common market and a European Atomic energy authority which were endorsed in the Rome Treaties in 1957. When Monnet left the European Coal and Steel Community in 1955 he set up an action committee to support integration. Despite being, in the words of his biographer François Duchêne, 'the first statesman of interdependence' (*Jean Monnet*, 1994) Jean Monnet was sidelined when de Gaulle returned to power and his influence (which remained considerable) was mainly indirect under the Fifth Republic.

Morgenthau, Henry Jr. (b. New York City, 11 May 1891; d. 6 Feb. 1967)
US; Secretary of the Treasury 1934–45

Morgenthau was the son of a German Jewish immigrant who had become a New York financier and served as US ambassador to Turkey 1913–16. He attended Philips Exeter Academy before entering Cornell University to study architecture. Finding this subject of little interest he left Cornell, began working with his father, became ill, and whilst recuperating in Texas became interested in agriculture. Returning to Cornell he studied agriculture for two years, 1909–10 and 1912–13, before buying a large farm on the Hudson River. During the First World War he served as a lieutenant in the US navy. After the war he returned to farming, and acquired the journal *American Agriculturalist*, which he published for eleven years, 1922–33.

Morgenthau's career in the public service began in 1929, when his farming neighbour and friend, Franklin D. *Roosevelt, then Governor of New York, appointed him chairman of the Agricultural Advisory Commission. Thereafter he was appointed a member, then chairman, of Taconic State Park Commission 1929–31, and a member of the New York State Conservation Commission 1931. When Roosevelt became President, Morgenthau became chairman of the Federal Farm Board and was assigned the task of reorganizing the existing farm lending agencies of the government. This was accomplished in the form of the Farm Credit Administration, of which he became governor in 1933. That same year he moved to the Treasury, serving first as acting secretary, then as Under-Secretary and finally, in 1934, as Secretary of the Treasury, a post which he continued to hold until 1945.

Morgenthau is chiefly remembered for his long tenure in this post. As Secretary of the Treasury he was in charge of US finances throughout the turbulent years of the New Deal and the Second World War. On taking office he faced the formidable task of stabilizing America's monetary system in the aftermath of abandoning the Gold Standard. During the war he played a key role in the planning and operation of the Lend-Lease scheme designed to support the Allied war effort. He was also instrumental in devising the plans for the post-war monetary system that eventually emerged from Bretton Woods in 1944. When, in 1945, his somewhat bizarre plans for the enforced 'pastoralization' of post-war Germany found little favour with *Truman, Morgenthau became marginalized and resigned.

After retiring from public life Morgenthau turned to the task of editing his detailed and controversial diaries and records of his time in the Treasury.

Morrison, Herbert (b. London, 3 Jan. 1888; d. 6. Mar. 1965)

British; deputy leader of the Labour Party 1951–5, Foreign Secretary 1951; Baron (life peer) 1959

Herbert Morrison was involved with the Labour Party from its creation until his death and a leading figure in its politics for over twenty-five years. He was the son of a policeman and largely self-educated. After holding various short-term jobs he became circulation manager of a Labour newspaper in 1912, a post which he held for three years. He then became part-time secretary of the London Labour Party, holding this post until 1947. Morrison had few links with the trade union movement and the early influences were the socialist societies, the Independent Labour Party, and the Social Democratic Federation.

Morrison was always interested in translating ideas into measures which would help people, particularly working people. In 1919 he became mayor of Hackney and in 1922 was returned as MP for Hackney South. He also became a member of the London county council (LCC) in 1922. He never lost this connection; he was council leader between 1934 and 1940, and a member until 1945.

Morrison's administrative talents were shown in the 1929 Labour government. As Minister for Transport he was responsible for the Road Traffic Act and the eventual establishment of the London Passenger Transport Board. This provided for the public management of the capital's bus and underground railway services. It also established the public corporation as the appropriate form for future nationalized industries. He expanded his ideas in a book; *Socialisation and Transport* (1933). Industries would be run by managers, not workers, and be answerable to parliament through ministers.

It was Morrison's misfortune that he was one of many Labour MPs swept away in the 1931 general election. Had he been returned, he would almost certainly have been elected party leader. When he returned to the Commons after the 1935 election, he was defeated in the party's leadership election by Clement *Attlee, who already held the post. For the next twenty years Morrison was never fully reconciled to his subordinate status.

In his years as LCC leader, Morrison displayed his vision in schemes of reclamation and an ambitious house-building programme. Labour in London showed what it could do in power. He was always conscious of Labour's need to appeal to the respectable working class and lower middle class. In parliament, he opposed schemes for rearmament and conscription to meet the rising menace of Nazi Germany. When Britain was at war, it was Morrison who moved the censure motion which eventually precipitated Neville *Chamberlain's resignation in 1940. During the wartime coalition, he was Minister of Supply, then Home Secretary and a member of the War Cabinet between 1942 and 1945.

Morrison was a key member of the 1945–51 Labour government. At the outset, he and his supporters challenged Clement Attlee's right to accept the monarch's invitation to form a government without first receiving party approval. Morrison hoped that he would be chosen as leader. The move failed, although he was made Deputy Prime Minister. The hostility of Ernest *Bevin, the Foreign Secretary, prompted Attlee to confine Morrison to Home Affairs. As Lord President of the Council, he co-ordinated domestic policy, although Stafford *Cripps took over economic policy in 1947. He was also leader of the House of Commons and deserves credit for getting so much radical legislation passed. He succeeded Bevin as Foreign Secretary for a few months in 1951 but damaged his reputation in the post. He lacked experience of foreign affairs. Morrison was acting Prime Minister (Attlee was in hospital), when *Bevan and Harold *Wilson resigned from the Cabinet.

Returned to political opposition after 1951, Morrison favoured consolidation rather than more radical measures, particularly on public ownership, and was the main influence on the 1951 election manifesto. The left detested him as a narrow-minded machine politician and he was voted off the party's national executive at the 1952 conference. Attlee hung on to the leadership and Morrison saw himself overtaken by younger men. As a long-serving deputy leader his opportunity had passed when Attlee resigned in late 1955 but it did not help when the latter called for his successor to be somebody born in the twentieth century. Morrison finished a poor third behind *Gaitskell and Bevan in the leadership election in December 1955 and bitterly refused the offer of deputy leadership. He retired in 1959 and took a peerage, as Morrison of Lambeth. He wrote an uninformative *Autobiography* in 1954.

Mosley, Sir Oswald Ernald (b. London, 16 Nov. 1896; d. 3 Dec. 1980)

British; Chancellor of the Duchy of Lancaster 1929–30, leader of British Union of Fascists 1931–40 and Union Movement 1948–66; 6th Baronet 1928

Born into a landed family, Mosley was educated at Winchester and Sandhurst. Invalided out of the army during the First World War, he was elected a Conservative MP in 1918, retained his seat as an Independent in 1922 and 1923, and in 1924 joined the Labour Party. On the formation of the second Labour government (1929–31) he was appointed Chancellor of the Duchy of Lancaster and one of a team of ministers commissioned to formulate solutions to the unemployment problem. But he resigned from the government after a year, when the Cabinet rejected the Keynesian proposals in his 'Mosley Memorandum', and formed the New Party. He lost his seat in the 1931 general election and rapidly gravitated towards non-parliamentary schemes for national economic reconstruction.

The British Union of Fascists, which Mosley founded in 1931, initially reflected his admiration for *Mussolini's Italian Fascism, but became heavily influenced by Nazism. Its increasingly anti-Semitic propaganda was paralleled by violence by black-shirted members organized on paramilitary lines. Their brutality at a rally at Olympia in 1934 and in street riots in 1936 prompted the passage of the Public Order Act banning the wearing of political uniforms.

Mosley's endorsement of *Hitler's policies after the outbreak of the Second World War led to his internment. His release, on health grounds, in 1943 was highly controversial. After the war, his candidature in the 1959 and 1966 general elections under the banner of his Union Movement was widely ridiculed. He lost his deposit on both occasions and disappeared from British politics.

Mossadeq, Muhammad (b. 1882; d. 5 Mar. 1967)

Iranian; Prime Minister 1951–3

Son of a Qajar dynasty Finance Minister and a Qajar princess, Mossadeq's shock at the terms of the Anglo-Persian Treaty of 1919 decided him on a policy of Persia for the Persians.

A member of the National Assembly from 1915, he held several brief government appointments between 1920 and 1924, but was forced out of public life by Reza Shah in 1928 until 1941. Upon his re-election in 1944, Mossadeq introduced a bill to prevent oil concessions to foreigners being made without the Assembly's approval. The Persian–USSR oil agreement went unratified as a result in 1947. In 1949 he formed the National Front from diverse factions opposed to foreign influence and increasing royal power. As chairman of the Assembly's oil commission, he secured rejection of the government's oil concession to the Anglo-Iranian Oil Company in 1950 and championed nationalization of the British-controlled oil industry. The Assembly implemented this in April 1951 and, after the assassination of the pro-Western Premier by Islamist National Front members, he became Prime Minister in May 1951 on a wave of nationalist fervour and opposition to misgovernment. A grave political and economic crisis then ensued; Mossadeq attacked the monarchy by seizing control of the armed forces and a world boycott of Iranian oil led by Britain resulted in almost total loss of oil revenues. After dismissing Mossadeq, the Shah was forced to reinstate him following street demonstrations in 1952. The crisis ended when Mossadeq was deposed in 1953 and the Shah restored to his throne in a military coup engineered by the CIA and the British Secret Service. Mossadeq was admired by nationalists and fundamentalists alike of later generations for his fervent, though unsuccessful, stand against the West and Iranian monarchy.

Moynihan, Daniel Patrick (b. Tulsa, 16 Mar. 1927)

US; US ambassador to India 1973–5, ambassador to the United Nations 1975–6; US Senator 1977–

Moynihan was educated at City College, New York. He graduated BA from Tufts University in 1948 and from Fletcher School of Law and Diplomacy he graduated MA in 1949 and Ph.D. in 1961. He is the recipient of numerous honorary degrees and awards and in 1950–1 was Fulbright Fellow at the London School of Economics.

In the 1950s he moved from an academic career to one in the public service. Serving first as acting secretary to the Governor of New York State 1955–8, and then after a two-year appointment on the Syracuse University government research project, he was appointed special assistant to the Secretary of Labor 1961–2, and promoted to executive assistant in 1962. A year later President *Johnson appointed him Assistant Secretary of Labor, a post which he held for two years. In 1966 he returned to an academic career, first in the post of professor of education and urban politics and then, in 1973, professor of government, at Harvard. Whilst at Harvard he continued to work for the federal government in the capacity of assistant to the President for urban affairs 1969–70 and counsellor to the President 1971–3. President *Nixon appointed him US ambassador to India in 1973, a post which he held until 1975 when President *Ford appointed him ambassador to the United Nations. His fervently pro-Israel stance whilst serving in the UN subsequently helped him to attract the Jewish vote, which helped him to gain election as US Senator for New York in 1976.

Moynihan, a Democrat who has specialized in family and welfare policies, has frequently been at the centre of controversy. He was accused of racism for views expressed in the 'Moynihan Report' prepared for President *Johnson in 1965. Intended to justify increased aid to black families, the report asserted that many of their problems were rooted in slavery, which had discouraged the emergence of strong father figures.

By the 1970s Moynihan shrugged off his former association with *Johnson's Great Society programme and embraced neo-liberalism. But in the 1980s he returned to his liberal roots and led a successful Senate fight against *Reagan's social security cutbacks. He also modified his past staunch anti-Communism, urging instead arms reduction and opposing *Reagan's interventions in Central America.

Moynihan's consistently independent and outspoken views were as irritating for Democrats as for Republicans.

Mubarak, Mohammed **Hosni** Said (b. Al-Minufiya, 4 May 1928)
Egyptian; Vice-President 1976–81, President 1981–

Born and raised in a Nile Delta village, Mubarak embarked on a military career, first graduating from the Military Academy in 1950 and subsequently from the Air Force Academy where he trained as a pilot. Combat experience early in the Yemen Civil War (1962–7) was followed by a rapid rise through the senior ranks of the Egyptian Air Force to become Air Chief of Staff in 1969 and Air Marshal in 1973. He commanded Egypt's military forces between 1972 and 1975, gaining considerable personal prestige from their victories in battle against Israel during the 1973 war.

President *Sadat appointed him Vice-President in 1975. Mubarak assumed the presidency in 1981 after Sadat's assassination and was subsequently re-elected in 1987 and 1993. He quickly established his political credentials, which until then had been in doubt, by declaring a state of emergency and vigorously suppressing the militant Islamists who had attempted to overthrow the government. He continued Sadat's key policies: 'open door' economic reforms were continued by accelerating privatization and developing a tourism infrastructure, while peaceful relations with Israel were maintained. Mubarak also sought to conciliate Arab leaders and end Egypt's isolation in the Arab world. By 1987, her gradual rehabilitation was virtually complete. Egypt's renewed leadership role was considerably enhanced during the Kuwait crisis of 1990–1 when Mubarak led Arab opposition to Saddam *Hussein and committed 35,000 Egyptian troops to the war against Iraq. The economy benefited greatly from the subsequent cancellation and rescheduling of debts. A renewed Islamist terrorist campaign in 1992 imperilled the Egyptian economy, especially its flourishing tourism industry, and threatened the regime—Mubarak's assassination was attempted in 1995. Extensive security counter-measures contained the insurgency, however, confining it mostly to remote parts of upper Egypt.

Mugabe, Robert Gabriel (b. Kutama, Northern Rhodesia, 21 Feb. 1924)
Zimbabwean; Prime Minister 1980–7, President 1987–

Born into the Shona ethnic group Mugabe worked as a teacher before becoming a founder-member of the Zimbabwe African People's Union (ZAPU) in 1960. In 1963 he spit from ZAPU to form the Zimbabwe African National Union (ZANU). From 1964 to 1974 he was held in detention for nationalist activities. On his release he went into exile in Mozambique, where he became president of ZANU and Commander-in-Chief of its guerrilla forces engaged in armed struggle against the white minority regime of Ian Smith. In 1979 he participated in the Lancaster House Conference which resulted in the end of the civil war and the agreement for Zimbabwean independence under majority rule. After the victory of his party in the pre-independence elections he became Prime Minister of the independent state in April 1980. Following constitutional change in 1987 he became the country's first executive President.

Although Zimbabwe retained a multi-party system Mugabe frequently adopted an intolerant, and at times brutal, style in his dealings with the opposition and in 1990 his desire to introduce a Marxist-Leninist single-party state was only prevented by his failure to win the support of the ZANU politburo. Although he favours radical Marxist rhetoric he has done little to disturb the capitalist system he inherited and has proceeded extremely slowly in dealing with the problem of the highly inegalitarian distribution of farming land in the country.

Displaying an aloof personality Mugabe tends to be respected or feared rather than loved by his people.

Muldoon, Robert David (b. Auckland, 25 Sept. 1921; d. 5 Aug. 1992)
New Zealand; Prime Minister 1975–84

Muldoon was brought up by his mother and grandmother in frugal circumstances. He scarcely knew his father except as an invalid visited in hospital after a stroke early in Muldoon's life. Muldoon was educated at Mt. Albert Grammar School, Auckland, and trained and worked as a Chartered Accountant and a Cost Accountant. He was elected National Party member for Tamaki in 1960. Prime Minister *Holyoake brought him into Cabinet as Minister for Finance in 1967.

From his first budget it was clear that Muldoon was in charge at the Treasury. His practice of adjusting the economy with mini-budgets not only allowed for changing conditions but brought him before the public. His capacity to use television to project himself with clear, direct answers soon made it obvious that he was very much part of the government. When he became leader of the Opposition in 1974 his unparalleled capacity for polarizing politics and for devastating criticism contributed to the Labour government's massive defeat in the 1975 elections.

Muldoon proved to be one of the most interventionist and most dominant Prime Ministers in New Zealand history. Holding both offices of Prime Minister and Minister for Finance gave him considerable power over all the other portfolios because he could approve or disapprove spending as he saw fit. His forceful personality was intimidating and Cabinet ministers had to buckle under or resign. Ironically, he introduced a programme of government regulation so comprehensive that his own National Party supporters, believers in private enterprise and free markets, began to question the government's policies. His bible was the election manifesto which was kept at hand for Cabinet meetings. If disagreement arose he would refer to it. He was perfectly clear that he had to stick to his election promises. The basis of his popular support was that people trusted him to keep his word.

Muldoon called a snap election in 1984 but the mood was for change and the Labour Party led by David *Lange won. Muldoon remained a member of parliament but was not appointed to Cabinet when National Party leader Jim *Bolger became Prime Minister after the defeat of Labour in the 1990 elections. He remained a truculent figure on the back bench and there were rumours of leadership challenges. In November 1991 he announced that he would quit politics in February 1992 in protest against the policies of the National government, at the same time denying that his intention had anything to do with his ailing health.

Müller, Hermann (b. Mannheim, 18 May 1876; d. 20 Mar. 1931)
German; Chancellor of Germany 1920, 1928–30, SPD chairman 1919–27

The son of a factory manager, Müller had been forced to leave grammar school early on the death of his father. He took up an apprenticeship as a salesman where he got involved in union activities. He joined the SPD and by 1899 was editor of a small SPD paper. Like *Ebert he was known more for his organizational talent than for his speaking ability and in 1905 he was a candidate for the post of secretary of the SPD, but was beaten by Ebert. He owed some of his success to backing from *Bebel. Because of his foreign language skills Müller was delegated to socialist congresses abroad. His most significant mission was to end in failure. In July 1914 he was sent to discuss the international situation with the French parliamentary group. Their leader Jean *Jaurès was murdered while Müller was still travelling and he arrived only to take part in the funeral. The two parties were unable to take joint action against the approaching war.

Müller remained with the majority SPD after the left-pacifist split in 1916, voting for the defence of Germany, but against annexations. When the revolution came, he was appointed Foreign Minister and then Chancellor to 1920. His popularity in the SPD was shown by his re-election year by year as party chairman from 1919 to 1927.

The break-up, in March 1930, of the coalition government led by Müller marked a decisive turning point in German politics, from which the democrats were unable to recover. The coalition fell apart because its members could not agree on measures to finance the unemployment insurance fund. The governments which followed it were less and less representative of the Reichstag until *Hitler was asked to form his government in 1933.

Mulroney, Martin Brian (b. Baie Comeau, Quebec, 20 Mar. 1939)
Canadian; Prime Minister 1984–93

Born and raised in a small community on the rugged north shore of the Gulf of St Lawrence, Mulroney attended St Francis Xavier University in Nova Scotia and then studied law at Laval University, Quebec City. He then practised as a Labour lawyer in Montreal, whilst becoming increasingly active in the Progressive Conservative Party. He was fluently bilingual, experienced in labour conciliation and in US–Canada economic relations.

In 1976 he failed to wrest the party leadership from Joe *Clarke and returned to business as president of a US-owned iron ore company. In 1983 he replaced Clarke and in September 1984 became Prime Minister when his party won a landslide victory over a tired Liberal administration. In close agreement with Robert Bourassa, premier of Quebec, he promoted two far-reaching measures—the 'Meech Lake Accord' aimed at settling disputes between the provinces and the federal government, which ultimately failed, and a free trade agreement with the United States concluded with Reagan's administration. One celebrated meeting between Mulroney and Reagan in Ottawa, between two men famed for their blarney and Irish pedigrees, was dubbed by the media 'the Shamrock Summit'. With the adhesion of Mexico, the US–Canada Free Trade Agreement was converted into the North American Free Trade Agreement (NAFTA).

Mulroney's Charlottestown Accord of September 1992—granting Quebec special status as 'a distinct society' whilst also changing the character of the Senate—was put to a national referendum on 26 October 1992 but decisively rejected. Mulroney failed to heal the constitutional rift and his popularity slumped to the lowest recorded for an incumbent Canadian Prime Minister. On 25 June 1993 he was replaced as party leader and Prime Minister by Kim *Campbell, who was herself decisively defeated by the Liberals under Jean *Chrétien in a federal election four months later. Much adverse criticism attached to the arrangements he made for his colleagues in his last months in office and these gave rise to Mulroney bringing an acrimonious libel suit, claiming heavy damages, after his retirement from political life.

Museveni, Yoweri Kaguta (b. Ntungamo, Uganda, 1944)
Ugandan; President 1986–

A Nyankole from south-west Uganda, Museveni was educated at the University of Dar-es-Salaam, then a leading centre of radical student activity in East Africa, and briefly joined the Ugandan civil service before going into exile after the *Amin coup of 1971. He organized the exiled opposition to Amin from Tanzania, and participated in the invasion that brought about Amin's overthrow, becoming briefly Minister of Defence in the subsequent interim government. He formed a party, the UPM, which contested the 1980 elections but won only one seat. Claiming (with some justice) that the elections had been rigged, Museveni organized a rural guerrilla movement, the National Resistance Army (NRA) which in January 1986 overthrew the incumbent government.

As President, Museveni sought to rescue Uganda from the shambles which had been bequeathed by Amin and exacerbated by a succession of weak regimes. His NRA was disciplined and efficient, and was widely welcomed as the best prospect for peace, though it faced opposition especially in northern Uganda. A broadly based government was formed, but Museveni remained hostile to multi-party elections, which he associated with ethnic competition and violence. He established good relations with Western states, but was on poor terms with most of his neighbours, who saw his reform programme as a threat to their own regimes, and probably sanctioned the RPF invasion of neighbouring Rwanda in 1990.

Mussolini, Benito (b. 29 July 1883; d. Dovia di Predappio, 28 Apr. 1945)
Italian; head of government 1922–43

Mussolini's father was a blacksmith, his mother a teacher, and his wider family small landowners in the foothills of the Apennines in Emilia-Romagna. His father was active in the revolutionary socialist movement, and Benito Mussolini grew up in the fervid atmosphere of the international socialist movement of the late nineteenth century. He was educated locally, and apparently distinguished himself both by his intelligence and by his ungovernable temper. He qualified as a teacher, but after a brief period in this profession he emigrated to Switzerland, where he was active in the socialist movement as a writer and self-procalaimed intellectual. He was expelled from the cantons of Berne and Geneva, and eventually in 1909 found work in Trento as a journalist and trade union organizer. When eventually he was expelled from the region by the Austrian authorities, he returned to Romagna, where he spent a period in prison for organizing a general strike.

He came to national prominence when in 1912 he was appointed editor of the Socialist party newspaper *Avanti!* His combination of revolutionary intransigence and ideological flexibility soon brought him into conflict with the reformist leaders of the Socialist Party. At the outbreak of the First World War, he was firmly neutralist and internationalist (unusually, since this was the official party line), but the break-up of international socialism led him quickly to support intervention, the ideological justification of which he found in the idea of the nation as an independent actor above the notion of class. After military service (1915–17) he became increasingly active in support of the economic demands of returning veterans and argued (as did others) that Italy's victory had been 'mutilated'.

His 'fasci di combattimento', one of several such groups from which the Fascist movement takes its name, were founded in Milan in March 1919. In the climate of revolutionary socialist fervour following the factory occupations in Turin, Fascists with their anti-parliamentary methods and radical nationalist demands increasingly appeared as protagonists in a potential civil war. After Mussolini's success in the elections of May 1921 and the formation of the National Fascist Party in October 1921, he moderated his rhetoric and sought to reassure the Court and the business community, both of his own moderation and of his capacity to control the Fascist squads. When the constitutional parties failed repeatedly to find a stable formula for government, Mussolini was asked by the King on 28 October 1922 to form a government. He marked the event several days later with his famous though unnecessary 'March on Rome' (10 November 1922).

His majority depended initially on the Liberals and on the Catholics, whose parliamentary leader was *De Gasperi. The support of the Catholics was particularly uncertain, and, to remedy this, Mussolini secured the acceptance in 1923 of a new electoral law giving the majority grouping two-thirds of the seats. Though controversial, this proved formally unnecessary, since in the elections of April 1924 Mussolini's 'big list' of approved candidates won 66 per cent of the votes. There is little doubt that the Italian establishment including the Court, the army, and the major industrialists expected Mussolini to content himself with this minimum of constitutional reform and to provide stable parliamentary government until a new Liberal leader emerged. In fact the pace of change accelerated. In June 1924, the Socialist leader Matteotti was murdered by a Fascist squad. In protest, the opposition parties left parliament, thereby granting Mussolini freedom from opposition and ensuring the collapse of liberal-democratic procedures. From this point on, both his formal authority and his effective power were unchallenged until his downfall in 1943.

During this nineteen-year period, Mussolini oscillated in domestic politics between economic innovation and social conservatism. His control of the media was complete, and was crucial to the social support of his regime. He promoted intervention in public works, particularly in the south, and pursued the development of the Corporatist state. He also achieved a settlement with the Vatican in the Lateran Pacts in 1929. In foreign affairs, his initial concern to avoid alienating the great powers gradually gave way to a more opportunistic line. After the success of the Abyssinian War (1935–6) he became more overtly pro-German, though this could be interpreted as a more noisy continuation of the traditional Italian foreign policy of manœuvring for advantage among unstable alliances. Mistrust of *Hitler and concern over Italy's lack of preparedness kept Italy out of the war until May 1940. The short triumphant campaign for which Mussolini hoped became a long series of fruitless military entanglements and defeats, in North Africa, Greece, and Russia. Northern Italy suffered mass aerial bombing from late 1942 on, and the first real stirrings of popular opposition began to show themselves in the northern factories. Mussolini sacked some of his senior Cabinet ministers in February 1943, thereby creating an internal opposition, which began to conspire against him. In May 1943 the Axis forces surrendered in North Africa, and on 9 July 1943 the Allies invaded Sicily. After secret negotiations between the Allies and the Court (via the Vatican), and after a damaging and dramatic air-raid on Rome, the Fascist Grand Council ousted Mussolini on 25 July 1943.

In September 1943, Mussolini was freed from his house arrest by a German raid, and was established by Hitler as the puppet head of the Italian Social Republic, based at Salo' on Lake Garda. Without the power to implement his decisions, Mussolini rediscovered the taste for verbal radicalism and nationalist republican rhetoric. When in April 1945 the German forces in Italy surrendered, Mussolini tried to escape into Switzerland. He was captured by Communist partisans and was executed by them. As a politician and national leader, Mussolini is remembered by almost all except the neo-Fascist Italian Social Movement as a symbol of what post-war Italy wanted to turn its back on.

Nagy, Imre (b. Kaposvár, southern Hungary, 7 June 1896; d. Budapest, 17 June 1958)
Hungarian; Prime Minister 1953–5, 1956

Nagy was the son of poor peasants who apprenticed him to a locksmith at the age of 10. Until 1914 he worked as a mechanic. During the First World War he was wounded on the eastern front and sent as a prisoner to Siberia. After the October Revolution of 1917, Nagy joined the Bolshevik Party and the Red Army. Later he became a Soviet citizen. He returned to Hungary in 1923 to develop the illegal Hungary Communist Party. He was imprisoned in 1927, but escaped to Austria the next year. From 1930 to 1944 he lived in Moscow, where he studied agriculture and worked for the Institute of Agrarian Sciences.

Nagy returned to Hungary in 1944 with the Red Army. In the first post-war coalition government, he was Minister of Agriculture, and was responsible for the implementation of far-reaching land reform, as the great noble estates were split up. In 1946 he was briefly Minister of the Interior, before *Rákosi removed him in favour of the more ruthless *Rajk and he became Speaker of Parliament. In 1949 *Stalin criticized Nagy for his opposition to the rapid collectivization of agriculture and he was removed from government office. Nagy's fortunes improved when *Malenkov became Soviet Prime Minister. In July 1953 Malenkov encouraged Rákosi's replacement as Hungarian Prime Minister by Nagy. Nagy cut back on Rákosi's harsh programme of agricultural collectivization, much reduced the terror of the secret police, and eased press censorship. In February 1955, eleven days after Malenkov's fall in the Soviet Union, Rákosi removed Nagy from office. Amid charges of 'Titoism', Nagy was expelled from the Communist Party in November 1955. After *Khrushchev's denunciation of Stalin at the 20th Party Congress of the CPSU, pressure mounted within Hungary for Nagy's reappointment. In October 1956 anti-Stalinist demonstrations in Budapest marked the start of the Hungarian Uprising. On 24 October the Communist Party reinstated Nagy as premier in an attempt mollify the population. From the start, Nagy was the prisoner of popular demands. He provided the Soviet Union with a pretext for intervention when he announced Hungary's withdrawal from the Warsaw Pact and desire for neutrality. On 4 November 1956 the Red Army invaded Hungary and Nagy took sanctuary in the Yugoslav Embassy, emerging after eighteen days under a Soviet safe conduct. He was seized and deported to Romania. In 1957 the Soviet authorities returned him to Budapest, where he was secretly tried. He was executed on 17 June 1958 and fully rehabilitated in 1989.

Nakasone Yasuhiro (b. Gumma, 27 May 1917)
Japanese; Prime Minister 1982–7

Nakasone was educated at Tokyo Imperial University and was first elected to the Diet in April 1947. He rose quickly in the Liberal Democratic Party (LDP), acquiring the reputation of being a strong Japanese nationalist and of being hawkish in defence matters. In 1959 he became director of the Science and Technology Agency (a post just below Cabinet level) and a protégé of *Tanaka Kakuei. Under *Satõ Eisaku he was Minister for Transport (1967–8), Director-General of the Defence Agency, the equivalent of Defence Secretary (1970–1), before becoming Minister of the powerful Ministry of International Trade and Industry (MITI) following Tanaka's appointment as Prime Minister (1972–4). He was secretary-general of the LDP from 1974 to 1976. In 1982, with support from the Tanaka faction, he became Prime Minister. His period in office was marked by a number or privatizations of state-controlled industries and attempts to reduce the role of the government and bureaucracy in the economy. He developed a close relationship with US President Ronald *Reagan as both shared a strong dislike of the Soviet Union, and the phrase 'Ron–Yasu Diplomacy' was coined to describe this. He pushed Japanese defence spending over the psychologically significant 1 per cent of GNP barrier for the first time.

Nakasone was forced to resign as Prime Minister in 1987 when he was implicated in the Recruit scandal, and was replaced by another Tanaka faction member, Takeshita Noboru. He rejoined the LDP in 1991 and remains active in the Diet.

Nasser, Gamal Abdul (b. Alexandria, 15 Jan. 1918; d. 28 Sept. 1970)
Egyptian; President 1954–70

Nasser joined the Fascist group, Young Egypt, as a schoolboy. He became an army officer in 1937, served with distinction in the Arab–Israeli War 1948–9 and reached the rank of colonel. The débâcle of the monarchist Arab armies and the resulting catastrophe for the Palestinian people convinced him of the need for revolution and elimination of foreign domination in Egypt.

Nasser led the Free Officer movement in the Egyptian armed forces which seized power in July 1952, under General Neguib. It abolished the monarchy a year later. Nasser ousted Neguib as head of state, Prime Minister, and chairman of the military junta (RCC) in 1954. His decision to nationalize the Suez Canal to finance the construction of the Aswan High Dam led directly to the second Arab–Israeli War of October–November 1956. The successful co-ordinated attacks upon Suez by Israel, France, and Britain were quickly halted and a ceasefire arranged after strong UN and USA pressure. Despite military defeat, Nasser was able to present the war as a great Arab victory over the forces of imperialism and Zionism and he was acclaimed as a great Arab hero.

From 1958, Egypt relied increasingly upon Soviet military and economic aid. This ended Egypt's non-aligned policy and she became the principal Soviet client state in the Middle Eastern Cold War. In the name of Arab socialism, Nasser carried out a domestic programme of extensive nationalization, income redistribution, subsidies on basic goods, and a reduction of rent, fares, and educational fees, in 1961. Nasser's post-Suez ascendancy lay chiefly in the wider Arab world, however. He inspired the pan-Arab union of Syria and Egypt, the United Arab Republic, in 1958, which lasted until 1961. Nasser sought the overthrow of Arab monarchies and the vestiges of European rule in the Arab world, by aiding revolutionary nationalist groups, as in Algeria, North Yemen, and Oman, and by supporting radical nationalist governments, like those of Nabulsi in Jordan and *Qadhafi in Libya. Nasser sponsored and sought to direct the Palestinian guerrilla groups al-Fatah in 1956 and the PLO in 1964. As Egypt, Syria, Iraq, and Jordan moved towards war with Israel, Israel destroyed the airforces of all four countries in pre-emptive airstrikes in June 1967. This enabled Israeli ground forces to win a rapid and crushing military victory in six days that destroyed Nasser's dreams of uniting the Arabs and annihilating Israel.

Nehru, Jawaharlal (b. Allahabad, 14 Nov. 1889; d. 27 May 1964)
Indian; President of Indian National Congress 1951–4, Prime Minister 1947–64

Son of a Kashmiri Brahmin lawyer, Nehru was educated at Harrow and Trinity College, Cambridge. He later qualified as a barrister at the Inner Temple. On returning to India he became involved in the Congress. The Jallianwala massacre left a deep impression on Nehru, who subsequently participated in the Non-Cooperation Movement (1919–22), which enabled him to become a popular leader, especially in Uttar Pradesh. He was imprisoned in 1921 and was to spend long periods in jail before 1947. Between the end of 1931 and September 1935 he was free for only six months.

The failure of the Non-Cooperation Movement led Nehru to move closer to socialism. During 1926–7 he visited Europe and was impressed by meetings with socialists and concerned by the rise of Fascism. His move to the left became permanent and he maintained his anti-Fascism throughout the 1930s.

In 1936–7 he steered the Congress to victories in the provincial elections and subsequently participated in the Quit India Movement (1942). In September 1946 Nehru was made the head of the Interim Government and Vice-President of the Governor-General's Executive Council. As Congress's chief spokesman in negotiations with the Muslim League and the colonial government, Nehru was a poor match for M. A. *Jinnah and squandered the opportunity to evolve a scheme for united India. Given his consistent opposition to the partition of India, his acceptance of the 3 June 1947 Plan, which created modern India and Pakistan, produced the outcome that he least desired.

After 15 August 1947, Nehru became the Prime Minister of India, a position he was to occupy until 27 May 1947. He was to lead the Congress to three successive general election victories (1952, 1957, and 1962) and following the death of Patel (1950) became the undisputed leader of the party.

Nehru was a prolific writer. He wrote extensively during spells in prison. Among his more prominent works are *Glimpses of World History* (1935), *Autobiography* (1936), and the *Discovery of India* (1946). Although influenced by Gandhian ideas, he was a modernizer who believed that the future of India lay with industry, science, technology, and state-led industrialization. Nehru was strongly influenced by the Soviet model of centralized planning and established the Planning Commission (1950) which oversaw the development and the implementation of Five-Year Plans. Centralized planning, however, was adapted to operate within the framework of a liberal democracy. The success of many of the elements of planning were made contingent upon the democratic mobilization of the poor, especially the rural poor.

During his tenure as Prime Minister Nehru also held the office of Foreign Minister. In 1954 he agreed a *Panch Shila* pact with China which asserted principles of peaceful coexistence and mutual non-aggression. Nehru's efforts to steer clear of the Cold War between the USA and Soviet Union led him to ally with other Third World leaders in a similar position. In 1955 he played a pre-eminent role at the Bandung Conference in Indonesia at which the Non-Aligned Movement was born. The following year Nehru visited USSR, followed by *Khrushchev's visit to India which established strong economic ties between the two countries. These initiatives, however, could not prevent growing border tension between India and China which eventually erupted into a full-scale war in October 1962.

In domestic politics Nehru nurtured political development by acting as a tutor to chief ministers. He wrote to them on a regular basis about issues of general and political concern. Following the defeat of Tandon (1951), Nehru became the President of Congress, a position he held until 1954. Nehru is accredited with establishing the 'Congress System'—a system of one-party dominance that combined democratic governance with the needs of political development. A particularly notable feature of the 'Congress System' was the high degree of autonomy given to provincial party bosses and the role of Nehru as national leader and mediator. This system worked well in the 1950s and managed the tensions generated for the linguistic reorganization of states and the imposition of Hindi as a national language.

In 1955 Nehru committed the Congress to a 'socialist pattern of society'. To further this aim the Second Five-Year Plan (1957–62) was formulated with the aim of collectivizing agriculture but this move was defeated at the annual conference of the Congress Party (1958). Nehru also suffered reversals with the dismissal of the Communist government in Kerala (1959) and increasing corruption within the party. His efforts to revive the Congress through the Kamaraj Plan (1963), which required leading Cabinet colleagues to return to the provinces, was widely interpreted as a move to prepare his daughter, Indira *Gandhi, for the succession.

Nehru was a towering personality who shaped the image of modern India. An intellectual statesman, he was ill at ease with the harsh realities of political life, either at home or abroad. His indecisions, romanticism, and patrician detachment led to fatal miscalculations that were best illustrated by the humiliation suffered by the Indian forces during the Indo-China war. Yet despite these limitations, Nehru provided stable leadership during dangerous years after the partition of India and established institutional structures that provided the basis of economic development.

Netanyahu, Binyamin (b. Tel-Aviv, 21 Oct. 1949)

Israeli; Prime Minister 1996–

Netanyahu attended an American high school from the age of 14. He returned to Israel in 1967 for military service, finishing as an officer in an élite anti-terrorist unit. He resumed his American education at MIT in 1972, graduating with degrees in architecture and business administration. A brief business career in the USA and Israel followed which ended when he became deputy to the ambassador in Washington in 1982. He was appointed UN ambassador from 1984 to 1988 and during this period Netanyahu acquired his considerable media skills.

In 1988 he was elected to the Knesset and straightway appointed deputy Foreign Minister. He relinquished the post in 1991 to serve in Prime Minister *Shamir's office as Israel's spokesman during the Gulf War. Later that year he was a member of the Israeli delegation to the Middle East peace talks which began at Madrid. Netanyahu succeeded Shamir as party leader in 1993 after Likud's electoral defeat the previous year. From the Oslo Accords (1993) onwards, he vehemently opposed the peace process with the Palestinians and played skillfully on the Israeli public's fears about personal security. These were accentuated after suicide bombings by Islamist terrorists in early 1996 and helped to secure his narrow victory in the direct election for Prime Minister later that year. Despite his party winning fewer seats than Labour in the simultaneous general election, Netanyahu successfully formed a Likud-led coalition government. After a year in power it had stalled the faltering peace process, violated the sanctity of Islam's Noble Sanctuary in Jerusalem (resulting in widespread violence and many deaths), alienated numerous allies, and nearly dragged Israel into war with Syria. Netanyahu narrowly escaped indictment for fraud and breach of trust in the Bar-On political scandal of 1997.

Ne Win, U or General (b. Paungde, 24 May 1911)

Burmese; Prime Minister 1958–60, head of state 1962–81

Born in a small town in the Pyi (Prome) division of the then British Indian province of Burma, and briefly educated at Rangoon University, before becoming involved in nationalist politics prior to the Second World War, General Ne Win governed Burma longer than any person since before the beginning of British colonization in 1824. As a member of a nationalist youth organization, he travelled, under Japanese auspices, to the island of Hainan in 1940 where he underwent military training with twenty-nine other young Burmese men. These became the nucleus of the Burma Independence Army which accompanied the Japanese when they invaded Burma in 1942.

Ne Win's subsequent career was centred on the army. He became deputy commander under General Aung San during the war. When the Burmese turned against the Japanese in 1945, he joined forces with British troops in retaking the country. Remaining in the army after independence, he was made commander of the armed forces in 1948 by Prime Minister *Nu. At the height of the civil war following independence, Nu turned to him as Deputy Prime Minister. Again, in 1958, Ne Win entered the Cabinet, this time as Prime Minister of an eighteen-month 'Caretaker Government' called to allow the anti-Communist politicians time to settle their Disputes.

Alarmed at the direction the re-elected Nu's government was taking the country in 1962, he conducted a coup which swiftly replaced the civilian government with a Revolutionary Council regime dedicated to the establishment of socialism by Burmese means. The Burma Socialist Programme Party became the sole legal party and assumed formal control of the state from the Revolutionary Council in 1974. Ne Win remained President until 1981 and party chairman until 1988. By then, the political consequences of the inability of the government's autarkic socialist policies pursued to create economic growth were evidenced by several months of demonstrations and strikes throughout the country. In an effort to lessen tensions, Ne Win resigned but in the face of continuing demonstrations, the military, under men trained by him, intervened, violently suppressing the demonstrators, and re-establishing military rule. Ne Win faded from the political scene at that time.

Though managing to keep Burma from becoming embroiled in the major international conflicts between India and China and the second Indochina War which surrounded the country during his years in office, Ne Win's political legacy is usually seen in the continuing underdevelopment of the country as a consequence of autarkic socialist policies. His earlier exploits in the nationalist movement and leadership of the armed forces against a number of internal Communist and separatist insurgent groups have been largely forgotten.

Nicholas II (Nikolai Romanov) (b. Tsarskoe Selo, near St Petersburg, 18 May 1868; d. Ekaterinburg, 17 July 1918)

Russian; last Tsar, reigning 20 Oct. 1894–2 Mar. 1917

Nicholas succeeded to the throne at the age of 26, following the death of his father Alexander III, who restored stability to the dynasty after the assassination of his reforming father by firmly suppressing dissent. Nicholas was inexperienced, immature, and without interest in military or political affairs. Influenced by his tutor and his father's mentor the arch-conservative Pobedonostsev he had an unshakeable commitment to the principles of autocracy and a dislike of reform. Soon after his accession he married the German Princess and grand-daughter of Queen Victoria Alix of Hesse-Darmstadt, who shared his conservative views. He had a very close and loving relationship with his wife and family and was never at ease outside the family circle. The health of his haemophiliac only son Alexei became a major preoccupation from 1904 and this, together with his wife's religious zeal, brought them increasingly under the influence of the unsavoury but charismatic monk Rasputin, which alienated the nobility, already resentful of Alexandra's German origins and dominant influence during the Great War. Nicholas was both indecisive and stubborn, temperamentally unsuited to being more than a constitutional monarch but never accepting that role.

For the first few years of his reign Nicholas maintained the ministers and policies of his father. *Witte, Minister of Finance and one of the ablest tsarist ministers of the nineteenth century, who had masterminded Russia's industrialization and railway development in the 1890s, was sacked in 1903 after personality clashes with the Tsar and criticism from the Tsar's conservative advisers. At the turn of the century Russia became involved in an adventuristic Far Eastern policy, actively promoted by the Tsar and Tsarina. This provoked a war with Japan in which Russia was comprehensively defeated in 1905. This defeat intensified a domestic political crisis, arising out of long-developing worker and peasant unrest dramatized by the bloody suppression of a workers' demonstration in St Petersburg in January 1905 ('Bloody Sunday'). With unrest amongst the non-Russian nationalities and mutinies in the navy, by the autumn the situation became so tense that Nicholas was forced to call on Witte to draft a manifesto of constitutional reforms (known as the October Manifesto), promising a legislative assembly (the Duma) with limited powers and basic civil rights. Witte became Prime Minister and a Duma was elected in 1906 dominated by the middle-class Kadet party, but even this proved too radical in its demands for the Tsar, who dissolved it in July and restricted the franchise to the property-owning classes. It became clear that Nicholas was not prepared to limit his autocratic prerogatives and tried to deal with the pressures for change by increasing police powers; there was brutal suppression of dissent and the civil rights granted in 1905 gradually restricted. Witte resigned and was replaced in July by *Stolypin, who combined ruthlessness in dealing with unrest with a thoughtful programme of agrarian reform which tried to remove the legacy of debt and land hunger and create a class of peasant farmers loyal to the regime. Stolypin had fallen out with the Tsar even before he was assassinated in 1911, and after this Nicholas's ministers were of limited ability. Even before the start of the First World War unrest was breaking out again, but the onset of war, and the rapidity and magnitude of Russian defeats, greatly weakened the political and economic structure of the country. In 1915 Nicholas unwisely chose to take personal charge of field operations, leaving his German wife with her dubious entourage in charge of affairs in the capital. By 1917 the regime was in a parlous state with revolutionary unrest spreading among the troops and workers, peasants seizing the large estates and (a decisive new factor compared with the events of 1905) signs of disunity and disaffection amongst the ruling élite and police, first shown in the murder of Rasputin by conservative nobles in 1916. In February 1917 disturbances increased and riot troops fraternized; an International Women's Day demonstration turned into a general strike. The Tsar dissolved the Duma, which had demanded a new government, but a group of deputies from the Duma's 'Progressive Bloc' who had formed themselves into a Provisional Committee demanded the abdication of the Tsar, who was still at the front. Eventually on 2 (15) March Nicholas agreed to abdicate in favour of his brother, but under pressure from the Committee the Grand Duke refused the throne. The royal family were put under arrest at their palace at Tsarskoe Selo; in August they were moved for safety to Tobolsk. After the Bolshevik Revolution in October their position became threatened, especially after the start of the civil war. As the war moved closer to Tobolsk they were moved to Ekaterinburg where they were murdered by local Bolsheviks acting on *Lenin's instructions. Nicholas had been exactly the wrong man to deal with the accumulated problems of the Romanov dynasty.

Nikolai Romanov *see* NICHOLAS II OF RUSSIA

Nimairi, Jafar Muhammed (b. Omdurman, 1930)
Sudanese; Head of State 1969–85

Born into a poor urban family, Nimairi joined the army in 1949, and participated in the coup led by General Abboud in 1958. In May 1969, having risen to the rank of colonel, he launched his own coup in association with radical elements and the Sudanese Communist Party, and subsequently ruled Sudan for far longer than anyone before or (as yet) since.

The initial imposition of socialist policies, involving considerable repression, lasted only two years; in July 1971, an attempted coup was launched with the support of the Communists, but was suppressed after three days. The Communists were purged, and Nimairi looked for support to the West. He resolved the civil war in southern Sudan by accepting southern regional autonomy in the March 1972 Addis Ababa agreement, and after the oil price rises of the mid-1970s sought to turn Sudan into the 'breadbasket of the Middle East' with aid from newly oil-rich Arab states.

These efforts failed. The ambitious development programme degenerated into massive corruption while producing negligible economic results, and Sudan itself became dependent on food aid. Nimairi himself undermined his own main achievement, the settlement of the war in the south, by unilaterally abrogating the Addis Ababa agreement, leading eventually to renewed war. In September 1983, he adopted Islamic law (whether out of personal religious conviction, or to improve his standing in Moslem northern Sudan, remains uncertain), thus further deepening the rift with the Christian south. In April 1985 he was overthrown while abroad by another military coup, and went into exile in Egypt.

Nixon, Richard Milhous (b. Yorba Linda, California, 9 Jan. 1913; d. 22 Apr. 1994)
US; US Senator 1951–2, Vice-President 1953–61, President 1969–74

Born to Quaker parents, Nixon was educated at Whittier High School and Whittier College, graduating in 1934. He then took a law degree at Duke University law school, where he was elected president of the student bar association, and was admitted to the California bar in 1937. He practised law in his home town of Whittier—he became a partner in a local law firm in 1939—and in 1940 married Thelma Catherine (Pat) Ryan. In 1941 he became assistant city attorney. His legal career was interrupted by war service. He served briefly in the type-rationing section of the Office of Price Administration in Washington, DC, before enlisting in the navy. His four-year stint in the navy included a fourteenth-month tour of duty in the Pacific. By the time he was discharged in 1946 he had reached the rank of lieutenant-commander.

On his return home he was persuaded to run for Congress. He had registered as a Republican in 1938 and was approached by some local Republicans to challenge a wall-entrenched liberal Democrat, Jerry Voorhis. Nixon took up the challenge, campaigned vigorously—characterizing Voorhis as voting the 'Moscow' line in Congress—and took on Voorhis in several debates. He won by more than 15,000 votes. Once in the House of Representatives, Nixon established a reputation as an aggressive conservative. Appointed to the Committee on Education and Labor, he helped draft the *Taft–Hartley Bill which outlawed the closed shop. As a member of the Committee on Un-American Activities, he achieved national fame for his questioning of witnesses, especially of a State Department official, Alger Hiss, who was later to be indicted and gaoled for perjury. Nixon's prominence gave him the basis for seeking election to the Senate and in 1950 he was elected as Senator for California. The contest had been hard fought—both candidates trading insults—but Nixon won by a wide margin, winning almost 60 per cent of the votes. The incumbent Senator resigned before the end of his term, allowing Nixon to gain seniority by taking his place a month ahead of other newcomers.

Nixon was touted as a possible vice-presidential candidate as soon as he was in the Senate. He had achieved national prominence, his election victory had been spectacular and he represented a new generation of Republicans. He was a forceful and energetic speech-giver. He supported Dwight *Eisenhower for the presidential nomination in 1952 and Eisenhower, acting on advice from senior party figures, chose Nixon as his running mate. During the campaign, allegations that Nixon had a private campaign 'slush fund' threatened his continued presence on the ticket. Nixon made an emotional speech on television—the 'Checkers speech'—defending his actions and claiming that the only personal gift he had accepted was a cocker spaniel named Checkers for his children. It proved an effective performance. With Eisenhower sweeping to victory in November, Nixon became Vice-President. He was 40 years old.

During his tenure as Vice-President, Nixon took a particular interest in foreign affairs and Eisenhower asked him to undertake a total of ten foreign visits, covering fifty-eight countries. His life was endangered by a mob during a visit to Venezuela. He chaired meetings of the Cabinet and National Security Council during Eisenhower's illnesses. He also served as the partisan voice of the administration, allowing Eisenhower to appear above the political fray. He fought and won a battle to remain

Eisenhower's running-mate in 1956. In 1960, after reaching agreement with his most likely challenger for the nomination, Governor Nelson *Rockefeller of New York, he won the Republican nomination for President by 1,321 votes to 10. He pursued a gruelling campaign itinerary and took on his Democratic opponent, John *Kennedy, in a televised debate. Most television viewers believed that the cool, attractive Kennedy had won the debate over the perspiring, shifty-looking Vice-President. Most radio listeners thought Nixon got the better of the exchange. In the election, Nixon was narrowly defeated, the gap between the two leading candidates being 0.2 per cent or just over 100,000 votes out of 68.8 million cast. Nixon returned to private life.

Two years after his unsuccessful bid for the presidency, Nixon re-entered the political fray and sought election as Governor of California. He lost, telling reporters that 'You won't have Richard Nixon to kick around any more, because, gentlemen, this is my last press conference.' He practised law again, this time in New York, and his law practice—along with royalties from the sale of his book *Six Crises* (1961)—provided him with an income he had not enjoyed before. He undertook trips to the Middle East, South America, and Europe—in France he was entertained by President Charles *de Gaulle—and began to plan a resumption of his political career. He campaigned for the Republican Barry *Goldwater in 1964 and in 1968 he sought the Republican nomination for President. He edged out his opponents and won the nomination at the Republican convention in Miami. An early lead over his Democratic opponent. Hubert *Humphrey, narrowed as the campaign progressed, but he emerged the victor, albeit by a narrow margin in the popular vote (43.4 per cent to 42.7 per cent). He was inaugurated as the 37th President on 20 January 1969.

Nixon's first term as President was to be dominated by foreign affairs. He achieved détente with both the Soviet Union and China, undertaking visits to both. His links with China pushed the Soviet Union into seeking a relationship. He signed the Strategic Arms Limitation Treaty (SALT), designed to deter the Soviet Union from launching a first strike, on his visit to Moscow. He re-established American influence in the Middle East. He sought to extricate the United States from Vietnam by placing greater emphasis on South Vietnamese forces. He also increased military attacks on North Vietnam—and authorized military incursions into Cambodia and Laos—in order to try to force North Vietnam to the negotiating table. The use of force attracted intense domestic opposition: four students were killed when members of the National Guard opened fire on demonstrating students at Kent State University. A peace agreement with North Vietnam, signed early in 1973, allowed the USA to extricate itself from Vietnam and for the President to claim 'Peace with Honour', though the terms were little different from those that could have been achieved earlier.

Nixon revolutionized American foreign policy by seeking disengagement and by placing greater emphasis on allies being responsible for their own protection. He conveyed that he had a sure feel for foreign affairs and by the time of the 1972 presidential election had an impressive record on which to run. In domestic affairs, the record was less impressive. He pursued a policy of 'New Federalism', manifested in the policy of revenue sharing, under which more federal funds than before were allocated to the states and municipalities. However, the main feature of his domestic politics was his clashes with a Democrat-controlled Congress. Nixon impounded funds voted by Congress. Congress twice rejected his nominee for a vacancy on the Supreme Court. President and Congress clashed over funding for the Vietnam War. The War Powers Act sought to limit the President's powers to commit troops abroad. Nixon adopted a stance of confrontation rather than conciliation. He created a Domestic Council, a form of super Cabinet. According to Arthur M. Schlesinger Jr., in *The Imperial Presidency*, Nixon sought to impose an imperial residency in the domestic as well as the foreign arena, creating a 'revolutionary presidency'. His ambitions were to be dashed by the Watergate affair. Nixon achieved an easy victory in the 1972 presidential election. His foreign policy had proved popular—the Nixon campaign ads on television constantly showed pictures of his trip to China—and the economy was in reasonable shape. His Democratic opponent, George *McGovern, had a disastrous campaign. Nixon was re-elected by 47 million votes to 29 million. Within days of his second inauguration he was able to announce the peace agreement reached with North Vietnam. Thereafter it was all downhill.

During the summer of 1972, the Democratic headquarters in the Watergate complex in Washington, DC, had been broken into. Though rumours of White House involvement circulated during the election campaign, they made little impact. However, early in 1973, the story began to achieve prominence. The men arrested for the break-in were convicted. In order to avoid a maximum sentence, one of them offered to break his silence. He claimed that certain White House officials had prior knowledge of the break-in. A Senate Committee, under Senator Sam *Ervin, began taking evidence. White House Counsel John Dean, implicated in the allegations, started giving evidence to Senate investigators. As the story moved closer to the Oval Office, the President requested and accepted the resignations of his two closest aides, H. R. 'Bob' Haldeman and John Ehrlichman, and dismissed Dean. In public testimony to the Senate Committee, Dean implicated the President in a cover-up. In July, a White House aide revealed that the President had a voice-activated recording system in the Oval Office. Various attempts were then made to subpoena the tapes of presidential conversations. Nixon initially resisted. In October, he fired the special prosecutor appointed by the Attorney-General as well as the Attorney-General and his deputy after they refused to fire him. Dubbed 'The Saturday Night Massacre', the firings undermined Nixon's credibility. Early in 1974, the House Judiciary Committee began to consider articles of impeachment against the President. In April, Nixon released edited transcripts—1,254 pages—of his conversations. On 24 July, the Supreme Court ruled that the President must hand over other tapes sought by the special prosecutor. Between 27 and 30 July, the House Judiciary Committee approved four articles of impeachment. On 5 August, the White House released transcripts sought by prosecutors, one of which—the 'smoking gun' transcript—revealed that the President authorized a cover-up shortly after the break-in. Republican leaders in Congress told the President that he did not have enough votes to avoid impeachment. In a televised address on 8 August, Nixon announced his resignation and the following day, after a tearful farewell to staff at the White House, his resignation took effect at noon.

During 1973, Nixon's problems had been compounded by the resignation of the Vice-President, Spiro *Agnew, after pleading 'no contest' to tax evasion charges. In his place, Nixon nominated a Republican member of the House of Representatives, Gerald R. *Ford. It was Ford who took the oath of office as Nixon's successor on 9 August. One of Ford's early acts in office was to pardon Nixon for any offence he may have committed.

Nixon retired to write his memoirs and rehabilitate his reputation. He wrote a number of books, including *The Real War*, and was variously consulted on a private basis by his successors. His standing as a 'disgraced' President dogged him. In the 1982 *Tribune* and Murray polls, he was rated by historians as one of the worst Presidents. The Murray poll rated him 34th out of 36. By the time of his death in 1994 he had achieved at least a partial rehabilitation. In the 1995 *Chicago Sun-Times* poll of presidential scholars, he was ranked 19th out of 38.

Nixon was one of the most controversial presidents in the twentieth century and the only one in history to resign. He adopted an adversarial approach and attracted the enmity of a great many opponents. He was shy and insecure, affected by the death of two of his brothers while still young, and awkward in his dealings with others. He was keen to win and adopted tactics that facilitated his winning. Towards the end of his presidency, he adopted a siege mentality. He was a man driven from within. Life was seen in terms of a series of crises—hence the title of his book, *Six Crises*—and he had an inherent tendency to rigidify. Watergate was the occasion when he rigidified and consequently sacrificed the presidency.

Nixon was also an individual of contradictions. A man who took an abrasive and partisan stance, he could be personally considerate and helpful. He adopted a friendly stance toward John Kennedy, a stance that was not reciprocated. Though waging war, he remained influenced by his Quaker beliefs. Though portrayed as a conservative Republican, he had a long-standing and consistent commitment to civil rights. Though declaring he was 'not a quitter', he quit. In international affairs, he was an internationalist and adopted far-sighted policies. Despite achieving much at an early age, his political life was a series of struggles. His perception of life as a series of crises had the air of a self-fulfilling prophecy. With the passage of years, a number of revisionist historians, including British MP Jonathan Aitken, have taken up his cause. His last struggle, to rehabilitate his name, is still being fought.

Nkrumah, Kwame Francis Nwia Kofie (b. Nkroful, Gold Coast, 28 Sept. 1909; d. 27 Apr. 1972)

Ghanaian; Prime Minister 1952–60, President 1960–6

Born into the small Nzima ethnic group Nkrumah studied and worked in the USA and Britain and became a significant figure in pan-Africanist circles in both. He returned home in 1947 to become general secretary of the newly established United Gold Coast Convention (UGCC). Following disagreements with more conservative members of the UGCC he broke away in 1949 to form his own Convention People's Party (CPP). Under his leadership the CPP built a mass base of support becoming the leading nationalist party in the territory. Following success in the 1951 elections he became leader of government business, and the following year Prime Minister. The CPP maintained its majority electoral support and at independence in 1957 he became Prime Minister of the new state of Ghana. Following constitutional change in 1960 he became the country's first President.

Nkrumah's career after independence combined an international and a domestic role. At the international level he was he most important African nationalist leader of his generation and was inspirational throughout Africa. He was the leading supporter of pan-African unity and worked tirelessly, but ultimately unsuccessfully, to bring about the political union of the emerging states of Africa. Domestically his rule was predominantly negative. He inherited one of the strongest economies in Africa but by the time he lost power Ghana was plunging towards economic collapse as a result of the inefficiency and corruption of its, predominantly state-run, economic enterprises. His regime became increasingly authoritarian. As early as 1958 he introduced a preventative detention act which allowed for arrest without charge and imprisonment without trial. Potential centres of opposition including the trade unions, the judiciary, and the universities were brought under tight government control and the media was rigidly censored. In 1964 he declared a single-party state and installed himself as 'President for Life'. His self-granted titles included 'the redeemer' and 'the initiator of the African personality'. He is credited with writing a large number of books but most (if not all) were ghost-written for him by his acolytes.

In 1966 he was overthrown by a military *coup d'état* whilst he was attending a meeting in Beijing. At the invitation of his close friend President Sekou *Toure he went into exile in Guinea and subsequently died of cancer in a Romanian hospital in 1972. His international reputation and prominence greatly outstripped his domestic political performance.

Norris, George (b. Ohio, 11 Jul. 1861; d. 2 Sept. 1944)

US; Senator

George Norris was the eleventh of twelve children. He studied and graduated in law while earning money as a schoolteacher. He moved to Nebraska in 1885 and practised law. He served time as an elected judge until 1902, when he was elected to

Congress as a Republican, serving until 1913. From the start he showed his independence. He was a key member of the insurgency group who curtailed the power of Speaker *Cannon, in 1910. He proposed that the membership of the powerful Rules Committee, which determined much of the business of the House, be increased and elected on a geographical basis, with the Speaker ineligible for membership. The proposal was carried and weakened the Speaker's power. He was elected in 1908 by a margin of only 22 votes and had received little help from the Republican Party. He considered himself a self-made candidate and that he might as well go it alone. He had also been denied committee assignments by Cannon. Norris was elected to Senate in 1912, displacing the incumbent Senator Brown, who had the support of the party establishment.

Norris is one of the great American legislators in the twentieth century. Remarkably many of his accomplishments came after he was over 70. He played a major role in the Rural Electrification Act (1936) which provided electricity to farming homes, and the Farm Forestry Act (1937). He was behind the amendment to the Nebraska constitution which made it the only state to have a unicameral system. He was behind one of the first New Deal measures, Tennessee Valley Authority Act, and author of the twentieth amendment to the American constitution, which abolished the short session of Congress and defined the terms of office of President, Vice-President, Senators, and representatives. He was an individualist, not a clubable or a party man. He supported Democratic candidates for the presidency in 1928, 1932, and 1936, but not the Democratic Party. In 1936 he defeated both Republican and Democratic opponents and was endorsed by the President. He was usually to be found supporting the rights of workers to form trade unions, conservation measures, constitutional reforms (including the abolition of the electoral college) and the public ownership of hydro-electric power. He stood as an independent in 1942 and lost.

Novotný, Antonín (b. Letnany, 10 Dec. 1904; d. Prague, 1 Feb. 1975)
Czech; First Secretary of the Communist Party of Czechoslovakia 1953–68

Novotný was the son of a bricklayer who worked in Prague in the Czech armaments industry in the 1920s and early 1930s. At the age of 17 he joined the CPCz upon its foundation in 1921 and started working in the party organization in 1929. In 1937 he moved to Moravia, where he took over the regional party organization. From 1941 to 1945 he was imprisoned in Mauthausen concentration camp.

In 1945 Novotný became Regional Secretary for Prague. He entered the Central Committee in 1946 and played an important part in the Communist seizure of power in February 1948. After the arrest of *Sláský in 1951 he entered the Presidium. Following *Gottwald's death in March 1953 he was appointed First Secretary of the CPCz. After the death of *Zápotocký in November 1957 he also became President of the Czechoslovak Republic. In his domestic policy, Novotný stood for a reduction of the repression of the *Stalin years, but for only a limited and discreet rehabilitation of the victims. He resisted proposals for economic reform. His position was weakened after *Dubček became First Secretary of the Slovak Party in May 1963. As a result of the revolt of the Slovak Party he was forced to drop two key supporters, Bacílek, a Slovak Party Secretary, and Široký, the Czechoslovak Premier, and clung on to power in 1963 only thanks to *Khrushchev's support. In January 1968 he lost the leadership of the CPCz to Dubček. In February 1968 he sought the backing of Czechoslovak army officers for a coup against Dubček's regime, but failed to secure Soviet backing. On 22 March 1968 he resigned as President and was replaced by *Svoboda. Shortly afterwards he was suspended from the party. He was reinstated to party membership in 1971, but played no further role in politics.

Nu, U Thakin (b. Wakema, 25 May 1907; d. Yangon, 1995)
Burmese; Prime Minister 1947–56, 1957–8, 1960–2

Born in the Irrawaddy Delta town of Wakema in British Burma, U Nu was the son of a small shopkeeper. Educated at Rangoon University, where he became involved in student and nationalist politics, he was closely associated with the major political movements of the country until ousted from office in 1962 in a military coup led by General *Ne Win.

A leading figure in the Thakin or *Do Bama* (We Burmese) nationalist movement of the late 1930s, he was chosen by Dr *Ba Maw to serve as Foreign Minister in his Japanese-sponsored government in 1942. Having to abandon politics for a career as an author in 1945 when Britain resumed control of the colony, Nu was made Deputy Chairman of the Anti-Fascist People's Freedom League (AFPFL), the popular organization with which Britain subsequently negotiated Burma's independence. On the assassination of General Aung San in 1947, Nu assumed the deputy chairmanship, effectively the prime ministership, on the eve of independence in January 1948.

Immediately the country was plunged into civil war between Nu's anti-Communist, neutralist government and a variety of Communist and ethnically-designated separatist and revolutionary groups. Dependent on the army under General Ne Win for support in the areas of greatest conflict, his government rested on support from various AFPFL political barons and local bosses in the parliament. Disgusted with their squabbling for spoils, Nu resigned in 1956 to 'clean up the party'. Resuming office in 1958, the AFPFL soon split between his 'Clean' and the two Deputy Prime Ministers' 'Stable' faction. This was the opening for an eighteen-month military 'caretaker government' under General Ne Win.

Though winning re-election in 1960, Nu was ousted in a coup by Ne Win in 1962. Attempting a comeback with the support of armed insurgents along the border with Thailand in the 1960s, Nu eventually slipped from political view, except for a brief resurgence at the time of the collapse of Ne Win's socialist regime in 1988. A devout Buddhist, Nu's years in government were noted for his attempts to bridge the gulf between the West and China at the height of the Cold War. While never a member of the Socialist Party, which formed the intellectual core of his governments, he advocated a set of political ideas which attempted to meld Theravada Buddhist and socialist concepts. His last major project, after accepting a pension from General Ne Win, was to embark on a major translation of Buddhist texts into English.

His autobiography, *U Nu: Saturday's Son* (1975), written in the third person by a fictitious nephew, provides a candid insight into his life.

Nujoma, Sam Daniel Saffishuna (b. Ogandjera, 12 May 1929)
Namibian; Leader of South West Africa People's Organization (SWAPO) 1960– , President 1990–

Born into the majority Ovambo ethnic group Nujoma worked in a variety of jobs before becoming involved in nationalist politics around the end of the 1950s. He was the founder and leader of SWAPO, which was the main organization opposing South African occupation of the territory. Until 1989 he lived mainly in exile in Tanzania from where he organized military and diplomatic pressure on the South Africans. In 1973 the United Nations recognized SWAPO as the legitimate authority for Namibia although the South Africans still controlled the territory. In 1989 a peace agreement was reached whereby South Africa relinquished control and Nujoma returned home to participate in the pre-independence elections. In the elections, held in November 1989, SWAPO won an overall majority of seats in the new legislature and, at independence in March 1990, Nujoma was installed as the country's first President. In the December 1994 elections SWAPO again won an overall majority of seats.

In power he has been a moderate reformist rather than a revolutionary. His earlier support for a Marxist-Leninist single-party state has been abandoned in favour of liberal-democracy and a predominantly free enterprise economy.

Nyerere, Julius Kambarage (b. Butiama, Tanganyika, Mar. 1922)
Tanzanian; Prime Minister 1961–2, President 1962–85

Nyerere initially trained and worked as a teacher but after studying at Edinburgh University from 1949 to 1952 he became the country's first graduate. On returning home he became involved in nationalist politics and founded the Tanganyika African National Union (TANU) in 1954. Following overwhelming TANU victories in the pre-independence elections he became Prime Minister at independence in 1961. In 1962, following the adoption of a republican constitution, he became President. In 1964 he negotiated the merger of mainland Tanganyika and the offshore island state of Zanzibar to form the united republic of Tanzania.

In 1965 he was instrumental in the introduction of a single-party state. He became a leading proponent of 'African Socialism', an ideology which was critical of both capitalism and Marxism, and wrote several influential books detailing his ideas. In 1967 he launched the Arusha Declaration which was designed to avoid the dominance of the single-party leading to abuse of office by establishing a strict leadership code. Although Nyerere has always retained an image of integrity and incorruptibility the code was only partially successful in curbing some of his colleagues. In 1977 he created a new party by merging TANU with the Zanzibari party to form Chama cha Mapinduzi (CCM—Party of the Revolution). By the late 1980s he had become increasingly critical of the single-party system and was one of the most influential figures in the restoration of a multi-party system in Tanzania.

During most of the post-independence period he supported high levels of state intervention in the economy although in later years he modified his views on this matter. During the 1970s the major expression of interventionism came with the compulsory establishment of 'ujamaa' (communal) villages in the rural areas but this policy, which involved high levels of coercion, was later recognized as a social and economic disaster and was abandoned.

Nyerere can be accurately regarded as one of Africa's leading international statesmen and was highly influential in the non-aligned and anti-apartheid movements. He was extremely critical of the abuses of power of other African leaders and in 1979 the Tanzanian army was instrumental in deposing Idi *Amin in neighbouring Uganda.

In 1985 he voluntarily retired from the Tanzanian presidency, although he remained leader of CCM until 1990. Since then he has remained an influential figure in both domestic and international politics. In spite of the problems that Tanzania experienced under his leadership 'Mwalimu' (KiSwahili for 'teacher') has continued to enjoy widespread respect at home and abroad as a man of great intelligence and personal humility, who retained a deep and genuine concern for the ordinary people.

Obote, Milton Apollo (b. Akoroko, Uganda, 1925)
Ugandan; Prime Minister 1962–6, President 1966–71, 1980–5

A member of the Langi ethnic group from northern Uganda, he graduated from Makerere University, and formed the Uganda People's Congress (UPC), which broadly represented northern interests, in 1958. He became Prime Minister of a coalition government at independence in 1962, and gradually imposed his control both over his own party and over his coalition partners, relying increasingly on the army commanded by Idi *Amin. In 1966, he arrested five of his ministers, suspended the constitution, deposed the President, and transferred all executive powers to himself. He pursued a socialist economic policy, and nationalist major companies, attempting to present himself as a populist through a programme called 'The Common Man's Charter'. In January 1971, he was deposed while abroad in a coup led by Amin, and went into exile in Tanzania.

As an old friend of Tanzanian President *Nyerere, he was the main beneficiary of Tanzania's invasion of Uganda to oust Amin in 1978–9. He returned in 1980 to participate in elections which were rigged in his favour, and became President again in December. His second term of office was even less successful than the first. The northerners who controlled the army were split between ethnic factions, while *Museveni's NRA was making increasing progress in the south. Brutal depopulation measures were taken especially against the NRA, with deaths possibly exceeding even the 300,000 under the Amin regime. Obote was however eventually overthrown by his ethnic rivals in the army in July 1985, six months before they in turn were ousted by Museveni. He fled to Kenya and later Zambia, where he continued to run the UPC from exile. His responsibility for Uganda's collapse was second only to Amin's.

Ojukwu, Chukwuemeka Odumegwu (b. Zungeru, Nigeria, 4 Nov. 1933)
Nigerian; leader of Biafra 1967–70

Born into a wealthy Ibo family Ojukwu was educated at Lincoln College, Oxford, and worked as a civil servant before joining the army in 1957. He served in the UN peacekeeping force in the Congo. Following his non-participation in the January 1966 *coup d'état* he was appointed military governor of the Eastern Region. After the July 1966 coup he refused to recognize the government of Yakubu *Gowon and was further alienated by the massacres of Ibo civilians in the north of the country. In May 1967 he led the secession of the Eastern Region to form the independent state of Biafra. This move precipitated the civil war which ended with the defeat of the Biafran forces in January 1970. Ojukwu went into exile in Côte d'Ivoire and remained there until 1982 when he returned home following a presidential pardon.

He joined the ruling National Party of Nigeria (NPN) and was elected national vice-chairman. In the 1983 elections he contested the Onitsha senate seat but lost in controversial circumstances. Following the coup later that year he was detained until October 1984. On his release he became a private businessman.

Ollenhauer, Erich (b. Magdeburg, 27 Mar. 1901; d. 14 Dec. 1963)
German; leader of the SPD 1952–63

Ollenhauer was one of the least charismatic but most honourable of the post-1945 German party leaders. Born in Magdeburg, a stronghold of the SPD, he was also born in the party; his father and his grandfathers were members. Although he completed an apprenticeship with a paint firm, at 18 Ollenhauer was already an SPD member and a trainee journalist on the local party newspaper. During the Weimar years he climbed the SPD ladder, serving as chairman of the Socialist Young Workers (SAJ) 1928–33. He was elected to the Executive of the SPD just after *Hitler's takeover and was sent by the party to carry on the fight from Prague.

The SPD exiles, generously received by their Czechoslovak comrades, remained in Prague until the Anschluss of Austria with Germany in 1938. From France many, including Ollenhauer, escaped just ahead of the Gestapo in 1940. Helped by the British Labour Party, and later Swedish comrades, Ollenhauer and his family remained until 1946 in London, where he carried on the propaganda war against Hitler.

On his return to Germany Ollenhauer helped Kurt *Schumacher rebuild the SPD in the western zones; in the Soviet Zone *Grotewohl had led the SPD into a forced merger with the Communists. They emphasized traditional SPD values and the restoration of German unity as their aims. In the elections of 1949, 1953, and 1957 Adenauer and his Christian Democrats stressed Western integration, NATO membership, and the social market economy, and won decisively. At Bad Godesberg (1959) the SPD adopted a new programme designed to put them in line with current reality. Ollenhauer, deputy chairman of the SPD from 1946 and, on Schumacher's death in 1952, chairman until his death, supported the change without enthusiasm.

O'Neill, Thomas Phillip **(Tip)** (b. Cambridge, Massachusetts, 9 Dec. 1912; d. 5 Jan. 1994)

US; representative in the Massachusetts State Legislature 1936–52, member of the US House of Representatives 1952–86, Speaker of the House 1977–86

The son of a bricklayer, O'Neill was educated in parochial schools and St John's High School, and graduated from Boston College in 1936. Thereafter he combined a career in politics with business interests in insurance and real estate. At the age of 21 he became a member of the State Legislature, serving as minority leader between 1947 and 1948 and Speaker 1949–52. In 1952 he succeeded to John F. *Kennedy's district in the US House of Representatives, when Kennedy moved to the Senate.

O'Neill, on the liberal wing of the Democratic Party, was more a pragmatist and political fixer, a representative of the old-style Tammany Hall politics, than a politician of philosophical convictions. His entry to Congress coincided with a temporary break in the dominance the Democrats had enjoyed since 1932. They regained their former ascendancy in 1955 and with it came promotion for O'Neill, who was appointed to the powerful House Rules Committee. In 1977, amid allegations of having accepted bribes from the South Koreans, he became Speaker of the House. He held this powerful and partisan office for the next ten years: longer than any previous one.

In the position of Speaker O'Neill displayed inspired and effective leadership in a decade of political upheaval. During his period in office the House adopted a new code of ethics, placed limits on outside income and introduced television coverage of its sessions. A charismatic and shrewd politician, O'Neill was careful never to neglect the needs of his constituents or forget his Irish working-class roots. He popularized the phrase 'all politics is local'. In 1987 he published a best-seller memoir: *Man of the House*.

Ordzhonikidze, Grigorii Konstantinovich (also known by first name **Sergo**) (b. Kutaisi province, Georgia, 12 (24) Oct. 1886; d. Moscow, 18 Feb. 1937)

Georgian; chair of Central Control Commission and of Rabkrin (Workers' and Peasants' Inspectorate) 1926–30, chair of Supreme Council of the National Economy 1930–37, Commissar for Heavy Industry 1932–7

The son of a minor nobleman, Ordzhonikidze graduated from a medical school in

Tiflis in 1905. He had been a Bolshevik member of the RSDLP since 1903 and in 1905 was arrested for smuggling arms. Thereafter he was regularly involved in revolutionary activity, both abroad and at home, especially in Transcaucasia (principally in Baku) and St Petersburg, where he was arrested in 1912 and sentenced to three years' hard labour followed by exile. He returned to Petrograd in June 1917. During the Civil War, when he established a close relationship with his compatriot *Stalin, he acted as an Extraordinary Commissar for the Soviet government on the southern front. In 1920–1 he was responsible for establishing Soviet power in Armenia and Georgia (where he removed an elected Menshevik government by methods which gave rise to a dispute between *Lenin and Stalin). From 1921 to 1926 he was in charge of the new Transcaucasian Republic. In 1926 Stalin brought him to Moscow, using his talents to purge the party and state bureaucracies as chair of the Central Control Commission and the Workers' and Peasants' Inspectorate (Rabkrin). In 1930 he was promoted to full membership of the Politbureau when he was appointed chair of the Supreme Council of the National Economy. In 1932 he was made Commissar for Heavy Industry, the post for which he is particularly known. However, he became increasingly disillusioned with Stalin and the purges (including the arrest of friends and relatives) and in 1937 he committed suicide (in 1956 *Khrushchev alleged that Stalin had forced him to do so).

Owen, David (b. Plymouth, 2 July 1938)

British; Foreign Secretary 1977–9, leader of the Social Democratic Party 1983–8; Baron (life peer) 1992

David Owen studied medicine at Cambridge and practised for a short time. He became an MP by winning Plymouth Sutton for Labour in 1966. He held this seat until February 1974 when it was largely reorganized as Plymouth Devonport, and remained its MP until he stepped down in 1992.

David Owen was given junior posts in health in the 1974 Labour government. He served for a year as No. 2 at the Foreign Office in 1976 and then succeeded Antony *Crosland as Foreign Secretary, when the latter died suddenly in 1977. This was an unexpected promotion for someone aged 39. Immediately he was talked of as a future leader of the Labour Party.

Owen was one of the original 'Gang of Four' which left the Labour Party to set up the Social Democratic Party in 1981. Owen probably had more to lose in career terms than the others. He was unhappy with the direction that Labour was taking, including the election of the party leader by a largely extra-parliamentary electoral college, its growing hostility to the European Community (he had resigned from the shadow Cabinet in 1972 on this issue), and its steady move to a unilateralist defence policy.

He and Roy *Jenkins contested the leadership of the new party. Owen was runner-up and became deputy leader. He was no admirer of Roy Jenkins and when the latter resigned the leadership after the 1983 general election, Owen was elected unopposed.

Owen was a jealous guardian of the SDP's independence during negotiations for an alliance with the Liberals in the 1983 parliament. The 1987 election campaign was not a happy experience. Far from there being an agreed strategy between the two Davids—*Steel of the Liberals and Owen—the two went their own ways. Journalists gleefully played the game of 'hunt the split'. While many Liberals talked of the possibility of an Alliance government, he dismissed such talk and campaigned for a hung parliament. He was still strongly anti-Labour and eager to dispel impressions that a vote for the Alliance might provide a backdoor entry for a Labour government. He admired Mrs *Thatcher as a leader more than Neil *Kinnock.

Following the election there were moves in both parties to effect a merger. Owen resisted, but when a ballot of SDP members showed strong support, he immediately resigned. He was elected leader of the rump of the SDP in 1988. In 1991 he met with John *Major and promised to declare his support if the Conservatives gave a clear run in the next general election to the two remaining SDP MPs. This was not possible. In the 1992 general election Owen still declared his support for the Conservative Party.

As a member of the House of Lords, Owen played a roving role as an international statesman. For some time he was engaged in trying to promote peace efforts in former Yugoslavia.

Owen was a headstrong character. He left the Labour Party, helped to split the SDP, and rejected any new merger. The SDP soon collapsed. He had a cross-bench mind, supporting a strong stand on defence and foreign policy while also supporting social market policies. His memoirs, *Time to Declare*, were published in 1991.

Pahlavi, Mohammed Reza (b. Tehran, 26 Oct. 1919; d. 27 Jul. 1980)
Iranian; Shah 1941–79

Iran was occupied by British and Soviet forces when Mohammed Reza succeeded his father as Shah in 1941. The autocratic regime he inherited disintegrated over the next twelve years under the pressure of foreign interference and mounting domestic unrest, culminating in the *Mossadeq government's challenge of 1951–3.

After his restoration to the throne in 1953, the Shah rebuilt the royal autocracy with American assistance. Organized opposition was crushed with the imprisonment of Mossadeq, the National Front's abolition and suppression of the Communist Tudeh party. Parliament was turned into a constitutional façade controlled by client landlords, government officials, and businessmen, in which only loyalist political parties were permitted. The Shah, however, took all important decisions. In 1975, he replaced the 'yes' and 'yes sir' parties by the National Resurgence Party to mobilize mass support for his regime, chiefly through propagandizing a monarchical form of nationalism. The central pillar of his regime's support was an extensive security apparatus that included SAVAK—formed in 1957 with CIA, FBI, and Mossad's assistance—as the front-line organization for intelligence gathering and destructive operations against the regime's opponents. When the security apparatus failed to repress internal opposition, as in 1963 and 1977–9, the armed forces were deployed to secure the regime's survival. (On the Nixon doctrine, they also had a regional gendarme role.)

From 1963, the Shah sought to modernize Iran on Western lines and mask his repressive, corrupt regime, principally through the non-violent 'White Revolution'. At its core was land redistribution to peasants, a campaign against rural illiteracy and female political emancipation. Extensive social welfare provisions were added later. These, and other measures, which included banning marriage until 15; giving women a right to divorce; allowing polygamy only with the wife's consent; the glorification of pre-Islamic Iran; and widespread Western fashions and consumer behaviour, by their perceived anti-Islamic character, helped to precipitate the Islamic revolution which overthrew the Shah in 1979.

Paisley, Ian Richard Kyle (b. Armagh, 6 Apr. 1926)
British; leader of the Democratic Unionist Party 1972–

The son of a Baptist pastor, Paisley was educated at the Ballymena Technical High School and the Belfast Reformed Presbyterian Theological College. He has represented North Antrim in the House of Commons since 1970, first as a Protestant Unionist and then as a Democratic Unionist.

As a minister in the Free Presbyterian Church, Paisley is fiercely opposed to Roman Catholicism. Politically, the Democratic Unionist Party—which he founded in 1972—represents extreme Loyalism and opposition to any consultation with the Republic of Ireland about the government of Northern Ireland. His fundamentalist approach has resulted in his imprisonment for action resulting in a riot in 1966, his temporary suspension from the House of Commons, and his eviction from a meeting with the Prime Minister at 10 Downing Street. He has also been involved in disorderly conduct in the European parliament, of which he has been a member since 1979.

Paisley's rasping voice, virulent invective, and preparedness to engage in public protest have made him the most widely recognized Northern Irish MP in Britain. He has written prolifically on religion and politics.

Palme, Sven **Olof** Joachim (b. Stockholm, 30 Jan. 1927; d. Stockholm, 28 Feb. 1986)
Swedish; Prime Minister 1969–76, 1982–6

The son of an insurance executive, Palme went to school in Stockholm and Sigtuna, then took his BA at Kenyon College, Ohio, followed by a law degree at Stockholm University. A fluent radical student debater and organizer, he was elected to the chair of the Swedish National Union of Students (1952–3). Travels to India and South East Asia in 1953 gave him an abiding interest in the problems of underdeveloped countries. On returning home he joined the Social Democratic Labour Party.

Palme's subsequent rapid political advance owed something to the impression he made on Prime Minister *Erlander as the result of a chance train encounter in 1951. In 1954 he became a full-time assistant in the Prime Minister's office; in 1958 he entered the Swedish parliament as its youngest MP. He worked closely with Erlander on a revamping of Social Democratic ideology based on the expansion of the welfare state and because of his intellectual sharpness and his problem-solving ability was eventually groomed for the succession to the party leadership.

In 1959–62 Palme chaired major commissions of inquiry into education (compulsory and universal comprehensive education) and into overseas aid. In 1961–3 he headed the Cabinet office, in 1963–5 was Minister without Portfolio, in 1965–7 Minister for Transport (overseeing the switch to right-hand traffic) and in 1967–9 Minister for Education.

In 1968 Palme hit the international headlines by leading a Stockholm demonstration against US policy in Vietnam. In 1969, on Erlander's retirement, he became Europe's youngest Prime Minister and put through a series of radical reforms on industrial democracy. Later, in opposition (1976–82), he helped *Brandt on the Socialist International with Third World problems and apartheid in South Africa, and he vainly sought to mediate in the Iraq–Iran War. Back as Prime Minister, he solved in 1983 the thorny and long-running issue of a scheme for wage-earner funds without putting the capitalist system in Sweden into jeopardy. He was shot at night in a Stockholm street walking home from the cinema: the murder remains unsolved.

Papandreou, Andreas G. (b. Chios, 5 Feb. 1919; d. 23 June 1996)
Greek; Prime Minister 1981–9, 1993–6

The son of Georgios Papandreou, a Liberal Greek politician who served as Prime Minister, Andreas Papandreou was educated in Athens and the USA where he gained his Ph.D. in economics from Harvard in 1943. He served as a non-combatant in the US navy during the Second World War and took US citizenship. He subsequently became an academic economist (heavily influenced by J. M. Keynes) teaching in Harvard, Minnesota, and Berkeley, where he also headed the School of Economics (1956–9).

Papandreou returned to Greece in 1959, to continue his academic career. Yet he entered parliament in 1964, and became Minister of Co-ordination in a government headed by his father. He developed his own political profile and as a radical left-winger, he was often at odds with the country's establishment (including the monarchy) and renounced his US citizenship. Arrested by the military dictatorship in April 1967, he was freed after the intervention of President *Johnson, who responded to pressure from American academics.

In exile in Canada and Sweden, he resumed an academic career and formed the socialist PAK (Panhellenic Liberation Movement) which constituted the basis of Pasok (the Panhellenic Socialist Movement), founded on his return to Greece in 1974. It was a one-man party and marked the beginning of a new era in Greek politics. Pasok quadrupled its percentage of the votes in seven years (from 13 per cent to 48 per cent) and in 1981 Papandreou formed his first socialist government. His government's policies were characterized by the development of the welfare state, designed to appeal to the less well off, public ownership, and leftist political rhetoric. He also adopted nationalist attitudes, demanding a renegotiation of Greece's terms of membership or withdrawal from the European Community, and promised Greek withdrawal from NATO and the removal of US bases in Greece. In government, however, these policies were moderated. The government was dogged by scandals and defeated in the 1989 elections, In 1989 he was indicted by Parliament to face charges of wire-tapping and involvement in a multi-million-dollar embezzlement of the Bank of Crete. In January 1992 he was acquitted by a single vote at a special tribunal. It seemed the end. Yet he made a spectacular comeback in the 1993 elections and returned to office for a third time. This final spell was a disaster. He was constantly shuffling his Cabinet and, in spite of ill-health, refused to delegate or name a successor. Scandal attached to the political role in his controversial third wife, a former air stewardess and thirty-nine years his junior, whom he made his Chief of Staff. He finally resigned, on the grounds of ill-health, in January 1996. He was probably the most charismatic Greek politician of his generation.

Parkinson, Cecil Edward (b. Lancashire, 1 Sept. 1931)

British; chairman of the Conservative Party 1981–3, 1997– , Secretary of State for Trade and Industry 1983; Baron (life peer) 1992

Educated at the Royal Lancaster Grammar School and Emmanuel College, Cambridge, where he achieved distinction as an athlete, Parkinson was a management trainee with the Metal Box Company before training as a chartered accountant. In 1967 he founded Parkinson Hart Securities Ltd. Though initially a Labour supporter, he became a committed Conservative and served as chairman of the Hemel Hempstead Conservative Association. In the 1970 general election he unsuccessfully contested Northampton but was elected at a by-election later that year as MP for Enfield West. He served as a parliamentary private secretary to Michael *Heseltine, the Aerospace Minister, for two years from 1972 to 1974 before entering the Conservative whips' office. In 1976 he was made an Opposition spokesman on trade and, following the Conservative election victory in 1979, he was appointed Minister of State for Trade. In 1981 he was plucked from relative political obscurity by Margaret *Thatcher and made chairman of the Conservative Party. He was given the ministerial post of Paymaster-General and then Chancellor of the Duchy of Lancaster. Reputedly promoted because of his good looks, he none the less proved a highly successful party chairman—he was popular with constituency parties—and was widely credited with having masterminded the Conservative victory in the 1983 general election. Following the election, he was appointed Secretary of State for Trade and Industry but was soon engulfed in a scandal about his private life, demonstrating indecisiveness when torn between staying with his wife or moving to be with a long-standing lover who had just given birth to his child. Press speculation about his future became intense during the Conservative Party conference that October and, despite the Prime Minister's support for him staying in his post, he resigned from the government. He was brought back by Margaret Thatcher in 1987, serving first as Energy Secretary (1987–9) and then Transport Secretary (1989–90), but provided a lacklustre performance, especially as Transport Secretary. He resigned from the government on the day that Margaret Thatcher gave up the premiership. He returned to business but did not abandon politics. He was a founder member of the Conservative Way Forward, a body set up to promote the principles espoused by Margaret Thatcher. He left the House of Commons in 1992, taking a life peerage. To great surprise William *Hague in 1997 recalled him to be party chairman.

Pasqua, Charles (b. 18 Apr. 1927)

French; Interior Minister 1986–8, 1993–5

The son of a policeman, and Corsican by origin, Pasqua fought in the Resistance and for twenty years combined a successful career in the Ricard drinks company with close involvement in the Gaullist organizations of the Fourth and Fifth Republics. He enjoyed the murkier elements of political activity and cultivated a reputation as a plain-speaking right-winger. He took up full-time politics in 1968, when he was elected to the Chamber of Deputies for the rich Paris suburb of Hauts-de-Seine, where he established a solid political base as Senator (from 1977) and president of the departmental council. A close ally of *Chirac, whose 1981 presidential campaign he organized, he was recognized as the strong man of the neo-Gaullist Rassemblement pour la Republique. His muscular nationalism made him the obvious choice for Interior Minister in Chirac's 1986 government with the task of winning back conservative support from the far right *Le Pen by emphasizing the toughness of the government's policy towards immigrants and terrorists. The failure of Chirac's 1988 presidential campaign led Pasqua, for the first time, to strike out on his own as the spokesman for populist Gaullism against the technocratic élite which he claimed had betrayed it. He built up his own power base within the RPR and, together with Seguin, led an effective campaign in 1992 against the ratification of the Maastricht Treaty which Chirac felt bound to support. Back at the Interior Ministry in the 1993 *Balladur government, with the same mission he had had in 1986, his plain man's rumbustiousness won him considerable popularity amongst an electorate obsessed with law and order issues. He did not hesitate to intervene in issues beyond his portfolio and was regarded as a Deputy Prime Minister. He made a serious miscalculation, however, in backing Balladur rather than his erstwhile champion Chirac for the 1995 presidential election. The latter's victory ensured his departure from office, though it did not consign him to the wilderness.

Patel, Vallabhbhai (b. Nadiad, 31 Oct. 1875; d. 15 Dec. 1950)

Indian; Home Minister and Deputy Prime Minister 1947–50

The son of an agriculturalist, Patel was educated at Karansad and Nadiad before qualifying as a barrister at Middle Temple in 1912. Upon return to India he became involved in local politics and was elected to Ahmedabad Municipal Committee in 1917. He was chairman of the committee between 1924 and 1928.

Patel came to prominence as the organizer of the Kheda *satyagraha* (1918) in which peasants sought exemption from land tax. He led another agitation of peasants against an increase in land revenue in Bardoli in 1928. Later he joined M. K. *Gandhi in the Salt *satyagraha* and was jailed for sixteen months. Following the 1937 provincial elections, Patel became the chairman of the Congress parliamentary board which supervised the work of Congress ministries in the provinces. Following the Quit India Movement he was imprisoned.

Patel was made Home Minister in the interim government (September 1946). After August 1947, he became Deputy Prime Minister and his portfolios included Home, the Indian States, and Information and Broadcasting. Patel's lasting achievement was the integration of 562 Indian (princely) states into the Indian Union. In this task Patel acted ruthlessly using force and persuasion alike.

As Minister for Home Affairs Patel was responsible for law and order and the rehabilitation of refugees displaced by the partition. He proved an able administrator and reorganized the public service with the launch of the Indian Administrative Service to replace the colonial Indian civil service.

Patel was a machine politician who, being close to the Bombay business community, did not share Nehru's socialist idealism. He was a Hindu conservative who was pragmatic by instinct. Patel's untimely death in 1950 removed the main challenge to *Nehru's leadership and enabled the latter to pursue socialist policies without substantial organized opposition from within the party.

Pătrăşcanu, Lucreţiu (d. Apr. 1954)

Romanian; member of the Romanian government 1944–8

Pătrăşcanu was active in the Romanian resistance during the Second World War. In April 1944 he organized a coalition between the Romanian Communist Party (RCP) and the Social Democrats known as the United Workers' Front (UWF). This provided the Communists with national legitimacy. In June 1944 he participated in the negotiations which led to the creation of the National Democratic Bloc (NDB)—a coalition including the two 'traditional parties', the National Liberal Party and the National Peasant Party. Pătrăşcanu was the main link between the court and the NDB. On 23 August 1944, the NDB took part in King Michael's successful coup against *Antonescu, which led to Romania's change to the Allied side in the war. In November 1944 Pătrăşcanu became Minister of Justice in General Sănătescu's government. Recognizing the numerical weakness of the RCP, he supported collaboration with the traditional parties. This led to tension with *Gheorghiu-Dej, who favoured a more aggressive role for the RCP. Pătrăşcanu and Gheorghiu-Dej were the only Communist ministers in the government which *Groza formed in 1945. Nonetheless, Pătrăşcanu disliked the heavy-handed Soviet intervention which had brought about the change of regime. He was described at this time as being 'the only genuine nationalist' in the Romanian party. In 1948 Pătrăşcanu and other 'local' Communists were purged from the party and imprisoned. He was tried and executed in April 1954. He was rehabilitated in 1968.

Pauker, Ana (b. Moldavia, 1894; d. *c.*8 June 1960)

Romanian; Foreign Minister 1947–52

Pauker was the daughter of a Moldavian rabbi. She joined the Social Democrat Party and took part in the revolutionary unrest in Romania in 1917–18. In 1920 she married Marcel Pauker and entered the Romanian Communist Party (RCP) with him. In 1922 she was appointed to its Central Committee. She was arrested in 1925, but escaped to the USSR and worked for the Comintern in the inter-war period. Pauker developed a passionate attachment to the Soviet Union, where she spent the Second World War.

Pauker returned to Romania in September 1944 after the fall of *Antonescu. In January 1945 she and *Gheorghiu-Dej were summoned to Moscow. Pauker tried to persuade *Stalin to use the Red Army immediately to install a government based on the RCP alone. Stalin instead chose Gheorghiu-Dej's strategy of maintaining a coalition government in Romania. From 1947 to 1952 Pauker was Foreign Minister. She played a major part in the collectivization of agriculture. In June 1952 Gheorghiu-Dej eliminated all Pauker's supporters in an anti-Jewish purge, which coincided with the wave of anti-Semitism which Stalin encouraged in the Soviet Union.

Paul (Pavle Karadjordjevic), Prince of Yugoslavia (b. St Petersburg, Russia, 27 Apr. 1893; d. Neuilly, France, 14 Sept. 1976)

Serb; Yugoslav Regent 1934–41

Nephew of the first Yugoslav King Peter I, Paul graduated in 1920 in Classics from Christ Church, Oxford—the origin of his Anglophile attitudes. When Peter's successor Alexander was assassinated in October 1934 Paul became chief Regent on behalf of the 11-year-old *Peter II. Paul's main aims were to strengthen national unity after the preceding Serb–Croat conflict and maintain neutrality amid the growing international tension, while keeping Yugoslavia as close to Britain as possible.

Considering a resolution of the Serb–Croat conflict to be the key to political stability, in August 1939 he succeeded in reaching an Agreement (*Sporazum*) which gave the Croats political autonomy. For the first time since the creation of the Yugoslav state the Croats were brought into government. But this, his greatest achievement, aroused resentment in the Serb-dominated military—the start of his undoing. In foreign policy he maintained good relations with Britain but also improved relations with Italy and reached a Concordat with the Vatican (1937), which helped to gain Croat trust. The Little Entente (with Czechoslovakia and Romania) and the Balkan Entente (with Greece and Turkey) were intended to strengthen Yugoslav security. But his diplomacy could not deal with mounting German pressure. After the Austrian *Anschluss* and Munich agreement in 1938 Paul's room for manœuvre disappeared. Despite dismissing his pro-German premier Stojadinovic in 1939, by 1941 he was internationally isolated. Given an ultimatum in March to join the Tripartite pact he reluctantly signed. The next day he was deposed by a military coup which placed the young Peter II on the throne. Branded unjustly as a traitor and barred from his beloved Britain, he settled in South Africa and later Paris, where he resumed his old passion, art collecting.

Pavle Karadjordjevic *see* Paul of Yugoslavia

Pearson, Lester Bowles (b. Toronto, 23 Apr. 1897; d. 27 Dec. 1972)
Canadian; Prime Minister 1963–8

After service in the First World War and a brief flirtation with law Pearson became a history lecturer at the University of Toronto. He then joined the diplomatic service, gaining top marks in the entrance exam for his year. As a diplomat he was a member of Canadian delegations at a number of international conferences. He had a talent for diplomacy, helped to draw up the United Nations Charter, and rose to become Canadian ambassador to the United States (1945–6). He entered parliament as Secretary of State for External Affairs, serving under St Laurent. In 1948 Mackenzie *King appointed Pearson as Secretary for External Affairs, in succession to St Laurent who now became Prime Minister. Pearson held this post until 1957 and also headed the Canadian delegation to the United Nations. He received the Nobel Peace Prize for his mediating role in the 1956 Suez crisis when he refused to support the French–British invasion of the Suez Canal without UN approval. He was also annoyed that Canada, although a member of the British Commonwealth, had not been consulted about the invasion.

In 1957 Pearson succeeded St Laurent as Liberal leader and led the party to a bad election defeat in 1958, which brought to an end its long spell of office. In the 1963 elections the party was expected to win by a large majority but instead Pearson was returned to head a minority Liberal government. He formed a second minority government after the 1965 elections. He was much criticized for his excessive loyalty to colleagues who showed political misjudgement or were tainted by scandals. On the positive side his ministry left behind a national Medicare plan, the Canada Pension Plan, and the new Canadian flag. He resigned in 1968.

Percy, Charles Harting (b. Pensacole, Florida, 27 Sept. 1919)
US; US Senator 1967–85, chairman of the Senate Committee on Foreign Relations 1981–5

Educated at the University of Chicago, Percy served in the navy during the Second World War and went on to an extremely successful career in business in the post-war years. On his appointment as president of Bell & Howell at the age of 30 he was named by the American Junior Chamber of Commerce as one of the ten most successful young men in America in 1949. In 1964 he was Republican candidate for Governor of Illinois. Although he ran a successful campaign, he fell victim to the sweep of Democratic triumphs and Republican defeats in the wake of the landslide victory of President *Johnson over Barry *Goldwater in the presidential election of 1964.

In 1966 he was elected Senator from Illinois and served three terms, winning re-election in 1972 and 1978. He was a consistent supporter of moderate Republican policies. He harboured ambitions to succeed to the presidency in 1976 if President *Nixon had completed his two terms. With Nixon's resignation in 1974 and the succession of President *Ford he supported Ford's re-election campaign in 1976 and by 1980 he felt that his chance to seek the presidency had passed.

With the victory of the Republicans in the Senate elections in 1980 he became chairman of the Senate Committee on Foreign Relations. He was a low-key chairman, seeking quietly but ineffectively to moderate the aggressive foreign policy standpoint of the *Reagan administration in the early 1980s. He found himself increasingly out of tune with the conservative policies of the Reagan administration on domestic as well as foreign issues. He was subjected to growing criticism from conservatives within the Republican party in Illinois and, although he won renomination as Republican candidate for the Senate in 1984, he lost to his Democratic opponent, Paul Simon, in a year when President Reagan was re-elected in a landslide on the Republican ticket.

He was a 'wunderkind' who never entirely lived up to his early promise. More significantly, he was representative of moderate liberal Republicanism in the mould of Nelson *Rockefeller, which became increasingly a minority position within the Republican Party in the 1970s and 1980s.

Peres, Shimon (b. Wolozyn, Poland, 16 Aug. 1923)
Israeli; Prime Minister 1977, 1984–6, 1995–6

Shimon Preski emigrated to Palestine in 1934, joined the nascent Israeli army in 1948, and headed the embryonic Israeli navy in the same year. He directed the Ministry of Defence until elected to the Knesset in 1959 as a member of the leftist Mapai party. After Golda *Meir's fall, Peres became Defence Minister in Yitzhak *Rabin's Labour government 1974–7 and Prime Minister on Rabin's resignation in 1977. Defeated in the general elections of the same year, Peres led Labour to electoral defeat in 1981 and to the inconclusive outcome of the 1984 elections. Under an agreement between Labour and Likud for their leaders to exchange offices after two years, Peres became Prime Minister in the National Unity government from 1984, with *Shamir as his Deputy Prime Minister. Although the popular withdrawal from Lebanon by the Israeli Defence Forces was completed in 1985, except for the border area 'security zone', the Palestinian uprising, which began in 1987, and the 1988 peace plan of US Secretary of State Schultz revealed deep divisions between Peres and Premier Shamir. These were to lead to the break-up of the second Likud-Labour government in 1990 over the peace plan of US Secretary of State Baker. After losing the leadership of Labour to Rabin, Peres became Foreign Minister in Rabin's Labour government after the elections of 1992 and was the architect of a historic peace agreement with the PLO in 1993. Following Rabin's assassination in November 1995, Prime Minister Peres defended its implementation against the opposition of Israeli right-wingers and Islamist Palestinians. Peres was narrowly defeated by Netanyahu in the new-style premiership election of May 1996 and consequently failed to form a Labour government for a fifth and final time.

Perkins, Frances (Mrs Paul Wilson) (b. Boston, Massachusetts, 10 Apr. 1882; d. 14 May 1965)
US; Secretary of Labour 1933–45

Perkins attended local schools before graduating BA from Mount Holyoke College in

1905. Thereafter she continued to study economics and sociology at the universities of Chicago, Pennsylvania, and Columbia, graduating MA from the latter in 1910. She became executive secretary of the Consumers' League in New York 1910–12, and in addition, from 1911, lectured in sociology at the Adelphi College. Between 1912 and 1933 she served on a variety of industrial boards including the New York Commission on Safety 1912–17; the State Factory Commission 1912–13; New York State Industrial Commission 1919–21; New York State Industrial Board 1923–9, becoming an Industrial Commissioner for New York 1929–33. During these years she established a reputation both as a reformer and as an expert on social problems, and she came to the attention of Franklin D. *Roosevelt, Governor of New York 1929–33. On becoming President he appointed her Secretary of Labour, the first American woman to hold Cabinet rank. She remained in post throughout Roosevelt's presidency and continued briefly under *Truman.

Perkins's period in office was notable for the introduction of wide-ranging reforms including the abolition of child labour, the introduction of unemployment insurance, minimum wage legislation, and a variety of measures to improve working conditions. She is also credited with devising and launching many of the New Deal initiatives aimed at stimulating employment.

After her retirement from the Department of Labour in 1945, she accepted an appointment from Truman to become a civil service commissioner, serving until 1953. At the same time she became a visiting lecturer in labour relations and political science at the University of Illinois and subsequently, in 1956, at Cornell University.

Perkins was not without her critics. That the Department of Labour was headed by a woman during the nation's most severe depression never disappeared as an issue. Some accused her of lack of economic expertise. Feminists were outraged by her suggestion that married working women should vacate jobs in favour of unemployed men. There were demands for her resignation from various quarters. Nevertheless, she is remembered for her shrewdness and for being a tireless and enthusiastic pioneer in the field of social and industrial reform. She is the author of several books including: *Life Hazards from Fire in New York Factories* (1912); *Women as Employers* (1919); *People at Work* (1934); *The Roosevelt I Knew* (1947).

Perón, Juan Domingo (b. Province of Buenos Aires, 8 Oct. 1895; d. 31 July 1975)
Argentine; President 1946–55, in exile 1955–73, 1973–5

The son of a small rancher, Perón entered the Military Academy in 1911. He later served as an instructor at the War Academy and in 1939 in *Mussolini's Italy, visiting Germany and Spain en route. These years of study and witness were the source of his later corporatist vision of politics.

Active in the 1943 coup, he was appointed to the National Labour Department. From this outpost he began to build a base within the working class which was to be the mainstay of the rest of his career. New unions were created, old ones were bought off, and hostile ones eliminated. The strategy paid off in October 1945 when, following splits within the regime, Perón was incarcerated but released following mass labour protest. The following year he was elected President on a populist, anti-American programme.

In his first term sweeping social legislation was enacted, foreign-owned companies were nationalized, and major public works begun. By 1950 war-accumulated reserves had run out and discontent with his caesaristic style was growing. Perón responded by tightening political control but after the death of Evita in 1952 he became increasingly isolated and in 1955 he was ousted by the military.

For the next eighteen years Perón skilfully manipulated the mass movement he had created. Confronting a Perónist electoral majority and rising guerrilla violence, the military allowed him back in 1973. This attempt at stabilization failed and his final term was characterized by political and economic chaos which culminated after his death in yet another coup.

Perón was a fine orator, individually persuasive and politically astute. But he was also intellectually overambitious and unnecessarily intolerant of opposition. His legacy is that to this day many Argentines classify themselves as *peronista* or *antiperonista*.

Pétain, Phillipe (b. Couchy à la Tour, 24 Apr. 1856; d. Île d'Yeu, 23 June 1951)
French; head of the French State 1940–4

Pétain came from a well-off peasant family, was educated by the Jesuits, and attended the French military academy Saint-Cyr. His army career in the infantry progressed slowly, and he was about to retire with the rank of colonel when the onset of the First World War transformed his destiny. By June he was head of the Second Army and in February 1916 was sent to command the French forces resisting the German attack on Verdun. The Pétain legend dates from his role as 'defender of Verdun'. He became known as a commander who did not, like so many others, waste the lives of his soldiers in useless attacks. His reputation was enhanced by his sensitive handling of the army mutinies which followed the disastrous Nivelle offensive of April 1917. Insiders regarded his caution as only one step away from pessimism and it was this that led him to being passed over in favour of Foch as Supreme Allied Commander in 1918. To the general public, however, he was a hero and at the end of the war he was promoted to the highest military rank, Marshal of France. In the inter-war years, Pétain's star shone brightly. He held the highest posts in the army and was the architect of the defensive military strategy whose symbol was the construction of the Maginot Line. Few shared the negative judgement of his strategic views held by his one-time protégé, Charles *de Gaulle. He served as Minister of War in the government of national unity formed by *Doumergue after the February 1934 riots and in 1939, after *Franco's victory in the Spanish Civil War, he became the Republic's ambassador to Madrid.

Public and politicians alike continued to regard the Peasant Marshal with a respect verging on veneration. This explains why in the crisis following the German attack of May 1940, he became Deputy Prime Minister. It was to prove a fateful appointment. The pessimism which some had noted in 1918 led him to believe that there was no alternative to an armistice; the authority he radiated meant that those in government who wished to continue the war were quite unable to combat his views; and the contrast between his reputation and that of the politicians gave him a free hand when *Lebrun appointed him Prime Minister on 16 June 1940. The following day he requested an armistice which the Germans signed on 22 June. Made invincible by defeat, Pétain now revealed the political ambitions which lay behind the dignified exterior. He appealed for a moral and intellectual reformation to extirpate the vices which had led to the defeat, and, in a remarkable phrase, offered his body to France to assuage its misfortunes. It is unlikely that he had already drawn up a plan for constitutional transformation. But he allowed *Laval, who had joined his government on 23 June, to put his name to a project of constitutional reform which culminated in the 10 July vote of the National Assembly abolishing the Third Republic and entrusting him with power. The next day Pétain became Head of the French State and the Vichy regime was born.

Pétain's 1940 apotheosis owed more to his legend than to any defined ideological position. Once in power he revealed his determination to overturn the political and social values of French democracy. He immediately launched an attack on the symbols of Republicanism by replacing the Revolutionary triptych Liberty Equality Fraternity with Order Authority Nation, and by stressing the need for obedience to the leader. He sought (despite his prior lack of religious conviction) to re-establish the authority of the Roman Catholic church and of the traditional social élites who had been excluded from national and local power by universal suffrage. Political parties and trade unions were banned; civil servants were required to take an oath of personal loyalty to the Head of State; the most prominent leaders of the defunct regime, including *Blum and *Daladier were arrested. Pétain also began the civic persecution of the 'enemies of France' amongst whom he numbered freemasons, Communists, and Jews. The anti-Semitism of the Vichy regime was not the result of Nazi pressure. It derived from the conservative, nationalist prejudices against the 'outsider' which forty years earlier had given rise to the Dreyfus Affair and had then re-emerged in the 1930s. Pétain's regime was indeed referred to as 'the revenge of the anti-Dreyfusards'. The core foreign policy ambition of Pétain was to keep France out of the war by a policy of collaboration with the victorious Nazi Germany. He met Hitler at a railway station at Montoire on the banks of the Loire. There is no evidence that he was playing a double game, preparing to rejoin the Allies, or that he knew in advance of the Allied landings in November 1942 in French North Africa. There is, by contrast, much to show that he authorized the brutal war waged against the interior Resistance by Vichy's security forces.

Pétain became the object of a veritable cult of personality as he travelled through France preaching his message of respect for authority and tradition. Soon, however, the fragility of the Vichy regime became apparent. The governments he appointed were no more stable than those of the despised Third Republic and his relations with Laval, the most able of his ministers, were bad. More important, the emergence of an internal Resistance and the German occupation of the whole of France in November 1942 destroyed whatever independence the regime had had. The continuing personal respect Pétain inspired was demonstrated by the crowds who greeted him in Paris shortly before Liberation. But he was decreasingly able to resist the demands of the Germans and the manœuvres of Laval. By the time he was carted off to Germany in August 1944 he had lost all semblance of power. He refused to take any part in the governments of exile established in Germany by the extreme collaborationists and at the end of the war insisted on returning to France. Put on trial for collaboration with the enemy, he was condemned to death. In view of his great age, the sentence was commuted by de Gaulle to life imprisonment and he was placed in a prison cell on the Île d'Yeu, where he died in 1951.

Pétain argued in his defence that his purpose in taking power was to protect France from the exactions of Occupation—to be, in other words, the shield that would prepare the ground for de Gaulle's sword. The argument fails to account for the facts that occupied France received no special favours from Nazi Germany, that Pétain contemplated with equanimity the defeat of Great Britain, that his regime persecuted those members of the national community whom it refused to regard as French, and that it co-operated in the destruction of France's pre-war Jewish population. The 1994 revelation of *Mitterrand's youthful admiration for Pétain shows how wide was the appeal of the National Revolution. Vichy's compromises and crimes, however, destroyed the legitimacy of the reactionary vision which Pétain tried to realize. He still has admirers; but he has never been rehabilitated.

Peter II (Petar Karadjordjevic) **of Yugoslavia** (b. Belgrade, 1923; d. Los Angeles, 5 Nov. 1970)

Yugoslav; King of Yugoslavia 1941–5

Peter was 11 years old when his father Alexander was assassinated in 1934. For the next six years his powers were exercised by a three-man regency headed by his uncle, Prince *Paul. On 27 March 1941 Paul was overthrown by a military coup the day after signing the Tripartite Pact, and Peter, though still a minor, was made King; Prince Paul left the country. The coup was greeted with popular enthusiasm as a demonstration of anti-Fascism and Yugoslav patriotism. A broadly based government was formed, but it was in a very weak position. The Germans invaded on 6 April and Peter was forced to flee the country, first to Greece, then to Britain in June, where he became titular head of the government-in-exile and *Mihailovic's Home Army, and a symbol of Serbian nationalism, anti-Fascism, and anti-Communism. But the young King was out of his depth in power politics. *Churchill's sympathies moved from Mihailovic to *Tito as the basis for resistance and after Tito formed a provisional government in November 1943 Peter was pressured by the British to sack Mihailovic, which he reluctantly did in June 1944, calling on Subasic to form a government and even broadcasting an appeal to his subjects to rally round Tito's Partisans. In November Tito reached an agreement with Subasic on a joint provisional government, whereby Peter would remain abroad but delegate his authority to an agreed regency. In February 1945 the government was formed despite Peter's objections. In August Peter withdrew his authority from the regents, claiming they could not exercise their powers. But by November the Communists were fully in control and the first act of the Constituent Assembly on 29 November was to abolish the monarchy. Peter was a sad figure: he tried to play a role beyond his skills or power, and remained a dupe of the politicians. He eked out his days in France and later the USA in declining fortunes and health.

Peter Karadjordjevic *see* PETER II OF YUGOSLAVIA

Petkov, Nikola (b. 1889; d. 23 Sept. 1947)
Bulgarian; peasant leader

Nikola was the son of Prime Minister Dimitur Petkov. After studying law at Paris, he entered the Bulgarian foreign service and was attached to the Bulgarian Embassy in Paris. Following the coup which overthrew *Stamboliiski's government in 1923 he was imprisoned, then went into exile in France. He returned to Bulgaria, where he led the left-wing of the Bulgarian Agrarian National Union. King Boris's regime interned him in 1942. In September 1944, after the fall of the monarchy, he became minister without portfolio in the provisional government. In July 1945 he left the government to lead the pro-Western opposition to the Communist takeover in Bulgaria and edited the peasant newspaper, the *National Agrarian Banner*. After the rigged election which brought the Communists to power in 1946 he attacked *Dimitrov as a Soviet puppet. As soon as the United States had ratified the peace treaty with Bulgaria, Dimitrov had Petkov arrested and tortured. He was executed after a show trial in which he refused to confess.

Pflimlin, Pierre (b. Roubaix, 5 Feb. 1907)
French; Prime Minister 1958

Born in Roubaix (Nord), Pflimlin moved as a young man to his future political fiefdom Strasbourg, where he practised law and was active in right-wing politics. Like many other inter-war European conservatives, he switched in 1945 to the more politically respectable cause of Christian Democracy, which in France was embodied by the Mouvement Républicain Populaire. He was an MRP representative in both Constituent Assemblies and in 1946 became a deputy for the Bas Rhin. His political hero was Robert *Schuman, the champion of European integration, who appointed him Minister of Agriculture in 1947. He subsequently held senior posts in a number of governments and became Prime Minister in May 1958, just as the events in Algeria boiled over into a full-scale crisis of civil–military relations and thus of the future of the Fourth Republic. Pflimlin was unable to persuade the army commanders in Algeria to accept the supremacy of the civil power and his proposals for constitutional reform were lost in the excitement produced by *de Gaulle's reappearance. A secret meeting between the two men failed to produce a solution to the constitutional crisis and had barely finished before de Gaulle announced that he was forming a government. Pflimlin resigned on 31 May. The following day he became Minister without Portfolio in de Gaulle's new government, where he intervened in the drafting of the Fifth Republic constitution to protect the parliamentary nature of governmental power. This was one indication of the limits of his acceptance of the Gaullist project for France. Another, more fundamental, disagreement emerged over the future shape of Europe. Pflimlin had been re-elected to the Chamber of Deputies in 1958 and the following year became mayor of Strasbourg, the city which was a symbol of the cause of European integration. In April 1962 he was appointed Minister of Co-operation in the new *Pompidou government. Four weeks later, he led the walkout of the MRP ministers in protest against de Gaulle's derisive rejection in a press conference of the cause of European integration. He then voted the censure motion against Pompidou's government which followed the announcement of a referendum on the direct election of the presidency. Unlike many of his MRP colleagues, he retained his seat in the 1962 parliamentary elections but gave it up five years later to concentrate on his two principal interests, Strasbourg (where he was mayor until 1983) and the European Community (whose parliament he presided over in 1984).

Pflimlin's career, like that of Lecanuet, demonstrated the persistence in France of a Christian Democratic family which could not accept the nationalist, and anti-parliamentarian, elements in Gaullism.

Phibun/Pibul/Bipul-songkhram/songgram, **Luang** (Plaek Kita-sangkha), otherwise known as 'Chomphon P.' (b. 14 July 1897; d. 11 June 1964)

Thai; premier 1938–44, 1948–57

Highly controversial internationally but his country's principal nation-builder, the 'Col. *Nasser of Thailand', Phibun emerged two decades before his Egyptian equivalent. His quarter-century see-saw career either side of the Far Eastern War 1941–5 illustrates the enormous dangers facing a small non-Western state with the decline of nineteenth-century Western imperial world hegemony.

Phibun's real heyday was the 1930s, culminating in the early years of his first premiership, 1938–41. He was no Fascist demagogue, but rather the mouthpiece of the Thai army seen increasingly since the beginning of the century as the best defence of Thai sovereignty. Western colonialism had left Old Siam's heartland intact, but even the absolute monarchy regime had not dared to rely on Western indifference alone. Princes monopolized the highest ranks but by the 1920s able commoners of very modest origins like Phibun could secure scholarships to train in the West.

It was study in France which brought Phibun first into contact with *Pridi Phanomyong, but only the second coup back in Bangkok in 1933 that featured him prominently. Indeed, it was this together with the suppression of a royalist counter-rebellion that established him as the saviour of the People's Party. By late 1934 he was Minister of Defence, and this led directly to his premiership in 1938.

A real balance of power in Eastern Asia promised 'Thailand' (a direct translation of the native name adopted in 1939) a more genuine independence. Moreover, pan-Asianist Japanese saw Phibun from the start as a likely sympathizer in their struggle against the West. Japan's entry into the war on 7/8 December 1941 led swiftly to an alliance between them, as Japan sought to use Thailand as the launchpad for its capture of British Singapore and invasion of the Dutch East Indies. Japanese troops also entered British Burma from Thailand, although their vain attempt at invasion of India was delayed until 1944. Not threatened even in the Philippines from this Japanese base-area, the United States sought simply to scapegoat Phibun as a collaborator with Tokyo. Britain categorized Thailand as an outright Axis enemy.

In July 1944, with the Japanese war effort failing, Phibun followed General *Tojo into retirement. Post-war, both were arraigned as war criminals, but the much shorter British occupation of Thailand made it possible for the Thai Supreme Court to free all the Thai accused. Phibun was only restored a degree of power by the military who overthrew the Pridi regime in November 1947, but, assisted by American aid, his second term as premier saw the beginnings of modern Thai economic development. In the end, however, the rivalry of Generals Phao and Sarit forced him into a final six years of exile in India and Japan.

Piłsudski, Józef Klimens (b. Zublów near Vilna, 5 Dec. 1867; d. Warsaw, 12 Mar. 1935)
Polish; Leader 1918–23, 1926–35

Piłsudski was born in Russian Poland into an impoverished noble family. He became a socialist when a student at Kharkov University. Exiled to Siberia in 1887 and released in 1892, he was a founder of the Polish Socialist Party in 1894 and editor of its newspaper, *Robotnik* ('The Worker') until its suppression in 1902. In 1904, during the Russo-Japanese War he went to Tokyo in an attempt to obtain Japanese support for a Polish uprising. After the Russian revolution of 1905 he was leader of the Polish Socialist Party's military wing, which mounted a terrorist campaign against the Tsarist administration. In the First World War he organized 10,000 volunteers into a Polish Legion which fought for Austria against the Russians. The Germans were suspicious of his national aims and refused to guarantee Polish independence after the war. They imprisoned him from July to November 1917.

From 1918 to 1921 Piłsudski was provisional head of the Polish Republic formed after the break-up of the Austrian, Russian, and German empires. Despite his socialist past he at no time intended to introduce social reforms. From 1918 to 1921 he was the army's Chief of Staff and led Poland to a decisive victory over the Bolsheviks in the Russo-Polish War of 1919–20. By the Treaty of Riga in 1921, Poland was granted large parts of Lithuania, Belorussia, and the Ukraine. In 1922 the Poles seized the Lithuanian capital, Vilnius, and held it until 1939. In 1923 Piłsudski retired from politics, in part because of his disillusion at the level of corruption. He returned to power in the military coup of 1926 and established an authoritarian regime which still permitted a multi-party system and some freedom of the press. Because of ill-health Piłsudski was incapable of providing consistent leadership. He was Minister of War from 1926 to 1935 and Prime Minister from 1926 to 1928 and again in 1930. In 1930 he ordered the arrest and torture of eighty members of parliament who opposed him. In the 1930s his regime became increasingly anti-Semitic. After Hitler came to power in 1933 he appreciated the threat to Poland and unsuccessfully proposed to the French a pre-emptive strike against Germany. Convinced of the weakness of the Western Powers, he made non-aggression pacts with Germany and the Soviet Union.

Pinay, Antoine (b. Saint-Symphorien-sur-Oise, 30 Dec. 1891; d. 15 Dec. 1994)
French; mayor of Saint-Chamond (Loire) 1929–79, Prime Minister Mar.–Dec. 1952

The son of a hat-maker, Pinay was educated at a Catholic church school, and became a leather-maker. A volunteer in the First World War, he was awarded the Croix-de-guerre medal. He voted full powers to Marshal *Pétain in 1940 but after the Liberation, in 1946, he was returned to the Constituent Assembly for the Loire and remained a deputy until 1958: he headed the Independents and Peasants Group for Social Action in the Assembly from 1956 to 1958. Pinay is now chiefly remembered for his brief government from 6 March 1952 to 22 December of the same year. He was hostile to public sector growth, planning, technocrats, and dirigisme, and sympathetic to business. Like most non-Gaullist conservatives he was Atlanticist but he was not a die-hard colonialist. His success in forming an avowedly right-wing administration was important because it showed that conservatives were no longer shut out of Republican government. France was then gripped by inflation and Pinay took the unpopular post of Finance Minister along with that of Prime Minister to enable the introduction of measures to deal with the crisis. He presented his plan as commonsensical and himself as the defender of the consumer and the franc and at the same time issued a government loan (*emprunt Pinay*) which was predictably popular as it enabled families to escape the tax net. When Pinay's government fell 56 per cent regretted his departure. However 1952 was a year of recession and the overheating of the world economy, which was the result of the Korean War, was being dissipated with falling wholesale and retail prices. The slowing down of the economy also reduced the demand for credit and this too brought down inflation. Although Pinay did restore faith in the franc he did so at the cost of a fall in investment, balance of payments problems, and the talk of a balanced budget was rhetoric. He tried several times to form another administration without success, although he was briefly Foreign Secretary in the government of Edgar *Faure from February 1955 to the end of that year and represented France at the Messina negotiations to promote European integration, to which he was well disposed. Pinay helped create the majority for de Gaulle's investiture. He was made Finance Minister in de Gaulle's government of June 1958 and was associated with de Gaulle's stabilization policies as well, although this time the position was more intricate even if his reputation was important in ensuring its success. He endorsed the overall plan even though he had opposed some of its key measures. Pinay's remaining time in de Gaulle's government was very uncomfortable. In a famous encounter Pinay raised the matter of de Gaulle's attitude to NATO at a Cabinet meeting. This, perfectly constitutional, request was met with 'Monsieur le Ministre des Finances is interested in foreign policy problems'. Pinay persisted so de Gaulle closed the meeting. De Gaulle later accused Pinay of being in the wrong Republic. Pinay was dismissed on 13 January 1960. Pinay thereafter played a secondary, if inspirational, role in French conservative politics.

Pinochet Ugarte, **Augusto** (b. Valparaíso, 23 Nov. 1915)

Chilean; President 1973–89

Pinochet, who began his military training at the Military Academy in 1936, rose steadily through the ranks: 1942 army lieutenant; 1946 captain; 1953 major; 1960 lieutenant-colonel; 1966 colonel; 1968 Subdirector of the War Academy, and head of the Army's 2nd Division; becoming Commander-in-Chief of the army in 1973.

Pinochet rejected the idea of an activist state and instead talked about the need to modernize Chile, with the exclusion of political liberties. Inspired by the works of Hayek and Friedman, and working with the so-called 'Chicago Boys', the military government introduced an austere and extremely radical neo-liberal economic plan. For Pinochet, this model of development meant freeing market forces, privatizing vast segments of the economy, the reversal of both *Frei and *Allende's land reforms, and withdrawing the state from its previous role in overseeing economic and social change. The economic liberalization model, however, was coupled with severe political repression and human suffering.

The violence unleashed by the Pinochet coup was horrendous. All political parties and trade unions were banned, and the traditional government houses, Congress, and the senate were closed down. Socialism had to be eradicated: members of the Popular Unity government were rounded up and either imprisoned or sent into exile. The military resorted to torture and killing; within a year, the Chilean left had been crushed at the cost of several thousand lives and the exodus of some 30,000 supporters of Popular Unity (conservative estimates). Although the economy grew between 5 and 6 per cent in 1985–8, the highest rate in the region, there was a huge human cost: wage levels remained extremely low, the top 5 per cent received over 80 per cent of the national income, and half the population lived below the poverty line.

The carefully controlled plebiscite of 1980 approved a constitution which installed Pinochet as President of the Republic until 1989. In October 1988, a year before the

1989 presidential elections, Pinochet held another plebiscite to determine whether or not the people wished him to stay on as President until 1997. He lost. However, safeguards built into the 1980 constitution would enable him to continue to preside over the national security council with powers to overrule the government on matters of national security. Finally, in 1989, military rule gave way to a civilian regime when the centre-left coalition led by Patricio Aylwin defeated the military's candidate in the presidential race.

Pittman, Key (b. Vicksburg, Mississippi, 19 Sept. 1872; d. 10 Nov. 1940)
US; US Senator 1913–40

Pittman was educated at Southwestern University and studied law, which he practised in Seattle, Washington. He was then drawn by the gold rush to Alaska before moving to Nevada in 1902.

Pittman's first try for the Senate was in 1910, before the direct election of Senators. The two candidates (Pittman and George Nixon) held a mock election to test their popularity, although the final choice rested with the state legislature. Nixon won but died in 1912, when the legislature chose Pittman to succeed him.

Pittman had specialized in mining law and much of his early career in the Senate involved promoting the interest of Nevada's silver mining industry. In 1933, as a delegate to the London Economic Conference, he helped devise the eight-power silver agreement which imposed restrictions on the production of silver and hence stabilized the silver market.

He also developed a strong interest in international affairs and served on the Foreign Relations Committee, which he came to chair for seven years, succeeding Thomas Walsh (who was appointed by Franklin *Roosevelt to be Attorney-General). Pittman had backed Woodrow *Wilson's abortive effort to secure ratification of the Versailles Treaty and in the 1930s he used his powerful committee chairmanship to support Roosevelt's foreign policy. He played a leading part in amending the United States neutrality legislation in order to make Lend-Lease possible.

In addition to his interests in silver and foreign affairs, Pittman, as a western Senator, was a strong advocate of environmental legislation. He was a stalwart Democrat who served from 1913 to 1917 as secretary of the Senate Democratic Caucus, as secretary of the Platform Committee of the Democratic National Convention in 1924, and as chairman of the Platform Committee in 1928. Although Pittman took an independent line on public land issues, he was in general a firm supporter of the New Deal and played a supporting role on the Judiciary Committee during Roosevelt's battle with the Supreme Court. He died after securing election for a fifth Senate term in 1940.

Podgorny, Nikolai Viktorovich (b. Karlovka, 18 Feb. 1903; d. 13 Jan. 1983)
Ukrainian; member of the Presidium of the CPSU 1958–65

Podgorny was the son of Ukrainian working-class parents. He worked first as a manual worker and then as an engineer in the Ukrainian sugar industry. His political career started in 1939 when he became Deputy Commissar for the food industry in the Ukraine. He held various posts connected with food production at the state and regional level until 1946, when he was made the Ukrainian government's representative in Moscow. He returned to the Ukraine in 1950, as First Secretary of the Kharkov regional party committee, and then became Second Secretary of the Ukrainian Communist Party, benefiting from the patronage of *Khrushchev. He entered the Central Committee in 1956 and the Presidium (later Politburo) in 1958, becoming a full member in 1960. In 1963 he moved to Moscow as a Secretary of the Central Committee. Podgorny's position weakened after Khrushchev's fall in 1964. In 1965 he was removed as Secretary of the Central Committee, and given the largely honorific post of chairman of the Presidium of the Supreme Soviet, the head of state. In 1977 he was sent into retirement.

Poher, Alain (b. Paris, 17 Apr. 1909)

French; President of the Senate 1968–92, Presidential candidate 1969

Born in the Paris region, Poher studied engineering and law and entered politics after the Second World War as a supporter of the Christian Democratic movement and in particular of Robert *Schuman, the architect of France's participation in the European Coal and Steel Community. He held a number of minor posts in the governments of the Fourth Republic but devoted most of his career to the causes of the French Senate and European integration. A fixture in the Senate from 1952, he also sat in the European Parliament and was its President from 1966 to 1969. His unthreatening anti-Gaullism was the reason for his election as Senate President in 1968 after the resignation of his predecessor, who had violently opposed *de Gaulle's exercise of power. His new position as second person in the state explains the one important intervention in French politics for which Poher is remembered. He opposed the 1969 referendum proposal to reform the Senate, and after its defeat and the resignation of de Gaulle, found himself acting President of the Republic. He moved into the Élysée Palace, made some changes in the presidential staff, and chaired a series of tense meetings of the Gaullist dominated Council of Ministers. The change in presidential style was dramatic and Poher's comfortable ordinariness made an initial appeal to a public grown weary of de Gaulle's authoritarianism. Urged on by party leaders of the centre and left, who saw him as a means of subverting Fifth Republic presidentialism, he decided to stand for the presidency against the obvious candidate *Pompidou. After initial successes, however, his campaign ran into the ground. The fragmented nature of his supporters, who were united only in their hostility to Gaullism, meant that he lacked a coherent programme. He failed to win the support of the most influential non-Gaullist Conservative *Giscard d'Estaing (who correctly regarded Pompidou as a more substantial figure) and of others who had no desire to return to the shambolic politics of the Fourth Republic. Although the 23 per cent of the vote Poher gained in the first round enabled him to go forward to the second, he was easily defeated by Pompidou and returned to his Senate presidency, which he held until 1992. When Pompidou died in 1974, he was once again acting President, but this time made no attempt to make the Élysée Palace his permanent residence. He was much better suited to the charms of regime dignitary than to the rigours of political leadership.

Poincaré, Raymond (b. Bar-le-duc, 20 Aug. 1860; d. 11 Oct. 1934)

French; Prime Minister of France 1912–13, 1922–4, 1926–9, President of the Third Republic 1913–20

Poincaré came from a middle-class family in Eastern France. Endowed with a prodigious memory and capacity for hard work, he trained as a lawyer and was elected to the Chamber of Deputies for his native Lorraine in 1887. He held a number of ministerial posts in the 1890s, but took no part in the agitated politics of the Dreyfus Affair and concentrated on his legal work until the years preceding the First World War. As a child, he had witnessed the occupation of the family home by German troops during the Franco-Prussian War of 1870–1 and it was the growing international tensions which propelled him centre stage. By now a Senator, he was appointed Prime Minister in 1912 and threw himself into the campaign for extending French military service from two to three years. The following year he stood for the presidency, presenting himself as the champion of military preparedness and advocating a stronger role for the President than had hitherto been the case. He was elected by the

National Assembly with the votes of the right, the first time this had happened since 1873.

Poincaré played an active role in the events which led to the outbreak of the First World War in 1914 and would subsequently be condemned by his left-wing critics as a warmonger. There is, however, no evidence that he encouraged France's Russian ally to declare war on Germany, or that he was able, once war broke out, to control policy; he himself complained of the impotence of his role. A committed supporter of France's war effort, he worked to maintain national morale and in November 1917 took the decisive step of making *Clemenceau Prime Minister. Clemenceau had been a savage critic of Poincaré throughout his career and his appointment showed a degree of self-restraint by a head of state renowned for his sensitivity to slights. Although the two men clashed repeatedly over war policy and over the preparation of the Versailles Peace Treaty, Poincaré never sought to challenge his Prime Minister's right to have the last word. On leaving office, he returned to the Senate but maintained a vigilant interest in foreign affairs and argued constantly for a rigorous implementation of the Versailles Treaty. It was this which led President *Millerand to invite him to be Prime Minister in 1922, after his predecessor *Briand had been thought to be too susceptible to the conciliatory policy of *Lloyd George. As Prime Minister, Poincaré was unswerving in his demands for German reparations and in 1924 caused a major international stir by sending in French troops to occupy the Rhineland after Germany defaulted on some repayments.

In the parliamentary elections of 1924, the right-wing majority elected in 1919 was defeated by a coalition of Radicals and Socialists. When the new majority forced Millerand to resign because of his excessively interventionist conception of the presidency, Poincaré demonstrated his belief in the parliamentary system of the Third Republic by declining to intervene on his behalf. Two years later, in the face of impending financial collapse, he again returned to office as head of a government of national union. His combination of political Republicanism and economic conservatism made him appear a safe leader. As Prime Minister, he successfully stabilized the franc (at 20 per cent of its pre-war value) and carried on the policy of prudent rapprochement with Germany inaugurated by his predecessors. He showed, however, the conservative's repugnance for the menace of Bolshevism by breaking off diplomatic relations with the Soviet Union. He led a successful centre-right coalition for the 1928 elections, but resigned through ill-health the following year. His last years, in which he wrote voluminous memoirs, were clouded by the resurgence of German militarism. He died in 1934.

Throughout his career, Poincaré inspired respect rather than affection. To his enemies he epitomized the vindictive narrowness of mind of the provincial middle classes from which he came. His diaries, however, reveal a much warmer personality—he was devoted to his wife and was an early supporter of animal rights. A champion of the interests of the small property owner, he was not attracted to the new forms of authoritarian politics which emerged in France and Europe in the early twentieth century, and his patriotism did not make him a militarist. Sixty years after his death, he remains the symbol of French Conservative Republicanism.

Pompidou, Georges (b. 5 July 1911; d. 2 Apr. 1974)
French; Prime Minister 1962–8, President 1969–74

The son of a primary schoolteacher, Georges Pompidou was born in the Centre France department of Cantal. He completed his education in Paris at the École Normale Supérieure, the élite training ground for *lycée* teachers, where he developed a lifelong interest in poetry and the classics. During the Occupation he taught at the Lycée Henri-IV. Unlike other future members of *de Gaulle's entourage, he took no part in the Resistance, but was introduced to his future leader in 1946 as 'a Normal Sup' graduate who knows how to write'. He quickly acquired the confidence of de Gaulle and his wife, and played an important backstage role organizing the political movement, the Rassemblement pour la France, which sought in the late 1940s and early 1950s to be the vehicle for de Gaulle's return to power. After the failure of the Rassemblement he stayed close to de Gaulle (he was treasurer of the charitable foundation de Gaulle established in memory of his handicapped daughter) while pursuing a new—and lucrative—career in Rothschilds Bank. He acted as de Gaulle's private secretary in the hectic months which followed the General's return to power in 1958 and became a member of the newly formed Constitutional Council. He continued to work for Rothschild, however, and was completely unknown to the general public. Thus his appointment as Prime Minister to succeed *Debré in April 1962 was a complete surprise and irritated the National Assembly, who regarded the nomination of someone who was not even a deputy as a deliberate snub. In October 1962, his government was overthrown by the Assembly in retaliation for de Gaulle's decision to introduce a referendum on the direct elections of the presidency.

The National Assembly was dissolved, the referendum was carried, and Pompidou remained in office. He quickly asserted his authority over his government and over the new Gaullist majority in the Assembly. Over the next six years, President and Prime Minister formed an effective governing diarchy. Pompidou made no attempt to challenge de Gaulle's high-profile, and controversial, foreign policy and concentrated instead on developing France's industrial strength and on building up the Gaullist Party as an electoral machine capable of existing one day without its founder. There is some evidence that de Gaulle was unhappy at his protégé's increasing authority and it is certain that he planned at one stage to replace him as Prime Minister after the 1967 parliamentary elections. The decisive moment in Pompidou's future career came, however, in the mass demonstrations of May 1968. The May events demonstrated the extent of popular dissatisfaction with de Gaulle's authoritarian style of leadership and led to a major crisis for the regime. Pompidou battled tirelessly to stem the tide of protest. Aided by the most energetic of his protégés, *Chirac, he organized round table negotiations between government and trade unions in an attempt to separate the fragile coalition of discontent that linked students and workers. The so-called Grenelle Agreements made substantial concessions to the trade unions. In the short run, they were unsuccessful and in the last week of May, President and Prime Minister looked helpless. There then occurred a crucial moment in the events. Without telling his Prime Minister what he was doing, de Gaulle flew to Germany to assure himself of the support of the commander of the French Army on the Rhine and returned to Paris to make a dramatic broadcast announcing his determination to fight to save the Fifth Republic. It was a turning point. The National Assembly was dissolved, the strikes faded away, and the Gaullists won a massive victory in the June elections. The regime was saved.

May 1968 was also a turning point in de Gaulle's relations with his erstwhile ally. Pompidou bitterly resented de Gaulle's actions in not forewarning him of his disappearance and was outraged at the way in which he was replaced as Prime Minister by *Couve de Murville after the elections. He correctly believed that he had played a decisive role in maintaining some semblance of governmental authority during the crisis and was no longer willing to conceal his own political ambitions. In November he announced that he would be a candidate for the presidency at some future occasion. De Gaulle sought to re-establish his own authority by staking it on a referendum but the damage had been done. Pompidou's availability as President reassured enough French conservatives that a vote against the founder of the Fifth Republic was not a vote for the political unknown. The referendum was defeated and de Gaulle immediately resigned.

Pompidou easily won the presidential campaign that followed. He campaigned on a slogan of 'change in continuity' and won the backing not only of the Gaullists but of a large part of the centrist electorate, and of its coming man *Giscard d'Estaing. He asked the dashing, and reform minded, president of the National Assembly, *Chaban Delmas, to form a government but quickly demonstrated that his conception of the presidency was every bit as interventionist as that of de Gaulle. Committed to the development of France's new status as a leading industrial power, he stage managed a successful devaluation of the franc in August 1969, oversaw a policy of company mergers, and indicated that he was prepared to accept Britain's membership of the European Economic Community. He made some attempts to restore France's relations with Washington and made an unsuccessful visit to the United States, during which he and his wife were, to his intense anger, jostled by a group of American Jews who disliked his pro-Arab policy.

The first two years of Pompidou's presidency were trouble free. France's economy boomed and the death of *de Gaulle in November 1970 removed his looming, if silent, presence. In 1972, however, things started to go wrong. Part of his difficulties stemmed from the revival of the Socialist and Communist parties and from the semi-failure of the referendum on British membership of the EEC which had been designed to split the newly formed Union of the Left. Another problem was the poor relations between President and Prime Minister. Pompidou grew increasingly irritated at what he regarded as the superficial reformism—and superficiality *tout court*—of Chaban Delmas. Egged on by advisers who detested Chaban as a threat to the Conservative electorate on which Gaullism depended, he blamed his Prime Minister for the failure of the referendum and for growing discontent on the backbenches. In a brutal display of presidential power, Pompidou sacked his Prime Minister in August 1972, replacing him with the ultra loyalist *Messmer. The new government failed to make much impact on public opinion and it was Pompidou himself who, in a strong television performance shortly before the 1973 Assembly elections, managed to swing the result his way by threatening not to co-operate with the Socialist–Communist alliance should it obtain a majority.

The old Gaullist threat—'me or chaos'—was once again successful. But by now Pompidou was a dying man. The victim of a rare blood cancer, in constant pain, he grew fat and lethargic but continued to assert his primacy, making exhausting visits to *Nixon in Reyjavik and *Brezhnev in Russia. He refused to contemplate resignation or even to allow his illness to become public knowledge, an act of concealment aided by the lack of independence of the French broadcast media. Thus his death in April 1974 came as a shock to the public, although not to the political class who had been preparing for it for some time.

Pompidou was an effective leader whose surface bonhomie concealed a tough, cold interior. If he lacked the visionary qualities of his mentor de Gaulle, he was committed to the model of strong presidential government created by the Fifth Republic and to the modernization of the French economy. The Pompidou Centre in central Paris, which he commissioned, is a fitting memorial to his fascination with high-tech culture and national grandeur.

Popov, Gavriil Kharitonovich (b. Moscow, 31 Oct. 1936)

Russian; mayor of Moscow 1991–2

Popov graduated from the Economics Faculty of Moscow State University in 1959 but stayed on there as a teacher and to study for his doctorate. From 1971 to 1980 he was the dean of the university's Economics Faculty and was responsible for the introduction of a management studies course. In 1987 he gained national prominence when he published an article in the journal *Nauka i zhizn'* ('Science and Life') attacking the totalitarian command economy. In 1988 he became editor of the journal *Voprosy ekonomikii* ('Economic affairs'). And the next year was elected to the Congress of People's Deputies. From 1990 to 1991 he was co-chairman of the Interregional Group of Deputies, which stood for greater democratization. In 1990 he became chairman of the Moscow city soviet following his success and that of the 'democratic platform' in the local election. In June 1991 he was elected mayor of Moscow. He protected the old Communist economic *nomenklatura* while retaining close ties with the reformers whom he appointed to executive positions. Later that year he became co-chairman of the Movement for Democratic Reform. He retired as mayor in 1992.

Poujade, Pierre (b. 1 Dec. 1920)
French; Political agitator

Pierre Poujade came from a lower-middle-class family established in the rural centre of France. A member of the Vichy youth organization, he crossed to Algeria in 1942, joined the air force, and returned to France in 1945 to set up a stationery business in the small south-western town of Saint Ceré. After 1950, small shopkeepers in France came under commercial pressure from retail chains and faced increasingly severe tax demands. Poujade launched a tax revolt against what he saw as an assault on the small man carried out by big government, big business, and big trade unionism. The Union des Commercants et Artisans (UDCA) which he founded in 1953 spread rapidly through agricultural regions and carried out a number of spectacular stunts designed to discredit the administration. With an expanding membership went a more radical rhetoric. Poujade denounced the corruptions of the political system, spoke out for the French settlers in Algeria, and called for the summoning of an Estates General. In the 1956 parliamentary elections, Poujade's candidates, to general astonishment, won fifty-two seats. This, however, was the high water mark of the movement which disappeared as a political force when *de Gaulle returned to power in 1958. Poujade retreated to Saint Ceré and his attempts at a comeback were unsuccessful.

Though opponents denounced Poujade as the voice of 'back of the shop Fascism', he was not ideologically driven and broke with erstwhile allies like *Le Pen who were. His ambition was simply to bring back the small town France which had enabled small men like him to survive. It is a measure of his initial impact that 'Poujadism' has become the generic term to describe the radical politics of social groups threatened by modernization.

Powell, Adam Clayton Jr. (b. New Haven, Connecticut, 29 Nov. 1908; d. 4 Apr. 1972)
US; member of the US House of Representatives 1945–66, 1969–70

Although Adam Clayton Powell was to become a flamboyant figure in black politics, he was descended from a white slave-owner on his father's side, was part-Cherokee Indian, and looked white. Powell grew up in New York where his father, a minister, built up the Harlem Abyssinian Baptist church into one of the largest black churches in the country. Educated at Colgate University and Columbia, Powell succeeded his father as minister at Abyssinian Baptist in 1931, where he organized relief programmes during the Depression.

In 1941 Powell was elected to the New York City Council and he built up a solid following in Harlem, where he led the militant People's Committee and also edited a weekly newspaper. In 1945 he was elected to the House of Representatives for New York's 19th District, which had the almost exclusively black Harlem at its core but which later took in parts of the affluent white Upper West Side. Powell was the first black to be elected to Congress from the East Coast and became a national celebrity in the twenty-five years he represented the district. An independent black determined to fight for racial justice, in his early years in Congress he sponsored a range of measures designed to remove segregation from American life. Between 1960 and 1967 he exercised real legislative influence as seniority brought him the chairmanship of the Education and Labour Committee and control over the range of anti-poverty programmes. He used his position to shape more than fifty pieces of reforming social legislation, including the 1961 Minimum Wage Bill.

Yet Powell's position was never entirely comfortable either in the black community or in Congress. Many blacks regarded him as arrogant and egocentric. He had always been seen as something of a maverick by the Democratic Party: in 1956 he voted for *Eisenhower as President over Adlai *Stevenson, a move which angered his party colleagues. He had a high absentee rate in Congress. And his personal life was more akin to that of a playboy than a serious politician.

In 1967 the House voted to exclude him from Congress following his attempt to evade a court judgment in a libel suit and allegations of the misuse of his staff payroll. He was re-elected in a special election but did not immediately attempt to reclaim the seat. He was re-elected again in 1968 and the House voted to reinstate him though it imposed a fine and a loss of seniority. (In 1969 the Supreme Court found his original exclusion from the House had been unconstitutional.) Although apparently vindicated, Powell's political career was gravely damaged. By 1969 Powell, who had also been suffering from cancer, seemed on the verge of retirement. Yet he decided to run again in 1970 despite strong opposition. In the Democratic primary in 1970, Charles Rangel, a black New York Assemblyman and former Powell supporter, narrowly defeated Powell. An attempt to get the primary declared invalid failed and Powell's political career ended. He died two years later.

Powell, Enoch (b. Birmingham, 15 June 1912)
British; Minister of Health 1960–3

Powell's parents were teachers in Birmingham. He was educated at King Edward School, Birmingham, and Trinity College, Cambridge, was a formidable scholar and won many prizes. He became professor of Greek at Sydney University at the age of 25 in 1937. Two years later he resigned to fight in the war. In the army he rose from private to brigadier. After the war he joined the Conservative Research Department and had for colleagues Reginald *Maudling and Iain *Macleod. He was returned as Conservative member for Wolverhampton South-West in 1950 and held the seat until 1964.

Powell's ministerial career was hardly impressive—a year as a junior minister at the Treasury and three years as Minister of Health, only one of which was in the Cabinet. Yet he proved to be one of the most dominating figures in post-war British politics, largely because of his controversial ideas. He was ahead of his time in breaking with the post-war consensus, defending the free market, warning about race, and opposing Britain's membership of the European Community.

Many of Powell's actions did not seem at first sight calculated to advance his career. He refused office in 1952, and resigned as part of the Treasury team in 1957 when the Cabinet refused to accept the Treasury's proposals for spending cuts. He was invited to join Lord *Home's Cabinet in 1963 but refused because he supported the claims of *Butler. Above all, his famous speech on 20 April 1968, warning of the consequences of immigration from the New Commonwealth, effectively ended his political career. Ted *Heath dismissed him as shadow spokesman on Defence. It was typical that Powell should be speaking on a subject quite outside his brief.

For at least the next two decades Powell was treated like a parliamentary leper and denied a platform in many parts of the country. Yet he was a popular figure in the country and his speech on race tapped popular feeling. It was a subject which the frontbenchers of both parties had chosen to ignore. Denied any chance of office under Heath, he broadened his differences with the leadership to cover the European Community and the U-turns which resulted in a statutory prices and incomes policy and intervention in industry.

Powell gave rise to his own 'ism'. His speeches dealt with the major issues of relations between the individual and the state, the tensions between state sovereignty, national identity, and the European Community, and the purpose of politics. Yet, having made his reputation as an advocate of free market economics after 1968, he was for long identified with race. Powell was not a simple right-winger. He opposed capital punishment, was suspicious of the United States, rejected Britain's claim to have a world role, believed in society, and deplored the Thatcher government's utilitarian approach to higher education.

When Mr Heath called an election in February 1974 Powell dismissed it as 'fraudulent', on the grounds that the election had been called to defend the statutory incomes policy but this would have to be abandoned to get the striking miners back to work. He also effectively disqualified himself from the Conservative Party by calling on his supporters to vote Labour in the future. Twelve months later, after Heath had lost another election and was challenged for the party leadership by Margaret *Thatcher, Powell was no longer available. In October 1974 he had been elected as an Ulster Unionist for Down, South, a seat which he held until his defeat in 1987.

Powell preached many of the ideas that later became identified with Thatcherism. His advocacy of the free market and monetarism only became fashionable over a decade after he advocated them. He stood in the 1965 leadership contest and came a poor third with only fifteen votes.

Prem Tinsulanon(da) (b. 26 Aug. 1920)

Thai; royalist Premier 1980–8

From the southern Thai town of Songkhla, Prem's career as a political healer took off as a consequence of a term as army commander in the north-east, based at Khorat, in the aftermath of the Vietnam War.

He was able to reconcile many students and intellectuals who had fled to the jungle either side of the Mekong following the collapse in 1976 of the so-called 'Student Revolution', and also establish links with the 'Palace', which supported such policies. He was similarly useful to General Kriangsak Chommanan, who seized power in 1977 to restore parliamentary government, and appointed him as Deputy Interior Minister 1977, army Commander-in-Chief 1978, and Defence Minister 1979. He succeeded as premier in early 1980 when Kriangsak's coalition fell apart. Royal support also ensured that his concurrent term as army chief was extended five years beyond the normal retirement age of 60, and was further cemented when he took refuge along with the royal couple at Khorat during the short-lived army 'Young Turk' coup of 1981.

Prem was the beneficiary of two major factors. First was the sense of shock that pervaded Buddhist Thailand following the unprecedented blood-letting of the years 1973–6. He was more compatible than Kriangsak with the desire for consensus, even if maintaining it was never easy. The Young Turk coup also implicated dissatisfied senior officers, and was a warning that the army feared he would forget his military loyalties. Yet Prem was only able to maintain his acceptability in the assembly through a coalition of all the major parties, declining when offered the leadership of one of them, and refusing to submit himself for election. In line with the tradition that had brought him to power, he also employed a number of technocrat ministers entirely dependent on his patronage.

The other advantage was that the Thai economy was entering a period of unprecedented growth averaging more than 6 per cent annually, and the stability of the era was crucial to its continuance. But there were no major initiatives, for instance in foreign policy, comparable with the 1967 hosting of the first ASEAN meeting, or the 1975 and 1977 reconciliations with Beijing and Hanoi.

Around 1986, Prem's unflappability began to wear thin. His efforts to break down divisive regional loyalties like his north-eastern and northern military predecessors Sarit and Thanom, by bringing fellow southerners into his administration, came under increased criticism from the Bangkok press. Also his continuing bachelorhood became notorious. However, his decision to step down in favour of an elected successor in 1988, and maintain only a distant influence as royal adviser, undermined the consensus, and led eventually to a new army regime in 1991, and the further blood-letting involved in its overthrow in 1992.

Preobrazhensky, Yevgeny Aleksandrovich (b. Bolkhoz, Central Russia, 1886; d. 1937)

Russian; 'Old Bolshevik' and political theorist

Preobrazhensky was the son of an Orthodox priest, and was a revolutionary sympathizer by the time he left school. He worked for the Bolsheviks inside Russia. After the February Revolution of 1917 he returned to his home territory east of the Urals, where he helped set up Soviet government. He fought in the Civil War against the Czech Legion and against Kolchaks' Whites. In 1919 he returned to Moscow where he worked for *Pravda* and helped draft the party's 1919 programme. In 1920 he became a secretary of the Party's Central Committee responsible for the finances of party and state institutions. He was a supporter of *Trotsky and campaigned for greater internal democracy within the party. He clashed with *Stalin and *Zinoviev, who in 1926 condemned him as a member of the 'New Opposition', and expelled him from the party. Jointly with Bukharin he wrote the *ABC of Communism*, which was to be an influential study of socialist theory. In 1927 he was exiled to Siberia. He conceded to Stalin and was readmitted to the party in 1929, but was subsequently expelled. He was arrested and imprisoned in 1935, appearing as a witness for the prosecution at Zinoviev's trial. He died in prison.

Prestes, Luís Carlos (b. Porto Alegre, Rio Grande do Sul, 1898; d. Rio de Janeiro, 7 Mar. 1990)

Brazilian; Revolutionary leader and head of 'Prestes Column' 1924–7, Secretary-General of the PCB

Luís Carlos Prestes was, for over six decades, the best-known, most charismatic leader of the left in South American politics, first as a military commander, then, for most of his life, as Secretary-General of the PCB, the Brazilian Communist Party. After long years of imprisonment, exile, and struggle, he was expelled from the PCB in 1984, but maintained his political commitment.

Prestes, like Getúlio *Vargas and Ernesto *Geisel, was a *gaúcho*, from Rio Grande do Sul, the son of an army officer. He was one of the leaders of the *tenente* movement, a group of young army officers opposed to the oligarchic government of the early 1920s. Because of a bout of typhoid, Prestes was not in the group of *tenentes* which seized the fort of Copacabana, in Rio de Janeiro, in 1922, leading to their heroic deaths on 5 July. He did, however, join the revolutionary movement, on 5 July 1924, which took control for three weeks of the city of São Paulo, centre of Brazil's coffee wealth.

Prestes, then jointly headed a column of troops which marched for over 14,000 miles through the interior of Brazil, from 1924 to 1927. The Prestes Column became a legend, fighting federal forces in over fifty battles, as well as the gunmen of landowners. The national press followed its progress and its demands for land and other social reforms, till it entered Bolivia in 1927.

Prestes was expected to become the military leader of the Vargas revolution of 1930, but he was suspicious of its bourgeois nature and went to the Soviet Union, joining the PCB. The PCB (Brazilian Communist Party) had been founded in 1922 with a notably élitist leadership and a membership heavily drawn from foreign immigrants. In March 1935, Prestes, now back in Brazil, became honorary president of the ANL (the National Liberation Alliance), a united front force, including the PCB. In July, Prestes called for a popular revolutionary government. In November 1935, instead of a massive uprising, there was only a series of barrack revolts, all swiftly subdued. Thousands of arrests, included that of Prestes. In April 1945, Vargas, seeking new allies, freed nearly 500 political prisoners, including Prestes, who, to the nation's surprise, declared the PCB's support for the Vargas government.

In the presidential elections of 1945, the candidates of the now legalized PCB won 10 per cent of the vote. This performance largely reflected the personal popularity of Prestes, but, in May 1947, the Dutra government declared the PCB illegal. Prestes, in August 1947, again went underground. Throughout the whole period till the coup of 1964, the PCB continued to be active in politics, especially through the trade union movement, but the party was riven by fierce debate over strategy and tactics.

Prestes claimed to be taken by surprise by the coup of 1964. He was now driven further undergound, losing contact with the party leadership. In February 1971, Prestes left the country for Moscow. He still kept up with events in Brazil, but, within the PCB, power was passing to Giocondo Dias. In August 1979, a political amnesty allowed Prestes and others to return to Brazil, to be received at the airport by about 10,000 people. Times, however, had changed and he could not recover ground already lost. He involved himself in wounding debates within the PCB, and, in May 1990, he was removed from his long-held post of Secretary-General.

Prestes remained untiring in his demands for social justice. Expelled from the PCB, in 1984, still he kept up his struggle, in newspaper articles, in interviews and on television, till his death in 1990.

Pridi Phanomyong/Banomyong, Luang Pradit/Pradisth (b. 11 May 1900; d. 2 May 1982)

Thai; premier 1946

Pridi has been Thailand's only really significant modern ideologue and international statesman, viewed by some as an important influence on *Mao Zedong's ideas, and even the inter-war Burmese nationalist movement. The high point of his career was attained in his mid-forties at the end of the Far Eastern War. This was succeeded by a final thirty-five years in exile, mostly in the People's Republic.

Pridi was born a Sino-Thai, son of a middle-rank official emerging from the growing Westernization of Old Siam in the latter years of the reign of King Chulalongkorn (1868–1910). Amongst the first commoners sent to study in the West on a government scholarship, he was fired by the intellectual ferment of Paris in the 1920s into forming a small secret society dedicated to the overthrow of the absolute monarchy regime.

Amidst the crisis of the Depression and its particularly severe effects on independent Asian states like Thailand, Pridi and his associates were able to make common cause with a group of army officers of similar status to his father, equally excluded from the highest positions in the kingdom, in an organization known as the 'People's Party'. However, their ambivalence produced a year of uncertainty before a second coup, just a year after the first in June 1932, put a final end to royal absolutism.

Much of Pridi's ideological reputation derives from this year of uncertainty. It saw him father the revolutionary manifesto, Siam/Thailand's first constitution, and in early 1933, a radical economic plan characterized by many of his opponents as communistic, following which, he was driven into exile. From 1934 to 1941 he was back to serve successively as Minister of the Interior, Foreign Affairs, and Finance. Executively he was not so effective and his role was complicated by his growing rivalry with his early Paris co-conspirator Colonel *Phibun over the direction of the revolution.

Ultimately this rivalry was played out against the background of the growing regional insecurity consequent upon the decline of the Western imperial hegemony in Asia. Neither Pridi nor Phibun regretted this, nor objected to the rise of Japan. However, Phibun was chosen as premier in 1938 as the figure best qualified to defend

Thailand's national interests, and their disagreement about the alliance with Japan in December 1941, seems to have stemmed principally from this. By 1943–4 Pridi was associating himself with the supposedly underground Free Thai movement, preparing for the expected Allied victory.

1945–6 saw a brief post-war British occupation of Thailand during which, with Phibun imprisoned, Pridi was able to establish a temporary ascendancy. In March 1946 he assumed the premiership, but resigned it in favour of an associate following the still mysterious death of the young King Anan in June. The subsequent fifteen months featured one further role of significance as a roving ambassador, amongst other things promoting a South East Asia League along with nationalist interests in neighbouring French Indochina. When an anti-Pridi army coup was mounted in November 1947, eventually restoring Phibun to power, the West did not immediately welcome his overthrow. But the strengthening of the Cold War meant that they came to oppose his return, and approve his increasing impotence in post-1949 China.

Prior, James Michael Leathers (b. Norfolk, 11 Oct. 1927)
British; Secretary of State for Northern Ireland 1981–4; Baron (life peer) 1987

Educated at Charterhouse and Pembroke College, Cambridge, Prior served as a farmer and land agent in Norfolk and Suffolk before entering politics. Elected as Conservative MP for Lowestoft in 1959, he served briefly as a parliamentary private secretary in the last year of the Conservative government (1963–4). His first significant appointment came in 1965 when the newly elected party leader, Edward *Heath, selected him as his PPS. He served as Heath's PPS throughout the period of Opposition and in 1970—despite having no previous front bench experience—was rewarded with Cabinet office, being made Minister for Agriculture, Fisheries, and Food. Two years later he was made Lord President of the Council and leader of the House of Commons and served until the end of the parliament. Heath in 1972 also appointed him as deputy chairman of the Conservative Party.

After Heath resigned the party leadership in 1975, following the result of the first ballot for the leadership, Prior contested the second ballot. He received a modest nineteen votes, coming third equal out of five candidates. Though prominently associated with Heath's leadership, he was nonetheless kept on the front bench as employment spokesman by the new leader Margaret *Thatcher. In 1979 she appointed him as Employment Secretary and later Northern Ireland Secretary (1981–4). Though kept in the Cabinet, his relationship with the Prime Minister was not always an easy one. She believed that his proposals for trade union reform were not sufficiently radical and she privately encouraged Conservative opponents of the legislation in the House of Lords to amend it. In 1981 she moved him from the post. He made public his reluctance to move but, after consultation with some of his supporters, he decided to accept the post of Northern Ireland Secretary. His public hand wringing, and failed attempt to pressure the Prime Minister to keep him in his present post, damaged his political credibility. As Northern Ireland Secretary, he was responsible for the policy of 'rolling devolution', but opposition in the province from the Social Democratic and Labour Party and Sinn Fein prevented it from being achieved. In 1984, he decided to give up ministerial office to pursue a business career. He accepted the chairmanship of the General Electric Company as well as becoming non-executive director of two other companies. He left the House of Commons at the end of the parliament and accepted a life peerage.

One of the most prominent 'Wets' in Margaret Thatcher's Cabinet, he argued his case but was frequently outmanœuvred by a determined Prime Minister. He was viewed as a decent man in politics, but one not destined for the highest offices—and certainly not a key economic ministry—during the Thatcher premiership.

Proxmire, William (b. Lake Forest, Illinois, 11 Nov. 1915)
US; member of the Wisconsin State Assembly 1951–2; US Senator 1957–88

The son of a wealthy doctor, Proxmire attended Hill School in Pottstown, Pennsylvania, Yale, and the Harvard Business School. He served in military intelligence in the Second World War and worked as a labour reporter in Madison, Wisconsin, as a preparation for a political career. In a surprise victory he was elected to the State Assembly in 1950 and then ran unsuccessfully for Governor in 1952, 1954, and 1956. Following the death of Wisconsin Senator Joseph *McCarthy he won a special election to fill the vacant seat and was regularly re-elected until retirement in 1989.

In the Senate Proxmire acquired a reputation for independence. Although a hawk in the Vietnam War, he was a scourge of excessive government spending, especially in the field of defence. His monthly 'Golden Fleece' award was given for conspicuous examples of projects which in his view were a waste of public money. As chairman of the Senate Banking Committee and Housing and Urban Affairs, he became a powerful influence both in the debates about the regulation of the banking industry and the financial problems of America's cities.

His dislike of unnecessary government waste was paralleled by personal austerity both in lifestyle and campaign spending. He was a strong advocate of improved consumer protection especially in the field of financial matters. Yet he was difficult to categorize on social issues. An early supporter of civil rights, he was nevertheless an opponent of bussing and abortion. In his last period in the Senate he successfully campaigned for Senate approval of a treaty outlawing genocide.

Pym, Francis Leslie (b. Abergavenny, 13 Feb. 1922)
British; Defence Secretary 1979–81, Foreign Secretary 1982–3; Baron (life peer) 1987

The son of a Conservative MP, Pym was educated at Eton and Magdalene College, Cambridge. He saw war service in Africa and Italy and was awarded the Military Cross. A traditional Tory landowner, he was elected as MP for Cambridgeshire in 1961. A year later he was appointed to the Whips' office and spent the next eleven years working his way up within that office: he was deputy chief in Opposition from 1967 to 1970 and became government chief whip following the Conservative election victory in 1970. An extremely patient and courteous man, his skills were put to the test by a stubborn Prime Minister, Edward *Heath, and an increasingly rebellious parliamentary party, Pym on occasion having to tell Heath that the did not have a majority to carry some votes. Heath did not always heed his advice, but Pym's careful handling of relations with backbenchers prevented Conservative backbench rebelliousness from being even greater than it was and he ensured the passage of the momentous and contentious European Communities Bill in 1972. He was promoted to the Cabinet as Northern Ireland Secretary in 1973, serving briefly before the Conservative defeat in the 1974 general election. Although he was a 'One-Nation' Tory, Margaret *Thatcher kept him on the front bench after her party leadership victory, but his position as shadow Foreign Secretary was not translated into the foreign secretaryship in 1979. Instead he was made Defence Secretary and upset the Prime Minister with his opposition to defence cuts. In 1981 he was shifted to become leader of the House of Commons, but the following year the departure of Lord *Carrington from the Foreign Office left the Prime Minister unable to resist pressure to appoint Pym as his successor. Largely out of step with the Prime Minister's thinking, his fate was sealed during the 1983 election campaign when he said that a massive Conservative majority might not be a good thing for the country. As soon as the election was over, Thatcher dismissed him from office. He left the House of Commons in 1987, taking a life peerage.

Pym was a gentleman of the old school, out of tune with the Thatcherite drift in the Conservative Party. After leaving office, he founded a body called Centre Forward to represent traditional Toryism, but it proved short-lived. He also expounded his beliefs in a short book, *The Politics of Consent* (1984).

Quayle, James **Danforth** (b. Indianapolis, 4 Feb. 1947)
US; US Senator for Indiana 1981–9, Vice-President 1989–93

Educated at De Pauw University in Indianapolis, Quayle worked in the family newspaper business in Indiana. In 1974 he was elected to the US House of Representatives at the age of 27. In 1980 he ran for the Senate at the age of 33 and defeated the incumbent liberal Democrat Birch Bayh. In 1986 he was easily re-elected to the Senate. From a wealthy background, he took a conservative standpoint on most issues. He was representative of the younger, conservative Republicans who came to dominate the Republican Party in the 1970s and 1980s.

In 1988 he was selected by George *Bush as the vice-presidential candiate on the Republican ticket. Aged 39, his youth and conservative outlook gave him strong credentials for this selection. In the campaign, however, he was inept, and his image was destroyed. A series of campaign gaffes won him a reputation of stupidity, while his Democratic rival for the vice-presidency, Senator Lloyd Bentsen, made him look foolish and unsuited for such high office. Though elected Vice-President on the successful Bush–Quayle Republican ticket in 1988, he failed to throw off his image as an inept bumbler. He had little influence as Vice-President. He was not close to President Bush and he was openly despised by some of Bush's closest advisers, such as Secretary of State James *Baker. Bush considered replacing him as vice-presidential candidate in 1992 but renominated him out of fear of offending conservatives and splitting the Republican Party by dumping him. In the 1992 campaign he compared unfavourably to his Democratic rival, Albert *Gore. With the Republican defeat in the presidential election of 1992, he resumed his career in the family newspaper business in Indiana.

From a privileged background, with boyish charm and good looks, he enjoyed a glitteringly successful early career, winning election to the House and Senate at a remarkably young age and becoming an influential voice of youthful conservative Republicanism. He advanced too far too fast, however, and, as one of the least successful vice-presidents in the history of the United States, he became a figure of ridicule. He published his view of his career and philosophy of government in *Standing Firm: A Vice-Presidential Memoir* (1995).

Qadhafi, Muammar *see* AL-QADHAFI, MUAMMAR

Queuille, Henri (b. 31 Mar. 1884; d. 17 June 1970)
French; Third and Fourth Republic politician and minister

Born in the rural department of the Corrèze, which he represented in the Chamber of Deputies and Senate for over forty years, Henri Queuille epitomized the provincial political class which found its natural home in the Radical Party and flourished in the parliamentary system of the Third and Fourth Republics. A country doctor, he became mayor of his home town of Neuvic in 1912 and was first elected to the Chamber in 1914. He held his first ministerial post in 1920 and became a near permanent feature of France's inter-war governments, particularly at the Agriculture Ministry, which he held on fifteen occasions, but also at Health and at Public Works (where he negotiated the nationalization of the railway network). Queuille's commitment to Republican democracy was demonstrated in 1940 when he refused to vote the handing over of power to *Pétain and again in 1943 when he abandoned occupied France for the Free French. He became Vice-President of *de Gaulle's government in exile in

Algeria. His support for de Gaulle did not, however, extend to support for constitutional Gaullism. One of the few Radicals to make a political comeback after 1945, he was appointed Prime Minister in 1948 of what would be the longest-lasting government (thirteen months) of the Fourth Republic. His administration managed to defuse the threat to the regime of the Communist and Gaullist parties. His brief second (1950) and third (1951) ministries were less successful and he opposed the new political agenda of *Mendès France and then of de Gaulle. He did not stand for re-election in 1958 and gave up the Neuvic town hall, which he had occupied for half a century, in 1965.

Rabin, Yitzhak (b. Jerusalem, 1 Mar. 1922; d. 4 Nov. 1995)
Israeli; Prime Minister 1974–7, 1992–5

At the age of 16 Rabin joined the Jewish Agency's clandestine military wing, Haganah, and was subsequently a commander in its élite Palmach force, during the Zionist revolt against Britain's Palestine Mandate. In the first Arab–Israeli War 1948–9 he superintended the ethnic cleansing of approximately 50,000 Palestinian Arabs. In the second Arab–Israeli (Suez) War of 1956, Rabin commanded the Israeli Defence Forces' northern front, but complained about the lack of action there. Rabin became Chief of Staff in 1963 and held this command during the victorious six-day was of 1967. He retired in the following year to become Israeli ambassador in Washington.

Within six months of his election to the Knesset for Labour in 1973, Rabin had become Minister of Labour in Golda *Meir's government and, after the débâcle of the Yom Kippur War of 1973, he replaced her as Prime Minister in 1974. A financial scandal forced Israel's first native born premier to resign in 1977. He remained in the political wilderness until he joined the Likud–Labour coalition government, formed in 1984 under the alternating premiership of *Peres and *Shamir, as Defence Minister. Rabin aquired international notoriety in the Palestinian *intifada* when IDF soldiers followed his instruction to 'break the bones' of demonstrators and by expelling 415 Palestinian Islamists to the exposed Lebanese border area in December 1992. Rabin's tough style proved reassuring to Labour, and to the electorate, in a critical phase of the peace process and he was chosen over Peres to lead the Labour Party in the 1992 general elections. The skilled diplomacy of Peres and Beilin enabled his government to reach a controversial peace agreement with the PLO in 1993. A Zionist extremist opposed to the peace accords assassinated Rabin in 1995.

Radek, Karl Bernhardovich (original name **Sobelsohn**) (b. Lemberg (Lvov), 1885; d. in prison camp ?1939)
Russian; secretary of the Communist International 1920–6; member of the Central Committee of the Russian Communist Party 1920–5

Never a top leader and never popular with his colleagues, Radek's strength was as a revolutionary activist and journalist in several countries and an adviser on foreign, especially German, affairs. Born in Polish Galicia (then Austria-Hungary), he was active in the Social Democratic Party there from 1901 and studied at Cracow University. Imprisoned for his participation in the 1905 events, he later worked in revolutionary circles in Poland, Switzerland, and Germany till the First World War. During the war he attended the Zimmerwald and Kienthal anti-war conferences in Switzerland. He developed contacts between the German government and the pacifist groups and in April 1917 accompanied *Lenin across Germany to Russia, where he took part in the Brest–Litovsk negotiations and directed the Central European Section of the Commissariat of International Affairs. In 1918 he worked in Berlin, helping to found the German Communist Party, and was imprisoned there in 1919. He returned to Russia in 1920 and became one of the leaders of the Communist International and a member of the party's Central Committee. He lost these positions in 1925 after siding with *Trotsky and became rector of the Sun-Yat-Sen Communist University in Moscow (for far-eastern students). He was expelled from the party in 1927 but was readmitted in 1930 after recanting and became a *Stalin apologist and a Foreign Affairs commentator for *Izvestiya*. But he was arrested in 1936, accused of treason and at a show trial in 1937 was sentenced to ten years' imprisonment. He died in the camps, probably in 1939. He was fully rehabilitated in 1988.

Rafsanjani, Ali *see* HASHEMI-RAFSANJANI, ALI

Rajk, Laszlo (b. near Budapest, 9 March 1909; d. Budapest, 15 Oct. 1949)
Hungarian; Minister of the Interior 1946–8, Foreign Minister 1948–9

Rajk was born into a middle-class Jewish family. He became a Communist while a student at Budapest University, and was expelled as a result. He became a building worker and trade unionist and in 1935 organized a major strike in the construction industry. He then fled arrest to Spain, where he served in the Civil War as party secretary of the Hungarian battalion of the International Brigades. After the collapse of the Republican cause in Spain in 1939 he fled to France, where he was interned. In 1940 he escaped to Hungary and served in the communist resistance, acting as a link between the Soviet leadership and the peace faction within *Horthy's government. In 1945 he was party secretary for Budapest, charged with building up the party's organization. In February 1946 he was appointed Minister of the Interior, which gave him oversight of the Communist secret police, the AVO. He was closely involved in the terror which accompanied the Sovietization of Hungary. In August 1948 he left the Ministry of the Interior to become Foreign Minister. In May 1949 he was arrested, tortured, and faced with the trumped-up charges of 'Titoism', of having worked for Horthy's secret police in the 1930s, and of intending to restore capitalism in Hungary. The real reason for his downfall was *Stalin's desire to control over-powerful Communist leaders in Eastern Europe following Yugoslavia's withdrawal from the Soviet Bloc in 1948. In September 1949 Rajk's trial was widely publicized throughout Eastern Europe. He pleaded guilty, allegedly on *Kádár's advice that he should act 'for the sake of the Party', and was hanged. He was rehabilitated in March 1956.

Rakhmonov (Rakhmanov), **Imomali** (Emomali) (b. Kulyab region, Tajikistan, 5 Oct. 1952)
Tajik; President (chair of Supreme Soviet) of the Republic of Tajikistan 1992–4; President of Tajikistan 1994–

After graduating in economics from Tajikistan State University Rakhmonov worked in trade union and party organizations before becoming Director of a state farm in the Kulyab region (1988–92). Soon after being appointed as chair of the Kulyab regional party committee in November 1992 he was elected chair of the Tajikistan Supreme Soviet (President) to replace the deposed Akbarsho Iskandarov. Rakhmonov was a safe Russian nominee installed when Russia and Uzbekistan jointly intervened in the Tajik civil war after Iskandarov had been forced to include members of the opposition (Democrats and Afghanistan-based Islamic Revivalists) in his government. After banning opposition parties and imposing controls on the press he won direct presidential elections in November 1994 (widespread vote-rigging was suspected). Similar legislative elections in February 1995 confirmed the domination of the Tajik Communist Party and its commitment to a one-party state.

Rákosi, Mátyás (b. Ada, Serbia, 9 March 1892; d. Gorky, USSR, 5 Feb. 1971)
Hungarian; leader of the Hungarian Communist Party 1940–56

Rákosi was born as Mátyás Rosenkrantz in Serbia, the son of middle-class Jewish parents, who moved to Budapest during his childhood. He showed early intellectual promise and a skill for foreign languages, of which he could speak eight. In the years immediately before the First World War he worked in a London bank. He was conscripted into the Austro-Hungarian army in 1914 and sent to the Eastern Front, where he was soon captured. He became a Communist while still a prisoner of war in 1918. In 1919 he was Commissar for Socialist Production in Béla *Kun's Soviet Republic of Hungary. He escaped to Russia, where he worked for the Comintern. In 1924 he secretly returned to Hungary with the task of developing the illegal Communist Party. He was arrested in 1925 and tried and imprisoned for eight years in 1927. Upon his release in 1934 he was rearrested and sentenced to life imprisonment. Were it not for an outcry by European intellectuals he would have been executed. In November 1940 *Horthy's regime exchanged Rákosi and another Communist for Hungarian national flags which had been held in Moscow since their capture in 1849. Upon his return to Moscow, Rákosi was made General Secretary of the Hungarian Communist Party.

Rákosi returned to Hungary with the Red Army in 1944. He later described the piecemeal destruction of his political opponents as 'salami tactics'. After 1947 he encouraged the forced collectivization of agriculture, which led to near famine in the countryside, and an all-pervading terror throughout Hungary. He moved to concentrate power in his own hands, becoming Prime Minister in 1952. Rákosi was weakened by *Stalin's death in 1953. In July 1953, at the instigation of *Malenkov, Imre *Nagy replaced Rákosi as premier, though he retained leadership of the party. After Malenkov's fall in 1955, Rákosi briefly regained power, dismissed Nagy, and reintroduced Stalinist policies. In July 1956, the Soviet leadership had him removed from all his offices, in order to please his enemy, *Tito. He was replaced as General Secretary by a fellow Stalinist, *Gerö. Later in 1956, as unrest in Hungary mounted, he went to the Soviet Union, apparently for a health cure. He never returned to Hungary. He was expelled from the party in 1962.

Ramgoolam, Seewoosagur (b. Belle Rive, 18 Sept. 1900; d. 15 Dec. 1985)
Mauritian; leader of the Mauritius Labour Party (MLP) 1958–82, Prime Minister 1968–82

Born into a poor Hindu family Ramgoolam qualified as a medical doctor in Britain. He joined the MLP in 1953, becoming its leader in 1958 and was the leading figure in the movement demanding an end to British colonial rule in Mauritius. At independence in 1968 he became the country's first Prime Minister. Under his rule the country was marked by democracy, stability, and significant levels of economic growth. A skilful politician, he was successful in dealing with the racial, ethnic, and religious cleavages within the Mauritian political system. In 1973 he was awarded the United Nations prize for Human Rights and from 1976 to 1977 he was Chairman of the Organization of African Unity (OAU).

Following defeat in the 1982 elections he stepped down in favour of the opposition (the first leader of an African state to do this). In 1983 he was appointed to the, largely ceremonial, position of Governor-General. A quiet and unspectacular political leader, he laid the solid foundations of modern Mauritius.

Rankin, John Elliott (b. Itawamba County, Mississippi, 29 Mar. 1882; d. 27 Nov. 1960)
US; member of the US House of Representatives 1920–52

Rankin worked for a time on a local newspaper but went to law school (at the local University of Mississippi) and thereafter practised as a lawyer. His political interests caused him to seek election to the House and he was elected for the first time in 1920. His career was marked by the fanatical espousal of segregation and opposition not only to blacks but also to Jews, liberals, organized labour, and Communists. (He served on the House Un-American Activities Committee.) He was a fervent supporter of the White Citizens Council Movement, formed to defend white supremacy. In this context Rankin was not only a stalwart opponent of civil rights but proposed legislation to ban racial intermarriage in Washington, DC.

Although Rankin's extremist views on race overshadowed his whole political career, his populism was on occasion of real benefit to his Mississippi constituency. He was an early advocate of the Tennessee Valley Authority and sponsored with Senator *Norris the legislation establishing it; and he promoted regional TVA systems to spread electrification through Mississippi.

Rankin served briefly in the war but gave great support to veterans' causes and became a member of the House Committee on Veterans Affairs, and later its chairman. In this capacity he sponsored the GI Bill of Rights which gave special privileges to returning servicemen in the job market, in housing, and in education.

Rankin lost his congressional seat as a result of the redistricting of 1952.

Rashidov, Sharaf Rashidovich (b. Uzbekistan, 6 Nov. 1917; d. 31 Oct. 1983)
Uzbek; Uzbek First Secretary 1959–83

Rashidov was born into a peasant family and educated at the University of Samarkand. He worked as a schoolteacher and journalist before the Second World War. He joined the Red Army in 1941. He was badly wounded and discharged the next year. He became editor of the Uzbek Communist Party's newspaper. From the 1940s to the early 1950s he held various posts in the Uzbek Supreme Soviet and writers' union, and entered the Uzbek party bureau in 1954. In 1959, under *Khrushchev he was made Uzbek party First Secretary. In 1961 he became a candidate member of the Presidium (the Politburo after 1966). Rashidov prospered under *Brezhnev, whom he enthusiastically supported. He approved of the central government's encouragement of Uzbek cotton production without diversifying the republic's economy and announced a constant increase in cotton production, based on falsified statistics. Rashidov further pleased Brezhnev by producing false statistics for the success of his linguistic policies which apparently had made the Uzbek population bilingual in their native language and Russian by the early 1980s. After Rashidov's death in 1983 the party and administration of Uzbekistan were subjected to a widespread purge to root out corruption. In 1986 *Gorbachev posthumously exposed Rashidov's crimes at the 27th Congress of the CPSU.

Rau, Johannes (b. Wuppertal, 16 Jan. 1931)
German; Minister-President of North Rhine-Westphalia 1978–

Rau was the son of an Evangelical pastor of the anti-Nazi Confessing church and followed his father's beliefs. He completed an apprenticeship in the book trade but developed an early interest in politics. Through personal association with *Heinemann he joined the GVP in opposition to German rearmament and when the party was dissolved he followed Heinemann into the SPD. In 1958 he was elected to the parliament (Landtag) of North Rhine-Westphalia and in 1962 to the executive of the SPD Landtag group, becoming the chairman in 1967. After serving briefly as mayor of Wuppertal he was appointed Minister of Science and Research in the SPD government of North Rhine-Westphalia. He was elected Minister-President in 1978. Successful regional election campaigns in 1980 and 1985 secured the SPD an absolute majority in the Landtag and helped his election as deputy chairman of the national SPD and adoption as the party's candidate to oppose *Kohl in the 1987 election. The SPD gained a smaller share of the vote than in 1983 and lost ground to the Greens, whom Rau had vigorously opposed. Rau, however, managed to maintain his, and the SPD's, grip on North Rhine-Westphalia, Germany's most populous region.

Rawlings, Jerry John (b. Accra, 22 June 1947)
Ghanaian; head of state 1979 and 1982–

Born to a Scottish father and a Ghanaian Ewe mother Rawlings joined the air force as a cadet in 1967 straight after leaving school. In 1978 he was promoted to the rank of flight lieutenant. In May 1979 he led an abortive *coup d'état* and was detained but the following month he was freed by his supporters within the military and ousted the incumbent military government. As chairman of the Armed Forces Revolutionary Council he served as head of state for three months before handing over power to an elected civilian government. On New Year's Eve 1981 he led a further coup to oust the civilian government, this time making it clear that there would be no rapid return to civilian rule.

As chairman of the Provisional National Defence Council (PNDC) he embarked on a radical populist phase with the declared aim of transforming Ghanaian society. He established a series of 'revolutionary' institutions including People's Defence Committees (PDCs) and Worker's Defence Committees (WDCs) but these were abandoned in 1984 by Committees for the Defence of the Revolution (CDRs). None of these committees enjoyed significant levels of autonomous power. From around 1983 Rawlings abandoned his left-wing economic policies, losing much of his student and trade union support in the process. Following a series of agreements with the International Monetary Fund (IMF) he adopted economic liberalism and introduced tough public austerity measures and a massive devaluation of the (significantly overvalued) Ghanaian currency. Although these measures were deeply unpopular in many circles they had the effect of reversing the chronic economic decline which had occurred continuously since independence.

In 1991, following a combination of domestic and international pressure, Rawlings agreed to reintroduce a civilian multi-party system. He retired from the air force and in the November 1992 presidential election he won over half of the popular vote as the candidate of the, newly created, National Democratic Congress (NDC). Although opposition parties claimed electoral fraud evidence suggests that Rawlings was genuinely supported by a majority of voters.

During his time in power the Ghanaian economy has unquestionably improved, and political stability has been maintained although at some cost to civil liberties and human rights. Rawlings has maintained his reputation as an honest and rather ascetic leader who has not used his position for personal enrichment.

Rayburn, Samuel Taliaferro (b. Roane County, Kingston, Tennessee, 6 Jan. 1882; d. 16 Nov. 1961)

US; member of the US House of Representatives 1913–61, Speaker of the House 1940–6, 1949–52, 1955–61

Sam Rayburn's parents were small farmers of Scottish-Irish descent and Primitive Baptist religion who moved to Texas from Tennessee in 1887. He studied education at East Texas State College (then the Mayo Normal School) and was employed as a teacher 1903–6. Elected to the Texas House of Representatives at the age of 24, he there displayed many of the talents including attention to detail and approachability that were to advance him in national legislative politics. While in the state assembly he studied law at the University of Texas and passed the state bar examinations in 1908. In his final two years in the Texas legislature, Rayburn was Speaker of the House.

Elected to the US House of Representatives in 1912, Rayburn became a member of the Interstate and Foreign Commerce Committee (which he chaired 1931–7). He quickly displayed a mastery of congressional procedures and acquired an unrivalled knowledge of its members. The close friendship with John Nance *Garner promoted Rayburn's career: he was campaign manager during Garner's 1932 presidential bid and an intimate associate both when Garner was Speaker (1931–3) and when he was Franklin *Roosevelt's Vice-President.

Rayburn was supportive of the New Deal (which accorded well with his own egalitarian philosophy) and helped steer many of its legislative measures through Congress. In foreign policy Rayburn supported Roosevelt's internationalism and had no truck with isolationism either before or after the Second World War. He made an unsuccessful bid to become Speaker in 1934 and became majority leader in 1936. He became Speaker in 1940 following the death of William Bankhead. His long tenure as Speaker enabled him to exert great influence over the shape of legislation, over the careers of congressmen, and over the politics of the Democratic Party.

The period of Rayburn's speakership was also the period of southern ascendancy in Congress. Rayburn well appreciated the role of the South in the Democratic coalition. He chaired the Democratic National Conventions of 1948, 1952, and 1956 and was Lyndon *Johnson's floor manager for his fellow Texan's 1960 attempt at the Democratic nomination. The leadership which he and Johnson provided in the Congress of the 1950s worked with and around both the conservative coalition and the *Eisenhower presidency. Inevitably by 1960 that leadership was criticized by some elements in the Democratic Party as too conservative and accommodationist.

Although he had backed Johnson for President, Rayburn deployed his support for President *Kennedy in the critical battle in 1961 to make the House Rules Committee more responsive to mainstream Democratic Party sentiment. The enlargement of the Rules Committee cleared the way for the passage of some of Kennedy's legislative agenda and reduced the power of the conservative minority to block legislation. Although himself no enthusiast for radical civil rights legislation, this action together with his help in the passage of the 1957 and 1960 civil rights bills underlined Rayburn's essentially pragmatic approach to politics.

Rayburn's political strength derived from his ability to understand his fellow legislators and from friendships across party and generation as well from his love of the procedures and prerogatives of the House. He was not an autocratic Speaker and the authority he exercised was more personal than institutional. 'Mr Sam', as he was popularly known, died in office from cancer.

Reagan, Ronald (b. Tampico, Illinois, 24 Apr. 1911)
US; President 1980–8

The son of a bankrupt store manager, Reagan was educated at Eureka College, Illinois, and became first a radio sportscaster in Davenport, Iowa, and then a film actor in Los Angeles after 1934. His role in the film *King's Row* gave him, finally, star status. Through the later 1930s he was an official of the Screen Actor's Guild. A liberal Democrat, he was a member of both Americans for Democratic Action and United World Federalists. Clashing with 'communists' in the Guild he became an active anti-Communist and appeared as a 'friendly witness' in the 1949 hearings of the House Un-American Activities Committee. With his film career declining after 1952 he became a paid speaker for the Gerneral Electric Corporation. He first appearance before the national public came in 1964 when he made a televised speech supporting Barry *Goldwater, the Republican candidate for President.

In 1966 Reagan defeated Pat *Brown to become the Republican Governor of California seeking to impose tax cuts of 10 per cent across the board. He found that budgets could be cut only slowly and went on to preside over the largest budgets and some of California's largest ever tax increases. Personally opposed to abortions, he had to accept an extension of abortion rights and, though enraged by student lifestyles and anti-Vietnam activities, he increased spending on higher education. He presided over a return to the use of the death penalty and sacked homosexuals on his staff, always denying that he did so. Re-elected in 1969, his second term was marked by a greater willingness to compromise with Democrats and, generally, to present the 'soft face' of conservatism. In part he did so in order to position himself to challenge President *Ford for the Republican nomination for President in 1976. He failed, but during a tough campaign he articulated growing official and public fears that the Russians were rearming during the period of détente while the USA was facing economic obsolescence because of business taxes and regulation and social dissolution because of welfare dependence. Three years later President *Carter's volte-face on defence and welfare gave these concerns legitimacy. Reagan campaigned on a platform of less government, lower taxes and balanced budgets, family values, and peace through military strength. He was able to ride to the White House on a tide of widespread, if shallow, 'conservative' sentiment, but his margin in the popular vote presaged difficulty in legislating his programme.

Reagan's accession ushered in a short-lived period of popular acceptance of supply-side economics at home and bellicosity abroad. The normal political 'honeymoon' given to a new President was lengthened by a failed assassination attempt in March of 1981. In domestic policy, with the support of conservative southern and western Democrats, a programme of large, phased tax cuts and increased defence expenditure was instituted. Cuts in welfare and education budgets were partially accepted by Congress as was a programme of business deregulation and tightened control over the supply of government information. Admirers of the British Official Secrets Acts, Reagan's staff contemplated similar legislation until they realized that they themselves would have to take loyalty oaths and lie detector tests.

In foreign policy allies and enemies alike were alarmed by the frank triumphalism of American rhetoric and the seeming determination of the administration to impose American leadership and priorities everywhere. NATO partners were pushed into increased defence expenditure and military readiness. Even Margaret *Thatcher, a staunch supporter, was affronted by Reagan's willingness to sell grain to Russia—pleasing his agribusiness sector—while trying to use subsidiaries of US companies in Europe and technology licences to prevent Western Europe importing much needed Russian natural gas. When such policies were accompanied by a potential invasion of Nicaragua and an actual invasion of Grenada—a British Commonwealth state—without informing London, North Atlantic relationships were in real disarray. Only when Reagan agreed to resume serious arms limitation talks with the Russians, and toned down bellicose rhetoric, did fears of nuclear was recede and matters improve. The summits with *Gorbachev at Geneva and Reykjavik marked this progress.

Reagan's domestic policies recessed the US economy and re-election seemed uncertain. By November 1984, however, a pre-election recovery gave him victory by bigger margins than in 1980 and began the longest peacetime economic boom in the twentieth century. With 'peace abroad and prosperity at home' Reagan seemed set to enjoy the most successful two-term presidency since *Roosevelt. He presided over the 1986 refurbishing of the Statue of Liberty, a very symbolic moment for him. Almost immediately the arms for Iran affair—later called Irangate—began to leak out. The Senate's Tower Report of March 1987 heavily criticized his involvement in the Iran affair and his general competence. It is possible that only his personal popularity and willingness 'to reign and not rule' kept him from further congressional action. His last months in office were clouded by this knowledge.

Reagan presided over the break-up of the USSR and claimed that he 'won the Cold War'. More a rhetorical and symbolic conservative than a systemic thinker his legacy was a long economic boom, a recapturing of national self-confidence, but a decay of community spirit as inequalities increased. History may remember him mostly for being the man who tripled the US national debt.

Renger, Annemarie (b. Leipzig, 7 Oct. 1919)

German; President of the Bundestag 1972–6

Renger was brought up in the SPD; her father was a full-time official of the workers' sport movement. For financial reasons she was forced to leave her grammar school and take a job in a printing firm, where she met her first husband. He was killed in the war, leaving her with a 7-year-old son. Renger found herself in Hanover in 1945 and answered an advertisement in the local paper for volunteers to help Kurt *Schumacher set up the new SPD. She responded enthusiastically and was soon

Schumacher's secretary and companion, remaining with him until his death in 1952. The SPD did not forget her and in 1953 she was elected to the Bundestag. She played an important part in the women's groups within the SPD but she was also elected to all the SPD's leading organs. She was a member of the Executive 1961–73, and the smaller Presidium 1970–3. In 1972, with the SPD in government and the biggest group in the Bonn parliament for the first time, she was elected President of the Bundestag. She served for four years and then as Vice-President. Renger was on the right of the SPD, the so-called 'canal workers', who felt the party was swinging too far to the left in the late 1970s. Keen on Germany being anchored in Western Europe, she remained in parliament until German unity was restored.

Reuter, Ernst (b. Apenrade, 29 July 1889; d. 29 Sept. 1953)
German; governing mayor of West Berlin 1950–3

In the Kaiser's Germany Reuter, as a Social Democrat, was banned from the public serivce and could not enter the teaching profession for which he had trained. He worked in the SPD's own educational service until called up for military service. Captured on the Russian front he sided with the Bolsheviks in 1917 and was appointed Commissar for the German minority in Russia. On his return to Germany in 1918 he rose rapidly in the newly formed Communist Party (KPD), becoming its General Secretary. He soon fell out with his KPD comrades and by 1922 was once again in the SPD. Through the SPD he was appointed head of the Berlin city transport department. He became known outside Germany for his excellent administration. Reuter served as mayor of Magdeburg from 1931 to 1933. He was arrested by the Nazis in that year and held in Lichtenberg concentration camp. After a second term in the same camp he left Germany. He worked as adviser on local government to the Turkish government and professor of local government at Ankara University.

Reuter returned to his old post in Berlin in November 1946. In 1947 the parliament of all four sectors of the city elected him by 89 votes to 17 as governing mayor. The Soviets refused to accept him and he stepped down in favour of SPD colleague Louise Schroeder. The Soviets cut off the road, rail, and waterway links between West Berlin and West Germany hoping to starve the 2 million West Berliners into submission. Remarkably, the Allies were able to fly in the minimum supplies to keep them alive, but the morale factor was vital and Reuter did much to maintain the fighting spirit of the Berliners, speaking at widely publicized mass demonstrations which inspired his fellow citizens. World attention was focused on Berlin. On 12 May 1949 the Soviets lifted the blockade.

Reuter wanted West Berlin to be integrated into the newly established Federal Republic of (West) Germany. This, which would have been an advantage for the SPD, was vetoed by the Western powers who exercised final authority in West Berlin. Elected to the Executive of the SPD in 1948, Reuter supported the integration of West Germany into the Western Alliance, but he continued to hope for the restoration of German unity. The victory of *Adenauer's Christian Democrats in September 1953 caused him to lose hope; he died in the same month.

Reynaud, Paul (b. Barcelonnette, 15 Oct. 1878; d. 21 Sept. 1966)
French; Prime Minister 1940, Deputy Prime Minister 1953

Born into a farming family which had made a considerable fortune in Mexico, Reynaud practised as a barrister and served in the army during the First World War (twice decorated) before entering the Assembly for Alpes de Haut Provence as a conservative in 1919–24. He was a campaigner for a Franco-German entente based on economic co-operation and was re-elected in 1928 for Paris and made his name as a representative of free-market conservatism on the one hand and (after the rise of *Hitler) a vigorous anti-Nazi foreign policy on the other. Although perceptive in his choice of issues, he advocated devaluation and intervention and was not clubable in an Assembly built on close networks (he was a forensic debater of brilliance, but arrogant and isolated). His opposition to appeasement and to the Munich agreement was forceful but ineffective and his plea for an alliance with *Stalin's Soviet Union also found no takers and made him enemies on the right. When the Popular Front fell he was made the Finance Minister in the *Daladier government and put into effect a liberal economic policy undoing much of Socialist Léon *Blum's work. Reynaud was made Prime Minister in March 1940 (by one vote) and tried to step up the war effort. He had inherited a situation of extreme weakness and ill preparation and tried to prosecute the war more vigorously but without taking up the attack on Germany itself. Reynaud concluded an agreement with Britain which stated that neither would sign a separate peace and he brought *de Gaulle in as a junior minister at the eleventh hour. However, while his courage was not in doubt, he had little room for manœuvre and made his own situation worse by bringing *Pétain and Weygand (capitulationists) into the Cabinet. Reynaud, through indecisiveness, more or less contributed to the growing demoralization but without enabling France to fight on (which it could have done). His curious behaviour in the face of invasion (at odds with his declared intentions and general outlook) is still unexplained. He could have continued the resistance either as a Gambetta or a *Clemenceau; instead he resigned in June and Pétain took over. He then went as French ambassador to Washington but was arrested in September 1940, imprisoned by Vichy after a fiasco of a trial, and handed over to the Germans on 20 November 1942. He was lucky to return alive in 1945. In the Fourth Republic Reynaud was a respected but marginal figure who presided for eleven years over the Assembly's powerful finance Committee. He was elected as deputy for the Nord and was briefly Finance Minister in 1948. A convinced Atlanticist, he contributed to the cause of European unity (on the Council of Europe 1949–57 and as an ECSC representative) and supported integration in the Assembly. He was not a colonialist and, a critic of the Fourth Republic's instability, argued for constitutional reform through the 1950s. He welcomed de Gaulle's return to power and took part in the drafting of the Fifth Republic's constitution, but he began to take issue with de Gaulle and campaigned against the Gaullist referendum of 1962. In 1965 he supported Jean *Lecanuet's presidential campaign against de Gaulle. Reynaud wrote a number of volumes of self-justificatory memoirs (one translated as *In the Thick of the Fight*) and other works. He was a connoisseur and collector of Chinese art.

Reynolds, Albert (b. Co. Roscommon, 3 Nov. 1932)

Irish; Taoiseach (premier) 1992–4

Reynolds made himself a millionaire as a ballroom proprietor and with his own dog-food business in the Irish midlands. He was elected to the Dáil as a Fianna Fáil deputy in 1977 and served as a minister in three governments, 1979–81, 1982, and 1987–92. He became Taoiseach and party leader in February 1992, on the resignation of Charles *Haughey. In his only general election as Taoiseach, that of November 1992, his party lost nine seats, but was saved in office by forming a coalition with Labour, with its leader, Dick Spring, as deputy premier (January 1993). His major achievement was the Downing Street Declaration of 15 December 1993, negotiated jointly with British premier John *Major, which set out a series of declaratory principles upon which the British and Irish governments would seek to create a lasting settlement of the Northern Ireland conflict. Subsequently Reynolds played a major part in coaxing the IRA into its ceasefire of 31 August 1994, including securing visas for the USA for leading Sinn Fein members. On 6 September 1994 Reynolds, with John Hume and Gerry Adams, took part in a historic handshake at government buildings, Dublin. Relations with his Labour coalition partners were always uneasy, however, and they broke down in November 1994 over a senior judicial appointment. Reynolds was obliged to resign on 17 November 1994. Essentially a non-ideological 'fixer' who had shown little interest in the Northern Ireland conflict before coming to the premiership, Reynolds had the advantage over his two immediate predecessors in the lightness of preconceptions brought by him to the problem. His unexpected loss of office however was a product of the mistrust engendered domestically by the dealer politics associated with his party. In particular Reynolds's reputation was dogged by a complicated imbroglio concerning state-provided export credit insurance for beef sales, negotiated during his period as Minister for Finance.

Richards, Ann (b. Lakeview, Texas, 1 Sept. 1933)
US; Governor of Texas 1990–4

Richards attended local school, graduated BA from Baylor University in 1954, and completed a postgraduate year at the University of Texas. In 1975 the reluctance of her lawyer husband, David Richards, to accept the Democratic nomination to run for county commissioner effected her political debut. He encouraged her to stand instead. She accepted the candidacy and won the election. County office was a stepping stone to state politics. In 1982 she was elected state treasurer, gaining re-election in 1986.

Richards came under the national political spotlight in 1988, when, as keynote speaker at the Democratic National Convention, she said of Republican presidential candidate George *Bush, 'Poor George, he can't help it, he was born with a silver foot in his mouth.' Two years later she entered the race for the Texan governorship a decided underdog and won, despite a highly acrimonious Democratic primary campaign, in which her history of alcoholism was used by her opponents to cast doubt on her fitness for office.

A liberal Democrat, as Governor Richards went some way towards fulfilling her electoral promises by appointing women and minorities to statewide offices and initiating an efficiency drive. But when she stood for re-election in 1994 her previous mockery of Bush came back to haunt her. His eldest son George W. Bush was selected as the Republican candidate and he succeeded in denying her a second term as Governor.

Richards co-authored with Peter Knobler *Straight from the Heart* (1989).

Rifkind, Malcolm Leslie (b. Edinburgh, 21 June 1946)
British; Secretary of State for Defence 1992–5, Foreign Secretary 1995–7

Educated at George Watson's College and Edinburgh University, Rifkind trained as an advocate. He went to Rhodesia in 1967 to spend a year lecturing at the University College of Rhodesia. He was called to the Scottish bar in 1970. The same year he sought election to parliament, unsuccessfully contesting the Edinburgh Central seat. He was returned to the House of Commons four years later, aged 27, as member for the Pentlands division of the city. An effective debater, his talents were soon rewarded with a frontbench post as deputy to the shadow Scottish Secretary. His tenure of the post was short-lived: a supporter of devolution, he resigned from the front bench in December 1976 in order to vote for the Scotland and Wales Bill. He was returned to partial favour in 1979 and made a junior minister at the Scottish Office, serving for three years before being appointed to the Foreign Office, first as Under-Secretary (1982–3) and then as Minister of State (1983–6). In 1986 he entered the Cabinet as Secretary of State for Scotland. After a four-year stint in the office, he was appointed Transport Secretary and then, two years later, was promoted to the post of Defence Secretary. Widely regarded as a highly effective parliamentarian—renowned for his capacity to speak without notes—he was none the less seen as a supporter of greater European integration at a time when the party was adopting a more sceptical stance on the issue. He gradually came to adopt a more sceptical position, in effect making him a viable candidate for the Foreign Office in succession to the committed European Douglas *Hurd. When Hurd stood down in July 1995, Rifkind was chosen to succeed him.

A gifted orator and respected administrator, he was seen by some supporters as a potential leader of the Conservative Party, combining a commitment to principle with a capacity to take a pragmatic stance where appropriate. It was his misfortune that he lost his marginal constituency in the 1997 general election and so was unable to stand for the party leadership when John *Major resigned. Both a plus and a minus in party circles is the fact that he was one of the most forceful of Cabinet ministers in urging Margaret *Thatcher to step down as leader following the first ballot in the leadership contest in 1990. With Kenneth *Clarke, he is reputed to have threatened to resign if she did not withdraw from the contest.

Robb, Charles S. (b. Phoenix, Arizona, 26 June 1939)
US; Governor of Virginia 1982–6, US Senator 1988–

Born to a family with long-established Virginia roots, Robb's childhood involved much relocation as a result of his father's varying business interests. Following a brief period at Cornell, Robb transferred to the University of Madison at Wisconsin and, after graduating, joined the Marines. As a military aide at the White House, he met and married Lyndon *Johnson's daughter Lynda Bird. Thereafter Robb studied law at Virginia and entered politics in 1977 when he ran for Lieutenant Governor of the state. Robb won, despite the Republican sweep of other state offices. In 1981 he was elected Governor, defeating state Attorney-General Marshall Coleman. In office he emphasized education spending and economic development, and promoted blacks and women to state offices.

Robb also managed to improve the unity of the faction-ridden Virginia Democratic Party and acquired further visibility as a co-founder of the conservative Democratic Leadership Council in 1985, becoming its second chairman in 1986.

Virginia law precludes a second consecutive gubernatorial term and Robb returned to law practice following his period of office. The popularity acquired as Governor encouraged him to run for the Senate in 1988. He won easily, breaking the trend of a state which had become increasingly Republican. Although he was sometimes mentioned as a possible presidential candidate, his reputation thereafter declined. In 1994 he faced real re-election difficulties both in the primary and in the three-way race between himself, Republican candidate Oliver North, and Marshall Coleman, who ran as an independent. Some of the difficulties encountered by Robb were political, reflecting opposition to the *Clinton administration and to Robb's increasingly erratic stance on policy issues. Others stemmed from allegations of personal impropriety, including drug use and sexual misdemeanours. Although Robb secured a narrow victory, he emerged from the race tarnished and in a much less impressive political position than six years earlier.

Robinson, Mary (née Bourke) (b. Ballina, Co. Mayo, 21 May 1944)
Irish; Senator 1969–76 and 1985–9, President of Republic of Ireland 1990–7

The daughter of a west of Ireland doctor, Mary Robinson became Reid Professor of Constitutional and Criminal Law at Trinity College, Dublin, in 1969 at the age of 25. Subsequently she was also lecturer in European common law. Elected to the Irish Senate by the University's graduates in 1969, she became a prominent champion of civil liberties and advocate of a more pluralist and secular state in Ireland, writing extensively on constitutional and family law issues. She stood twice, unsuccessfully, for the Dáil as a Labour candidate in 1977 and in 1981, and also served on Dublin City Council 1979–83. She played a prominent role in the New Ireland Forum of 1974. She resigned from the Labour Party in November 1985 in protest at its support for the Anglo-Irish Agreement, which she saw as having been negotiated over the heads of the Ulster Unionists. She served a further term as Senator from 1985 to 1989. In April 1990 she accepted the Labour Party's nomination in the forthcoming presidential election. Robinson campaigned as a 'president with a purpose' for an office which lacks all political power but which she believed could be employed to set a tone.

Mary Robinson's victory on 9 November 1990 came as a major surprise, being caused in part by the weakness of the Fine Gael candidate on the one hand and a serious political mishap to the otherwise popular Fianna Fáil frontrunner (who was alleged to have brought illegitimate influence to bear on the previous President some years earlier). The success was thus somewhat fortuitous and was by a relatively narrow margin (5.6 per cent), but it was hailed as a breakthrough for the modern liberal tendencies in Ireland she had symbolized, for a more understanding 'post-nationalist' attitude to the conflict in Northern Ireland, and, especially, for Irish women, who had, in the words of Robinson's inaugural address, 'felt themselves outside history' and would now be 'written back' into it. Robinson indeed proved energetic in expanding the possibilities of her office and made many visits outside the Republic, including to Belfast (where she shook the hand of Provisional Sinn Fein President Gerry Adams) and several to Warrington in the aftermath of the IRA bombing tragedy of 20 March 1993.

Rocard, Michel Louis Léon (b. Courbevoie, 23 Aug. 1930)

French; Prime Minister 1988–91, first secretary of the Parti Socialiste 1992–4

The son of a professor of physics and from a Protestant background, a member of the scout movement in France, Rocard moved to the Institut d'Études Politiques against his father's wishes and became a student socialist leader. He was national secretary during the crucial years of 1955–6 when the movement was dissolved for its sympathies with the Algerian insurgents. Shortly after graduating from the ENA he split with the SFIO over the *Mollet government's attitude to the war and became identified with the dissidents who were to become the Parti Socialiste Unifié (PSU). At the same time he progressed in the Ministry of Finance and in 1965 was made secretary-general for the Commission des Comptes et des Budgets. In 1967 he became national secretary of the PSU and in 1969 ran as PSU candidate in the presidentials polling a creditable 3.61 per cent (816,470 votes). In October 1969 he won the Yvelines by-election against the outgoing Prime Minister *Couve de Murville. As the exponent of *Mendésist realism in politics and economics, Rocard was ill at ease in a PSU where he had to jockey in between various left-wing and Trotskyite factions. The result was a 'social democratic' moderate imprisoned in an ultra-leftist party, a situation which was ultimately intolerable and in 1974 he quit the PSU to join the Socialist Party. Rocard was at first subdued but slowly began to mark himself out as the champion of the modern 'social democratic' left. In a remarkable speech at the PS Congress of 1977 he defined the 'two' cultures of the left, one state centred the other enabling and decentralizing. The disillusion with the *Mitterrand strategy in the defeat of 1978 enabled him to promote himself as the modernizer, challenge Mitterrand, and open a long civil war which persisted until the mid-1990s. Mitterrand won the presidentials of 1981 and, on Prime Minister *Mauroy's insistence, gave him the empty post of Planning Minister. In the 1983 reshuffle (a U-turn having been done) Rocard was made Agriculture Minister at which he was a success, but he resigned in 1985 over the introduction of proportional representation. His stance as the principal apostle of centrism in the Socialist Party made him popular and his help to get Mitterrand elected for a second term, with the need for allies in the centre, meant that he was made Prime Minister in 1988. After three years of barely concealed hostility to Rocard from the Élysée, he resigned but (despite rising unemployment and increased social problems) he remained popular. After the humiliating defeat of the

Socialists in 1993 Rocard took over the party in a coup but was faced with factional in-fighting (reminiscent of the PSU) and the Élysée's hindrance. A poor showing at the European elections of 1994 led to the resignation of the 'alternative presidential candidate' and the end to a career in the front rank. Rocard was elected to the Senate in 1995 and played a forthright role in Jospin's renovation of the party after the elections of 1995—an elder statesman of centre-left politics.

Rochet, 'Waldeck' Émile (b. Sainte-Croix, 5 Apr. 1905; d. 15 Feb. 1983)
French; Communist Party Central Committee member 1936–70, deputy 1936–73, Secretary-General of the Communist Party 1964–72

The son of a cobbler, a market garden worker and then mobilized, Rochet spent most of his life in the Communist movement. He joined the Young Communists at 18, was 'talent spotted', sent to the Comintern School in Moscow, and was promoted up the apparatus to become secretary for the Lyons region in 1932. He was, at the time, a hard-line sectarian agitator. In 1934 he became head of the party's farmers' section, in 1934 a Seine councillor, and then in 1936 a deputy for Saint-Denis 12th. In 1939 the Daladier government rounded up those who were opposed to the war and he was interned in North Africa. In 1943 he was liberated and made a member of the Consultative Assembly (1943–5). In 1944 he started editing *La Terre*, the party's journal for farming interests. In the Assembly Rochet took up farming questions and for a year chaired the agricultural committee (1946–7). Rochet was able to keep on good terms with the leadership despite (it seems) being more inclined to Khrushchev than was Secretary-General *Thorez. He became Secretary-General in 1964 and when Thorez died, Rochet soon came to be seen as the 'modernizing' impulse. When the Czechoslovak reforms started Rochet went to Prague to try to dissuade the Dubček government from persisting against Soviet advice. The party 'disapproved' of the invasion. Although re-elected Secretary-General in 1970 Rochet's health had deteriorated in 1969 and Marchais was in effect secretary-general. Often seen as the 'John 23rd' of French Communism, there is little evidence of his personal role. Rochet was vague and otherworldly in dealings so that his real feelings have remained unknown.

Rockefeller, Nelson (b. Bel Harbour, Maine, 8 July 1908; d. 27 Jan. 1979)
US; Vice-President 1974–7

The grandson of J. D. Rockefeller (the founder of the family fortune in oil), Nelson's grandfather and father were both prominent Republicans. He served as Assistant Secretary of State for Latin American Affairs from 1944 and for a year under President *Eisenhower. He was then elected Governor of New York State in 1958, winning election to that post four times in all. The 1958 election victory was significant because the Republicans did badly nationally. On the liberal wing of the party, he favoured advanced social programmes and civil rights for blacks, and sought to appeal to voters beyond the party. In 1960 he ran against Vice-President *Nixon, for the Republican presidential nomination, but lost. He was unhappy with Nixon's proposed platform and managed to reshape it. He was offered and turned down the vice-presidential slot. In 1964 he fought and lost a bitter campaign against the right-wing Barry *Goldwater for the party's nomination. Republican right-wingers detested him and his campaign was handicapped by his involvement in a messy divorce. In the presidential election he refused to campaign for Goldwater, the Republican candidate. He tried and failed again for the nomination in 1968.

As Governor of New York, he was criticized as the state encountered growing financial problems and for his handling of the prison riots in Attica in 1971 in which a number of people died. In 1974 President Gerald *Ford appointed him Vice-President, in spite of strong lobbying by George *Bush for the post. But Ford came under growing right-wing criticism for the appointment and Ronald *Reagan posed a serious threat to his renomination. Rockefeller was seen as a political liability and he eased Ford's problem by announcing that he would not be a candidate for the vice-presidency in the 1976 presidential election. His contacts and wealth enabled him to tap the expertise of a wide range of policy-makers. In his career he tried to combine private enterprise initiatives with a social conscience.

Rojas Pinilla, Gustavo (b. Tunja, Boyaca, Colombia, 12 Mar. 1900; d. 17 Jan. 1975)
Colombian; President of Colombia 1953–7

Rojas attended the Military Academy in Bogotá, and later studied engineering in the USA. He worked as a road engineer for a while, and then rejoined the army in 1932. He became Commander of the 3rd Brigade in Cali during the uprising in Bogotá, the *Bogatazo*, the wave of riots which hit Bogotá after the assassination of the populist Liberal leader, Jorge Eliecer Gaitan. Rojas remained in Cali for most of the years of the Colombian civil war, known as *la violencia*, which followed. In 1949 Rojas was promoted to lieutenant-general, and in 1952 he became Commander-in-Chief of the armed forces, Minister of Communications, and member of the Inter-American Defence Board.

On 13 June 1953 Rojas overthrew the then unpopular Conservative President of Colombia, Laureano Gomez, in a bloodless coup. He promised to end *la violencia* and establish political peace. His initial actions, like granting an amnesty for the Communist and Liberal guerrillas, were well received by almost everyone. His first Cabinet consisted almost entirely of Gomez's moderate opponents within the Conservative Party. However, he failed to establish full political peace. And in response Rojas became increasingly authoritarian, attempting to establish his own political party, which he described as 'Christian and Bolivarist'. He attempted to woo organized labour in the style of General Juan *Perón of Argentina. But these political moves alienated the two main Colombian political parties, the Liberals and the Conservatives, and worried both the Catholic Church and the business community. When Rojas secured a constitutional amendment to stand for a second term, and indicated he would not allow free elections, the above groups persuaded the heads of the armed forces to pressure him to go into exile. He did so on 10 May 1957, when it was clear that he had very little support in the country. He was replaced by a provisional military junta which in turn gave way to a 'National Front' government of Conservatives and Liberals.

Rojas later returned to Colombia in spite of being convicted of abuses of power by a national tribunal. In 1960s he established himself as leader of ANAPO, the populist and nationalist National Popular Alliance. He opposed the National Front, and narrowly lost the 1970 presidential elections. Many claim he was only deprived of victory through fraud. After his death his daughter became head of ANAPO, but the movement fell into insignifance.

Romney, George Wilcken (b. Chihuahua, Mexico, 8 July 1907; d. 26 July 1995)
US; Governor of Michigan 1963–9, Secretary of Housing and Urban Development 1969–72

George Romney was born in a Mormon settlement in Chihuahua, Mexico. He grew up in Idaho and Utah and himself spent two years as a Mormon missionary. Although he attended a number of different colleges, he never graduated. He started his career as speech writer for Massachusetts Senator David Walsh but became a lobbyist for Aluminium Corporation of America in the 1930s. He then moved to Detroit to work for the automobile industry, becoming in 1954 the chairman and general manager of American Motors, formed from two newly merged smaller companies—Nash Kelvinator and the Hudson Motor Car Corporation. He proved successful at rescuing the company, improving its market share and promoting its small car—the Midget. Romney also became involved in politics and headed a civic study group, Citizens for Michigan, to analyse Detroit's problems.

In 1962 Romney ran for Governor and won against an incumbent Governor, John Swainson, in part because of his appeal to organized labour. He was re-elected in 1964 and 1966 with increasingly comfortable majorities. As Governor, Romney's managerial expertise stood him in good stead. He reduced the state deficit by imposing new taxes and promoted progressive policies especially in the field of civil rights. A liberal Republican, Romney was the first candidate in the 1968 Republican nomination battle race; but he dropped out very early on in the race. *Nixon appointed Romney Secretary of Housing and Urban Development in 1969, a post in which Romney attempted to extend the amount of federally subsidized housing. Romney was only partially successful and his effort to extend subsidized housing to the suburbs was thwarted within the administration.

Romney did not serve in Nixon's second adminsitration and he instead devoted himself to promoting voluntary work and civic responsibility through the National Centre for Voluntary Activity which he founded.

Roosevelt, Franklin Delano (b. Hyde Park, New York, 30 Jan. 1882; d. 12 Apr. 1945)
US; Governor of New York 1929–32, President 1933–45

Born to well-to-do parents of Dutch and Flemish descent, Roosevelt was educated at Groton, Harvard University, and Columbia Law School. Each of his parents was independently wealthy and supportive, and he enjoyed a leisurely and liberal upbringing. Though he enjoyed reading, he did not apply himself to scholarship and coasted through his education, paying more attention to getting onto the football team at Harvard (he failed) than to his grades. At Harvard, he edited the student newspaper, but his educational career was undistinguished. He was married young—in 1905—to a distant cousin, Eleanor, and after taking his bar exams in 1907 practised law in a New York City firm.

A leisurely life as a lawyer soon lost its appeal and in 1910 he accepted an invitation by Democratic leaders in upstate New York to contest a seat in the state Senate. He threw himself into the race and achieved an unexpected victory. His spell in the New York Senate allowed him to develop his political skills and he showed some independence by leading a revolt against the choice of the party bosses in the selection of a candidate to a fill a vacancy for a US Senate seat. He was re-elected in 1912. The same year he attended the Democratic Convention and worked hard to deliver the New York delegation to Woodrow *Wilson, a task in which he was ultimately successful. Wilson rewarded him by appointing him Assistant Secretary of the Navy. Roosevelt was delighted. He loved the sea and it was a post once held by his distant cousin, Theodore *Roosevelt. He performed creditably in the post—he was an efficient administrator—and helped prepare a fleet ready for combat in the First World War. He continued in the post after contesting unsuccessfully the nomination for a US Senate seat in 1914. He was an observer at the Versailles Peace Conference. In 1920 he seconded the nomination of Alfred E. *Smith as Democratic candidate for President. The convention chose James E. Cox instead. Cox then chose Roosevelt as his running-mate. Roosevelt had a well-known name, experience in government, and helped balance the ticket, but 1920 was a Republican year and the pair went down to a heavy defeat. The contest nonetheless established Roosevelt as a national figure.

The following year Roosevelt was struck by personal tragedy. Suffering one evening from a chill after being in icy water, he went to bed and awoke in pain to find his legs would not support him. He was paralysed from the chest downwards, the victim—at the age of 39—of infantile paralysis. Recovery was initially slow but Roosevelt fought to regain some degree of independence and to rebuild his life. The effect of the illness was to galvanize him, to give him a determination that was previously lacking in his somewhat pampered existence. He learned to walk a few steps with the aid of leg braces. He drove a specially adapted car. He was later to develop a technique of appearing to walk while holding for support on aides. He resumed his legal career. Three years after being struck down he also briefly re-entered politics. He nominated Alfred E. Smith—the Governor of New York—as candidate for President at the 1924 Democratic convention. The convention again opted for another candidate but Roosevelt's powerful speech was greeted with a prolonged ovation. He had started his political comeback. When four years later, the Democratic nomination did nominate Smith, Smith urged Roosevelt to run for the governorship of New York. Roosevelt was reluctant—he hoped treatment would still allow him to walk without braces—but was nominated by acclamation by his party's state convention. After a vigorous campaign throughout the state, Roosevelt bucked the national Republican tide by winning election with a majority of 25,564 votes. Sixteen years after being elected to the state Senate, he was back in elective office. He proved to be an activist in office, pushing (not always successfully—the State Legislature was Republican-controlled) for new and radical programmes. Following the onset of the Depression, the political tide turned in his favour and he was re-elected by an overwhelming majority in 1930. His victory established him as a potential candidate for the presidency.

As Governor of New York he was to adopt practices and policies that were to be drawn on later when he entered the White House. He utilized a 'Brains Trust' of leading figures to advise him and he presented a range of measures—including unemployment relief, old-age pensions, and farm relief—to tackle the effects of the Depression. He instituted a Temporary Emergency Relief Administration to assist those in need in the state. He also stood up to party bosses and in his second term moved against the scandal-ridden New York city machine, achieving the resignation of the mayor.

Roosevelt built up his team of advisers and began planning a bid for the presidency. He was one of four candidates when the Democratic convention met in 1932. After some horse-trading, he was nominated on the fourth ballot. He accepted the nomination in person and made his famous declaration, 'I pledge you, I pledge myself, to a new deal for the American people.' He selected House Speaker John Nance *Garner, a Texan, as his running mate (a consequence of the convention horse-trading) and started out on a nationwide campaign. He advocated unemployment relief and tariff reform and was committed to a repeal of prohibition. He started to attack the powerful business corporations and to promote a more equitable distribution of wealth. Roosevelt offered hope against the tired administration of Herbert *Hoover and won an overwhelming victory by 22,809,638 votes to 15,758,901. Three months after his victory he survived an assassination attempt in Florida (five others were wounded, one fatally, by the shots from a deranged unemployed bricklayer) and was inaugurated on 4 March 1933. In his address, he declared that 'the only thing we have to fear is fear itself'. The country 'asks for action, and action now. Our greatest primary task is to put people to work'.

No sooner was he ensconced in the White House than he embarked on a hectic programme of reform. He closed the banks for four days. Congress was summoned into special session on 9 March and in a 100-day sitting was sent a raft of measures. Greater powers were taken to control the economy. The Emergency Banking Relief Act gave the President and the Treasury greater powers over the control of credit, currency, and foreign exchange. By resolution of Congress, the USA went off the gold standard. Public spending was reduced—the Economy Act cut federal salaries—and tax revenue increased: the Beer-Wine Revenue Act legalized the sale of the drinks and brought them within the tax mechanism. (Prohibition was repealed with the successful passage of the 21st Amendment.) The best-known measures were those providing federal relief. The Federal Emergency Relief Act gave direct relief to the states and localities, the Agricultural Adjustment Act subsidized farmers, the National Industrial Recovery Act established the Public Works Administration to create work in construction as well as protecting the rights of labour, and the Civilian Conservation Corps was founded to provide work for young men in public works projects. The Tennessee Valley Authority was created to administer a massive works programme throughout the Tennessee Valley, providing work for thousands, building dams, and generating an unprecedented public utility in the form of electricity.

The measures provided the basis for Roosevelt's New Deal. Even after the famous first '100 Days', Roosevelt was not finished. Later measures followed. Greater regulation of the economy and the stock market was introduced. More public works projects were established. Labour rights were extended. The Social Security Act of 1935 broke new ground in making provision for relief to the unemployed, the disabled, the needy, and for retirement payments to the elderly. Within three years of taking office, Roosevelt had changed dramatically the relationship between the public and private sector in making provision for the citizen.

Roosevelt's New Deal measures helped restore public confidence but they attracted opposition from significant sections of the business community and especially many in the financial community. Some of the measures also fell foul of the Supreme Court. In May 1935, the court struck down the National Industrial Recovery Act as unconstitutional, claiming that it imposed regulations on intrastate activity not permitted by the constitution. The Agricultural Adjustment Act and other acts were also later struck down.

Such setbacks did not prevent Roosevelt from sweeping to victory in the 1936 presidential election, carrying every state bar two against his Republican opponent, Kansas Governor Alf *Landon. He amassed almost 28 million votes against less than 17 million for Landon. Although he was to be elected to the presidency twice more, this election constituted Roosevelt's high point in the domestic politics of the USA. Thereafter, he was not to achieve the success he had in his first term. He sought to limit the Supreme Court by introducing a bill giving him power to appoint a new justice for every existing justice over the age of 70. Congress rejected his 'court packing' proposal. The measure appeared to achieve its purpose, even though it was not passed: members of the court were worried by what had happened and two of them switched sides in votes on subsequent New Deal measures (known as 'the switch in time that saved nine'). However, it served to sour relations between President and Congress and Roosevelt compounded the situation in 1938 by campaigning in the congressional elections against members who had opposed his plans. He failed in his efforts and the Republicans made significant gains. Though Roosevelt achieved passage of some measures in 1938, the outcome of the elections in November put an end to a continuation of the New Deal. Thereafter the President achieved the passage of no major domestic legislation.

The President's attention was being drawn more and more towards events in Europe and Asia. In 1937 and 1938 he warned of what was happening in Europe. Congress for its part passed in 1937 a Neutrality Act, imposing an arms embargo. Roosevelt responded to the Soviet-German non-aggression pact and the German invasion of Poland in 1939 by asking Congress to lift the arms embargo. Congress refused. In 1940 Roosevelt acted unilaterally, providing the United Kingdom with fifty old American destroyers in return for leases on military bases in the West Indies. As the Axis powers made further territorial gains, Roosevelt pressed for an increase in the production of planes. At the same time, a peacetime draft was introduced.

In pressing for help to the Allies, Roosevelt was running ahead of public opinion—there was widespread opposition to involvement in the war—and doing so at a time when a presidential election was imminent. Roosevelt defied tradition by seeking and gaining nomination for a third term. He remained popular but circumstances were not as propitious as in 1936. His decision to run was used against him and the Republicans nominated a popular and moderate candidate, Wendell *Willkie. Promising not to send Americans into foreign wars, Roosevelt won comfortably, but not as decisively as he had four years before. He won 27 million votes to 22 million for Willkie.

Roosevelt continued to take measures to help the Allies and to develop America's fighting capability. American forces were stationed in Greenland and Iceland. Ships belonging to Axis powers were seized in US ports after a Nazi submarine sank a US destroyer. Roosevelt, however, still faced a powerful 'America First' movement. The issue was resolved on 7 December 1941 when Japanese forces attacked the US fleet in Pearl Harbor. The following day Roosevelt addressed Congress—dubbing 7 December 'a date that will live in infamy'—and sought a declaration of war, which was duly forthcoming. Thereafter Roosevelt was transformed into a powerful war leader, his powers as Commander-in-Chief giving him a latitude in foreign affairs that was denied him in the domestic arena. The American war effort was stepped up dramatically, Roosevelt met with the British Prime Minister, *Churchill, and later with Churchill and the Soviet leader, *Stalin, to co-ordinate Allied strategy. Roosevelt was the most powerful figure—with America having a combination of economic power and manpower that could not be matched by Britain and (in economic terms) by Russia. Roosevelt was able to determine the broad strategy, leaving the implementation largely to some very able military leaders. His leadership was as important in the domestic arena as it was in the military. He provided the same inspiration to the American people in the war as he had done during the Depression. The war also served to bring the nation out of the Depression, rearmament providing the boost that had not been provided by Roosevelt's New Deal measures. The United States ended the war as the most powerful economic nation.

Roosevelt's wartime leadership put him in a powerful position to seek re-election in 1944. Though clearly ailing, he was leading the nation at time of war. He dumped his left-leaning Vice-President, Henry *Wallace, in favour of Senator Harry S *Truman, and together they won a race that was the closest of Roosevelt's career: 25.6 million votes to 22 million for the Republican, Thomas E. Dewey. Three months after the victory, Roosevelt met with Churchill and Stalin at Yalta to decide the post-war map of Europe, a map that was to prove highly controversial. In order to maintain Soviet support, Roosevelt and Churchill agreed to a disposition of forces that was later to be used by Stalin in imposing Soviet control in Eastern Europe.

Roosevelt looked unwell at Yalta, a fact commented upon by Churchill. On his return to the USA, the President addressed Congress but did so from a chair. He went to Warm Springs, Georgia—to a health resort which he had helped create—to rest. On 12 April, complaining of a headache, he collapsed, went into a coma, and—two hours later—died of a brain haemorrhage. He was 63 years of age.

Roosevelt is the outstanding President of the twentieth century. In polls of historians, conducted variously since 1948, he has always been voted among the three greatest presidents in US history, Lincoln always coming first and Roosevelt or George Washington coming second. Roosevelt transformed the office of the President and, indeed, transformed the economic and social structure of the United States. He built the presidential office into a powerful and organized unit of government. He established the Executive Office of the the President. He drew on many of the leading minds of the time. He transformed the President into Chief Legislator as well as—in the terminology of Emmet John Hughes—the Maker of World Peace. He not only made the President the most powerful person in the USA, he also made him the most powerful elected official in the world.

Roosevelt achieved all this despite being confined to a wheelchair. His disability was hidden from the public. Roosevelt was a great showman. He knew how to charm. He also knew how to act and recognized a good idea when he saw one. He was not an original thinker, but he brought in a team of first-rate thinkers and drew on their ideas as he saw fit. He was not averse to drawing on ideas originating from other sources. Many New Deal measures had their genesis in congressional bills. Roosevelt picked them up, revised them, and presented them as his own creation. He liked to be in control. He vetoed bills in order to demonstrate to Congress who was in charge. He appointed groups of advisers to provide advice on the same topic so that he could choose between them. He achieved a mastery of government unsurpassed in the history of the presidency.

At the personal level, Roosevelt achieved his ambitions despite his physical handicap, perhaps even because of it: his illness and recovery gave him a determination to succeed. He was a man who threw himself into his work and achieved a high level of emotional reward from it. He pushed as far as he could go—sometimes, in the eyes of critics, too far—and demonstrably enjoyed exercising power. He had a remarkable wife who became a public figure in her own right. More socially aware than Franklin, she showed him areas of social deprivation that shocked him. She busied herself in doing good works, both during the Depression and during the war. In many ways, she was Franklin's 'legs', visiting stricken communities and raising morale among the troops. Franklin's infidelity—he had an affair with Eleanor's social secretary, Lucy Mercer, who was to be at his side when he died—appeared to contribute to them leading separate lives, though Eleanor remained a powerful influence, once likened to a Minister without Portfolio. She has since served as an icon for many feminists.

Roosevelt's presidency has been subject to various revisionist interpretations, including those that argue that the New Deal should be credited to Congress and to Roosevelt's advisers, and that Roosevelt manipulated US entry into the Second World War. Such interpretations have not dented Roosevelt's standing. He is viewed as having been the right man for the right time—providing inspiration and leadership at a time when Americans cried out for it. His presidency has provided the benchmark for his successors.

Roosevelt, Theodore (Teddy) (b. New York City, 27 Oct. 1858; d. 6 Jan. 1919)
US; Governor of New York State 1899–1900, Vice-President 1901, President 1901–9

Born into a wealthy American family of Dutch descent, Roosevelt was related to a former President (Martin Van Buren 1837–41) as well as to a future one (Franklin D. *Roosevelt, 1933–45). His father was a merchant and banker. His mother was a descendant of Robert III, King of the Scots. As a child he was sickly and asthmatic. His parents took him on trips to Europe while he was young, initially in order to improve his poor state of health. He fought to strengthen his physical state by working out in a gymnasium (built for him by his father) and later by boxing and working as a rancher. He developed a love of travel and adventure as well as an interest in politics and writing.

He went to Harvard before studying law at Columbia Law School. While at law school, he was elected a member of the New York State Assembly, serving from 1881 to 1885. After the death of his first wife, shortly after giving birth to a daughter, in 1884 he retreated to Dakota for two years, returning to New York City in 1886 to seek the Republican nomination for mayor. He failed in his bid, then sailed to London to marry Edith Carow. He served as US civil service commissioner from 1889 to 1894, then spent two years as president of the New York City Police Board before being appointed Assistant Secretary of the Navy by President McKinley. His service as Assistant Secretary was short, lasting from 1897 until May of the following year, when he resigned in order to raise a cavalry regiment (the First United States Volunteer Cavalry) to fight in the Spanish-American War in Cuba. He led his men—an odd assortment of cowboys, college football players, and native Americans, dubbed Roosevelt's Rough Riders—in several sorties, most spectacularly in taking San Juan Hill, where Roosevelt led his men while under heavy fire. Returning to the USA later that year, he found himself a national hero.

His rise thereafter was rapid. He was elected Governor of New York State in the November of 1898, taking office the following January. The following year he was chosen as the vice-presidential candidate at the Republican convention in

Philadelphia, a nomination he had been persuaded to accept to prevent it going to someone else. In November 1990, McKinley and Roosevelt swept to victory, McKinley for a second term, with the party also taking control of both Houses of Congress. On 4 March 1901, Roosevelt took the oath as Vice-President. The assassination of McKinley six months later catapulted him into the presidency at the age of 42, the youngest—and at the time richest—ever holder of the office.

Roosevelt was by instinct an activist and a reformer. He had battled against corruption in New York and once in the White House battled against the power of the big corporations. Under the banner of 'A Square Deal', he enforced anti-trust legislation. He intervened in a coal strike in 1903. He was also responsible for the development of Forest Reserves throughout the country. He intervened in the Dominican Republic and began negotiations for the Panama Canal Zone. In 1904 he easily won election in his own right as President, gaining more than 7.6 million votes to just over 5 million for his Democratic opponent. The following year, he brought Russian and Japanese delegates together in Portsmouth, New Hampshire, to produce a peace treaty ending the war between the two countries. He played a role in bringing Germany and France together to resolve the issue of Morocco. For his work, he later received the Nobel Peace Prize. His extrovert leadership and an increasingly liberal stance nonetheless made him unpopular with many traditionalists within the Republican Party.

Stepping down from office in March 1909, he engaged in extensive travel, including hunting in Africa. In 1912, dismayed by the performance of his successor as President, William *Taft, he accepted nomination by dissident Republicans who had formed the Progressive Party. When he declared 'I feel fit as a Bull Moose' the party was instantly dubbed the Bull Moose Party. While speaking in Milwaukee he was shot in the breast but carried on talking. He got 4 million votes in the election, in effect letting in the Democratic candidate, Woodrow *Wilson. He then set off again on his travels, leading an expedition to Brazil. One of his sons died in Europe in 1918—Roosevelt himself had sought permission to lead men at the front but had been refused—and he died the following year at the age of 60.

Roosevelt was a man of great paradox. A gifted scholar—he penned over thirty books—and scion of a wealthy family, he was also a cowboy and populist. He was a great activist and optimist but also suffered from bouts of self-doubt. He was tough but sensitive. Though sometimes withdrawn, he was also flamboyant. He liked attention. He put the presidency on a new plane. He was the first President to travel abroad and he raised the profile of the office. He also had one other enduring legacy: the teddy bear is named after him—the result of a refusal while hunting to shoot a bear cub.

Root, Elihu (b. Clinton, New York, 15 Feb. 1845; d. 7 Feb. 1937)

US; Secretary of War 1899–1904, Secretary of State 1905–9, US Senator 1909–15

The son of a college professor, Root graduated BA from Hamilton College in 1864, LL B from New York City University in 1867, and was that same year called to the New York bar. He became a lawyer specializing in corporate law. He was appointed district attorney for New York Southern district, 1883–5. Thereafter he returned to private practice whilst assuming an active role in the Republican Party of New York City.

It was in 1899 that Root became a prominent national political figure and began a career in international diplomacy, when he was appointed Secretary of War by President McKinley. He remained in post when Vice-President Theodore *Roosevelt assumed office after McKinley's death. Root briefly returned to his private law practice in 1904 but by 1905 returned to the public service as Roosevelt's Secretary of State. In 1909 he gained election to the US Senate where he became an influential member of the prestigious Foreign Relations Committee. He declined to stand for re-election in 1915, returning instead to practising law.

Root remained an influential voice within the American foreign policy élite and served on numerous national and international bodies. In 1917, as President *Wilson's ambassador extraordinary, he headed a diplomatic mission to Russia, tasked with trying to persuade Russia to stay in the war. As chairman of the Republican Party national convention in Chicago in 1912, it was Root who presided over the historic division of the party that year, which led to the formation of the Progressive Party.

Root was noted for his brilliant analytical mind and a remarkable faculty for solving complicated problems of law, politics, and international affairs. His services in the cause of international peace were recognized in 1912 when he was awarded the Nobel Peace Prize. He is the author of several books including: *Experiment in Government and the Essentials of the Constitution* (1913); *Russia and the United States* (1917).

Runciman, Walter (b. South Shields, 19 Nov. 1870; d. 13 Nov. 1949)
British; president of the Board of Education 1908–11, Agriculture and Fisheries 1911–14, Board of Trade 1914–16 and 1931–7; Baron 1937

After a Cambridge education and a spell in the family shipping firm Runciman sought a political career in the Liberal Party. He won the seat of Oldham West in 1899 but lost it to Winston *Churchill the following year. In 1902 he re-entered parliament by winning Dewsbury at a by-election. He was on the fringe of the Cabinet when he was appointed Financial Secretary to the Treasury in the 1906 Liberal government. He had already shown a competence in financial and economic matters. Entry to the Cabinet followed a year later when he was made president of the Board of Education. He held a number of other posts before resigning along with Prime Minister *Asquith in 1916. He remained hostile to *Lloyd George.

The 1918 general election produced a landslide for Lloyd George's coalition government and Runciman, along with a number of other non-Lloyd George supporting Liberals, lost his seat. In 1924 he returned to the Commons as MP for Swansea West and in 1929 for St Ives. For most of these years he combined his interest in politics with a career in business. During the 1931 economic crisis he supported the national government and sat as a National Liberal until 1937 and was president of the Board of Trade in the government. On leaving the government in 1937 he was given a peerage. His mission to Czechoslovakia in 1938, designed to mend that country's relations with Germany, failed.

Runciman was prepared to treat some of his Liberal values lightly. In the 1914–18 war he accepted conscription and food rationing. Although the national government's adoption of tariffs in 1932 led to the resignation of a number of Liberals, Runciman remained.

Rusk, Dean (b. Cherokee County, Georgia, 9 Feb. 1909; d. 20 Dec. 1994)
US; Secretary of State 1961–9

Educated at Davidson College in North Carolina, Rusk was a Rhodes Scholar at Oxford University and taught government at Mills College in California 1934–40. After wartime service he embarked upon a career in the State Department, rising to the post of Assistant Secretary of State for Far Eastern Affairs in 1949. In 1952 he left the State Department to become president of the Rockefeller Foundation. Following the election of 1960, President *Kennedy appointed him Secretary of State, a post which he held throughout the entire administrations of Kennedy and of President *Johnson.

He took a strongly anti-Communist position. As Assistant Secretary of State for Far Eastern Affairs at the time of the Communist victory in China, he was virulently opposed to the Chinese Communists. Although critical of General Douglas MacArthur, he supported the invasion of North Korea led by MacArthur's United

Nations forces in October 1950 in an attempt to overthrow the North Korean Communist regime.

As Secretary of State he was a consistent supporter of American involvement in the war in Vietnam. He argued that the lessons of appeasement in the 1930s taught that there must be no appeasement of the Communists in Vietnam, whom he viewed as puppets of the Chinese and Soviet Communists in the relentless forward drive of international Communism in its aim of world domination. In his general conduct of foreign policy, he played a quiet, diplomatically professional role. He was criticized by some of Kennedy's advisers for lack of imagination and an overly low-key style, and it was rumoured that Kennedy intended to replace him as Secretary of State after the 1964 election. Following Kennedy's assassination in 1963 and his succession by President Johnson, he became increasingly influential. As a fellow southerner, he was much closer to Johnson then he had been to Kennedy, some of whose advisers had derided him. Moreover, since Johnson lacked experience in foreign policy and was interested mainly in domestic affairs, the President relied on him for advice on foreign policy to a much greater extent than Kennedy, whose main interest had lain in foreign affairs. He supported the escalation of American involvement in Vietnam throughout Johnson's presidency and sought to reassure the President that this would eventually lead to success.

As an intellectual in politics with a courteous professional manner he won wide respect. Rigidities of thinking from the 1930s and 1940s, however, led him to dogmatic adherence to a disastrous policy in Vietnam, of which he was one of the principal architects. With the assistance of his son Richard Rusk he wrote his memoirs, *As I Saw It* (1990).

Russell, Richard Brevard (b. Winder, Georgia, 2 Nov. 1897; d. 21 Jan. 1971)
US; Governor of Georgia 1931–3, US Senator 1933–71

Born into an established southern family, Russell was educated at the University of Georgia Law School, following a period at Gordon Military Institute and the Agricultural and Mechanical School in Powder Springs. After a brief stint in the navy, Russell began legal practice in Georgia and also started a political career. In 1920 he was elected to the Georgia State Assembly where he spent ten years, the last four as Speaker. From 1931 to 1933 Russell was Governor of Georgia and instituted a set of financially prudent policies which allowed Georgia to balance its budget. He also reformed the governmental structure and made major contribution to Georgia's agricultural sector. In 1932 Russell was elected to fill the Senate vacancy caused by the death of William Harris.

Russell's long tenure in the Senate was marked by steadfast adherence to the doctrine of states rights and a strong opposition to racial integration. It was also marked by devotion to the Senate as an institution (he became its president pro tem in 1969) and to the interests of Georgia, especially its farming and military businesses.

Although Russell started his career a supporter of F. D. *Roosevelt's New Deal (and was enthusiastic about many forms of federal support for agriculture and for rural electrification) like other southern Democrats he opposed the increasingly strong civil rights planks of Presidents *Truman, *Kennedy, and *Johnson. In 1935 Russell had opposed an anti-lynching bill and, although he did not join the Dixiecrat revolt of 1948, he was a key leader of the southern Democrats opposed to integration.

Russell was chair of the Armed Forces Committee from 1951 to 1969 and developed an expertise in the area of defence and national security policy which made him a significant participant in Democratic debates on these issues. Although anxious to maintain a strong American defence, he was not an uncritical 'hawk' and expressed his reservations about American involvement in Vietnam at an early stage of the conflict. He also won praise for his impartial chairing of the committee which investigated *Eisenhower's sacking of General MacArthur in the Korean War.

Russell made a bid for the presidential nomination in 1952 but it failed. Despite his ability as a legislator and administrator, his identification with the south and the cause of segregation proved a barrier to advance in national Democratic politics.

Rutskoi, Alexander Vladimirovich (b. Kursk, 16 Sept. 1947)
Russian; Russian Vice-President June 1991–Oct. 1993

A former air force officer, distinguished in Afghanistan (where as a colonel and deputy-commander of the 40th Army he was wounded), Rutskoi was promoted to major-general for his role in supporting *Yeltsin in the putsch of August 1991. He had been Yeltsin's Vice-President since June 1991. In 1990 he founded the political grouping 'Communists for Democracy' within the Russian Parliament (for which he was excluded from the CPSU) which later became the People's Party of Free Russia, part of the Civic Union coalition. He became increasingly critical of Yeltsin's economic reforms and style of government and, with *Khasbulatov, led the opposition against him. During the parliamentary crisis of October 1993 he was named President by the Parliament after it deposed Yeltsin but was arrested during the storming of the parliament building though charges of treason were later dropped. He later re-emerged as the founder and leader of a party originally called 'Free Russia' and later the 'Russian Socialists-Democratic People's Party'; this split and his wing became 'Derzhava-Rutskoi', but it never took off and his earlier popularity plummeted. He declared his intention to fight the 1996 presidential elections but withdrew his candidacy.

Rykov, Aleksei Ivanovich (b. Saratov, 1881; d. 15 Mar. 1938)
Russian; chairman of the Council of People's Commissars (Sovnarkom) 1924–30

Rykov's father was a merchant of peasant origin. He had a very impoverished childhood after his father's death when he was 8. In 1900 he entered the Law Faculty of Kazan University, where he became a Marxist and worked as a revolutionary for the RSDLP both inside Russia and abroad. In 1903 he joined the Bolsheviks, but broke with *Lenin in 1910 to lead the 'party-minded Bolsheviks' who were more tolerant of the Mensheviks. He supported the Bolshevik seizure of power in Moscow during the October Revolution of 1917 but thereafter advocated a coalition government of all socialist parties. Between 1918 and 1920 and 1923 and 1924 Rykov was chairman of the Supreme Council of the National Economy (VSNKh). From 1921 to 1924 he was deputy chairman of the Council of People's Commissars (Sovnarkom). After Lenin's death in 1924 he became chairman of Sovnarkom. Though he spoke for Party unity, *Stalin accused Rykov of being a member of the 'Right Opposition'. In 1930, he was forced to give up all his posts, but was then made Commissar for Transport. In 1937 he was arrested and executed the next year after a show trial. He was rehabilitated in 1988.

Ryzhkov, Nikolai Ivanovich (b. Donetsk region, Ukraine, 1929)
Russian; Soviet premier 1985–90

From the 1950s to the mid-1970s Ryzhkov worked for Uralmash, the vast engineering complex at Sverdlovsk. He rose from being a skilled worker to general manager of Uralmash as a whole in the period 1971 to 1975. He joined the Communist Party in 1956. In 1975 he embarked on a governmental career when he moved to Moscow as First Deputy Minister for Heavy and Transport Machine-Building. In 1979 under *Brezhnev he was first deputy chairman of the state's five-year plan (*Gosplan*). In 1982 *Andropov made him a secretary of the Party's Central Committee and head of its economic department. In April 1985, after *Gorbachev had become General Secretary of the CPSU, Ryzhkov was made full member of the Politburo. In September 1985 he became chairman of the Council of Ministers, replacing the elderly Brezhnevite, *Tikhonov. In this capacity he gained widespread respect for his integrity and industry, despite the failure of Gorbachev's economic reforms with which he was associated. In economic affairs he stood for cautious reform. In 1989 he became a member of the newly created Congress of People's Deputies, and the next year entered the Presidential Council of the USSR which Gorbachev had just formed. In June 1991 he was defeated by Boris *Yeltsin in the Russian Presidential elections.

Sadat, Anwar Mohammed (b. Mitabulkum, Egypt 25 Dec. 1918; d. 6 Oct. 1981)
Egyptian; President 1970–81

Sadat graduated from the Royal Military Academy, Cairo, in 1938. In 1942 he was imprisoned for pro-Axis activities. He became a leading member of the Free Officer group in 1949, though he was initially excluded from its inner circle by *Nasser for his perceived Islamic sympathies. Sadat, by then a close associate of Nasser, became chairman of Egypt's sole political party in 1957 and chaired the National Assembly from 1959 to 1969. He became a Vice-President in 1964 and sole Vice-President in 1969, in which capacity he took over the presidency in 1970 on Nasser's death.

Initially perceived as a weak leader, Sadat was to effect dramatic political changes within Egypt and in its external relations. The expulsion of Soviet military advisers in 1972 began the severance of close military and economic ties with the USSR which was completed in 1976. With his Syrian ally, Sadat renewed the war against Israel in October 1973, thereby ending years of stalemate and also considerably enhancing his personal reputation, both internally and internationally. In Egypt, his pre-eminence enabled him to amnesty political prisoners, lift press censorship, curb the police, and introduce a reform programme focused on economic reconstruction, attracting foreign investment and developing the private sector. Post-war Egypt also achieved a *rapprochement* with the USA in 1973–4. In 1977, Sadat paid a historic visit to Jerusalem at the invitation of Prime Minister *Begin, setting in motion a diplomatic process that culminated in the US-brokered Camp David Accords between Egypt and Israel of 1978 and the peace treaty of 1979. The settlement resulted in Egypt's isolation within the Arab world, heavier reliance on American economic and military aid, and Sadat's assassination by Islamic fundamentalists in 1981.

St Laurent, Louis (b. Compton, Quebec, 1 Feb. 1882; d. 25 Jul. 1973)
Canadian; Prime Minister 1948–57

St Laurent was brought up in Quebec and retained strong links with the province all his life. After graduating in law, he became a successful corporation lawyer. He entered politics in 1941 at the behest of Mackenzie *King, who was seeking a substantial Liberal politician in Quebec. His was a late start in politics. He joined the Cabinet as Minister of Justice and Attorney-General, aged 59, and entered the Canadian parliament in 1942. He was the only Liberal minister from Quebec to support King when conscription was imposed for overseas service in 1944. He originally agreed to serve in government only for the duration of the war but he became Minister for External Affairs and succeeded King as Liberal Party leader and Prime Minister on 15 November 1948. A few months later he led the party to election success and another victory in 1953. By 1957 the party had been in office for nearly twenty-two years and suffered from the electoral mood that it was time for a change. After defeat in the 1957 general election he soon retired from the leadership, to be succeeded by Lester *Pearson. His political life had been spent almost entirely in government and it was too late to learn the tricks of opposition. His successors struggled with growing problems of Canada's national identity and its changing relations with the British Commonwealth and with the United States.

Salazar, António de Oliveira (b. Beira, 28 Apr. 1889, d. 29 July 1970)
Portuguese; Finance Minister 1928–32, Prime Minister 1932–68

Salazar was born in the village of Santa Comba Dao, in the northern interior province of Beira. His parents were small farmers. In 1900 he joined the Catholic seminary of Viseu for his education. He remained there eight years and was deeply marked by this experience. Nevertheless, he did not decide to pursue an ecclesiastical career but went to the University of Coimbra where he became a professor.

In 1919 he was falsely accused by the Republic of conspiring against the state with three other colleagues. This led him to enter politics and become part of the Catholic opposition against the anticlerical Republican parties. In 1921, he was briefly a Member of Parliament. Disappointed with the politics in the First Republic, Salazar became co-founder of the extra-parliamentary Academic Centre for Christian Democracy (Centro Academico para a Democracia Crista—CADC) and a leading Catholic opponent of the Republican regime in the 1920s. He came to the forefront of Portuguese politics after the collapse of the First Republic in a military *coup d'état* on 28 May 1926. He refused a request from that military dictatorship to become Finance Minister, because he was not granted full control over the spending of all ministries. The economic pressures increased and he accepted a renewed invitation in April 1928. He imposed a very restrictive budget which stabilized the economy within two years, and was regarded as the saviour of the country.

After several political crises within the government, Salazar became Prime Minister in 1932. In 1933 and the following year his constitution created the Estado Novo, the New State, along corporatist lines. This concentrated power in the hands of the Prime Minister and the only legal political organization, the União Nacional. His authoritarian dictatorship formally lasted until 25 April 1974, but he was removed from office earlier in September 1968, after suffering a stroke. In his forty years at the helm, he attempted to preserve the way of life of a largely agrarian population and persecuted the opposition with his political police (PVDE and later PIDE). During the 1940s his dictatorship was sympathetic to Fascism, and his policies changed only slightly in the 1950s and 1960s. Portugal was neutral during the Second World War and was integrated into the North Atlantic Treaty Organization (NATO) in 1949 and into the United Nations Organization (UNO) in 1955. The invasion of the Portuguese enclaves in Goa and Damao Diu in December 1961, and the subsequent annexation by Indian troops, had a spillover effect in Portugal. The colonial wars in the Portuguese African empire, Angola, Mozambique, and Guinea-Bissau, imposed a considerable strain upon the budget. The international pressure coming from the democracies in Western Europe, the decolonization process, and the façade organic elections in the 1950s and 1960s forced Portugal to change both domestically and overseas. Salazar left this legacy to his successor Marcello *Caetano.

Salinas de Gortari, Carlos (b. Mexico City, 3 Apr. 1948)
Mexican; President of the Republic 1988–94

Carlos Salinas was born into the Mexican political élite. His father, Raul Salinas Lozano, was Minister of Industry and Commerce under President Lopez Mateos, 1958–64. After school in Mexico City Carlos studied economics at the National Autonomous University of Mexico (UNAM), from which he graduated in 1971. He then moved to Harvard University for postgraduate work, mixing his studies with terms of employment in the Ministry of Finance and the academic world in Mexico. He eventually graduated with three degrees from Harvard, including a doctorate in economics (1978).

He returned to Mexico and a typical two-track career, teaching at the Centre for Monetary Studies of Latin America (CEMLA) and working as an economic planner in the Treasury. In that ministry he worked under José López Portillo (President of the

Republic 1976–82) and Miguel de la Madrid (President of the Republic 1982–8). When the latter was selected as the governing party's candidate in 1981 he invited Salinas to help run his presidential campaign as director of the PRI's 'think tank', the Institute of Political, Economic, and Social Studies (IEPES). He was rewarded with the post of Minister of the Treasury for the whole of the de la Madrid term, that is, until his own nomination by the PRI in 1987.

The 1988 campaign proved to be a landmark in Mexico's electoral history. A group of leftists, led by Cuauhtemoc Cardenas, the son of a famous reformist president of the 1930s, had left the PRI in protest at the conservative policies being pursued by the government and the undemocratic way in which Salinas had been foisted on the party by the retiring president. Cuauhtemoc Cardenas as the National Democratic Front's (FDN) candidate attracted more votes than other previous opposition candidates and claimed that the government falsified the results in order to secure a victory for Salinas. Even so the victory was narrow, with less than half of the voters supporting Salinas, a drop from a level of 76 per cent in 1982.

The congressional elections were just as bad for the government. The PRI failed to win the two-thirds majority of seats required to confirm the President's election and to pass constitutional amendments. Salinas thus started his term in an unprecedentedly weak situation, that is, dependent upon the votes of opposition parties. Despite this handicap Salinas launched himself enthusiastically into a campaign of radical economic reforms. He was fully committed to the ideas of neo-liberal economics favoured by the International Monetary Fund and began the process of restructuring the Mexican economy. This involved efforts to reduce the size and scope of the state in economic life and an encouragement of foreign investment and free trade. He began negotiating the North American Free Trade Agreement (NAFTA) in order to facilitate commerce between Mexico and its northern neighbours, the USA and Canada. He thus sought to reverse the Mexican government's post-revolutionary commitment to nationalism, import substitution industrialization, and state-sponsored social protectionism.

At the macroeconomic level there was some early evidence of success but social and political costs were enormous. Unemployment, malnutrition, and the rate of business failure rose alarmingly. Opposition parties sought to take advantage of this situation and the National Action Party (PAN) gained the governorship of Baja California in 1989, the first opposition party victory at this level since 1929. The left-wing Democratic Revolutionary Party (PRD) fared less well, with its activists and vote suffering in the states where it challenged the governing party. Complaints about intimidation and electoral malpractice were common.

The final year of Salinas's term was disastrous. On 1 January, the day NAFTA became operative, a rebellion of poor and landless Indians was declared in the southern state of Chiapas. Salinas chose to negotiate rather than suppress, but the string of complaints made by the rebels were an embarrassing reminder of the deterioration of conditions in rural Mexico. In March the regime suffered another damaging blow when Salinas's choice as successor, Luis Donaldo Colosio, was assassinated while campaigning in Tijuana. There was suspicion that elements within the governing party were involved and the destabilizing prospect of growing political violence caused concern in financial circles. President* Clinton was forced to move quickly to support the Mexican peso. Despite these difficulties the presidential elections of July 1994 were held in calm conditions and with less electoral malpractice than ever before. In the interregnum before President Zedillo took office, however, political scandals began to surface with allegations of Salinas's involvement in assassination plots and financial irregularities. The economic collapse of December was perhaps the final nail in his political coffin and he left office with his reputation seriously damaged. He is now thought to be living in Eire.

Satõ Eisaku (b. Tabuse, 27 Mar. 1901; d. 3 June 1975)
Japanese; Prime Minister 1964–72

The son of a sake brewer, Satõ studied German Law at Tokyo Imperial University, graduating in 1924 and beginning a career in the Ministry of Railways and later the Ministry of Transport. In 1947 he was appointed Minister of Transport by the Occupation Authorities because of his handling of the 1947 General Strike, but took the post of Deputy Minister because of the difficulties surrounding his brother, Kishi Nobusuke (Prime Minister 1957–61), who was under suspicion of war crimes.

Satõ was a protégé of *Yoshida Shigeru and along with his brother Kishi Nobusuke rose quickly in the newly formed Liberal Democratic Party (LDP), becoming Prime Minister following the retirement through ill-health of Ikeda Hayato in 1964. He was the longest serving post-war Japanese Prime Minister, remaining in office for eight years until being forced to resign over the issue of recognizing the People's Republic of China (PRC) in May 1972. Satõ presided over a period of unprecedented growth in the Japanese economy, but had to deal with a series of serious international problems. He was torn between maintaining Yoshida's policy of supporting the USA and the unpopularity of the Vietnam War among the Japanese population. His greatest achievements were normalizing relations with the Republic of Korea (1965), negotiating the successful return of Okinawa to full Japanese sovereignty in 1972 and guaranteeing the removal of US nuclear weapons from Japanese soil.

Following the shock visit of US President Richard *Nixon to the PRC in 1971 Satõ moved hastily to improve relations with Beijing. However, because of his long-standing support for *Chiang Kai-shek and the Republic of China (ROC) on Taiwan he faced implacable opposition from *Mao Zedong and *Zhou Enlai. This led to widespread factional struggle within the LDP, forcing his resignation in 1972, when he was replaced as Prime Minister by *Tanaka Kakuei.

In 1974 Satõ was awarded the Nobel Peace Prize for his work in negotiating the Non-Proliferation Treaty and lifelong opposition to nuclear weapons, although rumours persist that Japanese business interests were instrumental in his nomination. He remained active in politics following his resignation, in particular in the pro-Taiwan lobby within the LDP, causing great anger in the PRC when he went to Taiwan to attend the funeral of Chiang Kai-shek in 1975. His son, Satõ Shinji, remains active in the LDP and in the pro-Taiwan Lobby.

Savage, Michael Joseph (b. Victoria, Australia, 23 Mar. 1872; d. 27 Mar. 1940)
New Zealand; Prime Minister 1935–40

Born in Australia to Irish immigrant parents, as a young man Savage had various labouring jobs in New South Wales. He emigrated to New Zealand in 1907 and became a trade union organizer. He played a part in forming the New Zealand Labour Party in 1916 and three years later became the party's national secretary, and succeeded Henry *Holland as leader on the latter's death in 1933.

Savage led Labour to its first general election victory in 1935; it was elected on a wave of disillusion with the outgoing government's failure to tackle the economic depression more energetically. Labour introduced a minimum wage, restored wage cuts, guaranteed prices for primary producers, expanded social welfare, and sponsored a public works programme. The policies established the domestic agenda of New Zealand politics until the mid-1970s. Savage was rewarded by an even greater victory in the 1938 election. He presented himself as a plain-speaking man, and was a reassuring figure to the middle class, although much of the press was strongly anti-socialist. He offered strong support to Britain on the outbreak of war in 1939, but died from cancer shortly afterwards, still in office.

Scheel, Walter (b. Höhschied, 8 July 1919)

German; President of the Federal Republic of Germany 1974–9, leader of the FDP 1968–74

After grammar school, Scheel completed a banking apprenticeship, before being called up for military service. He served as a lieutenant in the air force from 1939 to 1945. Then he worked in his stepfather's scissors factory in Solingen before acting as secretary for various trade associations. In 1946 Scheel joined the Liberal FDP, representing the party first (1950) in the parliament of North Rhine-Westphalia and then from 1953 in the Bundestag. In 1958 his party sent him to the European parliament, where he chaired the committee for co-operation with the developing countries. This led to his appointment as Minister for Economic Co-operation in the last *Adenauer government of 1961.

When the FDP lost office in 1966 Scheel identified himself with the liberal wing of his party and was elected chairman in 1968. He helped to persuade his colleagues to vote for *Heinemann (SPD) as President of West Germany in 1969. This paid off as it led to the formation of the SPD-FDP coalition in October 1969 in which Scheel was appointed Deputy Chancellor and Foreign Minister. He played his part with *Brandt in improving West Germany's relations with the Soviet bloc and in taking the Federal Republic into the UN in 1973. He was less successful in maintaining unity in his party and could do nothing to prevent a right-wing breakaway in 1970. He kept those who remained in the coalition with Brandt. In this the FDP prospered, increasing its vote from 5.8 per cent in 1969 to 8.4 per cent in 1972.

In 1974 Scheel was elected President of the Federal Republic and served until 1979.

Scheidemann, Philipp (b. Kassel, 26 July 1864; d. Copenhagen, 29 Nov. 1939)

German; Chancellor of Germany 1919, SPD co-chairman 1917–19

Scheidemann was a printer by trade and alter a journalist and editor of the SPD paper in Kassel. Due to his speaking skills and ambition he was elected to the SPD executive in 1911. Like Ebert, he supported the war in 1914, remaining in the leadership of the SPD and becoming co-chairman with *Ebert in 1917. He was a member of the last government of the Kaiser, under Prince Max of Baden, in 1918, becoming a member of the first Social Democratic government of Ebert in November of that year. On 9 November 1918 Scheidemann proclaimed the 'Free German Republic' from the balcony on the Reichstag in front of an excited crowd. He had no authority to do so, but his proclamation changed German history. Ebert, who had just taken over as head of government, would have settled for a constitutional monarchy, but Scheidemann was attempting to forestall the Lenin-inspired. Karl Liebknecht, who was about to proclaim a German Socialist Republic.

Scheidemann followed Ebert as Chancellor in February 1919 but resigned in June rather than agree to the Versailles Treaty. He was mayor of Kassel from 1920 to 1925. Like other SPD leaders he was subjected to a campaign of personal abuse and an attempted assassination. He left Germany when the Nazis took over in 1933, living the Copenhagen, where he continued his Social Democratic activities until his death in 1939.

Schlüter, Poul (b. Tønder, 3 Apr. 1929)

Danish; chairman of the Conservative People's Party 1974–7, 1981–93, Prime Minister 1982–93

The son of a wholesale merchant, Schlüter went to school in Copenhagen and then on to university there. He was active in student politics and chaired the youth wing of the Conservative People's Party 1952–5. In 1957 he obtained his degree in law and in 1960 set up in legal practice in Copenhagen. Schlüter was elected to parliament as one of the members for Copenhagen in 1964 and held his seat until retiring in 1994. From 1966 to 1971 he served on the municipal council and as deputy mayor for Gladsaxe. In 1971 he was elected to his party's national executive committee, in 1974–82 to the chair of its parliamentary group. In this latter capacity he rapidly established a reputation as a pragmatic and skilful politician.

In 1982 Schlüter became the first Danish Conservative Prime Minister this century when Anker *Jørgensen and the Social Democratic government resigned as a result of the economic crisis. Schlüter's political acumen helped him to stay in office at the head of successive and various non-socialist coalition governments for an uninterrupted span of eleven years. In 1993 however his incumbency came to an end as a result of the so-called Tamil affair, a refugee problem which eventually led to the prosecution of the former Minister of Justice.

Schlüter's international experience has included acting as a delegate to the United Nations General Assembly in 1965, as a member of the Council of Europe 1971–4, and as leader of the Danish delegation to the Nordic Council 1978–9. As Prime Minister he also of course served on the European Council of Ministers. Since 1994 he has been a member of the European Parliament, where he has been elected Vice-President.

Schmidt, Helmut (b. Hamburg, 23 Dec. 1918)

German; Chancellor of the Federal Republic 1974–82, deputy chairman of the SPD 1968–83

The son of a schoolteacher, Schmidt spent the war as a lieutenant in the anti-aircraft artillery. He studied economics at Hamburg University before taking up work in the transport department of the city, becoming its head in 1952. He became a committed Social Democrat at university, having been influenced by fellow prisoners of war. He was elected chairman of the Socialist German Students' League in 1947 and used the opportunity to build up international contacts. His professor, Karl Schiller, also a Social Democrat, helped his rise.

Schmidt was first elected to the Bundestag in 1953. He remained in parliament until 1961 when he took over as Senator (minister) for internal affairs in Hamburg. He won sympathy for his decisive leadership during the Hamburg floods of February 1962. In 1966 he took over as chairman of the SPD group in the Bundestag, declining a ministry in the grand coalition. In 1969 he was made Defence Minister, a key appointment. Schmidt had taken an interest in defence matters for many years as a colonel of the reserve, SPD spokesman, and writer on defence affairs. He had attempted to bring the SPD and the armed forces together against the opposition of the many pacifist-inclined SPD members. In 1972 he took over the Finance Ministry, where he remained until becoming Federal Chancellor in 1974. Both as Finance Minister and as Chancellor he had to deal with the two oil crises of 1973 and 1979/80 which ravaged the economies of the industrialized world. Inflation, increasing unemployment, and cuts in public expenditure were the results. Under Schmidt unemployment rose from a mere 582,000 to 1.8 million in 1982. Inflation also rose, though he got it down from its peak in 1974. Yet his government's achievements, despite the critics at home, were envied by other countries.

Another major concern which faced Schmidt was terrorism. Throughout his chancellorship the Red Army Faction (RAF) and other terrorist groups disturbed the peace in West Germany with a campaign of bombing, kidnapping, and murder in an effort to undermine the Federal Republic. The worst case for Schmidt was the hijacking of a Lufthansa airliner with ninety-one passengers and crew by a Palestinian group in October 1977. The pilot was killed and the plane landed at Mogadishu (Somalia). Schmidt took a tough stance and was prepared to resign if it failed. He ordered crack troops to storm the plane. This was successful, with no loss of life among either the hostages or the troops.

As Chancellor, Schmidt continued Brandt's *Ostpolitik*, taking every opportunity to meet the leaders of the Soviet Union, Poland, and East Germany. He was the first West German leader to visit the leader of the German Democratic Republic and developed a good working relationship with *Honecker. He developed a close personal friendship with the French President *Giscard d'Estaing, the two of them pushing forward the Franco-German alliance within the European Community. It was Schmidt who in 1978 proposed the introduction of European Monetary Union within the EC. In defence matters he got embroiled in the controversy over the modernization of NATO's nuclear deterrent in Europe. He hoped negotiations would persuade the Soviets not to deploy the medium range SS-20 rockets which were aimed at West European targets, but he believed that if they could not be convinced then NATO must respond. This was the so-called 'dual track' approach discussed by Schmidt with President *Carter, British Premier *Callaghan, and Giscard d'Estaing in January 1979 in Guadeloupe and later adopted by NATO.

Schmidt was regarded by many as the strongest Chancellor since *Adenauer but he faced much opposition. He had to consider his Liberal coalition partners in the FDP especially his Vice-Chanellor and Foreign Minister *Genscher. However, it is true that he had more trouble with the left wing of his own party than with the FDP. Although he maintained his position as deputy chairman of the SPD, a considerable section of the party was alienated from him. His tough line on terrorism, the economy, and defence won applause on the right-of-centre but lost the SPD support to the Greens. This opposition, and his health problems, caused him to retire from politics when the FDP decided to withdraw from his government in 1982. In retirement he remained a loyal supporter of the SPD, devoting much of his time to journalism, especially the prestigious weekly *Die Zeit*.

Helped by his excellent English, which enabled him to give informal speeches at many international gatherings, he increased the prestige of the Federal Republic.

Schroeder, Patricia Scott (b. Portland, Oregon, 30 July 1940)
US; Member of the US House of Representatives 1973–96

The daughter of an insurance adjuster, Schroeder was educated at the University of Minnesota and Harvard. She became a practising lawyer and law teacher before winning election in 1972. Her career in the House involved strong support for women's issues and civil liberties. (In the 104th Congress she sat on the Judiciary Committee and the National Security Committee and was co-chair of the Congressional Caucus on Women's Issues.) Her most notable legislative achievement was the 1993 Family and Medical Leave Act which President *Clinton signed into law as one of his first presidential acts. She has also been a consistent dove on foreign policy issues as well as an opponent of cost-cutting in government.

Despite Schroeder's high profile in Democratic national politics, her intervention in presidential politics has been limited. She chaired Gary *Hart's abortive campaign and made a brief bid for the nomination herself in 1988. She left Congress at the end of 1996 to assume a teaching position at Princeton University.

Schumacher, Kurt (b. Kulm, 13 Oct. 1895; d. 20 Aug. 1952)
German; leader of SPD 1946–52

Many Germans felt ill at ease with Schumacher because he seemed to personify the valour and the suffering of the few anti-Nazi resisters, in contrast to the complacency and cowardice of the many fellow-travellers. He had lost an arm in the 1914–18 war fighting for the Kaiser, and a leg as a result of his incarceration in a Nazi concentration camp. Because he was well known and on the verge of death, he was released in 1943, but it seemed to be sheer will power and sense of mission which kept him alive until 1952. He wanted to build up the SPD as the majority party to constitute a bulwark against political extremism, and he wanted to keep Germany united in a democratic Europe. The Allies found him a difficult man to deal with as he opposed the idea of the collective guilt of the Germans and the expulsion of millions from their homes as German territories were transferred to the Soviet Union and Poland.

The Social Democrats had the best record as consistent democrats of any of the German parties. The Communists already banned, they alone had voted against *Hitler's 'Enabling Act' in the Reichstag in 1933. The Communists had stood for a Soviet Germany, the SPD for a democratic Germany. Schumacher and his colleagues had warned that Hitler would bring about another war. They had been proved correct and they expected to be rewarded for their courage and vision when Germany was returned to democracy. They were to be disappointed. In the East many of their bastions were under Soviet control; there democratic elections could not be held. In the West the confessional structure of the voters was against them being more Catholic than Germany as a whole. Moreover, *Adenauer's Christian Democrats were ready to embrace integration with their neighbours, hoping that German reunification would come later. Schumacher urged that such integration should come *after* German unity had been restored. Strongly backed by the Catholic church and the Americans, Adenauer led his Christian Democrats to victory in 1949 and again in 1953 by which time Schumacher was dead. The jovial Rhinelander beat the austere Prussian.

Schumacher was born in Prussia beyond the Oder–Neisse line, and his home town became part of Poland after 1945. He grew up in a comfortable middle-class environment which was shattered by the outbreak of war in 1914. He volunteered for service but his wounds resulted in his discharge from the army in 1915. He took up the study of law and economics. His war experiences led him to side with the revolution in 1918. He joined the SPD and worked as a journalist for the party. By 1924 he was elected to the Württemberg parliament and in 1930 to the Reichstag. On a famous occasion in 1932 he interrupted *Goebbels, shouting, 'The entire National Socialist agitation is a constant appeal to the swine in man.' He became a marked man and was arrested in 1933. He was released from Dachau in 1943 only to be rearrested after the July 1944 plot against *Hitler. Released again, he was marked down for execution as the Allied advance in Germany continued. He went into hiding until the arrival of the British in Hanover. He immediately got to work building up the SPD and was elected chairman in 1946.

Schuman, Robert (b. Luxembourg, 29 June 1886; d. 4 Sept. 1963)
French; Prime Minister Nov. 1947–July 1950, Foreign Minister 1948–53

The son of a small farmer, Schuman attended Catholic secondary schools in Luxembourg and in German-occupied Metz and University in Bonn (where he met the young Konrad *Adenauer), Munich, Berlin, and Strasbourg. Elected deputy for Moselle when the provinces of Alsace and Lorraine were returned to France, he devoted himself to problems of reintegrating the departments into the Republic. He slowly but steadily ascended in the Assembly through specializing in financial affairs. He was noted by Paul *Reynaud, who made him under-secretary in the War Cabinet. Pétain reconfirmed him in that position but he was arrested by the Occupation authorities, freed, and then fled to Lyons. At the Liberation he was one of the founders of the French Christian Democratic Party (MRP) and returned to the Assembly. His great contribution was made over the next eight years as Prime Minister and as Foreign Minister. He became a liberalizing Finance Minister in 1946 and then, at the outbreak of the Cold War, Prime Minister. The government of 1947 was crucial to the future of France and Europe: it faced down the strike waves. During this year Schuman's government brought the United States back into the European arena and consolidated aid to the economies and he played a key role in securing the Atlantic Alliance. The other strand to Schuman's work was the development of European institutions on the basis of Franco-German rapprochement. This is where the famous 'Schuman Plan' (prepared by Jean *Monnet) to create a market in coal and steel across Germany and France was crucial. The Plan was approved by the Assembly and became the basis for future integration measures. The proposal for a defence community, which Schuman supported, failed in 1954 (and he resigned as Foreign Minister) but the Rome Treaties setting up the EEC were a success. Schuman was edged out of politics after 1958 by the return of de Gaulle and his party was also humbled by the General. He was, as has been said, a Luxembourger by birth, a German by education, Roman Catholic for ever, French at heart, and one of the princes of Europe.

Scott, Hugh Dogett (b. Fredericksburg, Virginia, 11 Nov. 1900; d. 21 July 1994)
US; Member of the US House of Representatives 1940–59, US Senator 1959–77

Scott was educated at Randolph-Macon College and at the University of Virginia where he studied law. After a period in private practice, he became in 1926 an assistant district attorney, a post he held until his election to the House of Representatives in 1941. Service in Congress was interrupted by a spell in the navy but in 1947 he returned to the House and in 1948 became chairman of the Republican National Committee, partly as a reward for help in getting Thomas *Dewey the nomination.

Elected to the Senate in 1958, Scott served on the Judiciary and Foreign Relations Committee. In 1969 Scott was made Republican whip and, when Everett *Dirksen died later that year, Scott was elected to succeed him as Republican Senate leader.

Scott was generally seen as being on the liberal wing of the Republican Party. For example, he was a reliable supporter of civil rights measures regardless of the partisan advantage to be gained increasingly from opposing such initiatives. Above all else he was a loyal party man who supported Republicans in the White House almost regardless of the impact of their policies on the congressional party. He took a long time to withdraw support from Richard *Nixon over Watergate; but in 1974 Scott was one of the Republican leaders who had to tell the embattled President that he could no longer survive impeachment.

Scott retired from the Senate in 1976 and returned to private practice in Washington, DC.

Semichastny, Vladimir Yefimovich (b. 1924)
Ukrainian; chairman of the KGB 1961–7

Semichastny left school with a secondary education. His political career started when he became First Secretary of the Ukrainian Communist Youth League (Comsomol) in 1947. In 1950 he was transferred to Moscow into the organization of the Soviet Comosomol. It was there that he became a client of his fellow Ukrainian, Aleksandr *Shelepin. From 1958 to 1961 he succeeded Shelepin as First Secretary of the Comsomol, head of the Central Committee's Department of Party Organs for the Union Republics, and chairman of the KGB. From 1959 to 1961 he was also Second Secretary of the Azerbaijani Party. By the time he became head of the KGB in 1961 he had the reputation of being a hard-line opponent of the West and Western culture. He was well-known for allegedly having made a crude denunciation of the writer Boris Pasternak in 1958. His appointment at the young age of thirty-seven and his lack of political status might, however, have been intended to stress the reduced status which the KGB had had since *Stalin's death in 1953. Semichastny and Shelepin were involved in the leadership plot which brought down *Khrushchev in 1964. Both were opposed to Khrushchev's relatively pro-Western policies. In 1966 Semichastny was seriously embarrassed by the defection of Stalin's daughter, Svetlana Alliluyeva to the West followed by a bungled attempt to kidnap her and bring her back to the Soviet Union. In May 1967 he was removed as head of the KGB and replaced by Yuri

*Andropov. He was demoted to deputy chairman of the Ukrainian Council of Ministers. In 1981 Semichastny was further demoted. He reappeared in public in the Gorbachev era in order to criticize *Brezhnev.

Senghor, Leopold Sedar (b. Joal, Senegal, 9 Oct. 1906)
Senegalese; President 1960–80

A Catholic in a heavily Moslem country and member of the minority Serer people, Senghor was educated at the Sorbonne, and emerged in the 1930s as a major poet in the French language, helping to develop the idea of 'negritude' which had a significant impact on the formation of a black consciousness; he founded the influential journal *Présence africaine* in 1947. As a member of the French Constituent and National Assemblies from 1945 to 1958, he built his political base by mobilizing rural Senegalese voters against the established urban élites, while disqualified by his religion from posing any threat to the autonomy of regional Islamic leaders. In 1955–6, he was briefly Minister of Education, not for Senegal but for France.

Becoming President of Senegal at independence in 1960, as leader of the Union Progressiste Sénégalaise, he combined a gentle and scholarly manner with a shrewd grasp of political power. He outmanœuvred his more radical opponents, both in the Mali Federation which linked Senegal and French Soudan in 1959–60, and in Senegal itself. He also used the support of rural Moslem potentates to control urban radicals in the capital, Dakar, and maintained close links with France including a military base near Dakar. Though initially he followed the common African pattern of a single party state, in 1976 he announced the formation of a three-party system based on competing ideologies—a device that allowed more open debate than in most African states, without threatening Senghor's Parti Socialiste, which was assigned the ideological centre and could also benefit from the advantages of office.

In keeping with his continuing cultural interests, he hosted the first world congress of black arts and culture in Dakar in the 1970s. He set a further precedent in December 1980, when he became the first African head of state voluntarily to leave office, retiring in favour of the Prime Minister, Abdou Diouf. He subsequently lived mostly in France. Though his rule was conservative, and left social inequalities especially in the countryside undisturbed or even enhanced, he is likely to be remembered as one of the most modest and benevolent post-independence African leaders.

Shamir, Yitzhak (b. Ruzinoy, Poland, 1915)
Israeli; Foreign Minister 1980–3, 1984–6, Prime Minister 1983–4, 1986–92

Yitzhak Yezernitsky became a revisionist Zionist and emigrated to Palestine in 1935. There he resumed his interrupted legal studies and joined the Irgun terrorist group in 1937. With its most militant members, he broke away in 1940 to form the extremist terrorist group LEHY (Lohamei Herut Yisrael), under the leadership of Abraham Stern. He was party to its notorious attempts at alliance with Fascist Italy, Nazi Germany, and the USSR and, after Stern's death in 1942, he led the fascistoid Stern Gang in its campaign of indiscriminate terrorism. Shamir continued his lethal career as head of Mossad's assassination unit between 1956 and 1964.

In 1970, Shamir joined *Begin's Herut party and was elected to the Knesset in 1973. As Foreign Minister in Begin's Likud government in 1980 he opposed the return of Sinai to Egypt under the 1979 peace treaty, but was overruled. He succeeded Premier Begin in 1983. In the Likud-Labour government of 1984, Shamir succeeded Prime Minister *Peres by arrangement in 1986, retaining the premiership in the new Likud-Labour government of 1988–90 and in the subsequent Likud government, until its defeat in 1992.

In office, Shamir implacably opposed trading territory occupied since 1967 for peace—he believed it part of the Land of Israel—and was equally intransigent in opposing Palestinian self-determination. He refused to negotiate with the PLO as a terrorist organization. Despite an 'iron first' attempt to suppress to the Palestinian *intifada*, which attracted international condemnation, his government's counter-insurgency policy failed to work. Shamir attended the Madrid peace conference of 1991, but later admitted trying to prolong peace negotiations for ten years to give time for a massive Jewish settlement of the West Bank and Gaza to become an irreversible fact. In retirement, Shamir urged the Oslo Accords with the PLO of 1993 be scrapped.

Shatalin, Stanislav Sergeyevich (b. Pushkin, Leningrad region, 24 Aug. 1934)
Russian; head of the economics division of the Academy of Sciences 1989–

Shatalin was an economist working in the State Committee of Science and Technology (GKNT) and at Moscow University. He was a member of the Soviet Academy of Sciences. After *Gorbachev came to power in 1985 he became the Soviet Union's most prominent radical economist, outspokenly advocating the establishment of a market economy. In 1989 he replaced Abel Aganbegyan as head of the economics division of the Academy of Sciences. In March 1990 he became a member of Gorbachev's Presidential Council upon its foundation. The powers of the council were imprecisely defined. As the Soviet Union's economic crisis worsened, Gorbachev and *Yeltsin united in an effort to produce a radical reform plan as soon as possible. In the summer of 1990 they appointed Shatalin as head of a team of radical economists who drew up a '500-Day Programme' for the transition to a market economy, which was also known as the 'Shatalin Plan'. However, the Soviet government refused to support the plan largely because it involved the devolution of economic power to the republics and it was abandoned. In summer 1991 Shatalin was a founder-member of the Movement for Democratic Reform.

Shcherbitsky, Vladimir Vasilyevich (b. Verkhnedneprovsk, Dnepropetrovsk region, 17 Feb. 1918; d. 16 Feb. 1990)
Ukrainian; First Secretary of the Ukrainian Communist Party 1972–89

Shcherbitsky was a graduate of the Dnepropetrovsk Chemical Technological Institute. He joined the Communist Party in 1941 and served in the Red Army during the Second World War. In 1945 he returned to the Dnepropetrovsk region, where he became a client of *Brezhnev. He progressed through the party organization until 1955 when he became First Secretary of the party organization for the Dnepropetrovsk region—a post which Brezhnev had previously held. From 1961 to 1963 he was candidate member of the Presidium of the Central Committee, but was removed at the end of the *Khrushchev era. When Brezhnev became leader his career was back on track and he re-entered the Presidium as a candidate member (known as the Politburo after 1966) in 1965; he attained full membership in 1971. In May 1972 he replaced Piotr *Shelest as First Secretary of the Ukrainian party. He was considerably less willing to assert Ukrainian interests than his predecessor and throughout the 1970s and early 1980s sought to repress local nationalism. He was honoured as a 'Hero of Socialist Labour' in 1974 and 1977 and awarded the Lenin Prize in 1982. He was unwilling to implement the new policies of glasnost and perestroika after *Gorbachev came to power in 1989, though he paid lip-service to them. He kept the Ukraine quiet when nationalist unrest was developing in the Baltic Republics and in the Caucasus. In 1989 he was elected unopposed for the Dnepropetrovsk seat in the Congress of People's Deputies, but when he was removed from office soon after, he was the last of the Brezhnevite 'old guard' to fall.

Shehu, Mehmet (b. 1913; d. Tirana, c.19 Dec. 1981)

Albanian; Minister of the Interior 1948–74, Minister of War 1974–80

Shehu was the son of prosperous Muslim parents. He was educated at the American school in Tirana then at an Italian military college, from which he was expelled for Communist activities. He fought with the International Brigades in the Spanish Civil War. In 1942 he became military commander of the Albanian National Liberation Army. After training at the Military Academy in Moscow, Shehu became Chief of Staff of the Albanian army in 1946. His fortunes slumped during the ascendancy of the pro-Yugoslav faction of the Albanian Party but picked up after the Tito–Stalin split in June 1948, when he replaced Koçi *Xoxe as Minister of the Interior. He was Prime Minister from 1954. In 1974 to 1980 he was Minister of War, conducting a purge of the officer corps. In 1981 Hoxa made it clear that Ramiz *Alia, not Shehu, was to be his successor. In December 1981 Shehu committed suicide in mysterious circumstances. It was rumoured that he had been murdered at a meeting of the Albanian Politburo. The Albanian leader, Enver *Hoxha denounced Shehu as an agent of the British, Yugoslav, US, and Soviet intelligence services. Over the next year his family and supporters were purged.

Shelepin, Aleksandr Nikolaevich (b. 1918)

Russian; chairman of the KGB 1958–61, member of the Politburo 1964–75

Shelepin graduated from the Moscow Institute of Philosophy and obtained a higher degree from the Moscow Institute of History. While still a student he expressed his ambition to become a party boss. He started his political career in the Communist Youth League (Comsomol). He served in the Red Army during the Russo-Finnish War of 1939 to 1940. During the Second World War he helped organize the partisan movement in the Moscow region. In 1943 he rejoined the Comsomol, working at its All-Union Secretariat in Moscow, and became its head in 1952. After 1954 he mobilized thousands of young Communists in support of *Khrushchev's 'Virgin Lands' programme. In 1958 he served briefly as Central Committee secretary in charge of the Party Organs Department. In December 1958 he replaced Ivan Serov as chairman of the KGB. His career outside state security and his higher education distinguished him from his predecessors and his appointment was probably intended to improve the image of the KGB. In November 1961 he left the KGB whose work he continued to oversee as chairman of the new Committee of Party and State Control within the Central Committee. The new head of the KGB was his client, Vladimir *Semichastny. Shelepin and Semichastny disliked their former patron Khrushchev's search for rapprochement with the West and participated in the plot which led to his fall in 1964. As a reward, Shelepin was made a full member of the Presidium (known as the Politburo after 1966). Shelepin soon aroused the suspicions of Leonid *Brezhnev, the new party leader. Brezhnev disliked Shelepin's ambition and his control of the security apparatus. He possibly also found his belligerent attitude an impediment to good East–West relations. In 1967 Shelepin was removed from the secretariat of the Central Committee and demoted to head of the Soviet trade unions. He was removed from the Politburo in 1975.

Shelest, Piotr (Petr) Yefimovich (b. 14 Mar. 1908)

Ukrainian; First Secretary of the Ukrainian Communist Party 1963–72, member of the Politburo 1966–73

Shelest was born into a poor peasant family. He graduated from the Mariupol Evening Metallurgical Institute, joined the Communist Party in 1928, and worked successively on a farm, for the railway, and in a factory before embarking on a party career. He was in charge of the industrial department of the Chelyabinsk regional party committee from 1941. In 1954 he entered the secretariat of the Kiev party organization, of which he became head in 1957. Thanks to *Khrushchev's patronage he was appointed a secretary of the Central Committee of the Ukrainian Communist Party, becoming its First Secretary in 1963. In December that year he was made a candidate member of the Presidium of the Central Committee of the CPSU, and was closely involved in the plot which led to Khrushchev's fall in 1964. Shelest became a full member of the Presidium in 1966. In 1968 he was one of the Soviet leaders most hostile to the reform Communists in Czechoslovakia, and was closely involved in negotiations with the Czechoslovak leaders. He was greatly concerned that the 'Prague Spring' might destabilize the Ukraine and was in favour of military intervention by the Warsaw Pact. At home Shelest vigorously repressed all signs of dissent, but sought to foster the development of Ukrainian culture. He increased the number of publications in Ukrainian, but failed to introduce tuition in that language into the Republic's higher educational system. He was an active defender of the Ukraine's economic interests within the Soviet Bloc. *Brezhnev came to see him as too soft on Ukrainian nationalism and replaced him in May 1972 as Ukrainian party leader with his own client, Vladimir *Shcherbitsky. In April 1973 he was removed from the Politburo.

Shevardnadze, Eduard Amvrosievich (b. Mamati, Georgia, 25 Jan. 1928)
Georgian; President of the Georgian Republic 1992–

The son of a schoolteacher, educated at a party school and a pedagogical institute in Georgia, Shevardnadze made his career in the local Comsomol and party apparatus. From 1964 to 1972 he worked in the Georgian Internal Affairs Ministry (from 1968 as Minister), when he exposed the criminal organization headed by the then Georgian First Secretary, V. P. Mzhavanadze, whom he replaced in 1972. As Georgian party leader Shevardnadze continued the fight against corruption but also pursued relatively liberal economic and cultural policies.

He had long had friendly contacts with *Gorbachev and shared his reformist orientation, but it was a surprise when Gorbachev made him Foreign Minister in July 1985. The assumption was that his inexperience would enable Gorbachev to control foreign policy himself, but this proved incorrect as Shevardnadze soon gained great respect and authority, especially amongst Western leaders, for his success in relaxing Cold War tensions. He restructured the Soviet Foreign Ministry after the dominance of Andrei Gromyko, promoted the withdrawal of Soviet troops from Afghanistan, and improved relations with Asian and Middle Eastern countries.

It was a great shock when he suddenly resigned in December 1990, alleging constant criticism and pressure from the Communist old guard against which he felt that he had failed to receive support from Gorbachev.

In 1991, while *Gamsakhurdia (whom he had once imprisoned) was still in charge in Georgia, he continued in political life in Moscow. But when Gamsakhurdia was ousted he returned to Georgia, where he became President in March 1992. He has pursued a more pro-Russian line, bringing to an end the conflict in Abkhazia and bringing Georgia into the CIS. He was re-elected President in November 1995.

Shinwell, Emanuel (b. London, 18 Oct 1884; d. 8 May 1986)
British; Minister of Defence 1950–1, chairman of the Parliamentary Labour Party 1964–7; Baron (life peer) 1970

The son of a clothing manufacturer, 'Manny' Shinwell became an apprentice tailor on leaving elementary school at the age of 11. Involvement in radical politics on Clydeside led to his imprisonment for several months in 1919. He entered parliament as MP for Linlithgow in 1992 but held only junior ministerial posts in the Labour governments of 1924 and 1929–31. However, his victory over Prime Minister Ramsay *MacDonald at Seaham Harbour in the 1935 general election made him nationally known.

During the Second World War, Shinwell became a pungent critic of the coalition government (in which he was reported to have declined Winston *Churchill's offer of a junior ministerial post). In 1945 he became Minister of Fuel and Power, with a seat in the Cabinet, in Clement *Attlee's Labour government (1945–51). His achievement in nationalizing the coal mines was overshadowed by a fuel crisis (for which he was largely held responsible) in the exceptional winter of 1946–7. In October 1947 he reluctantly accepted effective demotion to the non-Cabinet secretaryship of state for war. He re-entered the Cabinet in 1950 as Minister of Defence.

Too old for ministerial office in Harold *Wilson's Labour government (1964–70), he became chairman of the PLP. But he resigned in 1967 over a disagreement with the government's application to join the European Community and the chief whip's liberal approach to party discipline. He retired from the Commons in 1970 and subsequently became the first centenarian to sit in the House of Lords. The title of his autobiography, *Conflict without Malice* (1955), belied his renowned fieriness of temper.

Shore, Peter David (b. Liverpool, 20 May 1924)

British; Secretary of State for the Environment 1976–9

After education at Quarry Bank School, Liverpool, and King's College, Cambridge, Shore joined the Labour Party's Policy Research Department, becoming its head.

He entered the House of Commons in 1964 as MP for Stepney and (subject to boundary revisions) represented it continuously until 1997. After acting as Harold *Wilson's parliamentary private-secretary he rose rapidly and in 1967 joined the Cabinet as Secretary of State for Economic Affairs, later becoming Minister without Portfolio and deputy leader of the House of Commons. At this time many thought him over-promoted, and in spite of his patent intellectual capacity his performance in the House was often uncertain. This weakness was remedied during his membership of the shadow Cabinet while Labour was in Opposition (1970–4). When Labour returned to office he performed effectively in both Cabinet and parliament, first as Secretary of State for Trade (1974–6) and then as Secretary of State for the Environment (1976–9).

By 1980, Shore's stature was sufficient for him to be nominated as a candidate for the leadership in succession to James *Callaghan. He initially appeared to be a strong contender: he was not a left-winger but his opposition to membership of the European Community had gained him support on the left. But Michael *Foot, who appealed to the same electorate, then entered the contest and Shore came last. He was again a contender in 1983, but the domination of the extra-parliamentary party in the new electoral college operated against a man not widely known beyond Westminster. He remained in the shadow Cabinet until 1985. Afterwards, he participated actively in select committees and the Nolan Committee on Standards in Public Life, retiring as an MP in 1997.

Short, Edward Watson (b. Westmorland, 17 Dec. 1912)

British; Lord President of the Council and leader of the House of Commons 1974–6, deputy leader of the Labour Party 1972–6; Baron (life peer, Lord Glenamara) 1977

The son of a tailor, Short was educated at Bede College, Durham. During the Second World War he served in the army, reaching the rank of captain. He was elected to parliament in 1951 as MP for Newcastle upon Tyne, Central, which he represented continuously until 1976.

After serving in the Whips' office in opposition, Short was appointed government chief whip when Harold *Wilson formed his first administration in 1964. After that, he was made Postmaster-General (1966–8) and was then promoted to the Cabinet as Secretary of State for Education and Science. When Labour went into opposition, in 1970, he initially retained his frontbench responsibility for Education. However, in 1972 he was elected to the deputy leadership. Wilson appointed him Lord President and leader of the House in the government he formed in March 1974, but he was dropped when James *Callaghan assumed the premiership in 1976.

Short had a relatively low public profile as a minister, but he played an indispensable role for Labour behind the scenes at Westminster. As chief whip he had the onerous task of securing the passage of the government's legislation with a single-figure Commons majority and many ministers lacking experience of office. As the government's chief business manager between 1974 and 1976 he was initially faced with the even greater problems of a minority government. His autobiographical *Whip to Wilson* provides a fascinating insight into the difficulties of parliamentary party management in these circumstances.

Shultz, George Pratt (b. New York, 13 Dec. 1920)
US; Secretary of the Treasury 1972–4, Secretary of State 1982–9

Shultz took a BA at Princeton University and a Ph.D. at Massachusetts Institute of Technology. He pursued an academic career in industrial relations, serving as dean of the Graduate School of Business at the University of Chicago 1957–68. In the administration of President *Nixon he served as Secretary of Labor 1969–70, Director of the Office of Management and the Budget 1970–2, and Secretary of the Treasury 1972–4. He resumed his academic and business careers, becoming dean of the Graduate School of Business at Stanford University and president of the Bechtel Group, Inc.

In 1982 he was appointed Secretary of State by President *Reagan, following the resignation of Alexander *Haig. He served with great distinction and was one of the most influential and successful secretaries of state in American history. He worked quietly to tone down the virulently anti-Soviet rhetoric in which Reagan had engaged in the early 1980s and to resume talks with the Soviets after their breakdown in 1983. Following the accession to power in the Soviet Union of Mikhail *Gorbachev in 1985 he worked very closely with his Soviet counterpart, Eduard *Shevardnadze, to establish a remarkable thaw in US–Soviet relations. He encouraged regular summit meetings between Reagan and Gorbachev, while he engaged in frequent meetings with Shevardnadze. By the end of his tenure as Secretary of State the Cold War had virtually ended and the Soviet Union had embarked on the course which led to the collapse of Communist regimes in Eastern Europe and in the Soviet Union itself 1989–91. He was the single most important figure in transforming American foreign policy from confrontation to constructive engagement with the Soviet Union during the 1980s. He published his account of the remarkable developments during his tenure as Secretary of State in *Turmoil and Triumph: My Years as Secretary of State* (1993).

Simon, Paul (b. Eugene, Oregon, 29 Nov. 1928)
US; member of the US House of Representatives 1975–84, US senator 1985–96

Simon's parents were both heavily involved in the Lutheran church—his father as a minister and his mother as a missionary. Educated at the University of Oregon and Dana College in Blair, Nebraska, Simon's career started with a period as the editor and publisher of a small newspaper. After army service (where he worked in counter-intelligence) Simon ran successfully for the State Legislature. He served in the lower Illinois chamber 1954–62 and was elected to the state Senate in 1962, securing re-election in 1966. In 1968 Simon was elected Lieutenant Governor although the Democratic nominee for Governor was defeated. In 1972 Simon's own gubernatorial bid failed as he was beaten by Daniel Walker, who had chaired the Chicago Crime Commission.

Simon left politics briefly in 1972 for academic life but in 1974 he successfully ran for the Illinois 24th district following the incumbent's retirement. In 1984 Simon pulled off a surprise victory against Republican Charles Percy to win the Senate seat.

In Congress, Simon was generally regarded as a liberal and a reliable friend of organized labour. In the Senate he sat on the Labor and Human Resources Committee, Judiciary, Budget, and Foreign Relations. He was an opponent of the increased defence spending of the Reagan era, voting against new weapons systems such as MX, SDI, and the B1 bomber. He was also opposed to many of the Reagan judicial nominations and voted against Robert Bork's nomination to the Supreme Court in 1987.

In 1988 he made a bid for the Democratic presidential nomination. He made a virtue of his distinctive appearance (bow ties and horn-rimmed glasses) and his unpackaged self-presentation. However, he came fourth in a race which included not only Michael *Dukakis but also Albert *Gore and Jesse *Jackson. He retired from the Senate in 1996.

Slánský, Rudolf (b. Moravia, 1901; d. Prague, 3 Dec. 1952)
Czech; secretary-general of the Czechoslovak Communist Party 1945–51

Slánský was the son of middle-class Jewish parents. He belonged to the Czech intelligentsia. He joined the CPCz upon its foundation in 1921 and in 1929 became one of *Gottwald's main assistants in *Stalinizing the party on Moscow's instructions. He spent most of the Second World War in Moscow and in 1944 was flown to Slovakia to help lead the National Uprising. In 1945 he became Secretary-General of the CPCz—the party leader. In February 1948 he was primarily responsible for the planning of the Communist seizure of power and organized the brutal Sovietization of Czechoslovakia which followed. By the end of 1950 he had lost favour with Moscow and at Soviet instigation Gottwald, the Czechoslovak President, ordered the arrest of a number of Slánský's supporters. In September 1951 he gave up his post as secretary-general, but remained Vice-Premier. On 24 November 1951 Slánský was arrested by the secret police in Prague. Thirteen other senior Communists were also arrested, including the Foreign Minister, Vladimír Clementís; eleven of them were Jews. They were charged with Titoism, Trotskyism, Zionism, and with working for the West. The evidence was obviously fabricated. The real reasons for their arrest were Stalin's obsession with Titoism and his anti-Semitism as well as Gottwald's need for scapegoats to deflect public criticism from the economic failure of his regime. The Slánský Trial took place from 20 to 27 November 1952 amidst great publicity. Slánský was found guilty on all charges. On 2 December 1952 he and all but three of the accused were hanged. The others were sentenced to long terms of imprisonment. In 1963 Slánský was partially rehabilitated.

Smith, Al (b. New York, 30 Dec. 1873; d. 4 Oct. 1944)
US; Governor of New York

Smith was the first Roman Catholic to be nominated for the US presidency by a major political party. He was born and brought up in poverty on the lower East Side of New York City. After doing various menial jobs he was elected as a Democrat to the State Assembly in 1903 and served as Speaker 1913–15. He was a product of the Tammany Hall political machine but he was also interested in the progressive causes of the time. He was elected Governor of New York in 1918. He was defeated in 1920 in a landslide for the Republicans but was re-elected in 1922, 1924, and 1926. In office he compiled a strong record of reform, covering industrial relations, factory conditions, minimum wage, workmen's compensation, and slum clearance. As a successful New

York politician it was no surprise that his ambitions moved to the national stage. He nearly gained the Democratic nomination for the presidency in 1924 but was handicapped by being a Catholic, a 'wet'—opposing Prohibition—and personifying the big city politics which was bitterly opposed by the rural south. He managed to win the nomination in 1928 and was supported by F. D. *Roosevelt. In an attempt to unite the party Smith accepted Prohibition. The campaign was marred by bigotry and violence. The South turned against the Democratic candidate and the Ku-Klux-Klan also opposed Smith who went down to a heavy defeat, losing by 58 to 41 per cent of the vote to Herbert *Hoover. It seemed impossible for a Catholic to run successfully for the presidency. Smith sought and failed to win the nomination in 1932. He grew increasingly jealous of his protégé Roosevelt, who was now in the White House. He took up with business and conservative groups and joined the right-wing Liberty League which opposed the New Deal. Smith supported the Republican presidential candidates in 1936 and 1940.

Smith, Frederick Edwin *see* Birkenhead, Lord

Smith, John (b. Argyll, 13 Sept. 1938; d. 16 May 1994)
British; leader of the Labour Party 1992–4

Smith came from a hard-working, thrifty, ambitious family. His father was a head teacher. After attending a local grammar school and Glasgow University he became a lawyer, an advocate in Scotland. He was part of a strong Scottish contingent which came to the front ranks of the Labour Party in the late 1980s.

He became Labour MP for North Lanarkshire in 1970 and sat for that seat until 1983 when it was reorganized as part of Monklands East. Smith quickly showed himself to be a good debater. He was on the right of the political party and was one of the sixty-nine Labour MPs who defied the whip to vote to support the Conservative government's application to join the European Community in 1971.

In the 1974 Labour government he held junior posts in the Energy Department and in 1976 he was given responsibility for devolution. At the time, North sea oil and nationalization were high-profile issues in Scottish politics. He entered the Cabinet, at the age of 40, as Trade Secretary in 1978. These few months were to be his only spell in Cabinet.

After losing the general election in May 1979 Labour began the long period in Opposition. Smith was the only continuous member of the shadow Cabinet until his sudden death in 1994. He held a number of posts—Trade, Energy, Employment, Trade and Industry, and finally shadow Chancellor in the 1987 parliament. The best years of his political life were spent in Opposition, and this was not his natural forte.

Labour's sharp move to the left after 1979 and the exit of a number of his friends to the new Social Democratic Party made this a gloomy period for him and his brand of politics. Although on the political right he was never a factional politician. He was also able to escape from Westminster during the recess by resuming his law practice and hill climbing.

After another defeat in the 1983 election he was campaign manager for Roy *Hattersley, who was easily beaten by Neil *Kinnock for the party leadership. In the 1987 parliament, when Hattersley moved from the shadow post at the Treasury, John Smith replaced him. By now he was being widely regarded as a successor to Kinnock. His stocky figure, quick mind, and reassuring 'bank manager's' appearance seemed to appeal to voters. By 1989 he and Hattersley were the only members of the shadow Cabinet to have had Cabinet experience.

The talk of Smith's likely succession to Kinnock contributed to tensions between the two. Such talk increased every time Kinnock was judged to have made a mistake. Some of Kinnock's friends resented the good press that Smith had got and commented on his lack of strong engagement in battles to reform the party. Kinnock thought Smith was too cautious, particularly on tax policy; Smith in turn thought that his leader sometimes lacked consistency and was too influenced by opinion polls.

When Labour surprisingly lost the 1992 general election, Smith did not escape his share of criticism. His shadow budget was blamed for opening Labour to the charges that it was a party of high taxes. But when Kinnock resigned from the post, Smith easily won the leadership election, gaining over 90 per cent of the electoral college vote.

As a leader Smith was cautious. He would not take action to amend or remove Clause 4 from the party constitution. In contrast to Kinnock he opposed proportional representation but declared his willingness to abide by the result of a referendum on the matter. He was not as committed to the modernization of the party as his successor Tony *Blair. He did, however, stake his leadership on reforming the role of the trade unions in the party, in particular campaigning successfully for the introduction of one member one vote in party elections in 1993. He had vigorously supported Britain's membership of the ERM but escaped censure when membership proved to be an economic mistake.

Smith, Margaret Chase (b. Skowhegan, Maine, 14 Dec. 1897; d. 29 May 1995)
US; member of the US House of Representatives 1940–8, US Senator 1949–73

The daughter of the town barber, Smith received only a high school education before working as a teacher, telephonist, newspaperwoman, and office manager. In 1930 she married Clyde Harold Smith and became his secretary in 1937 when he was elected a Republican congressman. The sudden death of her husband in 1940 propelled Smith into a political career and transformed her into a role model for the present generation of American women politicians. That year she won a special election to complete her husband's unexpired term in the House. She went on to serve four full terms in her own right before, in 1948, gaining election to the Senate where she also served four full terms, until losing her seat in 1972.

Within a year of her Senate debut Smith gained national prominence with her 'Declaration of Conscience' (1950) in which she denounced fellow Republican Senator Joseph *McCarthy for his crusade against Communists. Throughout her long career in the Senate she continued to demonstrate that she was a Republican of independent mind.

Smith has been described as 'an inspiration' and 'a political trail-blazer'. She was the first woman elected to the Senate in her own right, the first woman to be elected to both the House of Representatives and to the Senate, and, in 1964, the first woman to have her name placed in nomination for President by either major political party.

After leaving the Senate in 1973, Smith spent the next twenty years lecturing in politics at dozens of universities and colleges across America. She was proud of her thirty-two years of public service and requested that her epitaph read: 'She served people.'

Smith published numerous papers and articles. She received ninety-five honorary degrees and in 1989 was awarded the Presidential Medal of Freedom.

Smuts, Jan Christian (b. Bovenplaats, 24 May 1870; d. 11 Sept. 1950)
South African; Prime Minister 1919–24 and 1939–48, Deputy Prime Minister 1933–9

Born into a leading Afrikaner family in Cape Province Smuts was educated at Christ's College, Cambridge, and was called to the bar in 1895. In 1898 he was appointed State Attorney of the Transvaal Republic. During the Anglo-Boer War he organized anti-British commando units in the Western Transvaal and led the Boer forces which attacked the British in the Cape Colony. In 1905 he was one of the founding leaders of the Afrikaner political party Het Volk (which later merged with others to form the

South African Party–SAP) and became Minister of Education in the Transvaal. He was a strong supporter of the Union of South Africa which was established in 1910. During the First World War he resisted calls for neutrality from some Afrikaner groups and was a strong supporter of participation on the British side. He fought with the British army, for whom he was the commander of operations in East Africa, and in 1916 was promoted to the rank of lieutenant-general in the British army. In 1917 he became a member of the British war Cabinet. Following the war he became Prime Minister until the SAP was defeated in the 1924 elections following his brutal suppression of the white mineworkers' strike on the Rand in 1922 which lost him the support of the Labour Party. Following the formation of a coalition government in 1933 he became Deputy Prime Minister. In 1934 the coalition partners, the SAP and the National Party, fused to form the United Party (UP) although hard-line Afrikaners in the National Party kept the latter going as a separate party. With the outbreak of the Second World War in 1939 Smuts became Prime Minister and again rejected Afrikaner nationalist calls for neutrality and pledged support for the Allies' war effort. In 1941 he was made a Field Marshal in the British army. Following UP victory in the 1943 election he became Prime Minister for a further five-year term. After the war he was a major participant in the establishment of the United Nations.

Smuts was a strong supporter of white political unity between Afrikaners and non-Afrikaners but in the 1948 election his UP was defeated by the (Afrikaner nationalist) National Party and he became leader of the Opposition in parliament. In 1948 he was elected chancellor of Cambridge University. In domestic politics he was ultimately outflanked by those who regarded him as an Afrikaner who was too accommodating to minority non-Afrikaner interests.

Snowden, Philip (b. Yorkshire, 18 July 1864; d. 15 May 1937)

British; Chancellor of the Exchequer 1924 and 1929–31

The son of a weaver, Snowden received only an elementary education. After clerical jobs, he became editor of a socialist newspaper. His skills as a propagandist were significant in the development first of the Independent Labour Party and then of the Labour Representation Committee (later Labour Party). He sat on the National Administrative Committee of the ILP for many years and was twice its chairman (1903–6 and 1917–20). However, he resigned from the ILP in 1927 in protest at its alleged extremism.

After entering the House of Commons as member for Blackburn in 1906 Snowden established a reputation as an expert on public finance. His opposition to the First World War resulted in electoral defeat in 1918, but he re-entered parliament in 1922. His first ministerial post was the chancellorship of the Exchequer in the first Labour government (1924). His cautious policy incurred criticism from Labour's left wing, but he shared Ramsay *MacDonald's determination to prove Labour 'fit to govern' by financial orthodoxy. He pursued the same line in the second Labour government (1929–31), but the policy exacerbated the economic depression and the unemployment problem.

In August 1931, Snowden was one of the few ministers to join MacDonald's national government when the Labour government collapsed. He continued as Chancellor and, after an emergency budget making further expenditure cuts, was compelled to respond to continuing pressure on sterling by suspending the gold standard. This was his final major decision as Chancellor. He did not contest the general election in October and went to the House of Lords as Lord Privy Seal. Early in 1932, differences arose over the introduction of a protectionist trade policy and Snowden was one of four 'free traders' whose resignations were averted only by the Cabinet's unprecedented adoption of an 'agreement to differ'. This proved only a temporary solution to the government's internal tensions and they resigned eight months later over imperial trade preference. Out of office, Snowden became an outspoken critic of the government and of MacDonald personally, though he never rejoined the Labour Party from which he and other Labour members joining the national government had been expelled. His two-volume *An Autobiography* (1937) is a useful account of the formative years of the Labour Party.

Soares, Mário Alberto Nobre Lopes (b. Lisbon, 29 Dec. 1924)
Portuguese; Prime Minister 1976–8, 1983–4, President 1986–96

Soares was born in Lisbon, the son of João Soares, a well-known minister of the First Portuguese Republic (1910–26) and opponent of the dictatorship of António *Salazar. This family background contributed substantially to his political education. One of his teachers was Alvaro Cunhal, who later became the secretary-general of the Portuguese Communist Party.

Mário Soares is probably, apart from António Salazar, the most significant Portuguese politician of the twentieth century. He first became politically active in the Communist-dominated MUNAF (Movimento de Unidade Nacional Anti-fascista—Movement of National Anti-Fascist Unity) after the Second World War. He then moved away from the Communist movement and became the leader of the small socialist opposition in Portugal. Nevertheless, he continued to co-operate with other opposition groups, particularly the Communists and republicans, for the occasional façade legislative elections. He was imprisoned twelve times and deported to the former Portuguese colony of São Tomé and Príncipe in 1968, for his political activities. In 1970 he was forced into exile in France.

After many attempts to refound the Portuguese Socialist Party, which had been established in 1875 and dissolved in 1933, his efforts succeeded on 19 April 1973 in the congress of the Socialist Opposition in Bad Munstereiffel, West Germany. The foundation of the Socialist Party (Partido Socialista—PS) was achieved with the help of the Socialist International (SI) and the German Social Democrats. After the collapse of the authoritarian regime on 25 April 1974, Soares returned to Portugal and was widely recognized as one of the major leaders of the Opposition. He took part in the first four provisional governments and sixth government. During 1974 and 1975 he became the major opponent of the attempts of the Communist Party to control the state apparatus, the media, and the economy, and played an important part in Portugal's successful transition to democracy. In the elections to the Constituent Assembly, the PS under his leadership achieved a relative majority of the vote. In the first elections of 1976, the Socialists again were the largest party and Soares became the first Prime Minister under the new constitution. Nevertheless, the instability of the minority government and its lack of a reliable majority in the parliament led to its downfall in 1978. In spite of some opposition inside the party, he became secretary-general again in 1980. Three years later he returned as Prime Minister leading a coalition with the PSD. In 1985 he was elected President and re-elected in 1991, acting more as a check on the absolute majority government.

Sobchak, Anatoly Aleksandrovich (b. Chit, 1937)
Russian; mayor of St Petersburg 1991–

Sobchak graduated from the law faculty of Leningrad State University in 1957. From 1959 to 1962 he worked as a lawyer in the Stavropol region. From 1959 to 1962 he was a secretary of the Communist Youth League (Comsomol). In 1973 he was lecturer and in 1982 a professor of economic law at Leningrad State University. In 1989 he became a member of the Congress of People's Deputies representing Leningrad, and was also a member of its inner body, the Supreme Soviet. He was a member of the Co-ordinating Council of the Interregional Group of Deputies, a pressure group for greater democratization, and headed the official inquiry into the violent repression of the demonstration in Tblisi in April 1989. In May 1990 he became chairman of Leningrad city soviet–the mayor of Leningrad. Soon afterwards he quarrelled with the Leningrad democrats who had come to power along with him on the radical reform platform. He began to rely on the old Communist economic bosses. In July 1990 he followed *Yeltsin in leaving the Communist Party. In June 1991 Sobchak was elected mayor of St Petersburg. In August 1991 he rallied the people of Leningrad against the conservative coup, which was a major factor behind its failure. In December 1991 he became co-chairman of the Movement for Democratic Reform jointly with *Popov, the mayor of Moscow. He became head of the Movement's Political Council. Sobchak was regarded as one of the leaders of the democratic movement in Russia. But among St Peterburg's radical reformers he acquired a reputation for incompetence, conservatism, and intellectual arrogance. He was believed to have aspirations to become President of Russia in succession to Boris Yeltsin. Sobchak published his version of events in his book *For a New Russia.*

Sobhuza the Second, King (b. Zombodze, 22 July 1899; d. 21 Aug. 1982)
Swazi; King of the Swazi 1921–82, King of Swaziland 1968–82

Sobhuza was recognized as King of the Swazi nation soon after his birth although his grandmother, Gwamile, acted as regent until his coronation in 1921. During the colonial period (Swaziland was a British protectorate) he maintained the traditional Swazi system, which included a dominant role for the *Ngwenyama* (the 'lion king') but was always willing to make adaptions to reflect changing conditions. Towards the end of colonial rule he was hostile towards British plans to set up a liberal-democratic system but then outmanœuvred all his opponents by establishing his own royalist party, the Imbokodvo National Movement, which won all the seats in the pre-independence elections.

Under the independence constitution he was legally a constitutional monarch but, in reality, he totally dominated the political system. In 1973, following the election of a small number of opposition MPs, he scrapped the constitution and ruled by decree as an absolute monarch. Under his rule Swaziland was politically stable and enjoyed relative economic prosperity.

At the time of his death he was the longest-reigning monarch in the world, having been King for over sixty years.

Spaak, Paul Henry (b. Schnebeck, 25 Jan. 1899; d. 31 July 1972)
Belgian; Prime Minister 1938–9, 1946, 1947–9

Spaak's importance extended beyond Belgium. As a key figure in the forging of West European institutions in the 1950s he earned the title 'Mr Europe'. He was interned by the Germans during the First World War when he was an adolescent, graduated in law from Brussels University, and practised as a lawyer. He was elected to the Belgian parliament as a Socialist in 1932, following his father who had been a renowned lawyer and left-wing MP. In 1936 he was Minister of Foreign Affairs and in 1938 became Prime Minister and held the post for nearly a year, while heading the Foreign Affairs Ministry. He tried to keep Belgium neutral when the Second World War broke out but after the German invasion in 1940 he went into exile. A prominent figure in the Belgian government in exile in London during the war years, Spaak returned to Belgium in 1944 and served variously as Prime Minister, Deputy Prime Minister, or Foreign Minister in several post-war coalition governments.

It was during these years that Spaak emerged as an international figure of major importance. He was one of the founders of the United Nations and the first president of the UN General Assembly (1946). More significant was his role as a founding father of a united Europe. He was convinced of the need for European unity, not least to prevent the outbreak of Franco-Geman rivalry leading to another war, and contributed to the creation of the early European Community institutions for coal and steel and atomic energy. He chaired the group that drafted the European Economic Community's founding Treaty of Rome and served as president of the Assembly of the Council of Europe (1949–51) and then of the General Assembly of the Council of Europe (1952). He also served as Secretary-General of NATO (1957–61). He was Belgian Foreign Minister from 1961 until his final resignation in 1966. As a strong supporter of Britain's entry to the European Community he was appalled by *de Gaulle's veto in 1963 of the British application for entry. At home, Belgian politics were increasingly bedevilled by tensions between the Flemish and Walloon communities and there was some criticism of Spaak's concentration on international affairs and relative neglect of domestic concerns.

Stalin, Yosif Vissarionovich (real name **Djugashvili**) (b. Gori, Georgia, 21 Dec. 1879; d. near Moscow, 5 Mar. 1953)

Georgian; People's Commissar for Nationalities 1917–22, General Secretary (later Secretary) of the CPSU 1922–53, chair of the Council of People's Commissars (later Council of Ministers) 1941–53

Born in the small Georgian town of Gori and losing his father, a poor cobbler, at the age of 10, Yosif Djugashvili was brought up by his pious mother. He was educated at an Orthodox elementary school and later at an Orthodox seminary, from which he was eventually expelled at the age of 20. This religious education, even though he rejected it, had an important influence in familiarizing him with Russian language and culture and producing lasting habits of thinking and expression. Developing an interest in Marxism, he soon became a political organizer in Transcaucasia, but fell out with the local Social Democrats because he supported the Bolshevik faction whereas most of them were Mensheviks. So 'Koba', as he was known, moved to St Petersburg in 1913 where he impressed the party enough to be brought onto the Bolshevik Central Committee and made an editor of *Pravda*. He visited *Lenin in Poland and at his suggestion wrote *Marxism and the National Question* which was published later in the year (under the pseudonym 'Stalin'—derived from the word 'Steel') and established his reputation with Lenin as the party expert on an important and contentious issue. He argued for a combination of political and economic centralism with national linguistic and cultural autonomy—the famous formula of 'national in form but socialist in content' which was to become the basis of Soviet federalism. In March 1917, after several years of arrest and exile, he returned to Petrograd (as St Petersburg had been renamed) from Siberia after the Tsar's abdication and re-established himself as an editor of *Pravda*. At this time he advocated co-operation with non-Bolshevik socialists in the Soviet and the provisional government and supported a defensive war and when Lenin returned in April and proposed a rejection of these positions Stalin was reluctant to agree. His natural caution was evident also in October when he was sceptical about the idea of armed insurrection.

In the new Council of People's Commissars Stalin became Commissar for Nationality Affairs. He played a major role in devising the state structure which formed the basis of the constitutions of the Russian Republic in 1918 and the Soviet Union in 1924. While his Georgian nationality made him sensitive to the feelings of the nationalities, his ingrained centralism and ruthlessness came out in the crushing of the Georgian Mensheviks in 1921, which first raised doubts in Lenin's mind about Stalin. During the Civil War Stalin served as a political commissar on several fronts, which brought him into frequent conflict with the Commissar for War *Trotsky. After the war his administrative capacities were recognized by Lenin in creating for him in 1922 the new post of General Secretary of the Central Committee, which Stalin was to make the basis of his political power through the control he exercised over appointments to key committees and his identification with the core of the party. Even before Lenin died in 1924 he had formed a ruling alliance with *Zinoviev and *Kamenev, isolating Trotsky. Stalin's reputation for unspectacular, business-like moderation enabled him to survive Lenin's recommendation in his 'Testament' that he be removed from his post because of his rudeness: the Central Committee agreed not to publish or act on the note.

Stalin gradually established his pre-eminence by astute political manœuvring, first sidelining Trotsky by stressing dogmatic loyalty to 'Lenin's behests' and then forcing Zinoviev and Kamenev into opposition through his development of Bukharin's idea of 'socialism in one country', which with its implication of national development rather than international revolution was popular amongst the party rank and file. By 1928 he was in control, having removed Zinoviev and Kamenev from the Politbureau and exiled Trotsky. He was then free to take up Trotsky's idea of rapid industrial development at the expense of the peasantry, which matched a general mood in the party of impatience with the consequences of NEP and worries about Soviet military preparedness, thus abandoning Bukharin's views of gradualist development which he had previously espoused.

But it was in 1929 that occurred the 'great change' that marked the onset of the 'Revolution from Above'. Faced with a grain crisis in the expanding industrializing cities, produced by the peasants' reluctance to sell grain at low state prices, he reintroduced limited grain requisitioning in 1928; when this made the situation worse, he decided in November 1929 to 'liquidate the kulaks [richer peasants] as a class' and to complete collectivization of farms in the term of the First Five-Year Plan (only 15 per cent collectivization was planned in 1928); at the same time the industrial targets of the plan were enormously increased, draconian work discipline introduced, and a massive anti-religious campaign started to break the church's hold over the peasantry. The coercion needed to carry through these campaigns caused a huge increase in the size and power of the secret police, the OGPU. Millions died in resistance or, as in Ukraine, in artificially induced famine; millions more stocked the rapidly expanding forced labour camps of the Gulag.

In 1933 the revolutionary excesses were terminated and a more ordered system established. This was a 'totalitarian' system in that it aspired to monopolistic political control of the whole of society—a centrally planned and nationalized economy; centrally controlled forms of education, association and expression, including intellectual and cultural life. This control was exercised not through perfect order but by classic 'divide and rule' methods of arbitrary central intervention, the use of terror as a means of government, and devolution of dictatorship to sectoral and regional leaders competing with each other for the favour of the Boss (*khozyain*). The whole was welded together by the formal and informal activities of the secret police and by the ritualistic use of 'Marxist-Leninist' ideological dogmas, supplemented by the consciously fostered 'personality cult' of the Leader (*vozhd'*). The values promulgated were not revolutionary-Bolshevik but traditional-peasant: hierarchy, nationalism (Russian), militarism, group tyranny and anti-individualism, brutal punishment and discipline, philistinism, pro-natalism, even serfdom (collective farms and the Gulag). Was it socialism? Stalin declared it was in the constitution of 1936 and undoubtedly believed that he had 'completed' and preserved the revolution by building up the power of the state in the face of 'capitalist encirclement'', a strong base from which 'socialism' could expand when the time was right. He also believed, like Lenin, that he was indispensable in this process.

The Purges and show trials of the 1930s had functional and traditional elements, but bore the hallmark of his pathologically suspicious and vengeful personality. Purges of the officer core greatly weakened the USSR before the war, but the crisis was postponed by the Nazi-Soviet pact of 1939, which gave the USSR control of the Baltic states, Karelia, eastern Poland, and Bessarabia. Stalin took the additional post of chair of the Council of People's Commissars, to ensure direct control of the state apparatus in case of war. He appears to have been surprised and temporarily panicked by the Nazi invasion of June 1941 (in spite of intelligence reports), no doubt because he thought he had outwitted *Hitler. He became chair of a war cabinet, the State Defence Committee, in addition to becoming People's Commissar for Defence and Supreme Commander of the Armed Forces. Initially his ruthless and arbitrary approach proved very costly, but as he allowed his generals more initiative and allowed free rein to Russian nationalism (including the revival of tsarist symbols and the Russian Orthodox Church), the tide turned in 1943 after Stalingrad and he proved an effective strategist and national leader. During the war he was a highly successful negotiator and representative of Soviet interests at the allied conferences in Tehran (1943), Moscow (1944), and Yalta and Potsdam (1945). As a result of Soviet military and diplomatic prowess not only were the illicit gains of 1939 allowed to stand but the USSR gained controls of a buffer zone in Eastern Europe which became its outer empire with the onset of the Cold War in 1947 (though *Tito's Yugoslavia broke away in 1948). Stalin emerged from the war with his military and political position much enhanced and as the head of a military super power, later with nuclear weapons, though with a devastated economy and catastrophic human losses. Reconstruction of the economy proceeded rapidly, through the exploitation of Eastern Europe, suppression of Soviet living standards, and resumption of police terror. In his final years Stalin was still contemplating grandiose schemes of 'transforming nature' and was about to launch another purge, mainly against Jews (the 'Doctors' Plot') before he was cut short by death in March 1953. His body was embalmed and placed next to Lenin's in the mausoleum, until it was removed and buried in the Kremlin Wall after *Khrushchev's attacks in 1961.

Revisionist historians have questioned the extent of his dictatorial control and the numbers of his victims, but recent archival research has broadly confirmed the traditional view of Stalin. Undoubtedly he presided over huge strides in industrial development, Russia's survival in the 'Great Patriotic War', and achievement of super-power status, but the methods used, involving enormous and needless human and material costs, fundamentally undermined the achievements. He suppressed all the libertarian and challenging aspects of Marxism-Leninism and carried to extremes the authoritarian and élitist aspects, which he combined with the traditions of Russian orthodoxy, the 'human engineering' of Peter the Great and his personal suspiciousness, ruthlessness, and vengefulness. He created a system which could not be maintained in modern conditions but could not be reformed without undermining its inner logic.

Stamboliiski, Petur (b. Slavovitsa near Radomir, 1 March 1879; d. near Slavovitsa, 15 June 1923)

Bulgarian; Prime Minster 1919–23

Stamboliiski was born into a wealthy peasant family, and studied agriculture in Germany. After returning to Bulgaria in 1897 he became an agrarian agitator. From 1906 he played a major part in the Bulgarian Agrarian Union. He was imprisoned in 1915 for opposing Bulgaria's entry into the First World War on Germany's side. In 1918 he led a march on Sofia which resulted in King Ferdinand's abdication. He was briefly President of a Bulgarian Republic before the army rallied to King *Boris. Becoming Prime Minister on October 1919 he represented Bulgaria in the peace negotiations at Versailles. At home Stamboliisky had near dictatorial powers. His regime drastically reduced taxation of the peasantry at the expense of the middle classes and workers. His goal was to turn Bulgaria into a model agricultural society. He was fiercely anti-Communist. His foreign policy was marked by an acceptance of the status quo. This included the improvement of relations with Yugoslavia culminating in 1923 with the Treaty of Niš. As a result, Stamboliiski was unpopular with the Macedonian separatist group IMRO. When he tried to suppress IMRO he was overthrown in a right-wing coup in June 1923. He was shot dead at the end of a dramatic escape.

Steel, David (b. Dumbarton, 31 Mar. 1938)

British; leader of the Liberal Party 1976–88; Baron (life peer 1997)

Steel's father was a clergyman and his early schooling was in Edinburgh and Nairobi, followed by Edinburgh University. He became a Liberal MP for Roxburgh, Peebles, and Selkirk at a by-election in 1965. He held the seat until 1983 and then sat for Tweedale. Ettrick, and Lauderdale. When he first entered parliament he was one of only ten Liberal MPs.

As a private member he sponsored the Abortion Act (1967) which legalized abortion up to twenty-eight weeks after gestation. This earned him the long-standing enmity of opponents of abortion. In the small Liberal Party he held a number of posts before becoming leader in 1976. The height of his influence was achieved during the Lib-Lab pact in which his party supported the minority Labour government, between 1977 and 1978. Many of his colleagues thought that Labour ministers were not sufficiently sympathetic to Liberal interests. During the pact he had to battle hard to keep his party in line and more than once threatened resignation.

Steel also worked hard to engineer the alliance between the new Social Democratic Party and the Liberals for the 1983 and 1987 general elections. Indeed, he had dissuaded Roy *Jenkins from joining the Liberals in 1980 and urged him to form the SDP. When the Alliance broke up after the 1987 general election and the two parties merged, Steel decided not to stand for the leadership of the new Liberal Democratic Party. However, he remained as foreign affairs spokesman.

Steel worked consistently for a realignment of the party system and hoped for a new centre-left party to emerge. At one time he thought that the Alliance would do this. His relations with the SDP leader David *Owen were difficult and he was overshadowed by the latter. Owen was more anti-Labour and Steel was more anti-Conservative.

Steel published his memoirs, *Against Goliath*, in 1987, and stood down as an MP in 1997.

Stennis, John (b. Kemper Co., Missouri, 3 Aug. 1901; d. 23 Apr. 1995)

US; Senator

Stennis served in the US Senate for forty-one years and at the time of his retirement only one Senator had served longer. He was one of the phalanx of conservative Democrats from the south who dominated the Senate. Committee chairmanships at this time were allocated on the basis of seniority. Because many southern seats were virtually one party constituencies they were able to collar most of the influential positions. Stennis served through the south's transition from being racially segregated to being integrated. He was brought up in Mississippi and eventually won his way to University of Virginia Law School, from which he graduated. He then practised law for a few years. As soon as he graduated in 1928, he was elected to the Mississippi legislature (1928–32). He served as district attorney (1932–7) and was appointed, in 1937, and then elected as a circuit judge in 1938, 1942, and 1946. In 1947 he filled a vacancy in the Senate for Mississippi. He eventually succeeded another southerner, Richard *Russell, as chairman of the Armed Services Committee in 1969. He shamelessly used his post to bring military installations to his state and the military had few stronger supporters for their demands for money and hardware. Though a firm supporter of racial segregation (indeed, it would have been impossible to get elected without such a policy) he was relatively liberal for Mississippi. But he ignored the plight of the many blacks in Mississippi and firmly believed that Washington should leave the states, particularly those in the south, alone. He came to terms only slowly with the consequences of the Civil Rights Act (1964). He was a signatory of the 'Southern Manifesto' (1954) which urged resistance to the Supreme Court's decision to end segregation. He voted against every piece of civil rights legislation until 1982.

He was the prime mover in the War Powers Bill (1971) to limit the President's power to commit American troops abroad without a formal declaration of war. It was said that the actor Charles Laughton modelled himself on Stennis's accent and manners in playing the Southern Senator in the film *Advise and Consent* (1962). He retired in 1988.

Stevens, Siaka Probyn (b. Tolobu, Sierra Leone, 1905; d. 29 May 1988)
Sierra Leonean; Prime Minister 1968–71, President 1971–85

Of mixed ethnicity, Stevens received a basic education in Freetown and joined the colonial police force, subsequently becoming a mineworkers' trade union activist. In 1951, he helped to found the Sierra Leone People's Party (SLPP), which represented the peoples of the interior against the coastal élite, but split from it in 1958, later founding the All People's Congress (APC), which represented northern and more radical elements against the southern and chief-dominated SLPP. This won the 1967 general election (the first occasion on which a governing party in independent Africa had been defeated by the opposition), but Stevens was prevented from taking power by a military takeover. In 1968, the military regime collapsed and Stevens became Prime Minister; he assumed the presidency in 1971, and held office until his voluntary retirement in 1985.

Such radical pretensions as he had shown in opposition rapidly disappeared in office. In 1971, he called in Guinean troops to protect himself against an attempted military coup, and in 1978 he created the single party state which he had virulently opposed when in opposition, On the whole, he preferred to co-opt his opponents rather than repress them, but several were executed either with or without formal trial. The patronage system fuelled largely by diamond revenues became his major instrument of rule, and he established close relations with diamond dealers of dubious repute. The OAU conference which he hosted in 1978 was a major drain on national revenues. He wrote an unrevealing autobiography, entitled *What Life Has Taught Me.*

Stevenson, Adlai (b. Los Angeles, 5 Feb. 1900; d. 14 July 1965)
US; Governor of Illinois 1949–53, Democratic presidential candidate 1952, 1956

Stevenson took a BA at Princeton University and an LL B at Northwestern University in Evanston, Illinois. He practised law in Chicago. Following the election of President *Roosevelt in 1932, he was appointed special counsel to the Agricultural Adjustment Agency. He took a keen interest in foreign policy issues. He was actively involved in the Council on Foreign Relations in Chicago. He opposed isolationism in the 1930s and became a member of the Committee to Defend America by Aiding the Allies.

In 1941 he was appointed special assistant to Secretary of the Navy Frank Knox. In 1945 he was appointed personal assistant to Secretary of State Edward Stettinns. He headed the American delegation to the meeting of the Preparatory Commission of the United Nations in London in 1945 and acted as senior adviser to the American delegation to the first session of the United Nations General Assembly in London in 1946.

In 1948 he was elected Governor of Illinois. He implemented important reforms of the corrupt state administration, substituting a merit system in place of political appointments. He attacked organized gambling interests, boosted education, and extended the state highway system.

In 1952 he became the Democratic nominee for President. He was reluctant to be the candidate, but his accomplishments as an effective reformer as Governor and his expertise in foreign affairs led him to be drafted. He lost heavily, however, to his Republican opponent, Dwight D. *Eisenhower. He resumed law practice in Illinois.

In 1956 he was again the presidential candidate of the Democratic Party. Although the Democrats had regained control of Congress in 1954 and increased their majority in Congress in 1956, he was overwhelmed in the presidential election by Eisenhower, who retained immense personal popularity.

In 1960 he again sought the Democratic nomination. He resented the ambitious drive for the Democratic nomination by John F. *Kennedy, while Kennedy's supporters resented his unwillingness to stand aside and give his full support to Kennedy. After the Democratic victory in 1960, Kennedy considered him as a candidate for Secretary of State, but, partly due to his hesitant support in the campaign, he was passed over in favour of Dean *Rusk. He was instead given the less significant post of American ambassador to the United Nations. He conducted himself with distinction at the United Nations. During the Cuban missile crisis in October 1962 he displayed great skill in demonstrating Soviet mendacity in their emplacement of nuclear missiles in Cuba with a dramatic presentation of photographic evidence. He played an important role in winning the support or at least neutrality of Third World countries in the Cuban missile crisis.

Stevenson was revered by liberal intellectuals in the 1950s. His self-deprecating wit and keen intelligence won him enthusiastic supporters in educated circles. He lacked the common touch, however, which was required to mount a successful presidential campaign. Moreover, his critique of the 1950s as a decade of complacency in domestic affairs and confrontation in foreign affairs had some merit, but his proposed alternative policies on such issues as civil rights and aid to developing countries were relatively limited.

Stewart, Robert **Michael** Maitland (b. London, 6 Nov. 1906; d. 10 Mar. 1993)

British; Foreign Secretary 1965–6, 1968–70; Baron (life peer) 1979

Stewart was educated at Christ's Hospital and St John's College, Oxford, before working as a schoolteacher and Workers' Educational Association lecturer in the 1930s. He served in the army during the Second World War, reaching the rank of captain.

After unsuccessful candidatures in 1931 and 1935 he entered the House of Commons in 1945 and sat as a Labour MP (first for Fulham and then Hammersmith) until 1979. He held several junior ministerial posts in Clement *Attlee's Labour government (1945–51) and was thus one of the limited number of members with ministerial experience when Labour again took office in 1964.

Stewart was a member of the Cabinet throughout Harold *Wilson's government (1964–70), and held numerous posts. His first appointment was as Secretary of State for Education and Science, but he remained there for only three months before being promoted to the foreign secretaryship in a reshuffle made necessary by Patrick *Gordon Walker's resignation. Seventeen months later he was moved again—this time to take George *Brown's place as First Secretary of State and Secretary of State for Economic Affairs. A year later, the latter post was transferred to Peter Shore, and after a further seven months in the non-portfolio first secretarship alone Brown's resignation resulted in his return to the Foreign Office.

The frequency with which Stewart was moved between departments precluded his making a major mark in any of them. He was known as a capable administrator and a 'safe pair of hands' rather than as a policy initiator. He also often had to defend the government's less popular policies, such as (at the DEA) the statutory regulation of prices and incomes and (at the Foreign Office) its stance on Vietnam. He lost his place as a frontbencher when Labour went into Opposition. Before retiring from the Commons in 1979 he served as a select committee chairman and, briefly, as a member of the European parliament.

Stikker, Dirk Uipko (b. Winschoten, 5 Feb. 1897; d. Wassenaar, 24 Dec. 1979)

Netherlandish; Foreign Minister 1948–52, Secretary-General of NATO

Having studied law in Groningen, Stikker occupied different functions in banking between 1922 and 1935. He then became a managing director of Heineken's Breweries in Amsterdam (1935–48). Engaged in international expansion, he was introduced to the word of international economical and political affairs. In that period he was also a member of the board of directors of the Nederlandse Bank and some other companies. From 1939 on he was chairman of the Netherlands Employer's Organization. During the war he was actively engaged in secret consultations with leaders of different employers' and workers' unions. This led to the establishment of the Netherlands Foundation of Labour under his presidency in 1945 which was to play a great role in improving labour relations and ensuring economic reconstruction in the Netherlands after 1945.

In 1945–6 he took the initiative for a reorganization of the pre-war Liberal Party into a new Partij van de Vrijheid (Party for Freedom). Two years later he led the merger of this party into the new Party for Freedom and Democracy (VVD). From 1945 till 1948 he was a member of the Upper House. In 1948 he was appointed Minister of Foreign Affairs in the first *Drees government, one of the first non-diplomats to serve in this post. From 1950 to 1952 he was chairman of the OEEC. During his four-year term as Cabinet minister the internationally minded Stikker increasingly clashed with his party on policies relating to the Netherlands Indies, and later concerning New Guinea. In 1952 Stikker left national politics for an international career. He became Dutch ambassador in London until 1958 (also representing the Netherlands in Iceland from 1954). In 1955 he was Chairman of the Netherlands delegation to the Economic and Social Council of the UN. From 1958 to 1961 he was the Netherlands Permanent Representative on the North Atlantic Council and to the OEEC in Paris. His international reputation grew. Notwithstanding French opposition, he became Secretary-General of NATO in 1961, a post he had to resign for health reasons in 1964. Thereafter he lived as a private citizen in Italy for some years. He returned to the Netherlands in 1972.

Stockton, Viscount *see* MACMILLAN, MAURICE HAROLD

Stolypin, Pyotr Arkadievich (b. Dresden, 14 Apr. 1862; d. Kiev, 18 Sept. 1911)
Russian; Minister of the Interior and Prime Minister 1906–11

A member of the provincial landowning nobility, Stolypin served as Governor of Grodno (1902) and Saratov (1903), where he attracted the Tsar's attention by his combination of understanding and firmness in dealing with peasant revolts. Made Interior Minister in May 1906, he became in addition Prime Minister in July at the early age of 44. An energetic, impressive man and a good orator, he appealed to the Tsar and to moderate conservatives. His moral prestige was enhanced by an attack on his home in August 1906, after which he instituted a series of summary trials of terrorists.

Failing to secure the co-operation of the deputies for his reforms he dissolved the Second Duma in June 1907 on the excuse of an alleged plot by Social Democrat deputies. He proceeded to drastically restrict the franchise, quite unconstitutionally, but the resultant Third Duma, though dominated by the centre-right, was not much more amenable. His arrogance and indifference to constitutionality were revealed again in March 1911. The Council of State (Upper Chamber) rejected a proposal to extend the Zemstva (local councils) to the Polish-Russian borderlands. Stolypin forced the Tsar, by threatening to resign, to prorogue both houses of the Duma for three days in order to pass his measure by emergency decree, while at the same time removing from the capital the measure's main opponents. This high-handed action brought Stolypin the hostility of the Duma and caused deep offence to the Tsar. Stolypin would probably soon have been dismissed, but was mortally wounded by a Socialist-Revolutionary terrorist at a theatre in Kiev in September 1911.

Although somewhat idealized by some contemporary Russians as the man who might have saved Russia from Bolshevism by his combination of reform and strong leadership, Stolypin was a highly contradictory character. His greatest achievements were in agricultural reform. He aimed at a 'wager on the strong', i.e. the creation of an independent peasantry which would become a bulwark for the reformed autocracy. He made it possible for ex-serfs to buy themselves out of the peasant commune and for small strips to be consolidated into capitalist farms, aided by loans from the Peasant Land Bank. About two million households (about one-eighth of the total) took advantage of these arrangements before 1916, many moving into the less populated Siberia and Central Asia. But the policy was not a panacea.

Other areas of his policy were more controversial. He made deliberate use of Russian nationalism to strengthen his support with the élite, especially in Poland and Finland, where Russification was stepped up. But his more 'liberal' reforms (extending religious freedoms to Jews and other groups; welfare legislation; changes in local government) alienated key groups in the nobility. He suffered from being neither a true conservative nor a true reformer and from having weak political skills, and his insensitivity to constitutionalism and democratic pressures frustrated the implementation of his reform programme.

Stoph, Willi (b. Berlin, 9 July 1914)

German; chairman of the Council of Ministers of the GDR 1964–73, 1976–89, head of state 1973–6

As chairman of the Council of Ministers (the government) of the German Democratic Republic (GDR) from 1964 to 1973, and again from 1976 to 1989, and head of state 1973–6, Stoph was prominent as the public face of the regime. Yet he was always overshadowed in real power by the general secretary of the ruling SED, first *Ulbricht and then *Honecker.

Born into a Berlin working-class family, after elementary school he completed an apprenticeship as a bricklayer. Although he had joined the Communist youth movement and the party (KPD), he served from 1935 to 1937 in the artillery of *Hitler's new Wehrmacht rising to the rank of corporal. During the war he served again and took advantage of Soviet 're-education' camps to secure early repatriation.

In 1945 Stoph joined the re-established KPD and was soon given a number of leading positions in the building and basic industries. By 1950 he was a member of the Central Committee of the ruling Socialist Unity Party (SED). Two years later he was appointed Minister of the Interior, where he remained until serving as first Minister of Defence, 1956–60. He was a member of the ruling Politburo from 1953 onwards. To have gone so far so fast Stoph must have enjoyed the confidence of the Soviets; he must also have been an Ulbricht supporter. It was Ulbricht who appointed him as chairman of the Council of Ministers in 1964.

Ulbricht reduced the power of the government in favour of the collective head of state, the Council of State, which he himself headed. The Council of Ministers was largely reduced to dealing with the economy. This helped to turn Stoph against Ulbricht. He threw in his lot with Honecker when the latter ousted Ulbricht in 1971. However, Honecker moved him to the chairmanship of the Council of State, with its powers trimmed, in 1973. Economic difficulties forced Honecker to reinstate Stoph at the Council of Ministers in 1976. The two remained rivals and Stoph was talked about as a possible successor. When *Krenz succeeded Honecker in 1989 he kept Stoph on for a few weeks until all the old guard were forced to retire.

Strauss, Franz Josef (b. Munich, 6 Sept. 1915; d. 3 Oct. 1988)

German; Minister-President of Bavaria 1978–88, leader of the CSU 1961–88

Strauss was one of the most colourful, respected, and feared of the post-war generation of German politicians. In the 1980 election he was the CDU/CSU candidate for German Chancellor. The party's vote fell from 48.6 per cent in 1976 to 44.5 per cent. Only in his native Bavaria did he improve their vote. His campaign was marked with violent and abusive rhetoric by him and against him.

The son of a Catholic butcher, Strauss achieved the best grammar school matriculation exam (*Abitur*) in the whole of Bavaria in 1935. He studied the classics as well as economics and qualified as a grammar schoolteacher. However, the war intervened and, like *Schmidt, he served as a lieutenant of anti-aircraft artillery. In 1945 he was a founder member of the (Bavarian) Christian Social Union (CSU). He rose rapidly and by 1948 was in charge of the party machine. In 1961 he was elected chairman of the CSU and retained this position until his death.

Strauss was elected to the Bundestag in 1949, and *Adenauer appointed him Minister for Special Tasks in 1953. His title changed in 1955 to Minister for Atomic Policy, in which capacity he achieved agreement that West Germany could build nuclear reactors for peaceful purposes. In 1956 he took over the (virtually new) Defence Ministry, playing an important role in building up the not very popular Bundeswehr. He had long been on bad terms with the influential weekly *Der Spiegel* and he initiated a police raid on the paper on alleged security grounds. This greatly shocked public opinion and he was dismissed in 1962. He bounced back in 1966 as Finance Minister in the *Kiesinger–*Brandt grand coalition. He clashed with Professor (of economics) Karl Schiller (SPD), Minister for Economic Affairs, but the two left the economy better than they found it in 1969.

In opposition, Strauss accused the leaders of the sister CDU of being too soft on the government. He threatened to set up the CSU throughout the Federal Republic, bullying his colleagues to propose him as their Chancellor candidate. After that failure Strauss fought on from Munich. He had been elected Minister-President of Bavaria in 1978 and he attempted to pursue an independent foreign policy, visiting Chile, South Africa, East Berlin, and Moscow. He had a personal relationship with the East German leader *Honecker, securing a massive loan for East Germany. He also attempted to influence the Bonn government through the Bundesrat, the upper chamber of the German parliament. Since 1989 rumours have circulated that he co-operated with the East German secret police, the *Stasi*. As yet no conclusive evidence has been made public to confirm them.

Stresemann, Gustav (b. Berlin, 10 May 1878; d. 3 Oct. 1929)

German; Chancellor 1923, Foreign Minister 1923–9

Stresemann was the youngest member elected to the Reichstag in 1908 but, although seen as a rising star of the National Liberals, he lost his seat in the election of 1912. In 1914 he was returned and, due to the absence on war service of the National Liberal Leader Ernst Bassermann, he was able to take over as leader of the parliamentary group. He supported the government's imperialist ambitions and Ludendorff's virtual dictatorship. He rejected the revolution of 1918 and looked for a restoration of the monarchy. These views very nearly ended his political career. By 1920 he had founded the German People's Party which, despite the name, represented only a section of the propertied middle class. In 1920 with 15.1 per cent of the vote it was the third largest party. It saw itself as a bridge between the National Right and the democrats.

Stresemann served briefly as Chancellor and Foreign Minister in 1923 and then under *Marx, Luther, and *Müller as Foreign Minister. He failed as Chancellor because he proved too right-wing for his SPD ministers. As Foreign Minister he was more successful. He wanted Germany restored to its frontiers of 1914, but sought to achieve this by patient diplomacy rather than by threats of violence. He hoped to win over the more conciliatory Americans and British against the French in his negotiations. The agreements over the *Dawes Plan (1924) and the Young Plan (1929), which regulated German reparations payments in exchange for Allied concessions over the occupation of the Rhineland, were seen as his successes even though they were bitterly opposed by the right in Germany. At Locarno in October 1925 the post-war frontiers between France, Belgium, and Germany were guaranteed. Agreement over the demilitarization of the Rhineland was also reached. The Kellogg–Briand Pact (August 1928) was initially an agreement between the foreign ministers of the USA (Frank *Kellogg) and France (Aristide *Briand) renouncing war as an instrument of national policy. It was subsequently signed by sixty-five states. Finally, under the Berlin Treaty (April 1926), Germany and the Soviet Union agreed to remain neutral in a conflict between either of them and a third party. Stresemann was recognized internationally, gaining (with Briand) the Nobel Prize for Peace in 1926. However, his achievements were short-lived. The Young Plan gave *Hitler and the nationalists the chance to wage a referendum campaign against the 'sell-out', which they lost, but which gave the Nazi leader more respectability among the monarchists.

Stroessner, Alfredo (b. Encarnación, Paraguay, 3 Nov. 1912)

Paraguayan; Commander-in-Chief of the armed forces 1951–4, President of the Republic 1954–89

The son of a German immigrant, Stroessner pursued a military career and fought in the Chaco War (1932–5) against Bolivia. He supported the victorious Partido Colorado during the 1947 Revolution and during the subsequent factional in-fighting in the party rose rapidly by adroitly switching his allegiances. In so doing, he capitalized on the United States Cold War fears about the spread of Communism. In May–June 1953 he visited the United States and the Panama Canal Zone at the invitation of the US Army. On 4 May 1954 he ousted Chaves from the presidency in a complex military uprising. He was chosen as the candidate of the Partido Colorado in presidential elections on 11 July in which he was the sole candidate. Significantly, on assuming the presidency he retained his position as Commander-in Chief of the armed forces.

The longevity of his regime depended on the tripartite alliance which he forged, as President of the Republic, with the armed forces and the Partido Colorado. Together they developed a symbiotic relationship, which was overseen by Stroessner in his capacity as Head of State, Commander-in-Chief of the Armed Forces, and Honorary President of the Colorado Party.

The regime dealt effectively with social discontent through an adroit mixture of co-option and repression. Stroessner maintained the façade of democracy in the form of a parliamentary system, comprising several political parties and regular elections. This was an important factor in its strategy of legitimization, both in the domestic and international arenas. Presidential elections were contested by legalized but tame opposition parties, the activities of which were severely circumscribed by the workings of the corporativist state. The consolidation of the regime was also facilitated by close relations with the United States which provided Stroessner with international support and substantial amounts of foreign aid. In return, Stroessner adopted a fierce anti-Communist posture internationally, which also provided a convenient pretext for harsh repression of dissidents at home.

A strong personality cult developed around the figure of Stroessner, despite his singular lack of charisma. However, Stroessner did not conform to the stereotyped image of the Latin American *caudillo*. The Stroessner cult emphasized not only his dull persona, but, more significantly, the importance of the alliance between the Colorado Party and armed forces to the maintenance of the 'peace and progress' of his regime. The most serious of several attempts on his life occurred in November 1974 when a car bomb was discovered near the headquarters of the Partido Colorado where he was due to attend an official reception.

The visit of Pope Paul in May 1988 focused international attention for the first time on the authoritarian nature of the Stroessner regime. Disagreements over the papal itinerary led to a sharp deterioration in relations with the Catholic church. The United States government became increasingly frustrated by Stroessner's refusal to engage in political liberalization. The economic situation also deteriorated, alienating the previously docile private sector, as growing corruption and over-staffing within the public administration led to a serious fiscal imbalance, inflationary spiral, and soaring foreign debt.

On 2 February 1989 he was overthrown in a putsch led by his military aide, General Andrés Rodríguez. He was allowed to fly to Brazil, where he was granted political asylum. He was the longest-serving head of state in Latin American history and the third longest-serving political leader in the world during the post-war period, after *Kim Il Sung of North Korea and Todor *Zhivkov of Bulgaria. He was also the longest-serving president in Paraguayan history.

Suárez González, Adolfo (b. Cebreros, Avila, 25 Sept. 1932)

Spanish; Prime Minister 1976–81

Widely seen as one of the principal architects of Spain's post-Franco transition to democracy, Adolfo Suárez first achieved political prominence as vice-secretary-general (1961–4) of the dictatorship's National Movement. Educated at the University of Madrid, from where he received a doctorate in law, he subsequently became director-general of the national broadcasting network (1965–73), before being appointed director of the National Movement on *Franco's death in 1975. A few months later, in July 1976, he was picked by King Juan Carlos to replace the Francoist loyalist Carlos Arias Navarro as Prime Minister. The move was greeted with considerable surprise, but turned out to be an inspired choice as Suárez set about dismantling the Franco dictatorship through a series of bold and imaginative initiatives. In particular, his Political Reform Law of November 1976 entailed the Francoist parliament voting itself out of existence and paved the way for free elections in June 1977, the first to be held in Spain in more than forty years.

His negotiating skills, allied to a telegenic image, helped ensure that he emerged victorious in the elections at the head of the Union of the Democratic Centre (UCD), a broad coalition of non-socialist forces, many of which had been associated with reformist elements within the Franco regime. As premier, Suárez steered through the 1978 constitution, a masterpiece of political compromise which laid the institutional foundations of Spain's successful transition to democracy. However, the constitutional settlement proved to be Suárez's political high point. Re-elected in 1979, he found it increasingly difficult to hold together the various strands which made up the UCD: once the goal of constitutional design had been achieved, increasingly bitter in-fighting developed within the party.

Although an accomplished negotiator face to face, Suárez was uncomfortable in parliamentary debates and came to avoid them, often going months without attending parliament, and even missing Cabinet meetings. Growing disillusionment with factionalism within the UCD led to his resignation as Prime Minister in January 1981. Soon after he left the UCD and set up a new party, the Democratic and Social Centre (CDS), to contest the 1982 general elections. In its first five years, the CDS tried to carve out a distinctive centre-left identity, then allied in municipal elections with the right-wing opposition against the now ruling Socialist Party, before claiming to stand to the left of the Socialists at the 1987 European elections. In 1990, Suárez—who had been elected a year earlier as president of the Liberal and Progressive International—entered an informal pact with the Socialist government, before resigning as party leader two years later and abandoning politics altogther. His descent into political obscurity was as unexpected as it was rapid, yet his contribution to the establishment of democracy in Spain remains extraordinary.

Suharto, Thojib N. J. (*also* Raden) (b. Kemusu, Yogjakarta, 8 June 1921)
Indonesian; President 1968–

Trained in the military school at Gombong (Central Java) for service in the Dutch colonial army, Suharto commanded a Japanese-sponsored defence force during the Japanese occupation (1942–5) and distinguished himself in the armed struggle against the Dutch (1945–9).

Under the Republic he rose to the rank of major-general in 1962 and Chief of Army Staff in 1965. Being strongly anti-Communist, he played a key part in the army's counter-coup against the attempt by the PKI (Communist Party) to seize power on 30 September 1965. During the following eighteen months of domestic violence, in which the death toll particularly amongst Communists and the Chinese community probably amounted to 500,000, Suharto consolidated his position, acquiring the powers of Achmed *Sukarno in two stages (March 1966 and February 1967) and assuming the title of President on 27 March 1968. Suharto then set about establishing a 'new order', to distinguish the regime from that of Sukarno, and he has been re-elected to office at five-yearly intervals.

As the 'new order' stabilized so the balance of Indonesian 'non-alignment' shifted from the Communist world. Suharto ended 'Konfrontasi' with Malaysia in March 1966, rejoined the UN, and worked closely with the USA as well as with neighbouring members of the Association of South East Asian Nations (formed in 1967). Western aid assisted economic recovery, which was further boosted by buoyant oil revenues from the mid-1970s. The collapse of the oil boom in the mid-1980s, however, led to inflation and government indebtedness, while expenditure on welfare programmes could not keep pace with demographic growth (the population is likely to be 220 million by the year 2000).

In response to the diversity of the Indonesian archipelago as well as economic grievances and social protest, Suharto has employed virtually dictatorial powers. Having eliminated the PKI in the late 1960s, he has purged the military and the bureaucracy, curbed Islamic fundamentalists, managed electoral success (through the *Selker Golkar*, joint secretariat of functional groups), manipulated corruption, detained thousands of political prisoners, and ruthlessly repressed regional unrest. He has also been impervious to international protests over deforestation, human rights, and military action in East Timor, the former Portuguese colony which was incorporated within the Indonesian Republic in 1975–6. Despite challenges to its authority, the regime of Raden Suharto has proved to be remarkably durable.

Sukarno, Achmed (b. Surabaya, 6 June 1901; d. 21 June 1970)
Indonesian; President 1945–68

Son of a Muslim Javanese teacher and his Balinese wife, Sukarno was educated in his father's school, in the European school system, and at the Technical College in Bandung (1921–6), where he trained as an engineer and became imbued with radical, secular nationalism against Dutch colonialism.

After the PKI (Communist Party) was crushed in 1926–7 and with the Islamic party in disarray, Sukarno formed the Indonesian Nationalist Party (PNI) in 1927. It was the first major party committed to the achievement of national unity and independence through mass participation and non-cooperation. Sukarno was interned by the Dutch in 1929–31 and rearrested in 1933 when he was exiled to Flores and later to Sumatra.

Released by the Japanese in 1942, Sukarno co-operated with them in the hope that they would assist the nationalist movement. Military reverses and Indonesian unrest forced the Japanese to make plans for the transfer of power but these were overtaken by Japan's surrender on 15 August 1945. On 17 August Sukarno and Dr Hatta proclaimed Indonesian independence.

In the subsequent four-year struggle against the restoration of Dutch control, Sukarno straddled divisions within the republican movement, oscillated between military and diplomatic methods, and benefited from the support of the USA and UN. When in December 1949 the Dutch surrendered claims to sovereignty, Sukarno continued the quest for national unity. His 'Pancasila' (five principles) were intended as an ideological umbrella under which all Indonesians might gather, while his sponsorship of the 'non-aligned movement' at the Bandung Conference (April 1955) was presented as a blow against European 'neo-colonialism' and the 'imperialism' of super powers.

The diversity of the vast archipelago, political factionalism, and rebellions in Sumatra and Sulawesi led Sukarno in 1957 to seek political balance through 'Guided Democracy'. Neither his charismatic leadership nor his manipulative skills, however, could achieve stability which was further undermined by galloping inflation. Increasingly hostile to Western capitalism, Sukarno embarked on foreign adventures (notably 'Konfrontasi' with Malaysia, 1963–6), withdrew from the UN (January 1965) and moved closer to China. Meanwhile, the contest between Communist and non-Communist forces in Indonesia culminated in the coup and counter-coup of September–October 1965 which brought the military to power and plunged the country into bloodshed. This crisis effectively ended Sukarno's regime, though it was not until March 1968 that he was formally replaced as President by General *Suharto.

Sun Yatsen (b. Xiangshan, Guangdong Province, 12 Nov. 1866; d. 12 Mar. 1925)

Chinese; Revolutionary leader and theoretician, first provisional President of post-Imperial China 1911, Founder and first leader of the Kuomintang

Sun Yatsen, who is widely regarded as being the father of modern Chinese nationalism, was originally named Sun Wen, and is known throughout the mandarin-speaking world as Sun Zhongshan. Sun was born in Xiangshan (now called Zhongshan in his honour) in the southern Chinese province of Guangdong on 12 November 1866. Xiangshan was fertile ground for a young revolutionary. The extreme poverty of the average peasant contrasted starkly with the ostentatious wealth of the foreigners and Chinese collaborators. Xiangshan had also provided many emigrants to the San Francisco gold rush. Despite constant complaints about the awful conditions on the transport ships (100 out of 500 'passengers' died on one shipment in 1854) and in America, the imperial system refused to intervene, which exacerbated existing anti-imperial sentiments. It also created a hostile overseas-Chinese community in America that Sun was later to able to exploit to support his revolutionary aims.

Xiangshan also provided shelter for many veterans of the Taiping Rebellion, an anti-imperial movement that defeated government forces across southern China and did much to weaken the Qing Dynasty between 1850 and 1864. Indeed, Sun's first teacher was a Taiping veteran, and he developed a lifelong admiration for the rebels, and especially for their leader Hong Xiuquan. Like Hong, Sun also became a Christian, and was educated in a Western Christian tradition, ultimately specializing in Western medicine in Hong Kong. In many ways Sun was remarkably atypically Chinese—he did not even speak particularly good mandarin Chinese, and always felt more at home with other East Asians or the overseas Chinese in America than he did with the Chinese in China. Furthermore, his political ideas owed much more to the French Revolution, Social Darwinism, and the Meiji Reformers in Japan, than they did to traditional Chinese political thought.

Whilst his revolutionary influence was enormous, Sun was not a particularly good revolutionary himself. His two attempts to lead anti-imperial uprisings in southern China in October 1895 and October 1901 were abject failures. After the first occasion, Sun was forced into exile in America and later Britain, where he was kidnapped/arrested by the Chinese legation. When the British government threatened severe diplomatic retribution, Sun was released. His story became international news, and Sun used his new-found fame to promote his political causes. Indeed, Sun's real political strengths lay in organization and mobilization for the revolutionary cause, primarily outside China. He spent years travelling the world trying to raise support (and funds) from the growing number of overseas Chinese, and from supportive foreign groups.

Sun recognized the need to establish as broad a political base as possible, and this in turn meant developing an inclusionary ideological basis for his revolution. This ideology became enshrined in 'The Three Principles of the People', which advocated the end of imperial rule and the promotion of nationalism, democracy, and people's livelihood (*min sheng*). The Three Principles remain the ideological basis of the Chinese nationalists (Kuomintang) in Taiwan, but the vagueness of particularly the third principle is shown by the way that the Chinese Communists equate people's livelihood with socialism. While Sun may not be happy that his portrait appears alongside those of *Mao, *Stalin, *Lenin, Marx, and Engels at official celebrations in Beijing, his ideas and principles were deliberately left open to different interpretations. Thus, for the British establishment, nationalism did not mean removing British influence from Hong Kong, but for radical Chinese and Japanese nationalists it did; for socialists, people's livelihood did indeed mean socialism, but for capitalists with money to support the revolution it meant something else.

In the end, however, nothing may have come from Sun's endeavours had it not been for support from Japan. By the end of the nineteenth century, Japanese authorities had decided that the best way of increasing their influence over China was to foster the next generation of Chinese leaders. Disillusioned and defeated Chinese reformers like Liang Qichao were joined in Japan by many of the brightest and best from all over China, who had been sent to Japan to learn the new skills of statecraft and military strategy. While in Japan, they came into contact with the works of Western political theories and theorists which they then sent back to their friends in China. It was in this political environment that Sun established the Chinese Revolutionary Alliance (*tongmenghui*) in July 1905 in exile in Japan, committed to both the establishment of a republic, and the removal of Western colonial influence in China.

It was the revolutionary alliance which nominally carried out the revolution in 1911 that overthrew the old imperial order. In reality, the empire had long ceased to function as an effective central government, and the real locus of power had passed to newly strong provincial leaders. What happened in 1911 was the final stage in a decade-long transfer of power from empire to province, and while the revolutionary alliance did help finally topple the empire, Sun Yatsen himself was not involved. However, Sun returned to China where he was elected as the first provisional President of the new republic based in Nanjing, and transformed the old revolutionary alliance into a new political party, the Kuomintang or Nationalist Party.

The Nationalists won the subsequent election, but the fledgling republic was thrown into chaos by Yuan Shikai, a key military leader who was determined to assume control. He declared the elections null and void, and ultimately declared himself the new Emperor, a title and position which few people ever acknowledged. The new system fell into chaos as Sun and the Kuomintang established their own rival provisional government in Guangdong. From 1913 to his death in 1925, Sun spent the remainder of his life fighting ever more divisive and destructive internecine warfare with various fragments of the Kuomintang as China slid into a period of warlordism where might, and not ideas, held sway. The fact that he managed to hold the party together at all says much about his organizational and tactical capabilities. The fact that Sun is still revered on both sides of the Taiwan Straits also bears testament to his significance. However, both China and the Kuomintang were in turmoil when Sun died, and it was left to others to build a new party and a new China after his death.

Suslov, Mikhail Andreevich (b. Saratov province, 21 Nov. 1902; d. Moscow, 25 Jan. 1982)

Russian; member of the Central Committee 1941–82 and Secretary 1947–50, 1952–82, 'Second Secretary' 1964–82

Born into a peasant family, Suslov was sent by the party to study in Moscow, later attending the Plekhanov Institute and the Institute of Red Professors. In 1931 he joined the party's Central Control Commission, helping to purge the Urals region. In 1937–9 he was secretary of the Rostov-on-Don Regional Committee and 1939–44 secretary of Stavropol Krai, in both areas being responsible for crushing dissent, in particular organizing the deportation of many 'disloyal' nationalities from the Caucasus. He headed the party Bureau in Lithuania 1944–6, where he organized mass executions and deportations. In 1947 *Stalin made him Agitprop Secretary and in 1948 a candidate member of the Politbureau. He drew up the indictment for Yugoslavia's expulsion from the Cominform and succeeded *Zhdanov as Soviet Cominform representative later in 1948. In 1949–50 he edited *Pravda* and in 1950 joined the Presidium of the Supreme Soviet. In 1952 he regained his post of Central Committee Secretary and became a full member of the Presidium (Politbureau).

After Stalin's death in 1953 he lost his seat on the Presidium, but in 1955 after the fall of *Malenkov regained full Politbureau membership, supervising policy on ideology and relations with foreign Communist parties. In 1956 he was responsible for crushing 'counter-revolution' in Eastern Europe, especially in Hungary, but in 1957 helped *Khrushchev defeat the 'Anti-Party Group'. He came to disagree with Khrushchev's style of government and policies and in 1964 plotted with *Brezhnev to oust him.

When Brezhnev became leader Suslov became *de facto* 'second secretary', wielding enormous influence on ideology, personnel, and foreign policy. He supported the crackdown on dissent but argued against military intervention in Czechoslovakia in 1968. He supported the invasion of Afghanistan in 1979 and the crackdown in Poland in 1981. On his death in 1982 he was buried next to Stalin.

Sverdlov, Yakov Mikhailovich (b. Nizhny Novgorod (Gorky), 4 June 1885; d. 16 Mar. 1919)

Russian; head of state 1917–19

Sverdlov was the son of a Jewish engraver. He joined the Russian Social Democratic Labour Party (RSDLP) in 1901 and became active in the underground, taking advantage of his father's printing facilities. He sided with *Lenin and the Bolsheviks after the RSDLP split in 1903, and became a member of the Party's Central Committee in 1913. Often under arrest, he was exiled in Siberia when the February Revolution broke out in 1917. He went to Petrograd where the Bolshevicks utilized his impressive organizational abilities. Sverdlov was completely loyal to Lenin and in the 'July Days' of 1917 was Bolshevik leader when Lenin and his associates were in hiding. After the October Revolution he became a party secretary and chairman of the Bolsheviks' All Russian Central Executive Committee (VTsIK) and as such head of state. He was closely involved in the organization of party control throughout Russia, and was a member of the commission which prepared the Soviet constitution of 1918. Habitually dressing in a leather coat, he set the fashion for the commissars of the 1920s. He died during the influenza epidemic in spring 1919.

Svoboda, Ludvík (b. near Bratislava, 15 Nov. 1895; d. 20 Sept. 1979)

Slovak; President of Czechoslovakia 1968–75

Svoboda fought in the Czech Legion on the Eastern Front at the end of the First World War. He joined the new Czechoslovak army after his return home in 1919. In

1939 he fled to the Soviet Union. At the end of 1943 he was appointed commander of the Czechoslovak Army Corps attached to the Red Army and his forces helped the Red Army liberate Czechoslovakia in 1944. He was appointed Minister of Defence in *Beneš's coalition government and held this post until 1950. Beneš and the non-Communist ministers of his government were not aware that Svoboda was a secret Communist. He played a part in the Communist seizure of power in February 1948, by keeping the army demobilized, and joined the Communist Party later in the year. Svoboda disappeared from public life at the beginning of 1952. *Stalin had become suspicious of him and he was briefly imprisoned. After his release he worked as an accountant in an agricultural collective. In 1963 *Khrushchev built up Svoboda's image as a Communist hero because of his exploits in the Second World War. In 1965 the *Brezhnev regime made him a Hero of the Soviet Union; he became a Hero of the Czechoslovak Republic at the same time. On 30 March 1968 he was elected President, replacing *Novotný, and worked closely with *Dubček in support of the reforms of the 'Prague Spring'. After the Warsaw Pact intervention in Czechoslovakia in August 1968 Svoboda was taken to Moscow along with the other reformist members of the party leadership, where they defended their reforms in the face of Brezhnev's threats. Svoboda remained in office until the beginning of 1975 when he retired on grounds of ill-health. Throughout this period he was only a figurehead.

Symington, William **Stuart** (b. Amherst, Massachusetts, 26 June 1901; d. 14 Dec. 1988)

US; Secretary of the Air Force 1947–50, US Senator 1953–76

Symington was born the son of an academic who later changed career to become a judge in Baltimore. After brief service in the First World War, Symington attended Yale but left without finishing his degree. He embarked on a successful business career and in 1939 he became chairman of the Emerson Electric Manufacturing Co. in St Louis.

Symington held a series of government positions in the *Truman administration: he was successively chairman of the Surplus Property Board, Assistant Secretary of War for Air, and the First Secretary of the Air Force. Symington was a powerful advocate for increased defence spending both within the Truman administration (when he resigned over cuts in the air force budget) and later in the Senate, where he criticized the *Eisenhower administration's defence spending cuts.

Symington was first elected to the Senate in 1952 when he defeated a candidate backed by Truman in the primary. Although Eisenhower carried Missouri in 1952, Symington easily beat the Republican candidate. He was part of a new group of Senate Democrats—liberal in outlook and wedded to the New Deal and Fair Deal platforms. Symington won re-election three more times.

In the Senate his major interests were foreign affairs, military issues, and defence policy. His early career in the Senate was marked by conflict with Senator Joseph *McCarthy. As a member of the Subcommittee on Investigations, Symington played a key role in deflating McCarthy's reputation during the army–McCarthy hearings.

Although a supporter of enhanced military expenditure, Symington was always conscious of the need to reconcile military imperatives with the requirements of a constitutional democracy. Originally supportive of American intervention in Vietnam, he became highly critical of the *Nixon administration's handling of the Vietnam War and especially its expansion into Laos and Cambodia. Part of his objection centred on the secrecy surrounding the Nixon administration's policy and he was an important influence in changing opinion in the Senate on the issue. He also came to believe that the United States was overcommitted in the world and that it should curtail its military and economic involvement.

On domestic issues he was a liberal, advocating enhanced walfare spending and measures such as gun control and a woman's right to an abortion.

Symington ran for President twice–in 1956 and in 1960 when he was also a strong contender for the vice-presidential slot. He retired from Congress in 1975.

Taft, Robert (b. Cincinnati, Ohio, 8 Sept. 1889; d. 31 July 1953)
US; US Senator 1939–53

The son of President William Howard *Taft, he bore the most famous name in Ohio politics. He took a BA at Yale University and graduated at Harvard Law School. He served as assistant counsel for the US Food Administration under Herbert *Hoover in 1917–18 and worked also with Hoover in the American Relief Administration in Europe in 1919. After his return from Europe, he practised law in Ohio. He was deeply involved in the politics of the Republican Party in Ohio throughout his life. He served in the Ohio House of Representatives 1921–6, becoming Speaker in 1926, and in the Ohio Senate 1930–2. In 1938 he was elected to the US Senate and was re-elected in 1944 and 1950.

He took a conservative position and firmly opposed the New Deal. He was hostile to the growing power of organized labour. In 1947 he sponsored the Taft–Hartley Act, which banned the closed shop, permitted employers to sue unions for breach of contract and for damages during a strike or secondary boycott, and required an eighty-day cooling-off period before a strike. In foreign policy he took an isolationist stance throughout the 1930s and vehemently opposed such policies of President Franklin *Roosevelt as Lend-Lease, which in his view were certain to take America into war. After Pearl Harbor he abandoned his isolationist position as unrealistic and supported American involvement in the war. He continued to support American involvement in international affairs after the Second World War but with considerable qualifications. He was a hesitant and reluctant supporter of such policies as the *Marshall Plan and NATO.

He sought the Republican nomination for president unsuccessfully on three occasions, in 1940, 1948, and 1952. In 1952 he appeared to be the front runner for the Republican nomination but lost to Dwight D. *Eisenhower, one of whose strongest reasons for entering the race was to prevent the nomination of a candidate with a foreign policy position not far removed from isolationism.

With the Republican victory in 1952 in the Senate elections as well as the presidential election, he became Senate majority leader and worked well with President Eisenhower despite their previous rivalry for the presidential nomination and their ideological differences on foreign and domestic policy. In the summer of 1953, however, he died of cancer.

Known as 'Mr Republican', he was the embodiment of conservative, Midwestern, isolationist Republicanism. He won respect for his intelligence and diligence. But he was somewhat cold in personality and too far to the right of the mainstream to succeed in his father's footsteps to the presidency.

Taft, William Howard (b. Cincinnati, Ohio, 15 Sept. 1857; d. 8 Mar. 1930)
US; Solicitor-General 1890–2, Governor of the Philippines 1901–3, President 1909–13, Chief Justice of the Supreme Court 1921–30

Born into a family involved in law and politics—his grandfather and father were judges, his father having served also as a Cabinet member—Taft was educated at high school in Cincinnati and took his first degree at Yale, graduating second in a class of 121. He studied law at Cincinnati Law School and was admitted to the bar in Ohio in 1880. He served in a number of positions, primarily legal posts, before being appointed a judge of the Superior Court of Cincinnati in 1887. Three years later he was appointed Solicitor-General of the United States. In 1892 he was appointed a US circuit judge. Four years later he became a law professor at his old law school.

His rise to public prominence began in 1900 when President McKinley appointed him to chair a commission to establish civil government in the Philippines. A year later he was appointed Governor-General of the Philippines, a post in which he served with some distinction. He served for three years and returned to take up a Cabinet post as Secretary of War. Well liked and trusted by the President, Teddy *Roosevelt, he was Roosevelt's chosen successor and in 1908 he was the Republican nominee for the presidency. He won with a convincing majority—achieving 7.6 million votes to William Jennings *Bryan's 6.4 million—and was inaugurated on 4 March 1909. As President, he maintained Roosevelt's campaign against monopolies and encouraged 'dollar diplomacy' abroad, relying on trade rather than military power to spread American influence. A number of important acts were passed and a constitutional amendment—introducing a federal income tax—was achieved. However, Taft lacked Roosevelt's clout and dynamism and had difficulty controlling the more conservative elements in the Republican Party. In the 1910 mid-term elections, the Republicans lost control of the House of Representatives. Progressives in the Republican Party became disillusioned with Taft and relations between the President and his predecessor became strained. In 1912, Roosevelt ran as a Progressive candidate for the presidency, effectively splitting the Republican vote and letting the Democrat, Woodrow *Wilson, into office. Taft finished third in the race.

After leaving the White House, Taft returned to academic life, taking up the post of law professor at Yale and serving briefly as joint chairman of the National War Labor Board. He returned to judicial life in 1921. The new Republican President, Warren *Harding, nominated him to be Chief Justice of the United States Supreme Court. It was a post in which he was to serve for nine years. Though not a great jurist, he was an effective administrator and achieved reform of the federal judiciary. He wrote some important opinions for the court and felt thoroughly at ease on the nation's highest court. He resigned in February 1930, at the age of 72, because of a heart ailment, and died just over a month later.

Taft was a great man physically—he weighed in excess of 20 stone, the heaviest man ever to occupy the presidency—but not a great man politically. His greatest love was the law and he was at his happiest when serving on the bench. What took him away from the bench so often was his sense of duty, as well as his wife's ambition for him. His wife was the daughter of a judge but she wanted her husband to achieve prominence; she was the first First Lady to travel with her husband from the inauguration to the White House. Above all, Taft was a man who believed in service to his country. When called upon by the President to serve in a particular post, Taft responded to the call. While in the Philippines, he twice turned down the offer of a place on the Supreme Court because his work was not finished. He disliked confrontation and was distraught when his old friend Roosevelt turned against him. He was a patrician—he treated the Filipinos as people for whom he had a special responsibility (he spoke of them 'as my little brown brothers')—and had a friendly disposition. He always took in good spirits jokes about his ample girth. When, in the Philippines, he cabled to the Secretary of War that he had ridden 25 miles on horseback, he received the reply: 'How is the horse?'

Taft was not cut out for the rough and tumble of national politics. When he lost office, he admitted to feeling relieved and told his successor, 'I'm glad to be going. This is the lonesomest place in the world.' His enduring love was for the law and he achieved contentment late in life when he became Chief Justice. 'I love judges and I love courts,' he once declared, and in 1925 he wrote 'The truth is that in my present life I don't remember that I was ever President.' As President, he fulfilled the ambitions of his wife. As Chief Justice, he fulfilled his own.

Tanaka Kakuei (b. Niigata, 4 May 1918; d. 16 Dec. 1993)
Japanese; Prime Minister 1972–4

Tanaka was born into a poor family and received little formal education. He was conscripted into the Japanese army and served briefly in Manchuria. On his return to Japan he started his own construction business, which was to make him his personal fortune in the post-war rebuilding boom.

Tanaka was elected to the Diet in 1948 as a member of the Democratic Party in his home Niigata Prefecture and rose quickly to become Deputy Minister of Justice as a member of the Democratic Liberal Party in Prime Minister *Yoshida Shigeru's second Cabinet in 1955. He served as Minister for Postal Services under Kishi Nobusuke in 1957 and became Minister of Finance under Ikeda Hayato in 1962. In 1965 he became secretary-general of the Liberal Democratic Party (LDP) and proved to be a very powerful party manager and faction builder, forming the power base that was to serve him until his stroke in 1985. In 1971 he became Minister of the powerful Ministry of International Trade and Industry (MITI). From this position he seized control of the LDP ahead of his rival Fukuda Takeo following the resignation of long-serving Prime Minister *Satõ Eisaku over the China recognition crisis and became Japan's youngest Prime Minister at the age of 54.

Tanaka quickly visited Beijing and normalized relations with the PRC, but remained Prime Minister for only two years as he was forced to resign following revelations over tax evasion and the manipulation of his private business interests. In 1976 he was implicated in the Lockheed Bribery Scandal and accused of having received a 500 million yen bribe to ensure that Lockheed aircraft were purchased by All Nippon Airways. He was found guilty by a Tokyo court in October 1983, and was sentenced to four years in prison, but remained free on appeal until his death in 1993.

Although forced to resign from the LDP he remained in the Diet as an independent, and also remained in control of his powerful faction within the LDP and was instrumental in the removal of Fukuda Takeo and Miki Takeo from the office of Prime Minister and the appointment of Ohira Masayoshi, Suzuki Zenko, and *Nakasone Yasuhiro to that position. His popularity in his native Niigata remained undiminished, where he is widely regarded as having rescued the region from poverty and obscurity.

Tanaka was arguably the most powerful individual political figure in post-war Japan whose 'machine politics' dominated the ruling LDP throughout the 1970s and 1980s.

Tebbit, Norman Beresford (b. Enfield, 29 Mar. 1931)
British; Secretary of State for Employment 1981–3, Trade and Industry 1983–5, chairman of the Conservative Party and Chancellor of the Duchy of Lancaster 1985–7; Baron (life peer) 1992

Norman Tebbit came from a working-class background and was employed as an airline pilot (and trade union official) before he became an MP. He expressed direct, even abrasive, right-wing views on immigration, Europe, capital punishment, and welfare shirkers. He articulated populist authoritarian attitudes. For much of his political career he was very close to Mrs *Thatcher.

He was first elected MP for Epping in 1970 and then Chingford from 1974 until his retirement in 1992. He seemed to represent what the media called the 'Essex Man'. Critics of his politics called him the 'Chingford skinhead'.

Mrs Thatcher made him Secretary of State for Employment in 1981. His predecessor Jim *Prior had favoured an incremental approach to the question of trade union reform and sought to carry the trade unions with him. Mrs Thatcher—and Tebbit—favoured a tougher approach. He was responsible for the 1982 Trade Union Act which further weakened the closed shop and made trade unions liable for damages arising from unlawful industrial action. In 1983 he became Secretary of State for Trade and Industry and further reduced subsidies to ailing industries.

Tebbit nearly lost his life when an IRA bomb blew up the Brighton Grand Hotel in which many Conservative ministers and delegates were staying during the 1984 party conference. His wife was permanently paralysed. In 1985 he became party chairman. Relations with Mrs Thatcher became uneasy; he was regarded as a possible successor and at times she seems to have thought that he had designs on her job.

After helping to organize the Conservative election victory in 1987 he retired from government. He needed to make money, in part to care for his sick wife. Mrs Thatcher tried and failed to tempt him back to office, at one point offering him Education. Tebbit was a doughty supporter when she faced a leadership challenge in 1990. When she stood down, he subsequently campaigned for John *Major. As a member of the House of Lords he joined with Mrs Thatcher in opposing the ratification of the Maastricht Treaty, describing the treaty as treason. Over time, Tebbit became more critical of John Major and claimed that he had not stood for the leadership in 1990 because he had thought that Major represented right-wing values.

Tebbit wrote a well-regarded memoir, *Upwardly Mobile*, and became a political commentator.

Templewood, Viscount *see* HOARE, SAMNEL

Teng Hsiao-p'ing *see* DENG XIAOPING

Thant, U (b. Pantanaw, 22 Jan. 1907; d. 25 Nov. 1974)

Burmese; Secretary-General of the United Nations 1962–72

Born in the delta of the Irrawaddy River in Lower Burma under British rule, U Thant was educated at Rangoon University after winning a national translation competition as a high-school student. At the university he became an associate of a number of the leading student politicians of the period including the Burmese nationalist hero General Aung San and the subsequent Prime Minister U *Nu. Older and less of an activist by nature than the nationalist leaders, he also worked with British Fabian intellectuals such as J. S. Furnivall in a number of educational and publishing ventures, including *The World of Books* magazine published in English in the early 1930s. He earned his living until the 1950s as a teacher in leading national high schools.

After Burma regained independence in 1948, Thant entered government service in the information ministry. There he worked closely with Prime Minister Nu. As a trusted associate, he represented Burma at the United Nations, becoming permanent representative in 1953. He was chosen acting Secretary-General after the death of Dag Hammarskjold in 1961. Following the Cold War dispute between the West and the Soviet Union over the future role of the United Nations and the Secretary-Generalship, he was elected in 1962 as Secretary-General in his own right as a neutral figure from one of the most active non-aligned states.

Thant's decade as Secretary-General was filled with a number of international crises. Those which were directly in the control of the two super powers, the United States and the Soviet Union, such as the Second Indochina War, he was less able to influence. However, during his first term, Thant had several remarkable successes. These included the transfer of Irian Jaya to Indonesian sovereignty from the Dutch (1962), the Cuban missile crisis (1962), the United Nations intervention in the civil war in the Congo (Zaire) (1963), the establishment of the UN peacekeeping force in Cyprus (1964) and the ending of an Indian–Pakistan border war (1965). His second term was marked by fewer successes as he faced seemingly intractable problems in Indochina, the Middle East, and South Asia. However, he headed the UN during the period when the organization began to become much more deeply involved in development and social justice issues in the Third World. These were issues to which he could clearly relate from his own personal experience in Burma.

A deeply religious man, he published a number of books in Burmese as well as a memoir of his days as Secretary-General.

Thatcher, Margaret Hilda (b. Grantham, 13 Oct. 1925)

British; leader of the Conservative Party 1975–90, Prime Minister 1979–90; Baroness (life peer) 1992

Margaret Thatcher was the longest continuously serving Prime Minister for over a century and a half, and the only one to have won three successive general elections. In addition, she was one of the few twentieth-century prime ministers to have lent her name to an 'ism'. She helped to change the political agenda in the 1980s in Britain and overseas and overturned much of the post-war conventional political wisdom. She is a model of a successful peacetime Prime Minister stretching the powers of the office to the limits.

Yet there was nothing remarkable about Margaret Roberts's background, apart from her intelligence and determination to succeed. Her father was a major influence. He was a shopkeeper and served as mayor of Grantham, a small Midlands town. She attended the local grammar school and Oxford, where she read chemistry. She became president of the university Conservative Association. Wishing to pursue a career in politics she then read for the bar. Her career was helped by marrying the wealthy Denis Thatcher.

Margaret Thatcher entered parliament as the member for Finchley in 1959 and remained its member until 1992. She held a number of junior posts but her breakthrough came when she was made shadow spokesman for Education in 1969 and entered the Cabinet in 1970 as Education Minister. She went along with the 'U-turns' in the 1970–4 government of Ted *Heath. As Education Minister she accepted a number of schemes for comprehensive reorganization and expanded nursery provision. She was not close to Heath nor a member of his inner Cabinet.

Like Sir Keith *Joseph she repented of her role in the Heath government, once the party was in Opposition. She stood against Mr Heath for the leadership in February 1975, in large part because nobody else of weight would. It was a surprise to many when she won the first ballot by 130 votes to 119; she went on to win the second ballot easily.

At the time she had few supporters and her views were not widely shared in the party. She also inherited a shadow Cabinet who were largely sympathetic to the views of the ousted leader Ted Heath. Conservative leaders usually came from the centre left. Mrs Thatcher, from the free market right, disturbed that continuity.

As Prime Minister from 1979 she faced a tough first two years. Unemployment soared, the government was deeply unpopular, and the policies did not seem to be working. The 1981 budget, which raised taxes at a time of economic recession, showed that the government was in earnest. The economy gradually improved, she brought more supporters into the Cabinet, and made her reputation as a successful war leader—recapturing the Falklands in 1982. She won a landslide election victory in 1983—helped by a weak Labour Party and the opposition forces being fragmented between Labour and the Alliance parties.

Mrs Thatcher was often lucky in her opponents—a weak Labour leader in Michael *Foot, unpopular trade union leaders, the Argentine General Galtieri. The Russians only added to her credibility when they named her the 'Iron Lady' in 1976 on account of her robust views on defence. She was also helped by the electoral system which gave her landslide majorities in parliament, with only 42 per cent of the vote.

As Prime Minister she had only a handful of close colleagues and never had a Cabinet which was largely Thatcherite. A succession of quarrels, and resignations of senior colleagues, at first stamped her as a strong leader but in the end proved to be her undoing. She was argumentative and forceful.

She was critical of many establishment institutions, notably the senior civil service, local government, the universities, the BBC, the Church of England, and even the professions. She was out to smash the consensus which had prevailed in post-1945 politics and, in her view, led to Britian's decline. Her abrasive attitude to the European Commission and much of the public sector, and her support for capital punishment, found a popular echo, although one which was not to the liking of many senior colleagues.

The government pursued radical policies of privatization for state-owned industries and utilities, reformed the trade unions, cut income taxes, and introduced more market-orientated mechanisms into health and education. The government, largely at her behest, also introduced an unpopular poll tax. The aim of the policies was to reduce the role of the government and make people more self-reliant and end the culture of dependency. Mrs Thatcher was also a commanding figure on the international stage and had good relations with Ronald *Reagan and Mikhail *Gorbachev.

It was her abrasive attitude to the European Community, however, which upset a number of her senior colleagues. This was the main reason that lay behind the resignation on 1 November 1990 of Sir Geoffrey *Howe. She was, at heart, a nationalist. Her view of Europe was that it would be a union of states co-operating in those areas where it was in their interests to do so. Howe and others believed that Britain's future lay in pooling its sovereignty with other states. Two weeks later he made a personal statement in the House of Commons which bitterly attacked her leadership and accused her of being a liability to her party and her country.

At her most vulnerable, she was challenged in a leadership election by Michael *Heseltine, who exceeded expectations by gaining 152 votes to 204 for Mrs Thatcher. Mrs Thatcher ended up four short of an overall majority. Many colleagues regarded her as an electoral liability, not least for her determination to retain the poll tax. Some 40 per cent of Conservative MPs wished for a change. Senior colleagues told her that she should stand down and in the end she accepted that advice. She announced to colleagues on 21 November that she was standing down. On 28 November, after the election of her preferred choice, John *Major, she tendered her resignation to the Queen. In subsequent years she made clear that John Major was failing to meet her expectations. In retirement she raised funds for her Thatcher Foundation, campaigned against closer British integration with Europe, and wrote her best-selling memoirs.

Thomas, James Henry (b. Monmouthshire, 3 Oct. 1874; d. 21 Jan. 1949)
British; Colonial Secretary 1924, 1935–6, Dominions Secretary 1930–5

The son of a domestic servant, Thomas worked on the railways after an elementary education. He became assistant general secretary of the National Union of Railwaymen in 1913 and then its parliamentary general secretary (1919–31).

Thomas entered the Commons in 1910. Having declined office in David *Lloyd George's wartime coalition government, his first ministerial appointment was as Colonial Secretary in the first Labour government (1924). In the second (1929–31) he was appointed Lord Privy Seal, heading a ministerial team responsible for dealing with unemployment. But in 1930 he was moved to the Dominions Office after his opposition to a Keynesian remedy had provoked Sir Oswald *Mosley's resignation. In 1931 he was one of the few Labour members to join the national government.

Political controversy often surrounded Thomas. His change of office in 1930 was precipitated by a petition signed by sixty Labour MPs and acrimony followed his decision to join the national government. Finally, in 1936, his ministerial and parliamentary career ended when an inquiry adjudged him responsible for a budget leak.

Thorez, Maurice (b. Noyelles-Godault, 28 Apr. 1900; d. 11 July 1964)

French; member of the Communist Party Central Committee 1925–64, Minister of State 1945–6, Deputy Prime Minister 1946–7

The son of a miner, a surface worker for a short time, Thorez rallied to the Communist cause in 1920. After a brief period of indecision (he was reflecting turmoil in the Kremlin) he rallied to *Stalin. Thorez was a loyal executor of instructions and was promoted by Moscow through the ranks of more talented (but less reliable) figures. Thorez was, despite the legend of the autodidact philosopher king whipped up in one of the most extraordinary personality cults ever seen in a Western society, typical of the 'prodigious mediocrities' of Communism. Thorez's contributions (if any) are difficult to disentangle from the history of Communism. The one time 'class against class' revolutionary became, abruptly as Stalin switched policies, the apostle of the Popular Front, then the opponent of 'imperialist war' between England and Germany (he had deserted the French army in October 1939 to spend the war in Moscow). Amnestied in 1944, he became a minister of 'bourgeois' rectitude at the Liberation. However, the Communists were evicted in 1947 and Cominform introduced an anti-bourgeois line. Thorez suffered a stroke in 1950 and spent the next three years in Russia, the party being run by *Duclos. After Stalin's death there was a drift back to alliance policies—the so-called 'peaceful road to power' line. Thorez then sought an alliance with the Socialists which became the union of the left. Where Thorez's influence was evident was in the party's refusal to join *Khrushchev's denunciation of Stalin. Thorez once had talent for the dramatizing phrase; this was soon replaced by the formulaic writing favoured by Communists.

Thorneycroft, George Edward **Peter** (b. Dunstan, Staffordshire, 26 July 1909; d. 4 June 1994)

British; Chancellor of the Exchequer 1957–8, Minister of Defence 1962–4; Baron (life peer) 1967

Educated at Eton and the Royal Military Academy, Woolwich, Thorneycroft trained as a barrister. Elected to parliament in 1938 (sitting for Stafford until 1945, when he was defeated, and then for Monmouth, being returned in a by-election later that year), he was a leading member of the Tory Reform Committee during the war years, pressing for acceptance of social reform by the party. He served briefly as a junior minister in 1945 and was recognized as a rising star in the party. In 1951, *Churchill appointed him to his new Cabinet as president of the Board of Trade. He held the post until January 1957, when the new Prime Minister, Harold *Macmillan, appointed him Chancellor of the Exchequer. However, he took a more austere stance on economic policy than the more expansionary Macmillan and in January 1958 unexpectedly resigned, along with his two junior ministers (Enoch *Powell and Nigel Birch), after the Cabinet refused to agree to an additional £50 million reduction in public expenditure. Macmillan, though deeply worried, dismissed the resignations as a 'little local difficulty' and appointed the more pliant Derick *Heathcoat-Amory as Chancellor. Thorneycroft was brought back to government two years later, serving as Aviation Minister and then Minister of Defence, presiding over a reorganization of the forces and the ministry. He served on the front bench in Opposition, but lost his seat in the 1966 general election. He was made a life peer the following year and pursued a number of business interests. He was unexpectedly brought back into politics in 1975, when the new party leader, Margaret *Thatcher, appointed him as party chairman. He proved effective in the post, enjoying the seniority and detachment necessary to make the position work, and served for six years before some independent comments on the state of the economy contributed to his departure.

Thorneycroft had an important influence on the Conservative Party over a period of four decades. Though Macmillan made various dismissive remarks about him, both before and after his 1958 resignation, Thorneycroft achieved a status as a respected elder statesman of the party.

Thorpe, Jeremy (b. London, 28 Apr. 1929)
British; leader of the Liberal Party 1967–76

Thorpe came from a well-to-do background. His father and grandfather had both been MPs. After Eton and Oxford University (becoming president of the Oxford Union) he won North Devon for the Liberals in 1959 and held the seat until he was defeated in 1979.

Thorpe succeeded Jo *Grimond as Liberal leader in 1967; the party then consisted of only six MPs. He was a witty debater but was not regarded as a serious political figure by commentators. There was, if anything, too much wit and humour. He gained praise for his conduct of the February 1974 general election campaign. Both the Labour and Conservative parties were unpopular and the Liberals saw their vote soar to over 19 per cent, then a post-war record, and nearly held the balance in the House of Commons. Indeed Ted *Heath offered a coalition to the Liberals, with a Cabinet seat for Thorpe. Under pressure from activists Thorpe turned the offer down. The Liberals failed to consolidate their position and gradually his leadership came under criticism. Colleagues were not sure what his long-term strategy was.

The last year of Thorpe's leadership was clouded by scandal. A male model made various allegations against him. Pressure from colleagues forced him to step down in May 1976. In August 1978 he was charged, along with three others, with conspiracy to murder. He was acquitted on all charges in June 1979. By then he had lost his seat.

Thurmond, James **(Strom)** (b. Edgefield, South Carolina, 5 Dec. 1902)
US; Governor of South Carolina 1947–51, US Senator 1954–64, 1964–

Thurmond's early career was as a teacher and school superintendent, though he later studied law and became a practising attorney in South Carolina. He served in the state Senate 1933–8 and became a circuit judge in 1938, holding that position until 1942. After war service in the army, he was elected Governor of South Carolina in 1947 and served a four-year term until 1951.

Initially, and by the standards of his time he was relatively progressive; but the mounting battle for civil rights took him into ever more extreme positions. In 1948 he led the Dixiecrat walkout from the Democratic ticket headed by Harry *Truman and himself stood as a presidential candidate on a states' rights ticket. He was originally appointed, as a Democrat, to the Senate in 1954 (following the resignation of Charles E. Daniel); but in 1956 he resigned and successfully ran for re-election, again as a Democrat.

Ever-widening divisions over civil rights in the Democratic Party pushed Thurmond closer to the Republican Party. In 1964 he switched parties and became a leading force in the emergent Republican Party in the south. Although Thurmond had long opposed racial integration, once it came he recognized the significance of the black vote for South Carolina politics and began to appoint blacks to his staff.

Republican captures of the Senate in 1981 and 1994 gave Thurmond enhanced influence. In 1981 he became chairman of the Judiciary Committee, a post which gave him scope to promote his support for harsh penal measures and his opposition to liberal jurisprudence. In 1995 he became chair of the Armed Services Committee, a post he relished because of his own opposition to cuts in defence spending and his state's interests in maintaining military bases. Despite his age, his ultra-conservative views seemed to give him an entrenched position in South Carolina politics and he was re-elected in 1996.

Tikhonov, Nikolai Aleksandrovich (b. Kharkov, 1905; d. 1 June 1997)
Ukrainian; Member of the Politburo 1978–85, chairman of the Council of Ministers 1980–5

Tikhonov was the son of a middle-class engineer and followed his father's profession, entering the Dnepropetrovsk Mining Institute in 1926 and graduating in 1930. He worked first as an engineer at the Lenin Plant of Dnepropetrovsk and was awarded the Order of Lenin in 1939. In the 1930s he became acquainted with his partron, Leonid *Brezhnev. During the Second World War he worked in industry east of the Urals. He joined the Communist Party in 1945. He returned to the Dnepropetrovsk region in 1947, serving as the manager of a tube plant in Nikopol. After 1950 Tikhonov followed a career in the governmental, not the party structure of the USSR. He joined the Ministry of Ferrous Metallurgy, becoming its Deputy Minister in 1955. In 1960 he returned to Moscow, serving consecutively until 1965 as vice-chairman of the State Scientific and Economic Council and vice-chairman of the State Planning Committee. In 1965 he was made a deputy chairman of the Council of Ministers, rising to first deputy chairman after 1976. In 1978 he was elected candidate member of the Politburo and full member the next year. When *Kosygin retired in 1980, the 75-year-old Tikhonov became chairman of the Council of Ministers—the head of the government. Gorbachev removed him from this post in September 1985, replacing him with *Ryzhkov.

Tiso, Josef (b. Bratislava, 13 Oct. 1887; d. Bratislava, 18 Apr. 1947)
Slovak; President of Slovakia 1939–45

Tiso was ordained as a Catholic priest in 1910. He became involved in politics after the creation of Czechoslovakia in 1918 because he resented Czech domination of the new state. Together with two other priests, Hlinka and Jehlička, he founded the Slovak People's Party, which called for Slovak autonomy. Following Hlinka's death in August 1938, Tiso became leader of the party. After the Munich Agreement of September 1938 he planned in collaboration with *Hitler for the dissolution of the rump of the Czechoslovak state. In October 1938 he became the premier of an autonomous Slovak government. On 14 March 1939, after the German invasion of Czechoslovakia, Tiso proclaimed Slovakia an independent republic, with himself as President. In October 1939 Slovakia became a protectorate of the Third Reich. In June 1941 Slovakia declared war on the Soviet Union, which lost Tiso support among Slovaks. At the end of 1944 Tiso's government was unable to control the Slovak National Rising and he called in German support. He was sentenced to death by a Czechoslovak court in April 1947. The non-Communist members of *Beneš's coalition government sought a reprieve, but at the insistence of the Communists Tiso was hanged on 18 April 1947.

Tito, Josip Broz (b. Kumrovec, Croatia, 7 May 1892; d. Ljubljana, Slovenia, 4 May 1980)
Croatian; Yugoslav Prime Minister and Defence Minister 1945–53, President 1953–80

Born into a peasant family, Josip Broz trained as a locksmith and became an itinerant worker in central Europe. Conscripted into the Austro-Hungarian army in the First World War he rose to the rank of sergeant, was wounded, and captured by the Russians. Released after the Revolution he joined the Red Army, fought in the Russian Civil War, and married a Russian woman. Returning to Croatia in 1920 he worked as a metalworker and joined the Communist Party. He became a trade union leader and strike organizer and secretary of the Zagreb Communists. In 1928 he was arrested and, after a trial at which he became famous for his outspoken defence of Communism and revolution, was imprisoned for five years. In 1934 he was co-opted onto the Central Committee and Politbureau of the decimated Yugoslav Communist

Party and adopted the underground name Tito. After the party was liquidated by *Stalin Tito worked for the Comintern in Moscow. He was sent back to Yugoslavia to reorganize the party as its General Secretary in 1937. He soon transformed it into an effective pan-Yugoslav revolutionary organization, which was to form the basis of the partisan army when the Germans invaded in April 1941.

In his July Declaration Tito called for national unity on the basis of equality of all ethnic groups; he advocated immediate resistance and downplayed socialist revolution. These appeals gained the Partisans much cross-national support. After the Italian surrender in September 1943 the Partisans acquired a considerable quantity of arms and were able to defeat the forces of *Mihailovic decisively and gain control of a large area of central Yugoslavia. In November Tito formed a provisional government and declared the creation of the Federal People's Republic of Yugoslavia. From this time he also gained the crucial support of *Churchill, who persuaded the government-in-exile to back him and drop Mihailovic. In 1944 Tito formed a provisional government with the royalist Subasic as Foreign Minister, but after the victorious Partisans entered Belgrade in 1945 the November elections ushered in a monolithic Communist government in which Tito was both premier and Foreign Minister and the monarchy was abolished.

Tito now established a tough Stalinist regime with harsh purges conducted by Rankovic's secret police. But the fact that his revolution had not been dependent on Soviet support encouraged him to take a more independent line from the USSR, as was seen in the negotiations on the Balkan Federation project. Disagreements with Stalin came to a head in 1948 when Tito refused to accept the total subservience now expected of the East European satellites in the new Cold War era and in February 1948 Yugoslavia was expelled from the Cominform. Massive US aid enabled Yugoslavia to survive the immediate trade embargo, but once Tito had accepted the break was final (which he did reluctantly) it was clear that Yugoslav strategy would have to be rethought if they were not to slip back into capitalism. With the help of *Kardelj and *Djilas he developed the alternative ideology of 'self-management' which he started to implement in 1950. In 1952 the name of the party was altered to the League of Communists of Yugoslavia and in 1953 a new constitution based on self-management was introduced. At the same time Djilas was arrested for criticisms of the leadership. After the death of Stalin in 1953 Khrushchev attempted to bring Yugoslavia back into the Communist fold but Tito remained wary and instead developed a new foreign policy role as leader of the Non-Aligned Movement. In the 1960s tensions in the country increased under the impact of the 1965 market-oriented reforms. In 1966 Tito was forced to sack security chief Rankovic because of his unpopularity with the other nationalities. In 1967 unrest developed in several republics which was resolved by devolutionary constitutional amendments, but nationalist pressure increased, especially in Croatia, coming to a head in the 'Croatian Spring' of 1971, when Tito replaced the Croatian party leadership. In 1974 a new constitution was introduced giving virtually confederal powers to the republics and provinces, nominally balanced by a reassertion of 'democratic centralism' in the party as a binding force, but this failed to stop the drift towards national particularism.

Tito's great achievements were as a resistance leader and a statesman who held his diverse country together for thirty-five years of peace and relative stability. On the other hand he had an inordinate vanity and love of luxury which ill accorded with his role as the socialist alternative to Stalinism.

Tojo Hideki (b. Tokyo, 30 Dec. 1884; d. 23 Dec. 1948)

Japanese; Prime Minister 1941–4

The son of an army officer, Tojo Hideki was educated at Tokyo Military Academy before starting a career in the army. Between 1919 and 1922 he was military attaché in Germany and Switzerland. After returning to Japan he taught at his Alma Mater before becoming Commander of the 1st Infantry Regiment in 1929. Tojo became involved in the complex factional politics of the times, siding with the *tōseiha* faction that promoted technological innovation in the Japanese military. In 1935 he was posted to Manchuria, returning to Tokyo as Army vice-Minister in 1938 and advocating the continuation of the war with China. In 1940 he became Minister for War, and advocated closer ties with Germany and Italy. In October 1941 he was appointed Prime Minister, where he pushed for a 'southward' strategy of taking over the colonies of the defeated European powers, and eventually the attack on Pearl Harbor. In 1944 Tojo resigned as Prime Minister because of the reverses suffered by the Japanese armed forces and the bombing raids on Tokyo.

He attempted suicide in September 1945 to avoid arrest by the Occupation authorities, but following his arrest he did all he could to exonerate Emperor *Hirohito of any blame for the war. He was found guilty of war crimes by the Tokyo Tribunal and was executed on 23 December 1948.

Touré, Ahmed **Sékou** (b. Faranah, Guinea, 1922; d. 26 Mar. 1984)
Guinean; President 1958–84

Born of poor peasant parents of Sousou and Malinke ethnicity, Touré claimed a probably fictitious descent from Almamy Samoure, the legendary leader of resistance to French colonialism. After secondary schooling, he worked as a clerk and trade union organizer, becoming a founder of the Rassemblement Democratique Africain in 1946. His political base in Guinea depended in part on unionized urban workers, in part on rural opposition to the system of administrative chieftaincy imposed by the French. This enabled him to lead the local section of the RDA, the Parti Democratique de Guinée (PDG), and to emerge as the most radical of the nationalist leaders in French West Africa.

The critical turning point came in 1958, when he successfully campaigned for a No vote in President *de Gaulle's referendum on continued association with France. Guinea was forced into abrupt independence and relations with France were cut. Touré sought support from Ghana's *Nkrumah and outside states including the USSR. Internally, he promoted a ruthless and radical single party state, nationalizing all assets except the international bauxite companies on whose revenues his regime relied. Plans for rapid socialist development through 'human investment' (which amounted in practice to forced labour schemes like those which he had earlier opposed) came to naught, and his rule became increasingly paranoid, with real or imagined plots followed by purges, jailings, and public executions. His suspicions of the Foulah ethnic group helped to produce an administration based on personal loyalties and run by members of his own group and indeed his family. Despite overtures to France and other Western states in the late 1970s, there was no political liberalization, and when Touré died after a heart attack in 1984, his regime was immediately overthrown by a military coup. He is remembered on the one hand for his heroic defiance of colonial rule, on the other for the failure of his paranoid and demagogic socialism.

Tower, John Goodwin (b. Houston, Texas, 29 Sept. 1925; d. 5 Apr. 1991)
US; US Senator 1961–85

The son of a methodist Church official, Tower spent a period in the navy before gaining a degree from Southwestern University in 1948. Between 1948 and 1951 he was employed as a radio announcer and as an insurance agent before continuing his education at Southern Methodist University in Dallas and at the London School of Economics. He then became a professor of political science at Midwestern University.

In 1960 he ran against Lyndon *Johnson for the Texas Senate seat. Although he lost, he achieved 41 per cent of the vote and in 1961 he won the seat in a special election. In the Senate Tower became a specialist in defence and security matters, serving as ranking member and then chairman of the Armed Services Committee. (He was later chief arms negotiator at Geneva.) A hard-line conservative, Tower was generally a fierce critic of expanding federal government responsibility. He was also an opponent of many federal civil rights initiatives including the work of the Civil Rights Commission. When Congress set up a commission to investigate the Iran-Contra affair, Tower chaired it.

In 1989 the newly elected President George *Bush nominated Tower as his Secretary of Defense. The Senate refused to confirm the nomination because of allegations about Tower's heavy drinking and sexual misconduct. Unwilling to lose Tower's expertise, Bush appointed him to chair his Foreign Intelligence Advisory Committee.

Tower was killed in a plane crash in 1991.

Trotsky, Lev Davidovich (real name **Bronstein**) (b. Yanovka, Ukraine, 26 Oct. 1879; d. Mexico City, 21 Aug. 1940)

Russian; People's Commissar for Foreign Affairs 1917–18, People's Commissar for Military Affairs 1918–25

Lev Bronstein was born into a family of prosperous Jewish peasants in the Ukraine. While attending secondary school he became interested in Populism but later, after leaving, joined a Marxist group, for which he was exiled to Siberia in 1900. He escaped abroad in 1902, adopting the name of his former gaoler—Trotsky. He soon became known for his incisive writing in the socialist press, being nicknamed 'The Pen'. At the 2nd Congress of the RSDLP in 1903 he supported Martov's views on party membership, though he saw the need for greater party discipline and supported the *Iskra* group (headed by *Lenin and Plekhanov) against the 'Economists' (advocates of incremental reform) and came to lead a group intermediate between the Mensheviks and the Bolsheviks. In 1904 he published *Our Political Tasks*, a critique of Lenin's *What is to be done?*, in which he warned prophetically of 'substitutism': with a Leninist organization the party would come to substitute itself for the working class; then the Central Committee would substitute itself for the Party; finally, a dictator would substitute himself for the Central Committee. He also applied the Marxian idea of 'permanent revolution' to Russia: since the Russian bourgeoisie was too weak to develop a democratic structure the workers would have to take over the revolution and move directly to socialism. Lenin rejected this idea as extremist, but came round to it in 1917, just as Trotsky came round to Lenin's idea of the party.

He returned to Russia in 1905 during the revolutionary events and with his fine oratory rapidly acquired a leading role, becoming chair of the Petrograd Soviet in September, but soon afterwards was arrested and exiled to Siberia, from where he again escaped abroad. In the next few years he tried to build bridges between the Bolshevik and Menshevik factions of the RSDLP, disliking Lenin's 'splitting' tactics, and lived by his writing, including a time as a war correspondent in the Balkans. In 1914 he became an advocate of the 'United States of Europe' idea, suggesting that a capitalist common market of European states could be transformed into a socialist federation as a step towards world socialist revolution. In 1917 he returned to Russia in the early summer and, attracted by Lenin's call for socialist revolution and disgusted with the Mensheviks' participation in the provisional government, in August joined the Bolsheviks and was elected to the Central Committee. In September he was once again elected chair of the Petrograd Soviet. He supported Lenin's plan for a seizure of power and chaired the Soviet's Military Revolutionary Committee which organized the overthrow of the provisional government in October. Trotsky supported Lenin's refusal to co-operate with other socialist groups in the new government.

Trotsky had now become Lenin's closest colleague and was made People's

Commissar for Foreign Affairs. In the negotiations with Germany and Austria he adopted a stalling tactic of 'neither war nor peace', but in January 1918 the Central Powers delivered an ultimatum and the Bolshevik government was forced into making a separate peace on disastrous terms in March. In the anticipation of civil war Trotsky was moved to the Commissariat for Military Affairs, where his talents as a mass orator and a brilliant, if often brutal and overbearing, organizer were displayed to their fullest advantage. In place of the voluntary militia of the first months of Soviet power he built the Red Army into a formidable and professional force, conscripting former tsarist officers to train and lead the peasant conscripts and personally directing operations and rallying the troops by touring the fronts in his sealed train. But his arrogant style earned him the hostility of colleagues, notably *Stalin, and in 1920, with the Civil War almost over, he was pressured into invading Poland by Lenin, who hoped to spread revolution by war, which ended in the Red Army's defeat.

With the end of hostilities Trotsky's role as Military Commissar declined in importance, although he set about developing a new structure for a standing army. The New Economic Policy, introduced in March 1921 and involving limited denationalization and resumption of an agricultural market, had been suggested by him in 1920, though he emphasized that this must be accompanied by planned industrialization. Relations with Lenin in his final years were often tense, though they remained close. Trotsky persistently refused Lenin's offer of a Vice-Premiership, hoping for some clearer role as Lenin's deputy. But his inaction allowed Stalin to bypass him by forming a ruling alliance with *Zinoviev and *Kamenev which was in place before Lenin died in 1924. Too late Trotsky started to mobilize a Left Opposition, advocating party democratization and a greater commitment to internationalism and rapid industrial transformation, in which he was joined by Zinoviev and Kamenev in 1926. But Stalin, whom Trotsky despised and underestimated, now held all the cards: Trotsky was forced to resign as War Commissar in 1925 and in 1927 was expelled from the party and exiled to Alma-Ata. Finally in 1928 he was deported, to spend the rest of his life in exile trying to organize opposition to Stalin through the optimistically named 'Fourth International'. In a series of major works, notably *The Revolution Betrayed* (1937), he attacked Stalinism, but his position was ambivalent since he approved of the policies of forced collectivization and industrialization and maintained that the USSR remained in essence a workers' state which should be supported. After many wanderings he ended up in Mexico, where he was assassinated in 1940 by an NKVD agent. Trotsky remains a highly controversial figure. Idealized by leftist groups in the west, in Russia he is regarded as quite as potentially dictatorial as Stalin. Lenin's assessment in his 'Testament' of 1923 was quite accurate: while admitting his outstanding abilities he said Trotsky was 'over-preoccupied with the administrative aspect of affairs'. A brilliant organizer, writer, and speaker, full of prophetic ideas, he lacked the skills and the inclination for the bargaining and compromise of politics and his assessments of political situations, domestic and international, were often totally unrealistic.

Trudeau, Pierre (b. Montreal, 18 Oct. 1919)
Canadian; Prime Minister 1968–79, 1980–4

Educated at Jesuit schools, the universities of Montreal, Harvard, and Paris and the London School of Economics, Trudeau was called to the bar of Quebec in 1944. He joined the Privy Council Office in Ottawa as Economic and Policy Adviser 1949, and practised law, specializing in Labour Law and Civil Liberties cases in Quebec. He was appointed Associate Professor of Law, University of Montreal, and member of staff of Institut de Recherches en Droit.

Trudeau was elected as a Liberal MP for Mount Royal (Montreal) in the general election of 1965. He was Minister of Justice under Lester *Pearson, whom he succeeded as

Prime Minister in 1968. His flamboyant, high-profile style appealed to the electorate, especially young voters, and he won a substantial majority at elections held ten weeks after taking office. Much of his premiership was concerned with efforts to curb separatism in Quebec and to renew Canadian federalism, which he conceived of in terms of a compact of bilingualism and biculturalism. His policies embraced firm handling of terrorist kidnappings with the encouragement of civil equality between English- and French-speaking communities. Initially critical of some of the features of the much-esteemed foreign policy of his Liberal predecessor Lester Pearson and employing the idiom of national interest, he none the less soon became active externally as a Liberal internationalist bent on promoting détente with the Soviet Union and China, and utilizing the United Nations and the Commonwealth, to the relative neglect of party organization and management.

Trudeau promoted the 1976 Olympic Games in Montreal, a costly enterprise which lost him much support in the elections of May 1979, when he went into Opposition for nine months. His skill in deflecting separatist threats from Quebec enabled him to bounce back to victory in the general election of February 1980 and to be Prime Minister for another four-and-a-half years, during which time he 'repatriated' and revised the Canadian constitution, formerly embodied in the British America Act of 1876 and its subsequent amendments. Trudeau's decision in 1977 to make Canada the first major country in the world to extend its jurisdiction over offshore fishing from 12 to 200 miles caused concern abroad and left problems—notably with Spain—which continued to reverberate long after his retirement from active politics in June 1984.

Trujillo, Rafael Leonidas (b. 24 Oct. 1891; d. 30 May 1961)

Dominican; President 1930–8, 1943–52

A former estate overseer, telegraph operator, and petty thief, Trujillo joined the Dominican army during the US occupation (1916–24) and rose rapidly, becoming national police chief in 1925 and army commander in 1927. He took political power in 1930, arranged rigged elections that year and brutally repressed all opposition within the Dominican Republic.

Famed for his megalomania, Trujillo had the capital city, Santo Domingo, renamed Ciudad Trujillo, christened himself 'the Benefactor', and authorized a personality cult based on terror. He also took personal control of large parts of the Dominican economy, expropriating the sugar estates and cattle ranches of opponents. In 1937 Trujillo ordered the massacre of some 20,000 Haitians living and working in the border area between the two countries. He organized an efficient network of informers and security forces, managing to suppress several planned uprisings.

In 1938 Trujillo handed over the titular presidency to Jacinto Peynado while remaining effectively in sole charge of the country. He resumed the title in 1943 and then in 1952 passed it to his brother, Héctor. In 1960 Joaquín Balaguer became puppet president.

Trujillo's human rights abuses began to attract international attention in the 1950s, and his regime became more isolated when in 1960 he ordered his agents to assassinate Venezuelan President Rómulo Betancourt, a long-time critic. The attempt failed and led to sanctions from the Organization of American States.

Trujillo was assassinated in 1961 by a group of army officers and civilians, allegedly with CIA backing. His brother, Ramfis, tried to hold on to power but was soon overthrown, ushering in a confused period of near civil war.

While Trujillo is mainly remembered for his dictatorial style and delusions of grandeur, many Dominicans recognize also that he provided a period of stability and reinforced the concept of Dominican nationhood after decades of chaos. Many of the country's institutions and much of its infrastructure can be traced back to his long reign.

Truman, Harry S (b. Lamar, Missouri, 8 May 1884; d. 26 Dec. 1972)

US; US Senator 1935–44, Vice-President 1945, President 1945–53

Born the son of a livestock salesman and farmer, Truman had the distinction of having a letter of the alphabet as part of his name. The families of his parents reputedly could not agree on a middle name—one wanting the family name of Shippe and the other Solomon—so his parents simply gave him 'S' as his middle name. His formal education was confined to high school. His father ran into financial difficulties, which prevented Harry from going to college. Harry also had poor eyesight—he wore glasses from the age of 8—and this prevented him from being admitted to West Point to pursue a military career. Instead he took up a number of clerical jobs before returning to work on the family farm. He was mobilized in 1917 and saw action during the First World War—showing leadership qualities that were admired by his men—and was demobilized with the rank of captain in 1919. Returning to Missouri, he married and with a friend set up a haberdasher's store. The store briefly flourished but then foundered. As the store hit hard times Truman began to take an interest in politics.

Truman began his political career in 1922 when he was elected to the administrative post of district judge. He lost a re-election bid in 1924 but was elected chief judge of Jackson County in 1926. He established a reputation for integrity and in 1934 the Democratic Party bosses in that state chose him to contest a Senate seat. They did so reluctantly after other potential candidates had turned them down. Truman won the election but had difficulty in making his mark in the Senate. He was associated with the party machine that had chosen him. What saved Truman's career was the decision of the Governor of Missouri, Lloyd Stark, to run against him for the Senate nomination in 1940. Truman had considered retiring—he had achieved little and found it difficult living in Washington—but he was stung into remaining in the race after President Franklin *Roosevelt offered him a federal appointment as a means of providing a clear field for Stark. Truman stumped the state to rally support and was successful especially in getting unions and many workers to support him. He won a narrow victory in the primary and a clear victory in the general election.

Once returned to the Senate, he was chosen to head a committee investigating how money was spent on defence. The committee was largely Truman's idea and it served to bring his name to national prominence. The committee revealed massive overspending and inefficiency, identifying how corporations were profiting at the expense of the war effort. The result was a significant improvement in efficiency and regulation, saving the country several billion dollars. Truman emerged as a leading figure in the Senate. It was a position that established him as a possible vice-presidential candidate. In 1944, Roosevelt dropped Vice-President Henry *Wallace from the ticket—Wallace was deemed too radical to be allowed to continue in the office—and Democratic Party chairman Bob Hannegan favoured Truman to succeed him. Truman, who had come to enjoy life in the Senate and supported James *Byrnes for the vice-presidency, had to be persuaded by Hannegan and Roosevelt to accept the nomination. Not for the first time, Truman was to ascend the political ladder because of the favours of a political boss.

Roosevelt's re-election to a fourth term in 1944, albeit it by a relatively narrow margin, resulted in Truman being sworn in as Vice-President of the United States. The swearing-in ceremony took place on 20 January. Truman had little contact with the President. He only recalled seeing him twice, on both occasions Cabinet meetings at which nothing important was discussed or decided. On 12 April, after chairing the Senate, he was asked to go to the White House. Eleanor Roosevelt informed him that the President was dead. Truman was sworn in as the 33rd President in the Cabinet Room. Although Roosevelt was clearly ill, Truman had had no idea how bad his condition was. His elevation to the presidency came as a massive shock.

Truman realized that there were many Americans who could do the job better than he could but that they were not the ones who had the job of President. He threw himself into the massive task that confronted him. Though not an original thinker, he had a grasp of history—he spent his early years reading history books—and was not afraid to take decisions. Once taken, he stood by them. Inasmuch as he had a problem in carrying out the job, it was not a reluctance to take decisions but rather the speed at which he took them. He did not always spend a great deal of time reflecting before reaching a decision. He was also prone to express himself in fairly plain terms. This sometimes aided communication but could undermine efforts at diplomacy. After giving Soviet Foreign Minister *Molotov a verbal dressing-down over the Soviet stance over Poland and the United Nations, Molotov complained that 'I have never been talked to in my life like this.' To which Truman retorted: 'Carry out your agreements and you won't get talked to like this.'

Truman had to take many decisions quickly. He authorized the dropping of the atomic bomb on Hiroshima and Nagasaki. He presided over America's response to the developing Cold War. He achieved perhaps his greatest success in ensuring, with the support of the Republican leader Senator Arthur Vandenberg, that America remained a military actor on the world stage rather than withdrawing within its own borders. In 1947 he proclaimed the Truman doctrine, prescribing a policy of containment for the Soviet Union. In 1948 he approved the Marshall Plan, developed by Secretary of State George *Marshall for the economic recovery of Europe. The same year he authorized the Berlin airlift, using planes to ship in supplies after the Soviets closed the road routes to Berlin.

Domestically, he faced many fights with Congress, especially after the Republicans gained control in 1946. His domestic programme was dubbed the Fair Deal but made little headway. His proposals to counter inflationary pressures failed to pass. Prices soared and industrial unrest increased. Congress passed the *Taft–Hartley Act, outlawing the closed shop, over Truman's veto. His liberal stance on social issues, including race, upset some of his own supporters, a number of whom—dubbed Dixiecrats—staged a walkout at the 1948 Democratic convention. Truman entered the 1948 presidential election as the underdog, most commentators expecting the Republican candidate Thomas E. *Dewey—who had fought Roosevelt in 1944—to win, a view shared by Dewey himself. Truman waged an energetic campaign, calling Congress into special session and then, when it failed to achieve anything, attacking it as the 'do-nothing 80th Congress'. On election night, early forecasts suggested that Truman had lost and the *Chicago Tribune* went to press with the headline 'Dewey defeats Truman', but by morning it was clear that Truman had won, winning 24.1 million votes against 21.9 for Dewey. Strom *Thurmond, the Dixiecrat States' Rights candidate won just over 1 million votes, as did Henry Wallace running as a Progressive.

Truman's second term was dominated by the Cold War and events in the Far East. After North Korean forces crossed the 38th parallel in Korea, Truman sent American forces to repel them, a move that was subsequently given United Nations sanction. General Douglas MacArthur was put in charge and he decided to pursue the fighting into North Korea, a tactic that prompted Chinese forces to intervene. MacArthur variously criticized both UN policy and that endorsed by his own President. After tolerating the General's insubordination for some months, Truman decided to act and dismissed MacArthur. MacArthur returned as a popular hero rather than a disgraced officer, though his popularity later waned.

MacArthur's dismissal came at a time when Truman was unpopular. Fears of Communists in government had led the Republicans to attack Truman for being 'soft on Communism'. Congress passed the McCarren Act in 1950, requiring Communists to register with the Justice Department; Truman vetoed it and Congress overrode the veto. Senator Joseph *McCarthy led the attack on Communists in public office. The threat of disruption to steel supplies by an industrial dispute led Truman to seize the steel mills in 1952, a move that was later declared unconstitutional by the Supreme

Court. With the Korean War still dragging on, Truman decided that he had had enough. Though eligible to seek re-election for a second term in his own right, he declined to do so. Instead, he retired to Independence, Missouri, to work on his memoirs and the Truman Library. He lived for almost another twenty years, doing some travelling and spending time with his family. In 1971 he declined the Congressional Medal of Honour on the grounds that he had not done anything to deserve it. He died on 26 December 1972 at the age of 88.

Truman was a man who was willing to lead and to accept responsibility. Down to earth in language and approach, he was willing to fight for what he believed was right. He was loyal to friends and family. If a reviewer criticized the performance of his daughter Margaret at a concert, a call from the White House would result, leaving the reviewer in no doubt as to the President's opinion of the review. However, he was also loyal to many old cronies—some of whom lacked his integrity—keeping them longer than was politically wise. He battled for his policies with a hostile Congress and was unpopular for most of his presidency. His reputation increased in the years after leaving the White House. In the 1962 poll of historians on US presidents, he was ranked as a near-great president and in subsequent polls has always figured in the list of the top ten presidents. In the 1995 *Chicago Sun-Times* poll of presidential scholars he was ranked sixth, behind Thomas Jefferson and ahead of Woodrow *Wilson. It was quite an achievement for the farm boy from Missouri.

Tubman, William Vacanarat Shadrach (b. Maryland, Liberia, Nov. 1895; d. 23 July 1971)

Liberian; President 1944–71

Born into a well-connected Americo-Liberian family in south-eastern Liberia, Tubman studied law and was elected in 1922 as the youngest ever member of the country's Senate. He was deputy president of the supreme court from 1937 to 1943, when he was chosen as the ruling True Whig Party candidate for the presidency; his election was a formality, and he took office in 1944.

He was an energetic and enterprising President, whose charm, folksy manner, and mastery of the intricacies of Liberian dynastic politics enabled him to gain a position of dominance. His declaration of war on Germany qualified Liberia for lend-lease aid from the United States, and his open-door policy for foreign investment, coupled with the adoption of the US dollar as domestic currency, brought investment especially in iron ore mining which led to rapid (if precarious) economic growth and swelled the government budget. Domestically, he sought to broaden the base of Liberian politics beyond the tiny coastal élite which had monopolized it since independence in 1847. He co-opted up-country people into positions of responsibility and expanded rural education, eventually extending full representation to the hinterland areas, though his government was still dominated by the old élite. He also amended the constitution, which had restricted presidential terms to eight years, to enable him to hold office indefinitely.

He adapted adroitly to the anti-colonial upsurge in neighbouring territories, holding a meeting with *Touré and *Nkrumah in 1959 and hosting a summit of independent African states in 1961, without allowing any radicalization of politics in Liberia itself. An inveterate drinker and womanizer, he ran Liberia in a highly personalized and generally easy-going fashion, while reacting sharply against any challenge to his authority. By the time of his death in office in 1971, the pressures of change which he had skilfully managed were undermining the élitist system of government which he had modernized and adapted but did not fundamentally alter.

Tudjman, Franjo (b. Veliko Trgovisce, Croatia, 14 May 1922)

Croatian; President of Croatia 1990–

After school Tudjman served in the Partisan army, rising to the rank of major, and from 1945 worked in the Political Division of the Yugoslav army headquarters. In 1955–7 Tudjman studied at the Higher Military Academy in Belgrade and in 1960, aged only 38, became a major-general.

In 1961 he left the army to become founder and director of the Institute of the History of the Workers' Movement in Zagreb, directing research on nationality questions and Yugoslavian socialism. In 1963 he became professor of socialist revolution and modern national history at the Faculty of Political Science, Zagreb University. In 1965 he completed his doctorate on monarchist Yugoslavia. In 1965–9, when he was a member of the Croatian parliament, Tudjman became increasingly nationalist and in 1967 was expelled from the League of Communists and dismissed from his posts for nationalist deviation.

After the failure of the 'Croatian Spring' of 1971, in which he had taken an active part, he was imprisoned for a year. After *Tito's death in 1980 he became increasingly critical of the Communist political system and was again imprisoned. Allowed to travel abroad again from 1987 Tudjman toured the Croatian diaspora to mobilize their support. In February 1989 he founded and became president of the Croatian Democratic Community Party which aimed at either a confederal Yugoslavia or Croatian independence. Legalized in 1990, his party won 42.5 per cent of the vote and 56 per cent of the seats in the Croatian parliament in the April 1990 elections and Tudjman became President of Croatia (from August 1992 directly elected). Leading his state to independence (in June 1991) and through a bloody war with the Yugoslav army and then in Bosnia, Tudjman is a major if controversial figure, whose strident nationalism and dismissive attitude towards the Serbian minority in Croatia undoubtedly escalated the conflict.

Tunku Abdul Rahman *see* ABDUL RAHMAN PUTRA AL-HAJ, TUNKU

Turner, John Napier (b. Richmond, England, 7 Jun. 1929)

Canadian; Prime Minister 1984

Turner came to Canada in 1932 and was educated in Ontario schools. After studying at the University of British Columbia, he won a Rhodes scholarship and read political science and law at Oxford. He then practised law in Britain and was called to the English bar, and later the bars of Quebec and Ontario, being made a QC in 1968. He entered the Canadian House of Commons in 1962 and was a junior minister in Lester *Pearson's government and later Attorney-General and Finance Minister under Pierre *Trudeau, but left the Trudeau administration in 1975 after a disagreement with the Prime Minister. Subsequently, Turner practised as a corporate lawyer resident in Toronto, avoiding public politics but retaining close personal ties with prominent Liberals.

When Trudeau retired Turner succeeded him as leader of the Liberal Party and Prime Minister on 30 June 1984. He inherited a party bereft of vigour and initiative after twenty-one years in office. Trudeau had neglected party organization, preferring to manage political affairs with the aid of a small group of advisers. Candidates had not been chosen for many ridings when Turner called the election, the party's finances were low, and it had no prepared electoral strategy and few new policies upon which to campaign. Twenty-three of the twenty-nine members of Turner's Cabinet were drawn from Trudeau's, which made it difficult for the new Prime Minister to be seen as inaugurating political change. Alleged abuse of patronage by the Liberals emerged as a leading issue during the election campaign, right up to polling day, 4 September 1984. Turner had promised Trudeau that he would appoint seventeen Liberal MPs who were not standing for re-election to posts on government boards, the judicial bench, or the nominated Senate. Large numbers of voters were outraged by these appointments, which Turner found difficult to justify at the hustings. It was widely believed that Trudeau, after more than fifteen years in office, had overstayed and overused his powers as Prime Minister. The Liberals went down to a crushing defeat in the 1984 election, which transformed the recent electoral patterns of Canadian politics.

Turner resigned office on 17 September, having led an administration that lasted for only eighty days, one of the shortest terms in Canadian history. He remained as party leader until 1990, and did not run in the 1993 general election.

Ubico y Castañeda, Jorge (b. Guatemala, 1878, d. New Orleans, 14 Aug. 1946)
Guatemalan; President 1931–44

Ubico served as interior minister and as envoy to the USA under President Justo Rufino Barrios. He also served in the army as a lieutenant during the 1906 border war with El Salvador, even though he had failed to graduate from the military academy. He was subsequently appointed political and military commander of the departments of Alta Verapaz (1907–9) and Retalhuleu (1911–19), where he gained a reputation for being both efficient and cruel. He became army Chief of Staff in 1920. Ubico was one of the first Guatemalan officers to receive US military training and after 1920 was instrumental in introducing US methods more widely into the army.

In 1920 Ubico took part in the coup which installed General José M. Orellana as President, and served as his minister of war between 1921 and 1923. In 1922 and 1926 he stood as a presidential candidate but failed to win on either occasion. Following a coup in 1930, the US government helped to install him as President following cosmetic elections.

Despite a constitutional ban on consecutive terms of office, Ubico employed various fraudulent means to extend his presidency to five terms. He was noted for the brutality of his regime, under which torture, exile, and summary execution were commonplace. He abolished municipal authorities; centralized government administration under his personal control; introduced a vagrancy law which compelled indigenous people to work 150 days a year on the plantations; and banned all political parties apart from his own Liberal Progressive Party (PLP). During the Second World War Ubico supported the Axis powers, but eventually US pressure forced him to expropriate German properties. He was finally forced out of office in 1944 by mass demonstrations and strikes led by students, teachers, and professionals. He died in exile in New Orleans. In 1963 his remains were returned to Guatemala and buried with full military honours.

Ulbricht, Walter (b. Leipzig, 30 June 1893; d. 1 Aug. 1973)
German; general first secretary of the SED 1950–71, head of the GDR 1960–73

By the late 1960s Walter Ulbricht had become the most experienced and long-serving European Communist leader yet his very success was to prove his undoing. The GDR which he headed had been planted in the Soviet Zone of Germany by the Soviets, not by the people, and remained dependent on the Soviet armed forces for its survival. Ulbricht seemed to forget this and sought more and more independence from the Soviets. At a secret meeting in August 1970 he told an astonished *Brezhnev, the CPSU leader, 'We're not Belorussia, we're not a Soviet republic.' Brezhnev found him arrogant and reckless. He thought Ulbricht was going too far too fast in his market-orientated economic reforms, introduced in 1963, and, even more so, in his attempts to draw closer to West Germany. At the time Ulbricht was seen in the West as an opponent of détente who was removed in a Moscow-engineered coup in May 1971. In reality Ulbricht had welcomed the change in government in Bonn in 1969 which brought in the *Brandt-led SPD-FDP coalition, believing that it would lead, in the long run, to German reunification and a united Communist Germany. Ulbricht was also vilified as the man who led the pack in the hunt against the Czechoslovak reform Communist Alexander *Dubček. In fact, at first he welcomed Dubček, partly because he had not got on with his predecessor, urging him to bring in a new generation of economic technocrats. Yet Ulbricht's image as an implacable enemy of 'revisionism' was correct. For all his new thinking in the early 1960s, he remained a strong exponent of Leninist democratic centralism and the leading role of the Marxist-Leninist party.

Born into a working-class family in Leipzig in 1893, Ulbricht worked as a cabinet maker before war service (1915–18). He was arrested for desertion, on political grounds, from the forces. A pre-war Social Democrat, he was a founder member of the Communist Party of Germany (KPD). As the KPD was Stalinized he rose rapidly and was elected to the Central Committee in 1927. Between 1928 and 1933 he served as a member of the German parliament. After the Nazi takeover in 1933 he emigrated to Moscow, surviving the murderous Stalinist purges of the exiled KPD by actively supporting them. Ulbricht returned to Germany with the Red Army in 1945 at the head of one of three groups ordered to build up the administration of the Soviet Zone. When the Socialist Unity Party of Germany (SED) was founded in 1946, by merging the KPD and the SPD, he was prominent in the leadership. In 1950 he became the General Secretary (later styled First Secretary), a post he retained until 1971. He fought off various challenges to his leadership, miraculously avoiding dismissal after the abortive revolt of June 1953. His extreme policies after 1958 helped to lead to the crisis which forced the building of the Berlin Wall in 1961. He pursued the 'cult of personality' and infuriated his colleagues by building up the Council of State, which he headed after the death of President Pieck in 1960, at the expense of the Politburo. His discreet removal in 1971, 'on health grounds', allowed him to remain chairman of the reduced Council of State until his death in 1973.

Ustinov, Dmitri Fedorovich (b. Samara (Kuibyshev), 30 Oct. 1908; d. 20 Dec. 1984)

Russian; member of the Politburo 1965–84, Minister of Defence 1976–84

Ustinov was the son of working-class parents, and joined the Communist Party in 1927. Thereafter he worked as a fitter and machine operator. He received a technical education first from the Bauman Higher Technical School in Moscow, then entered the Leningrad Institute of Military Mechanical Engineering, from which he graduated in 1934. From then until the outbreak of the Second World War he worked in the Leningrad armaments industry, attaining the post of factory manager. In June 1941, after the German invasion of the Soviet Union, he was appointed People's Commissar (i.e. Minister), though he was only 32 years old. His outstanding achievement was to supervise the wholesale transfer of Soviet industrial plant from areas threatened by the Germans to east of the Urals. In 1952 he entered the Central Committee of the CPSU. In 1953 he left the Ministry of Armaments to serve as Minister of the Defence Industry until 1957. Then he became a deputy chairman of the Council of Ministers, and was appointed first deputy chairman in 1963. He retained a supervisory brief for the defence industry. In 1965 *Brezhnev made Ustinov a secretary of the Central Committee, with oversight of the military, defence industry, and security organs. He became a candidate member of the Presidium (Politburo after 1966) that year and a full member in 1976. Later in 1976 Marshal *Grechko suddenly died and Ustinov replaced him as Minister of Defence and was made Marshal of the Soviet Union, even though he was a civilian. Ustinov effectively represented the interests of the military-industrial complex as Soviet defence expenditure grew every year in the 1970s, while the defence industry was the most efficient sector of the economy. In 1976 Ustinov supported Soviet military intervention in Afghanistan.

Van Karnebeek, Herman Adriaan (b. The Hague, 21 Aug. 1874; d. 29 Mar. 1942)
Dutch; Minister of Foreign Affairs 1918–27

Van Karnebeek studied law in Utrecht, and his career was strongly influenced by his father, A. P. C. Van Karnebeek, a prominent statesman, diplomat, deputy, and Minister of Foreign Affairs. The father introduced the son as clerk to the first Peace Conference in The Hague (1899). At the second Peace Conference (1907) Van Karnebeek was assistant delegate. He worked at the Ministry of Colonial Affairs from 1901 till 1911. His administrative qualities and his experience at the peace conferences contributed to his appointment as burgomaster of The Hague (1911–18), which housed the Permanent Court of Arbitration and the World Court.

Not belonging to a political party, he became Minister of Foreign Affairs in three successive Cabinets, mainly composed of the major religious parties (1918–27). His first task was to prepare the reorganization of the ministry, replacing a passive policy of neutrality with a more active international stance. His diplomacy did much to restore the international prestige of the Netherlands, which had fallen because of its neutrality in the First World War. Like his father he was a strong advocate of international arbitration. In his view arbitration, collective security, and disarmament were strongly connected. In 1921 Van Karnebeek led the Dutch delegation to the disarmament conference in Washington. He also was chairman of the Second Assembly of the League of Nations.

His political career ended when a proposed treaty with Belgium was defeated in the Upper House in 1927. He was appointed *Minister van Staat*. In 1928 he became Governor of the province of South Holland. Nationally and internationally he continued to play a role in arbitration matters. From 1930 till 1932 he was chairman of the Association for the League of Nations and Peace. In 1935 he became a member of the Permanent Court of Arbitration, and in 1936 chairman of the Carnegie-Foundation which administers the Peace Palace in The Hague.

Van Kleffens, Eelco Nicolaas (b. Heerenveen, 17 Nov. 1894; d. Almoçagême, Portugal, 17 June 1983)
Dutch; Minister of Foreign Affairs

After law study at Leiden, which he completed in 1918 with a dissertation on the relations between the Netherlands and Japan since 1605, Van Kleffens worked for a time in the secretariat of the League of Nations and then with the Shell group in London (1920–2). From 1922 until 1958 he served in the Ministry of Foreign Affairs, and from 1929 as head of the Division of Diplomatic Affairs. On the point of leaving the Netherlands as head of the Dutch Legation in Bern, he was asked to accept the portfolio of Foreign Affairs in the new De Geer Cabinet, which was to become the government in exile in 1940. During the war period he shared in international preparations for the establishment of the United Nations, generally acting as champion of the rights of smaller states over the great powers. He developed ideas about regional co-operation and security arrangements which foreshadowed the later establishment of NATO. He exchanged the Ministry for Foreign Affairs in the first post-war Cabinet for the post of Minister without Portfolio (1946) and Permanent Representative of the Netherlands at the Security Council (1946–7). The next three years he was Dutch ambassador in Washington. In 1950 he requested a quieter post, becoming ambassador in Portugal (1950–6). In 1954 he presided over the Ninth Session of the General

Assembly of the United Nations. In 1956 he became Permanent Representative for the Dutch government to NATO and the OEEC at Paris. For the last nine years of his public career he was Representative of the High Authority of the European Coal and Steel Community in the UK. He returned to Portugal on retirement.

Van Roijen, Jan Herman (b. Constantinople, 10 Apr. 1905; d. Wassenaar, 16 Mar. 1991)

Netherlandish; Minister of Foreign Affairs 1946

Van Roijen studied law in Utrecht. He followed his father in opting for a diplomatic career. His first station was Washington (1930). In 1933 he worked at the Ministry of Foreign Affairs in The Hague. At his next post (Tokyo 1937) he was involved in negotiations between the Netherlands Indies and Japan. He returned to The Hague in 1939 on his appointment as director of the Division of Diplomatic Affairs in the Ministry for Foreign Affairs.

During the German occupation he was arrested several times, and finally dismissed from the department. In 1944 he escaped to London to inform the government-in-exile of conditions prevailing in the occupied country. After the war he became Minister without Portfolio, charged with the reorganization of the department (1945–6). He attended several UN meetings, in San Francisco and in London. In March 1946 he changed roles with the Minister of Foreign Affairs, E. *Van Kleffens, who for various reasons preferred to be a Minister without Portfolio. After a few months Van Roijen returned to diplomatic life. He was ambassador in Ottawa (1947–50), in Washington (1950–64), and in London (1964–70). During these years he played an important role representing the Netherlands before the Security Council at the height of the Indonesian conflicts. He also played an important role in arriving at the so-called Van Roijen–Roem agreements which paved the way to the Round Table Conference resulting in the transfer of sovereignty in December 1949. He played an equally important role in the negotiations which led to the transfer of Dutch New Guinea to Indonesia (1962). After retirement he carried out an important special mission to Saudi Arabia (1973).

Vargas, Getúlio Dornelles (b. São Borja, Rio Grande do Sul, 1882; d. Rio de Janiero, 24 Aug. 1954)

Brazilian; Minister of Finance 1926, President of Rio Grande do Sul 1927, President of Brazil 1930–45, 1950–4

Getúlio Vargas, in his two terms as President, did more than any other politician to shape the modern Brazilian state, with its strong centralist, nationalist tradition, its long commitment to public ownership and to a formal, if not always effective, system of social welfare.

Vargas was a *gaúcho*, from the southernmost state of Rio Grande do Sul, deeply divided in the late nineteenth and early twentieth centuries by bloody civil war, from which emerged a centralist political system, influenced by positivism. Vargas helped to unite two of his state's most important political clans, becoming President of Rio Grande do Sul, then Minister of Finance in the federal government. He was already a seasoned politician, cautious, conciliatory, and with a strong dislike of conflict and confrontation, when he became President of Brazil, following the revolution of 3 October 1930. Vargas now drew on the centralizing tradition of his native state, supported by military leaders and industrialists, to weld the loose federation of the 'Old Republic' (1889–30) into a centralized state, with a stronger federal army, a stronger civil service and greatly enlarged social and economic powers and responsibilities. He confronted São Paulo in a civil war in 1932, defused other political opposition, from left and right, and pushed through political and social change under the corporatist constitution of the *Estado Novo*, 1937 to 1945.

In this process, he sought to break Brazil's economic dependence, however lucrative, on coffee and a handful of other primary products. He introduced measures for industrialization, including state control of the new steel industry, and sought to create a new industrial working class under corporatist controls, but protected, at least in law, by a detailed system of social and labour legislation, well in advance of its time. After Brazil entered the Second World War on the Allies' side, there was increased opposition to Vargas's corporatism, which he recognized by creating two political parties, the PTB (the Brazilian Labour Party), and the PSD (the Social Democratic Party), the first drawing on working-class support through the Ministry of Labour, the second largely on rural clientelism. He especially cultivated the urban working class and promised free elections, but was forced out of office in 1945 by united civilian and military opposition.

Vargas was elected as President in 1950 and committed himself to a programme of *trabalhismo*, namely, concerned with and for organized labour. This introduced, then increased, a minimum wage, offered wider social reforms, and sought to protect the national economy from what was perceived as an illegitimate degree of foreign intervention. Vargas's enemies on the right, in alliance with some leaders of the armed forces, partly inspired by Cold War ideology, accused him of 'populism' and wishing to follow a political trajectory similar to that of *Perón in Argentina. Under extreme pressure, Vargas shot himself on 24 August 1954.

Vargas remains an enigmatic figure, a supreme conciliatory politician, who died in political conflict, a social reformer, who imposed authoritarian controls, but was democratically elected with passionate popular support. The political tradition he introduced was inherited by President Kubitschek (1956–61), especially in promoting industrialization and infrastructure investment. The coup of 1964 and the subsequent military-backed regime (1964–85) were largely a reaction to Vargas and his policies. The key issues raised in his second period of government are still central to Brazilian political debate.

Veil, Simone Anne (b. Nice, 13 July 1927)
French; Minister of Health 1974–9, MEP 1979–

One of four children in a Jewish family from Nice, Veil was taken prisoner in the Occupation and sent to Auschwitz; her mother, father, and brother all died in captivity. She returned in 1945 and took up study of law and political science to qualify as a judge in 1956 but she entered the Ministry of Justice to become involved in a number of humanitarian and women's issues and adviser to the Minister of Justice in 1969. President *Giscard d'Estaing launched her political career by making her Minister of Health in 1974 in *Chirac's first Cabinet. As the first woman full Minister of the Fifth Republic she introduced the *Loi Veil* legalizing abortion. A law opening access to contraception and to information about birth control was passed in December of 1974. In January of 1975 the law legalizing abortion was passed, and was the start of an enduring popularity (and of venomous attacks). Mme Veil also undertook to reform or tackle other health issues and the reform of social security. No respecter of persons, a popular but not populist minister, she once noted that there is nothing more boring than an election meeting. She was a campaigner for women's issues and for the 'downtrodden in society' as well as a determined 'centrist' moderate (she set up the Club Vauban to bring together centrists who were, she felt, under pressure from party extremists). She became increasingly at odds with the politics of *Barre. She resigned in June 1979 to lead the centre Giscardian list for the European Parliament (against the Gaullists) and was immediately elected President of the new European Parliament. In 1984 she led a list of Gaullists and centrists (despite Giscard's pressure) and in 1989 led a centrist list against both the Gaullists and Giscard.

Velasco, Juan (b. Piura, 16 June 1910; d. 24 Dec. 1977)
Peruvian; President 1968–75

Originating from a poor family descended from Chinese immigrants, Velasco entered the Chorrillos military academy on the outskirts of Lima, rapidly rising to the rank of general. He became a supporter of the reformist current within the Peruvian armed forces, who on national security grounds argued that several decades of social change was rendering the oligarchic political system untenable, therefore socio-economic reforms aimed at increasing economic growth and enhancing national unity needed to be implemented—the gulf between the state and the population, especially the indigenous peasantry of the Andean highlands, made the nation vulnerable. Such attitudes were encouraged by the Cuban Revolution and the appearance of a guerrilla movement in the mid-1960s.

Given the inability of Fernando *Belaunde's government (1963–8) to address these issues, on 3 October 1968 Juan Velasco led a bloodless coup and in the following years pushed through key reforms aimed at fomenting industrialization, reducing the power of the oligarchy, minimizing external dependence and laying the foundations of a more modern democratic society. A comprehensive land reform was undertaken, strategic foreign interests in oil, mining, and telecommunications nationalized, as was the fishing industry and other activities. Multinationals engaged in the production of consumer durables were encouraged to invest. Worker participation in decision-making and profit distribution was introduced. Under Velasco, Peru became a prominent member of the non-aligned movement, education and social security provision was expanded, and Quechua made a second official language.

While this ambitious programme of reforms was being implemented, Velasco's health declined: he had a leg amputated in 1973 and it became increasingly difficult for him to run the government. Initially no move to oust him occurred due to the high regard with which he was held within the officer corps. Eventually, however, in August 1975 a bedridden Velasco was removed in a bloodless coup which ushered in the 'second phase' of the military government (1975–80). The new rulers reversed economic policy, pursuing IMF-style 'stabilization' programmes, and halted the reforms. Velasco eventually succumbed to his illness in December 1977. Several hundred thousand cramming the streets of Lima to accompany the funeral cortège to the cemetery, took control of the coffin and turned the procession into an impressive popular protest against the government's policies. Juan Velasco's administration proved a watershed in twentieth-century Peruvian politics; it changed everything while—paradoxically—changing nothing. He was an honest, sincere leader who inspired loyalty and affection; according to all recent opinion polls, by a large margin he remains the most popular president in living memory.

Velasco Ibarra, José María (b. Quito, 19 Mar. 1893; d. 30 Mar. 1979)
Ecuadorian; President 1934–5, 1944–7, 1952–6, 1960–1, 1968–72

Educated at a Jesuit College and at Quito's Central University where he studied law, Velasco Ibarra became a government official in 1922 and, despite sharing responsibility for the brutal suppression of the emerging labour movement, began to pose as the representative of the poor and the oppressed. He developed an ambivalent and vague 'populist' position based on a rejection of political parties, an emphasis on moral character, and tirades against the Ecuadorian élite.

After working as a journalist and studying in France at the Sorbonne he returned to enter Congress for the first time in 1932 as deputy for Pichincha. It was the beginning of a political career spanning fifty years during which he was elected President on five occasions, but only completed the alloted term of office once (1952–6).

Following his election in 1934 as a Liberal but with Conservative support, Velasco Ibarra's plan to establish a dictatorship was thwarted by an army coup. Fraud is believed to have robbed him of a return to governing the country in 1939, but five years later he reached the presidency for the second time. A familiar pattern followed: elected on a radical platform with left-wing support, he abruptly jettisoned his backers and installed a right-wing government with dictatorial powers. Overthrown and exiled in 1946 Velasco Ibarra returned to become president a third time in 1952. That he completed a full term for the first and only time is largely due to the prosperity generated by the banana boom and his rightward drift which met with oligarchical approval.

Elected again in 1960 only to be overthrown by his Vice-President a year later, Velasco Ibarra wore the presidential sash for the fifth time in 1968 only to repeat the pattern of the past. After assuming dictatorial powers the military removed him in 1972 and he slipped into exile for the last time.

Venizelos, Eleftherios (b. Mournies, Crete, 1864; d. Paris, 18 Mar. 1936)

Greek; Prime Minister 1910–15, 1917, 1918–20, 1924, 1928–32, 1932, 1933

Educated in Syros and Crete, Venizelos studied law in Athens, where he also gained his doctorate in 1886. Having participated actively in events that later led to the integration of his native Crete to Greece, Venizelos formed his first government in 1910. He immediately proceeded to the amendment of the constitution of 1864, thus establishing a bipolar system of government with a significant role for the monarch. The participation of Greece in the Balkan Wars under his inspirational leadership almost doubled the country's territory and population through the integration of Greek areas which until then had belonged to the Ottoman Empire. During the First World War he favoured Greek collaboration with the Entente forces, thus opposing King Constantine, who favoured a neutral stance (beneficial to Germany). This conflict also had a constitutional dimension, exacerbated by the King's open intervention in politics. Venizelos favoured a system of constitutional monarchy whereby the monarch would act within clearly defined limits. Constantine's departure in 1917 meant the collaboration of Greece with the Entente, which, after the end of the war, led to the significant expansion of Greece (Treaty of Sèvres, 1920). Venizelos led the Greek team that negotiated the Treaty of Lausanne, which settled a number of important disputes with Turkey. His second full term of office (1928–32) was marked by the consolidation of Greece's international position through the conclusion of important agreements with Italy (1928), Yugoslavia (1929), and Turkey (1930) aiming at the concentration of his efforts to modernize Greece.

Despite having participated in bitter political disputes Venizelos is now considered as the veritable Greek Leader of the Nation (*Ethnarchis*), whose action was characterized by an impressive mixture of vision, pragmatism, and resolve.

Verwoerd, Hendrik Frensch (b. Amsterdam, 8 Sept. 1901; d. 6 Sept. 1966)

South African; Prime Minister 1958–66

Born in the Netherlands to parents who emigrated to South Africa soon after his birth, Verwoerd enjoyed a successful academic career, becoming head of the sociology department at Stellenbosch University. He strongly identified with Afrikaner nationalism and edited the nationalist newspaper *Die Transvaler*, which was broadly sympathetic to the Nazi cause in Europe. In the 1948 elections he was narrowly defeated in his own parliamentary constituency but his standing in the National Party was such that he was appointed to the Senate and became its leader.

From 1950 he served in the Cabinet as Minister of Bantu Affairs and became the chief architect of the apartheid system. In 1958 he became leader of the National Party and Prime Minister, which placed him in an even more powerful position to push racial discrimination and segregation to its legal limits. In 1960 he banned the African National Congress and other anti-apartheid organizations, and in 1961 he withdrew South Africa from the Commonwealth, which he regarded as dangerously multi-racial. In 1962 he launched the Bantustan scheme under which black South Africans were to be allocated to 'independent' homelands and thereby deprived of any claims to South African citizenship. He recognized that black labour would continue to be essential for white prosperity but tried to ensure that they would have the status of migrant labourers with no civil rights. In 1966 Verwoerd was assassinated in parliament by a deranged white messenger who claimed to be acting on the orders of a giant tapeworm.

Ultimately Verwoerd's apartheid masterplan was to collapse but its impact on South Africa had deep and long-lasting consequences.

Vogel, Hans-Jochen (b. Göttingen, 3 Feb. 1926)

German; mayor of Munich 1960–72, SPD chairman 1987–91

The son of middle-class Bavarian Catholics, Vogel was a brilliant law student. Although his studies were interrupted by wartime military service he gained his doctorate in 1952. He had a successful career in the Bavarian legal service before becoming a professional politician. He joined the SPD in 1950, was elected to the SPD executive in 1970, and was mayor of Munich from 1960 to 1972. His greatest success there was to host the Olympic Games in 1972. He turned down re-election because of his disagreements with the left in the SPD in Munich.

Vogel was appointed by *Brandt Minister for Building and City Planning in 1972 but he failed to achieve his aim of reducing land speculation. From 1974 to 1981 he served as Minister of Justice. He was drafted by the SPD to take over as governing mayor of Berlin in 1981 at a time when the Berlin party was facing a crisis. Despite his many skills he could not stave off SPD defeat in the election in the same year, and then led the party in opposition until 1983 when he was drafted once again to challenge *Kohl in the federal election. The SPD suffered a resounding defeat, but he remained leader in the Bundestag until 1991. After Brandt gave up the chairmanship of the SPD in 1987 Vogel took over until 1991. In 1990 he opposed *Lafontaine's cautious approach to German reunification.

Von Bethmann Hollweg, Theobald (b. Hohenfinow, 29 Nov. 1856; d. 1 Jan. 1921)

German; German Chancellor 1909–17

Bethmann Hollweg was the son of a German landed estate owner whose family had produced a number of gifted lawyers, and a French Swiss officer's daughter. Having studied law he decided to join the civil service where his abilities were soon recognized. In 1905 he was appointed Prussian Minister of the Interior. He was known as a Conservative who encouraged the integration of the Social Democrats. On his resignation in 1909, *von Bülow recommended his appointment as Chancellor. At the same time he served as Prussian Minister-President and Foreign Minister and worked for an understanding with Britain. In return for a naval accord he wanted British neutrality in the event that Germany was involved in a European war. Grand Admiral Tirpitz opposed this and, despite goodwill on both sides, Lord *Haldane's mission of 1912 failed to bring about an Anglo-German understanding. This greatly increased the likelihood of war between the two states.

It appears that Bethmann Hollweg bore more responsibility than the Kaiser for the war which broke out in the summer of 1914. He saw Russia as the real danger to Germany and gambled on British neutrality in any German conflict with France and Russia. His mistake led to a general war. He believed the generals, who mistakenly thought the war would be short, and allowed himself to be convinced of the need for unrestricted submarine warfare, a major factor in the US declaration of war on Germany in 1917. Reactionaries brought about his downfall in July 1917 after he had successfully argued for electoral reform in the wake of growing political discontent.

Neither his reforms, nor opposition to them, could stop the revolutionary flood and Germany's defeat.

Von Bülow, Bernhard (b. 3 May 1849; d. 28 Oct. 1929)
German; Chancellor 1900–9

Von Bülow seemed to personify the spirit of the age. He wanted Germany to get its 'place in the sun' and become a world power. He followed his father into the diplomatic service, working in Vienna, Athens, Paris, and St Petersburg. Because he married a newly divorced woman he was banished to Romania from 1888 to 1893. During this time he became a convinced adherent of Treitschke, the historian who believed in the inevitability of Germany's rise to power. Von Bülow advocated close ties with Russia, indifference to Austria, caution *vis-à-vis* France, and hostility towards Britain. In 1893 he was appointed ambassador to Italy, and head of the Foreign Ministry in 1897. He was promoted to Chancellor in 1900, with a brief from the Kaiser to allay British suspicions of Germany's efforts to build a fleet, and finance its construction. This policy failed, causing fierce competition in naval building between Britain and Germany. The defeat of Russia in 1905 was also a blow to von Bülow, as Japan was an ally of Britain. Russia became allied to France and Britain.

In Germany Bülow gained Centre Party support for his programme and was the first Chancellor to attempt to govern through a parliamentary majority. He introduced tariffs which helped agriculture, especially the big landowners; when the Centre politicians criticized his colonialism, he dropped them and formed a Conservative–Liberal block which won the election of 1907. This fell apart after the left Liberals could not be appeased over political and financial reforms. He was already seriously damaged because he approved publication in the *Daily Telegraph* of an interview with the Kaiser which offended many in Britain and Germany alike. He was forced to resign in 1909.

Von Papen, Franz (b. Werl, 29 Oct. 1879; d. 2 May 1969)
German; Chancellor of Germany 1932, ambassador to Austria 1934–8, and to Turkey 1938–44

Born into a wealthy, aristocratic family Von Papen chose a military career, being promoted to captain and posted to the general staff in 1913. During the First World War he served in the German embassies in Mexico and Washington, where he was expelled for spying activities. With the rank of lieutenant-general he was then sent to Palestine to help Germany's ally Turkey. After the war he resigned from the army and took up politics. Although a member of the Catholic Centre Party he remained a monarchist and right-wing nationalist.

His links with industry and the military secured his appointment as German Chancellor on 1 June 1932. Totally unrepresentative of parliament, his government could only be a stop-gap. It lost a vote of confidence proposed by the Communists and supported by the Nazis. After the election of 6 November 1932 Von Papen's government fell and was eventually replaced by *Hitler on 30 January 1933. Von Papen agreed to serve as Deputy Chancellor in Hitler's first government, in which the Nazis were in a minority. Thus he gave respectability to Hitler in Germany's ruling circles. Hitler was able to outmanœuvre him at every turn and, when some of his closest associates were murdered in the Nazi blood purges of June 1934, he continued to serve. By 1936 he was banished as ambassador to Austria where he paved the way for its eventual takeover by Germany. From April 1939 he served as ambassador to Turkey.

Although Von Papen was acquitted by the International Military Tribunal at Nuremberg in 1946, he had played a decisive part in the rise of Hitler and remained identified with his regime to the end.

Von Weizsäcker, Richard (b. Stuttgart, 15 Apr. 1920)

German; President of Federal Republic of Germany 1981–4, governing mayor of West Berlin 1984–94

Richard von Weizsäcker completed his legal studies with a doctorate in law from Göttingen University. He turned to industry for employment but through his wife, Marianne von Kretschmann, he entered banking and became the head of her family's private bank. Other family contacts led to association with the pharmaceutical industry, Allianz insurance, Hill Samuel, and other firms.

Von Weizsäcker was greatly influenced by his wartime experiences. With his older brother he took part in the invasion of Poland on 1 September 1939. His brother was killed on 2 September and he was wounded but served until the end, reaching the rank of infantry captain. He had lost many of his illusions in the intervening campaigns. Worse was to come. His father Ernst von Weizsäcker was tried as a war criminal and sentenced to seven years' imprisonment by the Allies but released in a general amnesty in 1950. He had served the Nazi regime as a diplomat, his last posting being German ambassador to the Vatican, 1943–5.

Von Weizsäcker joined the CDU in 1954 and was elected to the executive of the party in 1964 and to the Bundestag in 1969. He was also, 1972–9, deputy chairman of the CDU/CSU joint parliamentary group. In 1979 he was elected one of four vice-presidents of the Bundestag. His political success was due in part to his chairmanship of the Synod of the Evangelical Church which he held from 1964 to 1970.

In 1981 von Weizsäcker beat *Vogel to be governing mayor of West Berlin. His election as President of the Federal Republic followed in May 1984. Vogel had advised his SPD colleagues to vote for von Weizsäcker. He remained President until 1994 and was well received by Germany's neighbours in East and West as a man of reconciliation.

Voroshilov, Kliment Yefremovich (b. Verkhne near Dnepropetrovsk, 4 Feb. 1881; d. Ukraine, 3 Dec. 1969)

Russian; Commissar of Military and Naval Affairs 1925–40, member of the Politburo 1926–60

Voroshilov was the son of working-class parents, and went to work in the mines at the age of 17. He joined the Bolshevik Party in 1903 and became a leader of the underground organization inside Russia, participating in the Revolution of 1905. During the Civil War he served under *Stalin, who gave him command of the Red Army at Tsaritsyn. He then served as a cavalry commander under Budenny and acquired a reputation for cruelty. From 1921 to 1925 he held important military commands. From 1925 to 1940 he was People's Commissar of Military and Naval Affairs with the rank of Marshal of the Soviet Union after 1935. He supported Stalin's purge of the Red Army at the end the 1930s and was appointed to the Main Military Council. He became a member of the *Stavka* (General Staff) just before the German invasion. He was, however, much more a general than a politician. He supported Stalin in his struggle against *Trotsky, opposing the latter's plans to reform the Red Army, and Tukhachevsky's plans to modernize the army. From 1926 to 1960 he was a member of the Politburo. During the war he served without distinction (described by a fellow Red Army general as 'incapable of understanding modern warfare') and accompanied Stalin to the Tehran Conference in 1943. From 1946 to 1953 he was Deputy Chairman of the Council of Ministers. But by 1948 Stalin suspected him, improbably, of being an English spy. After Stalin's death in 1953 he was appointed to the largely honorific post of chairman of the Presidium of the Supreme Soviet. In 1961 *Khrushchev denounced him as a sympathizer with the 'anti-party group' and dismissed him from office.

Vyshinsky, Andrei Yanuarovich (b. 11 Dec. 1883; d. 22 Nov. 1954)
Russian; Chief Procurator of the USSR 1935–9, Minister of Foreign Affairs 1949–53

Vyshinsky was of Polish extraction, the son of middle-class parents. He was educated as a lawyer. He joined the Russian Social Democratic Labour Party in 1902, and then the Mensheviks when the party split in 1903. He did not join the Bolsheviks until 1920. From 1921 to 1928 he was an academic lawyer at Moscow University, attaining the position of rector. From 1928 to 1931 he was head of the higher education section of the People's Commissariat for Education. Vyshinsky first came to public prominence in 1928 at the Shakhty trial in which a number of engineers were convicted on trumped-up charges of sabotage. He was either head of the court or chief prosecutor in subsequent show trials, notably the Industrial Party trial of 1930; the Metropolitan-Vickers trial of 1933; at the trials of *Zinoviev and *Kamenev in August 1936; of Marshal Tukhachevsky in 1937; and of *Bukharin, *Rykov, and *Yagoda in 1938. In all these cases Vyshinsky distinguished himself by his abusive, even vicious rhetoric. From 1935 to 1939 he was Chief Procurator of the USSR and in 1939 was elected member of the Soviet Academy of Sciences. From 1939 to 1955 he was a member of the Central Committee. In 1940 he moved to the post of Deputy People's Commissar (i.e. Deputy Minister) of Foreign Affairs. In 1949 he succeeded *Molotov as Minister of Foreign Affairs, holding this post until *Stalin's death in 1953. His vitriolic performances at the United Nations were reminiscent of his behaviour at the show trials and served to exacerbate East–West relations. After Stalin's death he was demoted to Deputy Minister of Foreign Affairs.

Wagner, Robert (b. Germany, 8 June 1877; d. 4 May 1953)
US; US Senator

Wagner emigrated with his family to New York in 1885. He was educated in New York and qualified as a lawyer. He made his reputation in fighting many high-profile labour cases. He was elected as a Democrat in the state Senate and became the party's floor leader. At the time he had to work with the notorious Tammany Hall political machine. As a pro-labour politician, he sponsored bills covering wages and working hours for women and children and workmen's compensation. He became a judge in 1918. In 1926 he was elected to the Senate for New York and he was re-elected three times until his retirement from ill-health in 1949. In the Senate he continued with his interest in labour and employment issues and was a strong supporter of Franklin *Roosevelt and the New Deal. He introduced the National Recovery Act (NRA), to provide for minimum wage and maximum hours and tackle unemployment by public works construction programmes. His Wagner Act (1935), passed after the Supreme Court struck down the NRA, protected workers' rights to organize and bargain collectively through their own representatives and forbade employers from discriminating against unions. He also helped to establish the National Labor Relations Board, to rule on disputes arising from the act and to settle inter-union disputes. Some of these gains for labour were later reversed by the *Taft–Hartley Act passed in 1947 by a Republican Congress. In his first term in the Senate, he sponsored a bill for a census of the unemployed, a scheme of public works, and the creation of an employment agency to assist in the transfer of labour from areas of high to low unemployment.

Wakeham, John (b. 22 June 1932)
British; chief whip 1983–7, leader of the House of Commons 1987–9 and House of Lords 1992–4; Baron (life peer) 1992

John Wakeham was an important member of Mrs *Thatcher's and John *Major's governments in the 1980s and 1990s. He was a successful accountant and already financially secure when he won the Malden consitutency in February 1974, a seat he held until 1983 when it was redrawn as Colchester South and Malden. He remained as MP for the seat until 1992.

Wakeham proved to be a skilful chief whip (1983–7), warning Margaret Thatcher that a number of her proposals, including the Shops Bill (allowing shops to trade on Sundays) and the sale of Austin Rover cars to General Motors in 1986, could not be carried in parliament. He nearly lost his life in October 1984 when the IRA bombed the Brighton Grand Hotel at the time of the annual party conference. His wife Roberta was among those who died. After a lengthy period of convalescence he returned to politics but was in pain and walked with some difficulty for the remainder of his life.

In the 1987 parliament Wakeham entered the Cabinet as Lord Privy Seal and Leader of the House of Commons. He managed to pilot through a number of controversial measures, including education reforms, the poll tax, and water privatization. He became Secretary of State for Energy in July 1989 and for the first time ran his own department. In this post he handled the privatization of electricity supply and distribution.

When Mrs Thatcher failed to win the party leadership on the first ballot in 1990 it was Wakeham's initiative for her to consult individually with Cabinet ministers.

Some of her supporters subsequently blamed him for arranging the meeting that finally persuaded her to step down. In the next round of the leadership election he supported John Major and remained at Energy in John Major's first government. He retired from the Commons in 1992.

In the new parliament Wakeham entered the House of Lords but remained in the Cabinet as Lord Privy Seal and leader of the Lords. He chaired a number of key Cabinet committees. He left the government in 1994 and became chairman of the Press Complaints Commission.

Wakeham was widely regarded as a skilled political fixer, operating behind the scenes. He was good at bringing people together and striking compromises between people of different viewpoints.

Waldheim, Kurt (b. 21 Dec. 1918)

Austrian; President 1986–92, Secretary-General of the UN 1972–82

Kurt Waldheim has the doubtful honour of being the only Austrian President, or indeed politician, since 1945, who is remembered outside Austria. He is remembered far more for his wartime service than for his service as UN Secretary-General.

Born in 1918 into a middle-class Catholic family in Lower Austria, Waldheim grew up in a country torn by political divisions and trying to come to terms with its decline from being a great empire in 1914 to being a small state in 1918. Waldheim studied law in Vienna with the intention of entering the diplomatic service, but the Nazi takeover of Austria in 1938 prevented him realizing this ambition. The war came and he was called up, serving in the German army as a lieutenant. After recovering from wounds sustained on the eastern front he was sent to occupied Greece and later Yugoslavia. He was an intelligence officer on the staff of General Alexander Löhr who, on *Hitler's birthday in 1945, presented his fellow Austrian Waldheim with a War Merit Cross, First Class, with Swords. Löhr was executed after the war as a war criminal. In his memoirs Waldheim wrote very little about his wartime activities.

As Austria was treated as a victim of Nazi Germany rather than a willing ally it was able to re-establish its own government and diplomatic service in 1945. Waldheim was accepted for the diplomatic service and rose rapidly, serving in Paris, Ottawa, at the UN, and as Minister for Foreign Affairs 1968–70. He stood unsuccessfully as the (Conservative) People's Party candidate for the Austrian presidency in 1971. As a seasoned diplomat from a small, neutral country he was elected Secretary-General of the UN in 1972, serving until 1982. On the second ballot, he was elected President of Austria in 1986, being the first non-Socialist since 1945 to hold this office.

It was during his election campaign that allegations were made about Waldheim's wartime role. He was accused of being involved in atrocities against civilians including the deportation of Jews to the death camps. Although an international commission of inquiry set up by the Socialist government found in his favour, it believed he had been unwise not to say more about his time in the German army. Simon Wiesenthal, the famous Nazi hunter, came to the same conclusion. Nevertheless, Waldheim's detractors were partly successful. He was largely ostracized during his presidency and decided not to seek a second term.

Wałęsa, Lech (b. Popowo, 29 Sept. 1943)

Polish; chairman of Solidarity, 1981– , President 1989–96

Wałęsa was the son of a carpenter. After elementary education and three years' vocational training he moved to Gdańsk, where he worked as an electrician in the Lenin Shipyards. He was determined to secure recognition for the workers shot by the regime after the food riots of 1970. In 1976 he joined in demonstrations against the government's watering-down of the economic concessions it had made in 1970 and as a result was dismissed from his job. From 1976 to 1980 he was unemployed and edited an underground newspaper. At the same time he was a prominent member of the Workers' Self-Defence Committee, an unofficial organization which had close links with the Catholic intelligentsia. In August 1980 the workers of Gdańsk went on strike at the government's raising food prices. Wałęsa climbed into the Lenin Shipyards where his former colleagues recognized him as leader of the strike which soon spread. At the end of the month, Wałęsa led a committee which negotiated with the Communist regime. On 30 August the government granted the workers' right to form independent trade unions and their right to strike as well as general freedom of expression. These concessions were unprecedented in the Soviet Bloc. In September 1980, Wałęsa became chairman of Solidarity, the newly created national organization of the independent trade unions. By the time of its first congress in September 1981, Solidarity had 9½ million members. Wałęsa tried to play a moderating role within the organization. A devout Catholic himself he was in close touch with the primate of Poland, Cardinal Glemp, and was advised by members of the Catholic intelligentsia, such as Tadeusz *Mazowiecki. He was unable to restrain the radical wing of Solidarity, which pushed for a greater share of political power. After General *Jaruzelski's declaration of martial law in December 1981, Wałęsa was put under house arrest for eleven months. Upon his release he resumed leadership of the now underground Solidarity organization. In 1983 he was awarded the Nobel Peace Prize for his defence of the Polish workers. He donated the money to charity. Solidarity refused to co-operate with Jaruzelski's programme of economic reform, which failed.

In January 1989 the Communist regime legalized Solidarity and Wałęsa played a key role in the negotiations between trade union, church, and state which led to the partially free elections of May 1989. In September 1989 Wałęsa's candidate, Mazowiecki, formed the first non-Communist government since the 1940s. In April 1990 Wałęsa was re-elected chairman of Solidarity. Over the year a split within Solidarity grew, partly because of Wałęsa's criticism of the slow pace of political reform and the harsh social consequences of rapid marketization. When Jaruzelski resigned as President in November he stood against Mazowiecki and Polish-born Canadian émigré, Tymiński. In the first electoral round he gained only 40 per cent of the vote against Tymiński's 23 per cent and Mazowiecki's 18 per cent. But in the second round he won a decisive victory with 74 per cent of the vote against Tymiński's 26 per cent, and became President in December 1990. His popularity continued to be eroded by austerity and he was narrowly defeated by the reformed Communist candidate in the presidential elections of January 1996.

Walker, Peter Edward (b. London, 25 Mar. 1932)

British; Secretary of State for the Environment 1970–2, Trade and Industry 1972–4, Welsh Secretary 1987–90; Baron (life peer) 1992

Educated at Latymer Upper School, Walker made his fortune early in life, as co-founder of the Slater-Walker companies, dealing in property and securities. He was chairman of the National Young Conservatives from 1958 to 1960 before he entered parliament in a by-election in 1961 as Conservative MP for Worcester. When the Conservative Party entered Opposition in 1964, he was appointed to the front bench and rose rapidly within party ranks. When the party was returned to power in 1970 he was made Minister of Housing and Local Government and then, in October, Secretary of State for the Environment. He was aged 38. Two years later, he was appointed to head the other 'super ministry', the Department of Trade and Industry. His career took a downward turn when Margaret *Thatcher was elected party leader in 1975. Walker, although a long-standing critic of the European Community, had been Edward *Heath's campaign manager in 1964 and was closely identified with him. Thatcher dropped him from the front bench. In 1979, he was nonetheless brought into government (much to his own surprise), serving first as Agriculture Minister, then Energy Secretary—presiding over the government's handling of the 1984–5 miners' strike—and, finally, as Secretary of State for Wales, before retiring from government in 1990. He left the House of Commons in 1992 and took his seat in the Lords as Lord Walker of Worcester.

Though out of sympathy with Margaret Thatcher's economic policies, he got on amicably with her in government. She preferred to have him in government rather than as an effective critic on the back benches and gave him her support in his un-Thatcherite running of the Welsh Office. By the time he left office, he and Margaret Thatcher were the only ministers who had held Cabinet office in every year of Conservative government since 1970.

Wallace, George Corley (b. Clio, Alabama, 25 Aug. 1919)

US; representative in the Alabama State Legislature 1946–50, Governor of Alabama 1962–6, 1970–8, 1982–6

The son of a farmer, Wallace graduated LL B from the University of Alabama in 1942 and that same year was called to the bar in Alabama. During the Second World War he served with the USAF 1942–5, after which he returned to Alabama and the appointment of assistant state attorney. A Democrat, he began an active political career in 1946 when he was elected to the State Legislature. He was re-elected for a seocnd term in 1948. It was as a judge of the Third Judicial Circuit of Alabama 1953–9 that Wallace first revealed what were to become the planks of his future political platform: states' rights and segregationalism. At this time he acquired the nickname the 'Fighting Judge' because of his intransigence in the face of the US Commission on Civil Rights investigations into discrimination in black voting rights.

It was as a racial moderate, however, that Wallace made a bid for the state governorship in 1958. His defeat at the hands of an undisguised segregationalist made him vow never to be 'outsegged' again. In 1962 he won the governorship after an openly racist campaign and at his inauguration in 1963 he pledged himself to segregation. He carried out this pledge to the extent of physically blocking the enrolment of black students at the University of Alabama, yielding only in the face of the federally deployed National Guard. In 1966 he was legally ineligible for re-election, but his wife successfully ran for office and replaced him as Governor. His wife died in 1968 and Wallace regained the governorship in 1970 in 1974.

Wallace was a populist leader with ambitions to become President. As an unashamedly segregationist candidate he attempted unsuccessfully to gain the Democratic nomination in 1964. He tried again in 1968, as candidate for the American Independent Party, attempting to capitalize on the white backlash against *Johnson's civil rights legislation. He failed to reach the White House but he did win 13.5 per cent of the popular vote and 46 electoral college votes. For his third try for the presidency, Wallace returned to the Democratic Party fold in 1972. On this occasion his campaign was brought to an abrupt end by an assassination attempt on 15 May 1972 at Laurel, Maryland. This left him permanently paralysed below the waist but, in 1976, from his wheelchair, he again contested the Democratic Party nomination but lost to Jimmy *Carter. In 1982 the indefatigable and charismatic Wallace, having recanted his former segregationalist policies, was again elected governor of Alabama. He retired from politics in 1987.

Wallace, Henry (b. Adair County, Iowa, 17 Oct. 1888; d. Nov. 1965)

US; Vice-President 1941–5

Henry Wallace graduated from college in animal husbandry and had a lifelong interest in farming matters. He was a breeder of rare plants and edited *Wallace's Farmer*. His father was Agricultural Secretary under Republican Presidents *Harding and

*Coolidge. Wallace switched from being a progressive Republican to supporting the Democrats in 1928 because of what he felt was the party's neglect of agriculture. F. D. *Roosevelt made him Secretary of Agriculture and he held this post in Roosevelt's first two administrations (1933–41). As Secretary, he helped farmers in the Depression by paying them to restrict their output and supplying credit through his Agriculture Adjustment Administration. He also brought in food stamps and school milk programmes. Roosevelt thought highly of him and supported him for the vice-presidential nomination at the 1940 Democratic convention. Wallace faced strong opposition but FDR declared that he would not serve unless Wallace was nominated.

During the war Wallace was also chairman of the Board of Economic Warfare (1942–5). In this post he was often in conflict with the Secretary of Commerce. At the 1944 Democratic convention there was even stronger opposition to his renomination, because party influentials feared for the health of the President and a Wallace succession. He was already an enthusiastic supporter of the USSR. In Roosevelt's fourth administration he was made Commerce Secretary, and advocated schemes of economic planning and full employment. As tensions developed between the United States and the USSR he was increasingly isolated within the administration. Following a speech critical of US foreign policy towards the Soviet Union, he was sacked by President *Truman.

Out of office, Wallace broadened his disagreements with the administration. He claimed that Truman was betraying the New Deal, and that the *Marshall Plan aid for reconstructing Europe was an instrument of US and big business influence. He blamed the United States for the coup in Czechoslovakia and for the worsening of relations with the USSR. In 1948 he ran as a liberal Progressive candidate for the presidency, although the main influences behind the campaign were Communist. His candidacy might have damaged Truman but he ended up with only 2 per cent of the vote and no electoral college votes. In his retirement he returned to farming. Wallace was a man of vision and great energy, but his lack of political judgement proved fatal.

Warren, Earl (b. Los Angeles, 19 Mar. 1891; d. 9 July 1974)

US; Governor of California 1942–53, Chief Justice of the Supreme Court 1953–69

Educated at the University of California in Berkeley, Warren practised law and became district attorney. He served as Attorney-General of California 1939–42. In 1942 he was elected Governor of California and was re-elected in 1946 and 1950. He was a very successful Governor as California boomed during the Second World War and in post-war years, enabling state expenditure to increase while taxes were lowered. He promoted the development of higher education in California. Although a moderate Republican he was not particularly liberal on issues of civil liberties. In particular, he supported the removal of Japanese Americans during the Second World War from their homes to camps inland in California.

In 1948 he was selected by Thomas *Dewey as vice-presidential candidate on the Republican ticket. Since President *Truman appeared to be extremely unpopular and the Democratic party was badly split, Republican victory and his election as Vice-President of the United States seemed assured. Surprisingly, however, Truman won re-election and the Dewey–Warren Republican ticket went down to defeat.

In 1952 he supported Dwight D. *Eisenhower for the Republican nomination for president in Eisenhower's contest with Robert *Taft. His support for Eisenhower was crucial in Eisenhower's success in winning the Republican nomination. In 1953, when a vacancy occurred for Chief Justice of the Supreme Court, Eisenhower appointed him to the post.

He became celebrated as a reforming liberal Chief Justice. In 1954, the Supreme Court ruling in the case of *Brown v. The Board of Education* declared segregation in schools to be unconstitutional and the court ordered the integration of schools as rapidly as practical. Other liberal rulings concerned reappointment of state legislatures on the basis of one person one vote and protection of the rights of the accused in criminal cases. He believed that the court should interpret the constitution in a manner which reflected contemporary political realities rather than rigidly adhering to narrow legal precedents. As Chief Justice he exercised his political skills to achieve a consensus on the court for his legal philosophy.

Washington, Harold (b. Chicago, 15 Apr. 1922; d. 25 Nov. 1987)

US; member of Illinois State Legislature 1966–80, member of the US House of Representatives 1981–2, mayor of Chicago 1983–7

The son of a Methodist minister and Democratic party activist, Washington spent his life immersed in the politics of Chicago. Following distinguished war service in the air force, Washington attended Roosevelt College and Northwestern Law School. Although he served as counsel for the Chicago corporation for a brief period, he was drawn to elective politics and ran successfully for the State Legislature in 1964. He served in the Illinois House of Representatives from 1966 to 1976 and in its Senate 1978–80. Initially he was part of the powerful political machine that supported Mayor Richard *Daley; but he later broke with the Cook County Democratic establishment and formed a coaltion of support built primarily on the black and growing Hispanic communities. In 1980 he ran as an independent candidate in the Illinois 1st District (the South Side) and defeated the official Democratic candidate.

In Congress, Washington became identified with black issues especially the battle to extend the protections against discrimination offered by the Voting Rights Act of 1965. Chicago politics reclaimed him when in 1983 he was persuaded to enter the Democratic primary race for mayor, a contest which acquired national significance. Washington's opponents were the incumbent mayor, Jane *Byrne (who had alienated her black support) and Richard M. Daley, the son of the former mayor (who was largely dependent on conservative ethnic voters). The contest opened up Democratic Party divisions as Walter *Mondale backed Daley and Edward *Kennedy backed Byrne. Washington received support from Jesse *Jackson, a long-time opponent of the Daley machine. Washington won the primary and the general election in which racial divisions polarized as many white Democrats switched their vote to Republican Bernard Epton. Washington thus became Chicago's first black mayor. While many regretted the role which race played in the campaigns, Washington became a symbol of black political achievement and one of a number of key elected black officials who could play a role in the national debate about urban policy.

In office Washington's record was mixed. He displayed caution in economic matters and attempted to reassure the financial community by balancing the budget. The intractable problems of housing, poverty, crime, and white flight to the suburbs posed challenges to his administration which he was only partially able to address. His own style of machine politics incorporated minorities but was by no means free of corruption. Moreover, it lacked the administrative efficiency of the defunct Daley machine.

Despite doubts about many aspects of Washington's policies, he was re-elected in 1987. Although race was still a factor, Washington had by that stage transcended much of the sectarianism associated with his first term. His unexpected death so soon after re-election deprived the black community of a formidable political operator.

Waverley, Viscount *see* ANDERSON, JOHN

Weaver, Robert Clifton (b. Washington, DC, 29 Dec. 1907)
US; black reformer

Educated at Harvard University (where he obtained a Ph.D. in economics), Weaver became an aide to Harold Ickes and played an increasingly important role advising on policy relating to black Americans, serving in the Interior Department 1933–7 and as special assistant to the administrator of the United States Housing Authority 1937–40. He spent time teaching and then from 1954 to 1959 became involved in the administration of housing policy in New York City as Deputy State Housing Commissioner and as vice-president of the City Housing and Redevelopment Board.

When John *Kennedy nominated Weaver to be administrator of the Housing and Home Finance Agency, the nomination had to overcome the objections of southern Democrats who were opposed to civil rights. Weaver's nomination succeeded but the Kennedy administration lost the battle to upgrade the agency to a Cabinet department not least because congressional conservatives thought that Weaver, a key figure in the National Association for the Advancement of Colored People, would be nominated to the post. Under Lyndon *Johnson a new department of Housing and Urban Development was created and Weaver was nominated to be its first secretary. He thus became in 1966 the first black member of an American Cabinet, a post in which he served until 1969. An able administrator and a committed reformer, Weaver advocated a number of new initatives including the demonstration cities programme. At the end of the Johnson administration, Weaver went into academic administration as president of Baruch College.

Webb, Sidney James (b. London, 13 July 1859; d. 13 Oct. 1947)
British; Secretary of State for the Colonies 1929–31; Baron (Lord Passfield) 1929

The son of an accountant, Webb was educated privately and then at the Birkbeck Institute and the City of London College.

Webb's House of Commons and ministerial career was brief and undistinguished. Entering the House of Commons at the age of 63, he became president of the Board of Trade in the first Labour government (1924) fifteen months later. He retired from the Commons when the government fell. He accepted a peerage to join the second Labour government (1929–31), as Secretary of State first for the Dominions and the Colonies (1929–30), then for the Colonies alone. He left office when the government collapsed in 1931.

It was as an intellectual that Webb made his greatest contribution to the Labour movement. One of its most prominent thinkers in its formative years, he played a dominant part in the Fabian Society in the 1890s and on the London county council for some twenty years before the First World War. First elected to the National Executive Committee of the Labour Party in 1915 and sitting on it for the next ten years, he drafted the manifesto for the vital 1918 general election, having already helped devise the new party constitution.

Webb was a prolific propagandist and first chairman of the editorial board of the weekly *New Statesman*. But he also undertook voluminous academic research into social issues, trade unionism, and local government. Much of this work was done in collaboration with his wife Beatrice. The most enduring memorial to their interest in education is the London School of Economics and Political Science, to whose establishment in 1895 they made an indispensable contribution.

Wehner, Herbert (b. Dresden, 11 July 1906; d. 1990)
German; deputy chairman of the SPD 1958–73, Minister for All-German Affairs 1966–9

Wehner was a brooding, enigmatic politician who was one of the founders of the Federal Republic of Germany. Rumours still surround this shoemaker's son from

Dresden largely because of his early activities in the Communist Party (KPD). After grammar school Wehner took up an apprenticeship as a commerical clerk but soon abandoned this for Communist journalism. He joined the KPD in 1927 and by 1930 was representing the party in the parliament of Saxony at the same time he was elected to the KPD's Central Committee. In 1935 he was in Moscow with the exiled KPD as a member of its Politburo. He was regarded as totally reliable and did not suffer in the Stalinist purges which decimated the KPD leadership. In 1941 he was sent as the Comintern's representative in neutral Sweden where he was imprisoned for unlawful political activity. It was during his Swedish sojourn that he broke with Stalinism and turned to social democracy.

Despite his past, in 1946 Wehner was welcomed into the SPD by *Schumacher, who saw him as a useful ally in the fight to keep the party free from KPD influence. In 1949 Wehner was elected to the first Bundestag and remained a member until he withdrew from politics in 1983. He led the SPD's group in the Bundestag from 1969 to 1983, serving also as deputy chairman of the SPD from 1958 to 1973. He was a key figure in the successful attempts to change the direction of the SPD by adopting the Bad Godesberg Programme (1958) and membership of NATO and the EEC. He also sought a coalition with the majority Christian Democrats which was achieved in 1966.

Wehner's home town had become part of the Soviet-occupied German Democratic Republic (GDR) and this is reason enough for his continuing interest in relations with the GDR and attempts to restore German unity. Between 1966 and 1969 he served in the grand coalition of Christian Democrats and Social Democrats as minister responsible for policy *vis-à-vis* the GDR. Although Wehner had been strongly denounced as a renegade and traitor in the GDR media, it fell to him to undertake delicate secret meetings with East German leader *Honecker.

In the West, Wehner was accused by some of having saved his own skin by denouncing his comrades to *Stalin's secret police in the 1930s; they regarded him as a Soviet Trojan horse. *Brandt believed he had been let down by Wehner when he was forced to resign in 1974. Wehner then backed Helmut *Schmidt as Brandt's successor.

Wheatley, John (b. Lanarkshire, 18 May 1869; d. 12 May 1930)
British; Minister of Health 1924

A labourer's son, Wheatley left elementary school at 11 and worked first in the coal mines and later as a shop assistant. He joined the Independent Labour Party in 1908. He followed the unpopular ILP line of opposition to the First World War, but was nevertheless only narrowly defeated when he stood at Glasgow, Shettleston, in the 1918 general election. He won the seat in 1922 and held it until his death.

In the Commons, Wheatley associated with other newly elected 'Clydeside Red' MPs in numerous disorderly scenes and was more than once suspended for obstructive behaviour. But he also rapidly established himself as a most able debater, particularly on issues concerned with housing and health. He assumed responsibility for both in the first Labour government (1924) when Ramsay *MacDonald appointed him to the Cabinet as Minister of Health. Despite the government's very brief lifespan, Wheatley secured the passage of a Housing Act providing for a substantial house-building programme.

When Labour returned to Opposition, Wheatley expressed increasing dissatisfaction with the gradualist approach of the party leadership and soon withdrew to the back benches, where he assumed the unofficial leadership of the party's left-wing MPs. They continued their independent activities after the formation of the second Labour government (1929–31)—from which Wheatley was, not surprisingly, excluded. Their strident criticisms of the government's approach to the problem of unemployment, with which Wheatley was closely identified, excited much ministerial anger.

The Parliamentary Labour Party was on the point of introducing its first comprehensive disciplinary code limiting the freedom of action permitted to Labour MPs, as a response to these activities, when Wheatley died.

Whitelaw, William Stephen Ian (b. Nairn, 28 June 1918)
British; deputy leader of the Conservative Party 1975–91, Home Secretary 1979–93; Viscount 1983

Whitelaw's father was killed in action shortly after he was born. Educated at Winchester and Trinity College, Cambridge, he saw action in the Scots Guards in the Second World War, and was awarded the Military Cross in 1944. A farmer and dedicated golfer, he initially showed little interest in politics, but after contesting East Dumbartonshire as the Conservative candidate in 1950, acquired a taste for political life. He was elected as Conservative MP for Penrith and the Border in 1955. He served briefly as a whip before being given junior ministerial office. In Opposition in 1964, he was appointed chief whip. In 1970 he was appointed to Cabinet as Lord President of the Council and leader of the House of Commons and then, following the suspension of the Northern Ireland government in 1972, Secretary of State for Northern Ireland. A natural conciliator, he was a popular chief whip and leader of the House and sought to use his skills to achieve a political settlement in Northern Ireland. He held all-party talks in order to achieve agreement on the creation of a new Northern Ireland Executive and Assembly. In 1973 he was appointed Energy Secretary, but the crucial negotiations with the miners during the industrial dispute at the time were handled by the Prime Minister, Edward *Heath.

In Opposition, Whitelaw served as a senior member of the shadow Cabinet. In 1975, after Heath withdrew from the party leadership contest, he contested the second ballot, but came second to Margaret *Thatcher. He was appointed deputy leader of the party and became both a loyal supporter and trusted adviser to the party leader. She relied on his judgement and support, especially on party and parliamentary matters. In office, she once declared, 'Every Prime Minister needs a Willy'. Whitelaw served as Home Secretary from 1979 to 1983, relying on his usually emollient disposition (though he was given to occasional bursts of temper) rather than an acute grasp of detail to see him through. During his tenure, he had to deal with a siege at the Iranian embassy, authorizing SAS action to bring it to an end, and riots in different parts of the country. He had to fend off calls for his resignation after an intruder managed to breach security at Buckingham Palace and enter the Queen's bedroom. In 1983, he was elevated to the Lords with a hereditary peerage. He continued as the elder statesman of government, holding office as Lord President of the Council and leader of the House of Lords. In 1988, he suddenly felt unwell during a church service, and a stroke was diagnosed. He retired from government.

Highly popular, Whitelaw was a High Tory who recognized that there were important pursuits other than politics (not least, for him, family and golf) and who placed stress on loyalty and integrity. A fairly shrewd judge of what would prove acceptable to the party, he proved indispensable to Margaret Thatcher during her period of leadership, his enforced departure from government denying her his counsel when she possibly needed it most. There was no other heavyweight figure in the party who enjoyed her confidence to the same degree.

Whitlam, Edward **Gough** (b. Melbourne, 11 July 1916)
Australian; Prime Minister 1972–5

Whitlam was the son of the Commonwealth Crown Solicitor, and spent much of his childhood in the young capital, Canberra. He was educated at Knox Grammar, Sydney, Canberra Grammar School, and Sydney University, where he completed degrees in arts and law.

He served briefly in the RAAF before practising law in New South Wales and federally. He entered parliament in 1952 and rose to prominence over the ten years following the Labor Party's disastrous split in 1955. Determined to reform decision-making within the Labor 'machine' and to present policy with popular appeal, he became party leader in 1967.

In 1972, when the Labor Party finally broke the twenty-three-year hold conservatives had on government, Whitlam became Prime Minister with a mandate for rapid reform. In his first two weeks of government he and his deputy constituted an interim Cabinet and they immediately ended military conscription and Australia's commitment in Vietnam; promised Papua New Guinea independence; recognized Communist China; provided greater services for Aborigines; abolished the imperial honours list; and supported equal pay for women. The rest of Whitlam's three-year reign (which included re-election in 1974) was characterized by tension between further sweeping reforms and the emergence of forces undermining his programmes. Amongst his other initiatives were universal health insurance (Medibank) and the abolition of tertiary education fees. However, externally, a global recession and boom in commodity prices saw Australia economically reeling from a new cocktail of high unemployment, high inflation, and low growth. Within Australia he met resistance from the Senate and from state governments suspicious of his centralism.

Whitlam was dismissed as Prime Minister on 11 November 1975 in what was Australia's greatest constitutional crisis. Opposition leader Malcolm *Fraser blocked supply in the Senate, and Whitlam refused to break the deadlock by holding an early election. The Governor-General, John Kerr, dismissed Whitlam as Prime Minister and appointed Fraser head of a caretaker government. In the ensuing election in December Whitlam was soundly defeated. After a second electoral defeat in 1977 he stepped down as Labor leader, and he resigned from parliament the following year. He quickly became an elder statesman, serving as ambassador to Unesco and chairing bodies such as the Australia–China Council.

In government Whitlam was renowned for his sense of humour and his allusions to classical history. He remains for many a public figure of political grandeur and tragedy.

Wilder, Lawrence **Douglas** (b. Richmond, Virginia, 17 Jan. 1931)
US; Governor of Virginia 1989–93

Wilder was the first black Governor of Virginia and indeed of any state. The son of an insurance salesman and the grandson of slaves, Wilder was educated at Union and Howard University where he studied law following war service in Korea. In 1969 Wilder was elected to the state senate and built up a reputation in the legislature as an aggressive but hard-working politician. Wilder stayed in the State Legislature until elected Lieutenant Governor in 1985 with 51 per cent of the vote.

In the legislature Wilder had advocated fair housing legislation and union rights in the public sector as well as greater opportunities for blacks. He had also opposed capital punishment though he later switched position on this sensitive electoral issue. Despite the fact that Virginia was becoming a solid Republican enclave, Wilder was narrowly elected Governor after a campaign in which only the abortion issue seemed to divide the pro-choice Wilder from his opponent Marshall Coleman.

The period of Wilder's governorship was not entirely happy. There was an open feud with former Governor Charles *Robb and the state was hit by a recession which required cuts in public spending. Although Wilder had been mentioned as a possible Democratic candidate in 1992, no campaign was launched. Wilder retired from the governorship in 1993.

Williams, Eric Eustace (b. 25 Sept. 1911; d. 29 March 1981)
Trinidadian; Chief Minister, Premier and Prime Minister 1956–81

An academic and much-respected historian, Oxford-educated Williams taught in the USA before working for the Anglo-American Caribbean Commission (1943–55). He founded the People's National Movement (PNM) in 1956 and won general elections that same year on a platform of anti-colonialist nationalism. Williams became Chief Minister and won considerable support through his popular style of oratory and appeal to Trinidad's majority black population. In 1958 Trinidad and Tobago joined the ten-state English-speaking West Indies Federation, whose headquarters were situated in Trinidad. But the federal experiment failed amidst inter-island disputes, and Williams was eager to leave the Federation and pursue the goal of Trinidadian independence from British rule. This was achieved in 1962 and Williams became the country's first Prime Minister.

Although widely recognized as an outstanding intellect, Williams began to lose the popular support that he had enjoyed in the 1950s. In 1970 an abortive 'black power' uprising and near mutiny shook his government and he was forced to declare a state of emergency. Increasingly reclusive and aloof, Williams announced in 1973 that he would stand down but then changed his mind. The main reason for his change of heart was the sudden and unexpected rise in world oil prices, which brought a huge windfall into oil-producing Trinidad. The oil boom restored Williams's political fortunes and he was able to preside over a period of rapid economic growth and extravagant consumerism. In 1976 the PNM was able to win another general election and Williams remained in office until his death in 1981, the year in which the oil boom came to an end.

The author of important works on slavery and other aspects of Caribbean history, Williams is commonly judged to be the most intellectually accomplished leader in the English-speaking Caribbean's history. Conversely, he is also widely believed to have been vain, autocratic, and lacking the 'common touch'.

Williams, Shirley (b. 27 July 1930)
British; Secretary of State for Education 1976–9; Baroness (life peer) 1993

Shirley Williams's parents were both involved in public affairs. They were the political scientist Professor George Catlin and the writer Vera Brittan. She was educated at Oxford and Columbia universities and her first employment was as a journalist. She was elected Labour MP for Hitchin in 1964 and held the seat until 1974, when she moved to Hertford and Stevenage and held the seat until 1979.

Mrs Williams was on the right of the Labour Party, a supporter of Hugh *Gaitskell. She favoured liberal social policies, the mixed economy, and redistribution. But, unlike Gaitskell, she was a pro-European. She held junior posts towards the end of Harold *Wilson's 1966–70 government. In Opposition she was elected to the shadow Cabinet in 1971. As a member of Wilson's 1974–6 Labour government she was Cabinet Minister for Prices and Consumer Protection. At the time the government had a 'social contract' with the trade unions, a key part of the government's anti-inflation policy. In this post she pressed for government subsidies to moderate increases in council house rents and food prices.

Under Wilson's successor, James *Callaghan, she was moved to Education and Science and continued to implement the party's policy of comprehensive education. But this was also a time when the political right made issues of educational standards and parental choice.

Labour lost the 1979 election and as the party moved to the left she was one of the original Gang of Four, along with *Owen and *Jenkins, who left Labour to form the Social Democratic Party. She was elected president of the new party in 1982. In 1981 she returned to parliament by capturing the safe Conservative seat of Crosby for the

SDP at a by-election. She lost the seat in the 1983 general election. She supported the merger of the Liberals and SDP to form the Liberal Democrats.

Subsequently, Shirley Williams took an academic post at Harvard University, USA, and continued to speak for the Liberal Democrats in the House of Lords, which she entered in 1993.

Willkie, Wendell (b. Elwood, Indiana, 18 Feb. 1892; d. 8 Oct. 1944)
US; Republican presidential candidate

Born to lawyer parents, Willkie also became a lawyer after graduating from Indiana University. In his early years he was a liberal Democrat. He made himself wealthy by a successful corporate legal practice and became head of the public utility Commonwealth and Southern Corporation (CSC). As a prominent businessman he broke with *Roosevelt's New Deal over the creation of the Tennessee Valley Authority which competed with his CSC.

Willkie's high media profile brought him to the attention of Republicans who were seeking a challenger to Roosevelt in the 1940 presidential election. Althought he only became a Republican in 1939 he gained the party's nomination after six ballots. In an election heavily influenced by the spectre of war, he lost by 55 per cent to 45 per cent of the popular vote. He campaigned for the USA to take a strong stand in support of Britain against *Hitler, and for the maintenance of the two-term limit to the presidency. (Roosevelt was trying for a third term.)

He sought the Republican nomination again in 1944, but the party had moved to the right and his liberal progressive views gained little support. He argued for a social security programme, opposed states' rights, and in the 1944 presidential election he failed to support the Republican candidate, Thomas *Dewey. Shortly before his death he received approaches from Roosevelt about realigning the liberal progressives in the Democratic and Republican parties into a new political force.

Wilson, James **Harold** (b. Huddersfield, 11 Mar. 1916; d. 24 May 1995)
British; Prime Minister 1964–70, 1974–76; Kt. 1976, Baron (life peer) 1983

Harold Wilson won more (four) general elections than any other Labour leader and is the party's longest-serving Prime Minister (eight years). His reputation fluctuated greatly during his life. At the time of his retirement and his death his stock was low. Yet in the mid-1960s he was regarded as a British John F. *Kennedy. Wilson reached the top in politics without any family connections and on his own merits. He was the son of a works chemist, educated at Wirral Grammar School, and an academic success at Oxford. As a wartime civil servant he drew on his economic background and by 1945 was director of economics and statistics at the Ministry of Fuel and Power. Although a successful career as a civil servant or university teacher beckoned, he opted for Labour politics. He was returned as MP for Ormskirk in 1945 and then for Huyton on Merseyside from 1950 until his retirement in 1983.

In parliament Wilson enjoyed a meteoric rise. Within two years of entering the Commons at the age of 31 he was president of the Board of Trade and in this post he removed many wartime controls on industry. In 1951 he resigned from Cabinet, along with *Bevan, in protest at *Gaitskell's budget, which proposed to finance a large armaments programme in part by cutting social spending. This act made Wilson's reputation as a man of the left and was reinforced in 1960 when he challenged Gaitskell in the annual election for the party leadership. In fact, Wilson was too much the pragmatist to be associated clearly with any ideology. Gaitskell was fighting to reverse the party conference vote for unilateral disarmament, a policy supported by the left. Wilson was not a unilaterist, but thought that Gaitskell was being divisive. He lost the contest by a two to one margin. Gaitskell looked set to lead Labour to victory at the next general election when he died, unexpectedly, in January

1963. Wilson, recently shadow Chancellor of the Exchequer, but now shadow Foreign Secretary, won the leadership on the second ballot by appealing to the centre. Labour's right had no credible standard bearer and the left was similarly bereft since the death of Bevan in 1960. He led the party to victory in the 1964 election, but by a majority of only four seats.

At the start of his premiership in October 1964, Wilson promised dynamic action, planning, economic growth, and the harnessing of science to the service of socialism. He was probably at his best in his first (1964–6) spell of office. Labour's tiny majority meant that he necessarily had to think of the short term, capture the press headlines, and create an impression of activity. In the 1966 general election he gained a landslide majority.

The government staked its reputation on maintaining the value of the pound. In spite of deflation and a statutory incomes policy the pound was eventually devalued in 1967, the economic plan collapsed, and the pursuit of economic growth abandoned. Planned reforms of the House of Lords and industrial relations were aborted and an attempt to enter the European Community also failed. Much time was spent in handling the unilateral declaration of independence in 1965 by Rhodesia (now Zimbabwe). Annual average economic growth in the six years 1964–70 was just over 2 per cent, worse than the rate during the much disparaged years of the previous years of Conservative administration. Among the achievements were the creation of the Open University, changes in laws affecting homosexuals and obscene publications, and the ending of capital punishment.

Wilson bore a heavy responsibility for the failures. It was his decision not to consider devaluation on taking office in October 1964 and when, almost inevitably, devaluation came in 1967, he refused the necessary follow-up measures to make it a success. He was deeply conservative about political institutions, the Commonwealth, and the Anglo-American relationship. Social programmes were sacrificed to protect the pound, and he hankered after an international role for Britain. He always seemed to be looking for scapegoats; party critics were dismissed as 'plotters' and other opponents as members of the 'sell Britain short' brigade. The left was disillusioned by his support for the American military campaign in Vietnam, incomes policies, and cuts to social spending.

In spite of the record, Labour's defeat in the 1970 general election came as a surprise. In Opposition, the left gained ground in the party and Wilson had to acquiesce in the repudiation of many of his government's policies. The party was split over Europe and his apparent change of mind over Britain's membership of the European Community cost him much credit with the pro-European wing of the party. Having ruled out a referendum on Britain's membership, he then accepted one. Keeping the party together meant accepting compromises, however unheroic they looked. Yet he led the party to an unexpected election victory in February 1974. This produced a minority government and another election victory in October 1979 produced only a small majority.

The government had to cope with an unenviable economic legacy from the *Heath government and deal with an international recession. It relied on a 'social contract' with the TUC to moderate wage claims. It had little success in reducing inflation while Wilson was in charge. He managed to stave off a party split on continued British membership of the European Community by holding a referendum in 1975; this convincingly backed British membership. In announcing his surprise resignation in March 1976, Wilson stated that he was bored with confronting the same problems he had dealt with a decade earlier. Colleagues had noted a marked decline in his energy and interest in major issues. His departure from office was marred by his controversial final honours list and complaints by party workers about the lucrative book contracts that he had negotiated. He left many problems to his successor as Prime Minister, *Callaghan.

Critics accused Wilson of being an opportunist and not standing for any principles beyond gaining and holding office and making Labour the natural party of government. After his resignation at the age of 60, he cut a lonely figure in the House of Commons, and even more so in the House of Lords, which he joined as Lord Wilson of Rievaulx after the 1983 general election.

Wilson, Pete (b. Lake Forest, Illinois, 23 Aug. 1933)
US; US Senator 1983–91, Governor of California 1991–

A lawyer educated at Yale and Berkeley, Wilson was elected to the California legislature in 1966 and served there until becoming mayor of San Diego in 1970, a post he occupied until 1983 and one which earned him a reputation as an able administrator. In 1982 Wilson was elected to the Senate, where he adopted a moderate approach to issues, but strongly supported the defence spending so crucial to the California economy. In 1988 he was re-elected to the Senate but chose to run for governor in a race against former San Francisco mayor Dianne *Feinstein in 1990. After a narrow victory in 1990, he was re-elected to a second gubernatorial term in 1994, gaining 55 per cent of the vote in a race against Kathleen Brown.

As governor Wilson had to deal with major budgetary problems, largely the effect of a recession which was especially marked in California because of cuts to the defence industry in the new environment created by the end of the Cold War. To solve revenue problems, Wilson supported tax rises and spending cuts which alienated both his Republican backers and the legislature. Wilson also had to cope with the effects of a series of natural disasters in California and with mounting concern about crime. Strong backing for law enforcement (including capital punishment) and for a tougher line on illegal immigrants helped Wilson to win re-election in 1994. On some of the most highly salient social issues in California (abortion and gay rights) he is a liberal.

As one of the Republican Party's most able and experienced politicians, Wilson has had presidential ambitions. In 1995 he announced he would seek the Republican nomination but he withdrew as Bob Dole's campaign gathered momentum.

Wilson, Thomas **Woodrow** (b. Staunton, Virginia, 28 Dec. 1856; d. 3 Feb. 1924)
US; Governor of New Jersey 1911–13, President 1913–21

The son of a presbyterian minister, Wilson's education was affected by his father's peripatetic calling and by his own ill-health. His studies at Davidson College in North Carolina were cut short by illness. When restored to health, he took his first degree at the College of New Jersey. Ill-health again cut short his studies after he entered the University of Virginia Law School and he continued his studies at home. He was admitted to the bar in Georgia and practised law briefly before entering Johns Hopkins University to pursue an academic career. Wilson published a book, *Congressional Government*, in 1885 that was to form the basis of his Ph.D. degree and was to become a classic work on American government. He took up posts at Bryn Mawr College, Pennsylvania, and Wesleyan University, Connecticut, before being appointed professor of jurisprudence and political economy at his old college, the College of New Jersey, in 1890. Six years later, the college became Princeton University. He published several books, including a five-volume history of the American people. In 1902, after variously declining the presidency of the University of Virginia, he was elected president of Princeton. He proved a reforming leader of the institution, battling—not always successfully—to achieve change.

He harboured an interest in the real world of politics. He toyed with the prospect of contesting a Senate race. In 1910, he obtained the Democratic nomination for Governor of New Jersey and won election in the November. Inaugurated in January 1911, he soon established a reputation as a reform Governor, distancing himself from the party bosses that had helped secure his election and battling successfully to reform the election process. He achieved the passage of social reform legislation. His political stance moved from proactive to reactive in 1912 after the Republicans won control of the state legislature. He vetoed fifty-seven measures. At the same time, he began campaigning for the presidential nomination. At the Democratic convention in July 1912, delegates were deadlocked and Wilson came from behind to win after forty-six ballots. In the election, he developed an effective campaigning style and was helped by the intervention of former President, Teddy *Roosevelt, on a Progressive ticket, effectively splitting the Republican vote. Wilson won over 6 million votes, Roosevelt just over 4 million, and *Taft 3 million. Wilson was inaugurated on 4 March 1913.

As President, Wilson launched a number of measures, dubbed the New Freedom programme, designed to promote competition and to remove the privileges of special interests. He achieved both tariff and banking reform. In 1916 he was nominated for a second term and won re-election with a clear but not overwhelming majority over his Republic opponent, Charles Evans *Hughes. (Wilson amassed 9.1 million votes to 8.5 million for Hughes.) Though he had maintained American neutrality in the opening years of the First World War, a fact used in his re-election campaign ('he kept us out of the war'), the resumption by Germany in 1917 of unrestricted submarine warfare led Wilson to sever diplomatic relations with Germany. He then authorized the arming of merchant ships and, after several American ships were sunk, sought a declaration of war by Congress. Though it took time for American forces to be marshalled and sent in strength, Wilson proved an effective wartime leader, aided by some competent military leaders.

Following the defeat of Germany, Wilson decided to lead the American delegation to the peace conference, a decision for which there was no precedent. Wilson had already enunciated his 'fourteen points' for achieving peace and set sail for Paris in order to achieve their realization. Despite his position and his forceful rhetoric, he had to fight with the other participants to achieve his goals and was not always successful. However, the resulting treaty, the Versailles Treaty, did incorporate his cherished goal, the creation of a League of Nations. He returned to the USA in July 1919 in order to campaign for its ratification. The Republicans had captured control of both Houses of Congress in the 1918 mid-term elections and many were not sympathetic to US involvement in the League. Some were adamantly opposed, others were prepared to compromise. For Wilson, it was the whole treaty or it was nothing and he set out on a speaking tour to rally popular support for it. Although he travelled 10,000 miles, he failed to complete his tour. On 26 September, in Colorado, he was taken ill: according to some accounts he suffered a mild stroke and, according to others, a nervous breakdown. On 2 October, back in Washington, DC, he had a serious stroke which left him partly paralysed. During the remaining months of his presidency, he was confined to his sick room, messages being transmitted through his wife Edith. So protective was his wife that it was unclear then, and since, what decisions were actually being taken by the President and what was being decided on his behalf by his wife. He was largely sidelined in the presidential election of 1920, the Democratic nominee, James Cox, losing to the Republican Warren G. *Harding. Wilson lingered another three years. He had another stroke early in 1924 and died on 3 February. His wife Edith, whom he had married in the White House after his first wife died, lived for nearly another forty years. She died in December 1961.

Though adopting liberal positions on trade and competition, Wilson was highly conservative in other respects. He failed to campaign for female suffrage and he approved segregation of the races in government offices. However, what raised him to particular prominence was his reputation as a reformer and, later, his wartime leadership. He believed in leading from the front. His essential failing was that he believed that he alone was capable of leading. He believed he knew what was right—his world-view was essentially religious and he came to see himself as God's representative on earth—and was not prepared to consider compromise in the battle to achieve the outcomes he wanted. Several measures that could have been saved by negotiation, including the Treaty of Versailles, were lost as a result of his intransigence. Principle was accorded precedence over friendship and political loyalty. He variously turned on those who had put him in positions of power. At the end of his tenure of office, he even turned against his most trusted lieutenant, 'Colonel' Edward M. House, who had been at his side since he entered the White House. His relations with the Republican leaders in Congress were frosty and he did not endear himself to the Allied leaders at the Paris peace conference. He suffered depression following the death of his first wife and by the time of the Paris conference had an almost Messianic view of himself. By the time he set sail for Europe, he was already exhausted both physically and mentally. He spent his last years believing that what he stood for would come about. 'You can't fight God!', he told visitors. He died with his dreams unfulfilled.

Witte, Sergei Yulevich (b. Tiflis, 17 June 1849, d. St Petersburg 13 Mar. 1915)
Russian; Russian Minister of Transport and of Finance 1892–1903, Prime Minister 1903–6

Witte was brought up in Tiflis, his father being of Dutch origin, his mother Russian, the daughter of a governor. He studied mathematics at university in Odessa and entered government service, becoming an expert on transport economics. Later he became a successful railway manager. In 1889 he was invited to set up a railway department within the Ministry of Finance to develop the construction of the Trans-Siberian Railway. In 1892 he was made Minister of Transport and then Minister of Finance, superintending the industrialization boom of the 1890s which made Russia a world industrial power. The 'Witte System' was a neo-mercantilist policy based on attracting foreign investment and loans by high protectionist tariffs, budgetary stability, putting the rouble on the gold standard (in 1897) and high taxation (he created the state spirits monopoly in 1894). He introduced labour legislation and urged (but never achieved) the abolition of the commune system in agriculture. In 1903 he became Prime Minister. He opposed the emperor's far-eastern policy which led to the war with Japan, but in 1905 negotiated the Treaty of Portsmouth which ended it. During the revolution of 1905 he combined suppression of popular unrest with advocacy of concessions to the middle classes. He compiled the 'October Manifesto' which prepared the way for Russia's first elected parliament, the Duma. He became Russia's first constitutional premier, but, increasingly criticized by the Tsar and his conservative allies and also by dissatisfied liberals, he was suddenly dismissed in 1906, and replaced by Stolypin. He remained politically active as an independent member of the State Council until his death in Petrograd in 1915. His remarkable talents were undermined by the mistrust of the Tsar and by the left-right polarization which made his moderate conservative position difficult to sustain.

Wofford, Harris (b. New York City, 26 Apr. 1926)
US; US Senator 1991–5

The son of an insurance company executive, Wofford grew up in New York and, after a spell of military service, attended Chicago, Yale, and the overwhelmingly black Howard University, specifically chosen to broaden his understanding of civil rights issues first-hand. Wofford published two books on world government while an undergraduate and spent a brief period as an aide to Chester Bowles before devoting himself to law practice. He joined John *Kennedy's presidential campaign and, together with Bowles, drafted the Democratic platform statement on civil rights. It was his initiative to get Kennedy to put through the symbolic telephone call to Martin Luther *King's wife when King was jailed, an electorally risky initiative which mobilized black voters in 1960.

Wofford was appointed special civil rights assistant in the Kennedy administration but became disillusioned by the pace of change and in 1962 moved to Ethiopia to head the operations of the Peace Corps.

From 1966 until 1978 Wofford was primarily engaged in academic life, first as president of SUNY's progressive Old Westbury campus and then as president of Bryn Mawr. He published his memoirs *Of Kennedys and Kings*. After a brief return to private practice in Philadelphia, Wofford served as chair of the Pennsylvania state Democratic Party and was then appointed by Governor Casey to be the state Secretary of Labor and Industry. His period in that post (1987–91) gave Wofford an opportunity to address a range of domestic issues including unemployment, training, and health care costs. In April 1991, when Pennsylvania Senator John Heinz was killed in an air crash, Casey appointed Wofford to fill the post until a special election could be held in November. In that election Wofford emphasized the health care issue and against the odds beat Richard Thornburgh, *Bush's former Attorney-General. The result was widely interpreted as an early indication of the Bush administration's weakness on domestic policy and the electoral salience of the health care issue. Democratic presidential candidates then addressed the theme of health care and for a time Wofford was spoken of as vice-presidential material for Clinton. However, Wofford himself was not able to entrench his position and in 1994 he lost the Senate seat to the young Republican candidate Rich Santorum.

Wood, Edward Frederick Lindley *see* HALIFAX, EARL OF

Wood, Howard **Kingsley** (b. Hull, 19 Aug. 1881; d. 21 Sept. 1943)

British; Chancellor of the Exchequer 1940–3; Kt. 1918

The son of a Wesleyan minister, Wood was educated at Central Foundation Boys' School and trained as a solicitor. An expert in insurance matters, he was appointed chairman of the Old Age Pensions Committee in 1915 and the London Insurance Committee in 1916. He entered parliament in 1918 as Conservative MP for Woolwich West and served in a number of junior minister posts between 1924 and 1931. In 1931 he was appointed Postmaster-General and raised to Cabinet rank in 1933. He was subsequently to serve as Minister of Health (1935–8) and Secretary of State for Air (1938–40). He was briefly Lord Privy Seal before being appointed Chancellor of the Exchequer, a post in which he proved highly competent. Wood died suddenly in office in September 1943.

As Air Secretary, he objected to plans to bomb German forests on the grounds that they were private property. A *Chamberlain supporter, in 1940 he told Chamberlain it was time for him to go. His most enduring legacy is his introduction, as Chancellor, of the Pay As You Earn (PAYE) scheme for income tax.

Woolton, Frederick James Marquis, **Lord** (b. Salford, 23 Aug. 1883; d. 14 Dec. 1964)

British; chairman of the Conservative Party 1946–55, Lord President of the Council 1951–2, Chancellor of Duchy of Lancaster 1953–5; Baron 1939, Viscount 1953, Earl 1956

Woolton was educated at Manchester Grammar School and Manchester University. In early life he served as a warden of a settlement in Liverpool dockland. Unfit for service in the First World War, he served as an economist in the War Office. He later joined the Lewis's retail firm, becoming eventually managing director and then chairman. His administrative and propagandizing skills were recognized by Sir Horace Wilson and he was brought into government in April 1940 as Minister of Food. He proved highly effective and in 1943 was brought into the War Cabinet as Minister for Reconstruction.

Though initially a Fabian, and a non-party figure in the wartime government, he joined the Conservative Party after the 1945 defeat. *Churchill in 1946 invited him to be party chairman. He proved an effective fund-raiser as well as recruiter: party membership doubled between 1947 and 1948. He also established the *Maxwell-Fyfe committee which led to candidates being recruited from a wider social base. He was made Lord President of the Council in 1951, then Chancellor of the Duchy of Lancaster, while retaining the party chairmanship. He served until 1955.

Though prone to pomposity, he was one of the successes of the wartime administration and his being made Conservative Party chairman was to prove one of Churchill's best political appointments. Woolton was one of the pivotal figures in the rejuvenation of the post-war Conservative Party.

Wright, Jim (b. Fort Worth, Texas, 22 Dec. 1922)

US; member of the US House of Representatives 1954–89, Speaker of the House of Representatives 1987–9

Wright was educated at Weatherford College and at the University of Texas. Originally seen as a liberal Democrat he gradually adopted a more conservative line on foreign policy issues (supporting American involvement in Vietnam) and environmental matters. His original political power base was the House Public Works Committee which enabled him to build broad support in the House. In 1976 Wright ran for the Democratic leadership and narrowly beat Richard Bolling and Phil Burton. When Tip *O'Neill announced his retirement in 1985 Wright's early announcement of his candidacy pre-empted the field.

A highly partisan politican, Wright took full advantage of a strengthened speakership. He spearheaded the opposition to the *Reagan administration in the 100th Congress (1987–8) and achieved a number of Democratic legislative victories including a tax rise and legislation on trade and health care. It seemed likely that the pattern would continue in the 101st Congress (1989–90); but allegations of financial impropriety (especially in relation to a book which Wright was selling at speaking engagements) had been made by Newt *Gingrich and the Republicans in December 1987 and had generated an investigation by the House Ethics Committee. In 1989 the House found eighty-nine occasions on which Wright had broken congressional rules and the Speaker's position became untenable. He resigned from the speakership and from the House in June 1989, the first Speaker to be forced from office in the middle of a Congress.

Xoxe, Koçi (b. 1917; d. 11 June 1949)
Albanian; Minister of the Interior 1945–8

Of working-class origin, Xoxe fought in the Albanian Communist resistance during the Second World War, when he became a protégé of *Tito. He was Minister of the Interior in the post-war government with responsibility for the secret police, the *Sigurimi*. He presided over the trials of 'war criminals' and the Albanian Labour Party's (ALP—the Communist party's) political opponents. He was the leader of the pro-Yugoslav faction of the ALP, which even considered union between Albania and Yugoslavia. He worked in close co-operation with the Yugoslav security service in conducting a purge of the Albanian party, in particular of all those who opposed Albania's close relationship with Yugoslavia. His position weakened after Yugoslavia was expelled from the Cominform in 1948. His rival, Enver *Hoxha, used Soviet support to eliminate his rivals from the party. In September 1948 Xoxe was removed from office. He was accused of 'Titoism' and, falsely, of having worked for British and US intelligence during the war. In May 1949 his supporters were put on the first Soviet-style show trial in Eastern Europe. On 11 June 1949 Xoxe was shot for treason.

Yagoda, Genrikh Grigoryevich (b. Lódź in Russian Poland, 1891; d. 15 Mar. 1938)
Chairman of the NKVD 1934–6

Yagoda was the son of a Jewish carpenter. After secondary education he became a statistician. He worked for the father of *Sverdlov and married into the Sverdlov family. He joined the Bolshevik Party in 1907 and was imprisoned for two years in 1911. He served in the army from 1915 to 1917 and helped organize the Red Guard in Petrograd in 1917. Yagoda served in the Cheka in the Civil War as well as holding some administrative posts. *Dzerzhinsky appointed him second deputy chairman of the GPU (secret police) in 1923, and he became deputy head of the GPU in 1926, serving under Vyacheslav Menzhinsky. As Menzhinsky's health declined after 1929, Yagoda was effectively in control of the secret police. He disapproved of Stalin's collectivization of agriculture though the secret police were closely involved in its implementation. From July 1934 to September 1936 he was chairman of the People's Commissariat of Internal Affairs (NKVD), and had overall control of the purges which took place after *Kirov's murder in 1934. It is generally believed that he had no prior knowledge of the murder. In 1936 he was replaced by *Yezhov and made Commissar for Communications. He was arrested in April 1937, accused of having been first a tsarist then a Nazi agent, and executed in 1938 after a show trial alongside Bukharin, *Rykov, and others. Yagoda always had a fearful reputation in the Soviet Union and was not rehabilitated.

Yakovlev, Aleksandr Nikolayevich (b. Koroleva, near Yaroslavl, 12 Feb. 1923)
Russian; member of the Politburo 1987–91

Yakovlev was born into a Russian peasant family. During the Second World War he served in the marines, commanding an intelligence platoon, but was seriously wounded in 1943 and discharged. He joined the Communist Party in 1944 and graduated from the Yaroslavl Pedagogical Institute in 1946. From 1948 to 1953 he worked as a party official in the Yaroslavl region, before being transferred to the apparatus of the Central Committee in Moscow. In 1956 he decided to follow a period of historical study at the Central Committee's Academy of Social Sciences. In 1960 he graduated from the Academy of Social Sciences with a doctorate and from then until 1973 he worked in the apparatus of the Central Committee. In 1972 he incurred official anger for publishing a newspaper article which attacked Russian nationalism and was sent into semi-exile in 1973 as Soviet ambassador to Canada. *Gorbachev organized his return to Moscow in 1983, where he was made Director of the Institute of World Economy and International Relations (IMEMO).

After Gorbachev came to power in 1985, Yakovlev was a key mover behind the introduction of the 'New Political Thinking', which reduced the role of Marxist-Leninist ideology in the Soviet Union, and of perestroika in general. He entered the Central Committee as secretary in 1985, becoming a full member the next year. In 1987 he became a full member of the Politburo and was a member of a commission investigating repression under *Stalin. He entered the Congress of People's Deputies in 1989 as one of the quota allotted to the CPSU but resigned from the party the next year and thus left the Politburo and Central Committee. In June 1991 he, along with *Shevardnadze and others, founded the Movement for Democratic Reform. After Gorbachev's fall in 1991 he became vice-president of the 'Gorbachev Fund'.

Yeltsin, Boris Nikolaevich (b. Sverdlovsk province, 1 Feb. 1931)

Russian; CPSU First Secretary for Sverdlovsk region 1976–85, First Secretary of Moscow Party Committee 1985–7, President of RSFSR Supreme Soviet 1990–1, President of the Russian Federation 1991–

Born into a poor peasant family in the Urals, Yeltsin studied engineering at Urals Polytechnical Institute, where he was a noted volleyball player. After graduation he worked in the construction industry as an engineer and later manager. In 1961 he joined the Communist Party and in 1968 became housing secretary of the Sverdlovsk regional party committee. In 1976 he became First Secretary of the Sverdlovsk party committee and in 1981 a full member of the CPSU Central Committee. In June 1985 he was brought to Moscow under the patronage of *Ligachev (also from Sverdlovsk), and became a Central Committee Secretary for a few months before being put in charge of the Moscow party organization and made a Candidate Member of the Politbureau. He proceeded to root out corruption in the Moscow party with great zeal and populist style, using public transport instead of limousines and openly attacking established bureaucrats. But this brought him into direct conflict with his patron Ligachev, who was in charge of the party apparatus. At a Central Committee Plenum before the 70th anniversary of the Russian Revolution he made a sensational speech criticizing Ligachev, warning of a developing personality cult round *Gorbachev, and resigning from his Moscow party post and the Politbureau. In early 1988, after recovering from a heart attack, he was transferred to the post of deputy chair of the State Construction Committee.

This seemed to be the end of his career, but in March 1989 his popularity as a trenchant critic of Gorbachev's half-measures secured him an overwhelming victory as a deputy for the Moscow constituency of the Congress of People's Deputies. He became a member of the USSR Supreme Soviet and, in 1990, of the RSFSR Supreme Soviet. He soon became a leader of the 'Inter-regional' group of liberal deputies in the USSR Supreme Soviet and a real thorn in Gorbachev's flesh when he was elected President of the Supreme Soviet of the RSFSR in May 1990. In August 1990 he publicly resigned from the Communist Party at the 28th CPSU Congress. The declaration of sovereignty made by the Russian Republic in 1990, along with the public rivalry between two leaders both based in Moscow, greatly destabilized the USSR. This was intensified when Yeltsin won a popular mandate (something Gorbachev never achieved) as directly elected President of the Russian Republic in June 1991. His finest hour came when, at great personal risk, he proclaimed from atop a tank the resistance of the Russian parliament to the coup of August 1991. Thereafter he called the tunes for the fatally weakened Gorbachev, banning the Communist Party in the Russian Republic and presiding over Russia's achievement of independence.

His ensuing years as Russian President were controversial. From November 1991 to June 1992 he was head of government as well as President, operating with a legislature elected as a subordinate part of the old system in 1990 and with a majority of unreformed Communists who had co-operated with him against Gorbachev but were deeply disappointed by the break-up of the USSR. Yeltsin tried to push through a programme of 'shock therapy' economic reform promoted by his deputy-premier *Gaidar, but this was resisted by an increasingly alienated parliament mobilized by the speaker *Khasbulatov and Yeltsin's Deputy-President, *Rutskoi. The constitution (a much amended version of the 1978 RSFSR Constitution) was not able to resolve the disputed precedence between President and parliament. Governmental paralysis continued even after *Chernomyrdin, a compromise choice, became Prime Minister. Tension increased in 1993 when, after winning a slender majority for reform in a referendum, Yeltsin tried to close down the Parliament; the Parliamentary forces resisted and security troops eventually stormed the Parliament and arrested the leaders. In December Yeltsin won narrow majority approval in a referendum for his constitution, which placed enormous power in the hands of the President. But in the elections for a new legislature, the Duma, the results were equivocal, associated with disillusionment with the harsh impact of economic reform, and included a strong showing for the extreme nationalists led by Zhirinovsky. The Duma, though much reduced in power compared with the old legislature, was not much easier to work with. This remained true of the new Duma elected in December 1995 in which the Communists made a strong showing and reformers did badly. Apart from continued resistance to marketization, which somewhat reduced the pace of reform, there were many disputes over the powers of the units of the new Russian Federation, producing a confused structure in which the centre increased its power. In 1995 Russian troops launched an incompetent and extremely bloody invasion of Chechnya which created a desert in the name of peace. Yeltsin's declining health from heart trouble and his unpredictable, often arrogant and tactless behaviour led to a loss of support at home and abroad. In foreign policy nationalist pressure pushed him into a more 'Eurasian' position on Bosnia, the expansion of NATO into Eastern Europe, and Russia's rule in the CIS, but Russia's continued parlous economic state made Yeltsin dependent on Western economic and political support and the West, and Russian metropolitan voters, continued to back Yeltsin for lack of a reliable alternative. Yeltsin played a heroic role in the break-up of the Communist party-state but has not been equal to the challenge of the consolidation of democracy and a market economy.

Yezhov, Nikolai Ivanovich (b. St Petersburg 1894; d. 1939)

Russian; Chairman of the NKVD 1936–8

Yezhov was of working-class origin. He joined the Bolsheviks before 1917 and became head of the Central Committee Secretariat's Cadres Department in 1930. By early 1935 he was Central Committee Secretary in charge of the Party Control Commission, which had oversight over the security police. In 1935 he was involved in the preparation of the show trial of *Zinoviev and *Kamenev and succeeded *Yagoda as head of the NKVD in 1936. In October 1937 he was made a candidate member of the Politburo. Yezhov presided over the high point of Stalinist repression in the Soviet Union, known in Russian as the *Yezhovshchina* (roughly, 'the evil times of Yezhov'). Yezhov apparently relished his job. An NKVD officer recalled: 'In my whole life I have never seen such a villain as Yezhov. He does it with pleasure.' The orders for increased repression undoubtedly came from *Stalin. The terror culminated in March 1938 with the last great show trial, that of Bukharin, *Rykov, and *Yagoda. Yezhov's disgrace followed on 8 December 1938, when he was replaced by *Beria as head of the NKVD and made Commissar for River Transport. Stalin used him as a scapegoat for the purges, executing him in 1939.

Yoshida Shigeru (b. Tokyo, 22 Sept. 1878; d. 20 Oct. 1967)

Japanese; Prime Minister 1946–7, 1949–55

Yoshida Shigeru was born into a large *samurai* family of the Tõsa Clan which had played an instrumental part in the Meiji Restoration of 1868 and later adopted into a powerful merchant family. He graduated from Tokyo Imperial University in 1906 and joined the Ministry of Foreign Affairs, and his first overseas posting was as consul-general to Mukden in Manchuria. In 1928 he was appointed Vice Minister for Foreign Affairs, and in 1930 he was posted to Rome as ambassador. In 1936 the army blocked his appointment to the position of Foreign Minister because they were critical of his liberal views, and instead he was appointed ambassador to London, where he remained until he retired in 1939, disillusioned at the direction that the military was taking Japan. He was arrested by the Japanese authorities in 1945 for calling for peace talks with the Allied powers.

Yoshida's credentials made him an ideal candidate for the Allied Occupation authorities to deal with. He was appointed Foreign Minister, and in May 1946 became

Prime Minister following the unexpected purge of Hatoyama Ichiro. Yoshida was out of office during the short period of the socialist Prime Minister Ashida, but returned to office from 1949 until 1955. In his joint role as Foreign Minister and Prime Minister, he was intimately involved in all the key issues of the Occupation, including the drafting of the 'Peace Constitution', the 'reverse course' where US policy moved away from the democratization and demilitarization of Japan to rebuilding the country as a Cold War ally, and negotiated on behalf of Japan during the San Francisco Peace Conference and negotiations over the Security Treaty in 1952. Growing dissatisfaction with his leadership and pro-American stance led to his being pushed from power in 1954 and replaced by his conservative rival Hatoyama. Yoshida vigorously defended Article 9 of the 1946 constitution which forbade Japan maintaining armed forces in the face of growing US pressure for Japan to rearm, though he later argued that he intended this position to be temporary until the time Japan was strong enough to afford such a role. Yoshida's view of post-war Japan was that it would be tied closely into the US security arena, and that it should follow the US lead on all foreign policy issues, a posture that was later called the 'Yoshida Doctrine', although Yoshida himself decried this appellation. As a consequence of his pro-US stance he put his name to the so-called 'Yoshida Letter', a note written by John Foster *Dulles in 1952 stating that Japan would recognize *Chiang Kai-shek's regime on Taiwan as the sole, legitimate government of China. Yoshida remained an advocate for Taiwan following his retirement.

Yoshida was one of the most important Japanese politicians of the twentieth century whose policies became the broad parameters of Japan's foreign policy up to the end of the Cold War. His *Memoirs* were published in English in 1961.

Young, Andrew Jackson, Jr. (b. New Orleans, Louisiana, 12 Mar. 1932)

US; member of the US House of Representatives 1973–7, ambassador to the United Nations 1977–9, mayor of Atlanta 1982–9

Andrew Yong's political career was forged in the heat of the civil rights movement. Educated at Dillard and Howard Universities and at Hartford Theological Seminary, he became a congregational minister and worked for a time organizing youth work for the National Council of Churches. He joined the Southern Christian Leadership Conference in 1960 and became its executive director 1964–70. His close association with Martin Luther *King and his own charismatic personality made him one of the key leaders of the black community in the south.

In 1972 Young was elected to Congress, the first black Congressman from Georgia in 100 years. In 1977, his fellow Georgian Jimmy *Carter appointed Young as ambassador to the United Nations. In that capacity Young excited controversy because of his support for Third World countries and he was forced to resign in 1979 following publicity given to a series of secret meetings with the Palestine Liberation Organization. He was elected as mayor of Atlanta in 1981 and served the full two terms allowed by the constitution.

Young's political stance was moderate and he was successful at building cross-community coalitions in Atlanta. In Democratic national politics, he translated that approach into support for mainstream liberalism. In 1984 he supported Walter *Mondale rather than the more radical black candidate Jesse *Jackson for the presidential nomination.

Yrigoyen, Hipolito (b. Buenos Aires 13 July 1850; d. 3 July 1933)

Argentine; President 1916–22, 1928–30

In 1896, following the suicide of his uncle, Yrigoyen inherited the leadership of the Radical Civic Union, a middle-class protest movement opposed to the prevailing oligarchical political system. Yrigoyen's declared goal was the establishment of a popular and 'ethical' democracy via free elections. His tactics included rebellion, electoral abstention, and 'intransigence' or refusal to compromise with other political actors.

Until 1912 he remained on the political sidelines but with the granting of universal male suffrage he was able to exploit the growing demand for a more representative political system. In 1916 he was narrowly elected President.

In his first term Yrigoyen showed that his commitment to reform was not only mild but also came second to party political advantage. He kept Argentina neutral during the First World War, reformed the university system, and nationalized the oil industry but never seriously threatened the economic and social power of the landed oligarchy. Nor did he deepen Argentina's fledgling democracy or address the burgeoning social problem, opting instead for controlling labour protest with military force and using his constitutional powers to oust his political opponents from provincial power. He also—fatefully—intervened in internal military affairs. His principal achievement was to use public patronage to convert the Radical Civic Union into an effective electoral machine.

Constitutionally prevented from succeeding himself in 1922, Yrigoyen was returned to the presidency with a sweeping majority in 1928. Popularly believed to be by now senile, his second term was largely devoid of policy initiatives. Following the Great Crash he was overthrown by a neo-Fascist group within the army in September 1930.

Though wealthy, Yrigoyen lived a very solitary and frugal life. He made no speeches and never appeared in public. Argentina's first democratically elected President, he did little to consolidate democracy.

Zapata, Emiliano (b. Anenecuilco, Mexico, 8 Aug. 1879; d. 10 Apr. 1919)
Mexican; revolutionary

Born into a large, relatively prosperous, peasant family in a village in the south-eastern state of Morelos, Zapata had little formal schooling. He was, however, able to read and write. He worked as a horse wrangler and sharecropper but became involved in a series of land disputes defending peasants against local landowners. He was elected president of his village council in 1909.

A year later the liberal reformer Francisco Madero called for the overthrow of the dictatorship of Porfirio Diaz and Zapata organized a band of disaffected young men and declared his support for the rebellion. By May 1911 he had captured the town of Cuautla in Morelos and his reputation as a skilled and inspiring peasant leader had been established. His relations with Madero, however, proved to be problematic. Zapata's prime, if not overwhelming, concern was with the distribution of land to the peasants. Madero, a landowner, on the other hand, was more concerned with the democratization of the political system. Zapata, described hysterically by the conservative Mexico City press as 'the Attila of the South', was now seen by Madero as a threat and ordered to disarm his band of guerrilla fighters. Zapata refused and retreated to the mountains of his home state, from where he issued, in November 1911, his Plan de Ayala.

This remarkable document called for a radical transformation of the landowning pattern in Mexico, demanding the return to the peasants of all lands stolen by the landowners and for the expropriation of one-third of all *hacienda* lands for distribution to landless peasants. His popularity grew amongst the peasants and his influence spread beyond the state of Morelos. By 1914 he commanded a large force of 25,000 armed men and was in position to threaten Mexico City. At this point he allied himself with the northern revolutionary Francisco 'Pancho' Villa, and together, with their bedraggled peasant armies, they entered Mexico City on 6 December to the misplaced consternation of its apprehensive inhabitants. The alliance, however, was short-lived and Zapata once again returned to Morelos where he attempted to apply the reforms outlined in his Plan de Ayala. His record, however, was marred by fighting between villages over land rights and by dissent within the *zapatista* ranks.

Meanwhile Villa's cavalry army was defeated at the Battle of Celaya and the more moderate General Carranza was therefore able to concentrate his attention on the irritating presence of Zapata's continuing rebellion in Morelos. Conventional warfare proved ineffective in the difficult terrain and against the fierce loyalty enjoyed by Zapata, but a meeting arranged by Colonel Jesus M. Guajardo, ostensibly to discuss his defection to the *zapatista* cause, turned out to be an ambush and Zapata was assassinated by government troops in Chinameca on 10 April 1919.

The influence of Zapata on Mexican history is difficult to assess. He injected the peasants' fierce demand for land into the *mélange* of ideas that informed the early days of the Revolution and is a powerful and inspiring icon for generations of peasants and peasant leaders since his death. The most recent example of this has been the rebellion of indigenous peasants in Chiapas in January 1994, which called itself the Zapatista Army of National Liberation.

Zápotocký, Antonín (b. Zakolany, 19 Dec. 1884; d. Prague, 13 Nov. 1957)
Czech; Czechoslovak premier 1948–53, President of Czechoslovakia 1953–7

Zápotocký was born in the mining region of Kladno to the west of Prague. He was the son of a founder of the Czech socialist movement, left school at 14, and started work as a stonemason. He joined the socialist youth movement in 1900 and from 1907 to 1911 was Social Democratic Party secretary in Kladno. He played a prominent role in the Czech trade union movement, organizing the unsuccessful general strike of 1920. In 1921 he was one of the founders of the Czechoslovak Communist Party (CPCz) and from 1922 to 1925 was secretary-general of the party. From 1929 to 1938 he was head of the Communist trade unions. Following imprisonment in a concentration camp during the Second World War he entered the CPCz's Presidium and became leader of the Revolutionary Trade Union Movement (ROH). Zápotocký and ROH played a major role in the Communist seizure of power in February 1948. From 1948 to 1953 he was Czechoslovak premier. He bore less responsibility for the purges in Czechoslovakia than *Slánský and *Gottwald and in March 1953 became President of Czechoslovakia after Gottwald's death. He did nothing to encourage reform in the post-*Stalin era.

Zhdanov, Andrei Aleksandrovich (b. 27 Feb. 1896; d. 31 Aug. 1948)

Russian; First Secretary of the Leningrad Party 1934–48, Central Committee Secretary for Ideology 1944–8

Zhdanov was of middle-class origin, the son of a school-inspector. He joined the Bolsheviks in 1915 and participated in the October Revolution. In the Russian Civil War he was a commissar attached to the Red Army. In 1924 he became head of the party in Novgorod and in 1928 went to the Volga region to supervise the collectivization of agriculture. In 1934 Zhdanov became secretary of the Central Committee and, after *Kirov's murder, head of the Leningrad Party. He supervised a bloody purge in the city. In 1935 he became a candidate member of the Politburo and a full member in 1939. In 1940 he oversaw the brutal Sovietization of Estonia immediately after its conquest. As head of the City Defence Council he played a major role in the siege of Leningrad from 1941 to 1944. In 1944 he became Central Committee Secretary responsible for ideology. In the immediate post-war years Zhdanov's influence within the Soviet Union was second only to *Stalin's. He led a campaign for the purification of Soviet society from the influence of Western cultural and scientific influence, strictly enforcing the principles of 'Socialist Realism' in the arts, and attacked the famous writers Mikhail Zoshchenko and Anna Akhmatova in 1946. In 1947 he presided over the Szklarska Poręba conference which resulted in the Soviet Bloc's declaration of ideological war on the West and the creation of the Cominform. He was noted for the violence of his anti-Western rhetoric. Zhdanov died suddenly in August 1948, and an extensive purge of the Leningrad party organization followed. In 1953 Stalin accused a group of Jewish doctors of his murder.

Zhivkov, Todor (b. 7 Sept. 1911)

Bulgarian; leader 1954–89

Zhivkov was the son of poor peasants. He moved to Sofia as a boy where he became a worker. He joined the illegal Bulgarian Communist Party in 1932 and had risen to senior rank within it by 1937. After 1941 he served in the pro-Soviet People's Liberation Insurgent Army, assisting the Red Army when it entered Bulgaria in September 1944. In 1945 he took charge of the Communist militia which was responsible for the arrest and murder of thousands of political opponents. Zhivkov entered the Bulgarian Politburo in 1951 and in 1954 received *Khrushchev's backing to replace the Stalinist *Chervenkov as party leader. From 1962 to 1971 he was also Prime Minister. He became Chairman of the Council of State in 1971, which made him effectively the President.

Zhivkov was devoted to his daughter Ludmila, a patron of the arts. Towards the end of her life she preached the virtues of mysticism and vegetarianism and other values at odds with Marxism–Leninism. She died in mysterious circumstances in 1981, aged 39. Thereafter Zhivkov became increasingly suspicious of his entourage.

In foreign policy Zhivkov unquestioningly followed the Soviet lead. At home, his regime greatly reduced the oppression of the Chervenkov years, but was set against any major political or economic reform. By 1989 Bulgaria was heavily indebted. In order to shift public opinion from the crisis, Zhivkov implemented nationalist policies against Bulgaria's Turkish minority. This led to economic collapse when 300,000 Turks fled Bulgaria. In November 1989 Zhivkov was overthrown by other members of his Politburo, led by the Foreign Minister, Petur *Mladenov, who replaced him as leader of the Bulgarian Communist Party. In 1990 Zhivkov was indicted on charges of 'especially gross embezzlement'. In September 1992 he was sentenced to eight years in prison.

Zhou Enlai (b. Huaian, Jiangsu Province, 5 Mar. 1898; d. 8 Jan. 1976)

Chinese; Prime Minister, *de facto* director of Chinese foreign affairs 1949–76

Zhou Enlai was probably the most respected of all China's Communist leaders. Within China, he is remembered for his restraining influence on Mao, particularly during the later years of the Cultural Revolution. Outside China, he is remembered as the sophisticated diplomat who was personally responsible for 'normalizing' Communist China's relations with many of her previous enemies after the 1949 revolution.

Zhou was born into a family with a long tradition of service in the imperial bureaucracy at a time when such families were becoming increasingly impoverished. Completing his middle school education at the prestigious Nankai Middle School in Tianjin, Zhou travelled to Japan in 1917 where he first became interested in Marxism whilst working to oppose Japanese encroachments on China. He returned to China in 1919, and continued his anti-colonialism campaigns by becoming a leading student activist in Tianjin, where he also met his future wife, Deng Yingchao, who also became an important post-1949 political leader in her own right. His political activity brought him to the attention of the Communist International, who sent him on a work-study tour to France in 1920, where Zhou organized Marxist study groups amongst Chinese students and workers in France and Germany.

During the period of Guomindang–Communist collaboration in 1924–5, Zhou was political director of the Nationalists' Whampoa Military Academy. Yet by 1927, Zhou was in conflict with his former allies, as the Nationalists moved to crush the April uprising of Shanghai workers that Zhou had organized and led. As the Nationalists stepped up their attacks, Zhou and Deng Yingchao abandoned their underground work in the cities, where Zhou soon became a key political figure and a crucial power broker. Despite initially opposing *Mao Zedong's revolutionary strategy, Zhou's decision to support Mao at the Zunyi conference in the midst of the Long March in January 1935 was crucial in assuring Mao's ascension to party leadership.

Throughout the revolutionary years, Zhou acted as the Communists' chief negotiator. When northern warlords kidnapped *Chiang Kai-shek in 1936, Zhou negotiated the Communists' role in the new United Front against the Japanese. He also spent much of the 1937–45 period in Chongqing as the Communists' representative in the exiled nationalist government, and held a number of talks with American and other foreign delegations. After the breakdown of talks with the Guomindang in 1946, he returned to the Communist base area in Yanan, where he helped formulate the successful revolutionary strategy, and laid the foundations for the post-revolutionary structure of political power. He was thus perhaps the natural choice to both take charge of China's international relations, and to oversee government administration as premier after 1949.

China was initially ostracized by the international community, with the Americans leading a trade embargo, and preventing the new People's Republic from taking

China's seat at the United Nations. Conflict with the American-dominated UN forces in the Korean War did little to ease the tension. It was Zhou in April 1954 who made the first steps towards reconciliation at the Geneva conference convened to discuss a solution to the Franco-Vietnamese War. Despite being cold-shouldered by John Foster *Dulles, Zhou impressed many the way he dealt with Dulles, as well as with his mediation skills.

The following year at the Bandung conference of African and Asian countries, Zhou made his first pitch for Chinese leadership of the Third World, claiming that the Americans were the main threat to instability in Asia. Despite continued revolutionary rhetoric, this marked the beginning of a process whereby China gradually became more a force for regime stability than for revolutionary insurgency in much of the Third World. Indeed, despite the continued shelling of the offshore islands occupied by the Taiwanese, Zhou persuaded his colleagues not to invade Quemoy and Matsu, and began to use the language of 'peaceful reunification' as early as May 1955.

Zhou spent much of the 1950s and 1960s travelling the world in pursuit of his diplomatic initiatives. He was a regular visitor to Third World capitals, and also spent more time in Moscow than any other Chinese leader as Sino-Soviet relations declined to the point of a short border war (officially skirmishes) in 1969. These initiatives came to fruition in the 1970s. His 'ping-pong' diplomacy with the United States (where the two traded sporting exchanges) laid the foundation for secret talks with *Kissinger in July 1971. It is no mere coincidence that the United Nations admitted the People's Republic of China and gave Zhou his world stage, on 25 October 1971. This was followed by *Nixon's visit to China the following February, and although Zhou died three years before the formal normalization of relations, the agreement that the two men signed on 28 February 1972 effectively took China's foreign relations into a new epoch, and was soon followed by the normalization of Sino-Japanese relations in September.

In domestic politics, Zhou was credited for being a voice of reason and pragmatism, for defending the victims of the Cultural Revolution where possible, and for persuading Mao to make a partial retreat from extreme radicalism between 1969 and 1971. Some historians have suggested that if Zhou's influence was so important in 1969, why didn't he do more to stop the excesses of 1966–9? Nevertheless, Zhou not only survived the Cultural Revolution without being purged, but also enhanced his reputation in the process.

His popular reputation was even further improved by his actions between 1973 (when he played a crucial role in rehabilitating *Deng Xiaoping) and his death in January 1976. Zhou shared the popular mistrust and hatred of the radical leftist Gang of Four who had risen to power during the Cultural Revolution. He was determined to block their influence (not least because of its potential damage to China's new found international respectability) and continued to control state affairs with his deputy Deng Xiaoping even after being hospitalized with terminal cancer in 1974.

After the radical left declined to attend Zhou's commemoration ceremony, the people of Beijing made their feelings clear by spontaneously massing in Tiananmen Square in support of Zhou (and by implication Deng Xiaoping) and against the left and the Gang of Four. If anything, the bloody suppression of this demonstration only served to raise Zhou's reputation higher still, and spawned an explosion of popular poems and eulogies in praise of the man that the Chinese still refer to as 'the people's premier'.

Zhukov, Georgi Konstantinovich (b. 11 Dec. 1896; d. 22 June 1974)

Russian; Deputy Commander-in-Chief of the Red Army 1942–6, Minister of Defence 1955–7

Zhukov was born into a poor peasant family and worked first as a craftsman in

Moscow. Starting as a conscript into the cavalry in August 1915 he had a distinguished wartime career, rising to the rank of NCO. In August 1918 he volunteered for the Red Cavalry and was made an officer. He joined the Bolshevik Party in March 1919. He remained in the Red Army after the Civil War and received senior officer training in 1924–5 and 1929–30. He was briefly attached to the Republican forces during the Spanish Civil War, returning to the USSR in 1937. In June 1939 Zhukov was sent to Outer Mongolia, where, in August, he routed the Japanese at the battle of Khalkin-Gol (Nomonhan). In June 1940 he commanded the troops which occupied the Romanian province of Bessarabia and became Chief of the General Staff, then Deputy Commissar for Defence.

When the Germans invaded the Soviet Union in June 1941 Zhukov commanded the reserve army. He held Leningrad in September 1941 and in the winter of 1941–2 drove the Germans back from Moscow. Becoming Deputy Supreme Commander-in-Chief, directly under Stalin, in August 1942, the Marshal of the Soviet Union in January 1943, he planned the Soviet counter-attack at Stalingrad at the beginning of 1943 and commanded at the battles around Kurst later in the year. Zhukov led the Red Army in the battle of Berlin and received the German surrender in May 1945.

In 1946 Stalin relieved Zhukov of his important offices and sent him to the Odessa Military District. In 1953 it was Zhukov who personally took *Beria into custody and, as a reward, *Khrushchev appointed him Defence Minister in 1955. In 1957 he gave Khrushchev vital support against the 'Anti-Party Faction' and was made a member of the Politburo. But in October 1957 Khrushchev dismissed him from all his offices. In 1964 *Brezhnev rehabilitated Zhukov, but left him in retirement.

Zia-ul-Huq, Mohammed *see* HUQ, ZIA-UL-

Zinoviev, Grigorii Yevseevich (b. Ukraine 24 Sept. 1883; d. Moscow 25 Aug. 1936)

Russian; chair of Petrograd Soviet Dec. 1917 (and of Leningrad Soviet 1924–6), first chair of Comintern Executive Committee 1919–26

Joining the RSDLP in 1901, Zinoviev met *Lenin in Switzerland in 1903 and became his close associate, helping to organize the Bolshevik faction. Returning to Russia, he became a member of the St Petersburg Central Committee, but went back to Western Europe in 1908 to become Lenin's chief assistant in party organization and propaganda. He worked with Lenin in Poland and Switzerland (where he studied at Bern University), editing the journal *Sotsial-Demokrat* and acting as his representative. In April 1917 he accompanied Lenin through Germany to Russia and went into hiding with him in Finland after July.

In October, after returning with Lenin to Russia, he publicly opposed (with *Kamenev) the seizure of power as premature and resigned from the Central Committee when Lenin refused to form a coalition socialist government. But he was soon reinstated and in December 1917 became chair of the Petrograd Soviet (remaining chair when it became the Leningrad Soviet in 1924). In 1919 he became a candidate member and in 1921 a full member of the Politbureau and from 1919 became chair of the newly formed Communist International's Executive Committee, to which Lenin attached great importance.

He formed part of the 'Triumvirate' (with *Stalin and Kamenev) which took over, when Lenin died, to oppose *Trotsky. However, in 1925 he attacked the then pro-NEP policy of Bukharin and Stalin and was dismissed as chair of the Leningrad Soviet in 1926. He then joined Trotsky's 'United Opposition' and was expelled from the Politbureau in July 1926 and from the Central Committee and the IKKI (Comintern) in October. He was dismissed from the party in 1927, but readmitted in 1928 after recanting and worked in the state apparatus. In 1932 he was again expelled but again readmitted in 1933. He spoke at the 'Congress of Victors' in 1934, but after the assassination of *Kirov in 1934 was arrested and sentenced to ten years' imprisonment in 1935 for alleged involvement. In 1936 was a subject of the first show trial, when he was found guilty and shot as the alleged organizer of terrorist groups. He was officially rehabilitated in 1988.

Zog I, King (b. Burgayet Castle, 8 Oct. 1895; d. Paris, 9 Apr. 1961)
Albanian; President 1925–8, King 1928–39

Born Ahmed Bey Zogolli, he was born in north-central Albania, the son of a wealthy Albanian landowner and leader of the Mati tribe. Educated in Constantinople, he entered politics before the First World War, becoming leader of the Nationalist party. During the war he served in the Austro-Hungarian army. From December 1921 until February 1924 he dominated most of the ministries of Albania's unstable governments. His aim was to end his country's tribal anarchy by creating a state centralized on himself. He believed that foreign investment was vital for Albania's economic development, but wanted to maintain Albania's independence. On becoming Prime Minister for the first time in 1922, he changed his name to Zog, considering 'Zogolli' to be too Turkified for an Albanian nationalist. In 1924, Zog had one of his political rivals assassinated, but had to flee the country as a result. Assisted by the Yugoslavs, he returned in December 1924 and made himself President the next year. He declared himself King Zog I (there was no Zog II) in 1928. It was not until 1929 that he had imposed order throughout the country. Thereafter he started a reform programme which included the introduction of a new civil code, the expansion and nationalization of education, and land redistribution. The reforms had only limited impact. After 1926 Zog developed close economic ties with Fascist Italy, while vainly hoping to restrict Italy's political influence in Albania. His regime achieved widespread unpopularity for its corruption and for allowing Italian economic exploitation of the country. By 1939, when *Mussolini invaded Albania, Italy controlled the Albanian economy. Zog fled to Britain, never to return to Albania. He formally abdicated in 1946. Zog lived the last years of his life in France, where he died in 1961.